WHAT IS THE INDIE BIBLE?

The Indie Bible is a valuable promotional tool for Independent Musicians and Songwriters that lists:

- 4200 publications that will REVIEW your music!
- 3500 radio stations that will PLAY your songs!
- 610 services that will help you to SELL your music!
- 400 sites where you can UPLOAD your band's MP3s or videos!
- and 50 articles that will help your music career to SUCCEED!

ALL styles of music are covered!

Pop, Rock, Hip Hop, Folk, Blues, Classical, Jazz, Punk, ALL Metals, Latin, Indie Rock, Electronic, Experimental, Christian, Dance, World Music, Soul, R&B, Women in Music, Country, Rap, Roots, Bluegrass, Reggae, Ska, Rockabilly, Ambient, Emo, Gothic, Industrial, Progressive Rock, Alternative, Americana, Oi, Jam Band, Hardcore, Garage, Avant-garde, House, Trip Hop, Celtic, EBM, Gospel, Space Rock, Noise, Alt-Country, Children's, New Age, Singer/Songwriter, Trance, Lo-Fi, Funk, Nu-Jazz ...

The Indie Bible also provides you with **50** insightful articles that will help you to succeed!

Articles Include:

- **How to Submit Your Music for Review**
- **How to Get Radio Airplay**
- **Getting Your Music into Film**
- **How to Copyright Your Music**
- **Why You Need an Entertainment Lawyer**
- **How to Create a Press Kit**
- **How Royalties Work**
- **How to Take Advantage of YouTube**

and MANY more!

COVER DESIGN
Warrior Girl Music www.warriorgirlmusic.com based on original art by gilli moon
www.gillimoon.com

ARTISTS PICTURED AND PHOTOGRAPHERS

From top left to right:

Markeisha Ensley - photo by Claire Gribbin
www.markeishaensley.com

gilli moon - photo by Larry Mah
www.gillimoon.com

Jocelyn Donegan - photo by Jeff Peterson
www.jocelyndonegan.com

Middle left to right:

J.Walker - photo by gilli moon
www.rhymecology.com

Myu - photo by Angry Steve
www.myumusic.com

Jimi Yamagishi - photo by Toni Koch
www.jimiyamagishi.com

Leave - photo by Laura Esmeijer
www.myspace.com/singersongwriterleave

Annette Conlon - photo by Kris Swenson
www.annetteconlon.com

Katie Garibaldi - photo by Marty Sconduto
www.katiegaribaldi.com

Bottom left to right:

Happy Ron - photo by Steve Covault
www.myspace.com/happyron

Bill Pere - photo courtesy of the Connecticut Songwriters Association
www.billpere.com

Lisa Jane Lipkin - photo by Kate Harper
www.lisajanelipkin.com

Copyright © 2009 by Big Meteor Publishing

This edition published 2009 by Big Meteor Publishing

ISBN 978-0-9686214-8-6

Printed in Canada by Bradda Printing

What people are saying about The Indie Bible...

"My press kit is full of positive press from around the WORLD because of The Indie Bible."
**- Terry Christopher,
Award Winning Singer/Songwriter**

"All the artists I work with personally are required to have a copy."
- Tim Sweeney, author of "Tim Sweeney's Guide To Releasing Independent Records"

"The Indie Bible provides a great service for artists and radio programmers."
- Kate Borger, WYEP FM

"I'm getting a nice chunk of radio play for my first CD and just received an label inquiry!"

- John Gordon, Recording Artist

"I can't thank you enough for this amazing summary of all your hard work and dedication. My heartfelt appreciation."

- David Culiner, LovethisLife

"It's great! The articles alone are worth the price."

- Beau Wadsworth, Recording Artist

"I bought the Indie Bible, and am still overwhelmed by it!"
- Michael Grady, The Strange Angels

"I have never seen as much relevent information in one publication. It is every thing I had hoped for!"

- John Morris, Recording Artist

"340 Pages of Pure Gold!"
– Guitar Player Magazine

TABLE OF CONTENTS

Dot On Shaft Guitars

Manufacturer, Distributors and *now Franchise Retail Store.*
Opening in a city near you!

We are original in many ways.
We sell only OUR brand of Guitars and Strings.
When you buy a guitar from our store, we give you
STRINGS FOR LIFE! Ask us how:)

We distribute the following products in Canada:
- Snap Jack Cables (www.snapjackcables.com)
- Carparelli HandWound Pickups
- KahlerUSA
- Decarlo HandMade Guitars
- Carparelli Guitars
- DOS-WYRES hand wound Telfon Coated Strings

Fastest growing Guitar company in Canada

DOT ON SHAFT GUITARS
37 Livingstone Street West
Barrie, Ontario L4N 7J2
705-812-1061 or 416-628-1467

**DOT ON SHAFT GUITARS &
SCHOOL OF MUSIC**
5875 Highway & Units 5 & 6
Woodbridge, Ontario L4L 1T9
(SE Corner of Highway 7 and 27)
416-249-PLEK

www.dotonshaft.com

SECTION SEVEN: HELPFUL RESOURCES FOR MUSICIANS AND SONGWRITERS

SECTION EIGHT: HELPFUL ARTICLES

overview

radio airplay

getting your music reviewed

tools

legal

Every independent musician knows the best way to make money is by selling your music. CD Poster Shop gets you started with 50 retail ready CDs for $99*†. Don't tie up all your money in 1000 CDs. Improve your cash flow now! All of our prices are low and our quality is outstanding. Visit www.cdpostershop.com today and **see what you have been missing.**

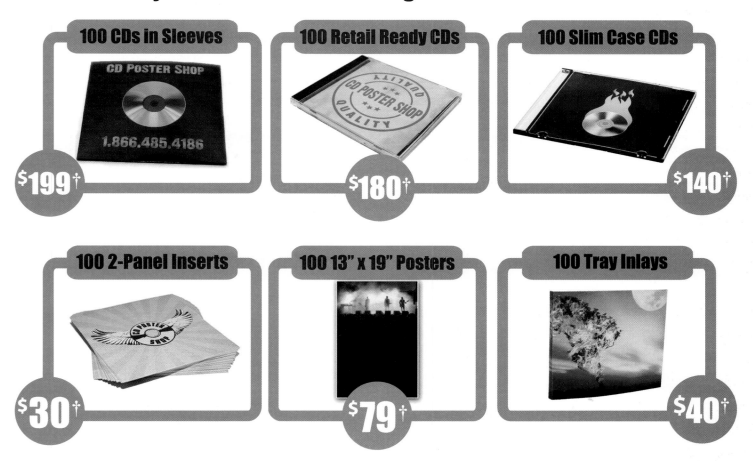

www.cdpostershop.com

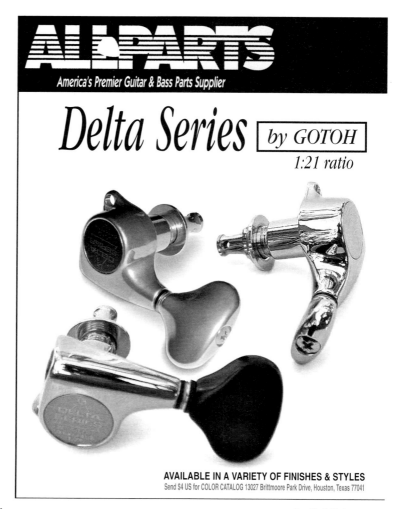

TIPS FOR USING THE INDIE BIBLE

How the listings are sorted

a) **TYPE OF SERVICE** (Publication, Radio Station, CD Vendor etc.)

  b) **Genre of Music**

   c) **Geographic Location**

The listings are set up this way so that you can quickly find a *specific* service in a *specific* area for a *specific* style of music. *ie:* Finding a **Hip Hop** magazine in **England** that will **REVIEW** your music.

How the various styles of resources are sorted

1. If a publication welcomes submissions from MANY genres, that publication will be listed in the **Mainstream** section. Publications in the Mainstream section welcome a *wide variety* of genres, but usually nothing too extreme. Common genres in this section are Pop, Rock, Indie Rock etc.

2. There is an unavoidable amount of *Genre Overflow* from section to section. For instance, if you are in a Punk band, you will not only find sites that will review your music in the **Punk** Section, but you will also find several sites that welcome your style of music in the **Metal** and **Goth** Sections.

Most publications review more than one style of music. The sites listed in the Indie Bible are placed in their respective sections based on the musical style that publication lists as their preference. For instance, if a publication states that they welcome Folk, Blues and Jazz music, that publication would be listed in the **Folk Music** section, because "Folk" was the first genre mentioned.

3. Quiz: Where would you find the listing of a magazine that reviews the music of **Christian Women New Age** artists that live in the **Chicago** area? Would you find it in the

  a. Christian Music section?
  b. New Age Music section?
  c. Women in Music section?
  d. The Local Music section under "Chicago"?

The answer is "d", the **Local Music** section. I'm using this example to point out that the LOCAL MUSIC SECTION OVERRIDES all other characteristics of any given resource. If it is a resource that provides a service for a *specific* area (country, city, town, state, province) then that resource is listed in the Local Music section (ie: a resource for Country Music bands based in Montana). The Indie Bible is arranged this way so that you can quickly look at the listings in your area to find out what kind of help is available for you locally. Please make sure to check out the Local Music section for your area (or those places that you will be passing through during your tour). You will be surprised at how many resources there are in your community that are willing to help you out.

4. The majority of the stations listed in the **Mainstream Radio** section are College, University and Community stations that have a weekly show catering to EVERY style of music, both mild and extreme (Country, Pop, Hip Hop, Death Metal, Goth, Classical etc.), so make sure that you CHECK THEM ALL!

About the articles

Before you start contacting the various resources listed in the Indie Bible, I STRONGLY RECOMMEND that you read the articles in **SECTION 8** to better understand how to submit your music for review, radio airplay etc. These articles are written by industry professionals who have a *wealth* of experience. They know what works, what doesn't work – and why. Reading the articles in SECTION 8 will save you an ENORMOUS amount of time and money and will help your career to move in a positive direction. In other words, you won't have to make the same mistakes that I and many others have made while trying to survive in the music business. Please take the time to read these articles. You will be glad that you did!

PLEASE READ THIS!!

I have received several complaints from music reviewers and radio hosts about high number of e-mails and CDs they are receiving **that have nothing to do with the style of music that their publication or show promotes**. PLEASE DO NOT SEND OUT MASS MAILINGS to the sites listed in this book telling them about your new release, latest invention, upcoming shows etc.

Instead of sending your e-mails and CDs out to everyone on the planet, take the time to read through The Indie Bible to find out who is actually looking for your specific style of music. RULE #1: Don't try and convert anyone! Respect that fact that different people have different tastes in music.

Put yourself in the position of a Magazine Editor. Let's say for example you are the Editor of a magazine that covers **Folk Music**. How irritating would it be continually getting blasted with e-mails from artists in **Metal** and **Punk** bands asking you to review their CD? How would you feel each day when you grab the truckload of CDs from your PO Box and find that about 1 in 30 are actually Folk CDs? You're going to feel irritated and frustrated.

Note that there are **49** articles in this edition. You will not find in ANY of the **49** articles a Radio Host or Magazine Editor saying that a *good* way for an artist to make initial contact is by sending out *mass e-mailings*. They all say the same thing, which is "take the time to do some research, and THEN contact the various services personally".

Remember, these are human beings you're dealing with. The recipient of your personalized e-mail or promo package will respect the time you have put in to find out about them and most often will get back to you quickly. On the other hand, a mass mailing is an insult to him/her and your e-mail will be deleted immediately and your CD chucked into the garbage.

The extra time you put in to do a bit of research and to personalize your initial contact will pay off for you in a BIG way in the end!

Final Notes

Please contact me with information on any broken links, outdated sites or mistakes of any kind. They will be addressed right away. Also, feel free to send your comments and suggestions to me. ALL suggestions will be taken into consideration. Thanks to your input, The Indie Bible continues to grow with each new edition.

I hope by utilizing the many contacts found in this book that you make some solid progress with your career. If you feel that you made a worthwhile investment by purchasing The Indie Bible, please tell your friends about it.

Also, remember to sign up for my monthly newsletter. Each month I send out 40 or so new listings of services that can help you to gain more exposure. Simply send an e-mail to **newsletter@indiebible.com** to sign up. Just put "newsletter" in the subject heading.

I wish you the very best with your music!

David Wimble
Editor, The Indie Bible
www.indiebible.com
Phone: 800-306-8167
david@indiebible.com

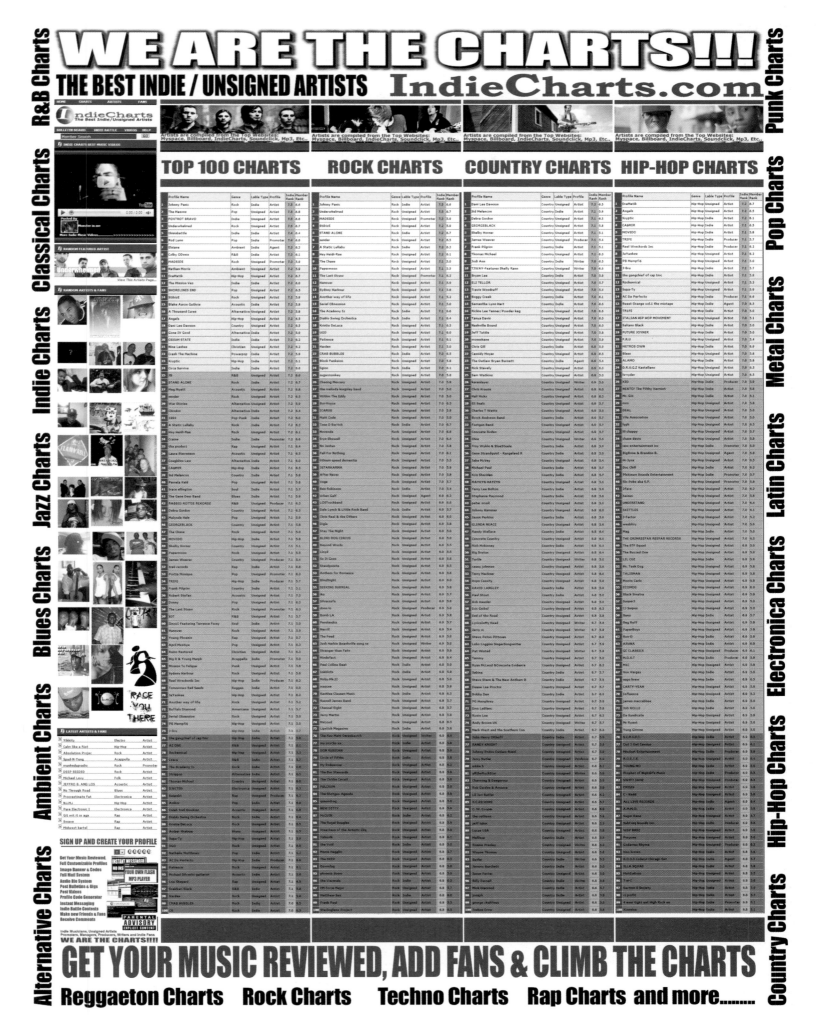

CD BABY™
INDEPENDENT MUSIC

SELL YOUR MUSIC EVERYWHERE.

CD Baby can get your music selling worldwide on cdbaby.com, the biggest independent music store online, Apple iTunes, Rhapsody, Napster, and over 2,400 retail stores. All for just a $35 setup fee.

CD Baby is based on the premise that anybody should be able to get worldwide distribution. Ten years later we are the world's largest online independent music store and we've paid indie musicians over $80,000,000!

Visit our store at cdbaby.com or sign up at cdbaby.net

SECTION ONE: REVIEWERS OF INDEPENDENT MUSIC

Mainstream Publications

Just to clarify, when I say mainstream, I'm not talking about Perry Como music. Mainstream is any sort of music that isn't too far "out there." That's not to say that publications in this section won't listen to all types of music, but they are more likely to enjoy Rock, Pop, Indie Rock etc. They are less likely to go for the Death Metal, Industrial, Hardcore etc....although some will accept those styles.

*Most of the newer music review sites are in **MP3 / Audioblog** format. Make sure to check out the MP3 / Audioblog area in **SECTION SIX** of this directory. You'll find hundreds of blogs that will feature your music in a variety of ways, including reviews along with audio and video clips. Several of them also do interviews.*

North America

United States

20th Century Guitar
135 Oser Ave. Hauppauge, NY 11788
PH: 800-291-9687 FX: 631-434-9057
www.tcguitar.com
CD reviews and features.

75 or Less
23 Laurel Ln. Warren, RI 02885
www.75orless.com
Will review anything in less than 75 words.

ADDreviews
PO Box 650113, Sterling, VA 20165-0113
crew@addreviews.com
www.addreviews.com
All music reviews are 20 words or less. It's about brevity. Terseness. Conciseness. You get the idea.

Advance Copy
Kenyon Hopkin kmhopkin@juno.com
advancecopy.blogspot.com
Blog in which music is reviewed and given a rating.

Agenda Magazine
3901 Scandia Way, Los Angeles, CA 90065
PH: 323-244-1140
agendamag@aol.com
www.Agendamag.com
A fashion ezine that also reviews music from independent artists.

Alarm Press
53 W. Jackson Blvd. #1256, Chicago, IL 60604
PH: 312-341-1290
music@alarmpress.com
www.alarmpress.com
We listen to thousands of CDs and attend live concerts in order to bring you inspirational artists who are fueled by an honest and contagious obsession with their art.

Alternative Addiction
PO Box 210369, Auburn Hills, MI 48321
Chad Durkee chad@alternativeaddiction.com
www.alternativeaddiction.com
Helps unsigned bands by offering promotional features and the possibility to have your song listed in our Top 10 Chart.

Alternative Press
1305 W. 80th St. #2F, Cleveland, OH 44102-1996
PH: 216-631-1510 FX: 216-631-1016
editorial@altpress.com
www.altpress.com
News, reviews, new releases etc.

American Songwriter
1303 16th Ave. S. 2nd Fl. Nashville, TN 37212
PH: 615-321-6096 FX: 615-321-6097
info@americansongwriter.com
www.americansongwriter.com
Interviews, writing tips, industry news, reviews, lyric contests and more.

Amplifier
5 Calista Ter. Westford, MA 01886
PH: 978-846-1177
Joe Joyce JoeJ@AmplifierMagazine.com
www.amplifiermagazine.com
Focuses on Pop, Melodic Rock and Roots Rock.

Angst Magazine
1770 Glendale Blvd. Los Angeles, CA 90026
PH: 323-953-1100
Laura Defelice angstmagazine@yahoo.com
www.myspace.com/angstmagazine
Our contributors are excellent music lovers and have a creative insight into the music scene.

Anthem Magazine
110 W. Ocean Blvd. 10th Fl.
Long Beach,
CA 90802-4605
info@anthem-magazine.com
www.anthem-magazine.com
Editorial coverage of emerging faces with some of the more well-known icons in film, music and art.

Ape Quake .|: Music Freak
918 Lake Court
Madison, WI 53715
PH: 608-250-2427
FX: 608-250-2427
Adam Mico
adammico@yahoo.com
apequake.blogspot.com
A frequently updated blog devoted to getting your music heard and viewed. Check the site for additional details!

Arthur Magazine
c/o Bull Tongue
PO Box 627
Northampton, MA 01061
www.arthurmag.com
Our Bull Tongue columnists review the latest emanations from the deep underground.

Auralgasms.com
Scott Zumberg szumberg@auralgasms.com
www.auralgasms.com
Reviews, sound samples, bios, discographies, tour dates and links.

The A.V. Club
c/o The Onion, 212 W. Superior St. #200
Chicago, IL 60610
www.avclub.com/content
Interviews, essays and reviews of movies, music and books.

BABBLE and BEAT
PO Box 327, Oconomowoc, WI 53066-0327
PH/FX: 888-512-7773
Stacy Sardelli admin@babbleandbeat.com
www.babbleandbeat.com
CD and concert reviews, musician interviews, music news, contests, and our general babble. We cover Indie, Pop, Goth, Electronic, Punk, Alternative, Industrial, New Wave, Folk, Rock and more!

Babysue
PO Box 15749, Chattanooga, TN 37415
PH: 423-285-8365
Don W. Seven LMNOP@babysue.com
www.babysue.com
Our website features continually updated music reviews as well as samples from the Babysue print magazine. All styles of music are considered for review from major and independent labels and bands as well as independent PR firms.

Bassics
PO Box 1178, Lewiston, NY 14092
PH: 888-223-3340
Ron Garant bassicsrg@aol.com
www.bassics.com
Each issue includes tracks from featured artists. All styles of music are covered.

Big TakeoverMagazine
Rm. 5-2, 1713 8ᵗʰ Ave. Brooklyn, NY 11215
www.bigtakeover.com
100 pages of indie music reviews.

The Biggest Letdown
Kevin Stoltz kevin@biggestletdown.com
biggestletdown.com
A continuation of articles, video projects, stories, ideas, and a pop-culture that is genuine.

Billboard
770 Broadway, New York, NY 10003
PH: 646-654-5549
Jonathan Cohen jacohen@billboard.com
www.billboard.com
International news weekly of music.

Blogcritics
Eric Olsen ecolsen2003@cs.com
blogcritics.org/music
An online magazine, a community of writers and readers from around the globe.

blue coupe
Linda Richards editor@bluecoupe.com
www.bluecoupe.com
Open to interviewing you about your music.

BLURT
140 Southwood Ave. Silver Spring, MD 20901
PH: 301-592-0006
Scott Crawford scrawford@blurt-online.com
Blurt-online.com
Combining insightful interviews with dozens of no-holds-barred reviews.

Buddyhead
PO Box 1268, Hollywood, CA 90078
FX: 801-684-1387
Travis Keller traviskeller@gmail.com
www.buddyhead.com
Can't even be defined at this point in the game.

BuddyHollywood.com
www.buddyhollywood.com
Your friend in entertainment!

buhdge
Alan Haber alan@buhdge.com
www.buhdge.com
Raging fiercely through the tangled media net to get to the bottom of that which we hold dear: our favorite new and old music.

Buzzine.com
5419 Hollywood Blvd. #C805
Hollywood, CA 90027
PH: 866-751-2899
contact@buzzine.com
www.buzzine.com
Interviews, concert reviews and up-to-date news.

Need Gigs?

A new live venue directory from the creators of The Indie Bible!

www.indievenuebible.com

CD Reviews by You
editor@cdreviewsbyyou.com
cdreviewsbyyou.com
Review any album you like! We're especially looking to showcase upcoming artists. Please check our submission details.

cdreviews.com
1929 Acari Ave. Sacramento, CA 95835
PH: 818-206-4245
www.cdreviews.com
Are you in a band? Do you have a CD out? If so let us know.

The Cheers
thecheers@thecheers.org
www.thecheers.org
Entertainment, opinion, politics, extreme sports.

The ChickenFish Speaks
PO Box 292168, Dayton, OH 45429-0168
PH: 937-609-9913
Grog Grog@theChickenFishSpeaks.com
www.theChickenFishSpeaks.com
All of our reviewers have eclectic tastes in music ... so send anything and everything!!!

Cityzen Entertainment
14 Manetto Hill Plaza, Plainview, NY 11803
PH: 516-384-5980 FX: 516-935-4674
info@cityzen.tv
www.cityzen.tv
We're always looking for new and exciting things to cover. You must send us (2) copies of your CD for review.

CMJ New Music Report
151 W. 25th St. 12th Fl. New York, NY 10001
PH: 917-606-1908 FX: 917-606-1914
www.cmj.com
All styles of music are welcome!

Comfort Comes
info@comfortcomes.com
www.comfortcomes.com
Would you like your band reviewed on our site?
Send us an e-mail!

The Consensus
www.c0nsensus.com
Brutally honest music reviews for all genres. Each
song gets listened to by five different reviewers.

concertlivewire.com
PO Box 2, Lake Geneva, WI 53147
PH: 262-949-8852
tonyb@concertlivewire.com
www.concertlivewire.com
Concert & CD reviews, artist interviews, free
exclusive MP3s and P2P ticket swap.

Copacetic Zine
PO Box 17321, Seattle, WA 98127
www.copacetic-zine.com
Please do us both a favor and look around the site
before sending us your CD. Make sure your music
fits.

Copper Press
PO Box 1601, Acme, MI 49610
steve@copperpress.com
www.copperpress.com
News, reviews, tours etc.

Crud Magazine
crudenquiries@crudmusic.com
www.2-4-7-music.com
All solicited material mailed us will be reviewed and
scheduled for inclusion.

Daily Vault
Jason Warburg editor@dailyvault.com
www.dailyvault.com
The longest running independent music review site
on the web. Reviews music of all genres.

Decentx.com
10 Thompson Ln. Edgewater, NJ 07020
PH: 201-313-1100
411@decentxposure.com
www.decentx.com
A social networking site that is geared to helping
emerging artists promote themselves. Bands that are
signed up for the site (which is free) have the
opportunity to submit their CDs for review.

Deep Water Acres
108 Ramblewood Rd.
Pennsylvania Furnace, PA 16865
www.dwacres.com
News, reviews, interviews and rants.

DemoCheck
democheck.com
An online paid service where you can have your
music or performance of music reviewed by some of
the top musicians, composers, and songwriters in
the industry. You send them your MP3 file, and
you'll get back a review of your music - it's that
simple.

Drawer B
PO Box 11726
Columbia, SC 29211-1726
www.drawerb.com
Unsolicited submissions are
accepted.

Erasing Clouds
415 S. 46th St. Apt. A,
Philadelphia, PA 19143
Dave Heaton
erasingclouds@gmail.com
www.erasingclouds.com
Where regular people write about
the music.

EvilSponge
brendan@evilsponge.org
www.evilsponge.org
We filter the cool stuff from the
garbage. Contact us for our mailing
address.

ExMogul Music
Susan White exmogul@gmail.com
www.exmogul.com
Do you want us to review your CD?
We'll listen and review it for your
press kit.

The Fader
info@thefader.com
www.thefader.com
Digging into the factual experiences
of music.

fakejazz
info@fakejazz.com
www.fakejazz.com
Submit material for review in our publication.

Filter Magazine
5908 Barton Ave. Los Angeles, CA 90038
PH: 323-464-4775
info@filtermmm.com
www.filter-mag.com
Exposure for credible artists.

Fingertips
letterbox@fingertipsmusic.com
www.fingertipsmusic.com
MP3 review site. For a review, you must be
"signed", even if it's to a small label.

Firesideometer
505 S. Main St., Frankfort, IN 46041
brent@firesideometer.com
www.firesideometer.com
Covering indie bands that make great music.

foxy digitalis
PO Box 700810, Tulsa, OK 74170
foxyd@digitalisindustries.com
www.digitalisindustries.com/foxyd
Everything received will be reviewed.

Front Row Fanz Magazine
webmaster@frontrowfanz.com
www.frontrowfanz.com
Interview magazine that will interview indie artists.

Garage Radio Magazine
John "RoadRash" Foxworthy
roadrash@garageradio.com
www.garageradio.com
From event and CD reviews to interviews and
industry news, GR Magazine features all the best
new music from the people that make it happen.

Groovevolt.com
Chauncy Jackson press@groovevolt.com
www.groovevolt.com
Features indie and upcoming artists.

Guaranteed Reviews
2400 NW 80th St. #154, Seattle, WA 98117-4449
info@guaranteedreviews.com
http://guaranteedreviews.com
Every reviewer at GuaranteedReviews is in some
way connected to the music business. Together we
have a combined 250 years in the industry. Our
advice to you is informed by decades worth of
success, mistakes and solid industry connections.
Please let us put that experience to work for you.
Reviews are $15 each.

Tired of promoting yourself???
Let us do it for you!

GET RADIO AIRPLAY and ONLINE REVIEWS

*Submit your music to radio stations,
music webzines, podcasts, blogs,
and directories in your genre!*

Over 10,000 stations & websites

42 genres served !!!

Since 2004
MusicSUBMIT.com
Internet promotion for musicians

Harp Magazine
8737 Colesville Rd. 9th Fl.
Silver Spring, MD 20910-3921
PH: 301-588-4114 FX: 301-588-5531
www.harpmagazine.com
In-depth features and reviews.

Hear/Say
PH: 800-227-2425 x110
Diane Singer diane@hearsay.cc
www.hearsay.cc
*America's College Music media for 11 years!
Distributed on 600 college campuses and 100 indie
music stores nationwide! Features artist spotlights,
CD reviews, artist interviews, streaming, podcast
interviews & more!*

HearYa
183 Fairchild Dr. Mountain View, CA 94043
hearyablog@yahoo.com
www.hearya.com
*An Indie music blog where we rely on band
recommendations from friends and like-minded
music enthusiasts to cut through the clutter.*

HitSession.com
6453 Pretti Rd. Corunna, MI 48817
dirtkahuna@michonline.net
www.hitsession.com
Small donation to get your music reviewed.

HYBRID Magazine
PO Box 9250, Denver, CO 80209
David DeVoe editor@hybridmagazine.com
www.hybridmagazine.com
We listen to every CD we receive.

impose magazine
PO Box 472, Village Stn. New York, NY 10014
Derek Evers derek@imposemagazine.com
www.imposemagazine.com
*Our goal is to articulately illustrate the common
sentiment that fans of all genres posses a love of
music.*

In Music We Trust
Alex Steininger alex@inmusicwetrust.com
www.inmusicwetrust.com
Exposes talented artists to a larger audience.

Independent Reviewer Darren Paltrowitz
45 Tudor City Pl. #906, New York, NY 10017
darren.paltrowitz@gmail.com
*I am open to everything, but Indie Rock, Punk,
Power Pop and other melodic and thoughtful music
takes precedence. Some Hip Hop is alright as well,
preferably old-school-influenced Hip Hop. But I
tend to receive too many submissions to be able to
listen to everything....*

Indie Ezine
5548 E. Gable Ave. Mesa, AZ 85206
PH: 480-981-5340
Jonathan Whitmer mail@indieezine.com
www.indieezine.com
*An online news magazine featuring independent
artists.*

Indie In-Tune Magazine
PO Box 355, Epping, NH 03042-0355
Attn: Reviews
www.myspace.com/Bob_D
*3 publications in 1! Indie IN-TUNE, Carpe
Nocturne & The Metal Horizon; all offering honest,
positive worldwide coverage. E-mail us first to tell
us what you do!*

Indie-Music.com
www.indie-music.com/
reviewpolicy.php
*You can request a certain
writer or you can simply
submit your package and it
will be distributed among
our current pool of
reviewers. You must be a
member of Indie-
Music.com in order to get a
review.*

**The Indie Music
Review**
Lisa Babick
indiemusicreview@
sbcglobal.net
myspace.com/
theindiemusicreview
*Focuses on talent in the
indie music scene including
Punk, Rock, Zen Jazz, Folk,
Alternative and more. As
long as it's not commercial
we cover it. Live
performance reviews/
interviews/CD reviews and
more.*

Indie Pages
7026 5th Ave. NW.
Seattle, WA 98117
chris@indiepages.com
www.indiepages.com
*Info about your favorite
indie bands and labels.*

The Indie Review
theindiereview.com
*Submissions MUST be
made through Sonicbids.
Check our website for
details.*

Indie Update Blog
www.indieupdate.com
*Here to keep you updated
on the world of the
independent musician.
We'll throw in reviews of
some of what we believe to
be some of the more
promising independent
bands and musicians out
there.*

Indieducky
indieducky@gmail.com
indieducky.com
*Providing music related
selections and reviews in
an attempt to introduce new
and upcoming artists.*

Ink 19
624 Georgia Ave.
Melbourne, FL 32901
www.ink19.com
*Accepts CDs and artist
bio's for review.*

inReview.net
www.inreview.net
*We write CD reviews,
compose feature articles
and conduct interviews
with our favorite artists.*

Issues Magazine
editors@issues-mag.com
www.issues-mag.com
Reviews any music good enough for radio! Please contact us before sending your CD.

Insulinfunk
429 Jarvis Rd. Greenville, KY 42345
PH: 270-543-8565
Wesley Johnson insulinfunk@gmail.com
www.insulinfunk.net
We cover tons of stuff, including music. Started by long time Buzzgrinder.com writer, Wes Johnson.

Junk Media
102 Sand Hill Rd. Shutesbury, MA 01072
Laura Sylvester laura@junkmedia.org
www.junkmedia.org
We strive to highlight music and musicians who have been overlooked by the mainstream music press as well as provide alternative viewpoints and opinions on "popular" artists.

Keyboard Magazine
1111 Bayhill Dr. #125, San Bruno, CA 94403
PH: 650-513-4671
Ernie Rideout erideout@musicplayer.com
www.keyboardmag.com
We are always interested in reviewing music by independent artists and producers. Features "The Unsigned Artist of The Month."

Kotori Magazine
info@kotorimag.com
www.kotorimag.com
Exposing subversive culture and showcasing underground sensations.

Kweevak Music Magazine
38 Oliver Pl. Ringwood, NJ 07456
PH: 973-556-5400
Rich Lynch mr_kweevak@yahoo.com
www.kweevak.com
We now guarantee CD reviews and a full 2-month main page artist spotlight feature for all bands that join our community!

LPM Voice Magazine
Jeremy contact@lpmvoice.com
lpmvoice.com
We are 100% dedicated to bringing you only the best nonpartisan Rock music from around the world. Band interviews, music news, music reviews, stories from bands on tour, playable songs, links to each band's webpage and much more!

La Famiglia Magazine
PO Box 19768, Detroit, MI 48219
PH: 313-544-0430
www.lafamigliazine.com
An art, music, and culture based magazine. Send us your CDs, DVDs, records, books etc.

Lab Productions
9655 Judi Dr. Baton Rouge, LA 70815
PH: 985-974-0792
albums@labproductions.com
www.labproductions.com
Send your demo to get reviewed/featured.

Listeners' Generation Music Reviews
www.listenersgeneration.com
We write subjective but mainly positive reviews of MP3s and CDs. We are selective of who we review, so please make sure your material is professional.

Luminous Flux Records
8 Forest Ave. Glen Cove, NY 11542
webmonkey@fluxnet.com
www.fluxnet.com/submiss.html
Reviews new music from new bands.

Magnet
1218 Chestnut St. #508, Philadelphia, PA 19107
PH: 215-413-8570 FX: 215-413-8569
Matthew Fritch matt@magnetmagazine.com
www.magnetmagazine.com
Gives attention to indie musicians.

Mean Street Magazine
6747-A Greenleaf Ave. Whittier, CA 90601
PH: 562-789-9455 FX: 562-789-9925
hello@meanstreet.com
www.meanstreet.com
Covers the independent music scene.

Metacritic
1223 Wilshire Blvd. #1240
Santa Monica, CA 90403-5400
www.metacritic.com/music
Reviews your music by assigning it a score.

Modern Drummer
12 Old Bridge Rd. Cedar Grove, NJ 07009-1288
PH: 973-239-4140 FX: 973-239-7139
mdinfo@moderndrummer.com
www.moderndrummer.com
Magazine focusing specifically on drummers.

Sign up for
The Indie Contact Newsletter
www.indiebible.com

Montgomery Guns Productions
14131 SE 86 Ter. Inglis, FL 34449
PH: 352-447-2560
Troy "Gun" Montgomery troygun@montgomery
gunproductions.com
www.montgomerygun productions.com
Send us material to review by using Sonicbids.com
www.sonicbids.com or mail us your press kit.

The Music Appraisal
matt@themusicappraisal.net
www.themusicappraisal.net
Want your band's CD reviewed? Want to have an
interview? We'd love to hear from you!

Music Box
PO Box 3911, Oak Park, IL 60303-3911
editor@musicbox online.com
www.musicbox-online.com
Concert and album reviews.

Music Connection
14654 Victory Blvd. 1st Fl. Van Nuys, CA 91411
PH: 818-995-0101
FX: 818-995-9235
contactmc@musicconnection.com
www.musicconnection.com
Interviews, reviews, critiques and more!

Music Korner
210 E. Middle St., Gettysburg PA 17325
Geoff Melton musccorn@aol.com
members.aol.com/musccorn
A webzine devoted to reviewing and interviewing
bands of almost every style.

Music Dish Reviews
editor@musicdish.com
www.musicdish.com
Check our site to find out which reviewer best suits
your style of music.

Music Industry Newswire
PMB 822 PO Box 7000
Redondo Beach, CA 90277-8710
support@neotrope.com
www.musicindustrynewswire.com
News, reviews, events and rants from the music
business. We do accept CDs for review. These should
be sent with cover letter and contact information to
our street address.

Musicgoat.com
www.musicgoat.com
I am a blogger who has been around music his
entire life and would like to do what I can to help
deserving bands and artists gain exposure. I like
many styles of music and try to keep an open mind.

MusicPlayers.com
637 Wyckoff Ave. #349, Wyckoff, NJ 07481-1442
PH: 201-303-8201
Scott Kahn info@musicplayers.com
www.musicplayers.com
The premiere online magazine for serious musicians.
We offer a ton of useful content for indie musicians.

music-reviewer.com
www.music-reviewer.com
One of the largest, longest-running independent
music review zines on the internet, specializing in
indie material.

MuzikReviews.com
Keith "MuzikMan" Hannaleck
info@muzikreviews.com
www.muzikreviews.com
Providing reviews & indie publicity. These are paid
services. Visit our site for details.

Nada Mucho
6200 6th Ave. NW. #8
Seattle, WA 98107
KOZ
kyle_kauz@hotmail.com
www.nadamucho.com
Entertaining and educating
the MTV generation.

New Directions Cello Assoc.
123 Rachel Carson Way
Ithaca, NY 14850
PH/FX: 607-277-1686
info@
newdirectionscello.com
www.newdirectionscello.com
A network for Alternative or
Non Classical cello.

NewBeats
David newbeats1@aol.com
www.newbeats.com
A music magazine that
covers all types of music
...the more eclectic the
better.

The Night Owl
editor@thenightowl.com
www.thenightowl.com
Music reviews covering
from Rock to Jazz.

Night Times
PO Box 1747
Maryland Hts, MO 63043
PH: 314-542-9995
Julia Gordon-Bramer
wordgirl@nighttimes.com
www.nighttimes.com
Offering CD reviews, show
previews and artist
interviews. We support
local, regional, national
and international
musicians.

Nine5Four The Magazine
www.nine5four.com
An online magazine for
ALL unsigned talent. It's
not WHERE we live, it's
HOW we live.

No-Fi Magazine
1316 El Paso Dr.
Los Angeles, CA 90065
Attn: Reviews
Chris Beyond
nofimag@hotmail.com
www.nofimagazine.com
Generally, we like to
receive 2 copies of
everything (1 for review
and one for possible airplay
on No-Fi "Radio"). DO
NOT send us MP3s via e-
mail!

NowOnTour.com
218 Main St. #748
Kirkland, WA 98033
www.NowOnTour.com
*Tour and show listings,
record reviews of indie
bands and more.*

Nuevo Revolution
Staff@
NuevoRevolution.com
www.
NuevoRevolution.com
*Various news, interviews,
reviews and download-
able music tracks.*

NYLON Magazine
110 Greene St. #607
New York, NY 10012
PH: 212-226-6454
FX: 212-226-7738
www.nylonmag.com
*Consistently features
emerging artists and
unique talent before they
hit the mainstream.*

OnlineRock
2033 Ralston Ave. #50
Belmont, CA 94002
PH: 650-649-2304
info@onlinerock.com
www.onlinerock.com
*We offer CD reviews
which are perfect for
your press kit and
website. All types of
music accepted. Please
note that we take
submissions via our
website and you must
send in two copies of
your CD.*

Paste Magazine
PO Box 1606
Decatur, GA 30031
letters@
pastemagazine.com
www.pastemusic.com
*Promotes lesser-known
indie musicians of all
genres.*

Pause & Play
gerry@pauseandplay.com
www.pauseandplay.com
*Weekly Pop/Rock artist
interview column.*

Perfect Porridge
PO Box 46515, Eden
Prairie, MN 55344
greg@
perfectporridge.com
www.
perfectporridge.com
*A news and review site
covering music, film,
literature and art.*

Perfect Sound Forever
perfectsoundweb@ furious.com
www. perfectsoundforever.com
*Home of musical underdogs of all
styles. We respond to every inquiry we get.*

Performer Publications
www.performermag.com
*Produces 3 monthly regional magazines that
highlight the best unsigned musical acts from the
US.*

Performing Songwriter
2805 Azalea Pl. Nashville, TN 37204
PH: 615-385-7796 FX: 615-385-5637
Jessica Draper jessica@performingsongwriter.com
www.performingsongwriter.com
*Interviews, reviews, release spotlights and more.
Please be patient and continue to send us your new
releases.*

Pitchfork Media
1834 W. North Ave. #2, Chicago, IL 60622
FX: 773-395-5992
www.pitchforkmedia.com
Covers all styles and genres of music.

PlugInMusic.com
PO Box 429, Parkerford, PA 19457
Corinne corinne@pluginmusic.com
www.pluginmusic.com
*Band profiles, reviews, interviews and more. Check
our site for submission details. We are currently
looking for Rock, Punk, Electronic, Industrial etc.*

Pop Culture Press
PO Box 4990, Austin, TX 78765-4990
pcpinfo@gmail.com
www.popculturepress.com
Pop and the rest of the musical spectrum.

PopMatters
1555 Sherman Ave. #324, Evanston, IL 60201
Sarah Zupko editor@popmatters.com
www.popmatters.com
CD/concert reviews, artist interview and profiles.

PopZine
540 Templeton Cemetery Rd.
Paso Robles, CA 93446
questions@popzineonline.com
www.popzineonline.com
*Reviews, interviews, features and more. Please do
not e-mail us electronic press kits!*

Prefix Magazine
80 Cranberry St. #5A, Brooklyn, NY 11201
Dave Park dave@prefixmag.com
www.prefixmag.com
Reviews CDs and concerts.

Prick
PO Box 381, Tucker, GA 30085
PH: 770-723-9824
Lisa Sharer lisa@prickmag.net
www.prickmag.net
Reviews on regional and national bands.

pucknation dot com
271 Salisbury Sq. #104, Louisville, KY 40207
pucknation@hotmail.com
www.pucknation.com
Send your demo, CD or comic to review.

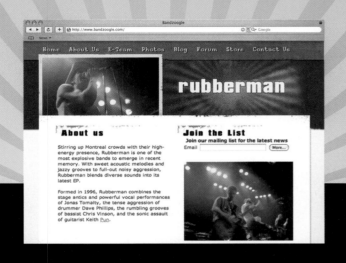

Online music community helping independent artists sell, promote and create ringtones with their own music!

MyMusicSite.com

Your Music! Your Site! MyMusicSite.com

MyMusicSite.com helps **You the independent artist sell your own music.** You can sell individual songs, albums or even have your fans, friends and family be able to instantly create ringtones for your original music. The next time a cell phone rings...have it be your song that is heard!

This is a FREE website and there are no contracts or commitments. Check it out for yourself at www.mymusicsite.com and take your career to the next level.

MyMusicSite.com also offers music lovers the ability to shop for independent music and discover new and hidden talent. Be the first to hear the hottest songs that will be tomorrow's mega hits at **www.mymusicsite.com.**

Ragazine
ragazine@oshradio.com
www.myspace.com/ragazine
Founded by music lovers and artists that believe together we can grow to be strong, successful and happy doing what we love.

Raised By The Music
302 Kentucky Ct. D-2, Lancaster, KY, 40444
PH: 606-669-7927
Gypsy Betty email@raisedbythemusic.com
www.RaisedByTheMusic.com
A blog that attempts to spread the word of indie artists to the general public through interviews and reviews. It serves to document the activities of unsigned, indie and newly signed musicians of all genres from around the world.

REAX Music Magazine
1614 N. 17th St. Ste. B, Tampa, FL 33605
PH: 813-766-1495 FX: 813-247-6975
reax@reaxmusic.com
www.reaxmusic.com
Published monthly and is available through local Tampa Bay businesses, music venues, restaurants, independent record stores and hotels.

The Red Alert
2118 Wilshire Blvd. #680, Santa Monica, CA 90403
Adam McKibbin info@theredalert.com
www.theredalert.com
Features interviews, album and concert reviews. See website for more explicit submission guidelines.

RetroRadar.com
401 E. Corporate Dr. #100, Lewisville, TX 75057
comments@retroradar.com
RetroRadar.com
Swing, Rockabilly, Surf, Lounge, Rock 'n Roll, Roots/R&B, Blues & Jazz standards. Send 2 copies of your CD.

Review You
www.ReviewYou.com
Have your album reviewed by a professional music journalist. This is a pay to get reviewed service.

Rocktober Magazine
1507 E. 53rd St. #617, Chicago, IL 60615
Jake Austen editor@roctober.com
www.roctober.com
Articles on obscure musicians in all genres of popular music.

Score! Music Magazine
Bands@ScoreMusicMagazine.com
www.scoremusicmagazine.com
To get your CD reviewed, fill out the submissions form on our website.

Shepizzle.com
1042 S. Anne Cir. Orem, UT 84058
jon@shepizzle.com
shepizzle.com
We dig music just as much as you do and we love the feeling of finding new music and sharing music that may be new to you.

Shotgun Reviews
Troy Brownfield psikotyk@aol.com
www.shotgunreviews.com
Special emphasis on Hip Hop, Britpop, Electronica and traditional Alternative.

The Silent Ballet
Jordan Volz.jordan@thesilentballet.com
thesilentballet.com
Online music zine with news and reviews. Contact me in regard to getting your material featured.

SIR Magazine
PH: 404-512-9741
FX: 678-556-9611
indie@sirmag.net
www.sirmag.net
We provide a totally unprecedented medium of exposure for highly talented artists and bands.

Skuawk!
moreinfo@skuawk.com
www.skuawk.com
A webzine where artists are creatively loud.

Slant Magazine
Sal Cinquemani
sal@slantmagazine.com
www.slantmagazine.com
Featuring reviews, editorials and critiques of a wide array of new and classic music and film.

Smother.Net
10835 Mayfield Trace Pl. Manassas, VA 20112
editor@smother.net
www.smother.net
Covers and reviews all genres of music. Please contact us before sending your material.

Southbound Beat
103 E. Main St.
Willow, OK 73673
PH: 580-287-3589
FX: 580-287-3590
Ray Carver
southboundbeat@yahoo.com
www.southboundbeat.com
CD reviews, interviews, columns & more. Please send (3) copies of your CD.

SOVIETPANDA
Peter
sovietpanda@gmail.com
www.sovietpanda.com
Rock 'n Roll news, reviews etc. Contact me for submission details.

sparkplugg.com
PO Box 5125
Richmond, VA 23220
sean@sparkplugg.com
sparkplugg.com
Please send all promotional materials to the above address.

SPIN Magazine
205 Lexington Ave. New York, NY 10016
PH: 212-231-7400 FX: 212-231-7312
feedback@spin.com
spin.com
Bringing you the absolute most in infotainment.

SquirrelFood.net
squirrelfoodmusic@gmail.com
www.squirrelfood.net
I'm just trying to share my love of great new music.

Static Multimedia
www.StaticMultiMedia.com
If you would like us to review a product, please send it our way.

Stomp and Stammer
PO Box 5440
Atlanta, GA 31107
PH: 404-880-0733
FX: 404-827-0905
www.stompandstammer.com
We cover a wide range of popular and not-so-popular music.

Stop Smiling
PO Box 577999
Chicago, IL 60657
PH: 773-342-1124
info@stopsmilingonline.com
www.stopsmilingonline.com
The magazine for high-minded lowlifes. Does one record review each issue.

The Synthesis
210 W. 6th St.
Chico, CA 95928
PH: 530-899-7708
www.thesynthesis.com
Thousands of pages of content, ranging from concert, CD and product reviews to MP3 downloads.

Synthesis Blog
210 W. 6th St., Chico, CA 95928
PH: 530-899-7708
Spencer Teilmann spencer@synthesis.net
blog.synthesis.net
We cover one new band every week day. It's available to all genres. Bands can submit themselves through Sonicbids www.sonicbids.com Our editors pick one artist per day to write about.

Talent in Motion Magazine
1011 Ave. of the Americas, 4th Fl.
New York, NY 10018
PH: 212-354-7189
talentinmotion@mindspring.com
timmag.com
Doesn't do reviews, but does feature a spotlight page on a new artist each issue.

Tiny Mix Tapes
submissions@tinymixtapes.com
www.tinymixtapes.com
For instructions on how and where to send materials, please e-mail us with a subject that reads "Interested in Submitting."

TotalFormat
www.totalformat.com/reviews
Covers a large variety of genres including Pop, Rock, Dance, Hip Hop, Metal etc.

The Tripwire
info@thetripwire.com
www.thetripwire.com
Supporting music for those in the industry that "genuinely care" and love music as much as we do.

Trouser Press
www.trouserpress.com
The "bible" of Alternative Rock since 1983.

Under the Radar
238 S. Tower Dr. #204, Beverly Hills, CA 90211
PH: 323-653-8705 FX: 323-658-5738
submissions@undertheradarmag.com
www.undertheradarmag.com
We're known for our in-depth and intelligent interviews and for our sharp photo shoots.

Unfinished
Hugh Miller hugh@liepaper.com
www.liepaper.com
I try to review everything I am sent, but cannot guarantee a write-up.

Upstage Magazine
PO Box 414, Stanhope, NJ 07874
PH: 908-391-0769
editor@upstagemagazine.com
www.upstagemagazine.com
Frequently features and reviews unsigned/independent artists.

Varla Magazine
PO Box 65978, Los Angeles, CA 90065-0978
PH: 213-484-6128
music@varla.com
www.varla.com
We cover everything. We will review your CDs.

Vintage Guitar
PO Box 7301, Bismarck, ND 58507
PH: 701-255-1197 FX: 701-255-0250
www.vintageguitar.com
Will review guitar oriented independent CDs.

West Coast Rockers
Leigh Davis leigh@westcoastrockers.com
www.westcoastrockers.com
We have helped many people along the way, and look forward to helping many more!

Wildy's World
152 Sunshine Dr. Amherst, NY 14228
Wildy wildysworld@gmail.com
wildysworld.blogspot.com
Whether we're giving you our insight into the latest in politics or introducing you to some of the best indie music out there, we're the place to be!

Canada

30music.com
#1404-10101 Saskatchewan Dr.
Edmonton, AB T6E 4R6
www.30music.com
We do our best to review everything received.

BangBang
355 Ste-Catherine W., 7th Fl.
Montréal, QB H3B 1A5
PH: 514-845-1658
info@bangbangtemort.com
bangbangtemort.com
Free alternative francophone cultural tabloid which follows both local and international scenes with equal treatment for all.

Being There Magazine
220 Viceroy Rd. #13, Concord, ON L4K 3C2
(US Office): Attn: Russell Bartholomee
PO Box 172174, Arlington, TX 76003-2174
PH: 647-881-8884 FX: 905-764-8367
Cari Crosby cari@beingtheremag.com
www.beingtheremag.com
An online music & film magazine for the literary minded. We include interviews, features and reviews.

Your whole world revolves around music.

That's why there's MusicPro.

Whether you're in the studio or on the road, protecting **your passion for music** has never been easier or more affordable. Thousands of music professionals rely on MusicPro to protect the tools of their trade.

We offer the advantage of one-stop shopping, low rates, flexible options and excellent service.

MusicPro offers specialized coverage for:
• Health Insurance
• Studio Liability
• Instrument & Equipment
• Classical Instruments
• Computers, Hardware & Software
• Tour Insurance
• Option to Cover Business Property

Our new website lets you effortlessly:
• Get a quick quote
• Manage your policy and account info
  in one convenient place
• Pay on-line for most insurance types

Get an affordable quote in seconds at:
WWW.MUSICPROINSURANCE.COM
or call 1.800.MUSICPRO

MusicPro INSURANCE®

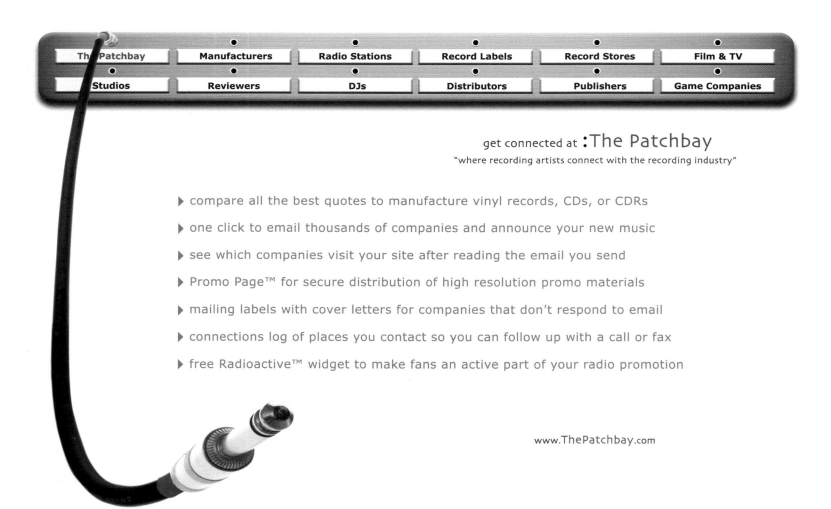

| The Patchbay | Manufacturers | Radio Stations | Record Labels | Record Stores | Film & TV |
| Studios | Reviewers | DJs | Distributors | Publishers | Game Companies |

get connected at :The Patchbay

"where recording artists connect with the recording industry"

▸ compare all the best quotes to manufacture vinyl records, CDs, or CDRs

▸ one click to email thousands of companies and announce your new music

▸ see which companies visit your site after reading the email you send

▸ Promo Page™ for secure distribution of high resolution promo materials

▸ mailing labels with cover letters for companies that don't respond to email

▸ connections log of places you contact so you can follow up with a call or fax

▸ free Radioactive™ widget to make fans an active part of your radio promotion

www.ThePatchbay.com

Broken Pencil
PO Box 203, Stn. P, Toronto, ON M5S 2S7
Sam Sutherland music@brokenpencil.com
www.brokenpencil.com
We cover zines, books, music, film/video and art produced with an indie attitude.

BullFrogMusic Reviews
PO Box 5041, Victoria, BC V8R 6N3
PH: 250-370-5448
Jeremiah Sutherland jeremiah@bullfrogmusic.com
frogblogreviews.bullfrogmusic.com
Comprises reviews of indie releases in Jazz, Blues, Folk, Pop, Early Music and Opera. Affiliated with BullFrogMusic.com.

Gasoline Magazine
www.bovineclub.com/gasoline
Covering the Rock & Roll community.

the GATE
www.thegate.ca
Reviews, interviews etc. Please contact us using our online form.

Guitar Noise
reviews@guitarnoise.com
www.guitarnoise.com
We review anything guitar related. Please check our site for submission guidelines!

Indieguitarists.com
PO Box 39174, 235 Dixon Rd.
Westown Plaza RPO, Etobicoke, ON M9P 3V2
Monica Yonge info@indieguitarists.com
www.indieguitarists.com
Contains spotlights, interviews, articles and news.

Indieville
PO Box 91017, 2901 Bayview Ave.
Toronto, ON M2K 1H0
PH: 514-262-2711
Matt Shimmer mattshimmer@gmail.com
www.indieville.com
Dedicated to independent music of all sorts. We review everything!

M Code Magazine
www.mcodeonline.com
Finally. A men's leisure magazine with market-wide appeal. As our tagline reads "every man has a code."

orcasound
5202 Mountain Sights, Montreal, QC H3W 2Y2
PH: 514-483-6722
info@orcasound.com
www.orcasound.com
Reports the hottest musical attractions and recordings.

Pulp Magazine
80 Glen Shields Ave. PO Box 49517
Concord, ON L4K 4P6
Tanya Bailey tanya@pulpmag.net
www.pulpmag.net
A shapeless, formless mass of rich media content that is adaptable to any change that exists outside of our control.

The Rock and Roll Report
rockandrollreport@gmail.com
www.rockandrollreport.com
If you're not sure if your music fits, send me a couple of MP3s using Dropload. Our preferred method of submission is through SonicBids
www.sonicbids.com

Soul Shine
Paul Whitfield
webmaster@soulshine.ca
www.soulshine.ca
News, features, reviews, gig listings and indie radio. E-mail us to set up a review.

Tambourine Magazine
tambourinemagazine.ca
Music: and everything nothing else is.

Tinfoil Music
Joe McGuire
theguy@tinfoil.net
www.tinfoilmusic.net
We review some CDs (depending on the genre). We also run press releases, tour info and CD release dates.

truth explosion magazine
538 Concord Ave. #3
Toronto, ON M6H 2R1
news@truthexplosion.com
www.truthexplosion.com
Indie Rock music reviews, interviews, gigs, news etc.

XS BS Magazine
PO Box 44145
6508 E. Hastings St.
Burnaby, BC V5B 4Y2
info@xs-bs.com
www.xs-bs.com
We are an independent Rock 'n Roll magazine covering major/indie artists from Europe, Canada and the US. We do features, interviews and reviews of new releases. Please visit our website for submission details.

Europe

Belgium

Keys & Chords
Alfons alfons.maes@keysandchords.com
www.keysandchords.com
Lots of reviews every issue. Covering Rock, Blues, Soul and Modern Jazz.

France

3AM Magazine
33 rue Jean Jaurès 93130
Noisy-le-Sec,
Paris, France
Andrew Gallix andrew@3ammagazine.com
www.3ammagazine.com
The hottest in online literature, entertainment and music. Please contact us before sending in your music.

Bokson
44 rue des Pyrénées, 75020 Paris, France
contact@bokson.net
www.bokson.net
Magazine des musiques Rock, Hip Hop Electro,
World. Interviews, chroniques, news.

bubblegum perfume
6 rue André Antoine, 75018 Paris, France
Violaine Schütz violaine.schutz@noos.fr
www.bubblegumperfume.ht.st
Fanzine in French about Twee Pop.

Dangerhouse
3 rue Thimonnier, 69001 Lyon, France
PH: 33-0-4-78-27-15-64 FX: 33-0-4-78-39-26-47
dangerhouse@numericable.fr
www.dangerhouse.fr
Comprehensive zine from a record store in France.

Inrockuptibles
24, rue Saint Sabin, 75011 Paris, France
PH: 01-42-44-16-16 FX: 01-42-44-16-00
www.lesinrocks.com
Online music and arts magazine.

Liability Webzine
6, allée de la Rance, 44 700 ORVAULT, France
Pondard Fabien fabien@liabilitywebzine.com
www.liabilitywebzine.com
Pop::Rock::Indé. Nous écoutons 90% des disques
que nous reçevons.

Nova Planet
33, rue du Faubourg Saint Antoine,
75011 Paris, France
PH: 01-53-33-22-94
webmaster@novaplanet.com
www.novaplanet.com
Consortium quotidien de culture underground.

POPnews
Guillaume Sautereau popscene@popnews.com
www.popnews.com
We are very keen on discovering new talents.

Premonition
12, rue Lapeyrère, 75018 Paris, France
PH: +33-1-4252-4205
www.premonition.fr
Our purpose is to give everyone the opportunity to
hear independent bands express themselves.

sefronia
info@sefronia.com
www.sefronia.com
A free CD review e-mail magazine.

Germany

CD-KRITIK.DE
Postfach 12 02 37, 27516 Bremerhaven, Germany
PH: 04706-41-28-13
redaktion@cd-kritik.de
www.cd-kritik.de
Wir beschreiben Ihnen die CDs, aber die Wahl
haben Sie.

Discover
Im Erpelgrund 80, 13503 Berlin, Germany
PH: +49-30-39932240
André Esch andre@discover.de
www.discover.de
CDs, stories, interviews ...

Flaming Youth
Marceese Trabus marceese@flamingyouth.de
www.flamingyouth.de
Rock musik magazin mit aktuellen album
rezensionen und veranstaltungstipps,
konzertberichten ...

Guitars Galore
Postfach 41 03 11, 12113 Berlin, Germany
Mike Korbik mail@twang-tone.de
www.twang-tone.de/gg.html
A flyer zine and monthly radio show as well.

Indie Music Review
Frobenstrasse 74, D-12249 Berlin, Germany
Don Nelson info@indiemusicreview.net
www.indiemusicreview.net
All genres of popular music including: Pop, Rock,
World music, Folk, Reggae, Hip Hop and New Age.
We are also looking for writers, reviewers and music
journalists.

indiepoprock.net
contact@indiepoprock.net
www.indiepoprock.net
Chroniques, interviews, live reports, labels etc.

Music-Scan Zine
Postbox 41 05 11, 34067 Kassel, Germany
info@music-scan.de
www.music-scan.de
Tons of news, reviews, interviews, contests, links and
information.

Plattentests Online
Grillparzerstraße 9, 81675 München, Germany
PH: 0176-24432675
Armin Linder armin@plattentests.de
www.plattentests.de
Das Beste aus Rock und independent!

PNG *(Persona Non Grata)*
Postfach 30 14 38, 04254 Leipzig, Germany
PH: 0341-49-25-178
Jana Klaus redaktion@png-online.de
png-online.de
News, reviews, interviews and more.

Rote Raupe*
Kirchenstr. 85, 81675 München, Germany
www.roteraupe.de
Indie webzine that does CD reviews, interviews,
concert photography and concert reviews.

TweeNet
c/o Peter Hahndorf, Pastorenweg 140, 28237
Bremen, Germany
www.twee.net
Submit your music and a press release to us.

VISIONS.de
Märkische Straße 115-117, 44141 Dortmund,
Germany
PH: 0231-557131-0 FX: 0231-557131-31
www.visions.de
Musikmagazin für Alternative musik

Greece

Scream Magazine
Saradaporou 45, 26223 Patra, Hellas, Greece
PH: 2610-422801
Spiros scream_zine@yahoo.com
www.scream.gr
Covers Rock, Jazz and Blues.

Italy

Rockit
artisti@rockit.it
www.rockit.it
Tutta roba Italiana.

Onda Rock
info@ondarock.it
www.ondarock.it
News and reviews.

Sodapop
www.sodapop.it
News, reviews, demos etc.

Three Monkeys
Via Tagliapietre 14, Bologna 40123, Italy
www.threemonkeysonline.com
Current affairs/music magazine with interviews and
reviews. Please submit your music using SonicBids
www.sonicbids.com

The Netherlands

3voor12
3voor12@vpro.nl
www.3voor12.nl
Features, shows, reviews etc.

Amsterdam Weekly
West-Indisch Pakhuis. 's-Gravenhekje 1A,
1011 TG Amsterdam, The Netherlands
PH: +31 (0)20-522-5200 FX: +31 (0)20-620-1666
info@amsterdamweekly.nl
www.amsterdamweekly.nl
Inside: Music, Film, Arts, Theatre.

HEAVEN
bladmanager@heaven.be
www.heaven.be
Popmagazine voor volwassenen.

Kinda Muzik You Like
Postbus 10614, 1001 EP Amsterdam,
The Netherlands
redactie@kindamuzik.net
www.kindamuzik.net
Giving Underground music the attention it deserves.

MusicRemedy.com
www.musicremedy.com
Send in your music so we can review it.

OOR
Postbus 9308, 1006 AH Amsterdam,
The Netherlands
info@oor.nl
www.oor.nl
News, reviews, events calendar and more.

Norway

Luna Kafe
PO Box 2175, Grunerlokka, 0505 Oslo, Norway
lunar@fuzzlogic.com
www.fuzzlogic.com/lunakafe
Record reviews, concert reviews, interviews and
more. We also have reviewers in the UK and the US
that you can send your CD to.

Spain

BuscaMusica.org
PO Box 440 - Jaen 23080, Spain
webmaster@buscamusica.org
www.buscamusica.org
Electronic magazine, band promotion and new indie
label. Upload your music!

La Ganzua, Radio Obradoiro
Preguntoiro, 29. 15702, Santiago de Compostela,
A Coruña, Spain
PH: 981-543766-64
www.laganzua.net
*E-zine de música independiente con noticias,
conciertos, festivales, crónicas, entrevistas, MP3,
discos, maquetas ...*

Indy Rock
info@indyrock.es
www.indyrock.es
News, reviews, concerts, festivals etc.

Manerasdevivir.com
info@manerasdevivir.com
www.manerasdevivir.com
*Punto de ecuentro de todos los amantes del
rocanrol. Noticias muy actualizadas, MP3 y
conciertos.*

Muzikalia.com
PO Box 5176, 47080 Valladolid, Spain
PH: 93-415-29-47
www.muzikalia.com
Completísima web de música independiente.

Space Rock Heaters
spacerockheaters@hotmail.com
spacerockheaters.com
*Webzine creado en Cáceres con las últimas noticias
sobre conciertos, grupos y festivales.*

thebellemusic.com
contacto@thebellemusic.com
www.thebellemusic.com
*Revista musical Independiente: crónicas de
conciertos, cometarios de discos, novedades,
noticias, entrevistas y mucho más.*

Sweden

melodic.net
Ola Hanssonsgatan 1, s-11252 Stockholm, Sweden
Johan Wippsson wippsson@melodic.net
www.melodic.net
Reviews, interviews and "Artist of the Week."

Musikermagasinet
PH: 031-775-65-54
Mats Grundberg mats@hansenmedia.se
www.musikermagasinet.com
The largest music magazine in Scandinavia.

Passagen
Gustav IIIs Boulevard 40, 169 87 Stockholm,
Sweden
www.passagen.se
Forum for indie artists.

Zero Music Magazine
Box 2002, 403 11 Gothenburg, Sweden
info@zeromagazine.nu
www.zeromagazine.nu
Pop and Electronica music magazine.

United Kingdom

AngryApe
info@angryape.com
www.angryape.com
*Music news, reviews, interviews. Do not attach
MP3s. Must be NEW material!*

Artrocker Magazine
43 Chute House, Stockwell Park Rd. Brixton,
SW9 0DW UK
artrockercontent@gmail.com
artrocker.com
*Rock n' Roll reviews, features, gigs, listings and
MP3s.*

Atomic Duster
nick.j@atomicduster.com
www.atomicduster.com
Music, news, reviews, interviews and competitions.

Audio Junkies
jedshepherd@gmail.com
www.audiojunkies.net
*One of The UK's largest online communities. News,
reviews, features etc.*

Beatmag
PO Box 4653, Worthing, BN11 9FG UK
PH: 0044-1903-539310
Thomas H. Green thomas@beathut.com
www.beatmag.net
*The official magazine for Beathut.com the
independent legal MP3 download site.*

Clash Magazine
29 D Arblay St., London, W1F 8EP UK
PH: 020-7734-9351
www.clashmusic.com
*Covering the best of breaking to established artists
alongside news, reviews, features, image gallery and
forums.*

Clown Magazine
Suite 3, Rosden House, 372 Old Street, London,
EC1V 9AU UK
office@clownmagazine.co.uk
www.clownmagazine.co.uk
*Thanks to all the folks you have contacted us and to
those in the industry for sending music material for
reviews. We say keep it coming!*

DirtyZine
dirtyzine.co.uk
*An Alternative Rock zine. Reviews, interviews,
downloads of the month. Contact us for mailing
info.*

Diskant
www.diskant.net
*A network of websites by independent fanzines,
bands and record labels. Please check our
submission details to see which reviewer fits your
music.*

Drowned in Sound
1 Chilworth Mews, London, W2 3RG UK
www.drownedinsound.com
Reviews, gigs, downloads, features and more.

Excellent Online.com
www.excellentonline.com
The home for North American fans of UK music.

Fact Magazine
info@factmagazine.co.uk
www.factmagazine.co.uk
*Provides a platform for talented young musicians,
artists and designers.*

FemaleFirst.co.uk
www.femalefirst.co.uk
*Women's lifestyle magazine that creates an unique
environment for women of all ages. Includes indie
music reviews, discussion board etc.*

get ready to ROCK!
www.getreadytorock.com
*Classic and Progressive Rock music news, reviews
and interviews.*

ilikemusic.com *Soundstage*
#404, Solent Business Ctr. Millbrook Road W.,
Millbrook, Southampton, Hampshire,
SO15 0HW UK
PH: +44 (0)845-430-8651
www.ilikemusic.com
*Reviews of unsigned talent, music promotion
articles, tips and links galore.*

is this music?
PO Box 13516, Linlithgow, EH49 6AS UK
Stuart McHugh editor@isthismusic.com
www.isthismusic.com
A Scottish music monthly that covers indie music.

Jamble Magazine
editor@jamblemag.co.uk
www.jamblemag.co.uk
*Music and travel zine focusing on the best up and
coming acts from around the world.*

The Line of Best Fit
www.thelineofbestfit.com
*Please feel free to contact using our online form
with any news, requests or material to review. Due
to the large amounts of email we receive, we are
unable to respond to every message, however every
single one is read.*

The Music Maker Association
28 Grafton Ter. London, NW5 4JJ UK
www.musicmakerassociation.co.uk
*Promotes the work of songwriters and independent
recording artists, covering all styles from Folk to
Country, Blues, Rock, Jazz and World music.
Members are profiled in our magazine and their
CDs reviewed by independent writers.*

Music News
17b Charteris Rd. London, N4 3AA UK
Marco Gandolfi marco@music-news.com
www.music-news.com
*News, reviews, interviews and the latest releases &
gossip from the current music scene.*

music week
Ludgate House, 245 Blackfriars Rd. London,
SE1 9LS UK
feedbackmusicweek@musicweek.com
www.musicweek.com
Music, news, charts, reviews, analysis, features.

MusicOMH.com
John Murphy john.murphy@musicOMH.com
www.musicomh.com
*Established reviews and interviews site. Contact us
before you send your music!*

New Music Express
news@nme.com
www.nme.com
Reviews, interviews, quotes…

noize makes enemies .co.uk
17 Haddeo Dr. Exeter, Devon, EX2 7PE UK
info@noizemakesenemies.co.uk
www.noizemakesenemies.co.uk
*Live and recorded music reviews, artist interviews
and news, focusing on innovative and cutting edge
new music while promoting a variety of musical
genres.*

Nunuworld
nunununa@nunuworldmusic.co.uk
www.nunuworldmusic.co.uk
Covers indie music with reviews, photos etc.

PHASE9 Entertainment
Nigel editorial@phase9tv.net
www.phase9.tv
Independent site for reviews and information on music and movies in the UK and USA.

Plan B Magazine
156-158 Grays Inn Rd. London, WC1X 8ED UK
PH: 020-7278-5070
Lauren Strain lauren@planbmag.com
www.planbmag.com
Reviews include all the music and culture we love, not just that being ignored elsewhere.

PLAYLOUDER
8-10 Rhoda St., London, E2 7EF UK
www.playlouder.com
Bringing you the very best in new music.

Popjustice
31 Chelsea Wharf, Lots Rd. London, SW10 0QJ UK
PH: 020-7352-9444
newmusic@popjustice.com
www.popjustice.com
Pop news, MP3s, single features etc. Also a monthly podcast.

rawkstar.net
www.rawkstar.net
Reviews of new releases, demos, live gigs, interviews etc.

Record Scout
17 High St., Southend on Sea, Essex, SS1 1JE UK
www.recordscout.com
We write music reviews for many magazines around the country and the bands we review will instantly receive national publicity.

Review Centre Indie *Music*
www.reviewcentre.com/products1684.html
Read about indie albums and contribute your comments or reviews, to help others discover new music.

reviewed4u.com
www.reviewed4u.com
Music, DVD, gig reviews and music news.

ROCK SOUND
Unit 22, Jack's Pl. 6 Corbet Pl. Spitalfields, London, E1 6NN UK
Rachel rachel.kellehar@rock-sound.net
www.rock-sound.net
Bringing you all the best new music from around the world.

Rock's Backpages
www.rocksbackpages.com
News, reviews and interviews of new artists.

rockcity.co.uk
8 Talbot St., Nottingham, NG1 5GG UK
amy@rock-city.co.uk
www.rock-city.co.uk
Reviews of both signed and unsigned recorded material and live shows.

RockFeedback.com
PO Box 704, High Wycombe, HP15 7GL UK
www.rockfeedback.com
Contact us to get featured on the site.

Shadders Online / Shadders? On me Lungs?
www.shaddersonline.com
We feature up and coming plus established UK artists.

Shindig
64 North View Rd. London, N8 7LL UK
info@shindig-magazine.com
www.shindig-magazine.com
Reviews Psych and Garage. No plain old indie/Alt-Rock.

Sonic Dice
contact@sonicdice.com
www.sonicdice.com
Our mission is to bring you reviews of recent gigs and tours, the latest album and single releases, as well as find out the inside track with plenty of band interviews.

state51
Rhoda St., London, E2 7EF UK
www.state51.co.uk
Showcasing the best new music in all genres.

Subba-Cultcha
www.subba-cultcha.com
CD, demo, live and DVD reviews, interviews, podcasts and more!

Tastyzine
submissions@tastyfanzine.org.uk
www.tastyfanzine.org.uk
Recommending the soundtrack for the revolution.

This Is Fake DIY
3rd Fl. 74 Great Eastern St., London, EC2A 3JL UK
editor@thisisfakediy.co.uk
www.thisisfakediy.co.uk
If you're desperate for us to listen to you or your pet hamster's band, get in touch.

Uncut Magazine
4th Fl. Blue Fin Bldg. Southwark St., London, SE1 0SU UK
PH: 020-3148-6985
John Robinson john_robinson@ipcmedia.com
www.uncut.co.uk/music
Reviews CDs of major and independent artists.

Unsung / Head Heritage
PO Box 1140, Calne, Wiltshire, SN11 8XQ UK
Julian Cope info@headheritage.co.uk
www.headheritage.co.uk/unsung
A repository for lost and unchampioned Rock'n' Roll.

Whisperin & Hollerin
Cosheen, Schull, Co Cork, Ireland
Tim Peacock tim@whisperinandhollerin.com
www.whisperinandhollerin.com
Music reviews and interviews with an Alternative bias - covers a huge range of genres.

worldwidereview.com
rudi@worldwidereview.com
www.worldwidereview.com
Anyone can write a review, anywhere in the world, about anything. It will appear on our site immediately.

The Indie Link Exchange

www.indielinkexchange.com/ile

Australia

Alternate Music Press
PO Box 2286, Ringwood N., VIC 3134 Australia
www.alternatemusicpress.com
Reviews, interviews etc. Please DO NOT send Rock, Alternative or Pop music!

Blunt Review
emily@bluntreview.com
www.bluntreview.com
We review indie music and interview musicians.

Buzz Magazine
psuttonh@ozonline.com.au
www.buzzmagazine.com.au
Features interviews with Australian and international artists, reviews and columns.

Long Gone Loser
damomusclecar@hotmail.com
www.myspace.com/longgoneloser
Feel free to send anything for review.

Sound the Sirens
brokenstar@gmail.com
www.soundthesirens.com
Send your CD in for review. Please check our submission policy.

Asia

BigO
PO Box 784, Marine Parade, Singapore 914410
PH: 63484007 FX: 63480362
mybigo@bigozine.com
www.bigo.com.sg
Features more than 150 reviews each issue.

Juice
www.juicemusic.com
Japanese based magazine featuring news and reviews.

Metropolis
3F Maison Tomoe Bldg. 3-16-1 Minami-Aoyama, Minato-Ku, Tokyo 107 Japan
PH: 81-3-3423-6932 FX: 81-3-3423-6931
letters@metropolis.co.jp
www.metropolis.co.jp
Japan's #1 English magazine. CD reviews and tour announcements in the music section.

Smashing Mag
Koichi Hanafusa info@smash-jpn.com
smashingmag.com
An independent Japanese online music magazine.

Blues

North America

United States

Blues Blowtorch
RR 2, Box 5, Clinton, IL 61727-9802
PH: 217-935-8603
Frank deltafrank@bluesblowtorch.com
www.bluesblowtorch.com
Promoting the Blues in all its forms.

Blues Bytes
Bruce Coen bluesbytes-info@bluenight.com
www.bluenight.com/BluesBytes
A monthly Blues CD review magazine.

Blues Guitar News
PO Box 2077, Benton, AR 72018
mike@bluesguitarnews.com
BluesGuitarNews.com
Read by thousands of discerning Blues enthusiasts worldwide.

Blues Music Now!
Jeff Stevens editor@bluesmusicnow.com
www.bluesmusicnow.com
Contact us about sending your CD in for review.

Blues Revue
Rte. 1, Box 75, Salem, WV 26426-9604
PH: 304-782-1971 FX: 304-782-1993
info@bluesrevue.com
www.bluesrevue.com
Artist profiles, interviews, reviews and more.

Blues Rocks The World
Paul Bondarovski editor@bluesrocks.net
www.bluesrocks.net
An international independent Blues music magazine.

Big City Rhythm & Blues Magazine
PO Box 1805, Royal Oak, MI 48068
PH: 248-582-1544 FX: 248-582-8242
blues@bigcitybluesmag.com
www.bigcitybluesmag.com
In-depth articles, interviews and CD reviews.

Bluesrockers
Tom Branson tom@bluesrockers.ws
www.bluesrockers.ws
Information and reviews on the best artists and recordings available.

Blueswax.com
www.blueswax.com
Reviews, industry news, interviews and MP3s.

Cross Harp Chronicles
PO Box 6283, Jackson, MI 49204
PH: 517-569-2615 FX: 517-569-8664
Dave King dking@crossharpchronicles.com
crossharpchronicles.com
Interviews with harmonica/Blues movers and shakers, concert news, CD reviews etc.

Electric Blues
PO Box 1370, Riverview, FL 33568-1370
herm@electricblues.com
www.electricblues.com
CD reviews, news and more.

Living Blues Magazine
PO Box 1848, 301 Hill Hall, University, MS 38677
PH: 800-390-3527 FX: 662-915-7842
www.livingblues.com
A bimonthly magazine for the Blues.

Mary4Music.com
blewzzman@aol.com
www.mary4music.com
Blues, Indie Rock & DIY music links, musician's resources, reviews and band listings.

Canada

Blues Reviewer Tim Holek
www.timholekblues.ca
Currently his writing and photography is regularly published in Living Blues magazine, Blues Beat magazine, Southwest Blues magazine, Blues Bytes website, Blues Art Journal website, Twoj Blues Magazine, Amazon.com, Chicago Blues Guide website, and The Great Lakes Blues Society newsletter and website.

Real Blues Magazine
PO Box 1201, Victoria, BC V8W 2T6
Andy andy@realbluesmagazine.com
www.realbluesmagazine.com
If you have a CD or DVD you would like considered for review, please send it to me.

Europe

Austria

BluesArtStudio
A-1223 Vienna, PO Box 54, Austria
bluesart@bluesart.at
www.bluesartstudio.at
Supporting and promoting the Blues.

Belgium

Back to the Roots
Joseph Wautersstraat 25, 8200 Sint-Michiels, Belgium
PH: 32-0-478-306-325 FX: 32-0-50-27-58-87
backtotheroots.franky@scarlet.be
www.backtotheroots.be
Is een nederlandstalig magazine voor Blues en aanverwante muziekstijlen.

Germany

Blues News Magazine
Verlag Dirk Föhrs, Freiherr-vom-Stein-Str. 28, D-58762 Altena, Germany
PH: 0-23-52-21-68-0
Redaktion@Blues-Germany.de
www.blues-germany.de
News, reviews, events etc.

Italy

Blues and Blues
info@bluesandblues.it
www.bluesandblues.it
The Italian Blues website.

Poland

Twoj Blues Magazine
ul. Klonowa 8, 41-506 Chorzów, Poland
PH: +48-032-246-25-26
twojblues@delta.art.pl
www.delta.art.pl
The only Polish magazine entirely devoted to Blues. Each issue brings CD, DVD and books reviews, interviews with Polish & foreign artists and feature articles.

Spain

La Hora del Blues Reviews
Apartado de Correos 12.085, 08080 Barcelona, Spain
Vicente P. Zumel zumel@lahoradelblues.com
www.lahoradelblues.com/criticas.htm
Reviews are done monthly. Send 2 copies.

Sweden

Jefferson
Solbergsgatan 16 A, 664 30 Grums, Sweden
Ingemar Karlsson 41451karlsson@telia.com
jeffersonbluesmag.com
Administered by the Scandinavian Blues Assoc.

United Kingdom

Blues In Britain
10, Messaline Ave. London, W3 6JX UK
PH: 44-0-20-8723-7376 FX: 44-0-20-8723 7380
Jon Taylor info@bluesinbritain.org
www.blueprint-blues.co.uk
Blues news, reviews and interviews and a four page gig guide to Blues events in the UK.

Blues Matters!
PO Box 18, Bridgend, CF33 6YW UK
PH: 44-0-1656-743406
info@bluesmatters.com
www.bluesmatters.com
Old, New, Traditional, Nu and any other type of Blues.

Juke Blues
PO Box 1654, Yatton, Bristol, BS49 4FD UK
juke@jukeblues.com
www.bluesworld.com/JukeBlues.html
Interviews, news, reviews, gig guide and more.

Children's

Children's Music that Rocks
Warren Truitt paulmccartney@teacher.com
www.kidsmusicthatrocks.blogspot.com
Music for kids that doesn't make adults want to rip their hair out.

Edutaining Kids *Guide to Children's Music*
stephanie@edutainingkids.com
www.edutainingkids.com/music.html
Articles, spotlights, reviews etc.

John Wood Revue
4841 Whitsett Ave. #11, Valley Village, CA 91607
john@kidzmusic.com
www.kidzmusic.com
A great place to find some of the best Children's music.

The Lovely Mrs. Davis Tells You What to Think
Amy Davis thelovelymrsdavis@gmail.com
thelovelymrsdavis.com
Submit children's music and media for review to the above address.

Zooglobble
Stefan Shepherd zooglobble@earthlink.net
www.zooglobble.com
Children and family music reviews. Music for the kids that parents won't hate!

THE **Indie**
VENUE
bible
32,000
Live Music Venues
in the US and Canada!!
www.indievenuebible.com

Christian

North America

United States

95one.com
Rick Summers rick@95one.com
95one.com
Helps promote Christian indie bands and artists.

Angelic Warlord
PO Box 83406, Phoenix, AZ 85071
Andrew angelicwarlord@hotmail.com
www.angelicwarlord.com
Your Christian Metal and Hard Rock resource!

ChristianMusicDaily.com
PO Box 654, E. Amherst, NY 14051
Mark Weber mark@christianmusicdaily.com
christianmusicdaily.com
Offers Christian and Gospel music news, reviews and interviews with famous and independent artists.

CatholicMusicNetwork.com
www.catholicmusicnetwork.com
Source for music by today's top Catholic artists.

Christianity Today
465 Gunderson Dr. Carol Stream, IL 60188
PH: 630-260-6200 FX: 630-260-0114
music@christianitytoday.com
christianmusictoday.com
News, interviews and reviews. We only review the best of what we receive.

ChristianRocker.com
ChristianRocker.com
A perfect way to share your gifts to the world. News, reviews, downloads and more.

Christian Rockers Online
C.W. Ross cw@christianrockersonline.com
www.christianrockersonline.com
We review all styles of Christian Music on our site. Everything from modern worship and contemporary to Rock, Punk and Metal.

Contemporary Christian Magazine
104 Woodmont Blvd. #300, Nashville, TN 37205
www.ccmcom.com
Supporting indie Christian bands.

CreatorsWeb
Ken Mowery ken@creatorsweb.com
www.creatorsweb.com
Reviews independent musicians.

Eager Magazine
contactus@eagermagazine.com
www.eagermagazine.com
Independent Gospel artists are encouraged to submit music to the magazine through email or press release links.

Gospel Engine *The Gospel Zone*
www.thegospelzone.com
Reviews, news, message boards and upcoming events.

Gospel Synergy Magazine
www.gospelsynergy.com
Stay in the know about new independent Gospel and Christian artists.

Gospel Today
286 Hwy. 314 Ste. C, Fayetteville, GA 30214
PH: 770-719-4825 FX: 770-716-2660
gospeltodaymag@aol.com
www.gospeltoday.com
New Gospel CDs, record sales charts etc.

GospelFlava.com
info@gospelflava.com
www.gospelflava.com
Reviews new CD and video Gospel releases.

Hip Hop For The Soul
TRu bdg@trudatmusic.com
hiphopforthesoul.com
To have your album considered for review, contact me.

HM Magazine
PO Box 367, Hutto, TX 78634
PH: 512-989-7309 FX: 512-670-2764
Doug Van Pelt dvanpelt@hmmag.com
www.hmmagazine.com
Features interviews, news and reviews of Hard Music. Send 2 copies (if possible).

Jesusfreakhideout.com
PO Box 559, Bethlehem, PA 18016-0559
www.jesusfreakhideout.com
One of the world's largest Christian music online resources. Our Indie Review Submission Service is $40.

Joy Comes E-Zine and Radio Show
Dr. Anita McLaughlin amministriesinc@aol.com
www.orgsites.com/ma/joycomesradio
A radio show and e-zine open to visual artists, poets, rappers, playwrights, creative people who need a place to display their gifts.

Music Spectrum
c/o Immanuel Lutheran Church,
13445 W. Hampton Ave. Brookfield, WI 53005
PH: 262-781-7140
Benjamin Squires benjamin@ musicspectrum.org
www.musicspectrum.org
Reviewing music across the spectrum of styles. Connecting secular and Christian music to the Christian faith.

NeuFutur
650 Morris #6
Kent, OH 44243
James McQuiston
editor@neufutur.com
www.neufutur.com
Covers anything from Christian praise to Death Metal. Fight on, little ones.

Opus' Album Reviews
www.opuszine.com
If you'd like to send in a demo, please contact me. Also, a brief bio about your band, influences etc. would be helpful.

Phantom Tollboth
W147N9991 Emerald Ln.
Germantown, WI 53022-6617
Shari Lloyd shari@tollbooth.org
tollbooth.org
Album, concert and movie reviews, interviews, features and resource links.

Power Source
PO Box 101336, Nashville, TN 37224
PH: 615- 742-9210 FX: 615-248-8505
Vickie Gardner vickie@powersourcemagazine.com
www.powersourcemusic.com
Official publication of The Christian Country Music Assoc.

RELEVANT Magazine
1220 Alden Rd. Orlando, FL 32803
PH: 407-660-1411 FX: 407-401-9100
www.relevantmagazine.com
Covering God, life and progressive culture.

Singing News Magazine
PO Box 2810, 330 University Hall Dr.
Boone, NC 28607
PH: 828-264-3700 FX: 828-264-4621
www.singingnews.com
Concerts, new recordings and the latest chart action.

SouthernGospelNews.com
220 Indian Park Dr. #1501
Murfreesboro, TN 37128
Attn: Reviews
sogospelnews.com
News, information, artist interviews, CD reviews and more!

Sphere of Hip Hop
3803 4th Pl. NW., Rochester, MN 55901
Attn: Josh Niemyjski
www.sphereofhiphop.com
Featured items: MP3, reviews, articles and more!

Tastyfresh
4380 Iris Brooke Ln. Snellville, GA 30039
www.tastyfresh.com
Christ centered DJ culture.

Transparent Chrstian Magazine
103 Orchard Valley Cir. Hendersonville, TN 37075
Jason Elkins Jason@TransparentYou.com
www.transparentchristianmagazine.com
When our lives reflect the brightest Light, we become transparent.

VictoryZine
victory@victoryzine.com
www.victoryzine.com
Your place on the internet to find the latest stuff about the Christian Metal scene.

Canada

FEED
400 Delaney Dr. Ajax, ON L1T 3Y7
PH: 647-722-4306 FX: 866-871-1914
editorial@feedstop.com
www.feedstop.com
Your source for the best in beats, rhymes & light.

GospelCity.com
1410 Stanley, #1020, Montreal, QC H3A 1P8
PH: 514-868-1600 FX: 514-868-1067
reviews@gospelcity.com
gospelcity.com
News, reviews, articles and more!

E u r o p e
Germany

BandsOnFire
www.bandsonfire.com
*It looks like Hardcore has almost lost its spirit and
has become more adapted to the norms of society
with its false ideals and values. BandsOnFire has
decided not to give in to this ongoing downward
spiral.*

United Kingdom

United by ONE
PO Box 3093, South Croydon, CR2 0YB UK
PH: +44 (0) 20-8681-8339
info@unitedbyone.co.uk
www.unitedbyone.co.uk
Urban Gospel site from the UK to the world.

Classical

N o r t h A m e r i c a
United States

andante.com
200 Park Ave. S. #910, New York, NY 10003
andante.com
News, reviews, concert reviews, essays and more.

Bass World
14070 Proton Rd. #100, Dallas, TX 75244
PH: 972-233-9107 x204 FX: 972-490-4219
info@isbworldoffice.com
www.isbworldoffice.com
Reviews recordings and music internationally.

Chamber Music Magazine
305 7th Ave. 5th Fl. New York, NY 10001
PH: 212-242-2022 FX: 212-242-7955
www.chamber-music.org
*Send new CDs and books, as well as press releases
by mail.*

Classical CD Review
bob@classicalcdreview.com
www.classicalcdreview.com
*We review CDs we feel are of particular interest to
us and to our readers.*

Classics Today
David Hurwitz dhurwitz@classicstoday.com
www.classicstoday.com
Five feature reviews per day.

The Detritus Review
Empiricus synapticsoup@gmail.com
detritusreview.blogspot.com
*Music's ivory tower laughs hard, falls over, soils
pants.*

Early Music America
2366 Eastlake Ave. E. #429, Seattle, WA 98102
PH: 206-720-6270 FX: 206-720-6290
info@earlymusic.org
earlymusic.org
Artist profiles, interview and record reviews.

La Folia
Mike Silverton editor@lafolia.com
www.lafolia.com
*We do review independent CDs. They MUST be
Classical, Old and New or Jazz other than
mainstream.*

The Horn Call
School of Music, W. Michigan U.
Kalamazoo, MI 49008
PH: 269-387-4692 FX: 269-387-1113
editor@hornsociety.org
www.hornsociety.org
News, feature articles, clinics, music and reviews.

NewMusicBox
30 W. 26th St. #1001, New York, NY 10010
editor@newmusicbox.org
www.newmusicbox.org
*Features any new CD that includes repertoire by
American composers.*

Online Trombone Journal
PO Box 1758, Starkville, MS 39760
PH: 662-325-8021
articles@trombone.org
www.trombone.org
*Provides trombonists a place to share information
about trombone pedagogy and performance.*

The Rambler
tim.johnson77@btopenworld.com
johnsonsrambler.wordpress.com
*As a rule, I like drones, thick chords, rich
production/orchestration, brashness/poor taste, and
a pinch of cultural significance.*

Renaissance Magazine
1 Controls Dr., Shelton, CT 06484
PH: 800-232-2224 FX: 800-775-2729
Jonathan Kantrowitz
ladyjanet@renaissancemagazine.com
renaissancemagazine.com
*We accept music from the Middle Ages and
Renaissance time periods for review.*

Sequenza21
340 W. 57th St. 12B, New York, NY 10019
PH: 212-582-3791
Jerry sequenza21@gmail.com
www.sequenza21.com
News, interviews and featured composers.

Strings Magazine
PO Box 767, San Anselmo, CA 94979
PH: 415-485-6946 FX: 415-485-0831
strings@pcspublink.com
www.stringsmagazine.com
For the violin, viola, cello, bass or fiddle.

Violinist.com
PH: 626-793-6577
www.violinist.com
*News, reviews and resources. Feel free to promote
your upcoming concerts or CD releases.*

World Guitarist
1000 W. Foothill Blvd. Glendora, CA 91741
Gunnar Eisel geisel@citruscollege.edu
www.worldguitarist.com
*Daily news coverage for the world Classical Guitar
community.*

Canada

La Scena Musicale
5409 Waverly, Montréal, QC H2T 2X8
PH: 514-948-2520 FX: 514-274-9456
info@scena.org
www.scena.org
Publishes reviews from independent artists.

E u r o p e
Czech Republic

His Voice
Besedni 3 118 00 Praha 1, Czech Republic
PH: 420-257-312-422 FX: 420-257-317-424
www.hisvoice.cz
Festivals and reviews of contemporary music.

France

Guitare Classique
www.myspace.com/guitareclassique
*Le magazine N°1 sur la guitare classique. Avec son
CD-ROM de vidéos pédagogiques et son CD audio.*

Germany

Crescendo
Senefelderstraße 14, 80336 München, Germany
PH: 49-0-89-74-15-09-0 FX: 49-0-89-74-15-09-11
crescendo@portmedia.de
www.crescendo-online.de
Deutschlands Klassik magazin

klassik.com
Lörracher Strasse 39a, D-79115 Freiburg, Germany
PH: +49-761-4587-317-0 FX: +49-761-4587-317-9
www.klassik.com
*Klassik-portal mit umfangreichen Informationen zur
Klassischen musik*

Klassik-Heute.com
Jägerstraße 17, Hörgertshausen, 85413, Germany
PH: 49-0-8764-92-09-42 FX: 49-0-8764-92-09-43
www.klassik-heute.com
*Musik, Festival, Konzert, Oper, Künstler, CD,
Komponist.*

Online Muzik Magazin
www.omm.de
*Das erste deutschsprachige musikmagazin im
internet.*

Oper&Tanz
Brienner Straße 52, 80333 München, Germany
PH: 089-34-35-59 FX: 089-34-35-60
redaktion@operundtanz.de
www.operundtanz.de
Zeitschrift für Opernchor und Bühnentanz.

Das Opernglas
Grelckstraße 36, 22529 Hamburg, Germany
PH: 040-58-55-01 FX: 040-58-55-05
info@opernglas.de
www.opernglas.de
Reviews and information.

Italy

PromArt
Viale San Lazzaro, 52, I - 36100 Vicenza, Italy
PH: 0039-0444564740 FX: 0039-0444285769
promart@promart.it
www.promart.it
News, reviews and an artist database.

Spain

FILOMUSICA Classical music and Opera
www.filomusica.com
We review all kinds of Classical music, including independent.

Goldberg
C/ Monasterio de Fitero, 34 bajo, 31011 Pamplona, Navarra, Spain
PH: 34-948-250-372 FX: 34-948-196-276
info@goldberg-magazine.com
www.goldberg-magazine.com
We review only CDs of early music before 1750.

Mundo Clasico
PH: 928-465-772
Xoán M. Carreira discos@mundoclasico.com
www.mundoclasico.com
Articles, interviews, reviews and news.

Ritmo
10 (Oficina95)-28050, Madrid, Spain
PH: 913588774 FX: 91-3588944
correo@ritmo.es
www.ritmo.es
Disfrute del mundo de la música clásica desde internet.

Sweden

Tidskriften OPERA
Box 4038, 102 61 Stockholm, Sweden
PH: 08-643-95-44 FX: 08-442-11-33
info@tidskriftenopera.nu
md.partitur.se
Sweden's foremost Opera magazine!

Switzerland

Musik & Theater
Postfach 1680, CH-8040 Zürich, Switzerland
PH: 41-1-491-71-88 FX: 41-1-493-11-76
musikundtheater@bluewin.ch
www.musikundtheater.ch
CD-Besprechungen, musik, theater, oper, interviews…

United Kingdom

BBC Music Magazine
BBC Radio 3, London, W1N 4DJ UK
PH: 087-00-100-100
radio3.website@bbc.co.uk
www.bbc.co.uk/music/classical
www.bbc.co.uk/radio3/classical
CD reviews, interviews, features, news etc.

Brass Band World
4ᵗʰ Fl. 117-119 Portland St., Manchester, M1 6FB UK
PH: 44-0-1298-812816 FX: 44-0-1298-815220
info@brassbandworld.com
www.brassbandworld.com
An independent monthly magazine for bands.

Classical Guitar Magazine
1 & 2 Vance Ct. Trans Britannia Enterprise Park, Blaydon on Tyne, NE21 5NH UK
PH: 44-0-191-414-9000 FX: 44-0-191-414-9001
classicalguitar@ashleymark.co.uk
www.classicalguitarmagazine.com
Features, interviews, news and reviews.

Classical Source
26 Great Queen St., London, WC2B 5BB UK
editor@classicalsource.com
www.classicalsource.com
Providing news and reviews.

ClassicalLink *MusicWeb*
40 Portman Sq. 4ᵗʰ Fl. London, W1H 6LT UK
PH: +44 (0) 20-7486-6300
FX: +44 (0) 20-7935-0922
info@classicall.net
www.classicall.net
We post about 12 new reviews a day. Also live Classical concerts, Film music and Jazz.

International Record Review
9 Spring Bridge Mews, London, W5 2AB UK
PH: +44 (0)20-8567-9244 FX: +44 (0)20-8840-5447
info@recordreview.co.uk
www.recordreview.co.uk
Actively seeks out CDs for review.

MUSIC & VISION
Flat D, 25 Oxford Rd. Ealing, London, W5 3SP UK
PH: +44 (0)20-8840-1564
www.mvdaily.com
Encouraging and educating young writers about serious music.

New Notes
4ᵗʰ Fl. St Margaret's House, 18-20 Southwark St., London, SE1 1TJ UK
PH: 020-7407-1640
spnm@spnm.org.uk
www.spnm.org.uk
Promoting New Music!

Opera Magazine
36 Black Lion Ln. London, W6 9BE UK
PH: +44 (0)20-8563-8893 FX: +44 (0)20-8563-8635
editor@opera.co.uk
www.opera.co.uk
News, letters, interviews, reviews and more.

Seen and Heard
www.musicweb.uk.net/SandH
The largest live music review site on the web.

The Strad
Ariane Todes thestrad@orpheuspublications.com
www.thestrad.com
We review CDs of string music and string musicians.

The Trombonist
www.trombone-society.org.uk
The magazine of The British Trombone Society.

Australia

Opera~Opera
ACN 001 713 319, PO Box R-361, Royal Exchange, NSW 1225 Australia
PH: 61-2-92472264 FX: 61-2-92472269
deg@opera-opera.com.au
www.opera-opera.com.au
We certainly have no qualms about reviewing releases emanating from independent quarters.

New Zealand

The Opera Critic
PO Box 99826, Newmarket, Auckland, NZ
PH: 64-9-525-3996
customers@theoperacritic.com
theoperacritic.com
Reviews, articles and news about opera worldwide.

Asia

CLASSICA JAPAN
iio@tka.att.ne.jp
www.classicajapan.com
Classical music news and links.

Country

Country, C&W, Americana, Bluegrass, Roots, Honky Tonk, Alt-Country, Old-Timey and Rockabilly

North America

United States

3ʳᵈ COAST MUSIC
237 W. Mandalay Dr. San Antonio, TX 78212
PH: 210-820-3748
John Conquest john@3rdcoastmusic.com
www.3rdcoastmusic.com
The essential newspaper for American Roots music. Published monthly in Central Texas it contains news, opinion, and reviews of musicians and their CDs. We ONLY review indie releases!

The 9513
PO Box 151264, Austin, TX 78715
editor@the9513.com
www.the9513.com
We work hard to promote and recognize excellent country music (in all of its forms), to be an outlet for new, undiscovered, and independent artists, and to provide a forum for open dialog between musicians and their audience.

Americana Roots
roots@AmericanaRoots.com
www.americanaroots.com
If you have a production quality CD (able to sell in a store) we will review it.

AngryCountry.com
angrycountry.com
All Country music related genres are covered including Bluegrass, Texas Country and Christian Country.

Blue Suede News
Box 25E, Duvall, WA 98019
PH: 425-788-2776
shakinboss@aol.com
www.bluesuedenews.com
We cover the entire spectrum of American Roots music.

The Bluegrass Blog
thebluegrassblog.com
News, interviews and reviews. Send in your news item, press release, radio update etc.

Bluegrass Music Profiles
PO Box 850, Nicholasville, KY 40340-0850
PH: 859-333-6465
info@bluegrassmusicprofiles.com
www.bluegrassmusicprofiles.com
Gettin' personal with Bluegrass music artists!

bluegrass now
PO Box 2020, Rolla, MO 65402
PH: 573-341-7336 FX: 573-341-7352
Deb Bledose bgn@fidnet.com
www.bluegrassnow.com
Reviews, interviews, profiles and more!

Bluegrass Unlimited
PO Box 771, Warrenton, VA 20188-0771
PH: 540-349-8181 FX: 540-341-0011
editor@bluegrassmusic.com
www.bluegrassmusic.com
Promotes Bluegrass and Old-time Country musicians.

Bluegrass Works
31 Oakdale Ave. Weston, MA 02493
lgeffen@mintz.com
www.bluegrassworks.com
Supports the musicians and other fans who help make the music.

Country Interviews Online
PO Box 558, Smyrna, TN 37167
PH: 815-361-3172 FX: 309-273-3965
Laurie Megan laurie@countryinterviewsonline.net
www.CountryInterviewsOnline.net
Reviews & interviews with major & indie label artists.

Country Line Magazine
9508 Chisholm Trail, Austin, TX 78748
T.J. Greaney tj@countrylinemagazine.com
www.countrylinemagazine.com
We are about Country music, born in Texas or raised in Nashville.

Country Standard Time
54 Ballard St., Newton Centre, MA 02459-1251
PH: 617-969-0331
Jeffrey B. Remz countryst@aol.com
countrystandardtime.com
Your guide to Roadhouse, Roots and Rockabilly.

Cybergrass
520 Carved Ter. Colorado Springs, CO 80919
www.cybergrass.com
News about Bluegrass music, artists and the music business. Promote your shows!

Flatpicking Guitar
PO Box 2160, Pulaski, VA 24301
PH: 540-980-0338 FX: 540-980-0557
info@flatpickingmercantile.com
www.flatpick.com
Presenting the art of flat picking the Acoustic guitar.

Freight Train Boogie
PO Box 4262, Santa Rosa, CA 95402
Bill Frater frater@freighttrainboogie.com
www.freighttrainboogie.com
News and reviews of Roots music.

Hillbilly-Music.com
PO Box 576245, Modesto, CA 95357-6245
Dave webmaster@hillbilly-music.com
www.hillbilly-music.com
We can't promise we'll review everything, but we'll try.

iBluegrass
1401 N. Lake Park Blvd. #46, Box 333
Carolina Beach, NC 28428
PH: 910-221-9474
Skip Ogden cwo@ibest.net
www.ibluegrass.com
We will accept unsolicited material for review. Check our site for submission details.

Mandolin Magazine
PO Box 13537, Salem, OR 97309
PH: 503-364-2100 FX: 503-588-7707
www.mandolinmagazine.com
We review CDs, books, videos and instruments.

MuseRevolution Magazine
Brandon Lynn Shane brandon@muserevolution.com
www.muserevolution.com
Indie Country music artists unite! Join the revolution today!

Nashville Country Music Blog
info@nashville95.com
www.nashville95.com
All about Country music including news and commentary. Country music CD reviews can be done here as well — just email us at to find out how we can review your CD.

No Depression
Peter Blackstock peter@nodepression.net
www.nodepression.net
Covers Alt-Country music (whatever that is).

The Old Time Herald
PO Box 51812, Durham, NC 27717-1812
PH: 919-419-1800 FX: 919-419-1881
info@oldtimeherald.org
www.oldtimeherald.org
Celebrates the love of Old-Time music - grassroots or homegrown music and dance.

Rockabilly Magazine
143 Dawson, Waterloo, IA 50703
PH: 888-516-0707 FX: 512-385-4300
www.rockabillymagazine.com
The ultimate source for Rockabilly info.

Roots Music Report
13501 Ranch Rd. 12 #103-327
Wimberley, TX 78676
PH: 877-532-2225
rmr@rootsmusicreport.com
Robert Bartosh rmr@rootsmusicreport.com
www.rootsmusicreport.com
Reviews and articles on Roots music and artists.

Roughstock
www.Roughstock.com
News, reviews, interviews, charts.

Canada

Fiddler Magazine
PO Box 101, North Sydney, NS B2A 3M1
PH: 902-794-2558
info@fiddle.com
www.fiddle.com
Feature articles, regular columns and more.

That's Country
906-7 Roanoke Rd. North York, ON M3A 1E3
PH: 615-692-1134
www.thatscountry.com
Created to help Country artists spread the word of their presence in the Country music community.

Uptown Bluegrass
George georgemcknight@telus.net
www.uptownbluegrass.com
CD review site and radio show.

E u r o p e

Belgium

BillyBop
www.billybop.be
Dedicated to Roots & Rockabilly music. Album reviews, contests, band promotion and much more.

Germany

Country Jukebox
Th. Dombart - Str. 5, 80805 München, Germany
Max W. Achatz info@countryjukebox.de
www.countryjukebox.de
Published monthly in Germany's Country Circle magazine as well as on the web.

CountryHome
Maiselsberger Str. 5, D-84416 Taufkirchen/Vils, Germany
PH: 08084-9166 FX: 08084-9165
iwde@iwde.de
www.countryhome.de
Das online magazin freier fachjournalisten.

The Netherlands

Alt Country NL
dutchtwang@yahoo.com
www.altcountry.nl
Er voor liefhebbers van Americana en Rootsmuziek.

United Kingdom

Americana UK
29 Avonmore Ave. Liverpool, L18 8AL UK
Mark Whitfield mark@americana-uk.com
www.americana-uk.com
UK home for Americana, Alt-Country and "No Depression" music. CDs only please. No CDRs or demos.

Country Music People
1-3 Love Ln. London, SE18 6QT UK
PH: 44-020-8854-7217 FX: 44-020-8855-6370
info@countrymusicpeople.com
www.countrymusicpeople.com
Reviews of latest CDs, features and interviews.

Fiddle On
info@fiddleon.co.uk
www.fiddleon.co.uk
A publication for the UK fiddle players.

Maverick
editor@maverick-country.com
www.maverick-country.com
Changing how Country music is perceived in the UK.

Metro Country
www.metrocountry.co.uk
Contact to get your CD reviewed and featured.

A u s t r a l i a

Capital News Country Music
Cheryl Byrnes cheryl.byrnes@ruralpress.com
www.capitalnews.com.au
Monthly magazine devoted to Country music in Australia.

Dance and Electronic

North America

United States

danceblogga
Dennis Romero chp@earthlink.net
www.dancemusic.blogspot.com
Dance music news and criticism.

DJ Times
25 Willowdale Ave. Port Washington, NY 11050
PH: 516-767-2500 FX: 516-767-9335
www.djtimes.com
*Considered the "bible of the industry" for the
professional DJ.*

Electrocore
PH: 918-852-7973
Reviews reviews@electrocore.com
Unsigned Artist Music Submissions
submitmusic@electrocore.com
www.electrocore.com
*Your avenue for information on everything
Electroclash / Disko Punk / Electro.*

Futuremusic
Columbus Circle Stn. PO Box 20888
New York, NY 10023
info@futuremusic.com
futuremusic.com
*The ultimate resource for Future music news,
technology, digital music etc. It's what's next!*

Igloo Magazine!
PO Box 307, Corona, CA 92878
Pietro Da Sacco editor@igloomag.com
www.igloomag.com
Online source for Electronic music coverage.

Independent Music Reviewer Eric Saeger
608 Lowell St. #1, Manchester, NH 03104
esaeger@cyberontix.com
*I am an Arts writer/CD reviewer for several local
(to Boston) and national publications. Currently my
work appears in Skope Magazine (Boston), Dayton
City Paper (Ohio), Virus Magazine (Germany),
Glide Magazine (NY/PA), Axis Magazine (Orlando,
FL), 168 Magazine (Nashua, NH) and the online
magazines Mouvement Nouveau (Germany),
Northeast In-Tune (NY/NJ/MA), Subculture
Magazine (London) and hippy.com. I mainly
specialize in Techno and Industrial, but all styles are
welcome.*

Iron Feather Journal
PO Box 1905, Boulder, CO 80306
Stevyn@IronFeather.com
www.ironfeather.com
*A wicked mega magazine about the subversive
HI-TEK underground, Techno + Jungle scenes.*

Jive Magazine
PO Box 2635, Lilburn, GA 30048
www.jivemagazine.com
*Extensive review section, events and more! Check
our site for submission details. Make sure to contact
us before you send anything in.*

Progressive Sounds
www.progressive-sounds.com
Bringing you the latest in Progressive Trance.

Sonic Curiosity
PO Box 28325, Philadelphia, PA 19149
Matt Howarth matt@soniccuriosity.com
www.soniccuriosity.com
Alternative/Electronic music review site.

Europe

Belgium

Beyondjazz
Braderijstraat 2 bus 2B, B-9000 Gent, Belgium
PH: +32-9-225-25-17
Lennart Schoors office@beyondjazz.net
www.beyondjazz.net
*A Future Jazz community, focusing on the exciting
sounds of Broken Beats, Future Jazz and Space
Funk.*

Estonia

Club Arena
www.clubarena.com
Promos will be reverberated.

Finland

Findance
info@findance.com
www.findance.com
Enimmäkseen muuta kuin kotimaista konemusiikkia.

France

Atome
atome@atome.com
www.atome.com
*Send us your charts, promo-copies, demos, news,
presents.*

Novaplanet.com
33, rue du Faubourg Saint Antoine,
75011 Paris, France
PH: 01-53-33-33-00
webmaster@novaplanet.com
www.novaplanet.com
News and reviews.

Yet Another Electro-Webzine?
www.yaew.com
Electronic music news, reviews and interviews.

Germany

BreakBeatz.de
Westerladekop 86a, 21635 Jork, Germany
PH: 0-41-62-91-32-63
www.breakbeatz.de
Your D n'B e-zine.

Couchsurfer.de
Schwabener Weg 14, D-85630 Neukerferloh-
Grasbrunn, Germany
Michael Kienzler mk@couchsurfer.de
www.couchsurfer.de
*A club culture portal. Send us your promos & mix-
CDs for review.*

Groove
Köpenicker Str. 178/179, 10997 Berlin, Germany
PH: 030-44-31-20-22 FX: 030-44-31-20-70
Thilo Schneider thilo@groove.de
www.groove.de
Reviews Electronica, Techno, House etc.

House-Beats.de
Nico Geisler mail@house-beats.de
www.house-beats.de
Deutschlands Housemusic community!

Motor
www.motor.de
News, releases, tours, reviews etc.

Norway

i:Vibes
webmaster@ivibes.nu
www.ivibes.nu
*Reviews of all the latest Trance and Electronica
tunes. Interviews with the biggest DJs.*

Portugal

The Connexion Bizarrre
info@connexionbizarre.net
www.connexionbizarre.net
*Electronic music from Synthpop to Noise, touching
everything in between.*

Russia

jungle.ru
mail@jungle.ru
www.jungle.ru
News, reviews, artist bio, streaming radio and more.

Sweden

trance.nu
trance.nu
The biggest Trance community on Earth!

United Kingdom

Blackout Audio
www.blackoutaudio.co.uk
Reviews and interviews of new sounds.

Dancemuzik.com
www.dancemuzik.com
News, reviews, features etc.

DJmag
The Old Truman Brewery, London, E1 6QL UK
PH: +44 (0) 20-7247-8855
Helene Stokes editors@djmag.com
www.djmag.com
*Up-front coverage of the Dance music scene. Check
for the reviewer covering your style.*

DogsOnAcid
Ben XO xo@dogsonacid.com
www.dogsonacid.com
*The world's largest D n'B and Jungle message
board and forum with news, reviews, audio etc.*

Drum n' Bass Arena
2nd Fl. 36-37 Featherstone St., London,
EC1Y 8QZ UK
PH: +44 (0) 207-741-0045
newtalent@breakbeat.co.uk
www.breakbeat.co.uk
The latest info on everything to do with D n'B.

M8 Magazine
Media Quarter, 111 Bell St., Glasgow, G4 0TQ UK
PH: 0141-553-0500 FX: 0141-553-5800
Kevin McFarlane kevin@m8magazine.com
www.m8magazine.com
The latest music reviews and news.

Ministry of Sound
103 Gaunt St., London, SE1 8DP UK
PH: 44-0-20-7740-8600 FX: 44-0-20-7403-5348
www.ministryofsound.com
Reviews of Dance albums and singles.

mixmag
90/92 Pentonville Rd. London, N1 9HS UK
PH: +207-520-8625 FX: +207 7833 9900
www.mixmag.net
The world's biggest selling clubbing magazine.

Nubreaks.com
www.nubreaks.com
Helps you get your DJ mix online.

Planetdnb
2ⁿᵈ Fl. 207 Cranbrook Rd. Ilford, Essex,
LG1 4TD UK
PH: 44-0-20-8554-4043 FX: 44-0-20-8554-4043
Andy Rayner mail@planetdnb.com
www.planetdnb.com
One of the leading Drum n' Bass resource sites.

Tunes.co.uk
Unit 4B Marsh Lane, Henstridge Trading Estate.
Henstridge, Somerset BA8 0TG UK
PH: +44(0)1963-364345
www.tunes.co.uk
*Dance music from Soul & Funk to House & Breaks:
reviews, real audio & worldwide mail order.*

Australia

Resident Advisor
www.residentadvisor.com.au
*Australian/Global Dance news, interviews and
reviews.*

TransZfusion
PO Box 2393, Richmond, NSW 3121 Australia
www.tranzfusion.net
Trusted voice in Electronica.

Experimental

*Experimental, Electronic, Ambient, Avant-garde,
Noise etc.*

North America

United States

aural innovations
2233 Edgevale Rd. Columbus, OH 43221
Jerry Kranitz jkranitz@aural-innovations.com
aural-innovations.com
Includes Psychedelia and related Electronic music.

disquiet.com
marc@disquiet.com
www.disquiet.com
*Focus on Ambient music, Electronica and Sound
Art. Interviews, recommended MP3s, reviews, news
and essays.*

Electro-music.com
electro-music.com
*Experimental, Electro-Acoustic and Electronic
music.*

Free City Media
Heidi@FreeCityMedia.com
www.freecitymedia.com
Psychedelic music and fresh perspectives.

Innerviews
Attn: Anil Prasad
PO Box 8548, Emeryville, CA 94662
www.myspace.com/innerviews
Music without borders.

Ptolemaic Terrascope
PO Box 18841, Oakland, CA 94619-8841
Pat Thomas normalsf@earthlink.net
www.terrascope.org
Unearthing Psychedelic/Folk nuggets.

SIGNAL to NOISE
operations@signaltonoisemagazine.org
www.signaltonoisemagazine.org
*The journal of Improvised and Experimental music.
You MUST contact us for approval before sending in
your work.*

Squid's Ear
160 Bennett Ave. #6K, New York, NY 10040
www.squidsear.com
*Experimental, Improvisation, Avant-garde and
unusual musical styles.*

Synthmuseum.com
399 School St. #2, Watertown, MA 02472
PH: 617-926-2298
jay@synthmuseum.com
www.synthmuseum.com
Our magazine features reviews of Synth music.

XLR8R
1388 Haight St. #105, San Francisco, CA 94117
Attn: Ken Taylor
PH: 415-861-7583 FX: 415-861-7584
Ken Taylor letterbox@xlr8r.com
www.xlr8r.com
Over 100 color pages. Internationally distributed.

Canada

Computer Music Journal
mitpress.mit.edu/e-journals/Computer-Music-Journal
*Covers digital audio signal processing and Electro
Acoustic music. When contacting, include "CMJ" in
your Subject line. Please visit our website for our
submission policy (you need to send your work to
(2) different addresses).*

Europe

Belgium

l'entrepot
Mesesstraat 6, 2300 Turnhout, Belgium
Tom Wilms tom.wilks@skynet.be
www.l-entrepot.blogspot.com
Resource center for unconventional tunes.

SIDE-LINE
Leuvenselaan 251, 3300 Tienen, Belgium
Stephane Froidcoeur stef@side-line.com
www.side-line.com
Magazine on the Underground genre.

Germany

de:bug
Schwedter Strasse 9a, 10119 Berlin, Germany
PH: 030-2838 4458 FX: 030-2838-4459
www.de-bug.de
News and reviews.

NMZ
www.nmz.de
*News, reviews, rezensionen, kulturpolitik,
musikwirtschaft, musikforen…*

re.fleXion
Zum Hasenkamp 8, 31552, Rodenberg, Germany
www.re-flexion.de
*Neuigkeiten, kritiken, interviews, kozerte, termine,
bands etc.*

spex
Köpenicker Str. 178/179, 0997 Berlin, Germany
PH: (030) 44312010 FX: (030) 44312019
redaktion@spex.de
www.spex.de
News and reviews.

synthetics
Enzianweg 7, 41836 Huckelhoven, Germany
PH: 02433-95-99-808 FX: 0721-151201169
contact@synthetics-magazin.de
www.synthiepop.de
BODY and SOUL come together.

Terrascope Online
63 Millers Close, Leominster,
Herefordshire HR6 8BP UK
Simon Lewis reviews@terrascope.co.uk
www.terrascope.co.uk
Unearthing Psychedelic/Folk nuggets.

Westzeit
Bahnhofstr. 6, 41334 Nettetal, Germany
PH: 02157-3858 FX: 02157-1760
Holger Seeling holger@westzeit.de
www.westzeit.de
Pop auf draht-musik, literatur, kunst und film.

Italy

Neural
Alessandro Ludovico a.ludovico@neural.it
www.neural.it
New media art and Electronic music.

United Kingdom

Computer Music
30 Monmouth St., Bath, BA1 2BW UK
PH: 01225-442244 FX: 01225-732353
www.computermusic.co.uk
Reviews of the latest gear/news as it happens.

Future Music
30 Monmouth St., Bath, BA1 2BW UK
PH: 01225-442244 FX: 01225-732353
futuremusic@futurenet.co.uk
futuremusic.co.uk
Making music at the cutting edge of technology.

Robots and Electric Brains
133 Green End Rd. Cambridge, CB4 1RW UK
Jimmy Possession rebzine@hotmail.com
www.robotsandelectronicbrains.co.uk
*Eclectic zine for music with that extra something
special.*

The Wire
23 Jack's Pl. 6 Corbet Pl. London, E1 6NN UK
PH: +44 (0)20-7422-5014 FX: +44 (0)20-7422-5011
www.thewire.co.uk
*Electronica, Breakbeat, Avant Rock, Free Jazz,
Classical, Global and beyond.*

Folk

Folk, Celtic, Singer/Songwriter, Roots, Acoustic, Traditional, Maritime

North America

United States

Acoustic Guitar Magazine
PO Box 767, San Anselmo, CA 94979
PH: 415-485-6946 FX: 415-485-0831
editors.ag@stringletter.com
www.acousticguitar.com
We only review recordings with widespread distribution or an established internet distribution channel.

Celtic Beat
4 Greenlay St., Nashua, NH 03063
PH: 603-880-3706
celt56@aol.com
www.mv.com/ipusers/celticbeat
Concert and CD reviews galore!

Dirty Linen
PO Box 66600, Baltimore, MD 21239-6600
PH: 410-583-7973 FX: 410-337-6735
office@dirtylinen.com
www.DirtyLinen.com
We welcome submission of audio Roots music.

eFolkMusic
101 Evans Ct. Carrboro, NC 27510
PH: 919-434-8349
artists@efolkMusic.org
www.efolkmusic.org
Traditional and Contemporary Folk music from around the world.

Folk & Acoustic Music Exchange
82 Leadmine Rd. Nelson, NH 03457
David N. Pyles dnpyles@acousticmusic.com
www.acousticmusic.com/fame/famehome.htm
Submit recordings and artist bio for review.

Folkwax
www.folkwax.com
Weekly Folk music e-zine with reviews.

Fret Knot Magazine
718 E. Seminary St. #4, Greencastle, IN 46135
PH/FX: 765-630-5123
info@fretknotmagazine.com
fretknotmagazine.com
Dedicated to the simple notion that music can change the world.

Green Man Review
82 Rackleff St., Portland, ME 04103
music@greenmanreview.com
www.greenmanreview.com
Focus on Folk music in all its aspects. You must send 2 copies of each CD that you want reviewed.

Minor 7th
PO Box 468, Manistee, MI 49660-0468
www.minor7th.com
Your CD must prominently feature acoustic guitar and be a recent release.

Puremusic
1708 21st Ave. S. #402, Nashville, TN 37212-3704
Frank Goodman frankgoodman@puremusic.com
www.puremusic.com
Bringing great music to the masses.

Rambles
1609 Ridgeview Ave. Lancaster, PA 17603
feedback@rambles.net
www.rambles.net
Folk & Traditional music.

Sing Out!
PO Box 5460, Bethlehem, PA 18015
PH: 610-865-5366 FX: 610-865-5129
info@singout.org
www.singout.org
Articles and interviews, tons of recording and book reviews.

Canada

CelticLife Magazine
Ste. 204, 1454 Dresden Row, Halifax, NS B3J 3T5
PH: 902-425-5716
Alexa Thompson editorial@CelticLife.ca
www.CelticLife.ca
Includes reviews of the latest in Celtic music, including independent labels. We also do reviews online.

Penguin Eggs
10942 80th Ave. Edmonton, AB T6G 0R1
PH: 780-433-8287 FX: 780-437-4603
penguineggs@shaw.ca
www.penguineggs.ab.ca
Canada's Folk, Roots and World music magazine.

Europe

France

Trad Magazine
1bis, impasse du Vivier - 91150, Etampes, France
PH: 01-69-58-72-24 FX: 01-60-83-21-46
tradmag@orange.fr
www.tradmagazine.com
Französisches magazin für Folk und Traditionelle musik.

Germany

Folker!
Postfach 300552, 53185 Bonn, Germany
PH: 0228-462424 FX: 0228-4298898
info@folker.de
www.folker.de
Das deutsche musikmagazin. Folk, Blues, Cajun ...

FolkWorld
reviews@folkworld.eu
www.folkworld.de
Contributions from you are welcome!

The Netherlands

Newfolksounds
info@newfolksounds.nl
www.newfolksounds.nl
Een Nederlands tijdschrift dat één keer in de twee maanden verschijnt.

The Real Roots Café
Lincolnstraat 2, 6566 CT Millingen aan de Rijn, The Netherlands
Jan Janssen rrc@realrootscafe.com
www.realrootscafe.com
Promotes fabulous American Roots music musicians.

United Kingdom

BBC Folk and Acoustic Page
www.bbc.co.uk/radio2/folk
Info, news, reviews, radio, events and more.

Folk and Roots
info@folkandroots.co.uk
www.folkandroots.co.uk
Gigs, reviews, interview featured artists and more.

Folk Roots
PO Box 337, London, N4 1TW UK
PH: 44-020-8340-9651 FX: 44-020-8348-5626
froots@frootsmag.com
www.frootsmag.com
Roots, Folk and World music magazine.

RootsMusic.co.uk
PO Box 23911, London, E12 5TD UK
PH/FX: 020-8553-1435
info@rootsmusic.co.uk
rootsmusic.co.uk
Bringing you some the best new and undiscovered Roots and Acoustic artists.

Trad Music / Music Maker Magazine
28 Grafton Terrace, London, NW5 4JJ UK
PH: 020-7424-0027
www.tradmusic.net
Dedicated to the promotion of independent labels, songwriters & performers. Folk to Country, Rock, Jazz and World music.

Australia

Trad&Now
PO Box 532, Woy Woy, NSW 2256 Australia
PH: (02) 4325-7369 FX: (02) 4325-7362
info@tradandnow.com
www.tradandnow.com
Promotes Traditional and Contemporary Folk music.

GLBT

Chicago Free Press
c/o Gregg Shapiro
3845 N. Broadway 2nd Fl. Chicago, IL 60613
gregg1959@aol.com
www.chicagofreepress.com
I also write for several other publications including afterelton.com, HX (NYC), Bay Area Reporter (SF), The Bottom Line (Palm Springs), In Newsweekly (Boston), Outsmart Magazine (Houston) and many others!

Freelance Reviewer - Jason Victor Serinus
PO Box 3073, Oakland, CA 94609-0073
Jason Victor Serinus healrmn@planeteria.net
www.jasonserinus.com
Writes and reviews for gay, alternative, New Age and audiophile publications nationwide.

Queerpunks.com
Jeremy jaffa@queerpunks.com
queerpunks.com/wordpress
Add your news, CD and show reviews etc. Covers Punk and all other Alternative genres.

Velvetpark Magazine
PO Box. 60248, Brooklyn, NY 11206-0248
info@velvetparkmagazine.com
velvetparkmagazine.com
Dyke culture in bloom!

Goth

Goth, Industrial, EBM, Ethereal, Synthpop, DeathRock, Darkwave and Pagan.

North America

United States

Absolute Zero Media
PO Box 717, Clayton, NC 27528-0717
gateway@absolutezeromedia.us
magazine.absolutezeromedia.us
Experimental, Dark Industrial/Ambient, Noise and Doom label, mail order, label and zine.

BiteMe!
6038 Hayes Ave. #1A, Los Angeles, CA 90042
PH: 626-359-5338
J j@bitemezine.net
www.bitemezine.net
Interviews, commentary. Also reviews demos.

Chaos Control Digizine
PO Box 1065, Hoboken, NJ 07030
PH: 201-610-0688
Bob Gourley chaoszine@gmail.com
www.chaoscontrol.com
Pioneering online zine focusing on, but not limited to, Electronic music. Features an extensive collection of interviews.

Dark Realms Magazine
4377 W. 60th St., Cleveland, OH 44144
goth@monolithgraphics.com
www.monolithgraphics.com/darkrealms.html
Visit our website for guidelines to submitting your music.

Gothic Beauty
4110 SE. Hawthorne Blvd. #501
Portland, OR 97214
FX: 503-249-8844
submissions@gothicbeauty.com
www.gothicbeauty.com
Send us your press kit.

Grave Concerns
PO Box 692, Valatie, NY 12184
PH: 518-755-0404
www.graveconcernsezine.com
An on-line magazine featuring Gothic, EBM, Industrial, Noise and Alternative music news, reviews, interviews and more. Now accepting submissions.

Horror Garage
PO Box 53, Nesconset, NY 11767
Pitch Black HorrorGarage@aol.com
www.horrorgarage.com
Combines he best in original dark fiction with the finest in horrific Rock n' Roll.

Outburn
PO Box 3187, Thousand Oaks, CA 91359-0187
outburn@outburn.com
www.outburn.com
In-depth interviews with popular musicians and established Underground favorites.

Regen Magazine
PO Box 14162, San Francisco, CA 94114-0162
PH: 415-420-8247
Nick Garland submissions@regenmag.com
www.regenmag.com
We feature IDM, Industrial, Goth, Synthpop etc.

Sentimentalist
madeline@sentimentalistmag.com
www.sentimentalistmag.com
Alternative music, art, film and fashion magazine.

Vampirefreaks.com
www.vampirefreaks.com
Online community featuring everything Gothic.

Canada

Morbid Outlook
772 Dovercourt Rd., PO Box 334
Toronto, ON M6H 4E3
Laura the Mistress McCutchan
submit@morbidoutlook.com
www.morbidoutlook.com
Feel free to send your CDs and press kits to us

Rue Morgue
2926 Dundas St. W., Toronto ON M6P 1Y8
PH: 416-651-9675
info@rue-morgue.com
www.rue-morgue.com
Reviews (no demos) Horror related music.

Europe

Belgium

Darker than the Bat
Peter Jan Van Damme pj.vandamme@scarlet.be
www.proservcenter.be/darkerthanthebat
CD reviews, interviews and airplay for indies.

De Kagan Kalender
info@kagankalender.com
www.kagankalender.com
Each promo is assured to get a review and will be played on our radio show.

Croatia

Elektronski Zvuk
info@elektronskizvuk.com
www.elektronskizvuk.com
We review Electronic music from bands around the world.

Czech Republic

teenage.cz
teenage.cz
School sucks. Music rocks!

France

D-Side
3 bis, rue Pasteur, 94270 Le Kremlin Bicetre, France
PH: 33-01-47-77-80-28 FX: 33-01-46-77-53-82
Monsieur Bruce ab@d-side.org
www.d-side.org
Gothic, Rock Metal, Electro, Industrial, Electronica, Darkwave.

Germany

Astan Magazine
PF 1247, 48629 Metelen, Germany
astanmagazin@t-online.de
www.astan-magazin.de
Gothic / Electro zine. News, reviews, interviews…

Back Again
Elbgaustr 118, 22547 Hamburg, Germany
Alexander Pohle sam@backagain.de
www.backagain.de
CD kritiken und Interviews aus dem independentbereich.

Black Rain
PO Box 300 130, 09033 Chemnitz, Germany
FX: 0049-(0)371-3899450
www.blackrain.de
Mail your demos in for review.

Crawling Tunes Magazine
www.myspace.com/crawlingtunesmagazine
Gothic, Dark-Wave, Shoegaze, Horrorpunk, Deathrock etc. NO Metal, Trash or EBM music, please!

The Dark Site
www.wavegothic.de
Schickt einfach euer Material an unsere Anschrift und gebt uns ein paar Wochen Zeit (wir müssen die CDs ja auch intern verteilen).

Dark Spy Magazine
Demo, Postfach 11 03 01, 46123 Oberhausen, Germany
PH: +49 (0) 208-635-397-60
FX: +49 (0) 208-635-398-00
redaktion@dark-spy.com
www.dark-spy.com
Mail your CD or e-mail us with the word "DEMO" in the subject heading. Stay Dark!

darkerradio
Ottostrasse 46, 47169 Duisburg, Germany
PH: +49(0)180-5-6-84-30-82-80
FX: +49(0)180-5-6-84-30-80-95
Falk Merten info@darkerradio.com
www.darkerradio.de
Tune in. Turn on. Burn out.

elektrauma
Andreas Romer andi@elektrauma.com
www.elektrauma.de
Musik als therapie für die seele.

Gothic Magazine
Hauptstraße 33, 72488 Sigmaringen, Germany
info@dark-media.de
www.gothic-magazine.de
News, reviews, newsletter, links and more!

Gothic World
Rainstrasse 3, D-77694 Kehl, Germany
PH: +49 (0)7853-87-34
Sir Ritchie gothicworld@ritchies.de
www.the-gothicworld.de
Unabhängiges internet-Magazin für die Gothicszene.

Medienkonverter
Johann-Clanze-Strasse 56, 81369 Munich, Germany
PH: (0)721-151-408442 FX: (0)721-151-408442
Bertram Uhner redaktion@medienkonverter.de
www.medienkonverter.de
Das eZine für die subkulturellen Töne. Darkwave, Wave, EBM, Gothic, Gothicrock …

NEROTUNES
Hebbelstraße 2, 30177 Hanover, Germany
PH/FX: 069-1-33-04-04-03-45
Jörn Sieveneck info@nerotunes.com
www.nerotunes.com
EBM, Gothic, Industrial music podcast and e-zine.

pandaimonix.de
Krokusweg 37, 76199 Karlsruhe, Germany
PH: 0721-98929933
Stefan Thiel staff@pandaimonix.de
www.pandaimonix.de
Provides information about Gothic, Metal and Dark music. News, reviews, stories…

Sonic Seducer
Postfach 14 01 54, 46131 Oberhausen, Germany
PH: 0208-699370 FX: 0208-6993715
www.sonic-seducer.de
Musicmagazin: Gothic, EBM, Alternative, Dark.

subKULTur.com
Postfach: 580664 - 10415 Berlin, Germany
PH: 030-446-780-86 FX: +49 (0) 721-151-281-383
Thomas Manegold redaktion@subKULTur.com
www.subkultur.com
Cd-kritiken, interviews, termine, MP3, galerien.

Zillo Musikmagazin
Sereetzer Weg 20, 23626 Ratekau, Germany
PH: 04504-606680 FX: 04504-60668-10
info@zillo.de
www.zillo.de
Darkwave, Alternative, Industrial music.

Greece

The Enochian Apocalypse
Vassago blackwidow79_drk@yahoo.com
www.enochianapocalypse.com
The best in Electro, EBM, Industrial, Darkwave and Goth music.

Italy

Angelic North-East Alternative Bands Club
www.angelic.it
Guide to the Dark Italian scene.

Chain D.L.K.
www.chaindlk.com
We have reviewers for each style and geographic location. Please check our site to see where to send your material.

Kronic.it
www.kronic.it
Encouraging music addiction since 2002.

Ver Sacrum
via Rosa Luxemburg 10/P,
56010 Orzignano (PI) - Italy
Marzia Bonato redazione@versacrum.com
www.versacrum.com
Rivista Gotica di letteratura, cinema, musica e arte.

Norway

Musique Machine
questions@musiquemachine.com
www.musiquemachine.com
Reviews, interviews, editorial columns and MP3s.

Russia

Russian Gothic Page
www.gothic.ru
An underground project promoting Gothic subculture in Russia.

Spain

Sonidobscuro
Pasaje de Briales 9, 2-I, 29009 Málaga, Spain
so@sonidobscuro.com
www.sonidobscuro.com
Webzine de musica oscura.

Sweden

Moving Hands
Sockenvägen 377, SE-122 63 Enskede, Sweden
Robert Eklind robert.eklind@movinghands.net
www.movinghands.net
We review Synth, Industrial, Electronica, EBM, Postpunk etc.

Release
V Stillestorpsg 23, S-417 Gothenburg, Sweden
PH: 46-31-775-00-83
info@releasemagazine.net
www.releasemagazine.net
Features, reviews, news, classified ads etc.

Switzerland

HeAvYmeTaL.ch
Im Trichtisal 8, CH-8053 Zürich, Switzerland
Roderick Zeig rzeig@gmx.ch
www.heavymetal.ch
The Metal / Gothic portal of Switzerland.

Sanctuary
www.sanctuary.ch
Promotes the musical alternative scene.

United Kingdom

DJ Martian's
altmartinuk@excite.com
djmartian.blogspot.com
Delivering cultural sound knowledge for the intelligent generation.

Hard Wired
www.hard-wired.org.uk
Send items for review (demos/albums etc.).

The Mick
mercermick@hotmail.com
www.mickmercer.com/themick.html
Online .pdf review zine. Contact me for our mailing address.

Ukraine

Ukrainian Gothic
www.gothic.com.ua
Supports the Ukrainian Gothic/Industrial/Independent scene.

Hip Hop

North America

United States

allhiphop.com
PH: 877-499-5111
Martin A. Berrios martin@allhiphop.com
www.allhiphop.com
Articles, audio, reviews, chat, boards etc.

Altrap.com
PO Box 4075, Tallahassee, FL 32315
A to the L mail@altrap.com
www.altrap.com
News, reviews, interviews and MP3s.

Bombhiphop.com
4104 24th St. #105, San Francisco, CA 94114
Attn: A&R Dept.
PH: 415-821-7965
usa@bombhiphop.com
www.bombhiphop.com
Artists, send in your demos for review.

ByronCrawford.com
Bol byron.crawford@gmail.com
www.byroncrawford.com
The mindset of a champion.

Concrete Loop
Brian blacksocialite@gmail.com
concreteloop.com
Urban entertainment news and reviews. Has spotlights featuring unsigned artists.

DaveyD's Hip Hop Corner
mrdaveyd@aol.com
www.daveyd.com
All the info on the Hip Hop scene.

Dork Magazine
www.dorkmag.com
Documenting the mundane, glamorous, funny, disturbing and just plain weird things that define our existence.

eJams
www.ejams.com
Let us feature your new CD.

The Elements
www.hiphop-elements.com
Your #1 source for Hip Hop related issues.

Grindahz
PH: 877-574-7463
www.grindahz.com
Grindahz.com and Grindahz Magazine are dedicated to giving Hip Hop, R&B and Reggae artists a play to showcase their talent.

Ground Lift Magazine
groundliftmag.com
Rare grooves, Hip Hop and Beats. Send your music to the above address for review consideration.

Hip Hop Linguistics
www.hiphoplinguistics.com
An underground-based Hip Hop website and online magazine created to give Hip Hop heads a portal into the positive, conscious, and thought-provoking Hip Hop ignored by mainstream media outlets.

Hip Hop Politics
HipHopPolitical@hotmail.com
hiphoppolitics.blogspot.com
Reflections, latest music, reviews, news and interviews from a 30-Something Hip Hop fan!

HipHopDX.com
www.hiphopdx.com
Hip Hop news, album reviews, links, release dates etc.

HipHopGame
730 mr730@tmail.com
www.hiphopgame.com
Daily information from around the world.

HipHopSite.com
4634 S. Maryland Pkwy. #107
Las Vegas, NV 89119
PH: 702-933-2120 FX: 702-947-2290
mistapizzo@hiphopsite.com
www.hiphopsite.com
Reviews and interesting items related to Hip Hop.

Hoodgrown Magazine
PO Box 733, Pocono Summit, PA 18346-0733
info@hoodgrownonline.com
www.hoodgrownonline.com
To get your product reviewed on the site you'll need to send 2 copies of your release.

Insomniac
insom@mindspring.com
www.insomniacmagazine.com
Features interviews, articles and reviews.

Murder Dog
164 Robles Dr. #257, Vallejo, CA 94591
PH: 707-553-8191
walkinbuffalo@murderdog.com
www.murderdog.com
America's #1 Rap magazine. Send us 2 copies of your CD for review.

Okay Player
c/o Reviews
84 Wooster St. #503, New York, NY 10012
promo@okayplayer.com
www.okayplayer.com
Artists, reviews, insights and much more.

OpenZine
PO Box 348515, Coral Gables, FL 33234
www.openzine.com
Submit articles, graffiti art pictures & many other outlets.

Pass the Mic
4130 Heyward St., Cincinnati, OH 45205
PH: 718-213-4176
www.passthemic.com
Community for independent Hip Hop artists.

Phatmag
thepublisher@phatmag.com
www.phatmag.com
Real news, interviews and reviews.

Rap Fanatic Magazine
www.rapfanatic.com
News, reviews, interviews as well as audio and video clips.

RapAttackLives
4750 Kester Ave. #11, Sherman Oaks, CA 91403
PH: 818-917-2217
Nasty-Nes nastynes1@aol.com
www.rapattacklives.com
The true voice of Hip Hop!

RapIndustry.Com
rapindustry.com
Showcase your talent!

Rapmusic.com
www.rapmusic.com
Your total source for Rap/Hip Hop.

rapreviews.com
Steve 'Flash' Juon dj.flash@rapreviews.com
www.rapreviews.com
An independent site dedicated to up-and-coming artists. Your music must be regionally distributed in stores or available on a widely recognized MAJOR retail website to get a review.

Riot Sound
PO Box 159, Landing, NJ 07850
PH: 973-343-2570
RiotSound@RiotSound.com
www.riotsound.com
Bringing together art, music and information from all corners of the globe in seamless harmony.

Shine Magazine
editors@planetshine.com
www.planetshine.com
Music, fashion, entertainment and more.

Siccness-Dot-Net
#105 8810-C Jamacha Blvd.
Spring Valley, CA 91977
PH: 619-690-7400
Nemo J. Mitchell contactnemo@hotmail.com
www.siccness.net
CD Vendors, reviews, interviews etc.

Soundslam
nick@soundslam.com
www.soundslam.com
The latest music news, reviews, artist info, contests and more!

Sphere of Hip Hop
3803 4th Pl. NW., Rochester, MN 55901
Attn: Josh Niemyjski
www.sphereofhiphop.com
Reviews positive Hip Hop.

Street Report Magazine
PO Box 725241, Atlanta, GA 31139
musiced@streetreportmagazine.net
www.streetreportmagazine.net
A Southern-based Hip Hop publication whose focal point is to give exposure to the independent artists.

Support Online Hip Hop
www.sohh.com
Connect with the online Hip Hop community.

ThugLifeArmy.com
Robert administrator@thuglifearmy.com
www.thuglifearmy.com
News, reviews, features etc.

The UIM *(Underwire Interactive Magazine)*
PO Box 261412, San Diego, CA 92196
Truth info@theuim.com
www.theuim.com
Hip Hop magazine that has been regarded amongst the industry as a great, unique outlet that combines text, video and audio features all in one.

underground sound
www.ugsmag.com
We post/review submitted Hip Hop MP3s.

Unsigned the Magazine
PO Box 165116, Irving, TX 75016
PH: 214-459-3199
reviews@unsignedthemagazine.com
www.unsignedthemagazine.com
Gives unsigned artists and labels maximum exposure.

URB
8484 Wilshire Blvd. #560
Beverly Hills, CA 90211-3234
promotions@urb.com
www.urb.com
Urban alternative culture!

Urban Newz
music@urbannewz.com
www.urbannewz.com
Provides its readers with daily Hip Hop and Urban entertainment newz, rumors, photos, music and interviews. Urban Newz not only works with major labels and artists, it also does a lot of work with independent artists, producers and DJ's all over the world.

Vapors Magazine
6725 Sunset Blvd. #320, Los Angeles, CA 90028
PH: 323-978-7920 FX: 323-978-7925
www.vaporsmagazine.com
We are also all about Hip Hop, skateboarding, art, fashion, sneakers (we love sneakers), parties and more!

Vice Magazine
97 N. 10th St. #202, Brooklyn, NY 11211
PH: 718-599-3101 FX: 718-599-1769
vice@viceland.com
www.viceland.com
We have offices around the world. Check our site for a contact near you.

XXL
1115 Broadway, New York, NY 10010
PH: 212-807-7100 FX: 212-620-7787
Leah Rose & Anslem Samuel xxl@harris-pub.com
www.xxlmag.com
Features eye candy, street team, articles and more.

Canada

A Rhyme and Melody Podcast
4172 Triumph St., Burnaby, BC V5C 1Z3
PH: 604-628-1624
Randy Ponzio rhymeandmelody@gmail.com
www.rhymeandmelody.com
Reviews Alt Hip Hop independent artists. We also offer weekly tips on how to promote yourself.

Earwaks.com
358 Dufferin St. #104, Toronto, ON M6K 1Z8
editor@earwaks.com
earwaks.com
We cover the full spectrum on Hip Hop with a strong emphasis on good music that is too often forgotten or underexposed. Please, no attachments!

Peace Magazine
PO Box 124, Stn. B, Toronto, ON M5T 2T3
PH: 416-406-2088
Harris Rosen info@peacemagazine.com
www.peacemagazine.com
Music. Fashion. Athletics. Lifestyle.

ThickOnline.com
reviewteam@thickonline.com
www.thickonline.com
Shedding light on unknown talent.

URBNET.COM
PO Box 10617, Toronto, ON M6H 1L8
PH: 647-271-7736 FX: 647-439-1411
info@urbnet.com
www.urbnet.com
Reviews, CDs and downloads of Techno, House etc.

Sign up for
The Indie Contact Newsletter
www.indiebible.com

Europe

Czech Republic

BBaRák CZ
Pribyslavska 10, 135 00 Praha 3, Czech Republic
PH: +420-222-714-285
info@bbarak.cz
www.bbarak.cz
Reviews local and international artists.

France

Just Like HipHop
97, Ave. Aristide Briand, 92120 Montrouge, France
PH: 33(0)1-58-07-04-85 FX: 33(0)1-58-35-00-53
service-client@justlikevibes.com
www.justlikehiphop.com
News, reviews, interviews, downloads etc.

Germany

Backspin
Hongkongstrasse 5, 20457 Hamburg, Germany
PH: 040-22-92-98-0 FX: 040-22-92-98-50
info@backspin.de
www.backspin.de
Marktplatz, forum, mail order etc.

hamburghiphop.de
Luisenweg 97, 20537 Hamburg, Germany
Philip Skupin redaktion@hamburghiphop.de
www.hamburghiphop.de
News, reviews, interviews and MP3s.

MK Zwo
Skalitzer Str. 97, 10997 Berlin, Germany
PH: +49 (0)30-616-27-414
FX: +49 (0)30-616-27-415
webmaster@mkzwo.com
www.mkzwo.com
Magazin für Hip Hop, Dancehall und Reggae.

Rap.de
Köpenicker Str. 178, 10997 Berlin, Germany
PH: 030-695-972-10 FX: 030-695-972-40
redaktion@rap.de
www.rap.de
Music, radio, video, shop, reviews, interviews.

WebBeatz
Auf dem Kamp 13, 42799 Leichlingen, Germany
PH/FX: +49-01212-5-59763024
Daniel Doege info@webbeatz.de
webbeatz.de
Hip Hop promotion platform.

Italy

HOTMC.COM
mail@hotmc.com
news.hotmc.com
News, articles and reviews, mainly on the Italian Hip Hop scene.

The Netherlands

Globaldarkness
Postbus 11173, 2301 ED Leiden, The Netherlands
www.globaldarkness.com
Jungle, Electro-Funk, Hip Hop & Reggae.

Hip Hop in je Smoel
Postbus 60, 2600AB Delft, The Netherlands
info@hiphopinjesmoel.nl
www.hiphopinjesmoel.nl
Reviews for everything Dutch in Hip Hop.

theBoombap
www.theboombap.nl
Nederlandsch meest gelezen Hip Hop magazine.

Urban Legends
www.urbanlegends.nl
For everything in Dutch Hip Hop. Local artists etc.

Spain

A Little Beat...
Avda.Malvarrosa 106-2 / 46011 Valencia, Spain
PH: 96-3275494
info@alittlebeat.com
www.alittlebeat.com
Hip Hop news, reviews, articles etc.

activohiphop.com
Apartado de correos 47050, 28080 Madrid, Spain
www.activohiphop.com
Send information on record launchings, concerts etc.

Hip Hop Directo
hhdirecto@gmail.com
www.hhdirecto.net
MP3 blog featuring news, reviews, video clips etc.

Hip Hop Yaik
www.hiphopyaik.com
Web dedicada al mundo del Hip Hop en Español.

RWHipHop.com
Apartado de Correos 559, Blanes, Girona, Spain
PH: +34-659-51-57-00
redaccion@rwhiphop.com
www.rwhiphop.com
I am Hip Hop, you are Hip Hop, we are Hip Hop.

Sweden

Street Zone
Flottbrovagen 23, 112 64 Stockholm, Sweden
Melin info@streetzone.com
www.streetzone.com
News, reviews, label and more.

Switzerland

Aight-Genossen
www.aight-genossen.ch
Swiss Hip Hop online.

Cosmic Hip Hop
27 ch. De Champ-Manon, 1233 Bernex, Switzerland
pub@cosmichiphop.com
www.cosmichiphop.com
Web mag exclusively dedicated to Hip Hop.

United Kingdom

Big Smoke Magazine
PO Box 38799, London, E10 5UZ UK
PH: 44-0-7966472051
Dirty Harry dirtyharry@bigsmokelive.com
www.myspace.com/bigsmokemagazine
Interviews, reviews, events, competitions and more!

Hip Hop Kings Entertainment
101 Aberdale Rd. Leicester, LE2 6GE UK
PH: +447526326748
info@Hip-HopKings.com
www.hip-hopkings.com
We are dedicated to bringing fans the latest news, reviews and interviews from around the world.

Knowledge
PO Box 56556, London, SW18 9EP UK
PH: (0) 207-183-0468
Colin Steven colin@kmag.co.uk
www.knowledgemag.co.uk
The magazine for Drum n' Bass, Jungle, Hip Hop, Breakbeat and Urban culture.

Spine Magazine
16 Kingly St., London, W1B 5PT UK
PH: +44 (0) 20-7494-4401
FX: +44 (0) 20-7494-4402
press@spinemagazine.com
www.spinemagazine.com
In-depth music reviews.

Australia

Stealth
www.stealthmag.com
Australia's premier Hip Hop magazine.

StreetHop.com
www.streethop.com
Promoting the Hip Hop culture: news, interviews, artist directory, music reviews ...

Africa

Africasgateway
PO Box 879, Strubensvalley, Gauteng,
South Africa 1735
www.africasgateway.com
Africa's largest platform for independent artists and record labels.

Asia

Luv Grooves Radio & Magazine
4-7-18-202 Sumiyoshi Heights, Konan-cho
Higashinada-ku, Kobe-shi Hyogo Japan 658-0084
PH: 011-81-505-532-5452
Gregory E. Williams luvgrooves@yahoo.co.jp
www.luvgrooves.com
Japan's only bilingual R&B/Hip Hop/Gospel magazine dedicated exclusively to indie artists.

Jam Band

Honest Tune
PO Box 1362, Oxford, MS 38655
PH: 662-281-0753 FX: 662-796-3056
www.honesttune.com
Mostly Jam bands, Americana, Alt-Country & Roots music.

High Times
mailbag@hightimes.com
www.hightimes.com
Presenting the true independent voice of today.

Hittin' the Note
customerservice@hittinthenote.com
www.hittinthenote.com
Americana sounds of Blues, Rock & Jazz.

JamBands.com
Dean Budnick dean@jambands.com
www.jambands.com
An online web zine devoted to Improvisational music.

KyndMusic
www.kyndmusic.com
We cover the national and regional Jam scene as well as Folk, World, Indie Rock, Jazz and Blues.

Relix Magazine
104 W. 29th St. 11th Fl. New York, NY 10001
PH: 646-230-0100 FX: 646-230-0200
www.relix.com
Covering other, non-mainstream, types of music.

Jazz

North America

United States

All About Jazz
761 Sproul Rd. #211, Springfield, PA 19064
PH: 610-690-0326
Michael Ricci mricci@allaboutjazz.com
www.allaboutjazz.com
Jazz & Blues magazine/resource.

All About Jazz Italian Version
302A W. 12th St. #204, New York, NY 10014
PH: 610-690-0326 FX: 240-359-2349
Luigi Santosuosso luigi@allaboutjazz.com
italia.allaboutjazz.com
All the info on the Italian Jazz scene.

American Rag
20137 Skyline Ranch Dr. Apple Valley, CA 92308
PH: 760-247-5145 FX: 760-247-5145
don@americanrag.com
www.americanrag.com
Commentary, news, articles of interest and reviews.

Cadence Magazine
Cadence Bldg. Redwood, NY 13679
PH: 315-287-2852 FX: 315-287-2860
Dave cadence@cadencebuilding.com
www.cadencebuilding.com
A thorough and honest guide to and through the current Jazz and Improvised music scenes.

Contemporary Jazz
PO Box 901362, Kansas City, MO 64190-1362
John Hilderbrand john@contemporaryjazz.com
www.contemporaryjazz.com
News, reviews, interviews and release listings.

Culturekiosque
164 Madison Ave. 5th Fl. New York, NY 10016-5411
editors@culturekiosque.com
www.culturekiosque.com
Worldwide A&E guide. We do Jazz and Classical music reviews.

DevraDoWrite
1828 Coolidge Ave. Altadena, CA 91001
PH: 626-398-7984 FX: 626-398-7563
Devra Hall devra@devradowrite.com
devradowrite.com
Blog featuring Jazz and book reviews. No Smooth Jazz!

Down Beat
102 N. Haven Rd. Elmhurst, IL 60126
editor@downbeat.com
www.downbeat.com
Send in your material for review.

FOJAZZ
423 Broadway #131
Millbrae, CA 94030
www.fojazz.com
Blog of Forrest Dylan Bryant, a freelance jazz journalist and broadcaster living in the San Francisco Bay Area. His reviews, profiles and interviews have been published in several leading jazz publications, including JazzTimes and Down Beat magazines, the websites All About Jazz and JazzWest, the Jazz Journalists Association's Jazz Notes journal, the Jazz Education Journal, and Jazz Improv magazine.

Jazz & Blues Music Reviews
jazzandblues.blogspot.com
A completely subjective blog of music reviews covering mostly Jazz and Blues.

Jazz & Blues Report
Bill Wahl billwahl@jazz-blues.com
www.jazz-blues.com
Features show listings and reviews.

Jazz Guitar Life
Lyle Robinson jazzguy@jazzguitarlife.com
www.jazzguitarlife.com
We focus on individuals who give their all to Jazz guitar music and thus, should be acknowledged and appreciated for what they do.

Jazz Improv
PO Box 26770, Elkins Park, PA 19027
PH: 215-887-8808
jazz@jazzimprov.com
www.jazzimprov.com
100 detailed Jazz CD reviews in each issue.

Jazz Monthly
PO Box 218362, Houston, TX 77218
PH: 832-439-3560
Baldwin "Smitty" Smith smitty@jazzmonthly.com
www.jazzmonthly.com
Interviews, news and entertainment that covers all genres of Jazz.

Jazz Times
8737 Colesville Rd. 9th Fl.
Silver Spring, MD 20910-3921
PH: 301-588-4114 x511 FX: 301-588-2009
www.jazztimes.com
World's leading Jazz publication.

Jazz USA
3527 NE 15th St. #126, Portland, OR 97212
PH: 503-715-2507
jazzusa.com
Submit music that you would like reviewed.

Jazziz
2650 N. Military Trail, Fountain Sq. II Bldg. #140
Boca Raton, FL 33431
PH: 561-893-6868 x303 FX: 561-893-6867
www.jazziz.com
The voice of a new Jazz culture.

JazzPolice
301 Oak Grove St. #101, Minneapolis, MN 55403
Don Berryman editor@jazzpolice.com
www.jazzpolice.com
If you would like your CD featured, send a copy to be reviewed and another copy for our give-away.

JazzReview.com
10101 Hunt Club Cir. Mequon, WI 53097
PH: 414-371-5820
Morrice Blackwell morrice@jazzreview.com
www.jazzreview.com
Promotes all styles of Jazz music.

Jus' Jazz
PO Box 2326, Stafford, TX 77497-2326
PH: 281-773-9346
www.jusjazz.com
Your best alternative source of information pertaining to pre-recorded Jazz music.

The Mississippi Rag
9448 Lyndale Ave. S. #120
Bloomington, MN 55420
PH: 952-885-9918 FX: 952-885-9943
editor@mississippirag.com
www.mississippirag.com
New bands are highlighted in each issue.

Point of Departure
Bill Shoemaker feedback@pointofdeparture.org
www.pointofdeparture.org
An online music journal focusing on Jazz and Experimental music.

Saxophone Journal
www.dornpub.com/saxophonejournal.html
Publishes reviews that are positive in nature. Visit our site to find which reviewer covers your style of music.

Smooth Jazz News
5858 Mt. Alifan Dr. #205, San Diego, CA 92111
PH: 858-541-1919
smoothjazznews@aol.com
www.smoothjazznews.com
News, reviews and interviews with both world-renown and cutting edge Jazz artists.

Smooth Jazz Vibes
PO Box 17060, Encino, CA 91416
PH: 818-981-3138
Jonathan Widran few522@aol.com
www.smoothvibes.com
The place to go if you are a fan of Contemporary or Smooth Jazz.

SmoothViews
PO Box 41507, Arlington, VA 22204
www.smoothviews.com
We only review Smooth Jazz CDs that are typically
no more that one year old.

Turbula.net
www.turbula.net
Talented people seem strangely compelled to send us
interesting works for others to enjoy.

Canada

eJazzNews
news@ejazznews.com
www.ejazznews.com
News, profiles, interviews, reviews and more.

Smooth Jazz Now
home@smoothjazznow.com
SmoothJazzNow.com
News, reviews and interviews. Also covers New Age
music.

Europe

Austria

jazzeit.at
Große Sperlgasse 2, A-1020 Wien, Austria
PH: 01-532-8560 FX: 01-532-8561
jazzzeit@jazzzeit.at
www.jazzzeit.at
Information and CD reviews.

Belgium

Dragon Jazz
Ave. du Forum n°17 / boîte 39, B-1020 Bruxelles,
Belgium
users.skynet.be/sky19290
Accent mis sur les productions Européennes et
Belges en particulier. Jazz, Blues, Avant-garde,
Fusion, World Jazz, Jazz Européen ...

Denmark

JAZZ SPECIAL
Havnegade 41, DK-1058 K, Denmark
PH: 45-33-33-87-60 FX: 45-33-33-87-30
www.jazzspecial.dk
The world's most distributed Jazz magazine!

France

Citizen Jazz
18, rue Dupetit-Thouars, 75003 Paris, France
redaction@citizenjazz.com
www.citizenjazz.com
CD review, articles, interviews, audio and radio.

Jazz Break
info@jazzbreak.com
www.jazzbreak.com
Covers the worldwide Jazz scene.

Jazz Hot
BP 405, 75969 Paris 20, France
PH: 33-01-43-66-74-88 FX: 33-01-43-66-72-60
jazzhot@wanadoo.fr
www.jazzhot.net
La revue internationale du Jazz depuis 1935.

Jazz Magazine
info@jazzmagazine.com
www.jazzmagazine.com
Interviews, articles, exhibitions, concert dates, news
reviews etc.

Germany

Jazz Pages
Friedrich Ebert Str 75, 69239 Neckarsteinach,
Germany
PH: 06229-28-20-7 FX: 06229-28-20-8
Frank Schindelbeck jazz@jazzpages.com
www.jazzpages.com
All about Jazz in Germany.

JAZZ PODIUM
Verlags GmbH, Vogelsangstrasse 32, 70197
Stuttgart, Germany
PH: 0711-99-33-778-0 FX: 0711-99-33-778-99
Frank Zimmerle frank.zimmerle@jazzpodium.de
www.jazzpodium.de
Die fachzeitschrift fuer den engagierten Jazz-
enthusiasten.

Jazz Thing
Verlag Azel Stinshoff, Sulzburgstr. 74,
50937 Koln, Germany
PH: 0221-941-488 FX: 0221-413-166
redaktion@jazzthing.de
www.jazzthing.de
Die Zeitschrift für weltoffene musikliebhaber von
heute.

Jazzdimensions
Postfach 36 03 10, 10973 Berlin, Germany
PH: 49-30-612-850-68 FX: 49-30-695-08-273
info@jazzdimensions.de
www.jazzdimensions.de
News, reviews, interviews and articles.

smooth-jazz.de
hbh@smooth-jazz.de
www.smooth-jazz.de
We would prefer to review albums of the Smooth
Jazz and Acid Jazz genre.

Greece

Jazz.GR
info@jazz.gr
www.jazz.gr
News and reviews.

Italy

Italian Jazz Musicians
largo S. Francesco d'Assisi, 25,
70052 Bisceglie BA Italy
PH: 39-080-3929215
marco.valente@jazzengine.com
www.ijm.it
News, reviews, MP3s and online CD sales.

Russia

Jazz News
home.nestor.minsk.by/jazz
A monthly magazine on Jazz and Blues.

Spain

Cuaderno de Jazz
PH: 91-308-03-02 FX: 91-308-05-99
cuadernos@cuadernosdejazz.com
www.cuadernosdejazz.com
Features articles about Jazz musicians.

United Kingdom

Jazzwise
2B Gleneagle Mews, Ambleside Ave. London,
SW16 6AE UK
PH: 44-020-8664-7222 FX: 4-020-8677-7128
www.jazzwise.com
From cutting-edge to Jazz club crossover and World
Jazz.

Smooth Jazz Therapy
Denis Poole denispoole2000@yahoo.com
www.smoothjazztherapy.com
The very best from the world of Smooth Jazz and
Classic Soul.

Asia

CyberFusion
webmaster@jazzfusion.com
jazzfusion.com
CD reviews, interviews, live reports.

Warta Jazz.com
info@wartajazz.net
www.wartajazz.com
The ultimate source for Indonesian Jazz lovers.

Latin

BoomOnline.com
PO Box 398752, Miami Beach, FL 33239
PH: 305-718-3612 FX: 305-468-1983
Gustavo Albán gustavo.alban@boomonline.com
www.boomonline.com
The community site for Latin Rock and Pop.

Brownpride Online
PO Box 3852, Fullerton, CA 92834
FX: 714-792-3806
info@digitalaztlan.com
www.brownpride.com
Everything about the Latino scene.

La Factoria del Ritmo
Apd. 647. CP 39080, Santander - Cantabria, Spain
info@lafactoriadelritmo.com
www.lafactoriadelritmo.com
El primer magazine musical en Español vía internet.

Flamenco-world.com
Concepción Jerónima 35, 3ºA, 28012 Madrid, Spain
magazine@flamenco-world.com
www.flamenco-world.com
Your one stop shop for anything and everything
Flamenco!

HispanicOnline.com
6355 NW 36th St., Virginia Gardens, FL 33166
PH: 305-774-3550 FX: 305-774-3578
Marissa Rodriguez
marissa.rodriguez@page1media.com
www.hispaniconline.com
Does reviews and has an artist-of-the-month feature.

Latin Beat Magazine
15900 Crenshaw Blvd. #1-223, Gardena, CA 90249
PH: 310-516-6767 FX: 310-516-9916
rudy@latinbeatmagazine.com
latinbeatmagazine.com
If you're a new singer or group, here's a chance for
some FREE publicity.

MUSICA SALSA
PH/FX: +49-40-6412902
Stefan Renz stefan.renz@musicasalsa.de
www.musicasalsa.de
*Events and Latin-American culture in Germany,
Colombia and more...*

'LA'Ritmo.com
www.laritmo.com
*Interviews and reviews of established and up-and-
coming artists.*

Musicas Del Mundo
2524 Cascadilla St., Durham, NC 27704-4406
info@musicasdelmundo.org
www.musicasdelmundo.org
News, reviews, interviews etc.

SalsaPower.com
2269 So. University Dr. #155, Davie, FL 33324
Jacira Castro & Julián Mejía jacira@salsapower.com
www.salsapower.com
*We only review artists who do Salsa, Timba and
other related Afro-Cuban rhythms.*

Timba.com
6800 Bird Rd. #267, Miami, FL 33155
www.timba.com
*News, some independent reviews and concert
information.*

Metal

*All styles of Metal as well as Hard Rock,
Modern Rock and Stoner Rock*

North America

United States

1340mag.com
PO Box 7182, 67 E. Main St.
Mount Jewett, PA 16740
Jim McDonald jmmcd@1340mag.com
www.1340mag.com
*Our primary focus is Metal and Punk and their
related genres.*

666metal.com / Harm Magazine
www.666metal.com
*If you are interested in reviews/interviews, please
contact the reviewer that matches your style.*

Absolut Metal
editor@absolutmetal.com
www.absolutmetal.com
Reviews, local tour dates/shows and more.

Adrenalin Metal Union
PO Box 296, Waunakee, WI 53597
Mike Burmeister mike@adrenalinfanzine.com
www.adrenalinmetalunion.com
Promotes bands of the various Metal styles.

APESHIT
www.apeshit.org
An extreme Metal e-zine. Reviews, interviews etc.

Aversion Online
andrew@aversionline.com
www.aversionline.com
*Exposure for all forms of Extreme/Underground
music.*

BallBusterHardMUSIC.com
PO Box 58368, Louisville, KY 40268-0368
PH/FX: 502-447-2568
general@ballbustermusic.com
www.ballbusterhardmusic.com
Without prejudice, 100% lead for your head!

Blabbermouth.net
PO Box 20143, Toledo, OH 43610
Keith Bergman bmouth@bellatlantic.net
www.blabbermouth.net
*All the latest Heavy Metal / Hard Rock news and
reviews. Updated daily.*

Buzzbin Magazine
PO Box 112, Dalton, OH 44618
www.buzzbinmagazine.com
*We feature Rock news, album reviews, download
cues and more from all areas of Rock music.*

Chronicles of Chaos
www.chroniclesofchaos.com
*Extreme music webzine. Updated daily! Contact the
reviewer in your region for our mailing address.*

Crave Magazine
www.cravemagazine.com
Your guide to extreme culture.

Dancing on the Edge
312 Estate Dr. Mt Juliet, TN 37122
Tommy Hash tommyhash@gmail.com
www.thatdevilmusic.com/Dancing
*This bombastic lil' corner o' cyberspace features
news, reviews and interviews from artists exploring
the limits of Progressive Rock, Heavy Metal and
Melodic Rock.*

Darksoul VII
Demian hagatha_xx@yahoo.com
www.darksoul7.net
*Extreme Metal brutality! News, reviews, interviews
etc.*

Doom-metal.com USA
1714 Bradford Dr. Arlington, TX 76010
Timothy Coleman reviews@doom-metal.com
www.doom-metal.com
*Please see submission guidelines before sending
your music.*

The DRP Music Source Webzine
Tony Sison, aka The Atomic Chaser
theatomicchaser@yahoo.com
atomicchaser.journalspace.com
*Great music hiding beyond what the mega-power
radio stations want you to hear.*

The Gauntlet
c/o Jason Fisher
174 W. Foothill Blvd. #235, Monrovia, CA 91016
PH: 310-909-8514 FX: 310-492-5172
www.thegauntlet.com
*Metal indie musicians, bi-weekly mailing list,
reviews, videos and more.*

Glam-Metal.com
Thomas S. Orwat glammetal@rock.com
glam-metal.com
*Bringing you the most updated information on the
best Hard Rock bands on the face of the planet.*

The Grimoire of Exalted Deeds
PO Box 1987, Clifton, NJ 07011
PH: 973-478-3743
www.thegrimoire.com
A Death Metal magazine for assholes, by assholes.

The Hard Rock Society
3201 20th St. S. #124, Fargo, ND 58104
"Metal Man" Dan mmd@hardrocksociety.com
www.hardrocksociety.com
*A Hard Rock/Heavy Metal site with reviews. Home
of Riff Radio.*

Hardrock Haven
John Kindred webmaster@hardrockhaven.net
www.hardrockhaven.net
*Contact us about submitting your material for
review.*

HMAS.org *Heavy Metal Appreciation Society*
John Brighenti jbrighenti@gmail.com
www.hmas.org
*We review ONLY Heavy Metal and its various sub
genres.*

Hyperblast
blood.shall.run@gmail.com
www.hyperblastmetal.com
*Contact us and we'll set you up with the appropriate
reviewer. No demos please!*

Jen's Metal Page
www.jensmetalpage.com
News, reviews, interviews, MP3s etc.

Loudside
3272 Motor Ave. Ste. G, Los Angeles, CA 90034
www.loudside.com
Send in your stuff for review.

Maelstrom
3234 Clay St., San Francisco, CA 94115
Roberto Martinelli giorgio75@hotmail.com
www.maelstrom.nu
Live/album reviews, interviews and more.

Maximum Metal
Frank Hill news@maximummetal.com
www.maximummetal.com
We will review every promo and demo we receive!

Metal Core
PO Box 622, Marlton, NJ 08053
metalczine@aol.com
www.metalcorefanzine.com
Review section for signed and unsigned bands.

Metal Crypt
www.metalcrypt.com
Submit your Metal CDs/demos for review.

Metal Fanatix
Jeffrey Adkins LEGION59@aol.com
www.metalfanatix.com
News, reviews, interviews of Metal music.

Metal Maniacs
104 W. 29th St. 11th Fl. New York, NY, 10001
PH: 646-230-0100 FX: 646-230-0200
www.metalmaniacs.com
News, reviews etc.

MetalBite Magazine
2503 Highland Dr. Lindenhurst, IL 60046
Chris Kloczko info@metalbite.com
www.metalbite.com
Providing insider information through interviews, reviews, editorials, articles and more.

MetalReview.com
www.metalreview.com
Album reviews, concert reviews, band interviews.

MetalReviews.com
www.metalreviews.com
Loads of reviews. Updated weekly!

metalunderground.com
9008 Harris St., Frederick, MD 21704
metalunderground.com
Send promo CDs, demos, stickers, t-shirts etc.

MUEN Magazine
PO Box 11446, Whittier, CA 90603
muentalk@gmail.com
www.muenmag.com
Music underground entertainment news. E-mail us at for interview requests or sending press releases/bios/photos etc.

Neo-Zine
116 E. Horner St., Ebensburg, PA 15931
Carnal neozine@verizon.net
www.myspace.com/neozine
We are involved in all kinds of Noise, Death Metal, Black Metal, Punk etc. Send an e-mail first to make sure that I have some space, and then when I return the e-mail, you can send away!!!

Nocturnal Hall USA
Jessie Gough jussie@nocturnalhall.com
www.nocturnalhall.de
We use a scale from 1 to 10 (1 = biggest crap ever to 10 = fucking brilliant).

On Track Magazine
1752 E. Ave. J #243, Lancaster, CA 93535
David Priest priest@ontrackmagazine.com
www.ontrackmagazine.com
Coverage of your favorite Hard music bands.

PiTRiFF Online
PO Box 1101, Twinsburg, OH 44087
PH: 206-202-5013
Chris richwithhatred@pitriff.com
www.pitriff.com
News, reviews, radio etc.

Revolver
149 5th Ave. 9th Fl. New York, NY 10010
PH: 800-266-3312
rvrcustserv@cdsfulfillment.com
www.revolvermag.com
The world's loudest Rock magazine!

RIFTrock
Jason Lutjen bassplayer@pitriff.com
www.riftrock.com
Rock promotion and daily news.

Rock In Review
www.rockinreview.com
We want to cover the bands you like so let us know who they are and we'll try to get to their show(s) and / or review their CD.

Rock My Monkey
PO Box 828, Olympia, WA 98507
PH: 360-789-0703
Mark mark@rockmymonkey.com
www.rockmymonkey.com
Covers any and all forms of abrasive Rock.

Rock On Request Magazine
PH: 919-889-5121
Christina Avina rockonrequest@lycos.com
www.rockonrequest.com
Focuses on promoting artists through interviews, concert coverage, CD reviews and up to date music news.

RockNet Webzine
Ste. 208 #169, Lewisville, TX 75067
Angela rocknetwebzine@earthlink.net
www.Rocknetwebzine.com
I am a huge fan of Rock and Metal music. One thing I enjoy doing is going out to shows and meeting people.

Rough Edge
PO Box 5160, Ventura, CA 93005
PH/FX: 805-293-8507
info@roughedge.com
www.roughedge.com
CD and live reviews, news, photos and more.

Satan Stole My Teddybear
John Chedsey john@ssmt-reviews.com
www.ssmt-reviews.com
Metal, Punk, Industrial and Rock music review archive. If your CD is Medicore or entirely generic, I'm not going to waste my time coming up with a halfhearted review that is equally generic.

Screachen Publications
PO Box 16352, Phoenix, AZ 85011-6352
president@screachen.com
www.screachen.com
Hard Rock news, interviews, reviews and more.

Silent Uproar
8516 Morgans Way, Raleigh, NC 27613
info@silentuproar.com
www.silentuproar.com
We cover a wide range of Alternative, Metal, Hardcore music.

Sleazegrinder
sleazegrinder@gmail.com
www.sleazegrinder.com
Preservation of full-tilt, high octane, blistering Rock!

SMNnews.com
www.smnnews.com
News, reviews, interviews.

Soul Killer
neil@soulburn3d.com
www.soulkillerwebzine.com
The very best in Death, Grind, Classic and New Metal.

stonerrock.com
PO Box 4, Tendoy, ID 83468
El Danno dan@stonerrock.com
www.stonerrock.com
If you're disgusted with the pathetic state of popular music, you've come to the right place. Please send TWO copies of your CD.

Strigl's Music News
Mark Strigl
PO Box 404, Maplewood, NJ 07040
Mark Strigl striglmark@gmail.com
striglsmusicnews.com
Please only send Hard Rock and Metal. No Emo, Punk etc. You must also create the mailing label as seen above (my name, address and city on different lines).

SugarBuzz
Lucky lucky@sugarbuzzmagazine.com
sugarbuzzmagazine.com
Looking in on today's up and coming Rock 'n Roll artists.

Transcending the Mundane
5 Hudson Ave. Bohemia, NY 11716
Ladd Everitt tmetal@verizon.net
basementbar.com
Quality reviews of newly-released Heavy Metal albums.

Treats from the Underground
PO Box 731, Phoenixville, PA 19460
Burt Wolf beowolfco@aol.com
www.myspace.com/beowolfproductions
Extreme music webzine.

Unchain the Underground
PO Box 15, Stony Point, NY 10980
Al Kikuras al@unchain.com
www.unchain.com
Reviews and interviews of all forms of Extreme music.

undiZcovered Magazine
1382 Wheatland Rd. Baskerville, VA 23915
Angel Hicks um@undizcovered.com
www.undizcovered.com
A Rock, Metal, Alternative and Gothic music magazine that features interviews, opportunities, contests and more!

VOXonline.com
PO Box 712412, Los Angeles, CA 90071
www.voxonline.com
We will listen to all submissions and publish reviews for those that we favor.

Canada

Blistering.com
43 Samson Blvd. #322, Laval, QC H7X 3R8
PH/FX: 450-689-7106
dgehlke@blistering.com
www.blistering.com
Submit your CDs and demos. Bands can sell their CDs at our store. We also feature downloads.

Brave Words and Bloody Knuckles
1057 Steeles Ave. W. #618, Toronto, ON M2R 3X1
PH: 416-229-2966 FX: 416-586-0819
bwbk@bravewords.com
www.bravewords.com
Metal news, features, columns, reviews…

The Metal Observer
71 Martinview Cres. NE., Calgary, AB T3J 2S5
lex@metal-observer.com
www.metal-observer.com
*Visit our website for instructions on sending your
promo/demo/CD in for review.*

Metallian.com
34 Okanagan Dr. #1129,
Richmond Hill, ON L4C 9R8
metallian@canada.com
www.metallian.com
Promotes all sub-genres of Heavy Metal.

Music Emissions.com
Brian Rutherford brian@musicemissions.com
www.musicemissions.com
*An independently run music review community. We
focus on independent labels and artists that fit into
the Alternative music category. We publish music
reviews of CDs on a daily basis as well as weekly
interviews and biographies.*

The PRP
wookubus@theprp.com
www.theprp.com
*We work relentlessly all year round providing news,
reviews and uncovering the very latest acts.*

PureGrainAudio.com
700 King St. W. #208, Toronto, ON M5V 2Y6
PH: 416-723-3911
mail@puregrainaudio.com
www.puregrainaudio.com
*We are looking for any Heavy music bands to send
us their material so that we may offer them some
free press. No demos please!*

Sleaze Roxx
PO Box 142, Minto, MB R0K 1M0
Skid skid55@sleazeroxx.com
www.sleazeroxx.com
Your Hard Rock and Heavy Metal resource.

UNRESTRAINED!
PO Box 42345, 128 Queen St. S.
Mississauga, ON L5M 4Z0
PH: 416-483-7917
vinylpillager@gmail.com
www.unrestrainedmag.com
*Every demo is taken into review/interview
consideration.*

E u r o p e

Austria

Arising Realm
Sechshauserstr. 59/6, A-1150 Vienna, Austria
PH: 0043-1-9665357
www.arisingrealm.at
Reviews, interviews etc.

DarkScene
Gumppstraße 77, 6020 Innsbruck, Austria
www.darkscene.at
*Metal and Gothic magazine with interviews, reviews
and more!*

deathmetal.at
www.deathmetal.at
Brutal Death Metal zine.

Denmark

Antenna
Lars Lolk lolk@antenna.nu
www.antenna.nu
News, reviews, interviews ...

RevelationZ Magazine
Gebauersgade 2, 4. sal, -3, 8000 Aarhus C, Denmark
Steen Jepsen steen@revelationz.net
www.revelationz.net
Your Heavy Metal and Hard Rock resource.

Finland

Imperiumi
tiedotteet@imperiumi.net
www.imperiumi.net
*Visit our website to see which reviewer covers your
particular style of Metal.*

Miasma
www.miasma.org
Blog featuring Metal reviews.

France

Burn Out
2, rue de la Colinette, 51110 Bourgogne, France
PH: 33-0-326-892-668
Phil Kieffer burn.out@wanadoo.fr
www.burnoutzine.net
Chroniques, interviews, concerts, distro ...

Decibels Storm
38 cours Gambetta 69007 Lyon, France
Christophe Noguès decibelsstorm@free.fr
www.decibels-storm.com
Le site de Metal par les fans, pour les fans.

Heavy Metal Universe
www.heavymetaluniverse.com
*From AOR to Grind Death. Please CONTACT US
before you send in your music.*

Leprozy.com
leprophil@aol.com
www.leprozy.com
*Send us news, tour dates, CDs etc. Contact us for
our mailing address.*

Les Immortels
lesimmortels@gmail.com
www.lesimmortels.com
Metal, Rock Prog etc.

Lords of Winter
Asgeirr serqueux@hotmail.com
www.lordsofwinter.com
News, reviews, articles etc.

Metalorgie.com
www.metalorgie.com
*Metal and Punk webzine. Check to see which
reviewer matches your style of music.*

ObsküR[e]
Emmanuel H. emmanuel.obskure@gmail.com
www.obskure.com
*Metal Gothique, Electro, Indus, Death, Black,
Progressif, Ambient, Heavy.*

Santagore
Pierre Noel pierrot@santagore.com
www.santagore.com
Chroniques, interviews, photos ...

Spirit of Metal
Kivan kivan@spirit-of-metal.com
www.spirit-of-metal.com
Reviews, biographies, reports etc.

Germany

Amboss
Postfach 1119, 32001 Herford, Germany
info@amboss-mag.de
www.amboss-mag.de
Heavy Metal and Gothic music magazine.

Ancient Spirit
Burdastr. 4, 77656 Offenburg, Germany
sascha@ancientspirit.de
www.ancientspirit.de
News, interviews, tour dates, live/CD reviews.

Bleeding for Metal
Bergpflege 41, 56218 Mülheim-Kärlich, Germany
Claudia Machwirth kruemel@bleeding.de
www.bleeding.de
*Please address demos, promo-materials etc. to the
above address.*

Bloodchamber
Postfach 30 13 55, 04253 Leipzig, Germany
Christian Rosenau info@bloodchamber.de
www.bloodchamber.de
CD and DVD reviews, interviews and MP3s.

Bright Eyes
Grunewaldstraße 49b, 22149 Hamburg, Germany
PH: +49 (0)40-69667832
info@brighteyes.de
www.bright-eyes.de
*Updates, interviews, reviews, tour dates, festival-
news und vieles mehr ...*

echoes-online.de
Ottmaringer Str. 1a, 92339 Beilngries, Germany
www.echoes-online.de
Metal review blog.

Eternity
StraBmannstr. 49, 10249 Berlin, Germany
redaktion@eternitymagazin.de
eternitymagazin.de
*News, interviews, specials, diskussionen,
festivalberichte, dates ...*

Evil Rocks Hard
Europastraße 3, 64569 Nauheim, Germany
Nils Manegold redaktion@evilrockshard.net
www.evilrockshard.de
*Wir sind ein musik magazin für Hard Rock, Metal,
Punk & Ska!*

Evilized
www.evilized.de
Death Metal, Swedish Metal, Melodic Death Metal.

FFM-Rock.de
www.ffm-rock.de
Interviews, CD reviews, live reviews etc.

Heavy-Magazine.de
Jahnstr.6, 85077 Manching/Oberstimm, Germany
Matt Stenner webmaster@heavy-magazine.de
www.heavy-magazine.de
*Habt Ihr Info Material , eine Promo CD , einen
Song oder ein neues Album? Dann nehmt Kontakt
per E-mail.*

Heavy-Metal.de
Amtsgerichtstr 10, 47119 Duisburg, Germany
PH: 49-0203-666-804 FX: 49-0203-66-93-253
mail@heavy-metal.de
www.heavy-metal.de
News, reviews, interviews, festival/tour dates…

Home of Rock
Kolumbusstr 17, 81543 München, Germany
Fred Schmidtlein webmaster@home-of-rock.de
www.home-of-rock.de
Rock, Heavy Metal news, reviews etc.

Metal District
Im Bauernfeld 30a, 96049 Bamberg, Germany
PH: +49 (0)951-2539843
Patrick Weinstein redaktion@metal-district.de
www.metal-district.de
We review all styles of Metal.

Metal Inside
Torben torben@metal-inside.de
www.metal-inside.de
News, reviews, interviews, tour dates & more.

METALMESSAGE.de
Brückenring 39a, 86916 Kaufering, Germany
PH: +49 (0)8191-6970
Markus Eck info@metalmessage.de
www.metalmessage.de
Reviews and interviews in German & English.

Metal1.info
www.metal1.info
Reviews, interviews und biografien aus der szene!

Metal2Metal
Jahnstr. 7, 46145 Oberhausen, Germany
Dennis Hemken ambiguity@metal2metal.de
www.metal2metal.de
The ultimate (online) Metal-fanzine / magazin.

Metal.de
Postfach 1130, 61451 Königstein i.Ts. Germany
PH: 06174-2939849
Dennis Walz contact@metal.de
metal-online.de
The dark site.

Metalglory
Im Moore 16 A, 30167 Hannover, Germany
metal@metalglory.de
www.metalglory.de
Heavy, Thrash, Black, Doom Metal reviews, interviews ...

Metalnews
www.metalnews.de
Metal, Heavy Metal, Blackmetal, Deathmetal, Darkmetal, Gothicmetal etc. Check our site to see which reviewer fits your style of music.

MyRevelations.de
www.myrevelations.de
Don't spit on those who chose to pose!

Nocturnal Hall
Schmale Strasse 8, 48149 Muenster, Germany
PH: +49 (0) 251-867493
Dajana Winkel office@nocturnalhall.com
www.nocturnalhall.de
We use a scale from 1 to 10
(1 = biggest crap ever to 10 = fucking brilliant).

Powermetal.de
Taunus Straße 44, 72622 Nürtingen, Germany
PH: +49-7022-951091 FX: +49-89-1488-171822
info@weihrauch-medien.de
www.powermetal.de
CD and show reviews and interviews.

Rock Hard Online
Postfach 11 02 12, 44058 Dortmund, Germany
PH: 0231-56-20-14-0 FX: 0231-56-20-14-13
Holger Stratmann Megazine@RockHard.de
www.rockhard.de
Ist sowohl in der Printausgabe als auch online das groesste Rock- und Metal-Magazin Europas.

Rock It!
Lüdinghauser Str. 23, 59387 Ascheberg, Germany
PH: ++49 (0) 2593-951063
FX: ++49 (0) 2593-951064
www.rock-it-magazine.de
*Das AOR * Hard Rock * Metal magazin.*

Schweres-Metall.de
Turnstr. 27, D-66976 Rodalben, Germany
info@schweres-metall.de
www.schweres-metall.de
Das Onlinemagazin für Rock und Metal.

Tinnitus
Holstenstraße 188, 22765 Hamburg, Germany
Haiko Nahm thetruthbeyond@hotmail.com
www.tinnitus-mag.de
Für adressen für demos und promos bitte die entsprechenden mitarbeiter kontaktieren.

Underground Empire Metal Magazine
Röthenbacher Hauptstr. 71,
90449 Nürnberg, Germany
PH: +49 (0)911-6421-924 FX: +49 (0)911-6421-923
info@underground-empire.com
www.underground-empire.de
Prasentiert Deutschlands fuhrendes Metal e-mag.

Vampster
Reichenberger Strasse 9, 71711 Steinheim, Germany
PH: 49-7144-894099 FX: 49-7144-894088
kontakt@vampster.com
www.vampster.com
Bands! labels! veranstalter! schickt daten, promos, demos etc.

Voices from the Darkside
www.voicesfromthedarkside.de
The magazine for brutal Death, Thrash and Black Metal!

Whiskey Soda
Postfach 42 01 02, 12061 Berlin, Germany
PH: 030-75-76-59-52
post@whiskey-soda.de
www.whiskey-soda.de
Alternative Rock/Metal music community.

Greece

Metal Eagle
info@metaleagle.com
www.metaleagle.com
News, reviews, interviews and more.

Italy

Babylon Magazine
www.babylonmagazine.net
Covering the Metal underground.

Shapeless Zine
PO Box 113, 20030 Senago (MI), Italy
Carlo Paleari hellvis@shapelesszine.com
www.shapelesszine.com
We review all Metal bands except nu-Metal bands.

The Netherlands

Aardschok
www.aardschok.com
You can send all CDs, demos and bios.

Art For The Ears
www.artfortheears.nl
Webzine focusing on Metal, Hard Rock, Heavy Alternative Rock, Hardcore and Punk Rock.

Blackfuel
www.blackfuel.nl
Metal & Hardcore e-zine.

Brutalism
Markiezaatpad 5, 5628 BR Eindhoven,
The Netherlands
PH: +31-6-231-33-859 FX: +31 (0) 847-16-59-67
Twan Sibon twan@brutalism.com
www.brutalism.com
Interviews, reviews etc. You can also have your band/label promoted on our site for free!

Lords of Metal
Postbus 756, 1780 AT Den Helder, The Netherlands
Horst Vonberg lordsofmetal@quicknet.nl
www.lordsofmetal.nl/english
CD reviews, gig reviews and new interviews.

Norway

Beat the Blizzard
Ostover, N-2730 Lunner, Norway
aj@beattheblizzard.com
www.beattheblizzard.com
Labels and bands are welcome to ship CDs for review.

Doom-metal.com
Strandvegen 150, 9006 Tromsø, Norway
Arnstein H. Pettersen reviews@doom-metal.com
www.doom-metal.com
Please see submission guidelines before sending your music.

Scream Magazine
www.screammagazine.com
Norway's biggest Metal magazine!

The Streets
Renvikveien 47, 8160 Glomfjord, Norway
PH: +47-480-93-990
Even Knudsen even@streetswebzine.com
www.streetswebzine.com
Dedicated to Heavy Metal music.

Poland

Department of Virtuosity
ul. Balkonowa 3/11, 03-329 Warsaw, Poland
Mikolaj 'Nicolo' Furmankiewicz
nicolo@hmpmag.pl
www.hmpmag.pl/dovmag
My editorial colleagues and I write mainly about traditional kinds of hard 'n'heavy music plus such genres like: Progressive Rock/Metal, Symphonic, Neoclassical Hard Rock/Metal, Shredding, AOR, Blues-Rock, Jazz/Fusion, Avant-garde, Techno-Thrash, Rock & Metal Operas and Classical Guitar-oriented music. My specialization is phenomenon of virtuosity in music.

HMP Magazine
ul. Balkonowa 3/11, 03-329 Warsaw, Poland
hmpmagazine@gmail.com
www.hmpmag.pl
A column with the reviews of virtuosos and virtuoso-like bands' releases - from Classical oriented music to instrumental Electric Guitar, from Neoclassical Metal to Jazz/Fusion.

rockmetal.pl
rockmetal@rockmetal.pl
www.rockmetal.pl
Rock i Metal po Polsku.

Russia

totalmetal.net
info@totalmetal.net
www.totalmetal.net
Russian's #1 Heavy Metal site.

Spain

Basa Rock
Rafa Basa info@rafabasa.com
www.rafabasa.com
Portal en Castellano dedicado al Heavy Metal.

Canedo Rock
Apartado de Correos: 1027, 32001 - Ourense, Spain
canedorock@canedorock.com
www.canedorock.com
Webzine dedicado al Rock en todas sus variantes Metal, Heavy, Punk etc.

Inside Out Webzine
correo@insideoutwebzine.com
www.insideoutwebzine.com
Musica, Metal, Rap-Metal, Nu-Metal, noticias, conciertos, discos, listas ...

The Metal Circus
Sergi Ramos sergi@themetalcircus.com
www.themetalcircus.com
Tu webzine de Metal.

NOIZZ
noizzweb@yahoo.es
personal.telefonica.terra.es/web/noizz
Dedicated to dark sounds. Metal, Gothic, Black, Death, Industrial, Pagan, Heavy, Rock, Dark, EBM...

Portaldelrock.com
comentariosportal@gmail.com
www.portaldelrock.com
Un portal de musica Rock y Metal.

Rock Circus
APDO. 146, 28820, Madrid, Spain
Iván Ortega rockcircus@arrakis.es
www.rockcircus.net
Tu revista de Rock en internet.

ROCK ESTATAL
rockestatal@rockestatal.com
rockestatal.com
Rock nacional estatal Heavy Metal y Punk.

XTREEM MUSIC
PO Box 1195, 28080, Madrid, Spain
info@xtreemmusic.com
www.xtreemmusic.com
Portal devoted to Extreme music.

Sweden

Close Up
PO Box 4411, SE-102 69, Stockholm, Sweden
PH: 46-8-462-02-14 FXA: 46-8-462-02-15
mail@closeupmagazine.net
www.closeupmagazine.net
A forum for all types of Extreme and Heavy music!

RockUnited.Com *A&R Dept.*
info@rockunited.com
rockunited.com
We review demos or independent releases of unsigned bands looking for promotion. Check our site to see which reviewer fits your style of music.

Tartarean Desire
Vincent Eldefors tartareandesire@yahoo.com
www.tartareandesire.com
Metal and Dark music with reviews, interviews etc. Please contact us to see which reviewer fits your style of music.

Switzerland

Swiss Metal Factory
PO Box 809, 5401 Baden, Switzerland
PH: 41-0-79-638-1021
metal@metalfactory.ch
www.metalfactory.ch
Reviews, interviews, concerts etc.

Turkey

Rock Vault
Hasam Basaram hasan@rock-vault.com
www.rock-vault.com
Raising its level of quality and performance higher by the time, Rock Vault continues to make firm steps towards becoming Turkey's fastest growing and most efficient webzine.

United Kingdom

Archaic Magazine
90 Methuen St., Wavertree, Liverpool, Merseyside, L15 1EQ UK
Dave Waite corpseplayer@hotmail.com
vampire-magazine.com
Covering the world of Underground Metal. Please send your promos, demos and other material to us for a fair review.

Black Velvet
editor@blackvelvetmagazine.com
www.blackvelvetmagazine.com
Features Glam, Punk, Rock, Metal and more.

Justin-Case.co.uk
justin@justin-case.co.uk
www.justin-case.co.uk
Rock album reviews.

Kerrang! Magazine
editor@kerrang.com
www.kerrang.com
The world's biggest selling weekly Rock magazine.

Live 4 Metal
PO Box 7626, Belper, DE56 9DQ UK
Steve Green Live4metalsteve@aol.com
www.live4metal.com
The best of the Metal world.

Metal Hammer
1 Balcombe St., London, NW1 6NA UK
Attn: Reviews editor
PH: +44 (0)870-444-8649
james.gill@futurenet.co.uk
www.metalhammer.co.uk
Send a copy of your latest demo.

Metal Mayhem
www.metal-mayhem.co.uk
Please contact us for the address to send stuff to.

Planet-Loud
PO Box 2581, Reading, Berks, RG1 7GT UK
info@planet-loud.com
www.planet-loud.com
The loudest music site on the net!

Powerplay
PO Box 227, Manchester, M22 4YT UK
PH: 0161-4914211
Mark Hoaksey powerplaymagazine@btinternet.com
www.powerplaymagazine.co.uk
Hard, Heavy, Power, Prog, Progressive, Speed, AOR, FM, Death, Extreme and Black.

Rock And Metal Domain
Matthew White
rock-metal-domain666@hotmail.com
www.rockandmetaldomain.co.uk
Rock and Metal website with news, reviews, bands and links.

Rock Midgets.com
www.rockmidgets.com
We focus on Rock, Metal and Punk.

ROCK SOUND
#22, Jack's Pl., 6 Corbet Pl., Spitalfields, London, E1 6NN UK
Darren darren.taylor@rock-sound.net
www.rock-sound.net
Monthly music magazine in the UK.

Australia

The Buzz
psuttonh@ozonline.com.au
www.ozonline.com.au/buzz
CD reviews, interviews and coverage of local artists.

FasterLouder.com.au
www.fasterlouder.com.au
Gig info, interviews, reviews etc.

MelodicRock.com
GPO Box 1770, Hobart, TAZ 7001 Australia
PH: +61-3-6229-3113
Andrew J. McNeice ajm@melodicrock.com
www.melodicrock.com
Reviews Melodic and Hard Rock.

PyroMusic
PO Box 6016, Marrickville South, NSW 2204 Australia
pyromusic@pyromusic.net
www.Pyromusic.net
If you're Metal we're happy to receive your material for review.

BOOK YOUR OWN GIGS!

32,000 Live Music Venues in the US and Canada - www.indievenuebible.com

New Age

Includes Ambient, Future Lounge, Downtempo and Chill-Out.

Amazing Sounds
amazingsounds@amazings.com
www.amazings.com
News, articles, interviews, album reviews...

Ambient Visions
Michael Foster editor@ambientvisions.com
www.ambientvisions.com
Reviews and interviews of Ambient, New Age, Electronica and Techno music.

Awareness Magazine
446 S. Anaheim Hills Rd. #183
Anaheim, CA 92807
PH: 714-283-3385 FX: 714-283-3389
info@awarenessmag.com
www.awarenessmag.com
Holistic magazine with music and video reviews.

The Harp Column
2101 Brandywine, #200B, Philadelphia, PA 19130
Attn: Jan Jennings
PH: 800-582-3021 FX: 215-564-3518
www.harpcolumn.com
Reviews, news, forum and announcements regarding the harp.

Innerchange
2329 Avent Ferry Rd. Holly Springs, NC 27540
PH: 919-552-3062
Diana Palmer dpalmer@innerchangemag.com
innerchangemag.com
Magazine website with music reviews.

Kindred Spirit
Unit 2, Lynher House, 3 Bush Park, Plymouth, Devon, PL6 7RG UK
PH: 01752-762-970 FX: 01752-772107
nigel.moore@metropolis.co.uk
www.kindredspirit.co.uk
The UK's leading guide for body, mind and spirit.

Mysteries Magazine
PO Box 490, Walpole, NH 03608-0490
PH: 603-352-1645 FX: 603-352-0232
Kim Guarnaccia editor@mysteriesmagazine.com
www.MysteriesMagazine.com
We review CDs of World music, New Age music, healing/meditation/yoga music etc.

New Age Retailer
2183 Alpine Way, Bellingham, WA 98226
PH: 800-463-9243 FX: 360-676-0932
www.newageretailer.com
Two independent music review columns.

New Age Reporter
650 Poydras #2523, New Orleans, LA 70130
www.newagereporter.com
We will review New Age, World, Celtic, Folk and Neo-Classical works.

New Renaissance
3A Cazenove Rd. London, N16 6PA UK
PH: +44-20-88064250
www.ru.org
Reviews of books, recordings and events.

Spirit of Change
2749 E. 17th St., Oakland, CA 94601
Jason Serinus jserinus@planeteria.net
www.spiritofchange.org
Welcomes independent music reviews and all music releases.

Writings by Serge Kozlovsky
ul.Kropotkina d.108 kv.11, 220123 Minsk, Belarus
serge_kozlovsky@tut.by
sergekozlovsky.com
Articles, interviews and reviews.

Yoga Journal
475 Sansome St. #850, San Francisco, CA 94111
PH: 415-591-0555 FX: 415-591-0733
www.yogajournal.com
The voice of yoga online.

Yoga Magazine
26 York St., London, W1U 6PZ UK
PH: 44-020-7729-5454 FX: 44-020-7739-0025
www.yogamagazine.co.uk
Willing to listen to anything you send.

Progressive Rock

Progressive Rock, AOR, Jazzrock, Melodic Rock, Progressive Metal, Spacerock, Krautrock, Psychedelic and Improvisational Rock

North America
United States

ghostland.com
chad@ghostland.com
ghostland.com
Your source for Progressive Rock on the web. Contact us for mailing address.

Ground and Sky
1743 Park Rd. NW., Washington, DC 20010
Brandon Wu webmaster@progreviews.com
www.progreviews.com
Do not e-mail us asking if it's OK to send us your CD. Just send it in and we'll make the judgment based on the music. Please, no MP3s!

Music Street Journal
Gary Hill
musicstreetjournal@musicstreetjournal.com
www.musicstreetjournal.com
News, reviews, interviews ...

Prog4you.com
PO Box 687, Coatesville, PA 19320
George Roldan info@prog4you.com
www.prog4you.com
We are always looking for new material, that we can listen to and review.

ProGGnosis
PO Box 27226, Golden Valley, MN 55427-0226
webmaster@proggnosis.com
www.proggnosis.com
Our goal is to further the success of Progressive and Fusion music genres.

Progression Magazine
PO Box 7164, Lowell, MA 01852
PH: 978-970-2728 FX: 978-970-2728
progmagazine@aol.com
www.progressionmagazine.com
News, reviews, interviews and features.

Progressive Ears
1594 6th St., Trenton, NJ 08638
Floyd Bledsoe floyd@progressiveears.com
progressiveears.com
Progressive Rock discussion, polls and reviews.

ProgressiveWorld.net
www.progressiveworld.net
Check our site to find out which reviewer accepts your style of Prog music.

ProgNaut.com
reviews@prognaut.com
www.prognaut.com
Vessel for Southern California Progressive music.

ProgScape.Com
www.progscape.com
Get your CD or DVD reviewed.

Sea of Tranquility
53 Old Country Rd. Monroe, NY 10950
www.seaoftranquility.org
Journal of Fusion and Progressive Rock.

Ytsejam.com
312 Estate Dr. Mt Juliet, TN 37122
Tommy Hash tommyhash@gmail.com
www.ytsejam.com
"Your Progressive Rock One Stop." The music genres I cover are Heavy Metal, Hard Rock, Progressive Rock, Melodic Rock, Classic Rock, and AOR. I do articles, conduct interviews, and review releases.

South America

Planeta-Rock
www.planeta-rock.com.ar
Based in Argentina. New, reviews, radio etc.

Progressive Rock & Progressive Metal
www.progressiverockbr.com
Based in Brazil. Reviews, interviews and much more.

Europe
Belgium

Prog-résiste
rue du Bordon, 36, B-5530, Durnal, Belgium
Olivier Delooz promos@progresiste.com
www.progresiste.com
We publish (in French only) a quarterly, 132 pages magazine with reviews, news, rumors, events ...

Rock Report
Collegestraat 129, B-8310 Assebroek, Belguim
PH: 32-050-35-87-72 FX: 32-050-35-87-72
info@rockreport.be
www.rockreport.be
A new medium, totally dedicated to AOR.

France

AmarokProg
webmaster@amarokprog.net
www.amarokprog.net
All about Progressive Rock, Metal, Alternative Rock and Electro with band pages, concert guides, news, reviews and much more!

Big Bang
redaction@bigbangmag.com
www.bigbangmag.com
Une revue Français consacrée aux musiques Progressives.

KOID'9
51 ave. du Président Wilson, 45500 Gien, France
Bernard Prevost ber.prevost@wanadoo.fr
koid9.fanzine.free.fr
Un fanzine trimestriel très complet, réalisé par des passionnés, traitant avec humour de l'actualité du Rock Progressif, Metal Progressif et Rock Alternatif.

Progressia.net
promotion@progressia.net
www.progressia.net
Rock Progressif, Metal Progressif, Jazz Expérimental, Fusion, Post-Rock.

Traverses
c/o Stéphane Fougère, 16, ave. d'Alfortville, 94600 Choisy le Roi, France
traversesmag.org
Musiques presque nouvelles et autrement Progressia neogressives.

Germany

Babyblaue Prog-Reviews
Grünwalder Straße 117, D-81547 München, Germany
PH: 089-64260946
Udo Gerhards promos@babyblaue-seiten.de
www.babyblaue-seiten.de
Die Prog-Enzyklopädie der mailing liste.

Progressive Newsletter
www.progressive-newsletter.de
Reviews, interviews, gig dates etc.

Italy

Arlequins
Via Paparoni 6, 53100 Siena, Italy
Alberto Nucci alberto@arlequins.it
www.arlequins.it
Covers the Progressive Rock underground scene.

MovimentiPROG
staff@movimentiprog.net
www.movimentiprog.net
Riflessioni scritte sulla musica che evolv.

The Netherlands

The Dutch Progressive Rock Page
www.dprp.net
Internet magazine on Progressive Rock.

The iO Pages
Postbus 67, 2678 ZH De Lier, The Netherlands
FX: +31-174-51-12-13
iopages@iopages.nl
www.iopages.nl
Magazine devoted to Progressive Rock and all its related genres.

Progwereld
Postbus 7069, 2701 AB Zoetermeer,
The Netherlands
www.progwereld.org
News, reviews, interviews, columns etc.

Norway

Tarkus
Mollefaret 48B, N-0750 Oslo, Norway
Sven Eriksen sven@tarkus.org
www.tarkus.org
We cover a wide spectrum of Progressive music.

United Kingdom

New Horizons
reviews@elrose.demon.co.uk
www.elrose.co.uk
Progressive, Classic and Melodic Rock on the web.

Uzbekistan

ProgressoR
PO Box 4065, Tashkent, 700100, Uzbekistan
Vitaly Menshikov vitt@glb.net
www.progressor.net
Send your CDs to us for review. Please, no demos!

Punk

Punk, Hardcore, Emo Oi, Garage and Anti-Folk

North America

United States

Absolute Punk
Linda linda@absolutepunk.net
www.absolutepunk.net
Submit your demo, album or EP to us.

Alarm Press
53 W. Jackson Blvd. #1256, Chicago, IL 60604
music@alarmpress.com
www.alarmpress.com
We listen to thousands of CDs and attend live concerts in order to bring you inspirational artists who are fueled by an honest and contagious obsession with their art.

American Music Press
PO Box 1070, Martinez, CA 94553
ampmagazine.com
Interviews, reviews, columns, articles etc.

Askew Reviews
PO Box 684, Hanover, MA 02339
denis@askewreviews.com
www.askewreviews.com
We cover, review and promote music.

Aversion.com
PO Box 271556, Fort Collins, CO 80527-1556
PH: 970-493-0585
www.aversion.com
Submit your press kits and demos. Rock, Punk and Indie Rock.

Bystander Fanzine
230 Myrtle Ave. Albany, NY 12202
Scott bystanderfanzine@gmail.com
www.bystanderfanzine.com
Covering the Hardcore scene.

centerfuse.net
reviews@centerfuse.net
www.centerfuse.net
Dedicated to the independent music scene.

Culture Bunker
PO Box 480353, Los Angeles, CA 90048
culturebunker@hotmail.com
www.culturebunker.com
Indiscriminate, wholesale, erotic, power-mad killing.

Decoy Music Magazine
PO Box 6078, Atascadero, CA 93423
aaron@decoymusic.com
www.decoymusic.com
Covering everything from Punk to Metal to Hip Hop. Industry revealing interviews and more.

Delusions of Adequacy
PO Box 1081, Drexel Hill, PA 19026
Jenn & Kyle doa@adequacy.net
www.adequacy.net
We primarily focus on independent music of various types with a focus on Rock, Metal, Folk and Punk.

emotionalpunk.com
PO Box 363, Littleton, CO 80160
Andrew Martin andrew.martin@emotionalpunk.com
www.emotionalpunk.com
If you are an artist or promoter and want a "guaranteed" review, be sure to e-mail me first.

Empyre Lounge
54 Montvale Rd. Woburn, MA 01801
label@empyrelounge.com
www.empyrelounge.com
Protecting endangered music.

How's Your Edge?
www.howsyouredge.com
News, reviews, shows etc.

ihateyour.com
560 Pine Ct. Sequim, WA 98382
John Himmelberger contact@ihateyour.com
www.ihateyour.com
Send us your press kit, along with your latest release.

Juice Magazine
2058 N. Sycamore Ave. Hollywood, CA 90068
PH: 310-399-5336 FX: 323-924-2363
Terri Craft info@juicemagazine.com
www.juicemagazine.com
Sounds, surf and skate.

Killwhat Fanzine
1797 Main St., Concord, MA 01742
Kelly Saux kelly@killwhat.com
www.killwhat.com
Send in your promo material.

Lollipop
PO Box 441493, Boston, MA 02144
PH: 617-623-5319
Scott Hefflon scott@lollipop.com
www.lollipop.com
We cover all that fiercely Alternative music.

Modern Fix
3368 Governor Dr. #318F, San Diego, CA 92122
PH: 715-514-1197
Eric Huntington eric.huntington@modernfix.com
www.modernfix.com
A cultural bib for those who enjoy music, video games and popular culture.

Mudsugar Magazine
107 S. West St. #463, Alexandria, VA 22314
www.mudsugar.com
We review Alternative music! "What is alternative music" you may ask? Who the hell knows anymore, but here's our definition: Alternative music is any Rock and Punk-Rock-based music genres that doesn't fit into current mainstream genres.

Neo-Zine
116 E. Horner St., Ebensburg, PA 15931
Carnal neo-zine@hotmail.com
www.myspace.com/neozine
We merge material from such diverse styles as Noise, Punk, Death Metal, Experimental, Gothic etc. Send an e-mail first to make sure that I have some space.

Neu Futur
650 Morris #6, Kent, OH 44243
James McQuiston editor@neufutur.com
www.neufutur.com
I review anything that comes across my desk.

Paranoize
PO Box 15554, New Orleans, LA 70175-5554
Bobby Bergeron bobby@paranoizenola.com
www.paranoizenola.com
Covers Sludge, Grindcore, Hardcore, Extreme Metal, Stoner Rock and non-Pop/Ska influenced Punk.

pastepunk
Jordan A. Baker jordan@pastepunk.com
www.pastepunk.com
Tons of reviews, interviews and columns.

Psychobilly Homepage
roy@wreckingpit.com
www.wreckingpit.com
Concerts, news, reviews interviews and more.

Punk Globe
PO Box 3064, Los Angeles, CA 90078
Ginger Coyote ginger@punkglobe.com
www.punkglobe.com
News, interviews, music & show reviews.

Punk Magazine
PMB 675, 200 E. 10th St., New York, NY 10003
Editor@punkmagazine.com
www.punkmagazine.com
Send all promo material, CDs and other hard copy to us. If you send us email asking us if we received your band's CD for review you risk our wrath!

punknews.org
39 Greenhaven Dr. Port Jefferson Stn., NY 11776
Attn: Brian Shultz
www.punknews.org
Submit your material for review.

ReadJunk.com
407 Regency Ct. Middletown, NY 10940
PH: 845-313-2516
Bryan Kremkau bryan@readjunk.com
www.readjunk.com
Entertainment website that features news, reviews, interviews, articles and more!

Redefine Magazine
Vivian Hua huav@redefinemag.com
www.redefinemag.com
An online magazine dedicated to Rock music, art and social commentary.

Redstar Magazine
www.redstarmag.com
Online magazine supporting music and modeling. New, reviews, interviews ...

Reviewer Magazine
PO Box 87069, San Diego, CA 92138
PH: 619-694-6680
Rob editor@reviewermagazine.com
www.reviewermag.com
We cover Indie and Punk Rock, social issues etc.

Rock n Roll Purgatory
PO Box 276258, San Antonio, TX 78227
rocknrollpurgatory@yahoo.com
www.rocknrollpurgatory.com
We review Rockabilly, Surf, Punk, Oi, Swing, Psychobilly and then some ...

Skratch Magazine
1085 N. Main St. Ste. N, Orange, CA 92867
www.SkratchMagazine.com
Covers Garage Rock, Punk, Hardcore and Emo.

Skyscraper
PO Box 486, Mamaroneck, NY 10543
skyscraperzine@hotmail.com
www.skyscrapermagazine.com
Music, print, live reviews and more.

Sonic Ruin Magazine
PO Box 752, Harvard, IL 60033
Carl Isonhart zombiezilla@yahoo.com
myspace.com/sonicruin
A print fanzine specializing in Glam/Rockabilly/Blues/Punk/Sleaze and basically straight up, good ol' Rock and Roll.

Soundnova.com
Corey Evans info@soundnova.com
www.Soundnova.com
Covering mainstream and underground acts.

Stereokiller.com
Chris Brickhouse
317 Washington Ave. Phoenixville, PA 19460
www.stereokiller.com
Reviews Hardcore, Emo, Punk and Metal CDs. Also, you can post your MP3s!

Substream Music Press
130 Griswold St., Delaware, OH 43015
PH: 614-370-0837
Jason McMahon jmac@substreammagazine.net
www.myspace.com/substreammagazine
Features Pop Punk, Emo and Indie Music. Our magazines go to retailers all over the US.

Super Bitch Magazine
John Davies superbitchmagazine@yahoo.com
www.superbitchmagazine.com
*Dedicated to girls, booze, music ...and more girls. Music reviews that don't follow the norm. *Contains adult content.*

Terminal Boredom
301 Tremaine Ave. Kenmore, NY 14217
Rich Kroneiss termibore@aol.com
www.terminal-boredom.com
Bands, labels and distros, please feel free to pick a reviewer who it seems might be the right person for your record and send it to them.

Tragic Endings
2 Stephanie Ln. Lakeville, MA 02347
Stephanie DeMoura
stephanie@silversteinmusic.com
www.tragicendings.net
We're not about money or being into the 'scene' or any of that nonsense. We love to help out the bands.

truepunk.com
www.truepunk.com
News, reviews, interviews and a message board.

Tweed Magazine
Stewart Smith stewart@tweedmag.com
tweedmag.com
Interviews with bands, artists and other influential members of society.

URPromotions Magazine
Dewey dewman92@hotmail.com
www.myspace.com/urpromotions
A magazine that supports independent labels and bands in Hard Rock, Punk, Metal and all genres in between.

UsedWigs
www.usedwigs.com
Current Indie Rock, Punk and other assorted quality music reviews.

Canada

Flex Your Head
www.flexyourhead.net
Reviews, audio samples, interviews, links and more.

Punk Me Up
PH: 514-659-6532
1652 Amherst, Montréal, QC H2L 3L5
Julien-Pierre Trudeau info@punkmeup.com
www.punkmeup.com
News, reviews and features.

Europe

Belgium

Mashnote.Magazine
Asstraat 4/2, 2400 Mol, Belgium
Jim Faes info@mashnote.net
www.mashnote.net
Interviews, reviews, news and more. Contact us before sending in your music.

PunkRockTheory
PO Box 79, Mechelen, Belgium 2800
PH: 0032-479-232-680
Thomas Dumarey thomas@punkrocktheory.com
www.punkrocktheory.com
We have tons of reviews, interviews, MP3s and label profiles.

Finland

Hardcoresounds
Kauppapuistikko 24 B 22, 65100 Vaasa, Finland
Arto Mäenpää crew@hardcoresounds.net
hardcoresounds.net
Send us an album or other material for review.

France

Dig It!
32, rue Pharaon, 31000 Toulouse, France
FX: 05-61-14-06-28
digitfanzine@gmail.com
www.chez.com/digitfanzine
Rawk 'n' Roll French fanzine!!!

Metalorgie.com
djou@metalorgie.com
www.metalorgie.com/punk
There are different contacts covering the various sub-genres of Punk.

Punksociety.fr
nico@punksociety.fr
punksociety.fr
News, reviews, gigs etc.

Sans Tambour ni Trompette
9, rue Bartholdi, 56700 Hennebont, France
info@stnt.org
www.stnt.org
Interactive ezine & radio show from France with news (a lot!), reviews, links, interviews…

Germany

Allschools Network
Nikolausstr, 107, 50937, Kohn, Germany
Torben Utecht torben@allschools.de
www.allschools.net
Online Hardcore fanzine. Send demos to the above address.

Between Evil And Peace
www.beap.de
Stoner Rock, Psychedelic Rock …

CORE Ground
RehmstraBe 119, #501, 49080 Osnabruck, Germany
Holger Straede holger@coreground.de
www.coreground.de
Hardcore fanzine. Send in your material.

Enough
info@enoughfanzine.com
www.enoughfanzine.com
DIY punk/HC/Ska/Indie e-zine for the scene!

FetzOrDie.com
Werner-Bock Str 9, D- 33602, Bielefeld, Germany
Raphael Gutberlet info@fetzordie.com
www.fetzordie.com
Send all CDs, tour information etc. to the above address.

Konzi-Tip.de
Schopenhauer Strasse 31, D-14467 Potsdam, Germany
PH: 030-70301911 FX: 0331-7482913
Martin R. Woicke webmaster@konzi-tip.de
www.konzi-tip.de
Punk, Emo, Hard Rock, Gothic …

Moloko Plus
Feldstr 10, 46286 Dorsten, Germany
info@moloko-plus.de
www.moloko-plus.de
News, dates, gigs, zines and more.

Online Zine
Aulgasse 131, 53721 Seigburg, Germany
Boguslaw Cala psychodad@onlinezine.de
www.onlinezine.net
The voice of subculture. Reviews, news and more.

Ox Fanzine
Postfach 11 04 20, 42664 Solingen, Germany
PH: +49 (0)212-38-31-828
FX: +49 (0)212-38-31-830
Joachim Hiller redaktion@ox-fanzine.de
www.ox-fanzine.de
Germany's biggest Punk Rock & Hardcore zine.

Plastic Bomb
Heckenstr. 35/HH, 47058 Duisburg, Germany
PH: 0203-3630334 Fx: 0203-734288
swebo@plastic-bomb.de
www.plastic-bomb.de
News, reviews, interviews and much more.

*poisonfree.com
Kronprinzenstr. 8b, 58511 Luedenscheid, Germany
Phil Penninger phil@poisonfree.com
www.poisonfree.com
Europe's oldest and best visited mag for Hardcore, Punk & related arts!

purerock.de
Diesterwegstr. 9c, 10405 Berlin, Germany
PH: 030-420-22-917 FX: 030-420-22-917
Steffen Lehmann webmaster@purerock.de
www.purerock.de
Your Alternative Rock community.

Scarred For Life
Muhlenstrasse 68, 13187 Berlin, Germany
info@scarred-for-life.de
www.scarred-for-life.de
Punk, Oi, Ska, Metal reviews, interviews etc.

Trust Fanzine
Postfach 11 07 62, 28087 Bremen, Germany
PH: 0421-49-15-88-0 FX: 0421-49-15-88-1
Dolf Hermannstädter dolf@trust-zine.de
www.trust-zine.de
Online resource for Hardcore, Punk Rock and Emo.

Waste of Mind
Reichenberger Str. 159, 10999 Berlin, Germany
Kai Wydra wom@wasteofmind.de
www.wasteofmind.de
News, reviews, tour dates, MP3s and much more.

Italy

Freak Out
C.P. 166 - 80059 - Torre del greco (Na), Italy
FX: 0039-081-8822687
Vittorio Emanule info@freakout-online.com
www.freakout-online.com
Independent music magazine. Postrock Noise, Emo, Metal …

In Your Eyes
Via n.cantalupo 15f, 17019 Varazze (SV) Italy
Simone Benerecetti simone@iyezine.com
www.iyezine.com
About what we think and what we feel.

komakino
Paolo yrkomakino@gmail.com
www.inkoma.com
If you can direct me to a couple of MP3s, I'll check them out and get in touch.

The Netherlands

Asice.net
Eerste Esweg 27A, 7642 BH Wierden, The Netherlands
David Brinks info@asice.net
www.asice.net
Get your stuff reviewed, promoted or whatever!

Norway

punkbands.com
Amy Meyer amyrebelyell@hotmail.com
www.punkbands.com
Promotes Punk, Ska and Oi bands from all over the world.

Spain

IPunkRock.com
PO Box 156.103, 28080, Madrid, Spain
escribenos@ipunkrock.com
www.ipunkrock.com
Online Punk- Rock n' Roll zine in Spanish.

RockCore
www.rockcore.com
Hardcore, Rock, Metal y Punk.

Sweden

Doomsday Magazine
Andreas Hedberg doomsday@home.se
www.doomsdaymag.com
News, interviews, reviews and more.

United Kingdom

Beat Motel
PO Box 773, Ipswich, IP1 9FT UK
poo@beatmotel.co.uk
beatmotel.co.uk
Kinda a Punk zine but our musical tastes are pretty broad and a bunch of our writing has chuff all to do with either Punk or music.

Big Cheese Magazine
Unit 7 Clarendon Bldg. 25 Horsell Rd. Highbury, London, N5 1XL UK
PH: +44 (0) 20-7607-0303
info@bigcheesemagazine.com
www.bigcheesemagazine.com
Featuring Punk, Metal and Rock.

Bubblegum Slut
27 Stores Ln. Tiptree, Essex, CO5 0LH UK
bubblegumslutzine@gmail.com
www.myspace.com/bubblegumslutzine
A glammy / sleazy / punky / gothy fanzine! This is NOT the place for Emo, Grunge and things ending in 'core' okay.

Organ Zine
19 Herbert Gardens, London, NW10 3BX UK
Sean organ@organart.demon.co.uk
www.organart.com
We're mostly interested in Punk/Metal/Alternative/ Prog and music of a left field guitar nature.

Punktastic.com
4 William St., Scunthorpe, North Lincs, DN16 1SZ UK
Mark mark@punktastic.com
www.punktastic.com
Send any goodies / releases / promos (no horses' heads please) to the above address.

R*E*P*E*A*T Online
PO Box 438, Cambridge, CB4 1FX UK
rosey@repeatfanzine.co.uk
www.repeatfanzine.co.uk
Focuses on the Underground music scene.

Suspect Device
PO Box 295, Southampton, SO17 1LW UK
suspectdevicehq@hotmail.com
www.suspectdevicehq.co.uk
We have diverse tastes and cover most styles of Punk Rock.

Voltcase
VM info@voltcase.co.uk
www.voltcase.co.uk
An online alternative culture magazine focusing on the Punk, Metal, Goth & Alternative scenes.

Africa

zapunx.com
www.zapunx.com
Alternative music community website. Share your views on CDs, EPs, LPs, VHS tapes, DVDs, anything!

Reggae

Reggae, Ska, Rocksteady, Dancehall and Caribbean.

The Beat Magazine
Chuck Foster cfoster907@yahoo.com
www.getthebeat.com
A bimonthly publication of Reggae, African, Caribbean and World music, providing information, news, reviews, interviews etc.

DerDude Goes SKA.de
Emser Straße 18, 56076 Koblenz, Germany
derdude@derdude-goes-ska.de
www.derdude-goes-ska.de
Ska nicht einfach eine muzik!

Dizzybeat *Australia*
dizzybeat.com
Ska, Reggae, Punk, Life. We encourage people to contribute photos, reviews, news and articles.

JahWorks.org
PO Box 9207, Berkeley, CA 94709
info@jahworks.org
jahworks.org
Portrays Caribbean and African-based music and culture with enthusiasm and integrity.

Jammin Reggae
niceup.com
The gateway to Reggae music on the internet!

Reggae in Germany
Peter Beckhaus peter@reggaenode.de
www.reggaenode.de
News, reviews, forums etc.

Reggae News
info@reggaenews.co.uk
www.reggaenews.co.uk
We review a very wide selection of Reggae music.

Reggae Report
PO Box 1823, Hallandale, FL 33008
PH: 305-933-9918 FX: 305-705-0448
info@reggaereport.com
www.reggaereport.com
All the info on the Reggae scene.

The Reggae Source
655 Deerfield Rd. #100-336, Deerfield, IL 60015
PH/FX: 773-785-7536
info@reggaesource.com
www.reggaesource.com
Solid information on this crucial music form.

Reggae Train.com
info@reggaetrain.com
reggaetrain.com
Comprehensive Reggae music portal on the web.

The Indie Contact Newsletter
www.indiebible.com

Reggae Vibes
Pieter Brueghelstraat 5, 6181 DJ Elsloo,
The Netherlands
PH: 31-46-4373228 FX: 31-46-4376427
info@reggae-vibes.com
www.reggae-vibes.com
Spread the "Reggae vibes"...anyway & anywhere!

Reggaefrance.com
33, rue de Trévise, 75009 Paris, France
redaction@reggaefrance.com
www.reggaefrance.com
Retrouvez la référence Reggae Dancehall, nombreuses interviews d'artistes Jamaïquains & Français.

The Ska Tipz
skatimail@neoska.com
neoska.com
A site for Japanese Ska bands and other Ska music.

Ska Wars
Gabriel gabriel@skawars.nu
www.skawars.nu
Guide to Ska, Reggae and Rocksteady.

Surforeggae
contato@surforeggae.com.br
www.surforeggae.com.br
All the info on the Reggae scene.

Soul / R&B

United States

BlackRadiolsBack.com
PO Box 2465, Waldorf, MD 20604-2465
Mary Nichols (DJ Fusion)
blackradioisback@gmail.com
www.blackradioisback.com
Submit your music, books, magazines, DVDs etc. for review.

RHYTHMflow.net
PO Box 130, Bronx, NY 10467
www.rhythmflow.net
If you are an artist and would like to have your project considered for an upcoming issue, please e-mail us your info.

RnB Music
www.rnbmusicblog.com
If you have a hot scoop, song, albums or you want this blog to promote your work, please send me an email.

Soul Strut
PO Box 174, Sellersville, PA 18960
ish415@soulstrut.com
www.soulstrut.com
All promotional material in the Hip Hop, Jazz, Funk, R&B vein can be sent to the above address. No MP3s!!

Soul Tracks
L. Michael Gipson lmgipson@earthlink.net
www.soultracks.com
Reviews, biographies and group updates.

Finland

Soul Express
Box 105, 02101 Espoo, Finland
PH: +358407461441 FX: +358975940401
postmaster@soulexpress.net
www.kolumbus.fi/soulexpr
Music magazine specialising in real Soul and Funk.

Germany

Groove Attack Magazine
Von-Huenefeld-Str. 2, 50829 Cologne, Germany
PH: +49 (0) 221-990750 FX: +49 (0) 221-99075990
www.grooveattack.com
News, new releases and profiles. We also deal with distribution and promotion.

SoulSite.de
Westring 249, 55120 Mainz, Germany
FX: +49 (0) 6131-26-87-64
info@soulsite.de
www.soulsite.de
The home of Soul in Germany.

The Netherlands

Soul of Amsterdam
2e Oosterparkstraat 59-D, 1091 HW Amsterdam,
The Netherlands
PH: +31-6-165-22229
Andreas Hellingh info@thesoulofamsterdam.com
thesoulofamsterdam.com
Resource centered around Soul music. We also provide coverage of R&B, Urban, Disco, Funk, Gospel and Jazz.

United Kingdom

Blues & Rhythm
82 Quenby Way, Bromham, Bedfordshire,
MK43 8QP UK
PH: +44 (0) 123-482-6158
www.bluesandrhythm.co.uk
Europe's leading Blues, R&B and Gospel mag.

Blues & Soul Magazine
153 Praed St., London, W2 1RL UK
PH: 0208-656-5651
editorial@bluesandsoul.com
www.bluesandsoul.com
Covers all the latest UK and US Urban music info, including news, charts, reviews, events and clubs, as well as in-depth interviews

funkjunkiez.biz
www.funkjunkiez.biz
Soul, R&B, Urban music etc. Reviews of the latest albums, singles and even live gigs.

futureboogie
www.futureboogie.com
Soul & Funk news, reviews and interviews. Send your demos to us (no attachments please).

In The Basement Magazine
193 Queens Park Rd. Brighton,
E. Sussex, BN2 9ZA UK
PH: 00-44-1273-601217 FX: 00-44-1273-601217
David Cole inthebasement@btinternet.com
www.basement-group.co.uk
60's, 70's-style Soul music specialist magazine. Happy to receive CDs for review.

Life & Soul Promotions
16B Albert Quadrant, Weston Super Mare,
BS23 2QY UK
PH: +44 (0)1934-642121
Mike Ashley mike@lifeandsoulpromotions.co.uk
indiesoulnews.blogspot.com
Independent Soul news and reviews.

The Indie Link Exchange
www.indielinkexchange.com/ile

Straight No Chaser
17D Ellingfort Rd. London, E8 3PA UK
PH: +44-020-8533-9999 FX: +44-020-8985-6447
Paul Bradshaw info@straightnochaser.co.uk
straightnochaser.co.uk
We review mostly "music from the African diaspora" - Jazz, Hip Hop, Latin etc.

Women in Music

Most of the publications in the section review exclusively Women's music. Solo artists, bands or female fronted bands.

United States

3BlackChicks Review
www.3blackchicks.com
Interested in submissions from Black artists.

The Beltane Papers
11506 NE 113th Pl. Kirkland, WA 98033
Lise Quinn editor@thebeltanepapers.net
www.thebeltanepapers.net
We're looking for Goddess/Pagan/Earth Spirit music. Please send your review material to the above address.

Bitch
4930 NE 29th Ave. Portland, OR 97211
PH: 877-212-4824
www.bitchmagazine.com
Covers all female music/musicians.

Cha Cha Charming
284 Lafayette St. #5D, New York, NY 10012
editor@chachacharming.com
www.chachacharming.com
Covering female Pop stars from Tokyo to Paris.

Collected Sounds
2751 Hennepin Ave. S. #630
Minneapolis, MN 55408
www.blog.collectedsounds.com
A site dedicated to women in music.

Cool Grrrls
PO Box 186, Balboa Island, CA 92662
PH: 714-960-2650 FX: 714-532-6829
Melody Licious editors@coolgrrrls.com
www.coolgrrrls.com
Show & CD reviews, interviews and more.

Cutting Edge Voices
c/o Reviews Editor, PO Box 539, Lucas, OH 44843
Michael Foster editor@cuttingedgevoices.com
www.cuttingedgevoices.com
Promoting female vocalists from around the world. Interviews, reviews, news etc. Please contact me before you send in your music.

Daily Diva
www.dailydiva.com
Fashion, music, culture and fine women of color. We review independent music.

Dish Magazine
info@dishmag.com
www.dishmag.com
An entertainment, fashion and style magazine for young women of all ages. Includes music features, news and reviews.

Ectophile's Guide
PO Box 30187, Seattle, WA 98113-0187
www.ectoguide.org
Submit your material for reviews.

GirlPunk.Net
www.girlpunk.net
News, reviews, articles, featured bands etc.

GoGirlsMusic.com
PO Box 16940, Sugar Land, TX 77496-6940
Madalyn Sklar info@gogirlsmusic.com
www.gogirlsmusic.com
Promoting women in music. You must be a GoGirls Elite member to get your CD reviewed. Info at www.gogirlselite.com.

Guitar Goddess Reviews
269 S. Beverly Dr. #513, Beverly Hills, CA 90212
PH: 310-882-1361
Lola Stewart info@guitargoddess.com
www.guitargoddess.com
We are a female guitarist webzine that promotes music by female singer/songwriters that play guitar. We do monthly reviews and hold an annual female guitarist competition.

Heartless Bitches International
bitchsupreme@heartlessbitches.com
www.heartless-bitches.com
Music for the heartless bitch in all of us.

MS. Magazine
433 S. Beverly Dr. Beverly Hills, CA 90212
www.msmagazine.com
We do publish music reviews, but not in every issue.

musical discoveries
rwelliot@hotmail.com
www.musicaldiscoveries.com
Reviews of Contemporary, Progressive and Crossover recordings.

On the Rag Zine
PO Box 251, Norco, CA 92860-0251
PH: 951-273-1402 FX: 951-273-1402
Renae Bryant webmistress@ontherag.net
www.ontherag.net
Webzine that features interviews, reviews, photos and show listings of Punk and Hardcore bands. Want to promote greater participation of women in both the Punk and Hardcore scenes.

PLUS Model Magazine
plusmodelmagazine.com
The premiere magazine celebrating and inspiring the plus size fashion and plus size modeling industry. Occasionally does music reviews.

Venus Magazine
2000 N. Racine #3400, Chicago, IL 60614
PH: 773-327-9790 FX: 773-296-6103
Sheba White sheba@venuszine.com
www.venuszine.com
Women in music, art, film and more.

Women of Country
www.womenofcountry.com
Features undiscovered female Country musical gems.

The Netherlands

Metal Maidens
PO Box 230, 4140 AE Leerdam, The Netherlands
metalmaid@globalxs.nl
www.metalmaidens.com
CDs, seven inches, demo tapes and concert reviews and dates.

Reviews of Women Composers
Patricia Werner Leanse patricia@dds.nl
www.patricia.dds.nl/cds.htm
Does reviews of Classical music CDs by women.

United Kingdom

AMP: IT'S THE TITS!
ampster@gmail.com
www.ampnet.co.uk
For chicks and dicks and ... just about anybody, really.

wears the trousers
17 Long Ridges, Fortis Green,
London, N2 9HN UK
editor@wearsthetrousers.com
wearsthetrousers.com
A resolutely anglocentric peek at the world of women in music. We are very happy to receive discs for review.

Australia

Femail Magazine
8 E. Concourse, Beaumaris, VIC 3193 Australia
femail@femail.com.au
femail.com.au
Please try to assist us by including a subject heading in your enquiry, ie: product reviews, competitions etc.

World Music

Allafrica.com
920 M St. SE., Washington, DC 20003
PH: 202-546-0777 FX: 202-546-0676
allafrica.com/music
Distributor of African news/music worldwide.

Global Rhythm
PH: 646-674-1744
bmurphy@globalrhythm.net
www.globalrhythm.net
World music, culture & lifestyle.

il giornale della musica
via Pianezza 17, 10149 Torino, Italy
PH: +39-11-5591811 FX: +39-11-2307035
gdm@giornaledellamusica.it
www.giornaledellamusica.it
Covering World, Jazz and Classical music.

Klezmer Shack
www.klezmershack.com
Good Klezmer and the music inspired by it.

Mondomix
9, Cité Paradis, 75010 Paris, France
PH: + 33 (0)1-56-03-90-89
FX: + 33 (0)1-56-03-90-84
info@mondomix.com
www.mondomix.com
The electronic media of reference for World music.

Musical Traditions
1 Castel St., Stroud, Glos, GL5 2HP UK
PH: 01453-759475
Rod Stradling rod@mustrad.org.uk
www.mustrad.org.uk
Traditional music throughout the world.

Songlines
PO Box 54209, London, W14 0WU UK
PH: +44 (0)20-7371-2777 FX: +44 (0)20-7371-2220
info@songlines.co.uk
www.songlines.co.uk
Packed full of the latest CD reviews, artist interviews, guides to particular world music traditions, concert-listings, travel stories and compilation CD.

Whispering Wind Magazine
PO Box 1390, Folsom, LA 70437-1390
PH: 985-796-5433 FX: 985-796-9236
www.whisperingwind.com
We offer Native American musicians a place to get their indie music reviewed.

World Music Central
2524 Cascadilla St., Durham, NC 27704-4406
www.worldmusiccentral.org
We accept news stories/articles/reviews and other contributions. There is an online form that you need to fill.

World Music Site at About.com
4203 Poydras Hwy. Breaux Bridge, LA 70517
PH: 337-332-1478
Megan Romer worldmusic.guide@about.com
worldmusic.about.com
I review all areas of World music, including Cajun/Zydeco, Celtic, African, Reggae, Caribbean etc.

SECTION TWO: "REGIONAL" PUBLICATIONS AND RESOURCES

The resources listed in this section can help you to gain exposure in your local area, whether it be a CD review, allowing you to post information about your band, post info on a new release, upcoming shows etc. Most of the organizations listed (Folk, Jazz, Blues etc.) publish a newsletter that will review your CD. Note that many of these resources will promote music from outside of their region, but give preference to local talent.

United States

Craigslist
www.craigslist.org
Now available for communities all over the world. Get the word out about your music, gigs etc.

donewaiting.com
2648 Deming Ave. Columbus, OH 43202
Robert Duffy rduffy@gmail.com
www.donewaiting.com
We currently have nine writers writing about their local scenes.

Home Town News
www.hometownnews.com
Providing direct links to more than 2,600 daily and weekly U.S. newspapers.

Loose Record
532 La Guardia Pl. #371, New York, NY 10012
www.looserecord.com
Focuses on the local scene of various cities. Please send all CDs and promotion materials to the above address.

NewsDirectory College Newspapers
www.newsdirectory.com/college_news.php
Links to hundreds of college newspapers.

Newspaper & News Media Guide
www.abyznewslinks.com
Links to over 12,000 newspapers worldwide.

Podbop
Taylor McKnight podbop@gmail.com
podbop.org
Fans type in a city, get MP3s, discover a band they like and go see them.

Spins.US
spins.us
An Electronic Dance music information resource and events calendar covering communities throughout the US.

United States Newspapers and News Media Database
www.abyznewslinks.com/unite.htm
Links to hundreds of US newspapers.

US Newspaper List
www.usnpl.com
Links to newspapers throughout the country.

Alabama

al.com
www.al.com/music
Online presence for the Birmingham News, Huntsville Times and Mobile Register. Local music section.

Alabama Bluegrass Music Assoc.
PO Box 220, Leeds, AL 35094
www.alabamabluegrass.org
Promoting Bluegrass music in the state of Alabama.

Alabama Blues Project
www.alabamablues.org
Dedicated to the preservation of Blues music as a traditional American art form.

Alabama Country & Gospel Music Assoc.
www.acgma.com
Dedicated to recognizing aspiring artists who may never be afforded the opportunity to perform for major recognition.

Alabama Jazz and Blues Federation
www.ajbf.com
We produce a myriad of events including concerts and jam sessions, one festival, River Jam, as many as 10 concerts a year and several musician clinics and workshops.

Alabama Roots Music Society
www.alabamarootsmusic.com
Formed to bring diverse musical genres into the central Alabama area.

Bama Hip Hop
1628 Christine Dr. Anniston, AL 36207
PH: 256-282-0799 FX: 925-475-7458
Ali Shabazz bamahiphop@yahoo.com
bamahiphop.homestead.com
Lists your bio, company profile, concert/festival schedule, release dates and booking contacts.

Birmingham Buzz
bhambuzz.com
Dedicated to covering the local Rock music scene in Birmingham.

Black & White
2210 2nd Ave. N. 2nd Fl. Birmingham, AL 35203
PH: 205-933-0460
www.bwcitypaper.com
Birmingham's city paper. Events, concerts and live music sections.

Cajun-Zydeco Connection of Huntsville
www.czdance.com
Dedicated to Cajun and Creole music, dancing and culture in the North Alabama area.

Crimson White
PO Box 2389, Tuscaloosa, AL 35403-2389
PH: 205-348-7845 FX: 205-348-8036
www.cw.ua.edu
University of Alabama newspaper.

fleabomb.com
www.fleabomb.com
Promotes local bands in Birmingham. We cover Punk, Grindcore, Indie Rock/Pop, Emo and Hip Hop.

Indie Community
9495 Brook Forest Cir. Helena, AL 35080
PH: 205-492-3284
Jennifer McConnell info@indiecommunity.com
www.indiecommunity.com
Alabama's network for independent Christian bands and artists.

Lagniappe
1407 Government St., Mobile, AL 36604
PH: 251-450-4466 FX: 251-450-4498
www.lagniappemobile.com
A&E publication covering the arts in Mobile.

Magic City Blues Society
www.magiccityblues.org
Encourages the performances of the Blues and develops an appreciation within the community.

MobileSucks
webmaster@mobilesucks.net
www.mobilesucks.net
Covering the Punk scene in Mobile.

The Planet Weekly
music@theplanetweekly.com
www.theplanetweekly.com
A&E publication covering the Tuscaloosa area.

The Valley Planet
203 Grove Ave. Huntsville, AL 35801
PH/FX: 256-533-4613
info@valleyplanet.com
www.valleyplanet.com
Covering A&E in Huntsville.

Alaska

Alaskan Folk Music And More!
gary@alaskafolkmusic.org
alaskafolkmusic.org
Comprehensive source for local and statewide Folk music happenings.

The Anchorage Press
PO Box 241841, Anchorage, AK 99524-1841
PH: 907-561-7737
www.anchoragepress.com
An A&E weekly newspaper.

Arizona

Acoustic Music Arizona
PO Box 1554, Queen Creek, AZ 85242
PH: 480-888-1692
info@acousticmusicaz.com
www.acousticmusicaz.com
Promoting Acoustic music and Arizona based Acoustic musicians.

The AMAZ Store
PO Box 1554, Queen Creek, AZ 85242
PH: 480-888-1692
Chris Masters info@theamazstore.com
www.theamazstore.com
Sells Acoustic music from Arizona artists.

Ariana Records
1312 S. Avenida Polar #A-8, Tucson, AZ 85710
PH: 520-790-7324
Mr. Jimmi jtiom@aol.com
www.arianarecords.net
Releases and promotes music from the US Southwest. Send me your finished project!

Arizona Bluegrass Assoc.
PO Box 8139, Glendale, AZ 85312-8139
www.azbluegrass.org
Up-to-date information about news, events, festivals and Bluegrass bands.

Arizona Folk
PH: 480-946-3936
www.azfolk.com
Dedicated to the advancement of the Folk arts in Arizona.

Arizona Irish Music Society
9867 Roundup Ct. Sun City, AZ 85373
www.azirishmusic.com
News, events, listings etc.

Arizona Music Club
9920 S. Rural Rd. #108, Tempe, AZ 85284
PH: 480-206-3435 FX: 480-753-7021
music@blackdogpromotions.com
www.arizonamusicclub.com
Help us spread the word about the great music of Arizona!

Arizona Old-Time Fiddlers Assoc.
7470 Derryberry Dr. Flagstaff, AZ 86004
www.arizonaoldtimefiddlers.org
Created to preserve and promote the art of Old-Time fiddling.

Arizona Open Mics
chris@azopenmic.com
azopenmic.com
Includes pictures and artist profiles.

ASU Web Devil
PO Box 871502, Tempe, AZ 85287-1502
PH: 480-965-2292 FX: 480-965-8484
webdevil@asu.edu
www.statepress.com
Arizona State University online publication.

AZPunk.com
PO Box 64862, Phoenix, AZ 85082-4862
Chris Lawson chris@azpunk.com
www.AZPunk.com
Arizona's #1 source for Punk Rock!

Desert Bluegrass Assoc.
www.desertbluegrass.org
Developing and promoting Bluegrass music in the Greater Tucson area.

Get Out
120 W. 1st Ave. Mesa, AZ 85210
PH: 480-898-6500
www.getoutaz.com/music
Arizona's premier entertainment and lifestyles guide.

MusicPHiX.com
support@musicphix.com
www.musicphix.com
Arizona's online resource for local musicians.

Phoenix Blues Society
www.phoenixblues.org
Promotes and perpetuates local and national Blues music.

Phoenix New Times
PO Box 2510, Phoenix, AZ 85002
PH: 602-271-0040 FX: 602-253-4884
www.phoenixnewtimes.com
Free weekly alternative paper. Thursday has local reviews.

Prescott Jazz Society
www.pjazz.org
Presenting, promoting and celebrating Jazz performance and education in Northern AZ.

Rock in Phoenix
PO Box 61432, Phoenix, AZ 85082
info@rockinphoenix.org
www.rockinphoenix.org
A Spanish Rock/Punk/Metal website dedicated to the Spanish Rock scene in Phoenix.

RockThis.net
PO Box 20783, Bullhead City, AZ 86439
PH: 928-444-6234
Nikki Reagan nikkireagan@gmail.com
www.rockthis.net
Serving Bullhead City, Kingman and Lake Havasu City. Local musicians forums, chat room, articles, photos and more!

So Much Silence
somuchsilence@gmail.com
www.somuchsilence.com
MP3 blog covering the Arizona music scene.

Stinkweeds Online
12 W. Camelback St., Phoenix, AZ 85013
PH: 602-248-9461 FX: 602-248-9471
kimber@stinkweeds.com
www.stinkweeds.com
Independent music store. Reviews of new music added weekly. You'll stay on top of everything indie.

Tucson Guitar Society
www.tucsongs.org
Organizes classic guitar concerts in the Tucson area for local, national and international talent.

Tucson Friends of Traditional Music
www.tftm.org
Sponsors and promotes concerts, dances, workshops and informal music sessions.

Tucson Jazz Society
www.tucsonjazz.org
Promotes Jazz across Southern AZ with concerts, festivals and media activities.

Tucson Weekly
PO Box 27087, Tucson, AZ 85726-7087
PH: 520-792-3630 FX: 520-792-2096
Stephen Seigel musiced@tucsonweekly.com
www.tucsonweekly.com
Free weekly paper. indie record reviews. Publish the annual "Tucson Musician's Register".

Zia Record Exchange
1940 W. Indian School Rd.
Phoenix, AZ 85015-5112
PH: 602-241-0313
www.ziarecords.com
Can set you up with a consignment arrangement.

Arkansas

Arkansas Jazz Heritage Foundation
arjazz.org
Sponsors jazz performances by musicians with Arkansas connections and educational clinics for high school and college musicians throughout the state.

Arkansas River Blues Society
www.myspace.com/arriverbluessociety
All the latest on Arkansas Blues.

Arkansas Times
PO Box 34010, Little Rock, AR 72203
PH: 501-375-2985 FX: 501-375-3623
arktimes@arktimes.com
www.arktimes.com
Alternative weekly. Covers local music.

Arkansas Bluegrass
www.arkansasbluegrass.com
Articles and information about various Bluegrass bands, promoters, festivals and events.

ArkansasRockers.com
www.arkansasrockers.com
It's a little bit MySpace, a little bit Craigslist and a little bit community message board.

Delta Boogie
1710 Henry St., Jonesboro, AR 72401
www.deltaboogie.com
Information about music, art and entertainment in NE Arkansas and the Mississippi Delta.

Fayetteville Free Weekly
PO Box 843, Fayetteville, AR 72702
PH: 479-521-4550
www.freeweekly.com
Entertainment weekly. Covers local music.

Hood Struck TV
www.myspace.com/hoodstrucktv
The first TV show in the state of Arkansas that put the spotlight on the local artists in the Arkansas area. Hood Struck grew into the voice of the streets spotlighting everything that goes on in the hood.

Midsouth Metal Society
midsouthmetal.com
Online community where you can post shows, news, releases etc.

Nightflying
PO Box 250276, Little Rock, AR 72225
PH: 501-354-8577 FX: 501-354-1994
pr@nightflying.com
www.nightflying.com
Free monthly alternative magazine. Live music guide, CD reviews, features and previews.

North Arkansas Jazz Society
www.digjazz.com
Bringing world class Jazz to NW Arkansas.

Northeast Arkansas Bluegrass Assoc.
www.neabluegrass.bravehost.com
Designed keep you informed of Bluegrass happenings in our area.

Spa City Blues Society
www.myspace.com/spacityblues
Preserving and promoting Blues music and musicians.

California

Alive & Kicking
www.myspace.com/alivekicking
Sacramento's finest music 'zine with a cow logo!!!

All Access Magazine
15981 Yarnell St. #122
Rancho Cascades, CA 91342
PH: 818-833-8852
Debra Stocker allaccessmgzn@aol.com
www.allaccessmagazine.com
Bridges the gap by featuring national touring acts and "NEW" breaking acts performing in and around the local club scene.

The Almanac
3525 Alameda de las Pulgas
Menlo Park, CA 94025-4455
PH: 650-854-2626
www.almanacnews.com
The community news and information service for Menlo Park, Atherton, Portola Valley and Woodside.

PLANNING A TOUR?

32,000 Live Music Venues
in the US and Canada!!

Whether you're playing around town or planning a national tour, we can help you find the perfect fit! Thousands of venues in every major city and ALL points in between!

clubs   colleges   festivals   coffee shops   halls   bookstores
open mics   churches   record stores   community centers
restaurants   house concerts   jams   booking agents

www.IndieVenueBible.com

Amoeba Music *Home Grown*
www.amoebamusic.com
Our Home Grown artists are nominated by Amoeba staff and must be local to Berkeley, Hollywood or San Francisco.

American Guitar Society
library.csun.edu/igra/ags
Provides an opportunity for you to perform before an appreciative audience.

Bakotopia / BakersfieldBands.com
PO Box 2454, Bakersfield, CA 93303
PH: 661-395-7660
www.bakotopia.com
www.bakersfieldbands.com
Covering the latest and greatest music in Bakersfield.

Barflies.net
PO Box 1367, Orange, CA 92856-1367
www.barflies.net
Weekly concert calendar, weekly CD/show reviews and a bi-monthly features magazine.

bohemian.com
www.bohemian.com
News, music, movies, restaurants & wine culture in Sonoma, Marin and Napa counties.

Butte Folk Music Society
www.bfms.freeservers.com
Supports traditional and Folk music through concert venues and other music-related activities.

CaBands.com
PO Box 661254, Sacramento, CA 95866
PH: 916-247-9024
Robert Michael Lockwood II robert@cabands.com
www.cabands.com
We do concert and CD reviews and list over 7,000 local CA bands.

California Aggie
25 Lower Freeborn, 1 Shields Ave.
Davis, CA 95616
PH: 530-752-0208
www.californiaaggie.com
UC Davis Student paper is distributed free on the UC Davis campus and in the Davis community.

California Bluegrass Assoc.
www.cbaontheweb.org
Dedicated to the furtherance of Bluegrass, Old-Time and Gospel music.

California Hardcore
PO Box 271765, Concord, CA 94527-1765
info@calihardcore.com
www.calihardcore.com
The latest information on the bands, zines, record labels, distros and more from the Bay area.

California Lawyers for the Arts
cla@calawyersforthearts.org
www.calawyersforthearts.org
Provides lawyer referrals, dispute resolution services, publications and a resource library.

California State Old-Time Fiddler's Assoc.
www.fiddle.com/calfiddle
Dedicated to the preservation of Old-Time fiddle music.

California Traditional Music Society
www.ctmsfolkmusic.org
Dedicated to the preservation and dissemination of traditional Folk music and related Folk arts.

California Newspapers
www.usnpl.com/canews.php
Links to newspapers throughout the state.

Carmel Classic Guitar Society
www.starrsites.com/CarmelClassicGuitar
Promotes the Classical guitar through education, recitals and gatherings.

Catz Go Round Records
1730 Baines Ave., Sacramento, CA 95835
PH: 916 501-9558
Nancy Nickle nanlvscats@yahoo.com
www.myspace.com/catzgoroundrecords
Small indie label that works with Hip Hop artists in Oakland, Sacramento, Los Angeles and San Diego.

Celtic Society of the Monterey Bay
www.celticsociety.org
Encouraging an awareness of all aspects of the Celtic culture with a special emphasis on the rich musical tradition.

Central Valley Blues Society
www.cvblues.org
Covering all things Blues in the Fresno area.

CentralCali.com
www.centralcali.com
Covers the Hip Hop scene in California, featuring message boards and news on local events.

Chico News and Reviews
353 E. 2nd St., Chico, CA 95928
PH: 530-894-2300 FX: 530-894-0143
www.newsreview.com/chico/home
Provides extensive coverage of grassroots issues and the local music scene.

chico underground show info
chicolist@synthesis.net
www.chicolist.com
Promotes the local Indie Rock/Punk/Hardcore scene in the Chico area. Emphasizes unity in the scene.

DIG Music
1831 V St., Sacramento, CA 95818
PH: 916-442-5344 FX: 916-442-5382
ben@digmusic.com
www.digmusic.com
Independent record label and artist management company. We mainly have relationships with local/regional acts.

East Bay Express
1335 Stanford Ave. Emeryville, CA 94608
PH: 510-879-3700 FX: 510-601-0217
Rachel Swan rachel.swan@eastbayexpress.com
www.eastbayexpress.com
Extensive coverage of local music including weekly reviews and gig listings.

Easy Reader
PO Box 427, Hermosa Beach, CA 90254
PH: 310-372-4611
easyreader@easyreader.info
www.easyreader.info
The South Bay's hometown news.

The Fresno Bee
1626 E. St., Fresno, CA 93786-0001
PH: 559-441-6356 FX: 559-441-6457
features@fresnobee.com
www.fresnobee.com
Central California's leading daily newspaper. Local entertainment section.

Fresno Folklore Society
home.pacbell.net/ckjohns
Preserves Folk arts, especially traditional music, in California's San Joaquin Valley.

Good Times
1205 Pacific Ave. #300, Santa Cruz, CA 95060
PH: 831-458-1100 x223 FX: 831-458-1295
www.gtweekly.com
Santa Cruz news and entertainment weekly. Extensive coverage of the local music scene.

Humboldt Folklife Society
www.humboldtfolklife.org
Working to bring together Folk dancers, musicians and music lovers.

HumboldtMusic.com
mike@humboldtmusic.com
www.humboldtmusic.com
Provides an extensive and searchable directory of local musicians and music resources.

Inland Empire Weekly
2175 Sampson Ave. #118, Corona, CA 92879
PH: 951-284-0120 FX: 951-284-2596
www.ieweekly.com
We are the Inland Empire's first and only FREE weekly A&E publication!

inTUNE: SoCal Bluegrass News
www.socalbluegrass.org
Profiles regional Bluegrass folks. The DISCoverings column lets you know which CDs to buy.

Jazz Connection
jazzconnection@hotmail.com
jazzconnectionmag.com
Celebrating the fine art of Jazz music in Northern CA.

Jazz Society of Santa Cruz County
santacruzjazz.org
Promotes Jazz with a bulletin board, musician's directory service and news and views of Jazz.

Kings River Bluegrass Assoc.
www.krblue.net
Dedicated to the preservation, promotion and performance of Bluegrass, Old-Time and Gospel acoustic music.

The List
skoepke@stevelist.com
jon.luini.com/thelist
stevelist.com
Features SoCal Funk-Punk-Thrash-Ska upcoming shows of interest.

The Living Tradition
PH: 949-559-1419
www.thelivingtradition.org
Sponsors regular contra dances, Folk music concerts and Folk music jams in Bellflower and Anaheim.

Mach Turtle
FX: 305-768-6224
agentwahine@yahoo.com
www.machturtleprods.com
Listing of live Surf music events in Southern CA.

MetroSantaCruz
115 Cooper St., Santa Cruz, CA 95060
PH: 831-457-9000 FX: 831-457-5828
www.metcruz.com
Free weekly alternative paper. Indie music reviews.

Modesto Area Musician Assoc.
4300 Finch Rd. Modesto, CA 95357
FX: 209-572-0221
mama@modestoview.com
www.modestoview.com/mama
News, reviews, MP3s etc.

The Modesto Bee
1325 H St., Modesto, CA 95352
PH: 209-578-2284
www.modbee.com
Serving California's Central Valley. Covers local music.

Moshking.com
PO Box 1605, Glendora, CA 91740
moshking@moshking.com
www.moshking.com
Info on all Metal and Hard Rock concerts, events and bands in the SoCal area.

Mountain View Voice
655 W. Evelyn Ave. PO Box 405
Mountain View, CA 94042
PH: 650-964-6300
mv-voice.com
A&E publication serving the San Francisco Peninsula community of Mountain View and surrounding areas.

Mr. Gig Presents
PH: 951-818-9601
Jason Gokei mrgigpresents@yahoo.com
www.mrgigpresents.com
Promoting the most cutting edge bands for over 30 years.

mydesert.com
PO Box 2734, Palm Springs, CA 92263
PH: 760-322-8889
www.mydesert.com
Palm Springs news, community, entertainment, yellow pages and classifieds.

New Times
505 Higuera St., San Luis Obispo, CA 93401
PH: 805-546-8208 FX: 805-546-8641
www.newtimes-slo.com
San Luis Obispo County's news & entertainment weekly.

North Bay Bohemian
216 E. St., Santa Rosa, CA 95404
FX: 707-527-1288
www.metroactive.com/sonoma
Arts and entertainment weekly. Covers the local music scene.

North Coast Journal Weekly
145 G St. Ste. A, Arcata, CA 95521
PH: 707-826-2000 FX: 707-826-2060
ncjournal@northcoastjournal.com
www.northcoastjournal.com
Politics, people and art!

Northern California Bluegrass Society
www.scbs.org
Events calendar, news, messages and more about Bluegrass, Old-Time and related music in NoCal.

OC Punk
www.ocpunk.com
A resource for Orange County Punk bands and their fans.

OC Weekly
1666 N. Main St. #500, Santa Ana, CA 92701-7417
PH: 714-550-5950 FX: 714-550-5903
submissions@ocweekly.com
www.ocweekly.com
Orange County A&E weekly. Lots of local music coverage.

The Orange County Register
625 N. Grand Ave. Santa Ana, CA 92701
PH: 714-796-7866
www.ocregister.com
Entertainment section covers local music.

The Orion
CSU, Chico, CA 95926-0600
PH: 530-898-5625 FX: 530-898-4799
www.orion-online.net
California State U. Chico's student publication.

Pacific Sun
PO Box 8507, San Rafael, CA 94915
PH: 415-485-6700 FX: 415-485-6226
www.pacificsun.com
North Bay's weekly paper.

Palo Alto Weekly
703 High St., Box 1610, Palo Alto, CA 94302
PH: 650-326-8210 FX: 650-326-3928
www.paloaltoonline.com
Semi-weekly newspaper. Post your events online.

PARADIGM magazine
PO Box 9541, Brea, CA 92835
Kari Hamanaka ParadigmMag@aol.com
www.myspace.com/paradigmmagazine
Distributed to records stores throughout SoCal. Half of the zine is devoted to interviews of local, unsigned bands.

Pasadena Weekly
50 S. DeLacey Ave. #200, Pasadena, CA 91105
PH: 626-584-1500 FX: 626-795-0149
www.pasadenaweekly.com
Pasadena's A&E weekly. Lists gigs by local bands, reviews CDs, writes features etc.

Pleasanton Weekly
5506 Sunol Blvd. #100, Pleasanton, CA 94566
PH: 925-600-0840
www.pleasantonweekly.com
Alternative weekly. Covers local music.

Powerslave.com
1610 Blossom Hill Rd. #7F, San Jose, CA 95124
PH: 408-266-0300 FX: 408-266-0303
info@powerslave.com
www.powerslave.com
NoCal underground Metal scene with show and album reviews.

Random Lengths News
1300 S. Pacific Ave. San Pedro, CA 90731
PH: 310-519-1016 FX: 310-832-1000
www.randomlengthsnews.com
The only newspaper covering the entire harbor area.

Reviewer Magazine
PO Box 87069, San Diego, CA 92138
PH: 619-992-9211
editor@reviewermagazine.com
www.reviewermagazine.com
Southern California music, entertainment and lifestyle magazine.

Rose Street Music
1839 Rose St., Berkeley, CA 94703
PH: 510-594-4000 x687
rosestbooking@yahoo.com
www.rosestreetmusic.com
A Berkeley house concert venue featuring women musicians and songwriters.

Sacramento Guitar Society
www.sacguitar.net
Provides education and performance opportunities to all cultures, ages, abilities and economic means.

Sacramento News & Review
1015 20th St., Sacramento, CA 95814
PH: 916-498-1234 FX: 916-498-7920
www.newsreview.com/sacto
Independent A&E news resource.

Sacramento Punk Shows
www.myspace.com/sacramentopunkshows
A place to list and find out about Punk/Hardcore/Thrash/Metal/Garage and Art Punk shows in and around Sacramento.

San Luis Obispo County Jazz Federation
www.slojazz.org
Supporting the performance and appreciation of Jazz, both professionally and educationally.

San Luis Obispo New Times
505 Higuera St., San Luis Obispo, CA 93401
PH: 805-546-8208 FX: 805-546-8641
www.newtimesslo.com
The largest circulated paper in the region, covering local news and entertainment each week.

Santa Barbara Blues Society
www.sbblues.org
Dedicated to keeping the African-American Blues tradition alive in the Santa Barbara area.

Santa Barbara Choral Society
www.sbchoral.org
Provides qualified singers with an opportunity to study and perform great works of music.

Santa Barbara Independent
122 W. Figueroa St., Santa Barbara, CA 93101
PH: 805-965-5205 FX: 805-965-5518
www.independent.com
The county's news and entertainment paper.

Santa Clara Valley Fiddlers Assoc.
www.scvfa.org
Dedicated to the preservation of traditional American music such as Old-Time, Bluegrass and Gospel.

Santa Clarita Valley Blues Society
www.scvblues.org
Preserving and promoting Blues music.

Santa Cruz Sentinel
207 Church St., Santa Cruz, CA 95060
PH: 831-423-4242
www.santacruzsentinel.com
Entertainment section includes a calendar of music events.

Santa Maria Sun
3130 Skyway Dr. #603, Santa Maria, CA 93455
PH: 805-347-1968 FX: 805-347-9889
www.santamariasun.com
Covering local news and entertainment each week.

Seven South Record Shop
7 S. Quarantina St., Santa Barbara, CA 93103
PH: 805-965-4983
Ed Layola edion2@hotmail.com
sevensouth.com
*Sell recordings at our shop if you're from the Santa
Barbara / Ventura area.*

Skinnie
10184 6th St. Ste. A Rancho Cucamonga, CA 91730
PH: 909-476-0270 FX: 909-476-5931
www.skinniezine.com
*A monthly entertainment and lifestyles magazine
based out of Rancho Cucamonga.*

Sonoma County Blues Society
www.sonomacountybluessociety.com
*Interviews and CD reviews in our monthly
newsletter.*

Sonoma Tunes
webmaster@sonomatunes.com
www.sonomatunes.com
*Dedicated to live Blues in Northern CA in general
and Sonoma County in particular.*

Southern California Blues Society
www.socalblues.org
*Presentation of Blues music through teaching,
publications, festivals and concerts.*

Southern California Early Music Society
www.earlymusicla.org
*Supports the study, performance and enjoyment of
Medieval, Renaissance, Baroque and Classical
music.*

Southland Blues
6475 E. Pacific Coast Hwy. #397
Long Beach, CA 90803
PH: 562-498-6942 FX: 562-498-6946
info@southlandblues.com
www.southlandblues.com
The hub of the Blues in Southern CA.

Southwest Bluegrass Assoc.
www.s-w-b-a.com
*Bi-monthly newsletter with information about
festivals and house jams. Members get free web
page.*

Supergiant Productions
2109 W. St. #4, Sacramento, CA 95818
PH: 916-317-1156
Gina Azzarello gina@supergiantproductions.com
www.supergiantproductions.com
*We promote and book bands in the Sacramento
area.*

The Switchboard
Lady Noir ladynoir@socalgoth.com
www.socalgoth.com
*Southern California Goth directory. Contact us to be
included on the site.*

Valley Scene Magazine
6520 Platt Ave. #336, West Hills, CA 91307
PH: 818-888-2114 FX: 818-888-7142
contact@valleyscenemagazine.com
www.valleyscenemagazine.com
*Provides the most current information on
entertainment, restaurants, retail, services and more.*

Ventura Reporter
700 E. Main St., Ventura, CA 93001
PH: 805-658-2244 FX: 805-658-7803
Bill Lascher editor@vcreporter.com
www.vcreporter.com
*Ventura County's news and entertainment weekly.
Covers local music with articles and show listings.*

webookbands.com
7095 Hollywood Blvd. #794, Hollywood, CA 90028
PH: 323-651-1582 FX: 323-651-2643
info@webookbands.com
www.webookbands.com
*Books talent and promotes for over 30 venues, both
club and theatre, in California and Seattle.*

West Coast Performer
1278 20th Ave. Ste. C-1, San Francisco, CA 94122
PH: 415-742-0775
Katherine Hoffert wcpeditorial@performermag.com
www.performermag.com/wcperformer.php
*Want your CD reviewed? Send your CDs and press
releases.*

Westcoast Worldwide
Mike xhatex@earthlink.net
www.myspace.com/westcoastworldwiderecords
*Covers the Punk/Hardcore scene. Has a message
board, zine, CD reviews, gig listings, bookings etc.*

White Rock Blues Society
www.myspace.com/whiterockbluessociety
*Created to advance Blues and related music in our
community. In that, we plan to establish and
promote White Rock as a regional epicenter for
quality music and music venues.*

Your Music Magazine
105 Pioneer St. Ste. I, Santa Cruz, CA 95060
PH: 831-465-1305
mikelyon@yourmusicmagazine.com
www.yourmusicmagazine.com
Metal magazine distributed throughout SoCal.

The Bay Area

Bay Area Blues Society
www.bayareabluessociety.net
*Dedicated to the preservation, promotion and
representation of Blues, Jazz and Gospel.*

Bay Area Ska Page
PO Box 3092, San Leandro, CA 94578
www.bayareaska.com
*Reviews are broken up between albums or demos by
a band, compilations and shows.*

baymusicscene.com
633 Renfrew Rd. El Sobrante, CA 94803
PH: 925-768-6994
www.baymusicscene.com
*Provides free resources for musicians including an
online store, show listings and club information.*

BayProg
don@till.com
www.bayprog.org
San Francisco area Progressive Rock community.

Bluegrass by the Bay
134 Serrano Dr. San Francisco, CA 94132
deirdre@deirdre-cassandra.com
www.scbs.org/bbb.htm
*Contains reviews and articles about shows, venues,
albums, artists and upcoming Bluegrass event.*

Cruzin' the Bluz
Onnie Heaney cruzinbluz@earthlink.net
www.cruzinbluz.com
*Blues news and reviews from Santa Cruz and the
Bay Area.*

Dub Beautiful Collective
Maer Ben-Yisrael maer@dub-beautiful.org
www.dub-beautiful.org
*Presents live Electronic music events. We record all
of our shows and stream the best recordings.*

East Bay Recorder Society
www.sfems.org/ebrs
*Hosts monthly meetings for amateur recorder
players to play Renaissance and Baroque music.*

Flavorpill SF
sf_editor@flavorpill.net
sf.flavorpill.net
*A publishing company that seeks out the best in arts,
music and culture and delivers its findings.*

Iron Tongue of Midnight
Lisa Hirsch sunbear@well.com
irontongue.blogspot.com
Blog covering the Bay Area Classical music scene.

KFOG's Local Scene
55 Hawthorne St. #1000, San Francisco, CA 94105
PH: 415-817-5364 FX: 415-995-6867
kfog@kfog.com
www.kfog.com/music/local_scene
*Turning the spotlight on up and coming Bay Area
musicians.*

KUSF Entertainment Calendar
2130 Fulton St., San Francisco, CA 94117
kusf@usfca.edu
kusf.org/calendar.shtml
Please send only calendar listings to this address.

Laughing Squid
PO Box 77633, San Francisco, CA 94107
hello@laughingsquid.com
www.laughingsquid.org
*An online resource for underground art and culture
of San Francisco and beyond.*

Mesh Magazine
617 Oak St., San Francisco, CA 94117
PH: 415-845-9979
www.meshsf.com
*Free entertainment magazine. Our musical coverage
focuses on independent Rock, Hip Hop and Punk.*

Metro San Jose
550 S. 1st St., San Jose, CA 95113
PH: 408-298-8000 FX: 408-298-0602
www.metroactive.com/metro
Silicon Valley's leading weekly newspaper.

No Left Turn Records
633 Renfrew Rd. El Sobrante, CA 94803
PH: 925-768-6994
www.noleftturnrecords.com
*We search for the best talent in California for record
contracts and compilation albums.*

North Bay Music
info@northbaymusic.com
www.northbaymusic.com
*An online guide to live music in the San Francisco
area.*

On The Tip of My Tongue
Cecilia Gin ceemoon@yahoo.com
www.tipofmytongue.net
*We produce a cable video show in San Francisco
that focuses on local Bay Area talent.*

Outsound
www.outsound.org
*Tries to raise public awareness of music by
presenting public performance, promotion and
education.*

The Owl Mag
829 27th Ave. #206, Oakland, CA 94601
info@theowlmag.com
theowlmag.com
Written specifically for the Bay Area's vibrant and diverse music scene.

Pacific Noise Video Podcast
pacificnoise@gmail.com
www.pacificnoise.com
Each week we capture some element of San Francisco's hidden art and music scene and broadcast it.

Redwood Bluegrass Associates
www.rba.org
Serving the Bay area to promote Bluegrass and related Acoustic music through concerts and workshops.

San Francisco Bay Area Early Music Concert Listings
1071 Blair, Sunnyvale, CA 94087
FX: 408-245-6901
Jonathan Salzedo listings@albanyconsort.com
www.albanyconsort.com/concerts
A resource for working musicians and concert-goers.

San Francisco Classical Guitar Society
www.sfcgs.org
Promoting the awareness, understanding and appreciation of the Classical guitar.

San Francisco Classical Voice
225 Bush St. #500, San Francisco, CA 94104
Editor@SFCV.org
www.sfcv.org
The Bay Area's website journal of Classical music criticism. Features reviews of musical performances.

San Francisco Early Music Society
www.sfems.org
Creates a supportive environment for the performance of Medieval, Renaissance and Baroque music.

San Francisco Traditional Jazz Foundation
www.sftradjazz.org
Helps foster live, high quality traditional Jazz, regionally and worldwide.

San Jose Jazz Society
www.sanjosejazz.org
Presents free concerts, festivals, hands-on workshops, clinics and master classes.

San Jose Mercury News
750 Ridder Park Dr. San Jose, CA 95190
PH: 408-920-5027 FX: 408-288-8060
Ron Kitagawa rkitagawa@mercurynews.com
www.mercurynews.com
Entertainment section covers the local music scene.

SF Bay Guardian
135 Mississippi, San Francisco, CA 94107-2536
PH: 415-255-3100 FX: 415-255-8762
www.sfbg.com
Free weekly alternative paper. Local indie music, concert reviews and artist interviews.

SF JAZZ
www.sfjazz.org
Devoted to Jazz at the highest level, with concert performers ranging from acknowledged masters to the newest and most promising talents.

SF Weekly
185 Berry #3800, San Francisco, CA 94107
PH: 415-536-8100 FX: 415-541-9096
Jennifer Maerz feedback@sfweekly.com
www.sfweekly.com
San Francisco's smartest publication. Local music section.

SFBlues.net
Rich Piellisch peach@sfblues.net
www.sfblues.net
Your source of information on San Francisco's Blues scene.

sfcelticmusic.com
jim@sfcelticmusic.com
www.sfcelticmusic.com
Traditional Celtic music of Ireland, Scotland, Cape Breton and Brittany in the Bay Area.

sfgoth.com
www.sfgoth.com
Provided for free to the SF net.goth community for hosting Gothic or Industrial club pages.

SFist
sfist.com
Online A&E zine that covers the local music scene.

SFMPB.com
e@sfmpb.com
www.sfmpb.com
Exists to promote Brazilian music in the San Francisco Bay Area.

sfstation.com
3528 17th St., San Francisco, CA 94110
PH: 415-552-5588 FX: 415-552-5587
www.sfstation.com
San Francisco's independent information resource.

Sister SF
PO Box 6, 1001 Page St., San Francisco, CA 94117
www.myspace.com/sistersf
Providing a supportive, friendly platform for any female DJ, MC or live performer.

South Bay Folks
contact-sbf@SouthBayFolks.org
www.SouthBayFolks.org
Dedicated to promoting Folk music in the greater San Jose area.

South Bay Guitar Society
www.sbgs.org
Promotes Classical and related guitar music by providing performance opportunities to professional and amateur musicians.

Thrasher Magazine
1303 Underwood Ave. San Francisco, CA 94124
PH: 415-822-3083 FX: 415-822-8359
greg@thrashermagazine.com
www.thrashermagazine.com
Covers SF Punk and Hardcore music scene.

Transbay Creative Music Calendar
1510 8th St., Oakland, CA 94607
PH: 510-893-2840
mail@transbaycalendar.org
transbaycalendar.org
Concert listings for non-commercial, adventurous new music in the Bay Area.

True Skool
Ren dj_ren@true-skool.org
true-skool.org
Dedicated to preserving Hip Hop and Funk. Covering the Bay Area's musicians and events.

urban delicious
Alex Pleasant alex@urbandelicious.com
www.urbandelicious.com
San Francisco event calendar.

West Coast Songwriters
1724 Laurel St. #120, San Carlos, CA 94070
PH: 650-654-3966 FX: 650-654-2156
info@westcoastsongwriters.org
www.westcoastsongwriters.org
Promotes, educates and provides tools and opportunities to songwriters from Alaska to California.

Zero Magazine
12 S. 1st St. #300, San Jose, CA 95113
PH: 408-971-8510 FX: 408-971-0139
Larry Trujillo larry@zero.cc
www.zeromag.com
Alternative record reviews & interviews. Please CONTACT me before sending your music.

Los Angeles

The Americana Music Circle
Lauren Adams americanacircle@yahoo.com
www.americanacircle.com
A place for songwriters to enjoy themselves, stretch out and meet new comrades each month.

The Axe Shop
10962 Ventura Blvd. Studio City, CA 91604
PH: 818-755-9851
www.theaxeshop.net
We're looking to add CDs from Los Angeles guitar-based bands of all genres to our inventory. For consideration, drop you CD off to the above address.

Flavorpill LA
la_events@flavorpill.net
la.flavorpill.net
A publishing company that seeks out the best in arts, music and culture and delivers its findings.

folkWorks
PO Box 55051, Sherman Oaks, CA 91413
PH: 818-785-3839
folkworks@frognet.net
www.folkworks.org
A newspaper dedicated to promoting Folk music, dance and other folk arts.

Inflight At Night
info@inflightatnight.com
www.inflightatnight.com
MP3 blog covering the LA, Long Beach, Orange County music scene.

JesusJams.com
PH: 301-289-5635
news@jesusjams.com
www.jesusjams.com
L.A. area Christian music concerts and events.

LA CityBeat
5209 Wilshire Blvd. Los Angeles, CA 90036
PH: 323-938-1700 FX: 323-938-1661
www.lacitybeat.com
Alternative weekly. Covers local music.

LA Times BuzzBands
Kevin Bronson kevin.bronson@latimes.com
latimesblogs.latimes.com/buzzbands
Blog covering the music scene in Los Angeles and beyond.

LA Weekly
PO Box 4315, Los Angeles, CA 90078
PH: 323-465-9909
www.laweekly.com
LA arts and entertainment. Local music coverage includes spotlight artists, reviews and gig listings.

LAist
www.laist.com
Online A&E zine that covers the local music scene.

LAmusic.com
dean@lamusic.com
www.lamusic.com
Promotes artists with little or no access to airwaves due to economic rather than creative reasons.

LAReggaeClubs.com
10008 National Blvd. #144, Los Angeles, CA 90034
www.lareggaeclubs.com
Your one stop for Reggae entertainment in Los Angeles.

LOL Records
PO Box 5148, Beverly Hills, CA 90209
PH: 310-790-5689 FX: 208-460-2903
Gerry Davies info@lolrecords.com
www.lolrecords.com
A record label gearing up to sign more music and help indie artists get their careers off the ground.

Los Angeles Goes Underground
lagu.somaweb.org
Showcasing Los Angeles based Underground, Alternative & Indie Rock bands.

Los Angeles Jazz Society
www.lajazzsociety.org
Keeps its members informed through its quarterly newsletter, "Quarter Notes."

Los Angeles Songwriters' Network
PH: 626-818-0047
Jimi Yamagishi, jimi@songnet.org
www.songnet.org
Career-minded artists supporting each other through network events, seminars and collaboration.

Los Angeles Times
202 W. 1st St., Los Angeles, CA 90012
PH: 213-237-5000
www.latimes.com
Covers local and national music scene.

LosAngeles.com
www.losangeles.com/music
Our insider's look at the L.A. music scene.

Losanjealous
wassup@losanjealous.com
www.losanjealous.com
Covering culture and music in Los Angeles.

Music Glob
Dan dan@musicglob.com
www.musicglob.com
An MP3 blog about Rock music. E-mail me MP3s, videos etc. you would like to share.

Music Plus TV
517 N. Alvarado St., Los Angeles, CA 90026
PH: 213-572-0240 FX: 213-572-0241
Marc Cubas marc@musicplustv.com
www.musicplustv.com
We air undiscovered and indie artists of all genres 24/7 on our cable and web TV stations.

NoHo Arts District Magazine
nancy@nohoartsdistrict.com
www.nohoartsdistrict.com
Covering the North Hollywood arts scene.

Planet Shark Productions
333 N. Hayworth Ave. Los Angeles, CA 90048
www.planetsharkproductions.com
Produces, markets and promotes film, record and DVD release parties & other industry events.

QCLA
4013 Sequoia St., Los Angeles, CA 90039
Brian McKinney brian@qcla.net
www.qcla.net
We cover any good shows in Charlotte or LA as well as national music news.

Radio Free Silver Lake
www.radiofreesilverlake.com
Blog covering LA's fantastic independent music scene ... and beyond.

Rewriteable Content
rewriteablecontent@gmail.com
www.rewriteablecontent.com
Los Angeles music blog with tons of new music reviews, concert listings and photography/video from all the best LA shows.

Rock City News
7030 De Longpre Ave. Hollywood, CA 90028
PH: 323-461-6600 FX: 323-461-6622
Ruben webmaster@rockcitynews.com
www.rockcitynews.com
Covering local bands, clubs and other social gatherings.

Rock Insider
PO Box 1314, Hollywood, CA 90078
JAX jax@rockinsider.com
www.rockinsider.com
A Hollywood music scene MP3 blog. News, downloads, concerts etc.

Venice Magazine
PO Box 1, Venice, CA 90294-0001
venicemag@venicemag.com
www.venicemag.com
Los Angeles A&E magazine.

Webookbands.com
7095 Hollywood Blvd. #794, Hollywood, CA 90028
PH: 323-651-1582 FX: 323-651-2643
info@webookbands.com
www.webookbands.com
A booking service giving local talent easy access to clubs throughout LA.

WHERE Magazine
3679 Motor Ave. #300, Los Angeles, CA 90034
PH: 310-280-2880 FX: 310-280-2890
art@wherela.com
www.wherela.com
List your upcoming events.

You Set the Scene
2632 Crestmoore Pl. Los Angeles, CA 90065
Duke Logan dukeufo@hotmail.com
yousetthescene.blogspot.com
Keeping track of the massive Los Angeles music scene. Primarily focusing on Indie Rock.

YourLocalScene.com Los Angeles
PO Box 41669, Long Beach, CA 90853
Eric eric@yourlocalscene.com
la.yourlocalscene.com
Los Angeles' home on the internet for local music information, bands, venues and more!

San Diego

Accretions
PO Box 81973, San Diego, CA 92138
PH: 619-299-5371
sounds@accretions.com
www.accretions.com
An artist-based label with an ear towards Experimental, Improvisational and Global sounds.

Blues Lovers United of San Diego
www.blusd.org
Presenting and supporting local and national Blues artists and culture.

Good Blues Update
Chet BluShouter@aol.com
www.goodbluesupdate.com
San Diego's independent Blues publication.

Lo-CaL
www.lo-cal.com
Supporting the San Diego music scene. News, concerts, MP3s ...

Oly's San Diego Open Mic Schedule
PH: 720-985-7423
Scott "Oly" Olson olyjams@yahoo.com
webspawner.com/users/sdopenmic
A comprehensive list of various open mic events in the San Diego area.

San Diego Acoustic Music Scene
Kelley Martin kelley@acousticpie.com
www.acousticpie.com/SanDiego.html
San Diego is becoming a hotbed of Acoustic Singer/Songwriters and a springboard for national talent.

San Diego CityBEAT
3550 Camino Del Rio N. #207
San Diego, CA 92108
PH: 619-281-7526 FX: 619-281-5273
www.sdcitybeat.com
Has "locals only" section.

San Diego Early Music Society
www.sdems.org
Showcasing the musical treasures of Europe's Medieval, Renaissance and Baroque periods.

San Diego Local Metal
raymond@sdmetal.com
www.sdmetal.com
Presenting the best of San Diego's local Metal bands.

San Diego Magazine
1450 Front St., San Diego, CA 92101
PH: 619-230-9292 FX: 619-230-0490
www.sandiego-online.com
We welcome information on upcoming events in the San Diego area.

San Diego NSAI
PH: 619-884-1401
Liz Axford pianopress@pianopress.com
www.pianopress.com/nsai.htm
We do writing exercises as well as group song critiques. We host special events with pro-writers and industry pros.

San Diego Reader *Hometown CDs*
c/o Music Editor, PO Box 85803
San Diego, CA 92186
PH: 619-235-3000 FX: 619-231-0489
e-music@sdreader.com
www.sandiegoreader.com
Does reviews of local artists.

San Diego Songwriter's Guild
sdsongwriters@hotmail.com
www.sdsongwriters.org
Exposing original songs to the recording, TV and movie industries via pitch sessions with entertainment professionals.

San Diego Swings
PO Box 460084, Escondido, CA 92046-0084
FX: 760-740-1732
www.sandiegoswings.com
Your source for Swing and Big Band music in America's finest city.

San Diego Troubadour
PO Box 164, La Jolla, CA 92038
info@sandiegotroubadour.com
www.sandiegotroubadour.com
A free publication specializing in Alt-Country, Folk, Gospel and Bluegrass.

San Diego Union-Tribune *Under the Radar*
PO Box 120191, San Diego, CA 92112-0191
PH: 619-718-5200 FX: 619-260-5081
Anna Maria Stephens
annamaria.stephens@uniontrib.com
entertainment.signonsandiego.com/section/music
Takes a look at the independent arts and music scene.

SandiegoMix.com
SandiegoMix.com
Your San Diego guide to nightlife, clubs, bars and more!

SanDiegoPunk.com
cole@sandiegopunk.com
www.sandiegopunk.com
Coverage includes show listings, pictures, interviews, places to hang out and buy records and more.

sdmetal.org
webmaster@sdmetal.org
www.sdmetal.org
San Diego's online realm for Metal.

Colorado

Black Rose Acoustic Society
www.blackroseacoustic.org
Dedicated to the education, performance and preservation of all types of traditional music.

Boulder Weekly
690 S. Lashley Ln. Boulder, CO 80303
PH: 303-494-5511 FX: 303-494-2585
www.boulderweekly.com
Free weekly alternative paper. CD and concert reviews, club listings.

Classical Guitar Society of Northern Colorado
www.coloradoguitar.com
Brings both Classical and Acoustic guitar players and friends together each month in a pleasant cafe.

Colorado Bluegrass Music Society
www.coloradobluegrass.org
Promotes and encourages the development, performance and preservation of Bluegrass.

Colorado Blues Society
www.coblues.com
Creating a wider appreciation of the American indigenous art form, the Blues.

Colorado Friends of Cajun/Zydeco Music and Dance
cfcz.org
Your guide for the best in Cajun and Zydeco music in the front range area of Colorado.

Colorado Music Assoc. *(COMA)*
www.coloradomusic.org
Presents music festivals showcasing and celebrating local talent.

Colorado Springs Independent Newsweekly
235 S. Nevada, Colorado Springs, CO 80903
PH: 719-577-4545 FX: 719-577-4107
www.csindy.com
Colorado Springs weekly A&E paper.

Fort Collins Music Index
studio@seldomfed.com
www.seldomfed.com/fcmusic.htm
We list musician's pages, artists, music projects, venues, stores and more. Learn about the music biz.

Fort Collins Now
400 Remington St. Ste B, Fort Collins, CO 80524
PH: 970-493-1011
www.fortcollinsnow.com
Alternative weekly. Covers local music.

GJLive.com
PH: 800-340-6545
Sean Gibbs info@GJLive.com
www.GJLive.com
Your source for the latest on the Grand Junction music scene!

Hapi Skratch Entertainment
1151 Eagle Dr. #324, Loveland, CO 80537-8020
PH: 970-613-8879 FX: 775-256-2501
info@hapiskratch.com
www.hapiskratch.com
Offers a complete line of service essential to the growth and development of any band.

Independent Records and Video
3030 E. Platte Ave. Colorado Springs, CO 80909
PH: 719-473-0882
independent@beindependent.com
www.beindependent.com
Since 1978, fulfilling Southern Colorado's music needs.

Kaffeine Buzz
PO Box 181261, Denver, CO 80218
PH: 303-394-4959
kowens@kaffeinebuzz.com
www.kaffeinebuzz.com
An online music and entertainment source for Colorado and beyond.

KGNU's Bluegrass Calendar
Cuz'N Nickles bluegrass@kgnu.org
www.kgnu.org/bluegrass
List your upcoming Bluegrass event.

MileHighMusicStore.com
1151 Eagle Dr. #324, Loveland, CO 80537-8020
PH: 970-613-8879
info@milehighmusicstore.com
MileHighMusicStore.com
We want to sell all CDs that have a Colorado and Rocky Mountain connection.

Northern Colorado Traditional Jazz Society
www.fortnet.org/tradjazz
A group of Jazz enthusiasts who enjoy and support traditional and other forms of Jazz in this region.

Rock on Colorado!
1550 Larminer St. #608, Denver, CO 80202
David Webmaster@RockOnColorado.com
www.rockoncolorado.com
A celebration of Colorado's music scene!

Rocky Mountain Jazz
www.rockymountainjazz.com
Covering the Colorado Jazz scene. Post your shows!

Scene Magazine
PO Box 489, Fort Collins, CO 80522
PH: 970-490-1009 FX: 970-490-1266
Danielle Cunningham editor@scenemagazine.info
www.scenemagazine.info
Ft. Collins arts and music information covering local and national acts. Profiles bands and reviews CDs.

D e n v e r

Core Magazine
11347 Eliot Ct. Denver, CO 80234
PH: 303-458-0486
www.core-media.org
The premiere online guide to entertainment in Denver. Covers local music.

Denver Musicians Association
1165 Delaware St., Denver, CO 80204
PH: 303-573-1717
www.dmamusic.org
We help improve the quality of life in Colorado by making traditional jazz an integral part of that life.

DenverBoulderMusic.com
info@denverbouldermusic.com
www.denverbouldermusic.com
The finest site on the web to find the best music in Denver, Boulder and all over Colorado.

KTCL's Locals Only Calendar
4695 S. Monaco St., Denver, CO 80237
PH: 303-713-8000
www.area93.com
Post your upcoming shows.

MileHighNights.com *Denver Nightclubs*
www.milehighnights.com
Lists Denver nightclubs by genre.

Swallow Hill Music Assoc.
www.swallowhill.com
Denver's home for Folk and Acoustic music. Publishes the Swallow Hill Quarterly.

Underground Network
www.undergroundnet.net
Submit events, club nights, links, event reviews, CD or DJ reviews and much more.

Westword
PO Box 5970, Denver, CO 80217
PH: 303-296-7744 FX: 303-296-5416
www.westword.com
Denver free weekly alternative paper. Reviews CDs and normally does a full bio on one local band each week.

Connecticut

Club CT Live Bands
24 Wilfred Rd. Manchester, CT 06040
PH: 860-680-4756
clubct2@clubct.com
www.clubct.com/bands.htm
Submit your band if playing in Connecticut. Also contains a band of the month feature.

Connecticut Bluegrass Music Assoc.
www.ctbluegrass.org
Preserves Bluegrass music in Connecticut and the surrounding area.

Connecticut Blues Society
www.ctblues.org
Promoting a sense of community through our newsletters and special events.

Connecticut Classical Guitar Society
www.ccgs.org
Serving Classical guitarists by providing a forum for listening, learning, performing and teaching.

Connecticut Songwriters Assoc.
PO Box 511, Mystic, CT 06355
Bill Pere info@ctsongwriters.com
www.ctsongs.com
Weekly newsletter full of helpful information, news, classified ads and upcoming events.

CT Punx
www.ctpunx.com
News, reviews, profiles and MP3s.

CTFolk.com
www.ctfolk.com
Current info on the Connecticut Folk music scene.

CTMusicScene.com
Kim kim@ctmusicscene.com
www.ctmusicscene.com
Comprehensive guide covering the Connecticut music scene.

entertainment.ctcentral.com
Weekend, New Haven Register, 40 Sargent Dr.
New Haven, CT 06511
FX: 203-865-7894
entertainment.ctcentral.com
CTCentral's hub for entertainment news. Phone or fax your shows. Do not send by e-mail!

Fairfield County Weekly
350 Fairfield Ave. #605, Bridgeport, CT 06640
PH: 203-382-9666 FX: 203-382-9657
www.fairfieldweekly.com
Free weekly paper. CD and concert reviews, previews shows, interviews bands.

Hartford Advocate
121 Wawarme Ave. 1st Fl. Hartford, CT 06114
PH: 860-548-9300 FX: 860-548-9335
www.hartfordadvocate.com
CD reviews. Local Bands and Happenings. Updated every Thursday.

Hartford Courant
285 Broad St., Hartford, CT 06115
PH: 860-241-6200
www.ctnow.com
Accepts CD for review if playing in Connecticut. Previews shows and interviews bands.

Hartford Jazz Society
www.hartfordjazzsociety.com
Improves Jazz as America's gift to the music world and fosters an appreciation and love for Jazz.

Media Factory TV / Media Factory Radio Show
718 Enfield St. Space B, Enfield, CT 06082
PH: 860-741-8801
netshows@aol.com
www.netshows.us
TV and radio shows. Musicians, send us your videos and CDs.

New Haven Advocate
900 Chapel St. #1100, New Haven, CT 06510
PH: 203-789-0010 FX: 203-787-1418
www.newhavenadvocate.com
New Haven's weekly newspaper. Local bands and happenings, updated every Thursday.

openmikeonline.com
www.openmikeonline.com
Features pictures and news from CT open mics. Site includes a "featured artist".

Soundwaves
PO Box 710, Old Mystic, CT 06355
PH: 860-572-5738 FX: 860-572-5738
David L. Pottie editor@swaves.com
www.swaves.com
Southern New England's entertainment guide. In-depth band & club info.

Delaware

Brandywine Friends of Old-Time Music
www.brandywinefriends.org
Preserving and presenting traditional American music.

Delaware Friends of Folk
www.delfolk.org
Furthering the cause of Folk music and Folk musicians in our area.

DelawareOnline
PO Box 15505, Wilmington, DE 19850
PH: 302-324-2500
www.delawareonline.com/entertainment
Concerts, clubs and local nightlife around Delaware and Philadelphia.

Delaware Today
3301 Lancaster Ave. #5-C, Wilmington, DE 19805
PH: 302-656-1809 FX: 302-656-5843
www.delawaretoday.com
List your upcoming events.

Diamond State Blues Society
www.diamondstateblues.com
Supporting local Blues artists as well as to bring national acts to the Diamond State.

freedelaware.com
PH: 302-421-9377 FX: 302-421-8365
info@freedelaware.com
freedelaware.com
Includes a message board, MP3 service area and search engine.

Newark Arts Alliance
100 Elkton Rd. Newark, DE 19711
PH: 302-266-7266
info@newarkartsalliance.org
www.newarkartsalliance.org
Community A&E calendar accepts events.

Project Unity
PO Box 129, Hockessin, DE 19707
xprojectunityx@hotmail.com
www.projectunity.cjb.net
We have a spot for local up and coming bands to play and gain exposure.

Spark Weekly
www.sparkweekly.com
Alternative weekly. Covers local music.

Florida

Apalachee Blues Society
www.apalacheebluessociety.com
Created to preserve, nurture and promote the Blues in the Tallahassee region.

Axis Magazine
116 S. Orange Ave. Orlando, FL 32801
PH: 407-839-0039
www.axismag.com
Orlando's A&E magazine.

BackStage Pass Magazine
info@backpassmag.com
www.backpassmag.com
Your news and entertainment connection serving Florida's East Coast.

Broward Folk Club
www.browardfolkclub.com
Promotes Folk and Acoustic music.

Central Florida Bluegrass Assoc.
centralfloridabluegrass.com
Promoting Bluegrass in Central Florida, from the Gulf Coast to the Space Coast.

Central Florida Rocks
centralfloridarocks@yahoo.com
www.centralfloridarocks.net
This site is updated weekly with new music reviews, interviews, articles and full-length streaming audio tracks from unsigned acts for your listening pleasure.

City Link
PO Box 14426, Fort Lauderdale, FL 33302
PH: 954-356-4943
www.citylinkmagazine.com
Your link to news, A&E in Broward & Palm Beach County.

Creative Loafing Sarasota
1383 5th St., Sarasota, FL 34236
PH: 941-365-6776 FX: 941-365-6854
Wade wade.tatangelo@creativeloafing.com
sarasota.creativeloafing.com
Weekly alternative paper. Covers local scene and reviews indie CD releases.

Creative Loafing Tampa
810 N. Howard Ave. Tampa, FL 33606
PH: 813-739-4800 FX: 813-739-4801
tampa.creativeloafing.com
Weekly alternative paper. Covers local scene and reviews indie CD releases.

Fla.vor Alliance
7809 N. Orleans Ave. Tampa, FL 33604
PH: 813-935-8887 FX: 813-935-0535
info@flavoralliance.com
www.flavoralliance.com
Supports local Christian Hip Hop music and artists.

Florida Harpers and Friends
www.florida.harper.org
An organizing force for Florida harpers and other instrumentalists.

Florida State Fiddlers Assoc.
www.nettally.com/fiddler
Hold a yearly convention and fiddle contest.

Folio Weekly
9456 Philips Hwy. #11, Jacksonville, FL 32256
PH: 904-260-9770 FX: 904-260-9773
www.folioweekly.com
Jacksonville free weekly alternative paper with complete concert calendar.

Fort Myers Beach Bulletin
19260 San Carlos Blvd. Bldg. C
Fort Myers Beach, FL 33931
PH: 239-463-4421
www.beach-bulletin.com
Alternative weekly. Covers local music.

Fort Pierce Jazz Society
www.jazzsociety.org
A cultural, educational and entertainment resource for Jazz.

Friends of Florida Folk
www.foff.org
Publicizes, sponsors and produces newsletters, film, records, festivals and other events.

Gainesville Friends of Jazz and Blues
www.gnvfriendsofjazz.org
Promotes and supports Jazz and Blues music in Gainesville and surrounding area.

GainesvilleBands.com
info@gainesvillebands.com
www.gainesvillebands.com
Your source for local music in Gainesville.

GlassKiss Promotions
www.myspace.com/glasskisspromotions
Dedicated to promotions and supporting local Orlando music/talent. Our primary goal is to make sure deserving bands get the exposure that they wouldn't have the opportunity to receive anywhere else.

Gulf Coast Bluegrass Music Assoc.
www.gcbma.com
Bringing Bluegrass music to Northwest Florida and Southern Alabama.

Heat Beat
2020 NW 32ⁿᵈ St., Pompano Beach, FL 33064
PH: 954-972-6373 FX: 954-972-8141
info@heatbeat.com
www.heatbeat.com
Florida's entertainment magazine for over 10 years!

Hiphopelements
PH: 954-977-7886 FX: 775-249-0062
webmaster@hiphopelements.com
www.hiphopelements.com
Supporting the Florida Hip Hop scene.

Independent News
PO Box 12082, Pensacola, FL 32591
PH: 850-438-8115 FX: 850-438-0228
www.inweekly.net
Provides the Pensacola area with local news, events and reviews.

INsite Magazine
PO Box 15192, Gainesville, FL 32604
FX: 352-377-6602
www.insitegainesville.com
The #1 entertainment magazine in Gainesville!

JaxBands
PO Box 14315, Jacksonville, FL 32238-1315
webmaster@JaxBands.com
www.jaxbands.com
Dedicated to supporting Jacksonville local bands!

Jazz Arts Music Association of Palm Beach
www.jamsociety.org
Formed to encourage the performance, promotion, preservation and perpetuation of America's original art form - JAZZ.

Jazz Club of Sarasota
www.jazzclubsarasota.com
Provides Jazz and community programs for Florida's West Coast.

Jazz Society of Pensacola
www.jazzpensacola.com
Working together for the purpose of advancing Jazz music.

JungleTV
info@jungletv.com
www.jungletv.com
TV program featuring the best in South Florida music.

Movement Magazine
1650-302 Margaret St. PMB 132
Jacksonville, FL 32204
movementmagazine@aol.com
www.movementmagazine.com
Underground music magazine. Interviews with local and world renowned musicians.

MusicPensacola.com
tiger@gulfbreeze.net
www.musicpensacola.com
Pensacola's weekly live entertainment guide. Local artists, concerts, festivals and services.

New Times Broward Palm Beach
PO Box 14128, Ft. Lauderdale, FL 33302-4128
PH: 954-233-1600 FX: 954-233-1521
www.newtimesbpb.com
Weekly paper with local music coverage. Reviews and previews bands playing the area.

North Central Florida Blues Society
www.ncfblues.org
Supporting the Blues in North Central Florida on all levels and in multiple venues.

North Florida Bluegrass Assoc.
www.nfbluegrass.org
Promotes and preserves Bluegrass music.

Orlando Weekly
100 W. Livingston St., Orlando, FL 32801
PH: 407-377-0400 FX: 407-377-0420
www.orlandoweekly.com
Free weekly alternative paper. Covers local music scene, reviews new CD releases.

OrlandoBands.com
PH: 321-202-0011
www.orlandobands.com
Our mission is simple. Taking independent artists and supplying them with educational content that can further their music lifestyles.

OrlandoCityBeat.com
www.orlandocitybeat.com/citybeat/music
The definitive guide to the Orlando music scene.

OrlandoSwing.com
info@OrlandoSwing.com
www.orlandoswing.com
Delivers the latest swing news and events.

Rag Magazine
8930 State Rd. 84 #322, Ft. Lauderdale, FL 33324
PH: 954-234-2888 FX: 954-727-1797
info@ragmagazine.com
www.ragmagazine.com
South Florida's music magazine.

Realitysnap.com
5401 65ᵗʰ Ter. N. Ste. A, Pinellas Park, FL 33781
PH: 727-520-7540
Ken Thomas Ken@realitysnap.com
www.realitysnap.com
A comprehensive Tampa Bay music resource.

Rivot Rag
www.myspace.com/rivotrag
Tampa Bay's ONLY Underground Metal magazine.

Sarasota Folk Club
www.sarafolk.org
Keeping the traditions of Folk music a living part of the Sarasota community.

Somebody Cares Tampa Bay
2140 Range Rd. Clearwater, FL 33765
PH: 727-536-2273 FX: 727-461-3985
Daniel Bernard daniel@sctb.org
www.sctb.org
A Christian ministry that networks the Tampa Bay area to impact the community with a demonstration of the Gospel. We do several big concerts each year as well as many smaller church events.

South Florida Bluegrass Assoc.
www.southfloridabluegrass.org
Dedicated to preserving the heritage of acoustic Bluegrass music and educating the public about this unique genre.

South Florida Blues Society
www.soflablues.org
Promoting, teaching and advancing the Blues through networking with fans and musicians.

South Florida JAZZ
southfloridajazz.org
Offering performance venues for musicians local, regional, national and international, whom we regard as treasured talents.

The Southern Rock Society
southernrocksociety.com
A place to go for information, to post your upcoming shows and to share information.

Southwest Florida Bluegrass Assoc.
www.southwestfloridabluegrass.org
Preserving, encouraging and promoting traditional Bluegrass music.

Space Coast Jazz Society
www.spacecoastjazzsociety.com
Promotes, preserves and educates Jazz-music lovers and Jazz-music makers.

Suncoast Blues Society
www.suncoastblues.org
Dedicated to upholding the traditions of the Blues.

Swept Away TV
4915 Oxford Cr. Boca Raton, FL 33434
PH: 561-241-9110 FX: 561-241-4422
www.sweptawaytv.com
A TV program that airs in more than 60 markets. We are now accepting electronic submissions from unsigned artists to be featured on our show. You MUST submit your press kit electronically through Sonicbids www.sonicbids.com

Tampa Bay Entertainment Guide
PO Box 17674, Clearwater, FL 33762
info@usaentertainment.com
tampabayentertainment.com
Promoting Tampa Bay's entertainment industry.

tampahiphop.com
kramtronix@tampahiphop.com
www.tampahiphop.com
Covering the local scene.

TheIndieOutie.com
admin@theindieoutie.com
theindieoutie.com
Selling the music of Central Florida artists.

Miami

CityLink Online
PO Box 14426, Fort Lauderdale, FL 33302
PH: 954-356-4943
www.citylinkonline.com
South Florida's alternative news magazine.

CLOSER Magazine
623 Selkirk St., West Palm Beach, FL 33405
Steve Rullman steev@thehoneycomb.com
www.closermagazine.com
Networks for you. Meet artists from Palm Beach to Miami.

GoPBI.com
PO Box 24700, West Palm Beach, FL 33416
PH: 561-820-3700 FX: 561-820-3722
Leslie Gray Streeter lstreeter@pbpost.com
www.gopbi.com/events/music
Music guide for the Palm Beaches and South Florida.

Miami New Times Online
PO Box 011591, Miami, FL 33101-1591
PH: 305-576-8000 FX: 305-571-7677
www.miaminewtimes.com
Online paper with local music section.

Miami Unsigned
PH: 610-348-0705
Eric Shenkman miamiunsigned@gmail.com
myspace.com/miamiunsigned
We feel that Miami's live music scene could be 100% better if properly organized. Our strategy is to act as the driving force for communication between artists, venues and the music industry at large. Mind Your Music because Your Music Minds You!

Sun Post
PO Box 191870, Miami Beach, FL 33139
PH: 305-538-9700 FX: 305-538-6077
www.miamisunpost.com
Alternative weekly. Covers local music.

Slammie Productions
PO Box 5891, Lake Worth, FL 33461
PH: 954-532-4333
feedback@slammie.com
www.Slammie.com
An independent concert promoter presenting club shows in South Florida.

South Florida Jams
13855 Langley Pl. Davie, FL 33325
PH: 954-424-8728 FX: 954-424-8902
ethanschwartz@southfloridajams.com
www.southfloridajams.com
Bringing the best live music to South Florida.

South Florida Zydeco Society
www.soflozydeco.com
Educating and encouraging Zydeco music in South Florida.

TheHoneyComb.com
623 Selkirk St., West Palm Beach, FL 33405
Steven Rullman steev@thehoneycomb.com
thehoneycomb.com
This site is an "underground" music resource module for the So-Fla area.

Georgia

Athens Blur Magazine
editorial@athensblur.com
www.athensblur.com
Georgia's premier free monthly music/variety magazine.

Athens Exchange
196 Alps Rd. #2-133, Athens, GA 30606
editor@athensexchange.com
www.athensexchange.com
Online A&E magazine.

Athens Folk Music and Dance Society
www.uga.edu/folkdance
Promotes Folk music by providing an opportunity to perform in the area.

Athensmusic.net
www.athensmusic.net
Covering the Athens music scene with news, interviews, downloads etc.

Blank Crisis
Neal blankcrisis@yahoo.com
blank-crisis.blogspot.com
MP3 Blog covering the Georgia music scene.

Cherokee County Music Society
www.cherokeecountymusicsociety.org
Our mission is to create opportunities for musicians and songwriters within Cherokee County by developing more opportunities to increase visibility while preserving integrity and striving for excellence in the music community.

The Coastal Jazz Association of Savannah
www.savannahjazzfestival.org
Offering performance opportunities for local, regional, national and international Jazz musicians.

Connect Savannah
1800 E. Victory Dr. #7, Savannah, GA 31404
PH: 912-231-0250 FX: 912-231-9932
www.connectsavannah.com
Weekly news, A&E publication. Extensive coverage of local music.

Connect Statesboro
1 Proctor St., Herald Sq. Statesboro, GA 30458
PH: 912-764-9031 FX: 912-489-8181
www.connectstatesboro.com
Alternative weekly. Covers local music.

Decatur CD
356 W. Ponce de Leon Ave. Decatur, GA 30030
PH: 404-371-9090
decaturcd@bellsouth.net
www.decaturcd.com
Music store that features lots of in-store performances as well as a local music blog.

Georgia Music Industry Assoc.
www.gmia.org
Educates the songwriter and performer on all aspects of the music industry.

Georgia Music Magazine
484 Cherry St., Macon, GA 31201
PH: 478-744-9955 FX: 678-559-0263
info@georgiamusicmag.com
www.georgiamusicmag.com
Profiles of the state's artists, pioneers and colorful characters related to music.

Georgia Soul
georgiasoul.blogspot.com
An interactive way to share the wealth of great Soul records from Georgia.

Gospel Music Productions
PO Box 7317, Warner Robins, GA 31095
PH: 478-997-1734 FX: 478-218-2720
www.gospelmusicproductions.net
Provides aspiring local Gospel artists the opportunity to use their gifts and promote their musical talents.

Livewire Recordings
21 S. Main St. Ste. B, Alpharetta, GA 30004
PH: 678-624-1770 FX: 678-624-1774
Mark Pollock info@livewirerecordings.net
www.livewirerecordings.net
Label focusing on up and coming acts in all Rock genres that share the same passion for great songs, performances and love for the scene.

Lokal Loudness
734 Hickory Oak Hollow, Augusta, GA 30901
PH: 706-836-5683
John "Stoney" Cannon info@lokalloudness.com
www.myspace.com/lokalloudnesslive
Covering the Augusta music scene.

Metropolitan Spirit
700 Broad St., Augusta, GA 30901
PH: 706-738-1142 FX: 706-733-6663
Stacey Hudson stacey.hudson@metrospirit.com
www.metrospirit.com
Augusta's most popular newsweekly.

Middle Georgia Bluegrass Assoc.
www.middlegeorgiabluegrass.org
Promoting, preserving and perpetuating Bluegrass music throughout central Georgia.

Nuçi's Space
396 Oconne St., Athens, GA 30601
PH: 706-227-1515 FX: 706-227-1524
space@nuci.org
www.nuci.org
A resource center for musicians.

redandblack.com
540 Baxter St., Athens, GA 30605
PH: 706-433-3000 FX: 706-433-3033
www.redandblack.com
U. Georgia's student publication.

Savannah Underground
Jon jkolko@gmail.com
www.savannahunderground.com
The definitive resource for the Savannah music scene.

Southeast Performer
449 ½ Moreland Ave. #206 Atlanta, GA 30307
PH: 404-582-0088
Leila Regan-Porter sepeditorial@performermag.com
www.performermag.com
Want your CD reviewed? Do you have news on your band? Send your CDs and press releases.

South Eastern Bluegrass Assoc.
www.sebabluegrass.org
Promotes Bluegrass activities through a newsletter.

Atlanta

ATLmetal.com
www.atlmetal.com
Covering all things Metal in Atlanta.

Art Rock in Atlanta
www.gnosisarts.org/aria
News, references and resources for the Atlanta Art Rock community.

Atlanta Blues Society
www.atlantablues.org
Keeping the Blues alive.

Atlanta Journal
PH: 404-522-4141
www.accessatlanta.com
Arts and entertainment online resource.

Atlanta Magazine
260 Peachtree St. #300, Atlanta, GA 30303
PH: 404-527-5500 FX: 404-527-5575
www.atlantamagazine.com
List your upcoming events online.

Atlanta Music Guide
878 Peachtree St. NE. #504, Atlanta, GA 30309
PH: 404-892-1533 FX: 404-254-2749
www.atlantamusicguide.com
Atlanta bands, news, concerts, reviews, venues and radio stations.

Atlanta Music Scene
info@atlantamusicscene.com
www.atlantamusicscene.com
Your source for regional talent and related services.

Atlanta Street Vibe Magazine
Patrick atlantastreetvibe@yahoo.com
www.atlantastreetvibe.com
Atlanta's hottest source for Urban music, fashion and entertainment.

AtlantaGothic.NET
jfoster@atlantagothic.net
www.atlantagothic.net
We are the top resource for information in the Gothic scene in Atlanta.

AtlantaJarnz.com
4514 Chamblee Dunwoody Rd. #279
Atlanta, GA 30338
PH: 678-476-3726
info@atlantajamz.com
atlantajamz.com
Online store, full service promotion and marketing.

AtlantaJazz Discussion Group
groups.yahoo.com/group/AtlantaJazz
Supports and encourages the proliferation of Jazz music.

atlantashows.com
www.atlantashows.com
Information on how to get recognition for your band.

atlantashows.org
www.atlantashows.org
Listing of Metro Atlanta and surrounding area shows.

Cable and Tweed
cableandtweed@gmail.com
cableandtweed.blogspot.com
MP3 blog with news and reviews. Submissions are welcome, especially from Atlanta/Athens bands.

captains dead
gregor@captainsdead.com
captainsdead.com
MP3 Blog covering the Atlanta music scene.

Celtic Atlanta
celticatlanta.com
Covering the local Celtic music scene.

Confessions of a Music Addict
265 Ponce de Leon Ave NE #3509
Atlanta, GA 30308
Ally Allen ally.allen@gmail.com
confessionsofamusicaddict.blogspot.com
If you want me to review your CD, send me a copy.

Creative Loafing Atlanta
384 Northyards Blvd. #600
Atlanta, GA 30313-2454
PH: 404-688-5623 FX: 404-614-3599
www.atlanta.creativeloafing.com
Free weekly alternative paper. Covers local music scene and reviews CDs.

DeadJournalist.com
deadjournalist@gmail.com
www.deadjournalist.com
Atlanta blogger that reports on the local music scene and interviews bands playing in town.

Drive a Faster Car
PO Box 79257, Atlanta, GA 30357
Tessa Horehled contact@driveafastercar.com
www.driveafastercar.com
MP3 Blog about music, art, restaurants, and pretty much anything that excites us enough to write about.

DryerBuzz
PH: 866-576-2899 FX: 877-576-1895
support@dryerbuzz.com
www.dryerbuzz.com
Atlanta's Urban entertainment magazine.

Flagpole Magazine
PO Box 1027, Athens, GA 30603
PH: 706-549-9523 FX: 706-548-8981
music@flagpole.com
flagpole.com
The color bearer of Athens' art, entertainment, music, politics and just about anything else.

KISSatlanta
Preston preston@kissatlanta.com
www.kissatlanta.com
MP3 Blog covering the Atlanta music scene.

Ohmpark
www.ohmpark.com
Blog covering the Atlanta music scene.

Sounds Atlanta
PO Box 49266, Atlanta, GA 30359
PH: 404-329-9438 FX: 404-325-8401
Bill Tullis SoundsAtlanta@aol.com
soundsatlanta.com
Studio & remote recording and mastering.

The Sunday Paper
PH: 404-351-5797 FX: 404-351-2350
Kevin Moreau kevinmoreau@sundaypaper.com
www.sundaypaper.com
Covers the local music scene.

Underneathica
manyjars@gmail.com
underneathica.blogspot.com
MP3 Blog covering the Atlanta music scene.

Hawaii

Aloha Joe
PO Box 4777, Lakewood, CA 90711
PH: 562-925-3711
alohajoe@alohajoe.com
www.alohajoe.com
Will review or play any music created on the Island.

Bluegrass Hawaii Traditional & Bluegrass Society
www.bluegrasshawaii.com
Dedicated to connecting fans and musicians all over the Hawaiian Islands.

BuyHawaiianMusic.com
1145 Kilauea, Hilo, HI 96720
PH: 888-652-2212 FX: 808-935-7761
info@buyhawaiianmusic.com
www.buyhawaiianmusic.com
All your favorite Hawaiian CDs and new releases.

Chamber Music Hawaii
www.chambermusichawaii.com
Created to promote appreciation, understanding, and learning of Chamber music in Hawaii.

Hawaii Island Journal
116 Kamehameha Ave. #3, Hilo, HI 96720
PH: 808-961-1200 FX: 808-961-1202
www.hawaiiislandjournal.com
The LARGEST independent news publication on Hawaii Island.

Hawaiian Steel Guitar Assoc.
www.hsga.org
Promotes traditional Hawaiian music.

HawaiiEventsOnline.com
www.hawaiieventsonline.com
Includes listings of live shows going on throughout Hawaii.

Honolulu Advertiser *TGIF*
PO Box 3110, Honolulu, HI 96802
PH: 808-525-8056 FX: 808-525-8037
tgif@honoluluadvertiser.com
www.honoluluadvertiser.com/tgif
Weekly arts section. Covers local music and events.

Honolulu Weekly
1200 College Walk #214, Honolulu, HI 96817
PH: 808-528-1475 FX: 808-528-3144
www.honoluluweekly.com
Honolulu's A&E weekly.

Maui Time Weekly
33 Market St. #201, Wailuku, HI 96793
PH: 808-661-3786 FX: 808-661-0446
www.mauitime.com
Maui weekly A&E paper.

mele.com
PO Box 223399, Princeville, HI 96722
www.mele.com
The internet's largest in-stock catalog of Hawaiian music CD titles.

Idaho

The Arbiter
1910 University Dr. Boise, ID 83725
PH: 208-345-8204 FX: 208-426-3198
www.arbiteronline.com
Boise State U's student newspaper.

Argonaut
301 Student Union, Moscow, ID 83844
PH: 208-885-8924 FX: 208-885-2222
Ryli Hennessey arg_arts@sub.uidaho.edu
www.argonaut.uidaho.edu
U. of Idaho's student paper.

Boise Blues Society
www.boiseblues.org
Promoting the Blues as an American art form.

Boise Local Music Group
www.blmg.org
The primary goal is to get local musicians better exposure, and hopefully help put a little cash in their pockets.

Boise Weekly
523 Broad St., Boise, ID 83702
PH: 208-344-2055 FX: 208-342-4733
Amy Atkins amy@boiseweekly.com
www.boiseweekly.com
Entertainment publication that covers the local music scene.

HelloBoise.com
www.helloboise.com/music
Local bands can post their MP3s.

Idaho Bluegrass Assoc.
www.smithfowler.org/bluegrass/IdahoBGindex.htm
Promoting Bluegrass music in Idaho.

Idaho Sawtooth Bluegrass Assoc.
www.idahosawtoothbluegrass.org
Created to promote the education and the enjoyment of Bluegrass music.

Zidaho
www.zidaho.com
Everything in Idaho from A to Z. Add your event listing.

Illinois

Blues Blowtorch Society
www.bluesblowtorch.com/society
Promotes local artists as well as regional and national talents.

Carbondale Nightlife
nightlif@midwest.net
www.carbondalerocks.com
Southern Illinois's weekly alternative.

Central Illinois Jazz Society
www.midil.com/cijs.html
Provides opportunities for Jazz artists to play.

Holy Ground Coffee House
304 W. Allen St., Springfield, IL 62704
PH: 217-391-0450 FX: 217-585-1534
Don Hunt don@cggm.org
www.cggm.org
A place for Christian indie artists to share their gifts.

Illinois Music Promotions
illinois.newmusicpromote.com
I started this website to make it easier for booking agents and talent managers to find LOCAL Statewide talent.

Illinois Times
PO Box 5256, Springfield, IL 62705
PH: 217-753-2226 FX: 217-753-2281
www.illinoistimes.com
Springfield's A&E weekly.

IllinoisMusicians.com
www.illinoismusicians.com
Online community with classifieds, gig postings etc.

Northern Illinois Bluegrass Assoc.
www.nibaweb.org
Promotes Bluegrass music by sponsoring events.

Peoria Shows
Melvin Malone peoriashows@hotmail.com
www.peoriashows.net
Everything you need to know about the Peoria music scene.

River City Blues Society
www.rivercityblues.com
Submit news items, CD reviews and articles for the newsletter.

River City Times
www.rctimes.net
Peoria's original alternative newspaper.

Tank's Place
www.tanksplace.com
Promoting live music entertainment in Central Illinois.

Chicago

American Gothic Productions
PMB 258, 2506 N. Clark St., Chicago, IL 60614
PH: 773-278-4684
scaryladysarah@aol.com
www.americangothicprod.com
Send your recordings for review.

Assoc. for the Advancement of Creative Musicians
aacmchicago.org
Dedicated to nurturing, performing and recording serious, original music.

Bluegrass Chatterbox Discussion Group
launch.groups.yahoo.com/group/bgrass-chatbox-illinois
Join for info on bands, musicians, festivals, jam sessions, concerts and more.

CenterstageChicago.com
350 N. Orleans St., 10th Fl. Chicago, IL 60654
PH: 312-944.0032 FX: 773-442.0190
centerstagechicago.com/music
Chicago's original online city guide. Covers local music.

chi-improv Discussion Group
launch.groups.yahoo.com/group/chi-improv
Discussion about the Chicago creative and Improvised music scene.

Chicago Classical Guitar Society
www.chicagoclassicalguitarsociety.org
Sponsors recitals, master classes, evaluated recitals and lectures.

Chicago Classical Music
www.chicagoclassicalmusic.org
An online community for Classical music enthusiasts. Membership is free and open to anyone with an interest in Classical music.

Chicago Flame
222 S. Morgan #3E, Chicago, IL 60607
PH: 312-421-0480 FX: 312-421-0491
chicagoflame@chicagoflame.com
www.chicagoflame.com
Independent student newspaper of the U. Illinois.

Chicago Harmony and Truth
PO Box 578456, Chicago, IL 60657
www.chatmusic.com
Creates a more hospitable music business environment.

Chicago Jazz Magazine
PO Box 737, Park Ridge, IL 60068
PH: 847-322-3534
reviews@ChicagoJazz.com
www.chicagojazzmagazine.com
News, reviews, shows etc.

Chicago Music Promotions
www.chicagomusicpromotions.com
Created to help independent artists with better internet promotions and exposure.

Chicago Reader
11 E. Illinois St., Chicago, IL 60611
PH: 312-828-0350
musiclistings@chicagoreader.com
www.chicagoreader.com
Free weekly paper. Chicago's essential music guide.

Chicago Singer Spotlight
www.singerspotlight.com
Produces three singer showcases in the Chicago area.

Chicago Songwriter's Collective
info@chicagosongwriters.com
chicagosongwriters.com
Our purpose is to work for the community of artists by networking, showcases and educational seminars.

Chicago Stoner Rock
1573 N. Milwaukee Ave. PMB 488
Chicago, IL 60622
PH: 773-276-4474
www.chicagostonerrock.com
Reviews Heavy, Stoner, Drug Metal and Space Rock CDs and live shows.

ChicagoGigs.com
PO Box 2419, Palatine, IL 60078-2419
chicagogigs@gmail.com
www.Chicagogigs.com
Covers both local and national touring acts.

ChicagoGroove.com
2318 S. Oakley, #3, Chicago, IL 60608
info@chicagogroove.com
www.chicagogroove.com
Pics and audio sets from local DJs.

Chicagoist
chicagoist.com
Online A&E zine that covers the local music scene.

ChicagoJazz.com
Contact@ChicagoJazz.com
www.chicagojazz.com
Online version of Chicago Jazz magazine.

ChicagoReggae.com
PH: 773-793-4008
chicagoreggae@chicagoreggae.com
www.chicagoreggae.com
Chicago's premier guide to Reggae entertainment.

ChiCds.com
63 E. Lake St., Mail Box 17, Chicago, IL 60601
PH: 312-884 8341 FX: 312-884-8342
chiradio@hotmail.com
www.chicds.com
Rap and Soul online CD store.

Early MusiChicago
www.earlymusichicago.org
*Covering this captivating but strangely under-
appreciated art form that we call Early Music.*

Emerging Improvisers / The Hungry Brain
c/o EIO Jazz Series, 2319 W. Belmont Ave.
Chicago, IL 60647
contact@emergingimprovisers.org
www.emergingimprovisers.org
*Nurturing experimentation and artistic growth
among Chicago's Jazz musicians.*

Entertainment Law Chicago
PO Box 558023, Chicago, IL 60655
PH: 773-882-4912 FX: 708-206-1663
info@entertainmentlawchicago.com
www.entertainmentlawchicago.com
*Entertainment, music and intellectual property legal
issues.*

Gothic Chicago
davidb@gothicchicago.com
www.gothicchicago.com
*We want to be your resource to events in the
Chicago Gothic community.*

Greenleaf Music Blog
greenleafmusic.com
*A new music company that supports artists fully and
fairly. The focus is on Jazz, Post-Jazz and World
music.*

Illinois Entertainer
124 W. Polk St., Chicago, IL 60605
Attn: CD Reviews
PH: 312-922-9333 FX: 312-922-9369
service@illinoisentertainer.com
www.illinoisentertainer.com
*Chicago A&E weekly. Loads of local music
coverage!*

Jazz Chicago
Brad Walseth bwalseth60@aol.com
www.jazzchicago.net
*CD and concert reviews. Photos, club directory and
free classifieds.*

Jazz Institute of Chicago
410 S. Michigan Ave. Chicago, IL 60605
PH: 312-427-1676 FX: 312-427-1684
www.JazzInstituteOfChicago.org
Preserving and perpetuating Jazz.

JstreetZine.com
PO Box 126, Waukegan, IL 60079
PH: 847-589-1396
Jesse Mendoza jesse@jstreetzine.com
www.jstreetzine.com
Focuses on unsigned, talented, hardworking artists.

Live Music Chicago
2328 W. Touhy Ave. Chicago, IL 60645
PH: 312-698-8995
info@livemusicchicago.com
www.livemusicchicago.com
*The premier source for Chicago live music
entertainment and DJs for all occasions.*

The Methods Reporter Music Blog
www.methodsreporter.com/chicago/music
*A group blog manned by graduate students at the
Medill School of Journalism in Evanston, IL.*

Metromix,com
metromix.chicagotribune.com/music
Supports the local music scene.

Newcity Chicago
770 N. Halsted #306, Chicago, IL 60622
www.newcitychicago.com
Chicago's free A&E publication.

Oh My Rockness Chicago
chicago@ohmyrockness.com
chicago.ohmyrockness.com
*Your one-stop shop for Indie Rock show listings in
Chicago. If you think people should know more
about you e-mail us and tell us.*

Revolutionslive.com
2521 N. Artesian Ave. #2, Chicago, IL 60647
Sean seanorr@revolutionslive.com
www.revolutionslive.com
*Online provider of tour dates , show reviews, venue
info and more for the Chicago area.*

Rock Out Chicago
pete@rockoutchicago.com
www.rockoutchicago.com
Chicago's premier online music community.

RushAndDivision.com
www.rushanddivision.com
*Designed to be your central source for Chicago
nightlife.*

Silver Wrapper Productions
5352 N. Lockwood Ave. Chicago, IL 60630
heynow@silverwrapper.com
www.silverwrapper.com
*Concerts, Jazz, Funk, Electronic, Creole and Soul
music.*

Start A Revolution
1635 W. Julian, Chicago, IL 60622
www.startarevolution.com
*Focuses on the Chicago Jam Band and Prog Rock
scene.*

Suburban NiteLife
PO Box 428, West Chicago, IL 60186
PH: 800-339-2000 FX: 630-653-2123
www.nitelife.org
Chicago entertainment magazine.

Triple Dot MAS
2549 Waukegan Rd. #178
Bannockburn, IL 60015-1510
PH: 312-223-0088
Davan Sand davan@3dmas.com
www.3dmas.com
*A movement towards unity and harmony amongst
creative people through our multimedia events.*

UR Chicago Magazine
213 W. Institute Pl. #305, Chicago, IL 60610
PH: 312-238-9782 FX: 312-238-9838
editorial@urchicago.com
www.urchicago.com
New releases, local shows and more.

Windy City Media Group
5443 N. Broadway, Chicago, IL 60640
PH: 773-871-7610 FX: 773-871-7609
www.wctimes.com
*The voice of Chicago's gay, lesbian, bisexual and
transgender community. Has a music section. Post
your upcoming shows.*

Windyhop
www.windyhop.org
Covering the Chicago swing scene.

Women With Guitars
contact@womenwithguitars.com
www.womenwithguitars.com
*Submit your promotional materials to be considered
for a WWG showcase slot.*

Indiana

BandNut
www.bandnut.com
*Local band connection for the Evansville Tri-State
area local bands.*

**Central Indiana Folk Music & Mountain
Dulcimer Society**
www.indianafolkmusic.org
*Promoting and preserving American Folk music and
Acoustic instruments.*

EvansvilleScene.com
Adam Ferguson webmaster@evansvillescene.com
www.evansvillescene.com
Promoting local talent in the area.

FortWayneHipHop.com
PO Box 13591, Fort Wayne, IN 46869
admin@fortwaynehiphop.com
www.fortwaynehiphop.com
*Keeping you informed of upcoming Hip Hop related
events in the Fort Wayne and surrounding areas.*

FortWayneMusic.com
feedback@fortwaynemusic.com
www.fortwaynemusic.com
*Exposing as many people as possible to the
excellent Fort Wayne music scene.*

Indiana SKAlendar
thomska@yahoo.com
php.indiana.edu/~tgatkins/ska.html
Upcoming Ska shows in the Indiana area.

Indiana45s
indiana45s@yahoo.com
www.indiana45s.com
*A resource dedicated to the documentation and
preservation of music and the history of Hoosier
artists.*

IndianaBluegrass.com
www.indianabluegrass.com
The Hoosier Bluegrass network.

Indianapolis Musicians
www.indymusicians.com
Promoting the music profession in Indiana.

IndianapolisMusic.net
5260 Hinesley Ave. Indianapolis, IN 46208
indianapolismusic.net
*Sparking interest in local music. Features Indy MP3
project.*

Midwest BEAT Magazine
2613 41st St., Highland, IN 46322
PH: 219-972-9131
Tom Lounges tom@midwestbeat.com
www.midwestbeat.com
A&E weekly publication throughout the Midwest.

Naptown Reggae
the_lioness@naptownreggae.com
www.naptownreggae.com
Covering the Indianapolis Reggae scene.

News4U
www.news-4u.com
Evansville's entertainment guide.

Northern Indiana Bluegrass Assoc.
www.bluegrassusa.net
Info on Bluegrass and all Acoustic music in a 200 mile radius of Fort Wayne.

NUVO Newsweekly
3951 N. Meridian St., Indianapolis, IN 46208
PH: 317-254-2400 FX: 317-254-2405
www.nuvo.net
Indianapolis free weekly alternative paper. Covers local music scene!

NWiLive.com
PO Box 551, Schererville, IN 46375
www.nwilive.com
Northwest Indiana's premium source for local music info.

Ric Elson Music
PH: 260-470-4204 FX: 260-470-4204
Derrick Ellison
derrickellison@ricelsonmusicltd.com
www.ricelsonmusicltd.com
Indy's indie music connection. Offers marketing, advertising, online radio play and online sales.

Southwest Indiana Bluegrass Assoc.
www.freewebs.com/tri-statebluegrassassociation
Dedicated to preserving Bluegrass and Old-Time music.

TheMuncieScene.com
PH: 765-215-5440
Phantom phantom@TheMuncieScene.com
themunciescene.com
Assisting local artists in the creation and distribution of their music.

Whatzup Magazine
2305 E. Esterline Rd. Columbia City, IN 46725
PH: 260-691-3048
www.whatzup.com
Indianapolis based entertainment magazine. Show listings and reviews of local bands.

Iowa

Celtic Music Assoc.
www.thecma.org
Bringing quality Celtic entertainment to the Des Moines area.

Central Iowa Blues Society
www.cibs.org
Keeping the Blues alive through appreciation and education.

Cityview
414 61st St., Des Moines, IA 50312
PH: 515-953-4822 FX: 515-953-1394
www.dmcityview.com
Central Iowa's independent weekly.

Des Moines Music Coalition
PO Box 41490, Des Moines, IA 50311
PH: 515-309-2314
info@desmoinesmc.com
www.desmoinesmc.com
Become a part of Central Iowa's music revolution. Create an online account and join our growing community.

Des Moines Register
PO Box 957, Des Moines, IA 50304-0957
PH: 515-284-8000
www.desmoinesregister.com
Daily A&E paper. Covers new music and indie bands.

Iowa HomeGrown Music
PO Box 23265, Nashville, TN 37202
PH: 615-244-0570 FX: 615-242-2472
bronson@iowahomegrown.com
www.iowahomegrown.com
Represents songwriters and artists with a variety of musical styles.

Linn County Blues Society
www.lcbs.org
Preserving Blues music in Eastern Iowa.

Lizard Creek Blues Society
www.lizardcreekblues.org
Promoting the local Blues scene.

Mississippi Valley Blues Society
www.mvbs.org
Educating the general public about the Blues through performances.

Quad City Music
quadcity@gmail.com
www.quadcitymusic.com
We focus on Eastern Iowa and Western Illinois, but can help any musician.

River Cities' Reader
532 W. 3rd St., Davenport, IA 52801
PH: 563-324-0049 FX: 563-323-3101
www.rcreader.com
Davenport news & entertainment weekly.

Siouxland Weekender
PO Box 3616, Sioux City, IA 51102
PH: 712-224-4200 FX: 712-255-7301
www.siouxland.net
Siouxland's first source for community news, events and information.

Stars For Iowa
Randy RozeRocks@aol.com
www.stars4iowa.com
Central Iowa's Rock connection.

Kansas

Afrodisiac Productions
PO Box 1631, Lawrence, KS 66044-9998
PH: 785-749-7475 x110
info@afrodisiac.biz
www.afrodisiac.biz
A multifaceted consulting firm that specializes in the facilitation of events and performances. We have worked with a wide range of performing artists and unique gatherings, from large-scale events to street level promotions and marketing.

Chillfactor Productions
PH: 913-636-8100
Aaron Waters djex4@chillfactorproductions.com
www.chillfactorproductions.com
Promotions label specifically in the area of Electronic Dance music. Long term goal for the biz is to become a record label for the Midwest DJ scene.

Kansas Folk Music and Dance
www.kansasfolk.org
Seeks to showcase traditional music and dance, past and present, in Kansas communities.

Kansas Old-Time Fiddlers, Pickers and Singers
www.kofps.org
Dedicated to promoting and preserving the enjoyment of the art form known as "Old-Time" music.

Kansas Prairie Pickers Assoc.
www.accesskansas.org/kppa
Preserving Bluegrass and Old-Time Acoustic music.

Lawrence.com
645 New Hampshire St., Lawrence, KS 66044
PH: 785-832-7270
www.lawrence.com
Good coverage of local music scene.

LawrenceReggae.com
shows@lawrencereggae.com
www.lawrencereggae.com
Coverage of the Lawrence and Kansas City Reggae scene.

Manhattan Mercury
PO Box 787, Manhattan, KS 66505
PH: 785-776-8808 FX: 785-776-8807
www.themercury.com
Contact us if you would like your band showcased.

Pipeline Productions
c/o The Bottleneck, 737 New Hampshire St.
Lawrence, KS 66044
Julia julia@pipelineproductions.com
www.pipelineproductions.com
Presents concerts in Lawrence & Kansas City. Visit our site for submission details.

Topeka Tonight
topekatonight@aol.com
topekatonight.smugmug.com
Features upcoming shows and photos of local talent.

Wichita City Paper
2100 E. Douglas Ave. Wichita, KS 67214
PH: 316-219-5835 FX: 316-269-2555
www.wichitacitypaper.com
Alternative weekly. Covers local music.

WichitaBandScene.com
www.wichitabandscene.com
Providing free schedule and bio listings to local musicians.

Kentucky

AceWeekly
486 W. 2nd St., Lexington, KY 40507
www.aceweekly.com
Alternative weekly. Covers local music.

Amplifier
PO Box 90012, Bowling Green, KY 42102
PH: 270-781-1700 x378 FX: 270-783-3221
Kim Mason amplifier@bgdailynews.com
www.amplifier.bgdailynews.com
Bowling Green monthly music & entertainment magazine.

Kentuckiana Blues Society
kbsblues.org
Accepts and lists CDs from local acts.

Kentucky Friends of Bluegrass Music Club
www.kyfriends.com
Dedicated to preserving and furthering Bluegrass Music.

LEO Weekly
640 S. 4th St. #100, Louisville, KY 40402
PH: 502-895-9770 x224 FX: 502-895-9779
leo@leoweekly.com
www.leoweekly.com
Your complete guide to the city's musical goings-on.

Louisville Bluegrass Music Assoc.
www.bluegrass-anonymous.org
Dedicated to promoting and supporting bluegrass music, preserving its traditions, and nurturing its growth.

Louisville Music Industry Alliance
www.lmiacentral.com
Supporting and furthering of the Louisville original music scene.

Louisville Music News
3705 Fairway Ln. Louisville, KY 40207
PH: 502-893-9933 FX: 502-721-7482
www.louisvillemusicnews.net
Free monthly music paper. Covers regional music scene.

Louisville Scene
www.louisvillescene.com
Extensive music review section.

LouisvilleHardcore.com
louisvillehardcore.com
Cataloging the Underground music scene of Louisville.

Northern Kentucky Bluegrass Music Assoc.
www.nkbma.com
Fostering and promoting the tradition and well being of Bluegrass music.

Serious Bizness Records
PH: 859-433-9280 FX: 859-971-2328
Joe Fields seriousbiz@holyhiphop.com
www.myspace.com/myspacebiggie
An independent label that promotes events in Central Kentucky for Holy Hip Hop.

W Weekly
434 Old Vine St., Lexington, KY 40507
PH: 859-266-6537
info@lexweekly.com
lexweekly.com
Alternative weekly. Covers local music.

Louisiana

225 Magazine
445 North Blvd. #210, Baton Rouge, LA 70802
PH: 225-214-5225
editor@225batonrouge.com
225batonrouge.com
We're dedicated to bringing you the best coverage of local arts, culture, entertainment and more.

Absinthe Promotions
7836 Jay St., Metairie, LA 70003
PH: 504-458-3129
Katy Kuntz absinthepromo@yahoo.com
www.myspace.com/absinthepromotions
Booking & promotional service for local and national bands in the New Orleans area. Metal, Punk and Rock.

Baton Rouge Blues Society
batonrougeblues.org
Our society strives to educate the general public about Blues related music by performance, appreciation and knowledge.

Cajun French Music Assoc.
www.cajunfrenchmusic.org
Preserves and promotes traditional French Cajun music.

Cajunfun.com
www.cajunfun.com
List your show or event.

Country Roads Magazine
728 France St., Baton Rouge, LA 70802
PH: 800-582-1792
www.countryroadsmagazine.com
A cultural reporting publication focusing on the communities of the Great River Road region between Natchez, Mississippi, and New Orleans.

Cox.net NewOrleans.com *Music*
neworleans.cox.net
Got a show? Let us know!

EntertainLouisiana.com
12551 Lockhaven Ave. Baton Rouge, LA 70815
PH: 225-270-1137 FX: 225-612-6709
www.entertainlouisiana.com
We are proud to be promoting, booking, and managing some of the best musical talent in the country.

The Forum Newsweekly
1158 Texas Ave. Shreveport, LA 71101
PH: 318-222-0409
www.theforumnews.com
Alternative weekly. Covers local music.

Gambit Weekly
3923 Bienville St., New Orleans, LA 70119
PH: 504-486-5900
www.bestofneworleans.com
New Orleans' alternative weekly magazine.

Gris Gris Rouge
715 Spanish Town Rd.
Baton Rouge, LA 70802-5363
PH: 225-383-1489
grisgrisrouge.com
Alternative weekly. Covers local music.

The Independent Weekly
P.O. Box 4307, Lafayette, LA 70502
PH: 337-988-4607 FX: 337-983-0150
www.theind.com
Lafayette alternative weekly magazine.

LiveNewOrleans.com
jason@liveneworleans.com
www.LiveNewOrleans.com
Dedicated to covering the New Orleans music scene with reviews and photographs.

Louisiana Blues Preservation Society
www.geocities.com/Bluespreserve
Preserving and supporting Blues music throughout.

Louisiana Folk Roots
www.lafolkroots.org
Nurturing the unique Folk art scene in Louisiana.

Louisiana Music Factory
210 Decatur St., New Orleans, LA 70130
PH: 504-586-1094
www.louisianamusicfactory.com
Resources for artists in Louisiana.

Mothership Entertainment
1403 Annunciation St., New Orleans, LA 70130
PH: 504-488-3865 FX: 504-488-1574
funk@mothershipentertainment.com
www.MotherShipEntertainment.com
Aids artists by building a strategy designed for success.

New Orleans Bands.com
1609-D Hesiod St., Metairie, LA 70005
Thaddeus Frick thaddeus@nolabands.com
www.neworleansbands.com
Providing a network to help New Orleans talent become successful.

New Orleans Bands.net
4453 E. Falk St., New Orleans, LA 70121
dantheman@neworleansbands.net
www.neworleansbands.net
Bringing a new dimension to the local music scene in the Big Easy.

NewOrleansOnline.com
www.neworleansonline.com/neworleans/music
Extensive coverage of local music.

NOLA Underground
www.nolaunderground.com
Supporting the New Orleans Alternative music scene.

NOLA.com
jdonley@nola.com
www.nolalive.com/music
News and reviews of local music.

NOLADIY
trey@dephex.org
noladiy.org
Supporting the New Orleans DIY scene. Post your upcoming shows.

Offbeat
421 Frenchmen St. #200
New Orleans, LA 70116-2506
PH: 504-944-4300 FX: 504-944-4306
offbeat@offbeat.com
www.offbeat.com
Louisiana's music and entertainment magazine.

Pershing Well's South Louisiana Music Site
150 Shady Arbors Cr. #17-D, Houma, LA 70360
PH: 985-209-2229
info@pershingwells.com
www.pershingwells.com
Provide free listings for Louisiana artists.

Satchmo.com
Greg Hardison gregh@satchmo.com
www.satchmo.com
New Orleans & Louisiana music news, CD reviews, listings etc.

South Louisiana Bluegrass Assoc.
www.southlouisianabluegrass.org
Promoting and preserving Bluegrass music.

Times of Acadiana
1100 Bertrand Dr. Lafayette, LA 70502
PH: 337-289-6300 FX: 337-289-6443
Arsenio Orteza arsenioort@aol.com
www.timesofacadiana.com
Lafayette A&E weekly.

Times of Southwest Louisiana
720 Kirby St., Lake Charles, LA 70601
PH: 337-439-0995 FX: 337-439-0418
www.timessw.com
A&E weekly that reaches 47,000 people.

Where y'at Magazine
5500 Prytania St. #248, New Orleans, LA 70115
PH: 504-891-0144 FX: 504-891-0145
Ashley Curren ashley@whereyat.com
www.whereyat.net
New Orleans' monthly entertainment magazine.

Maine

Bluegrass Music Assoc. of Maine
www.bmam.org
Supports local Bluegrass musicians.

Entertainment in Maine Today.com
390 Congress St., Portland, ME 04104
PH: 207-822-4060 FX: 207-879-1042
entertainment.mainetoday.com
Maine music resource including reviews and previews.

The Maine Blues Society
mainebluessociety.com
Our mission is to encourage, promote and expand the enjoyment, development, performance and preservation of the Blues.

Maine Songwriters Assoc.
www.mesongwriters.com
Supporting songwriters and their art.

MaineList.com
www.mainelist.com
Submit your Maine-based website.

MaineMusic.Org
997 State St., Bangor, ME 04401
PH: 207-775-9056
info@maineperformingarts.org
www.mainemusic.org
Supporting artists of all genres throughout Maine.

Partridge Records and Music
submisions@partridgerecords.com
www.partridgerecords.com
Established to support independent artists and song writers in the local New England market.

Portland Phoenix
16 York St. #102, Portland, ME 04101
PH: 207-773-8900 FX: 207-773-8905
www.portlandphoenix.com
Local band coverage including MP3s from locally based musicians.

PortlandatNight.net
www.portlandatnight.net
Features bars, clubs, nightlife & entertainment in The Old Port.

Song of the Sea
www.songsea.com
Celtic and Folk music resource enabling people to add music to their lives.

Maryland

A Day in the Life of a Hip Hop Heroine
theurbanuderground.blogspot.com
Blog covering the Baltimore Hip Hop scene.

Any Given Tuesday
PH: 443-955-5382
blawk359@gmail.com
www.anygiventuesday.info
Your source for music news, album reviews, concert updates, concert reviews and artist information. Also covers the Baltimore music scene.

Baltimore Blues Society
www.mojoworkin.com
Reviews CD releases by national, regional and local artists.

Baltimore City Paper
812 Park Ave. Baltimore, MD 21201
PH: 410-523-2300 FX: 410-523-2222
www.citypaper.com
A&E publication with news and opinions on local politics, communities, culture and the arts.

Baltimore Classical Guitar Society
www.bcgs.org
Organizes concerts for local and national Classical guitarists.

BaltimoreBands.com
www.baltimorebands.com
Classifieds, gigs, plus the ultimate list of Baltimore and Maryland's finest music makers.

Cajun/Zydeco in the Mid-Atlantic Region
Pat Yaffe patyaffe@yahoo.com
www.wherewegotozydeco.com
Cajun and Zydeco music and dance guide for the Baltimore-Washington area.

Chesapeake Music Guide
PO Box 1029, Stevensville, MD 21666
PH: 410-643-0613 FX: 410-643-0614
Becky Cooper becky@chesapeakemusicguide.com
www.chesapeakemusicguide.com
News, reviews, show dates and more!

Frederick Blues Society
www.frederickblues.org
Supporting the Blues in the Frederick area.

Government Names
Al Shipley shipley.al@gmail.com
governmentnames.blogspot.com
A music blog covering the Baltimore Hip Hop scene.

Instrumental Analysis
instanalysis@aol.com
instrumentalanalysis.blogspot.com
Covering Baltimore, DC and PA. We love receiving tips on new artists. If we don't know about it, we can't write about it.

Maryland Night Life.com
PH: 410-239-2817
www.marylandnightlife.com
Free online entertainment guide with local music section.

MarylandParty.com
409 Lee Dr. Baltimore, MD 21228
PH: 410-869-9348 FX: 443-697-0210
www.mdparty.com
Guide to live music in Maryland and surrounding states.

Music Monthly
2807 Goodwood Rd. Baltimore, MD 21214
PH: 410-426-9000 FX: 410-426-4100
kcmusicmonthly@comcast.net
www.musicmonthly.com
Baltimore monthly music magazine. Register your band.

Potomac River Jazz Club
www.prjc.org
Encouraging and promoting traditional Jazz.

RNR TV
244 Leppo Rd. Westminster, MD 21158
sightbringer@yahoo.com
www.rnrtv.com
Weekly show featuring all genres of Rock music videos from Blues to Heavy Metal. If you are a band searching for exposure and coming through the Baltimore area, please email us and we'll try to set up an interview.

Static Chain
PO Box 30, Owings Mills, MD 21117
PH: 443-857-7096
Jason McKay jason@staticchain.com
www.staticchain.com
Networking Baltimore area artists, venues and listeners, to create a true music community.

StatiQ Records
11221 Grouse Ln. Hagerstown, MD 21742
PH: 301-992-9889
Natasha A. Smith-Hazzard tasha@statiqrecords.ws
www.statiqrecords.ws
Record company with virtual music recording studio, music production & publishing and video production.

Walther Productions
PO Box 116, Jefferson, MD 21755
FX: 301-834-3373
info@walther-productions.com
www.walther-productions.com
Hosts tons of awesome Jam Band shows in the Baltimore & DC areas.

Massachusetts

Cambridge Society for Early Music
www.csem.org
Enlightening, educating and promoting the rich musical culture of five centuries.

capecodmusic.com
info@capecodmusic.com
www.capecodmusic.com
Extensive listing of events in the area. Post yours.

Country Dance and Song Society
www.cdss.org
Celebrating English and Anglo-American Folk dance and music.

Folk Arts Center of New England
www.facone.org
Promoting traditional Dance, music and related Folk arts.

MassConcerts
MassMediaGirl@aol.com
www.massconcerts.com
Find information about music and entertainment events in the Northeast US.

Music For Robin
www.music-for-robin.org
Folk & Celtic resources covering Mass.

New England Country Music Club
www.necmc.homestead.com
Promoting Country music and local talent!

New England Entertainment Digest
PO Box 88, Burlington, MA 01803
Julie Ann Charest jacneed@aol.com
www.jacneed.com
Covering all of New England and New York.

New England Jazz Alliance
www.nejazz.org
Celebrating and perpetuating the tradition of Jazz in New England.

NewEARS
www.newears.org
A community dedicated to sharing and promoting Progressive Rock in the New England area.

NoMaSoNHa
www.myspace.com/nomasonha
Greater Merrimack Valley music magazine with coverage from Lowell, MA to Manchester, NH and from Nashua, NH to Salem, NH ...and beyond.

Northeast Performer
24 Dane St., Somerville, MA 02143
PH: 617-627-9200 FX: 617-627-9930
Adam Arrigo nepeditorial@performermag.com
www.performermag.com
Want your CD reviewed? Send your CDs and press releases.

PACE Arts Center
pioneerarts.org
Supporting the arts in Massachusetts.

The Pulse Magazine
84 Winter St., Worcester, MA 01604
PH: 508-756-5006
thepulsemag.com
Worcester's arts & entertainment magazine.

TRP/NME Wreckidz
9 Hutchins Ct. Gloucester, MA 01930
PH: 978-394-0751
Mr. Dilligence mrdilligence@aol.com
www.NMEwreckidz.com
Indie record label/grassroots distributor for Massachusetts (and beyond) Rappers/R&B singers.

Valley Advocate
116 Pleasant St., Easthampton, MA 01027
PH: 413-529-2840 FX: 413-529-2844
www.valleyadvocate.com
Springfield free weekly alternative paper. Local bands and happenings section.

Worcester County Jazz Scene
Don Ricklin don@donricklin.com
www.donricklin.com/worcjazz
Everything you want to know about Jazz in Worcester County.

Worcester Magazine
PH: 508-749-3166 FX: 508-749-3165
www.worcestermag.com
Alternative weekly. Covers local music.

Wormtown
www.wormtown.org
Info on the Worcester, MA scene. Free listings.

B o s t o n

All That She Surveys
PO Box 53011, Medford, MA 02153
watchinginkdry@hotmail.fr
queenofnotes.blogspot.com
MP3 blog featuring music that comes through my area, or just my head.

Arts & Culture in Bostonia
petthebunny@gmail.com
under21inboston.typepad.com
Boston guide to UnPop-culture hot spots.

Band in Boston
bandinboston@gmail.com
bandinbostonpodcast.com
Blog covering the Boston music scene. Features live performances.

Boston Beats
195 Tower St., Dedham, MA 02026
PH: 781-381-2856 FX: 206-237-2473
artists@bostonbeats.com
www.bostonbeats.com
Your guide to Boston's music scene.

Boston Bluegrass Union
www.bbu.org
Promoting and supporting the wealth of regional bands.

Boston Blues Society
www.bostonblues.com
Preserving and promoting the Blues.

Boston Classical Guitar Society
www.bostonguitar.org
Bimonthly newsletter. Submit your info to get posted.

BostonGeek
admin@bostongeek.com
www.bostongeek.com
MP3 blog by a geeky resident of Boston who sits around, drinks beer, and ruminates on the topics of the day.

The Boston Hip-Hop Alliance
askdarcie@hotmail.com
bostonhha.tripod.com
Helping to make the experience of Hip Hop artists, producers, promoters etc. better in the city of Boston.

Boston Jazz Fest
Chris Allen centralarteryproject@yahoo.com
bostonjazzfest.com
Promoting Jazz in the Boston area.

Boston Phoenix
126 Brookline Ave. Boston, MA 02215
PH: 617-536-5390 FX: 617-536-1463
www.bostonphoenix.com
Entertainment magazine covering the New England region.

BostonBands.com
www.myspace.com/bostonbands
Covering the Boston music scene.

Bostonist
bostonist.com
Online A&E zine that covers the local music scene.

Bradley's Almanac
bradleysalmanac@gmail.com
www.bradleysalmanac.com
Covers the Boston music scene. If you want to send me something drop me an email and I'll let you know my mailing address.

The Brilliant Mistake
mail@thebrilliantmistake.com
www.thebrilliantmistake.com
MP3 and video blog covering the Boston scene.

Exploit Boston!
343 Medford St. #2A, Somerville, MA 02145
PH: 781-420-9660
www.exploitboston.com
Event calendar and guide to interesting happenings around Boston: art, books, music, theater etc.

Folk Song Society of Greater Boston
www.fssgb.org
Providing opportunities for everyone to make, enjoy and support this music.

GyrlsRock Boston
1238 Comm Ave. #36, Boston, MA 02134
Sara Hamilton webmaster@gyrlsrock.com
www.gyrlsrock.com
100% devoted to female musicians in Boston.

Improper Bostonian
142 Berkeley St., Boston, MA 02116
PH: 617-859-1400
music@improper.com
www.improper.com
Boston's A&E magazine.

JazzBoston
www.jazzboston.org
Spreading the word about Boston's thriving Jazz scene and keeping it growing.

The Noise
74 Jamaica St., Boston, MA 02130
PH: 617-524-4735
www.thenoise-boston.com
If you're a New England band, we'll review your music!

On the Download
onthedownload@phx.com
thephoenix.com/onthedownload
The Phoenix's MP3 blog with hundreds of downloads plus news, reviews and scene reports.

Onward Charles
onward.charles@gmail.com
onwardcharles.blogspot.com
MP3 blog covering the Boston music scene.

Purerockfury.com
Deek deek@purerockfury.com
www.purerockfury.com
Covering the Hard Rock/Metal scene. Includes a local band spotlight.

SalsaBoston.com
salsaboston.com
Boston's premiere Latin music and dance website.

thewicked
Ashley Wicked ashley@the-wicked.org
www.the-wicked.org
Listing of upcoming Boston gigs.

WBUR Online Arts
890 Commonwealth Ave. 3rd Fl. Boston, MA 02215
PH: 617-353-0909
www.wbur.org
Covers the local Boston music scene.

Michigan

Ann Arbor Classical Guitar Society
www.society.arborguitar.org
Bringing performances of Classical guitar music to Michigan.

Ann Arbor Council for Traditional Music and Dance
www.aactmad.org
Dedicated to the promotion and preservation of Acoustic Folk, Traditional and Ethnic music only.

The Ark
316 S. Main St., Ann Arbor, MI 48104
PH: 734-761-1818
www.theark.org
Presenting and encouraging Folk, Roots and Ethnic music.

Arts League of Michigan
www.artsleague.com
Develops, promotes, presents and preserves the African and African American cultural arts traditions within our multicultural community.

Capital Area Blues Society
www.cabsblues.com
Reviews of new album releases every month.

City Pulse
2001 E. Michigan Ave. Lansing, MI 48912
PH: 517-371-5600 FX: 517-371-5800
citypulse@lansingcitypulse.com
www.lansingcitypulse.com
Lansing's Alternative weekly. Covers local music.

Current Magazine
212 E. Huron St., Ann Arbor, MI 48104
PH: 734-668-4044 FX: 734-668-0555
music@ecurrent.com
ecurrent.com
Free monthly A&E magazine. Covers local music scene, news and reviews.

Flint Folk Music Society
www.flintfolkmusic.org
Promoting Folk music through performances and workshops.

Folk Alliance Region Midwest
www.farmfolk.org
Promotes the growth of Folk music and dance.

Grand Rapids Hip Hop Coalition
www.myspace.com/grandrapidshiphopcoalition
Launching all Hip Hop, Rap and R&B artists in the area that believe in themselves and the organization.

Grand River Folk Arts Society
www.grfolkarts.org
Contact to perform in West Michigan.

Great Lakes Acoustic Music Assoc.
www.greatlakesacoustic.org
Promoting Bluegrass and Acoustic music.

Hearts On Fire Records
PO Box 852, Marshall, MI 49068
PH: 800-381-1063
www.heartsonfirerecords.com
Kalamazoo, Michigan Rock!

Kalamazoo Valley Blues Assoc.
www.kvba.org
Preserving Blues music around Kalamazoo.

K'zoo Folklife Organization
www.geocities.com/Vienna/Studio/5893
Promotes multi-cultural, traditional and contemporary Folk music.

Lansing Indie Music Project
3435 Dietz Rd. Williamston, MI 48895
PH: 517-512-9259
Ryan Ridenour lansing@indiemusicproject.com
lansing.indiemusicproject.com
An e-zine helping to bring Michigan artists to the world stage. Affiliated with The Insomnia Radio Network & The Bush Radio!

Magazine of Country Music
PO Box 1412, Warren, MI 48090
PH: 586-755-0471
countrymusicmag@yahoo.com
www.magazineofcountrymusic.com
Monthly publication. Features national and local Country music.

Michigan Artists
contactus@michiganartists.com
www.michiganartists.com
Supporting Michigan artists with postings of history, bios, pictures and more!

Michigan Bands dot Com
www.michiganbands.com
Submit news and press releases and add links to your band page.

Michigan Bluegrass Network
www.myspace.com/michiganbluegrassnetwork
Includes upcoming gigs, message board etc.

The Michigan Musician's Network
www.myspace.com/mimusicnetwork
Resources for up-and-coming working singers, musicians, bands, songwriters, producers, managers etc.

Michigan Television Network
PO Box 765, Royal Oak, MI 48068-0765
PH: 248-376-4162
MichiganTV@hotmail.com
www.myspace.com/michiganmadetv
Increasing public awareness of Michigan's homegrown talent.

MichiganMetal
webmaster@michiganmetal.com
www.michiganmetal.com
Michigan's Heavy Metal resource. Downloads, gigs and more!

MLive
www.mlive.com
Michigan's home on the net. CD and concert reviews, music news.

Northern Express
PO Box 209, Traverse City, MI 49685-0209
PH: 231-947-8787 FX: 231-947-2425
www.northernexpress.com
Covering Northern Michigan. Does features on local musicians.

Northern Michigan Update
northernmichiganupdate.com
Any new CD releases or big events, you would like me to promote?

On-The-Town
PO Box 499, Jenison, MI 49429-0499
PH: 616-669-1366 FX: 616-662-4060
www.on-the-town.com
The Arts and Entertainment magazine of West Michigan.

Review Magazine
318 S Hamilton St., Saginaw, MI 48602
PH: 989-799-6078 FX: 989-799-6162
www.aftershockmultimedia.com/review-mag
Bars, nightclubs and what's happening!

Southeast Michigan Jazz Assoc.
www.semja.org
Monthly newsletter and free online listings.

State News
435 E. Grand River Ave. East Lansing, MI 48823
PH: 517-432-3000
www.statenews.com
Michigan State U's student paper.

Tawas Bay Blues Society
www.bluesbythebaytawas.com
Promoting and preserving Blues music and culture.

West Michigan Bluegrass Music Assoc.
www.wmbma.org
Proud to help keep the tradition of Bluegrass and Acoustic music alive in our W. Michigan area.

West Michigan Blues Society
www.wmbs.org
Promotes Blues appreciation by sponsoring concerts, festivals and community events.

West Michigan Jazz Society
www.wmichjazz.org
Promotes numerous events and local artists.

West Michigan Music
listen@westmichiganmusic.com
www.westmichiganmusic.com
The area's one-stop place for the best information on the unique and exciting West Michigan music scene.

Wheatland Music Organization
www.wheatlandmusic.org
Resource center for the preservation and presentation of traditional music and arts.

Detroit

DetMusic.com
www.detmusic.com
A local artist boards community. Promote your CD or upcoming shows.

Detroit Blues Society
www.dbsblues.com
Promotes the Blues to the general public.

Detroit Metro Times
733 Saint Antoine, Detroit, MI 48226
PH: 313-961-4060 FX: 313-961-6598
www.metrotimes.com
Free weekly alternative. CD reviews, concert reviews and previews.

Detroit Reggae
www.detroitreggae.com
Complete coverage of the Detroit Reggae scene.

DetroitCountryMusic.com
11449 Fleming St., Hamtramck, MI 48212
larry@detroitcountrymusic.com
www.detroitcountrymusic.com
Promotes and showcases local talent.

Motor City Rocks
PH: 313-982-0607 FX: 313-982-0607
Gary Blackwell gary@motorcityrocks.com
www.motorcityrocks.com
Our mission is to promote Detroit musicians and Detroit music venues.

Nestor in Detroit
hectop@peoplepc.com
www.nestorindetroit.com
News, releases and show reviews of the local Punk scene.

Online Bands
joe@onlinebands.com
www.onlinebands.com
Visit our site where you will find exciting fresh music from Detroit area bands.

Real Detroit Weekly
359 Livernois Ave. 2ⁿᵈ Fl. Ferndale, MI 48220
PH: 248-591-7325 FX: 248-544-9893
www.realdetroitweekly.com
Detroit's entertaining source for music, nightlife, movies and all other things under the pop culture umbrella.

Renaissance Soul Detroit
PMB #323, 23205 Gratiot Ave.
Eastpointe, MI 48021
Kelly "K-Fresh" Frazier djkfresh@rensoul.com
rensoul.com
The Detroit Urban alternative. Dedicated to Detroit Hip Hop.

Minnesota

City Pages MN Music Directory
401 N. 3ʳᵈ St. #550, Minneapolis, MN 55401
PH: 612-372-3792
mmd@citypages.com
www.citypages.com/mmd
Magazine resource for local musicians.

The Current Music Blog
minnesota.publicradio.org/collections/special/
columns/music_blog
The staff of 89.3 The Current to talk to you about local music.

KXXR's Loud & Local Page
2000 SE. Elm St., Minneapolis, MN 55414
PH: 612-617-4000
Patrick loudandlocal@93xrocks.com
www.93x.com/loudnlocal.asp
Submit news on your local band.

Midwest Movement
2804 Silver Ln. NE #202, Minneapolis, MN 55421
Brad Gunnarson contact@midwestmovement.com
www.midwestmovement.com
Covering the Midwest Punk scene. Reviews, interviews, spotlight bands etc.

Minnesota Bluegrass and OT Music Assoc.
www.minnesotabluegrass.org
Host's Bluegrass and Old-Time music events and celebrations.

MusicScene
1998 Bluestem Ln. Shoreview, MN 55126-5013
PH: 612-747-0894 FX: 612-605-1299
Conal "Reverend Gonzo" Garrity
gonzo@musicscene.org
www.musicscene.org
Submit your band, gig, news etc. Send your demos and CDs for review.

Southeast Minnesota Bluegrass Assoc.
www.semba.tv
Created to promote traditional Country and Bluegrass music in the area.

Springboard for the Arts
www.springboardforthearts.org
Provides affordable management information for indie artists.

Minneapolis/St. Paul

Blues On Stage
PO Box 582983, Minneapolis, MN 55458-2983
Ray Stiles mnblues@aol.com
www.mnblues.com
Covering Blues in the Twin Cities & around the world. Send 2 copies of your CD for review.

Downtown Journal
1115 Hennepin Ave. S., Minneapolis, MN 55403
PH: 612-825-9205 FX: 612-825-0929
www.downtownjournal.com
Covers the Twin Cities music scene.

Greater Twin Cities Blues Music Society
www.gtcbms.org
Created to enhance and celebrate the existing Blues music environment in our area.

HowWasTheShow.com
2751 Hennepin Ave. S. #245
Minneapolis, MN 55408
David de Young david@howwastheshow.com
www.howwastheshow.com
Covering the Twin City music scene. Send us your promotional CDs and press releases to the above address.

Minneapolis Fucking Rocks
Attn: Reviews, 222 W. 25ᵗʰ St.
Minneapolis, MN 55404
info@minneapolisfuckingrocks.com
minneapolisfuckingrocks.blogspot.com
A daily music column by the guys who run slivermagazine.com.

Minneapolis Reggae Connection
Paul McGee paul@mplsreggae.com
www.mplsreggae.com
Keeping you plugged into the Minneapolis Reggae scene.

MinneapolisMusic.com
www.minneapolismusic.com
Find all the latest gossip, gab and news right here!

MinneapolitanMusic
Andrea andrea.j.myers@gmail.com
minneapolitanmusic.blogspot.com
Blog that covers the local music scene.

More Cowbell
301 Shelard Pkwy. #226, St. Louis Park, MN 55426
Kyle Matteson kyle@morecowbell.net
www.morecowbell.net
Covering the Twin Cities' scene.

Pulse of the Twin Cities
3200 Chicago Ave. S., Minneapolis, MN 55407
PH: 612-824-0000 FX: 612-822-0342
Dwight Hobbes musiceditor@pulsetc.com
pulsetc.com
Weekly alternative paper. CD reviews and concert previews.

Rake Magazine
800 Washington Ave. N. #504
Minneapolis, MN 55401
PH: 612-436-2880 FX: 612-436-2890
www.rakemag.com
Provides entertaining reading for the Twin Cities.

Twin Cities Acoustic Music Calendar
www.tcacoustic.com
Includes major events in the upper Midwest, including Wisconsin, Iowa, ND and SD.

Twin Cities Jazz Society
www.tcjs.org
Sponsors local Jazz concerts, workshops and education programs.

Twin Cities Music Network
23 SE. 4ᵗʰ St. #213, Minneapolis, MN 55414
PH: 612-605-7960
email@tcmusic.net
www.tcmusic.net
List performances, band info and sell your CDs online.

TwinCitiesBands.com
www.twincitiesbands.com
Dedicated to the Twin Cities music scene. Gigs, venues, open stages etc.

Vita.mn
www.vita.mn
Your ultimate guide to what's going on in the Twin Cities. Covers local music.

Mississippi

The Burger
PO Box 1169, Hattiesburg, MS 39403-1169
PH: 601-529-9993
editor@theburger.org
www.theburger.org
Hattiesburg's one and only alternative press!

Ground Zero Blues Club Clarksdale
groundzerobluesclub.com
Promoting the Clarksdale, Mississippi Blues scene.

Jackson Free Press
PO Box 2047, Jackson, MS 39225
PH: 601-362-6121 FX: 601-510-9019
www.jacksonfreepress.com
The alternative newsweekly of Jackson.

Magnolia State Bluegrass Assoc.
www.geocities.com/magnoliabluegrass
Promotes Bluegrass music in the Deep South.

Mississippi Link
2659 Livingston Rd. Jackson, MS 39213
PH: 601-355-9103 FX: 601-355-9105
www.mississippilink.com
Jackson weekly paper.

The Reflector
www.reflector-online.com
Mississippi State U's student paper.

Missouri

Blues Society of the Ozarks
www.ozarksblues.org
Encourages performance of the Blues at clubs, at festivals and on radio.

CapeScene.com
scott@capescene.com
www.capescene.com
Covering upcoming events in the Cape Girardeau music scene.

Central Plains Jam Band Society
www.cpjs.org
Promotes the arts, music and spirit of Jam Band music.

Columbia360.com
www.columbia360.com
List your band, event, news etc.

COMOmusic
www.comomusic.com
Columbia's definitive guide to local music. Post your profile, CD and show reviews etc.

GO Magazine
www.springfieldgo.com
Springfield's premier source for music, movies, dining and living the active lifestyle.

Heart of the Ozarks Bluegrass Assoc.
www.heartoftheozarksbluegrass.com
Created to further the enjoyment of Bluegrass music and to bring together Bluegrass musicians.

Heavy Frequency
13415 15th St., Grandview, MO 64030
PH: 816-995-0460
Heather Bashaw
heather.bashaw@heavyfrequency.com
www.heavyfrequency.com
Features promising Heavy Metal and Hardcore acts emerging from the depths of the Midwest underground.

Kirksville Rocks!
Royce Kallerud manager@kvrocks.com
www.kvrocks.com
Information about all the great live music community in and around Kirksville.

Missouri Area Bluegrass Committee
www.bluegrassamerica.com
Promoting Bluegrass music across the US.

MO Blues Assoc.
www.moblues.org
Artist photos, merchandise, CD reviews and more!

MOrawk.com
318 ½ Park Central W. #204, Springfield, MO 65806
PH: 417-832-9795
aaron@morawk.com
www.morawk.com
Supporting independent music in Missouri.

Springfield Music Scene
3055 S. Lakeside Ave. Springfield, MO 65804
James Kavanaugh james@gufbal.com
springfieldmusicscene.com
Springfield's source for live music and music hosting.

Tri-State Bluegrass Assc.
tsbafestivals.org
Publishes both a yearly festival guide and quarterly newsletter.

Unsigned Hype
PH: 206-984-4973
info@unsignedhype.org
www.unsignedhype.org
Hip Hop artist promotion and services.

Voxmagazine
320 Lee Hills Hall, Columbia, MO 65211
PH: 573-882-6432 FX: 573-884-1870
vox@missouri.edu
www.voxmagazine.com
Columbia's weekly guide to area new, arts and entertainment.

Yellowstone Bluegrass Assoc.
www.yellowstonebluegrass.com
Created to promote the education and enjoyment of Bluegrass and Old-Time music.

Kansas City

Banzai Magazine
PO Box 7522, Overland Park, KS 66207
PH: 913-642-2262
Jim Kilroy jimkilroy@bizkc.rr.com
www.banzaimagazine.net
Kansas City's Rock n' Roll headquarters.

Club Wars
PO Box 7522, Overland Park, KS 66207
PH: 913-642-2262
Jim Kilroy clubwars@hotmail.com
www.clubwars.net
Held at venues in Kansas City the and surrounding region since the Spring of 2002.

eKC online
www.kcactive.com
Metro Kansas City news and entertainment.

Heart of America Bluegrass and Old-Time Music
www.banjonut.com/habot
Performances, jam sessions, newsletter, gigs etc.

Heat Advisory Records
PO Box 300317, Kansas City, MO 64130
Bryan B. Brooks bryan@heatadvisoryrecords.com
heatadvisoryrecords.com
Hip Hop label currently looking for new artists.

HipHopKC.com
hiphopkc@gmail.com
www.hiphopkc.com
The virtual Hip Hop community of Kansas City.

Kansas City Blues Society
www.kcbluessociety.com
Keeping the Blues alive.

Kansas City Folk Arts Alliance
www.crosscurrentsculture.org
We produce concerts, plays and community events, and welcome all talent.

Kansas City Guitar Society
www.kansascityguitarsociety.org
Encourages artistry of the Classical guitar.

Kansas City Infozine
PO Box 22661, Kansas City, MO 64113
PH: 913-432-2661
www.infozine.com
Post your show information on the music page.

Kansas City Jazz Ambassadors
PO Box 36181, Kansas City, MO 64171
PH: 913-967-6767
www.jazzkc.org
Publishes Jam Magazine. Submit CDs for review.

Kansas City Music
2510 Grand Ave. #603, Kansas City, MO 64108
PH: 816-520-8430
valentine@boxofchalk.com
www.kansascitymusic.com
Find musicians, their gigs, as well as posting your own.

King Cat Music
17300 Gray Dr. Pleasant Hill, MO 64080
PH: 816-540-4197
info@kingcatmusic.com
www.kingcatmusic.com
Provides a safe place for Christian artists to network, fellowship, encourage and pray for each other.

Missouri Valley Folklife Society
www.mvfs.org
Provides opportunities for local, regional and international Folk musicians to perform.

Pitch Weekly
1701 Main St., Kansas City, MO 64108
PH: 816-561-6061 FX: 816-756-0502
Jason Harper jason.harper@pitch.com
music.pitch.com
Kansas City free weekly alternative. Reviews new CDs. Focuses on local music scene.

Songwriters Circle of Kansas City
www.songwriterscircle.org
Supporting local indie songwriters.

St. Louis

Entertainment St. Louis
PO Box 1354, St. Louis, MO 63188
PH: 314-771-0200 FX: 314-771-0300
editor@slfp.com
www.slfp.com
Internet based publication. Post your event.

gtp-inc.com
shaunbrooks@gtp-inc.com
www.gtp-inc.com
Dedicated to the St. Louis music scene.

playback
PO Box 9170, St. Louis, MO 63117
PH: 314-952-6404 FX: 877-204-2067
Laura Hamlett editor@playbackstl.com
www.playbackstl.com
St. Louis pop culture. Send your info and news.

Riverfront Times
6358 Delmar Blvd. #200
St. Louis, MO 63130-4719
PH: 314-754-5966 FX: 314-754-5955
Annie Zaleski Annie.Zaleski@riverfronttimes.com
www.rftstl.com
St. Louis free weekly A&E paper. Covers local music scene.

St. Louis Gothic
stlouisgothic@yahoo.com
www.stlouisgothic.com
Your source for St. Louis Darkwave events and information!

St. Louis Magazine
1600 S. Brentwood St. #550, St. Louis, MO 63144
PH: 314-918-3000 FX: 314-918-3099
www.stlmag.com
What's happening in the arts, music, politics, the media and more.

St. Louis Punk Page
PO Box 63207, St. Louis, MO 63163
jerome@stlpunk.com
www.stlpunk.com
Post your band info and events.

STLBlues
11469 Olive Blvd. #163, St. Louis, MO 63141
publisher@stlblues.net
www.stlblues.net
E-mail us to get your band listed here!

STLHipHop.com
PH: 314-732-4045
info@stlhiphop.com
www.stlhiphop.com
Every year we draft the best of the best - artists that we support with our blood, sweat & tears.

STLtoday.com
www.stltoday.com/entertainment
Extensive local music coverage. News, reviews, spotlights etc. Submit your band's info.

Montana

The BoZone
PO Box 3548, Bozeman, MT 59772-3548
PH: 406-586-6730 FX: 406-582-7676
info@bozone.com
www.bozone.com
Designed to inform you of Bozeman community events.

Exponent
www.exponent.montana.edu
Montana State U.'s student newspaper.

Lively Times
1152 Eagle Pass Trail, Charlo, MT 59824
PH: 406-644-2910
www.livelytimes.com
Montana's most complete A&E calendar.

Missoula Folklore Society
www.montanafolk.org
Preserving contemporary and traditional music.

Missoula Independent
PO Box 8275, Missoula, MT 59807
PH: 406-543-6609 FX: 406-543-4367
www.missoulanews.com
Free weekly alternative paper. CD and concert reviews, interviews and previews.

Montana Kaimin
Journalism 206, U. Montana, Missoula, MT 59801
PH: 406-243-6541 FX: 406-243-4303
www.montanakaimin.com
U. Montana's student paper.

Montana Rockies Bluegrass Assoc.
www.mtbluegrass.com
Dedicated to performing, promoting and preserving Bluegrass music.

Nebraska

1% Productions
Mario & Jim info@onepercentproductions.com
www.onepercentproductions.com
Puts on Rock and Punk shows in Omaha.

Blues Society of Omaha
omahablues.com
Promoting Blues music in the greater Omaha-Lincoln area. News, reviews, newsletter, upcoming shows…

Great Plains Bluegrass & Old-Time Music Assoc.
gpbotma.homestead.com
Promoting Bluegrass and Old-Time music in and around Omaha.

Homer's Music & Gifts
info@homersmusic.com
www.homersmusic.com
Several stores throughout Nebraska that promote local artists. Runs an online shop as well.

Lazy-i
743 J.E. George Blvd. Omaha, NE 68132
Tim McMahan tim@lazy-i.com
www.timmcmahan.com/lazyeye.htm
Interviews and band profiles, reviews and hype.

Lincoln Assoc. for Traditional Arts
www.lafta.net
Our mission is to preserve and promote Folk & Traditional music in the Lincoln area.

Night Moves Magazine
info@nightmovesmag.com
www.nightmovesmag.com
Lists Omaha bands, clubs, gigs etc.

Omaha City Weekly
1307 Leavenworth St., Omaha, NE 68102
PH: 402-933-8338 FX: 402-934-2956
www.omahacityweekly.com
Weekly A&E magazine. List your upcoming shows.

Omaha Concerts
www.myspace.com/omahaconcerts
Info and video on upcoming shows.

OMAHAMUSIC.com
www.omahamusic.com
Official website of the Omaha Musician's Assoc.. Band and event listings.

OmahaNightlife.com
PH/FX: 402-933-6573
www.omahanightlife.com
Covers local gigs, venues, bands etc.

The Reader
5015 Underwood Ave. #101, Omaha, NE 68132
PH: 402-341-7323 FX: 402-341-6967
www.thereader.com
Alternative news zine. Submit your info/events.

SLAM Omaha
PO Box 391264, Omaha, NE 68139-1264
Bubba bubba@slamomaha.com
www.slamomaha.com
Local music, featured bands, new releases etc.

Starcityscene.com
Tery info@astropopweb.com
www.starcityscene.com
Your guide to the Lincoln music scene.

Nevada

Northern Nevada Bluegrass Assoc.
www.nnba.org
Dedicated to promoting and preserving Bluegrass, Old-Time and related Folk music.

Las Vegas

Guitar Society of Las Vegas
www.gslv.org
Promoting the art of Acoustic guitar.

IndieKrush
spaceywolfe@hotmail.com
www.indiecrush.org
If you are an artist, promoter, designer, or music/clothing label and have fresh material, mixes, artwork, events or products you would like for us to feature on our site, please contact us.

Jazzlasvegas.com
jazzlasvegas@lvcoxmail.com
www.jazzlasvegas.com
Emphasis on Jazz in the Las Vegas area.

Las Vegas City Life
1385 Pama Ln. #111, Las Vegas, NV 89119
PH: 702-871-6780
Mike Prevat mprevatt@lvcitylife.com
www.lvcitylife.com
Extensive music section with profiles and reviews of musicians.

Las Vegas Jam Band Society
www.lvjbs.org
Creating a supportive music community in Southern Nevada for the musicians of the Jam Band genre.

Las Vegas Jazz Society
www.vegasjazz.org
Publishes and reviews concerts, club dates and special events.

Las Vegas Weekly
PO Box 230040, Las Vegas, NV 89123-0011
PH: 702-990-2411 FX: 702-990-2400
www.lasvegasweekly.com
Extensive coverage of both local and touring bands.

Neon
1111 W. Bonanza Rd. PO Box 70
Las Vegas, NV 89125
PH: 702-383-0211
www.reviewjournal.com/neon
Entertainment section of the Las Vegas Review-Journal.

The Vegas Hustler
www.thevegashustler.com
Your underground guide to Sin City.

Vegas Rocks Magazine
PO Box 231447, Las Vegas, NV 89105
PH: 702-252-0532 FX: 702-252-0532
Sally Steele sally@vegasrocksmag.com
www.vegasrocksmag.com
Las Vegas Rock City news!

Reno

Reno Blues Society
www.renoblues.org
One stop source for the Blues in Reno.

Reno News & Review
708 N. Center St., Reno, NV 89501
PH: 775-324-4440 x3520
Peter Thompson petert@newsreview.com
www.newsreview.com/reno
Reno's news and entertainment weekly.

New Hampshire

Blues Audience Newsletter
www.bluesaudience.com
Supports New England's fine Blues musicians and clubs.

Foster's Online *Showcase Magazine*
333 Central Ave. Dover, NH 03820
showcase@fosters.com
www.fosters.com
Dover weekly A&E magazine.

Hippo Music and Nitelife
49 Hollis St., Manchester, NH 03101
PH: 603-232-7569
Erica Febre efebre@hippopress.com
www.hippopress.com
I write profile and preview articles on local musicians as well as mainstream musicians that come to the area to perform.

Monadnock Folklore Society
www.monadnockfolk.org
Offering support to local musicians' projects.

New Hampshire Country Music Assoc.
www.nhcma.com
Country music is alive and kickin' in New Hampshire!

Peterborough Folk Music Society
pfmsconcerts.org
Supporting musicians in the Monadnock region.

Spotlight Magazine
spotlight@seacoastonline.com
www.seacoastonline.com/calendar/nightlife.htm
Portsmouth's A&E magazine.

New Jersey

All-Access-Minus
87 Gless Ave. 2nd Fl. Belleville, NJ 07109
PH: 732-266-9828
M. Pimentel minus@minusp.com
www.minusp.com
Site for upcoming Hip Hop artists in the Tri-State area.

Aquarian Weekly
52 Sindle Ave. PO Box 1140, Little Falls, NJ 07424
PH: 973-812-6766 FX: 973-812-5420
www.theaquarian.com
Covers the area of New York, New Jersey and Connecticut.

Bluegrass & Oldtime Music Assoc. of NJ
www.newjerseybluegrass.org
Dedicated to the preservation and perpetuation of Bluegrass and Old-Time music.

Casa Bonita Productions
410 E. Center Ave. Maple Shade, NJ 08052
PH: 856-482-0285
Jim Santora Jr. jim@casabonitaproductions.com
www.casabonitaproductions.com
Provides booking services for the NJ/Philadelphia area. A&R/film/TV submission opportunities, radio submission and tracking services, website development, CD creation/duplication, artwork and photography.

Central NJ Song Circle
www.jerseysongs.com
A friendly, in-the-round get-together for testing out new songs.

Chorus and Verse
editor@chorusandverse.com
www.chorusandverse.com
Provides exposure and insight into the New Jersey scene.

Composers Guild of New Jersey
www.cgnj.org
Focuses on local contemporary music.

Crooked Beat
feedback@crooked-beat.com
www.crooked-beat.com
Band pages and gig listings for NY and NJ bands.

Eastside
Cherry Hill HS East, 1750 Kresson Rd.
Cherry Hill, NJ 08003
www.eastside-online.org
We're seeking indie CDs to review and publicize in our paper.

Folk Project
www.folkproject.org
Sponsors Folk music and dance activities in the NJ area.

House 38 Productions
225 Adams Ave. Williamstown, NJ 08094
PH: 856-629-6055
Christopher Willis Deepelmdesciple@yahoo.com
www.myspace.com/sparktherevolution
Promotional services for promoters who book shows in our local area. Also a label strictly for securing distribution deals for local bands.

Jersey Beat
418 Gregory Ave. Weehawken, NJ 07086
jim@jerseybeat.com
www.jerseybeat.com
Will accept all CDs, but local releases get the highest priority.

Jersey Jam
www@jerseyjam.com
www.jerseyjams.com
We'll visit your website, listen to your music, see what you're up to and decide if you should be the "Spotlight Artist of the Month!"

Jersey Shore Jazz and Blues Foundation
www.jsjbf.org
Formed to preserve, promote and perpetuate Jazz, Blues and other indigenous music forms in New Jersey.

JERSEYMUSIC.COM
jerseymusic.com
Connect to the local music scene.

jerseyshows.com
Dan Fulton dan@jerseyshows.com
www.jerseyshows.com
We try to link up local music fans with local and touring bands.

New Jersey Jazz Society
www.njjs.org
Monthly magazine with feature articles, reviews and event calendar.

Night & Day
PO Box 202, Spring Lake, NJ 07762
PH: 732-974-0047 FX: 732-974-0163
info@ndmag.com
www.ndmag.com
Covers movies, concerts, local bands and more.

NorthJerseyMusic.com
www.northjerseymusic.com
Northern New Jersey's premiere live music resource.

Princeton Folk Music Society
www.princetonol.com/groups/pfms
Encourages the growth of Folk music.

Steppin' Out Magazine
21-07 Maple Ave. Fairlawn, NJ 07410-1524
stepoutmag@aol.com
www.steppinoutmagazine.com
North Jersey/NYC music weekly.

Tri-State Punk
Stumpy stumpy@tristatepunk.com
www.tristatepunk.com
Promoting/presenting the Tri-State area with musical events for all ages.

Upstage Magazine
PO Box 140, Spring Lake, NJ 07762
PH: 732-280-3305
Gary Wien info@upstagemagazine.com
www.upstagemagazine.com
Supporting the original arts scene of Central NJ.

WFMU's Beware of the Blog
blog.wfmu.org
Covering music in New York and New Jersey.

New Mexico

Alibi
2118 Central Ave. SE. #151
Albuquerque, NM 87106-4004
PH: 505-346-0660 x260 FX: 505-256-9651
Laura Marrich lauram@alibi.com
alibi.com
Albuquerque's weekly A&E paper. Extensive local music coverage.

Local IQ
PO Box 7490, Albuquerque, NM 87194
PH: 505-247-1343 FX: 505-243-8173
iq@local-iq.com
local-iq.com
Alternative weekly. Covers local music.

Mitch's New Mexico Music Connection
Mitch Mitch@NMMusic.com
www.nmmusic.com
Band listings, events, classifieds etc.

New Mexico Folk Music & Dance Society
www.folkmads.org
Promoting and teaching traditional music and dance.

NewMexicoEvents.com
5104 Gaviota NW., Albuquerque, NM 87120
FX: 505-922-8775
Mark Hendricks mark@nmevents.com
www.newmexicoevents.com
Submit events and band info to get listed.

Santa Fe Reporter
132 E. Marcy St., Santa Fe, NM 87504
PH: 505-988-5541 x217 FX: 505-988-5348
Trisha Sauthoff culture@sfreporter.com
www.sfreporter.com
Weekly news and culture paper. Covers local music scene.

Southwest Traditional and Bluegrass Music Assoc.
www.southwestpickers.org
Promoting Acoustic music through jams and workshops.

taosmusic.com
PO Box 2627, Taos, NM 87571
www.taosmusic.com
Supporting the Taos music scene. News, CD/DVD sales, gigs etc.

New York

AcousticMusicScene.com
www.acousticmusicscene.com
Uniting musicians of the Hudson Valley region in support of a music community coming together to celebrate human experience through song.

albanyjazz.com
info@albanyjazz.com
www.albanyjazz.com
Covering the Albany Jazz scene with news, CD reviews, show reviews etc.

Artvoice
810-812 Main St., Buffalo, NY 14202
PH: 716-881-6604 FX: 716-881-6682
editorial@artvoice.com
www.artvoice.com
Buffalo free weekly A&E paper. Reviews album releases and profiles new bands.

Bands of New York State
ableals@juno.com
www.yrbook.com/music
Supporting upstate NY groups and artists.

The Blues Society of Western New York
www.wnyblues.org
Promoting Blues events, record releases and club scenes.

Buffalo Friends of Folk Music
folkmusic.bfn.org
Supports Folk music in the Buffalo area through local events including concerts and sing-arounds.

Buffalo Music Online
www.wnymusic.com
Submit your band news, info and events.

Buffalo Punx
www.myspace.com/buffalopunx716
Dedicated to the Buffalo Punk scene promoting local shows in the area, helping out your band, getting people involved, setting up shows, D.I.Y. whatever.

Buffalobarfly.com
162 Elmwood Ave. Buffalo, NY 14201
PH: 716-886-4785 FX: 716-886-5481
info@buffalobarfly.com
www.buffalobarfly.com
Promoting nightlife and entertainment in the Buffalo area.

BuffaloBluegrass.com
www.buffalobluegrass.com
Dedicated to promoting Bluegrass music in the Buffalo area.

Bushwick is Beautiful
bushwickisbeautifulblog@yahoo.com
bushwickisbeautiful.blogspot.com
Covering the Bushwick, NY music scene.

Capital Region Unofficial Musicians and Bands Site
guzzo@crumbs.net
www.crumbs.net
Online music resource for the Albany area.

Central New York Bluegrass Assoc.
www.cnyba.com
News, calendar, classifieds, jams, festivals etc.

Central New York Friends of Folk
www.folkus.org/fof
Supporting Folk and Acoustic music.

City Newspaper
250 N. Goodman St., Rochester, NY 14607
PH: 585-244-3329
rochester-citynews.com
Alternative weekly. Covers local music.

CNY Jazz
www.cnyjazz.org
Created to positively affect the quality of life in our region by preserving, supporting and advancing the art form of American Jazz.

Folkus Project
www.folkus.org
Presents Folk and Acoustic music. Includes artist spotlight.

Freetime Magazine
850 University Ave. Rochester, NY 14607
PH: 585-473-2266
www.freetime.com
Rochester A&E mag. Covers local and national music.

Funkyside.com
PO Box 885, Ithaca, NY 14850
PH: 607-269-0632 FX: 607-256-8829
info@funkyside.com
www.funkyside.com
Sells music from the Fingerlakes in New York.

Garagista Music
PO Box 238, Dobbs Ferry, NY 10522
www.garagistamusic.com
Our mission is to showcase Rivertown artists through online and local distribution.

Golden Link
www.goldenlink.org
Rochester publication containing everything about Folk music.

Hudson Valley Bluegrass Assoc.
www.hvbluegrass.org
Contains Bluegrass news, show schedules, CD reviews, newsletter etc.

Hudson Valley Folk Guild
www.hudsonvalleyfolkguild.org
Produces events and nurtures new Folk artists.

INSIDEOUT Magazine
PO Box 165, Athens, NY 12105
PH: 518-943-9200 FX: 518-943-9201
info@insideouthv.com
www.insideouthv.com
The Hudson Valley magazine for the GLBT community.

Ithaca Times
PO Box 27, Ithaca, NY 14851
PH: 607-277-7000 FX: 607-277-1012
Jessica del Mundo jdelmundo@ithacatimes.com
www.ithacatimes.com
Free weekly alternative paper. Local concert reviews, accepts CDs for review.

Metroland *Rough Mix*
419 Madison Ave. Albany, NY 12210
PH: 518-463-2500 x143 FX: 518-463-3712
www.metroland.net
Albany's alternative newsweekly local music section.

Mohawk Valley Bluegrass Assoc.
www.mvbga.com
Building a base of members in an area that is rich in musicians.

Music 315
PO Box 4796, Rome, NY 13442
FX: 866-851-3851
thedude@music315.com
www.music315.com
Area code 314 bands contact us to get your site listed.

MyRochester.com
www.myrochester.com
Rochester's ultimate online music guide.

New York Newspapers
www.usnpl.com/nynews.php
Links to newspapers throughout the state.

New York/Tri-State Area Bluegrass/ Old Time Music Scene
www.banjoben.com
Send details of your gig to get posted.

Northeast Blues Society
www.timesunion.com/communities/nebs
Exposing regional Blues talent to the largest possible audience.

PRIMO PR 716
PO Box 654, East Amherst, NY 14051
Mark Weber primopr716@adelphia.net
www.primopr.com
Specializes in getting the word out to Buffalo and beyond about upcoming concerts and events put on by Christian artists.

The Refrigerator
editor@therefrigerator.net
www.therefrigerator.net
Rochester A&E online zine.

Rkstar.com
1699 W. Glenville Rd. Amsterdam, NY 12010
Dan Goodspeed editor@rkstar.com
www.rkstar.com
Covering the capital district of NY and the national music scenes. All genres.

Rochester Groove
16 Norway Dr. Rochester, NY 14616
webmaster@rochestergroove.com
www.rochestergroove.com
An effort to promote local Groove/Jam Bands who are making the effort & playing around the region.

Rochester Music Coalition
PO Box 26378, Rochester, NY 14626
rochestermusiccoalition.org
Supports and promotes artists of all genres.

Rochester Punk
www.myspace.com/rocpunk
Keeping Rochester Punk rock alive, keep you updated on the latest shows and other cool stuff in Rochester.

Rochester Ska
www.myspace.com/rocska
The beat is BACK in the 585!

Society For New Music
438 Brookford Rd. Syracuse, NY 13224
www.societyfornewmusic.org
Commissioning new works, through advocacy by featuring regional composers alongside guest composers, by providing regional musicians an opportunity to perform the music of their peers in order to gain new skills and techniques which they then share with their students, and by bringing new music to as broad an audience as possible, through performances, broadcasts and cable TV.

The Stencil
caps@thestencil.com
www.thestencil.com
MP3 blog covering Buffalo music and upcoming shows.

Syracuse Bands
www.syracusebands.net
News, classifieds, gigs and more!

Syracuse New Times
1415 W. Genesee St., Syracuse, NY 13204-2156
PH: 315-422-7011 FX: 315-422-1721
www.syracusenewtimes.com
Provides extensive A&E information for the Syracuse area.

Syracuse Ska Scene
skadanny@gmail.com
syracuseska.com
Shows, classifieds, MP3s and more!

Tribal Jams Magazine
stepheninfo@tribaljams.com
www.tribaljams.com
Information on festivals and venues for the "tie-die" Jam Band music in the NE U.S.

Tribes Hill - Kindred Folk
www.tribeshill.com
Uniting musician of the lower Hudson Valley region and their patrons in support of a music community that aspires to common goals and beliefs.

Upstate NY Reggae
Ras Adam Simeon rasadam@yahoo.com
go.to/NYreggae
Postings for concerts, radio shows, shops, venues, contacts etc.

WestchesterRocks.com
PH: 914-374-1589
Lauren westchesterrocks@hotmail.com
www.westchesterrocks.com
Offers band booking services, band and gig promotions and more!

AURAL FIX
PO Box 6054, North Babylon, NY 11703
PH: 631-943-3213
Mike Ferrari auralfix@optonline.net
www.auralfix.com
We are the ONLY publication that covers the Long Island music scene exclusively!!!

Club Long Island
info@clublongisland.com
www.clublongisland.com
Has a Local Band feature.

Island Songwriter Showcase
www.islandsongwriters.org
Support original music through workshops and showcases.

Long Island Blues Society
www.liblues.org
Band listings, newsletter, events etc.

Long Island Classical Guitar Society
www.licgs.us
Hosts a quarterly mixer to showcase local talent.

Long Island Press
1103 Stewart Ave. Garden City, NY 11530
PH: 516-629-4327 FX: 516-992-1801
www.longislandpress.com
Bi-weekly A&E paper. Reviews concerts, profiles and interviews bands.

LongIsland.com *Nightlife*
nightlife.longisland.com
Long Island band pages, calendar, interviews, bulletin boards and more.

longislandmusicscene
groups.yahoo.com/group/longislandmusicscene
Discussing the LI original music scene.

longislandmusicscene.com
PO Box 417, E. Rockaway, NY 11518-0417
PH: 516-887-0923 FX: 516-887-0923
webguy@longislandmusicscene.com
www.longislandmusicscene.com
Provides free exposure and resources for musicians.

5th Floor Artist Management
Jen Carlson info@5thFloor.org
5thFloor.org
Are you a band in need of management, booking and PR?

Acoustic Live!
51 MacDougal St. PO Box #254
New York, NY 10012
riccco@earthlink.net
www.acousticlive.com
Monthly newsletter showcasing all Acoustic performances in NY.

Antifolk.net
PO Box 20469, Tompkins Sq. Stn.
New York, NY 10009
info@antifolk.net
www.antifolk.net
The home for the NYC Antifolk scene.

Associated Musicians of Greater New York
www.local802afm.org
Musicians union fighting for your well-being.

Booking Live Shows Has Never Been So Easy!

www.IndieVenueBible.com

BadmintonStamps
SkinnySlim skinnyslim@badmintonstamps.com
www.badmintonstamps.com
Covering the NYC music scene.

Battle Of The Boroughs
www.kicknote.com
*A search for New York City's most talented
independent artists.*

The Battering Room
batteringroom@gmail.com
batteringroom.blogspot.com
Blog covering music in and around NYC.

Big Apple Jazz
Gordon Polatnick gordon@bigapplejazz.com
www.bigapplejazz.com
*Reinvigorating the Jazz scene in NYC, by
introducing fans to the more authentic and hidden
Jazz events that occur.*

Big Apple Music Scene
Devorah Klein bigapplemusicscene@gmail.com
www.bigapplemusicscene.com
Writings on the music scene in New York.

Black Rock Coalition
PO Box 1054, Cooper Stn. New York, NY 10276
PH: 212-713-5097
Earl Douglas edouglas@blackrockcoalition.org
www.blackrockcoalition.org
*Represents a united front musically and politically
progressive Black artists and supporters.*

Brooklyn Bodega
info@brooklynbodega.com
www.brooklynbodega.com
*Covering the Hip Hop scene. The Brooklyn Bodega
crew will do their best to serve it up to you daily.*

Brooklyn Vegan
brooklynvegan@hotmail.com
www.brooklynvegan.com
Music, photos & news from a vegan in Brooklyn.

Chicks With Guitars
PH: 917-969-6409
Jeanette Palmer info@chickswithguitars.com
chickswithguitars.com
*Provides publishing and performing opportunities
for emerging and established musicians.*

Crackers United
crackersunited@gmail.com
crackersunited.com
*Covers NYC music scene. We welcome records and
promotional materials for consideration.*

Crashin' In
204 Powers St. #1, Brooklyn, NY 11211
www.crashinin.com
Reviews, interviews and online listening parties.

D1 Music
244 5th Ave. #2547, New York, NY 10001
PH: 646-312-0115 FX: 646-312-0240
Peter McLean d1mc@d1music.biz
www.d1music.biz
*New York's premiere boutique house music label
producing soundtracks, demos, remixes and music -
always - all ways!!!*

Danger Vision *Manhattan Neighborhood
Network*
PO Box 1615, Morningside Stn.
New York, NY 10026-9998
Tommy Danger info@tommydanger.net
www.tommydanger.net
*A Hip Hop video show featuring some of the hottest
Underground Hip Hop and Rap artists, producers
and video directors.*

The Deli
37 W. 20th St. #1006, New York, NY 10011
info@thedelimagazine.com
www.thedelimagazine.com
*Provides news, reviews and in-depth interviews with
NYC bands, analyses of where the scene is headed.*

East Coast Hardcore
nycore@hardcorewebsite.net
www.hardcorewebsite.net
*New York Hardcore direct from where it all
happens.*

Elizabeth Records
PO Box 22049, Brooklyn, NY 11202
PH: 212-330-7082
info@elizabethrecords.com
www.elizabethrecords.com
Promotes indie Folk artists.

Fearless Music TV Show
mail@fearlessmusic.tv
www.fearlessmusic.tv
Weekly show featuring indie bands.

Flavorpill NYC
594 Broadway #1212, New York, NY 10012
PH: 212-253-9309 FX: 212-313-9833
nyc_events@flavorpill.net
flavorpill.net
*A publishing company with a weekly e-mail events
list.*

Free Williamsburg
311 Graham Ave. Brooklyn, NY 11211
PH: 718-393-7510
mail@freewilliamsburg.com
www.freewilliamsburg.com
Providing you with cutting edge music.

GigApple.com
www.gigapple.com
*The place to find out where to go and see and listen
to live independent music in NYC.*

Gothamist
Prince Street Stn. PO Box 510
New York, NY 10012
Jen Chung jen@gothamist.com
www.gothamist.com
*A website about NYC and everything that happens
in it.*

GothamJazz
www.gothamjazz.com
Shedding light on lesser known, indie performers.

Greenwich Village Gazette
PO Box 1023 Island Hts., NJ 08732
www.nycny.com
Complete listing of NYC Jazz, Folk and Rock events.

HelloBrooklyn.com
PH: 917-754-3537
info@hellobrooklyn.com
www.hellobrooklyn.com
Send your calendar listings by e-mail.

HUGE!
hugemassif@gmail.com
www.hugemassif.com
Focuses on the NYC rave scene.

i rock i roll
irockiroll@gmail.com
irockiroll.blogspot.com
NYC blog about music, gigs and other assorted stuff.

Indie Sounds NY
pete@indiesoundsny.com
indiesoundsny.com
*We cover the people that make up one of the most
creative and vibrant artistic communities on the
planet.*

JACKMUSIC
332 Bleecker St. G7, New York, NY 10014
PH: 212-279-3941
info@jack-music.com
www.jack-music.com
*We represent the music of NYC's best small label
and unsigned talent.*

The L Magazine
20 Jay St. #207, Brooklyn, NY 11201
PH: 718-596-3462
livemusic@thelmagazine.com
thelmagazine.com
*A distillation of the best music and special events
the city has to offer.*

Mass Appeal
261 Vandervoort Ave. Brooklyn, NY 11211
PH: 718-858-0979 FX: 347-365-2159
Gavin Stevens gavin@massappealmag.com
www.massappealmag.com
Focuses on urban culture, music, art and fashion.

melodynelson.com
Audrey audrey@melodynelson.com
www.melodynelson.com
Information about the NYC music scene.

Metal Injection
hatemail@metalinjection.net
www.metalinjection.net
*TV and radio show representing Metal and
Hardcore in its truest nature.*

The Modern Age
Miss Modernage edit@themodernage.org
www.themodernage.org
*A cheat sheet for those who can only pretend they're
cool enough to live in Williamsburg, Brooklyn.*

multidimensions.net *People Talk*
Paris K. paris@multidimensions.net
www.multidimensions.net/PeopleTalk/PeopleTalk.php
*If you have a video or an article that you would like
to exhibit for free, then email us.*

Music Snobbery
musicsnobbery@comcast.net
www.musicsnobbery.com
*I go to gigs, interview bands and musicians. I like
Brit Pop, but will check out most styles of music.*

The New York Art Ensemble
640 W. 139th St. #60, New York, NY 10031
www.nyae.org
*A non-profit organization that specializes in the
performance and presentation of new American
music.*

New York Blues and Jazz Society
www.nybluesandjazz.org
Blues and Jazz news, reviews, listings etc.

New York Blade
333 7th Ave. 14th Fl. New York, NY 10001
PH: 212-268-2701 FX: 212-268-2069
www.nyblade.com
A weekly newspaper covering the New York Gay communities.

New York City Area Bluegrass Music Scene
banjoben.com
A calendar of Bluegrass events. Submit your info.

New York City Classical Guitar Society
www.nyccgs.com
Providing a dynamic community for Classical guitarists in New York City.

New York City is my Kind of Town
www.newyorkismykindoftown.com/music
How many musical artists are there in New York City? A lot! Lucky for you that we're listing some of the best right here.

New York Cool
Wendy R. Williams wendy@newyorkcool.com
www.newyorkcool.com
Entertainment site that gives great coverage of local musicians and events.

New York Metro
444 Madison Ave. 4th Fl. New York, NY 10022
www.newyorkmetro.com/arts/theweek/music
A&E magazine. Covers local music.

New York Metropolitan Country Music Assc.
www.nymcma.org
We produce a series of free concerts in public parks during the summer. These concerts feature at least one local band.

New York Pinewoods Folk Music Club
www.folkmusicny.org
Concerts and events plus a monthly newsletter.

New York Press
333 7th Ave. 14th Fl. New York, NY 10001
PH: 212-244-2282 FX: 212-244-9864
www.nypress.com
Free weekly A&E paper. Reviews CDs and concerts by indie artists.

New York Times *Music Section*
directory@nytimes.com
www.nytimes.com/pages/arts/music
Send a blank e-mail for an automated response including mailing address and departmental e-mail addresses.

New York Underbelly
RSVP@NewYorkUnderbelly.com
www.newyorkunderbelly.com
DJ events and live music shows around the city.

NewYorkCity.com
235 Pinelawn Rd. Melville, NY 11747-4250
PH: 516-843-2000
ndstaff@newsday.com
www.nyc.com
Guide to New York music and clubs.

Night After Night
ssmith66@sprynet.com
nightafternight.blogs.com
Conspicuous consumption of Classical music, live and otherwise in New York City.

Notorious Marketing & Promotion
31-15 30th St. #3R, Astoria, NY 11106
PH: 718-545-9816
Notorious L.I.Z. notorious@notoriousradio.com
www.notoriousradio.com
Promotes Alternative/Rock indie bands and artists.

NY JAZZ REPORT
WillWolf@NYJazzReport.com
www.nyjazzreport.com
News and links about jazz in NYC. Musicians, clubs, concerts, poetry, music, interviews etc.

NY Rock
PO Box 563, Gracie Stn. New York, NY 10028
PH: 212-426-4657
www.nyrock.com
Reviews full length CDs.

NY Waste
PO Box 20005, W. Village Stn.
New York, NY 10014
FX: 212-243-7252
info@newyorkwaste.com
www.newyorkwaste.com
New York's Punk Rock newspaper. News, reviews and attitude.

NYC Music Places
61 W. 23rd St. 4th Fl. New York, NY 10010-4205
PH: 212-886-2503 FX: 212-737-1496
info@nycmusicplaces.org
www.nycmusicplaces.org
Find rehearsal and performance spaces in NYC.

NYPunkScene
www.nypunkscene.com
This site is for the Punk/Hardcore Scene, and its many variations. The kind of Rock and Roll that requires a deeper commitment.

NYC Reggae
Ras Adam rasadam@yahoo.com
web.syr.edu/~affellem/nycshows.html
Covering concerts, shows and dances in the NYC area.

Oh My Rockness
PO Box 720337, Jackson Heights, NY 11372
shows@ohmyrockness.com
ohmyrockness.com
Your one-stop shop for Indie Rock show listings in NYC. If you think people should know more about you, e-mail us and tell us.

Other Music NYC
15 E. 4th St., New York, NY 10003
PH: 212-477-8150
www.othermusic.com
An unparalleled selection of Underground and Experimental music. We are all about supporting independent music, so we do consign the music of NYC artists.

PAPERMAG
365 Broadway, New York, NY 10013
PH: 212-226-4405 FX: 212-226-0062
edit@papermag.com
www.papermag.com
Guide to urban culture, events, people, news and entertainment.

Pop Tarts Suck Toasted
poptartssucktoasted@gmail.com
poptartssucktoasted.blogspot.com
If you'd like to send me some music please send it digitally via e-mail. I will accept some CDs but I'd like to do it on a case by case basis.

Product Shop NYC
productshopnyc@gmail.com
www.productshopnyc.com
Blog covering NYC entertainment. Local shows, articles etc.

punkcast.com Podcast
PO Box 2016 Madison Sq. Stn.
New York, NY 10159-2016
PH: 212-608-1334
joly@dti.net
punkcast.com
Videos of the NYC underground music scene.

Real Magic TV
PO Box 264, Bedford Hills, NY 10507-0264
PH: 917-495-0741
info@RealMagicNY.com
www.realmagictv.com
Send your band's material in for a chance to get booked.

Roulette Television
228 W. Broadway, New York, NY 10013
PH: 212-219-8242 FX: 212-219-8773
roulette@roulette.org
www.roulette.org
Presents New Jazz, World music, Experimental Rock, Improvisation, Traditional and Hybrid ensembles from NYC and around the world.

The Simple Mission
Elliot Aronow elliot@thesimplemission.com
www.thesimplemission.com
Blog about the NYC music scene.

So More Scene
Miss Modernage edit@somorescene.com
www.somorescene.com
It's so more scene than you'll ever be.

Solid Goldberger
solidgoldberger@gmail.com
solidgoldberger.blogspot.com
Blog covering music happenings in New York and elsewhere.

Songwriter's Beat
PO Box 20086, W. Village Stn.
New York, NY 10014
songwritersbeat.com
Create an environment where musicians can share their experiences.

SoundArt
www.soundart.org
New York City's source for information on concerts of contemporary music.

stereogum
tips@stereogum.com
www.stereogum.com
MP3 blog with local band news, tracks etc.

subinev blog
172 5th Ave. PMB #14, Brooklyn, NY 11217
bryan@subinev.com
www.subinev.com
Bands! Get in touch! If I like what I hear and plan on checking you out I'll add your shows here.

Sucka Pants
suckapants.com
MP3 blog from Brooklyn. If you would like to send music, contact me via e-mail.

The Swift Chancellor Report
Wes Jack info@brooklynbodega.com
swiftchancellor.blogspot.com
Observations, reviews and ramblings about Hip Hop culture.

This Twilight Garden
chris@thechristophereffect.com
thistwilightgarden.blogspot.com
Musical adventures in New York City.

Time Out New York
475 10th Ave. 12th Fl. New York, NY 10018
PH: 646-432-3000 FX: 646-432-3010
music@timeoutny.com
www.timeoutny.com
The obsessive guide to impulsive entertainment.

Tiswas Records
332 Bleecker St. #G11, New York, NY 10014
tiswas2002@aol.com
www.tiswasnyc.com
Exposing exciting NYC music to a larger audience and growing their fan base.

UMO Music
www.umo.com
Provides online artist promotional accounts, live music events and compilation CDs.

Urban Folk
www.myspace.com/urbanfolkzine
Stories of the bohemians, bums and poet troubadours out there trying to explain the universe or at least entertain it for awhile.

Video City TV
PO Box 1607, New York, NY 10013
Attn: A&R Department
PH: 212-613-0072
videocitytv@aol.com
www.videocity.tv
Cable show that spotlights indie music.

Village Indian
417 E. 6th St. #20, New York, NY 10009
Amrit villageindian@gmail.com
www.villageindian.com
Musings on music, art and life in the East Village. Send in your music!

Village Voice
36 Cooper Sq. New York, NY 10003
PH: 212-475-3333
www.villagevoice.com
Alternative weekly newspaper. Extensive A&E section.

Vocal Area Network
www.van.org
Dedicated to the advancement of vocal ensemble music in the New York City area.

Volunteer Lawyers for the Arts
1 E. 53rd St. 6th Fl. New York, NY 10022-4201
PH: 212-319-2787 FX: 212-752-6575
www.vlany.org
Pro bono legal services for artists.

Webtunes
39-37 50th St., Woodside, NY 11377
FX: 718-426-6346
John Elder tunemaster@webtunes.com
www.webtunes.com
New York City's premier music guide.

ZydecoRoad.com
2450 Marshall Ave. North Bellmore, NY 11710
PH: 516-643-7231
K-Paule Pachter zydecoroad@yahoo.com
www.zydecoroad.com
Covering Zydeco and Cajun music in NYC and Long Island.

North Carolina

910 Noise Collective
www.myspace.com/910noise
A platform to showcase Noise & Experimental artists from the local area code as well as out of town (or country).

Amps 11
David Kiser david@ampseleven.com
www.ampseleven.com
Taking Charlotte's music scene to the next level!

Asheville Citizen Times
PO Box 2090, Asheville, NC 28802
PH: 828-232-5855
tkiss@citizen-times.com
www.citizen-times.com
Reviews CDs and interviews bands if playing in the area.

AshevilleRock.com
sean@ashevillerock.com
www.ashevillerock.com
Online forum promoting the local Alternative music scene.

Banjo in the Hollow
banjointhehollow.org
Preserving and promoting Bluegrass and Old-Time music.

Blues Society of the Lower Cape Fear
www.capefearblues.org
Welcomes listeners, musicians and Blues enthusiasts.

Bootleg Magazine
PO Box 7811, Wilmington, NC 28406
www.myspace.com/avenuemagazinepresents
An independent monthly music, art, fiction & culture publication. Send CDs, books etc. for review.

Cape Fear Songwriters Guild
capefearsongwritersguild.com
Created to promote the craft of songwriting and music composition.

Central Carolina Songwriters Assoc.
www.ccsa-raleigh.com
Promotes songwriting and music in NC.

Chamber Music Wilmington
www.chambermusicwilmington.org
Brings world-class Chamber music concerts to Southeastern NC.

Charlotte Blues Society
www.charlottebluessociety.org
Presents Blues concerts, forums, workshops and educational programs.

Charlotte Chapter NSAI
www.secondwindmusic.com/NSAICLT
Supporting songwriters through workshops, festivals and concerts.

Charlotte Folk Society
www.folksociety.org
Promoting contemporary Folk music, dance and crafts.

CharlotteMusician.com
PO Box 241502, Charlotte, NC 28224-1502
PH: 704 953-7358
Brian Hartzog info@charlottemusician.com
www.CharlotteMusician.com
Our goal is to find ways the local music community can work together to create a true music scene.

Classical Voice of North Carolina
www.cvnc.org
Features Classical music news, reviews, show dates etc.

Creative Loafing Charlotte
820 Hamilton St. #C-2, Charlotte, NC 28206
PH: 704-522-8334 FX: 704-522-8088
charlotte.creativeloafing.com
Free weekly alternative paper. Covers local and national music.

Dalloway Records
www.myspace.com/dallowayrecords
Headed by a lawyer and a shrink - we've found that both professions are much needed in the industry.

Down East Folk Arts Society
www.downeastfolkarts.org
Sponsors programs in music, dance and community arts.

East Carolinian
2nd Fl. Old Cafeteria Complex,
Greenville, NC 27858
PH: 252-328-6366 FX: 252-328-6558
www.theeastcarolinian.com
East Carolina U's student paper.

Eastern North Carolina Bluegrass Assoc.
encbluegrass.freeservers.com
Promoting Bluegrass music as clean, wholesome entertainment for the entire family.

Encore
PO Box 12430, Wilmington, NC 28405
PH: 910-791-0688 FX: 910-791-9177
www.encorepub.com
Covers local music with interviews, previews and reviews.

Fiddle & Bow Society
www.fiddleandbow.org
Preserving Folk music, dance and related arts.

Friends of Bluegrass
www.friendsofbluegrass.org
Dedicated to the preservation, education and promotion of Bluegrass music in the Holly Springs, NC and surrounding area.

Friends of World Music
www.friendsofworldmusic.org
Help preserve Folk traditions by providing venues for artists to share their cultural heritage.

goTriad.com
www.gotriad.com
Covering A&E in Greensboro.

Guitartown
webmaster@guitartown.org
www.guitartown.org
Features news of the thriving NC Roots music scene.

High Lonesome Strings Bluegrass Assoc.
www.highlonesomestrings.org
Celebrate Bluegrass music.

Independent Weekly
PO Box 2690, Durham, NC 27715
PH: 919-286-1972 FX: 919-286-4274
indyweek.com
Interviews bands, previews and reviews CDs and concerts.

Lumber River Regional Bluegrass Assoc.
www.lrrba.com
Keeping alive the Bluegrass traditions of our country.

Mountain Xpress
2 Wall St., Asheville, NC 28801
PH: 828-251-1333 FX: 828-251-1311
mountainx.com/ae/music.php
Has music section covering the Asheville area music scene.

musicomet
PO Box 31725, Charlotte, NC 28231
PH: 704-527-7570
Samir Shukla cometriderx@yahoo.com
www.musicomet.com
I am the current listing editor and music writer for Creative Loafing (Charlotte).

NC Goth DOT COM
steve@ncgoth.com
www.ncgoth.com
All the info on the NC Goth scene.

NCMusic.com
www.ncmusic.com
Online community covering music in NC.

NCScene.com
63 John Lewis Rd. Walstonburg, NC 27888
webmaster@ncscene.com
www.ncscene.com
Rock, Metal Hardcore and more!

North Carolina Mountain Acoustic Music Assc.
www.ncmama.org
Enriching the mountain Acoustic music culture by serving its musicians and their supporters!

North Carolina Songwriters Co-op
www.ncsongwriters.org
Promoting songwriters in NC.

Nothing but Drums
John Ehlers john@nothingbutdrums.net
www.nothingbutdrums.net
A Charlotte TV show featuring local area drummers.

Pamlico Musical Society
www.pamlicomusic.org
Based our of Oriental, NC, our purpose is to increase access to professional music by sponsoring concerts in the county.

Piedmont Blues Preservation Society
www.piedmontblues.org
Preserving the fine art of American Blues.

PineCone *(Piedmont Council of Traditional Music)*
www.pinecone.org
Showcasing the many traditions and musical styles that are a part of North Carolina's culture.

Raleigh Underground
dj-joey@raleighunderground.com
www.raleighunderground.com
Lists info on Raleigh's Underground music scene.

Raleighmusic.com
joanna@raleighmusic.com
www.raleighmusic.com
Marketing local artists to a regional audience.

SleeplessInCharlotte.com
www.sleeplessincharlotte.com
Information on artists, events, venues etc. in Charlotte. Send us your photos, flyers, events listing.

This Week Magazine
PO Box 1679, Morehead City, NC 28557
FX: 252-726-6016
twm@thenewstimes.com
www.thisweekmag.com
The ultimate authority in entertainment for more than 26 years!

Triangle Guitar Society
www.triangleguitar.org
Inspired by love for the musical arts and dedicated to nurturing an appreciation for the guitar.

Village Idiot Magazine
PO Box 6969, 197 New Market Ctr.
Boone, NC 28607
the-village-idiot.com
All bands/labels looking for exposure in NC, whether your from here or are just passing through you need to get up with us.

Wilkes Acoustic Folk Society
www.wilkesfolks.org
Focused on nurturing musical appreciation and talent in the Wilkesboro area.

YES! Weekly
5500 Adams Farm Ln. #204, Greensboro, NC 27407
PH: 336-316-1231
www.yesweekly.com
The largest circulated newsweekly in the Triad! Covers arts, entertainment and news.

ZSpotlight
PH: 919-215-5000
www.zspotlight.com
Information on who's playing where in the Triangle.

North Dakota

BismanLIVE.com
www.bismanlive.com
Bismarck Mandan's music and performance destination. Post your shows!

Fargo Bands
PO Box 145, Moorhead, MN 56561-0145
contact@fargobands.com
www.fargobands.com
Promoting live music in the Fargo-Moorhead area.

North Dakota State U. Spectrum
Mike Honl Mike.Honl@ndsu.edu
PH: 701-231-6287
www.ndsuspectrum.com
Campus publication. Covers local music.

Saboingaden.com
www.saboingaden.com
Fargo Electronica community & center of the Electronica earth. Dedicated to news and events in the ND and MN region.

Ohio

AcousticOhio.com
contact-us@acousticohio.com
www.acousticohio.com
An emphasis on singers, songwriters, acoustic guitarists, Folk singers and like-minded artists.

Athens Musician's Network
amn@frognet.net
www.athensmusician.net
Covers the local music scene around Athens.

The Athens NEWS
PO Box 543, Athens, OH 45701
PH: 740-594-8219 FX: 740-592-5695
news@athensnews.com
athensnews.com
Twice weekly paper. Covers local music.

BGMusicians.com
www.bgmusicians.com
Covering the Bowling Green music scene.

Blues, Jazz & Folk Music Society
www.bjfm.org
Promoting Blues, Jazz & Folk music in the Mid-Ohio Valley.

Buckeye Bluegrass
www.buckeyebluegrass.com
Celebrating Bluegrass music in Ohio.

Central Ohio Bluegrass Assoc.
www.centralohiobluegrass.com
Preserving Bluegrass in the central Ohio area.

CowTownMusic.com
PO Box 144, Orient, OH 43146
sixis@columbus.rr.com
www.cowtownmusic.com
Source for live entertainment in central Ohio.

Highlands of Ohio Folk & Celtic Music Society
www.highlandsofohio.com
Keeps the local community informed of Celtic concerts and other events.

Midwest Mixtapes
midwestmixtapes.com
Bringing you the hottest mixtapes from the Midwest.

Ohio Bands Online
PH: 330-206-0564
ohiobandsonline@yahoo.com
www.ohiobandsonline.com
A listing of Ohio bands by city and genre.

Ohio Hystairical Musick Society
ohms.nu
We list the shows and venues where bands can get gigs. Send in your band and gig info.

Ohio Online Magazine
Peanuts hostofthenorthcoast@yahoo.com
www.ohioonline.com
Supporting the local music scene around the state of Ohio.

T-TownMusic.com
Scott Stampflmeier scott-stamp@t-townmusic.com
www.t-townmusic.com
Covering NW Ohio's Hip Hop scene.

Cincinnati

Cincinnati CityBeat
811 Race St. 5th Fl. Cincinnati, OH 45202
PH: 513-665-4700 FX: 513-665-4368
Mike Breen letters@citybeat.com
www.citybeat.com
Covers news, A&E, reviews CDs and posts gigs.

Cincinnati Music Online
PO Box 54096, Cincinnati, OH 45254
cincymusic.com
Free promotion of Cincinnati artists and music.

Cincinnati Shows
PO Box 42815, Cincinnati, OH 45242-0815
cincyshows@niceguyrecords.com
www.cincinnatishows.com
Show listings, downloads, links, pictures etc. of Cincinnati bands.

Greater Cincinnati Blues Society
www.cincyblues.org
Advancing the culture and tradition of Blues music.

Greater Cincinnati Guitar Society
www.cincinnatiguitarsociety.org
Get in touch with the local Acoustic scene.

LocalMetal.com
localmetal@gmail.com
www.localmetal.com
Supporting the Cinci Metal scene.

The Wheel's Still in Spin
thewheelsstillinspin@gmail.com
www.thewheelsstillinspin.com
Cincinnati blog focusing on new music releases and reviews of individual albums as original, fictional short stories.

Cleveland

ClePunk
clepunk@gmail.com
www.clepunk.com
All the info on the local Punk scene.

Cleveland Composers Guild
my.en.com/~jaquick/ccg.html
Promoting the music of composers living in Northeast Ohio.

Cleveland Metal Connection
jjodon@clevmetalconn.org
www.clevmetalconn.org
Connect to the Metal scene. Features a band of the month.

Cleveland Scene
1468 W. 9th St. #805, Cleveland, OH 44113
PH: 216-241-7550
www.clevescene.com
Alternative news weekly.

cleveland.com *Local Band Section*
www.cleveland.com/music
www.cleveland.com/friday
Have your band's bio, audio clips and gigs listed online.

Cool Cleveland
14837 Detroit St. #105, Cleveland, OH 44107
www.coolcleveland.com
Blog and weekly newsletter with cool events, news, reviews and interviews.

Dark Cleveland
www.darkcleveland.com
Local music events, menus and new releases.

Starvation Army Zine
11124 Clifton Blvd. #9, Cleveland, OH 44102
www.myspace.com/starvationarmyzine
All things in the DIY world!!! Mostly Cleveland shite.

Columbus

Buckeye Country Music Organization
www.bcmoa.com
Helps local entertainers in their pursuit to secure a future in the Country, Bluegrass and Gospel music industries.

Columbus Alive
34 S. 3rd St. Columbus, OH 43215
PH: 614-221-2449 FX: 614-221-2456
www.columbusalive.com
Covers local indie music with concert previews and reviews.

Columbus Blues Alliance
www.colsbluesalliance.org
Encourages ties between traditional and electric Blues.

ColumbusArts.com
www.columbusarts.com
Resource for Central Ohio culture and arts.

Cringe
PO Box 10276, Columbus, OH 43201
PH: 614-421-7589
webmaster@cringe.com
www.cringe.com
Accepts nearly all submissions from the Columbus area.

musicohio
5579 Valencia Park Blvd. Hilliard, OH 43026
PH: 614-771-4243
Jason Perlman jason@musicohio.com
www.musicohio.com
Un-known artists get recognition. Covers mostly the Columbus area.

The Other Paper
5255 Sinclair Rd. Columbus, OH 43229
PH: 614-847-3800 FX: 614-848-3838
www.theotherpaper.com
Covers indie music with band interviews, CD and concert previews and reviews.

U Weekly
PO Box 623, Columbus, OH 43216
PH: 614-488-3226 FX: 614-488-4402
www.uweekly.com
If you are a local band or in a band coming through Columbus, get in touch.

Dayton

Dayton Band Resource Page
2948 Robin Rd. Dayton, OH 45409
PH: 937-838-5800
Jeremy Knedler info@daytonbands.com
www.daytonbands.com
Helping indie local musicians become successful.

Dayton City Paper
322 S. Patterson Blvd. Dayton, OH 45402
PH: 937-222-8855 FX: 937-222-6113
contactus@daytoncitypaper.com
www.daytoncitypaper.com
Alternative weekly. Covers local music.

H.M.D. Music Resource Guide
251 W. Central Ave. #292
Springboro, OH 45066-1103
PH: 937-903-1250
Sonny Thomas contact@thehmd.com
www.thehmd.com
Gem City resource where "unsigned" means you're a star here!

NiteOnTheTown.com
3430 S. Dixie Dr. #200, Dayton, OH 45439
PH: 937-297-3052 FX: 937-293-4523
www.niteonthetown.com
Guide to local nightlife. Includes local music listings.

WXEG's Local Band Page
101 Pine St., Dayton, OH 45402
PH: 937-224-1137 FX: 937-224-9965
Jericho jericho@wxeg.com
www.wxeg.com/pages/local_bands.html
Always keeping you up to date on the music that you love.

Toledo

Toledo City Paper
1120 Adams St., Toledo, OH 43624
PH: 419-244-9859 FX: 419-244-9871
www.toledocitypaper.com
Alternative weekly. Covers local music.

Toledo Jazz Society
www.toledojazzsociety.org
Increasing the appreciation of Jazz.

The Toledo Wire
thetoledowire.com
Created to connect Toledo's underground music and art communities, promote awareness, growth and interest.

T-townmusic.com
www.t-townmusic.com
Your source for Northwest Ohio and Southeast Michigan's local music scene.

Oklahoma

BestofTulsa.com *Music*
4821 S. Sheridan #228, Tulsa, OK 74145
PH: 918-632-0000
info@bestoftulsa.com
bestoftulsa.com/html/music.shtml
Listings, spotlights, events etc.

Greater Oklahoma Bluegrass Music Society
www.gobms.org
Continuing the tradition of Bluegrass music in Oklahoma and the Southwest US.

Green Country Bluegrass Assoc.
www.gcba.homestead.com
Promoting Bluegrass in Northeast OK.

MidwestVenues.com
Pat O'Reilly Midwestvenues@aol.com
www.midwestvenues.com
Providing the music community with info on thousands of venues in the greater Midwest region.

NormanMusicScene.com
511 Highland Pkwy. Norman, OK 73069
pchelp@normanmusicscene.com
www.normanmusicscene.com
Linking local musical artists, events & venues.

NormanNow.com
www.normannow.com
Post your band info and upcoming shows.

OKC Live
4215 NW 51ˢᵗ St., Oklahoma City, OK 73112
PH: 866-465-5483
www.okclive.com
Oklahoma City's online entertainment source.

Oklahoma Blues Society
www.okblues.org
CD reviews, news, gig listings etc.

Oklahoma Bluegrass Events
myweb.cableone.net/cdonaghe/bgrassfest.htm
Add information about your upcoming shows.

Oklahoma City Traditional Music Assoc.
www.octma.org
Learning, teaching and playing Acoustic Folk music.

Oklahoma Country Music Assoc.
www.oklahomacma.com
Created to promote and advance Country & Western music and its artists in Oklahoma.

Oklahoma Gazette
3701 N. Shartel, Oklahoma City, OK 73118
PH: 405-528-6000
Joe Wertz jwertz@okgazette.com
www.okgazette.com
Alternative weekly. Covers local music.

Oklahoma Hardcore
www.oklahomahardcore.com
We are here to support the DIY ethic, and give light to all things Hardcore in Oklahoma.

OklahomaPunkscene.com
Barb spano25@hotmail.com
www.oklahomapunkscene.com
Articles, interviews, photos, reviews and more!

OklahomaRock.com
Ryan LaCroix ryan@oklahomarock.com
www.oklahomarock.com
Helping others to realize what great talents are out there in Oklahoma. News, reviews etc.

Southwest Songwriters Assoc.
PH: 580-354-1402
music@sirinet.net
www.swsongwriters.com
Place for musicians looking for bands or bands looking for musicians.

Stillwater Scene
916 N. Duck, Stillwater, OK 74075
PH: 405-762-9733
www.stillwaterscene.com
Magazine with local music news, reviews, interviews etc.

Tulsa Music Pulse
jordanius@tulsamusicpulse.com
www.tulsamusicpulse.com
Tulsa Bands heard here. Cuz every band was local at some point. Protect endangered music.

Tulsa Rock 'n' Roll
4116 E. 30ᵗʰ St., Tulsa, OK 74114
Emmett Lollis Jr. emmett@tulsarocknroll.com
www.tulsarocknroll.com
If you would like to be considered for a CD review or interview please mail us your press kit .

TulsaBands.com
tulsabands.com
Oklahoma's #1 website for Tulsa bands and music!!!

Tulsa Music Pulse
jordanius@tulsamusicpulse.com
tulsamusicpulse.com
Listings of Metal, Rock and Punk shows.

TulsaMusicScene.com
www.tulsamusicscene.com
Showing the world the sea of musical talent that Tulsa has to offer.

Urban Tulsa Weekly
710 S. Kenosha, Tulsa, OK 74120
PH: 918-592-5550 FX: 918-592-5970
urbantulsa@urbantulsa.com
www.urbantulsa.com
Free weekly A&E paper. Covers local music scene.

Oregon

Cascade Blues Assoc.
www.cascadeblues.org
Promoting Blues and Roots music in the Northwest.

Creative Music Guild
PO Box 40564, Portland, OR 97240-0564
PH: 503-772-0772
www.creativemusicguild.org
Promotes new music that advances the art of composition.

Early Music Guild of Oregon
www.emgo.org
Bulletin board of news and events related to Early music.

Eugene Weekly
1251 Lincoln, Eugene, OR 97401
Molly Templeton molly@eugeneweekly.com
www.eugeneweekly.com
Eugene's A&E publication.

IndieAvenue.com
8152 SW. Hall Blvd. #103, Beaverton, OR 97008
PH: 503-961-2998 FX: 717-828-8257
www.indieavenue.com
Database of Northwest musicians, bands and venues.

Jazz Society of Oregon
www.jsojazzscene.org
Promotes Jazz musicians, Jazz education and Jazz appreciation.

Kingbanana
kngbanana@aol.com
www.kingbanana.net
Covering the Portland Punk/Hardcore/Metal scene.

Local Cut
2220 NW Quimby, Portland, OR 97210
Casey Jarman cjarman@wweek.com
localcut.wweek.com
Portland's music journal.

Lyay.net
86279 Lorane Hwy. Eugene, OR 97405
PH: 541-515-0101
www.lyay.net
A social network for West Coast rappers. Artists can stream and sell their music for free.

NAIL Distribution
14134 NE. Airport Way, Portland, OR 97230
PH: 888-6245-462 FX: 503-257-9061
info@naildistribution.com
www.naildistribution.com
Placing independent music in Northwest stores.

Oregon Bluegrass Assoc.
www.oregonbluegrass.org
Promotes, encourages, fosters and cultivates bluegrass. The Bluegrass Express is our bi-monthly newsletter.

Oregon Live
www.oregonlive.com/music
All the info on the Oregon music scene.

Portland Folklore Society
www.portlandfolklore.org
Promoting Folk music and arts in the greater Portland area.

Portland Mercury
605 NE. 21ˢᵗ Ave. #200, Portland, OR 97232
PH: 503-294-0840 FX: 503-294-0844
www.portlandmercury.com
Portland's A&E weekly. Submit your info.

Portland Songwriters Assoc.
www.portlandsongwriters.org
Developing the talents of our members.

Rainy Day Blues Society
www.rainydayblues.org
Based in Eugene, we feature regularly scheduled showcases where artists can perform before a live audience.

The Source
704 NW Georgia, Bend, OR 97701
www.tsweekly.com
Alternative weekly. Covers local music.

Willamette Week
2220 NW. Quimby, Portland, OR 97210
PH: 503-243-2122 FX: 503-243-1115
www.wweek.com
A weekly calendar of live music in venues throughout the city.

Pennsylvania

AK Music Scene
www.akmusicscene.com
Based in the Alle-Kiski Valley, we provide free resources to help promote unsigned bands, including: show calendar, an affiliation with Indie Band Radio and much more!

Appalachian Fiddle and Bluegrass Assoc.
www.afbawindgap.org
Promoting Bluegrass in the Wind Gap area.

Billtown Blues Assoc.
www.billtownblues.org
Providing opportunities for area residents to experience Blues music. Our newsletter is the Blues Note.

BilltownLive.com
507 W. 4ᵗʰ St., Williamsport, PA 17701
PH: 570-329-0228
billtownlive@gmail.com
www.billtownlive.com
Dedicated to promoting Williamsport's vibrant scene, by offering a valuable resource to our musical & cultural community.

Bucks County Blues Society
www.bucksbluessociety.com
Keeping the Blues alive in Bucks County!

Bucks County Folk Song Society
www.bucksfolk.org
Furthering the interest and appreciation of Folk music.

Central PA Friends of Jazz
www.pajazz.org
Presenting and promoting local and national Jazz artists.

Central Pennsylvania Blues Calendar
www.delta-blues.com/PABLUES.HTM
Listing Blues events in & around central PA.

Electric City/Diamond City
149 Penn Ave. Scranton, PA 18503
www.ecweekend.com
Northeast PA's free entertainment weekly.

ErieShows.com
Mike Torti miketorti@erieshows.com
www.erieshows.com
Covering the Erie Punk scene.

Fly Magazine
22 E. McGovern Ave. Lancaster, PA 17602
PH: 717-293-9772 FX: 717-295-7561
info@flymagazine.net
www.flymagazine.net
Central PA's most complete guide to entertainment.

Gallery of Sound
www.galleryofsound.com
Monthly publication reviewing CDs plus interviews with new musicians.

Harrisburg Online
PO Box 360, Steelton, PA 17113
PH: 717-649-1330
info@hbgonline.com
www.hbgonline.com
Central PA's entertainment guide.

Lehigh Valley Blues Network
www.lvbn.org
Promoting the Blues in the Lehigh Valley area.

Lehigh Valley Folk Music Society
lvfolkmusicsociety.org
Promoting the appreciation of the Old-Time American Folk music.

Northeast Gospel Music
www.northeastgospelmusic.net
Dedicated to promoting Gospel music in the Northeast US.

Out On the Town
100 Temple Blvd. Palmyra, NJ 08065
PH: 856-786-1600 FX: 856-786-1450
Michael Vagnoni ootme2@aol.com
www.ootweb.com
Entertainment trade paper covering PA and NJ.

The PA Jazz Alliance
www.pajazzalliance.com
Created out of a strong desire to present top professional Jazz, Blues, Latin and World musicians to a number of communities currently alive with interest in such musical experiences.

PABands.com
info@pabands.com
www.pabands.com
Sign your band up today. Free unlimited listing.

PaMidstate
www.pamidstate.com
Your A&E guide to the Midstate region of PA.

Patriot News
2214 Market St., Camp Hill, PA 17011-4600
PH: 717-255-8161 FX: 717-255-8456
www.patriot-news.com
Interviews bands, previews and reviews CDs and concerts.

Pennsylvania Arts & Music
www.artsandmusicpa.com
Guide to the arts, music and local cultures of PA.

Pulse Weekly
930 N. 4th St. #205, Allentown, PA 18102
PH: 610-437-7867 FX: 610-437-7869
Michael Faillace michaelf@pulseweekly.com
www.pulseweekly.com
Covering the A&E scene in the Lehigh Valley and beyond.

Rock in PA
www.rockinpa.com
Information about local bands, concerts, clubs etc.

Rockerie
www.rockerie.com
Covering live music events in the Erie area.

ROCKPAGE
www.rockpage.net
We're doing our best to serve the local and regional music community here in PA. Set up your own band page, list gigs etc.

Seven Mountains Bluegrass Assoc.
www.sevenmountainsbluegrass.org
Preserving and promoting Bluegrass music.

Susquehanna Folk Music Society
www.sfmsfolk.org
Preserving and encouraging the traditional arts in Central PA.

The Weekender
15 N. Main St., Wilkes-Barre, PA 18711
PH: 570-829-7101
www.timesleader.com
Free weekly A&E paper. Interviews bands and previews concerts.

West Chester Folk
www.westchesterfolk.org
Concerts, dances and other gatherings featuring traditional Folk music.

Philadelphia

BadmintonStamps Philadelphia
Philabuster philabuster@badmintonstamps.com
www.badmintonstamps.com
Covering the Philly music scene.

Call me Mickey
callmemickey@gmail.com
callmemickey.blogspot.com
MP3 blog covering the local music scene.

Jazz Events in Philly
jazzeventsinphilly.com
Features upcoming Philadelphia Jazz concerts.

Jazzmatazz
4 E. Mt. Pleasant Ave. Philadelphia, PA 19119
Alan Lankin lankina@att.net
www.Jazzmatazz.info
I concentrate on Jazz and Jazz-related releases. List of upcoming shows.

MW Sound Promotions
Megan Wetzel megan_wetzel24@yahoo.com
www.myspace.com/mwsoundpromotions
Local music promotions for Philadelphia area bands looking to get their name out in the public eye.

Origivation Magazine
249 Market St., Philadelphia, PA 19106
Dominic Nicosia dominic@origivation.com
www.origivation.com
All original music publication and hosts Philadelphia's most popular message board.

Philadelphia City Paper
123 Chestnut St. 3rd Fl. Philadelphia, PA 19106
PH: 215-735-8444
Patrick Rapa pat@citypaper.net
citypaper.net
Free weekly alternative paper. Covers all music styles.

Philadelphia Classical Guitar Society
www.phillyguitar.org
Encouraging Classical guitar activities in the area.

Philadelphia Folksong Society
www.pfs.org
Dedicated to the encouragement, dissemination, enjoyment of Folk music and related expressions of folklore.

Philadelphia Songwriters Project
www.phillysongwriters.com
Local artists can showcase their music and advance their career.

Philadelphia Weekly
1500 Sansom St. 3rd Fl. Philadelphia, PA 19102
PH: 215-563-7400
www.philadelphiaweekly.com
Free weekly alternative paper. Does CD reviews.

Philebrity
tips@philebrity.com
www.philebrity.com
A city blog covering the arts, gossip and media in Philadelphia. We'll be here long after you move back to New York.

Philly Blues
phillyblues@comcast.net
www.phillyblues.com
A comprehensive list of Blues bands, events and websites.

Philly Future
www.phillyfuture.org
Information about local shows in the music section.

Philly Jazz Blog
LoHo phillyjazzblog@verizon.net
www.phillyjazzblog.blogspot.com
The forum to heighten the level of conversation about Jazz in Philadelphia and to focus on the state of the music in the "City of Brotherly Love and Sisterly Affection."

philly.com
www.philly.com/mld/philly/entertainment/nightlife
Entertainment section covers local music.

Phillyist
phillyist.com
Online A&E zine that covers the local music scene.

phillymusic.com
www.phillymusic.com
All the latest on the Philly music scene.

Urban Web Link
PO Box 38922, Philadelphia, PA 19104
PH: 888-628-2618
www.urbanweblink.com
Your source for Urban Christian events in the Philadelphia area.

Wonkavision Magazine
PO Box 63680, Philadelphia, PA 19147
PH: 215-413-2136 FX: 775-261-5247
Jeff Meyers jeff@wonkavisionmagazine.com
www.wonkavisionmagazine.com
Entertainment magazine covering Rock and Punk in the Philly area.

Pittsburgh

PghLocalMusic.com
PO Box 17970, Pittsburgh, PA 15235
info@pghlocalmusic.com
www.pghlocalmusic.com
All the info on the local music scene.

pittpunk.com
2803 Fitzhugh Way, Pittsburgh, PA 15226
Adam Rahuba adam.rahuba@gmail.com
www.pittpunk.com
CD and show reviews, event calendar and MP3s.

Pittsburgh Beat.com
www.pittsburghbeat.com
Discussion board for all things music in Pittsburgh

Pittsburgh City Paper
650 Smithfield St. #2200, Pittsburgh, PA 15222
PH: 412-316-3342 FX: 412-316-3388
Aaron Jentzen ajentzen@steelcitymedia.com
www.pghcitypaper.com
Free weekly A&E paper.

Pittsburgh Folk Music Society
www.calliopehouse.org
Promotes traditional and contemporary Folk music.

Pittsburgh Jazz Society
www.pittsburghjazz.org
Preserving and perpetuating local Jazz music.

Pittsburgh Live Music
mediawebsource@yahoo.com
www.mediawebsource.com/pittsburghlive
Band websites, event and concert listings, venue directory etc.

Renaissance and Baroque Society of Pittsburgh
www.rbsp.org
Presents performances of the music of the middle ages.

Rhode Island

Lotsofnoise
www.lotsofnoise.com
Devoted to Providence-area indie shows, leaning towards Noise and Punk Rock.

Rhode Island Songwriters Assoc.
www.risongwriters.com
An organization dedicated the art of songwriting.

South Carolina

The Beat
PO Box 26924, Greenville, SC 29616
Vince Harris vince@upstatebeat.com
www.metrobeat.net
Alternative weekly. Covers local music.

Charleston City Paper
1049 B Morrison Dr. Charleston, SC 29403
PH: 843-577-5304 x118 FX: 843-853-6899
T. Ballard Lesemann
ballard@charlestoncitypaper.com
www.charlestoncitypaper.com
Free weekly A&E paper. CD and concert previews and reviews.

Free Times
c/o Music Editor
PO Box 8295, Columbia, SC 29202
music@free-times.com
www.free-times.com
Free A&E paper. CD and concert previews and reviews. Include a one page bio.

GRITZ
24 Vardry St. #101-G, Greenville, SC 29601
PH/FX: 864-467-1699
Michael Buffalo Smith editor@gritz.net
www.gritz.net
A national print magazine with a sister e-zine. We review CDs, DVDs, books - all Southern flavored.

Rivertown Bluegrass Society
www.rivertownbluegrasssociety.com
Supports local Bluegrass musicians/events.

SCbands.com
devin@scbands.com
www.scbands.com
Dedicated to promoting and supporting the SC music community. Browse hundreds of bands, find local venues and events, join thousands of others in our forums, and tune in to the largest local band site in the Carolina's!

South Carolina Bluegrass and Traditional Music Assoc.
www.sebabluegrass.org
Host's Bluegrass concerts and workshops to promote the art.

Southeastern Bluegrass Assoc. of South Carolina
www.sebga.org
Preserving the love of Bluegrass music.

Weekly Surge
www.weeklysurge.com
Myrtle Beach's free alternative for entertainment, news and lifestyle information.

South Dakota

Babafest.com
Cornell Costa cornellcosta@hotmail.com
www.babafest.com
Music promotion site for independent artists in the Midwest.

C-Sharp Productions
421 N. Edgerton, Mitchell, SD 57301
PH: 605-996-0232
live@sharpmusic.com
www.sharpmusic.com
Production company and label that signs and develops acts.

Joeisapunk Inc.
jiap.s2.bizhat.com
Helping to keep the Sioux City music scene alive and thriving.

Rapid City Journal
507 Main St., Rapid City, SD 57701
PH: 605-394-8300
www.rapidcityjournal.com
Covers local music scene with CD and concert reviews.

Sioux Falls Jazz and Blues Society
www.sfjb.org
Promoting Jazz and Blues through events and education.

SiouxReview.com
www.siouxreview.com
Your guide to Sioux Falls. Post info about your band, shows etc.

South Dakota Friends of Traditional Music
www.fotm.org
Promoting traditional music for generations of South Dakotans.

Wipe Your Eyes and Face the Day
811 S. Minnesota, Sioux Falls, SD 57104
PH: 605-728-4635
Jayson jweihs@hotmail.com
wye.slyink.com/board
Report of the local Punk scene.

Tennessee

BlueHighways TV
111 Shivel Dr. Hendersonville, TN 37075
PH: 866-454-2488
feedback@bluehighwaystv.com
bluehighwaystv.com
Fresh and original Roots music that combines new faces and places with our library of original programming.

Chattanooga Pulse
PO Box 4070, Chattanooga, TN 37405
PH: 423-648-7857 FX: 423-648-7860
www.chattanoogapulse.com
Chattanooga's alternative news weekly featuring what's now, what's local, what's next.

Down-South.com
PO Box 1295, Mt. Juliet, TN 37121
www.down-south.com
Reviews local and major Hip Hop albums.

Enigma Online
PO Box 825, Chattanooga, TN 37401
PH: 423-267-6072 FX: 423-265-0120
enigmathemagazine@yahoo.com
www.enigmaonline.com
We support the local indie music scene.

GoTricities
108 E. Main St. #202, Kingsport, TN 37660
PH: 423-392-1756 FX: 423-245-4910
www.gotricities.com/music
Covers local music including a local music podcast. Post your MP3s.

Ground Zero Blues Club Memphis
groundzerobluesclub.com
Promoting the Memphis Blues scene.

jungleroom.com
www.jungleroom.com
Memphis local music notes. Post news about your upcoming release.

Knox Scene Coalition
knoxscenecoaliti@aol.com
www.knoxscenecoalition.zoomshare.com
We strive to bring more exposure to our local music scene.

KnoxGothic.com
www.knoxgothic.com
Features a forum and events calendar.

KnoxNews.com
2332 News Sentinel Dr. Knoxville, TN 37921-5761
PH: 865-523-3131
www.knoxnews.com
Covers local music. Post your MP3s!

KnoxNightlife.com
www.myspace.com/knoxnightlife
Knoxville's premier nightlife and concert guide.

Knoxville Metro Pulse
602 S. Gay St., Knoxville, TN 37902
PH: 865-522-5399 FX: 865-522-2955
Kevin Crowe crowe@metropulse.com
www.metropulse.com
A&E section allows local bands to list info and post MP3s.

KnoxShows.com
www.knoxshows.com
Post band info, upcoming events, links etc.

Live From Memphis
PH: 901-523-9763
Christopher Reyes info@livefrommemphis.com
www.livefrommemphis.com
We support and promote local musicians, filmmakers and artists who are the lifeblood of the Memphis creative scene.

Memphis Acoustic Music Assoc.
www.mamamusic.org
Sponsors Acoustic music, both American Folk and Celtic.

Memphis Area Bluegrass Assoc.
www.memphis-bluegrass.org
Info on the Bluegrass scene. Reviews CDs.

Memphis Blues Society
www.memphisbluessociety.com
Created to help preserve a deep rich part of Memphis' heritage.

Memphis Commercial Appeal
495 Union Ave. Memphis, TN 38103
PH: 901-529-2345
www.commercialappeal.com
Covers the tri-state music scenes. Profiles touring bands, reviews CDs.

Memphis Flyer
460 Tennessee St., Memphis, TN 38103
PH: 901-521-9000 FX: 901-521-0129
Chris Herrington herrington@memphisflyer.com
www.memphisflyer.com
Free weekly paper. Covers local scene and bands playing the area.

The Memphis Mojo
www.memphismojo.com
Focusing on local music, where it's played and by whom.

Memphis Music Foundation
431 S. Main #201, Memphis, TN 38103
PH: 901-527-1029 FX: 901-527-1049
Cameron Mann
cameron@memphismeansmusic.com
www.memphismeansmusic.com
Our programs and services provide guidance, education, connections and resources to help our members earn a living at the business of music while maintaining their professional independence.

Memphis Songwriters Assoc.
www.memphissongwriters.org
All the resources local songwriters need.

MemphisRap.com
PO Box 30337, Memphis, TN 38130
PH: 901-332-3504
feedback@memphisrap.com
www.MemphisRap.com
Artists can submit news, links, demos, audio files and more!

Ramblin' Man
Randall Brown brownr@knews.com
blogs.knoxnews.com/knx/brown
A blog about Knoxville-area music and other entertainment happenings.

Rebourne Entertainment
1102 Llano Cove, Memphis, TN 38134-7908
PH: 901-388-2988
Bill & Holly Simmers simmers@rebourne.net
www.rebourne.net
A network of musicians and songwriters who are committed to using their talents to make a positive impact on the world around them.

Smoky Mountain Blues Society
www.smokymountainblues.com
Serving Maryville, Knoxville and all of East Tennessee.

Southern Fried Magazine
www.southernfriedmagazine.com
Southern Rock and Roots music webzine complete with intimate interviews, exclusive photos, contests and hot new band reviews.

Tennessee Jazz & Blues Society
www.jazzblues.org
Submit news, articles, CDs for review and more.

Nashville

Hays Entertainment / Songwriters Anonymous
602 S. 15th St., Nashville, TN 37206
PH: 615-730-8877
Gary Hays haysentertainment@gmail.com
www.songwritersanonymous.net
Nashville based booking & promotions agency.

Music City Blues
www.musiccityblues.org
Hosts performances and programs to sustain this music.

Music Row
1231 17th Ave. S., Nashville, TN 37212
PH: 615-321-3617 FX: 615-329-0852
info@musicrow.com
www.musicrow.com
Nashville's music industry publication.

Nashville Ear
4636 Lebanon Pike #144, Hermitage, TN 37076
Steve McNaron smac@NashvilleEar.com
NashvilleEar.com
A venue for songwriters and singers to get their music out on the internet to gain exposure.

Nashville Gothic
djneph@nashvillegothic.com
www.nashvillegothic.com
Serving the needs of the Gothic community in the area.

The Nashville Muse
PO Box 121456, Nashville, TN 37212
PH: 615-354-6400
Doak Turner doakt@comcast.net.
www.nashvillemuse.com
A must-read weekly reference for Music City's songwriting community.

Nashville Music Guide
PO Box 100234, Nashville, TN 37224-0234
PH: 615-244-5673 FX: 615-244-5645
nmg@net-serv.com
www.nashvillemusicguide.com
Free publication dedicated to promoting the performing artist, musician and songwriter.

Nashville Scene
2120 8th Ave. S., Nashville, TN 37204-2204
PH: 615-244-7989
Tracy Moore editor@nashvillescene.com
www.nashscene.com
Free weekly alternative paper. Covers local music scene.

Nashville Songwriter's Assoc. International (NSAI)
www.nashvillesongwriters.com
Protecting the rights and serving songwriters in all genres.

NashvilleConnection.com
9 Music Sq. S. #210, Nashville, TN 37203
PH: 615-826-4141
info@nashvilleconnection.com
www.NashvilleConnection.com
Your source for info about the business of music in Nashville.

NashvilleRock.net
PH: 615-319-1773
nashvillerock.net
The latest local Rock news, reviews and concert information.

The Rage
1100 Broadway, Nashville, TN 37203
PH: 615-664-2270 FX: 615-664-2280
www.nashvillerage.com
Nashville free A&E weekly.

Songhenge
Gary Hays songhenge@hobojoes.net
www.hobojoes.net
A comprehensive site for songwriters in Nashville or those wishing to be there. Links, advice, forum and much more.

Tunesmith / Tunesmith Media / Tunesmith PRO
Nan Cassidy info@tunesmith.net
www.tunesmith.net
Tunesmith offers networking and referral services for songwriters wanting to make connections in Nashville. Tunesmith Media offers record promotion, artist management services and PR. Tunesmith PRO offers a private message board, song referrals to Nashville Publishers and Labels.

Writer/Artist Showcase
PO Box 1346, Hendersonville, TN 37077
PH: 615-826-9550
Jack Scott mail@writerartist.com
www.writerartist.com
A tool for success for aspiring songwriters and artists.

Texas

The Academy of Texas Music
www.academyoftexasmusic.com
Contact us about becoming eligible for sanctioned awards, getting funding for your education project, applying for a scholarship, or applying for assistance under our musician benevolence fund.

The All-You-Can-Eat Texas Music Cafe
TMC/Media Communications
3801 Campus Dr. Waco, TX 76705
Paula Unger texasmusiccafe@hot.rr.com
www.texasmusiccafe.com
Variety music television and radio program.

The Bulletin
PO Box 2219, Conroe, TX 77305
PH: 936-539-2200
www.thebulletin.com
The weekly alternative for Montgomery County.

CD TEX
8806 Lockway, San Antonio, TX 78217
PH: 210-654-8773 FX: 210-654-8895
bill@bgmnetwork.com
www.cdtex.com
CD store for Texas and Americana music.

Central Texas Bluegrass Assoc.
www.centraltexasbluegrass.org
Post events and get your CD reviewed.

Conexion Rockera
Alicia Zertuche aliciaz@conexionrockera.org
www.conexionrockera.org
The ultimate online resource for Latin musical goings on in Central Texas and beyond.

corpusmusic.com
corpusmusic.com
Band information, show dates and song downloads of local artists.

Country Line Magazine
16150 IH 35, Buda, TX 78610
PH: 512-295-8400 FX: 512-295-8600
TJ Greaney tj@countrylinemagazine.com
www.countrylinemagazine.com
A Country music magazine distributed throughout Texas. Special ad rates for indies.

Denton Rock City
www.dentonrockcity.com
An information source for Denton musicians, bands, venues and music writers.

El Paso Music Scene
11705 Coral Palm, El Paso, TX 79936
Charles Hurley bigcheese@elpasomusicscene.com
www.elpasomusicscene.com
Covering the local scene with news, reviews, interviews etc.

El Paso Scene
PO Box 13615, El Paso, TX 79913
PH: 915-542-1422 FX: 915-542-4292
Brian Chozick epscene@epscene.com
www.epscene.com
Free monthly A&E paper. Concert previews and CD reviews.

ElDoradoUnderground.com
www.eldoradounderground.com
Resource for the local music scene. Post your news, MP3s etc.

Extreme Texas Metal
contact@extremetexasmetal.com
www.extremetexasmetal.com
Supporting the Texas underground Metal scene.

Galveston Music Scene
PH: 409-621-2099
David Stanowski
drs2211@GalvestonMusicScene.com
www.galvestonmusicscene.com
Provides a complete picture of the Galveston live music scene!

GrindLab.tv
PO Box 3215, Temple, TX 76505
PH: 888-675-2659 FX: 888-675-2659
Moni Johnson webmaster@thegrindlab.com
www.grindlab.tv
An independent artist video sharing community built upon the same formula as YouTube. Our primary focus is the independent Rap culture of central Texas.

Gruene With Envy
PO Box 92722, Austin, TX 78709
Katie Lytle katie@415e.com
www.gruenewithenvy.com
Texas/Americana music reviews plus a radio show.

Harmonica Organization of Texas
www.hoottexas.com
Promoting the art of playing the harmonica.

Hill Country Scene
PH: 702-340-6748
Roy Al Rendahl royalrendahl@thefaro.com
www.hillcountryscene.com/
Music, arts, & visitor info for the central Texas Hill Country.

Left Ear Entertainment
2611 N. Beltline Rd. #111, Sunnyvale, TX 75182
PH: 469-233-9563
Chaz@LeftEarRadio.com
www.myspace.com/texasradio1
Dedicated to supporting local music from The Lone Star State!

Lone Star Music
1243 Gruene Rd. New Braunfels, TX 78130
PH: 830-627-1992 FX: 830-624-0976
customerservice@lonestarmusic.com
www.lonestarmusic.com
Reviews, tour dates, contests, prizes and much more.

MyTexasMusic.com
PO Box 148, Linden, TX 75563
PH: 903-846-9919
Lucky Boyd MyTexasMusic@aol.com
www.mytexasmusic.com
We are doing more for musicians in Texas than other online vendors could ever pretend to do.

musicTX.com
musictx.com
Show postings for Texas Underground/Alternative bands.

North Texas Blues Society
dentonblues.com
Preserving, promoting and performing our musical heritage!

SA Music Scene
PH: 210-367-2572
www.samusicscene.net
Promotes Texas bands and all acts touring through there.

San Antonio Blues Society
www.sanantonioblues.com
Preserving various styles of Blues music.

San Antonio Current
1500 N. St. Mary's St., San Antonio, TX 78215
PH: 210-227 0044
www.sacurrent.com
San Antonio's free, award-winning, alternative newsweekly.

San Antonio Rocks
www.sanantoniorocks.fr.st
Covering the local Christian Rock scene.

San Antonio Weekly Music News
PO Box 201090, San Antonio, TX 78220
PH: 210-227-4821 FX: 210-225-5009
editor@sambe.org
sambe.org
An online newsletter with all that's going on in the SA music scene.

Southwest Bluegrass Club
www.southwestbluegrassclub.org
Created to preserve and promote Bluegrass music as an original art form.

Spring Creek Bluegrass Club (SCBC)
www.springcreekbluegrass.com
An organization dedicated to preserving the wonderful tradition of Bluegrass music.

State of Texas Gospel Announcers Guild
www.texasgag.com
Increasing the penetration of Gospel music in cities in America.

Texarkana Blues Society
www.texarkanablues.com
Preserving Blues history, supporting Blues education and promoting the ongoing development of Blues music.

Texarkanarocks.com
webmaster@texarkanarocks.com
www.texarkanarocks.com
Providing useful information about music related issues and events in and around Texarkana.

Texas Music Chart
2500 Tanglewilde #106, Houston, TX 77063
PH: 713-952-9221 FX: 713-952-1207
katie@shanemedia.com
www.texasmusicchart.com
The industry standard weekly compilation of radio airplay for Texas artists and their fans.

Texas Music Connection
Grady Smith texasmusicconnection@yahoo.com
www.texasmusicconnection.com
Home of The Texas Music Search Engine. Dedicated to uniting the Texas music community.

Texas Music Magazine
PO Box 50273, Austin, TX 78763
PH: 512-472-6630 FX: 208-485-0347
info@txmusic.com
www.txmusic.com
Promoting original indie Texas music.

Texas Music Office
www.governor.state.tx.us/music
Listing of Texas born or based recording artists.

Texas Music Promotions
texas.newmusicpromote.com
I started this website to make it easier for booking agents and talent managers to find LOCAL Statewide talent.

Texas Music Round-Up
PO Box 49884 Austin, TX 78765-9884
PH: 512-480-0765 FX: 512-499-0207
info@texasmusicroundup.com
www.texasmusicroundup.com
Your independent Texas music superstore!

texasmetalundeground.com
admin@texasmetalundeground.com
www.texasmetalunderground.com
Band profiles, interviews, articles etc.

TexasMusicGuide.com
PO Box 2032, Allen, TX 75013-0036
www.texasmusicguide.com
Texas music festivals, events, venues, CD releases and artist links.

TexasReggae.org
www.texasreggae.org
Covering all things Reggae in Texas.

This Is Texas Music
2311 Westforest Dr. Austin, TX 78704
PH: 512-638-6410
Patrick Nichols patrick@thisistexasmusic.com
www.thisistexasmusic.com
Reviews, profiles, interviews etc.

Tylermusic.com
www.tylermusic.com
Resource for Acoustic music in East Texas.

West Texas Country
www.westtexascountry.com
Dedicated to the preservation and promotion of our Cowboy/Western heritage through Texas style music.

Austin

Austin 360 *Ultimate Austin Band List*
PO Box 670, Austin, TX 78767
PH: 512-912-2591 FX: 512-912-2926
Steven Smith ssmith@statesman.com
www.austin360.com
List your band, events etc.

Austin Celtic Assoc.
www.austincelts.org
Promoting Celtic culture through music, dance and the arts in Central Texas.

Austin Classical Guitar Society
www.austinclassicalguitar.org
Link between amateur and professional guitarists and the community.

Austin Chronicle
PO Box 49066, Austin, TX 78765
PH: 512-454-5766 FX: 512-458.6910
www.austinchronicle.com
Music section covers local music.

Austin Friends of Traditional Music
www.aftm.us
Preserving all genres of traditional music.

Austin Hip Hop Scene
Minto Tsai emptyonline@gmail.com
austinhiphopscene.blogspot.com
Blog covering all things Hip Hop in Austin.

Austin Indie Alliance
PO Box 19661, Austin, TX 78760
PH: 512-912-8863 x4634
www.austinindiealliance.com
Advancing the state of the musical arts of Austin by supporting independent musicians.

Austin Metro Entertainment
PO Box 1583, Pflugerville, TX 78691-1583
PH: 512-251-1882 FX: 512-251-1909
info@austinmetro.com
www.austinmetro.com
An entertainment guide for Austin and Central Texas.

Austin Music Download
2013 Wells Branch Pkwy. #302, Austin, TX 78728
PH: 512-388-1998 FX: 512-251-1107
Carolyn Holzman info@austinmusicdownload.com
www.austinmusicdownload.com
A digital consignment website for MP3s featuring diverse music recorded, marketed or performed in Texas.

Austin Music Foundation
www.austinmusicfoundation.org
Professional development and economic advancement of local musicians.

Austin Showlist
showlistaustin@yahoo.com
www.showlistaustin.com
Lists upcoming shows in Austin. Post your gigs!

Austin Sound
PO Box 4028, Austin, TX 78765-4028
theaustinsound@gmail.com
www.austinsound.net
Seeks to provide a space for information about independent local artists with thoughtful, independent writing and MP3 samples.

Austinist
austinist.com
Online A&E zine that covers the local music scene.

austinlivemusic.com
music@austinlivemusic.com
www.austinlivemusic.com
Post your upcoming shows.

Both Sides of the Mouth
bothsidesofthemouth.blogspot.com
bothsidesofthemouth@gmail.com
A dual-authored MP3 blog based in Austin, Texas.

Burnt Orange Juice
reggie@burntorangejuice.com
burntorangejuice.com
The Daily Texan's official and oh-so-fresh music and entertainment blog.

Covert Curiosity
covertcuriosity@gmail.com
covertcuriosity.blogspot.com
Created to help promote the Austin music scene.

Do512.com
do512@do512.com
do512.com
An interactive event calendar for Austin. What to do in Austin and who is doing it.

INsite Magazine
1704 ½ S. Congress Ste. J, Austin, TX 78704
PH: 512-462-9260 FX: 512-326-4923
mail@insiteaustin.com
www.insiteaustin.com
Features with local up-in-coming acts.

Jupiter index
PO Box 2024, Austin, TX 78768-2024
Gabrielle Burns mail@jupiterindex.com
www.jupiterindex.com
Helping musicians by connecting them with a wider audience.

MusicAustin
www.musicaustin.com
A catalog of the Austin music scene.

Party Ends
John and Luther partyends@gmail.com
partyends.com
If you would like to have your music, film, or other material reviewed or talked about by us, please contact us through e-mail.

Ultra 8201
JoelRichardson.Austin@gmail.com
ultra8201.com
An Austin, TX based music blog.

Unlock Austin
www.unlockaustin.com
Your key to the Austin live music scene.

Dallas/Fort Worth

Dallas Hardcore
www.dallashardcore.com
Promoting the local Hardcore scene.

Dallas Music Guide
660 Preston Forest Ctr. #218, Dallas, TX 75230
PH: 214-739-5300 FX: 214-696-6249
Paul Salfen psalfen@dallasmusicguide.com
www.dallasmusicguide.com
Online music magazine in the Dallas/Ft. Worth area.

Dallas Songwriter's Assoc.
www.dallassongwriters.org
Enhancing the overall personal growth and professionalism of our members.

dallasmusic
4912 Wedgeview Dr. Hurst, TX 76053
Darin Wakely dallasmusic@hotmail.com
www.dallasmusic.com
Live reviews, CD reviews, interviews and more!

Dallas Observer
PO Box 190289, Dallas, TX 75219-0289
www.dallasobserver.com
Night & Day section covers the local music scene.

Fort Worth Songwriters Assoc.
www.fwsa.com
Improving musical work through fellowship, workshops and education.

Fort Worth Weekly
3311 Hamilton Ave. Fort Worth, TX 76107
PH: 817-321-9700 FX: 817-335-9575
www.fwweekly.com
Fort Worth's A&E weekly.

ftworthmusic.com
1912 River Bend Rd. Arlington, TX 76104
ftworthmusic@hotmail.com
ftworthmusic.com
Live reviews, CD reviews, interviews and more!

GuideLive.com
508 Young St., Dallas, TX 75202
PH: 214-977-5603
Christy Robinson carobinson@dallasnews.com
www.guidelive.com
Covers the local music scene. Post your shows and events.

Harder Beat
PO Box 59711, Dallas, TX 75229
PH/FX: 972-484-8030
Linda Hollar linda@harderbeat.com
www.harderbeat.com
Local band features, show and CD reviews and more.

Pegasus News
8140 Walnut Hill Ln. #605, Dallas, TX 75231
PH: 214-764-9663 FX: 214-363-9304
www.pegasusnews.com
Covers the local music scene in Dallas.

Southwest Blues
PO Box 710475, Dallas, TX 75371
PH: 214-887-1188 FX: 972-642-6999
joanna-iz@southwestblues.com
www.southwestblues.com
We feature and spotlight Blues artists that deserve the recognition.

Spune Productions
PH: 817-637-8199
info@spune.com
www.spune.com
Promotes quality artists. Reviews demos, posts events and more.

Houston

Bay Area Bluegrass Assoc.
www.bayareabluegrass.org
Promotes Bluegrass music in the Houston area and beyond.

Best In Texas Magazine
2500 Tanglewilde, #106, Houston, TX 77063
PH: 713-952-9221
Ed Shane ed@bestintexasonline.com
www.bestintexasonline.com
News, reviews and profiles, plus reports on new releases, live shows, events etc.

Free Press Houston
PH: 713-527-0014
editors@freepresshouston.com
www.freepresshouston.com
Alternative weekly. Covers local music.

Guitar Houston
www.guitarhouston.org
Supports developing artists through free concerts.

Houston Band Coalition
www.hbclive.com
Includes a forum for musicians, fans and industry pros.

Houston Beat
www.houstonbeat.com
List your bands, shows and special events.

Houston Blues Society
www.houstonbluessociety.org
Blues education, special events and a monthly jam session.

Houston Calling
David A. Cobb dacobb@gmail.com
www.donewaiting.com/houston
Musings and witticisms on music and all things music-related ... from Houston, Texas and beyond.

Houston Folklore & Folk Music Society
www.houstonfolkmusic.org
Promoting folklore and Folk music.

Houston Songwriters Assoc.
www.houstonsongwriters.com
Supports and encourages the art and craft of songwriting.

Houston Press
1621 Milam #100, Houston, TX 77002
PH: 713-280-2400 FX: 713-280-2444
John Nova Lomax john.lomax@houstonpress.com
www.houstonpress.com
Major news and entertainment weekly.

houstonbands.net
10250 Lands End #304, Houston, TX 77099
Mark Landrum webmaster@houstonbands.net
www.houstonbands.net
The network for Houston bands on the internet. Send your CDs for review.

Houstonist
houstonist.com
Online A&E zine that covers the local music scene.

HoustonSoReal
www.houstonsoreal.blogspot.com
MP3 blog covering the Houston Hip Hop scene.

Jazz Houston
Kelly kel@jazzhouston.com
www.jazzhouston.com
Gig listings, profiles, recordings, news and more.

Silver Dragon Records
3452 Palmer Hwy. PMB #308
Texas City, TX 77590
PH: 409-939-0897 FX: 409-948-4409
info@silver-dragon-records.com
www.silver-dragon-records.com
Helping to promote the Houston music scene. Send us your news!

Space City Rock
PO Box 541010, Houston, TX 77254
gaijin@spacecityrock.com
www.spacecityrock.com
Covering the Houston music scene.

Utah

In Utah This Week
www.inthisweek.com
Alternative weekly. Covers local music.

Intermountain Acoustic Music Assoc.
www.iamaweb.org
Preserving Acoustic music, including Bluegrass, Folk etc.

LDS Music World
www.ldsmusicworld.com
News, reviews, features, music downloads, internet radio and more.

LDSMusicians.com
www.ldsmusicians.com
Discussion forum for LDS musicians and fans.

Salt Lake City Weekly
248 S. Main St., Salt Lake City, UT 84101
PH: 801-575-7003
www.slweekly.com
Free weekly alternative paper. Band interviews, CD and concert previews and reviews.

Salt Lake Under Ground (*SLUG*)
351 W. Pierpont Ave. 4B, Salt Lake City, UT 84101
PH: 801-487-9221 FX: 801-487-1359
info@slugmag.com
www.slugmag.com
Covers local music scene with concert and indie CD reviews.

Utah Blues
info@utahblues.com
www.utahblues.com
Information, news, gigs etc.

Vermont

Deerfield Valley News
PH: 802-464-3388 FX: 802-464-7255
events@vermontmedia.com
www.dvalnews.com
Southern Vermont's source for entertainment.

Early Music Vermont
www.earlymusicvermont.org
Connecting artists and fans of Early music.

Seven Days
PO Box 1164, Burlington, VT 05402
PH: 802-864-5684 FX: 802-865-1015
Dan Bolles dan@sevendaysvt.com
www.sevendaysvt.com
Weekly A&E paper. Accepts CDs for review.

Vermont Music Shop
215 College St., 3rd Fl. Burlington, VT 05401
PH: 802-865-1140
info@vmls.org
www.vermontmusicshop.com
Selling local musicians CDs. Consign your CDs with us.

Virginia

804noise
PO Box 4296, Richmond, VA 23220
info@804noise.org
www.804noise.org
A collective of artists & enthusiasts dedicated to making the Richmond community more receptive to Experimental, Noise, and Avant-garde art/ideas.

Americana Rhythm
PO Box 450, Dayton, VA 22821
PH: 540-746-0360
Greg E. Tutwiler greg@americanarhythm.com
www.americanarhythm.com
Reviews CDs of regional artists and those touring through the area. Americana, Roots, Bluegrass and Folk.

Bandbo
PO Box 7147, Fairfax, VA 22039
Ben Osterhaus ben@bandbo.com
www.bandbo.com
Free resources, promotion and networking for musicians. We are a one-stop shop for everything needed to get your band started.

Bluegrass Connection
9908 Brightlea Dr. Vienna, VA 22181
PH: 703-927-1875
pmilano@bgstate.com
www.gotech.com
Band, performer and festival home pages for the Virginia area.

Bluegrass in Galax
www.bluegrassingalax.com
Dedicated to promoting Bluegrass music since 1996.

The Breeze
G1, Anthony-Seeger Hall, MSC 6805,
Harrisonburg, VA 22807
PH: 540-568-3151
ae@thebreeze.org
www.thebreeze.org
James Madison U. student paper.

C-Ville Weekly
106 E. Main St., Charlottesville, VA 22902
PH: 434-817-2749 FX: 434-817-2758
www.c-ville.com
Charlottesville free weekly paper. Covers local music scene.

Charlottesville Monthly
301 E. Market St., Charlottesville, VA 22902
PH: 804-295-9004 FX: 434-293-5618
info@artsmonthly.com
artsmonthly.com
Monthly A&E magazine. Covers local music scene.

City Magazine
206 Market Sq. SE, Roanoke, VA 24011
PH: 540-345-6300 FX: 540-345-9666
citymagazineonline.com
The premier arts & leisure guide of Roanoke and Southwest Virginia.

Dan River Region Blues and Folk Society
www.danriverregion.com/bluessociety
Supports local artists. Gig calendar, artist info etc.

Fredericksburg Songwriters' Showcase
122 Laurel Ave. Fredericksburg, VA 22408
PH: 540-898-0611
Bob Gramann showcase@bobgramann.com
www.webliminal.com/songwrite
A forum for local songwriters with monthly showcases.

GetRockedOut.com
www.getrockedout.com
Helping the music scene in Blacksburg and surrounding areas. Shows, band listings etc.

HamptonRoads.com
150 W. Brambleton Ave. Norfolk, VA 23510
PH: 757-446-2989
www.hamptonroads.com
News, information, calendars, reviews and more.

The Hook
100 2ⁿᵈ St., Charlottesville, VA 22902
PH: 434-295-8700 FX: 434-295-8097
www.readthehook.com
A&E weekly. Covers local music scene.

Invisible Youth
PO Box 5125, Richmond, VA 23220
PH: 804-543-5995
services@invisibleyouthpr.com
www.invisibleyouthpr.com
We work with Punk/Hardcore bands. We use our extensive knowledge of music and the music community to aid in spreading the word about the great music and music related materials with which our clients work.

James River Blues Society
www.jamesriverblues.org
Promoting and preserving Blues music in the area.

MEONA
meona@verizon.net
www.meona.net
Supporting the local music scene in the SE Virginia area.

Natchel Blues Network
www.natchelblues.org
Blues newsletter, reviews, gig listings and a "spotlight artist" feature.

Port Folio Weekly
258 Granby St., Norfolk, VA 23510
PH: 757-222-3939 FX: 757-363-1767
www.portfolioweekly.com
The alternative voice of The Seven Cities.

Reload
3729 Colonial Pkwy. Virginia Beach, VA 23452
Don Womack webmaster@710.com
www.710.com/reload
Promoting the local talent of Hampton Roads and Richmond.

Richmond.com
1427 W. Main St., Richmond, VA 23220
PH: 804-355-4500 FX: 804-355-3110
www.richmond.com
Online guide to Richmond events. Submit your gig.

Richmond Jazz Society
www.vajazz.org
Promotes Jazz through performances, lectures and workshops.

Richmond Music Journal
www.mindspring.com/~rmjournal
Covering local music in Richmond. Please do NOT send us CDs if you are not from Richmond!

River City Blues Society
www.rivercityblues.com
Educating and enlightening the metropolitan area on the Blues.

Roanoke Times
201 W. Campbell Ave. PO Box 2491,
Roanoke, VA 24010-2491
PH: 800-346-1234
www.roanoke.com
Covers Southern Virginia music scene.

RVA
3512 Floyd Ave. #1, Richmond, VA 23221
PH: 804-349-5890
parker@rvamag.com
www.rvamag.com
We are a magazine focused on showing you Richmond's progressive arts and culture.

ShenandoahMusic.com
www.shenandoahmusic.com
Covering the music scene of Virginia and West Virginia.

Style Weekly
1707 Summit Ave. #201, Richmond, VA 23230
PH: 804-358-0825 FX: 804-358-1079
Brent Baldwin info@styleweekly.com
www.styleweekly.com
Richmond's magazine of news, culture and opinion.

The Undersound
Alex Winfield questions@theundersound.com
theundersound.com
Virginia Beach local music scene. Punk, Hardcore ...all types of music.

Tidewater Bluegrass Music Assoc.
www.geocities.com/tidewaterbluegrassmusic
Preserving the Bluegrass music that we love.

Tidewater Classical Guitar Society
www.tcgs.cx
Concert schedule features local performers.

Tidewater Friends of Folk Music
www.tffm.org
Promotes traditional and contemporary Folk music in SE Virginia.

Tidewater Rocks!
edrocker@tidewaterrocks.net
www.tidewaterrocks.net
Get the lowdown on Hampton local bands.

VaRockBands.com
812 Moorefield Park Dr. #300,
Richmond, VA 23236
Jason Smith staff@varockbands.com
www.myspace.com/varockbands
Linking fans with Virginia's best bands.

Virginia Bluegrass
www.vabluegrass.com
Resources for the Virginia Bluegrass/Folk/Acoustic music scene.

Virginia Organization of Composers and Lyricists
www.vocalsongwriter.org
Promoting the art and craft of songwriting and musical composition.

Washington

Bellingham Independent Music Assoc.
www.bima.com
Independent musicians and music supporters promoting local arts.

The Blues Lamp
www.blueslamp.com
Shining its light on Blues in the Northwest corner of Washington State.

Blues to Do
PO Box 22950, Seattle, WA 98122-0950
PH: 206-328-0662
calendar@bluestodo.com
www.bluestodo.com
Source of information about live Blues in the Northwest!

Cascadia Weekly
PO Box 2833, Bellingham, WA 98227-2833
PH/FX: 360-647-8200
Carey Ross carey@cascadiaweekly.com
cascadiaweekly.com
Alternative weekly. Covers local music.

ForceWeb.com
www.forceweb.com
Puget Sound live music.

Inland Empire Blues Society
www.ieblues.org
Promoting the Blues in the Northwest.

Inland Northwest Bluegrass Assoc.
www.spokanebluegrass.org
Host's Bluegrass concerts, jams, festivals and other events.

Northwest Christian Music
Nwchristianmusic.com
Our mission is to promote Northwest Christian artists and impact this region with inspirational music.

Northwest Dance Music Assoc.
www.nwdma.org
The premier record pool covering the Pacific Northwest.

Northwest Folklife
www.nwfolklife.org
The most visible advocate of the traditional arts in the Northwest region.

Northwest Music Network
PO Box 46401, Seattle, WA 98146
info@northwestmusic.net
www.northwestmusic.net
Online guide to all things musical in the Northwest!

Northwest Tekno
www.nwtekno.org
Electronic music community.

Old Time Music in Portland
www.bubbaguitar.com
Lists Old-Time music gigs and music gatherings in the Portland area.

Olymusic.com
www.olymusic.com
Site for Olympia musicians.

Pacific Northwest Inlander
1020 W. Riverside Ave. Spokane, WA 99201
PH: 509-325-0634 x228
www.inlander.com
Spokane weekly that reviews and covers local music.

Songwriters of the Northwest Guild
www.songnw.com
Helps songwriters define and pursue their artistic goals.

Spokane Folklore Society
spokanefolklore.org
Dedicated to the celebration of Folk Arts, particularly music and dance.

Spokanebands.com
PH: 509-701-0333
Shane Zaborac, Brian Knight
info@spokanebands.com
www.spokanebands.com
Events, bands, news, forums, venues and much more.

Three Rivers Folklife Society
www.3rfs.org
Promoting Folk music in the Tri-Cities area.

Track10
14201 SE. Petrovitsky Rd. Ste. A3-338,
Renton, WA 98058
PH: 206-686-7700
info@track10.com
track10.com
Connecting the best talent the Northwest Christian music scene has to offer.

Walla Walla Blues Society
www.wwbs.org
Keeping the public in touch with our American musical heritage.

Washington Bluegrass Assoc.
www.washingtonbluegrassassociation.org
Promotes understanding and enjoyment of Bluegrass and other closely related music.

Washington Blues Society
www.wablues.org
News, CD reviews, classifieds etc.

Weekly Volcano
weeklyvolcano.com
South Puget Sound's arts & entertainment authority!

Seattle

Early Music Guild of Seattle
www.earlymusicguild.org
Supports Early music artists through concerts and programs.

Earshot Jazz
www.earshot.org
Supports Jazz and increases awareness in the community.

Gospel Music Workshop of America Pacific
www.pacificnwchapter.com
Promoting Gospel and all its beliefs in the community.

Seaspot.com
info@seaspot.com
www.seaspot.com
Covering the entertainment scene in the Seattle area.

Seattle Chamber Music Society
www.seattlechambermusic.org
Created to foster the appreciation of chamber music in our region by presenting performances featuring world-class musicians in accessible and inviting formats.

Seattle Classic Guitar Society
www.seattleguitar.org
Events calendar, local news, articles of interest and more.

Seattle Composer's Alliance
www.seattlecomposers.org
Uniting Seattle composers to share ideas.

Seattle Drummer
Aaron aarongrey@seattledrummer.com
www.seattledrummer.com
Helping musicians achieve their personal and professional goals.

Seattle Folklore Society
seafolklore.org
Promoting Folk and traditional arts in the Seattle area.

Seattle Gay News
1605 12th Ave. #31, Seattle, WA 98122
PH: 206-324-4297 FX: 206-322-7188
sgn2@sgn.org
www.sgn.org
Post your shows and events.

Seattle Post-Intelligencer *SeattleNoise*
101 Elliott Ave. W., Seattle, WA 98119
PH: 206-448-8000
seattlepi.nwsource.com/bands
Covers local music with news and interviews.

Seattle Sinner
Brook Hatch brook@theseattlesinner.com
www.theseattlesinner.com
Seattle's only true monthly alternative.

Seattle Weekly
1008 Western Ave. #300, Seattle, WA 98104
PH: 206-623-0500 FX: 206-467-4338
music@seattleweekly.com
www.seattleweekly.com
Covers local music scene with artist interviews, CD and concert previews and reviews.

SeattleDIY Collective
www.seattlediy.org
A collective whose mission is to promote and support the DIY ethos and its associated growing community in Seattle.

Seattlest
seattlest.com
Online A&E zine that covers the local music scene.

Songspace
Richard Middleton editor@songspace.net
www.songspace.net
Your connection to Seattle's Singer/Songwriter community.

The Stranger
1535 11th Ave. 3rd Fl. Seattle, WA 98122
PH: 206-323-7101 FX: 206-323-7203
music@thestranger.com
www.thestranger.com
Seattle free weekly alternative paper. Covers local music with concert previews and CD reviews.

Three Imaginary Girls
PO Box 20428, Seattle, WA 98102
www.threeimaginarygirls.com
Seattle's sparkly Indie Pop press.

Washington DC

Baby, You Got a Stew Goin'!
steve@babystew.com
rogo2000.blogspot.com
Audioblog covering the DC music scene.

Blues Alley Jazz Society
www.bluesalley.org
About all things Jazz here in our Nation's Capitol.

**Capitol Area Bluegrass and
Old-Time Music Assoc.**
www.caboma.org
Dedicated to preserving and promoting Bluegrass and Old-Time music in the DC area.

DC Bluegrass Union
www.dcbu.org
Promoting and supporting Bluegrass music in the area.

DC Blues Society
www.dcblues.org
Dedicated to preserving and promoting the Blues.

DC Hip Hop Network
launch.groups.yahoo.com/group/dchiphopnetwork
Share music, drop rhymes, post show info and more.

DC Rock Club
DCRockClub@gmail.com
www.dcrockclub.com
Blog covering the DC music scene.

DCGoGo.COM
5814 Clay St. NE. Washington, DC 20019
PH: 202-257-7992 FX: 202-398-8299
www.dcgogo.com
Source for Go Go music in our nations capital.

DCist
dcist.com
Online A&E zine that covers the local music scene.

DCjazz.com
www.dcjazz.com
MP3s, videos, CD store and more!

dcMusicNews
www.dcmusicnews.com
Resource sites for independent musicians in the area.

DCShows.net
www.dcshows.net
Local Punk, Metal and Hardcore shows for the mid-Atlantic.

District Records
3453 Sherbourg Ave. Las Vegas, NV 89141
PH: 202-494-1297
David Ridgeway ridgeway@districtrecords.com
www.districtrecords.com
Our goal is to nurture and help musicians, adding their unique contributions to the musical tradition of Washington and the surrounding area.

Exotic Fever Records
PO Box 297, College Park, MD 20741-0297
Sara sara@exoticfever.com
www.exoticfever.com
Supports local and regional independent music/writing/art.

Folklore Society of Greater Washington
www.fsgw.org
Promoting the traditional Folk music and folklore of the American people.

Girls Need Guitars
girlsneedguitars.net
We would like to provide guitars, rhythm instruments, and music lessons for all the at-risk teenage girls in Whatcom County that want to participate.

House of Musical Traditions
7040 Carroll Ave. Takoma Park, MD 20912
PH: 301-270-9090 FX: 301-270-3010
hmtmail@hmtrad.com
www.hmtrad.com
We have one of the most extensive collections of recordings done by musicians local to the DC area.

Mantis Magazine
PO Box 9566, Silver Spring, MD 20916
submissions@mantismagazine.com
www.mantismagazine.com
Promoting local artists and writers. E-mail us to let us know you've sent your music.

Metro Distortion
metrodistortion@hotmail.com
www.metrodistortion.blogspot.com
Providing reviews and news on the DC, Baltimore and NYC live music scene.

MetroMusicScene.com
Jeff Campagna jeffc@lastsecondcomeback.com
www.metromusicscene.blogspot.com
A source for music news and community for the DC metro area.

On Tap
4238 Wilson Blvd. #3078, Arlington, VA 22203
PH: 703-465-0500 FX: 703-465-0400
www.ontaponline.com
Arts & entertainment magazine for the DC area.

Phat Cats Entertainment
1220 L St. NW. #100-483
Washington, DC 20005-4018
PH: 202-415-9268
www.phatcats.com
Management/entertainment company that brings the best talent to the DC, MD and VA area.

Society of Art Rockers
www.dc-soar.org
Promoting the musical form called Art Rock or Progressive Rock in the Metropolitan Washington, DC area.

Songwriters' Assoc. of Washington
saw.org
Resource for professional songwriters to further their careers.

Washington Area Lawyers for the Arts
901 New York Ave. NW. Ste. P-1
Washington, DC 20001-4413
PH: 202-289-4440 FX: 202-289-4985
legalservices@thewala.org
www.thewala.org
Provides legal service to the arts community.

Washington Area Music Assoc.
wamadc.com
Promotes local music regardless of genre.

Washington City Paper
2390 Champlain St. NW., Washington, DC 20009
PH: 202-332-2100 FX: 202-332-8500
www.washingtoncitypaper.com
Covers the local music scene and previews upcoming A&E events.

Washington Post
1150 15th St. NW., Washington, DC 20071
PH: 202-334-7582
www.washingtonpost.com
Considers indie albums for review. Covers local music scene.

washingtonpost.com MP3
mp3@wpni.com
mp3.washingtonpost.com
Self-publishing by and for the Metro region's music community.

West Virginia

Caustic Eye Productions
www.myspace.com/causticeyeproductions
An independent music label and promotions company that is in place to help bands get their music into people's hands and take some of the stress out of self-promotions.

The Daily Athenaeum
1374 VanVoorhis Rd. Lot D14,
Morgantown, WV 26505
www.da.wvu.edu
West Virginia U's daily paper. We're always looking for new things to write about. My next article could be your CD review!

Graffiti
519 Juliana St., Parkersburg, WV 26101
PH: 304-485-1891
www.grafwv.com
Covers local music scene with interviews, concert and CD reviews.

Nation Full of Ivy
nationfullofivy.wordpress.com
I love everything about music and writing and this site is my creative outlet. I am a musician and I've always thought that my area (Eastern panhandle of West Virginia) was in desperate need of a music site of some kind.

WVRockscene
Nick Harrah wvrockscene@gmail.com
wvrockscene.blogspot.com
Started as a way to highlight cool bands in West Virginia. Nobody covers local music better.

Wisconsin

Brave the Cold
Dawn dawners13@gmail.com
www.myspace.com/bravethecold
Supporting local/regional music in the Midwest area and beyond. What do you need??? We can hook you up or get it done for you.

City Pages
300 3rd St. Washington Sq. Wausau, WI 54403
PH: 715-845-5171
citypages@dwave.net
www.thecitypages.com
Alternative weekly. Covers local music.

Cty Murph's Music Page
ctymurph@netwurx.net
www.ctymurph.com
Listing of Wisconsin bands and show dates.

FolkLib Index
PO Box 1447, Oshkosh, WI 54903-1447
henkle@pobox.com
www.folklib.net/index/wi
Information of Wisconsin Folk, Bluegrass, Celtic, Acoustic and Blues artists.

Fondy Acoustic Music Alliance
www.fondyacoustic.org
Providing listening and playing opportunities for fans of Acoustic music.

Isthmus
101 King St., Madison, WI 53703
PH: 608-251-5627
www.thedailypage.com
Madison's news & entertainment weekly.

mad.city.hard.core
www.MadHC.com
A Madison/Milwaukee area music site focusing on Punk, Metal, Hardcore and Rock.

Madison Blues Society
www.madisonbluessociety.com
Keeping the Blues alive in the Madison area.

Madison Folk Music Society
www.madfolk.org
Dedicated to fostering Folk music in the Madison area.

Madison Jazz Society
www.madisonjazz.com
Preserving and promoting Jazz music.

MadisonSongwriters.com
www.madisonsongwriters.com
Provides education and networking opportunities within the music business.

MadisonMusicians.Net
admin@madisonmusicians.net
www.madisonmusicians.net
Connect with the local music scene.

Maximum Ink
PH: 608-245-0781 FX: 608-245-0782
Rokker Rokker@maximumink.com
www.maximumink.com
Music magazine featuring interviews/stories, CD reviews, events and more.

Milwaukee Area Bluegrass Music Assoc.
www.mabma.org
Dedicated to the preservation and promotion of Bluegrass music in SW Wisconsin.

Milwaukee Journal Sentinel
PH: 414-223-5250
Dave Tianen dtianen@journalsentinel.com
www.jsonline.com/music
Your LIVE guide for Wisconsin music.

Milwaukee Shows
www.myspace.com/milwaukeeshows1
I thought there should be a space that lists Milwaukee shows, so here it is.

The Music Review
Elvis Aaron Presley Sheehan
the.music.review@gmail.com
www.myspace.com/themusicreview
Helping local Rock, Jam and Metal bands spread original music and live concerts. Check our website for submission details!

Muzzle of Bees
Ryan Matteson uwmryan@yahoo.com
www.muzzleofbees.com
Blog covering the Madison music scene.

OnMilwaukee.com
1930 E. North Ave. 2nd Fl. Milwaukee, WI 53202
PH: 414-272-0557
www.onmilwaukee.com
Milwaukee music guide. Add your band to our local music database.

Rick's Cafe
836 E. Johnson St., Madison, WI 53703
PH: 608-250-2565
Rick Tvedt rick@rickscafe.org
www.rickscafe.org
Created because of the lack of coverage being given to Madison-area musicians coupled with his desire to contribute to the local music community.

Rock Wisconsin
www.rockwisconsin.com
A social network for Wisconsin musicians.

Shepherd Express
207 E. Buffalo St. #410, Milwaukee, WI 53202
Attn: Evan Rytlewski
PH: 414-276-2222 x218 FX: 414-276-3312
www.shepherd-express.com
Milwaukee free daily alternative paper. Covers local music scene.

Southern Wisconsin Bluegrass Music Assoc.
www.swbmai.org
News about Bluegrass events, profiles of area bands and reviews.

Up the Downstair
bish_tim_archer@yahoo.com
www.upthedownstair.net
MP3 blog focussing on the Madison music scene.

Volume One
17 S. Barstow St., Eau Claire, WI 54701
PH: 715-552-0457
mail@volumeone.org
www.volumeone.org
Pouring down from the heavens, soaking your clothes with culture and entertainment while lightening flashes, igniting the childlike glee in your eyes.

WISCONLINE
www.wisconline.com
Everything Wisconsin. Submit your music event.

Wisconsin Area Music Industry
www.wamimusic.com
Our purpose is to educate and recognize the achievements and accomplishments of individuals in the Wisconsin music industry.

Wisconsin Musical Groups
regent@execpc.com
www.execpc.com/~regent
Wisconsin's music resource! Submit your band/gig info.

Wyoming

Jackson Hole Online
610 W. Broadway, WY 83001
PH: 377-733-5681
www.jacksonholenet.com
Entertainment section covers local music.

Planet Jackson Hole
Box 3249, Jackson, WY 83001
PH: 307-732-0299 FX: 307-732-0996
www.planetjh.com
Alternative weekly. Covers local music.

Wyoming Blues and Jazz Society
www.wyobluesandjazz.org
Created to promote and perpetuate Blues and Jazz music across the state of Wyoming.

Canada

A Better World
182-4936 Yonge St., Toronto, ON M2N 6S3
mastermail@abetterworld.ca
www.abetterworld.ca
Created to encourage artists to convey 'Better World' themes through their art form.

acousticroof.ca
Julian West contact@acousticroof.ca
www.acousticroof.ca
A network that aims to facilitate the growth of house concerts in communities for the benefit of music artists, and audiences.

Assoc. of Canadian Women Composers
www.acwc.ca
Active in the promotion of music written by Canadian women composers and endeavors to help these composers achieve a higher profile in the community.

AtlanticSeabreeze.com
1276 Nelligan Rd. R.R. #4, Tignish, PE C0B 2B0
PH: 902-882-2364
John Gavin john@atlanticseabreeze.com
www.atlanticseabreeze.com
Supports Celtic, East Coast and Country music in Canada.

BandMix.ca
PH: 877-569-6118
bandmix.ca
We promote your music. Make a profile and get exposure from our daily traffic. Post your gigs on your calendar.

Borealis Recording Company
225 Sterling Rd. #19, Toronto, ON M6R 2B2
PH: 416-530-4288 FX: 416-530-0461
info@borealisrecords.com
www.borealisrecords.com
The best in Canadian Folk music.

Brockway Entertainment
PO Box 90014, Ottawa, ON K1V 1J8
PH: 888-267-7568
Troy Neilson troy@brockwayent.com
www.brockwayent.com
Our mission is to assist independent Canadian Hip Hop artists in exposing their music via radio, press & print throughout North America.

Bullfrog Music
Box 5041, 1625 Fort St., Victoria, BC V8R 6N3
PH: 250-370-5448
Jeremiah Sutherland jeremiah@bullfrogmusic.com
www.bullfrogmusic.com
Bringing independent Canadian music artists to the world. We get you "out there" and help you sell your CD to an unlimited global audience. We don't expect exclusivity. In fact, it's better for you to have your CDs for sale in as many places as possible.

Canada.com
www.canada.com
Post your event news! (check for the contact e-mail for your city).

Canada Jams
PH: 647-225-2243
Steve L'Espérance steve@canadajams.ca
www.canadajams.ca
A cross section of the music scene in Canada, with video, audio, reviews and information on our artists and our industry.

Canadian Academy of Recording Arts and Sciences *(CARAS)*
345 Adelaide St. W. 2nd Fl. Toronto, ON M5V 1R5
PH: 416-485-3135 FX: 416-485-4978
info@carasonline.ca
www.carasonline.ca
Development of opportunities to showcase and promote Canadian artists and music.

Canadian Amateur Musicians
www.cammac.ca
Creating opportunities for musicians of all levels.

Canadian Celtic Music
Kimberley kimberley@islandviewcreations.com
members.shaw.ca/kimberleyw/canadaceltcmusic
Musician's websites, tour date, news and more.

Canadian Copyright Act
Legislative Services, 284 Wellington St. SAT-4, Ottawa, ON K1A 0H8
PH: 613-957-4222 FX: 613-954-0811
webadmin@justice.gc.ca
laws.justice.gc.ca/en/C-42
Important information on the Canadian copyright act.

Canadian Country Music Assoc.
www.ccma.org
Developing Canadian Country music.

Canadian Cowboy Country Magazine
#4, 9343- 50th St., Edmonton, AB T6B 2L5
PH: 800-943-7336
www.canadiancowboy.ca
Features a Country music review in each edition.

Canadian Electroacoustic Community
cec.concordia.ca
Network for the flow and exchange of information and ideas.

Canadian Gospel Music Assoc.
www.cgmaonline.com
Promoting the growth and ministry of the Christian music arts in Canada.

Canadian Guitar Players Assoc.
www.guitarassociation.org
Sharing information and helping one another in developing individual talents.

Canadian Intellectual Property Office
50 Victoria St. Rm. C-229, Gatineau, QC K1A 0C9
PH: 819-953-7620
cipo.contact@ic.gc.ca
strategis.gc.ca/sc_mrksv/cipo
Responsible for intellectual property (copyright and trademarks) in Canada.

Canadian Music Center
20 St. Joseph St., Toronto, ON M4Y 1J9
PH: 4160961-6601 FX: 416-961-7198
info@musiccentre.ca
www.musiccentre.ca
Collecting, distributing and promoting music by Canada's composers.

Canadian Music TV
1 Yonge St. #1801, Toronto, ON M5E 1W7
Jack Tasse canadianmusictv@gmail.com
www.canadianmusictv.ca
Free service that allows indie artists to gain further exposure for their music via traditional television and the web.

Canadian Musical Reproduction Rights Agency (CMRRA)
56 Wellesley St. W. #320, Toronto, ON M5S 2S3
PH: 416-926-1966 FX: 416-926-7521
inquiries@cmrra.ca
www.cmrra.ca
Represents the vast majority of music copyright owners (usually called music publishers) doing business in Canada. Issues licenses and collects royalties for the use of music on CDs and other products.

Canadian Musician
23 Hannover Dr. #7, St. Catharines, ON L2W 1A3
PH: 905-641-3471 FX: 905-641-1648
mail@nor.com
www.canadianmusician.com
Showcases unsigned Canadian acts.

Canadian Newspaper and News Media Database
www.abyznewslinks.com/canad.htm
Links to hundreds of Canadian newspapers.

Canadian Society for Traditional Music
www.yorku.ca/cstm
Articles, notices and reviews on all aspects of Canadian Folk music.

CanadianBands.com
4110 51st Ave. Cold Lake, AB T9M 1A2
Dan Brisebois canconrox@excite.com
www.canadianbands.com
Submit band info, gigs, reviews etc.

Canuck Blues
admin@canuckblues.ca
www.canuckblues.ca
Created for the promotion of Canuck Blues music.

CBC Records
PO Box 500 Stn. A, Toronto, ON M5W 1E6
PH: 416-555-1212 FX: 416-205-2139
www.cbcrecords.cbc.ca
Making the music of Canadian performers available to music lovers around the world.

Chart Magazine
41 Britain St. #200, Toronto, ON M5A 1R7
PH: 416-363-3101 FX: 416-363-3109
chart@chartattack.com
www.chartattack.com
Canadian college radio and retail charts, reviews and lots more.

Choose The Blues Productions
65 Williams St. W., Smiths Falls, ON K7A 1N5
PH: 613-283-8830 FX: 613-283-3273
info@choosetheblues.ca
www.choosetheblues.ca
Bringing you the best in the Blues with a focus on Canadian talent. Artist management, event production etc.

CMC Distribution
590 York Rd. Niagara-On-The-Lake, ON L0S 1J0
PH: 905-641-0631 FX: 905-641-8824
oe@cmcdistribution.com
cmcmusic.ca
Features resources for Canadian Christian artists.

Collective Of Black Artists COBA
2444 Bloor St. W. 2nd Fl. Toronto, ON M6S 1R2
PH: 416-658-3111 FX: 416-658-9980
info@cobainc.com
www.cobainc.com
Dedicated to the creation and production of dance and music while preserving cultural traditions of the African Diaspora.

Concept Entertainment Ltd.
3146 Patullo Cres. Coquitlam, BC V3E 2R3
PH: 604-552-2170 FX: 604-552-2175
Mario Brox mario@conceptentertainment.net
www.conceptentertainment.net
West Coast based promotion agency featuring Canadian talent in Europe.

EventInfo.ca
www.eventinfo.ca
We'll list any type of event in Canada for free. We also list artist profiles, venue locations, event promoter profiles etc.

!*@# Exclaim!
7-B Pleasant Blvd. #966, Toronto, ON M4T 1K2
PH: 416-535-9735
Ian Danzig ian@exclaim.ca
www.exclaim.ca
Coverage of new music across all genres of Canadian cutting-edge artists.

Federation of Canadian Music Festivals
www.fcmf.org
An umbrella organization for 230 local and provincial festivals.

Festival Distribution
1351 Grant St., Vancouver, BC V5L 2X7
PH: 604-253-2662 FX: 604-253-2634
fdi@festival.bc.ca
www.festival.bc.ca
Distributor of Canadian indie music of all genres.

Folk Alliance Canada
www.folkalliance.ca
Helps you create, perform and market your Folk music here and internationally.

GuitarsCanada
www.guitarscanada.com
Helps out any up and coming Canadian bands. Submit your info.

HERIZONS
PO Box 128, Winnipeg, MB R3C 2G1
PH: 888-408-0028
Penni Mitchell editor@herizons.ca
www.herizons.ca
Feminist magazine. We focus on Canadian female indie musicians.

hiphopcanada.com
532 Montreal Rd. #493, Ottawa, ON K1K 4R4
PH: 613-749-7777 FX: 613-747-9317
info@hiphopcanada.com
www.hiphopcanada.com
Send artist press kits, new updates etc.

Indie Band Canada
162 St. John's Rd. Toronto, ON M6P 1T9
www.indiebandcanada.com
Community for bands to network and display their music. Free artist website and internet radio exposure.

Indie Can Music
50 Cordova Ave. #2102, Toronto, ON M9A 4X6
PH: 416-239-8737
Joe Chisolm info@indiecan.com
www.indiecan.com
Online community where fans, bands and industry insiders meet.

Indie Pool
118 Berkeley St., Toronto, ON M5A 2W9
PH: 416-424-4666 FX: 416-424-4265
mail@indiepool.com
www.indiepool.com
Provides an affordable distribution alternative.

IndieTV
116C Hazelton Ave. Toronto, ON M5R 2E5
PH: 416-561-6536 FX: 416-944-3191
indiepipe.ca
A national television channel devoted 100% to Canada's amazing music.

jambands.ca
www.jambands.ca
Bringing together great bands and appreciative fans.

JamHub.ca
www.jamhub.ca
Canada's online Jam Bands community.

Jazz Elements
cindy@jazzelements.com
www.jazzelements.com
Jazz and Blues music, news, reviews, interviews and shop with a Canadian focus.

JazzPromo.com
650 Dupont St. #503, Toronto, ON M6G 4B1
jazz@jazzpromo.com
www.jazzpromo.com
Showcasing Canadian artists. Artist of the Month feature.

Joni Daniels - Fund Me
www.myspace.com/fundme
If you're Canadian I can help you apply for money from funding organizations for your album, video, tour, promotion, etc. Many bands find that the application and completion processes for FACTOR money and other government funds are impossibly time-consuming and complicated. I'm an expert!

Linear Reflections
647 Kelly Rd. Victoria, BC V9B 2A6
PH: 250-474-0692
Naomi de Bruyn naomi@linearreflections.com
www.linearreflections.com
An arts review e-zine, which deals with all genres of music.

LiveTourArtists
1451 White Oaks Blvd. Oakville, ON L6H 4R9
PH: 905-844-0097 FX: 905-844-9839
info@livetourartists.com
www.livetourartists.com
International booking agency representing talented artists.

MapleMusic
230 Richmond St. W. 11th Fl. Toronto, ON M5V 3E5
PH: 877-944-5144 FX: 416-961-1040
justcurious@maplemusic.com
www.maplemusic.com
Submit your info, gigs, sell your CD from our site and more.

Metalworks Production Group
3611 Mavis Rd. #21, Mississauga, ON L5C 1T7
PH: 905-890-4500 FX: 905-890-1150
info@metalworksproductiongroup.com
www.metalworksproductiongroup.com
With vast experience ranging from concerts and live theater to corporate and special events, our technical directors and event personnel are ready to provide personalized, custom service. As a single-source production integrator, the Metalworks team can manage projects of any scope. Offering the newest technologies, as well as the latest inventory of top-of-the-line sound, lighting, video and staging equipment, Metalworks Production Group is on the cutting edge of live production.

Music By Mail Canada
rob_mcintyre@excite.com
www.musicbymailcanada.com
Canadian source for music.

Music For Coffee Beings
www.musicforcoffeebeings.com
This is a promotional CD that will not be sold and will get Canadian and original music out there and into the ears of the general public. By playing our CDs, coffee shops can play an important part in nurturing the growth of Canadian Music.

Music is My Business
music.gc.ca
We'll help you better understand the inner workings of the Canadian music industry.

North by Northeast Music and Film Festival Conference
189 Church St., Toronto, ON M5B 1Y7
PH: 416-863-6963 FX: 416-863-0828
Gillian Zulauf info@nxne.com
www.nxne.com
Canada's #1 showcase for new independent music, where fans can catch great local and international performers at intimate venues.

Opera.ca
www.opera.ca
Keeps members abreast of issues relating to artistic quality and creativity, education and audience development.

Orchestras Canada
www.oc.ca
The national service organization for all Canadian orchestras.

PhemPhat
Ebonnie Rowe phemphat@hotmail.com
www.phemphat.com
Created to foster the growth, education and promotion of women in all aspects of the Canadian Urban entertainment scene.

R&J Music Canada
PH: 604-649-6960
www.randjmusic.com
We enjoy working with talented musicians and writers. We strive to create fresh new songs that will reach a wide audience and suit a variety of projects.

RUN! RUN! RUN! Records
Davide Di Saro' runwithrunner@yahoo.ca
www.000runrunrun000.com
Motion graphics, design company and record label. The aim of this alternative visual factory is to help independent productions to reach the media as major labels do.

Songwriters Assoc. of Canada
26 Soho St. #340, Toronto, ON M5T 1Z7
PH: 416-961-1588 FX: 416-961-2040
Don Quarles don@songwriters.ca
www.songwriters.ca
Exclusively for Canadian composers, lyricists and songwriters.

stillepost.ca
stillepost.ca
Online music community with information from cities across Canada.

School Alliance of Student Songwriters
sass@sasscanada.net
www.sasscanada.net
Supporting young people as they express themselves through songwriting in a safe environment.

Supernova.com
PH: 416-635-8885 x333 FX: 416-638-6333
www.supernova.com
Free service where Canadian bands upload their music and create profiles.

Urban Music Assoc. of Canada
www.umacunited.com
Domestic and international promotion and development of Canadian Urban music.

We Go To Shows Magazine
editorial@wgtsmagazine.com
www.wgtsmagazine.com
Covering the Canadian live music scene. News, interviews, features etc.

The Wedge
muchmail@muchmusic.com
www.muchmusic.com/tv/thewedge
A weekly showcase of Alternative/Indie music videos on MuchMusic.

West49 Music
info@west49.com
www.west49music.com
Supporting the thriving Canadian music scene. Download some of the best in Canadian indie music!

Words & Music
socan@socan.ca
www.socan.ca
SOCAN's publication. Music news and bios are done on a few members each month. New releases are also listed.

Zone Francophone
www.francoculture.ca
A site dedicated to francophone culture and arts.

Zoilus.com
c/o The Globe and Mail
444 Front St. W., Toronto, ON M5V 2S9
Carl Wilson caligariscabinet@gmail.com
www.zoilus.com
I am an editor and critic at the Toronto Globe & Mail. My music column Overtones appears there every Saturday. Send me your CDs for review.

Alberta

ALBERTA Metal
www.albertametal.net
Canadian Metal bands may submit a profile and MP3.

Calgary Jazz Assc.
www.calgaryjazz.com
Our mandate is to strengthen, support and promote Jazz in Calgary.

CalgaryJazz.com
calgaryjazzgigs@yahoo.ca
www.calgaryjazz.com
Calgary's most comprehensive Jazz listings.

CalgaryPlus.ca
www.calgaryplus.ca
Post your music events.

Dose Calgary
www.dose.ca/getout/calgary.html
A free daily online magazine. One of the key areas of our website is promotion of indie bands.

Dose Edmonton
www.dose.ca/getout/edmonton.html
A free daily online magazine. One of the key areas of our website is promotion of indie bands.

Edmonton Composers' Concert Society
www.eccsociety.com
Our vision is to ensure that the musical works of composers from Edmonton, as well as Alberta, Canada and the rest of the world, are made fully accessible to and for the Canadian public.

EdmontonPlus.ca
PH: 403-228-1800 FX: 403-240-5669
www.edmontonplus.ca
Online A&E magazine covering the local music scene.

Failsafe Productions
www.myspace.com/failsafeproductions
We are here to make life easier for starting bands We provide top of the line management phenomenal designs and non stop promotions.

FFWD
206-1210 20th Ave. SE., Calgary, AB T2G 1M8
PH: 403-244-2235 FX: 403-244-1431
Peter Hemminger phemminger@ffwd.greatwest.ca
www.ffwdweekly.com
Calgary's news and entertainment weekly.

Foothills Bluegrass Music Society
www.foothillsbluegrass.com
Promoting Bluegrass music in Calgary.

Full Moon Folk Club
www.fmfc.ca
We are committed to producing Edmonton Folk music events which feature top quality acts as well as up and coming artists.

Jazz Is Society of Alberta
www.jazzis.org
Exists to present Jazz music forms to the public.

MediaKinesis.com
www.MediaKinesis.com
A site for Alberta bands with MP3s, charts, spotlights, band stores, biographies, contacts ...

Megatunes
CAL: customer.service@megatunes.com
EDM: edmt.customer.service@megatunes.com
www.megatunes.com
An independent music store located in Calgary and Edmonton.

Northern Bluegrass Circle Music Society
www.bluegrassnorth.com
Created to play and promote Bluegrass music in Edmonton.

The Northern Lights Folk Club
www.northernlightsfc.ca
Dedicated to the promotion of live Acoustic Roots music in the Edmonton area.

Red Mitten Collective
289 Bannister Dr. Calgary, AB T0L 1T2
Liam, Anne and Josh
redmittencollective@hotmail.com
www.myspace.com/redmittencollective
All ages promoter in Calgary. We are always looking to book local and touring bands coming through the Calgary area.

SEE Magazine
10275 Jasper Ave. #200, Edmonton, AB T5J 1X8
PH: 780-430-9003 FX: 780-432-1102
info@see.greatwest.ca
www.seemagazine.com
Edmonton's weekly source for news, arts and entertainment.

Waskasoo Bluegrass Music Society
www.waskasoobluegrass.com
Promoting Bluegrass in Red Deer, AB. News, reviews, jams etc.

British Columbia

B.C. Country Music Assoc.
www.bccountry.com
Promotes the BC Country music community.

BC Touring Council
PO Box 547, Nelson, BC V1L 5R3
PH: 250-352-0021 FX: 250-352-0027
fyi@bctouring.org
www.bctouring.org
Expands touring opportunities for artists.

Blues Underground Network
bluesnorth.com
We bring in many great Canadian Blues acts for dances / concerts while helping raise money for young musicians in the Prince George area.

Brand X Media
1219 Pembroke St., Victoria, BC V8T 1J6
Jesse Ladret jesse@brandxmedia.ca
www.brandxmedia.ca
Reviews music predominantly from Western Canada, covering all genres of music.

Bulkley Valley Folk Music Society
www.bvfms.org
Promoting a greater appreciation of Folk music in the Bulkley Valley and Northwestern region of BC.

Cd Isle
1527 Extension Rd. Nanaimo, BC V9X 1A6
PH: 250-754-3170
Ric Lafontaine info@cdisle.ca
www.cdisle.ca
A CD store & archive of artists living on Vancouver Island, the Sunshine Coast and all islands in BC.

Cosmic Debris
PO Box 90, Duncan, BC V9L 3X1
Guy Langlois cosmic@cvnet.net
www.cvnet.net/cosmic
Entertainment magazine covering the local music scene.

Cowichan Folk Guild
www.folkfest.bc.ca
Preserves and promotes local Folk artists.

Gothic BC
www.gothic.bc.ca
British Columbia's Gothic source.

GothVic.com
www.gothvic.com
Covering all things Goth in Victoria.

Hornby Island Blues Society
www.hornby-blues.bc.ca
Connects listeners and players of Blues music.

Kamloops Jazz Society
www.kamloopsjazz.com
Our mission is to bring Jazz to the High Country, through performance, advocacy and education.

KelownaGigs
www.kelownagigs.com
Your local, up to date concert listings.

liquidbeat.com
www.liquidbeat.com
Underground Dance community site catering to the BC interior.

Monday Magazine
818 Broughton, Victoria, BC V8W 1E4
PH: 250-382-6188 x132
Amanda Farrell amandaf@mondaymag.com
web.bcnewsgroup.com/portals/monday
Victoria's weekly entertainment magazine.

MusicBC
www.musicbc.org
Supports and promotes the spirit, development, and growth of the BC music community.

The Nerve Magazine
508-825 Granville St., Vancouver, BC V6Z 1K9
PH: 604-734-1611 FX: 604-684-1698
contact@thenervemagazine.com
www.thenervemagazine.com
The Northwest's Rock n' Roll magazine.

Okanagan Music Online
4140 Hwy. 6, Lumby, BC V0E 2G7
PH: 250 547-2312
tim@okanaganmusic.ca
www.okanaganmusic.com
The largest and most established music website in the Okanagan Valley.

The Pacific Music Industry Assoc.
www.musicbc.org
Supports and promotes the spirit, development and growth of the BC music community.

Pique Newsmagazine
#103-1390, Alpha Lake Rd. Whistler, BC V0N 1B1
PH: 604-938-0202 FX: 604-938-0201
entertainment@piquenewsmagazine.com
www.piquenewsmagazine.com
Alternative weekly. Covers local music.

Rave Victoria
www.ravevictoria.com
Provides DJ sets for download by the community.

Victoria Bluegrass Association
www.victoriabluegrass.ca
Bringing people together for the enjoyment and advancement of Bluegrass music.

Victoria Fiddle Society
www.bckitchenparty.com
A fiddle community for all persons interested in fiddle music in the Victoria region.

Victoria Jazz Society
www.jazzvictoria.ca
Presenting high quality Jazz to the community.

Vancouver

Beyond Robson
beyondrobson.com/music
Blog covering Vancouver arts and entertainment.

City In Tune
Randy Gaudreau randy@cityintune.com
www.cityintune.com
An all-in-one resource dedicated to empowering independent artists and unifying the Vancouver music scene.

Coastal Jazz & Blues Society
www.coastaljazz.ca
Covering the Jazz scene both locally and nationally.

DISCORDER
c/o CITR, #233-6138 SUB Blvd.
Vancouver, BC V6T 1Z1
PH: 604-822-3017 x3
discorder.citr.ca
An indie review magazine published by CITR FM.

Dose Vancouver
www.dose.ca/getout/vancouver.html
A free daily online magazine. One of the key areas of our website is promotion of indie bands.

File Under: Music
#275-167 W. 2nd Ave. Vancouver, BC V5Y 1B8
PH: 604-628-5275 FX: 604-737-3602
info@fileundermusic.com
www.fileundermusic.com
*An artist manager, an independent label, film &
television placement house, a tour manager, a
production house, a merch supplier, a booking
agency, and whatever else we decide we want to be
or need to be for our artists.*

From Blown Speakers
Quinn quinn.omori@gmail.com
itcameoutmagical.blogspot.com
*MP3 blog covering the Vancouver and Pacific NW
music scene.*

Georgia Straight
1701 W. Broadway, Vancouver, BC V6J 1Y3
PH: 604-730-7000 FX: 604-730-7010
www.straight.com
Mag covering the active urban West Coast lifestyle.

Live Music In Vancouver
Kristine Morrison
kristine@livemusicinvancouver.com
www.livemusicinvancouver.com
*The main focus of the website is photos of local
bands.*

LiveMusicVancouver.com
PH: 604-871-0477
Sati Muthanna sati@LiveMusicVancouver.com
livemusicvancouver.com
Covering local music with news, gigs, resources etc.

Open Mic Vancouver
openmicvancouver.com
*A listing of open mics in the Greater Vancouver
area.*

oscillations.ca
comments@oscillations.ca
oscillations.ca
*The source for New Music events and performances
in Vancouver and the surrounding region.*

Rogue Folk Club
www.roguefolk.bc.ca
Vancouver area folk dancing, jam sessions etc.

VanCityBands.com
www.vancitybands.com
Showcasing unsigned Vancouver indie music!

Vancouver Courier
1574 W. 6th Ave. Vancouver, BC V6J 1R2
PH: 604-738-1411
www.vancourier.com
*Vancouver news and entertainment. Covers local
music.*

Vancouver World Music Collective
www.vancouverworldmusic.org
Promoting our music and city internationally.

VancouverBands.com
info@vancouverbands.com
www.vancouverbands.com
Promoting Vancouver's music scene.

vancouverJazz.com
www.vancouverjazz.com
Reviews, news, interviews etc.

Westender
1490 W. Broadway #200, Vancouver, BC V6H 4E8
PH: 604-742-8686
www.westender.com
Vancouver's urban voice. Covers local music.

Western Front Society
303 E. 8th Ave. Vancouver, BC V5T 1S1
PH: 604-876-9343 FX: 604-876-4099
Debbie Boyko newmusic@front.bc.ca
www.front.bc.ca
Produces and promotes contemporary media.

Manitoba

Backstage Winnipeg
500 Carlaw Ave. Winnipeg, MB R3L 0V1
Kristie Allen backstagewinnipeg@yahoo.com
www.backstagewinnipeg.com
*Dedicated to promoting the indie scene. We offer
monthly interviews, show reviews, CD reviews and
more!*

Manitoba Audio Recording Industry Assoc.
www.manitobamusic.com
Helps anyone involved with music in Manitoba.

Manitoba Blues Society
www.mbblues.mb.ca
*Promotes, fosters and supports the Blues in
Manitoba.*

Manitoba Metal
www.myspace.com/manitoba_metal
*Manitoba Metal bands and promoters, send me your
show info, posters etc. and I'll add it to the page.*

Manitoba Old-Tyme & Bluegrass Society
www.manitobabluegrass.ca
All the info on the local Bluegrass scene.

Musicians Network
90 Greensboro Sq. Winnipeg, MB R3T 4L1
Mike Garbutt riffvandal@mts.net
www.bytes4u.ca
*Join a band, form a band, tour, record or jam and
more.*

Uptown Magazine
1465 St. James St., Winnipeg, MB R3H 0W9
PH: 204-949-4370 FX: 204-949 4376
www.uptownmag.com
*Winnipeg's online source for arts, entertainment &
news.*

Winnipeg Classical Guitar Society
www.winnipegclassicalguitarsociety.org
Promoting the Classical guitar in Winnipeg.

Winnipeg Early Music Society
www.winnipegearlymusic.com
Gives members opportunities to perform.

Winnipeg Metal
winnipegmetal.cjb.net
*Online Metal community. Post shows, reviews, news
etc.*

Winnipeg Punk
Starblubber winnipegpunk@gmail.com
www.winnipegpunks.com
*A non profit community driven website that exists to
promote the local music scene.*

Winnipeg Underground
www.myspace.com/thewinnipegunderground
*Your source for news, reviews, interviews and event
listings for the underground scenes in Winnipeg.*

New Brunswick

Argosy
152 Main St., Sackville, NB E4L 1B3
PH: 506-364-2236
William Gregory wpgrgry@mta.ca
argosy.mta.ca
Mount Allison U. independent student journal.

canadaeast.com
www.canadaeast.com
Local music covered in the entertainment section.

giraffecycle.com
www.giraffecycle.com
Dedicated to the Saint John Hardcore music scene.

Maritime Metal
www.discorporatemusic.com/MessageBoard
*A forum is meant exclusively for Maritime Metal
bands.*

monctonlocals.com
admin@monctonlocals.com
www.monctonlocals.com
Covering the local music scene. Post your info!

Music New Brunswick
www.musicnb.org
*Promoting and developing the New Brunswick
music industry.*

Newfoundland

AtlanticCanadianMusic.com
PO Box 847, Mount Pearl, NL A1N 3C8
PH: 709-744-5037 FX: 709-737-0912
atlanticcanadianmusic@gmail.com
www.atlanticcanadianmusic.com
*We offer over 300 titles of music and audio books
from Atlantic Canada.*

**Bluegrass and Oldtime Country Music
Society of NFLD & Labrador**
www.bluegrass-nl.ca
*Fosters the awareness, development and growth of
Bluegrass & Oldtime Country music in the province.*

MUSICNL
www.musicnl.ca
*Provides opportunities for local bands to grow. Our
newsletter, "The Measure" features local artists.*

nflocals.com
Dan Murray admin@nflocals.com
www.nflocals.com
The very best in underground culture.

Nova Scotia

Castlebay Music
PO Box 6266, Marion Bridge, NS B1K 3T8
PH: 902-727-2850
info@castlebaymusic.com
www.castlebaymusic.com
Cape Breton and East Coast music.

cblocals.com
Eli Richards bands@cblocals.com
www.cblocals.com
Covering the Cape Breton underground culture.

Celtic Music Interpretive Centre
www.celticmusicsite.com
*Promoting the traditional music of Cape Breton
Island through education and performance.*

The Coast
5435 Portland Pl. Halifax, NS B3K 6R7
PH: 902-422-6278 FX: 902-425-0013
www.thecoast.ca
Submit info about your event, performance or gig to us.

East Coast Catalogue Company Ltd.
45 Madeira Cr. Dartmouth, NS B2W 6G7
PH: 800-461-3361 FX: 902-492-8770
www.eastcoastcatalogue.com
Mail order retailer of Atlantic Canadian products.

Halifamous Music Forum
2570 Sherwood St., Halifax, NS B3L 3G8
PH: 902-499-4682
Greg Bates greg@halifamous.com
www.halifamous.com
Hip Hop community where you can post music, images, lyrics etc. for evaluation by other members.

halifaxlocals.com
Sean MacGillivray admin@halifaxlocals.com
www.halifaxlocals.com
Connect to the Halifax underground culture.

JazzEast
www.jazzeast.com
Presents live Jazz concerts and workshops.

Music Industry Assoc. of Nova Scotia
www.mians.ca
Promotes the local music industry in Nova Scotia.

Music Nova Scotia
www.musicnovascotia.ca
We'll get you "in the know" regarding the industry mover and shakers and educate you on the business of music.

Rock In Halifax
www.rockinhalifax.net
News, updates, show listings etc.

Saltscapes
saltscapes.com
Regional magazine that occasionally features East Coast artists.

Ontario

Angel Wing Entertainment
Sam Cook sam@angelwingentertainment.com
www.angelwingentertainment.com
We help independent artists get work across Southern Ontario whether it's a festival, wedding, corporate event, private function or club opening.

Barrie Folk Society
www.barriefolk.com
Supports artistic talent, style and creative vision.

BayToday.ca
664 Sherbrooke St., North Bay, ON P1B 2C6
PH: 705-497-9619 FX: 705-497-9671
www.baytoday.ca
North Bay A&E publication. Post your news and events.

Brantford Folk Club
www.brantford.folk.on.ca
Keeping the tradition alive!

Brock Press
Alumni Students' Ctr. 204A, 500 Glenridge Ave.
St. Catharines, ON L2S 3A1
PH: 905-688-5550 x3269 FX: 905-641-7581
www.brockpress.com
Brock U. campus paper.

Bronte Sound Project
2366 Yolanda Dr. Oakville, ON L6L2H8
PH: 905-465-0246
info@brontesound.ca
www.brontesound.ca
Welcome to the home of songwriting in Ontario.

Canada South Blues Society
www.bluessociety.ca
Helping to keep the Blues alive in SW Ontario.

Cuckoo's Nest Folk Club
www.cuckoosnest.folk.on.ca
Promoting traditional Folk music in London.

Dogbus Music
14 Oak St., Lindsay, ON K9V 5K4
dogbus@gmail.com
www.dogbusonline.com
We're always looking for new Punk bands to support and help grow their message.

ECHO Weekly
19 King St. E. 2nd Fl. Kitchener, ON N2G 2K4
PH: 519-220-1594 FX: 519-743-7491
www.echoweekly.com
Weekly alternative magazine covering the greater Kitchener/Waterloo/Cambridge/Guelph area.

Georgian Bay Folk Society
www.summerfolk.org
Promoting Folk music through concerts, dances and Folk clubs.

Grand River Blues Society
www.grandriverblues.org
Encouraging a greater appreciation of the music being created in our community.

Great Lakes Blues Society
www.greatlakesbluessociety.com
Created to unite the Blues community in the London area and give it a central voice.

Haliburton County Folk Society
www.haliburtonfolk.com
Promoting Folk and Acoustic Roots music opportunities.

Hamilton Folk Club
www.hamiltonfolkclub.ca
Hosting regular Folk music evenings for more than 25 years.

The Humm
PO Box 1391, Almonte, ON K0A 1A0
PH: 613-256-5081
Kris Riendeau editor@thehumm.com
www.thehumm.com
We only review CDs that are produced by Ottawa Valley artists. We cover the communities of Perth, Carleton Place, Almonte, Westport, Arnprior, Carp and surrounding areas, but we don't cover Ottawa.

Imprint
Student Life Center, Rm. 1116, U. Waterloo
Waterloo, ON N2L 3G1
PH: 519-888-4048 FX: 519-884-7800
imprint.uwaterloo.ca
U. Waterloo's student paper.

Kingston Blues Society
843 Ludgate Cr. Kingston, ON K7M 6C7
PH: 613-384-8168
www.kingstonbluessociety.ca
Dedicated to the promotion and preservation of local and international Blues artists.

Kingston Jazz Society
www.kingstonjazz.com
Preserving Jazz music in the Limestone City.

London INDIE
www.londonindie.com
We are attempting to re-establish the London scene.

London Jazz Society
londonjazzsociety.ca
Promotes Jazz music by presenting live concerts and jazz radio programs covering local, regional and international jazz related activities.

The London Musicians' Assoc.
www.londonmusicians.com
Benefits include our Booking Referral Service.

London Ontario Rox
930 N. Park Rd. PO Box 33044
Brampton, ON L6S 3Y0
Josie info@londonontariorox.com
www.londonontariorox.com
Advertise your band, post your events.

LondonPunkRock.Kicks-Ass.org
Laurie ljwedge@shaw.ca
londonpunkrock.kicks-ass.org
If you would like to submit photos, add a link, promote a band, a CD or an upcoming gig, get in touch with us.

Loyal Blues Fellowship
www.loyalblues.ca
Created to bring the Blues to the Quinte area on an ongoing basis and to encourage local Blues musicians.

MyGigList.com
Box 1883, London, ON N6A 5J4
PH: 519-670-5066
Cora Linden webmistress@mygiglist.com
www.mygiglist.com
Promoting gigs, artists and venues in Southwestern Ontario... for free!

Niagara Blues & Jazz Society
www.niagarabluesandjazz.com
Enriching lives through a mutual appreciation of Blues and Jazz music and the preservation of its roots.

The Northern Bluegrass Committee
www.northernbluegrass.com
Promoting the local Bluegrass scene.

Northern Blues
225 Sterling Rd. #19, Toronto, ON M6R 2B2
PH: 416-536-4892 FX: 416-536-1494
info@northernblues.com
www.northernblues.com
Bringing you the best in world class Blues.

Ontario Council of Folk Festivals
www.ocff.ca
Website includes a list of upcoming Folk festivals.

Open Mics in Ontario
www.openmikes.org/calendar/ON

Orillia Folk Society
www.geocities.com/liveatjives/ofs1.html
Focus on local contemporary and traditional Folk music.

PartyInKingston.com
www.partyinkingston.com
Submit gig info, album reviews etc.

PeterboroughJams.ca
14-1548 Newlands Cres. Burlington, ON L7M 1V6
musicianlisting@peterboroughjams.ca
www.peterboroughjams.ca
This is your best online source for entertainment, the music scene and nightlife in the Kawarthas.

Pulse Niagra
243 Church St. #208, St. Catharines, ON L2R 3E8
PH: 905-682-5999 FX: 905-682-1414
www.pulseniagara.com
The Niagra region's weekly alternative paper.

Rock Crew Productions
14 Garrett St., Kingston, ON K7L 1H6
PH: 613-539-8438
Bryan Dewar bryan@rockcrew.ca
www.rockcrew.ca
Presenting local, Canadian and international talent in Kingston's premier live venues.

royalcitymusic.ca
info@royalcitymusic.ca
www.royalcitymusic.ca
An online community for artists and fans from a variety of genres in the Guelph area.

Scene Magazine
PO Box 2302, London, ON N6A 4E3
PH: 519-642-4780 FX: 519-642-0737
music@scenemagazine.com
www.scenemagazine.com
London arts & entertainment magazine.

Scotia Entertainment
589 Parkview Cres. Cambridge, ON N3H 4Z9
PH: 519-591-2725
terry@scotiaentertainment.com
www.scotiaentertainment.com
Artist management & bookings, showcase events and event planning.

Shout! London
439 Ferndale Ave. London, ON N6C2Z2
PH: 519-852-8141 FX: 519-936-8852
Shawn shout@shoutlondon.com
www.shoutlondon.com
London, Ontario's FREE source for local arts, indie music, news, lifestyle, events and more! Includes our 24-7 "ALL London artist - All the Time" streaming radio station!

Steel City Music
www.steelcitymusic.ca
Website dedicated to the promotion of the Hamilton, Ontario music scene.

tbshows.com
www.tbshows.com
Covering the Thunder Bay Punk scene.

Thames Valley Bluegrass Assoc.
www.tvba.ca
Dedicated to the preservation and promotion of Acoustic Roots music throughout the SW Ontario region.

Thunder Bay Blues Society
www.thunderbaybluessociety.ca
Supports local, national and international Blues artists.

Traditions Folk Club
www.acoustictraditions.com/folkclub.html
Showcases local performers.

The Underground
1265 Military Trail, Rm. 207, Students Ctr.
Scarborough, ON M1C 1A4
PH: 416-287-7054 FX: 416-287-7055
info@the-underground.ca
the-underground.ca
U of T Scarborough student publication.

Upfront Magazine
325 Chatham St. W., Windsor, ON N9A 5M8
PH: 519-254-5268 FX: 519-254-6110
info@upfrontwindsor.com
www.upfrontwindsor.com
Windsor's independent news, music and art culture magazine.

VIEW Magazine
370 Main St. W., Hamilton, ON L8P 1K3
PH: 905-527-3343 FX: 905-527-3721
www.viewmag.com
Greater Hamilton's weekly alternative.

Wow! Sudbury
info@wowsudbury.com
www.wowsudbury.com
Sudbury's entertainment website. Covers local music.

Ottawa

The Algonquin Times
1385 Woodroffe Ave. Ottawa, ON K2G 1V8
PH: 613-727-4723 x5459
www.myspace.com/sawed_off_half_spic
Algonquin College's campus newspaper. This year select local indie bands will be chosen to be profiled in the entertainment section.

Dark Ottawa
darkottawa@gmail.com
community.livejournal.com/darkottawa
An alternative guide to Canada's capital.

>Dial 6-1-3_
dial613@gmail.com
dial613.blogspot.com
Blog covering the Ottawa music scene.

Dose Ottawa
www.dose.ca/getout/ottawa.html
A free daily online magazine. One of the key areas of our website is promotion of indie bands.

Dummy Cream
Clem Lee dummycream@hotmail.com
myspace.com/dummycream
Local Punk zine full of local events, music reviews, poetry, stories, interviews and just any kind of crap I come up with.

LOCKS - A Guide to Music on the Rideau
PO Box 71, Merrickville, ON K0G 1N0
PH: 613-797-7823
Maren marenscommunications@yahoo.ca
www.rideauguide.blogspot.com
I try to review and point out local bands and concerts with original music to an international tourist/visitor audience.

Music On McLean House Concerts
12 McLean Blvd. Perth, ON K7H 2Z3
PH: 613-267-7902
Steve & Sue Tennant tennants@sympatico.ca
www.perthhouseconcerts.com
Hosts house concerts for artists and bands that are located from, or are touring the Perth/Ottawa Valley area.

National Capital Rock
Andrew Carver andcarver@hotmail.com
www.natcaprock.blogspot.com
I work on the opinion pages and review music for The Ottawa Sun, as well as take photographs at local gigs.

Opus Pocus
www.opuspocus.ca
Covering the Ottawa Classical music scene.

Ottawa Blues Society
www.ottawabluessociety.com
Concert reviews and information on the scene.

Ottawa Chamber Music Society
www.chamberfest.com
Dedicated to presenting Chamber music of the highest possible artistic standard.

Ottawa Hardcore
www.myspace.com/ottawahxc
We are here to help support our music scene and encourage others to do the same.

The Ottawa Musician
www.theottawamusician.com
With continuing support, The OM site has a NEW feature promoting talented artist MP3s from the greater Ottawa area.

Ottawa Valley Bluegrass Music Assoc.
www.valleygrass.ca
Promotes and publicizes Bluegrass music and activities.

Ottawa XPress
309 Cooper St. #401, Ottawa, ON K2P 0G5
PH: 6133-237-8226 FX: 613-237-8220
www.ottawaxpress.ca
Weekly paper. Coverage of local music.

OttawaJazz.com
kgrace@entrenet.com
www.ottawajazz.com
Lists upcoming gigs and special events.

Outaouais Rock
outaouaisrock@hotmail.com
www.outaouaisrock.org
Covering the local Rock, Punk, Metal and Alternative scene.

OverdoseTV
contact@overdosetv.com
www.overdosetv.com
Based in Ottawa-Gatineau region, the members of OverDoseTV dedicate this site to the promotion of local bands.

punkottawa.com
PO Box 57043, 163 Bell St., Ottawa, ON K1R 6P0
PH: 613-234-7869
info@punkottawa.com
www.punkottawa.com
Covers the local Punk scene.

Revolution Rock
revolutionrock@punkottawa.com
www.myspace.com/revolutionrock
Production company specializing in Punk, Rock, Hardcore, Ska, Indie and Experimental...whatever.

Rockin' the Blues from Canada
DD Rocker ddrocker@yahoo.com
rockintthebluesfromcanada.blogspot.com
Blog covering the Ottawa Blues scene.

SKAttawa
skattawa@hotmail.com
www.skattawa.com
Covering the Ottawa Ska scene. News, shows, festivals etc.

Sounds Unlikely
PH: 613-565-1661
sounds.unlikely@gmail.com
www.myspace.com/soundsunlikely
Ottawa's newest independent record shop.

Upfront
PO Box 4389, Stn. E., Ottawa, ON K1S 5B4
PH: 613-321-3353 FX: 740-422-4163
info@upfrontottawa.com
www.upfrontottawa.com
Ottawa's independent news, music, art and culture magazine.

VOIR Ottawa/Gatineau
309 Cooper St. #401, Ottawa, ON K2P 0G5
PH: 613-237-8226 FX: 613-237-8220
www.voir.ca
A&E magazine. In French.

Toronto

The Ambient Ping
2141 Kipling Ave. PO Box 30119
Etobicoke, ON M9W 6T1
info@theambientping.com
www.theambientping.com
Weekly musical performance event. Ambient, Soundscapes, Downtempo etc.

ARRAYMUSIC
60 Atlantic Ave. #218, Toronto, ON M6K 1X9
PH: 416-532-3019 FX: 416-532-9797
info@arraymusic.com
www.arraymusic.com
Site for composers of all levels.

blogTO
info@blogto.com
www.blogto.com/music
Covers Toronto music, film, the arts, bars, restaurants, people, places and more.

Citygigs *Toronto*
toronto@citygigs.com
www.citygigs.com
Reviews, interviews, concert previews and more!

Classic Jazz Society of Toronto
www.classicjazztoronto.com
Promotes the original form of Jazz.

Daughters of Invention
Jaime sin.jaime@gmail.com
daughtersofinvention.blogspot.com
MP3 blog with tracks, news and upcoming shows.

Dose Toronto
1450 Don Mills Rd. Toronto, ON M3B 2X7
info@dose.ca
www.dose.ca/toronto
A free daily online magazine. One of the key areas of our website is promotion of indie bands.

Eye Weekly
625 Church St. 6th Fl. Toronto, ON M4Y 2G1
PH: 416-596-4393
Dave Morris dmorris@eyeweekly.com
www.eye.net
Toronto's A&E weekly. Local music covered.

The Eyeopener
Student Campus Ctr. 55 Gould St. 2nd Fl.
Toronto, ON M5B 1W7
PH: 416-979-5262 x2342
www.theeyeopener.com
Ryerson's independent student newspaper.

Flying Cloud Folk Club
www.flyingcloudfolk.ca
Information about the Toronto Folk music scene.

Guitar Society of Toronto
www.guitar-toronto.on.ca
Promoting the Classical guitar and artists.

IndieEh.com
www.indieeh.com
Weekly features of Toronto bands.

Jazz in Toronto
3 St. Patrick St., Toronto, ON M5T 1T9
PH: 416-599-5486
jazz@jazzintoronto.com
www.jazzintoronto.com
The official guide to Jazz in Toronto.

Maple Blues
www.torontobluessociety.com/maple.htm
Toronto Blues Society's magazine promoting local artists.

Meg-a Music Toronto
Mary-Elizabeth Gilbert
mary@megamusictoronto.com
www.megamusictoronto.com
Whether you are a musician located right here in Toronto or coming to Toronto, I want to know about it. So come on in and lets have some fun!

Music Gallery
www.musicgallery.org
Center for new and unusual music.

New Adventures in Sound Art
401 Richmond St. W. #358, Toronto, ON M5V 3A8
PH: 416-910-7231 FX: 905-454-7662
Nadene naisa@soundtravels.ca
www.soundtravels.ca
Produces performances and installations spanning the entire spectrum of Electroacoustic and Experimental Sound Art.

Nocturnal
info@nocturnalmagazine.net
www.nocturnalmagazine.net
Guide to the music and artists of Toronto.

NOW
189 Church St., Toronto, ON M5B 1Y7
PH: 416-364-1301
music@nowtoronto.com
www.nowtoronto.com
Extensive coverage of local music.

Omy minimag
Spazz omyminimag.com
www.omyminimag.com
Covering the Toronto music scene. News, reviews, articles...

Rotate This
620 Queen St. W., Toronto, ON M6J 1E4
ilovespam@rotate.com
www.rotate.com
One of Toronto's best known independent record stores. We stock new releases from independent bands and artists from around the world.

Skylar Entertainment
www.myspace.com/skylarentertainment
Whether you have an upcoming CD release, a tour to promote or you need to create a buzz about your company or event, we can provide local, regional and national publicity services.

Small World Music
29 Gwynne Ave. Toronto, ON M6K 2C2
PH: 416-536-5439 FX: 416-536-2742
Alan Davis alan@smallworldmusic.com
www.smallworldmusic.com
Created to promote World music activity in Toronto.

Soundproof Magazine
PH: 647-293-4405
Chris Stevenson soundproofmagazine@gmail.com
www.soundproofmagazine.com
Features a mix of artist interviews, features, concert and CD reviews.

Spill
3055 Harold Sheard Dr. Mississauga, ON L4T 1V4
PH: 905-677-8337 FX: 905-677-9705
info@spillmagazine.com
www.spillmagazine.com
Concert listings, show and CD reviews and more.

TOFLO.com
75 Bayly St. W., PO Box 14554, Ajax, ON L1S 7K7
info@toflo.com
www.toflo.com
Your source for Toronto Urban life. News, reviews etc.

Toonage Magazine
PO Box 69014, 12 St. Clair Ave. E.
Toronto, ON M4T 3A1
features@toonage.ca
toonage.ca
Covers everything music, without pretension, whether commercial or independent and regardless of genre.

Toronto Blues Society
www.torontobluessociety.com
Promoting and preserving the Blues.

Toronto Downtown Jazz
82 Bleecker St., Toronto, ON M4X 1L8
PH: 416-928-2033 FX: 416-928-0533
tdjs@tojazz.com
www.torontojazz.com
Our missions is to promote the art of Jazz. Devoted to year round activities and initiatives.

Toronto Early Music Players Organization
www.chass.utoronto.ca/~dresher/TEMPO
Nurtures and encourages all early music.

Toronto-goth.com
tg@toronto-goth.com
www.toronto-goth.com
Resource for Toronto's Gothic/Industrial scene.

Toronto Hip Hop Online
RR #3, Parkhill, ON N0M 2K0
FX: 519-238-1224
Matt Eagleson matt@megacityhiphop.com
www.megacityhiphop.com
Gets exposure for your work. Reviews CDs.

ToRonTo HisPaNo.com
PH: 416-694-1834
info@torontohispano.com
www.torontohispano.com
Covering music in the Toronto Hispanic community.

Toronto Music Scene
1-857 Bloor St. W., Toronto, ON M6G 1M3
TJ Liebgott tj@torontomusicscene.ca
www.torontomusicscene.ca
Interviews, reviews, live show listings and other
music news in Toronto.

Torontoist
torontoist.com
Online A&E zine that covers the local music scene.

Toronto Musicians' Assoc.
www.torontomusicians.org
Our experience and support can help you achieve
your goals.

toronto.com
www.toronto.com
Covers the local music scene.

The Varsity
21 Sussex Ave. Toronto, ON M5S 1J6
PH: 416-946-7600 x205
Jordan Brimm review@thevarsity.ca
www.thevarsity.ca
U. Toronto's student newspaper.

Wavelength
PO Box 86010, 670 Bloor St. W.
Toronto, ON M6G 1L2
booking@wavelengthtoronto.com
www.wavelengthtoronto.com
Underground music from Toronto and beyond.

Word Magazine
4-2880 Queen St. E. #123, Brampton, ON L6S 6H4
PH: 905-799-1630 FX: 905-799-2788
happenings@wordmag.com
www.wordmag.com
Toronto's urban culture magazine.

Prince Edward Island

Alchemy Music
www.alchemymusic.net
PEI's leading music news and discussion website.

The Buzz
PO Box 1945, Charlottetown, PE C1A 7N5
PH: 902-628-1958 FX: 902-628-1953
buzzon@isn.net
www.buzzon.com
What's going on in the lively cultural scene of PEI.

East Coast Music Assoc.
www.ecma.ca
Promote/celebrates music locally and globally.

peilocals.com
admin@peilocals.com
www.peilocals.com
The very best in the PEI underground scene.

Quebec

FOLQUÉBEC
www.folquebec.com
Increases recognition of Québec's Folk music and
dance culture.

Quebec Hardcore
c/o Jeff Lambert
898 Short #2, Sherbrooke, QC J1H 2G2
www.qchc.com
Promoting local bands, labels and organizations.

Quebec Punk Scene
469, boul. Langelier, #3, Québec City, QC G1K 5P3
info@quebecpunkscene.net
www.quebecpunkscene.net
La source #1 de la scène Punk Québécoise.

Rimouski Metal
106 St. Germain E. #16, Rimouski, QC G5L 1A6
www.rimouskimetal.net
News, reviews, gig dates etc.

SOPREF
info@sopref.org
www.sopref.org
Société pour la promotion de la relève musicale de
l'espace francophone.

SubQuebec.com
186 Boul. Indutriel #201
Saint-Eustache, QC J7R 5C2
PH: 450-974-9339
www.subquebec.com
Covering the Hard Music scene in Quebec.

Sur Scene
www.surscene.qc.ca
Quebec music and arts scene.

Thirty Below
1108 rue Dollar, Val-Belair, QC G3K 1W6
FX: 418-847-9815
thirtybelow@trentesouszero.com
www.trentesouszero.com
Quebec traditional and Folk music site.

Trois-Rivieres Metal
584 rue Principale, St-Boniface, QC G0X 2L0
PH: 819-535-3777
info@troisrivieresmetal.com
www.troisrivieresmetal.com
Ce site est une référence Metal pour la région de
Trois-Rivières.

Voir
internet@voir.ca
www.voir.ca
A&E magazine covering Quebec City.

Montreal

33-MTL.com
645 Wellington St. W. #418
Montréal, QC H3C 1T2
PH/FX: 514-990-3160
Benjamin Trottier benjamin@33mag.com
www.33mag.com
Covering the Montreal Urban music scene.

Bandeapart.fm
1400 boul. Rene-Levesque E. 8e etage
Montreal, QC H2L 2M2
PH: 514-597-5909 FX: 514-597-7373
bap@radio-canada.ca
www.bandeapart.fm
Magazine internet sur les musiques Alternatives
francophones.

Hour
355 W. St. Catharine 7th Fl. Montreal, QC H3B 1A5
PH: 514-848-0777 FX: 514-848-9004
info@hour.ca
www.hour.ca
Weekly news. Extensive coverage of local music.

Jazz Montréal
www.jazzmontreal.com
A site devoted to Jazz in Montreal.

Midnight Poutine
midnightpoutine.ca/music
Blog covering the Montreal arts and entertainment
scene.

Montreal Blues Society
C.P. 72010, Bois-des-Filions, QC J6Z 4N9
PH: 514-990-1769
www.bluesmontreal.com
Our mission is to perpetuate, promote, share and
advance Blues music and its culture among our
members in the Montreal region.

Montreal Mirror
465 McGill St. 3rd Fl. Montreal, QC H2Y 4B4
PH: 514-393-1010 FX: 514-393-3173
www.montrealmirror.com
Weekly A&E paper. Covers local music.

Montrealgroove
3750 Cremazie E. #305, Montreal, QC H2B 1A6
PH: 514-727-2737 FX: 514-727-2737
info@montrealgroove.com
www.montrealgroove.com
CD vendor for local Montreal artists.

MontrealMusicScene.com
info@montrealmusicscene.com
www.montrealmusicscene.com
Informing locals about the Montreal music scene.

Voir
internet@voir.ca
www.voir.ca
A&E magazine covering Montreal.

Vu d'ici / Seen From Here
Marie-Chantale Turgeon mcturgeon@gmail.com
www.mcturgeon.com/blog
Blogging about Montreal, music, the arts and pop
culture.

Saskatchewan

The Carillon
377 Main St., Steinbach, MB R5G 1A5
PH: 204-326-3421 FX: 204-326-4860
www.thecarillon.com
U. Regina's student publication.

Planet S Magazine
308-220 3rd Ave. S., Saskatoon, SK S7K 1M1
PH: 306-651-3423 FX: 306-651-3428
www.planetsmag.com
Saskatoon's city magazine. Covers local music.

Regina Jazz Society
www.reginajazz.ca
Our newsletter covers local Jazz events.

Saskatoon Bluegrass Society
www.saskatoonbluegrasssociety.org
Created to promote Bluegrass music and provide a
forum for pickers to get together and jam.

Saskatchewan Country Music Assoc.
www.scma.sk.ca
Promoting Saskatchewan Country music.

Saskatchewan Recording Industry Assoc.
www.saskrecording.ca
The sound recording industries of Saskatchewan.

The Saskatoon Blues Society
www.saskatoonbluessociety.ca
Celebrates Blues music throughout Saskatchewan.

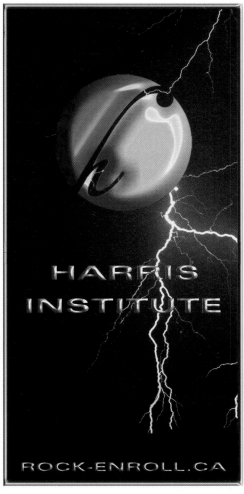

BRYAN FARRISH
RADIO PROMOTION

(310) 998-8305

www.radio-media.com

SECTION THREE: RADIO STATIONS AND SHOWS THAT ARE WILLING TO PLAY INDEPENDENT MUSIC

*Following a DJ's set list is **mandatory**. I find it annoying when someone contacts me asking if I have received their CD, when I have already played them once or twice. It shows me that they would rather bother me than do the work to find out themselves. - **Angela Page, Host of Folk Plus on WJFF Radio***

Promotional Services

United States

Advanced Alternative Media
7 W. 22nd St. 4th Fl. New York, NY 10010
PH: 212-924-3005 FX: 212-929-6305
justin@aaminc.com
www.aampromo.com
The number one choice in independent marketing and college radio promotions nationwide since 1982.

AirPlay Direct
Music Upload Ctr. 200 Corporate Lake Dr.
Columbia, MO 65203-7172
PH: 678-318-1900
www.airplaydirect.com
A cost effective way to securely deliver your music to radio industry professionals across the world.

AirplayAccess
www.airplayaccess.com
The music industry's answer for fast, secure music delivery, enabling registered industry professionals, records labels, artist/bands to get their promotional music directly to radio as broadcast quality digital files.

Backstage Entertainment
2530 Atlantic Ave. Ste. C, Long Beach, CA 90806
PH: 310-325-9997
staff@backstageentertainment.net
www.backstageentertainment.net
A marketing information company which focuses its management abilities throughout all aspects of the music industry.

Bill Wence Promotions
PO Box 39, Nolensville, TN 37135
PH: 615-776-2060 FX: 615-776-2181
www.billwencepromotions.com
Hundreds of singles and albums have been charted for our clients.

Bryan Farrish Radio Promotion
1828 Broadway, 2nd Fl. Santa Monica, CA 90404
PH: 310-998-8305 FX: 310-998-8323
airplay@radio-media.com
www.radio-media.com
Indie airplay promotion to commercial, commercial specialty and college radio stations in the U.S. and Canada.

Casa Bonita Productions
410 E. Center Ave. Maple Shade, NJ 08052
PH: 856-649-3351
Jim Santora info@casabonitaproductions.com
www.casabonitaproductions.com
Provides a radio promotion and distribution service for all genres of music. We also have several promotional CD projects for interested artists. Please e-mail or call prior to submission.

Creativity In Music
PO Box 3481
Bridgeport, CT 06605
Gi Dussault
npsfunk@optonline.net
www.creativityinmusic.com
Radio Promotion of all genres, concert promotion and submission of press releases.

Howard Rosen Promotion
5605 Woodman Ave. #206
Van Nuys, CA 91401
PH: 818-901-1122
FX: 818-901-6513
musicsubmissions@howiewood.com
www.howiewood.com
Since 1985 We have been helping artists reach their goals of obtaining radio airplay, expanding their fan base, and creating awareness throughout the industry.

Jerome Promotions & Marketing
2535 Winthrope Way, Lawrenceville, GA 30044
PH: 770-982-7055 FX: 770-982-1882
Bill Jerome hitcd@bellsouth.net
www.jeromepromotions.com
We call the music directors and program directors of over 250 stations several times a week in order to help our artists get airplay and the recognition that they deserve with the goal of helping them make a deal with a major label.

Jerry Lembo Entertainment Group
742 Bergen Blvd. 2nd Fl. Ridgefield, NJ 07657
PH: 201-840-9980 FX: 201-840-9921
Jerry Lembo jerry@lemboentertainment.com
www.lemboentertainment.com
Specializing in radio promotion, artist management, music publishing and publicity.

7KDM Promotion
4002 SW. Webster St., Seattle, WA 98136
PH: 206-938-6679 FX: 206-938-6379
Kathleen Monahan kdmpromo@mindspring.com
www.mc-kdm.com
We introduce new music and artists to radio stations focusing on Jazz, Blues, World, Celtic, Ambient, Acoustic and Folk programming.

Loggins Promotion
2530 Atlantic Ave. Ste. C, Long Beach, CA 90806
PH: 310-325-2800
promo@logginspromotion.com
www.logginspromotion.com
Most advanced system for tracking radio airplay.

Mediaguide
640 Freedom Business Ctr. #305
King Of Prussia, PA 19406
PH: 610-578-0800
music@mediaguide.com
www.mediaguide.com
Music monitoring company that provides radio airplay information products on nearly 2,500 stations.

MiaMindMusic
259 W. 30th St. #12FR, New York, NY 10001-2809
PH: 212-564-4611 FX: 212-564-4448
MiMiMus@aol.com
www.miamindmusic.com
Radio tracking and working with CMJ and R&R surveyed radio stations.

Nice Promotion
PO Box 352, Portland, OR 97207
PH: 866-475-3820 FX: 503-848-8448
info@nicepromo.com
www.nicepromo.com
Providing college radio promotion to labels and indie musicians alike. Experimental/Indie Electronic, Hip Hop, Alt-Country or Folk.

Pirate! Promotion and Management
145 Columbia St., Cambridge, MA 02139
PH: 617-256-8709
Steve Theo steve@piratepirate.com
www.piratepirate.com
Services college and non-commercial radio stations across North America to gain airplay for our artists.

Planetary Group
PO Box 52116, Boston, MA 02205
PH: 617-451-0444 FX: 617-451-0888
www.planetarygroup.com
Full promotional services as well as targeted radio mailing services.

Powderfinger Promotions
47 Mellen St., Framingham, MA 01702
PH: 800-356-1155 x234
radio@powderfingerpromo.com
www.powderfingerpromo.com
We have solid connections at over 500 college and AAA stations across the U.S. and Canada and hundreds of press contacts.

Radio & Retail Promotions
PH: 323-876-7027
Jon Flanagan promotions@radioandretail.com
www.radioandretail.com
Build a fan base through radio airplay and retail promotion.

RadioSubmit.com
13501 Ranch Rd. 12 #103-327
Wimberley, TX 78676
PH: 866-432-7965
Robert Bartosh rs@radiosubmit.com
www.radiosubmit.com
Allows artists to submit their music directly to radio stations around the world.

RadioWave
radiowavemonitor@radiowavemonitor.com
www.radiowavemonitor.com
A suite of services that will help you to get your music heard by potentially thousands of internet radio listeners.

RAM *(Realtime Airplay Metrics)*
151 W. 25th St. 12th Fl. New York, NY 10001
PH: 917-606-1908 FX: 917-606-1914
ram@cmj.com
www.cmj.com/ram
A revolutionary airplay tracking service.

South Beach Marketing (SBMP)
7332 Erin Ct.
Longmont, CO 80503
PH: 303-952-0249
Amanda Alexandrakis
info@MusicPromotion.com
www.musicpromotion.com
Specializes in the Adult Contemporary radio format.Our expertise has helped many artists attain national radio airplay and has been highly successful in charting our clients on national radio charts. Helping our clients succeed in commercial radio is a top priority. SBMP utilizes our extensive network of individual and label relationships within the music industry to help elevate your project to the next level of promotion. From the established artist on a major label to the indie band, SBMP can work for you.

Space 380
2008 Swindon Ave.
Columbia, MO 65203-8985
PH: 573-446-7221
FX: 309-210-9037
www.space380.com
We develop name recognition for independent artists & labels of ALL genres.

The Syndicate
1801 Willow Ave.
Weehawken, NJ 07086-6614
PH: 201-864-0900
Matt college@thesyn.com
musicsyndicate.com
We work mainly with artists and labels that are completely ready, with all the puzzle-pieces in place.

Tinderbox Music
3148 Bryant Ave. S.
Minneapolis, MN 55408
PH: 612-375-1113
FX: 612-341-3330
Krista Vilinskis
krista@tinderboxmusic.com
www.tinderboxmusic.com
Music promotion and distribution company.

Trakheadz
PO Box 1304
Teaneck, NJ 07666-1304
questionsandcomments@trakheadz.com
www.trakheadz.com
Our patented music distribution system called Direct Digital Distribution (DDD™), allows labels and artists to get their music into the hands of record pools, internet and college radio stations, trade magazines and other music industry professionals.

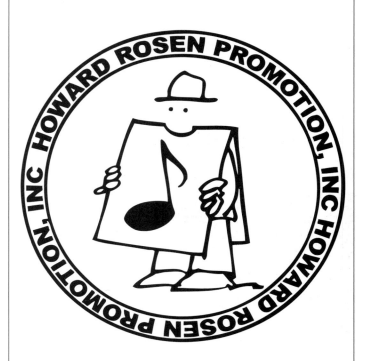

Triplearadio.com
228 Commercial St., Nevada City, CA 95959-2507
PH: 530-477-2224 FX: 530-477-5599
Dave Chaney dave@triplearadio.com
www.triplearadio.com
Helps anyone who will be working their music to Triple A radio.

Twin Vision
261 5ᵗʰ Ave. #1F, Brooklyn, NY 11215
PH: 718-369-1370
Peter Hay TwinVision@aol.com
twinvision.net
Offers radio promotion services to artists and labels with proven strategies that create exposure and awareness with national audiences. We are specialists in working with independently created projects, from artists putting out their own recordings to major independent labels, as well as foreign labels looking for a niche in the American market. For the last seventeen years, Twin Vision has provided promotion services to artists, managers, publishers and labels whose projects required special attention at radio formats that embrace new and emerging artists.

Canada

AM to FM Promotions
56 Empire Ave. Toronto, ON M4M 2L4
PH: 416-469-1314
Andrea Morris andrea.morris@sympatico.ca
www.amtofm.com
While the primary focus of the company is radio promotion, clients have also been provided with international label contacts and tour promotion.

dB Promotions & Publicity
1365 Yonge St. #204
Toronto, ON M4T 2P7
PH: 416 928 3550
FX: 416 928 3401
Dulce Barbosa
info@dbpromotions.ca
www.dbpromotions.ca
National radio promotion and artist publicity.

RadioDirectX
650 Dupont St. #503
Toronto, ON M6G 4B1
PH: 888-746-7234
radio@radiodirectx.com
www.radiodirectx.com
We've focused on developing a service that offers artists the opportunity to gain an international listening audience.

Spincycle Direct
1187 W. 16ᵗʰ Ave. Vancouver, BC V6H 1S8
Geoff Goddard geoff@spincycledirect.com
www.spincycledirect.com
Service provider for artists to securely distribute singles to radio for airplay consideration.

United Kingdom

Matchbox Recordings
Old Road A&R Dept., PO Box 1467,
Oxford, OX3 3BH UK
PH: 01865-741-802
demos@matchboxrecordings.co.uk
www.matchboxrecordings.co.uk
Plugging dept specializes in delivering and plugging new release singles and albums to Alternative DJ's in the U.K.

Stations that Play a Variety of Genres

Most stations listed in the Variety section have weekly shows that cater to every style of music – Pop, Rock, Folk, Jazz, Various Metals, Punk, Goth, Industrial, Electronic, Hip Hop, Country, Blues etc. As one Music Director pointed out, when contacting these stations, it is **crucial** *to add:* **ATTENTION - MUSIC DIRECTOR** *in the Subject: heading of your e-mail, as well as on the* **package** *you mail to the station.*

North America

United States

Alabama

Alabama Public Radio
PO Box 870370, Tuscaloosa, AL 35487-0370
PH: 205-348-6644 FX: 205-348-6648
www.apr.org

WALW
531 Walnut St., Moulton AL 35650
PH: 256-905-4400
cieradio@aol.com
www.walw.org

WBLZ *U. Alabama*
HUC 151, 1530 3ʳᵈ Ave. S.
Birmingham, AL 35294-1150
PH: 205-975-9259 FX: 205-975-9261
www.blazeradio.org

WEGL
116 Foy Union Blvd. Auburn U. AL 36849-5231
PH: 334-844-4113 FX: 334-844-4118
wegl@auburn.edu
wegl.auburn.edu

WLJS *Jacksonville State U.*
700 Pelham Rd. N. Jacksonville, AL 36265
PH: 256-782-5571 FX: 256-782-5645
www.jsu.edu/92j

WVUA *U. Alabama*
PO Box 870152, Tuscaloosa, AL 35487
PH: 205-348-6461
wvuamusic@sa.ua.edu
www.newrock907.com

Alaska

KBBI
3913 Kachemak Way, Homer, AK 99603
PH: 907-235-7721 x227
Paulette Wellington paulette@kbbi.org
www.kbbi.org

KBRW
PO Box 109, Barrow, AK 99723
PH: 907-852-6811
info@kbrw.org
www.kbrw.org

KCAW
2 Lincoln St. Ste. B, Sitka, AK 99835
PH: 907-747-5877 FX: 907-747-5977
www.ravenradio.org

KCHU
PO Box 467, Valdez, AK 99686
PH: 800-478-5080
kchu@cvinternet.net
www.kchu.org

KEUL
PO Box 29, Girdwood, AK 99587
PH: 907-754-2489
radio@glaciercity.us
glaciercity.us

KHNS
PO Box 1109, Haines, AK 99827
PH: 907-76-2020 FX: 907-766-2022
www.khns.org

KMXT
620 Egan Way, Kodiak, AK 99615-6487
PH: 907-486-5698 FX: 907-486-2733
Mike Wall gm@kmxt.org
www.kmxt.org

KRUA *U. Alaska Anchorage*
PSB Rm. 254, 3211 Providence Dr.
Anchorage, AK 99508
PH: 907-786-6802
aykrua9@uaa.alaska.edu
www.myspace.com/krua

KSTK
PO Box 1141, Wrangell, AK 99929
PH: 907-874-2345 FX: 907-874-3293
www.kstk.org

KSUA *U. Alaska Fairbanks*
PO Box 750113, Fairbanks, AK 99775
PH: 907-474-7054 FX: 907-474-6314
ksua.uaf.edu

KTOO
360 Egan Dr. Juneau, AK 99801-1748
PH: 907-586-1670 FX: 907-586-3612
www.ktoo.org

KUHB
PO Box 905, St. Paul, AK 99660
PH: 907-546-2254 FX: 907-546-2367
www.kuhb.org

Arizona

KAMP *U. Arizona*
PO Box 3605, Tucson, AZ 85722
Attn: Music Director
PH: 520-626-4460 FX: 520 626-5986
Matt Ritzel headmd@kamp.arizona.edu
kamp.arizona.edu

KASC *Arizona State U.*
Stauffer Hall A231, Tempe, AZ 85287-1305
PH: 480-965-4163
Becky Bartkowski md@theblaze1260.com
www.theblaze1260.com

KBRP *Radio Free Bisbee*
PO Box 1501, Bisbee, AZ 85603
PH: 520-432-1400
kbrp@kbrp.org
www.kbrpradio.com

KFHX
12645 E. Saguaro Blvd. PO Box 17228
Fountain Hills, AZ 85269
PH: 602-260-1620 FX: 480-837-2820
info@kfhx.org
www.kfhx.com

KJACK *N. Arizona U.*
PO Box 5619, Flagstaff, AZ 86011
PH: 928-523-4554 FX: 928-523-1505
Chuck Garton kjackattack@gmail.com
www.jackcentral.com/kjack

KRIM
HC4 Box 4C, Payson, AZ 85541
PH: 928-468-5746 FX: 928-468-5746
Kit McGuire krimfm@gmail.com
www.krim-fm.com

KWSS
PH: 480-551-1067
radioinfo@kwss1067.com
www.kwss1067.com

KXCI
220 S. 4th Ave. Tucson, AZ 85701
PH: 520-622-5924
www.kxci.org

Arkansas

KABF
2101 S. Main St., Little Rock, AR 72206
PH: 501-372-6119 FX: 501-376-3952
kabf@acorn.org
www.kabfradio.org

KHDX *Hendrix College*
506 Oak St., Conway, AZ
PH: 501-327-8129 FX: 501-327-5073
khdx@hendrix.edu
students.hendrix.edu/orgs/khdx

KUAF *U. Arkansas*
747 W. Dickson St., Fayetteville, AR 72701
PH: 479-575-6574 FX: 479-575-8440
PJ Robowski pjrobows@uark.edu
www.kuaf.com

KXUA *U. Arkansas*
A665 Arkansas Union, Fayetteville, AR 72701
PH: 479-575-5883
charts@uark.edu
www.kxua.com

California

Demolisten *KXLU*
1 LMU Dr. Los Angeles, CA 90045
PH: 310-338-5958 FX: 310-338-5959
demolisten@yahoo.com
www.demolisten.org
Submit your homemade music on cassettes and CDRs. We expose the unexposable.

Free Radio San Diego
PO Box 33430, San Diego, CA 92163-3430
Attn: (name of DJ)
PH: 619-544-0918
www.pirate969.org
Just burn MP3s onto a CD and mail it to whatever DJ you think will care and want to play it.

Free Radio Santa Cruz
PO Box 7507, Santa Cruz, CA 95061
PH: 831-427-3772
frsc@freakradio.org
www.freakradio.org

Indie 103
5700 Wilshire Blvd. #250, Los Angeles, CA 90036
PH: 877-452-1031
feedback@indie1031.fm
indie1031.fm

iRADIO Los Angeles
PO Box 1403, Covina, CA 91722
PH: 818-627-6819
Contact: Mark Maverick
www.iradiola.com
If you would like to submit a song for airplay please go to our website and click on "Submit Music" on the right side. All songs submitted through this means will be added to rotation as long as they follow our terms of airplay.

KALX *U. California Berkeley*
26 Barrows Hall #5650, Berkeley, CA 94720-5650
PH: 510-642-1111
music@kalx.berkeley.edu
kalx.berkeley.edu

KAPU *Azusa Pacific U.*
PO Box 9521, #5168 Azusa, CA 91702
musicdirector@kapuradio.com
kapu.apu.edu

KBeach
1212 Bellflower Blvd. USU #110
Long Beach, CA 90815
PH: 562-985-2282
www.kbeach.org

KCHO *Cal State U.*
Chico 95929-0500
PH: 530-898-5896 FX: 530-898-4348
info@kcho.org
www.kcho.org

KCPR *California Poly State U.*
Graphic Arts Bldg. 26 #201
San Luis Obispo, CA 93407
PH: 805-756-2965
www.kcpr.org

KCR *San Diego College*
5200 Campanile Dr. San Diego, CA 92182
PH: 619-594-7014 FX: 619-594-6092
md.kcr.sdsu@gmail.com
kcr.sdsu.edu

KCRW
1900 Pico Blvd. Santa Monica, CA 90405
PH: 310-450-5183 FX: 310-450-7172
www.kcrw.org

KCSB *U. California*
PO Box 13401, Santa Barbara, CA 93107-3401
PH: 805-893-3757
Maggie Muldoon external.music@kcsb.org
www.kcsb.org

KCSC *Cal State U. Chico*
Chico, CA 95929
PH: 530-898-6229
promo@kcscradio.com
kcscradio.com

KCSN *Cal State U. Northridge*
18111 Nordhoff St., Northridge, CA 91330-8312
PH: 818-677-3090
www.kcsn.org

KCXX
242 E. Airport Dr. #106, San Bernardino, CA 92408
PH: 909-384-1039 FX: 909-888-7302
Bobby Sato programming@x1039.com
www.x1039.com

KDVS *U. California*
14 Lower Freeborn, Davis, CA 95616
PH: 530-752-2777
Jessica & Sean musicdept@kdvs.org
www.kdvs.org

KFCF
PO Box 4364, Fresno, CA 93744
PH: 559-233-2221
rwithers@kfcf.org
www.kfcf.org

KFJC
12345 El Monte Rd. Los Altos Hills, CA 94022
PH: 650-949-7092 FX: 650-948-1085
John Burns music@kfjc.org
www.kfjc.org

KFOK
PO Box 4238, Georgetown, CA 95634
PH: 530-333-4300
4info@kfok.org
www.kfok.org

KFSR *Cal State U. Fresno*
Mail Stop SA #119, 5201 N. Maple
Fresno, CA 93740
PH: 559-278-4082 FX: 559-278-6985
kfsr_musicdirector@yahoo.com
www.csufresno.edu/kfsr

KGFN *Grossmont College*
8800 Grossmont College Dr. El Cajon, CA 92020
PH: 619-644-7287
kgfnfm@yahoo.com
www.grossmont.net/kgfn

KHUM *Humboldt State U.*
PO Box 25, Ferndale, CA 95536
PH: 707-786-5104 FX: 707-786-5100
info@khum.com
www.khum.com

KISL
PO Box 1980, Avalon, CA 90704
PH: 310-510-7469 FX: 310-510-1025
contact@kisl.org
www.kisl.org

KITS *Soundcheck*
865 Battery St. 2nd Fl. San Francisco, CA 94111
PH: 415-478-5483
www.live105.com

KKSM *Palomar College*
1140 W. Mission Rd. San Marcos, CA 92069
PH: 760-744-1150 x2183
www.palomar.edu/kksm

KKUP
933 Monroe St., PMB 9150, Santa Clara, CA 95050
PH: 408-260-2999
webmeister@kkup.org
www.kkup.com

KMUD
PO Box 135, 1144 Redway Dr.
Redway, CA 95560-0135
PH: 707-923-2513 x109 FX: 707-923-2501
kmud.org

KNAB *Chapman U.*
1 University Dr. Orange, CA 92866
PH: 714-516-5622
Lani Nguyen musicdirector@chapmanradio.com
www.ChapmanRadio.com

KOZT
110 S. Franklin St., Fort Bragg, CA 95437
PH: 707-964-7277 FX: 707 964-95FM
thecoast@kozt.com
www.kozt.com

KPCC *Pasadena City College*
1570 E. Colorado Blvd. Pasadena, CA 91106-2003
PH: 626-585-7000
www.kpcc.org

KPFA
1929 MLK Jr. Way Berkeley, CA 94704
PH: 510-848-6767 x219 FX: 510-848-3812
music@kpfa.org
www.kpfa.org

KRBS
PO Box 9, Oroville, CA 95965
PH: 530-534-1200
krbs@cncnet.com
www.radiobirdstreet.org

KRCB
5850 Labath Ave. Rohnert Park, CA 94928
PH: 707-585-8522 FX: 707-585-1363
listener@krcb.org
www.krcb.org/radio

KRFH *Humboldt State U.*
c/o Dept. of Journalism, HSU, Arcata, CA 95521
PH: 707-826-6077
krfh@humboldt.edu
www.humboldt.edu/~krfh

KRSH
3565 Standish Ave. Santa Rosa, CA 95407
PH: 707-588-9999
studio@krsh.com
www.krsh.com

KSAK *Mt. San Antonio College*
1100 N. Grand Ave. Walnut, CA 91789
PH: 909-594-5611 x5725
ksak@mtsac.edu
www.ksak.com

KSCR *U. Southern California*
STU 404, Los Angeles, CA 90089-0895
PH: 213-740-1486
music@kscr.org
kscr.org

KSCU *Santa Clara U.*
SCU 3207, 500 El Camino Real,
Santa Clara, CA 95053
PH: 408-554-4907
music@kscu.org
www.kscu.org

KSDT *U. California San Diego*
9500 Gilman Dr. #0315, La Jolla, CA 92093-0315
PH: 858-534-5738
scw.ucsd.edu

KSFS *San Francisco State U.*
1600 Holloway Ave. San Francisco, CA 94132
PH: 415-338-1532
Francis Basbas diyanggo@hotmail.com
ksfs.sfsu.edu

KSJS *San Jose State U.*
Hugh Gillis Hall #132, San Jose, CA 95192-0094
PH: 408-924-5757 FX: 408-924-4558
ksjs@ksjs.org
www.ksjs.org

KSPB *Stevenson H.S.*
3152 Forest Lake Rd. Pebble Beach, CA 93953
PH: 831-625-5078
www.kspb.org

KSPC *Pomona College*
Thatcher Music Bldg. 340 N. College Ave.
Claremont, CA 91711
PH: 909-621-8157 FX: 909-607-1269
www.kspc.org

KSSU *California State U.*
c/o ASI, 6000 J St., Sacramento, CA 95819
PH: 916-278- 3666 FX: 916-278-6278
music@kssu.com
www.kssu.com

KSUN *Sonoma State U.*
1801 E. Cotati Ave. Rohnert Park, CA 94928
PH: 707-664-2623
Eric Ritz gmksun@yahoo.com
www.sonoma.edu/ksun

KUCI *U. California*
PO Box 4362, Irvine, CA 92616
PH: 949-824-6868
Kyle Olson music@kuci.org
www.kuci.org

KUCR *U. California*
Riverside, CA 92521
PH: 951-827-3838
Walter Douglas walter@kucr.org
www.kucr.org

KUSF *U. San Francisco*
2130 Fulton St., San Francisco, CA 94117
PH: 415-386-5873
kusfmusic@yahoo.com
www.kusf.org

KUSP
203 8th Ave. Santa Cruz, CA 95062
PH: 831-476-2800
Rob Mullen rmullen@kusp.org
kusp.org

Need Gigs?

A new live venue directory from the creators of The Indie Bible!

Tour locally, regionally or nationally!

Our regional guides (featuring 32,000 venues in the US and Canada) will help you to find gigs perfectly suited to your touring needs.

Also includes 3,500 booking agents!

www.indievenuebible.com

KVMR
401 Spring St., Nevada City, CA 95959
PH: 530-265-5531 FX: 530-265-9077
Alice MacAllister music@kvmr.org
www.kvmr.org

KWMR
PO Box 1262, 11431 State Rt. One #8
Point Reyes Station, CA 94956
PH: 415-663-8492
music@kwmr.org
www.kwmr.org

KXLU *Loyola - Marymount U.*
1 LMU Dr. Los Angeles, CA 90045
PH: 310-338-5958 FX: 310-338-5959
Lauren Villa laurenkxlu@gmail.com
www.kxlu.com

KZFR
PO Box 3173, Chico, CA 95927
PH: 530-895-0131 FX: 530-895-0775
www.kzfr.org

KZSC *U. California*
1156 High St., Santa Cruz, CA 95064
PH: 831-459-2811 FX: 831-459-4734
Ben Cruz music@kzsc.org
kzsc.org

KZSU *Stanford U.*
PO Box 20510, Stanford, CA 94309
PH: 650-723-9010 FX: 650-725-5865
Murray Jason music@kzsu.stanford.edu
kzsu.stanford.edu

KZYX
PO Box 1, Philo, CA 95466
PH: 707-895-2324 FX: 707-895-2451
Mary Aigner mary@kzyx.org
www.kzyx.org

Morning Becomes Eclectic *KCRW*
1900 Pico Blvd. Santa Monica, CA 90405
PH: 310-450-5183 FX: 310-450-7172
Nic Harcourt music@kcrw.org
www.kcrw.com/show/mb
*We attempt to mark the next new sound and bring to
the public eye a range of music and artists.*

New Ground *KCRW*
1900 Pico Blvd. Santa Monica, CA 90405
PH: 310-450-5183 FX: 310-450-7172
www.kcrw.com/show/gz
*Host Chris Douridas features the best new music in
current and forthcoming releases.*

The Open Road *KUSP*
203 8th Ave. Santa Cruz, CA 95062
PH: 831-476-2800
kusp@kusp.org
kusp.org
*Weekday show featuring both a variety of genres
and hosts.*

Penguin Radio *Dominican U. California*
50 Acacia Ave. San Rafael, CA 94901
PH: 482-3587
radio@dominican.edu
radio.dominican.edu

Pirate Cat Radio
2781 21st St., San Francisco, CA 94110
PH: 415-341-1199
monkey@piratecatradio.com
www.piratecatradio.com

Play it as it Lays *KUCI*
PO Box 4362, Irvine, CA 92616
PH: 949-824-5824
Sean Boy Walton playit889@yahoo.com
playit.blogspot.com
Indie-Hip-Pop-Rock 'n' Soul.

Proper Social Etiquette *KSCU*
DJ Bardot dj_bardot@hotmail.com
soundinwater.blogspot.com
*Indie, Lounge/Electronica, No Wave, New Wave,
Synthpop and whatever suits my fancy.*

Titan Radio *Cal State U. Fullerton*
PO Box 6868, Fullerton, CA 92834-6868
PH: 714-278-5505 FX: 714-278-5514
Nick Trevino ijustwannamisabehave@msn.com
tir.fullerton.edu

UCLA Radio
118 Kerckhoff Hall, 308 Westwood Plaza
Los Angeles, CA 90024
PH: 310-825-9999
music@UCLAradio.com
www.uclaradio.com

The Unsigned Artist *KFOK*
PO Box 4238, Georgetown, CA 95634
PH: 530-333-4300
Trapper info@kfok.org
www.kfok.org
*A hip music program dedicated to the music of
unsigned artists.*

Western Addition Radio
www.westaddradio.com
Features shows covering a variety of genres.

WPMD *Cerritos College*
11110 Alondra Blvd., Norwalk, CA 90650
PH: 562-860-2451 x2626 FX: 562-467-5005
wpmd@cerritos.edu
www.cerritos.edu/wpmd

Colorado

Castle Rock Radio
210 Fifth St., Ste. A, Castle Rock, CO 80104
PH: 888-321-7234
gary@garydeansmith.com
www.castlerockradio.com
Providing an opportunity for artists to be heard.

etown
207 Canyon #302, Boulder, CO 80302
PH: 303-443-8696 FX: 303-443-4489
Nick & Helen Forster info@etown.org
www.etown.org
*Syndicated show featuring a variety of musical
styles. Live performances and interviews.*

iSAMI
1420 Austin Bluffs Pkwy. PO Box 7150
Colorado Springs, CO 80933-7150
radio.uccs.edu

KAFM
1310 Ute Ave. Grand Junction, CO 81501
PH: 970-241-8801 x5 FX: 970-241-0995
Jon Rizzo pd@kafmradio.org
www.kafmradio.org

KASF *Adams State*
110 Richardson Ave. Alamosa, CO 81102
PH: 719-587-7871
Matthew Clark clarkmm@adams.edu
kasf.asf.adams.edu

KBUT
PO Box 308, Crested Butte, CO 81224
PH: 970-349-5225 x15 FX: 970-349-6440
Chad Reich music@kbut.org
kbut.org

KCSU *Colorado State U.*
Student Ctr. Box 13, Lory Student Ctr.
Fort Collins, CO 80523
PH: 970-491-7611 FX: 970-491-7612
kcsumusic@gmail.com
kcsufm.com

KDNK
PO Box 1388, Carbondale, CO 81623
PH: 970-963-0139 FX: 970-963-0810
Luke Nestler luke@kdnk.org
www.kdnk.org

KDUR *Ft. Lewis College*
1000 Rim Dr. Durango, CO 81301
PH: 970-247-7288
kdur_st1@fortlewis.edu
www.kdur.org

KGNU
4700 Walnut St., Boulder, CO 80301
PH: 303-449-4885
www.kgnu.org

KMSA *Mesa State College*
1100 N. Ave. Grand Junction, CO 81501-3122
PH: 970-248-1718 x1
Jeff Paris froparis@msn.com
www.mesastate.edu/kmsa

KOTO
PO Box 1069, 207 N. Pine St., Telluride, CO 81435
PH: 970-728-4334
Suzanne Cheavens suzanne@koto.org
koto.org

KRCC *Colorado College*
912 N. Weber St., Colorado Springs, CO 80903
PH: 719-473-4801
Jeff Bieri jeff@krcc.org
www.krcc.org

KRCX *Regis U.*
3333 Regis Blvd. Denver, CO 80221
PH: 303-964-5396
krcx@regis.edu
academic.regis.edu/krcx

KSJD
PO Box 970, Cortez, CO 81321
PH: 970-564-0808 FX: 970-564-0434
www.ksjd.org

KSRX *U. Northern Colorado*
928 20th St., Greeley, CO 80639
PH: 970-351-1256 FX: 305-489-8256
uncstudentradio@yahoo.com
www.unco.edu/ksrx

KSUT
PO Box 737, 123 Capote Dr. Ignacio, CO 81137
PH: 970-563-0255 FX: 970-563-0399
www.ksut.org

KTSC *U. Southern Colorado*
2200 Bonforte Blvd. Pueblo, CO 81001
719-549-2820
rev89@colostate-pueblo.edu
www.colostate-pueblo.edu/rev89

KVCU *U. Colorado*
Campus Box 207, Boulder, CO 80309
PH: 303-492-7405 FX: 303-492-1369
Pat Collins pat@radio1190.org
www.radio1190.org

KVDU *U. Denver*
2055 E. Evans Ave. Denver, CO 80208
PH: 303-871-2020
kvdu.du.edu

KVNF
PO Box 1350, Paonia, CO 81428
PH: 970-527-4868 FX: 970-527-4865
kvnf@kvnf.org
www.kvnf.org

KWSB *Western State College*
Taylor Hall, Rm. 111, Gunnison, CO 81230
PH: 970-943-3033
www.myspace.com/kwsb

Connecticut

Offbeat *WPKN*
244 U. Ave. Bridgeport, CT 06604
PH: 203-331-9756
Rich Kaminsky wpkn@wpkn.org
www.wpkn.org
Reviewing sounds and styles that fly just beneath the radar of commercial radio stations.

Upper Room with Joe Kelley
PO Box 3481, Bridgeport, CT 06605
Gi Dussault or Joe Kelley npsfunk@optonline.net
www.upperroomwithjoekelley.com
Interviews, in-house concert series and support of indie artists of all genres. E-mail us before sending a CD.

WACC *Asnuntuck College*
170 Elm St., Enfield, CT 06082
PH: 860-253-9222
waccfm@yahoo.com
www.acc.commnet.edu/WACC

WCNI *Connecticut College*
PO Box 4972, 270 Mohegan Ave.
New London, CT 06320
PH: 860-439-2850 FX: 860-439-2805
www.wcniradio.org

WECS *Eastern Connecticut State U.*
83 Windham St., Willimantic, CT 06226
PH: 860-456-2164
WECS@hotmail.com
www.easternct.edu/depts/wecs

WESU *Wesleyan U.*
Wesleyan Stn. 45 Wyllys Ave.
Middletown, CT 06459
PH: 860-685-7700 FX: 860-704-0608
wesu@wesufm.org
www.wesufm.org

WFCS *Central Connecticut State U.*
1615 Stanley St., New Britain, CT 06050
PH: 860-832-1077 FX: 860-832-3757
WFCS1077@yahoo.com
clubs.ccsu.edu/wfcs

WHUS *U. Connecticut*
Student Union Rm. 412, 2110 Hillside Rd. #3008R
Storrs, CT 06268-3008
PH: 860-429-9487
Hanna Niklewicz whus.musicdirector@gmail.com
whus.org

WNHU *U. New Haven*
300 Boston Post Rd. West Haven, CT 06516
PH: 203-479-8801 FX: 203-931-6055
info@wnhu.net
www.wnhu.net

WPKN
244 U. Ave. Bridgeport, CT 06604
PH: 203-331-9756
wpkn@wpkn.org
www.wpkn.org

WRTC *Trinity College*
300 Summit St., Hartford, CT 06106
PH: 860-297-2450
www.wrtcfm.com

WSIN *Southern Connecticut State U.*
Student Ctr. Rm. 210, 501 Crescent St.
New Haven, CT 06456
PH: 203-392-5353
wsin@southernct.edu
radio.southernct.edu

WVOF *Fairfield U.*
1073 N. Benson Rd. Box R
Fairfield, CT 06430-5195
PH: 203-254-4144 FX: 203-254-4224
Lauren Cesiro wvofmusicdirector3@yahoo.com
www.wvof.org

WWUH *Hartford U.*
200 Bloomfield Ave. West Hartford, CT 06117
PH: 860-768-4701 FX: 860-768-5701
Andy Taylor wwuh@hartford.edu
www.wwuh.org

WXCI *Western Connecticut State U.*
181 White St., Danbury, CT 06811
PH: 203-837-9924
www.myspace.com/wxci

Delaware

WVUD *U. Delaware*
Perkins Student Ctr. Newark, DE 19716
PH: 302-831-2701 FX: 302-831-1399
Bill Russo wvudmusic@gmail.com
www.wvud.org

Florida

Pop Garden Radio *WMEL*
PO Box 560351, Rockledge, FL 32956-0351
Adam Waltemire adam@popgardenradio.com
www.PopGardenRadio.com
5 hours of great Pop music from all ends of the genre.

WBUL *U. South Florida*
4202 E. Fowler Ave. CTR 2487, Tampa, FL 33620
PH: 813-974-3285
wbul_md@yahoo.com
wbul.usf.edu

WFCF *Flagler College*
PO Box 1027, St. Augustine, FL 32085-1027
PH: 904-829-6940
wfcf@flagler.edu
www.flagler.edu/news_events/wfcf.html

WGKN *U. Central Florida*
PO Box 161344, Orlando, FL 32816-1344
PH: 407-823-4151 FX: 407-823-6360
Matt Spikes wgknmusic@yahoo.com
wnsc.ucf.edu

WIKD *Embry-Riddle Aeronautical U.*
SGA Office, 600 S. Clyde Morris Blvd.
Daytona Beach, FL 32114
PH: 386-226-6272 FX: 386-226-6083
www.eaglesfm.com

WKNT *U. Central Florida*
PO Box 163230, Orlando, FL 32816
PH: 407-823-4584 FX: 407-823-5899
Carmen Serrano carmen@knightcast.org
www.knightcast.org

WMNF *Tampa College*
1210 E. MLK Blvd. Tampa, FL 33603-4449
Attn: Music Director <your genre>
PH: 813-238-9663 FX: 813-238-1802
Lee Courtney "Flee" flee@wmnf.org
www.wmnf.org

WNSU *Nova Southeastern U.*
3301 College Ave. Ft. Lauderdale, FL 33314
PH: 954-262-8457 FX: 954-262-3928
wnsu@nova.edu
www.nova.edu/radiox

WOSP *U. North Florida*
4567 St. John's Bluff Rd. S., Jacksonville, FL 32224
PH: 904-620-2908 FX: 904-620-1560
www.unf.edu/groups/wosp

WOWL *Florida Atlantic U.*
777 Glades Rd. U. Ctr. #207D
Boca Raton, FL 33431
PH: 561-297-2842 FX: 561-297-3771
wowl@fau.edu
wowl.fau.edu

WPBZ *Smith College*
701 Northpointe Pkwy. #500
West Palm Beach, FL 33407
PH: 561-616-4600
www.buzz103.com

WPRK *Rollins College*
1000 Holt Ave. 2745, Winter Park, FL 32789
PH: 407-646-2915 FX: 407-646-1560
wprkfm@rollins.edu
www.rollins.edu/wprk

WRGP *Florida International U.*
11200 SW. 8th St., U. Park, GC 319
Miami, FL 33199
PH: 305-348-3575 FX: 305-348-6665
Ashley Russell wrgpmusic@gmail.com
wrgp.fiu.edu

WSLR
PO Box 2540, Sarasota, FL 34230
PH: 941-894-6469
info@wslr.org
www.wslr.org

WVFS *Florida State U.*
420 Diffenbaugh Bldg. Tallahassee, FL 32306-1550
music@wvfs.fsu.edu
www.wvfs.fsu.edu

WVUM *U. Miami*
PO Box 248191, Coral Gables, FL 33124
PH: 305-284-3131 FX: 305-284-3132
music@wvum.org
wvum.org

Georgia

Just Off the Radar *WUGA*
U. Georgia, 1197 S. Lumpkin St., Athens, GA 30602
PH: 706-542-9842 FX: 706-542-6718
Joe Silva justofftheradar@yahoo.com
justofftheradar.com
*The best of Folk to Techno and everything in
between.*

SCAD Radio *Savannah College of
Art and Design*
Student Media Ctr. PO Box 3146
Savannah, GA 31402
PH: 912-525-5541 FX: 912-525-5509
radiomd@scad.edu
www.scadradio.org

WMRE *Emory U.*
PO Drawer AG, Atlanta, GA 30322
PH: 404-727-9673 FX: 404-712-8000
Corey Licht execstaff@learnlink.emory.edu
www.students.emory.edu/WMRE

WRAS *Georgia State U.*
PO Box 4048, Atlanta, GA 30302-4048
PH: 404-413-9727
www.wras.org

WREK *Georgia Tech*
350 Ferst Dr. NW. #2224, Atlanta, GA 30332-0630
PH: 404-894-2468 FX: 404-894-6872
music.director@wrek.org
www.wrek.org

WRFG
1083 Austin Ave. NE, Atlanta, GA 30307-1940
PH: 404-523-8989
info@wrfg.org
www.wrfg.org

WUOG *U. Georgia*
Box 2065 Tate Student Ctr. Athens, GA 30602
PH: 706-542-8466 FX: 706-542-0070
info@wuog.org
wuog.org

WVVS *Valdosta State U.*
2ⁿᵈ Fl. University Union, 1500 N. Patterson St.
Valdosta, GA 31698
PH: 229-333-7314
www.valdosta.edu/wvvs

WWGC *West Georgia U.*
1600 Maple St., Carrollton, GA 30118
PH: 770-836-6500
wwgc@westga.edu
www.westga.edu/~wwgc

Hawaii

KKCR
PO Box 825, Hanalei, HI 96714
PH: 808-826-7771
Ken Jannelli ken@kkcr.org
www.kkcr.org

KTUH *U. Hawaii*
2445 Campus Rd. Hemenway Hall #203
Honolulu, HI 96822
PH: 808-956-7261 FX: 808-956-5271
music@ktuh.org
ktuh.hawaii.edu

Idaho

KRFP
#201-116 E. 3ʳᵈ St., Moscow, ID 83843
PH: 208-892-9200
info@radiofreemoscow.com
www.radiofreemoscow.com

KISU *Idaho State U.*
Campus Box 8014, Pocatello, ID 83209
PH: 208-282-5939
www.kisu.org

KUOI *U. Idaho*
3ʳᵈ Fl. Student Union Bldg. Campus Box 444272
Moscow, ID 83844-4272
PH: 208-885-6433 FX: 208-885-2222
kuoi@uidaho.edu
kuoi.asui.uidaho.edu

Illinois

Jstreet Radio
PO Box 126, Waukegan, IL 60079
PH: 847-546-9757
radio@jstreetzine.com
www.jstreetzine.com/radio
*Spinning independent music, on-air interviews and
more!*

The Perfect Face for Radio *WLUW*
6525 N. Sheridan Rd. Chicago, IL 60626
PH: 773-508-9589 FX: 773-508-8082
Nicole mcnicole@gmail.com
www.theperfectfaceforradio.com
Music and interviews. The best in Indie Rock.

SHINE.fm *Olivet Nazarene U.*
1 University Ave. Bourbonnais, IL 60914-2345
PH: 800-987-9668 FX: 815-939-5087
shine@olivet.edu
www.shine.fm

UIC Radio *U. Illinois Chicago*
750 S. Halsted, Rm. 386, 118 M/C
Chicago, IL 60607
PH: 312-413-2191
uicradio@uic.edu
uicradio.pages.uic.edu

WCSF *U. St. Francis*
500 N. Wilcox St., Joliet, IL 60435
PH: 815-740-3217
webmaster@stfrancis.edu
www.stfrancis.edu/theedge
Rock/Alternative format.

WCRX *Columbia College*
600 S. Michigan Ave. Chicago, IL 60605
Attn: Virginia Lozano
PH: 312-663-1693 FX: 312-344-8007
www.colum.edu/crx/snoble

WDBX
224 N. Washington St., Carbondale, IL 62901
PH: 618-457-3691 FX: 618-529-5900
Brian Powell wdbx@globaleyes.net
www.wdbx.org

WEFT
113 N. Market St., Champaign, IL 61820
PH: 217-359-9338
music@weft.org
www.weft.org

WEIU *Eastern Illinois U.*
PH: 217-581-6954
Jeff Owens jeff@weiu.net
hitmix@weiu.net
www.weiufm.org

WESN *Illinois Wesleyan U.*
PO Box 2900, Bloomington, IL 61701
PH: 309-556-2949 FX: 309-556-2949
Jeff Curran jcurran@iwu.edu
www.wesn.org

WHPK *U. Chicago*
5706 S. U. Ave. Chicago, IL 60637
PH: 773-702-8424 FX: 773-834-1488
whpk-pd@uchicago.edu
whpk.uchicago.edu

WIDB *Southern Illinois U.*
Mailcode 4428, Carbondale, IL 62901
PH: 618-536-2361
Travis Past pd@widb.net
www.widb.net

WIIT *Illinois Inst. Tech*
3300 S. Federal St., Chicago, IL 60616
PH: 312-567-3088 FX: 312-567-7042
md.wiit@iit.edu
radio.iit.edu

WIUS *Indiana U.*
326 Sallee Hall, Macomb, IL 61455
PH: 309-298-3218
www.wiu.edu/thedog

WJMU *Millikin U.*
1184 W. Main St., Decatur, IL 62522
PH: 217-424-6377
wjmu@mail.millikin
www.millikin.edu/wjmu

WLTL *Lyons Township H.S.*
100 S. Brainard Ave. La Grange, IL 60525
PH: 708-482-9585 FX: 708-482-7051
www.wltl.net

WLUW *Loyola U.*
6525 N. Sheridan Rd. Chicago, IL 60626
PH: 773-508-9589 FX: 773-508-8082
musicdept@wluw.org
www.wluw.org

WMCR *Monmouth College*
700 E. Broadway Monmouth, IL 61462
PH: 309-457-3060 FX: 309-457-2141
department.monm.edu/wmcr

WNTH *New Trier H.S.*
385 Winnetka Ave. Winnetka, IL 60093
PH: 847-501-6457
wnth@newtrier.k12.il.us
www.wnth.org

WNUR *Northwestern U.*
1920 Campus Dr. Evanston, IL 60208-2280
PH: 847-491-7102 FX: 847-467-2058
rock-md@wnur.org
www.wnur.org

WONC *North Central College*
30 N. Brainard St., Naperville, IL 60540-4690
PH: 630-637-5965 x1 FX: 630-637-5900
Nick Devlin feedback@wonc.org
www.wonc.org

WPCD *Parkland College*
2400 W. Bradley Ave. Champaign, IL 61821
PH: 217-373-3790
www.parkland.edu/wpcd

WQNA *Springfield*
2201 Toronto Rd. Springfield, IL 62712
PH: 217-529-5431 x164 FX: 217-529-7861
www.wqna.org

WQUB *Quincy U.*
1800 College Ave., Quincy, IL 62301-2699
PH: 217-228-5410
Mick Freeman mick@wqub.org
www.wqub.org

WRDP *DePaul U.*
2250 N. Sheffield Ave. #317, Box #640
Chicago, IL 60614
PH: 773-325-7341 FX: 773-325-7399
radiodepaulmusicdirector@gmail.com
radio.depaul.edu

WRRG *Triton College*
2000 5th Ave., River Grove, IL 60171
PH: 708-583-3110
info@wrrg.org
www.wrrg.org

WRSE *Elmhurst College*
190 Propect Ave. Elmhurst, IL 60126
PH: 630-617-5683
webmaster@wrse.com
www.wrse.com

WSIE *S. Illinois U.*
0141 Dunham Hall, Box 1773
Edwardsville, IL 62026
PH: 618-650-2228
www.siue.edu/WSIE

WVJC *Wabash Valley College*
2200 College Dr. Mount Carmel, IL 62863
PH: 618-262-8989 FX: 618-262-7317
Glenda Raber raberg@iecc.edu
www.iecc.cc.il.us/wvjc

WVKC *Knox College*
PO Box K-254 2 E. S. St., Galesburg, IL 61401
PH: 309-341-7441
mimielsk@knox.edu
deptorg.knox.edu/wvkc

WXAV *St. Xavier U.*
3700 W. 103rd St., Chicago, IL 60655
PH: 773-298-3386 FX: 773-298-3381
wxavmusic@yahoo.com
web.sxu.edu/wxav

WZND *Illinois State U.*
007 Fell Hall, Normal, IL 61790-4481
PH: 309-438-5490 FX: 309-438-2652
z106music@hotmail.com
www.wznd.com

WZRD *Northeastern Illinois U.*
5500 N. St. Louis Ave. Chicago, IL 60625-4699
PH: 773-442-4578 FX: 773-442-4665
wzrd.promotions@gmail.com
www.myspace.com/wzrd

Indiana

City of Music Radio Hour
7399 N. Shadeland Ave. #284
Indianapolis, IN 46250
PH: 317-471-3333
information@cityofmusic.com
www.cityofmusic.com
Searching the world for the best new music!

WBAA *Purdue U.*
712 3rd St., W. Lafayette, IN 47907-2005
PH: 765-494-5920
wbaa@wbaa.org
www.purdue.edu/wbaa

WBDG *Ben Davis H.S.*
1200 N. Girls School Rd. Indianapolis, IN 46214
PH: 317-244-9234 FX: 317-243-5506
www.wayne.k12.in.us/bdwbdg

WBKE *Manchester College*
MC Box 19, North Manchester, IN 46962
PH: 260-982-5272 FX: 260-982-5043
Chris Greenwood WBKEmusic@gmail.com
wbke.manchester.edu

WCCR *Purdue U.*
Box M, 1016 W. Stadium Ave.
West Lafayette, IN 47906-4243
PH: 765-494-9773
wccr@expert.ics.purdue.edu
purdue.edu/wccr

WCRD *Ball State U.*
BC 132, Muncie, IN 47306
PH: 765-285-2473
George McKibben gsmckibben@bsu.edu
wcrd.net

WECI *Earlham College*
801 National Rd. W. Dr. 45, Richmond, IN 47374
PH: 765-983-1246 FX: 765-983-1641
www.weciradio.org

WFHB
PO Box 1973, Bloomington, IN 47402
PH: 812-323-1200 FX: 812-323-0320
ionman@wfhb.org
www.wfhb.org

WGCS *Goshen College*
1700 S. Main St., Goshen, IN 46526
PH: 574-535-7488 FX: 574-535-7293
globe@goshen.edu
www.goshen.edu/wgcs

WGRE *DePauw U.*
609 Locust St., Greencastle, IN 46135
PH: 765-658-4637
www.depauw.edu/univ/wgre

WISU *Indiana State U.*
217 Dreiser, Terre Haute, IN 47809
PH: 812-237-FM90 FX: 812-237-8970
Dave Sabaini MrRadio@indstate.edu
wisu.indstate.edu

WMHD *Rose-Hulman Inst. Tech*
5500 Wabash Ave. Terre Haute, IN 47803
PH: 812-877-8350
Stephen Dupal musicdir@wmhdradio.org
wmhdradio.org

WNDY *Wabash College*
301 W. Wabash Ave. Crawfordsville, IN 47933
PH: 765-361-6038
Homer Twigg twiggh@wabash.edu
www.wabash.edu/orgs/wndy

WPUM *St. Joseph's College*
US Hwy. 231, PO Box 870, Rensselaer, IN 47978
PH: 219-866-6000 x6905
wpum@saintjoe.edu
www.saintjoe.edu/~wpum

WQHU *Huntington College*
2303 College Ave. Huntington, IN 46750
www.wqhu.net

WUEV *U. Evansville*
1800 Lincoln Ave. Evansville, IN 47722
PH: 812-479-2020 FX: 812-479-2320
wuevfm@evansville.edu
wuev.evansville.edu

WVFI *U. Notre Dame*
200 LaFortune Hall, Notre Dame, IN 46556
PH: 574-631-6400
wvfi@nd.edu
www.nd.edu/~wvfi

WVUR *Valparaiso U.*
32 Schnabel Hall, 1809 Chapel Dr.
Valparaiso, IN 46383
PH: 219-464-6683
www.valpo.edu/student/wvur

Iowa

KALA *St. Ambrose U.*
518 W. Locust St., Davenport, IA 52803
PH: 563-333-6216 FX: 563-333-6218
kala@sau.edu
sau.edu/kala

KBVU *Buena Vista U.*
610 W. 4th St., Storm Lake, IA 50588
PH: 712-749-1234 FX: 712-749-2037
Scott Beck becksco@bvu.edu
edge.bvu.edu

KDPS *Grand View College*
1200 Grandview Ave. Des Moines, IA 50309
PH: 515-263-2985
kdpsradio@gvc.edu
www.kdpsradio.com

KDRA *Drake U.*
9 Meredith Hall, Des Moines, IA 50311
PH: 515-271-2766 FX: 515-271-2798
Cody Gough csg003@drake.edu
www.drakebroadcasting.com

KICB *Iowa Central College*
330 Ave. M, Fort Dodge, IA 50501
PH: 515-576-0099 ext. 2353
www.iccc.cc.ia.us/kicb

KMSC *Morningside College*
1501 Morningside Ave. Sioux City, IA 51106
PH: 712-274-5331
Libby Green kmscmusic@morningside.edu
webs.morningside.edu/masscomm/KMSC

KRNL *Cornell College*
810 Commons Cir. Mount Vernon, IA 52314
PH: 319-895-5765
www.cornellcollege.edu/krnl

KRUI *U. Iowa*
379 IMU, Iowa City, IA 52242
PH: 319-335-7215 FX: 319-335-9526
krui.music@gmail.com
kruiradio.org

KULT *U. Northern Iowa*
L045 Maucker Union, Cedar Falls, IA 50614
PH: 319-372-5858
kult@uni.edu
www.uni.edu/kult

KURE *Iowa State U.*
1199 Friley Hall, Ames, IA 50012
PH: 515-294-9292 FX: 515-294-4332
Neal Buchmeyer music@kure885.org
www.kure885.org

KWAR
100 Wartburg Blvd. Waverly, IA 50677
PH: 319-352-8306
music@kwar.org
www.kwar.org

KWLC *Luther College*
700 College Dr. Decorah, IA 52101-1045
PH: 563-387-1571 FX: 563-387-2158
kwlcam@luther.edu
kwlc.luther.edu

KZOW *Waldorf College*
106 S. 6th St., Forest City, IA 50436
PH: 515-923-3210
www.kzowfm.com

Kansas

KBCU *Bethel College*
PO Box 88, North Newton, KS 67117
PH: 316-284-5228
kbcu@bethelks.edu
www.bethelks.edu/KBCU

KFHS *Fort Hays State U.*
600 Park St., Hays, KS 67601
PH: 785-628-4198
kfhs@fhsu.edu
www.fhsu.edu/int/kfhsradio

KJAG
624 Sonora Dr. McPherson, KS 67460
PH: 620-960-4929
airplay@kjagradio.com
www.kjagradio.com

KJHK *U. Kansas*
1301 Jayhawk Blvd. Kansas Union, Rm. 427
Lawrence, KS 66045
PH: 785-864-5483
Nick Spacek kjhkmusic@ku.edu
kjhk.org

KSDB *Kansas State U.*
105 Kedzie Hall, Manhattan, KS 66506-1501
PH: 785-532-0919
radio@ksu.edu
wildcatradio.ksu.edu

Kentucky

WFPK
619 S. 4th St., Louisville, KY 40202
PH: 502-814-6500
studio@wfpk.org
www.wfpk.org

WMMT
91 Madison St., Whitesburg, KY 41858
PH: 606-633-1208
wmmtfm@appalshop.org
www.appalshop.org/wmmt

WRFL *U. Kentucky*
777 U. Stn. Lexington, KY 40506-0025
PH: 859-257-4636 FX: 859-323-1039
www.wrfl.fm

WWHR *Western Kentucky U.*
College Heights, 1 Big Red Way
Bowling Green, KY 42101
PH: 270-745-5350
Justin Pitt music@revolution.fm
www.wku.edu/revolution917

Louisiana

KGRM *Grambling U.*
Dunbar Hall, Rm. 220, PO Box K
Grambling, LA 71245
PH: 318-274-6343 FX: 318-274-3245
Joyce Evans evansjb@gram.edu
www.gram.edu/kgrm

KLPI *Louisiana Tech*
PO Box 8638, Tech Stn. Ruston, LA 71272
PH: 318-257-4851 FX: 318-257-5073
general@891klpi.org
www.latech.edu/tech/orgs/klpi

KLSP *Louisiana State Penitentiary*
Angola, LA 70712
www.corrections.state.la.us/LSP/KLSP.htm
The only licensed radio station to operate from within a prison by inmate DJs.

KLSU *Louisiana State U.*
B-39 Hodges Hall, Baton Rouge, LA 70803
PH: 225-578-4038 FX: 225-578-1698
Randy Faucheux music.director@klsu.fm
www.klsu.fm

KSCL *Centenary College*
2911 Centenary Blvd. Shreveport, LA 71104
PH: 318-869-5296
Tyler Davis TDavis@centenary.edu
www.kscl.fm

KSLU *Southern Louisiana U.*
D. Vickers Rm. 112, SLU 10783
Hammond, LA 70402
PH: 985-549-5758 FX: 985-549-3960
kslu@selu.edu
www.selu.edu/kslu

WTUL
Tulane U. Ctr., New Orleans, LA 70118
PH: 504-865-5885 FX: 504-463-1023
Rob Rioux md1@wtul.fm
www.wtul.fm

Maine

WBOR *Bowdoin College*
Smith Union, Brunswick, ME 04011
PH: 207-725-3210
Mark Nason mark@nescom.edu
studorgs.bowdoin.edu/wbor

WERU
PO Box 170, 1186 Acadia Hwy.
East Orland, ME 04431
PH: 207-469-6600 FX: 207-469-8961
info@weru.org
www.weru.org

WHSN *Husson College*
1 College Cir. Bangor, ME 04401
PH: 207-941-7116 FX: 207-947-3987
whsn@nescom.edu
www.whsn-fm.com

WMEB *U. Maine*
5748 Memorial Union, Orono, ME 04469-5748
PH: 207-588-2333 FX: 207-581-4343
www.umaine.edu/wmeb

WMHB *Colby College*
4000 Mayflower Hill, Waterville, ME 04901
PH: 207-872-3686
info@wmhb.org
www.colby.edu/wmhb

WMPG *U. Southern Maine*
96 Falmouth St., Portland, ME 04104-9300
PH: 207-780-4976
Ron Raymond musicdepartment@wmpg.org
www.wmpg.org

WRBC *Bates College*
Lewiston, ME 04240
PH: 207-777-7532 FX: 207-795-8793
Bill Morse lmorse@gwi.net
www.bates.edu/people/orgs/wrbc

WUMF *U. Maine*
111 South St., Farmington, ME 04938
PH: 207-777-7353 FX: 207-778-7113
Kelly Basley wumf@umf.maine.edu
wumf.umf.maine.edu

WUPI *U. Maine Presque Isle*
PO Box 525, 181 Main St., Presque Isle, ME 04769
PH: 207-768-9742
www.umpi.maine.edu/~wupi

Maryland

WFWM *Frostburg State U.*
Frostburg, MD 21532
PH: 301-687-7096
wfwm@frostburg.edu
www.wfwm.org

WMBC *U. Maryland*
U. Ctr. 101, 1000 Hilltop Cir. Baltimore, MD 21250
PH: 410-455-26582 FX: 410-455-3067
Chris Pierce indie@wmbc.umbc.edu
wmbc.umbc.edu

WMUC *U. Maryland*
3130 S. Campus Dining Hall
College Park, MD 20742-8431
PH: 301-314-7868
Rohan Mahadevan rorawks@umd.edu
www.wmuc.umd.edu

WXSU *Salisbury U.*
PO Box 3151 Salisbury, MD 21801
PH: 410-548-4760
wxsu@salisbury.edu
orgs.salisbury.edu/wxsu

XTSR *Towson U.*
8000 York Rd. Media Ctr. Rm. 005,
Towson, MD 21252
PH: 410-704-5309
xtsr@hotmail.com
wwwnew.towson.edu/xtsr
Towson's commercial free Rock station.

Massachusetts

Local Music Café *mvy Radio*
PO Box 1148. Tisbury, MA 02568
Alison Hammond alisonh@mvyradio.com
www.mvyradio.com/local_musicafe
The mighty acorn of radio shows. Introducing you to today's grassroots artists who will be tomorrow's towering oaks.

Three Ring Circus *WMBR*
3 Ames St., Cambridge, MA 02142
PH: 617-253-8810
Joan Hathaway circus@wmbr.org
www.audioe.com/circus
Roots Rock, Indie Rock, Blues, Garage, Surf/instro and all the billies (Rocka, Hill and Psycho).

WAMH *Amherst College*
AC #1907 Campus Ctr. Amherst, MA 01002-5000
PH: 413-542-2288
wamh@amherst.edu
wamh.amherst.edu

WBIM *Bridgewater College*
109 Campus Ctr. Bridgewater, MA 02325
PH: 508-531-1303 FX: 508-531-1786
Tim Marciano wbimmd@hotmail.com
www.bridgew.edu/wbim

WBRS *Brandeis U.*
Shapiro Campus Ctr. 415 South St.
Waltham, MA 02453-2728
Attn: (genre)
PH: 781-736-4786
music@wbrs.org
www.wbrs.org

WBTY *Bentley College*
175 Forest St., Waltham, MA 02452
PH: 781-891- 3473
wbtyinfo@bentley.edu
www.wbty.com

WCFM *Williams College*
Baxter Hall, Williamstown, MA 01267
PH: 413-597-2373 FX: 413-597-2259
wcfmbd@wso.williams.edu
wcfm.williams.edu

WCHC *College of the Holy Cross*
1 College St., Worcester, MA 01610
PH: 508-793-2474
wchc@holycross.edu
college.holycross.edu/wchc

WCUW
910 Main St., Worcester, MA 01610
PH: 508-753-2274
www.wcuw.com

WDOA
128 Mechanic St., Spencer, MA 01562
FX: 253-323-1606
wdoainfo@wdoa.com
www.wdoa.com

WERS *Emerson College*
120 Boylston St., Boston, MA 02116
PH: 617-824-8891
Sam Citron music@wers.org
www.wers.org

WHHB *Holliston H.S.*
370 Hollis St., Holliston, MA 01746
PH: 508-429-0681
ProgramDirector@whhbfm.com
www.whhbfm.com

WIQH
500 Walden St., Concord, MA 01742
PH: 978-369-2440
Dan Babai wiqh@colonial.net
www.colonial.net/wiqh

WMBR *Mass Inst. Technology*
3 Ames St., Cambridge, MA 02142
PH: 617-253-7777
music@wmbr.org
wmbr.mit.edu

WMFO *Tufts U.*
PO Box 65, Medford, MA 02155
PH: 617-627-3800
Sam Obey md@wmfo.org
www.wmfo.org

WMHC *Mt. Holyoke College*
Blanchard Student Ctr. South Hadley, MA 01705
PH: 413-538-2044 FX: 413-538-2431
Megan Chen chen20m@mtholyoke.edu
www.mtholyoke.edu/org/wmhc

WMUA *U. Massachusetts*
105 Campus Ctr. Amherst, MA 01003
PH: 413-545-3691 FX: 413-545-0682
Erika Patsy music@wmua.org
wmua.org

WMWM *Salem State College*
352 Lafayette St., Salem, MA 01970-5353
PH: 978-745-9170
wmwmsalem@gmail.com
www.wmwmsalem.com

WOMR
494 Commercial St., Provincetown, MA 02657
PH: 508-487-2619
www.womr.org

WOZQ
Campus Ctr. Northampton, MA 01063
PH: 413-585-4977
sophia.smith.edu/org/wozq

WPAA *Phillips Academy*
180 Main St., Andover, MA 01810
PH: 978-749-4384
WPAA@aol.com
users.aol.com/wpaa

WRBB *Northeastern U.*
360 Huntington Ave. Boston, MA 02115
PH: 617-373-4339 FX: 617-373-5095
Marybeth Miller wrbb_program@yahoo.com
wrbbradio.org

WRNX
98 Lower Westfield Rd. Holyoke, MA 01040
PH: 413-536-1009 FX: 413-536-1153
info@wrnx.com
www.wrnx.com

WRSI
15 Hampton Ave. PO Box 268
Northampton, MA 01060
PH: 413-585-8939 FX: 413-585-8501
Johnny Memphis johnny@wrsi.com
www.wrsi.com

WSHL *Stonehill College*
320 Washington St., North Easton, MA 02357
PH: 508-565-1913 FX: 508-565-1974
www.stonehill.edu/wshl

WSKB *Westfield State College*
577 Western Ave. Westfield, MA 01086
PH: 413-572-5579 FX: 413-572-5625
wskbgm@yahoo.com
www.wsc.ma.edu/wskb

WTBU *Boston U .*
640 Commonwealth Ave. Boston, MA 02215
PH: 617-353-6400 FX: 617-353-6403
www.wtburadio.com

WTCC *Springfield Tech*
#1, PO Box 9000, Springfield, MA 01102-9000
PH: 413-736-2781 x13 FX: 413-755-6305
Sonya Barber musicwtcc@stcc.edu
www.wtccfm.org

WUML *U. Massachusetts*
1 U. Ave. Lowell, MA 01854
PH: 978-934-4975
Chris Gilroy md@wuml.org
wuml.org

WWPI *Worcester Polytechnic Inst.*
100 Institute Rd. Worcester, MA 01609
PH: 508-831-5956
radio.wpi.edu

WXOJ
Florence Community Ctr. 140 Pine St.,
Florence, MA 01062
Rikk Desgres WXOJ@catseyesoup.com
info@valleyfreeradio.org
www.valleyfreeradio.org

WXPL *Fitchburg State*
160 Pearl St., Fitchburg, MA 01420
PH: 978-665-4848
falcon.fsc.edu/~wxpl

WZBC *Boston College*
McElroy Commons, 107 Chestnut Hill, MA 02467
PH: 617-552-4686 FX: 617-552-1738
Chris Collins wzbcmusic@gmail.com
www.wzbc.org

WZLY *Wellesley College*
Schneider Ctr. 106 Central St., Wellesley, MA 02481
PH: 781-283-2690
md@wzly.net
wzly.net

Michigan

Detroit Riot Radio
PO Box 15001, Detroit, MI 48215
PH: 313-459-6309
Rein detroitriotradio@gmail.com
www.officialriotradio.com
An internet radio station and on-air live show aired Thursdays at 8pm on WHPR (Detroit). We are looking for new indie music for airplay and internet rotation.

Lake FX Radio *Muskegon College*
221 S. Quarterine Rd. Muskegon, MI 49437
PH: 231-777-0330
lakefxradio.com

WCBN *U. Michigan*
530 Student Activities Bldg.
Ann Arbor, MI 48109-1316
PH: 734-763-3501
music@wcbn.org
www.wcbn.org

WHFR *Henry Ford College*
5101 Evergreen Rd. Dearborn, MI 48128
PH: 313-845-9783 FX: 313-317-4034
Bernadette Balleza whfr-md@hfcc.edu
whfr.hfcc.net

WIDR *Western Michigan U.*
1501 Faunce Student Service Bldg.
Kalamazoo, MI 49008-6301
PH: 269-387-6306
Jessica Kizer widr.music@gmail.com
www.widr.org

WLBN *Albion College*
611 E. Porter St., Albion, MI 49224
PH: 517-629-1000
wlbn@albion.edu
www.albion.edu/wlbn

WLSO *Lake Superior State U.*
680 W. Easterday Ave. Sault Ste. Marie, MI 49783
PH: 906-635-2107 FX: 906-635-2111
wlso@lssu.edu
www.lssu.edu/wlso

WMHW *Central Michigan U.*
183 Moore Hall, Mt. Pleasant, MI 48859
PH: 989-774-7287
wmhw@cmich.edu
www.bca.cmich.edu/WMHW

WMTU *Michigan Tech U.*
G03 Wadsworth Hall, 1703 Townsend Dr.
Houghton MI 49931-1193
PH: 906-487-2333 FX: 906-483-3016
wmtu@mtu.edu
wmtu.mtu.edu

WNMC *NW Michigan College*
1701 E. Front St., Traverse City, MI 49686
PH: 231-995-1135
www.wnmc.org

WOES *Ovid-Elsie Area Schools*
8989 Colony Rd. Elsie, MI 48831
PH: 989-862-4237
woes@oe.k12.mi.us
oe.edzone.net/~woes

WQAC *Alma College*
614 W. Superior St., Alma, MI 48801
PH: 989-466-4359
wqaccharts@gmail.com
www.alma.edu/organizations/wqac

WUMD *U. Michigan Dearborn*
4901 Evergreen Rd. Dearborn, MI 48128
PH: 313-593-5167 FX: 313-593-3503
www.umd.umich.edu/wumd

WUPX *Marquette U.*
1204 U. Ctr. Marquette, MI 49855
PH: 906-227-1844 FX: 906-227-2344
www.wupx.com

WXOU *Oakland U.*
69 Oakland Ctr. Rochester, MI 48309
PH: 248-370-2845 FX: 248-370-2846
wxoumusic@yahoo.com
www.oakland.edu/org/wxou

WYCE
711 Bridge St. NW, Grand Rapids, MI 49504
PH: 616-459-4788 x110 FX: 616-742-0599
Pete Bruinsma pete@wyce.org
www.wyce.org

Minnesota

KAXE
260 NE. 2nd St., Grand Rapids, MN 55744
PH: 218-326-1234 FX: 218-326-1235
kaxe@kaxe.org
www.kaxe.org

KBSB *Bemidji State U.*
1500 Birchmont Dr. NE, Bemidji, MN 56601-2699
PH: 218-755-4120 FX: 218-755-4048
fm90@bemidjistate.edu
www.fm90.org

KFAI
1808 Riverside Ave. Minneapolis, MN 55454
PH: 612-341-0980 FX: 612-341-4281
Dan Richmond richmond@kfai.org
www.kfai.org

KGSM *Gustavus Adolphus College*
800 W. College Ave. St. Peter, MN 56082
PH: 507-933-8000 x8783
www.gustavus.edu/orgs/kgsm/blog

KJNB *College of St. Benedict*
37 S. College Ave. St. Joseph, MN 56374
PH: 320-363-3380 x4
www.csbsju.edu/kjnb

KMSC *Minnesota State U. Moorhead*
Owens Hall Box 138, Moorhead, MN 56563
PH: 218-477-2116
Megan Amot kmsc1500am@yahoo.com
www.dragonradio.org

KMSU *Minnesota State U.*
AF 205, Mankato, MN 56001
PH: 507-389-5678 FX: 507-389-1705
Shelley Pierce shelley215@juno.com
www.mnsu.edu/kmsufm

KORD *Concordia College*
901 8th St. S., Moorhead, MN 56562
www.cord.edu/dept/kord

KQAL
PO Box 5838, Winona, MN 55987
PH: 507-453-5229 FX: 507-457-5226
www.kqal.org

KRLX
300 N. College St., Northfield, MN 55057
PH: 507-646-4127
www.krlx.org

KSMR *St. Mary's U.*
2500 Park Ave. Minneapolis, MN 55404-4403
PH: 507-457-1613
ksmr@smumn.edu
www2.smumn.edu/studorg/~ksmr

KSTO *St. Olaf College*
1500 St. Olaf Ave. Northfield, MN 55057
PH: 507-646-3603
ksto@stolaf.edu
www.stolaf.edu/orgs/ksto

KUMM *U. Minnesota*
600 E. 4th St., Morris, MN 56267
PH: 320-589-6076
Joe Gold kumm@kumm.org
www.kumm.org
Hard Alternative music.

KUOM *U. Minnesota*
610 Rarig Ctr. 330 21st Ave. S.
Minneapolis, MN 55455
PH: 612-625-5304 FX: 612-625-2112
Pushkar Ojha music@radiok.org
www.radiok.org

KVSC *Saint Cloud State U.*
720 4th Ave. S. 27 Stewart Hall
St. Cloud, MN 56301-4498
PH: 320-308-3126 FX: 320-308-5337
Chris Hontos music@kvsc.org
www.kvsc.org

WELY
133 E. Chapman St., Ely, MN 55731
PH: 218-365-4444
www.wely.com

WMCN *Manchester College*
1600 Grand Ave. Saint Paul, MN 55105
PH: 651-696-6082
wmcn@macalester.edu
www.macalester.edu/wmcn

WTIP
PO Box 1005, Grand Marais, MN 55604
PH: 218-387-1070 FX: 218-387-1120
info@wtip.org
wtip.org

Mississippi

WMSV *Mississippi State U.*
PO Box 6210 Student Media Ctr. MS 39762-6210
PH: 662-325-8034 FX: 662-325-8037
wmsv@msstate.edu
www.wmsv.msstate.edu

Missouri

3WK Undergroundradio
PO Box 160161, St. Louis, MO 63116
Wanda wandagm@3wk.com
www.3wk.com

The Growl
901 S. National, Springfield, MO 65804
PH: 417-836-6286
Daniel Walters dan@dankevinandliz.com
thegrowl.missouristate.edu

KCFV *Florissant Valley College*
3400 Pershall Rd. St Louis, MO 63135-1499
PH: 414-595-4463 FX: 314-595-4217
showmemusic@yahoo.com
www.stlcc.edu/fv/kcfv

KCLC
Lindenwood U. 209 S. Kingshighway
St. Charles, MO 63301
PH: 636-949-4880
fm891@lindenwood.edu
www.891thewood.com

KCOU *U. Missouri*
101F Pershing Hall, Columbia, MO 65201
PH: 573-882-7820
Keith Kelley dkk3kf@mizzou.edu
kcou.missouri.edu

KDHX
3504 Magnolia, St. Louis, MO 63118
PH: 314-664-3955 x301 FX: 314-664-1020
musicdepartment@kdhx.org
www.kdhx.org

KKFI
PO Box 32250, Kansas City, MO 64171
PH: 816-931-3122 x106
www.kkfi.org

KMNR *U. Missouri*
113E U. Ctr. W. 1870 Miner Cir.
Rolla, MO 65409-1440
PH: 573-341-4273 FX: 573-341-6021
web.umr.edu/~kmnr

KOPN
915 E. Broadway St., Columbia, MO 65201
PH: 573-874-1139 FX: 573-499-1662
md@kopnmusic.org
www.kopn.org/artist_sub.htm

KSLU *St. Louis U.*
20 N. Grand Blvd. St. Louis, MO 63108
PH: 314-977-1574 FX: 314-977-1579
kslu@slu.edu
kslu.slu.edu

KTBG
Wood 11, Warrensburg, MO 64093
PH: 660-543-4491
Jon Hart jhart@ktbg.fm
ktbg.fm

KTRM *Truman State U.*
100 E. Normal St., Student Union Bldg. LL
Kirksville, MO 63501
PH: 660-785-5876 FX: 660-785-7261
Harry Burson ktrm.music@gmail.com
ktrm.truman.edu

KWUR *Washington U.*
Campus Box 1205, 1 Brookings Dr.
St. Louis, MO 63105
PH: 314-935-5952
Sarah Duve music1@kwur.com
www.kwur.com

Retro Red-Eye Express *KKFI*
PO Box 32250, Kansas City, MO 64171-2250
Attn: Sunshine
Sunshine retroredeye@gmail.com
www.myspace.com/retrosunshine
*To be reviewed for station airplay, please send a
CD. If you'd like Sunshine to review your music,
please contact her via MySpace or email.*

Montana

KBGA *U. Montana*
U. Ctr. Rm. 208, Missoula, MT 59812
PH: 406-243-5715
kbgamd@kbga.org
www.kbga.org

KDWG
Campus Box 119, 710 S. Atlantic St.
Dillion, MT 59725
PH: 406-683-7394
kdwg@umwestern.edu
www.umwestern.edu/kdwg

KGLT
MSU Box 17424, Bozeman, MT 59717-4240
PH: 406-994-6483 FX: 406-994-1987
wwwkglt@montana.edu
www.kglt.net

Nebraska

KDNE *Doane College*
1014 Boswell Ave. Crete, NE 68333
PH: 402-826-8677
webcast.doane.edu

KLPR *U. Nebraska*
109 Thomas Hall, Kearney, NE 68849
PH: 308-865-8217
klpr.unk.edu

KRNU *U. Nebraska*
147 Andersen Hall, PO Box 880466
Lincoln, NE 68588-0466
PH: 402-472-8277
krnu-music@unl.edu
krnu.unl.edu

KZUM
941 "O" St., Lincoln, NE 68508
PH: 402-474-5086 FX: 402-474-5091
Jesse Starita programming@kzum.org
www.kzum.org

Nevada

It Hurts When I Pee *KXTE*
6655 W. Sahara Ave. #C-202, Las Vegas, NV 89146
homie@xtremeradio.com
www.myspace.com/ithurtswhenipeemusic
*The new music show with a really goofy name.
Local and indie bands.*

New Hampshire

Radio SNHU *S. New Hampshire U.*
2500 N. River Rd. Manchester, NH 03106-1045
PH: 603-629-4695
radiosnhu@snhu.edu
radio.snhu.edu

Seldom Heard Radio *WSCS*
DJ Frederick singinggrove@conknet.com
seldomheardradio.blogspot.com
*My occasional program comprised (mostly) of
tracks over ten minutes in length in all genres
including Rock, Jam Bands, Jazz, Classical, avant-
garde, Folk, and anything that fits and is music to
the ears.*

WDCR *Dartmouth College*
PO Box 957, Hanover, NH 03755
PH: 603-643-1340 FX: 603-646-7655
Rob Demick rob.demick@webdcr.com
www.webdcr.com

WKNH *Keene State College*
229 Main St., Keene, NH 03435
PH: 603-358-2420
Sam Sudhalter music@wknh.org
www.wknh.org

WSCA
PO Box 6532, Portsmouth, NH 03802
PH: 603-430-9722 FX: 603-430-9822
Chad Beisswanger
music@portsmouthcommunityradio.org
www.wscafm.org

WSCS *Colby-Sawyer College*
541 Main St., New London, NH 03257
PH: 603-526-3443
www.colby-sawyer.edu/wscs

WUNH *U. New Hampshire*
MUB Durham, NH 03824
PH: 603-862-2222
music@wunh.org
wunh.org

New Jersey

All Mixed Up *WDHA*
55 Horsehill Rd. Cedar Knolls, NJ 07927
Jim Monaghan AllMixedUpRadio@aol.com
www.myspace.com/allmixedupradio
*A little Rock, Folk, Country, Soul, Jazz - all custom-
blended for your Sunday morning.*

Anything Goes
PO Box 314, Rutherford, NJ 07070
PH: 212-613-6163
Lise Avery info@anythinggoesradio.com
www.anythinggoesradio.com
*An eclectic mix of Jazz standards and classic Pop
with a little bit of anything else thrown into the mix.*

Carnival of Song *WFDU*
Metropolitan Campus, 1000 River Rd.
Teaneck, NJ 07666
Lynn Crystal lynncrystal@carnivalofsong.com
carnivalofsong.com
*I play music from artists who deserve to be heard
because of the emotional honesty of their work.*

WBZC *Burlington County College*
601 Pemberton Browns Mills Rd.
Pemberton, NJ 08068-1599
PH: 609-894-9311 x1592 FX: 609-894-9440
staff.bcc.edu/radio

WFDU *Fairleigh Dickinson U.*
Metropolitan Campus, 1000 River Rd.
Teaneck, NJ 07666
PH: 201-692-2806 FX: 201-692-2807
Barry Sheffield barrys@fdu.edu
wfdu.fm

WFMU
PO Box 5101, Hoboken, NJ 07030
PH: 201-521-1416
www.wfmu.org

WGLS *Rowan U.*
201 Mullica Hill Rd. Glassboro, NJ 08028
PH: 856-863-9457 FX: 856-256-4704
wgls.rowan.edu

WJTB *New Jersey Inst. of Tech.*
323 MLK Blvd. Newark, NJ 07102
PH: 973-596-5816
www.wjtb.org

WMCX *Monmouth U.*
400 Cedar Ave. W. Long Branch, NJ 07764
PH: 732-571-5229 FX: 732-263-5145
Steve Paravati wmcxmusic@monmouth.edu
hawkmail.monmouth.edu/~wmcx

WMSC *Montclair State U .*
1 Normal Ave. Upper Montclair, NJ 07043
PH: 973-655-4587 FX: 973-655-7433
www.wmscradio.com

WNTI *Centenary College*
400 Jefferson St., Hackettstown, NJ 07840
PH: 908-979-4355
Spider Glenn Compton spiderglenn@hotmail.com
www.wnti.org

WPRB *Princeton U.*
030 Bloomberg Hall, Princeton U. NJ 08544
PH: 609-258-1033 Fx: 609-258-1806
music@wprb.com
www.wprb.com

WPSC *William Patterson U.*
300 Pompton Rd. Wayne, NJ 07442
PH: 973-720-3669
Rob Quicke music@wpscradio.com
www.wpscradio.com

WRNU *Rutgers U.*
350 MLK Blvd. Rm. 315, Newark, NJ 07102
PH: 973-353-5746 FX: 973-353-5187
staff@wrnu.net
wrnu.net

WRPR *Ramapo College*
505 Ramapo Valley Rd. Mahwah, NJ 07430
wrpr@ramapo.edu
phobos.ramapo.edu/wrpr

WRSU *Rutgers U.*
126 College Ave. New Brunswick, NJ 08901
PH: 732-932-7800 x23 FX: 732-932-1768
Tom Nunziata music@wrsu.org
wrsu.rutgers.edu

WSOU *Seton Hall U.*
400 S. Orange Ave. South Orange, NJ 07079
PH: 973-761-7546 FX: 973-761-7593
Leanne Kohlbecker wsoumusic@hotmail.com
www.wsou.net

WTSR *College of New Jersey*
Kendall Hall, PO Box 7718, Ewing, NJ 08628
PH: 609-771-2420 FX: 609-637-5113
tsrmusic@tcnj.edu
www.wtsr.org

WVPH *Rutgers U. Livingston*
#117 Student Ctr. 84 Joyce Kilmer Ave.
Piscataway, NJ 08854
PH: 732-445-4100
Robert Drucker programdirector@thecore.fm
www.thecore.rutgers.edu

WVRM
615 Valley Rd. Upper Montclair, NJ 07043
PH: 973-746-4999 FX: 973-746-4749
info@villageradio.com
www.villageradio.com

New Mexico

KRUX *New Mexico State U.*
Corbett Ctr. Box 30004, Las Cruces, NM 88003
PH: 505-646-4640 FX: 505-646-5219
music@kruxradio.com
www.krux.nmsu.edu

KTEK *New Mexico Tech.*
SAC Rm. 219, 801 Leroy Place
Socorro, NM 87801
PH: 505-835-6013
ktek@nmt.edu
infohost.nmt.edu/~ktek

KUNM *U. New Mexico*
MSC06 3520, Onate Hall 1
Albuquerque, NM 87131-0001
PH: 505-277-5615
music@kunm.org
www.kunm.org

New York

106 VIC *Ithaca College*
118 Roy H. Park Hall, Ithaca, NY 14850
PH: 607-274-1059
vic@ithaca.edu
www.vicradio.org

Emotional Rescue *WJFF*
4765 State Rt. 52, PO Box 546
Jeffersonville, NY 12748
PH: 845-482-4141 FX: 845-482-9533
Kae Kotarski rescue@wjffradio.org
www.wjffradio.org
A weekly, 90 minute music show covering most genres.

Fast Forward Reverse *East Village Radio*
TimmyG fastfwdrev@yahoo.com
www.myspace.com/fastforwardreverse
Shoegaze, Indie Rock, Pop, BritPop, Dreampop, Post Punk/New Wave, Alt-Rock ...

Fredonia Radio *SUNY Fredonia*
115 McEwen Hall, Fredonia, NY 14063
PH: 716-673-3420
Vince Quatroche quat1776@fredonia.edu
www.fredoniaradio.com

RocklandWorldRadio.com
1 Wood Ln. Suffern, NY 10901
PH: 845-364-9473
www.RocklandWorldRadio.com
Download our release form and send it with your CD.

Sandy Acres Sound Lab *East Village Radio*
DJ Matilda von Crumbcake sugartown@gmail.com
girljukebox.typepad.com
Indie, New Wave, Post Punk & more!

This is Only a Test *WFUV*
Bronx, NY 10458
PH: 718-817-4550 FX: 718-365-9815
Rich McLaughlin test@wfuv.org
www.wfuv.org/programs/test.html
It's a kind of laboratory where we'll experiment with diverse genres and sounds as we build a unique, full-time web and radio service made right here in New York City.

The Tuesday Night Rock & Roll Dance Party *WUSB*
Stony Brook Union 266
Stony Brook, NY 11794-3263
PH: 631-632-6501 FX: 631-632-7182
music@wusb.fm
wusb.fm/rockandroll
Contact us to lay down a set of music.

WAIH *SUNY Potsdam*
9050 Barrington Dr. Potsdam, NY 13676
PH: 315-267-2511
Jess Mitchell surly_blonde@yahoo.com
www2.potsdam.edu/WAIH

WALF *Alfred U.*
1 Saxon Dr. Alfred, NY 14802
PH: 607-871-2200
Irene Brown icb3@alfred.edu
www.walfradio.org

WAMC
PO Box 66600, Albany, NY 12206
PH: 518-465-5233 FX: 518-432-6974
mail@wamc.org
www.wamc.org

WBAI
120 Wall St.10th Fl. New York, NY 10005
PH: 212-209-2800 FX: 212-747-1698
editor@wbai.org
www.wbai.org

WBAR *Barnard College*
3009 Broadway, New York, NY 10027-6598
PH: 212-854-6538 FX: 601-510-7683
wbar@columbia.edu
www.wbar.org

WBER
2596 Baird Rd. Penfield, NY 14526-2333
PH: 585-419-8190
wber.monroe.edu

WBMB *Baruch College*
55 Lexington Ave. #3-280, New York, NY 10010
PH: 646-312-4720
WBMBOnline@gmail.com
www.wbmbradio.com

WBNY *Buffalo State U.*
1300 Elmwood Ave. Buffalo, NY 14222
PH: 716-878-3080 FX: 716-878-6600
wbnymd@gmail.com
www.wbny.org

WBSU *SUNY Brockport*
135 Seymour Union, Brockport, NY 14420
PH: 716-395-2580 FX: 585-395-5534
www.891thepoint.com

WCDB *U. Albany*
Campus Ctr. 316 1400 Washington Ave.
Albany, NY 12222
PH: 518-442-5262 FX: 518-442-4366
Seth Tillinghast wcdbpd@gmail.com
www.wcdbfm.com

WCWP *Long Island U.*
720 Northern Blvd. Brookville, NY 11548-1300
PH: 516-299-2627 FX: 516-299-2767
wcwp@cwpost.liu.edu
www.liu.edu/cwis/cwp/radio/wcwp

WDFH
21 Brookside Ln. Dobbs Ferry, NY 10522
PH: 914-674-0900
Tom Jones music@wdfh.org
wdfh.org

WDST
PO Box 367, Woodstock, NY 12498
PH: 845-679-7266 x12 FX: 845-679-5395
Dave Doud daved@wdst.com
www.wdst.com

WDYN
2844-46 Dewey Ave. Rochester, NY 14616
PH: 585-621-6270 FX: 585-621-6278
wdyn@wdyn.net
dynamicradio.net

WERW *Syracuse U.*
Schine Student Ctr. Rm. 126G, 303 University Pl.
Syracuse, NY 13210
PH: 315-443-2021
Drew Mitnick werwmusic@gmail.com
www.werw.org

WETD *Alfred State College*
10 Upper Campus Dr., Alfred NY 14802
PH: 607-587-2907
wetd@alfredstate.edu
web.alfredstate.edu/wetd

WFNP *SUNY*
SUB 413, New Paltz, NY 12561-2443
PH: 845-257-3041 FX: 845-257-3099
wfnpmusic@newpaltz.edu
www.newpaltz.edu/wfnp

WFUV *Fordham U.*
Bronx, NY 10458
PH: 718-817-4550 FX: 718-365-9815
www.wfuv.org

WGFR *Adirondack College*
640 Bay Rd. Queensbury, NY 12804
PH: 518-743-2300 x2376
www.wgfr.org

WGSU *SUNY Geneseo*
Blake B 104, 1 College Cir. Geneseo, NY 14454
PH: 585-245-5488
onesun.cc.geneseo.edu/~wgsu

WHCL *Hamilton College*
198 College Hill Rd. Clinton, NY 13323
PH: 315-859-4200
mngrwhcl@hamilton.edu
www.whcl.org

WHPC *Nassau College*
1 Education Dr. Garden City, NY 11530-6793
PH: 516-572-7438 FX: 516-572-7831
whpc@ncc.edu
www.ncc.edu/About/WHPC

WHTZ
PO Box 7100, New York, NY 10150
PH: 800-242-0100 FX: 800-386-2329
zvip@z100.com
www.z100.com
Visit our website for details on how to get your music on-air.

PLANNING A TOUR?

32,000 Live Music Venues
in the US and Canada!!

Whether you're playing around town or planning a national tour, we can help you find the perfect fit! Thousands of venues in every major city and ALL points in between!

clubs   colleges   festivals   coffee shops   halls   bookstores
open mics   churches   record stores   community centers
restaurants   house concerts   jams   booking agents

www.IndieVenueBible.com

WICB *Ithaca College*
118 Park Hall, Ithaca, NY 14850
PH: 607-274-1040 FX: 607-274-1061
www.wicb.org

WITR *Rochester Institute of Tech.*
32 Lomb Memorial Dr. Rochester, NY 14623-0563
PH: 585-475-5643 FX: 585-475-4988
witr.rit.edu

WJFF
4765 State Rt. 52, PO Box 546
Jeffersonville, NY 12748
PH: 845-482-4141 FX: 845-482-9533
wjff@wjffradio.org
www.wjffradio.org

WKRB *Kingsborough College*
2001 Oriental Blvd. Brooklyn, NY 11235
PH: 718-368-4572 FX: 718-368-4776
gm@wkrb.org
www.wkrb.org

WKZE
7392 S. Broadway, Red Hook, NY 12571
PH: 845-758-9811 FX: 845-758-9819
info@wkze.com
www.wkze.com

WLIX
PO Box 594, Ridge, NY 11961
PH: 631-345-3946
programming@radiox.fm
www.radiox.fm

WNYO *SUNY Oswego*
9B Hewitt Union, Oswego, NY 13126
PH: 315-312-2101 FX: 315-312-2907
wnyo@oswego.edu
www.oswego.edu/~wnyo

WNYU *New York U.*
194 Mercer St. 5th Fl. New York, NY 10012
PH: 212-998-1658 FX: 212-998-1652
Robby Morris music@wnyu.org
www.wnyu.org

WONY *SUNY Oneonta*
Alumni Hall, Oneonta, NY 13820
PH: 607-436-2712
wonymusic@gmail.com
organizations.oneonta.edu/wony

WQKE *Plattsburgh State U.*
110 Angell College Ctr. Plattsburgh, NY 12901
PH: 518-564-6566
Chelsea Vogg chelsamuffin@yahoo.com
wqke.org

WRAJ *Bohemia*
FX: 413-521-5976
www.wrajradio.com

WRCU *Colgate U.*
13 Oak Dr. Hamilton, NY 13346
PH: 315-228-7901 FX: 315-228-7028
Joel Feitzinger wrcumusic@mail.colgate.edu
wrcufm.com

WRHO *Hartwick College*
1 Hartwick Dr. Oneonta, NY 13820
PH: 607-431-4555 FX: 607-431-4064
wrho@hartwick.edu
users.hartwick.edu/wrho

WRHU *Hofstra U.*
Rm. 127, Hempstead, NY 11549-1000
PH: 516-463-3674
Jessica Weisensell wrhumusic@wrhu.org
www.wrhu.org

WRPI *Rensselaer Polytechnic Inst.*
1 WRPI Plaza, Troy, NY 12180
PH: 518-276-6248 FX: 518-276-2360
wrpi-md@rpi.edu
www.wrpi.org

WRUB *SUNY U. Buffalo*
174/175 MFAC. Buffalo, NY 14261
PH: 716-645-3370
www.myspace.com/wrub

WRUR *U. Rochester*
PO Box 277356, Rochester, NY 14627
PH: 585-275-6400 FX: 585-256-3989
wrur.rochester.edu

WSBU *Bonaventure U.*
Drawer O, St. Bonaventure, NY 14778
PH: 716-375-2332 FX: 716-375-2583
wsbufm.net

WSIA *College of Staten Island*
2800 Victory Blvd. Rm. 1C-106
Staten Island, NY 10314
PH: 718-982-3057 FX: 718-982-3052
music@wsia.fm
wsia.fm

WSPN *Skidmore College*
815 N. Broadway, Saratoga Springs, NY 12866
PH: 518-580-5787
wspn@skidmore.edu
www.skidmore.edu/~wspn

WSUC *SUNY Cortland*
PH: 607-753 2936
wsucsecretary@yahoo.com.
web.cortland.edu/wsuc

WTSC *Clarkson U.*
PO Box 8743, Potsdam, NY 13699
PH: 315-268-7658
radio@clarkson.edu
radio.clarkson.edu

WUSB *SUNY Stoneybrook*
Stony Brook Union 266,
Stony Brook, NY 11794-3263
PH: 631-632-6501 FX: 631-632-7182
music@wusb.fm
wusb.fm

WVBR
957 Mitchell St. Ste. B, Ithaca, NY 14850
PH: 607-273-4000 FX: 607-273-4069
www.wvbr.com

WVKR *Vassar College*
Box 726, 124 Raymond Ave.
Poughkeepsie, NY 12604
PH: 845-437-5476 FX: 845-437-7656
www.wvkr.org

WXXE
826 Euclid Ave. Syracuse, NY 13210
PH: 315-455-0850 FX: 315-701-0303
www.wxxe.org
*Check to make sure that they are accepting music
submissions before sending in your CD.*

North Carolina

Wake Radio *Wake Forest U.*
PO Box 7760, Winston-Salem, NC 27109
PH: 336-758-4894 FX: 336-758-4562
radio.wfu.edu

WASU *Appalachian State U.*
Wey Hall #332, Boone, NC 28608
PH: 828-262-3170 FX: 828-262-6521
Daniel Earney music@wasurocks.com
www.wasurocks.com

WCOM
201 N. Greensboro St., Carrboro, NC 27510
PH: 919-929-9601
volunteer@communityradio.coop
www.communityradio.coop

WKNC *North Carolina State U.*
Mail Ctr. Box 8607, Raleigh, NC 27695-8607
PH: 919-515-2400 FX: 919-513-2693
wknc.org

WNCW *Isothermal College*
PO Box 804, Spindale, NC 28160
PH: 828-287-8000 x349 FX: 828-287-8012
info@wncw.org
www.wncw.org

WPVM
75 Haywood St., Asheville, NC 28801
PH: 828-258-0085
music@wpvm.org
www.wpvm.org

WQFS *Guilford College*
17714 Founders Hall, 5800 W. Friendly Ave.
Greensboro, NC 27410
PH: 336-316-2352
Tim May tmay@guilford.edu
www.guilford.edu/wqfs

WSGE *Gaston College*
201 Hwy. 321 S. Dallas, NC 28034
PH: 704-922-6273 FX: 704-922-2347
Cliff Anderson anderson.cliff@gaston.edu
www.wsge.org

WSOE *Elon College*
Campus Box 2700, Elon, NC 27244
PH: 336-278-7211 FX: 336-278-7298
Eric Navarro enavarro@elon.edu
www.elon.edu/wsoe

WUAG *U. North Carolina Greensboro*
402 Tate St. Brown Blg. Rm. 210, UNCG
Greensboro, NC 27412
PH: 336-334-5688
Travis Diehl wuagmd@gmail.com
www.wuag.net

WVOD
637 Harbor Rd. Wanchese, NC 27981
PH: 252-475-1888
www.991thesound.com

WXDU *Duke U.*
PO Box 90689, Duke Stn. Durham, NC 27708
PH: 919-684-2957
music@wxdu.org
www.wxdu.duke.edu

WXYC *U. North Carolina*
CB 5210 Carolina Union, Chapel Hill, NC 27599
PH: 919-962-7768
David Harper md@wxyc.org
www.wxyc.org

WZMB *East Carolina U.*
Mendenhall Basement, Greenville, NC 27858
PH: 252-328-4751 FX: 252-328-4773
www.ecu.edu/wzmb

Ohio

ACRN *Ohio U.*
1 Park Place Suite (Baker Center) 329
Athens, OH 45701
PH: 740-593-4910
Ty Owen music@acrn.com
www.acrn.com

BearCast Radio *U. Cincinnati*
2217 Mary Emery Hall, PO Box 210003,
Cincinnati, OH 45221
PH: 513-556-6578
bearcastprogramming@gmail.com
www.BearcastRadio.com

The Cream of Broccoli Radio Hour *WRUW*
11220 Bellflower Rd. Cleveland, OH 44106
PH: 216-368-2208
Brandt md@wruw.org
wruw.org/guide/show.php?show_id=164
*The best in Indie Rock and Pop and your requests —
how can you refuse?*

KBUX *Ohio State U.*
1849 Cannon Dr. Columbus, OH 43210
Attn: New Music
PH: 614-688-3780 FX: 614-688-5788
Adam Carrington carrington@ohio.fm
ohio.fm

Radio U *Westerville*
PO Box 1887, Westerville, OH 43086
PH: 614-839-7100 FX: 614-839-1329
www.radiou.com

WAIF
1434 E. McMillan Ave. Cincinnati, OH 45206
PH: 513-961-8900
www.waif883.org

WBGU *Bowling Green State U.*
120 West Hall, Bowling Green, OH 43403
PH: 419-372-2820 FX: 419-372-9449
Mike Hertz music@wbgufm.com
www.wbgufm.com

WBWC *Baldwin-Wallace College*
275 Eastland Rd. Berea, OH 44017
PH: 440-826-2145 FX: 440-826-3426
Cynthia Luna music@wbwc.com
www.wbwc.com

WCSB *Cleveland State U.*
Rhodes Tower 956, 2121 Euclid Ave.
Cleveland, OH 44115-2214
PH: 216-687-3721 FX: 216-687-2161
Ryan Kuehn musicdirector@wcsb.org
wcsb.org

WCWS *College of Wooster*
Wishart Hall, Wooster, OH 44691
PH: 330-263-2240 FX: 330-263-2690
wcws_music@wooster.edu
www.wooster.edu/wcws

WJCU *John Carroll U.*
20700 North Park Blvd.
University Heights, OH 44118
PH: 216-397-4937
wjcu.info@gmail.com
www.wjcu.org

WKSR *Kent State U.*
C306 Music & Speech, Kent, OH 44242
PH: 330-672-2131
www.blacksquirrelradio.com

WLHS *Lakota H.S.*
6840 Lakota Ln. Liberty Township, OH 45044
PH: 513-759-4864
info@wlhsradio.com
www.wlhsradio.net

WMCO *Muskingum College*
163 Stormont St., New Concord, OH 43762
PH: 740-826-8907
wmco@muskingum.edu
muskingum.edu/~wmco

WMSR *Miami U.*
221 Williams Hall, Oxford, OH 45056
PH: 513-529-1985
Sandy Boyer boyersg@muohio.edu
www.orgs.muohio.edu/wmsr

WOBC *Oberlin College*
Wilder Hall 319, 135 W. Lorain St.
Oberlin, OH 44074
PH: 440-775-8107 FX: 440-775-6678
music.wobc@oberlin.edu
www.wobc.org

WOBO
PO Box 338, Owensville, OH 45160
PH: 513-724-3939
listener.support@wobofm.org
www.wobofm.com

WONB *Ohio Northern U.*
525 S. Main St., Ada, OH 45810
PH: 419-772-1194 FX: 419-772-2794
wonb@onu.edu
www.onu.edu/wonb

WOXY
700 W. Pete Rose Way, Cincinnati, OH 45203
PH: 513-621-0012
Matt Shiv shiv@woxy.com
www.woxy.com

WRDL *Ashland U.*
401 College Ave. Ashland, OH 44805
PH: 419-289-5678 FX: 419-289-5329
www.myspace.com/wrdl

WRMU *Mount Union College*
1972 Clark Ave. Alliance, OH 44601
PH: 800-992-6682 x3777 FX: 330-823-4913
Jeremy Miller millerjd@muc.edu
www.muc.edu/wrmu

WRUW *Case Western Reserve U.*
11220 Bellflower Rd. Cleveland, OH 44106
PH: 216-368-2207 FX: 216-368-5414
Roger Weist md@wruw.org
www.wruw.org

WSLN *Ohio Wesleyan U.*
HWCC Box 1366, Delaware, OH 43015
PH: 740-368-2239
wsln.owu.edu

WUDR *U. Dayton*
300 College Park K.U. #215, Dayton, OH 45409
PH: 937-229-3058
Katie Sunday sundayke@notes.udayton.edu
flyer-radio.udayton.edu

WWCD *Independent Playground, Indie
Playground Deux*
503 S. Front St. #101, Columbus, OH 43215
PH: 614-221-9923 FX: 614-227-0021
Tom Butler & Rudy Gerdeman tbutler@cd101.com
myspace.com/independentplayground
Award winning independent music shows.

WWSU *Wright State U.*
018 Student Union, Dayton, OH 45435
PH: 937-775-5554 FX: 937-775-5553
wwsuprogramming@yahoo.com
www.wright.edu/studentorgs/wwsu

WXUT *U. Toledo*
2801 W. Bancroft, SU2515, Toledo, OH 43606
PH: 419-530-4172 FX: 419-530-2210
Bryan Crist bryan.crist@utoledo.edu
wxut.utoledo.edu

WZIP *U. Akron*
302 E. Buchtel Ave. Akron, OH 44325-1004
PH: 330-972-7105 FX: 330-972-5521
wzip@uakron.edu
www.wzip.fm

Oklahoma

KRSC *Rogers State U.*
1701 W. Will Rogers Blvd. Claremore, OK 74017
PH: 918-343-7913
www.rsu.edu/rsuradio

WIRE *U. Oklahoma*
395 W. Lindsey, Norman, OK 73019
PH: 405-325-0121 FX: 405-325-7565
John Cope wiremusic@ou.edu
wire.ou.edu

Oregon

In Suspect Terrane *KPSU*
PO Box 751-SD, Portland, OR 97207
PH: 503-725-4071 FX: 503-725-4079
Judith music@kpsu.org
www.kpsu.org
A mix of World, Blues, Americana and Metal.

KBVR *Oregon State U.*
210 Memorial Union E. Corvallis, OR 97331
PH: 541-737-2008 FX: 541-737-4545
Nick Lilja fmprogdir@oregonstate.edu
oregonstate.edu/dept/kbvr/html

KEOL *Eastern Oregon State College*
1 University Blvd. La Grande, OR 97850
PH: 541-962-3698
keol@eou.edu
www3.eou.edu/~keol

KLC *Lewis and Clark College*
0615 SW. Palatine Hill Rd. Portland, OR 97219
PH: 503-768-7133 FX: 503-768-7130
Josh Schield music@klcradio.net
www.lclark.edu/~klc

KPSU *Portland State U.*
PO Box 751-SD, Portland, OR 97207
PH: 503-725-4071 FX: 503-725-4079
Aaron Reyna music@kpsu.org
www.kpsu.org

KRVM *Eugene*
1574 Coburg Rd. PMB 237, Eugene, OR 97401
PH: 541 687-3370
Ken Martin ken@krvm.org
www.krvm.org

KTEC
PO Box 2009, Klamath Falls, OR 97601
PH: 541-885-1840 FX: 541-885-1857
Ryan Martin ryan.martin@oit.edu
www.oit.edu/d/ktec

KWVA *U. Oregon*
PO Box 3157, Eugene, OR 97403
PH: 541-346-4091 FX: 541-346-0648
kwva@uoregon.edu
kwva.uoregon.edu

Pennsylvania

Radio Show Host Stewart Brodian
PO Box 1253, Easton, PA 18044
Stewart Brodian sbrodian@yahoo.com
www.webspawner.com/users/brodianpage
*I am a radio DJ at three area radio stations: WDIY
(+WXLV 90.3 FM) Allentown, WMUH Allentown
and WLVR Bethlehem. Check my playlists to see if
your music fits!*

WARC *Allegheny College*
520 N. Main St. Box C, Meadville, PA 16335
PH: 814-332-3376
warc@allegheny.edu
warc.allegheny.edu

WBUQ *Bloomsburg U.*
1250 McCormick Ctr. 400 E. 2nd St.
Bloomsburg, PA 17815
PH: 570-389-8632 FX: 570-389-2718
orgs.bloomu.edu/wbuq

WCLH *Wilkes U.*
84 W. South St., Wilkes Barre, PA 18766
PH: 570-408-2908 FX: 570-408-5908
wclh.org

WCUR *West Chester U.*
237 Sykes Student Union, West Chester, PA 19383
PH: 610-436-2414
wcurmd@gmail.com
www.wcur.fm

WDCV *Dickinson College*
PO Box 1773, Carlisle, PA 17013
PH: 717-245-1444
usherh@dickinson.edu
alpha.dickinson.edu/storg/wdcv

WDIY
301 Broadway, Bethlehem, PA 18015
PH: 610-694-8100 FX: 610-954-9474
Neil Hever neil@wdiy.org
www.wdiyfm.org

WDNR *Widener U.*
Box 1000, 1 University Pl. Chester, PA 19013
PH: 610-499-4439
Kris Gill krgill@mail.widener.edu
www.wdnr.com

WDSR *Duquesne U.*
1345 Vickroy St., CMC #2500500
Pittsburgh, PA 15219
PH: 412-396-5085
wdsr97@yahoo.com
www.wdsr.org

WEHR *Penn State*
120 S. Burrowes St. Box 30, U. Park, PA 16801
PH: 814-865-0897
Evan Raffel esr5006@psu.edu
www.clubs.psu.edu/wehr

WERG *Gannon U.*
University Sq. Erie, PA 16541
PH: 814-871-5841 x3
Katie Gabelman gabelman001@gannon.edu
www.wergfm.com

WESS *East Stroudsburg U.*
200 Prospect St., E. Stroudsburg, PA 18301-2999
PH: 570-422-3512
wess@po-box.esu.edu
www.esu.edu/wess

WHRC *Haverford College*
370 Lancaster Ave. Haverford, PA 19041
PH: 610-896-2920
www.whrcradio.com

WIUP *U. Pennsylvania*
121 Stouffer Hall, Indiana, PA 15705
PH: 724-357-7971
www.coe.iup.edu/wiupfm

WIXQ *Millersville U.*
Student Memorial Ctr. Millersville, PA 17551-0302
PH: 717-872-3333 FX: 717-872-3383
music.director@wixq.com
www.wixq.com

WJRH *Lafayette College*
Farinon Ctr., PO Box 9473, Easton, PA 18042
PH: 610-330-5316 FX: 610-330-5318
www.lafayette.edu/~wjrh

WKDU *Drexel U.*
3210 Chestnut St., Philadelphia, PA 19104
PH: 215-895-2580
musicdir@wkdu.org
www.wkdu.org

WKPS *Penn State U.*
125 HUB-Robeson Ctr. U. Park, PA 16802-6600
PH: 814-865-7983 FX: 814-865-2751
lion-officers@thelion.fm
www.thelion.fm

WKVR *Juniata College*
1005 Juniata College, Huntingdon, PA 16652
PH: 814-641-3341 FX: 814-643-4477
wkvr@juniata.edu
clubs.juniata.edu/wkvr

WLVR *Lehigh U.*
39 University Dr. Bethlehem, PA 18015
PH: 610-758-3000
inwlvr@lehigh.edu
www.wlvr.org

WMSS *Middletown HS*
215 Oberlin Rd. Middletown, PA 17057
PH: 717-948-9136
music@wmssfm.com
www.wmssfm.com

WMUH *Muhlenberg College*
2400 Chew St., Allentown, PA 18104
PH: 484-664-3239 FX: 484-664-3539
wmuh@muhlenberg.edu
www.muhlenberg.edu/cultural/wmuh

World Café *WXPN*
3025 Walnut St., Philadelphia, PA 19104
David Dye wxpndesk@xpn.org
www.xpn.org
*Daily interviews and live in-studio performances
featuring Blues, Rock, Folk and Alt-Country. Send
TWO CDs!*

WPPJ *Point Park College*
201 Wood St., Pittsburgh, PA 15222
PH: 412-392-4724
www.pointpark.edu/default.aspx?id=350

WPTC *Pennsylvania College of Tech.*
DIF 48, 1 College Ave. Williamsport, PA 17701
PH: 570-326-3761 x7214
wptc@pct.edu
www.pct.edu/wptc

WPTS *U. Pittsburgh*
411 William Pitt Union, Pittsburgh, PA 15260
PH: 412-648-7990 FX: 412-648-7988
Seth Ballentine wptsmusicdirector@gmail.com
www.wpts.pitt.edu

WQHS *U. Pennsylvania*
Rm. 504 Hollenback Ctr. 3000 South St.
Philadelphia, PA 19104
PH: 215-898-3500
Mike Murphy music@wqhs.org
www.wqhs.org

WQSU *Susquehanna U.*
514 University Ave. Selinsgrove, PA 17870
PH: 570-372-4030
pulserequest@susqu.edu
www.susqu.edu/wqsu-fm

WRCT *Carnegie Mellon U.*
1 WRCT Plaza, 5000 Forbes Ave.
Pittsburgh, PA 15213
PH: 412-621-0728
Alberto Guzman intmusic@wrct.org
www.wrct.org

WRFT *Temple U.*
580 Meetinghouse Rd. Ambler, PA 19002
PH: 215-283-1280
www.temple.edu/wrft

WRLC *Lycoming College*
700 College Pl. Williamsport, PA 17701
PH: 570-321-4054
Melissa King kinmeli@lycoming.edu
www.lycoming.edu/orgs/wrlc

WRKC *Kings College*
133 N. Franklin St., Wilkes Barre, PA 18711
PH: 570-208-5931
wrkc@kings.edu
www.kings.edu/wrkc

WSRN *Swarthmore College*
500 College Ave. Swarthmore, PA 19081
PH: 610-328-8335
www.wsrnfm.org

WSYC *Shippensburg U.*
3rd Fl. CUB, 1871 Old Main Dr.
Shippensburg, PA 17257
PH: 717-532-6006 FX: 717-477-4024
wsyc@wsyc.org
www.wsyc.org

WUSR *U. Scranton*
800 Linden St., Scranton, PA 18510
PH: 570-941-7648 FX: 570-941-4628
wusrfm@scranton.edu
playlist.wusr.scranton.edu

WVBU *Bucknell U.*
Box C-3956, Lewisburg, PA 17837
PH: 570-577-1174
Tara Hankinson wvbumd@yahoo.com
www.wvbu.com

WVYC *York College*
339 Country Club Rd. York, PA 17405-7199
PH: 717-815-1932 FX: 717-849-1602
music@wvyc.org
wvyc.org

WXPN *U. Pennsylvania*
3025 Walnut St., Philadelphia, PA 19104
PH: 215-898-6677 FX: 215-898-0707
wxpndesk@xpn.org
xpn.org
.

WXVU *Villanova U.*
210 Dougherty Hall, 800 Lancaster Ave.
Villanova, PA 19085-1699
PH: 610-519-7200
wxvufm.com

WYBF *Cabrini College*
610 King of Prussia Rd. Radnor, PA 19087
PH: 610-902-8457
modernrock@wybf.com
www.wybf.com

WYEP
67 Bedford Sq. Pittsburgh, PA 15203
PH: 412-381-9900 FX: 412-381-9126
info@wyep.org
www.wyep.org

Rhode Island

WBRU *Brown U.*
88 Benevolent St., Providence, RI 02906-2046
PH: 401-272-9550 FX: 401-272-9278
heydj@wbru.com
wbru.com

WBSR *Brown U.*
PO Box 1930, Providence, RI 02912
PH: 401-863-9600
music.director@bsrlive.com
www.bsrlive.com

WDOM *Providence U.*
549 River Ave. Providence, RI 02918-0001
PH: 401-865-2460 FX: 401-865-2822
wdomdj@yahoo.com
studentweb.providence.edu/~wdom

WJMF *Bryant U.*
Box 6, 1150 Douglas Pike, Smithfield, RI 02917
PH: 401-232-6150
www.wjmf887.com

WQRI *Roger Williams U.*
1 Old Ferry Rd. Bristol, RI 02809-2923
PH: 401-254-3283
programdirector_wqri@hawks.rwu.edu
wqri.rwu.edu

WRIU *U. Rhode Island*
326 Memorial Union, Kingston, RI 02881
PH: 401-874-4949 FX: 401-874-4349
comments@wriu.org
www.wriu.org

WXHQ
PO Box 3541, Newport, RI 02840
PH: 401-847-1955
info@radionewport.org
www.radionewport.org

WXIN *Rhode Island College*
600 Mt. Pleasant Ave. Providence, RI 02908
PH: 401-456-8541 FX: 401-456-1988
www.ricradio.org

South Carolina

WSBF *Clemson U.*
315 Hendrix Ctr. Clemson, SC 29634
PH: 864-656-4010 FX: 864-656-4011
music@wsbf.net
wsbf.clemson.edu

WUSC *U. South Carolina Columbia*
RHUU Rm. 343, 1400 Greene St.
Columbia, SC 29208
PH: 803-777-5124
Ashley Blewer wuscmd@gwm.sc.edu
wusc.sc.edu

South Dakota

KBHU *Black Hills State U.*
1200 University St. #9003, Spearfish, SD 57799
PH: 605-642-6265
KBHUFM@gmail.com
www.bhsu.edu/bh/studentlife/organizations/kbhu

KTEQ *SD School of Mines and Tech.*
Surbeck Ctr. 501 E. St. Joseph St.
Rapid City, SD 57701
PH: 605-394-2233
kteq@sdsmt.edu
www.hpcnet.org/kteq

Tennessee

Eclectic Cuts *WMTS*
PO Box 331775, Murfreesboro, TN 37133-1775
Jane Elizabeth mail@eclecticcuts.com
www.radio.eclecticcuts.com
Features interviews and CD reviews. Focuses on a different genre each show.

The Funhouse *WUTK*
Derek & Rob funhouserock@gmail.com
www.funhouserock.com
Featuring everything from old school Punk and Funk to College Rock and Americana to all the best in local music.

WAWL *Chattanooga State Tech*
4501 Amnicola Hwy. Chattanooga, TN 37406-1097
Don Hixson don.hixson@chattanoogastate.edu
www.wawl.org

WEVL
PO Box 40952, Memphis, TN 38174
PH: 901-528-0560
wevl@wevl.org
wevl.org

WMTS *Middle Tennessee State U.*
Box 58, 1301 E. Main St., Murfreesboro, TN 37132
PH: 615-898-2636 FX: 615-898-5682
Brad Wilson brad@wmts.org
www.wmts.org

Writer's Block *WDVX*
PO Box 18157, Knoxville, TN 37928
PH: 865-494-2020
Karen E. Reynolds writersblockinfo@aol.com
www.writersblockonline.com
Interviews, a new live performance series and in studio performances.

WRLT
1310 Clinton St. #200, Nashville, TN 37203
PH: 615-242-5600 FX: 615-523-2199
www.wrlt.com

WRVU *Vanderbilt U.*
PO Box 9100, Stn. B, Nashville, TN 37235
PH: 615-322-3691 FX: 615-343-2582
wrvumd@gmail.com
wrvu.org

WTTU *Tennessee Tech.*
1000 N. Dixie Ave. UC Rm. 376
Cookeville, TN 38505
PH: 931-372-3688
davewttu@gmail.com
www.tntech.edu/wttu

WUMC
PO Box 9, Milligan College, TN 37682
PH: 423-461-8464
Madison Mathews memathews@milligan.edu
www.milliganradio.com

WUTK *U. Tennessee*
P103 Andy Holt Tower, Knoxville, TN 37996-0333
PH: 865-974-2229 FX: 865-974-2814
wutk@utk.edu
www.wutkradio.com

WUTM *U. Tennessee*
220 Gooch Hall, U. St. Martin, TN 38238
PH: 731-587-7000
wutm@utm.edu
www.utm.edu/organizations/wutm

WUTS *Sewanee U.*
735 University Ave. Sewanee, TN 37383
PH: 931-598-1206
wuts@sewanee.edu
www.wuts913.org

WVCP *Volunteer State College*
1480 Nashville Pike, Ramer Bldg. #101
Gallatin, TN 37066
PH: 615-230-3618 FX: 615-230-4803
holly.nimmo@volstate.edu
www2.volstate.edu/wvcp

XNRock
1824 Murfreesboro Rd. Nashville, TN 37217
Addison addison@xnrock.com
xnrock.com
Taking Rock to an Xtreme! Want your CD/EP/demo reviewed? Email me to find out how to submit your CD to us.

Texas

High Plains Morning *HPPR*
101 W. 5th St. #100, Amarillo, TX 79101
PH: 806-367-9088
Johnny Black music@hppr.org
www.hppr.org
Singer/Songwriters, Bluegrass, Contemporary Folk, World, Jazz and much more. Includes a performance studio.

KACC
3110 Mustang Rd. Alvin, TX 77511
PH: 281-756-3897
comments@kaccradio.com
www.kaccradio.com
Rock format.

KACV *Amarillo College*
PO Box 447, Amarillo, TX 79178
PH: 806-371-5222
kacvfm90@actx.edu
www.kacvfm.org

KANM *Texas A&M U.*
Student Services Bldg. 1236 TAMU
College Station, TX 77843-1236
PH: 979-862-2516 FX: 979-847-8854
Chris Sakaguchi md@kanm.tamu.edu
kanm.tamu.edu

KEOS *College Station*
PO Box 78, College Station, TX 77841
PH: 979-779-5367 FX: 979-779-7259
John Roths jroths@mail.tca.net
www.keos.org

KFAN
PO Box 311, Fredericksburg, TX 78624
PH: 830-997-2197 FX: 830-997-2198
musicandprogramming@ctesc.net
www.texasrebelradio.com

KGSR
8309 N. IH 35, Austin, TX 78753
PH: 512-832-4000 FX: 512-908-4902
Susan Castle scastle@kgsr.com
www.kgsr.com

KNON
5353 Maple Ave. Dallas, TX 75235
PH: 214-828-9500 x234
Christian Lee md@knon.org
www.knon.org

KOOP
PO Box 2116, Austin, TX 78768-2116
PH: 512-472-1369 FX: 512-472-6149
Paul Borelli music@koop.org
www.koop.org

KPFT
419 Lovett Blvd. Houston, TX 77006
PH: 713-526-4000 x313 FX: 713-526-5750
www.kpft.org

KRTU *Trinity U.*
One Trinity Pl. San Antonio, TX 78212
PH: 210-999-8313
Aaron Prado aprado@trinity.edu
www.krtu.org

KSAU *Stephen F. Austin State U.*
1936 North St., Nacogdoches, TX 75961
PH: 936-468-4000
ksaumusic@yahoo.com
www.sfasu.edu/ksau

KSHU *Sam Houston State U.*
PO Box 2207, Huntsville, TX 77341
PH: 936-294-1111
thekatkshu@yahoo.com
www.kshu.org

KTAI *Texas A&M U.*
Campus Box 178, Kingsville, TX 78363
PH: 361-593-5824 FX: 361-593-3402
ktai@tamuk.edu
www.tamuk.edu/ktai

KTCU *Texas Christian U.*
Box 298020, Fort Worth, TX 76129
PH: 817-257-7631
ktcu@tcu.edu
www.ktcu.tcu.edu

KTRU *Rice U.*
PO Box 1892, Houston, TX 77251
PH: 713-348-5878
noise@ktru.org
www.ktru.org

KTSW *Southwest Texas State U.*
601 University Dr. Old Main Rm. 106
San Marcos, TX 78666
PH: 512-245-3485 FX: 512-245-3732
ktswmusic@txstate.edu
www.ktsw.net

KTXT *Texas Tech*
PO Box 43081, Lubbock, TX 79409
PH: 806-742-3916 FX: 806-742-3906
ktxtfm@yahoo.com
www.ktxt.net

KUT/KUTX *U. Texas*
1 University Stn. A0704, Austin, TX 78712
PH: 512-471-1631 FX: 512-471-3700
music@kut.org
www.kut.org

KVRX *U. Texas/Austin*
PO Box D, Austin, TX 78713-7209
PH: 512-471-5431
music@kvrx.org
www.kvrx.org

KWTS *West Texas A&M U.*
2501 4th Ave. Canyon, TX 79016-0001
PH: 806-651-2000
kwts@mail.wtamu.edu
www.wtamu.edu/kwts

KYSM *San Antonio College*
1300 San Pedro Ave. San Antonio, TX 78212
PH: 210-733-2800
Leora Uribe ksymmd@yahoo.com
www.ksym.org

Rock Menagerie *KTCU*
Box 298020, Fort Worth, TX 76129
PH: 817-257-7631
Dale Gleitz RockMenagerie@netscape.net
www.ktcu.tcu.edu
*Up tempo music including Heavy Metal, Bubble
Gum, Jazz Fusion, New Wave, Stadium Rock,
Country Rock, Psychedelic etc.*

Texas Online Radio
190 Satterfield Rd. Lake Dunlap
New Braunfels, TX 78130
PH: 830-627-2547
Jeff@TexasOnlineRadio.com
www.texasonlineradio.com
*We're not limited to Texas artists! We support the
growth and promotion of new artists everywhere!*

Utah

KAGJ *Snow College*
150 E. College Ave. Ephraim, UT 84627
PH: 435-283-7007
www.snow.edu/~kage

KOEZ *Dixie State College*
225 S. 700 E., St George, UT 84770
PH: 435-634-2040
thedisc@dixie.edu
thedisc.dixie.edu

KPCW
PO Box 1372, Park City, UT 84060
PH: 435-645-7629
letters@kpcw.org
www.kpcw.org

KRCL
1971 W. N. Temple, Salt Lake City, UT 84116
PH: 801-363-1818 FX: 801-533-9136
Ryan Tronier ryant@krcl.org
www.krcl.org

KSUU *Southern Utah U.*
351 W. Ctr. Cedar City, UT 84720
PH: 435-865-8224 FX: 435-865-8352
ksuu@suu.edu
www.suu.edu/ksuu

KWCR *Weber State U.*
2188 University Cir. Ogden, UT 84408
PH: 801-626-8800
kwcrradio@mail.weber.edu
www.weberfm.org

KZMU
PO Box 1076, 1734 Rocky Rd. Moab, UT 84532
PH: 435-259-8824 FX: 435-259-8763
www.kzmu.org

Vermont

Download *WEQX*
PO Box 102.7 Manchester, VT 05254
PH: 802-362-4800 FX: 802-362-5555
Crista Leigh cristaleigh@gmail.com
www.weqx.com
3 Hours of the new music every Sunday night!

Early Warning *WBTZ*
PO Box 999, Burlington, VT 05402
PH: 877-893-2899
mailbag@999thebuzz.com
www.999thebuzz.com
New music from new artists and unheard of bands.

WGDR *Goddard College*
PO Box 336, Plainfield, VT 05667
PH: 802-454-7367
wgdrmusic@goddard.edu
www.wgdr.org

WNCS
169 River St. Montpelier, VT 05602
PH: 802-223-2396 FX: 802-223-1520
feedback@pointfm.com
www.pointfm.com

WOMM
PO Box 428, 215 College St. #301
Burlington, VT 05402-0428
PH: 802-865-1140
music@theradiator.org
www.theradiator.org

WRMC *Middlebury College*
Middlebury, VT 05753
PH: 802-443-6324 FX: 802-443-5108
Jordan Nassar jnassar@middlebury.edu
wrmc.middlebury.edu

WRUV *U. Vermont*
Billings Student Ctr. UVM Burlington, VT 05405
PH: 802-656-0796
wruv@wruv.org
www.myspace.com/wruv

WWPV *Saint Michael's College*
Box 274, Winooski Park, Colchester, VT 05439
PH: 802-654-2334 FX: 802-654-2336
Andrew Reid areid@smcvt.edu
personalweb.smcvt.edu/wwpv

Virginia

The Electric Croude *WCVE*
23 Sesame St., Richmond, VA 23235
PH: 804-560-8172
George Maida George_Maida@wcve.pbs.org
www.wcve.org/wcvefm
*As far as music goes, the show is very eclectic. I
play both acoustic and electric. The only genre I
don't play is Rap.*

Sans Serif *WTJU*
PO Box 400811, Charlottesville, VA 22904-4811
PH: 434-924-0885 FX: 434-924-8996
DJ Danger Dimples & D-Mo wtju@virginia.edu
sansserifradio.blogspot.com
*Celebrating the content, the certainty and whimsy of
audiophilia and atmosphere.*

WCWM *College of William and Mary*
Campus Ctr. PO Box 8793
Williamsburg, VA 23186
PH: 757-221-3287 FX: 757-221-2118
wcwmmd@wm.edu
www.wcwm.org

WDCE
Box 85, U. Richmond, VA 23173
PH: 804-289-8698 FX: 804-289-8996
wdce@richmond.edu
www.wdce.org

WEBR
2929 Eskridge Rd. Ste. S, Fairfax, VA 22031
PH: 703-573-8255 FX: 703-573-1210
webr@fcac.org
www.fcac.org/webr

WFFC *Ferrum College*
Ferrum, VA 24088
PH: 540-365-4483
wffc@ferrum.edu
www.ferrumradio.com

WGMU *George Mason U.*
4400 University Dr. MS4B7
Fairfax, VA 22031-4444
PH: 703-993-2940 FX: 703-993-2941
www.wgmuradio.com

WLUR *Washington & Lee U.*
Early-Fielding Ctr. 204 W. Washington St.
Lexington, VA 24450-2116
PH: 540-458-4995 FX: 540-458-4079
wlur@wlu.edu
wlur.wlu.edu

WMWC *Mary Washington College*
Box WMWC, 1301 College Ave.
Fredericksburg, VA 22401
PH: 540-654-1152
station@wmwc.org
www.wmwc.org

WODU *Old Dominion U.*
2102 Webb Ctr. Norfolk, VA 23529
PH: 757-683-3441
manager@woduradio.com
www.woduradio.com

WRIR *Richmond Indie Radio*
PO Box 4787, Richmond, VA 23220
PH: 804-649-9737 FX: 804-622-1436
Paul Ginder music@wrir.org
wrir.org

WTJU *U. Virginia*
PO Box 400811, Charlottesville, VA 22904-4811
PH: 434-924-0885 FX: 434-924-8996
wtju@virginia.edu
wtju.net/cpages/musub
Please visit our website for music submission guidelines.

WUVT *Virginia Tech*
350 Squires Student Ctr.
Blacksburg, VA 24061-0546
PH: 540-231-9880 FX: 208-692-5239
wuvtamfm@vt.edu
www.wuvt.vt.edu

WVCW *Virginia Commonwealth U.*
PO Box 842010, Richmond, VA 23284-2010
PH: 804-828-1058
wvcw@hotmail.com
www.wvcw.cc

WVRU *Radford U.*
PO Box 6973, Radford, VA 24142
PH: 540-831-6059 FX: 540-831-5893
wvru@radford.edu
www.wvru.org

WWHS *Hampden-Sydney College*
PO Box 128, Hampden-Sydney, VA 23943
PH: 434-223-6009
wwhs@wwhsfm.org
www.wwhsfm.org

WXJM *James Madison U.*
983 Reservoir St., Harrisonburg, VA 22801-4350
PH: 540-568-3425
wxjm@jmu.edu
orgs.jmu.edu/wxjm

Washington

KAOS *Evergreen State College*
CAB 301 2700 Evergreen Pkwy.
Olympia, WA 98505
PH: 360-867-6896
kaos_music@evergreen.edu
www.kaosradio.org

KBCS
3000 Landerholm Cir. SE.
Bellevue, WA 98007-6484
PH: 425-564-2424
office@kbcs.fm
kbcs.fm

KCCR *Pacific Lutheran U.*
Pacific Lutheran U. Tacoma, WA 98447
PH: 253-535-8860
kccr@plu.edu
www.plu.edu/~kccr

KCWU *Central Washington U.*
400 E. U. Way, Ellensburg, WA 98926-7594
PH: 509-963-2283 FX: 509-963-1688
www.881theburg.com

KEXP *U. Washington*
113 Dexter Ave. N., Seattle, WA 98109
PH: 206-520-5833 FX: 206-520-5899
info@kexp.org
www.kexp.org

KGRG *Green River College*
12401 SE. 320th St., Auburn, WA 98092-3699
PH: 253-833-9111 ext.2192 FX: 253-288-3439
www.kgrg.com

KNDD
1100 Olive Way #1650, Seattle, WA 98101
PH: 206-622-3251
www.1077theend.com
Rock format.

KOHO
7475 KOHO Place, Leavenworth, WA 98826
PH: 509-548-1011 FX: 509-548-3222
www.kohoradio.com

KSER
2623 Wetmore Ave. Everett, WA 98201
PH: 425-303-9070 FX: 425-303-9075
www.kser.org

KSUB *Seattle U.*
901 12th Ave. PO Box 222000, Seattle, WA 98122
PH: 206-296-2255
Will Johnson ksubmd@seattleu.edu
www.seattleu.edu/ksub

KSVR *Skagit Valley College*
2405 E. College Way, Mount Vernon, WA 98273
PH: 360-416-7711
mail@ksvr.org
www.ksvr.org

KUGS *Western Washington U.*
700 Viking Union MS 9106, Bellingham, WA 98225
PH: 360-650-2936
Christopher Mak music@kugs.org
www.kugs.org

KUPS *U. Puget Sound*
1500 N. Warner, Tacoma, WA 98416
PH: 253-879-2974
kupsprogramming@ups.edu
kups.ups.edu

KVTI *Clover Park College*
4500 Steilacoom Blvd. SW.
Lakewood, WA 98499-4098
PH: 253-589-5884 FX: 253-589-5797
i-91fm@cptc.edu
www.i91.ctc.edu

KWCW *Whitman College*
200 E. Boyer Ave. Walla Walla, WA 99362
PH: 509-527-5285
www.kwcw.net

KWRS *Whitworth College*
300 W. Hawthorne Rd. Spokane, WA 99251
PH: 509-777-4575
Caleb Knox kwrsmd@whitworth.edu
www.whitworth.edu/KWRS

KYVT
1116 S. 15th Ave. Yakima, WA 98902
PH: 509-573-5013.
Ryan ricigliano.ryan@ysd.wednet.edu
kyvtradio.com
Rock format.

KZUU *Washington State U.*
CUB Rm. 311, Pullman, WA 99164
PH: 509-335-2208
Brielle Schaeffer md@kzuu.org
www.kzuu.org

Nite Life *KEXP*
113 Dexter Ave. N., Seattle, WA 98109
PH: 206-520-5833 FX: 206-520-5899
DJ Michele michele@kexp.org
www.myspace.com/djmichele
Features Alt-Rock, Brit Pop, Trip-Hop, Soul, Indie Rock, Pop…

Rainy Dawg Radio *U. Washington*
SAO 254, Box 352238, Seattle, WA 98195
PH: 206-543-7675
Kyle Hargus top200md@rainydawg.org
www.rainydawg.org
Visit our website to find the e-mail address for your style of music.

Washington DC

Radio CPR
radiocpr@riseup.net
www.radiocpr.com

WCUA *Catholic U. America*
129 Pryzbyla Ctr. Washington, DC 20064
PH: 202-319-5106
cua-radio@cua.edu
wcua.cua.edu

WGTB *Georgetown U.*
432 Leavey Ctr. Washington, DC 20057
PH: 202-687-3702 FX: 202-687-8940
wgtb.music@gmail.com
georgetownradio.com

WRGW *George Washington U.*
800 21st St. NW. #G02, Washington, DC 20052
PH: 202-994-7554 FX: 202-994-4551
Glenn Sleasman music@gwradio.com
www.gwradio.com

WVAU *American U.*
Mary Graydon Ctr. 256, 4400 Massachusetts Ave.
NW, Washington, DC 20016
PH: 202-885-1212
Colin Fleming music@wvau.org
www.wvau.org

West Virginia

WMUL *Marshall U.*
1 John Marshall Dr. Huntington, WV 25755-2635
PH: 304-696-2295 FX: 304-696-3232
wmul@marshall.edu
www.marshall.edu/wmul

WSHC *Shepherd U.*
PO Box 3210, Shepherdstown, WV 25443
PH: 304-876-5369 FX: 304-876-5405
wshc@shepherd.edu
www.897wshc.org

WVWC *West Virginia Wesleyan*
Box 167, 59 College Ave.
Buckhannon, WV 26201-2999
PH: 304-473-8292
www.wvwc.edu/c92

WWVU *West Virginia U.*
PO Box 6446, Morgantown, WV 26506-6446
PH: 304-293-3329 FX: 304293-7363
www.wvu.edu/~u92

Wisconsin

KUWS *U. Wisconsin*
PO Box 2000, Superior, WI 54880
PH: 715-394-8530 FX: 715-394-8404
kuwsmd@yahoo.com
kuws.fm

WBCR *Beloit College*
Box 39, 700 College St., Beloit, WI 53511
PH: 608-363-2402 FX: 608-363-2718
www.beloit.edu/wbcr

WCCX *Carroll College*
100 N. East Ave. Waukesha, WI 53186
PH: 262-524-7355
wccx@cc.edu
wccx.cc.edu

WIPZ *U. Wisconsin*
900 Wood Rd. Kenosha, WI 53141
PH: 262-595-2527
webmaster@wipzradio.com
wipzradio.com

WLFM *Appleton*
Music Ctr. 420 E. College Ave. Appleton, WI 54911
PH: 920-832-6567 FX: 920-832-6904
wlfm.top200@gmail.com
www.lawrence.edu/sorg/wlfm

WMMM
7601 Ganser Way, Madison, WI 53719
PH: 608-826-0077 FX: 608-826-1245
1055triplem@entercom.com
www.1055triplem.com

WMSE *Milwaukee School of Engineering*
1025 N. Broadway, Milwaukee, WI 53202
PH: 414-277-7247 FX: 414-277-7149
Mike Bereiter bereiter@msoe.edu
www.wmse.org

WMUR *Marquette U.*
1131 W. Wisconsin Ave. #421
Milwaukee, WI 53233
PH: 414-288-7541 FX: 414-288-0643
marquetteradio.mu.edu

WORT
118 S. Bedford St., Madison, WI 53703-2692
PH: 608-256-2001 FX: 608-256-3704
wort@wort-fm.org
www.wort-fm.org
Our Friday afternoon show features interviews with independent artists.

WRFW *U. Wisconsin*
306 N. Hall, 410 S. 3rd St., River Falls, WI 54022
PH: 715-425-3689 FX: 715-425-3532
www.uwrf.edu/wrfw

WSUM *U. Wisconsin Madison*
PO Box 260020, Madison, WI 53726
music@wsum.wisc.edu
wsum.wisc.edu

WSUP *U. Wisconsin Platteville*
42 Pioneer Tower, 1 U. Plaza, Platteville, WI 53818
PH: 608-342-1165 FX: 608-342-1290
Ryan Whipple music@wsup.org
www.wsup.org

WSUW *U. Wisconsin Whitewater*
1201 Anderson Library, Whitewater, WI 53190
PH: 262-472-1323 FX: 262-472-5029
wsuw@wsuw.org
www.wsuw.org

WWSP *U. Wisconsin Steven's Point*
105 CAC Reserve St., Stevens Point, WI 54481
PH: 715-346-3755 FX: 715-346-4012
www.uwsp.edu/stuorg/wwsp

Canada

Canadian Satellite Radio
161 Bay St. #2300, PO Box 222
Toronto, ON M5J 2S1
PH: 416-203-6666
public.relations@xmradio.ca
www.cdnsatrad.com
Formed to provide subscription-based satellite radio service to Canadians.

Creative Radio
1147 Homewood Dr. Burlington, ON L7P 2M3
PH: 905-315-9032
cradio@creativeradiocentral.com
www.creativeradiocentral.com
Get the exposure you deserve.

Galaxie - The Continuous Music Network
PO Box 3220, Stn. C, Ottawa, ON K1Y 1E4
PH: 877-425-2943 FX: 613-562-8889
information@galaxie.ca
www.galaxie.ca
We recognize Canadian talent by supporting the development and promotion of our home-grown musicians. Our "Rising Stars" program encourages Canada's up-and-coming stars.

radioKAOS
1067 Bruce Ave. Windsor, ON N9A 4Y1
PH: 519-984-2377
radiokaos.com
Featuring many live shows and welcomes requests 24/7.

RadioMOI
#1-1555 Dublin Ave. Winnipeg, MB R3E 3M8
PH: 204-786-3994 FX: 204-783-5805
www.radiomoi.com
We accept submissions from independent artists.

THAT RADIO
www.thatradio.com
PH: 416-204-9951 FX: 416-204-9723
D'Anise danisestar@gmail.com
www.thatradio.com
Canada's #1 internet radio station with the World's biggest playlist including YOUR music!

Alberta

CJSR *U. Alberta*
0-09 Students' Union Bldg. Edmonton, AB T6G 2J7
PH: 780-492-2577 x232 FX: 780-492-3121
music@cjsr.com
www.cjsr.com

CJSW *U. Calgary*
#127 MacEwan Hall, Calgary, AB T2N 1N4
PH: 403-220-3902 FX: 403-289-8212
Myke Atkinson cjswfm@ucalgary.ca
www.cjsw.com

CKXU *U. Lethbridge*
SU 164, 4401 University Dr. W.
Lethbridge, AB T1K 3M4
PH: 403-329-2335 FX: 403-329-2224
www.ckxu.com

CKUA
10526 Jasper Ave. Edmonton, AB T5J 1Z7
PH: 780-428-7595 FX: 780-428-7624
music.director@ckua.org
www.ckua.org

Jim's Basement
87 Tuscany Springs Way NW, Calgary, AB T3L 2N4
jim@bignote.net
www.myspace.com/jimsbasement
All songs are from artists I have met, seen live, grown up listening to or just had their CD handed to me.

British Columbia

Breakfast With The Browns *CITR*
#233-6138 SUB Blvd. Vancouver, BC V6T 1Z1
PH: 604-822-2487 FX: 604-822-9364
breakfastwiththebrowns@hotmail.com
www.citr.ca
Plays all the best new and old Downtempo- Electro-Pop- Lounge- Core in an exciting eclectic blend of aural delights.

CFBX *U. College of the Cariboo*
900 McGill Rd. House 8 Kamloops, BC V2C 5N3
PH: 250-377-3988 FX: 250-852-6350
Steve Marlow radio8music@yahoo.com
www.thex.ca

CFML *BC Inst. Tech*
Building SE-10, 3700 Willingdon Ave.
Burnaby, BC V5G 3H2
PH: 604-432-8510
allofus@evolution1079.com
www.evolution1079.com

CFRO
110-360 Columbia St., Vancouver, BC V6A 4J1
PH: 604-684-8494 x250
music-department@coopradio.org
www.coopradio.org

CFUR *UNBC*
3333 University Way, Prince George, BC V2N 4Z9
PH: 250-960-7664
Bryndis Ogmundson cfurradio@hotmail.com
www.cfur.ca

CFUV *U. Victoria*
PO Box 3035, Victoria, BC V8W 3P3
PH: 250-721-8704
Justin Lanoue cfuvmd@uvic.ca
cfuv.uvic.ca

CHLY *Malaspina U. College*
#2-34 Victoria Rd. Nanaimo, BC V9R 5B8
PH: 250-716 3410
George Millar music@chly.ca
www.chly.ca

CITR
#233-6138 SUB Blvd. Vancouver, BC V6T 1Z1
PH: 604-822-8733 FX: 604-822-9364
Luke Meat citrmusic@club.ams.ubc.ca
www.citr.ca

CJLY
Box 767, Nelson, BC V1L 5R4
PH: 250-352-9600 FX: 250-352-9653
Zoe Creighton md@kootenaycoopradio.com
www.kics.bc.ca/kcr

CJSF *Simon Fraser U.*
TC 216, Burnaby, BC V5A 1S6
PH: 604-291-3076 FX: 604-291-3695
www.myspace.com/cjsffm

CKMO *Camosun College*
3100 Foul Bay Rd. Victoria, BC V8P 5J2
PH: 250-370-3658 FX: 250-370-3679
Doug Ozeroff doug@village900.ca
www.village900.ca

CVUE
PO Box 2288, Sechelt, BC V0N3A0
PH: 604-885-0800 FX: 604-885-0803
cvuemail@yahoo.ca
www.civu.net

Manitoba

CJUM
Rm. 308 U. Ctr. Winnipeg, MB R3T 2N2
PH: 204-474-7027 FX: 204-269-1299
Michael Elves program.director@umfm.com
www.umfm.com

CKIC *Red River College*
W-106, 160 Princess St., Winnipeg, MB R3B 1K9
heyeverybody@kick.fm
www.kick.fm

CKUW *U. Winnipeg*
Rm. 4CM11, 515 Portage Ave.
Winnipeg, MB R3B 2E9
PH: 204-786-9782 FX: 204-783-7080
ckuw@uwinnipeg.ca
www.ckuw.ca

Native Communications Inc.
1507 Inkster Blvd. Winnipeg, MB R2X 1R2
PH: 204-772-8255 FX: 204-779-5628
www.ncifm.com
An Aboriginal service organization offering radio programming throughout Manitoba.

New Brunswick

CHMA *Mount Allison U.*
152-A Main St. #303, Sackville, NB E4L 1B4
PH: 506-364-2222
chma@mta.ca
www.mta.ca/chma

CHSR *U. New Brunswick*
PO Box 4400, Fredericton, NB E3B 5A3
PH: 506-453-4985 FX: 506-453-4999
Andrew Robinson chsrmd@unb.ca
www.unb.ca/web/chsr

CJPN
715 rue Priestman, Fredericton, NB E3B 5W7
PH: 506-454-2576 FX: 506-453-3958
cjpn@nbnet.nb.ca
www.centre-sainte-anne.nb.ca/cjpn

CJSE
96 rue Providence, Shédiac, NB E4P 2M9
PH: 506-532-0080 FX: 506-532-0120
cjse@cjse.ca
www.cjse.ca

CKUM *U. Moncton*
Centre Etudiant, Moncton, NB E1A 3E9
PH: 506-858-5772
Carolynn McNally musiqueradioj935@yahoo.ca
www.umoncton.ca/ckum

Olive's Brain Independent Radio
17 Vaughan Dr. Nauwigewauk, NB E5N 6T9
Brad Stevenson olivesbrain@hotmail.com
www.olivesbrain.gotdns.com
An online radio station that plays only independent music.

Newfoundland

CHMR *Memorial U. Newfoundland*
Box A-119 St. John's, NL A1C 5S7
PH: 709-737-4777 FX: 709-737-7688
chmr@mun.ca
www.chmr.ca

The Songwriters *CHMR*
Box A-119 St. John's, NL A1C 5S7
PH: 709-737-4777 FX: 709-737-7688
chmr@mun.ca
www.chmr.ca
If you are a Singer/Songwriter and would like to be a guest, contact me.

Nova Scotia

CFXU *St. Francis Xavier U.*
PO Box 948, Antigonish, NS B2G 2X1
PH: 902-867-2401
cfxumd@stfx.ca
radiocfxu.ca

CKDU *Dalhousie U.*
Dalhousie Stud. Union Bldg. 6136 U. Ave.
Halifax, NS B3H 4J2
PH: 902-494-6479
Laura Peek music@ckdu.ca
www.ckdu.ca

Ontario

C101.5 *Mohawk College*
135 Fennell Ave. W. PO Box 2034
Hamilton, ON L8N 3T2
PH: 905-575-2175 FX: 905-575-2385
www.mohawkcollege.ca/msa/cioi/index.htm

CFBU *Brock U.*
500 Glenridge Ave. St. Catharines, ON L2S 3A1
PH: 905-346-2644
md@cfbu.ca
www.cfbu.ca

CFFF *Trent U.*
715 George St. N., Peterborough, ON K9H 3T2
PH: 705-748-4761
info@trentradio.ca
www.trentu.ca/trentradio

CFMU *McMaster U.*
Student Ctr. Rm. B119, Hamilton, ON L8S 4S4
PH: 905-525-9140 x22053
Olga Kirgidis cfmumusic@msu.mcmaster.ca
cfmu.mcmaster.ca

CFRC *Queens U.*
Carruthers Hall Kingston, ON K7L 3N6
PH: 613-533-6000 x74849 FX: 613-533-6049
Scott Stevens cfrcmusic@ams.queensu.ca
www.cfrc.ca

CFRE
3359 Mississauga Rd. Mississauga, ON L5L 1C6
PH: 905-569-4712 FX: 905-569-4713
Tenni Gharakhanian tenni@cfreradio.com
www.cfreradio.com

CFRL *Fanshawe College*
1460 Oxford St. E., London, ON N5V 1W2
PH: 519-453-2810 x201
www.1069fm.ca

CFRU *U. Guelph*
U.C. Level 2 Guelph, ON N1G 2W1
PH: 519-824-4120 x56919 FX: 519-763-9603
info@cfru.ca
www.cfru.ca

CHRW *U. Western Ontario*
Rm. 250 UCC, UWO, London, ON N6A 3K7
PH: 519-661-3601 FX: 519-661-3372
Alicks Girowski chrwmp@uwo.ca
www.chrwradio.com

CHRY *York U.*
Rm. 413, Student Ctr. Toronto, ON M3J 1P3
PH: 416-736-5293 x20185 FX: 416-650-8052
www.yorku.ca/chry

CHUO *U. Ottawa*
65 University Pvt. #0038, Ottawa, ON K1N 9A5
PH: 613-562-5800 x2720 FX: 613-562-5969
Joni Sadler music@chuo.fm
www.chuo.fm

CILU *Lakehead U.*
955 Oliver Rd. Rm. UC2014A
Thunder Bay, ON P7B 5E1
PH: 807-766-7207
David Ivany musicdirector@luradio.ca
www.luradio.ca

CIUT *U. Toronto*
91 St. George St., Toronto, ON M5S 2E8
PH: 416-978-0909 x214 FX: 416-946-7004
Ron Burd r_burd@ciut.fm
www.ciut.fm

CJAM *U. Windsor*
401 Sunset Ave. Windsor, ON N9B 3P4
PH: 519-253-3000 x2527 FX: 519-971-3605
cjammd@uwindsor.ca
www.uwindsor.ca/cjam

CJIQ *Conestoga College*
Rm. 3B15, 299 Doon Valley Dr.
Kitchener, ON N2G 4M4
PH: 519-748-5220 x3223
Mike Thurnell mthurnell@conestogac.on.ca
www.cjiq.fm

CJLX *Loyalist College*
PO Box 4200, Belleville, ON K8N 5B9
PH: 613-966-0923 FX: 613-966-1993
www.91x.fm

CKCU *Carleton U.*
Rm. 517 U. Ctr., 1125 Colonel By Dr.
Ottawa, ON K1S 5B6
PH: 613-520-2898
Christian Rosplesch music@ckcufm.com
www.ckcufm.com

CKDJ *Algonquin College*
1385 Woodroffe Ave. Ottawa, ON K2G 1V8
PH: 613-727-4723 x2408
crockfd@algonquincollege.com
www.ckdj.net

CKHC *Humber College*
205 Humber College Blvd. Toronto, ON M5W 5L7
PH: 416-675-6622 x4913
radio.humber.ca

CKLN *Ryerson*
55 Gould St. 2nd Fl. Toronto, ON M5B 1E9
PH: 416-979-5251 x2374 FX: 416-595-0226
Tim May music@ckln.fm
www.ckln.fm

CKLU *Laurentian U.*
935 Ramsey Lake Rd. Sudbury, ON P3E 2C6
PH: 705-673-6538 FX: 705-675-4878
Mark Browning md@cklu.ca
www.cklu.ca

CKMS *U. Waterloo*
200 University Ave. W., Waterloo, ON N2L 3G1
PH: 519-886-2567 x204 FX: 519-884-3530
www.ckmsfm.ca

CKRG *Glendon College*
2275 Bayview Ave. Toronto, ON M4N 3M6
PH: 416-487-6739
Nadia Ouellet nadia@ckrgfm.com
www.ckrgfm.com

CKON *Akwesasne Mohawk Nation Radio*
PO Box 1496, Cornwall, ON K6H 5V5
PH: 613-575-2100 FX: 613-575-2566
ckonfm@yahoo.com
www.ckonfm.com

CKVI *Kingston Collegiate*
235 Frontenac St., Kingston, ON K7L 3S7
PH: 613-544-7864 FX: 613-544-8795
Max Lienhard ckvi@limestone.on.ca
www.thecave.ca

CKWR
375 University Ave. E. Waterloo, ON N2K 3M7
PH: 519-886-9870 FX: 519-886-0090
general@ckwr.com
www.ckwr.com

CSCR *U. Toronto*
1265 Military Trail, Scarborough, ON M1C 1A4
PH: 416-287-7049
info@fusionradio.ca
www.fusionradio.ca

Indie Hour *CFNY*
PH: 416-408-3343 FX: 416-847-3300
www.edge102.com/station/sp_indie_hour.cfm
We do NOT ACCEPT CDs anymore. Send us one MP3 for the show.

Off the Beaten Track *CKCU*
PH: 613-520-2898
Dave Aardvark daardvark@yahoo.com
www.offthebeatentrackradio.com
Far reaching Underground Rock based, general music show with an emphasis on "organic" sounds. Contact me for the mailing address.

Radio Laurier
3rd Fl. Fred Nichols Campus Ctr. WLU
75 University Ave. W., Waterloo, ON N2L 3C5
PH: 519-884-0710 x2191
Joy Ghosh radiolaurier@wlusu.com
www.radiolaurier.com

Spirit Live Radio *Ryerson Polytechnic U.*
350 Victoria St., Toronto, ON M5B 2K3
PH: 416-979-8151 FX: 416-979-5246
spiritlive.net@gmail.com
www.spiritlive.net

ThatRadio.com
600 Bay St. #405, Toronto, ON M5G 1M6
PH: 416-204-9951 FX: 416-204-9723
D'Anise danisestar@gmail.com
www.thatradio.com
Members can promote their businesses, projects, organizations, or ideas to other members of the community. If you'd like to get interviewed on Liquid Lunch or any other ThatRadio.com show, please call or e-mail us.

Up for Sale *CHRY*
Rm. 413, Student Ctr. Toronto, ON M3J 1P3
PH: 416-736-5656 FX: 416-650-8052
Daria info@upforsaleradio.com
www.upforsaleradio.com
Indie Rock show. Feel free to drop me a line or send your music to the station!

Quebec

CFAK *U. Sherbrooke*
2500, boul. de l'Université
Sherbrooke, QC J1K 2R1
PH: 819-821-8000 FX: 819-821-7930
musik@cfak.qc.ca
www.cfak.qc.ca

CFLX
67, rue Wellington nord, Sherbrooke, QC J1H 5A9
PH: 819-566-2787 FX: 819-566-7331
cflx@cflx.qc.ca
www.cflx.qc.ca

CFOU
3351, boul. des Forges,
Trois-Rivières, QC G9A 5H7
PH: 819-376-5184 FX: 819-376-5239
Alain Lefebvre progcfou@uqtr.ca
www.cfou.ca

CHAA
91, rue St. Jean, Longueuil, QC J4H 2W8
PH: 450-646-6800 FX: 450-646-7378
info@fm1033.ca
www.fm1033.ca

CHGA
163 Laurier, Maniwaki, QC J9E 2K6
PH: 1-819-449-3959 FX: 819-449-7331
chga@bellnet.ca
www.chga.qc.ca

CHYZ *U. Laval*
Local 0236, Pavillon Pollack, QC G1K 7P4
PH: 418-656-2131 FX: 418-656-2365
Catherine Couture chyz-fm@public.ulaval.ca
www.chyz.qc.ca

CIBL
1691, boul Pie IX, Montréal, QC H1V 2C3
PH: 514-526-2581 FX: 514-526-3583
info@cibl.cam.org
cibl1015.com

CISM *U. de Montréal*
2332 Edouard Montpetit, C-1509 C.P. 6128
Montréal, QC H3C 3J7
PH: 514-343-CISM FX: 514-343-2418
mroussy@cism893.ca
www.cism.umontreal.ca

CJLO
7141 Sherbrooke St. Ouest, #CC-430
Montreal, QC H4B 1R6
PH: 514-848-7401 FX: 514-848-7450
Omar Husain md-alt@cjlo.com
www.cjlo.com

CJMQ *Bishops U.*
Box 2135, Lennoxville, QC J1M 1Z7
PH: 819-822-9600 x2689
cjmqnews@yahoo.ca
www.cjmq.fm

CKRL *Québec City*
405, 3e Ave. Québec City, QC G1L 2W2
PH: 418-640-2575 FX: 418-640-1588
ckrl@ckrl.qc.ca
www.ckrl.qc.ca

CKUT *McGill U.*
3647 U. St., Montreal, QC H3A 2B3
PH: 514-398-6787 FX: 514-398-8261
music@ckut.ca
www.ckut.ca

Mohawk Radio
PO Box 1743, Kahnawake
Mohawk Territory via QC J0L 1B0
PH: 450-632-5050
Daniel Kirby danielk@mohawk-radio.com
www.mohawk-radio.com
Giving indie bands the recognition they deserve.

Muzik Paradise
C.P. 151, Bromont, QC J2L 1A9
www.muzikparadise.org
La radio internet du top chrétien francophone!

Saskatchewan

CFCR
PO Box 7544, Saskatoon, SK S7K 4L4
PH: 306-664-6678
Zach Low tracking@cfcr.ca
www.cfcr.ca

Mexico

e-reverenc!a
ereverencia@gmail.com
www.e-reverencia.net
Para quienes expresarse no es una falta de respeto (New Rock, Alternative, Indie Rock).

Eufonia Radio
Postal 2146 Sucursal de Correos "J" 64841
Monterrey, N.L. México
PH: 5281-8387-0665
programa@eufonia.net
www.eufonia.net
2hrs weekly of Indie Rock and other non commercial genres.

XHUG *Radio U. de Guadalajara*
#976, PISO 12A.P. 4-29 C.P. 44100 Guadalajara,
Jalisco, México
PH: 0133-3825-6000 FX: 0133-3826-1848
www.radio.udg.mx

South America

Radio Ufscar
Rodovia Washington Luis KM 235 - Monjolinho -
CEP 13565-905 - São Carlos - SP - Brasil
PH: 55-16-3351-8099 FX: 55-16-3351-8119
Ricardo Rodrigues ricardo@ufscar.br
www.ufscar.br/radio
*Brazilian University radio that play independent
music of all genres. Send your music for instant
airplay!!!*

Europe

Austria

FM4 *Linz U.*
A-1136 Wien, Austria
PH: +43-1-505-22-55 FX: 01-50101-16449
fm4@orf.at
fm4.orf.at

Freier Rundfunk Oberösterreich
GmbH Kirchengasse 4 A-4040 Linz, Austria
PH: 43-732-71-72-77 FX: 43-732-71-72-77 -155
fro@fro.at
www.fro.at

Orange 94.0 *Free Radio in Wien*
Klosterneuburger Str. 1, A-1200 Wien, Austria
PH: 43-1-3190999 FX: 43-1-3190999-14
programm@o94.at
www.orange.or.at

Radio 1476
ORF, 1476 Argentinierstr. 30a A-1040 Wien, Austria
1476@orf.at
1476.orf.at

Belgium

Belgischer Rundfunk
Kehrweg 11, 4700 Eupen, Belgium
PH: 087-591111 FX: 087-591199
musik@brf.be
www.brf.be

FM Brussel
Eugène Flageyplein 18, Bus 18 - 1050 Elsene,
Belgium
PH: 02-800-0-808 FX: 02-800-0-809
muziekredactie@fmbrussel.be
www.fmbrussel.be

Kinky Star Radio
Vlasmarkt 9 9000 Gent, Belgium
PH: +32-9-223-48-45
radio@kinkystar.com
www.kinkystar.com
Features indie music, news and reviews.

Radio 1
Auguste Reyerslaan 52 1043, Brussels, Belgium
PH: 02-741-38-93 FX: 02-736-57-86
info@radio1.be
www.radio1.be

Radio 101
PO Box 2, B-4851 Gemmenich, Belgium
radio101.de

Radio Campus Bruxelles
22 av. Paul Héger 1000 Bruxelles, Belgium
PH: 32-2-640-87-17 FX: 32-2-650-34-63
rcampus@ulb.ac.be
radiocampus.ulb.ac.be

Radio Panik
Rue Saint Josse, 49, 1210 Bruxelles, Belgium
PH/FX: +32 (0)2-732-14-45
cp@radiopanik.org
www.radiopanik.org

Radio Scorpio
Naamsestraat 96, 3000 Leuven, Belgium
PH: 32-016-222-300
mail@radioscorpio.com
www.radioscorpio.com

RUN
OREFUNDP ASBL, Rue du Séminaire, 22/15 5000
Namur, Belgium
run@fundp.ac.be
www.run.be

Urgent FM *U. Ghent*
Sint-Pietersnieuwstraat 43, 9000 Gent, Belgium
PH: 09-264-79-09
muziek@urgent.fm
urgent.fm

Czech Republic

THC Radio
submit@thcradio.net
www.thcradio.net

Denmark

DR Barometer
TV Byen, Pavillion 22, 2860 Søborg, Denmark
barometer@dr.dk
www.dr.dk/skum/barometer
Denmark's Alternative radio channel.

Radio Holstebro
PH: 40193355
Henrik Højbjerg henrik@radioholstebro.dk
www.radioholstebro.dk

Station 10
Stationsvej 10 9400 Nørresundby, Denmark
PH: 98-19-47-91
Else Petersen else@station10.dk
www.station10.dk

Universitetsradioen Nalle Kirkväg
Krystalgade 14, 1172 København K, Denmark
PH: 35-32-39-39 FX: 35-32-39-38
info@universitetsradioen.dk
www.uradio.ku.dk

Radio Østsjælland
Vinkældertorvet 2A Postboks 34 4640 Fakse,
Denmark
PH: 56-71-30-03 FX: 56-71-39-51
fakse@lokalradio.dk
www.lokalradio.dk

Finland

Radio Robin Hood
Itäinen Rantakatu 64 20810 Turku, Finland
PH: 02-2773-666 FX: 02-2500-905
info@radiorobinhood.fi
www.radiorobinhood.fi/rrh

France

Alternantes FM
Blvd. des Poilus, BP 31 605,
44 316 Nantes cedex 3, France
PH: 02-40-93-26-62 FX: 02-40-93-04-98
musique@alternantesfm.net
www.alternantesfm.net

Le Biplan
19 rue Colbert 59000 Lille, France
PH: 33-03-20-420-227
lebiplan.programmation@wanadoo.fr
www.lebiplan.org

Canal B Rennes
BP 7147, 35171 Bruz, France
PH: 33-0-2-99-52-77-66 FX: 33-0-2-99-05-39-07
canalb@rennet.org
www.rennet.org/canalb

Coloriage
Ferme de la Vendue 21500 Fain les Moutiers,
France
PH: 03-80-96-40-76 FX: 03-80-96-34-99
coloriage@coloriage.fr
coloriage.free.fr

Couleur 3 Lausanne
Av. du Temple 40, case postale 78, CH-1010
Lausanne, France
PH: +41-21-318-15-42
www.couleur3.ch

C'rock radio
BP 231, 38201 Vienne, France
PH: 04-74-53-28-91 FX: 04-74-31-59-07
www.crockradio.com

L'Eko des Garrigues
BP5555 34070 Montpellier 3, France
PH: 04-67-70-80-86 FX: 04-67-70-93-65
www.ekodesgarrigues.com

FMR
9 bd. Minimes, 31200 Toulouse, France
PH: 05-61-58-35-12 FX: 05-61-58-37-04
www.radio-fmr.net

JetFM
11 rue de Dijon 44800 St., Herblain, France
PH: 02-40-58-63-63 FX: 02-40-43-68-05
www.jetfm.asso.fr

Ocean Radio
2, place du Foirail 81220 St Paul Cap de Joux,
France
eole@ocean-music.com
www.ocean-music.com

Planet Claire
denis@planet-claire.org
planet-claire.org

Planet of Sound
planet_of_sound@lemoneyes-radio.com
www.lemoneyes-radio.com/music

Radio 666
BP 666, 14201 Hérouville Saint Clair, France
PH: 02-3194-6666
www.radio666.com

Radio Alpine Meilleure
Rue du Sénateur Bonniard 05 200 Embrun, France
PH: 04-92-43-37-38 FX: 04-92-43-54-43
ram05@wanadoo.fr
perso.wanadoo.fr/jb.oury/RAM.htm

Radio Beton
90, ave. Maginot, 37100 Tours, France
PH: 02-47-51-03-83
info@radiobeton.com
www.radiobeton.com

Radio Campus
16 rue degeorges 63000 Clermont-FD, France
PH: 04-73-140-158 FX: 04-73-902-877
clermont@radiocampus.org
clermont.radio-campus.org

Radio Campus Grenoble
av. Centrale Domaine universitaire 38402
Saint Martin d'Hères, France
PH: 04-56-52-85-20
contact@campusgrenoble.org
www.grenoble.radio-campus.org

Radio Campus Lille
campus@campuslille.com
www.campuslille.com

Radio Campus Paris
50, rue des Tournelles, 75 003 Paris, France
PH: 01-49-96-65-45
www.radiocampusparis.org

Radio Canut
24, rue Sergent Blandan 1er arrdt - BP 1101 -
69201 Lyon, France
PH: 04-78-39-18-15 FX: 04-78-29-26-00
radio@radiocanut.org
regardeavue.com/radiocanut

Radio Dio
BP 51, 42002 St-Etienne, France
PH: 0477250594 FX: 0477417916
nokilldio@yahoo.fr
radiodio.org

Radio En Construction
BP124, 67069 Strasbourg, France
PH: 33-0-3-88-600-915
Emilie emilie@radioenconstruction.com
www.recfm.com

Radio Grenouille
41, rue Jobin, 13003 Marseille, France
PH: 04-95-04-95-15 FX: 04-95-04-95-00
radio@grenouille888.org
www.grenouille888.org

Radio Grésivaudan
94, rue du Brocey, 38920 Crolles, France
PH: 04-76-08-91-91
webmaster@radio-gresivaudan.org
www.radio-gresivaudan.org

Radio Pluriel
BP 106 69801 Saint-Priest, France
PH: 04-78-21-83-49 FX: 04-78-21-46-58
prog@plurielfm.org
www.plurielfm.org

Radio Primitive
13, rue. Flodoard BP 2169 51081 Reims, France
PH: 33-03-26-02-33-74 FX: 33-03-26-02-68-30
radio.primitive@wanadoo.fr
perso.wanadoo.fr/primitive

Radio Pulsar
15, rue. des Feuillants 86035 Poitiers, France
PH: 05-49-88-33-04 FX: 05-49-88-07-99
info@radio-pulsar.org
www.radio-pulsar.org

RCT
BP 2001-69603 Villeurbanne, France
PH: 33-04-78-89-59-48 FX: 33-04-72-44-34-42
rctworld@radio-rct.com
www.radio-rct.com

RCV
41 Bis Bd Vauban, 59046 Lille, France
PH: 05-56-00-87-02 FX: 33-03-20-30-40-51
Nicolas Pradeau nico@radio-sauvagine.com
www.rcv-lille.com

Sauvagine
15 rue Rode, 33000 Bordeaux, France
PH: 05-56-00-87-00 FX: 05-56-90-07-57
info@radio-sauvagine.com
www.radio-sauvagine.com

Germany

Alooga Radio
Westerwaldstr.35, D-53489 Sinzig, Germany
PH: +49-2642-43385 FX: +49-30-484983193
Gerd Hoeschen aka DJ Ottic info@alooga.de
www.alooga.de
Features Alternative music.

ALPHAbeat Radio
Westerwaldstr.35 D-53489 Sinzig, Germany
PH: 49-2642-43385 FX: 49-30-484983193
DJ Ottic info@ottic.de
www.ottic.de

Bayerischer Rundfunk
Rundfunkplatz 1 80300 München, Germany
PH: (089) 59-00-01
radio@br-online.de
www.br-online.de

bigFM
Kronenstrasse 24, im Zeppelin Carré, 70173
Stuttgart, Germany
PH: 07-11-28-420-0 FX: 07-11-28-420-490
music@big-fm.de
www.bigfm.de

Campus-Welle Köln
Albertus-Magnus-Platz 50923 Köln, Germany
PH: 0221-470-4831 FX: 0221-470-6712
musik@koelncampus.com
www.koelncampus.com

coloRadio
Jordanstraße 5 01099 Dresden, Germany
PH: 0351-317-9227 FX: 0351-317-9226
info@coloradio.org
www.freie-radios.de/coloradio

Eins live
WDR, 50600 Köln, Germany
PH: 0180-5678-111
einslive@wdr.de
www.einslive.de

elDOradio!
Vogelpothsweg 74, 44227 Dortmund, Germany
PH: 0231-755-7474 FX: 0231-755-7476
musik@elDOradio.de
www.eldoradio.de

Freies Radio für
Rieckestr. 24 70190 Stuttgart, Germany
PH: 0711-64-00-444 FX: 0711-64-00-443
info@freies-radio.de
www.freies-radio.de

FRITZ Radio
Postfach 90 9000 14439 Potsdam, Germany
PH: 0331-70-97-110 FX: 0331-731-39-83
fritz@fritz.de
www.fritz.de

HSF Studentenradio
Max-Planck-Ring 8b, 98693 Ilmenau, Germany
PH: +49-3677-694222 FX: +49-3677-694216
info@radio-hsf.de
www.hsf.tu-ilmenau.de

ju: N ai
UNI, radio über Otto-von-Guericke-Universität PF
4120 39016 Magdeburg, Germany
adminuniradio-magdeburg.de
www.uniradio-magdeburg.de

Kontrast Radio
Postfach 36 03 36, 10973 Berlin, Germany
PH: +49-30-61107895
www.kontrastradio.net
Berlin's finest Alternative radio. Does reviews too.

M945
Schwere-Reiter-Str. 35 Gebäude 40a 80797
München, Germany
PH: 089-360-388-0 FX: 089-360-388-59
info@m945.de
m945.afk.de/m

Oldenburg Eins
Bahnhofstr.11 26 122 Oldenburg, Germany
PH: 0441 21-888-44 FX: 0441 21-888-40
info@oeins.de
www.oeins.de

POPSCENE with J*A*L*A*L
Elisabethstr.120, 28217 Bremen, Germany
www.popscenewithjalal.com
One of the leading indie radio shows in Europe.

QUERFUNK
Steinstraße 23 76133 Karlsruhe, Germany
PH: 0721 38-50-30 FX: 0721 38-50-20
info@querfunk.de
www.querfunk.de

Radio Blau
V.i.S.d.P Paul-Gruner-StraBe 62 04107 Leipzig,
Germany
PH: 0341-301-00-97 FX: 0341-301-00-07
musik@radioblau.de
www.radioblau.de

Radio C.T.
Ruhr-Universität 44780 Bochum, Germany
PH: 0234-971-90-80 FX: 0234-971-90-82
info@radioct.de
www.radioct.de

Radio Dreyeckland
Betriebs GmbH Adlerstr. 12, D - 79098 Freiburg,
Germany
PH: 0761-31028 FX: 0761-31868
verwaltung@rdl.de
www.rdl.de

radioeins
Marlene-Dietrich-Allee 20, 14482 Potsdam -
Babelsberg, Germany
PH: 0331-70-99-888 FX: 0331-70 99 333
www.radioeins.de

Radio Flora
Zur Bettfedernfabrik 1 30451 Hannover, Germany
PH: 0511-219-79-0 FX: 0511-219-79-19
postbox@radioflora.de
radioflora.apc.de

Radio Mittweida
Leisniger Straße 9, 09648 Mittweida, Germany
PH: 03727-581022 FX: 03727-581454
musik@radio-mittweida.de
www.radio-mittweida.de

Radio Neckarburg
August-Schuhmacher-Straße 10, 78664 Eschbronn-
Mariazell, Germany
PH: 07403-8000 FX: 07403-8002
info@radio-neckarburg.de
www.radio-neckarburg.de

Radio Rheinwelle
Postfach 4920 65039 Wiesbaden, Germany
PH: 0611-609-9333 FX: 0611-609-9334
musik@radio-rheinwelle.de
www.radio-rheinwelle.de

Radio SIRUP
AVMZ Adolf-Reichwein-Str.2 57068 Siegen,
Germany
PH: 0271-2-383-666 FX: 0271-740-25-26
musik@radio-sirup.de
www.radio-sirup.de

Radio T
Karl-Liebknecht-Str. 19 09111 Chemnitz, Germany
PH: 0371-350-235 FX: 0371-350-234
info@radiot.de
www.radiot.de

Radio Wüste Welle
Hechingerstr. 203, 72072 Tübingen, Germany
PH: 07071-760204 FX: 07071-760347
www.wueste-welle.de

RadioActiv
Rhein-Neckar e.V.U. Mannheim Schloß, Postfach
144 68131 Mannheim, Germany
PH: 0621-1-81-18-11 FX: 0621-1-81-18-12
www.radioaktiv.org

uniRadio
Malteser Str. 74-100/ Haus M 12249 Berlin,
Germany
PH: 030-841-727-101 FX: 030-841-727-109
redaktion@uniradio.de
www.uniradio.de

Uniwelle Tübingen
Gmelinstr. 6/1 72076 Tübingen, Germany
PH: 07071-297-7688 FX: 07071-29-5881
uniradio@uni-tuebingen.de
www.uni-tuebingen.de/uniradio

YOU FM
60222 Frankfurt a.M. Germany
PH: 069-55-30-40 FX: 069-55-88-06
studio@you-fm.de
www.youfm.de

Greece

ERA Aigaiou
nk@aegean.gr
www.aegean.gr/era_aegean

Hot Station
info@hotstation.gr
www.hotstation.gr

Hungary

Tilos Rádió
1462 Budapest, Pf: 601, Hungary
PH: +36-1-476-8491 FX: +36-1-476-8492
radio@tilos.hu
tilos.hu

Italy

Kristall Radio
Via Lodovico il Moro n. 165, 20142 Milano, Italy
PH: 0039-02-8912 FX: 0039-02-0212
info@kristallradio.it
www.kristallradio.it

Novaradio
viale Redi 45/b – 50144 Firenze, Italy
PH: 055-3215143 FX: 055-3219325
redmus@novaradio.info
www.novaradio.info

Radio Beckwith
Via Fuhrmann, 25, 10062 - Luserna San Giovanni
(TO) Italy
PH: 0121-954194
promozione@rbe.it
www.rbe.it

radiocitta'fujiko
PH: +39051346458
rc103@rc103.it
radiocittafujiko.it

RadioLina
PH: 0817340853
radiolina@bastardi.net
www1.autistici.org/radiolina

Radio Onda d'Urto
via Luzzago 2/b, 25126 Brescia, Italy
PH: 030-45670 FX: 030-3771921
info@radiondadurto.org
www.radiondadurto.org

TRS The Radio Station
c/o DJ Box s.r.l., Via Re Enzo 20, 00131,
Rome, Italy
PH: +39-334-80-18-398 FX: +39-06-41400962
Luigi airplay@trsradio.net
www.trsradio.net
Broadcasting since 1975. We are now offering
selected airplay to independent bands and singers.

Radio Onda Rossa
Via dei Volsci 56 00185 Rome, Italy
PH: 06-491-750 FX: 06-446-3616
www.ondarossa.info

Luxembourg

Eldoradio Dortmund
B.P. 1344 L-1013, Luxembourg
PH: 352-409-509-1 FX: 352-409-509-509
program@eldoradio.lu
www.eldoradio.lu

Radio ARA
3, rue principale, L-9183 Schlindermanderscheid,
Luxembourg
PH: 00352-22-22-89
radioara@pt.lu
www.ara.lu

The Netherlands

3FM
Postbus 26444 1202 JJ Hilversum, The Netherlands
3fm.omroep.nl

3voor12
Postbus 6, 1200AA Hilversum, The Netherlands
3voor12lokaal@vpro.nl
3voor12.vpro.nl

B92
Bulevar AVNOJ-a 64 11000 Beograd,
The Netherlands
PH: 381-11-301-2000 FX: 381-11-301-2001
www.b92.net

Internet Radio Zeeland
djrudy@zeelandnet.nl
www.internetradiozeeland.nl

Kink FM - The Alternative
Postbus 22300, 1202 CE Hilversum,
The Netherlands
PH: 0909-3001900
radio@kinkfm.com
www.kinkfm.com

Radio Hoorn
Stichting Lokale Omroep Hoorn, Postbus 214, 1620
AE Hoorn, The Netherlands
PH: 0229-210301 FX: 0229-247046
info@radiohoorn.nl
www.radiohoorn.nl

Radio Patapoe
patapoe@freeteam.nl
freeteam.nl/patapoe

Radio Rietveld
Frederik Roeskestraat 96, 1076 ED Amsterdam,
The Netherlands
PH: 003120-5711600 FX: 003120-5711654
www.myspace.com/rietveldradio

Radio Winschoten
Mr. D.U. Stikkerlaan 39, 9675 AA Winschoten,
The Netherlands
PH: 0597-424200 FX: 0597-424221
www.radiowinschoten.nl

StadsRadio Almere
Edestraat 18, 1324 KB Almere Stad,
The Netherlands
PH: 036-534-15-02 FX: 036-534-43-79
info@StadsOmroep-almere.nl
www.stadsomroep-almere.nl/radio

Radio & TV Arnhem
Dullertstraat 27, 6828 HJ Arnhem, The Netherlands
PH: 026-4422282 FX: 026-4431547
info@rtv-arnhem.nl
www.rtv-arnhem.nl

Norway

Radio Nova
Slemdalsveien 15, Postboks 1162 Blindern, 0317
Oslo, Norway
PH: 22844187
Carline Tromp carline@radionova.no
www.radionova.no

Radio Tango
Hegdehausveien 24, 0352 Oslo, Norway
PH: 23-33-35-76 FX: 23-33-35-71
www.radiotango.no

Studentradioen i Bergen
Parkveien 1, 5007 Bergen, Norway
PH: 47-55-54-51-29 FX: 47-55-32-84-05
musikkredaktor@srib.no
studentradioen.uib.no

Studentradio'n i Trondheim
Elgesetergt. 1 7030 Trondheim, Norway
PH: 47-73-51-88-88 FX: 47-73-89-96-69
post@studentradion.no
www.studentradion.no

Poland

Radio Akademickie
INDEX ul. Podgórna 50 DS 1 65-246 Zielona Góra,
Poland
PH: 0-68-328-22-25 FX: 0-68-324-55-93
muzyczna@index.zgora.pl
www.index.zgora.pl

Radio Sfera
U. Mikolaja Kopernika Rozglosnia U. Gagarina 17,
87-100 Torun', Poland
PH: 48-56-611-49-00 FX: 48-56-611-45-84
www.radiosfera.pl

Portugal

Rádio Universitária do Minho
Apartado 3061, 4711-906 Braga, Portugal
PH: +351253200637
programacao@rum.pt
www.rum.pt

Russia

Special Radio
PO Box 424, Moscow, 119017, Russia
admin@specialradio.ru
www.specialradio.ru

Serbia and Montenegro

Alternatives Show Radio 021
Brace Ribnikar, 65a, 21000 Novi Sad,
Serbia & Monte Negro
Predrag Strazmester silver@ns.sbb.co.yu
www.radio021.info
*I have been promoting independent music for over
10 years.*

Radio FEDRAE
Dositeja Obradovica 48, Zrenjanin, Serbia
PH: +381-23-589-470
fedraradio@sezampro.yu
www.fedraradio.org.yu

Sound and Music
Grmecka 14, 11080 Zemun, Serbia
PH/FX: +381 (11) 3163-469
public@soundnmusic.net
www.soundnmusic.net
Covers Electronica, Rock and Hip Hop.

Slovakia

Radio Mars
Gosposvetska cesta 83, 2000 Maribor, Slovakia
PH: 386-2-228-19-20 FX: 0386-2-25-25-489
mars@radiomars.si
www.radiomars.si

Slovenia

Radio Student Ljubjana
PO Cesta 27. aprila 31 1000 Ljubljana, Slovenia
PH: 01/24-28-814
luka.zagoricnik@radiostudent.si
www.radiostudent.si

Spain

Radio Contadero
C/ Granada 45, 18198 Huétor Vega, Granada, Spain
PH: 958-301048
radiocontadero@huetorvega.com
www.radiocontadero.com

Ràdio Despí
Avda. Barcelona, 64, 08970 Sant Joan Despí,
Barcelona, Spain
PH: 93-373-43-40 FX: 93-373-87-54
info@radiodespi.com
www.radiodespi.com

Radio PICA
PO Box 9242, 08080 Barcelona, Spain
radio.pica@gmail.com
www.radiopica.net

Sweden

DemoRadio
Eklandagatan 54 D, 412 61 Göteborg, Sweden
PH: 556586-8667
info@voolife.se
www.voolife.se

K103 Göteborgs Studentradio
Götabergsgatan 17, 411 34 Göteborg, Sweden
PH: 031-182250
therese@gfs.se
www.k103.se

Radio AF
Sandgatan 2, S-223 50 Lund, Sweden
PH:+46 (0)46-2115020
mc@radioaf.se
www.radioaf.se

Rocket Radio
THS 10044 Stockholm, Sweden
PH: 468-790-9869
eric@rocket.fm
www.rocket.fm

Umeå Studentradio
Box 7652 907 13 Umeå, Sweden
PH: 090-786-90-40 FX: 090-13-09-28
msn@umeastudentradio.se
www.umeastudentradio.se

Switzerland

Frequence Banane
Centre Est, EPFL 1015 Lausanne, Switzerland
PH: 41-0-21-693-40-25 FX: 41-0-21-693-40-24
fbwww.epfl.ch

Radio Lora
Militärstrasse 85a, 8004 Zürich, Switzerland
PH: 044-567-24-10 FX: 044-567-24-17
musik@lora.ch
www.lora.ch

radio RaBe
Randweg 21 Postfach 297 3000 Bern 11,
Switzerland
PH: 031-330-99-90 FX: 031-330-99-92
rabe@rabe.ch
www.rabe.ch

United Kingdom

2010fm.com
PO Box 212, Baldock, SG7 6ZR UK
info@2010fm.com
www.2010fm.com
Live webcasts of unsigned bands and DJs.

209radio
Citylife House, Sturton St., Cambridge,
CB1 2QF UK
PH: 01223-488418 FX: 01223-488419
getinvolved@209radio.co.uk
www.209radio.co.uk

6 Music Unsigned *BBC 6*
6 Music, Western House, 99 Great Portland St.,
London, W1A 1AA UK
PH: 08700-100-600
Steve Lamacq lamacq.6music@bbc.co.uk
www.bbc.co.uk/6music/shows/steve_lamacq
*Each Thursday Steve plays a demo by an unsigned
band.*

ArtistBoost
PH: +3725169765
Siim Einfeldt reviews@artistboost.com
www.artistboost.com
*A full-featured portal for unsigned musicians.
Register (for free) to be eligible for a review or
submit your own reviews.*

BBC Radio 1 *Indie*
www.bbc.co.uk/radio1/alt
*Home page of the BBC Radio 1's various indie
music shows. Info, shows, contacts etc.*

BBC Radio 2 *Rock and Pop*
www.bbc.co.uk/radio2/r2music/rockandpop
*Home page of the BBC Radio 2's various Rock and
Pop shows. Info, shows, contacts etc.*

BCB Radio
11 Rawson Rd. Bradford,
West Yorkshire, BD1 3SH UK
PH: 01274-771677 FX: 01274-771680
info@bcbradio.co.uk
www.bcbradio.co.uk

BLAST 1386 *Thames Valley U.*
Thames Valley U., Crescent Rd. Reading,
Berkshire, RG1 5RQ UK
PH: 0118-967-5090 FX: 0118-967-5083
www.blast1386.com

BLAST FM *Thames Valley U.*
Grove House, 1 The Grove, Ealing,
London, W5 5EP UK
PH: 020-8758-8500 FX: 020-8566-5562
www.blastfm.co.uk

Cambridge U. Radio
Churchill College, Cambridge, CB3 0DS UK
PH: 01223-501004 FX: 01223-336180
Sandy Mill sandy.mill@cur1350.co.uk
new.cur1350.co.uk

Castledown Radio
Tidworth Rd. Ludgershall, Wiltshire, SP11 9RR UK
PH: 01264-841047
www.castledownradio.info

Celtica Radio Wales
PO Box 48, Bridgend, CF32 9ZY UK
PH: 07005-963770
info@celticaradio.com
www.celticaradio.com
*A platform for artists who have been denied
elsewhere.*

Cheshire FM
Verdin Exchange, Winsford,
Cheshire, CW7 2AN UK
PH: 01606-555-925
Dave Brierley-Jones
dave.brierleyjones@cheshirefm.com
www.cheshirefm.com

The Chris Slight Show *209 Radio*
Citylife House, Sturton St.,
Cambridge, CB1 2QF UK
PH: 01223-488418 FX: 01223-488419
Chris slight.chris@209radio.co.uk
www.209radio.co.uk
An eclectic mix of music supporting unsigned bands.

Clare FM
Abbeyfield Ctr. Francis St.
Ennis, Co. Clare, Ireland
PH: 353-0-65-68-28-888 FX: 353-0-65-68-29-392
info@clarefm.ie
www.clarefm.ie

Downtown Radio
Kiltonga Ind. Est. Newtownards,
County Down, BT23 4ES UK
PH: 028-9181-5555 FX: 028-9181-5252
www.downtown.co.uk

Earwax
PO Box 155, Sidcup, DA15 8XT UK
www.wax-music.com
Focused on bringing you the best in new and local talent as well as tracks from more established artists.

errorFM
PH: 310-878-4890
www.errorfm.com
A listener-controlled radio station.

Fame Games
PH: +34-951-239-617
Paul info@famegamesradio.com
www.meermusic.com
An informational program about new music with on-air critiques. The show features the best of unsigned talent from all over the world, focusing on music in any style but with strong crossover potential. Selections are done by means of a weekly contest with current top prize being regular rotational airplay on Fame Games and collaborating stations.

Forest of Dean Radio
Rheola House, Belle Vue Ctr. Belle Vue Rd.
Cinderford, GL14 2AB UK
PH: 01594-820722 FX: 01594-820724
contactus@fodradio.org
www.fodradio.org

Fresh Air FM
5/2 Bristo Sq. Edinburgh, EH8 9AL UK
PH: 44-0-131-650-2656 FX: 44-0-131-668-4177
Jonny Brick music@freshair.org.uk
www.freshair.org.uk

Future Radio
Neighbourhood Ctr. 168b Motum Rd. Norwich,
Norfolk, NR5 8EG UK
PH: 01603-455250
info@futureradio.co.uk
www.futureradio.co.uk

Gideon Coe *BBC 6*
6 Music, Western House, 99 Great Portland St.,
London, W1A 1AA UK
PH: 08700-100-600
Gideon Coe gideon.6music@bbc.co.uk
www.bbc.co.uk/6music/shows/gideon_coe
Features music from a variety of styles as well as in-studio sessions.

Hertbeat FM
The Pump House, Knebworth Park,
Hertfordshire, SG3 6HQ UK
PH: 0845-090-1069
www.hertbeat.com

HFM Radio
PO Box 1055, Market Harborough,
Leicestershire, LE16 7ZL UK
PH: 01858-464666 FX: 01858-464678
Simon Parry simon.parry@harboroughfm.co.uk
www.harboroughfm.co.uk

Imperial College Radio
Beit Quad Prince Consort Rd. S. Kensington,
London, SW7 2BB UK
PH: 020-7594-8100 FX: 020-7594-8101
manager@icradio.com
icradio.su.ic.ac.uk

In New Music We Trust *BBC 1*
Radio 1 London, W1N 4DJ UK
Steve Lamacq steve.lamacq@bbc.co.uk
www.bbc.co.uk/radio1/innewmusicwetrust/
stevelamacq
Steve Lamacq is acknowledged as one of the UK's most committed supporters of new bands.

Indiepop Radio
dan@indiepopradio.co.uk
www.indiepopradio.co.uk
I am always happy to receive CDs for review. Before getting in touch, please have a listen to the station to get a feel for the music.

Inspiration FM *Northampton*
PH: 01604-250544 FX: 01604-250573
info@inspirationfm.com
www.inspirationfm.com

Jimmy Possession's Radio Show
c/o r+eb 133 Green End Rd.
Cambridge, CB4 1RW UK
rebzine@hotmail.com
www.robotsandelectronicbrains.co.uk
Band demos, unreleased tracks and (as yet) undiscovered bands from all over the world.

jockrock radio
PO Box 13516, Linlithgow, EH49 6WB UK
FX: 070-92-011-439
jockrock@vacant.org.uk
www.vacant.org.uk/jockrock/jockrock.html

Jon Holmes *BBC 6*
6 Music, Western House, 99 Great Portland St.,
London, W1A 1AA UK
PH: 08700-100-600
Jon Holmes jon.6music@bbc.co.uk
www.bbc.co.uk/6music/shows/jon_holmes
Music show and more, as Jon and cohorts get up to radio mischief, mess around and often mess up.

Junction11 *U. Reading*
Reading, Berkshire, RG6 6AZ UK
PH: 0118-378-4152
www.1287am.com

KCC Live *Knowsley College*
Rupert Rd. Liverpool, Lancashire, L36 9TD UK
PH: 0151-477-5080
studio@kcclive.com
www.kcclive.com

KIAC Internet Radio
16 Russell Ave. Dunchurch, Rugby, CV22 6PX UK
PH: 07790957028
Stephen Parfitt radio@kerascene.com
www.kerascene.com
Showcases the best independent music. Covers all genres. Contact us about being included in an upcoming broadcast.

Kick FM
The Studios 42 Bone Ln. Newbury Berkshire,
RG14 5SD UK
PH: 01635-841000 FX: 01635-841010
studio@kickfm.com
www.kickfm.co.uk

Kooba Radio
54 Maltings Pl. 169 Tower Bridge Rd.
London, SE1 3LJ UK
submissions@koobaradio.co.uk
www.KoobaRadio.co.uk
Internet radio exclusively for the unsigned.

KUSU *Keele U.*
Newcastle-under-Lyme, Staffordshire, ST5 5BH UK
PH: 01782-583700 FX: 01782-712671
sta15@kusu.keele.ac.uk
www.kusu.net

Last.fm
Karen House, 1–11 Baches St.,
London, UK N1 6DL
PH: +44 (0) 20-7780-7080
labels@last.fm
www.last.fm/labels
The listeners decide what's great music and what's rubbish.

LCR *Loughborough U.*
Union Bldg. Ashby Rd.
Loughborough, LE11 3TT UK
studio@lcr1350.co.uk
www.lcr1350.co.uk

LiveIreland
www.liveireland.com
Five stations that play Irish influenced music.

Livewire *U. East Anglia*
Union House, Norwich, Norfolk, NR4 7TJ UK
PH: 01603-592512
www.livewire1350.com

LSR FM *Leeds U.*
PO Box 157, Leeds, LS1 1UH UK
PH: 0113-380-1280 FX: 07845-13-83-16
info@lsrfm.com
www.lsrfm.com

Marc Riley's Brain Surgery *BBC 6*
6 Music, Western House, 99 Great Portland St.,
London, W1A 1AA UK
PH: 08700-100-600
Marc Riley marc.6music@bbc.co.uk
www.bbc.co.uk/6music/shows/brain_surgery
Mission to educate and entertain. Music and in-studio guests.

NEAR FM
Northside Civic Ctr. Bunratty Rd. Dublin 17 Ireland
PH: 867-1016 FX: 848-6111
arts@nearfm.ie
www.nearfm.ie

Northern Broadcasting *Halifax*
www.northernbroadcasting.co.uk

OneMusic *BBC Radio 1*
London, W1A 7WW UK
huwstephens@bbc.co.uk
www.bbc.co.uk/radio1/onemusic
Resources for unsigned bands – articles, downloads, radio shows etc.

Original 106fm
Roman Landing, Kingsway,
Southampton, SO14 1BN UK
PH: 08454-660-106 FX: 023-8082-9844
studio@original106.com
www.original106.com
The quality threshold is the key for us – we avoid boy bands, overtly manufactured Pop music and novelty acts. It's about credible artists and class songs.

Oxide Radio *Oxford U.*
Thomas Hull House, 1 New Inn Hall St., Oxford,
Oxfordshire, OX1 2DH UK
PH: 01865-288458
Will Tooke william.tooke@some.ox.ac.uk
www.oxideradio.co.uk

Phantom FM
12 Camden Row, Dublin 8 Ireland
PH: 353-1-478-0363 FX: 353-1-476-2138
phoenixfm@iolfree.ie
www.phantomfm.com

Phoenix FM
Unit 333 The Blanchardstown Centre,
Blanchardstown, Dublin 15 Ireland
PH: 822-72-22 FX: 822-72-09
phoenixfm@iolfree.ie
www.iolfree.ie/~phoenixfm

Phoenix FM
The Baytree Centre, Brentwood, CM14 4BX UK
PH: 01277-849931
www.phoenixfm.com

Pipeline Radio
pipelineradio.org
Shows featuring Rock, Pop, Soul, Jazz, Funk ...

Priory FM *Grantham*
webfeedback@prioryfm.co.uk
www.prioryfm.co.uk

Pulse Unsigned
Enterprise House, Woodgreen Industrial Estate,
Salhouse, Norwich, NR13 6NY UK
PH: +44 (0) 870-1423456 FX: +44 (0) 1603-735160
info@pulseunsigned.com
www.pulseunsigned.com
*You must fill out our online submission pack to be
considered for airplay.*

PURE FM *Portsmouth U.*
Student Ctr. Cambridge Rd.
Portsmouth, PO1 2EF UK
PH: 02392-84-3987
purefm.com

Pure Play Music
Cavell House, Stannard Place, St. Crispins Rd.
Norwich, NR3 1YE UK
PH: 01603821057
Roschan Thompson rosch@pureplaymusic.com
www.pureplaymusic.com
*Europe's leading internet radio station playing only
the very best music from new, unsigned and
emerging artists worldwide.*

QualityBeatsRadio UK
#11E The Wren Centre, Westbourne Rd. Emsworth,
Hants, PO10 7SU UK
PH: 01243-373660
www.qualitybeatsradio.com
Providing quality DJs and shows of all genres.

Queens of Noize *BBC 6*
333 Old St., London, C1V 9LE UK
PH: 08700-100-600
queens.6music@bbc.co.uk
www.bbc.co.uk/6music/shows/queensofnoize
*Each week we forage through the musical
undergrowth to track a particular genre.*

Queens Radio *Queens U.*
Students' Union, University Rd.
Belfast, Ireland BT7 1NF
PH: (028) 90-97-1065
music@queensradio.org
queensradio.org

Radio Gets Wild
Rose Cottage, Grimston Rd. Gayton,
Norfolk, England
PH: +441553636 1169
Tim Daymond tim@radiogetswild.com
www.radiogetswild.com
*Radio airplay / artist promotion / sell your CDs /
live interviews / advertising / reviews and much
more. Live DJs from around the world.*

Radio Six International
PO Box 600, Glasgow, G41 5SH, Scotland
letters@radiosix.com
www.radiosix.com

Radio Telefís Éireann
Donnybrook, Dublin 4, Ireland
PH: 353 (0) 1-208-3111
info@rte.ie
www.rte.ie/radio
*The Irish national public service broadcasting
organization.*

Radio Warwick *U. Warwick*
Student's Union Coventry, CV4 7AL UK
PH: 024-765-73077
studio@radio.warwick.ac.uk
www.raw.warwick.ac.uk

RadioReverb
170 North St., Brighton, East Sussex, BN1 1EA UK
PH: +44 (0) 1273-323-040
music@radioreverb.com
radioreverb.com

RamAir
Communal Bldg. U. Bradford, BD7 1DP UK
PH: 01274-233267
info@ramair.co.uk
www.ramairfm.co.uk

rare FM
UCL Union 25 Gordon St.,
London, WC1H 0AY UK
PH: 44-020-7679-2509
Lucy Dearlove hom.rarefm@ucl.ac.uk
www.rarefm.co.uk

Reptor Productions Radio
PO Box 198, Abergele, Conwy, LL22 9WZ UK
PH: 44-0-1745-343-777
submissions@reptorproductions.co.uk
www.reptorproductions.co.uk
We offer radio play online to UK and US artists.

Shock Radio *U. Salford*
University House, Salford,
Manchester, M5 4WT UK
PH: 0161-295-6303 FX: 07765-65-38-62
Vickie Scullard music@shockradio.co.uk
www.shockradio.co.uk

SirenFM *U. Lincoln*
Imanuel Votteler mad_hatter@blueyonder.co.uk
www.sirenonline.co.uk
*I produce 3 radio shows on the Uni's radio station.
Send us CDs, t-shirts and posters for give-aways to
promote you and your music.*

Smoke Radio *U. Westminster*
Students Union, Harrow Campus,
London, HA1 3TP UK
PH: 020-79115000 x4413
studio@smokeradio.co.uk
smokeradio.co.uk

Spirit FM
9-10 Dukes Ct. Bognor Rd. Chichester,
West Sussex, PO19 8FX UK
PH: 01243-539000 FX: 01243-786464
www.spiritfm.net

S. R. Effej Radio
PH: 07774717199
chip@sreffejradio.com
www.sreffejradio.com

Star FM *St. Andrews U.*
Students Union, St. Mary's Pl, KY16 9UZ Scotland
radio@st-andrews.ac.uk
standrewsradio.com

Subcity Radio *Glasgow U.*
John McIntyre Bldg. University Ave.
Glasgow, G12 8QQ Scotland
PH: 0141-341-6222 FX: 0141-337-3557
music@subcity.org
subcity.org

Sure Radio *U. Sheffield*
University House, Western Bank,
Sheffield, S10 2TG UK
PH: 0114-2228750
www.sureradio.com

SURGE *U. Southampton*
Students' Union, Southampton, SO17 1BJ UK
PH: 023-8059-8852 FX: 023-8059-5252
studio@surgeradio.co.uk
surgeradio.co.uk

thesunmachine.net radio
234/5 Marionville Rd. Edinburgh,
Midlothian, EH7 6BE UK
www.thesunmachine.net/radio
Discover a whole new world of music.

Today FM
124 Upper Abbey St., Dublin 1, Ireland
PH: 01-8049000
www.todayfm.com

totallyradio
170 North St., Brighton, BN1 1EA UK
www.totallyradio.com
Packed with new music across the board.

UCA Radio *U. Paisley*
U. Campus Ayr, Beech Grove,
Ayr, KA8 0SR Scotland
PH: 01292-886385
Marcus.Bowman@paisley.ac.uk
www.ucaradio.paisley.ac.uk

University Radio York
c/o Vanbrugh College, U. York, Heslington,
York, YO10 5DD UK
PH: 01904-433840 FX: 01904-433840
head.of.music@ury.york.ac.uk
ury.york.ac.uk

URB *U. Bath*
Students' Union, Claverton Down,
Bath, BA2 7AY UK
PH: 01225-38-66-11 FX: 07890-160-839
urb-music@bath.ac.uk
www.1449urb.co.uk

URF *U. Sussex*
Norwich House, Falmer, Brighton,
Sussex, BN1 9QS UK
PH: 01273-678-999
music@urfonline.com
www.urfonline.com

URN *U. Nottingham*
Students Union U. Park Nottingham, NG7 2RD UK
PH: 0115-846-8722 FX: 0115-846-8801
Tom Aldridge music@urn1350.net
urn1350.net

The Vibe *U. Radio York*
c/o Vanbrugh College, Heslington,
York, YO10 5DD UK
PH: 01904-433840 FX: 01904-433840
Zara head.of.music@ury.york.ac.uk
ury.york.ac.uk/music
*A new music review show. Also includes music news,
interviews and gig guide.*

WCR *Wolverhampton College*
Newhampton Ctr. Newhampton Rd. E.,
Wolverhampton, WV1 4AP UK
PH: 01902-572260 FX: 01902-572261
www.wcrfm.com

Weekend Breakfast Show *BBC 6*
6 Music, Western House, 99 Great Portland St.,
London, W1A 1AA UK
PH: 08700-100-600
Natasha natasha.6music@bbc.co.uk
www.bbc.co.uk/6music/shows/natasha
*The show features a wide variety of music from
Choral to Goth.*

XFM
30 Leicester Sq. London, WC2H 7LA UK
PH: 020-7766-6000
xfm.co.uk

XFM Scotland
The Four Winds Pavilion, Glasgow, G51 1EB UK
www.xfmscotland.co.uk

Xpress Radio *Cardiff U.*
Students Union, Park Place, Cardiff,
Wales CF10 3QN
PH: 02920-781530 FX: 07722-263888
studio@xpressradio.co.uk
www.xpressradio.co.uk

Xpression *U. Exeter*
c/o Devonshire House, Stocker Rd. Exeter,
Devon, EX4 4PZ UK
PH: 01392-26-3568
music@xpressionfm.com
xpression.ex.ac.uk

Xtreme Radio *Swansea U.*
Union House, Singleton Park,
Swansea, SA2 0AE UK
www.xtremeradio.org

Yugoslavia

Radio Free Belgrade
B92 Bulevar AVNOJ-a 64 11000 Beograd,
Yugoslavia
PH: 381-11-301-2000 FX: 381-11-301-2001
www.b92.net

Australia

1ART
PO Box 3573, Manuka, ACT 2603 Australia
PH: 02-6295 8444 FX: 02-6295 8499
onair@artsoundfm.asn.au
www.artsoundfm.asn.au

1VFM
Post: PO Box 112, Erindale, ACT 2903 Australia
PH: 041-775-2494 FX: 02-6292-0332
Chris Moy valleyfm895@optusnet.com.au
www.valleyfm.com

2AAA
PO Box 2019, Wagga Wagga, NSW 2650 Australia
PH: 61-02-6925-3000 FX: 61-02-6925-2300
fm107@2aaa.net
www.2aaa.net

2BAY
PO Box 1003, Cleveland, QLD 4163 Australia
PH: 07-3821-0022 FX: 07-3286-9166
bayfm@bayfm.org.au
www.bayfm.org.au

2BBB
52 Wheatley St., Bellingen, NSW 2454 Australia
PH: 02-6655-0718 FX: 02-6655-1888
radio@2bbb.net.au
www.2bbb.net.au

2BCR
PO Box 659, Padstow, NSW 2211 Australia.
PH: 02-9771-2846 FX: 02-9774-5292
bfm1009@bigpond.net.au
www.2bfm.com

2BLU
PO Box 64, Katoomba, NSW 2780 Australia
PH: 02-4782 2490 FX: 02-4782 6699
info@blufm.org.au
blufm.org.au

2CCC
PO Box 19, Gosford, NSW 2250 Australia
PH: 02-4322-0072 FX: 02-4322-0075
twoccc@tac.com.au
www.2ccc.net

2CCR
PO Box 977, Baulkham Hills, NSW 1755 Australia
PH: 9686-3888 FX: 9639-5618
www.2ccrfm.com

2CHY
30 Orlando St., Coffs Harbour, NSW 2450 Australia
PH: 02-6651-1104 FX: 02-66513-100
sales@chyfm.com
www.chyfm.midcoast.com.au

2EAR
PO Box 86, Moruya, NSW 2537 Australia
PH: 02-4474-3443 FX: 02-4474-3500
earfm@earfm.com
www.earfm.com

2FBI
PO Box 1962, Strawberry Hills, NSW 2012
Australia
PH: 02-8332-2999 FX: 02-8332 2901
music@fbiradio.com
www.fbi.org.au

2GLF
306 Macquarie St., Liverpool, NSW 2170 Australia
PH: +61-2-9822 8893 FX: +61-2-9602-3232
office@893fm.com.au
www.893fm.com.au

2MAX
Old Newell Hwy. PO Box 158w, Narrabri,
NSW 2390 Australia
PH: (02) 6792-4884 Fx: (02) 6792-4582
maxfm@2maxfm.com.au
www.2maxfm.com.au

2MCE
Panorama Ave. Bathurst, NSW 2795 Australia
PH: +61-2-6338-4790 FX: +61-2-6338-4402
2mce@csu.edu.au
www.2mce.org

2MCR
PO Box 1420, Campbelltown, NSW 2560 Australia
PH: 02-4625 2768 FX: 02-4627 0670
feedback@2mcr.org.au
www.2mcr.org.au

2MIA
Groongal Ave. Griffith, NSW 2680 Australia
PH: 02-69641033 FX: 02-69644046
2miafm@dragnet.com.au
www.2mia.dragnet.com.au

2NCR
PO Box 5123, E. Lismore, NSW 2480 Australia
PH: 02-66203-929 FX: 02-66-203884
fm2ncr@scu.edu.au
www.2ncr.org.au

2NSB
PO Box 468, Chatswood, NSW 2057 Australia
PH: 02-9419-6969 FX: 02-9413-1684
Barbara Peters bpeters@fm993.com.au
www.fm993.com.au

2NUR *U. Newcastle*
University Dr. Callaghan, NSW 2308 Australia
PH: 61-2-4921-5555 FX: 61-2-4921-7158
contact@2nurfm.com
www.2nurfm.com

2RRR
PO Box 644, Gladesville, NSW 1675 Australia
PH: 61-29816-2988 FX: 61-2-9817-1048
www.2rrr.org.au

2SER
PO Box 123, Broadway, NSW 2007 Australia
PH: 61-2-9514-9514 FX: 61-2-9514-9599
info@2ser.com
www.2ser.com

2TEN
PO Box 93, Tenterfield, NSW 2372 Australia
PH: 02-6736-3444 FX: 02-6736-2197
twotenfm@halenet.com.au
www.halenet.com.au/~twotenfm

2UNE
UNE, Armidale, NSW 2351 Australia
PH: 02-677-323-99 FX: 02-677-27-633
radio@tunefm.net
www.tunefm.net

2VOX
PO Box 1663, Wollongong, NSW 2500 Australia
PH: 02-4227-3436 FX: 02-4226-5922
office@voxfm.org.au
www.voxfm.org.au

2VTR
11 Fitzgerald St., Windsor, NSW 2756 Australia
PH: 02- 45-775-662 FX: 02-45-878-865
www.hawkradio.org.au

2XX
PO Box 812, Canberra, ACT 2601 Australia
PH: 02-6230-0100 FX: 02-6248-5560
info@2xxfm.org.au
www.2xxfm.org.au

3CR
PO Box 1277, Collingwood, Melbourne,
VIC 3065 Australia
PH: 03-9419-8377 FX: 03-9417-4472
programming@3cr.org.au
www.3cr.org.au

3MBR
PO Box 139, Murrayville, VIC 3512 Australia
PH: 03-5095-2045 FX: 03-5095-2346
3mbr@riverland.net.au
www.riverland.net.au/~3mbr

3MGB
PO Box 555, Mallacoota, VIC 3892 Australia
PH: 03-5158-0929 FX: 03-5158-0079
home.vicnet.net.au/~cootafm

3PBS
PO Box 2917, Fitzroy MDC, VIC 3065 Australia
PH: 61-3-8415-1067 FX: 61-3-8415-1831
info@pbsfm.org.au
www.pbsfm.org.au

3RIM
PO Box 979, Melton, VIC 3337 Australia
PH: 03-9747-8500 FX: 03-9747-0405
info@979fm.net
www.979fm.net

3RPP
PO Box 602, Somerville, VIC 3912 Australia
PH: 03-5978-8200 FX: 03-5978-8551
rpp@peninsula.hotkey.net.au
www.3rpp.asn.au

3RRR
221 Nicholson St., PO Box 2145, Brunswick East,
Melbourne, VIC 3057 Australia
PH: +61-3 9388-1027 FX: +61-3-9388-9079
3rrr@rrr.org.au
www.rrr.org.au

3SCB
PO Box 2132, Moorabbin, VIC 3189 Australia
PH: 03-9553-5444 FX: 03-9553-5244
info@southernfm.com.au
www.southernfm.com.au

3SER
PO Box 977, Cranbourne DC, VIC 3977 Australia
PH: 03-5996-6977 FX: 03-5996-6900
David Lentin dlentin@3ser.org.au
www.3ser.org.au

3WAY
PO Box 752, Warrnambool, VIC 3280 Australia
PH: 03-55612666 FX: 03-55612585
3wayfm@hotkey.net.au
www.3wayfm.org.au

4CCR
PO Box 891, Manunda, QLD 4870 Australia
PH: 61-7-4053-6891 FX: 61-7-4053-2085
info@cairnsfm891.org
cairnsfm891.org

4CLB
PO Box 2101, Logan City DC, QLD 4114 Australia
PH: 07-3808-8101 FX: 07-3808-7787
admin@101fm.asn.au
www.101fm.asn.au

4CRM *Mackay*
PO Box 1075, Mackay, QLD 4740 Australia
PH: 07-49531411
4crm@4crm.com.au
www.4crm.com.au

4RED
PO Box 139, Redcliffe, QLD 4020 Australia
PH: 07-3284-5000 FX: 07-3283-4527
station@red997.com.au
www.red997.com.au

4ZZZ
PO Box 509, Fortitude Valley, QLD 4006 Australia
PH: 07-3252-1555 FX: 07-3252-1950
charlie@4zzzfm.org.au
www.4zzzfm.org.au

5PBA
PO Box 433, Salisbury, SA 5108 Australia
PH: 61-8-8250-3735 FX: 61-8-8281-7495
pbafm@pbafm.org.au
www.pbafm.org.au

5UV
228 N. Terrace, Adelaide, SA 5000 Australia
PH: 61-8-8303-5000 FX: 61-8-8303-4374
Kat McGuffie katrina.mcguffie@adelaide.edu.au
radio.adelaide.edu.au

96.5 Family FM
PO Box 965, Milton BC, QLD 4064 Australia
PH: 07-3217-5999 FX: 07-3217-5888
www.96five.org.au

ABC Radio
www.abc.net.au/radio
*Produces national shows as well as local shows
throughout the network.*

ArtSound FM
PO Box 3573, Manuka, Canberra,
ACT 2603 Australia
PH: 612-6295-8444 FX: 612-6295-8499
onair@artsoundfm.asn.au
www.artsound.com.au

AwesomeRadio
www.myspace.com/awesomeradio_net
*Working hard to promote new artists of all genre.
Feel free to contact us if you want your music put in
rotation on our station.*

Bondi FM
PO Box 7588, Bondi Beach, NSW 2026 Australia
PH: 61-0-2-9365-55-88
team@bondifm.com.au
www.bondifm.com.au

Boost Digital Indie Radio
PO Box 578, Crows Nest, NSW 1585 Australia
PH: +61-2-9959-4405 FX: +61-2-9460-0044
Ian MacRae ian@boostdigital.com
www.boostdigital.com
*Dedicated to giving independent artists a platform
to expose their talent. Please include a copy of our
online submission form.*

City Park Radio
PO Box 1501, Launceston, TAS 7250 Australia
PH: 03-6334-7429
cityparkradio@cityparkradio.com
www.cityparkradio.com

Contact! *2RDJ FM*
contact2001@bigpond.com
members.westnet.com.au/celt1969
*International Indie Rock/Alternative/New Wave Pop,
broadcast across Australia. Demos too.*

fat planet *FBI*
Stuart Buchanan mail@fatplanet.com.au
www.fatplanet.com.au/blog
*We LOVE getting new music, so please do feel free
to send material our way.*

ISON Live Radio
PO Box 532, Newcastle, NSW 2300 Australia
PH: 6102-49270290 FX: 6102-49270290
www.isonliveradio.com

JOY Melbourne
PO Box 907, S. Melbourne, VIC 3205 Australia
PH: 61-03-9699-2949 FX: 61-03-9699-2646
pm@joy.org.au
www.joy.org.au

Nova 969
Locked Bag 2009, Broadway, NSW 2007 Australia
PH: 13-24-10
www.nova969.com.au

QBN FM
PO Box 984, Queanbeyan, NSW 2620 Australia
PH: 02-6299-6899 FX: 02-6299-6804
admin@qbnfm.com.au
www.qbnfm.com.au

RelaxRadio
43 Federal St., Karlgarin, WA 6358 Australia
PH: 618-98895050
Ron Trigwell music_submission@esat.net.au
www.relaxradio.net.au
*Supporting independent artists worldwide. We play
most genres of music except Heavy Alternative.*

RTR FM
PO Box 842, Mt. Lawley, WA 6929 Australia
PH: +61-8-9260-9200 FX: +61-8-9260-9222
rtrfm@rtrfm.com.au
www.rtrfm.com.au

RUM Radio *(Radio Upper Murray)*
programs@radiouppermurray.com
www.radiouppermurray.com
Folk, Country and Roots radio.

Three D Radio
PO Box 937, Stepney, SA 5069 Australia
PH: 61-8-83633937
mail@threedradio.com
www.threedradio.com

TiN Radio
#7, Level 1, Civic Arcade, 401 Hunter St.,
Newcastle, NSW 2300 Australia
PH: 02-49271668
programs@tin.org.au
www.tin.org.au

Triple H
PO Box 2055, Hornsby Westfield,
NSW 1635 Australia
PH: (02) 9987-1800
info@triplehfm.com.au
triplehfm.com.au

Triple J
PO Box 9994, Canberra, ACT Australia
PH: 1300-0555-36
www.abc.net.au/triplej

Triple U
12 Berry St., Nowra, PO Box 884, Nowra,
NSW 2541 Australia
PH: +612-44221045
pres@tripleu.org.au
www.shoalhavenfm.org.au

UMFM
3 / 14 Fitzroy St., St. Kilda, VIC 3182 Australia
radio@umfm.net
www.umfm.net
*If you are a band, musician, DJ, producer or other
musical artist, we would love to hear your music.*

WOW FM
PO Box 1041, St. Marys, NSW 1790 Australia
PH: 9833-1444 FX: 9833-4539
wowfm1007@uvtc.net.au
www.wowfm1007.com.au

Yarra Valley FM
PO Box 991, Woori Yallock, VIC 3139 Australia
PH: 03-5961 5991 FX: 03-5964 6662
info@yarravalleyfm.com
www.yarravalleyfm.com

New Zealand

95b FM
PO Box 4560, Shortland St.,
Auckland 1001 New Zealand
PH: 64-9-309-4831 FX: 64-9-366-7224
www.95bfm.co.nz

Radio Active
PO Box 11-971, Wellington, New Zealand
PH: 64-4-801-9089
studiolive@radioactive.co.nz
www.radioactive.co.nz

Radio Kidnappers
PO Box 680, Hastings, New Zealand
PH: 06-876-6914 FX: 06-876-6914
David Teesdale kidnap.am@xtra.co.nz
www.radiokidnappers.org.nz

Radio One
PO Box 1436, Dunedin, New Zealand
PH: 03-477-1969
Tom Bell tom@r1.co.nz
www.r1.co.nz

RDU *U. Canterbury*
PO Box 31-311, Ilam, Christchurch, New Zealand
PH: 03-348 8610 FX: 03-364-2509
station@rdu.org.nz
www.rdu.org.nz

Asia

Gone Fishing for Blue Skies
bigfoot@gonefishingforblueskies.com
www.gonefishingforblueskies.com
*An internet show based in Japan, introducing
quality independent music from around the globe.
Delivering melodious music of all genres. Contact
us for submission details.*

music-islands.com web-radio
2-19-20-603 Mizusawa, Miyamae, Kawasaki,
Kanagawa 216-0012 Japan
PH: 044-979-1124 FX: 044-979-1124
Masayoshi Yamamiya info@fishthemusic.com
music-islands.com/radio
Playing a variety of styles.

Radio Oxigen
Emin Vafi Korusu Muallim Naci cad. No 61/5
Ortaköy 80840, Turkey
PH: 0212-236-5436 FX: 0212-236-5440
info@radiooxigen.com
www.radiooxigen.com

Yellow Beat Shonan Beach FM
Gremlin and Baby Magic
ciao_babies@yellowbeat.net
www.yellowbeat.com
*We can be a key step to introducing your into the
Japanese market.*

Internet Radio and Syndicated Shows

12StepRadio.com
11452 El Camino Real, #401, San Diego, CA 92130
www.12stepradio.com
*We are always looking for new recovery oriented
music suitable to play on the "air". We are very
selective.*

440MUSIC.COM
3200 N. Lake Shore Dr. #1103
Chicago, IL 60657-3919
www.440music.com
*We play only original music from independent
bands. Please fill out our online submission form.*

AccuRadio
400 N. Wells St. #404, Chicago, IL 60610
PH: 312-527-3879
feedback@accuradio.com
www.accuradio.com
Featuring over 280 channels of really cool music.

Alexa Digital Internet Radio
alexadigitalradio@yahoo.com
alexadigitalmusic.com
The best mix of indie music on the web.

All Indie Radio
PO Box 420933, San Diego, CA 92142-0933
www.allindieradio.com
*A portal where music fans can learn about there
favorite indie artists and help those artists get their
music to their fans.*

All Songs Considered *NPR*
635 Mass. Ave. NW., Washington, DC 20001
Bob Boilen allsongs@npr.org
www.npr.org/programs/asc
*Full versions of the music snippets played on NPR's
afternoon news program. Check our site for
submission details.*

All Songs Considered
Open Mic
NPR, Attn. Robin Hilton
635 Mass. Ave. NW.
Washington, DC 20001
www.npr.org/programs/asc
*A showcase for independent
artists. Print, fill out and sign
the online submission form and
send it in along with your CD.*

Allan Handelman Show
PH: 704-363-8326
Allan rocktalk@ifitrocks.com
ifitrocks.com
*Rock n' Roll and the Rock
culture. The talk show that
rocks!*

Altrok Radio
www.altrok.com
*We're paying attention to scenes all over the world,
watching the energy build and waiting to see what it
creates.*

American Radio Network *ARN*
5287 Sunset Blvd. Hollywood, CA 90027
PH: 323-464-4580
kclafm@kclafm.com
www.kclafm.com

ArtistFirst Internet Radio
1062 Parkside Dr. Alliance, OH 44601
PH: 330-823-2264
info@artistfirst.com
www.artistfirst.com
*If you have a CD, you can have a 1hr prime-time
radio show here.*

Artists International Independent Radio
www.aiiradio.net
Featuring worldwide independent recording artists.

AudioRealm.Com
504 N. Hockley Main, Ropesville, TX 79405
PH: 806-562-3838
www.audiorealm.com
*Operates the AudioRealm Broadcast Network with
currently over 800 active stations.*

ArtistLaunch.com
23905 Clinton Keith 114-155, Wildomar, CA 92595
PH: 951-551-5502
Moses de los Santos info@artistlaunch.com
www.artistlaunch.com
*Live showcases, internet and real-world radio
outlets, reviews and artist pages.*

Artists Without a Label Radio
PO Box 879, Ojai, CA 93024
PH: 805-640-7399 FX: 805-646-6077
www.awal.com
Discover great new music and artists.

AURICAST
235 W. 56th St. #31D, New York, NY 10019
PH: 212-307-1333 FX: 212-246-2329
media@auricast.com
www.auricast.com
*Would you like your sound in rotation at thousands
of retail locations?*

BAGeL Radio
209 11th Ave. San Francisco, CA 94118-2101
Ted feedback@bagelradio.com
www.bagelradio.com
*Playlists include Indie & Alternative Rock and
Noisy Pop. Mostly guitar music ...no testosterock.*

Big Dumb Fun Show
PH: 888-832-7561
www.bigdumbfunshow.com
You can submit your songs to us in MP3 format to the above address. If we use your music, we will let you know.

BlackLight Radio
11975 Gun Smoke Dr.
Collinsville, OK 74021
Gene Savage postmaster@blacklightradio.com
www.blacklightradio.com
We WILL play independent artists and if requested we can review CDs. We welcome submissions in all genres.

BreakThru Radio
954 Lexington Ave. #199
New York, NY 10021
PH: 917-463-4811
FX: 212-671-1341
info@breakthruradio.com
www.breakthruradio.com
An internet radio station with a listenership of 5 million per week. We play only indie label and unsigned artists!

The BZT Weekly
buzzcat.net
It's Rock & Roll mixed with a little Blues, Folk, Punk and other odds and ends.

Cactus Radio
411 W. Buena Vista Dr.
Tempe, AZ 85284-5221
www.cactusradio.com
Shows featuring Power Pop, Emo and otherwise Alternative artists. Visit our website for submission details.

CoolStreams
www.CoolStreams.com
You must fill out our online artist submission form before sending your CD.

Crossfire Radio
www.myspace.com/crossfireradio
Play music of all genres from around the world!

Cygnus Radio
www.cygnusradio.com
Bringing the best of independent music to a wider audience.

Dark Side of the Radio
2288 Sharon Depoy Rd.
Greenville, KY 42345
hollywood@kih.net
www.dsotr.8m.com/indy.htm
No MP3s. See submission guidelines.

D'Art Radio
PO Box 303, W. Long Branch, NJ 07764
Arlene Smith info@dartradio.com
www.dartradio.com
Playing Rock, Techno, Pop, R&B, Rap and Hip Hop. An artist may submit one MP3 for free.

Elvii Radio
PO Box 272014, Columbus, OH 43227
email@elvii.com
www.Elvii.com
Upload your MP3s for airplay.

eoRadio
PH: 303-808-8140
Ryan Smith webmaster@eoradio.com
www.eoradio.com
The best free music from unsigned artists from around the globe. We require all artists to register online and sign a release form before submitting. Visit online for details.

The Epicenter
PO Box 90440, Tucson, AZ 85752
www.myspace.com/theepicenter
THE source for the best of the best in independent music. You love music and we love you for it.

erika.net
PO Box 2168, Royal Oak, MI 48068
programming@erika.net
erika.net
Sounds and styles you won't hear on other radio stations.

Evolving Artist Entertainment
Attn: Programming Department CODE: EA
18 Mill St., Southbridge, MA 01550
PH: 508-764-3865
info@evolvingartist.com
www.evolvingartist.com
Internet radio & television, providing the best new music to a worldwide audience. Submission guidelines available on our website.

Excellent Radio Online
www.excellentonline.com
The home for North American fans of UK music.

eXtreme Indie Radio
www.extremeindieradio.com
Unsigned music without Limits! Playing the best in the independent and unsigned music.

FatCat Radio Network
Swede or Jennifer fatcatradio@gmail.com
www.fatcatradio.com
We have one goal - to help get indie artists more exposure. Visit our website for submission details.

Fevered Brain Radio
PO Box 2631, Austin, TX 78768-2631
Mike Perazzetti mike@feveredbrainradio.com
www.thefeveredbrainofradiomike.com
Our mission is to make the world safe for good music.

Flat Cat Radio
www.myspace.com/flatcatradio
Featuring interviews and music from independent artists on MySpace.

FreshBlend Radio
PO Box 85, Bell Buckle, TN 37020
requests@freshblendradio.com
www.freshblendradio.com
The latest music from a variety of styles.

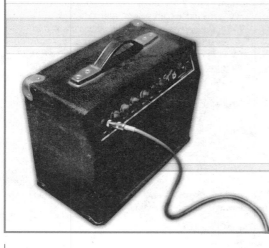
Gator Broadcasting
6101 Metrowest Blvd. Orlando, FL 32835
PH: 813-695-5976 FX: 407-292-2049
Scott Beaty infor@gatorbroadcasting.com
www.gatorbroadcasting.com
An online radio station dedicated to the very best unsigned and indie artists.

GotRadio
8100 Mulrany Way, Antelope, CA 95843
programmer@gotradio.com
www.gotradio.com
Send your CD to our address and mention the STATION you are contacting ie: "New Age".

Growth House Radio
Package Receiving, 2215-R Market St. #199
San Francisco, CA 94114
PH: 415-863-3045
info@growthhouse.org
www.growthhouse.org
Created to improve the quality of compassionate care for people who are dying. We offer several different channels with music and easy-listening education features on end-of-life care.

Harley Radio
PH: 704-212-2405
DJ Clone clone880@hotmail.com
www.harleyradio.com
Internet radio featuring a variety of styles.

Harris Radio
www.harrisradio.com
Created to offer "intelligent music for intelligent minds".

Hot Rocks Radio
www.hotrocksradio.net
We are proud to pay performance royalties to artists affiliated with ASCAP, BMI, SESAC and Sound Exchange. We are fully DMCA and RIAA compliant.

iChannel
PH: 314-983-6000
www.ichannelmusic.com
An online radio station unlike any other. We play the best unsigned music from around the world.

iLike2Rock.net
www.iLike2Rock.net
Free indie band promotion and internet radio station. Your online source for new music. Please use our web form to get in touch. Make sure you check the list of genres that we accept.

IMC Radio
PO Box 2366, Madison, MS 39130-2366
PH: 601-605-9691
www.imcradio.com
Open format internet radio station. The home of "The Better Music Mix!"

InYourFaceRadio.net
PH: 858-952-0991
iyfr@inyourfaceradio.net
www.inyourfaceradio.net
A Voice for the People!

Independent Nation
www.independentnation.net
Great independent music, interviews and some really off beat comedy.

Indie Life Radio
indieliferadio.com
The best music you've never heard!

The Indie Show
www.theindieshow.com
Broadcasting live every Sunday morning from the entertainment capital of the world, Las Vegas.

InRadio
PO Box 6882, Minneapolis, MN 55406
PH: 612-332-9606 FX: 612-338-6043
info@inradio.net
www.inradio.net
Encourages music and ideas not found on mainstream FM radio.

Insomnia Radio Network
34 W. 2nd St., Maysville, KY 41056
Jason Evangelho jason@insomniaradio.net
insomniaradio.net
Our hosts scour the independent music scene discovering unknown artists.

Jack and Jill Radio
PO Box 901345, Homestead, FL 33090
DJ Rambler dj_rambler@yahoo.com
www.jackandjillradio.com
Acoustic, Folk, Blues, Bluegrass, Country and Light Pop.

Kill Radio
mail@killradio.org
www.killradio.org
Anti corporate internet radio.

K-IRB
www.K-IRB.com
Ninja pirate radio!

Kool Rock Radio
kool@koolrockradio.com
www.koolrockradio.com
Formed by international DJs. Featuring the best Underground radio shows with the best indie music.

Kulak's Woodshed
5230½ Laurel Canyon Blvd.
North Hollywood, CA 91607
PH: 818-766-9913
Paul Kulak paulkulak@earthlink.net
www.kulakswoodshed.com
Live internet video webcasts and Acoustic music showcases.

Lisa's Walk The Talk Show
3160 Wellner Dr. NE #300, Rochester, MN 55906
PH: 507-536-4082
www.myspace.com/lisaswalkthetalk
Syndicated one hour radio show featuring all genres. Heart-to-hear talk with artists. They get 5-7 songs played on at least six stations. We WANT MORE INDIE artists!

Little Radio
scott@littleradio.com
littleradio.com
A variety of shows that welcome submissions.

Live365.com
950 Tower Ln. #400, Foster City, CA 94404
PH: 323-469-4582 FX: 650-345-7497
www.live365.com
Over 3 million visitors per month and 5,000 radio stations.

LoudCity
PO Box 1487, Somerville, MA 02144
support@loudcity.net
www.loudcity.net
An online broadcasting company with nearly one million unique listeners tune in each month.

LuxuriaMusic
PO Box 26290, San Francisco, CA 94126-6290
feedback@luxuriamusic.com
www.luxuriamusic.com
Featuring Outré Lounge and Latin Jazz, breezy swinging instrumentals and vocals, groovy 60's Go-Go, Psychedelia etc.

M3 Radio
259 W. 30th St. 12th Fl. New York, NY 10001
PH: 917-351-1021
Tony-O m3newmusic@yahoo.com
www.m3radio.com
Gets independent musicians airplay.

Monks Media Radio Network
5751 Bruce Blvd. Noblesville, IN 46062
PH: 317-565-1392
Jeffrey S. Monks jeff@monksmedia.com
www.monksmedia.com
A weekly show that showcases indie artists.

Moozikoo Radio
PO Box 50322, Nashville, TN 37205-0322
Anthony Bates radio@moozikoo.com
www.MoozikooRadio.com
An online retail site and radio station with an international customer/listener base. Our reputation and business is built upon the premise that we play and sell ONLY THE BEST of today's indie music - which assures exposure within the U.S. and abroad.

Music Business Radio *Dave's Demo Derby*
1310 Clinton St. #200, Nashville, TN 37203
www.MusicBusinessRadio.com
In this section on the show, your music will be heard by host David Hooper and his guests for the first time, live on the air. It will then be reviewed.

MUSIC CHOICE
Attn: Unsigned Material
328 W. 34th St., New York, NY 10001
www.musicchoice.com
44 genre specific non-stop digital quality music channels.

Music Highway Radio with Sheena Metal
15030 Ventura Blvd. #843
Sherman Oaks, CA 91403
PH: 818-785-7144
Sheena Metal sheena@musichighwayradio.com
www.musichighwayradio.com
The playlist is 100% fan/listener requested. That means that an artist's fans will be responsible for picking the show's music each week. Visit our website for submission details.

The Music Shoppe with Joanne Ledesma
www.myspace.com/themusicshoppe
A weekly radio show about the music industry. Visit our website for CD submission instructions.

Musical Justice
justice@musicaljustice.com
www.MusicalJustice.com
We welcome your submissions. Please note that we prefer to get CDs or links to MP3s. E-mailing us MP3 files just fills up our in-box and makes us grumpy.

Musictogousa.com
32 McKinley Ave. Bristol, CT 06010
PH: 860-490-0542
Bert Gagnon neonproductions@sbcglobal.net
www.musictogousa.com
The broadcast home of Neon Productions Radio playing all genres of indie music. Musictogousa.com also accepts member artists music store players and video coding for display on our site. Membership is free and all services to member artists are also free.

MusicWorld3D
36008 Poinsettia Ave. Fruitland Park, FL 34731
PH: 866-841-0089 FX: 321-206-4874
Mr. Heid admin@musicworld3d.com
www.musicworld3d.com
Indie radio/TV embedded in 3D virtual reality. Artist websites and more. A unique promotional service.

MyMusicStream
Andrew Drake andrew.drake@mymusicstream.com
www.mymusicstream.com
Streaming internet radio and music video site for bands, solo artists and music fans!

MyRealBroadcast
myrealtalent.com
Talk and music radio shows promoting undiscovered talent.

NEKKID Radio
info@nekkidradio.com
www.nekkidradio.com
DJs from around the world and the widest mix of music anywhere on the NET!

Netradio100
programming@netradio100.com
www.Netradio100.com
Rock, Jazz, Indie, Folk and Comedy.

NeverEndingWonder Radio
16 SW. 3rd #18, Portland, OR 97204
PH: 503-219-6741
Lee Widener neverendingwonder@hotmail.com
www.neverendingwonder.com/radio.htm
Plays a wide variety of music & comedy. NOT interested in Rap, Hip Hop or Dance.

New Artist Radio.net
www.newartistradio.net
We are the only station that can guarantee airplay for all genres of music! A FREE service offered to any band or independent artist that would like to get airplay worldwide. We feature 6,887 on-demand streams & 13 radio shows.

On The Horizon *New Artist Radio*
PO Box 92, Canton, NC 28716
Elly & John theonthehorizonradioshow@yahoo.com
www.theothnetwork.com
A weekly show that plays independent music and interviews independent artists.

Outsight Communications
5224 Shoreline Blvd. Waterford, MI 48329-1670
PH: 248-842-5850
Tom Schulte outsight@usa.net
www.new-sounds.com
Brings to light non-mainstream music.

Pandora
Attn: Music Genome Project Indie Submission
360 22nd St. #390, Oakland, CA 94612
pandora-support@pandora.com
www.pandora.com
A music discovery service designed to help clients find and enjoy music that they love. Along with your CD, send in your bio, tour dates, press clippings etc.

Peace and Pipedreams
Jimmy Peace peace@fearlessradio.com
www.myspace.com/peaceandpipedreams
From the depths of insanity comes a show that defies all convention. One troubled young man, on a quest to rid the world of stupid jerks, has taken to the airwaves, unleashing a treasure chest of fun, revenge and new music.

The Penguin
PO Box 140, Spring Lake, NJ 07762
PH: 732-280-3305
Gary Wien lightgrw@verizon.net
www.ThePenguinRocks.com
We largely play indie artists in our current playlist. We feature 200 songs each month in current rotation and then have several other rotations of older songs that combine to about 8,000 tunes.

PittRadio
PH: 202-483-6864
pittradio.bottomlesspitt.com
Streaming the cutting edge artistry of the independents. Upload your music today!

Pop Garden Radio
PO Box 560351, Rockledge, FL 32956-0351
adam@popgardenradio.com
www.popgardenradio.com
Each week you'll hear unsigned artists from around the globe and all aspects of the Pop genre.

Popbang.com
PO Box 6522, St. Paul, MN 55106
Jay Anderson jay@popbang.com
www.popbang.com
Newer power Pop and other Rock!

Pro Flow Radio & M3 Records
Mike V. Mosley m3@maxheat.com
www.maxheat.com
International radio broadcasting & pro audio production hosted by MaD MaXxx and featuring the best indie music.

Radio Artistopia
12955 Buck Board Ct. Woodbridge, VA 22192
radio.artistopia.com
To have your music aired you will need to begin by establishing your presence on Artistopia.com, which is free as well.

Radio Contraband
contact@radiocontraband.com
www.radiocontraband.com
We are continuously looking for new artists to feature on our music streams and podcasts.

Radio Crystal Blue
3655 Shore Pkwy. #1F, Brooklyn, NY 11235
PH: 718-646-0158
Dan Herman cblue456@optonline.net
www.radiocrystalblue.com
Featuring the best of the independents. Send your latest CD to the above address.

Radio Free David
PO Box 555, Tijeras, NM 87059
PH: 505-281-0800 FX: 505-281-0110
www.radiofreedavid.com
We play music to rock to - music to groove to... and everything in between.

Radio Free World
PO Box 444, Idyllwild, CA 92549
information@radiofreeworld.com
www.radiofreeworld.com
Almost 12 hrs of indie music per day.

Radio Indie
www.radioindie.com
Independent, streaming radio station dedicated to your music and your fans.

Radio Indie Pop
175 E. 2ⁿᵈ St. #1B, New York, NY 10009
Rob Sacher LunaSeaRecords@nyc.rr.com
www.radio-indie-pop.com
Music by independent label artists with no commercial radio airplay.

Radio Muse
1111 Davis Dr. #1-456, Newmarket, ON L3Y 9E5
Jodi Krangle jodi@musesmuse.com
www.musesmuse.com/radiomuse.html
Bringing together the very best indie music. Please visit our site for submission details!

Radio Nowhere
Christopher radionowhere@hotmail.com
www.radionowhere.org
Alternative, Electro and indie music show.

Radio Paradise
PO Box 3008, Paradise, CA 95967
bill@radioparadise.com
www.radioparadise.com
We welcome CDs from artists & record labels.

Radio Free Buzzine
5419 Hollywood Blvd. #C805
Hollywood, CA 90027
www.buzzine.com/radio
With over 4.7 million opt-in viewers on Buzzine, we can give bands an audience they could never get otherwise.

Radio Free Tunes
radiofreetunes@yahoo.com
www.radiofreetunes.com
Your gateway to new music!

Radio Sunset Entertainment
1133 Broadway #708, New York, NY 10010
PH: 877-542-6664
www.Radio-Sunset.com
Radio format where every song played is the live version.

Radio Ugly
42 Sewell St., Lake George, NY 12845
PH: 518-932-6751
Ken Lytle kenlytle@gmail.com
www.radiougly.com
Rock genre internet radio station playing the music of independent artists.

RadioINDY.com
PO Box 230581, Encinitas, CA 92023
support@radioIndy.com
www.radioindy.com
Home for independent music on the web.

radioio
5025 W. Lemon St. #200, Tampa, FL 33609
PH: 800-884-8634
www.radioio.com
Alternative Rock, cutting-edge Pop, contemporary Folk, Blues and Jazz.

RadioU
PO Box 1887, Westerville, OH 43086
PH: 614-839-7100
radiou.com
We play the stuff corporate radio doesn't.

RadioXY
Chaos aceking@pobox.com
radioxy.com
Underground Alternative music.

Rock Solid Pressure *KWTF*
4254 Whistlewood Cir. Lakeland, FL 33811
Patty Yagtu rocksolidpressure@yahoo.com
rocksolidpressure.com
The only independent music game show on the net! Focusing exclusively on 'Rock' music.

Scrub Radio
info@scrubradio.com
www.scrubradio.com
A station dedicated to unsigned artists.

Sirius Satellite Radio
1221 Ave. of the Americas, New York, NY 10020
PH: 212-584-5100
www.siriusradio.com
The best music you've ever heard and never heard.

Skope Radio
radio@skopemagazine.com
www.skopemagazine.com/html/radio.html
An opportunity for artists to submit MP3s directly to the Skope website. From there, as long as all the prerequisites are in place, the song will appear on the station.

Sloth Radio
slothradio@gmail.com
www.slothradio.com
Playing the best in modern and classic Synthpop and New Wave.

SMtv/The Samantha Murphy Show
PH: 323-284-5988
Samantha Murphy sm@smtvmusic.com
www.smtvmusic.com
A traveling music show for Singer/Songwriters and Pop/Rock bands.

SomaFM
1890 Bryant St. #303, San Francisco, CA 94110
(channel name)
Shawn shawn@somafm.com
www.somafm.com
Internet broadcasts that reach around the world.

Songtiger.com
6415 Oliver Ave. S., Richfield, MN 55423
PH: 952-200-6255
st-staff@songtiger.com
www.songtiger.com
Covers most genres of music.

SongPlanet.com
radioinfo@songplanet.com
www.songplanet.com/artists/signup.html
We offer free artist pages, live DJs (who select the music for airplay), artist forums, and other great tools for Indie artists. We're based in Seattle, and have DJs in Canada, Sweden, the US, and the UK, as well as world-wide artists and listeners.

SongVault.fm
2260 Rutherford Rd. #111, Carlsbad, CA 92008
support@songvault.fm
www.songvault.fm
Artists upload 3 songs for free to have listeners filter out the best of the best in order to get permanent radio airplay and featured on one of our daily podcast shows. Please do NOT send CDs to our address!

The Sound of Young America
720 S. Normandie Ave. #505
Los Angeles, CA 90005
Jesse Thorn jesse@maximumfun.org
www.maximumfun.org
Syndicated show with in-depth discussions with personalities from the world of entertainment. If you think that you would fit, get in touch. We're all ears!

Spider Radio
Donnie spiderradio@cableone.net
www.spiderradio.net
Broadcasting indie music on the world wide web!

StardustRadio.com
stardust@stardustradio.com
www.stardustent.com
Internet radio supporting the US troops. All genres welcome.

StreetBlast Radio
PH: 502-442-7378
www.streetblastradio.com
Underground music, popular culture, rants and raves.

The Trans-Atlantic Underground
www.myspace.com/transatlanticunderground
Takes you around the world of Shoegaze, Indie Rock, Psychedelia and other movements within a vast body of underground music.

TribecaRadio.net
PH: 212-941-5857
Leigh Crizoe tribecar@tribecaradio.net
www.tribecaradio.net
Internet radio station featuring a variety of shows.

Unknown Radio
Erik D. erik@unknownradio.com
www.unknownradio.com
Innovative talk programing includes great indie music ranging from Folk to Hard Rock and everything in between — even Indie Rock.

Unsigned Artists Radio
Julian Bankston julian@uaradio.net
www.uaradio.net
Our primary goal to provide you with a new revenue and distribution model for your music. You will also be featured on our internet radio station which is broadcast globally.

Unsigned Musicians Internet Radio
Deb unsignedmusicians@hotmail.com
www.myspace.com/unsignedmusicians
Created to feature the original songs of incredibly talented unsigned musicians who are not getting the recognition they deserve. The song title and artist will always be provided and information about how to purchase downloads and CDs will be provided as well.

Virtual Party Zone Radio
www.vpzradio.com
Supports and works with indie artists to get there music exposed to the world.

Way Out There Radio
Kysses kysses@wayoutthere.net
www.wayoutthere.net
You can be sure to hear our DJs play local bands and unsigned artists from their area and everywhere.

WCH Radio
GW Carver House, 3035 Bell Ave.
St. Louis, MO 63106
PH: 314-457-3560
John O'Day wchradio@gmail.com
www.wchradio.net
We try to play as much indie music as possible.

WebRadioPugetSound.com
PO Box 1801, Eatonville, WA 98328
wrps1@comcast.net
www.webradiopugetsound.com
See website for submission guidelines/forms.

Westsidewill Radio
333 Cottonwood Ln. Naperville, IL 60540
PH: 630-309-4423
Will westside@westsidewill.com
www.westsidewill.com
*We specialize in promoting unsigned artists. We
allow artists to post songs, sell merchandise as well
as promote upcoming events.*

Wild Side Radio
10662 De La Roche, Montreal, QC H2C 2P5
Station@WildSideRadio.com
www.WildSideRadio.com
*A variety of shows featuring the best in indie music.
Send in a CD or a link to your music.*

WorldRock Radio
PH: 580-371-2101
CSC worldrockradio2@gmail.com
www.worldrockradio.com
*An internet radio station that plays Rock & Indie
Rock 24 hours a day.*

WSVN Radio
PO Box 132, Thornton, IL 60476-0132
wsvnradio@yahoo.com
www.wsvnradio.net
Send your CD and additional info.

X-Site Radio
22447 Hartland St., West Hills, CA 91307
818-985-2464
info@xmradio.la
www.xsiteradio.com
Upload your music. The world is listening!

XM Satellite Radio
1500 Eckington Place NE,
Washington, DC 20002-2194
Attn: Billy Zero
FX: 202-380-4065
xmu43@xmradio.com
xmu.xmradio.com
Submit your CD with genre labeled. No MP3s.

XND Radio
PH: 312-924-0460
www.xndradio.com
*24/7 internet radio station playing the best in
independent music.*

You Rock Radio
8539 W. Sanna St., Peoria, AZ 85345
PH: 623-266-0309
Uncle Indie yourock@yourockradio.com
www.YouRockRadio.com
*We accept Rap, Hip Hop, Rock, Metal, Gospel,
Country, Acoustic, Folk and Electronica. Your music
will appear on shows with similar music styles.
There is a theme style for every episode. If you are
in a "band", we can only have one of you as guest
host. We will need (3) high quality songs for the
show from a guest co-host.*

YourOnLive.com
www.youronlive.com
Rock and talk only the internet can handle.

Zero Art Radio
1560 Corinth Rd. Mount Juliet, TN 37122
www.zeroartradio.com
*A consortium of Alternative musicians, artists and
people in general who are enthused by creativity
and free thought.*

Podcasts

*Podcasts listed in this section feature a variety
of musical styles. Other more genre-specific
podcasts can be found in the appropriate
sections of this book. Most podcasters don't
mind if you send MP3s via e-mail, but there are
some will DELETE any attachments sent to
them and insist that you send a LINK to your
song file. So just to be safe, make sure to
check the submission details for each show.*

*Many podcasts feature what is called "podsafe
music". To find out what podsafe music is, read
the article in SECTION EIGHT of this book
called "What is Podsafe Music?"*

United States

A1 Artist Spotlight .Com
1605 Zurich Dr. St. Louis, MO 63031
PH: 206-984-3002
A1 Mark A1BandSpotlight@gmail.com
www.A1ArtistSpotlight.com
*25 minute podcast spotlighting one artist for the
whole show. Electric Rock n' Blues.*

Accidental Hash
PO Box 367, Milford, MA 01757
PH: 617-934-0545
C.C. Chapman cc.chapman@gmail.com
www.accidenthash.com
Playing the best in podsafe music Visit the website for submission details.

Adam Curry's Daily Source Code
adam@podshow.com
www.dailysourcecode.com
Podfather Adam Curry scours the globe for the hottest new mashups, podcast highlights and podsafe music.

Alaska Podshow
PO Box 221856, Anchorage, AK 99522-1856
Scott Slone media@alaskapodshow.com
www.alaskapodshow.com
Local news, events and introducing independent music from artists around the world.

American Cliche
PH: 323-285-5219
Scott TheAmericanCliche@gmail.com
americancliche.net
Bizarre news stories, politics and undiscovered music all served up with a heaping dose of sarcasm. We want to hear from you!

America Unsigned
americaunsigned.com
Featuring the best independent musicians in the country. Send us an e-mail with a short bio and the names of the songs you would like played.

Amplified Podcast
PO Box 151, Seattle, WA 98111
Eric Hoglund eric@amplifiedpodcast.com
www.amplifiedpodcast.com
Podcasting great indie bands from around the globe.

Ash Radio
PH: 203-389-1736
csr@froppo.com
www.ashradio.com
Dedicated to giving you the best exposure we possibly can. Visit our site for submission details.

Assoc. of Music Podcasting *(AMP)*
Ed Roberts ed@kcweather.org
musicpodcasting.org
Consider submitting your music to AMP's music library, which our members use to fill their unique podcasts with hot new acts.

Audio Popcorn
PH: 763-390-5051
audiopopcorn@gmail.com
www.audiopopcorn.net
Small musical shows focusing on one artist or group.

Bald Guy Show
8594 88th St. S., Cottage Grove, MN 55016-4708
AJ Janssen baldguyshow@gmail.com
www.BaldGuyShow.net
I play 3 or 4 songs from a CD I've received and talk about what I think of the music. There may also be an interview with the artist or band.

Band Weblogs Podcast
Jenny & Dave info@bandweblogs.com
www.bandweblogs.com/podcastshow.html
Playing podsafe and independent music with the occasional special guest dropping by.

Bands Under the Radar
kami@viperroom.com
bandsundertheradar.com
Featuring unsigned bands and indie artists.

Barefoot Radio
barefootradio.com
Nobody does more to promote independent bands and musicians. We work hard to sell your music.

BFN Networks
Justin Holt aka "Bob Dubilina"
webmaster@bfninyourears.com
www.bfninyourears.com
Bold declarations, risky propositions, dark humor, angry rants, wild interviews and great music!

Big Daddy Dan Podcast
PH: 206-333-0090
dannyt@hintonet.net
okieradio.com
Podsafe music, random banter, humor, technology, events.

BinaryStarCAST
PO Box 650246, Miami, FL 33265
PH: 888-457-2209 FX: 786-206-0657
Henry A. Otero starcast@binarystarmusic.com
www.binarystarcast.com
Features only the best in Alternative, Pop, Rock, Hip Hop and R&B. Contact us, we want to play your stuff!

The Bitterest Pill
8939 S. Sepulveda Blvd. #110-713
Los Angeles, CA 90045
PH: 206-309-7455
Dan Klass pill@danklass.com
www.thebitterestpill.com
Commentary and music from a stay-at-home dad/shut in.

Buckeye Drive Time
buckeyedrivetime@gmail.com
www.buckeyedrivetime.com
A drive time alternative. 3 Songs, 3 Promos, no idiots!

The Buddy Culver Show
Darren Proctor darrenproctor@gmail.com
www.buddyculver.com
Coming to you from the bowels of a basement in Dearborn, MI. Highlighting indie bands from all decades.

bumrocks
andre@bumrocks.com
www.bumrocks.com
Podcast featuring a wide variety of music.

BZoO HomeGrown Radio
cafeRg@gmail.com
www.bzoo.org
Where political pundits, artists, poets and fans play!

C.C. Chapman's U-Turn Cafe
PO Box 367, Milford, MA 01757
PH: 206-984-2233
C.C. Chapman uturncafe@gmail.com
u-turncafewp.podshow.com
A special focus on mellow, chilled Acoustic music. Grab a seat and enjoy!

Celebrate Radio
PO Box 72174, Oakland, CA 94612
PH: 510 464-4677
Don Fass info@celebrateradio.com
www.celebrateradio.com
Positive music, social justice commentary, culture and spirituality features.

Chillcast
375 Redondo Ave. #326, Long Beach, CA 90814
thechillcast.podshow.com
Music ranging from Downtempo to Deep House, Trip Hop to Dream Pop, Electro Lounge to old school Jazz and Blues.

The Closet Geek Show
Brent closetgeekshow@gmail.com
www.closetgeekshow.com
A mix of Trance, Drum n' Bass, Rock, Metal and mashups that will make you want to dance, mosh or both at once.

CoolerPodcasts.com
PO Box 26272, Akron, OH 44319
PH: 330-807-5236
Dave Jackson musicianscooler@gmail.com
www.coolerpodcasts.com
Where musicians come to trade advice and music.

Coverville
PMB 12, 15400 W. 64th Ave. #E-9
Arvada, CO 80007
PH: 206-222-2683
Brian Ibbott coverville@gmail.com
www.coverville.com
A podcast that focuses on new renditions of previously recorded songs.

CriticCAST | SongCritic.com
JD Atkinson songcritic@comcast.net
www.SongCritic.com
A weekly podcast of guest critics reviewing songs posted at SongCritic.com.

Deliberate Noise
admin@deliberatenoise.com
PH: 206-202-9973
www.deliberatenoise.com
Music from independent record labels and unsigned artists.

Digital Detroit Radio
www.digitaldetroitradio.com
Our mission is to promote independent bands that aren't associated with the RIAA. I love spreading the word about indie bands that people might not have heard of yet.

DigiVegas
PH: 702-425-3263
Paulie Podcaster paulie@digivegaspodcast.com
www.digivegaspodcast.com
Bringing you the very best indie music from Las Vegas, as well as from all over the world.

Eclectic Mix
eclecticmix@gmail.com
eclecticmix.com
Offers the best from a mixture of musical styles. A single artist will be highlighted during each show so that the listener can absorb what is offered.

Get Jacked!
Jack Elias getjackedpodcast@gmail.com
www.getjackedpodcast.com
I play what I like. Say what I like. Show up when I like.

High Orbit
matthewebel.com/podcast
Music, news and feedback from all over the quadrant with Matthew Ebel.

The Home Made Hit Show
Tony Butterworth homemadehitshow@gmail.com
www.homemadehitshow.com
Featuring exciting and original Rock, Acoustic, Blues and Pop music made by home based artists.

Indie500Show
Jamey Wilson indie500show@gmail.com
indie500show.podomatic.com
"The Lucky 13" features the top 13 songs in independent and unsigned music every month as determined by our panel and the ratings of listeners.

IndieFeed
Chris MacDonald info@indiefeed.com
www.indiefeed.com
Your music must be unique, high impact, high energy and compelling. Your songs must push the envelope and resonate, stimulate and perhaps even challenge the audience.

Jason Knows
PH: 641-985-7800 pin 858057
knows.jason@gmail.com
www.jasonknows.com
Deals in indie music and interviews.

The Jersey Toddshow
85 Castleton Rd. Princeton, NJ 08540
PH: 609-924-3948
Todd Wachtel jerseytoddshow@gmail.com
www.jerseytoddshow.com
A podcast that was featured on Sirius and a nominee for an Asbury Park Music Award for Best Personality. Bringing the best indie music and scathing rants from the mind of a warped Joisey lawyer.

Little Radio
scott@littleradio.com
www.littleradio.com
Broadcasts several shows that feature independent music.

Looking out the Window
PH: 206-666-5665
artist@lookingoutthewindow.com
lookingoutthewindow.com
Highlights the inspiration behind the music. Peak inside the musicians studio and you just may be inspired yourself!

Love House Radio
PH: 206-202-5666
PD Love LoveHouseRadio@gmail.com
www.lovehouseradio.com
Fresh music and personal interviews.

Lunatic Radio
theshow@lunaticradio.com
lunaticradio.com
Interviews with independent artists and their music.

Lying Media Bastards
PO Box 4705, San Diego, CA 92164
Jake lmbradio@gmail.com
www.lyingmediabastards.com
Couples excellent music with angry news commentary (and the occasional interview). If you've got songs for us send MP3s via e-mail.

Mashup of the Week
www.mashuptown.com
Promoting the brilliance, creativity and hard work of DJs, producers, Mashup artists and the original artists whose music is mashed.

The MastanMusic Hour
1028 SE Water St. #230, Portland, OR 97214
PH: 503-889-8646
Jeremy Wilson mastan@comcast.net
www.mastanmusic.com/podcast
A podcast that features Americana, Rock, Psychedelic, Alternative, Alt-Country and Punk music.

Most People Are DJs
PO Box 1231,
Union Lake, MI 48387
PH: 206-666-3248
Mikel O.D.
mostpeopleredjs@gmail.com
mostpeopleredjs.libsyn.com
Send me stuff for my show!!

musicNerve.com
Weekly Podcast
PO Box 67405,
Albuquerque, NM
87193-7405
Peter Mezensky
podcast@musicnerve.com
www.musicnerve.com
We seek out the best Indie Rock, the weirdest outsider music and the most ground breaking of the Experimental and Avant-garde.

MusicRebellion.com
Paul Mahern
paulm@musicrebellion.com
www.musicrebellion.com
Our podcasts feature information about up and coming artists.

Next Big Hit
300 W. 43rd St. #303, New York, NY 10036
music@nextbighit.com
www.nextbighit.com
Submit your music for us to consider for our podcast programming and for Indie Airplay Internet Radio!

Notes From The Underground
music@notesunderground.com
notesunderground.com
New music recommendations, music news, film reviews and more.

The Obtuse Angle
PH: 206-350-0790
Steve Dupont obtuseangle@stevedupont.com
obtuseangle.libsyn.com
Brought to you by the hardest working brain cell in America!

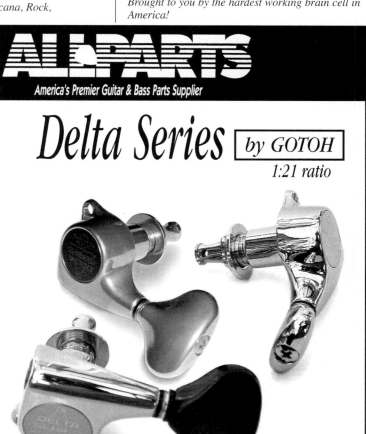

Off the Beat-n-Track
PO Box 1190, Sheffield, MA 01257
PH: 413-229-9939
info@offthebeat-n-track.com
offthebeatntrack.libsyn.com
The best in indie music from across the country and beyond. Live performances, interviews, CD spotlights and more.

The Open Mike Cafe
32712 Cardinal Ln. Wayne, MI 48184
Michael Stephens mike8657@gmail.com
openmikecafe.blogspot.com
Weekly podcast. Most of the music is Folk/Acoustic, though we are starting to play more Blues, Jazz and Alternative.

PEACEPOD
Jason Brock peacepod@songserverworldwide.com
www.songserverworldwide.com
A cutting edge way for activists, artists and the audience to connect. For music submissions please sign the guest book with a link to your music.

The PhiLL(er)
PO Box 1345, Issaquah, WA 98027
phill@thephiller.com
www.thephiller.com/podcast
Weekly independent music showcase.

Pod Music Countdown (PMC Top10)
www.podmusiccountdown.com
A weekly countdown show featuring the top tunes being spun by podcasters.

The Podcast Network
www.thepodcastnetwork.com
One of the best resources for quality audio content that people can listen to when they want, where they want and on any device they want.

The Podcast Network's Rock Show
Ewan ewanspence@gmail.com
rock.thepodcastnetwork.com
Walking the dark corners of the internet to find the best underground and unnoticed Rock bands.

Podsafe Music Daily
www.podsafemusicdaily.com
Your daily dose of 100% podsafe music to make your day go by just that much faster.

podsafe music network
music.podshow.com
The best in new music and music podcasts. Submit your music and watch your fans and CD sales grow!

Podshow Music Rewind
Marcus Couch podshowmusicrewind@gmail.com
rewind.podshow.com
The best independent music from the best independent music podcasts.

Podshow Radio
PH: 415-287-3763
www.podshowradio.com
Where we talk about music and more!

Radio Orphans Podcast
radioorphanspodcast@gmail.com
radioorphans.blogspot.com
Weekly music podcast dedicated to bringing you original independent music from around the world. Each episode is hosted by Jaw Knee and Finneaus of the Radio Orphans.

Radio QRM
PH: 206-666-7760
barryj@radioqrm.com
radioqrm.com
Noise traditional radio can't ignore.

Random Signal
PH: 206-984-2461
Jason Adams randomsignal@gmail.com
randomsignal.libsyn.com
Tangential transmissions from a disorganized mind.

Reaching for Lucidity
PH: 206-339-9452
ebancrawford@gmail.com
reachingforlucidity.net
The condom for your ears in the fight against STD's (sonically transmitted diseases).

The Robot 40 Podcast
12040 Lake Ave. #203, Lakewood, OH 44107
PH: 216-759-4131 FX: 319-856-7726
Brad Makula bands@robot40.com
www.robot40.com
A one hour weekly podcast featuring independent artists trying to break through.

Rock and Roll Geek Indie Show
PH: 706-621-7625
Michael Butler rockandrollgeek@gmail.com
www.rockandrollgeek.org
Playing the best in podsafe independent Rock.

Rock and Roll Jew Show
David Jacobs rockandrolljew@gmail.com
www.rockandrolljew.com
The best Indie Rock 'n Roll from all over the world. A special spotlight is put on bands from Israel or with Jewish heritage.

The Rock and Roll Report Podcast
rockandrollreport@gmail.com
www.rockandrollreport.com
Specializes in unsigned and independent Rock and Roll that should be heard on commercial Rock radio - if only commercial Rock radio wasn't so lazy and focused on selling cars and plasma TVs.

Shifted Sound
www.shiftedsound.com
Showcasing great independent and small label music.

The Sounds in My Head
daniel@thesoundsinmyhead.com
www.thesoundsinmyhead.com
A weekly show featuring songs and bands you might have missed.

The Soupy Gato Show
532 ½ W. Center, Essexville, MI 48732
PH: 206-203-4286
Daniel J. Harris soupygato@gmail.com
soupygato.com
Showcases original music by independent artists of all genres. Mail your CD or e-mail me your MP3s.

Tracks Up the Tree
contact@upthetree.com
www.upthetree.com
We play artists we connect to, so bio's and photographs are strongly suggested. I also post reviews occasionally.

The Tripwire
info@thetripwire.com
www.thetripwire.com/podcast
We always aim to support and highlight music for those in the industry that "genuinely care" and love music as much as we do.

UC Radio
PH: 323-319-4230
www.ucradiopodshow.com
Always on the look out for anything that is good and that hasn't been tainted by corporate baggage.

The Unharshed Mellow
PO Box 30849, Philadelphia, PA 19104
Seuss & BJ theunharshedmellow@gmail.com
www.theunharshedmellow.com
Like a wet willy of independent music.

Unsigned Underground
261 S. Main St. #319, Newtown, CT 06470
Darryl Gregory info@unsignedunderground.net
www.unsignedunderground.net
Take a listen to one or two of the shows and you make the decision. If you think your music is a fit and you are an unsigned artist or band then send me a CD and tell me what your website address is.

Well-Rounded Radio
59 Forest Hills St., Jamaica Plain, MA 02130-2933
PH: 617-233-6613
Charlie McEnerney charlie@wellroundedradio.net
www.wellroundedradio.net
An interview program that finds what inspires and influences artists work.

Zaldor's World
www.zaldor.com
Detroit based show playing a wide variety of music.

Canada

Audio Popcorn
14 St-Georges St., Oka, QC J0N 1E0
PH: 763-390-5051
Krash Coarse audiopopcorn@gmail.com
audiopopcorn.net
Featuring a single artist (2-3 songs) per program. Maximum tunes, minimum "blabla."

Cadence Revolution
843 Ludgate Cr. Kingston, ON K7M 6C7
contact@cadencerevolution.com
www.kingstonbluessociety.ca
A weekly sixty minute mix of music to work out to. We're always open to new artists and music of just about every genere although the shows leans towards something with a good driving beat to work out to.

The Kaflooey Podcast
Chris Sherry kaflooey@gmail.com
www.kaflooey.com
A comedy and music podcast featuring comedy sketches and independent podsafe music.

mostlytunes.com
PO Box 87, Ste-Marthe-sur-le-Lac, QC J0N 1P0
PH: 267-220-3701
media@mostlytunes.com
www.mostlytunes.com
We're always looking for new music!

My Living Room!
www.myspace.com/mylivingroomradioshow
A fresh, funny and funky look at indie and commercial pop-culture through the eyes of a self-confessed pop culture, music obsessed, MySpace-living junkie! I am interested in meeting independent bands and solo artists to interview on the show from all spectrums of the industry!

Space Junk Radio
filmjunk@gmail.com
www.spacejunk.org
News and reviews from the world of movies and pop culture plus the best in Indie Rock and Electronic music.

France

Meltingpod
Annie Viglielmo meltingpod@free.fr
meltingpod.free.fr
A melting pot of music, colors and cultures.

Germany

Uwe Hermann's Music Podcast
PH: +49-931-663927-408
uwe@hermann-uwe.de
www.hermann-uwe.de/podcast
Playing freely available (podsafe) music by various artists and from most music genres.

Italy

RockCast Italia
dok@rockcastitalia.com
www.rockcastitalia.com
Il podcast n'1 per gli amanti del rock in Italia.

United Kingdom

Bitjobs for the Masses!
54 Briery Rd. Halesowen, West Mids, B63 1AS UK
PH: 206-350-1228
Phil Coyne phil@bitjobs.net
bfm.btpodshow.com
An independent music podcast playing the very best music from around the world.

Dark Compass
Rowland ro@darkcompass.com
www.darkcompass.com
With the knowledge that regular radio will almost never play or support indie music, we are giving you a free and valuable service.

Darkhorse Radio
darkhorse@podomatic.com
www.darkhorseradio.co.uk
Plays only the BEST independent music from around the world - no fillers, just great music.

The Flashing 12
55 Marlborough Pk. Ave. Sidcup,
Kent, DA15 9DL UK
PH: 07767-443536
Paul & Janet Parkinson flashing12@gmail.com
www.theflashing12.com
We are known as "The Richard and Judy of podcasting". We both talk about stuff and nonsense and tech and anything else that drifts past the window.

Homegrown
Nic Treadwell nic@homegrownpodcast.co.uk
homegrown.libsyn.com
Music, poetry and prose featuring an eclectic mix of artists from all over the world.

My Silver Mount Zion
12 St Michael's Mount, Northampton, NN1 4JH UK
PH: 206-888-6769
Rob & Steve mysilvermountzion@gmail.com
robular.libsyn.com
We welcome you to something you haven't heard before.

Not Your Usual Bollocks
www.notyourusualbollocks.squarespace.com
An on-demand refuge from main-stream radio featuring the best independent artists from the Rock and Electronic music genres.

Radio Clash
PH: +44-700-598-1731
radioclash@mutantpop.net
www.mutantpop.net/radioclash
From remixes to DJ mixes, bootlegs to Electronica, Experimental weirdness to aural oddities and insane covers.

Short Attention Span Radio
shortattentionspan_radio@yahoo.co.uk
sasradio.blogspot.com
If you hear your favourite bands on here, let us know - well see it doesn't happen again.

TheDogBox
PH: 206-666-6637
Bruce woof@thedogbox.info
www.thedogbox.info
A regular round-up of motor sport news plus great music.

Three From Leith
Grant Mason threefromleith@gmail.com
www.threefromleith.com
Send an e-mail submission, attaching a track or two, along with a few paragraphs about yourself or the band.

Unsigned at The Podcast Brewery
hello@podcastbrewery.com
www.podcastbrewery.com
Looking to help get some more exposure, awareness and increase your listenership? Then you can become part of our growing niche podcasts.

The Voodoo Quota Show
19 Ridgewalk Way, Worsbrough, Barnsley, S.,
Yorkshire, S70 6TH UK
PH: 44-7905-052307
Izzie Kirk izie@voodooquotashow.co.uk
www.voodooquotashow.co.uk
A weekly radio/podshow introducing you to excellent new music from over the place. Each show brings you 20-30 minutes of delicious new music to get your teeth into without putting up stupid genre barriers.

Xan Phillips Presents
admin@xan.co.uk
www.xan.co.uk
Due to the high volume of excellent new music we are being sent we have put them into a half-hour show called The New Music Collection.

Japan

...My cup of tea...
mail@mycupoftea.cc
www.mycupoftea.cc
Music, talk, creative commons and more.

podshower.com
2-19-20-603 Mizusawa, Miyamae, Kawasaki,
Kanagawa 216-0012 Japan
PH: 044-979-1124 FX: 044-979-1124
Masayoshi Yamamiya info@fishthemusic.com
www.podshower.com
Podcast for Japanese music made in Japan.

Blues Radio

Internet, Syndicated Shows and Podcasts

United States

Beale Street Caravan
66 Monroe Ave. #101, Memphis, TN 38103
PH: 901-527-4666 FX: 901-529-4030
info@bealestreetcaravan.com
www.bealestreetcaravan.com
Aired weekly on over 280 public, community and college radio stations nationwide.

Blues Before Sunrise
PO Box 272, Forest Park, IL 60130
PH: 708-771-2135
Steve Cushing doublnot@inil.com
www.bluesbeforesunrise.com
Nationally syndicated public radio program explores, preserves and popularizes the various eras and genre of Blues heritage.

Cybro Radio
Larry Lowe info@cybroradio.us
www.cybroradio.com
Broadcasting Blues, Jazz, Country Gospel and Hip Hop music and featuring emerging new stars.

ElectricBlues Radio
GoodBlues@ElectricBluesRadio.com
web.tampabay.rr.com/ebradio
Sizzlin' electric Blues guitar.

Mark Kerr's Blues Nation
bluesboy747@yahoo.com
www.markkerrltd.com/bluesnation.htm
Dedicated to promoting the music of indie Blues. Must be a studio quality CD of your own music.

Murphy's Saloon
PH: 312-239-0678
murphyssaloon@gmail.com
www.murphyssaloon.com
Podcast home of the Blues!

The Roadhouse
Tony Steidler-Dennison
tony@roadhousepodcast.com
www.roadhousepodcast.com
A weekly podcast of great Blues music by unknown artists. The finest Blues you've never heard!

California

Ann the Raven's Blues Show *KCSN*
18111 Nordhoff St., Northridge, CA 91330-8312
PH: 818-885-5276
Ann the Raven anntheraven@aol.com
www.kcsn.org/programs/anntheraven.html
Delivering the best Blues sounds in SoCal for over 20 years.

Blues Evening Train *KKUP*
933 Monroe St., PMB 9150, Santa Clara, CA 95050
PH: 408-260-2999
www.kkup.org/dj/conductor.html
The Conductor hips listeners to the best in Blues, whether it's hot off the presses or a scratchy vinyl LP.

Damn Traffic! *KKUP*
933 Monroe St., PMB 9150, Santa Clara, CA 95050
PH: 408-260-2999
Jammin Jim jammin_jim@sbcglobal.net
www.kkup.org/dj/farris.html
Features up-and-coming Blues artists, the Youngbloods of the Blues.

Rollin' and Tumblin / Two Steps from the Blues *KUSP*
203 8th Ave. Santa Cruz, CA 95062
PH: 831-476-2800 FX: 831-476-2802
kusp@kusp.org
www.kusp.org
Send any promotional items for airplay, giveaway or review.

Colorado

Strictly Blues *103.5 The Fox*
4695 S. Monaco, Denver, CO 80237
www.thefox.com/pages/strictlyblues-index.html
Host Kai Turner features the best of national, international & local Blues as well as interviews and live in-studio performances.

Florida

Smokestack Lightnin' Blues Radio *WUCF*
PO Box 162199, Orlando, FL 32816-2199
PH: 407-823-0899
Bluesman Tommy blues@smokestacklightnin.com
www.smokestacklightnin.com
Features the very best New Blues and newly reissued Classic Blues, Adult R&B, Adult Soul, Blues Rock, Zydeco Blues and Gospel.

Indiana

The Blues Revue *WVPE*
2424 California Rd. Elkhart, IN 46514
PH: 888-399-9873
Ole Harv oleharve@att.net
www.wvpe.org/blues_revue.html
Celebrating over 20 years of the Blues!

Minnesota

Rollin & Tumblin *KFAI*
1808 Riverside Ave. Minneapolis, MN 55454
PH: 612-341-0980 FX: 612-341-4281
Jacquie Maddix diamondblue@qwest.net
www.kfai.org
A synthesis of Blues and Big Band.

Mississippi

WMPR
1018 Pecan Park Cir. Jackson, MS 39286
PH: 601-948-5950 FX: 601-948-6162
DJ@wmpr901.com
www.wmpr901.com
Blues and Gospel station.

Nebraska

Mystic Mile *KZUM*
941 "O" St., Lincoln, NE 68508
PH: 402-474-5086 FX: 402-474-5091
Mike Flowers mflowers@lps.org
www.kzum.org/mystic
Nothing but the very best of Blues with the classics and new releases.

New York

Across the Tracks *WFDU*
Metropolitan Campus, 1000 River Rd.
Teaneck, NJ 07666
PH: 201-692-2806 FX: 201-692-2807
Richy Harps richyharps@aol.com
wfdu.fm
Blends both classic Blues and Soul with new artists who perform in the traditional style.

Big Road Blues *WGMC*
32 Lomb Memorial Dr. Rochester, NY 14623-0563
PH: 585-475-2271 FX: 585-475-4988
sundayblues.org
We span the history of the Blues bringing you everything from Barrelhouse Piano to searing Electric Blues.

Sunday Night Blues *WAER*
795 Ostrom Ave. Syracuse, NY 13244-4601
PH: 315-443-4021 FX: 315-443-2148
Tom Townsley waer@syr.edu
waer.org/blues.html
For over 12 years supplying Blues fans a healthy dosage of both national and local Blues talent.

Ohio

Woodchopper's Ball *WRUW*
11220 Bellflower Rd. Cleveland, OH 44106
PH: 216-368-2208
Chip md@wruw.org
wruw.org
An exploration of the Blues. Specializing in Traditional, Delta and Piedmont styles.

Oklahoma

The Weekend Blues *KGOU*
Copeland Hall, Rm. 300, U. Oklahoma
Norman, OK 73019-2053
PH: 405-325-3388 FX: 405-325-7129
'Hardluck' Jim jjhardluck@ou.edu
www.kgou.org
The best in Blues, Roots Rock, & down home Soul... old & new!

Pennsylvania

Bandana Blues with Beardo & Spinner
Spinner spinner.blues@gmail.com Beardo
thebeardo@gmail.com
www.bandanablues.com
Podcast playing all things Blues.

Texas

The Casbah *KYSM*
1300 San Pedro Ave. San Antonio, TX 78212
PH: 210-733-2800
Brian Parrish casbahradio@yahoo.com
www.ksym.org
Featuring Surf-Instrumentals, Garage, Blues and more!

On the Roadside *KMBH*
PO Box 2147, Harlingen, TX 78551
PH: 800-839-6771 FX: 956-421-4150
Chris Maley kmbhkhid@aol.com
www.kmbh.org/radio/roadside.htm
The best in classic & latest Blues.

Virginia

Nothin' But the Blues *WTJU*
PO Box 400811, Charlottesville, VA 22904-4811
PH: 434-924-0885 FX: 434-924-8996
Peter Welch wtju@virginia.edu
wtju.net/cpages/musub
Featuring the best of Mississippi and Chicago acoustic and electric Blues.

The Indie Link Exchange

www.indielinkexchange.com/ile

Canada

At the Crossroads
PO Box 20027, Stn. Sahali Mall
Kamloops, BC V2C 6X1
Brant Zwicker brant@atcblues.ca
www.atcblues.ca
A syndicated program that focuses upon Blues music and many various genres – Soul, R&B, Swing, Delta, Zydeco etc.

The Blues Never Die *CHRW*
Rm. 250, UCC, UWO, 1151 Richmond St.
London, ON N6A 3K7
PH: 519-661-3600 FX: 519-661-3372
John tbnd@rogers.com
www.chrwradio.com/tbnd
Featuring the latest Blues releases.

Code Blue *CITR*
#233-6138 SUB Blvd. Vancouver, BC V6T 1Z1
PH: 604-822-2487 FX: 604-822-9364
codeblue@buddy-system.org
www.citr.ca
All the Blues, all the time. From the classics to the newest Bluest notes.

Eclectic Blues *CFBU*
500 Glenridge Ave. St. Catharines, ON L2S 3A1
PH: 905-346-2644
Debbie Cartmer pd@cfbu.ca
www.cfbu.ca
A fusion of Blues blending Chicago, Delta, Jump, Memphis, Louisiana, Folk, Rock, Country and Punk Blues. A special focus on homegrown talent and Canadian women in Blues.

Natch'l Blues *CKUA*
10526 Jasper Ave. Edmonton, AB T5J 1Z7
PH: 780-428-7595 FX: 780-428-7624
Holger Petersen holger.petersen@ckua.org
www.ckua.org
Canada's longest running Blues program. Over 33 years old!

Saturday Night Blues *CBC*
PO Box 555, Edmonton, AB T5J 2P4
PH: 780-468-7472
www.cbc.ca/snb
Host Holger Petersen presents concerts, interviews, artist features and new releases.

France

Midnight Special Blues Radio
14, rue Olier, 75015 Paris, France
PH: +33-1-45323893 FX: 2062030639
www.ms-blues.com
Host Paul Bondarovski provides support for independent artists. Keeping the Blues alive!

Spain

La Hora del Blues *Radio PICA*
Apartado de Correos 12.085, 08080 Barcelona, Spain
Vicente P. Zumel zumel@lahoradelblues.com
www.lahoradelblues.com
Each CD received is listed and rated on our website.

United Kingdom

Digital Blues *Phoenix FM*
www.digitalblues.co.uk
The voice of the Blues in Essex.

The Raven 'n' the Blues *REM FM*
Koraki, Taggs Island, Hampton, TW12 2HA UK
Dave Raven dave@raven.dj
www.raven.dj
60 minutes of the best in Blues, every Saturday evening.

Australia

BluesBeat *5EFM*
PO Box 1008, Victor Harbor, SA 5211 Australia
Geoff Pegler info@bluesbeatradio.com
www.bluesbeatradio.com
Labels & indie artists CDs welcome for airplay.

Salty Dog Blues n Roots Podcast
PO Box 159, Elwood, VIC 3184 Australia
PH: 613-9531-7578
Salty saltyblues@gmail.com
www.salty.com.au
Playing Blues, Roots and Alt-Country.

Saturday Blues *5UV*
228 N. Terrace, Adelaide, SA 5000 Australia
PH: 61-8-8303-5000 FX: 61-8-8303-4374
radio.adelaide.edu.au
The longest running Blues show in Australia.

Children's Radio

United States

All-Ages Show *WPRB*
030 Bloomberg Hall, Princeton U. NJ 08544
PH: 609-258-1033 Fx: 609-258-1806
Paddy allagesshow@wprb.com
www.wprb.com
Music, a story time, banter and frolic for all ages with Paddy and his partner, Eddap (species unrevealed).

Buck Howdy's Cow Pie Radio
PO Box 28700, San Diego, CA 92198
PH: 888-826-9743 FX: 858-674-1114
Buck Howdy cowpie@cox.net
www.buckhowdy.com
We air roughly 20 minutes of music in each program, so we have a voracious appetite for material.

Castle Cottage *KUSP*
203 8th Ave. Santa Cruz, CA 95062
Attn: Rob Mullen
PH: 831-476-2800
Susan Freeman kusp@kusp.org
www.kusp.org/shows/cottage
Stories and Folk oriented music for preschoolers with host Susan Freeman.

Chickens R People 2 *WMPG*
PO Box 9300, Portland, ME 04104
PH: 207-780 4916 FX: 207-780 4590
Kelsey Perchinski wmpg_kids@yahoo.com
www.wmpg.org/shows/sat5.htm
I accept all materials for review: Books, music, spoken word etc.

Children's Corner *KUFM*
MPR, 32 Campus Dr. U. Montana
Missoula, MT 59812-8064
PH: 406-243-4931 FX: 406-243-3299
www.kufm.org
Delightful stories and music for children.

Children's Hour *KRZA*
528 9th St., Alamosa, CO 81101
PH: 719-589-8844
music@krza.org
www.krza.org
Music and stories for preschoolers.

Children's Hour *KUNM*
MSC06 3520, Onate Hall, 1 UNM
Albuquerque, NM 87131-0001
PH: 505-277-5615
kunmkids@unm.edu
www.kunm.org
Music and stories for children of all ages.

Children's Radio Funhouse *WCRF*
9756 Barr Rd. Cleveland, OH 44141
PH: 440-526-1111
Mark Zimmerman wcrf@moody.edu
www.mbn.org
Christian show featuring stories and Children's music.

Children's Stories & Music *KMUD*
PO Box 135, 1144 Redway Dr.
Redway, CA 95560-0135
PH: 707-923-2513 FX: 707-923-2501
Kate Klein md@kmud.org
www.kmud.org
An inspirational blend of stories and music for children of all ages.

Crazy Dave's Kid Show *KDPS*
Grand View College, 1200 Grandview Ave.
Des Moines, IA 50316
crazydave@crazydaveradio.com
www.crazydaveradio.com
Our goal is to provide an opportunity for youth to use their imagination and to realize how wonderful and important they are to the world.

Enchanted Island *KMXT*
620 Egan Way, Kodiak, AK 99615
PH: 907-486-3181
Mike Wall kmxtmusic@yahoo.com
www.kmxt.org
Music for preschoolers with Children's music, family music and stories.

Family Groove *KFAI*
1808 Riverside Ave. Minneapolis, MN 55454
PH: 612-341-0980 FX: 612-341-4281
Will Hale groove@willhale.com
www.kfai.org
Well produced, upbeat, positive music in diverse styles are always welcome.

Funky Phantom Tollbooth *KDNK*
PO Box 1388, Carbondale, CO 81623-1388
PH: 970-963-0139 FX: 970-963-0810
www.kdnk.org
Host Andrea Marsh features Children's music and stories.

Gooney Bird Kids *Live365*
PH: 678-358-4206
Gwyneth Butera gbkids@butera.org
gooneybirdkids.blogspot.com
We play a set list of music that appeals to kids and adults. Submissions are welcome.

Greasy Kid Stuff
Belinda & Hova stuff@greasykidstuff.net
greasykidstuff.vox.com
Radio that stays crunchy ... even in milk!

Halfway Down the Stairs *KPFK*
3729 Cahuenga Blvd. W.
North Hollywood, CA 91604
PH: 818-985-2711 FX: 818-763-7526
Uncle Ruthie Buell uncleruthie@aol.com
www.kpfk.org
A multicultural FUN program for the whole family.

Hickory Dickory Dock *WUVT*
350 Squires Student Ctr.
Blacksburg, VA 24061-0546
PH: 540-231-9880 FX: 208-692-5239
wuvtamfm@vt.edu
www.wuvt.vt.edu
Music and stories for preschoolers.

HIS KIDS RADIO
PO Box 151515, Grand Rapids, MI 49515-1515
hiskidsradio.gospelcom.net
A Christian station for the young heart.

HYP Radio
1828 N. Winona Blvd. #2, Los Angeles, CA 90027
PH: 323-662-3894 FX: 323-662-3894
Amy Trulock trulock@miscamy.com
www.hipyoungparent.com
Especially looking for artists that appeal to parents as well as kids.

Kids Cookie Break *WJTL*
PO Box 1614, Lancaster, PA 17608
PH: 717-392-3690 FX: 717-390-2892
Lisa Landis cookiebreak@wjtl.com
www.kidscookiebreak.com
A music/talk atmosphere welcoming to listeners of all ages.

Kids Corner *WXPN*
3025 Walnut St., Philadelphia, PA 19104
PH: 215-898-6677 FX: 215-898-0707
kidscorner.org
Entertaining and educational programming for children.

Kids Kamp *WDBX*
224 N. Washington St. Carbondale, IL 62901
PH: 618-529-5900 FX: 618-529-5900
Momma C wdbx@globaleys.net
www.wdbx.org
We have a very diverse format from Experimental music (I personally like the balloons squeaking) to Opera.

Kids Play *WLUW*
6525 N. Sheridan Rd. Chicago, IL 60626
PH: 773-508-9589 FX: 773-508-8082
Sheila Donlan kidsplay@wluw.org
wluw.org
Features new and old releases of Kids' music.

Kids Radio Mania *KDPS*
1200 Grandview Ave. Des Moines, IA 50309
PH: 515-263-2985
Crazy Dave kidsradio@gvc.edu
www.kdpsradio.com/kidsradio
The most mixed-up, crazy kid-fun anywhere on the planet.

The Kids Show *WTUL*
Tulane U., New Orleans, LA 70118-5555
PH: 504-865 5667 FX: 504-463 1023
Uncle Chris Trochez unclechris@thekidsshow.com
www.thekidsshow.com
Your music has to be something both kids and their parents can enjoy.

Learn Along Radio Show *WHRU*
Box 154, Huntington, NY 11743
PH: 631-421-2231 FX: 631-421-1050
Janice Buckner janicekidmusic@worldnet.att.net
home.att.net/~janicekidmusic//radio.htm
*Interviews children and performing artists
(musicians and story tellers).*

Mah Na Mah Na *WEFT*
113 N. Market St., Champaign, IL 61820
PH: 217-359-9338
Mark & Travis Morenz weftkids@yahoo.com
wiki.weft.org/Mah_Na_Mah_Na
*Think Mister Rogers meets Doctor Demento. Don't
be shy about sending us something off-beat or
novelty.*

MASSIVE Radio *Live365.com*
3204 19th Ave. S., Seattle, WA 98144
PH: 206-290-8826 FX: 206-616-5721
Greg Crowther greg@science-groove.org
www.science-groove.org/MASSIVE
*Science and math songs only, please! And the focus
is on somewhat older kids, so songs about counting,
colors, etc. probably won't be used.*

Mundo Infantil *KBBF*
PO Box 7189, 410 Finley Ave.
Santa Rosa, CA 95407 Attn: Margarita Rosas
PH: 707-545-8833 FX: 707-545-6244
kbbf-radio.com
Music and stories for preschoolers.

Nacho Celtic Hour *KPBX*
2319 N. Monroe St., Spokane, WA 99205
PH: 509-328-5729
Carlos Alden kpbx@kpbx.org
www.kpbx.org/programs/nacho.htm
First half Folk music, second half Children's music.

Over the Rainbow *WERU*
PO Box 170, 1186 Acadia Highway
East Orland, ME 04431
PH: 207-469-6600 FX: 207-469-8961
Rhonda Nichols info@weru.org
www.weru.org
Children's music and stories.

Pea Green Boat *KUFM*
MPR, 32 Campus Dr. Missoula, MT 59812-8064
PH: 406-243-4931 FX: 406-243-3299
Ann Garde peagreen.boat@yahoo.com
www.kufm.org
Stories, songs, poetry and special guests for kids.

Penelope's Radio
305 Dickens Way, Santa Cruz, CA 95064
PH: 831-427-3980
childrensmusic.org/penelope.html
*Various children's radio programs in both Spanish
and English. Use the form at the bottom of our main
page to submit material.*

The Playground *WERS*
120 Boylston St., Boston, MA 02116
PH: 617-578-8890 FX: 617-824-8804
Leah Labrecque playground@WERS.org
www.wers.org/playground
*3 hours of the best in Children's music. Live local
and national artists every month.*

Pot o' Gold *KVNF*
PO Box 1350, Paonia, CO 81428
PH: 970-527-4868 FX: 970-527-4865
kvnf@kvnf.org
www.kvnf.org
Mostly stories with some music.

Redwood Earlines *KHSU*
1 Harpst St., Arcata, CA 95521
PH: 707-826-4807
Kim Shank khsu@humbolt.edu
www.khsu.org
*Music for preschoolers, Children's music and
stories.*

The Sandbox *KOEZ*
225 S. 700 E., St George, UT 84770
PH: 435-652 7825 FX: 435-656 4032
Matt Smith lahrman@dixie.edu
thedisc.dixie.edu
Features stories and Children's music.

Saturday Morning Cartoons *WBRS*
Shapiro Campus Ctr. 415 South St.
Waltham, MA 02453-2728
PH: 781-736-5277
Josh Segal music@wbrs.org
www.wbrs.org
The best Children's music on the airwaves.

The Saturday Morning Cereal Bowl *WAWL*
SMCB, 1437 Elm St., Chattanooga, TN 37415
PH: 423-697-4470
Dave Loftin saturdaycerealbowl@yahoo.com
smcb.blogspot.com
*I'm open to all styles of music. I want to keep the
show as diverse as possible.*

Skinnamarink *KMUN*
PO Box 269, Astoria, OR 97103
PH: 503-325-0010
Debbie Twombly trollradio@coastradio.org
www.coastradio.org/skinnamarink.html
*An hour of songs, stories and children's issues for
kids of all ages.*

Spare the Rock, Spoil the Child
140 Pine St., Florence, MA 01062
Bill Childs show@sparetherock.com
sparetherock.com
*Kid-friendly music that wont make parents gouge
out their ears.*

Tell Us a Tale *WTJU*
PO Box 7344, Charlottesville, VA 22906-7344
Attn: Review
PH: 434-978-3603 FX: 434-978-4935
Peter Jones radio@tellusatale.com
www.tellusatale.com
*Send us your CDs for radio airplay consideration or
review.*

The Tweenlight Zone *WMPG*
PO Box 9300, Portland, ME 04104-9300
Attn: Kelsey Perchinski
PH: 207-780-4916 FX: 207-780-4590
Rick & Elaine Colella wmpg_kids@yahoo.com
www.wmpg.org
*Music is accepted for this show, but should go
through the Children's music director for review
first.*

We Kids Radio
PO Box 444, Paradise, CA 95969
Mr.Nick@WeKids.org
www.wekids.org
Pointing little people and their families to God.

We Like Kids! *KTOO*
360 Egan Dr. Juneau, AK 99801-1748
PH: 907-463-6425 FX: 907-586-3612
Jeff Brown jbrown@alaska.net
www.ktoo.org
Weekly Children's music show.

XM Kids
PH: 866-328-2345
xmkids@xmradio.com
www.xmradio.com/onxm/channelguide.xmc?ch=116
We host a variety of Children's music shows.

Yes All Ages Radio *WBCR*
PO Box 152, Great Barrington, MA 01230
Scott Marks listlessscott@gmail.com
www.berkshireradio.org
A weekly kid-focused radio show.

**The Zucchini Brothers, Live! at the
Clubhouse**
206A Lake Ave. Saratoga Springs, NY 12866-2627
PH: 518-583-9835
Sam Zucchini sam@zucchinibrothers.com
www.zucchinibrothers.com/radio.htm
*A zany half hour filled with songs, stories and
educational tidbits. Targets 7-13 year olds.*

Canada

CBC 4 Kids Music
PO Box 500 Stn. A, Toronto, ON M5W 1E6
PH: 866-306-4636
kids@cbc.ca
www.cbc.ca/kids
*Features interviews and music from Canadian music
stars.*

Kids' Stuff *Galaxie*
PO Box 3220, succ. C, Ottawa, ON K1Y 1E4
PH: 613-288-6205
Mira Laufer information@galaxie.ca
www.galaxie.ca/en
*Features the world's best Children's entertainers
and storytellers.*

Kids' Time! *CFRU*
U. Guelph, Guelph, ON N1G 2W1
PH: 519-829-3731
Michele McMillan cfrukids@yahoo.ca
www.freewebs.com/kidstimeradio
*We play music, read stories, and talk about issues
that are important to children.*

Radio Enfant
855 boul de la Gappe pièce 310,
Gatineau, QB J8T 8H9
PH: 819-827-3146
info@radioenfant.ca
radioenfant.ca
Radio shows produced by children ages 5-16.

United Kingdom

FUN Radio
One Passage St., Bristol, BS2 0JF UK
funradio@funradiolive.com
www.funradiolive.com
*Children's station playing the best sing-a-long music
and stories with great presenters.*

The Radio Children Show
111 Queen's Cres. London, NW5 4EY UK
PH: 0044-7711-007471
Natasha Seery natasha@radiochildren.com
www.radiochildren.com
*A mad, funny, contemporary, cultural and
informative programme beamed out of London to
children all over the world.*

Radio Lollipop
6 St Andrew St., London, EC4A 3LX UK
PH: 44-0-208-661-0666
info@radiolollipop.org
www.radiolollipop.org
*Providing smiles and laughter to children during
their stay in the hospital.*

Takeover Radio
PO Box 2000, Leicester, LE1 6YX UK
PH: 0116-2999615
Graham Coley solo@bandreg.co.uk
www.takeoverradio.co.uk
Only children's station in the UK broadcasting on the web and on FM.
Australia/New Zealand

Boost Digital Kids Radio
36 Emmett St., Crows Nest, NSW 2065 Australia
PH: +61-2-9460-1400 FX: +61-2-9460-0044
Graeme Logan kids@boostdigital.com
www.boostdigital.com
Please send your submission to the above address. Make sure to include a completed copy of our online submission form.

Follow the Rainbow *Yarra Valley FM*
Wattle Valley Rd. Mt Evelyn, VIC 3796 Australia
Marcella Sharp marcedd@bigpond.com.au
www.magicalteddies.com.au
Looking for Children's published music and stories as well as original material which is uplifting, self-affirming, joyful and fun!

That's the Story
PO Box 6626. Wellelsley St.
Auckland New Zealand
FX: 021-055-6877
www.thatsthestory.co.nz
Mostly New Zealand stories and songs for children, but 10% is music from around the world.

Christian Radio
Promoters

HMG-Nashville Radio Promotions
PO Box 101336, Nashville, TN 37224
PH: 615-248-8105 FX: 615-248-8505
info@powersourcemusic.com
hmgnashville.com
We are one of the top voted radio promotion companies in the industry. The categories we focus on are Christian Country, Country, Southern Gospel, Bluegrass, Praise and Worship, and Christian Rock.

Ministry Networks
www.ministrynetworks.rockofages.ca
Digital Download and promotional programs available to get your song to Christian radio. Radio lists for Christian radio also available starting at $24.99 Indie Bible purchasers can have their songs submitted to digital download to Christian radio stations in Canada and U.S for just $35.00 per song.

Stations and Shows
United States

Abundant Life Radio
300 Euclid Sq. Mall, Euclid, OH 44132
PH: 216 767-0000
info@abundantlifeccci.org
www.abundantlifeccci.org
If you're an artist that needs exposure and wants to sell albums, we would love to interview you.

After Midnight *WQME*
1100 E. 5th St. Anderson, IN 46012
PH: 765-641-3800
www.myspace.com/aftermidnight987
We play the best in Christian Rock, Hardcore, Emo and Hip Hop.

Air 1
5700 W. Oaks Blvd. Rocklin, CA 95765
PH: 888-937-2471 FX: 888-329-2471
www.AIR1.com
If you have something with exceptional sound quality, contact us.

Almighty Metal Radio
Steve Roush steve@almightymetalradio.com
www.almightymetalradio.com
The finest Christian Metal, classic Christian Rock and rockin' Blues in a unique new mix!

BBS Radio
5167 Toyon Ln. Paradise, CA 95969
PH: 530-876-3222
Douglas Newsom doug@bbsradio.com
www.bbsradio.com
The largest online spiritual network featuring 60 different talk shows, free readings and consultations and the hottest in new independent music.

BCMP-God Jam
212 Village Way, Mount Airy, MD 21771
PH: 301-829-3986
bobcouchenour@godjam.u
www.bcmp.us
Podcast featuring Christian Rock, Prog, Blues, Bluegrass, Country, New Age and World music.

Bigloo Christian Radio
Attn: Louis Rivera
PO Box 182, West Chester, OH 45071
www.biglooradio.com
A mix from the best contemporary Christian to Christian Rock to Inspirational to the best in Christian indie artists!

Black Gospel Radio
4142 Ogletown-Stanton Rd. #138
Newark, DE 19713
PH: 215-227-5026
dj@blackgospelradio.net
www.blackgospelradio.net
Playing the best in Black Gospel music on the internet.

The Bored-Again Christian Podcast
PH: 512-533-0655
Just Pete boredagainchristian@gmail.com
www.boredagainchristian.com
Christian music for people who are tired of Christian music.

Bread-n-Jam *WRXV*
www.breadnjam.net
Rock n' Roll 2 feed your soul!

Caribbean Gospel Surf
PO Box 32507, Newark, NJ 07102
PH: 973-856-7115
Delroy Souden wcgsradio@yahoo.com
www.ensound.org/radio
An internet radio station playing Gospel music from the Islands.

Catholic Music 24/7
music@cm247.com
www.catholicmusic247.com

ChargeRadio.com
PO Box 671, Lebanon, OH 45036
PH: 513-255-8477
www.chargeradio.com
We are a Christian CHR station with a sound that is competitive with a mainstream Top 40 station.

Christian Blues Radio
37637 Five Mile Rd. #218, Livonia, MI 48154-1543
CustomerService@ChristianBlues.net
www.christianblues.net
The web's most complete resource for Christian Blues music and Christian Blues artists.

Christian Rock Radio
online@christianrockradio.com
www.christianrockradio.com
We also do album and concert reviews.

ChristianRock.net / Christian-HipHop.Net
333 Park Central E. #610, Springfield, MO 65806
PH: 417-865-1283 x41 FX: 417-865-9062
Bryan Whitaker mail@christian-hiphop.net
www.christianrock.net
The music we play features bands who are taking the Gospel to people all over the world.

Classic Christian Rock Radio
PH: 661-878-7692
mrbill@classicchristianrock.net
www.classicchristianrock.net
Features Rock music from artists who proclaim themselves to be Christians and who have demonstrated Christian attributes in their lives.

CMRadio.Net
PO Box 687, Allentown, PA 18105-0687
FX: 610-746-4053
musicmakers@cmradio.net
www.cmradio.net
Worldwide source of Christ inspired music.

The Corner Church Podcast
Rick Massey masseysmusic@podomatic.com
masseysmusic.podomatic.com
A varied collection of locally based independent Christian artists. No big names here!! Just great music.

Cornerstone *KXUL*
130 Stubbs Hall, ULM Monroe, LA 71209-8821
PH: 318-342-5662
kxul.com
A non-sectarian presentation of contemporary Christian music.

CrosswalkPlus.com
www.crosswalkplus.com
Features stations with various styles of commercial free web broadcasting.

Daily Devotions
1 Congress Sq. Portland, ME 04101
PH: 207-523-2945 FX: 207-828-6620
Peter Panagore peter@dailydevotions.org
www.dailydevotions.org
The music we play is eclectic and falls generally into the category of "music I like."

DeltaWav
c/o WEJF Radio, 2824 Palm Bay Rd.
Palm Bay, FL 32905
PH: 800-973-3398
Rick Cupoli rickc@deltawav.com
deltawav.com
Dedicated to playing indie artists. We are bringing indie Christian music to the air waves.

Drama Free Radio
PH: 877-891-3117
www.dramafreeradio.com
Your favorites styles of music, talk and news without the drama!

Effect Radio
PO Box 271, Twin Falls, ID 83301
PH: 208-734-2049 FX: 208-736-1958
www.effectradio.com
We play music as led by the spirit of the living God of The Bible.

En Sound
PO Box 32507, Newark, NJ 07104
PH: 973-856-7115
Delroy info@ensoundentertainment.com
ensoundentertainment.com/radio.htm
News, interviews and reviews of Gospel music.

The Fish 95.9
PO Box 29023, Glendale, CA 91209
PH: 818-956-5552
fishfeedback@thefish959.com
www.TheFish959.com
The hottest Christian radio station on the planet!

The Gospel Connection *WRBB*
360 Huntington Ave. #174, Curry Student Ctr.
Boston, MA 02115
PH: 617-373-4339 FX: 617-373-5095
wrbbradio.org
The longest running Gospel show in Boston!

The Gospel Experience *KPFA*
1929 MLK Jr. Way Berkeley, CA 94704
PH: 510-848-4425 FX: 510-848-3812
Emmit Powell emmitap@aol.com
kpfa.org
One of the longest running Gospel music shows in the Bay Area.

The Gospel Hiway
PO Box 34321, Houston, TX 77234-4321
Attn: Music Director
www.thegospelhiway.org
Submissions must be on CD, professionally produced along with a bio on the group or artist so we can know more about you.

Gospel Jazz Podcast
21901 Mada Ave. Southfield, MI 48075
PH: 734-658-9482 FX: 248-356-2021
gospeljazzsite.mypodcasts.net
Giving the Lord praise through Jazz music and poetry.

Gospel Jazzations *WFDU*
Metropolitan Campus, 1000 River Rd.
Teaneck, NJ 07666
PH: 201-833-0694
Tony Smith gospeljazzations@yahoo.com
www.gospeljazzations.com
Focuses on the instrumental side of Gospel Jazz.

Gospel Revelations *WFDU*
Metropolitan Campus, 1000 River Rd.
Teaneck, NJ 07666
PH: 201-692-2806 FX: 201-692-2807
Stacy Wendell gospelrevelations@gmail.com
www.wfdu.fm
Bringing you the very best variety of traditional Gospel music.

The Gospel Sound
1825 Pelican Rd. DeRidder, LA 70634
info@kdla1010.com
thegospelsound.com
Southern Gospel music featuring quartet-style singing and close harmony.

The Gospel Truth *WNCW*
PO Box 804, Spindale, NC 28160
PH: 828-287-8000 x328 FX: 828-287-8012
programming@wncw.org
www.wncw.org
Bluegrass Gospel. Send 2 CDs to the attention of the music director. Make sure to include a one-sheet bio.

Gospel Vibrations *WFDU*
1402 Teaneck Rd. #105, Teaneck, NJ 07666
PH: 201-833-0694 FX: 201-837-0611
Floyd Cray info@GospelVibrations.org
www.gospelvibrations.org
Features a large variety of contemporary Gospel music.

Gospel's Glory Road *KOHO*
7475 KOHO Pl., Leavenworth, WA 98826
PH: 509-548-1011 FX: 509-548-3222
www.kohoradio.com
Host John T. Humphreys presents an exciting blend of music and artists.

HCJB World Radio
PO Box 39800, Colorado Springs, CO 80949-9800
PH: 719-590-9800 FX: 719-590-9801
info@hcjb.org
www.hcjb.org
Broadcasts the Gospel in nearly 120 languages.

Holy Culture Radio
DJ MVP hcrdotfm@gmail.com
www.holycultureradio.com
The platform for Holy Hip Hop. Your chances of getting rotation increase dramatically by sending your music to all of our mixshows.

Holy Hip Hop Radio
PO Box 1023, Pine Lake, GA 30072
www.holyhiphop.com/radio
Over 200 domestic & international markets. Please send 2 CDs!

Honor & Glory Music
PO Box 18930, Atlanta, GA 31126
G-Wade honorandglorymusic@yahoo.com
honorandglorymusic.com
We play Gospel Hip Hop music videos from some of the hottest national and underground Hip Hop artists.

HOPE 107.9
PO Box 278, Albany, OR 97321
PH: 541-926-2431 FX: 541-926-3925
Paul Hernandez paul@hope1079.com
www.hope1079.com

Intense Radio
PO Box 1477, Mt. Juliet, TN 37121-1477
www.IntenseRadio.com
Christian Rock. Programs, great music, interviews and more.

The Johnny Mack
Gospel Music Show *WNAH*
44 Music Sq. E., Nashville, TN 37203
PH: 615-254-7611
Johnny Mack johnniemackjones@yahoo.com
www.wnah.com
I also interview up and coming Singer/Songwriters in the Gospel genre.

KCMS
19303 Fremont Ave. N., Seattle, WA 98133
PH: 206-546-7350 FX: 206-546-7372
Sarah Taylor sarah@spirit1053.com
www.spirit1053.com

KCWJ
4240 Blue Ridge Blvd. #530,
Kansas City, MO 64133
PH: 816-313-0049 FX: 816-313-1036
www.1030thelight.com

Kingdom Keys Network
PO Box 8088, Amarillo, TX 79114-8088
PH: 806-359-8855 FX: 806-354-2039
kjrt@kingdomkeys.org
www.kingdomkeys.org
Teaching, preaching, music, news, talk and commentaries.

KLRC *John Brown U.*
2000 W. University, Siloam Springs, AR 72761
PH: 479-524-7101 FX: 479-524-7451
www.klrc.com

KOBC *Ozark Christian College*
1111 N. Main Joplin, MO 64801
PH: 417-781-6401 FX: 417-782-1841
www.kobc.org

KTIS *Northwestern College*
3003 Snelling Ave. N., Saint Paul, MN 55113-1598
PH: 651-631-5000
studio@ktis.org
www.ktis.org

KTCU *Texas Christian U.*
TCU Box 298020, Fort Worth, TX 76129
PH: 817-257-7631
ktcu@tcu.edu
www.ktcu.tcu.edu

KWCB
1905 10h St., Floresville, TX 78114
PH: 830-393-4703
kwcb89fm@yahoo.com
www.wcn-online.com/kwcb

Lifespring!
PH: 951-232-7923
steve.lifespring@gmail.com
LifespringMedia.com
A host of Christian shows, with music as an integral part.

The Pillar Cast
2422 N. 100th St., Omaha, NE 68134
PH: 402-319-5095
Jon Tucker thepillarcast@gmail.com
www.thepillarcast.com
Podcast playing the best in podsafe and independent Christian music.

Power FM
11061 Shady Trail, Dallas, TX 75229
PH: 214-353-8970
Drue Mitchell drue@kvrk.com
897powerfm.com
A full time Christian Rock station in North Texas.

Power Praise Radio
promo@powerpraiseradio.com
www.indieheaven.com/powerpraiseradio
Syndicated radio show dedicated to independent Christian music artists, fans and those who support them. The music is inspirational, uplifting and powerful and our goal is to tell the world about this incredible music.

The Praise House
PO Box 1113, Conley, GA 30288
PH: 404-381-0722
thepraisehouse@comcast.net
www.thepraisehouse.com
Gospel webcast network.

Rebourne Radio
1102 Llano Cove, Memphis, TN 38134
PH: 901-388-2988
Bill Simmers radio@rebourne.net
www.rebourneradio.com
Indie positive CD submissions are welcome!

Renegade Radio
PO Box 490, Wadsworth, NV 89442
PH: 775-575-7777 FX: 775-575-7737
William E. Bauer email@renegaderadio.org
www.renegaderadio.org
Christian Rock, Hip Hop, Metal and Electronic Beat. We accept MP3s, but please contact us BEFORE you send an attachment.

RevFM
925 Houserville Rd. State College, PA 16801
PH: 814-867-1922
info@revfm.net
www.revfm.net
Encouraging believers to grow spiritually and to share the message of Jesus with unbelievers.

SGM Radio
rob@sgmradio.com
www.sgmradio.com
Today's best Southern Gospel and Christian Country music. We'll also review your album.

Silent Planet Radio *WCLH*
8466 TR 166, West Liberty, OH 43357
PH: 661-878-7764
tracking@silentplanetradio.com
www.silentplanetradio.com
Progressive Christian music.

Solid Gospel
402 BNA Dr. #400, Nashville, TN 37217
PH: 615-367-2210 FX: 615-367-0758
info@solidgospel.com
www.solidgospel.com

Spin 180
6400 N. Beltline Rd. #210, Irving, TX 75063
Matt Mungle info@spin180.net
www.spin180.net
Submit your CD, bio and lyric sheet to the above address. Christian Rock and Alternative only.

The Spirit Radio
9241 W. Rising Sun Dr. Pendleton, IN 46064
PH: 317-501-2242 FX: 317-536-8447
info@thespiritradio.com
www.thespiritradio.net
Christian artists ranging from Easy Listening to Heavy Metal.

Spiritco1.com Radio
6178 Oxon Hill Rd. #101, Oxon Hill, MD 20745
PH: 301-567-5349
www.spiritco1.com
Spreading the Gospel ministry of music and messages to the internet radio community.

Star93fm.com
PO Box 4048, Clinton, MS 39058
PH: 601-925-3548 FX: 601-925-3337
www.star93fm.com

Sunday Night Gospel Show
PO Box 1184, Crockett, TX 75835
PH: 936-546-8291 FX: 270-837-1977
submissions@24hourgospelnetwork.org
www.24hourgospelnetwork.org
Accepting Black Gospel and Gospel Jazz music for airplay consideration.

Three Angels Broadcasting Network
PO Box 220, W. Frankfort, IL 62896
PH: 618-627-4651 FX: 618-627-2726
www.3abn.org

Train to Glory *KUNM*
MSC06 3520, Onate Hall 1 U. New Mexico
Albuquerque, NM 87131-0001
PH: 505-277-5615
music@kunm.org
www.kunm.org
Black Gospel music featuring traditional, contemporary and local church choirs.

Uncle Samoo's Zoo *WITR*
32 Lomb Memorial Dr. Rochester, NY 14623-0563
PH: 585-475-2271 FX: 585-475-4988
Pastor Samme sammep@aol.com
www.myspace.com/thelivingrock
Featuring independent & import artists from all around the globe!

WAY-FM
1012 McEwen Dr. Franklin, TN 37067
PH: 615-261-9293 FX: 615-261-3967
waym.wayfm.com
We use radio to encourage youth and young adults in their Christian walk.

WAWZ
PO Box 9058, Zarephath, NJ 08890
PH: 732-469-0991 x3132
Dave Moore dave@star991fm.com
www.991HD3.com
We are only interested in Christian Rock, Christian Indie, Christian Alternative, Christian Hip-Hop etc.

WCDR *Cedarville College*
251 N. Main St., Cedarville, OH 45314
PH: 800-333-0601 FX: 937-766-7927
www.thepath.fm

WCNO
2960 SW. Mapp Rd. Palm City, FL 34990
PH: 772-221-1100 FX: 772-221-8716
wcno@wcno.com
www.wcno.com
Adult Contemporary Christian music and programming.

WCSE
126 Sharp Hill Rd. Uncasville, CT 06382
PH: 860-848-7400
info@wcse.org
www.wcse.org
A Christian station that plays the music of independent artists.

WDYN
1815 Union Ave. Chattanooga, TN 37404
PH: 423-493-4382 FX: 423-493-4526
wdyn@wdyn.com
www.wdyn.com

wePRAISE.fm
7101 Deshon Bend Cove, Lithonia, GA 30058
PH: 678-526-0592 FX: 678-526-2533
Winston A. Walker admin@wepraise.fm
www.wePRAISE.fm
We play Gospel videos and songs that we feel uplifts and edifies the body of Christ.

WETN *Wheaton College*
501 College Ave. Wheaton, IL 60187
PH: 630-752-5074
wetn@wheaton.edu
www.wheaton.edu/wetn

WFCA *French Camp Academy*
Rte. 1, Box 12, French Camp, MS 39745
PH: 662-547-6414 FX: 662-547-9451
events@wfcafm108.com
www.wfcafm108.com
All Southern Gospel radio.

WGEV *Geneva College*
c/o Dept. of Communication, 3200 College Ave.
Beaver Falls, PA 15010
PH: 724-846-5100
thughes@geneva.edu
www.wgev.net

WGJB *(World Gospel Jazz Broadcast)*
21901 Mada Ave. Southfield, MI 48075
PH: 734-658-9482 FX: 248-356-2021
Norvell Molex Jr. spiritaldance@comcast.net
xianz.com/Norvell
We play Jazz artists that choose to give God praise through the gift of music.

WGTS *Columbia U. College*
7600 Flower Ave. Takoma Park, MD 20912
PH: 301-270-1800 FX: 301-270-9191
wgts@wgts919.com
www.wgts.org

What's the Buzz *WCNI*
Box 4972 Connecticut College, 270 Mohegan Ave.
New London, CT 06320
PH: 860-439-2850
John the Baptist buzzradiowcni@aol.com
www.wcniradio.com
Christian Rock, Pop & Hip Hop. I am happy to play the music of independent artists.

Whitedove Radio
HCR 82 Box 62-A, Salem, MO 65560
PH: 573-729-6144
Crystal Clear crystalclear@whitedoveradio.com
www.whitedoveradio.com
Featuring Christian music of all styles.

WJTL
PO Box 1614, Lancaster, PA 17608-1614
PH: 717-392-3690 FX: 717-390-2892
contact@wjtl.com
www.wjtl.com
We have a responsibility to our listeners to play the best artists, regardless of whether they are local, national, independent or major label.

WMHK *Columbia International U.*
PO Box 3122, Columbia, SC 29230
PH: 803-754-5400 FX: 803-714-0849
wmhk@wmhk.com
www.wmhk.com

WOCG *Oakwood College*
7000 Adventist Blvd. Huntsville, AL 35896
PH: 256-726-7420 FX: 256-726-7417
wocg@wocg.org
www.wocg.org

WRCM *Columbia International U.*
PO Box 17069, Charlotte, NC 28227
PH: 704-821-9293 FX: 704-821-9285
info@newlife919.com
www.newlife919.com
Featuring family friendly Christian music.

WRVL *Liberty U.*
1971 U. Blvd Lynchburg, VA 24502
PH: 434-582-3688 FX: 434-582-2994
wrvl@liberty.edu
www.liberty.edu/wrvl

WSAE *Spring Arbor College*
106 E. Main St., Spring Arbor, MI 49283
PH: 517-750-9723 FX: 517-750-6619
info@home.fm
www.home.fm

WTBC
PO Box 371, Berrien Springs, MI 49103
PH: 269-487-6652
info@wtbcradio.com
www.wtbcradio.com
Gospel and Holy Hip Hop. Please submit your music using Sonicbids www.sonicbids.com.

WTLC Radio
Box 20205, Springfield, IL 62708
PH: 217-487-4321
www.wtlcradio.com
We only play Christian indie music and programs. We are looking for Christian indie artists to submit completed works for consideration of airplay.

Canada

CHRI
1010 Thomas Spratt Pl. #3, Ottawa, ON K1G 5L5
PH: 613-247-1440 FX: 613-247-7128
chri.ca

Christian Punk Experience *WORLD FM*
5915 Gateway Blvd. Edmonton, AB T6H 2H3
PH: 780-438-1017 FX: 780-437-5129
www.worldfm.ca
Weekly show featuring 3 hours of Christian Punk.

eJNM.net
6550 Maurice-Duplessis,
Montréal-Nord, QC H1G 6K9
PH: 514-324-2190
ejnm@ejnm.net
eJNM.net
A source of blessing for independent Christian artists. We have programming in English, French, Italian & Spanish.

The MAD Christian Radio Show
Kristen McNulty madradioshow@hotmail.com
www.madradioshow.net
A syndicated youth radio show that is making a difference in the lives of youth around the world. Christian Rock artists can send their material to the above address.

United Kingdom

Branch FM
17 Halifax Rd. Dewsbury,
West Yorkshire,
WF13 2JH UK
PH: +44 (0)1924-454750
studio@branchfm.co.uk
www.branchfm.co.uk
Christian music 24/365 available across the globe.

Cross Rhythms Radio
PO Box 1110
Stoke on Trent,
ST1 1XR UK
PH: 44-8700-118-008
FX: 44-8700-117-002
radio@crossrhythms.co.uk
www.crossrhythms.co.uk/radio
Predominantly contemporary Christian music.

Australia

Rhema FM
PO Box 886, Belmont, VIC 3216 Australia
PH: 61-3-5241-6550 FX: 61-3-5241-6552
rhema@rhemafm.org.au
www.rhemafm.org.au
A station that can change lives for good and the promotion of family values.

Classical Radio

Radio Promoters

Art of the States
PO Box 390046, Cambridge MA 02139
Matthew Packwood matthew@artofthestates.org
www.artofthestates.org
For the past 14 years we have collected performances and recordings of a wide range of music from across the United States, focusing on new, unusual, and lesser-known repertoire. We present selected works in monthly program offerings which are organized thematically and accompanied by notes on the music, composers, and performers.

Stations and Shows

North America

United States

beethoven.com
1039 Asylum Ave. Hartford, CT 06105
PH: 860-525-1069 FX: 860-246-9084
www.beethoven.com
The World's Classical Station! Our goal is to be the best place on the internet for lovers of classical music to listen, read, learn, play and interact with each other.

Brass Band Podcast
Peter brasscast@gmail.com
www.brasscast.com
Produced for your entertainment and to keep you informed of events in the world of Brass Band music.

Classical Excursions *KTCU*
TCU Box 298020, Fort Worth, TX 76129
PH: 817-257-7631
Rosemary Solomons R.Solomons@tcu.edu
www.ktcu.tcu.edu/classical.asp
Two uninterrupted hours of music from the Baroque to the present.

Classical Music *WBHM*
650 11th St. S. Birmingham, AL 35294
PH: 205-934-2606 FX: 205-934-5075
Alan Chapman info@wbhm.org
www.wbhm.org
Features music by acknowledged Classical masters as well as emerging composers of merit.

ClassicalMusicAmerica.com
PH: 248-324-2600 FX: 248-324-0439
Pat McElroy
patmcelroy@classicalmusicamerica.com
www.classicalmusicamerica.com
Local events, music and recording artists are prominent in the mix.

Colorado Public Radio
7409 S. Alton Ct. Centennial, CO 80112
PH: 303-871-9191 FX: 303-733-3319
cpr.org
Presents the full range of Classical music.

The Composer's Voice *MPR*
480 Cedar St., Saint Paul, MN 55101
PH: 651-290-1212
John Zech mail@mpr.org
music.minnesota.publicradio.org/programs/composersvoice
The program that asks current composers "Who are you? What does your music sound like? Why does it sound the way it does?"

Contemplation Connection *KKUP*
933 Monroe St., PMB 9150, Santa Clara, CA 95050
PH: 408-260-2999
Roger Werner wernerr@pacbell.net
www.kkup.com
Visionary and Classical music for contemplation. Quotes for self-awareness.

Dawn's Early Light *WTJU*
PO Box 400811, Charlottesville, VA 22904-4811
PH: 434-924-0885 FX: 434-924-8996
John Delehanty wtju@virginia.edu
wtju.net/cpages/musub
An array of periods and styles, never forgetting the musicality of the human voice.

From the Top
295 Huntington Ave. Boston, MA 02115
PH: 617-437-0707 FX: 617-262-4267
www.fromthetop.org
Showcases the nation's most exceptional pre-college age Classical musicians.

Gamut *WTJU*
PO Box 400811, Charlottesville, VA 22904-4811
PH: 434-924-0885 FX: 434-924-8996
Ralph Graves wtju@virginia.edu
wtju.net/cpages/musub
No repeat programming since 1984 and no end in sight!

Harmonia *WFIU*
1229 E. 7th St., Bloomington, IN 47405
PH: 812-855-1357
Emily Blacklin harmonia@indiana.edu
www.indiana.edu/~harmonia
Brings the music of these earlier periods to life.

Here of a Sunday Morning *WBAI*
120 Wall St., New York, NY 10005
PH: 212-209-2900
Chris Whent mail@hoasm.org
www.hoasm.org
The very best in Early music.

Iridian Radio
PO Box 80427, Goleta, CA 93118
mail@iridianradio.com
www.iridianradio.com
An intelligently mellow New-Music station.

KANU
1120 W. 11th St., U. Kansas, Lawrence, KS 66044
PH: 785-864-4530 FX: 785-864-5278
Rachel Hunter rhunter@ku.edu
kansaspublicradio.org
We do play music by independent Classical musicians.

KBIA
409 Jesse Hall, Columbia, MO 65211
PH: 573-882-3431 FX: 573-882-2636
kbia@kbia.org
www.kbia.org
We love to play music from new and independent Classical artists.

KBPS
515 NE. 15th Ave. Portland, OR 97232
PH: 503-916-5828 FX: 503-916-2642
music.info@allclassical.org
www.allclassical.org
Happy to receive any CDs by indie performers of standard Classical.

KBYU *Brigham Young U.*
2000 Ironton Blvd. Provo, UT 84606
PH: 800-298-5298
www.kbyu.org
New material is reviewed and aired if deemed appropriate.

KCME
1921 N. Weber St., Colorado Springs, CO 80907
PH: 719-578-5263 FX: 719-578-1033
jazz@kcme.org
www.kcme.org
We play independent labels Classical and Jazz music.

KCSC *U. Central Oklahoma*
100 N. University Dr. Edmond, OK 73034
PH: 405-974-3333 FX: 405-974-3844
kcscfm@ucok.edu
www.kcscfm.com

KDFC
201 3rd St. #1200, San Francisco, CA 94103
PH: 415-764-1021
Rik Malone rmalone@kdfc.com
www.kdfc.com
We don't discriminate against struggling musicians!

KEDM
ULM 225 Stubbs Hall Monroe, LA 71209-6805
PH: 318-342-5565 FX: 318-342-5570
classical@kedm.org
kedmjazz@ulm.edu
www.kedm.org
We do play Classical and Jazz music by independent musicians/composers/producers.

KFUO
85 Founders Ln. St. Louis, MO 63105
PH: 314-725-0099 FX: 314-725-3801
John Roberts jroberts@classic99.com
www.classic99.com

KHSU *Humboldt State U.*
1 Harpst St., Arcata, CA 95521
PH: 707-826-6086
khsuplay@humboldt.edu
www.khsu.org

KING
10 Harrison St. #100, Seattle, WA 98109
PH: 206-691-2981 FX: 206-691-2982
Tom Olsen tomo@king.org
www.king.org
We do air independent musician's recordings.

KNAU *Northern Arizona U.*
Bldg. 83 Box 5764, Flagstaff, AZ 86011
PH: 928-523-5628
knauradio.org

KNPR *Nevada Public Radio*
1289 S. Torrey Pines Dr. Las Vegas, NV 89146
PH: 702-258-9895 FX: 702-258-5646
Dave Becker davebecker@knpr.org
www.knpr.org
I try to play as many independents as I can.

KRPS
PO Box 899, Pittsburg, KS 66762
PH: 620-235-4288
Tim Metcalf tmetcalf@pittstate.edu
www.krps.org
Any music received is first reviewed by our program director.

KSUI
710 S. Clinton St., Iowa City, IA 52242-1030
PH: 319-335-5746 FX: 319-335-6116
Dennis Reese dennis-reese@uiowa.edu
ksui.uiowa.edu
We welcome the music of independent Classical musicians.

KUAT
PO Box 210067, Tucson, AZ 85721-0067
PH: 520-621-5828 FX: 520-621-3360
radio.azpm.org/classical
A "serious" Classical station. NO recordings from New Age noodlers.

KUFM *Morning Classics*
U. Montana, Missoula, MT 59812-8064
PH: 406-243-4931 FX: 406-243-3299
www.kufm.org
We play a wide variety of Classical music.

KUHF
4343 Elgin, 3rd Fl. Houston, TX 77204-0887
PH: 713-743-0887 FX: 713-743-0868
communications@kuhf.org
www.kuhf.org
As long as your performances and recordings are of professional quality, we'll play 'em.

KUSC
PO Box 77913, Los Angeles, CA 90007-0913
PH: 213-225-7400
kusc@kusc.org
www.kusc.org
Making Classical music a more important part of more people's lives.

KWAX *U. Oregon*
Agate Hall, Eugene, OR 97403
PH: 541-345-0800
kwax@qwest.net
www.kwaxradio.com
Classical music 24-hour a day.

KWIT *West Iowa Tech College*
4647 Stone Ave. PO Box 5199
Sioux City, IA 51106
PH: 712-274-6406 FX: 712-274-6411
www.kwit.org

KXMS *Missouri Southern State U.*
3950 E. Newman Rd. Joplin, MO 64801-1595
PH: 417-625-9356 FX: 417-625-9742
kxms@mssu.edu
www.kxms.org
Happy to highlight independent Classical CDs. Please send only Classical music!

KXPR *California State U.*
7055 Folsom Blvd. Sacramento, CA 95826-2625
PH: 916-278-5299 FX: 916-278-8989
classical@capradio.org
www.capradio.org/programs

Millennium of Music
2775 S. Quincy St., Arlington, VA 22206
radman@weta.com
www.classicstoday.com/mom
Features the evolution of Sacred music, East and West. Our one-hour national weekly program is heard on over 190 public radio stations across the country.

A Musical Meander *KRCU*
1 University Pl. Cape Girardeau, MO 63701
PH: 573-651-5070 FX: 888-651-5070
Jake McCleland jmccleland@semo.edu
www.semo.edu/sepr
The basic theme is Classical music in the broadest sense.

MUSICclassical *Live365.com*
musiclassical@yahoo.com
www.musicclassical.com
Stations featuring Classical music - most of it from independent artists.

The New Edge *WMBR*
3 Ames St., Cambridge, MA 02142
PH: 617-253-8810
Ken Field newedge@wmbr.org
newedge.home.att.net
Creative and innovative, mostly instrumental new music, composed and improvised at the intersection of Classical, Jazz and World styles.

New Sounds *WNYC*
160 Varick St., New York, NY 10013
PH: 212-669-3333 FX: 212-669-3312
John Schaefer newsounds@wnyc.org
www.wnyc.org/shows/newsounds
New works from the Classic and Operatic to Folk and Jazz.

Pipedreams *MPR*
480 Cedar St., Saint Paul, MN 55101-2217
PH: 651-290-1212
Michael Barone mail@americanpublicmedia.org
pipedreams.mpr.org
The finest organ music from around the world.

Saint Paul Sunday *MPR*
480 Cedar St., Saint Paul, MN 55101-2217
PH: 651-290-1212
www.stpaulsunday.org
Host opens the studio to the world's best Classical artists.

Sound and Spirit *WGBH*
PO Box 200, Boston, MA 02134
PH: 617-300-5400
www.wgbh.org/pages/pri/spirit
Blends Classical, Traditional and World music.

Sunday Baroque *WSHU*
5151 Park Ave. Fairfield, CT 06825
PH: 203-365-0425
Suzanne Bona sundayb@wshu.org
www.sundaybaroque.org
An exploration of Baroque and Early music.

Thursday Evening Classics *WWUH*
Attn: Music Director, 200 Bloomfield Ave.
West Hartford, CT 06117
PH: 860-768-4701 FX: 860-768-5701
Steve Petke sdpetke@comcast.net
www.wwuh.org
Offers a broad range of music from the Middle Ages to the present, highlighting Renaissance Choral music and lesser-known works by familiar and obscure composers.

Vermont Public Radio
365 Troy Ave. Colchester, VT 05446
PH: 802-655-9451 FX: 802-655-2799
www.vpr.net

WBACH
15 Monument Sq. 3E, Portland, ME 04101
PH: 207-553-9000 FX: 207-553-9005
Scott Hooper shooper@nassaubroadcasting.com
www.wbachradio.com

WBJC
6776 Reisterstown Rd. #202, Baltimore, MD 21215
PH: 410-580-5800
jpalevsky@wbjc.com
www.wbjc.com
The Baltimore region's only Classical music station.

WCLV
26501 Renaissance Pkwy. Cleveland, OH 44128
PH: 216-464-0900
wclv@wclv.com
www.wclv.com
Spotlights new Classical CDs.

WCNY *Syracuse*
506 Old Liverpool Rd. Liverpool, NY 13088-6259
www.wcny.org
Features performances by numerous local musical institutions.

WCPE
PO Box 897, Wake Forest, NC 27588
PH: 919-556-5178
William Woltz music@TheClassicalStation.org
www.wcpe.org
Makes great Classical music available to the public.

WDAV
PO Box 7178, 423 N. Main St.
Davidson, NC 28035-7178
PH: 704-894-8900 FX: 704-894-2997
wdav@davidson.edu
www.wdav.org
We have numerous independently produced recordings as part of its regular music rotation.

WDPR
126 N. Main St., Dayton, OH 45402
PH: 937-496-3850 FX: 937-496-3852
Charles Wendelken-Wilson cww@dpr.org
dpr.org
The voice for our region's performing and fine arts organizations.

WEKU
102 Perkins Bldg. 521 Lancaster Ave.
Richmond, KY 40475-3102
PH: 800-621-8890 FX: 859-622-6276
weku@eku.edu
www.weku.fm

WETA
2775 S. Quincy St., Arlington, VA 22206
PH: 703-998-2600 FX: 703-998-3401
info@weta.org
www.weta.org
Feel free to submit your music.

WETS *East Tennessee State U.*
PO Box 70630, Johnson City, TN 37614-1709
PH: 423-439-6440 FX: 423-439-6449
www.wets.org

WFCR *U. Massachusetts*
Hampshire House, 131 County Cir.
Amherst, MA 01003-9257
PH: 413-545-0100 FX: 413-545-2546
John Montanari jm@wfcr.org
www.wfcr.org

WFMR
5407 W. McKinley Ave.
Milwaukee, WI 53208-2540
PH: 414-978-9000 FX: 414-978-9001
Steve Murphy smurphy@wfmr.com
www.wfmr.com

WFMT
5400 N. St. Louis Ave. Chicago, IL 60625-4698
PH: 773-279-2020
www.wfmt.com
We do play some self-produced CDs.

WGUC
1223 Central Pkwy. Cincinnati, OH 45214
PH: 513-241-8282 FX: 513-241-8456
www.wguc.org

WHRO
5200 Hampton Blvd. Norfolk, VA 23508
PH: 757-889-9400 FX: 757-489-0007
info@whro.org
www.whro.org
Will consider any independent Classical recordings for possible airplay.

WILL
Campbell Hall 300 N. Goodwin Ave.
Urbana, IL 61801-2316
PH: 217-333-0850 FX: 217-244-9586
willamfm@uiuc.edu
www.wcny.org/classicfm
Send us your Classical, Jazz and Traditional/Ethnic music.

WITF
4801 Lindle Rd. Harrisburg, PA 17111
PH: 717-704-3000
Craig Cohen craig_cohen@witf.org
www.witf.org
Offering Classical music and news.

WKAR *Michigan State U.*
283 Communication Arts Bldg.
East Lansing, MI 48824-1212
PH: 517-432-9527 FX: 517-353-7124
curt@wkar.org
wkar.org/90.5

WKSU *Kent State U.*
PO Box 5190, Kent, OH 44242-0001
PH: 330-672-3114 FX: 330-672-4107
letters@wksu.org
www.wksu.org

WMNR
PO Box 920, Monroe, CT 06468
PH: 203-268-9667
info@wmnr.org
www.wmnr.org
Non-commercial Classical and Fine Arts music.

WMUH *Muhlenberg College*
2400 Chew St., Allentown, PA 18104-5586
PH: 484-664-3239 FX: 484-664-3539
wmuh@muhlenberg.edu
www.muhlenberg.edu/cultural/wmuh
We play independent Classical 4 hrs/week.

WNPR
1049 Asylum Ave. Hartford, CT 06105
PH: 860-278-5310 FX: 860-244-9624
info@wnpr.org
www.wnpr.org
We welcome the music of independent Classical musicians.

WQED
4802 5th Ave. Pittsburgh, PA 15213
PH: 412-622-1300 FX: 412-622-1488
music@wqed.org
www.wqed.org
You are more than welcome to send CDs for consideration.

WQXR
122 5th Ave. New York, NY 10011
PH: 212-633-7600 FX: 212-633-7730
listener.mail@wqxr.com
www.wqxr.com
Welcomes submissions from independent artists.

WRR
PO Box 159001, Dallas, TX 75315-9001
PH: 214-670-8888
Kurt Rongey krongey@wrr101.com
www.wrr101.com

WRTI
1509 Cecil B. Moore Ave. 3rd Fl.
Philadelphia, PA 19121-3410
PH: 215-204-3393 FX: 215-204-7027
www.wrti.org
Plays some Classical/Jazz independent music.

WSCL
PO Box 2596, Salisbury, MD 21802
PH: 410-543-6895
prd@salisbury.edu
publicradiodelmarva.net
Will accept quality indie submissions.

WSKG/WSQX
PO Box 3000, Binghamton, NY 13902-3000
PH: 607-729-0100 FX: 607-729-7328
www.wskg.com/radiowskg.htm

WWFM
PO Box B, Trenton, NJ 08690
PH: 609-587-8989 FX: 609-586-4533
www.wwfm.org
Playing the finest Classical music available.

WXPR
303 W. Prospect St., Rhinelander, WI 54501
PH: 715-362-6000 FX: 715-362-6007
wxpr@wxpr.org
www.wxpr.org

WXXI
280 State St. PO Box 30021
Rochester, NY 14603-3021
PH: 585-258-0200
wxxi@wxxi.org
www.wxxi.org
We do play the music of independent artists.

XLNC1 Radio
1690 Frontage Rd. Chula Vista, CA 91911
PH: 619-575-9090 x452
www.xlnc1.org

Yellowstone Public Radio
1500 U. Dr. Billings, MT 59101
PH: 406-657-2941 FX: 406-657-2977
mail@ypradio.org
www.yellowstonepublicradio.org

Canada

Shades of Classics *CKUW*
Rm. 4CM11 U. Winnipeg, 515 Portage Ave.
Winnipeg, MA R3B 2E9
PH: 204-786-9782 FX: 204-783-7080
John Iverson shades@mts.net
www.jliverson.com/ckuw
Promoting the music of local musicians/ensembles.

Symphony Hall *CBC*
PH: 403-521-6109 FX: 403-521-6232
www.cbc.ca/symphonyhall
Host Katherine Duncan presents a showcase for Canadian orchestras and their musicians.

Europe

Czech Republic

Cesky rozhlas 3 - Vltava
Vinohradská 12 120 99 Prague, Czech Republic
PH: 420-221-552-647 FX: 420-221-552-676
info@rozhlas.cz
www.rozhlas.cz/vltava
Live broadcasts Opera, Classical music and Jazz from all over the world.

The Netherlands

AVRO Klassiek
Postbus 2, 1200 JA Hilversum, The Netherlands
PH: 035-671-79-11
klassiek@avro.nl
www.avro.nl

Classic FM
Postbus 1088 1400 BB Bussum, The Netherlands
PH: 035-699-79-99 FX: 035-699-79-98
classicfm@classicfm.nl
www.classicfm.nl

The Concertzender
PO Box 275, 1200 AG Hilversum, The Netherlands
PH: +31-35-677-31-02 FX: +31-35-677-31-04
concert.post@concertzender.nl
www.concertzender.nl
Presenting remarkable programs with lots of genuine Jazz and Classical music.

Norway

NRK - NRK Alltid Klassisk
PH: 815-65-900
info@nrk.no
www.nrk.no/kanal/nrk_alltid_klassisk
The Classical station of the Norwegian Public Radio.

United Kingdom

BBC Radio 2 *Easy Listening and Classical*
www.bbc.co.uk/radio2/r2music/easy
Home page of the BBC Radio 2's various Easy Listening and Classical shows. Info, shows, contacts etc.

BBC Radio 3
London, W1N 4DJ UK
PH: 087-00-100-100
www.bbc.co.uk/radio3/classical
The mother of all Classical radio stations!

Hear and Now *BBC*
Radio 3, London, W1N 4DJ UK
PH: 087-00-100-100
www.bbc.co.uk/radio3/hearandnow
Features live concerts, studio sessions from the best new music groups.

Lyric FM
Cornmarket Sq. Limerick, Ireland
PH: 353-0-61-207300 FX: 353-0-61-207390
lyric@rte.ie
www.lyricfm.ie
Irish Classical music station.

Australia

2MBS
76 Chandos St., St Leonards, NSW 2065 Australia
PH: 9439-4777 FX: 9439-4064
info@2mbs.com
www.2mbs.com
Programs of Classical, Jazz and Contemporary music.

ABC Classical Music
PO Box 9994, Melbourne, VIC 3001 Australia
PH: 03-9626-1600 FX: 03-9626-1633
www.abc.net.au/classic
Programs that feature new Australian Classical music.

The Chamber Music Hour *5UV*
228 N. Terrace, Adelaide, SA 5000 Australia
PH: 61-8-8303-5000 FX: 61-8-8303-4374
Bryan Glennon radio@adelaide.edu.au
radio.adelaide.edu.au
Make your Chamber our Chamber with beautifully intimate music.

Music Box *ArtSound FM*
PO Box 3573, Manuka, Canberra,
ACT 2603 Australia
PH: 612-6295-8444 FX: 612-6295-8499
onair@artsoundfm.asn.au
www.artsound.com.au
Classical music journeys.

Country Radio

Radio Promoters

Airplay Specialists
1100 18th Ave. S., Nashville, TN 37212
PH: 615-364-5145 FX: 615-321-2244
airplay4U@aol.com
www.airplayspecialists.com
We have a personal relationship with the 1300+ stations that collectively comprise the secondary Country radio marketplace.

Billy James Productions
PO Box 5496
Deptford, NJ 08096
PH: 856-468-7889
Billy
gobillygo@netzero.com
www.wnjc1360.com/Shows/
Billy_James/
billy_james.html
We offer promotion for artists and bands.

E. H. King Music
PO Box 40, Santa Fe, TX 77517
PH: 409-925-4539
Ed & Barbara Ekingehk@cs.com
www.wingnut.net/ehk.htm
We'll mail out your CDs for you!! We get airplay!!

Jerry Duncan Promotions
PO Box 40471, Nashville, TN 37204
www.duncanpromo.com
Has successfully promoted 60 #1 country hits including breakthrough singles for some of today's biggest stars including Tim McGraw, Toby Keith, Martina McBride, Brad Paisley and Alison Krauss.

Marco Promotions
620 16th Ave. S., Nashville, TN 37212
PH: 615-269-7071 FX: 615-269-0131
info@marcopromo.com
www.marcopromo.com
Our radio marketing strategy provides the artist an opportunity to make an impact at secondary Country radio by establishing an audience base and creating product awareness in targeted sales markets.

North America

United States

Internet, Syndicated Shows and Podcasts

Abbott's Bluegrass Habit
PO Box 54668, Cincinnati, OH 45254-0668
Vicki Abbott abbottsbluegrasshabit@yahoo.com
www.geocities.com/abbottsbluegrasshabit
Do you have material that you would like to be considered for airplay? Contact me!

Always Country
www.alwayscountry.net
A blend of old and new Country, with the family at heart.

Americana Roots Review
www.americanaroots.com
Podcast featuring music from some great unsigned Americana artists.

Bluegrass Review
PH: 651-690-1508
Phil Nusbaum pnusbaum@bitstream.net
www.bluegrassreview.com
Includes Bluegrass classics as well as the current wave.

BluegrassRadio.org
293 JC Saunders Rd. Moultrie, GA 31768
PH: 229-890-2506
Clyde Scott cscott229@alltel.net
bluegrassradio.org
If you would like to have your project considered for "wire play" please submit it to the above address.

Boulton Beach Studios / Green Mountain Music Productions
PO Box 436, Manlius, NY 13104
Mark Bee markbee@greenmountainmusic.com
www.greenmountainmusic.com
Syndicated radio programs featuring indie artists in the genres of Bluegrass, Country, Rock and Pop.

Cowboy Cultural Society
1110 Main St. #16, Watsonville, CA 95076
www.cowboyculturalsociety.com
No great social upheaval or revolutionary insights, just classic Cowboy music.

The Doo Wop Cafe Radio
furjack@iname.com
www.doowopcaferadio.com
Dedicated to preserving the best music that there is, vocal group harmony.

FHR Radio Entertainment
PO Box 139091, Hialeah, FL 33013-9091
DJ Jeremy djfirehouse@fhrradio.com
www.fhrradio.com
We are a licensed online radio station that plays Country music.

Frank's Americana
frank@franksamericana.com
www.franksamericana.com
Cooking the music of the world in the melting pot of American life!

Gruene With Envy Radio
c/o 415 Entertainment, PO Box 92722
Austin, TX 78709
Dave Lytle dave@415e.com
www.gruenewithenvy.com
Playing music from all of your favorite Texas and Americana artists.

HounddogRadio.net
750 Hunters Ln. Loganville, GA 30052
Frank Coon frank@hounddogradio.net
www.hounddogradio.net
We present a mix of Country, Bluegrass, Rock and Blues. We also host a variety of live, interactive shows on most nights of the week.

Independent Music Network
8424 Santa Monica Blvd. S. #776
West Hollywood, CA 90069
PH: 323-951-0674
Gary Hendrix gary@independentmusicnetwork.com
independentmusicnetwork.com
Featuring the best independent artists in the universe!

Into the Blue
Attn: Production/Jon Weisberger
701 Amy Ct. Cottontown, TN 37048
www.bluegrassradio.com
Longest running commercial Bluegrass syndication in the country.

Muldoon in the Afternoon *World Wide Bluegrass Radio*
PO Box 95, Marathon, OH 45145
PH: 513-724-1440
Gracie Muldoon gracie@worldwidebluegrass.com
www.freewebs.com/muldoon_til_noon
Featuring the best Bluegrass music on Earth. Bluegrass radio with live Bluegrass shows and interviews. We are still spinnin' tons of Bluegrass indies.

The Nashville Nobody Knows
Candace Corrigan candace@candacecorrigan.com
www.nashvillenobodyknows.com
Interview and performance podcast featuring Country, Folk, Acoustic and Roots artists. Great music and in depth interviews.

Olde Surber Station
3578 Old Rail Rd. Eagle Rock, VA 24085
PH: 540-567-2000
Jack W. Lewis JackLewis@surberstation.com
www.surberstation.com/radio
Music and interviews covering Bluegrass, Old-Time and Gospel music.

Pickin' in the Pines
1401 N. Lake Park Blvd. #46, Box 333
Carolina Beach, NC 28428
PH: 910-221-9474
Skip Ogden cwo@ibest.net
www.pickininthepines.com
Bluegrass radio. Please check the site for submission details.

Red Dirt Radio
2579 Hwy. 252, Laurens, SC 29360
PH: 513-255-8477
airplay@reddirtradio.com
reddirtradio.com
We're searching for the BEST new Red Dirt music to add to our playlist.

Red Truck Radio
Charlotte Ryerson charlotte@redtruckradio.com
www.redtruckradio.com
About the songs that got written because they were aching inside somebody to come out!

Rockin' Roundup Rodeo
DJ Jody eagle_dreamspromo2@yahoo.com
www.rockinrounduprodeo.com
Spinning independent Country and Southern Rock music.

Roots Rock Radio
PO Box 397, Sykesville, MD 21784
PH: 202-470-3299
Richard Taylor RootsRockRadio@gmail.com
RRRadio.com
Showcases the best indie Roots Rock, Americana, Alt-Country, Indie Pop/Rock etc.

Sugar in the Gourd
4639 Hazel Ave. Philadelphia, PA 19143-2103
John Salmon john@sugarinthegourd.com
sugarinthegourd.com
Bluegrass and Old-Time music. View the website for submission details.

Taproot Radio
123 Nolen Ln. Chapel Hill, NC 27516
Calvin Powers director@TaprootRadio.com
www.taprootradio.com
A blend of Alt-Country, Roots Rock, 60's era Soul and deep Blues. Contact us for our mailing address.

Traditional Country Music Radio
Dusty Owens dusowens@hotmail.com
www.tcmradio.com
Presents the most qualified work from artists.

Twangtown USA
610 Maple Acres, Holladay, TN 38341
PH: 731-584-0398
Dick Shuey dick@dickshuey.com
www.twangtownusa.com
Broadcasting a variety of Country music shows.

Western Beat Radio
PO Box 128105, Nashville, TN 37212
PH: 615-665-8772 FX: 615-665-8977
billy@westernbeat.com
www.westernbeat.com
The only nationally syndicated program devoted to the Americana side of the Country spectrum.

X Country *XM Radio*
PH: 866-964-8439
xcountry.xmradio.com
Honors the roots of Country while infusing a sonic personality that is unmistakably NOW!

Alaska

The Arctic Cactus Hour *KNBA*
3600 San Jeronimo Dr. #480, Anchorage, AK 99508
PH: 907-793-3500
Eric Smith & Jim Stratton stratto@alaska.net
www.alaska.net/~stratto
Covering all that Rocks and honky tonks.

Arizona

M-PAK Radio
PO Box 3262, Gilbert, AZ 85299-3262
Mike Mikels mikemikels@cox.net
www.mpakproductions.com
Plays Country/Texas Country/and Americana artists. We also review or recommend certain CDs.

California

Bluegrass, Etc. *KCSN*
18111 Nordhoff St., Northridge, CA 91330-8312
PH: 818-885-5276
Frank Hoppe fhoppe@kcsn.org
kcsn.org/programs/bluegrassetcetera.html
Features traditional Bluegrass, Old-Time and Early Country music to move your heart and your feet.

Bluegrass Signal *KALW*
500 Mansell St., San Francisco, CA 94134
PH: 415-841-4134 FX: 415-841-4125
Peter Thompson bgsignal@comcast.net
www.kalw.org
A unique synthesis of Blues and Old-Time Country music, with elements of Celtic, Jazz and a variety of Folk music.

Boot Liquor Radio
1890 Bryant St. #303, San Francisco, CA 94110
roy@somafm.com
bootliquor.com
American Roots music for saddle-weary drunkards.

Carefree Highway *KVMR*
401 Spring St., Nevada City, CA 95959
PH: 530-265-9555 FX: 530-265-9077
Gary Harrison carefreehighway@kvmr.org
www.kvmr.org/personalities/g_harrison.html
Folk, Americana, Cowboy & Native American. Send 2 CDs (one is for our library).

Cupertino Barndance *KKUP*
933 Monroe St., PMB 9150, Santa Clara, CA 95050
Stompin' Steve Hathaway steve@westernswing.com
www.westernswing.com/barndance.html
Classic Country, Honky Tonk, Western Swing,
Bluegrass and Rockabilly. The middle hour features
a current release of either a new artist or reissue.

Down Home *KCSN*
18111 Nordhoff St., Northridge, CA 91330-8312
PH: 818-885-5276
Chuck Taggart chuck@downhome.org
kcsn.org/programs/downhome.html
Folk, Roots, Traditional base and beyond.

Down On the Pataphysical Farm *KUSP*
203 8th Ave. Santa Cruz, CA 95062
PH: 831-476-2800
Leigh Hill bluegrass@kusp.org
www.kusp.org/playlists/pharm
If it's good, Acoustic and Country I'll play it.

Freight Train Boogie Radio
PO Box 4262, Santa Rosa, CA 95402
Bill Frater frater@freighttrainboogie.com
www.freighttrainboogie.com
An emphasis on Alt-Country or Americana music.
Please send 2 copies of your CD.

Howdylicious!
PO Box 4362, Irvine, CA 92616
PH: 949-824-6868
Wanda wanda@kuci.org
www.howdylicious.com
The best in new and old Twangy music.

Jeff's Roadhouse *KFOK*
PO Box 4238, Georgetown, CA 95634
PH: 530-333-4300
Jeff Dunn 4info@kfok.org
www.kfok.org
Americana including Blues, Rockabilly, Western
Swing, Honkytonk, Cajun, New Orleans Jazz and
Zydeco.

Lunch on the Back Porch *KZYX*
PO Box 1, Philo, CA 95466
PH: 707-895-2324 FX: 707-895-2451
Diane Hering kzyx@kzyx.org
kzyx.org/show_profiles/lunch_on_porch.htm
Traditional and contemporary Bluegrass.

Semi-Twang
4623 T St., Sacramento, CA 95819-4743
PH: 916-456-8600 FX: 916-451-9601
Paul A. Hefti semitwang@yahoo.com
www.angelfire.com/indie/semitwang
Classic Country show.

Sunny Side Up *KZSU*
PO Box 20510, Stanford, CA 94309
PH: 650-723-9010 FX: 650-725-5865
Bruce Ross country@kzsu.stanford.edu
kzsu.stanford.edu
Features Bluegrass and Old-Time music.

Tangled Roots *KCSN*
18111 Nordhoff St., Northridge, CA 91330-8312
PH: 818-885-5276
Pat Baker pat@kcsn.org
kcsn.org/programs/tangledroots.html
Alt-Country, Folk, Folk/Rock, Gospel, Blues and
music from the Singer/Songwriter tradition.

Wildwood Flower *KPFK*
3729 Cahuenga Blvd. W.
North Hollywood, CA 91604
PH: 818-985-2711 FX: 818-763-7526
Ben Elder weissenben@earthlink.net
www.kpfk.org
Your music MUST be Bluegrass, Old-Time or
Traditional Country to be considered for airplay.

Colorado

The Conman Radio Show
8200 S. Akron St. #103, Englewood, CO 80112
Chris Conn conman@newhitcountry.com
www.conmanradio.com
Bar Bands & Basement Tapes is one our special
features.

Honky Tonk Heroes / Old Grass GNU Grass
4700 Walnut St., Boulder, CO 80301
PH: 303-449-4885
www.kgnu.org
Old and new Country & Western music!

KCUV
1201 18th St. #250, Denver, CO 80202
PH: 303-296-7025
Doug Clifton dclifton@kcuvradio.com
www.kcuvradio.com
Americana music.

KSUT
PO Box 737, 123 Capote Dr. Ignacio, CO 81137
PH: 970-563-0255 FX: 970-563-0399
beth@ksut.org
www.ksut.org
An eclectic Triple A and Americana music mix.

Route 78 West *KVCU*
6968 ½ S. Boulder Rd. Boulder, CO 80303
PH: 303-492-1190
Uncle Jeff Holland jeff@obliq.net
www.route78west.com
Spinning down the by-ways and blind alleys of
Americana's past and future.

Connecticut

Go Kat Go! *WNHU*
PO Box 5392, Milford, CT 06460
PH: 203-479-8807
Michelle gokatgo13@hotmail.com
www.gokatgoradio.com
Spinning the latest and greatest Rockabilly and
Psychobilly.

Swingin' West *WVOF*
Fairfield U. 1073 N. Benson Rd.
Fairfield, CT 06824
PH: 203-254-4111
Mike Gross mike@swinginwest.com
www.swinginwest.com
Western Swing and Western music (not Country).

U-H Radio Bluegrass *WWUH*
200 Bloomfield Ave. West Hartford, CT 06117
PH: 860-768-4701 FX: 860-768-5701
Kevin Lynch KLbgrass@aol.com
www.wwuh.org
Traditional to contemporary Bluegrass music as
well as occasional live performances.

Delaware

Rural Free Delivery *WVUD*
Perkins Student Ctr. U. Delaware
Newark, DE 19716
PH: 302-831-2701 FX: 302-831-1399
wvudmusic@gmail.com
www.wvud.org
Devoted to Bluegrass, Old-Time and Classic
Country music.

Florida

CountryBear.com
PO Box 758, Lake Placid, FL 33862
PH: 863-531-0102 FX: 863-531-0103
sbc48@hotmail.com
www.countrybear.com
All material must be licensed through one of the
licensing companies.

This is Bluegrass *WMNF*
1210 E. MLK Blvd. Tampa, FL 33603-4449
PH: 813-238-9663 FX: 813-238-1802
Tom Henderson TomH@wmnf.org
www.wmnf.org
Old and new Bluegrass.

Sonic Detour *WMNF*
1210 E. MLK Blvd. Tampa, FL 33603-4449
PH: 813-238-9963 FX: 813-238-1802
Denny Reisinger wmnf@wmnf.org
www.wmnf.org
Roots Rock, Rockabilly, Zydeco, Blues and Honky
Tonk.

Illinois

Live-N-Kickin Bluegrass *WLUW*
6525 N. Sheridan Rd. Chicago, IL 60626
PH: 773-508-9589 FX: 773-508-8082
Billy J. Ivers BillyJ@wluw.org
www.wluw.org
Recorded and live Bluegrass music in the studio
with featured artist.

Strictly Bluegrass *WDCB*
College of DuPage, 425 Fawell Blvd.
Glen Ellyn, IL 60137
PH: 630-942-4200 FX: 630-942-2788
Larry Robinson RobinsonL@wdcb.org
wdcb.org
Presenting the music I love, along with information
on local groups and Bluegrass concerts.

WWHP
407 N. Main St., Farmer City, IL 61842
PH: 309-928-9876 FX: 309-928-3708
wwhp@farmwagon.com
www.wwhp.com
Blues, Bluegrass, Rock, Gospel and American Roots
music.

Indiana

Roots For Breakfast *WFHB*
PO Box 1973, Bloomington, IN 47402
PH: 812-323-1200 FX: 812-323-0320
Mark Richardson rootsforbreakfast@hotmail.com
www.wfhb.org
The usual assortment of Old-Time, Blues, Alt-
Country, Bluegrass and Folk songs/tunes are played.

Kansas

Rockabilly Mood Swing *KKFI*
PO Box 9332, Shawnee Mission, KS 66201
PH: 816-931-5534
Lynne Greenamyre kcrockabilly@yahoo.com
launch.groups.yahoo.com/group/KCRockabilly
*A revved up trip down the Rockabilly speedway!
With side trips to Jump Blues, Psychobilly, Punk,
Hillbilly and Old-Time Country Twang.*

Trail Mix *KPR*
1120 W. 11th St. U. Kansas, Lawrence, KS 66044
PH: 785-864-4530 FX: 785-864-5278
Bob McWilliams radiobob@ku.edu
kpr.ku.edu/trailmix.shtml
Celtic, Folk, Old-Time and Bluegrass.

Kentucky

Americana Crossroads *WMKY*
UPO Box 903, MSU, Morehead, KY 40351
PH: 606-783-2001 FX: 606-783-2335
Sasha Colette wmky@moreheadstate.edu
www.myspace.com/americanacrossroads
*Blending Folk, Bluegrass, Alt-Country and Acoustic
Blues in a music format known as Americana.*

Barren River Breakdown *WKYU*
W. Kentucky U., 1906 College Heights Blvd.
#11035, Bowling Green, KY 42101-1035
PH: 270-745-5489 FX: 270-745-6272
Erika Brady & Mark Hayes wkyufm@wku.edu
www.wkyufm.org
*The best of American music with roots, including
plenty of Bluegrass.*

Blue Yodel #9 *WRFL*
777 University Stn. Lexington, KY 40506-0025
PH: 859-257-4636 FX: 859-323-1039
Joe Takacs shadygrove@prodigy.net
www.wrfl.fm
Country and Americana.

The Cecilian Bank Bluegrass Hour *WLVK*
PO Box 1092, Ashland, KY 41105-1092
PH: 606-831-1266
theboman@theboman.com
www.theboman.com/cecilian.html
*Once Bluegrass music gets into your body, life as
you know it will change forever.*

H. Perkins Bluegrass *WBRT*
106 S. 3rd St., Bardstown, KY 40004
PH: 502-348-3943 FX: 502-348-4043
Howard Perkins h.perkins@juno.com
www.1320wbrt.com
*I play a lot of independent music. I have live bands
drop by as well.*

Roots n' Boots *WFPK*
619 S. 4th St., Louisville, KY 40202
PH: 502-814-6500
Michael Young myoung@wfpk.org
www.wfpk.org/programs/rootsandboots.html
*There's room for outlaws, preachers, rockers and
prophets.*

Sunday Bluegrass *WFPK*
619 S. 4th St., Louisville, KY 40202
PH: 502-814-6500
Berk Bryant bbryant@wfpk.org
www.wfpk.org/programs/bluegrass.html
If it fits the format of the show, I'll play it.

WHAY
PO Box 69, Whitley City, KY 42653
PH: 606-376-2218 FX: 606-376-5146
whayradio@highland.net
www.hay98.com

Louisiana

American Routes *
501 Basin St. Ste. D, New Orleans, LA 70112
Nick Spitzer mail@amroutes.org
amroutes.org
*Presenting a broad range of American music –
Blues, Jazz, Gospel, Soul, Old-Time Country,
Zydeco ...*

Old Time Country and Bluegrass *WWOZ*
PO Box 51840, New Orleans, LA 70151-1840
PH: 504-568-1234 FX: 504-558-9332
Hazel The Delta Rambler hazeldelt@yahoo.com
www.wwoz.org

Maine

The Blue Country *WMPG*
96 Falmouth St., Portland, ME 04104-9300
PH: 207-780-4909
Blizzard Bob blizbob@maine.rr.com
www.wmpg.org
*Where the Bluegrass grows high, under a clear
country sky.*

Massachusetts

Bluegrass Junction *WICN*
50 Portland St., Worcester, MA 01608
PH: 508-752-0700 FX: 508-752-7518
Tom Banyai T.Banyai@worldnet.att.net
www.bluegrassjunction.org
*Back to days when the radio was the center of
family entertainment.*

Bradford Street Bluegrass *WOMR*
PO Box 975, Provincetown, MA 02657
PH: 508-487-2619
Bob Seay bob@womr.org
www.womr.org

Hillbilly at Harvard *WHRB*
389 Harvard St., Cambridge, MA 02138
PH: 617-495-4818
mail@whrb.org
www.whrb.net
The best Country/Western show in New England.

Lost Highway *WMBR*
3 Ames St., Cambridge, MA 02142
PH: 617-253-8810
Doug Gesler highway@wmbr.org
wmbr.mit.edu
*Americana, Alt-Country, Blues, Bluegrass, Cajun,
Zydeco and Hawaiian.*

Michigan

Progressive Torch and Twang *WDBM*
G-4 Holden Hall, MSU East Lansing, MI 48825
PH: 517-353-4414
Doug Neal nealdoug@msu.edu
www.myspace.com/torchandtwang
Home of hip-shakin', soul-swayin' music!

Minnesota

Good 'n' Country *KFAI*
1808 Riverside Ave. Minneapolis, MN 55454
PH: 612-341-0980 FX: 612-341-4281
Ken Hippler vintagecountry@hotmail.com
www.kfai.org
*One of KFAI's oldest programs. Traditional, classic
and vintage American Country music.*

Missouri

Bluegrass Breakdown *KDHX*
3504 Magnolia St. Louis, MO 63118
PH: 314-664-3688 FX: 314-664-1020
Walter & Willa Volz bluegrassbreakdown@kdhx.org
www.kdhx.org/programs/bluegrassbreakdown.htm
*Part of each show will be dedicated to Homegrown
Grass.*

Country Function Bluegrass Junction *KDHX*
3504 Magnolia, St. Louis, MO 63118
PH: 314-664-3688 FX: 314-664-1020
Gene & Larry cfandbj@kdhx.org
www.kdhx.org/programs/
countryfunctionbluegrassjunction.htm
Featuring local artists and unknown artists.

Down Yonder *KDHX*
3504 Magnolia, St. Louis, MO 63118
PH: 314-664-3688 FX: 314-664-1020
Keith Dudding, downyonder@kdhx.org
www.kdhx.org/programs/downyonder
Bluegrass and Old-Time music.

Fishin' with Dynamite *KDHX*
3504 Magnolia, St. Louis, MO 63118
PH: 314-664-3688 FX: 314-664-1020
Fred Friction fishinwithdynamite@kdhx.org
www.kdhx.org/programs/fishinwithdynamite.htm
*Features the finest Alt-Country, Cow-Punk and
Roots Rock.*

New Jersey

Honky Tonk Roadhouse *WDVR*
PO Box 191, Sergeantsville, NJ 08557
PH: 609-397-1620 FX: 609-397-5991
Ted Lyons tlyons@blast.net
www.wdvrfm.org

WDVR
PO Box 191 Sergeantsville, NJ 08557
PH: 609-397-1620 FX: 609-397-5991
host@wdvrfm.org
www.wdvrfm.org
Quite a few of the DJ's play indie artists.

New Mexico

The Santa Fe Opry *KSFR*
PO Box 31366, Santa Fe, NM 87504-1366
PH: 505-428-1527 FX: 505-428-1237
Stephen W. Terrell robotclaww@msn.com
steveterrell.blogspot.com
*Hardcore, Alternative, Outlaw, Insurgent, No
Depression.*

New York

Bluegrass Ramble *WCNY*
PO Box 2400, Syracuse, NY 13220-2400
Bill Knowlton udmacon@aol.com
www.wcny.org

Salt Creek Show *WVBR*
957 Mitchell St., Ithaca, NY 14850
PH: 607-273-2121 FX: 607-273-4069
Peter Fraissinet pf13@cornell.edu
wvbr.com
*Old-Time, Bluegrass, Old and Alt-Country with a
sprinkling Cajun, Blues and Gospel.*

String Fever *NCPR*
St. Lawrence U. Canton, NY 13617-1475
PH: 315-229-5356 FX: 315-229-5373
Barb Heller barb@ncpr.org
www.northcountrypublicradio.org/programs/local/
string.html
Instrumental finger picking guitar for GREAT musicians.

North Carolina

The Good-Tyme Bluegrass Show *WFSS*
1200 Murchison Rd. Fayetteville, NC 28301
PH: 910-672-1919 FX: 910-672-1964
Bob and Sara Barden monkous@nc.rr.com
www.wfss.org

This Old Porch *WNCW*
286 ICC Loop Rd. Spindale, NC 28160
PH: 828-287-8080 FX: 828-287-8012
Joe Cline kilocycles@carolina.rr.com
www.wncw.org
Features classic music from the Old-Time Country music tradition.

WPAQ
PO Box 907, Mount Airy, NC 27030
PH: 336-786-6111 FX: 336-789-7792
info@wpaq740.com
www.wpaq740.com
Bluegrass and Gospel Bluegrass station.

The Wrecking Ball *WCOM*
201 N. Greensboro St., Carrboro, NC 27510
PH: 919-929-9601
Jayson thewreckingballradioshow@gmail.com
www.myspace.com/progressivespirit
Roots, Americana, Alt-Country etc. If yours is a CD that might fit the format of my show, send it to me for review.

Ohio

Connie's Country Roadhouse
4109 Cedar Ridge Rd. Dayton, OH 45414
PH: 937-274-2924
Connie Bennington blackwolfshadovv@aol.com
I play indie music on my show. I am looking for any of you who want your music heard throughout the world.

D28+5 *WOUB*
9 S. College St., Athens, OH 45701
PH: 740-593-1771 FX: 740-593-0240
radio@woub.org
woub.org/bluegrass
Bluegrass Roots radio for SE Ohio.

Down Home Bluegrass *WYSO*
795 Livermore St., Yellow Springs, OH 45387
PH: 937-767-6420
Joe Colvin jcolvin6740@yahoo.com
www.wyso.org
Bluegrass and Old-Time music. Please e-mail me before sending in your music.

Rise When the Rooster Crows *WYSO*
795 Livermore St., Yellow Springs, OH 45387
PH: 937-767-6420
Joe Colvin jcolvin6740@yahoo.com
www.wyso.org
Old-Time Gospel and Bluegrass. Please e-mail me before sending in your music.

Roots 'n' Offshoots *WCBE*
540 Jack Gibbs Blvd. Columbus, OH 43215
PH: 614-821-9223 FX: 614-365-5060
Maggie Brennan mbrennan@wcbe.org
www.wcbe.org
Folk, Bluegrass, Rockabilly and more.

Oregon

Early Morning Gumbo *KBOO*
20 SE. 8th Ave. Portland, OR 97214
PH: 503-231-8187 FX: 503-231-7145
Diane Karl dkarl@ipns.com
www.kboo.fm
Features Acoustic Blues, Texas Folk, Cajun, Old-Time, Bluegrass etc.

The Long & Dusty Road *KBOO*
20 SE. 8th Ave. Portland, OR 97214
PH: 503-231-8187 FX: 503-231-7145
Don Jacobson donj@dslnorthwest.net
www.kboo.fm
Americana, Alt-Country, Roots etc.

Pennsylvania

The Bluegrass Jam Session *WYEP*
67 Bedford Sq. Pittsburgh, PA 15203
PH: 412-381-9900 FX: 412-381-9126
Bruce Mountjoy mtjoypgh@aol.com
www.wyep.org
Explores Bluegrass music from its 1940's creation by Kentuckian Bill Monroe into the new century.

Mountain Folk
PO Box 2266, Sinking Spring, PA 19608
mtnfolk@aol.com
www.mountainfolk.com
Indie artists are encouraged to send material.

Roots and Rhythm Mix *WYEP*
67 Bedford Sq. Pittsburgh, PA 15203
PH: 412-381-9900 FX: 412-381-9126
Kate Borger kateb913@hotmail.com
www.wyep.org
As well as playing Roots and Alt-Country, I'm also into any regional rhythms - Tex-Mex, Zydeco, Latin etc.

Traditional Ties *WYEP*
67 Bedford Sq. Pittsburgh, PA 15203
PH: 412-381-9900 FX: 412-381-9126
John Trout johntrout91@hotmail.com
www.wyep.org
New Bluegrass releases and old favorites.

South Carolina

The Bluegrass Sound *ETV*
1101 George Rogers Blvd.
Columbia, SC 29201-4761
PH: 803-737-3420
www.etvradio.org/bgs
Host Larry Klein presents a mix of both traditional and contemporary Bluegrass music, some occasional Old-Time Mountain music.

Tennessee

Bluegrass Breakdown *WPLN*
630 Mainstream Dr. Nashville, TN 37228-1204
PH: 615-760-2903 FX: 615-760-2904
Dave Higgs bluegrass@wpln.org
www.wpln.org/bluegrass
Our goal is to edify, educate and entertain. We leave no instrument unpicked, no song unsung and no interview undone.

The Bluegrass Special *WDVX*
PO Box 18157 Knoxville, TN 37928
PH: 865-494-2020
Alex Leach alex899@comcast.net
www.wdvx.com
The best in Bluegrass music, old and new.

Clinch River Breakdown *WDVX*
PO Box 27568, Knoxville, TN 37927
PH: 865-494-2020
Amy Campbell campbellcreative@charter.net
Charlie Lutz charlie_lutz@comcast.net
www.wdvx.com
Bluegrass, Old-Time and Classic Country.

Cumberland Sunday Morning *WDVX*
PO Box 27568, Knoxville, TN 37927
PH: 865-494-2020
Mike Kelly bluegrassmike@hotmail.com
www.wdvx.com
The best in Bluegrass Gospel. I enjoy spreading the word about musicians that folks may not be familiar with.

WDVX
PO Box 27568, Knoxville, TN 37927
PH: 865-494-2020
studio@wdvx.com
www.wdvx.com
We play all types of Country, Celtic and Folk.

Texas

The Bluegrass Zone *KPFT*
419 Lovett Blvd. Houston, TX 77006
PH: 713-526-5738 FX: 713-526-5750
Chris Hirsch cshirsch@alltel.net
www.bluegrasszone.com
Houston's Bluegrass radio program.

The LoneStar JukeBox *KPFT*
419 Lovett Blvd. Houston, TX 77006
PH: 713-526-5738
Rick Heysquierdo lonestarjukebox@kpft.org
www.lonestarjukebox.com
Promotes Americana and Alt-Country genres.

Random Routes *KEOS*
PO Box 78, College Station, TX 77841
PH: 979-779-5367 FX: 979-779-7259
John Roths jroths@mail.tca.net
www.keos.org
All-American, regional & Texas Roots music.

Third Coast Music Network *KSYM*
7519 Dell Oak, San Antonio, TX 78218-2634
PH: 210-733-2800
David Ludwig ihod7519@yahoo.com
www.tcmnradio.com

Utah

The Amarillo Highway *KZMU*
PO Box 1076, 1734 Rocky Rd. Moab, UT 84532
PH: 435-259-5968 FX: 435-259-8763
www.kzmu.org
Hillbilly, Alt-Country, Alterna-Twang, No Depression, Country, Honky Tonk.

Monday Breakfast Jam *KRCL*
1971 W. North Temple, Salt Lake City, UT 84116
PH: 801-359-9191 FX: 801-533-9136
Doug Young dougy@krcl.org
www.krcl.org
Eclectic mix of Insurgent Country, contemporary Singer/Songwriter, Folk and Rock.

Vermont

Fellow Travelers *WOMM*
PO Box 428, 215 College St. #301
Burlington, VT 05402-0428
PH: 802-861-9666
Rik Palieri rik@banjo.net
www.theradiator.org
A mix of Americana, C&W, Hillbilly, Blues, Folk and World music.

Virginia

Allegheny Mountain Radio
Rt. 1, Box 139, Dunmore, WV 24934
PH: 304-799-6004
Cheryl Kinderman ckamr@frontiernet.net
www.alleghenymountainradio.org
Country, Bluegrass, Gospel, Rock, Classical and Jazz.

Bluegrass Sunday Morning *WNRN*
2250 Old Ivy Rd. #2, Charlottesville, VA 22903
PH: 434-979-0919
wnrn.rlc.net
Host Scott Buchanan features 4 hours of Bluegrass music.

Fitzgrass *WEBR*
2929 Eskridge Rd. Ste. S, Fairfax, VA 22031
PH: 703-573-8255 FX: 703-573-1210
Mike Fitzgerald mfitzgerald21@cox.net
www.fcac.org/webr
Keepin' the Bluegrass flowin' from Northern Virginia.

WGRX
4414 Lafayette Blvd. #100
Fredericksburg, VA 22408
PH: 540-891-9696 FX: 540-891-1656
Jerome Hruska: jhruska@959wgrq.com
www.thunder1045.com
We air an Americana/Bluegrass/Texas Country show on Sunday nights that incorporates independent artists.

Washington

Front Porch Bluegrass *KPBX*
2319 N. Monroe St., Spokane, WA 99205
PH: 509-328-5729 FX: 509-328-5764
Kevin Brown bluegrass@kpbx.org
www.kpbx.org/programs/frontporch
Classic Bluegrass and its progressive offshoots.

Road Songs *KBCS*
3000 Landerholm Cir. SE.
Bellevue, WA 98007-6484
Attn: Music Director
PH: 425-564-2424
Hal Durden asubdude@att.net
kbcs.fm
A journey down the highways of Alt-Country, Folk, Classic Country and Country Rock.

Washington DC

Bluegrass Overnight *WAMU*
A.U. 4400 Mass. Ave. NW.
Washington, DC 20016-8082
PH: 202-885-1200
www.wamu.org
Six lively hours of Bluegrass every week.

bluegrasscountry.org
4000 Brandywine St. NW., Washington, DC 20016
bluegrasscountry.org
Traditional and contemporary Bluegrass.

The Ray Davis Show *WAMU*
A.U. 4400 Mass. Ave. NW.
Washington, DC 20016-8082
PH: 202-885-1200
www.wamu.org/programs/rd
Traditional and Gospel Bluegrass.

Stained Glass Bluegrass *WAMU*
A.U. 4400 Mass. Ave. NW.
Washington, DC 20016-8082
PH: 202-885-1200
www.wamu.org/programs/sgbg
Receives and considers material from anyone.

WAMU *American U.*
4400 Mass. Ave. NW., Washington, DC 20016-8082
PH: 202-885-1200
www.wamu.org

West Virginia

Sidetracks
151 S. Mineral St., Keyser, WV 26726
PH: 304-788-7878
Ed McDonald sidetracks@eioproductions.com
www.wvpubcast.org
A weekly syndicated program of Bluegrass, Folk, Country, Blues and related styles of contemporary Acoustic music.

Wisconsin

Bluegrass Saturday *WXPR*
303 W. Prospect Ave. Rhinelander, WI 54501
PH: 715-362-6000 FX: 715-362-6007
Henry Galvin wxpr@wxpr.org
www.wxpr.org
Four big hours of Bluegrass every Saturday afternoon.

Wyoming

Clear Out West
PO Box 1547, Pinedale, WY 82941
PH: 307-360-8776
cowboys@clearoutwest.com
clearoutwest.com
A weekly syndicated cowboy radio show dedicated to introducing the cowboy culture to new folks and bringing back some great memories to some old cowboys.

Canada

Angel Radio Bluegrass
Stormin Norman norm@angelradio.net
angelradio.net
Bluegrass old and new.

The Back Forty *CKCU*
56-121 Buell St., Ottawa, ON K1Z 7E7
PH: 819-827-0068
Ron Moores ron.moores@back40.ca
www.back40.ca
Traditional Country, Western and Bluegrass music.

Brave New Frontiers Podcast
radio.weblogs.com/0146182
Host Randall Cousins presents a weekly peek into the on-the-edge Country influenced indie scene.

Daybreak In Dixie *CJAM*
401 Sunset Ave. Windsor, ON N9B 3P4
PH: 519-253-3000 x2527 FX: 519-971-3605
www.uwindsor.ca/cjam
Bluegrass music.

Fire on the Mountain *CKUA*
10526 Jasper Ave. Edmonton, AB T5J 1Z7
PH: 780-428-7595 FX: 780-428-7624
Craig Korth craig.korth@ckua.com
www.ckua.org
From the roots of Bluegrass to the new Acoustic frontier.

Good 'n Country *CFFF*
715 George St. N., Peterborough, ON K9H 3T2
PH: 705-748-4761
Barb Holtmann restorix@nexicom.net
www.trentu.ca/trentradio
Blending the old, the new and the unusual in Country music. News, views and interviews with local and area artists.

Pacific Pickin' *CITR*
#233-6138 SUB Blvd. Vancouver, BC V6T 1Z1
PH: 604-822-2487
Arthur & Andrea Berman pacificpickin@yahoo.com
www.citr.ca
Bluegrass, Old-Time music and its derivatives.

Radio Boogie *CKLN*
55 Gould St. 2nd Fl. Toronto, ON M5B 1E9
PH: 416-979-5251 FX: 416-595-0226
Steve Pritchard s.pritchard1@sympatico.ca
www.ckln.fm
Bluegrass, Old-Tyme, Acoustic and Traditional Country.

Uptown Bluegrass
PO Box 1372, Kamloops, BC V2C 6L7
PH: 250-852-0595
George georgemcknight@telus.net
www.uptownbluegrass.com
Syndicated radio show.

Wide Cut Country *CKUA*
10526 Jasper Ave. Edmonton, AB T5J 1Z7
PH: 780-428-7595 FX: 780-428-7624
Allison Brock allison.brock@ckua.org
www.ckua.com
Traditional Hillbilly to Pop Country of today.

Europe

Austria

Go West Go Country *Radio Ostttirol*
Hans Mair hans.mair@gmx.at
www.radio.osttirol.net/gowest.htm
Send your promotional CDs to the above address.

Denmark

Absolute Country
Gammel Strandvej 426, 3060 Espergaerde, Denmark
Per Kildahl per-kildahl@adslhome.dk
www.radiohelsingor.dk
A mix of old and new Country music.

Bornholms Stemme
Gammeltoft 36 – 25, 3790 Hasle, Bornholm, Denmark
Lulu and Arne Andersen arne_lulu@country-vaerkstedet.dk
www.country-vaerkstedet.dk
On the local radio we air Country music 2 hours a week, plus entertain every second Saturday with mixed music for 3 hours.

Estonia

Bluegrass Radio 108
bluegrassradio@hot.ee
www.hot.ee/bluegrassradio
Devoted to the American Bluegrass and Grassroots music.

France

Keep It Country!
B.P. 6101, 75061 Paris Cedex 02, France
Mathias Andrieu mathiasandrieu@yahoo.com
www.keepitcountryfrance.com
*A weekly program based on the history and reality
of authentic Country music.*

Germany

Country Special Radio *Countrymusic24*
Postfach 480146, 12251 Berlin, Germany
PH: +49 (0) 30-710-93334
band@countrymusic24.com
www.countrymusic24.com
*A weekly show that plays independent Country
music.*

Hillbilly Boogie
Saarstraße 8, 72070 Tübingen, Germany
PH: +49(0)7073-2250 FX: +49(0)7073-2134
Rainer Zellner zellner@musiccontact.com
www.musiccontact.com
*We cover many musical genres related to Country or
Hillbilly.*

Hillbilly Jukebox *Radio Rhein Welle*
Hauptstrasse 62, 65396 Walluf, Germany
FX: 012-126-744-372-84
Rolf Hierath cashville@gmx.de
www.cashville.de

Hillbilly Rockhouse *Countrymusic24*
Postfach 480146, 12251 Berlin, Germany
PH: +49 (0) 30-710-93334
DJ Gerd Stassen g.stassen@t-online.de
www.countrymusic24.com

Luxembourg

Country Club Music Show
2, rue de la Boucherie, L-1247 Luxembourg
Mam Lexy lexyzen@pt.lu
www.ara.lu

Country Music Show *Radio Ara*
2 rue de la Boucherie, L-1247, Luxembourg
Willie Jervis radioaracountryshow@yahoo.com
www.ara.lu
*We're seeking new music to play on our show. I'm
seeking Country, Bluegrass, American Native music
and Folk. Artists can mail their CD and press kit to
the above address.*

The Netherlands

B.R.T.O.
Burgemeester van Hasseltstraat 7,
4611 BG Bergen op Zoom, The Netherlands
PH: 0164-211030 FX: 0164-211032
redactie@brto.nl
www.brto.nl
*Bluegrass, Gospel, Cajun, Zydeco, Tex Mex,
Rockabilly and Modern Country.*

Country Express Radio Rucphen
Zwaard 27 4871 DL Etten-Leur, The Netherlands
Ries & Johan verwijmerenries@zonnet.nl
www.home.zonnet.nl/verwijmerenries
Please send me material (CDs & Bio) for my show.

Countryland Radio Barneveld
Postbus 285, 3770 AG Barneveld, The Netherlands
PH: 0342-422-411 FX: 0342-422-345
Dick Brink & Timen van Ark
info@radiobarneveld.nl
www.radiobarneveld.nl
*Bluegrass, Old-Time Country, New Country,
aandacht aan de Nederlandse artiesten en in mei
geen artiest van de maand, maar Bluegrass maand!!*

Paul Van Gelder's Americana Music Show
Paul gelder@paulvangelder.com
www.americanaradio.nl
*Features Americana, Folk, Country, Jazz, Blues,
Bluegrass etc.*

PeelGrass
Akelei 10 5803 CA Venray, The Netherlands
Rein Wortelboer peelgras@xs4all.nl
www.xs4all.nl/~peelgras
*Send a promotional CD for review and possible
airplay.*

proRadio4
Postbus 86, 5900 AB Venlo, The Netherlands
PH: 01805-7834-24001 FX: 001831-677-9141
Dean Grunwald info@proradio4.com
www.proradio4.net
*Playing high quality independent music of all
genres, with a particular emphasis on Country, Rock
and Dance music.*

United Kingdom

AmericanaOK
26 Buie Brae, Kirkliston, EH29 9FB Scotland
PH: +44(0)7765898260
Tom Fahey americanaok@btinternet.com
www.americanaok.com
*A syndicated radio show playing the best in
independent Americana & Alt-Country.*

Bob Harris Country *BBC 2*
PH: 08700-100-200
www.bbc.co.uk/radio2/shows/bobharriscountry
*The best in Country, from cowboy classics to the
newest sounds coming out of Nashville.*

CMR Nashville
51 Union St., Farnborough, Hants, GU14 7PX UK
PH: +44 (0) 845-8901-913
FX: +44 (0) 870-3612-913
Lee Williams info@cmrnashville.net
www.cmrnashville.net
*Europe's hottest 24/7 Country music service.
Dedicated to promoting and assisting in several
fields of artist promotion.*

The Comfort Zone
gail_comfort@hotmail.com
www.myspace.com/gailcomfort
Americana, Alt-Country and Bluegrass music.

Country Corner Radio Show *Claire FM*
Abbeyfield Ctr. Francis St., Ennis Co. Clare, Ireland
PH: 353-0-65-682-8888 FX: 353-0-65-682-9392
Mike Gardiner mgardiner@clarefm.ie
www.clarefm.ie
*Features Irish, American and European Country
music, new and old.*

Metro Country
ray@metrocountry.co.uk
www.metrocountry.co.uk
E-mail to submit your material.

Twangfest *U. Radio York*
10 Heworth Hall Dr. Heworth, York,
Yorkshire, YO31 1AQ UK
Allan Nelson allan@allan70.wanadoo.co.uk
ury.york.ac.uk
Roots, Americana, Folk, Country etc.

Australia

Bay Breeze Country *Bay FM*
PO Box 1003, Cleveland, QLD 4163 Australia
Bob Atkins bob_atkins@iprimus.com.au
www.bayfm.org.au
Weekly show featuring independent artists.

Bluegrass Unlimited *5UV*
228 N. Terrace, Adelaide, SA 5000 Australia
PH: 61-8-8303-5000 FX: 61-8-8303-4374
Bill Lawson lawson@chariot.net.au
radio.adelaide.edu.au
*Covers the whole Bluegrass spectrum from the
earliest days to the latest overseas and local
releases.*

Chicken Hot Rod *2RRR*
PO Box 644, Gladesville, NSW 1675 Australia
Lindsay Mar chickenhotrod@bluegrass.org.au
www.2rrr.org.au
*3 hours of Bluegrass, Old Timey and other
forbidden delights.*

MCR Radio
PO Box 1420, Campbelltown, NSW 2560 Australia
PH: 02-4625-2768 FX: 02-4627-0670
feedback@2mcr.org.au
2mcr.org.au/country
*Our station features a variety of Country music
shows.*

Music from Foggy Hollow *Hawk Radio*
20 Hale Cres. Windsor, NSW 2756 Australia
PH: 02-45-775-662
atalkingdog.com
Our show is a new releases Bluegrass show.

Saturday Night Country *ABC*
PO Box 694 Townsville, QLD 4810 Australia
PH: +61-7-4722-3050 FX: 07-4722-3099
www.abc.net.au/snc
*Your gateway to the best in Australian Country
music.*

Slinga's Independent Country *WYN*
PO Box 4221 MDC, Hoppers Crossing,
VIC 3029 Australia
PH: 61-1-03-9742-1868 FX: 61-1-03-9742-1868
slinga.com
Indie Country music from all over the world!

Stone Cold Country *Yarra Valley FM*
85 Rathmullen Rd. Boronia, VIC 3155 Australia
PH: 61-0419-346230
Rod Bradey rod@austadhesives.com.au
www.yarravalleyfm.com
*Featuring mainly independent Country music
artists.*

New Zealand

Best of Bluegrass *Radio Kidnappers*
PO Box 680, Hastings, New Zealand
PH: 06-876-6914 FX: 06-876-6914
Trevor Ruffell comus@xtra.co.nz
www.radiokidnappers.org.nz
*Two hours of contemporary and Old-Time Bluegrass
music.*

New Zealand Country Music Network
PO Box 352, Stratford, Taranaki 4352 New Zealand
music@countrymusic.net.nz
www.nzcountrymusic.net
We welcome CDs from most sources for air play on the five LPFM stations we currently operate in.

Dance and Electronic Radio

North America

United States

Absolute Technoise Radio
www.technofor.us
Techno radio and online community.

Abstract Science *WLUW*
6525 N. Sheridan Rd.Chicago, IL 60626
PH: 773-508-9589
Kim Schlechter kim@abstractscience.net
abstractscience.net
Explores what we refer to as 'Future Music'. The constant evolution of modern Electronic music in its varied forms, to its roots in Funk, Jazz, Dub and Soul.

astralwerks Radio
101 Ave. of the Americas, 4th Fl.
New York, NY 10013
a&r@astralwerks.net
www.astralwerks.com
Limit your demo to your 3 best tracks. Please, no phone calls!

BassDrive
Zew info@bassdrive.com
www.bassdrive.com
The best of Drum n' Bass & Jungle music.

Beats in Space *WNYU*
194 Mercer Str. 5th Fl. New York, NY 10012
PH: 212-998-1660 FX: 212-998-1652
Tim Sweeney tim@beatsinspace.net
www.beatsinspace.net
The sounds you'll hear are not limited to one style.

Bentwave *WNYU*
194 Mercer Str. 5th Fl. New York, NY 10012
PH: 212-998-1660 FX: 212-998-1652
Miss Eleanor bentwave@wnyu.org
wnyu.org
Brings the experimental side of Electronic music to radio in a format you can dance to.

Beta Lounge Radio Show
1072 Illinois St., San Francisco, CA 94107
feedback@betalounge.com
www.betalounge.com
Send a sample of your material.

Darkside Radio Internet Program *(DRiP)*
PO Box 1905, Boulder, CO 80306
Stevyn stevyn@ironfeather.com
www.ironfeather.com
We welcome Dance & Electronica CDs, demos etc.

Dave's Lounge
daveslounge@gmail.com
www.daveslounge.com
A weekly podcast that showcases the best in Chillout, Trip Hop and Downtempo Electronica. If you make any of these styles of music e-mail your artist info and MP3 files (or links to MP3 files) to me.

Digitally Imported Radio
demos@di.fm
www.di.fm
E-mail to get submission instructions.

dnbradio.com
info@dnbradio.com
www.dnbradio.com
Drum n' Bass, Jungle and Liquid Funk. If you would like to submit your work, please contact us.

Future Breaks FM *KUSF*
2130 Fulton St., San Francisco, CA 94117
PH: 415-751-5873
dj PUSH djpush@futurebreaks.fm
www.futurebreaks.fm
21st Century Breakbeat music, pioneering Underground music and DJ culture on the airwaves.

Gruvsonic Dance Radio
720 Two Mile, Wisconsin Rapids, WI 54494
www.gruvsonic.com
Willing to spin any Dance material via live mix shows.

The Hitchhiker's Dance Guide *WEVL*
PO Box 40952, Memphis, TN 38174
PH: 901-528-1990
Buddy buddy@wevl.org
www.wevl.org
Guest hosts present Progressive to Breaks, House to Trip Hop and just about everything in between.

KNHC *Nathan Hale H.S.*
10750 30th Ave. NE, Seattle, WA 98125
PH: 206-421-8989 FX: 206-252-3805
www.c895fm.com
A recognized leader in Dance music.

Metropolis *KCRW*
1900 Pico Blvd. Santa Monica, CA 90405
PH: 310-450-5183 FX: 310-450-7172
Jason Bentley metroweb@kcrw.org
www.kcrw.org/show/mt
The hypnotic pulse of modern city life.

milk.audio
gani@milkaudio.com
www.milkaudio.com
If you would like to send CDs or vinyl, e-mail me.

Mixin' It Up
DJ Baddog djbaddog@mixinitup.com
www.myspace.com/djbaddog
A showcase for signed & unsigned artists alike. Latin beats & rhythms, Hip Hop, Dance, House, Club music & all its many genres.

ND Lounge
www.ndlounge.com
An internet radio station streaming you the best in Lounge, Downtempo, Ambient and Trip Hop music.

Phuture Frequency Radio
www.pfradio.com
Online music community and D n'B radio station.

Proton Radio
Sam Packer sam@protonradio.com
www.protonradio.com
The internet's gold standard for underground Dance music. Visit our site for submission details.

SectionZ Radio
2513 W. Superior St. 1st Fl. Chicago, IL 60612
Joshua 'Z' Hernandez z@sectionz.com
www.sectionz.com
We have a bunch of different DJs hand picking the tracks for the wire waves. Upload all the tracks you want and get feedback from thousands of other artists.

The "So Very" Show *KTUH*
Honolulu, Hemenway Hall #203, 2445 Campus Rd.
Honolulu, HI 96822.
PH: 808-956-7261 FX: 808-956-5271
thesoveryshow@gmail.com
www.sovery.org
Groove to the sounds of Deep House.

Streetbeat *WNUR*
1920 Campus Dr. Evanston, IL 60208-2280
PH: 847-866-9687 FX: 847-467-2058
streetbeat-md@wnur.org
streetbeat.wnur.org
Dance music that doesn't get exposure elsewhere.

Technomusic.com Radio
www.technomusic.com
Broadcasting live DJ Mixes, 24/7. Also does music reviews.

Trance Lab Radio
DJ Lord Bass lordbass@trancelab.com
www.trancelab.com
Podcast featuring new flavors of German Tech-House, Glitch and fuzzy Electro grooves with an interest in exposing new music and dusting off old cuts.

The Underground Sounds Show *KTUH*
PO Box 12073, Honolulu, HI 96828-1073
PH: 808-591-3500
info@double-o-spot.com
www.double-o-spot.com
The hottest and latest Dance tracks with a mix of past recordings, combining House, Trance, D n'B, Trip Hop etc.

WMPH *Mt. Pleasant H.S.*
5201 Washington St. Ext. Wilmington, DE 19809
PH: 302-762-7199 FX: 302-762-7042
www.wmph.org
We accept indie releases.

Canada

The Groove *CKCU*
Rm. 517 U. Ctr. 1125 Colonel By Dr.
Ottawa, ON K1S 5B6
PH: 613-520-2898
Elorius Cain music@ckcufm.com
www.ckcufm.com
Canada's longest running Disco show playing every variation.

Higher Ground *CIUT*
91 St. George St., Toronto, ON M5S 2E8
PH: 416-978-0909 x214 FX: 416-946-7004
Jason Palma jasonpalma@rogers.com
www.highergroundradio.com
Along with the music I love, we also feature information on upcoming events.

Shadow Jugglers *CITR*
#233-6138 SUB Blvd. Vancouver, BC V6T 1Z1
PH: 604-822-2487 FX: 604-822-9364
tobydyc3@hotmail.com
www.citr.ca
Bringing you the sounds of DnB and Jungle.

Tongue and Groove CKUA
10526 Jasper Ave. Edmonton, AB T5J 1Z7
PH: 780-428-7595 FX: 780-428-7624
Kevin Wilson kevin.wilson@ckua.org
www.ckua.com
Oasis of everything that grooves.

E u r o p e
Belgium

Beyondjazz Radio Show
Lange Boomgaardstraat 114a, b9000 Gent, Belgium
PH: +32-9-225-25-17
Jurriaan Persyn office@beyondjazz.net
www.beyondjazz.net
We play, review and discuss on the show whatever we like and love. Broken Beats, Future Jazz, Space Funk ...

France

Galaxie Radio
BP 21-59392 Wattrelos, France
PH: 03-20-83-57-57 FX: 03-20-75-09-87
info@galaxiefm.com
www.galaxiefm.com

MaXXima
contact@maxxima.org
www.maxxima.org
Electronic, NuJazz, Lounge, Downtemp, DeepHouse, House, TekHouse ...

Radio FG Paris
51 rue de Rivoli - 75001, Paris, France
PH: 01-40-13-88-00
webmaster@radiofg.com
www.radiofg.com
Broadcasting a variety of Dance music shows.

Radio Nova
33, rue du Faubourg Saint Antoine, 75011 Paris, France
PH: 01-53-33-33-15
radionova@radionova.com
www.novaplanet.com
Broadcasting on various stations throughout France.

Germany

Back to the Basics
NDR, Rothenbaumchaussee 132 20149 Hamburg, Germany
PH: 040-41-56-2788 FX: 040-41-56-3018
websta@vinylizer.net
www.vinylizer.net
Presents new releases and exclusively recorded sessions by DJs from all over the world.

Klub Radio
Caseler Str. 4A, 13088 Berlin, Germany
PH: 030-27-59-60-41
www.klubradio.de
Brings you the worlds best DJs live from the best clubs in Germany.

Nova Radio
Postbox 40 13 51, 80713 Munich, Germany
PH: 089-3715645-67 FX: 089-3715645-27
www.novaradio.de
Club sound network.

Radio Quintessenz
Lörenskogstr. 4, 85748 München/Garching, Germany
PH: +49 (0)89-24408713 FX: +49 (0)89-24408712
Wolfgang Droszczack
wolfgang@radioquintessenz.de
www.radioquintessenz.de
Videostream of Electronic music live in the Mix. Party.

The Netherlands

Radio X-Clusief
Reepstraat 33, 2583 XG 'S-Gravenhage, The Netherlands
PH: +316-12136870
info@exclusieffm.nl
www.exclusieffm.nl
The #1 Trance station of the Hague.

Slovenia

DRUGATRON Radio Mars
Gosposvetska 83, 2000 Maribor, Slovenia, EU
PH: +386-2-25-25-495 FX: +386-2-25-25-490
Matjaz Ploj mars@radiomars.si
www.radiomars.si
Electronic music scene promotion. Presenting & representing 'best' releases & authors. NuBreaks, D'n'B, Mash Ups, Hip Hop and BreakBeat.

Switzerland

Basic.ch
Boulevard St-Georges 21 PO Box 166, CH1211 Geneva 8, Switzerland
PH: +41-22-800-22-32 FX: +41-22-800-22-33
basic@basic.ch
live.basic.ch
Covering quality Electronic music and more.

lounge-radio.com
Heimstrasse 13 CH-5430 Wettingen, Switzerland
PH: +41-56-221-63-66
Thomas Zumbrunnen dj@lounge-radio.com
www.lounge-radio.com
Fresh beats of NuJazz - dipped with a smile of Brazil and served with a breath of Ambient. We play lot of stuff from independent artists.

Radio Couleur 3
Av. du Temple 40, Case Postale 78, CH-1010 Lausanne, Switzerland
PH: +41(21) 318-11-11 FX: +41(21) 652-37-19
www.couleur3.ch

SwissGroove
Bahnhofstrasse 14, CH-9450 Altstätten, Switzerland
PH: +41 (0)71-755-08-22
Peter Böhi mail@swissgroove.ch
swissgroove.ch
Our sound is a mix of Acid, Nu, Smooth-Jazz, Trip-Hop, Funk, Soul, R&B, Lounge & Latin.

United Kingdom

B2B Radio
PO Box 41, Tipton, DY4 7YT UK
PH/FX: 44 (0) 121-520-1150
www.back2basicsrecords.com
The best in up front D n'B.

BBC Radio 1 *Dance Music*
PH: 03700-100-100
www.bbc.co.uk/radio1/dance
Home page of the BBC Radio 1's various Dance music shows. Info, shows, contacts etc.

BBC Radio 1xtra *Drum & Bass*
DJ Bailey 1xtra@bbc.co.uk
www.bbc.co.uk/1xtra/drumbass
Home page of the BBC 1xtra's various D n'B shows. Info, shows, contacts etc.

BBC Radio 1xtra *Garage*
1xtra@bbc.co.uk
www.bbc.co.uk/1xtra/garage
Home page of the BBC 1xtra's various Garage shows. Info, shows, contacts etc.

Breaks FM
www.breaksfm.com
Playing host to the worlds leading breaks DJs/labels & artists.

DJ AZ Productions
PH: 07990626729
DJ AZ djazproductions@toucansurf.com
www.artistserver.com/DJAZPRODUCTIONS
Music production and unsigned artist promotion. I also host a UK internet radio show that plays Trance, Techno, House, Garage etc.

ministryofsound radio
103 Gaunt St., London, SE1 6DP UK
PH: 44-0-20-7740-8600 FX: 44-0-20-7403-5348
label@ministryofsound.com
www.ministryofsound.com/radio
The biggest digital dance floor on the planet.

Power FM
68 Parkwest Enterprise Ctr. Dublin 12 Ireland
PH: 353-76-6700883 FX: 353-16296085
studio@powerfm.org
www.powerfm.org
Streaming live Dance music from Dublin.

Radio Magnetic
Argyle House, 7B Left Argyle Ct. 1103 Argyle St., Glasgow, G3 8ND UK
PH: 44-141-226-8808 FX: 44-141-226-8818
Tony Black tony@radiomagnetic.com
www.radiomagnetic.com
Covers the UK and Scottish Dance music scenes.

Universal Vibes
info@universalvibes.com
www.universalvibes.com
Hosts a variety of shows. Has interviews and guest DJs.

A u s t r a l i a

Australian Underground Dance Station
Ison Live Radio, PO Box 532, Newcastle, NSW 2300 Australia
PH: 02-40164290
www.isonliveradio.com
Underground Dance music from all around the world!

Fat Planet *FBi*
PO Box 1962, Strawberry Hills, Sydney, NSW 2012 Australia
Stuart Buchanan mail@fatplanet.com.au
www.fatplanet.com.au
Downloads, videos and podcasts looking at Alternative, Electronic & Urban music from around the world.

Fresh FM
Unit Level 2, 230 Angas St., Adelaide, SA 5000 Australia
PH: (08) 8232-7927 FX: (08) 8224-0922
manager@freshfm.com.au
www.freshfm.com.au
The rhythm of Adelaide's youth.

In the Mix Podcast
PO Box 1964, Strawberry Hills,
NSW 2012 Australia
PH: 02-9282-4000 FX: 02-9282-4099
www.inthemix.com.au/podcast
Features cutting edge Dance music tracks.

Mix Up
PO Box 9994, Sydney, NSW 2001 Australia
www.abc.net.au/triplej/mixup/default.htm
Grab your clubbin' outfit, your water bottle and jump into your fav dancing shoes.

PsyKe Out
www.psykeout.net
All the very best and latest Psy-Trance.

Spraci
PH: +61-(0) 415-802-648 FX: +61-1300-300-374
support@spraci.com
spraci.cia.com.au
An extensive list of weekly Dance music radio shows heard around the Sydney area.

Experimental Radio

North America

United States

420 Train Wreck
rocksanne@420trainwreck.com.
www.420trainwreck.com
Psychedelic, Stoner Rock, Space & Heavy Groove.

Aural Innovations SpaceRock Radio
1364 W. 7th Ave. Ste. B, Columbus, OH 43212
jkranitz@aural-innovations.com
www.aural-innovations.com/radio/radio.html
Space Rock, Psychedelia and eclectic forms of Progressive Rock.

Bohemian Radio
BohemianRadio@comcast.net
www.bohemianradio.com
An eclectic selection of Electronic music, mixed in with Sci-Fi tunes.

Cyberage Radio *KUNM*
237 Cagua NE, Albuquerque, NM 87108
PH: 505-277-5615
Tommy T tommyt@dsbp.cx
www.cyberage.cx
Electronic music and Underground sounds.

DIGITAL::NIMBUS *KUCI*
PO Box 4362, Irvine, CA 92616
Freakquency Modulator
feedback@digitalnimbus.com
digitalnimbus.com
Electronica, Post-Industrial, Electro, IDM/Ambient and all the debris in between, as well as live in-studio performances.

Dr. Demento On the Net
PO Box 884, Culver City, CA 90232
DrDemento@drDemento.com
www.drdemento.com
Mad music and crazy comedy heard on over 100 stations coast to coast. It's a free-wheeling unpredictable mix of music and comedy.

Electronic Periodic Podcast
submission@electronicperiodic.com
www.electronicperiodic.com
Mixes and live recordings of Ambient, IDM, Electro, Trance and Experimental music. Fill out our online submission form.

Esoterica *WQNA*
PO 1233, Springfield, IL 62705
PH: 217-528-8466
Ted Keylon eted@blowingthewhistle.org
www.wqna.org
Experimental, Electronica, unsigned and unusual.

Galactic Travels *WDIY*
PO Box 632, Nazareth, PA 18064-0632
Bill Fox billyfox@soundscapes.us
wdiy.org/programs/gt
An Electronic, Ambient, Progressive and Space music show. Inquire by e-mail before submitting music! I just want to make sure your music is one of the above genres.

The Greatest Show From Earth *WWUH*
Attn: Music Director
200 Bloomfield Ave.
West Hartford, CT 06117
PH: 860-768-4701 FX: 860-768-5701
Mark DeLorenzo teltanman@cox.net
www.teltan.org
Focuses on Psychedelic, Electronic and Progressive music.

Green Arrow Radio *WSUM*
5205 Kroncke Dr. Madison, WI 53711
MisterG greenarrowradio@hotmail.com
www.greenarrowradio.com
Music programmed for open minds and thirsty ear-holes!

H.A.R.M. *WRUW*
11220 Bellflower Rd. Cleveland, OH 44106
PH: 216-368-2208
DJ Fair Use md@wruw.org
wruw.org
Show your true enthusiasm for college radio and your glut for pain in all its varied forms. Tune in. I dare you!

Hollow Earth Radio
PO Box 70147. Seattle, WA 98127
PH: 206-905-1250
hollowearthradio@gmail.com
www.hollowearthradio.com
We seek out content that is raw and undiscovered such as found sound from answering machine tapes scavenged from yard sales or bedroom recordings that have never seen the light of day or old gospel records found at thrift stores or stories from everyday life from people in our neighborhood, or music from bands that mostly play house shows.

The Indie Show *WZNZ*
190 Belfort Rd. #450, Jacksonville, FL 32216
John Maycumber john@1460.us
www.1460.us
The show's emphasis is on edgier, Experimental Rock and Electronic music.

Lord Litter's Magic Music Box
Pariser Str. 63, 10719 Berlin, Germany
LordLitter@LordLitter.de
www.lordlitter.de
*I have reduced my radio show production to presenting *only extremely unique microcosm creations of all styles* - whenever I have enough releases with this *future sound seeking real quality music* I produce the next show.*

marvin suicide podcast
marvin@marvinsuicide.org
marvinsuicide.org
Do you like the smell of goats? Spend every day thinking about fun? Don't like using public toilets? Then try listening our 30 minutes of eclectic music.

Music For Nimrods *KXLU*
1 LMU Dr. Los Angeles, CA 90045
PH: 310-338-5958 FX: 310-338-5959
Reverend Dan reverenddan@hotmail.com
www.musicfornimrods.net
Looking for degenerate music of all styles.

New Dreamers *KLCC*
136 W. 8th Ave. Eugene, OR 97401
PH: 541-463-5522 FX: 541-463-6046
Chris Owen music@klcc.org
www.klcc.org
Electronic and Synthesized sounds from this world and beyond. The full spectrum of Electronic music, from Classical to Progressive Rock, Avant-garde to Space music.

No Pigeon Holes Radio Show *KKUP*
933 Monroe St., PMB 9150, Santa Clara, CA 95050
PH: 408-260-2999
Don Campau campaudj@comcast.net
www.doncampau.com
I accept all styles. However, I do give original, home recorded music precedence.

Other Music *KZUM*
941 "O" St., Lincoln, NE 68508
PH: 402-474-5086 FX: 402-474-5091
Thad, Erik, Malcom & Jeff om_kzum@yahoo.com
www.myspace.com/omkzum
We mostly delve into Experimental types of Jazz, Electronica, Rock, Spoken Word and Freeform Improvisation.

Postclassic Radio
www.live365.com/stations/kylegann
Weirdly beautiful new music from composers who've left the Classical world far behind.

Press the Button *WRUW*
11220 Bellflower Rd. Cleveland, OH 44106
PH: 216-368-2208 FX: 216-368-5414
www.wruw.org
An Experimental radio show of found sound collage.

Psych-Out *WREK*
350 Ferst Dr. NW. #2224, Atlanta, GA 30332-0630
PH: 404-894-2468 FX: 404-894-6872
music.director@wrek.org
www.wrek.org
Specializing in the best Psychedelic music from around the globe.

Pushing The Envelope *WHUS*
Student Union Rm. 412, 2110 Hillside Rd. #3008R
Storrs, CT 06268-3008
PH: 860-429-9487
Brendan Sudol whus.musicdirector@gmail.com
www.whus.org
The finest in Avant Ephemera.

Robot Sanctuary *WTJU*
PO Box 400811, Charlottesville, VA 22904-4811
PH: 434-924-0885 FX: 434-924-8996
Morgan & Matt wtju@virginia.edu
wtju.net/cpages/musub
A weekly blend of Atmospheric Rock, Experimental Beats, and Electronic music of all kinds.

Some Assembly Required
2751 Hennepin Ave. S. #145
Minneapolis, MN 55408
PH: 612-990-0460
Jon Nelson assembly@detritus.net
www.some-assembly-required.net
Please feel free to send anything which creatively recycles recognizable bits of sound from the media environment - whether it's mashed up, cut-up, turntablism or whatever - as long as it's sample based music and/or audio art, we'd be happy to listen!

Something Else *WLUW*
6525 N. Sheridan Rd. Chicago, IL 60626
PH: 773-508-9589 FX: 773-508-8082
Philip von Zweck somethingelse@wluw.org
www.wluw.org
A weekly radio program of Sound Art & New/Experimental music.

Spartacus Roosevelt Podcast
www.spartacusroosevelt.com/podcast.php
Obscure Noise, glitchy Electropop, fake nostalgia, bastardized Exotica, tweaky Lounge, creepy Ambient and musical non sequitors.

The Stone Zone Show
Big Daddy D d@thestonezoneshow.com
www.thestonezoneshow.com
Giving artists more chances to have their music aired to SMOKERS around the world!!! Send us your tunes for consideration, and come listen to the PREMIERE show for smokers!

Strange Music in Small Doses
inkxpotter.libsyn.com
Podcast featuring a three cut collision to the avant extremes of sound.

Transfigured Night *WKCR*
2920 Broadway Mailcode 2612
New York, NY 10027
PH: 212-854-9920
newmusic@wkcr.org
www.wkcr.org
An overnight exploration of Experimental music, with an emphasis on Electronic works

Weirdsville!
PO Box 936, Northampton, MA 01061
weirdo@weirdsville.com
www.weirdsville.com
We are constantly on the hunt for strange, bizarre and righteous music to blow your minds.

Canada

Adventures In Plasticland *CKWR*
19 Norfolk Ave. Cambridge, ON N1R 3T5
Spaceman Stan spacedman40@hotmail.com
www.romislokus.com/eng/stan.html
Progressive, Acid, Stoner, Psychedelic, Garage and Rock music of the 60's up to now.

ANoiZE *CITR*
#233-6138 SUB Blvd. Vancouver, BC V6T 1Z1
PH: 604-822-2487 FX: 604-822-9364
Luke Meat lukemeat@hotmail.com
www.myspace.com/lukemeat
Avant Rock, Noize, Plunderphonic, Psychedelic, and Outsider aspects of audio.

Cranial Explosions: Sounds That Blow Minds! *CJTR*
PO Box 334 Stn. Main, Regina, SK S4P 3A1
PH: 306-525-7274 FX: 306-525-9741
kcolhoun@cjtr.ca
www.cjtr.ca
Submit your impacting music to us and if it moves us, we will play it on our show!!

Do Not Touch This Amp *CFBX*
House 8, U. College of the Cariboo, 900 McGill Rd.
Kamloops, BC V2C 5N3
PH: 250-377-3988 FX: 250-372-5055
Steve Marlow dntta@yahoo.ca
www.geocities.com/dntta
An Experimental/Electronic/Industrial program that runs every Friday night.

Synaptic Sandwich *CITR*
#233-6138 SUB Blvd. Vancouver, BC V6T 1Z1
PH: 604-822-2487 FX: 604-822-9364
Dj Cyber and Ryan Fantastic
Synaptic_Sandwich@telus.net
www.citr.ca
Every show is full of electro bleeps, retrowave, computer generated, synthetically manipulated aural rhythms.

Europe

Germany

Radio Future 2
webmail@radiofuture2.de
www.radiofuture2.purespace.de
Electro, Industrial, Crossover, Darkwave…

The Netherlands

MeMbus
info@membus.nl
www.membus.nl
Podcast featuring Soundscapes, Rough Radio, Tape Distortion.

United Kingdom

BBC Radio 3 *New Music*
David Ireland david.ireland@bbc.co.uk
www.bbc.co.uk/radio3/newmusic
Home page of the BBC Radio 3's various New Music shows. Info, contacts etc.

Flat four radio
14 Torrington Park, London, N12 9SS UK
dan@flatfourradio.co.uk
www.mcld.co.uk/flatfour
We broadcast Indie Rock and Experimental music. We like to support independent-minded artists - so send us your stuff!

Freak Zone *BBC 6*
Rm. 2018, BBC Manchester, Oxford Rd.
Manchester, M60 1SJ UK
PH: 08700-100-600
Stuart Maconie stuart.6music@bbc.co.uk
www.bbc.co.uk/6music/shows/freakzone
We want to hear about all your Freak-tastic musical discoveries.

Resonance FM
144 Borough High St., London, SE1 1LB UK
PH/FX: 020-7403-1922
Ed Baxter info@resonancefm.com
www.resonancefm.com
Radio art station, brought to you by London Musicians' Collective.

Australia

Sideways Through Sound
PO Box 1330, Neutral Bay, NSW 2089 Australia
Thee Sonic Assassin
sidewaysthroughsound@hotmail.com
www.sidewaysthroughsound.com
Welcome to the realm where shadowy Folk songs and supernatural ballads join hands with the soundtrack to the new dark ages. We will chant a mantra to our psychic musical expansion, our perception bathed in the ancient haze of oblivion.

Sound Quality *ABC*
GPO Box 9994, Sydney, NSW 2001 Australia
PH: 02-8333-2051 FX: 02-8333-1381
www.abc.net.au/rn/soundquality
Host Tim Ritchie presents the interesting, the evolutionary, the inaccessible and the wonderful.

Folk Radio

North America

United States

Internet, Syndicated Shows and Podcasts

Acoustic Café
PO Box 7730, Ann Arbor, MI 48107-7730
Rob Reinhart rob@acafe.com
www.acafe.com
Rare Acoustic cuts and classic tracks with a strong commitment to indies. Heard on 60+ stations.

Acoustic Pie Radio
Kelley Martin kelley@acousticpie.com
www.acousticpie.com/Radio.htm
Devoted to Acoustic Singer/Songwriters.

Art of the Song
HC 81 Box 6033, Questa, NM 87556
PH: 575-586-1996 FX: 575-586-1778
John & Viv info@artofthesong.org
www.artofthesong.org
Syndicated show with music and interviews exploring inspiration and creativity through songwriting and other art forms.

Cleveland Celtic Podcast
itsmewendylee@yahoo.com
www.clevelandcelticpodcast.com
Featuring Celtic music from around the world.

The Folk Sampler
PO Box 520, Siloam Springs, AR 72761
Mike Flynn mike@folksampler.com
www.folksampler.com
Folk, Traditional, Bluegrass and Blues.

FolkScene
PO Box 707, Woodland Hills, CA 91365
PH: 818-883-7557
Roz & Howard folkscene@folkscene.com
www.folkscene.com
Live music, interviews and remote recordings.

GidaFOLK
multithd@hotmail.com
gida.tzo.net/RadioDB
Playing whatever sounds good.

Grassy Hill Radio
c/o Submissions Mgr.
PO Box 160, Lyme, CT 06371
ghradio@grassyhill.org
radio.grassyhill.org
Streaming lesser known/self released songs.

Highlander Radio
www.CelticRadio.net
Scottish, Irish and Celtic music.

Hober Radio
PO Box 5748, Takoma Park, MD 20913
PH: 301-270-1734
Gregor Markowitz gregor@hober.com
hober.com
*An attempt to bring human warmth to the computer
environment. Hober brings unvarnished sounds into
a glossy space.*

Internet Folk Festival
PO Box 331173, Elmwood, CT 06133-1173
feedback@internetfolkfestival.com
www.internetfolkfestival.com
Send your CDs and information to us.

Irish & Celtic Music Podcast
PH: 512-470-4866
Marc Gunn music@celticmusicpodcast.com
www.celticmusicpodcast.com
Digital submissions must be podsafe music.

Online Folk Festival
6333 Well Fleet Dr. Columbus, OH 43231
PH: 614-257-9379
Greg Grant greg@onlinefolkfestival.com
www.onlinefolkfestival.com
Freeform Folk and Folk related music.

radiowayne
PO Box 17742, Shreveport, LA 71138
Wayne Greene radiowayne@att.net
www.radiowayne.com
*An eclectic mix of Folk, Singer/Songwriter, Acoustic,
Swing and more.*

Renradio
600 Barwood Park Rd. #1623, Austin, TX 78753
Michael Harris rengeek@renradio.com
renradio.com
*The music and spirit of Renaissance and Celtic
Festivals.*

The Village / Songs to Hang on Stars *XM*
1500 Eckington Pl. NE., Washington, DC 20002
Mary Sue Twohy marysue.twohy@xmradio.com
www.xmradio.com/onxm/channelpage.xmc?ch=15
Singer/Songwriter, Acoustic and Folk music.

Whole Wheat Radio
15528 E. Birch Creek Blvd. HC89 Box 8109
Talkeetna, AK 99676
PH: 907-733-2452 FX: 907-733-2934
www.wholewheatradio.org
*We focus on independent music. Do not ask if you
can send your music – JUST SEND IT!*

Woodsongs Old-Time Radio Hour
PO Box 200, Lexington, KY 40588
Attn: Submissions
FX: 859-225-4020
radio@woodsongs.com
www.woodsongs.com/wotrh.html
*Exploring the beautiful world of Folk, Bluegrass
and Songwriting. Submit TWO CDs and a press kit
with a brief cover letter.*

Your Folk Connection *KRCU*
1 U. Plaza, Cape Girardeau, MO 63701
PH: 573-651-5070 FX: 888-651-5070
comments@yourfolkconnection.org
www.yourfolkconnection.org
Folk artists, performers and songwriters.

Alaska

Acoustic Accents
PO Box 89, Tok, AK 99780
Bud Johnson info@acousticaccents.net
www.acousticaccents.net
*In-depth interviews and songs from some of the best
performers around.*

It's All Folk *KEUL*
PO Box 29, Girdwood, AK 99587
PH: 907 754-2489
Karen Rakos keulkaren@hotmail.com
www.glaciercity.us
I play Folk, Roots, Bluegrass and Old-Time music.

Arizona

Acoustic Alternative *KXCI*
220 S. 4th Ave. Tucson, AZ 85701
PH: 520-622-5924
Betsi Meissner meissner@ccp.library.arizona.edu
www.kxci.org
*Celtic (first hour), Folk, Swing, Blues, Jazz,
Bluegrass etc.*

Arkansas

From Albion and Beyond *KUAR*
2801 S. University, Little Rock, AR 72204
PH: 501-569-8485 FX: 501-569-8488
Len Horton lholton@swbell.net
home.swbell.net/lholton/fromalbionandbeyond.html
Traditional, revival and contemporary Folk music.

California

Back Roads *KVMR*
401 Spring St., Nevada City, CA 95959
Larry Hillberg walkinglarry@yahoo.com
www.kvmr.org
*A musical journey through Folk, Acoustic, Singer-
Songwriter and more, new and old.*

Celtic Quest
6872 Panamint Row #4, San Diego, CA 92139
PH: 619-475-4484
Doug Shaw info@celticquest.info
www.celticquest.info
*Playing traditional and contemporary music from
Scotland, Ireland, other Celtic regions of the world.*

Click Your Heels Together *KVMR*
401 Spring St., Nevada City, CA 95959
PH: 530-265-9555 FX: 530-265-9077
Ruby Slippers rubyslippers@kvmr.org
www.kvmr.org
*Americana, Folk, Blues etc. with a focus on
humorous, fun and clever music...and music with a
message.*

Cool As Folk *KDVS*
14 Lower Freeborn Hall, UC, Davis, CA 95616
PH: 530-752-2777
Michael Leahy coolasfolk@hotmail.com
www.myspace.com/coolasfolk
*Folk, Bluegrass, Americana, Singer/Songwriter and
other Acoustic based music. I also welcome weekly
in-studio guests.*

Don't Get Trouble on Your Mind *KMUD*
PO Box 135, 1144 Redway Dr.
Redway, CA 95560-0135
PH: 707-923-2513 FX: 707-923-2501
Ed Denson md@kmud.org
www.kmud.org
Each show I play 25 or so Folk and Blues songs.

Don't Panic (It's Just Us Folks) *KKUP*
933 Monroe St., PMB 9150, Santa Clara, CA 95050
PH: 408-260-2999
Lisa Atkinson latkinson@rcn.com
www.kkup.com
Folk, Country, Bluegrass, Irish and Blues.

Folk Music & Beyond *KALW*
500 Mansell St., San Francisco, CA 94134
PH: 415-841-4134 FX: 415-841-4125
JoAnn & Bob kalwfolk@rahul.net
www.kalwfolk.org
Folk, traditional and original music.

Folk Roots *KSBR*
28000 Marguerite Pkwy. Mission Viejo, CA 92692
PH: 949-582-5727 FX: 949-347-9693
Marshall Andrews tomarshall@aol.com
www.ksbr.net
*A wide range of Bluegrass, Old-Time, Celtic, Gospel
and Folk.*

Friday Folk Off *KKUP*
933 Monroe St., PMB 9150, Santa Clara, CA 95050
PH: 408-260-2999
David Stafford davstaff@ix.netcom.com
www.kkup.org
*An unpredictable mix of live music, acoustic
recordings and a healthy dose of Celtic, English,
and American melodies.*

KPIG
1110 Main St. #16, Watsonville, CA 95076
PH: 831-722-9000
sty@kpig.com
www.kpig.com
*Great music and serious fun - Folk, Rock, Acoustic,
Roots, Blues.*

Heaven's Bar 'n Grill *KZSC*
1156 High St., Santa Cruz, CA 95064
PH: 831-459-5972 FX: 831-459-4734
Clytia Fuller clytia@cruzio.com
members.cruzio.com/~clytia
Showcases live guests playing in the area.

Music Along The Feather *KRBS*
PO Box 9, Oroville, CA 95965
PH: 530-534-1200
Erv krbs@cncnet.com
www.radiobirdstreet.org
*Contemporary Folk. Bluegrass, Country and new
Folk.*

New Wood *KKUP*
933 Monroe St., PMB 9150, Santa Clara, CA 95050
PH: 408-260-2999
Peter Schwarz kkup.folk@gmail.com
www.kkup.com
American, Celtic and Bluegrass. Find your roots.

Please Stand By *KPIG*
1110 Main St. #16, Watsonville, CA 95076
PH: 831-722-9000
Sleepy John sty@kpig.com
www.kpig.com
Live music on THE PIG, every Sunday morning.

The Roadtunes Sessions *KCSB*
PO Box 13401, Santa Barbara, CA 93107-3401
PH: 805-893-3757
Andrew Doerr roadtunes@cox.net
www.kcsb.org
Songs and tunes for days spent on the road and back'round the kitchen table.

Saturday Morning Folks Show *KDVS*
1 Shields Ave., U. Cal, Davis, CA 95616
PH: 530-752-2777
Bill Wagman wjwagman@ucdavis.edu
www.kdvs.org
Folk music of all kinds!

Two Penny Opera *KZFR*
PO Box 3173, Chico, CA 95927
PH: 530-895-0131 FX: 530-895-0775
Laurie Niles laurish@yahoo.com
www.kzfr.org
We weave our way through the acoustic musical world of Folk, Bluegrass, Celtic and Americana.

Wild River Radio *KMUD*
PO Box 135, 1144 Redway Dr.
Redway, CA 95560-0135
PH: 707-923-2513 FX: 707-923-2501
Kate Klein md@kmud.org
www.kmud.org
Sometimes we play independent Folk artists. Looking for songs that promote social justice.

Colorado

The Folk Show *KRFC*
619 S. College Ave. #4, Fort Collins, CO 80524
PH: 970-221-5065
Dennis Bigelow dennis@krfcfm.org
krfcfm.org
Send your music in!

Sounds from the Mother Road *KSUT*
PO Box 737, 123 Capote Dr. Ignacio, CO 81137
PH: 970-563-0255 FX: 970-563-0399
Jamie Hoover jamie_h54@msn.com
www.ksut.org
A slice of Americana.

Zesty Ranch *KSJD*
33051 Hwy 160, Mancos, CO 81328
PH: 970-564-0808 FX: 970-564-0434
Jamie Hoover jamie_h54@msn.com
www.ksjd.org
An hour of Roots music.

Connecticut

AcousticConnections *WSHU*
5151 Park Ave. Fairfield, CT 06825
PH: 203-365-0425
Walt Graham graham@wshu.org
www.wshu.org
Acoustic music, Folk, Celtic and Bluegrass.

Caterwaul *WWUH*
Attn: Music Director
200 Bloomfield Ave. West Hartford, CT 06117
PH: 860-768-4701 FX: 860-768-5701
Ed McKeon emckeon@aol.com
www.wwuh.org
The "Father" of the Folk Next Door concert series. Our most unusually progressive and eclectic Folk show.

Passenger Side Folk Show / Oh Bury Me Not *WESU*
Wesleyan Stn. 45 Wyllys Ave.
Middletown, CT 06459
PH: 860-685-7700 FX: 860-704-0608
Ken W. folkmd@wesufm.org
www.wesufm.org
I look forward to review for airplay your upcoming Folk releases.

Profiles in Folk *WSHU*
5151 Park Ave. Fairfield, CT 06825-1000
PH: 203-365-0425 FX: 203-365-0425
Steve Winters winters@wshu.org
wshu.org
Traditional and Celtic Folk with Bluegrass.

Sunday Night Folk Festival
Student Union Rm. 412, 2110 Hillside Rd. #3008R
Storrs, CT 06268-3008
PH: 860-429-9487
Susan Forbes Hansen flkczarina@aol.com
whus.org
Has held down the end-of-the-weekend spot on WHUS for over 28 years.

Florida

Acoustic Highways *WPRK*
1000 Holt Ave. Winter Park, FL 32789
PH: 407-646-2915 FX: 407-646-1560
Rich Pietrzak rapietrzak@hotmail.com
www.rollins.edu/wprk
A free-wheeling show devoted to bringing Folk music, performing songwriters and other guitar-based acoustic music to the airwaves.

Folk & Acoustic Music *WLRN*
172 NE. 15th St., Miami, FL 33132
PH: 305-995-2207 FX: 305-995-2299
Michael Stock mstock@wlrn.org
www.wlrn.org
Playing songs ignored by other stations.

Folk, Bluegrass and More *WFIT*
150 W. University Blvd. Melbourne, FL 32901-6975
PH: 321-674-8140 FX: 321-674-8139
Bill Stuart ukidnme@aol.com
www.wfit.org
Weekly Acoustic music show.

Our Kind of Folk *WSLR*
PO Box 2540, Sarasota, FL 34230
PH: 941-894-6469
Craig Huegel huegelc55@aol.com
www.wslr.org
Features a wide variety of Singer/Songwriters.

Progressive Roots *WZNZ*
190 Belfort Rd. #450, Jacksonville, FL 32216
Ken Connors kenconnors@bellsouth.net
www.1460.us
We make the effort to include a good deal of topical or political material in our mix.

The Shuffle *WFIT*
150 W. University Blvd. Melbourne, FL 32901
PH: 321-674-8140 FX: 321-674-8139
Todd Gross service@theshuffle.org
www.wfit.org
I feature a wide variety of music, but my heart is in Folk and Acoustic music.

Georgia

Fox's Minstrel Show *WRFG*
1083 Austin Ave. NE., Atlanta, GA 30307-1940
PH: 404-523-8989
Harlon Joye sheartfiel@aol.com
www.wrfg.org
A mixture of Folk, Blues, Country, some Rock and even some early Jazz.

Green Island Radio Show *WSVH*
12 Ocean Science Cir. Savannah, GA 31411
PH: 912-598-3300 FX: 912-598-3306
Harry O'Donoghue wsvhirish@earthlink.net.
www.wsvh.org/giarchive.htm
The very best Irish and Celtic music.

Illinois

Celtic Connections *WSIU*
Southern Illinois U. Carbondale, IL 62901-6602
PH: 618-453-1884
Bryan Kelso Crow bcrow@siu.edu
www.celticconnectionsradio.org
The finest selections from new releases.

Continental Drift *WNUR*
1920 Campus Dr. Evanston, IL 60208-2280
PH: 847-491-7102 FX: 847-467-2058
Allie Silver drift-producer@wnur.org
www.wnur.org/drift
Roots and Folk music of cultures around the world.

Folk Fiasco *WDBX*
224 N. Washington St., Carbondale, IL 62901
PH: 618-529-5900 FX: 618-529-5900
Randy Auxier drauxier@yahoo.com
www.wdbx.org
Weekly Singer/Songwriter show.

The Joshua Tree Inn *WEFT*
113 N. Market St., Champaign, IL 61820
PH: 217-359-9338
Kevin Elliott kelliott28@hotmail.com
www.folkplaylist.blogspot.com
The best in contemporary Folk, Country & Bluegrass and all those regions in between!

Midnight Special *WFMT*
5400 N. St. Louis, Chicago, IL 60625
PH: 773-509-1111
www.midnightspecial.org
Host Rich Warren presents Folk music with a sense of humor.

Somebody Else's Troubles *WLUW*
6525 N. Sheridan Rd. Chicago, IL 60626
PH: 773-508-9589
Tom Jackson musicdept@wluw.org
www.wluw.org
Open to all kinds of Acoustic music.

T.G.I.Folk *WDBX*
224 N. Washington St., Carbondale, IL 62901
PH: 618-457-3691 FX: 618-529-5900
Gaye Auxier tgifolk@yahoo.com
www.wdbx.org
Mainly Singer/Songwriter, mostly contemporary, independent touring musicians. Occasional live interviews.

Indiana

The Back Porch *WVPE*
2424 California Rd. Elkhart, IN 46514
PH: 888-399-9873
Norm Mast nmast@wvpe.org
www.wvpe.org/backporch.html
The best of Folk and Bluegrass.

Crossings *WGCS*
1700 S. Main St., Goshen, IN 46526
PH: 574-535-7488 FX: 574-535-7293
www.goshen.edu/wgcs
Folk music show, 10 years strong. Features live in studio performances.

Iowa

KUNI's Folk Music
U. Northern Iowa, Cedar Falls, IA 50614-0359
PH: 319-273-6400 FX: 319-273-2682
Karen Impola karen.impola@uni.edu
www.kuniradio.org/kufolk.html
Traditional and contemporary Acoustic music.

Louisiana

Hootenanny Power *WRKF*
3050 Valley Creek Dr. Baton Rouge, LA 70808
www.hootenannypower.com
Folk and Acoustic music.

Maine

Us Folk *WMPG*
96 Falmouth St., Portland, ME 04104-9300
PH: 207-780-4909
Chris ctdarlin@maine.rr.com
www.wmpg.org
Promotes independent Folk artists from around the world.

Maryland

Detour *WTMD*
Towson U. 8000 York Rd. Towson, MD 21252
Paul Hartman wtmd@towson.edu
www.detourradio.com
An eclectic blend of Folk and World music.

Just Folks *WSCL*
PO Box 2596, Salisbury, MD 21802
PH: 410-543-6895 FX: 410-548-3000
John Kalb jdkalb@salisbury.edu
www.wscl.org
Contemporary Folk music (mostly Acoustic).

Roots and Wings *WMUC*
3130 S. Campus Dining Hall,
College Park, MD 20742-8431
PH: 301-314-7868
thedigitalfolklife.org
Folk and Bluegrass.

Massachusetts

A Celtic Sojourn *WGBH*
PO Box 200, Boston, MA 02134
PH: 617-300-5400
www.wgbh.org
Traditional and contemporary music from the Celtic countries.

The Fiddle & the Harp *WOMR*
494 Commercial St., Provincetown, MA 02657
PH: 508-487-2619
Dinah Mellin dinah164@capecod.net
www.womr.org
Irish, Scottish and Canadian Maritime music.

Folk 'n Good Music Show *WMFO*
PO Box 65 Medford, MA 02155
PH: 617-625-0800
Morgan Huke morganhuke@yahoo.com
www.wmfo.org
An experience of Acoustic and Electric tunes live from our studios. Features up and coming artists.

Folk on WGBH
PO Box 200, Boston, MA 02134
PH: 617-300-5400
www.wgbh.org
New and traditional Folk music by local and national musicians.

The New Song Library
PO Box 295, Northampton, MA 01061
PH: 413-586-9485
Johanna Halbeisen JH@newsonglibrary.org
www.newsonglibrary.org
A unique song resource library that collects and preserves songs about people's lives, hopes and struggles, and helps performers, teachers and community activists share these songs with a wide variety of audiences. NSL's main purpose is to get your songs out to people who can use your music in their work and to do this in ways that support you as an artist.

The Old Songs' Home *WOMR*
PO Box 2171, Orleans, MA 02653
Bob Weiser theoldsongshome@hotmail.com
www.womr.org
I will gladly review CDs for airplay. Folk and Acoustic music, traditional and contemporary.

Sounds of Erin Radio
Box 12, Belmont, MA 02428
soundoferinradio@comcast.net
soundoferinradio.com
Features interviews, music, book reviews, sports and other items of interest for the world-wide Celtic community.

Watch City Coffeehouse *WBRS*
Shapiro Campus Ctr. 415 South St.
Waltham, MA 02453-2728
PH: 781-736-5277
Bob Weiser theoldsongshome@hotmail.com
www.wbrs.org
I will gladly review CDs for airplay. Folk and Acoustic music, traditional and contemporary.

WUMB *U. Mass Boston*
100 Morrissey Blvd. Boston, MA 02125-3393
PH: 617-287-6900 FX: 617-287-6916
wumb@umb.edu
www.wumb.org
The only full-time listener funded Folk station in the US.

Michigan

Folks Like Us *WEMU*
4600 Cass Ave. Detroit, MI 48201
PH: 313-577-1019
Matt Watroba matt@watrobanetwork.com
www.folkslikeus.org
Traditional and contemporary Folk music.

The Folk Tradition *WKAR*
283 Comm Arts Bldg. Michigan State U.
East Lansing, MI 48824-1212
PH: 517 432-9527 FX: 517-353-7124
Bob Blackman blackman@wkar.org
wkar.org/folktradition
Traditional Folk songs, Celtic tunes and more.

Old Front Porch *WXOU*
69 Oakland Ctr. Rochester, MI 48309
PH: 248-370-4274
wxoumusic@yahoo.com
www.wxou.org
Pioneering progressive Folk, holding fast to Traditional Roots. We promote and support Michigan and regional artists.

Minnesota

Folk Migrations *KUMD*
130 Humanities Bldg. 1201 Ordean Ct.
Duluth, MN 55812
PH: 218-726-7181 FX: 218-726-6571
kumd@kumd.org
www.kumd.org
If you would like your CDs considered for airplay, please send them to me at the above address.

Thirsty Boots *WTIP*
PO Box 1005, Grand Marais, MN 55604
PH: 218-387-1070 FX: 218-387-1120
info@wtip.org
wtip.org
Three hours of Folk, Americana and protest songs.

Missouri

The Acoustic Edge *KCLC*
Lindenwood U. 209 S. Kingshighway
St. Charles, MO 63301
PH: 636-949-4891
Naomi & Terry acoustic.edge@yahoo.com
www.geocities.com/nstm1/acousticedge.html
Cool tunes each Sunday.

Blue Highways/No Limit *KOPN*
915 E Broadway, Columbia, MO 65201
PH: 573-874-5676
md@kopnmusic.org
www.kopn.org
We cruise the back roads to track down great Folk, Jazz, Blues and Rock music. Please e-mail me before you send in your material.

Coffeehouse Radio Show *KKFI*
PO Box 32250, Kansas City, MO 64171
PH: 816-931-3122 x106
Jeanne Jasper kcpegasus@aol.com
www.kkfi.org
Contemporary Singer/Songwriter. Local when possible.

Family Reunion *KDHX*
3504 Magnolia, St. Louis, MO 63118
PH: 314-664-3688 FX: 314-664-1020
Judy Stein ashehi@kdhx.org
www.kdhx.org/programs/familyreunion.htm
Often featuring artists who will be performing locally.

Foolkiller Folk *KKFI*
PO Box 32250, Kansas City, MO 64171
PH: 816-931-3122 x106
Valerie Andruss mandr0328@aol.com
www.kkfi.org
Weekly Folk show with various hosts.

Sunday Morning Coffeehouse *KOPN*
1713 Rose Dr. Columbia, MO 65202-3234
PH: 573-874-5676 FX: 573-499-1662
Steve Jerrett steve@sundaymorningcoffeehouse.org
www.sundaymorningcoffeehouse.org
Traditional Folk, Bluegrass, Country, Celtic and Singer/Songwriter expressions of the ever-evolving Folk process.

Montana

The Folk Show *KUFM*
MPR, 32 Campus Dr. U. Montana
Missoula, MT 59812-8064
PH: 406-243-4931 FX: 406-243-3299
www.kufm.org
Host Beth Anne Austein presents a potpourri of Folk music from around the world.

New Hampshire

Ceili *WUNH*
MUB Durham, NH 03824
PH: 603-862-2222
Roland Goodbody goodbody@unh.edu
www.ceili.unh.edu
Features music in the living traditions of the Celtic countries and England.

The Folk Show *NHPR*
207 N. Main St., Concord, NH 03301-5003
PH: 603-228-8910 FX: 603-224-6052
Kate McNal folkshow@nhpr.org
www.nhpr.org
Traditional and contemporary Acoustic and Folk music. In-studio guests as well.

Writers in the Round *WSCA*
c/o Portsmouth Radio, PO Box 6532
Portsmouth, NH 03802
PH: 603-430-9722 FX: 430-9822
Deidre Randall talk@witrhome.org
witrhome.org
A weekly showcase of live music with two songwriters and one poet.

New Jersey

Legacy *WTSR*
2000 Pennington Rd. Ewing, NJ 08628-0718
PH: 609-771-2554
Peter Kernast wtsrlegacy1@cs.com
www.wtsr.org
Expanding the boundaries of Folk music.

Music You Can't Hear On the Radio *WPRB*
030 Bloomberg Hall, Princeton U. NJ 08544
PH: 609-258-1033 Fx: 609-258-1806
John Weingart radio@veryseldom.com
www.veryseldom.com
Features Folk music, String Band music, Bluegrass, Blues and humor.

Traditions / The Session *WFDU*
Metropolitan Campus, 1000 River Rd.
Teaneck, NJ 07666
PH: 201-692-2806 FX: 201-692-2807
Ron Olesko wfdutraditions@aol.com
www.ronolesko.blogspot.com
Sharing the unique and expansive world of Folk music. Continuing its long "tradition" of introducing new artists to its audience.

New York

A Thousand Welcomes *WFUV*
Fordham U. Bronx, NY 10458
PH: 718-817-4550 FX: 718-365-9815
www.wfuv.org/programs/athousandwelcomes.html
Celtic traditional music.

Ballads and Banjos *WJFF*
PO Box 546, Jeffersonville, NY 12748
PH: 845-482-204141
Sonja Hedlund sonja@applepondfarm.com
www.wjffradio.org
Folk and Acoustic music.

Bound for Glory *WVBR*
957 B Mitchell St., Ithaca, NY 14850
PH: 607-273-2121
Phil Shapiro bfg@wvbr.com
www.wvbr.com
Guest artists perform three half-hour sets in front of a live audience and for the pleasure of the "audio radiance" of Central New York.

Common Threads *WAER*
795 Ostrom Ave. Syracuse, NY 13244-4601
PH: 315-443-4021 FX: 315-443-2148
Larry Hoyt newfolknow@netscape.net
waer.org/threads.html
Traditional Folk and Acoustically-based music.

Dancing on the Air *WAMC*
PO Box 66600, Albany, NY 12206
PH: 800-323-9262 FX: 518-432-6974
Jay Ungar & Molly Mason mail@wamc.org
dancingontheair.com
Live musical performances. Folk, Celtic, Swing, Cajun, Old-Time Country, Bluegrass and more.

Folk Plus *WJFF*
PO Box 797, Jeffersonville, NY 12748
PH: 845-482-4141
Angela Page folkplus@wjffradio.org
www.wjffradio.org/FolkPlus
I explore the music and artists that I call FOLK.

Folk, Rock & Roots *WVKR*
Box 726, Vassar College, 124 Raymond Ave.
Poughkeepsie, NY 12604
PH: 845-437-7178 FX: 845-437-7656
Andrew Tokash aptokash@aol.com
www.FolkRockandRoots.org
Playing Folk, Alt-Country, Rock, Blues, guitar instrumentals and Roots Rock.

The Folk Show *WSLU*
St. Lawrence U. Canton, NY 13617
PH: 315-229-5356 FX: 315-229-5373
Mike Alzo folkshow@ncpr.org
www.northcountrypublicradio.org/programs/local/folk.html
Traditional and contemporary Folk music.

Hootenanny Cafe *WTBQ*
87 Ronald Reagan Blvd. Warwick, NY 10990
PH: 845-651-1110 FX: 845-986-7760
Jon Stein musicnow@frontiernet.net
www.wtbq.com
Acoustic music show.

Hudson River Sampler *WAMC*
PO Box 66600, Albany, NY 12206
PH: 800-323-9262 FX: 518-432-6974
Wanda Fischer wanda@wamc.org
www.wamc.org/prog-hudson.html
Folk, Bluegrass and Blues.

It's For Folks *WBNY*
Buffalo State College, 1300 Elmwood Ave.
Buffalo, NY 14222
PH: 716-878-5104
Kevin slatkd64@mail.buffalostate.edu
www.wbny.org
Features Folk and Acoustic Singer/Songwriters on independent and self-published labels.

Light Show *WBAI*
120 Wall St. 10th Fl. New York, NY 10005
PH: 212-209-2917 FX: 212-747-1698
Evan Ginzburg lightshow@wbai.org
www.wbai.org
Folk songs, tale of struggle, people's poetry, drama, liturgy, theology, professional wrestling — narrative forms that proclaim the values of a civilization striving to be born.

Nonesuch *WVBR*
957 Mitchell St. Ste. B, Ithaca, NY 14850
PH: 607-273-2121 FX: 607-273-4069
nonesuch@wvbr.com
wvbr.com
Music in the Folk tradition.

Sunday Street *WUSB*
Stony Brook Union 266,
Stony Brook, NY 11794-3263
PH: 631-632-6501 FX: 631-632-7182
wusb.fm
An Acoustic-oriented program on the air since 1978.

A Variety of Folk *WRUR*
PO Box 277356, Rochester, NY 14627
PH: 585-275-6400 FX: 585-256-3989
Tom Bohan rbaumler@rochester.rr.com
wrur.rochester.edu
Folk, Bluegrass, Old-Time, Singer Songwriter etc.

North Carolina

Acoustic Planet *WFSS*
1200 Murchison Rd. Fayetteville, NC 28301
PH: 910-672-1919 FX: 910-672-1964
www.wfss.org
Featuring Acoustic and Folk music.

Back Porch Music *WUNC*
120 Friday Ctr. Dr. Chapel Hill, NC 27517
PH: 919-966-5454 FX: 919-966-5955
Freddy Jenkins fjenkins@wunc.org
wunc.org/programs/backporchmusic
A wide range of Acoustic-based Folk music.

Ohio

Below the Salt *WOUB*
9 S. College St., Athens, OH 45701
PH: 740-593-1771 FX: 740-593-0240
Keith Newman belowthesalt@woub.org
woub.org/belowthesalt
An eclectic mix of Folk music.

The Dear Green Place *WYSO*
795 Livermore St., Yellow Springs, OH 45387
PH: 937-767-6420
Cindy Funk cindy@cindyfunk.com
cindyfunk.com
Top names in the world of Celtic music, as well as local acts and performers you've never heard of ...but need to meet.

Detours *WYSO*
795 Livermore St., Yellow Springs, OH 45387
PH: 937-767-6420
Norm Whitman nwhitman@msn.com
www.wyso.org/detours.html
Mainly Folk and Celtic music, but sometimes I throw in a bit from some other genre.

FolkAlley.com
1613 E. Summit St., Kent, OH 44242-0001
Linda Fahey linda@folkalley.com
www.folkalley.com
The online gateway to the world of Folk music!

Folk Music *WKSU*
PO Box 5190, Kent, OH 44242-0001
PH: 330-672-3114 FX: 330-672-4107
letters@wksu.org
www.wksu.org/folk
We air 13 hours of Folk music weekly!

Roll Away The Dew *WRUW*
11220 Bellflower Rd. Cleveland, OH 44106
Jimmie Wilson md@wruw.org
PH: 216-368-2208
www.myspace.com/cousinjimmie
Playing Folk, Country, Bluegrass and Traditional for over 25 years.

Toss the Feathers *WCBE*
540 Jack Gibbs Blvd. Columbus, OH 43215
PH: 614-821-9223 FX: 614-365-5060
www.wcbe.org
Featuring the best of Celtic and British Folk - Rock.

Visiting The Folks *WJCU*
20700 North Park Blvd.
University Heights, OH 44118
PH: 216-397-4937
Fred Dolan dolan@en.com
www.wjcu.org
Folk, Acoustic, Celtic, Classic Country, & Bluegrass vocals.

Oklahoma

Different Roads *KCSC*
100 N. University Dr. Edmond, OK 73034
Kent Anderson kentd30@sbcglobal.net
www.differentroads.org
An eclectic acoustic radio mix of Folk, Traditional, Classical, New Age and World music.

Folk Salad *KWGS*
U. Tulsa, 600 S. College Ave. Tulsa, OK 74104
PH: 918-836-4354
Richard & Scott folksalad@kwgs.org
kwgs.org/folksalad.html
Contemporary and traditional offerings in Folk.

Oregon

The Saturday Cafe *KLCC*
136 W. 8th Ave. Eugene, OR 97401
PH: 541-463-6004 FX: 541-463-6046
Frank Gosar fgosar@efn.org
www.klcc.org
Mostly Acoustic, Folk and Singer/Songwriter music.

Texas Chainsaw Acoustic Hour *KWVA*
PO Box 3157, Eugene, OR 97403
PH: 541-346-0645 FX: 541-346-0648
kwva.uoregon.edu
Voted the Tri-County area's number one radio program in a poll of people who begin drinking before 9 a.m.

Pennsylvania

In The Tradition *WDIY*
301 Broadway, Bethlehem, PA 18015
PH: 610-694-8100 FX: 610-954-9474
info@wdiy.org
www.wdiy.org
It's healthy dose of Cajun, Blues, Old-Time, Texas and New England Folk, with stops at all points in between.

Roots *WVUD*
PO Box 701, Unionville, PA 19375
PH: 302-831-2701 FX: 302-831-1399
Suzi Wollenberg rivrhors@dca.net
www.wvud.org
All kinds of Folk, for all kinds of folks.

The Saturday Light Brigade *WRCT*
PO Box 100092, Pittsburgh, PA 15233
PH: 412-761-5144 FX: 412-761-3625
slb@slbradio.com
www.slbradio.com
Acoustic music and family fun.

Transitions Radio Magazine *KBAC*
17 Alondra Rd. Santa Fe, NM 87508
Alan Hunter & Elizabeth Rose
hosts@transradio.com
www.transradio.com
Music crosses over typical industry classifications to provide a wide range of vocals and instrumentals, Acoustic and Electronic styles, from the familiar to the unique.

Rhode Island

Traditions *WRIU*
326 Memorial Union, Kingston, RI 02881
PH: 401-874-4949 FX: 401-874-4349
folk@wriu.org
www.wriu.org
The place to hear new Folk & Roots releases.

Texas

Folk Fury *KTEP*
500 W. U. Ave. #200, El Paso, TX 79968-0001
PH: 915-747-5152 FX: 915-747-5641
Dan Alloway ktep@utep.edu
www.ktep.org
Unique blends of Bluegrass, Blues, Western Swing, Progressive Country and of course, Folk music.

Folkways *KUT*
1 University Stn. A0704, Austin, TX 78712
PH: 512-471-2345 FX: 512-471-3700
Ed Miller edmiller@io.com
www.kut.org
Six hours of assorted Folk music.

Some Call it Folk *KEDT*
4455 S. Padre Island Dr. #38
Corpus Christi, TX 78411-4481
PH: 361-855-2213 FX: 361-855-3877
Pam Stakes prstakes@aol.com
www.kedt.org/fm/pamstakesbio.htm
Featuring today's Singer/Songwriters and yesterday's Folk legends.

Utah

Fresh Folk *UPR*
8505 Old Main Hill, Utah State U.
Logan, UT 84322-8505
Blair Larsen blair_larsen@yahoo.com
www.upr.org/folk.html
Folk, Blues, Bluegrass and Celtic new releases.

Saturday Sagebrush Serenade *KRCL*
1971 W. N. Temple, Salt Lake City, UT 84116
PH: 801-359-9191 FX: 801-533-9136
Dave davesa@krcl.org
www.krcl.org/programs/satsage.htm
Folk and Acoustic Rock to ease you from your morning cup of coffee through your Sunday afternoon.

Sunday Sagebrush Serenade *KRCL*
1971 W. North Temple, Salt Lake City, UT 84116
PH: 801-359-9191 FX: 801-533-9136
Phil phill@krcl.org
www.krcl.org/programs/sunsage.htm
Folk and Acoustic Rock every Sunday.

Thursday Breakfast Jam *KRLC*
1752 S. 600 E., Salt Lake City, UT 84105
PH: 801-359-9191 FX: 801-533-9136
Dave M. davem@krcl.org
www.krcl.org
Folk, Jazz, world, eclectic mix.

Vermont

All the Traditions *Vermont Public Radio*
20 Troy Ave. Colchester, VT 05446
PH: 802-655-9451 FX: 802-655-2799
Robert Resnik rresnik@vpr.net
www.vpr.net
Features Folk, Country, Old-Time etc.

The Folk Show *WWPV*
St. Michael's College, Box 274,
Winooski Park, Colchester, VT 05439
PH: 802-654-2334 FX: 802-654-2336
John Sheehey wwpv@smcvt.edu
personalweb.smcvt.edu/wwpv
Contemporary Folk, Celtic, Blues and more.

Virginia

Out O' the Blue Radio Revue *WCVE*
PO Box 1117, Mechanicsville, VA 23111-6117
PH: 804-559-8855 FX: 804-559-0516
Page Wilson page@pagewilson.com
www.ideastations.org/radio
Folk, Blues, Bluegrass, Country, Cajun/Zydeco, Rock n' Roll, Irish and more.

Sunset Road *WTJU*
PO Box 400811, Charlottesville, VA 22901-4811
Terry Carpenter etc56@aol.com
wtju.net/cpages/musub
Folk show featuring local, regional, national and international artists. Also, what's happening at local and regional venues, new releases, interviews, featured artists and more.

Walk Right In *WTJU*
PO Box 400811, Charlottesville, VA 22904-4811
PH: 434-924-0885 FX: 434-924-8996
Rebecca wtju@virginia.edu
wtju.net/cpages/musub
Plenty of acoustic staples: Folk, Old-Time, Country Blues and Bluegrass.

Washington

Inland Folk *KWSU*
PO Box 3, Pullman, WA 99163-003
PH: 509-332-5047
Dan Maher dmaher@wsu.edu
www.kpbx.org/programs/inlandfolk.htm
Music of local and national Folk artists.

Lunch With Folks *KBCS*
3000 Landerholm Cir. SE,
Bellevue, WA 98007-6484
PH: 425-564-2424
John Sincock john.sincock@verizon.net
kbcs.fm
Every weekday a different host features 3 hours of flavorful Folk music.

Our Saturday Tradition *KBCS*
3000 Landerholm Cir. SE,
Bellevue, WA 98007-6484
PH: 425-564-2424
Hal Durden asubdude@att.net
kbcs.fm
Traditional Folk music including Bluegrass, Old-Time, British and American contemporary.

Sunday Brunch *KMTT*
1100 Olive Way #1650, Seattle, WA 98101
PH: 206-233-1037 FX: 206-233-8978
Drew Dundon studio@1037themountain.com
www.kmtt.com
Selections from the lighter side of the music library.

Washington DC

Traditions *WETA*
2775 S. Quincy St., Arlington, VA 22206
PH: 703-998-2600 FX: 703-998-3401
Mary Cliff traditions@weta.com
www.marycliff.net
*A mix of traditional, revival, Singer/Songwriter,
Ethnic and World music.*

Wisconsin

Acoustic Revival *WWSP*
105 CAC UWSP Reserve St.
Stevens Point, WI 54481
PH: 715-346-4029 FX: 715-346-4012
Granddad granddad90fm@hotmail.com
www.uwsp.edu/stuorg/wwsp
*The best selections of Acoustic music in Central
Wisconsin.*

Diaspora *WORT*
118 S. Bedford St., Madison, WI 53704
PH: 608-256-2695 FX: 608-256-3704
Terry O'Laughlin diaspora@terryo.org
diaspora.terryo.org
Folk and World music.

Folkways *WOJB*
13386 W. Trepania Rd. Hayward, WI 54843
PH: 715-634-2100 FX: 715-634-4070
Mark Pedersen pedersen@chibardun.net
www.wojb.org
*From American Roots music to contemporary
Singer/Songwriters.*

Northwoods Cafe *WXPR*
303 W. Prospect Ave. Rhinelander, WI 54501
PH: 715-362-6000 FX: 715-362-6007
Marcia Barkus wxpr@wxpr.org
www.wxpr.org
Folk, Roots, World, Blues, Cajun, Zydeco…

Simply Folk *Wisconsin Public Radio*
821 University Ave. Madison, WI 53706
PH: 800-747-7444
Tom Martin-Erickson martin-erickson@wpr.org
www.wpr.org/simplyfolk
Bringing you concerts recorded here in Wisconsin.

Wyoming

Morning Music With Don Woods *WPR*
U. Wyoming, Dept: 3984 1000 E. U.
Laramie, WY 82071
PH: 307-766-4240 FX: 307-766-6184
Don Woods dwoods@uwyo.edu
uwadmnweb.uwyo.edu/wpr/mm
Daily 3 hour show.

US Virgin Islands

The Doug Lewis Show *WVGN*
PO Box 6786, St. Thomas, VI 00804-6786
PH: 340-777-6035
Doug Dick cddick@viaccess.net
www.wvgn.org
Blues, Folk, Classic Rock n' Roll and Country.

Canada

Acoustic Roots *CHUO*
65 University Pvt. #0038, Ottawa, ON K1N 9A5
PH: 613-729-1106
JC Bouchard ljbouchard@rogers.com
www.chuo.fm
*We play acoustic guitar-focused Singer/Songwriters,
traditional music from Celtic to Americana, Acoustic
Blues, Old-Timey music, World music - on occasion,
Newgrass, Bluegrass, (some) Country.*

Acoustic Routes *CKLN*
168 Combe Ave. Toronto, ON M3H 4K3
PH: 416-979-5251 FX: 416-595-0226
Joel Wortzman jwortzman@sympatico.ca
www.ckln.fm
Contemporary Acoustic Singer/Songwriter.

Before the Deluge *CJSR*
0-09 Students' Union Bldg. Edmonton, AB T6G 2J7
PH: 780-492-2577 x232 FX: 780-492-3121
Sandy Stift & Richard Thornley
before.the.deluge@gmail.com
before-the-deluge.blogspot.com
*Traditional music from around the world:
Quebecois, Celtic, Klezmer, Bluegrass,
Scandinavian, African and lots more.*

The Celtic Show *CKUA*
10526 Jasper Ave. Edmonton, AB T5J 1Z7
PH: 780-428-7595 FX: 780-428-7624
Andy Donnelly andy.donnelly@ckua.org
www.ckua.com
Traditional ballads to hard-driving Rock tunes.

Folk Roots/Folk Branches *CKUT*
235 Metcalfe Ave. #402, Westmount, QC H3Z 2H8
PH: 514-398-4616 FX: 514-398-8261
Mike Regenstreif mike@ckutfolk.com
www.ckutfolk.com
Broadly-defined Folk-oriented program.

Folk Routes *CKUA*
10526 Jasper Ave. Edmonton, AB T5J 1Z7
PH: 780-428-7595 FX: 780-428-7624
Tom Coxworth tom.coxworth@ckua.org
www.ckua.org
Tracing Folk music from around the world.

For the Folk *CHRW*
Rm. 250, UCC, UWO, London, ON N6A 3K7
PH: 519-661-3600 FX: 519-661-3372
chrwradio.com
*Host Allison Brown plays Folk, Roots, Traditional,
Celtic and Singer/Songwriter.*

Freewheeling Folk Show *CFMU*
16 Penlake Ct. Hamilton, ON L9C 5Y7
Jim Marino jlmarino@mountaincable.net
cfmu.mcmaster.ca
*Folk and Celtic music with a touch of Bluegrass and
an emphasis on local talent.*

Galaxie Folk/Roots Channel *Galaxie Network*
93 Fieldrow St., Nepean, ON K2G 2Y8
Roch Parisien roch@rocon.ca
www.galaxie.ca
*Please send submissions for broadcast
consideration to the above address.*

The Gaelic Hour *CHIN*
Austin austin@thegaelichour.ca
www.thegaelichour.ca
*Our Monday show has a magazine format while the
Tuesday show presents a varied selection of music,
particularly Irish music.*

Jigs and Reels *CKWR*
6-130 Columbia St. W., Waterloo, ON N2L 3K9
PH: 519-886-9870 FX: 519-886-0090
Dean Clarke general@ckwr.com
www.ckwr.com
East Coast style music show.

Prairie Ceilidh *CKJS*
96 Erlandson Dr. Winnipeg, MB R3K 0G8
Lyle Skinner pceilidh@shaw.ca
members.shaw.ca/pceilidh
Traditional and contemporary Celtic music.

Regina's Mighty Shores *CJTR*
PO Box 334, Stn. Main, Regina, SK S4P 3A1
Roman & Brenda Tacik mightyshores@hotmail.com
regie2.phys.uregina.ca
Featuring Folk, Roots, Celtic, Bluegrass etc.

Roots and Wings *CBC*
PO Box 500, Stn. A, Toronto, ON M5W 1E6
PH: 416-205-3700 FX: 416-205-6040
www.cbc.ca/rootsandwings
*Hosted by Philly Markowitz. Send in any and all
music.*

Roots & Writers *UMFM*
153 Emerson Ave. Winnipeg, MB R2G 1E8
Len Osland lennytunes@shaw.ca
www.umfm.com
*A weekly cocktail of Roots/ Blues/ Country &
rockin' Folk tunes served up by artists you may
never have heard of before.*

The Saturday Edge *CITR*
#233-6138 SUB Blvd. Vancouver, BC V6T 1Z1
PH: 604-822-2487
Steve Edge steveedgeonfolk@telus.net
www.citr.ca
*Send me a link with samples I can check it out. If I
like what I hear I'll request a copy of your CD.*

Steel Belted Radio
126 Meadow Lake Dr. Winnipeg, MB R2C 4K3
PH: 204-224-1663
steelbeltedradio@shaw.ca
www.steelbeltedradio.com
*Specializing in Roots, Country and all the down and
dirty stuff those wimps at other radio stations won't
play!*

Sunday Coffee House *CJLX*
PO Box 4200, Belleville, ON K8N 5B9
PH: 613-966-2559 FX: 613-966-1993
Greg Schatzmann sundaycoffeehouse@yahoo.ca
www.91x.fm
Folk/Acoustic/Celtic/Roots music & beyond.

Tell the Band to Go Home
A-136 Spence St., Winnipeg, MB R3C 1Y3
Jeff Robson bandgohome@shaw.ca
www.tellthebandtogohome.com
*Weekly Singer/Songwriter radio show. I also review
CDs and write music articles for local publications.*

Waxies Dargle *UMFM*
Rm. 308 U. Ctr. Winnipeg, MB R3T 2N2
PH: 204-474-7027 FX: 204-269-1299
Lyle Skinner waxies@shaw.ca
www.umfm.com
*Traditional and Contemporary Celtic-edged
Folk/Pop/Rock music from near and afar.*

Window of Opportunity *CKCU*
61 Highmont Ct. Kanata, ON K2T 1B2
Laurie-Ann Copple lcopple@ncf.ca
www.ncf.ca/~eh202/window.html
*We support up-and-coming Folk, Blues and Jazz
artists. Bluegrass, Celtic and World artists are often
featured as well.*

Europe

Belgium

Psyche van het Folk
PO Box 28, 2570 Duffel, Belgium
PH: 0472-769207
Gerald Van Waes
psychevanhetfolk@radiocentraal.be
psychevanhetfolk.homestead.com
World progressive music, Acoustic crossovers, Acid Folk …

Germany

Keine Heimat *Radio Dreyeckland*
Lehener Str. 31, 79098 Freiburg, Germany
PH: 49-761-35329 FX: 49-761-35329
Christian Rath info@keine-heimat.de
www.keine-heimat.de
Euro-Folk show.

Radio ISW
Mozartstraße 3a, 84508 Burgkirchen/Alz, Germany
PH: 08679-9827-0 FX: 08679-9827-30
info@inn-salzach-welle.de
www.inn-salzach-welle.de
Folk & Country music.

Radio ZuSa
Scharnhorststr. 1, 21335 Lueneburg, Germany
Juergen Kramer j.kramer@zusa.de
www.zusa.de
Folk, Acoustic and Traditional music from around the world.

Italy

"Highway 61" and "Un Mondo Di Musica"
PO Box 12, 15040 San Michele, Alessandria, Italy
PH: 39-131-225791 FX: 39-131-225791
Massimo Ferro info@highway61.it
www.highway61.it
Highway 61 plays Folk, Country, Bluegrass, Blues, Roots Rock, Americana, Alt-Country etc. Un Mondo Di Musica deals with every form of Folk, Roots & World music.

The Netherlands

Crossroads Radio *BRTO*
Smitsstraat 13, 4623 XP Bergen op Zoom,
The Netherlands
Jos van den Boom crossroadsradio@home.nl
www.crossroadsradio.nl
Roots and Singer/Songwriter music. Once a month musicians from all over the world are invited to record an acoustic session in front of an audience of about 50 people.

United Kingdom

BBC Radio 2 *Folk and Acoustic*
www.bbc.co.uk/radio2/r2music/folk
Home page of the BBC Radio 2's various Folk and Acoustic shows. Info, shows, contacts etc.

BBC Radio 2 *Folk and Country*
www.bbc.co.uk/radio2/r2music/folkandcountry
Home page of the BBC Radio 2's various Folk and Country shows. Info, shows, contacts etc.

The Late Session *RTÉ*
PH: 01-2082040 FX: 01-2083092
Áine Hensey brownep@rte.ie
www.rte.ie/radio1/thelatesession
Irish traditional and Folk music.

The Miller Tells Her Tale
Karen karen@themillertellshertale.co.uk
www.themillertellshertale.co.uk
Singer/Songwriter, Alt-Country, Americana, Contemporary Folk, Power Pop and some Blues. PLEASE e-mail me before you send any music!

Roots Around the World *Spirit FM*
The Barn, Fordwater Ln. Chichester, W. Sussex,
PO19 6PT UK
PH: 01243-774641 FX: 01243-789787
rootsaroundtheworld@btopenworld.com
rootsaroundtheworld.info
The best in Folk, Blues, World and Country music, including the latest gig news, exclusive airplays and interviews.

Australia

A Dog's Breakfast
Glenn Morrow glen@saturdaybreakfast.com
saturdaybreakfast.com
Playing a mixture of Blues, Folk, Roots, Country and World music.

Acoustic Soup *2AIR*
PO Box 1809, Coffs Harbour, NSW 2450 Australia
PH: 0411-603-913
Laura Summerfield laura.summerfield@gmail.com
Features Folk, Acoustic and Roots music.

Come All Ye *2MCE*
Panorama Ave. Bathurst, NSW 2795 Australia
PH: 02-6338-4790 FX: 02-6338-4402
Bruce Cameron cameron@ix.net.au
www.2mce.org
The longest running Folk program on Australian radio. Preview CDs are welcomed.

Danny Watson's Folk Show *2MAX*
191 Teston Ln. Maules Creek, NSW 2382 Australia
PH: (02) 6792-4884 FX: (02) 6792-4582
Danny dannywatson2000@hotmail.com
www.2maxfm.com.au
Features traditional and contemporary Folk music & Folk Song.

Folk on Sunday *ArtSound FM*
PO Box 365, Jamison, ACT 2614 Australia
Graham McDonald
Graham.McDonald@nfsa.afc.gov.au
www.artsound.com.au
The focus of this program is on traditional music in all its forms.

The Folk Show *5UV*
228 N. Terrace, Adelaide, SA 5000 Australia
PH: 61-8-8303-5000 FX: 61-8-8303-4374
Julie Cavanagh yarrahpark@bigpond.com
radio.adelaide.edu.au
For the last 30 years presenting the best of Anglo-Celtic, Australian and Contemporary Folk music to entertain you.

Folk till Midnight / Good Morning Folk *5EB*
10 Byron Pl. Adelaide, SA 5000 Australia
FX: 8231-1456
Henk de Weerd hdeweerd@hotkey.net.au
www.5ebi.com.au
Please send in your promotional CDs.

On the Right Track *KLFM*
PO Box 2997, Bendigo, VIC 3554 Australia
Phil Knipe phillipknipe@aapt.net.au
www.klfm.com.au
Featuring a selection of the best Roots Rock, C&W, Blues, Folk, Gospel and more.

Patchwork *ArtSound FM*
PO Box 3573, Manuka, Canberra,
ACT 2603 Australia
PH: 612-6295-8444 FX: 612-6295-8499
onair@artsoundfm.asn.au
www.artsound.com.au
Folk music from near and far.

Worlds of Trad
Fred Fredlive365@aol.com
www.live365.com/stations/oneworldmusic
Folk, Ethnic, World, Roots, Blues, Old Time Country and even early Jazz!

New Zealand

Folk on Sunday
1214 Louie St., Hastings, New Zealand 4201
PH: 64-6-8785395
Mitch and Robyn Park mfpark@xtra.co.nz
www.radiokidnappers.org.nz
Ballads, Shanties, Blues, Gospel, Bluegrass etc.

GLBT Radio

After Hours *KPFT*
400 Westmoreland #2, Houston, TX 77006
PH: 713-526-5738 FX: 713-526-5750
www.kpft.org
Queer weekly variety show, generally 6-8 GLBT songs per show.

Amazon Country *WXPN*
3025 Walnut St., Philadelphia, PA 19104
PH: 215-898-6677. FX: 215-898-0707
Debra D'Alessandro amazon@xpn.org
www.xpn.org
One of the longest-running gay and lesbian/feminist radio shows in America.

Bear Radio Network
136D Clintwood Ct. Rochester, NY 14620-3551
Joe Maulucci Poetbear@BearRadio.net
www.BearRadio.Net
We're looking for submissions from artists in the GLBT community and those musicians who are gay friendly.

Dykes on Mics *3CR*
PO Box 1277, Collingwood, Melbourne,
VIC 3065 Australia
PH: 03-9419-8377 FX: 03-9417-4472
dykes_on_mics@yahoo.com
www.myspace.com/dykesonmics
News, music, interviews and community announcements from the perspective of women who love women.

Dykes On Mykes *4ZZZ*
PO Box 509, Fortitude Valley, QLD 4006 Australia
dykesonmykes@hotmail.com
www.queerradio.org/dykesonmykes.html
100% women-presented and women-focused.

Dykes on Mykes *CKUT*
3647 U. St., Montreal, QC H3A 2B3
PH: 514-398-4616 FX: 514-398-8261
music@ckut.ca
www.ckut.ca
Dyke radio for everyone. Even Barbie listens.

Face the Music *WCUW*
910 Main St., Worcester, MA 01610
PH: 508-753-1012
www.wcuw.com
Syndicated lesbian/feminist music program.

Fresh Fruit *KFAI*
1808 Riverside Ave. Minneapolis, MN 55454
PH: 612-341-0980 FX: 612-341-4281
Leigh Combs peaceluv@bitstream.net
www.kfai.org
Interviews with activists, authors and musicians from all over the country. It offers recorded music, live music, news and more.

Gay Spirit *WWUH*
200 Bloomfield Ave. West Hartford, CT 06117
PH: 860-768-4701 FX: 860-768-5701
wwuh@hartford.edu
www.wwuh.org
Greater Hartford's only gay news program featuring contemporary issues, music and special guests.

GaydarRadio.com
PH: +44-700-4429-327
stationmanager@gaydarradio.com
www.gaydarradio.com
Featuring great music and interviews.

Generation Q *WRSU*
126 College Ave. New Brunswick, NJ 08901
PH: 732-932-8800 FX: 732-932-1768
music@wrsu.org
wrsu.rutgers.edu
Out music, interviews & conversation. On the air for over 25 years!

Highest Common Denominator *WRSU*
126 College Ave. New Brunswick, NJ 08901
PH: 732-932-8800 FX: 732-932-1768
Bill Stella realman@att.net
wrsu.rutgers.edu
Champions great under appreciated musicians. Gay/Queer/Out music + political & passionate songs.

Homo Radio *WRPI*
51 Park Ave. Albany, NY 12202-1722
PH: 518-276-6248
Sean McLaughlin HomoRadio@yahoo.com
www.myspace.com/homoradio
Mix of talk and music by GLBT artists of all genres.

Homophobic *PlanetOut Radio*
PO Box 500, San Francisco, CA 94104-0500
PH: 415-834-6500 FX: 415-834-6502
www.planetout.com/pno/radio
A music show bringing you interesting, hip and relevant artists from the past, present and future.

IMRU Radio *KPFK*
11333 Moorpark St. PMB 456
Studio City, CA 91602
imru@kpfk.org
www.imru.org
Focusing on issues affecting the GLBT community in SoCal. We welcome CD submissions from all "out" LGBT artists. We do CD reviews as well.

Lesbian Radio
PO Box 13-0021, Christchurch, New Zealand
info@lesbianradio.org.nz
www.lesbianradio.org.nz
A weekly half-hour magazine that is primarily focused on lesbians and queer women. Usually 3 songs per show but every few weeks a whole show is dedicated to new and old music.

Out, Loud, & Queer *WJFF*
4765 State Rt. 52, PO Box 546
Jeffersonville, NY 12748
PH: 845-482-4141 FX: 845-482-9533
Kathy Rieser kathy@trashq.com
www.wjffradio.org
Showcasing local talent and issues whenever possible.

PrideNation
pridenation.com/radio.htm
24 hour Dance music with Trance, House, Techno and more.

Queer Corps *CKUT*
3647 U. St., Montreal, QC H3A 2B3
PH: 514-398-4616 FX: 514-398-8261
music@ckut.ca
www.ckut.ca

Queer FM *CITR*
#233-6138 SUB Blvd. Vancouver, BC V6T 1Z1
PH: 604-822-2487 FX: 604-822-9364
Heather Kitching queerfmradio@gmail.com
www.geocities.com/iwantmyqueerfm
Combines in depth analysis of GLBT current events with human interest stories, arts coverage and great music by artists of all sexual orientations.

Queer Radio *4ZZZ*
82 Main Ave. Wavell Heights, QLD 4012 Australia
PH: +61-7-3350-1562
John Frame jvframe@ozemail.com.au
www.queerradio.org
Support, talk, music and news for GLBT.

Queer Voices *KPFT*
PO Box 66075, Houston, TX 77266-6075
PH: 713-526-5738 FX: 713-529-6929
JD Doyle jack@queervoices.org
www.queervoices.org
It's a public affairs show but that doesn't stop me from slipping in a number of new songs each week.

Queer Waves *KOOP*
2819 Foster Ln. F122, Austin, TX 78757
PH: 512-472-1369 FX: 512-472-6149
Taylor Cage cagetaylor@aol.com
www.koop.org
A weekly showcase for GLBT and just plain queer musicians.

Q'zine *WXPN*
3025 Walnut St., Philadelphia, PA 19104
PH: 215-898-6677. FX: 215-898-0707
Robert Drake qzine@xpn.org
www.xpn.org
Celebrates queer arts and culture with a mix of interviews, commentary and music from out artists worldwide.

Rainbow World Radio
Len len@stonewallsociety.net
www.rainbowworldradio.com
Promoting GLBT artists, GLBT music and the GLBT community with music choices and interviews!

SIRIUS OutQ
1221 Ave. of the Americas, New York, NY 10020
PH: 212-584-5334 FX: 212-584-5200
www.sirius.com/outq
America's only 24/7 radio station for the gay, lesbian, bisexual and transgender community. Provocative, entertaining-even titillating! Plus news, interviews and music from GLBT recording artists.

Think Pink *WLUW*
6525 N. Sheridan Rd. Chicago, IL 60626
PH: 773-508-9589 FX: 773-508-8082
Erik & Ali thinkpink@wluw.org
www.wluw.org
Focuses on music made by the GLBT community but will also include music with queer themes and music targeting the queer audience.

This Way Out
PO Box 38327, Los Angeles, CA 90038-0327
PH: 818-986-4106
Greg Gordon tworadio@aol.com
www.thiswayout.org
Internationally syndicated news magazine. Plays music between segments. Particularly interested in "out" songs that are relevant to current events.

Tranny Wreck
trannywreck@gmail.com
www.trannywreck.com
I do occasional comedy skits, interviews and play a good dose of podsafe music.

Windy City Queercast *WCKG*
5443 N. Broadway, Chicago, IL 60640
PH: 773-871-7610 FX: 773-871-7609
Peter Mavrik & Amy Matheny
noise@radiopeter.com
www.radiopeter.com
A fun program that allows for a new and creative outlet to cover the GLBT community.

Goth Radio

North America

United States

A Feast Of Friends *KTUH*
Hemenway Hall #203, 2445 Campus Rd.
Honolulu, HI 96822
PH: 808-956-7261 FX: 808-956-5271
www.myspace.com/djnocturna
Features Gothic, Industrial, Ethereal, Darkwave, Death Rock and Dark Narrative Rock music. The music is dark and we de our best to keep it there.

A Place In The Dirt
DJ Silvermyth rockstar.ate.my.hamster@gmail.com
www.a-place-in-the-dirt.com
I play Industrial, Gothic, Metal and all the other stuff you didn't know you had forgotten.

Bats in the Belfry *WMBR*
3 Ames St., Cambridge, MA 02142
PH: 617-253-8810
Mistress Laura bats@wmbr.org
www.myspace.com/bats_in_the_belfry
Moody, dark and atmospheric – beginning with ancient music and chant, to the newest Gothic Rock, Darkwave, Goth-Industrial and Dark-Ambient.

The Black Cauldron *KUCI*
PO Box 4362 Irvine, CA 92616
PH: 949-824-6868
Dr. Raven morven@byz.org
www.kuci.org/~mbrown/cauldron.html
Goth, Industrial, Pagan, Ethereal, Electronica and Darkwave.

Closed Caskets for the Living Impaired *KUCI*
PO Box 4362 Irvine, CA 92616
PH: 949-824-5824
Dach dach@kuci.org
www.closedcaskets.com
The most popular Goth radio show of all time.

Dark Horizons *WMNF*
6006 N. Branch Ave. Tampa, FL 33604
PH: 813-238-9663
dj@darkhorizonsradio.com
www.darkhorizonsradio.com
Ethereal, Gothic, Industrial and Synthpop bands.

Dark Nation Radio *Live365.com*
DJ Cypher cypher@bound.org
www.live365.com/stations/cypheractive
Features a mix of Gothic, Industrial, Deathrock and Ambient.

Darkfield Imagery *WRUW*
Box #30, 11220 Bellflower Rd.
Cleveland, OH 44106
PH: 216-368-2208
DJ E.C. & the Mystery Dancer
baldwin-c@ sbcglobal.net
www.myspace.com/darkfieldimagery
Featuring Alternative, Electronic, Synthpop and Industrial-Dance!

Digital Gunfire
shirow@digitalgunfire.com
www.digitalgunfire.com
Industrial, EBM and Electronic. Please submit our online release form with your music.

EBM-Radio.com
www.ebm-radio.com
The best Industrial, EBM, Futurepop, Synthpop, Darkwave, Goth and Dark Electronic.

Factory 911 *WEGL*
116 Foy Union Bldg. Auburn U., AL 36849-5231
PH: 334-844-4113 FX: 334-844-4118
wegl.auburn.edu
An Industrial and Electronic show.

Goth Metal Radio
www.gothmetal.net
20,000 listeners per day. When did your band last get a chance to play for an audience like this?

Gothic Paradise Radio
info@gothicparadise.com
www.Gothicparadise.com
Gothic, Industrial, Darkwave, EBM, Ethereal and Synthpop.

In Perpetual Motion Radio
314 Kensington Ave. Ferndale, MI 48220-2359
G. R. Perye III ipm@ipmradio.com
www.ipmradio.com
Indie artists of the Gothic, Industrial and Electronic genres.

Industrial Radio
industrialradio.org
Podcast featuring the very best Industrial music, news and interviews.

Lance and Graal Podcast
info@lanceandgraal.com
www.lanceandgraal.com
Pagan talk radio with attitude! Has yearly music awards show.

Malice Radio
PO Box 6685, Harrisburg, PA 17112-6685
PH: 717-798-8413
reverendmalice@gmail.com
www.maliceradio.com
Darkwave has a voice!

Murphy's Magic Mess *KZUM*
941 "O" St., Lincoln, NE 68508
PH: 402-474-5086 FX: 402-474-5091
Murph sidri.geo@yahoo.com
www.geocities.com/Athens/Parthenon/5412/mess.html
A pagan radio show with music, interviews and fun stuff.

Radio Free Satan
tiberia_nine@yahoo.com
www.radiofreesatan.com
Corrupting the minds of the youth since 2000.

Radio Satan 666
www.radiosatan666.com
Various shows including Goth, Metal etc.

Regen Podcast
PO Box 14162, San Francisco, CA 94114-0162
PH: 415-420-8247
submissions@regenmag.com
www.regenmag.com
Playing the best in IDM, Industrial, Goth and Darkwave.

Second Shifters
Atnevon atnevon@secondshifters.com
www.secondshifters.com
We seek out music that appeals to the darker side of us.

Seismic Radio
Teri teri@comcast.net
www.seismicradio.com
Have your band featured/interviewed.

sursumcorda Radio
5115 Excelsior Blvd. #235, Minneapolis, MN 55416
FX: 612-677-3272
www.sursumcorda.com
New directions in Electronic organic groove.

This is Corrosion
4317 Harlem Rd. Amherst, NY 14226
legion@thisiscorrosion.com
www.thisiscorrosion.com
Please send only CDs.

Canada

The Electric Front
djlee@theelectricfront.com
www.theelectricfront.com
Industrial, Electronic, Synth, Goth and Dark-Rock songs.

Real Synthetic Audio
2515 Bathurst St. #B01, Toronto, ON M6B 2Z1
Todd Clayton todd@synthetic.org
www.synthetic.org
The most listened to Industrial net-radio show.

Rue Morgue Radio
2926 Dundas St. W., Toronto, ON M6P 1V8
Tomb Dragonmir tomb@ruemorgueradio.com
www.ruemorgueradio.com
Sounds of Horror.

What The...? CHUO
65 University Pvt. #0038, Ottawa, ON K1N 9A5
PH: 613-562-5800 x2720 FX: 613-562-5969
The Thorn what-the@email.com
www.myspace.com/the_thorn
The purpose of the show is to expose listeners to artists or material they wouldn't otherwise discover.

Europe

Belgium

Darker than the Bat
ZRO, Pierets-De Colvenaerplein 7a, 9060 Zelzate, Belgium
PH: 32-0-9-345-54-55 FX: 32-0-9-342-99-38
DJ Peter-Jan pj.vandamme@scarlet.be
www.proservcenter.be/darkerthanthebat/radio.html
Featuring Gothic, Industrial, Electro, EBM ...

Kagan *Radio Scorpio*
Geerdegemstraat 23, 2800 Mechelen, Belgium
PH: +32 (0)15-424363
Wim Troost radio@kagankalender.com
www.kagankalender.com
Wave, Gothic, Electro, Industrial. Each promo is assured a review and airplay.

France

Coquille Felee Radio
coquille-felee.net
Goth, Industrial and Electronica music.

Meiose
Meiose RCT, BP 2001 69603 Villeurbanne, France
PH: 04-78-94-37-37
kb69@free.fr
meiose.free.fr
Industriel, Gothique, Expérimental, Electro Dark, Dark Folk and Médiéval.

Germany

Black Channel Radio Show
An der Lehmgrube 4, D-79312 Emmendingen, Germany
PH: 49-160-8532545 FX: 49-7641-9373-13
Tobias Kuechen info@blackchannel.org
www.blackchannel.org
Wave, Gothic, Industrial, Dark Techno, Electro, Ritual etc.

(((EBM Radio)))
Fritz-Reuter-Str. 69, 18057 Rostock, Germany
www.ebm-radio.de
Strange music 4 strange people.

Radio Morituri
Wiesenstr. 17, D-47169 Duisburg, Germany
PH: +49-(0)176-21242202
Madrego madrego@radio-morituri.de
radio-morituri.de
Featuring Goth and Industrial music.

Ultra Dark Radio
Lievelingsweg 129, D-53119 Bonn, Germany
PH: 0178-378-29-03
www.ultradarkradio.com
Dark, Elektro, New Wave, Darkwave, Industrial ...

Italy

Chain the Door Radio Show
c/o Ferruccio Milanesi, Via G. Jannelli 45/D, 80131 Napoli, Italy
www.chaindlk.com
Promote your music through our show. Please check our submission guidelines.

Radio Blackout
Via Cecchi 21-A 10100 Torino, Italy
PH: 0112495669
blackout@ecn.org
www.radioblackout.org
L'unica Radio libera In piemonte. Sostieni la frequenza libera!

United Kingdom

DARKLIFE Podcast
The Small House, 138b Brownlow Rd.
London, GB-N11 2BP UK
Gianfranco Sciacca darklifezine@gmx.de
www.darklifezine.de
Spreading the latest sounds pertinent to the varied world of Dark and Experimental music.

TotalRock
1 Denmark Pl. London, WC2H 8NL UK
Tony Wilson tw@totalrock.com
www.totalrock.com
Featuring Rock, Metal and Industrial releases.

Australia

Darkwings Radio Show *RTR*
PO Box 842, Mt. Lawley, WA 6929 Australia
PH: +61-8-9260-9210 FX: +61 8 9260 9222
rtrfm@rtrfm.com.au
www.rtrfm.com.au
For all your Industrial and Gothic wants.

Dawntreader *RTR*
PO Box 842, Mt. Lawley, WA 6929 Australia
PH: +61-8-9260-9210 FX: +61 8 9260 9222
rtrfm@rtrfm.com.au
www.rtrfm.com.au
Post-Punk, Industrial and more.

Hip Hop Radio
Radio Promoters

Mo' Better Music
77 Bleecker St. #C115, New York, NY 10012
PH: 212-388-0597 FX: 212-388-0592
retail@mobettermusic.com
www.mobettermusic.com
A National marketing and promotion company.

Looking4airplay
PO Box 630372, Houston, TX 77263
PH: 281-277-6626 FX: 281-277-6626
Michael Matthews support@looking4airplay.com
www.looking4airplay.com
Urban radio & record pool marketing (Rap/Hip-Hop/R&B Format). We will digitally deliver your next hit directly to radio today!

Shocksound Promotions
PO Box 3441, Norfolk, VA 23514-3441
PH: 252-435-6589
Greg Burke shocksoundpromo@yahoo.com
www.shocksoundpromotions.com
We specialize in national radio promotions, email blast, brand marketing and consulting.

Stations and Shows

North America
United States

2hot4radio
700 N. Calhoune St. Ste B-10
Tallahassee, FL 32313
PH/FX: 407-902-4228
J. A. Myrick jovanmyrick@yahoo.com
www.2hot4radio.us
We specialize in underground Hip Hop promotions marketing pirate radio. We are more than just a station, we are the underground force behind the movement!

Apex Express *KPFA*
1929 MLK Way, Berkeley, CA 94704
PH: 510-848-6767 x464
apex@apexexpress.org
apexexpress.org
If you have music that you'd like featured on our show, HOLLA!!! Preferably music created by Asian/Pacific Islanders.

Beatsauce *KUSF*
2130 Fulton St., San Francisco, CA 94117
PH: 415-386-5873
J. Boogie justin@jboogie.com
www.kusf.org
San Francisco's premier Underground Hip Hop mix show. We create a positive vibe for local and out of town artists to showcase their talent and promote their skills for the entire Bay Area and beyond.

Chiradio.com
63 E. Lake St., Mail Box 17, Chicago, IL 60601
PH: 800-683-8200
chiradio@hotmail.com
www.chiradio.com
Features a Rap and Soul station.

Cipha Sounds
20 W. 38th St. #403, New York, NY 10018
PH: 212-239-2855
DJ Cipha Sounds djcipha@ciphasounds.com
www.ciphasounds.com
DJ Cipha Sounds is one of the select few trailblazers with the natural ability to discover and develop new talent.

The City *XM Radio*
PH: 866-388-6767
thecity@xmradio.com
thecity.xmradio.com
The hottest Hip Hop, Reggae and R&B from your favorite artists and the newcomers to watch.

DREADXX.com
PO Box 647, Boynton Beach, FL 33425
PH: 561-503-1513
music@dreadxx.com
dreadxx.com
A Hip Hop station that also promotes music through different record pools and A&R.

Earthbound Radio
7580 Trade St. Ste. C, San Diego, CA 92126
PH: 858-366-4327
submissions@twelvez.com
www.twelvez.com
From Hip Hop to Jazz and Acoustic to Electronic. No limits and no boundaries.

egRadio
info@egradioonline.com
www.egradioonline.com
Featuring some of the hottest music in Underground Hip-Hop, Reggaeton and R&B.

The Fresh Connection *KPSU*
1825 SW. Broadway #443, Portland, OR 97201
PH: 503-752-2541
DJ Fresh fresh3122000@yahoo.com
freshconnection.cjb.net
Portland's hottest Hip Hop show!

Hiphop Philosophy.com Radio
1008 E. Pacific Coast Hwy.
Long Beach, CA 90803-5017
www.myspace.com/theprogramdirector
The first 24-hour real hardcore Hip Hop radio format on Earth!

Hoodhype.com
PO Box 1453, Brighton, MI 48116
music@hoodhype.com
www.HoodHype.com
An all Urban podcast focusing on underground artists.

ILLVIBE
PO Box 35072, Philadelphia, PA 19128
Statik info@illvibe.net
illvibe.net
You can expect to hear anything from Funk to Traditional Jazz, from Hip Hop to Bossanova and Soulful House.

KMEL
340 Townsend St. 4th Fl. San Francisco, CA 94107
Big Von Johnson bigvon@clearchannel.com
www.106kmel.com
Plays both independent and mainstream music.

OnPoint.FM
PH: 336-273-7323
www.onpoint.fm
Hip Hop radio for your soul!

Outside The Box Radio
530 Main St. #653, New Rochelle, NY 10801
PH: 914-879-8837
admin@otbradio.com.
www.otbradio.com
The tri-states' #1 station for Underground and unsigned Hip Hop.

Planet X Radio
1011 NE. 109th St., Portland, OR 97218
nbnusa@hotmail.com
www.planetxradio.com
Underground Hip Hop sounds. Download the release form from our website and send it in with your CD.

The Pro Flow Fa-Sho Show
PO Box 8287, Akron, OH 44320
PH: 330-431-1680
MaD MaXxx M3@maxheat.com
maxheat.com
The show has a strong Hip Hop origin.

Rapdreams Radio
rapdreamsradio@aol.com
rapdreamsradio.ning.com
We are currently looking for new music, drops & interviews. Hip Hop, R&B and Reggaeton artists wanted.

RAW *XM Radio*
PH: 866-280-4729
Leo G. 66raw@xmradio.com
raw.xmradio.com
All about living on the cutting edge of today's Hip Hop scene.

Slum Radio
3542 Fruitvale Ave. #331, Oakland, CA 94602
PH: 510-281-2718
Tunsi tunsi@comcast.net
www.paranarecords.net
Featuring Underground Hip Hop.

SOL of HIPHOP Radio *TIR*
PO Box 6868, Fullerton, CA 92834-6868
PH: 714-278-5505 FX: 714-278-5514
DJ Buddhabong buddhabong@solofhiphop.com
www.solofhiphop.com
Streamin' live every Friday 4-7 PM pst.

Sunday Night Jams *KTXT*
Texas Tech U. PO Box 43081, Lubbock, TX 79409
PH: 806-742-3916 FX: 806-742-3906
ktxtfm@yahoo.com
www.ktxt.net
The #1 rated Urban show in Lubbock!!

Thug Life Army Radio
2753 E. Broadway Rd. Ste. 101-109
Mesa, AZ 85204-1573
PH: 866-887-3405
music@TLARadio.com
www.tlaradio.com
Our main focus is on less-heard and more deserving Hip Hop, Rap and R&B.

The Underground Railroad *WBAI*
120 Wall St., 10th Fl. New York, NY 10005
PH: 212-209-2800 x2931
Jay Smooth jsmooth@hiphopmusic.com
www.hiphopmusic.com
The first DJ on radio to explore mixing classic Jazz cuts with the latest underground Hip Hop.

Unified Sounds
www.unifiedbeats.com
Supports Underground music. Get recognition!

Urban Newz Radio
UrbanNewzRadio@gmail.com
www.urbannewz.com
Yeah you heard it right, UrbanNewz has its own LIVE Hip Hop radio show. Send us your Hip Hop MP3s!

Urban State of Brainwashing *WRUW*
11220 Bellflower Rd. Cleveland, OH 44106
PH: 216-368-2208
Harry T. Blackmann & Sonia Glass md@wruw.org
wruw.org
We play Hip Hop, Breakbeats, Turntablism, Freestyle, DnB, Jungle and Rap.

WBCR *Brooklyn College*
Rm. 306, Whitehead Hall, 2900 Bedford Ave.
Brooklyn, NY 11210
PH: 718-951-4515
brooklyncollegeradio@gmail.com
brooklyncollegeradio.org

WHTD
3250 Franklin St., Detroit, MI 48207
PH: 313-259-2000 FX: 313-259-7011
\www.hot1027detroit.com

WKXN
PO Box 369, Greenville, AL 36037
PH: 334-613-1071 FX: 334-382-7770
Roscoe Miller wkxn@wkxn.com
www.wkxn.com
Hip Hop, Gospel and R&B.

YP's Crunk House Radio Show
PO Box 45793, Atlanta, GA 30320
PH: 770-843-2559
Sheryl Brown ypscrunkhouse@hotmail.com
www.myspace.com/ypscrunkhouse
An online radio show which features independent artists by way of interviews and music airplay.

Canada

Deadbeat Radio
deadbeatradio@gmail.com
deadbeatradio.com
An alternative to mainstream radio featuring the most diverse selection of Hip Hop, R&B and Drum n' Bass.

Hip Hop 101 *UMFM*
Rm. 308 U. Ctr. Winnipeg, MB R3T 2N2
PH: 204-474-7027 FX: 204-269-1299
Kinetik kinetikaljoints@hotmail.com
www.umfm.com
The best in independent and underground Hip Hop. Constantly introducing the city to brand new artists and flavas!

in over your head
PH: 206-202-3291
inoveryourhead@gmail.com
inoveryourhead.net
Hip Hop podcast, culture and wrath from Montreal.

Keep it Surreal *CJUM*
Rm. 308 U. Ctr. Winnipeg, MB R3T 2N2
PH: 204-474-7027 FX: 204-269-1299
DJ Brace brace@umfm.com
www.djbrace.com
An eclectic mix of turntable related music. From breaks to the music that sampled them. Focusing heavily on turntablism galore, breaking it down and playing it.

The Lounge *CKUW*
Rm. 4CM11, 515 Portage Ave.
Winnipeg, MB R3B 2E9
PH: 204-786-9782 FX: 204-783-7080
Jay Boogie uptownsreq@mts.net
www.ckuw.ca
Online radio show playing Hip Hop, R&B and Dancehall Reggae.

Off the Hook *CKUT*
3647 U. St., Montreal, QC H3A 2B3
PH: 514-398-4616 FX: 514-398-8261
yourbeat2008@gmail.com
www.myspace.com/offthehookradio
Montreal's Underground + independent Hip Hop source.

The Wax Jungle *CKMS*
200 University Ave. W., Waterloo, ON N2L 3G1
PH: 519-886-2567 FX: 519-884-3530
www.ckmsfm.ca
The show focuses on Hip Hop and R&B beats.

E u r o p e

France

Skyrock
Skyrock.com, 37 bis rue Grenéta 75002 Paris, France
www.skyrock.com
Rap, Hip Hop, R&B…

Sweden

P3 Hip-Hop
Sveriges Radio, 211 01 Malmö, Sweden
www.sr.se/p3/hiphop
Y'all need to peep this, because it's slammin! Nuff said!

United Kingdom

BBC Radio 1xtra *Hip Hop*
www.bbc.co.uk/1xtra/hiphop
Home page of the BBC 1xtra's various Hip Hop shows. Info, shows, contacts etc.

BBC Radio 1 *Urban Music*
www.bbc.co.uk/radio1/urban
Home page of the BBC Radio 1's various Urban Music shows. Info, shows, contacts etc.

Conspiracy UK
montana1099@hotmail.com
www.conspiracyuk.com
Hip Hop, Old Skool, Jungle, DnB, Garage, Tekno, Soul, Reggae and much much more!

Innacity Radio
dubs@innacityfm.com
innercityfm.com
Only a few of us have any real heart, any real intention of making a chance or trying to make a difference. Only a few of us understand what it's all about.

New Zealand

True School Hip Hop Show *95bFM*
PO Box 4560, Shortland St.
Auckland 1001 New Zealand
PH: 64-9-309-4831 FX: 64-9-366-7224
music@95bfm.com
www.95bfm.co.nz
The phattest coverage of local and international Hip Hop.

A s i a

Japan

The Mixtape Show
kucrdex@gmail.com
www.mixtapeshow.net
Broadcasting from Tokyo, Japan by way of Los Angeles, this is the most popular Hip Hop podcast on the internet. This is your opportunity to be featured right next to some heavy hitters.

A f r i c a

Bay FM
PO Box 70371, Greenacres 6000 South Africa
PH: 041-363-6788 FX: 041-363-7085
www.bayfm.co.za
We have several regular Hip Hop shows.

Jam Band Radio

Dead to the World *KPFA*
484 Lake Park Ave. #102, Oakland, CA 94610-2730
PH: 510-848-4425
David Gans david@trufun.com
dttw.gdhour.com
A mix of various Americana and Jam Bands in the second hour.

Endless Boundaries
www.endlessboundaries.com
Music in and around the Jam scene.

Finding The Groove *KUMD*
130 Humanities Bldg. 1201 Ordean Ct.
Duluth, MN 55812
PH: 218-726-7181 FX: 218-726-6571
kumd@kumd.org
www.kumd.org
A collection of Jam Bands from all over the U.S. & the world.

Home Grown Radio
PO Box 340, Mebane, NC 27302
PH: 919-563 4923
leeway@homegrownmusic.net
www.homegrownmusic.net/radio.html
Discover new bands and kind music.

Honest Tunes Radio Show *KXUA*
618 E. Edna St., Fayetteville, AR 72703
Daniel Gold goodgold@gmail.com
www.dgold.info/radio
Covering a wonderful array of Songwriters, Jam Bands and Roots music, including Blues, Jazz, Bluegrass, Folk, Improv and live Electronic. Please send CD's and press kits.

Jam Band Extravaganza *KIWR*
2700 College Rd. Council Bluffs, IA 51503
PH: 712-325-3254 FX: 712-325-3391
Brock Turner jamband897@gmail.com
www.897theriver.com/jam.asp
Specializing in automated hydro phonic growing systems and the cutting edge of Rock.

Jamnation *WXPN*
3025 Walnut St., Philadelphia, PA 19104
PH: 215-898-6677. FX: 215-898-0707
Matt Reilly online@xpn.org
www.xpn.org
Dedicated to the broad variety of musical output often grouped under the "Jam Band" umbrella.

The Music Never Stops *KPFK*
c/o Nomenclature Records,
419 N. Larchmont Blvd. #15,
Los Angeles, CA 90004
Barry Smolin shmo@well.com
www.mrsmolin.com/radio.php
Contemporary Jam-Rock and miscellaneous Psychedelia.

The Side Trip *WQNR*
6622 Vermont Ave. 1st Fl. St. Louis, MO 63111
PH: 314-832-5529
James Mullin jamesm@thesidetrip.com
www.thesidetrip.com
Groove and Jam music.

Stumble In The Dark *KDHX*
3504 Magnolia St. Louis, MO 63118
PH: 314-664-3688 FX: 314-664-1020
James Mullin stumbleinthedark@kdhx.org
www.kdhx.org/programs/stumbleinthedark.htm
An eclectic mix of Rock, Jazz, Funk and Bluegrass. Features some of the best live music from today's best Jam Bands.

The Wildman Steve Show *WQNR*
2514 S. College St. #104, Auburn, AL 36830
Wildman Steve wildmansteve@wildmansteve.com
www.WildmanSteve.com
An eclectic mix of deep-catalog Classic Rock and new 'good' music.

Jazz Radio

North America

Promotional Services

United States

ASL Developing Artists Promotion Campaign
121 S. Martel Ave. Los Angeles, CA 90036
PH: 323-934-0333
info@aslmusicmedia.com
www.aslmusicmedia.com
Offers a comprehensive promotion package for new and developing artists. Delivers incredible exposure in one efficient and cost-effective program.

Sign up for
The Indie Contact Newsletter
www.indiebible.com

Lisa Reedy Promotions
275 Bonnie Briar Pl. Reno, NV 89509
PH: 775-826-0755
Lisa Reedy reedylm@aol.com
www.jazzpromotion.com
Works with 500+ radio stations throughout the United States and Canada on a weekly basis to solicit radio airplay, interviews to promote new releases & artist tour-dates, Charting at JazzWeek & CMJ, and other special promotions such as station IDs, CD giveaways, special program features and obtaining quotes from radio personalities.

Internet, Syndicated Shows and Podcasts

aTTeNTioN sPaN raDiO
dj@attentionspanradio.net
www.attentionspanradio.net
The hippest, coolest mix of Jazz, Funk and Rock instrumentals available.

BendingCorners
PO Box 1487, San Bruno, CA 94066
bendingcorners@gmail.com
www.bendingcorners.com
Podcast featuring Jazz and Jazz-inspired grooves. If you enjoy the groove side of all things "Jazz", this is your thang.

Beyond Bop
Tom tom@beyondbop.com
www.beyondbop.com
An internet Jazz radio station created for musicians by musicians showcasing some of the best kept secrets in Jazz. Most of these tracks are relatively unknown and are not likely to be heard on commercial radio. Nonetheless, they're from some of the coolest cats on the planet today, bar none.

Big Band Jump
PH: 800-377-0022 FX: 404-231-7990
Don Kennedy don@bigbandjump.com
www.bigbandjump.com
Featuring both original and later Swing music.

Broke N' Beat Radio
2217 Fitzwater St. #2, Philadelphia, PA 19146
brokenbeatradio@gmail.com
www.brokenbeatradio.com
Podcast featuring the latest Broken Beat and Nu Jazz sounds.

Cat Galaxy
catprotector@catgalaxymedia.com
www.catgalaxymedia.com
A station for cats to enjoy. Our format is what we call feline freeform as our station is for cats by cats. It is my hope that all of you cats and your humans will enjoy this station. Smooth Jazz, Classic Rock, Alternative, Funk, R&B and Swing.

Chill With Chris Botti
Chris info@chillwithchrisbotti.com
www.chillwithchrisbotti.com
Syndicated show playing NY Chill music. Chris also posts recommended CDs on his website.

CIM Radio
PH: 212-461-4838
www.cimradio.com
Smooth Fusion 24 hours a day!

Groove Suite
3861 Chapparal Dr. Fairfield, CA 94534
DJ Walker groovin@groovesuite.com
www.Groovesuite.com
Smooth Jazz and R&B internet radio station.

Jazz After Hours
729 N. 66th St., Seattle, WA 98103
Jim Wilke jim@jazzafterhours.org
www.jazzafterhours.org
New and well-established Jazz artists regularly drop in for a chat.

The Jazz Suite
21901 Mada Ave. Southfield, MI 48075
PH: 734-658-9482 FX: 248-356-2021
Norvell Molex Jr. nmolexjr@aim.com
thejazzsuite.mypodcasts.net
Podcast playing Contemporary, Progressive & Acid Jazz from independent artists.

Jazz, Then and Now *Healthy Life Radio*
16787 Beach Blvd. #454
Huntington Beach, CA 92647
PH: 949-231-8476
Bill Tannebring info@jazzthenandnow.com
www.jazzthenandnow.com
Showcases mainstream Jazz of all genres from around the world. I also invite established and up and coming players to talk about their careers and their music.

Jazz with Bob Parlocha
1216 Post St., Alameda, CA 94501
Bob bob@jazzwithbobparlocha.com
www.jazzwithbobparlocha.com
Information about Jazz recordings, publications, musicians and live gigs.

JazzSet
Dee Dee Bridgewater jazzset@npr.org
www.npr.org/programs/jazzset
Jazz radio series presenting today's artists.

Jazztrax
611 S. Palm Canyon Dr. #7-458
Palm Springs, CA 92264-7402
PH: 760-323-1171 FX: 760-323-5770
info@jazztrax.com
www.jazztrax.com
The very best songs, from the very best Smooth Jazz albums.

LuxuriaMusic.com
PO Box 61036, Pasadena, CA 91116
Chuck Kelley support@luxuriamusic.com
www.luxuriamusic.com
Outré lounge and Latin Jazz, breezy swinging instrumentals and vocals, Psychedelia, quirky oddities, Retro Pop and Surf music.

New Orleans Radio
nospam@lagniappe.la
www.neworleansradio.com
Produces and delivers regional custom music.

NPR Jazz
635 Massachusetts Ave. NW.
Washington, DC 20001
www.nprjazz.org
Submit your CD for review consideration.

Quietmusic.com
www.quietmusic.com
Host Nick Francis brings you Smooth Jazz.

Smoothjazz.com
PO Box 982, Pacific Grove, CA 93950
feedback@smoothjazz.com
www.smoothjazz.com
For on-air consideration, record representatives may e-mail our music department.

SoulfulSmoothJazz.com Radio
PO Box 660-100, Flushing, NY 11366
Blackwell contact@SoulfulSmoothJazz.com
www.SoulfulSmoothJazz.com
*The world's hot spot for Soulful Smooth Jazz &
R&B where you can request your music and hear it
instantly. Commercial free all day, every day!*

WCJZ World's Cool JazZ
www.wcjz.com
*Our goal is to help the new Jazz artists get exposure
for their music. Submit your info via our online
artists music submission form.*

WNJL.com
1040 Riverview Dr. Florence, NJ 08518
PH: 609-922-1620 FX: 609-499-1971
wnjl@wnjl.com
www.wnjl.com
The home of Smooth Jazz On the internet.

Alabama

Alabama Public Radio Evening Jazz
PO Box 870370, Tuscaloosa, AL 35487-0370
PH: 205-348-6644 FX: 205-348-6648
Alisa Beckwith abeckwith@apr.org
www.apr.org

WJAB *Alabama A&M*
PO Box 1687, Normal, AL 35762
www.aamu.edu/wjab

WVSU *Samford U.*
Birmingham, AL 35229-2301
PH: 205-726-2934 FX: 205-726-4032
wvsu@samford.edu
www.samford.edu/groups/wvsu

Arizona

KJZZ
2323 W. 14th St., Tempe, AZ 85281
PH: 480-834-5627 FX: 480-774-8475
Blaise Lantana mail@kjzz.org
www.kjzz.org

KYOT
PH: 480-966-6236
www.kyot.com
Featuring lots of known & unknown Jazz artists.

Arkansas

KASU *Arkansas State U.*
PO Box 2160, State U. AR 72467
PH: 870-972- 2200
www.kasu.org

KXRJ
Hwy 7 N., Russellville, AR 72801
PH: 479-964-0806 FX: 479-498-6024
broadcast.atu.edu/broadcasting.shtml

California

Capital Public Radio
7055 Folsom Blvd. Sacramento, CA 95826
PH: 916-278-8900 FX: 916-278-8989
jazz@capradio.org
www.capradio.org

FreeFall *KUSF*
1131 Diamond St., San Francisco, CA 94114
PH: 415-386-5873
David Bassin playlist@freefallradio.com
www.freefallradio.com
*Playing Jazz, Electronica, Downtempo & World.
Please, no New Age or Smooth Jazz!*

In the Groove *KUSP*
203 8th Ave. Santa Cruz, CA 95062
PH: 831-476-2800
Mike Lambert kusp@kusp.org
www.kusp.org
*Send any promotional items for airplay, giveaway or
review.*

In Your Ear *KPFA*
1929 MLK Jr. Way, Berkeley, CA 94704
PH: 510-848-4425 FX: 510-848-3812
Art Sato music@kpfa.org
www.kpfa.org
*A cool fusion of Jazz and Latin music, giving voice
to musicians deserving wider recognition.*

Jazz Beat Radio
1801 Jefferson St., Oakland, CA 94612
PH: 510-444-6673
www.jazzbeatradio.tv
*Classic Jazz mixed with occasional today's and old
school R&B, Blues, Afro Cuban, Latin Jazz and
Caribbean music.*

KCBX
4100 Vachell Ln. San Luis Obispo, CA 93401
PH: 805-549-8855
Neal Losey nlosey@kcbx.org
www.kcbx.org

KCLU *California Lutheran College*
60 W. Olsen Rd. #4400, Thousand Oaks, CA 91360
PH: 805-493-3900
Jim Rondeau jrondeau@clunet.edu
www.kclu.org

KCSM Jazz 91
1700 W. Hillsdale Blvd. San Mateo, CA 94402
PH: 650-524-6945
www.kcsm.org
E-mail Jesse to set up submissions etc.

KKJZ *California State U.*
1288 N. Bellflower Blvd. Long Beach, CA 90815
PH: 562-985-5566 FX: 562-597-8453
www.jazzandblues.org

KKSF
340 Townsend St., San Francisco, CA 94107
Attn: Music Director
PH: 415-975-5555 FX: 415-975-5573
Ken Jones kenjones@clearchannel.com
www.kksf.com
*Send your CD to the music director at the above
address. You will notified if we add it to rotation.*

KPFK
3729 Cahuenga Blvd. W.,
North Hollywood, CA 91604
PH: 818-985-2711 FX: 818-763-7526
Armando Gudiño pd@kpfk.org
www.kpfk.org

KRVR
961 N. Emerald Ave. Ste. A, Modesto, CA 95351
PH: 209-544-1055
theriver@krvr.com
www.krvr.com

KSBR *Saddleback College*
28000 Marguerite Pkwy. Mission Viejo, CA 92692
PH: 949-582-5727 FX: 949-347-9693
www.ksbr.net

KSDS
1313 Park Blvd. San Diego, CA 92101
PH: 619-388-3068 FX: 619-230-2212
Joe Kocherhans joek@jazz88online.org
www.jazz88online.org

KXJZ *California State U.*
7055 Folsom Blvd. Sacramento, CA 95826-2625
PH: 916-278-5299 FX: 916-278-8989
jazz@capradio.org
www.capradio.org

Madly Cocktail *KCSN*
18111 Nordhoff St., Northridge, CA 91330-8312
PH: 818-885-5276
Kat Griffin madlycocktail@aol.com
www.kcsn.org/programs/madlycocktail.html
*An excellent mix of Cocktail Jazz, Latin Soul and
Big Band mayhem all done up with a healthy dose
of class.*

No Cover, No Minimum *KZSU*
423 Broadway #131, Millbrae, CA 94030
Host: Forrest Dylan Bryant.
www.fojazz.com
*Take 3 parts Jazz, 1 part Blues, 1 part World music.
Shake with ice and pour into a martini glass.
Garnish with live interviews with local and national
artists.*

Outstanding Music *Kbeach Radio*
PO Box 2111, Huntington Beach, CA 92647
PH: 714-377-7447
Earl Beecher Beecher@OutstandingMusic.com
www.outstandingmusic.com
*Jazz oriented radio. I play anything and anyone, as
long as it's good in my opinion.*

Radio Sausalito
PO Box 397, Sausalito, CA 94966
PH: 415-332-5299
info@radiosausalito.org
www.radiosausalito.org
*Several locally produced, Jazz oriented programs
every week.*

Tony Palkovic's Jazz Show *KSPC*
Thatcher Music Bldg. 340 N. College Ave.
Claremont, CA 91711-6340
PH: 909-626-5772 FX: 909-621-8769
Tony tpjazzshow@cs.com
www.kspc.org
A mix of Jazz-Fusion, Straight Ahead and Latin.

Colorado

KAJX
110 E. Hallam #134, Aspen, CO 81611
PH: 970-925-6445 x19 FX: 970-544-8002
Mike Rosenbaum music@kajx.org
www.kajx.org

KCME
1921 N. Weber St., Colorado Springs, CO 80907
PH: 719-578-5263 FX: 719-578-1033
Lenny Mazel jazz@kcme.org
www.kcme.org

KRFC
619 S. College Ave. #4, Fort Collins, CO 80524
PH: 970-221-5075
Dennis Bigelow musicdirector@krfcfm.org
krfcfm.org

KRZA
528 9th St., Alamosa, CO 81101
PH: 719-589-8844 FX: 719-587-0032
Mike Sisneros music@krza.org
www.krza.org

KUNC *U. Northern Colorado*
822 7th St. #530, Greeley, CO 80631-3945
PH: 970-378-2579
mailbag@kunc.org
www.kunc.org

KUVO
PO Box 2040, Denver, CO 80201-2040
PH: 303-480-9272 x17
Arturo Gomez arturo@kuvo.org
www.kuvo.org

Connecticut

In The Groove, Jazz and Beyond *WHUS*
Student Union Rm. 412, 2110 Hillside Rd. #3008R
Storrs, CT 06268-3008
Ken Laster ken@lasternet.com
www.lasternet.com/inthegroove
From Jazz masters of past and present to emerging new artists performing Jazz, Fusion and Funk.

Out Here & Beyond *WWUH*
200 Bloomfield Ave. West Hartford, CT 06117
PH: 860-768-4701 FX: 860-768-5701
Chuck Obuchowski cobuchow@aol.com
www.wwuh.org
I attempt to capture the diversity of the modern Jazz realm. I frequently feature interviews with the music-makers.

Florida

WDNA
PO Box 558636, Miami, FL 33255
PH: 305-662-8889 FX: 305-662-1975
Michael Valentine info@wdna.org
www.wdna.org
Send in your serious Jazz.

WFIT *Florida Tech*
150 W. University Blvd. Melbourne, FL 32901
PH: 321-674-8949 FX: 321-674-8139
wfit@fit.edu
www.wfit.org

WLOQ
2301 Lucien Way #180, Maitland, FL 32751
PH: 407-647-5557 FX: 407-647-4495
www.wloq.com
CD Reviews-'Smooth Jazz' shows all day.

WLRN
172 NE. 15th St., Miami, FL 33132
PH: 305-995-2207 FX: 305-995-2299
info@wlrn.org
www.wlrn.org

WSJT
9721 Executive Ctr. Dr. N. #200
St. Petersburg, FL 33702-2439
PH: 727-563-8830 FX: 727-568-9758
Kathy Curtis kcurtis@wsjt.com
wsjt.com
CD Reviews, concerts, interviews. Note that it's more difficult to get music on the air if you don't have any representation.

WUCF *U. Central Florida*
PO Box 162199, Orlando, FL 32816-2199
PH: 407-823-0899
Dave Martin dpmartin@mail.ucf.edu
wucf.ucf.edu

WUFT *U. Florida*
PO Box 118405, Gainesville, FL 32611
PH: 352-392-5200 FX: 352-392-5741
radio@wuft.org
www.wuft.org/fm

Georgia

The Jazz Spot *Georgia Public Radio*
260 14th St. NW., Atlanta, GA 30318
PH: 404-685-2400 FX: 404-685-2684
Masani jazz@gpb.org
www.gpb.org/public/radio/jazzspot
Mainstream and progressive contemporary impressions of Jazz music.

WBCX *Brenau U.*
PH: 770-538-4744
Scott Fugate sfugate@brenau.edu
www.brenau.edu/about/wbcx
Promotes and supports local Jazz musicians.

WCLK *Clark Atlanta U.*
111 James P. Brawley Dr. SW., Atlanta, GA 30314
PH: 404-880-8273
wwilliam@cau.edu
www.wclk.com

Hawaii

Jazz with Don Gordon *KIPO*
738 Kaheka St., Honolulu, HI 98614
PH: 808-955-8821 FX: 808-942-5477
Don Gordon dgordon@hawaiipublicradio.org
dongordon.net
Jazz is a very thick tree with deep roots and many branches and I try to cover the gamut.

The Real Deal *KIPO*
738 Kaheka St. #101, Honolulu, HI 96814
PH: 808-955-8821 FX: 808-942-5477
Seth Markow realdeal@lava.net
www.hawaiipublicradio.org
I do play independent music, namely Jazz (likely to expand soon to include more diverse Roots music).

Idaho

BSU Radio Network *Boise State U.*
1910 University Dr. Boise, ID 83725-1915
PH: 208-947-5660 FX: 208-344-6631
radio.boisestate.edu
Radio Vision and Idaho's Jazz station.

Illinois

New Vintage *WDCB*
College of DuPage, 425 Fawell Blvd.
Glen Ellyn, IL 60137
PH: 630-942-4200 FX: 630-942-2788
Bill O'Connell OConnellB@wdcb.org
wdcb.org
Celebrating the many successes of today's band leaders dedicated to furthering and promoting America's greatest contribution to world music history.

WBEZ
Navy Pier, 848 E. Grand Ave.
Chicago, IL 60611-3462
PH: 312-948-4855
questions@chicagopublicradio.org
www.wbez.org

WDCB *College of DuPage*
425 Fawell Blvd. Glen Ellyn, IL 60137
PH: 630-942-4200 FX: 630-942-2788
wdcb.org
We're known for our eclectic music programming.

WGLT
8910 Illinois State U. Normal, IL 61790-8910
PH: 309-438-7871 FX: 309-438-7870
Jon Norton j.norton@ilstu.edu
www.wglt.org

WILL *U. Illinois*
Campbell Hall, 300 N. Goodwin Ave.
Urbana, IL 61801-2316
PH: 217-333-0850 FX: 217-244-9586
Jake Schumacher willamfm@uiuc.edu
www.will.uiuc.edu
Send us your Classical, Jazz and Traditional/Ethnic music.

Indiana

Jazz By The Border *WVPE*
2424 California Rd. Elkhart, IN 46514
PH: 888-399-9873
Lee Burdorf lburdorf@wvpe.org
www.wvpe.org/border.html
We love to receive music from independent artists!

WBAA AM *Purdue U.*
712 3rd St. W. Lafayette, IN 47907-2005
PH: 765-494-3961
David Bunte dpbunte@wbaa.org
www.purdue.edu/wbaa

WFIU *Indiana U.*
1229 E. 7th St., Bloomington, IN 47405
PH: 812-855-1357 FX: 812-855-5600
wfiu@indiana.edu
www.indiana.edu/~wfiu

WSND *U. Notre Dame*
315 LaFortune Student Ctr. Notre Dame, IN 46556
PH: 574-631-4069
wsnd@nd.edu
www.nd.edu/~wsnd

Iowa

KCCK *Kirkwood College*
6301 Kirkwood Blvd. SW., Cedar Rapids, IA 52406
PH: 319-398-5446 FX: 319-398-5492
Bob Stewart bobs@kcck.org
www.kcck.org

KHKE *U. Northern Iowa*
U. Cedar Falls, IA 50614-0359
PH: 319-273-6400 FX: 319-273-2682
kuni@uni.edu
www.khke.org

WOI *Iowa State U.*
2022 Comm. Bldg. Iowa State U.
Ames, IA 50011-3241
PH: 515-294-2025 FX: 515-294-1544
Karen Bryan kbryan@iastate.edu
www.woi.org

Kansas

Jazz in the Night *U. Kansas*
1120 W. 11th St. U. Kansas, Lawrence, KS 66044
PH: 785-864-4530 FX: 785-864-5278
Bob McWilliams radiobob@ku.edu
kansaspublicradio.org/jazz.php

KMUW *Wichita State U.*
3317 E. 17th St. N., Wichita, KS 67208-1912
PH: 316-978-6789
info@kmuw.org
www.kmuw.org

Kentucky

WKMS *Murray State U.*
2018 U. Stn. Murray, KY 42071
PH: 270-809-4744 FX: 270-762-4667
Mark Welch mark.welch@murraystate.edu
www.wkms.org

WMKY *Morehead State U.*
132 Breckinridge Hall, Morehead, KY 40351
PH: 606-783-2001 FX: 606-783-2335
wmky@moreheadstate.edu
www.wmkyradio.com

WNKU *Northern Kentucky U.*
PO Box 337, Highland Heights, KY 41076
PH: 859-572-7897 FX: 859-572-6604
radio@nku.edu
www.wnku.org

Louisiana

KRVS *U. Southern Louisiana*
PO Box 42171, Lafayette, LA 70504
PH: 337-482-5787 FX: 337-482-6101
David Spizale dspizale@krvs.org
www.krvs.org

WWOZ
1008 N. Peters St., New Orleans, LA 70116
www.wwoz.org

Maryland

WTMD *Towson U.*
8000 York Rd. Towson, MD 21252
PH: 410-704-8938
wwwnew.towson.edu/wtmd

WYPR *Johns Hopkins U.*
2216 N. Charles St., Baltimore, MD 21218
PH: 410-235-1660 x1061 FX: 410-235-1161
Andy Bienstock bienstock@wypr.org
www.wypr.org

Massachusetts

Jazz Safari *WFCR*
Hampshire House, U. Mass, 131 County Cir.
Amherst, MA 01003-9257
PH: 413-545-0100 FX: 413-545-2546
Kari Njiiri kari@wfcr.org
www.wfcr.org/about/jsafari.php
African, Afro-Latin, Afro-Caribbean and other
international Jazz styles.

WGBH
PO Box 200, Boston, MA 02134
PH: 617-300-5400
www.wgbh.org

WHRB *Harvard U.*
389 Harvard St., Cambridge, MA 02138
PH: 617-495-4818
mail@whrb.org
www.whrb.net

WICN
50 Portland St., Worcester, MA 01608
PH: 508-752-0700 FX: 508-752-7518
Tyra Penn tyra@wicn.org
www.wicn.org
Many hours of Jazz, CD release parties and more!

Michigan

Nightside Jazz and Blues *CMU Public Radio*
1999 E. Campus Dr. Mt. Pleasant, MI 48859
PH: 989-774-3105 FX: 989-774-4427
John Sheffler sheff1j@cmich.edu
www.wcmu.org/radio/cmuradioproductions/
nightside.html
Artists/Labels submit your music for airplay.

WDET *Wayne State U.*
4600 Cass Ave. Detroit, MI 48201
PH: 313-577-4146 FX: 313-577-1300
wdetfm@wdetfm.org
www.wdetfm.org

WEMU *Eastern Michigan U.*
PO Box 980350, Ypsilanti, MI 48198
PH: 734-487-2229
www.wemu.org

WGVU
301 W. Fulton Ave. Grand Rapids, MI 49504-6492
PH: 616-331-6666
www.wgvu.org/radio

WLNZ *Lansing College*
400 N. Capitol #001, Lansing, MI 48933
PH: 517-483-1710 FX: 517-483-1894
www.lcc.edu/wlnz

Minnesota

KBEM
1555 James Ave. N., Minneapolis, MN 55411
PH: 612-668-1752 FX: 612-668-1766
Kevin O'Connor kevino@jazz88fm.com
www.jazz88fm.com

Mississippi

WJSU *Jackson State U.*
PO Box 18450, Jackson, MS 39217
PH: 601-979-2140 FX: 601-979-2878
www.wjsu.org

WUSM *U. Southern Mississippi*
118 College Dr. #10045, Hattiesburg, MS 39406
PH: 601-266-4287 FX: 601-266-4288
wusmmik@yahoo.com
www.usm.edu/wusm

Missouri

KSMU
901 S. National, Springfield, MO 65804-0089
PH: 417-836-5878 FX: 417-836-5889
ksmu@missouristate.edu
www.ksmu.missouristate.edu

KWWC *Stephens College*
1200 E. Broadway, Columbia, MO 65215
PH: 573-876–7272
www.stephens.edu/campuslife/kwwc

Nebraska

KIOS
3230 Burt St., Omaha, NE 68131
PH: 402-557-2777 FX: 402-557-2559
listener@kios.org
www.kios.org

Nevada

KUNV *U. Nevada Las Vegas*
1515 E. Tropicana Ave. #240, Las Vegas, NV 89119
PH: 702-798-8797
kunv.unlv.edu

New Jersey

The Groove Boutique
41 Watchung Plaza #387, Montclair, NJ 07042
Rafe Gomez music@thegrooveboutique.com
www.thegrooveboutique.com
An exhilarating listening experience that melds
vibrant Jazz musicianship with dynamic, irresistible
rhythms.

WBGO
54 Park Pl. Newark, NJ 07102
PH: 973-624-8880 FX: 973-824-8888
www.wbgo.org

WBJB *Brookdale College*
765 Newman Springs Rd. Lincroft, NJ 07738
PH: 732-224-2492
www.wbjb.org

New Mexico

KGLP
200 College Rd. Gallup, NM 87301
PH: 505-863-7626 FX: 505-863-7633
kglp@kglp.org
www.kglp.org

KRWG *New Mexico State U.*
PO Box 3000, Las Cruces, NM 88003-3000
PH: 505-646-4525 FX: 505-646-1974
krwgfm@nmsu.edu
www.krwgfm.org

KSFR *Santa Fe College*
PO Box 31366, Santa Fe, NM 87504-1366
PH: 505-428-1527 FX: 505-428-1237
info@ksfr.org
www.ksfr.org

New York

WAER
795 Ostrom Ave. Syracuse, NY 13244-4610
PH: 315-443-4021 FX: 315-443-2148
Eric Cohen escohen@syr.edu
www.waer.org

WBFO *U. Buffalo*
205 Allen Hall, 3435 Main St.
Buffalo, NY 14214-3003
PH: 716-829-6000
Bert Gambini bgambini@wbfo.org
www.wbfo.buffalo.edu

WDWN *Cayuga County College*
197 Franklin St., Auburn, NY 13021
PH: 315-255-1743 x2284 FX: 315-255-2690
wdwn@hotmail.com
www.wdwn.fm

WEOS *Hobart and William Smith Colleges*
300 Pulteney St., Geneva, NY 14456
PH: 315-781-3812 FX: 315-781-3916
Jamie Agnello weosmusic@hws.edu
www.weos.org

WGMC
1139 Maiden Ln. Rochester, NY 14615
PH: 585-966-2404 FX: 585-581-8185
Derrick Lucas derrick@jazz901.org
www.jazz901.org

WLIU *Long Island U.*
239 Montauk Hwy. Southampton, NY 11968
PH: 631-591-7005 FX: 631-287-8392
Bonnie Grice bonnie@wliu.org
www.wliu.org

WQCD
395 Hudson St. 7th Fl. New York, NY 10014
PH: 212-352-1019 FX: 212-929-8559
cd1019@cd1019.com
www.cd1019.com
Playing NY Chill. CD reviews, live events and
concert series.

North Carolina

WSHA *Shaw College*
118 E. South St., Raleigh, NC 27601
PH: 919-546-8430 FX: 919-546-8315
wsha@shawu.edu
www.wshafm.org

WZRU
232 Roanoke Ave. Roanoke Rapids, NC 27870
PH: 252-308-0885 FX: 252-537-3333
www.wzru.org

Ohio

The Fusion Show *WCSB*
2121 Euclid Ave. Cleveland, OH 44115-2214
PH: 216-687-3515 FX: 216-687-2161
Randy Allar fusion893@earthlink.net
thefusionshow.com
Fusion, Progressive, Instrumental music.

Mama Jazz *WMUB*
Williams Hall, Miami U. Oxford, OH 45056
PH: 513-529-5885 FX: 513-529-6048
Phyllis Campbell mamajazz@yahoo.com
www.wmub.org/mamajazz
The best in Jazz from the classics to today.

WAPS
65 Steiner Ave. Akron, OH 44301
PH: 330-761-3098 FX: 330-761-3240
Bill Gruber billgruber@913thesummit.com
www.wapsfm.com

WJZA
4401 Carriage Hill Ln. Columbus, OH 43220
PH: 614-451-2191 FX: 614-451-1831
www.columbusjazz.com
Live Jazz concerts listing, lots of Jazz programming.

WMUB *Miami U.*
Williams Hall, Miami U. Oxford, OH 45056
PH: 513-529-5885 FX: 513-529-6048
wmub@wmub.org
www.wmub.org

WNWV
PO Box 4006, Elyria, OH 44036
PH: 440-236-9283 FX: 440-236-3299
www.wnwv.com
Great Jazz and local concert listings for the area.

WYSO *Antioch U.*
795 Livermore St., Yellow Springs, OH 45387
PH: 937-767-6420
Niki Dakota ndakota@wyso.org
www.wyso.org

WYSU *Youngstown State U.*
1 University Plaza, Youngstown, OH 44555
PH: 330-941-3363
info@wysu.org
www.wysu.org

Oregon

KLCC
136 W. 8th Ave. Eugene, OR 97401
PH: 541-463-6004 FX: 541-463-6046
www.klcc.org

KMHD *Mt. Hood College*
26000 SE. Stark St., Gresham, OR 97030
PH: 503-491-7633 FX: 503-491-6999
Greg Gomez music_director@kmhd.fm

KMUN
PO Box 269, Astoria, OR 97103
PH: 503-325-0010
Elizabeth Menetrey Grant elizm@coastradio.org
www.kmun.org

Pennsylvania

WDUQ *Duquesne U.*
Pittsburgh, PA 15282
PH: 412-396-6030 FX: 412-396-5061
music@wduq.org
www.wduq.org

WPSU *Pennsylvania State U.*
102 Wagner Bldg. University Park, PA 16802
PH: 814-865-9778 FX: 814-865-3145
Kristine Allen kta1@outreach.psu.edu
wpsu.org/radio

WRDV
PO Box 2012, Warminster, PA 18974
PH: 215-674-8002
info@wrdv.org
www.wrdv.org
Jazz, Big Band, R&B.

Tennessee

WFHC *Freed-Hardeman U.*
158 E. Main St., Henderson, TN 38340
PH: 731-989-6691
Ron Means remeans@fhu.edu
www.fhu.edu/radio

WFSK *Fisk U.*
Nashville, TN 37208-3051
PH: 615-329-8754
Xuam Lawson xlawson@fisk.edu
www.fisk.edu/wfsk

WMOT *Middle Tenn. State U.*
PO Box 3, Murfreesboro, TN 37132
PH: 615-898-2800 FX: 615-898-2774
Greg Lee Hunt ghunt@mtsu.edu
www.wmot.org

WUOT *U. Tennessee*
209 Comm. Bldg. Knoxville, TN 37996
PH: 865-974-5375 FX: 865-974-3941
wuot@utk.edu
sunsite.utk.edu/wuot

WUTC *U. Tennessee*
104 Cadek Hall, Dept. 1151, 615 McCallie Ave.
Chattanooga, TN 37403
PH: 423-265-9882 FX: 423-425-2379
Mark Colbert mark-colbert@utc.edu
www.wutc.org

Texas

KACU *Abilene Christian U.*
PO Box 27820, Abilene, TX 79699
PH: 325-674-2441
John Best bestj@acu.edu
www.kacu.org

KNTU *U. North Texas*
PO Box 310881, Denton, TX 76203
PH: 940-565-3688 FX: 940-565-2518
www.kntu.unt.edu

KTXK *Texarkana College*
2500 N. Robison Rd. Texarkana, TX 75599
PH: 903-838-4541 x3269 FX: 903-832-5030
Jerry Atkins jbbop@aol.com
www.tc.cc.tx.us/ktxk

KVLU *Lamar U.*
PO Box 10064, Beaumont, TX 77710
PH: 409-880-8164
Joe Elwell joe.elwell@lamar.edu
dept.lamar.edu/kvlu

KWBU *Baylor U.*
1 Bear Pl. #97296, Waco, TX 76798-7296
PH: 254-710-3472 FX: 254-710-3874
www.baylor.edu/kwbu/index.php

Morning Jazz *KTEP*
500 W. University Ave. Cotton Memorial #203
El Paso, TX 79968
PH: 915-747-5152 FX: 915-747-5641
www.ktep.org
Mainstream Jazz, Big Band, Traditional and up and coming Jazz artists.

Utah

KUER *U. Utah*
101 S. Wasatch Dr. Salt Lake City, UT 84112
PH: 801-581-4997
Steve Williams swilliams@media.utah.edu
www.kuer.org

Virginia

Soundwaves *WDCE*
PO Box 85, U. Richmond, VA 23173
PH: 804-289-8790 FX: 804-289-8996
Herb King wdce@richmond.edu
www.wdce.org
Purist prepare for an expansive look at the Jazz idiom.

Washington

KPLU
12180 Park Ave. S., Tacoma, WA 98447-0885
PH: 253-535-7758 FX: 253-535-8332
Joey Cohn jcohn@kplu.org
www.kplu.org

Washington DC

WPFW
2390 Champlain St. NW. 2nd Fl.
Washington, DC 20009
PH: 202-588-0999 x357
Bobby Hill hill_bobby@wpfw.org
www.wpfw.org

Wisconsin

WOJB *Lac Courte Oreilles Ojibwa College*
13386 W. Trepania Rd. Hayward, WI 54843
PH: 715-634-2100 FX: 715-634-4070
Nicky Kellar programdirector@wojb.org
www.wojb.org

Wisconsin Public Radio *WPR*
821 University Ave. Madison, WI 53706
PH: 800-747-7444
Vicki Nonn NonnV@wpr.org
www.wpr.org/regions

Canada

African Rhythms Radio *CITR*
319 W. Hastings St., Vancouver BC V6B 1H6
PH: 604-822-2487
David Jones david@africanrhythmsradio.com
www.africanrhythmsradio.com
Jazz, Nu Jazz, Soul, Latin, Hip Hop.

Café Jazz Radio Show
669 Fairmont Rd. Winnipeg, MB R3R 1B2
PH: 204-777-5200 FX: 204-777-5323
ted@jazzlynx.net
www.jazzlynx.net
Exposes and support new artists from around the world.

In a Mellow Tone *CKCU*
Rm. 517, U. Ctr., 1125 Colonel By Dr.
Ottawa, ON K1S 5B6
PH: 613-520-2898
Ron Sweetman ronsweetman@kalixo.com
inamellowtone.blogspot.com
Jazz from every era and in every style.

jazz for a sunday night *CHRW*
Rm. 250, UCC, UWO, London, ON N6A 3K7
PH: 519-661-3600 FX: 519-661-3372
Barrie Woodey jazz4a@yahoo.ca
chrwradio.com/shows/jazz.htm
Covers the whole spectrum of Jazz.

The Jazz Show *CITR*
#233-6138 SUB Blvd. Vancouver, BC V6T 1Z1
PH: 604-822-2487 FX: 604-822-9364
Gavin Walker citrmusic@club.ams.ubc.ca
www.citr.ca
Features Jazz music that is respectful of its tradition and influential to the future.

JAZZ.FM91
4 Pardee Ave. #100, Toronto, ON M6K 3H5
PH: 416-595-0404 FX: 416-595-9413
info@jazz.fm
www.jazz.fm
Latest Jazz and Blues styles, artists and their music.

Swing is in the Air *CKCU*
Jacques Émond jre@radiojazz.ca
www.ckcufm.com
On the air for over 20 years. Featuring a wide spectrum of Jazz, including Traditional, Blues, Bop, Latin as well as Contemporary Jazz.

Time for Jazz *CKUA*
10526 Jasper Ave. Edmonton, AB T5J 1Z7
PH: 780-428-7595 FX: 780-428-7624
Don Berner don.berner@ckua.com
www.ckua.com
Blending all eras of popular Jazz into three hours.

Europe

Belgium

The Global Jazz Scene
Peter Maguire
pmaguire@jazz-clubs-worldwide.com
www.jazz-clubsworldwide.com/netradio/
jazzhalfhour.htm
Please e-mail me and I will send you submission details.

Germany

department deluxe
Blutenburgstraße 82, d-80636, Munich, Germany
PH: +49 (0) 170-14-77-039
Jan Siegmund info@department-deluxe.org
www.department-deluxe.org
NuJazz and Freestyle with a touch of Jazz. I always request some MP3 samples to see if your music fits our format.

JazzRadio.net
Kornaue 1, 14109 Berlin, Germany
PH: 030-80692050 FX: 030-80692051
info@jazzradio.net
www.jazzradio.net
Covering the world of Jazz - from Jazz news and reviews to the Jazz lifestyle.

The Netherlands

Jazz & Blues Tour
PO Box 471, 2400 Al Alphen a/d Rijn,
The Netherlands
www.jazzbluestour.nl
Send any promotion material for airplay.

NPS Radio
www.omroep.nl/nps/output
Jazz, World and beyond.

Portugal

The Jazz Picante Radio Show
Largo dos Fornos - nº3 - 2ºESQ, Paço de Arcos -
2770-067 Portugal
Daniel info@jazzpicante.com
www.jazzpicante.com
Broken Beat, Nu Jazz, Nu Soul, Hip Hop ...

Spain

All that Jazz Radio
Apartado de Correos 445, San Pedro de Alcantara,
29670, Malaga, Spain
PH: 34-95-278-56-16 FX: 34-95-278-39-04
Brian Parker bp@jazz-radio.fm
www.jazz-radio.fm
Online 24 HOURS A DAY with the best Jazz on the net.

Switzerland

Smooth Vibes Radio
Peter Böhi pboehi@boehi.ch
www.smoothvibes.com/swissgroove.html
The best of Smooth Jazz the way you always wanted it to get but never received due to Broadcast Architecture's limiting effect.

United Kingdom

BBC Radio 2 *Jazz and Big Band*
www.bbc.co.uk/radio2/r2music/jazz
Home page of the BBC Radio 2's various Jazz and Big Band shows. Info, shows, contacts etc.

BBC Radio 3 *Jazz*
www.bbc.co.uk/radio3/jazz
Home page of the BBC Radio 3's various Jazz shows. Info, shows, contacts etc.

Gilles Peterson Show *BBC Radio 1*
London, W1N 4DJ UK
PH: 08700-100-100
Gilles Peterson gilles.peterson@bbc.co.uk
www.bbc.co.uk/radio1/gillespeterson
Features cutting edge Jazz.

JazzDJ Podcast
PO Box 2128, Leigh on Sea, Essex, SS9 1YU UK
PH: +44 (0) 203-239-8770
www.jazzdj.co.uk
Explorations in Jazz. Exploring the many essences of that Jazz juice groove!

Jazz FM
26-27 Castlereagh St., London, W1H 5DL UK
www.jazzfm.com
Latin Jazz, world Jazz, fusion, vocalists and more.

Australia

3MBS
St. Euphrasia, 1 St Heliers St., Abbotsford,
VIC 3067 Australia
PH: 03-9816-9355 FX: 03-9817 3777
info@3mbs.org.au
www.3mbs.org.au
Jazz and Classical music.

Latin Radio

United States

Al Lado Latino *KBCS*
3000 Landerholm Cir. SE.,
Bellevue, WA 98007-6484
PH: 425-564-2424
Johnny Conga kbcsdj@ctc.edu
www.kbcs.fm
A lively fusion of Latin music showcasing the diversity of the Latin music community of yesterday and today.

Alma del Barrio *KXLU*
1 LMU Dr. Los Angeles, CA 90045
PH: 310-338-5958 FX: 310-338-5959
www.kxlu.com
Authentic and traditional Latin music.

Alma Latina *KDHX*
3504 Magnolia, St. Louis, MO 63118
PH: 314-664-3688 FX: 314-664-1020
Lydia and Carlos almalatina@kdhx.org
www.kdhx.org/programs/almalatina.htm
Caribbean beats, classic Boleros and Latin-style Rock 'n Roll.

Arriba *WDVR*
PO Box 191 Sergeantsville, NJ 08557
PH: 609-397-1620 FX: 609-397-5991
www.wdvrfm.org
Featuring Latin rhythms.

Batanga.com
2007 Yanceyville St., Greensboro, NC 27405
Attn: Programming
www.batanga.com
Plays several Hispanic genres.

The Best of Brazil *KZUM*
941 "O" St., Lincoln, NE 68508
PH: 402-474-5086 FX: 402-474-5091
Randy Morse somdobrasil@alltel.net
www.kzum.org/brazil
Featuring Brazilian musicians and composers.

Cafe Brasil *WDNA*
PO Box 558636, Miami, FL 33255
PH: 305-662-8889 FX: 305-662-1975
info@wdna.org
www.wdna.org
Brazilian Jazz/Bossa Nova music in all styles , interviews and special in-studio musical guests.

Canto Tropical *KPFK*
3729 Cahuenga Blvd. W.
North Hollywood, CA 91604
PH: 818-985-2711 FX: 818-763-7526
Hector Resendez hector@westsiderc.org
www.kpfk.org
Focusing on Salsa, Mambo, Afro-Cuban, & Latin Jazz from around the world.

Need Gigs?

A new live venue directory from the creators of The Indie Bible!

Tour locally, regionally or nationally!

Our regional guides (featuring 32,000 venues in the US and Canada) will help you to find gigs perfectly suited to your touring needs.

Also includes 3,500 booking agents!

www.indievenuebible.com

Chicano Radio Network
7336 Santa Monica Blvd. #800,
Hollywood, CA 90046
PH: 480-636-8853 FX: 612-465-4500
info@crnlive.com
www.crnlive.com
Submit your recordings to be included for possible rotation.

Con Clave *KPOO*
PO Box 423030, San Francisco, CA 94142
PH: 415-346-5373 FX: 415-346-5173
Chata Gutierrez conclave@kpoo.com
www.kpoo.com
Celebrating 30 years of Salsa music on the airwaves.

Con Sabor *KPFA*
1929 MLK Jr. Way, Berkeley, CA 94704
PH: 510-848-4425 FX: 510-848-3812
Luis Medina music@kpfa.org
www.kpfa.org
Afro-Caribbean Dance music. A mix of Salsa, Afro-Cuban and Latin Jazz.

Con Salsa *WBUR*
890 Commonwealth Ave. 3rd Fl. Boston, MA 02215
PH: 617-353-0909
Jose Masso jmasso@consalsa.org
www.consalsa.org
Afro-Cuban music, Salsa, Latin-Jazz, Merengue, Nueva Trova and World music.

Corriente *KGNU*
4700 Walnut St., Boulder, CO 80301
PH: 303-449-4885
www.kgnu.org
Music, news, poetry and features.

Cyber Station FM
info@cyberstationfm.com
www.cyberstationfm.com
En este link hay Salsa 24 horas desde New York, el sonido es muy bueno.

Danza Latina *WTJU*
PO Box 400811, Charlottesville, VA 22904-4811
PH: 434-924-0885 FX: 434-924-8996
M.I.G. & DJ Rafael wtju@virginia.edu
wtju.net/cpages/musub
Lo mejor de Salsa, Merengue, Cumbia, Reggeaton, y Rock en Espanol.

Dimension Latina *WLUW*
6525 N. Sheridan Rd. Chicago, IL 60626
PH: 773-508-9589 FX: 773-508-8082
musicdept@wluw.org
wluw.org
Four hours of Latin music with occasional news.

El Viaje *WRTI*
1509 Cecil B. Moore Ave. 3rd Fl.
Philadelphia, PA 19121-3410
PH: 215-204-3393 FX: 215-204-7027
davidortiz@phillysalseros.com
www.wrti.org
David Ortiz spins the classics alongside the currents in the ever-growing field of Latin Jazz.

EnFiltro.com
enfiltro@gmail.com
www.enfiltro.com
Podcast featuring independent music from around the globe.

Horizontes *KUT*
1 University Stn. A0704, Austin, TX 78712
PH: 512-471-2345 FX: 512-471-3700
Michael Crockett music@kut.org
www.kut.org
Travel the musical airways of Latin America.

In the Pocket *WTJU*
PO Box 400811, Charlottesville, VA 22904-4811
PH: 434-924-0885 FX: 434-924-8996
El Gordito wtju@virginia.edu
wtju.net/cpages/musub
In search of the holy groove!

Jazz Tropicale *WDCB*
College of DuPage, 425 Fawell Blvd.
Glen Ellyn, IL 60137
PH: 630-942-4200 FX: 630-942-2788
Marshall Vente VenteM@wdcb.org
wdcb.org
From traditional to contemporary and Brazilian to Caribbean. It's a Jazz show with palm trees.

KBBF
PO Box 7189, 410 Finley Ave.
Santa Rosa, CA 95407
PH: 707-545-8833 FX: 707-545-6244
kbbf-radio.com
Our programs reflect all segments of the community, from the Latino and Anglo cultures.

KDNA
121 Sunnyside Ave. PO Box 800,
Granger, WA 98932
PH: 509-854-1900
kdna.org
Addressing the needs and interests of Spanish speaking audiences.

KHDC
5005 E. Belmont, Fresno, CA 93727
PH: 559-455-5777 FX: 559-455-5778
www.radiobilingue.org
The only national distributor of Spanish-language programming in public radio.

KTUZ
5101 Shields Blvd. Oklahoma City, OK 73129
PH: 405-616-9900 FX: 405-616-0328
ktuz@tylermedia.com
www.ktuz.com

Latino America Sonando *KMUD*
PO Box 135, 1144 Redway Dr.
Redway, CA 95560-0135
PH: 707-923-2513 FX: 707-923-2501
Kate Klein md@kmud.org
www.kmud.org
The latest in Salsa, Songo, Latin Jazz, Afro-Cuban Folkloric, music from all over Latin America, plus interviews and other specials.

The Mambo Machine *WKCR*
2920 Broadway, Mailcode 2612,
New York, NY 10027
PH: 212-854-9920
Jose "Cheo" Diaz latin@wkcr.org
www.columbia.edu/cu/wkcr
The longest running Salsa show in New York City.

Night Latin Jass y Mucho Mas in the Morning
3504 Magnolia, St. Louis, MO 63118
PH: 314-664-3955 x301 FX: 314-664-1020
Carlos G. Jove carlos@kdhx.org
www.kdhx.org
Your way of staying asleep while you wake up. With a fine layer of Jazz, you pile on a sheet of beats, over the broad foundation of Rock and Roll, top it all off with that Latin touch..... & you gave a stack of great music.

Onda Nueva *WUSB*
Stony Brook Union 266,
Stony Brook, NY 11794-3263
PH: 631-632-6501 FX: 631-632-7182
Felix Palacios music@wusb.fm
wusb.fm
Everything from Sun to Salsa, Plena, Afro-Antillean, Latin-American music, interviews, history, live in-studio jams and critique.

Opportunity Radio
16815 Woodridge Rd. Clermont, FL 34714
PH: 407 860-8160
Jhonny Mercedes jhonnymercedes@yahoo.com
www.opportunityradio.net
A new talents internet radio station for Spanish speaking unsigned artists.

Radio Tierra
PO Box 859, Hood River, OR 97031
PH: 541-387-3772 FX: 510-740-3637
main@radiotierra.org
www.radiotierra.org

Raices *KUNM*
MSC06 3520, Onate Hall, 1 U. NM,
Albuquerque, NM 87131-0001
PH: 505-277-5615
Henry Gonzales music@kunm.org
www.kunm.org
All genres of Hispanic music.

Raizes Radio Show *KBCS*
3000 Landerholm Cir. SE,
Bellevue, WA 98007-6484
PH: 425-564-2424
Paula Maya paulamaya@yellowhouserec.com
kbcs.fm
Explores the music and culture of Brazil and its neighbors.

The Red Zone Indie *103.1*
www.myspace.com/theredzone
Cha Cha spins the hottest music being made by Latin artists from around the globe - spanning the alternative, Rock, Hip Hop, Punk, Ska, Electronic, Reggae and other cool music genres.

Ritmo Latino
www.ritmolatino.org
An hour of eclectic Latin music that will leave you shaking your booty and speaking in tongues. (Really.)

Ritmos Latinos *KRBS*
PO Box #9, Oroville, CA 95965
Mike Coranado krbs@cncnet.com
www.radiobirdstreet.org
Music from The Americas, Europe and the Caribbean.

Rock Sin Anestesia *WLUW*
6525 N. Sheridan Rd. Chicago, IL 60626
PH: 773-508-9589 FX: 773-508-8082
spanishrock@wluw.org
wluw.org
Latin Alternative radio show featuring Indie-Rock, Electronica, Surf, Fusion, Ska and more!

Sabor Tropical *KIPO*
738 Kaheka St. #101, Honolulu, HI 96814
PH: 808-955-8821 FX: 808-942-5477
Ray Cruz salsaymas@aol.com
www.hawaiipublicradio.org
Tropical programming with emphasis on Salsa, Afro-Cuban & Latin Jazz.

Salsa *WNHU*
300 Boston Post Rd. West Haven, CT 06516
PH: 203-479-8807 FX: 203-931-6055
newmusic@wnhu.net
www.wnhu.net

The Salsa and Latin Jazz Show *KVMR*
401 Spring St., Nevada City, CA 95959
PH: 530-265-9555 FX: 530-265-9077
Leon Reyes elleon@kvmr.org
www.kvmr.org
The best in Salsa, Salsa Jazz, Latin Jazz and those other Latin musical surprises.

Salsa Sabrosa *KUNM*
MSC06 3520, Onate Hall, 1 U. New Mexico,
Albuquerque, NM 87131-0001
PH: 505-277-5615
Wellington Guzman music@kunm.org
www.kunm.org
Friday nights are hot hot hot!

Son del Caribe *WRTU*
PO Box 21305, San Juan, Puerto Rico 00931-1305
PH: 787-763-8500
Elmer González sondelcaribe@hotmail.com
www.wrtu.org
Afro-Caribbean, Latin Jazz, Salsa.

Son Pacifica *KPFT*
419 Lovett Blvd. Houston, TX 77006
PH: 713-526-5738
Alfonso Rivera alfonso@sonpacifica.com
www.sonpacifica.com
The best of independent Latino music!

The Sounds of Brazil
5250 Grand Ave. 14/111, Gurnee, IL 60031
PH: 847-855-8546 FX: 240-358-3096
www.connectbrazil.com
The best and the latest sounds from Brazil.

Su Tumbao Por La Manana *WVKR*
Box 726, Vassar College, 124 Raymond Ave.
Poughkeepsie, NY 12604
PH: 845-437-7178 FX: 845-437-7656
Jorge Quintana tumbao@wvkr.org
www.wvkr.org
Salsa, Latin Jazz, and Afro Cuban rhythms, featuring the artists of today, the past, and those who are impacting the music of tomorrow.

¡Tertulia! *WFCR*
Hampshire House, U. Mass, 131 County Cir.
Amherst, MA 01003-9257
PH: 413-545-0100 FX: 413-545-2546
www.wfcr.org
Latin Jazz, Boleros, Salsa, Merengue, Nueva Trova, Tango and Folk music.

WHCR
138th & Convent, Nac Building, Rm. 1515,
New York, NY 10031
PH: 212-650-7481
whcr903fm@yahoo.com
www.whcr.org
Hosts many Latin music shows.

WKCR *Columbia U.*
2920 Broadway, Mailcode 2612,
New York, NY 10027
PH: 212-854-9920
latin@wkcr.org jazz@wkcr.org
www.wkcr.org
A leader in Latin and Jazz music broadcasting.

WRTE *Mexican Fine Arts Center*
1401 W. 18th St., Chicago, IL 60608
PH: 312-455-9455 x201 FX: 312-455-9755
Carlos Mendez carlos.mendez@radioarte.org
www.wrte.org
Bilingual youth-operated, urban, community radio.

WWGC
State U. W. Georgia, 1600 Maple St.,
Carrollton, GA 30118
PH: 770-836-6500
wwgc@westga.edu
www.westga.edu/~wwgc
Features several Latin music shows.

La X Estereo
laxestereo@hotmail.com
www.laxestereo.com
100% Pura Salsa - Con el Sabor de Cali - Colombia.

Canada

The Latin Train/El Tren Latino *CHUO*
65 University Pvt. #0038, Ottawa, ON K1N 9A5
PH: 613-562-5967 FX: 613-562-5969
Michael Bongard latintrain@yahoo.com
www.myspace.com/latintrainradio
Weekly show featuring Latin Jazz, Salsa, Timba and Cuban Son.

The Leo Ramirez Show *CITR*
#233-6138 SUB Blvd. Vancouver, BC V6T 1Z1
PH: 604-822-2487 FX: 604-822-9364
Leo Ramirez leoramirez@canada.com
www.citr.ca
The best mix of Latin American music.

Viejoteca *CFRU*
U.C. Level 2 Guelph, ON N1G 2W1
PH: 519-837-2378 FX: 519-763-9603
DJ Gury Gury djgurygury@yahoo.ca
www.cfru.ca
The best in old school Salsa, along with the hottest new performers. Que Viva la Salsa!

Greece

Sonido Bestial
Basilio Stamatiou stamatiou@latinmusic.gr
www.sonidobestial.net
Online Latin Radio from Greece!

Turkey

Latino Time *Radio Oxigen*
Emin Vafi Korusu Muallim Naci cad. No 61/5
Ortaköy 80840, Turkey
PH: 0212-236-5436 FX: 0212-236-5440
Ayhan Sicimoglu info@radiooxigen.com
www.radiooxigen.com

United Kingdom

Brasil Brasil *209 Radio*
Citylife House, Sturton St., Cambridge,
CB1 2QF UK
PH: 01223-488418 FX: 01223-488419
Inacio Vieira brasilbrasil@209radio.co.uk
www.209radio.co.uk
Brings you the joy and vibrancy of Brazilian music.

Metal Radio

Radio Promoters

Skateboard Marketing
1150 Agnes Ct. Valley Stream, NY 11580
Attn: Munsey Ricci
PH: 516-328-1103 FX: 516-328-1293
Munsey excuseking@aol.com
www.skateboard-marketing.com
Commercial and college Metal radio promotion.
Commercial active Rock promotion and marketing.

Stations and Shows

North America

United States

Auditory Demise *WBGU*
120 West Hall, Bowling Green, OH 43403
PH: 419-372-8657 FX: 419-372-9449
www.myspace.com/auditorydemise
Steve Lazenby plays the latest and best of the Metal genre plus interviews with some up-and-coming bands.

Axecaliber *WITR*
32 Lomb Memorial Dr. Rochester, NY 14623-0563
PH: 585-475-2271 FX: 585-475-4988
geno@heavyrock.com
www.heavyrock.com/radioshow.html
Promotes undiscovered Heavy Rock artists.

Bad Attitude Radio
PO Box 604, Kewaskum, WI 53040
cormws@charter.net
www.kissthis.com
Send your music and info and a written letter stating that you give us permission to air your music.

Beyond the Grave *WKNH*
Attn: Paul Weston, 229 Main St., Keene, NH 03435
PH: 603-358-8863
www.btgrave.com
Weekly Metal show.

Braingell Unsigned
vboogieman@braingell.com
www.myspace.com/bgrunsigned
Are you in a Metal/Hard Rock band? Want to get your music heard on Braingell Unsigned show? Are you part of a non-major record company and wanting to promote your bands?

CottonRock Radio Podcast
PO Box 3646, Meridian, MS 39303-3646
www.myspace.com/cottonrock
Gives exposure to some of the best Rock, Hard Rock, Metal and indie bands.

Children of the Metal Movement *WRUW*
11220 Bellflower Rd. Cleveland, OH 44106
PH: 216-368-2208
Roger md@wruw.org
wruw.org
Metal of the 80's, 90's and today, plus local Metal bands.

ChroniX Radio
www.chronixradio.com
Metal/Hard Rock/Alternative internet radio station.

CrossFire-Radio
DJ Fire bands@crossfire-radio.com
www.crossfire-radio.com
We currently play around 180+ unsigned Hard Rock bands on our station. In order to get airplay, we have a small form for you to fill out.

Dark Cloud Radio
darkcloudradio@yahoo.com
www.darkcloudradio.net
Heavy, Hard, Dark … or just anything that Rocks!

Darksoul VII Radio
US: 209 S. Monte Vista Ave. San Dimas, CA 91773
Canada: 501-1251 Jervis St.,
Vancouver, BC V6E 2E1
www.darksoul7.net
We play only Black, Death, Gore, Guttural, Grind, Thrash, Hybrid and Progressive Metal.

Dementia Radio
www.dementiaradio.com
We encourage indies to submit their music to us.

Doom Metal Radio
info@doom-metal.com
www.doom-metal.com/radio.html
All Doom and closely related music 24 hours a day, 7 days a week.

DrunkMonkeyRadio
music@drunkmonkeyradio.com
www.myspace.com/311236430
We're always looking for new music to play on our station. If you are in a Hard Rock band and would like to get your music played just email your song to us.

Embrace of the Darkness & Metal *WMUA*
105 Campus Ctr. U. Mass, Amherst, MA 01003
PH: 413-545-3691 FX: 413-545-0682
DJ Solveig embraceofthedarkness@yahoo.com
www.wmua.org
European Metal (Death, Black etc.) Sunday nights.

From the Depths *KTRU*
PO Box 1892, Houston, TX 77251
PH: 713-348-5878
Wes Weaver fromthedepths666@hotmail.com
www.myspace.com/fromthedepths
Extreme Death and Black Metal radio program.

Full Metal Contact *WOBC*
Wilder Hall 319, 135 W. Lorain St.
Oberlin, OH 44074
PH: 440-775-8107 FX: 440-775-6678
John Raab music.wobc@oberlin.edu
www.wobc.org
Best of Hardcore, Death and local Metal.

Greasy Kids' Stuff *WRUW*
11220 Bellflower Rd. Cleveland, OH 44106
PH: 216-368-2208
Ace md@wruw.org
wruw.org
Features Metal, Punk and Hard Rock.

HardDrive XL with Lou Brutus
www.myspace.com/harddriveradio
The nation's premiere new Rock radio show for over 10 years. Each week the show features the best new rock and conversation with the people who make it.

HeavyMetalRadio.com
www.heavymetalradio.com
The loudest site on the internet!!!

Into the Pit *KUPD*
c/o Marcus Meng, 1900 W. Carmen
Tempe, AZ 85283
www.98KUPD.com
The shit your mama don't want you to hear.

JJ-Overdrive *WJJO*
PH: 608-321-0941
www.wjjo.com
The loudest, hardest and fastest Metal on Earth.

K666 Radio /StonerRock.com
PO Box 4, Tendoy, ID 83468
El Danno dan@stonerrock.com
www.stonerrock.com
If you're disgusted with the pathetic state of popular music, you've come to the right place. Please send TWO copies of your CD.

The Last Exit for the Lost *WVBR*
PO Box 224, Ovid, NY 14521-0224
PH: 607-273-2121 FX: 607-273-4069
lastexit@thelastexit.org
www.thelastexit.org
Supports indie Metal, Goth, Punk, Industrial etc.

Livehardrock.com
www.livehardrock.com
Carries Hard Rock shows with DJs from around the world.

Mayhem and Rage Metal Radio Show
www.myspace.com/mayhemragemetalradio
Syndicated show featuring Metal, Thrash and Death Metal.

Metalradio.com
1321 Campbell Ave. La Salle, IL 61301
FX: 815-780-6001
www.metalradio.com
The only station for a Metal Nation! Send us your demos or press releases and we'll get 'em up on the site.

Mosh Pit *WORT*
118 S. Bedford St., Madison, WI 53703
matt@moshpitradio.com
www.moshpitradio.com
A Heavy Metal radio show. Send your CDs or demos to our address for airplay.

Radio xXx
www.radio3x.com
Rock/Metal station who focus on both popular and undiscovered artists from around the world.

Rampage Radio *KUSF*
2130 Fulton St., San Francisco, CA 94117
Dirty Sanchez rampageradio@hotmail.com
kusf.org
The Bay Area's heaviest radio show since 1981. Send any CDs to the address above. If your band wants to be interviewed on the show, e-mail me.

RIFF Radio
3201 20th St. S. #124, Fargo, ND 58104
"Metal Man" Dan mmd@hardrocksociety.com
www.hardrocksociety.com
A 24/7 high quality streaming radio station.

The Root Of All Evil *KFAI*
1808 Riverside Ave. Minneapolis, MN 55454
PH: 612-341-0980 FX: 612-341-4281
Earl Root root@rootofallevil.com
www.rootofallevil.com
Molten Metal meltdowns, demented and deranged. Totally tasteless. Rotten mean and nasty.

Rough Edge Radio
PO Box 5160, Ventura, CA 93005
PH/FX: 805-293-8507
R. Scott Bolton info@roughedge.com
roughedgeradio.com
Features 2 weekly Metal shows.

Scene Zine Podcast
PH: 312-239-0057
Marcus Couch thescenezine@gmail.com
www.thescenezine.com
Featuring independent Hard Rock artists.

Spider Bite Radio
435 Elm S. Manchester, NH 03101
PH: 603-645-1449 x113 FX: 603-657-7202
Myke mykel@spiderbiteradio.com
www.spiderbiteradio.com
Independent music from around the globe!

Spread Radio Live
Dave Navarro spreadradiolive@6767.com
www.spreadradiolive.com
We play anything and everything we think is good! Alternative, Electro, Metal, Punk and Goth.

STEEL 93
adamz@steel93.com
www.steel93.com
All forms of Rock. Hard, Metal, Punk, Glam etc. We would love to play your songs!

StrongArm Radio *WRBB*
www.strongarmradio.com
www.myspace.com/strongarmradio
Loud, heavy and all about the local and underground. If your band wants to be played, let us know and send us some music.

Talking Metal
Mark Strigl
PO Box 404
Maplewood, NJ 07040
Mark Strigl talkingmetal@yahoo.com
www.talkingmetal.com
"Metal's reigning podcast champs!" Please only send Hard Rock and Metal. No Emo, Punk etc. You must also create the mailing label as seen above (my name, address and city on different lines).

The Tink's Metal Show *WVUD*
PO Box 9284, Wilmington, DE 19809
PH: 302-798-0144
The Tink tink@thetinksinc.com
www.thetinksinc.com
The TINK is Metal incarnate. Radio, video, online…and in person. He is the Godfather. He is the man, the myth, the legend and the entity that makes it possible for the rest of us to be Metal.

Tundra Trash Radio
PO Box 657, Soldotna, AK 99669
Beth dj@tundratrashradio.com
www.tundratrashradio.com
Voted Best Metal Station for 2004. A venue to some of the best independent artists you will ever hear!

WFLM Radio
691 NW 59th Ave. Ocala, FL 34482
Pamela submissions@wflmradio.com
wflmradio.com
Your home for the best indie & mainstream Metal on the web.

Wylde Radio
6125 N. Mason Ave. Chicago, IL 60646
PH: 773 775-6596
Tom Wylde tom@wylderadio.com
www.wylderadio.com
An internet radio show dedicated to the support and promotion of independent and underground Metal.

Canada

94.9FM The Rock
1200 Airport Blvd. #207, Oshawa, ON L1J 8P5
Vanessa Murphy vanessa@therock.fm
www.therock.fm
I like guitar solos in music so if you like the honky tonk badonkadonk don't bother.

Anger Management *CJIQ*
299 Don Valley Dr. Kitchener, ON N2G 4M4
www.myspace.com/883angermanagement
Weekly Metal show with host Gruesome Geddes.

Bourreau Metallique *CIBL*
1691, boul Pie IX, Montréal, QC H1V 2C3
PH: 514-526-2581 FX: 514-526-3583
www.myspace.com/bourreau
Metalizing the airwaves for over 20 years.

Hellbound Radio *CIOI*
www.myspace.com/hellboundradio
A weekly metal radio show in Hamilton.

High Voltage Rock
highvoltagepodcast@gmail.com
www.highvoltagerock.ca
The best place to hear kick-ass high energy Rock!!!

Metal Canvas *CHUO*
65 University Pvt. #0038, Ottawa, ON K1N 9A5
PH: 613-562-5967 FX: 613-562-5969
metalcanvas@yahoo.com
www.chuo.fm
If you send it, Metal Canvas will broadcast it!

Métal Pesant *CFLX*
67 rue Wellington nord, Sherbrooke, QC J1H 5A9
PH: 819-566-2787 FX: 819-566-7331
metalpesant@hotmail.com
www.cflx.qc.ca
Where the word Metal finds all its meaning.

METALLICITY Radio Hour *CFBU*
www.myspace.com/metallicityfm
Everything heavier than everything else!

MetalNetRadio.com
1 Selkirk Rd. W., Lethbridge, AB T1K 4N4
programdirector@metalnetradio.com
www.metalnetradio.com
We maintain our independence and play only what we think is good and what our listeners think is good.

Mind Compression *CJSR*
Rm. 0-09 Students' Union Bldg. U. Alberta,
Edmonton, AB T6G 2J7
PH: 780-492-2577 x232 FX: 780-492-3121
Metal John & DJ Temptress music@cjsr.com
www.cjsr.com
Canada's longest running Heavy Metal show! Metal John plays Old School Metal, Hardcore, Classic Metal and anything else he wants.

Powerchord *CITR*
#233-6138 SUB Blvd. Vancouver, BC V6T 1Z1
PH: 604-822-2487 FX: 604-822-9364
citrmusic@club.ams.ubc.ca
www.citr.ca
Vancouver 's longest running Metal show.

Pure Grain Audio Radio
700 King St. W. #208, Toronto, ON M5V 2Y6
PH: 416-723-3911
Chris Gonda gonda@puregrainaudio.com
www.puregrainaudio.com
Send us an e-mail and we'll arrange to have your music featured on our amazing indie show or all of our weekly shows.

Rock and Roll Report Podcast
rockandrollreport@gmail.com
www.rockandrollreport.com
I play Rock & Roll that both floats my boat and that I think should be played on commercial Rock radio if only it had the balls to do so.

Sounds of Steel *CKUT*
3647 U. St., Montreal, QC H3A 2B3
PH: 514-398-6787 FX: 514-398-8261
www.myspace.com/soundsofsteel
Montreal's best stop for ball-smashin', riff-lovin' headbangin' Metal-Heads who are in need of a 2 hour Metal fix on the radio.

Space in Your Face *CKMS*
200 University Ave. W., Waterloo, ON N2L 3G1
PH: 519-886-2567 FX: 519-884-3530
siyf@gto.net
ckmsfm.uwaterloo.ca
Features Metal news, interviews, give-aways and more!

Mexico

Mi Mama Me Mima
losmimados@gmail.com
www.mimamamemima.com.mx
Internet radio with a Rock format.

Europe

Andorra

KWFM.net
c/o Prat De La Creu, 16 - AD500 Andorra La Vella,
Andorra
J-E je.henley@kwfm.net
www.kwfm.net
International Rock and Metal radio. All submissions are welcome without restriction of country and language!

France

Kerosene Radio
6 bis, rue d'Echange, 35000 Rennes, France
kfuel@kfuel.org
www.kfuel.org
Rock, Noise, Hard/Emo Core, Experimental, Punk, Pop ...

Germany

InfraRot
Amtsgericht HRA 10032 Memmingen, Germany
PH: 49-0-8333/93113 FX: 49-0-8333/93114
Jörg Wolfgram gott@infrarot.de
www.infrarot.de
Fresh music for rotten people.

Radio Melodic
Postfach 3144, 70777 Filderstadt, Germany
PH: +49-7158-956611 FX: +49-7158-956611
radio@radiomelodic.de
www.radiomelodic.de
Each show is full of new CDs, news, interviews, concert reports and more.

Rock of Ages *Bermuda-Funk*
PH: 0621-300-97-97 FX: 0621-33-688-63
Georg Lögler rockofages@gmx.de
www.bermudafunk.org
All styles of Rock/Metal. No Death Metal. My emphasis is on UNKNOWN bands.

Rock Station Kiel
von Lüttwitz-Heinrichstr. 18, 24802 Emkendorf,
Germany
Heiko Mangels rockstation@kielfm.de
www.rockstationkiel.de
We play all styles from AOR to Metal in 2 shows. Please send promotional stuff to the above address.

Rockin` Radio
Banderbacher Str. 24, 90513 Zirndorf, Germany
PH/FX: 0911-60-95-95
info@rockin-radio.de
www.rockin-radio.de
Das beste fur franken in sachen Rock.

Stahlwerk-Hannover *Radio Flora*
Zur Bettfedernfabrik 1, D-30451 Hannover,
Germany
PH: 49-511-219790 FX: 49-511-2197919
info@stahlwerk-hannover.de
www.stahlwerk-hannover.de
Different bands without a recent record deal are featured.

The Netherlands

Art For The Ears Radio *Radio 90FM*
www.artfortheears.nl
Webzine focusing on Metal, Hard Rock, Heavy Alternative Rock, Hardcore and Punk Rock.

Norway

Metal Express Radio Show
Ovrefoss 14, N-0555 Oslo, Norway
Stig. G. Nordahl stig@metalexpressradio.com
www.metalexpressradio.com
Streaming radio, news, reviews, interviews…

Portugal

S.O.S Heavy Metal Radio Show
PO Box 408, 4703 Braga Codex, Portugal
PH: +351-919051581
Filipe Marta sosradio@hotmail.com
www.myspace.com/sosmetalradio_show
Online and screaming fucking loud!

United Kingdom

4Q Radio
PH: +44-7793868611
andy@4qradio.com
www.4qradio.com
Station with a Metal and Punk Rock show.

Rock Show *BBC 6*
6 Music, Western House, 99 Great Portland St.,
London, W1A 1AA UK
PH: 08700-100-600
Craig Charles funk.6music@bbc.co.uk
www.bbc.co.uk/6music/shows/funk_soul
Your chance to hear the latest, greatest new Hard Rock and Metal.

The Rock Show
Ewan Spence ewanspence@gmail.com
rock.thepodcastnetwork.com
If you think you should be in a future show, then you need to let me know. I'll be happy with a URL pointing to a demo or even a small MP3 file.

Sex to 9 with María *TotalRock*
1 Denmark Pl. London, WC2H 8NL UK
maria@sexto9.com
www.sexto9.com
*Rock and Metal like you've never heard it before
...with a touch of exotic Latin passion.*

Australia

Critical Mass Radio Show *RTR FM*
PO Box 842, Mt. Lawley, WA 6929 Australia
PH: (08) 9260-9210
www.myspace.com/criticalmassradio
Stay Heavy Metal and bang your heads.

Full Metal Racket *Triple J*
GPO Box 9994, Melbourne, VIC 3000 Australia
PH: 1-800-0555-36
Andrew Haug fullmetalracket@triplej.abc.net.au
www.triplej.abc.net.au/racket
*Covering a wide range of the latest and greatest
heavy sounds with news updates, interviews, local
and international tour announcements and tonnes
more. Send in your demo CDs and tapes.*

New Age Radio

United States

Alpha Rhythms *WYSO*
2287 Schenley St., Dayton, OH 45439
Jerry Kenney allank@earthlink.net
www.wyso.org
4 hours of Ambient and New Age music.

Ambience *WWUH*
200 Bloomfield Ave. West Hartford, CT 06117
PH: 860-768-4701 FX: 860-768-5701
Susan teltanman@cox.net
www.teltan.org
*Ambient and Atmospheric Electronic music to drift
into Sunday morning with.*

The AM/FM Show (Saturday edition) *WMUH*
PO Box 632, Nazareth, PA 18064-0632
Bill Fox billyfox@soundscapes.us
soundscapes.us/amfm
*Electronic, Ambient, Space, Acoustic, Electric, Pop,
New Age and whatever strikes my fancy. Inquire by
e-mail BEFORE submitting your music!*

Astreaux World
www.astreauxworld.com
*Ambient/ New Age / Space music. Visit our website
to find out submission details.*

Audioscapes *KCPR*
Graphic Arts Bldg. 26, Rm. 201, CPSU
San Luis Obispo, CA 93407
PH: 805-756-2965
audioscapes@yahoo.com
www.geocities.com/audioscapes
*A Classical, Electronic and Progressive music
merge.*

Audiosyncracry *KTEP*
500 W. University Ave. Cotton Memorial #203
El Paso, TX 79968
PH: 915-747-5152 FX: 915-747-5641
www.ktep.org
*Host Jamey Osborne covers a wide range of music,
from Acoustic to Electronica. A good deal of Jazz
and Classical is played with an occasional dash of
World music.*

The Autopsy Report
Gramie Pompous.Brit@gmail.com
www.myspace.com/autopsyreport
*If you are heavy, true and seriously minded, you
WILL be played. I will contact you if you are good
enough for the show. Send a CD/bio. Good MP3s
are perfectly acceptable.*

BRAINWAVES *KXCI*
220 S. 4th Ave. Tucson, AZ 85701
PH: 520-623-1000
www.kxci.org
*New Age, Ambient, Experimental, Electro-Acoustic
Classical, World music.*

CheezMuzik *WTUL*
Tulane U. Ctr., New Orleans, LA 70118
PH: 504-865-5885 FX: 504-463-1023
www.wtul.fm
*One of the longest running shows in New Orleans'
radio history. Over 30 years & still going strong!*

Cosmic Island
Kevin kevin@thecosmicisland.com
TheCosmicIsland.com
*The best mix of New Age and Ambient music. Please
do NOT send MP3s!*

Earth Tones *KVLU*
PO Box 10064, Beaumont, TX 77710
PH: 409-880-8164
Elizabeth French kvlu@hal.lamar.edu
dept.lamar.edu/kvlu
*Two hours of New Age, Acoustic, Ambient and
World music.*

Echoes
PO Box 256, Chester Springs, PA 19425
FX: 610-827-9614
www.echoes.org
*Send submissions for airplay (CDs only). Do NOT
attach MP3s!*

ethnosphere *KRCL*
450 S. 300 W., Salt Lake City, UT 84101
PH: 801-359-9191 FX: 801-533-9136
Sohrab Mafi peace@krcl.org
www.krcl.org/~sohrabm
*A meditative journey into the world of consciousness
through music.*

Galactic Voyager *KCSN*
18111 Nordhoff St., Northridge, CA 91330-8312
PH: 818-885-5276
Meishel Menachekanian meishel@kcsn.org
www.kcsn.org/programs/galacticvoyager.html
A blend of Electronic and New Age music.

Gift of Peace *WJFF*
4765 State Rt. 52, PO Box 546
Jeffersonville, NY 12748
PH: 845-482-4141 FX: 845-482-9533
Lisa Brody jimandlisa@pronetisp.net
www.wjffradio.org
*The New Age music has to have a certain feel to it. I
guess you could call it spiritual, but not sappy. The
World music is usually very mellow.*

Groovera Chilled Web Radio
groovera.com
*Future Lounge, Nu-Jazz, Downtempo, Soft Techno,
Chill-Out music. To get started, please send us a
message with links to online music samples via our
contact page.*

Hearts of Space Radio
454 Las Gallinas #333, San Rafael, CA 94903
PH: 415-499-9901 FX: 415-499-9903
radio@hos.com
www.hos.com/radio.html
Submit your music, send CD & promo info.

Idyllic Music
idyllicmusic@cox.net
www.idyllicmusic.com
*Podcast featuring Trip Hop, Ambient, Jazz, Dub and
Downtempo songs by outstanding bands from
around the globe.*

Inner Visions *WNMC*
1701 E. Front St., Traverse City, MI 49686
PH: 231-995-2562
www.wnmc.org
*A mix of sounds and textures that could not be more
appropriate for a Sunday morning.*

Instrumental Saturdays *WMSE*
1025 N. Broadway, Milwaukee, WI 53202
PH: 414-277-6942 FX: 414-277-7149
Mary Bartlein meab@execpc.com
my.execpc.com/~meab
New Age, Ambient and World music.

Iridium Radio *KZYX/KZYZ*
PO Box 1, Philo, CA 95466
PH: 707-895-2324 FX: 707-895-2451
Kitty & Creek Iridiumradio@starband.net.
www.kzyx.org
*Currently we are interested in exploring your
offerings in New Age, World and Cool Jazz.*

Kozmik Radio
Koz kozmik@charter.net
kozmikradio.com
*A neo symphonical journey through time, space and
evolution.*

The Lighthouse *KCHO*
Cal State U. Chico 95929-0500
PH: 530-898-5896 FX: 530-898-4348
info@kcho.org
www.kcho.org
Mellow and uplifting music.

Limbik Frequencies
320 E. Buffalo St. #605, Milwaukee, WI 53202
djsam@limbikfreq.com
www.limbikfreq.com
*Our mix of Ambient, Downtempo, Ethereal,
Industrial and intelligent Techno, is an active
exploration into deep and uncharted modes of
existence.*

Lucid Sounds *WZBC*
Boston College, McElroy Commons 107
Chestnut Hill, MA 02467
PH: 617-552-4686 FX: 617-552-1738
Victor V. wzbcmusic@gmail.com
www.wzbc.org
Expanding awareness.

Midnight Light *KKUP*
933 Monroe St., PMB 9150, Santa Clara, CA 95050
PH: 408-260-2999
Joseph Leight kkup.folk@gmail.com
www.kkup.com
*Soundscapes, spoken words, occasionally taped
interviews with the thoughts to foster peaceful states
of mind*

Morning Breeze *KSBR*
28000 Marguerite Pkwy. Mission Viejo, CA 92692
PH: 949-582-5727 FX: 949-347-9693
Donna Jo Thornton themorningbreeze@gmail.com
www.ksbr.net
A mixture of New Age, World, Acoustic Instrumental and Spacey Electronic music.

The Morning Fog *WVUD*
Perkins Student Ctr. U. Delaware
Newark, DE 19716
PH: 302-831-2701 FX: 302-831-1399
wvudmusic@gmail.com
www.wvud.org
Early morning Ambience for sleeping or waking.

Music From Beyond the Lakes *WDBX*
224 N. Washington St., Carbondale, IL 62901
PH: 618-457-3691
Jerry & Namdar wdbx@globaleyes.net
www.wdbx.org
New Age music show.

Music from the Cosmic Wheel *WSCS*
Postmaster, E. Andover, NH 03231
PH: 603-735-5586
Brad Hartwell brad@cosmicwheel.net
www.colby-sawyer.edu/wscs
New Age, Ambient/Electronic/Space, World Fusion, Native, Celtic etc. Taped interviews and live performances are an occasional feature.

Music of the 21st Century with Chris Hickey *WXXI*
280 State St. PO Box 30021
Rochester, NY 14603-3021
PH: 585-258-0200
wxxi.org
New Age, Celtic, Jazz and World music that is energetic, rhythmic and melodic. It is a journey through a pleasing, surprising and sometimes startling musical landscape.

Musical Starstreams
Forest & Madison info@starstreams.com
www.starstreams.com
Mid to Downtempo, exotic Electronica. If you think your stuff fits, send your release on regular CD only (no MP3s) to our mailing address and then watch our playlists to see if it worked for us.

Mystic Music *KKUP*
933 Monroe St., PMB 9150, Santa Clara, CA 95050
Eric Mystic admin@kkup.com
www.kkup.com/ericm.html
Something special and out of the ordinary. Lifts and awakens you above normal consciousness.

Mystic Soundscapes
PO Box 50128, Albuquerque, NM 87181-0128
www.mysticsoundscapes.com
We make it our mission to promote your music to our large listener base. If your music fits the New Age, World music, Celtic, Ambient or Instrumental genre, we'd love to hear from you.

Neptune Currents *KKUP*
933 Monroe St., PMB 9150, Santa Clara, CA 95050
Steve Davis & Carol Joyce
neptuneradio@earthlink.net
www.kkup.org
Tranquil, expressive, meditative. Emphasis on electronic & Electro-Acoustic music, plus music of the Far East and other World music.

New Age Collage *SDPR*
555 Dakota St. PO Box 5000, Vermillion, SD 57069
PH: 800-456-0766
Jerry Cooley programming@sdpb.org
www.sdpb.org/radio/newage
2 hours of modern instrumental music.

The New Edge *WMBR*
3 Ames St., Cambridge, MA 02142
PH: 617-253-8810
Ken Field newedge@wmbr.org
wmbr.mit.edu
Mostly instrumental creative new music, composed and improvised at the intersection of Classical, Jazz and World styles.

New Frontiers *WXDU*
PO Box 90689, Duke Stn. Durham, NC 27708
Attn: Marty
PH: 919-684-2957
music@wxdu.org
www.wxdu.duke.edu
Two hours of Space music. Almost Ambient, almost Trance & almost Folk.

New Music Gallery *WMNR*
PO Box 920, Monroe, CT 06468
PH: 203-268-9667
info@wmnr.org
www.wmnr.org

Night Breeze *KCCK*
6301 Kirkwood Blvd. SW, Cedar Rapids, IA 52406
PH: 319-398-5446 FX: 319-398-5492
Mark Jayne nightbreeze@kcck.org
www.kcck.org
The most relaxing evening in radio. An exotic blend of mellow Jazz with new Instrumental and Ambient sounds.

Night Tides *KCUR*
4825 Troost Ave. #202, Kansas City, MO 64110
PH: 816-235-1551 FX: 816-235-2864
Renee Blanche blanchea@umkc.edu
www.kcur.org/nighttides.html
Instrumental & Electronic music that combines upbeat grooves and dubs with soothing melodies that whisper (softly) to the soul.

Nightcrossings *Radio Kansas*
815 N. Walnut #300, Hutchinson, KS 67501-6217
PH: 620-662-6646
comments@radiokansas.org
www.radiokansas.org/nc.cfm
New Age music with light Jazz and Classical.

Nightstreams *KASU*
PO Box 2160, State University, AR 72467
PH: 870-972- 2200
Marty Scarbrough kasu@astate.edu
www.kasu.org
Relaxing, contemporary instrumental music.

Nocturnes *KEDM*
ULM 225 Stubbs Hall, Monroe, LA 71209-6805
PH: 318-342-5556 FX: 318-342-5570
Adrainne LaFrance classical@kedm.org
kedm.ulm.edu
Mixes Acoustic and Classical music forms.

Oasis *Montana Public Radio*
U. Montana, Missoula, MT 59812-8064
PH: 406-243-4931 FX: 406-243-3299
www.mtpr.net
Electronic and Acoustic New Age music with host Joan Richarde.

Open Space District *KRCB*
5850 Labath Ave. Rohnert Park, CA 94928
PH: 707-584-2000 FX: 707-585-1363
John Katchmer listener@krcb.org
www.krcb.org/radio
A weekly slide through the dreamy, dopey, sexy world of contemporary Electronica.

SeeQ Radio
www.myspace.com/seeqradio
The web's number one Posi Music internet radio station.

Soundscape *WSKG*
PO Box 3000, Binghamton, NY 13902
PH: 607-729-0100 x315
Crystal Sarakas Crystal_Sarakas@wskg.pbs.org
wskg.com/Soundscape/soundscape.htm
New Age & World music.

Star's End *WXPN*
PO Box 22, Upper Darby, PA 19082-0022
Chuck van Zyl info@starsend.org
www.starsend.org
A non-stop drifting blend, drawing from many genres including Ambient, Space music, Chillout, New Age etc.

Sunday CD Spotlight *WSHU*
5151 Park Ave. Fairfield, CT 06825
PH: 203-365-0425
Julie Freddino jfred@wshu.org
wshu.org
New Age and Space music.

Sunday Session *WKZE*
7392 S. Broadway, Red Hook, NY 12571
PH: 845-758-9811 FX: 845-758-9819
Steve Utterback info@wkze.com
www.wkze.com
An interesting mix of Contemporary Jazz, Native, World Beat and New Age music.

Sunday Sunrise *KRVR*
961 N. Emerald Ave. Ste. A, Modesto, CA 95351
PH: 209-544-1055
Jim Bryan theriver@krvr.com
www.krvr.com
Acoustic, New Age and World music.

Sunrise *WUTC*
615 McCallie Ave. Dept. 1151
Chattanooga, TN 37403
PH: 423-265-9882 FX: 423-425-2379
Rabbit rabbit@celticradio.org
www.wutc.org
Soothing Acoustic, New Age and World music. Quiet and reflective moments provide an opportunity to begin your weekend with a peaceful atmosphere of relaxing music.

Tangents *KALW*
301 Gambier St., San Francisco, CA 94134-1341
PH: 415-841-4134 FX: 415-841-4125
Dore tangentsradio@gmail.com
www.tangents.com
A program that explores the bridges connecting various styles of music, such as World and Roots music and creative Jazz hybrids.

Tonal Vision *WICN*
50 Portland St., Worcester, MA 01608
PH: 508-752-0700 FX: 508-752-7518
Karen Mungal karen@wicn.org
www.wicn.org
New Age, Acoustic, Ambient and World music.

Visionary Activist *KPFA*
PO Box 94, Cabin John, MD 20818
PH: 510-848-4425 FX: 510-848-3812
Caroline W. Casey info@visionaryactivism.com
www.visionaryactivism.com
Insights on the nature of magic and reality.

VoyagerRadio
547 Gayley Ave. #1, Los Angeles, CA 90024
Harold J. Johnson voyagerradio@gmail.com
www.voyagerradio.com
The only internet radio station in the known universe webcasting Downtempo from outer space. Send your demos to the above address.

Canada

Deep Intense Radio *CHLY*
c/o Music Dept. #242, 1-5765 Turner Rd.
Nanaimo, BC V9T 6M4
info@deepintense.com
www.deepintense.com
We're looking for Downtempo Electronica music artists to submit their music for airplay.

Germany

Sounds of Syn
Steffen Thieme redaktion@sounds-of-syn.de
www.sounds-of-syn.de
A program for Synthesizer music.

The Netherlands

Time Trek
Jelke Bethlehem jelkeb@xs4all.nl
timetrek.nl
Het programma neemt u mee op een ontspannende reis door de wereld van de New Age muziek.

Sound Sounding
Ronald promotiekk@boortman.presenteert.nl
boortman.presenteert.nl
Smooth moods, which one can bring spiritual emotions.

Norway

SZ Radio
info@svdv-photography.net
svdv-photography.net/szradio
We focus on New Age, Jazz, Classical and Piano music.

Australia

Ambient Moods *ArtSound FM*
PO Box 3573, Manuka, Canberra,
ACT 2603 Australia
PH: 612-6295-8444 FX: 612-6295-8499
onair@artsoundfm.asn.au
www.artsound.com.au
Music to relax, transcend & inspire.

Sirius Music
1/22 The Avenue, Corrimal, NSW 2518 Australia
PH: 42-853691
Paul Headon pheadon@tpg.com.au
www.emanationsinsound.com
Ambient/Meditational/World Fusion. The best from around the world. Please e-mail first.

Ultima Thule *2MBS*
PO Box 633, Potts Point, NSW 1335 Australia
information@ultimathule.info
www.ultimathule.info
Enthralling audiences with a unique, entrancing melange of Ambient and Atmospheric music from around the world.

Japan

Earth Feeling *Love FM*
2-18-1-501 Kusagae, Chuo-ku, Fukuoka,
810-0045, Japan
PH/FX: 81-92-716-8848
Jeffrey Martin earthfeeling@yahoo.com
www.lovefm.co.jp
Features relaxing kinds of sounds that is described in Japan as "healing music," known more popularly in Europe and America as New Age.

Progressive Rock Radio

North America

United States

Afterglow *WMUH*
PO Box 632, Nazareth, PA 18064-0632
Bill Fox billyfox@soundscapes.us
soundscapes.us/afterglow
Progressive Rock. Inquire by e-mail before submitting music!

Aural Moon
admin@auralmoon.com
www.auralmoon.com
A large portion of our playlist is from independent artists.

The Canvas Prog Hour
411 Lorraine Blvd. Pickerington, OH 43147
Matt Sweitzer canvas@insight.rr.com
www.canvasproductions.net
We welcome promos that fall under the rather broad category of Jazz Fusion, Prog and/or Art Rock.

Cosmic Chaos *WOBC*
Wilder Hall 319, 135 W. Lorain St.
Oberlin, OH 44074
PH: 440-775-8107 FX: 440-775-6678
Cosmic Charlie music.wobc@oberlin.edu
www.wobc.org
The best of Psychedelic, Progressive, Krautrock, Spacerock and Classic Rock.

Delicious Agony
Don Cassidy dcass21@optonline.net
deliciousagony.com
We have added more live DJs and many live shows, each with a different flavor.

Dreams Wide Awake *WOSP*
11800 UNF Dr. HB #2565, Jacksonville, FL 32224
Jason Ellerbee jeller@unf.edu
www.unf.edu/~jeller/dreams.html
Features Progressive Rock and related music.

Epic Rock Radio
Kailef kailef@epicrockradio.com
www.epicrockradio.com
We regularly feature independent artists, as long as the style (Symphonic / Melodic / Power Metal) matches with what we play.

Gagliarchives *WBZC*
645 S. Forklanding Rd. #18
Maple Shade, NJ 08052
PH: 609-332-2019 FX: 609-894-9440
Tom Gagliardi gagliarchives@yahoo.com
gagliarchives.com
A Progressive and Art Rock program.

New World Enigma Radio *Live365.com*
radio.nwemusic.com
Broadcasts a unique blend of great music from many genres, mostly Rock, but much more.

Night Vision *WITR*
32 Lomb Memorial Dr. Rochester, NY 14623-0563
PH: 585-475-2271 FX: 585-475-4988
Jack Luminous jluminous@hotmail.com
witr.rit.edu
The best in Progressive Rock from all across the globe! If you have a band looking for a new audience, get in touch with us about airplay.

Peace and Pipedreams
Jimmy Peace peace@fearlessradio.com
www.myspace.com/peaceandpipedreams
We are looking for artist and bands in the Rock, Modern Rock and Experimental Rock genre to submit their release.

The Pit *WYBF*
610 King of Prussia Rd. Radnor, PA 19087
PH: 610-902-8457
Joe Stevenson loudrock@wybf.com
www.wybf.com
The authority on Progressive Rock, Jazz, Jam and New Age music.

Planet Prog
PO Box 04512, Milwaukee, WI 53204
Mark Krueger markakrueger@hotmail.com
planetprog.com
You are invited to send your promotional discs and information for airplay consideration to the above address.

The Point of No Return
stevec@thedividingline.com
www.thedividingline.com/ponr.html
There are amazing Prog artists out there who can now be heard!

Prog Palace Radio
PO Box 3538, Gaithersburg, MD 20885
Greg Stafford gregstaf@progpalaceradio.com
www.progpalaceradio.com
If you feel your music fits our format, send us your CD.

Progressive Positivity Radio
moses@progpositivity.com
www.progpositivity.com
We are very proud to feature the best (and most positive) independent Progressive Rock.

The Progressive Rock Radio Network
www.progradio.net
Discover the joys of Progressive music.

ProgRockRadio
PO Box 8335, Red Bank, NJ 07701
www.progrockradio.com
Send a CD with press kit to the above address.

ProgScape Radio
www.progscaperadio.com
Host Michael Ostrich exposes listeners to music that they simply wouldn't hear anywhere else.

The Prog-Rock Diner *WEBR*
2929 Eskridge Rd. Ste. S, Fairfax, VA 22031
PH: 703-573-8255 FX: 703-573-1210
Debbie Sears webr@fcac.org
www.fcac.org/webr
Prog from all over the world.

progrock.com
www.progrock.com
Can only accept Ogg Vorbis files with the quality set to 5 for playback.

Progulus Radio
www.progulus.com
Poised to make a name for ourselves in the Progressive / Metal arena.

Rogues' Gallery
Frans Keylard frans@thedividingline.com
www.thedividingline.com/rg.html
A wide swath of Progressive-influenced music from the unknown to the infamous.

The Trip *WRFL*
777 University Stn. Lexington, KY 40506-0025
Clay Gaunce thetrip@uky.edu
www.uky.edu/~wrfl/trip/trip.html
Send us your music.

Canada

The Dividing Line
#593-1027 Davie St., Vancouver, BC V6E 4L2
management@thedividingline.com
www.thedividingline.com
Promotes artists by playing their music and broadcasting interviews.

La Villa Strangiato *CHUO*
Gary Lauzon & Gilles Potvin
complexmusic@gmail.com
www.yantz.com/lavilla
Are you in a Prog band wanting airplay on the radio to get the recognition you deserve? Drop me an e-mail and I will be glad to give you my address and play your material on my show!

South America

The Musical Box *Argentina*
eventos@themusicalbox.com.ar
www.themusicalbox.com.ar
Progressive Rock radio show.

Europe

Germany

Progdependent *Rockin` Radio*
Banderbacher Str. 24, 90513 Zirndorf, Germany
PH/FX: 0911-60-95-95
progdependent@rockin-radio.de
www.rockin-radio.de

The Netherlands

Mark From Holland Radio Show
Anna Blamanhof 37, 1962 HK Heemskerk,
The Netherlands
PH: ++31-251-246497
Mark C. Deren mcd@wanadoo.nl
www.markfromholland.com
It is recommended to "follow-up" submissions of music with a request via e-mail for a Sunday night "on air" interview. The conversations usually last 5-7 minutes.

Paperlate
Andre Steijns andre.steijns@planet.nl
www.paperlate.nl
Concentrates on Classic, Progressive and Psychedelic Rock.

Psychedelicatessen Radio Patapoe
Feddo Renier f.renier@kennisnet.nl
launch.groups.yahoo.com/group/psychedelicatessen
Psychedelic and Progressive music show.

Symfomania
www.symfomania.com
Progressive, Symphonic & Melodic Rock show. If you have new material that you would like us to play, get in touch!

United Kingdom

Rush Radio
NMB, City Campus, Pond St., Sheffield,
South Yorkshire, S1 2BW UK
Ken Shipley ken@rushradio.org
www.rushradio.org

Punk Radio

North America

United States

@ntiRADIO *KGNU*
Sin bleedingright@gmail.com
www.myspace.com/antiradio
Features everything from old-school Punk and 80's New Wave to Goth and Horror-Punk, Hardcore, Metal, Industrial, Lounge.

The Anti-Emo Empire! *WNHU*
PO Box 5392, Milford, CT 06460
PH: 203-479-8807
Jeff Terranova theantiemoempire@earthlink.net
www.theantiemoempire.com
Spinning the best rare old school and new school Hardcore/Punk.

The Cherry Blossom Clinic *WFMU*
PO Box 5101, Hoboken, NJ 07030
www.wfmu.org/playlists/TT
Hosted by Terre T. Please DON'T send any attached files (flyers, MP3s etc.). Also, DON'T contact me and ask if I played your CD or demo. Check my playlist to find out.

DIY Radio *WAPS*
65 Steiner Ave. Akron, OH 44301
PH: 330-761-3098 FX: 330-761-3240
www.diyradio.net
A Punk Rock radio show. It's best to send your actual released product rather than a few songs burnt to a CD.

DJ Rossstar's Punk Rock Show
djrossstar@yahoo.com
www.myspace.com/djrossstar
With an audience of more than 20,000 people per broadcast, the show has remained one of the leading internet radio shows since its creation in 2002.

GaragePunk.com
PH: 206-339-9281
www.garagepunk.com
To get your music played on our podcasts, don't send us your CDs. Just rip MP3s of your songs (you probably have done this for your MySpace page already, anyway) and upload them to the Podsafe Music Network.

Hussieskunk
PO Box 1599, Reynoldsburg, OH 43068
Matt mattg@hussieskunk.com
www.hussieskunk.com
Every CD we receive is reviewed and promoted on our site, as well as featured on our show.

idobi.com Radio
1941 Vermont Ave. #2
Washington, DC 20001-4125
pr@idobi.com.
www.idobi.com/radio
Broadcasts Alternative Rock and Punk music. We are committed to bringing you the best of the known (and not-so-well-known) artists from around the world.

Mohawk Radio
10862 Coronel Rd. Ste. B, Santa Ana, CA 92705
Rich Z. richz@mohawkradio.com
www.mohawkradio.com
Punk, Psychobilly, Hardcore and Alternative music community. New and unsigned Bands.

Music to Spazz By *WFMU*
PO Box 5101, Hoboken, NJ 07030
PH: 201-521-1416
www.wfmu.org/~spazz
Host Dave the Spazz presents this Punk Rock R n' B Surf Garage radio show!

The Next Big Thing *KALX*
26 Barrows Hall #5650, Berkeley, CA 94720-5650
PH: 510-642-1111
Marshall Stax robins@ix.netcom.com
kalx.berkeley.edu
Showcase for demo and pre-released music. I want Punk, Hardcore, Emocore ...anything with an edge, passion or purpose.

The No Show *KDHX*
3504 Magnolia, St. Louis, MO 63118
PH: 314-664-3688 FX: 314-664-1020
Brett Underwood noshow@kdhx.org
www.kdhx.org
Punk, Post-Punk, No-Wave and more.

Planet Verge
planetverge@gmail.com
www.planetverge.com
All female staff featuring interviews up-and-coming Punk/Rock bands.

Punk University *WSOU*
400 S. Orange Ave. South Orange, NJ 07079
PH: 973-761-9768 FX: 973-761-7593
wsoumusic@hotmail.com
www.wsou.net
Underground Punk and Ska.

Punk Up the Volume *KIWR*
2700 College Rd. Council Bluffs, IA 51503
PH: 712-325-3254
Chayse 897theriver@iwcc.edu
www.897theriver.com/punk.asp
Punk music every Sunday night!

Rock Hell Radio
104 Lake Ct. Chapel Hill, NC 27516
James Saltzman rockhellradio@yahoo.com
www.rockhellradio.com
We play Street, Oi, Old School, Hardcore, Thrash and other Punk indiscretions.

Sonic Overload
PO Box 2746, Lynn, MA 01903
Al sonicoverload@earthlink.net
www.myspace.com/sonicoverload
Punk, Hardcore, Garage and other loud music from the past and present.

The Subculture Collective
wicked13@gmail.com
subculturecollective.com
Playing the best Psycho/Rockabilly, Alt-Country, Cow Punk, Surf and even some Bluegrass.

Super Fun Happy Hour *KDHX*
3504 Magnolia, St. Louis, MO 63118
PH: 314-664-3688 FX: 314-664-1020
Tim, Matt & Heather superfunhappyhour@kdhx.org
www.kdhx.org/programs/superfunhappyhour.htm
*Punk Rock from the 70's to the latest independent
and major label releases of today.*

The Tragically Nameless Podcast
denbez@gmail.com
tnppodcast.libsyn.org
*Want your music played on the show? Send me an
email with a couple MP3s!*

Troy's Room Radio Show
137 E. Anaheim St., Wilmington, CA 90744
PH: 310-308-2920
Troy Spiropoulos Troysroom@hotmail.com
www.myspace.com/troysroomradioshow
*An internet Rock show featuring the best in
unsigned Rock from around the world. Garage,
Psychedelia, Indie, Punk, Metal submissions
accepted only. Send press packages or MP3
attachments.*

WDOA.com
128 Mechanic St., Spencer, MA 01562
FX: 253-323-1606
wdoainfo@wdoa.com
wdoa.com
*We actively encourage independent bands and
artists to send us their music.*

Whiskey N' Waterbeds
Joey Fuckup & WhiskeyBrian
whiskeynwaterbedspodcast@gmail.com
www.myspace.com/whiskeynwaterbeds
*A podcast that plays a melting pot of Garage
Rock/Punk, 70&80's era/style Punk, Rockabilly,
some old school Hardcore, and possibly some
paisley underground stuff.*

Canada

Equalizing X Distort *CIUT*
35 Raglan Ave. #204, Toronto, ON M6C 2K7
PH: 416-978-0909 FX: 416-946-7004
Stephe Perry equalizingxdistort@ciut.fm
www.ciut.fm
Dedicated to the underground Hardcore Punk scene.

Flex Your Head Radio Show *CITR*
#233-6138 SUB Blvd. Vancouver, BC V6T 1Z1
PH: 604-822-2487 FX: 604-822-9364
www.flexyourhead.net
Long running Hardcore/Punk radio program.

Generation Annihilation *CITR*
PO Box 48116, 595 Burrard St.
Vancouver, BC V7X 1N8
PH: 604-822-2487
Aaron Kid generationannihilation@yahoo.com
streetpunkradio.com
Punk and Hardcore, both old and new.

Punk101
506 King Edward St., Winnipeg, MB R3J 1L8
PH: 204-885-5792
DJ Kris djkris@punk101.net
www.punk101.net
*Punk radio streaming Punk, Emo, Ska and Metal,
24/7. Forum, contests and more!*

PunkRadioCast
6-295 Queen St. E. #388, Brampton, ON L6W 4S6
PH: 905-495-6003
info@punkradiocast.com
www.punkradiocast.com
Features a variety of Punk related shows.

Sous les Pavés *CHUO*
65 University Pvt. #0038, Ottawa, ON K1N-9A5
www.myspace.com/souslespavesradio
Plays mostly Francophone Punk.

Europe

Austria

Chilibox Rocks! *Radio Orange*
Klosterneuburger Strasse 1, A-1200 Wien, Austria
PH: 01-319-09-99
chilibox@gmx.at
www.chilibox.net
Punk, Ska and Hardcore.

France

Ecrasons La Vermine *Radio Campus Lille*
59656 Villeneuve d'Ascq, France
pa@chpunk.org
chpunk.org
Punk, Hardcore, Oi, Crust, Ska…

Italy

dirtywaves radio *Radio Onda d'Urto*
c\o cs Leoncavallo via Watteau 7, 20125 Milano,
Italy
dirtywaves@hotmail.it
dirtywaves.blogspot.com
Music, interviews etc.

United Kingdom

hungbunny podcast
satanicholiness@hotmail.com
www.hungbunny.co.uk
Fisting your ears with my noise.

Reggae Radio

United States

BigUp Radio
US: 4096 Piedmont Ave. #407, Oakland, CA 94611
info@bigupradio.com
www.bigupradio.com
*If you want airplay on our Roots or Dancehall
stations please forward us your CD for
consideration.*

Dub Mixture *KDHX*
3504 Magnolia, St. Louis, MO 63118
PH: 314-664-3688 FX: 314-664-1020
DJ Ranx dubmixture@kdhx.org
www.kdhx.org/programs/dubmixture.htm
*The hottest Reggae in the classic Dub style with DJ
Ranx.*

Dub Session
DJ Chill Will dubsession@gmail.com
www.dubsession.com
*Podcast of progressive Reggae, Dub and
Downtempo grooves.*

Everything Off Beat *WLUW*
6525 N. Sheridan Rd. Chicago, IL 60626
PH: 773-508-9589 FX: 773-508-8082
DJ Chuck Wren musicdept@wluw.org
wluw.org
The world's premier Ska oriented radio show.

Ithaska *WVBR*
957 Mitchell St. Ste. B, Ithaca, NY 14850
PH: 607-273-2121 FX: 607-273-4069
wvbr.com
Despite our name, we play all sorts of music.

Jammin Reggae Radio
eznoh@niceup.com
niceup.com
The gateway to Reggae music on the internet!

The Night Shift *KDHX*
3504 Magnolia, St. Louis, MO 63118
PH: 314-664-3688 FX: 314-664-1020
Kevin Straw roots@kdhx.org
www.kdhx.org/programs/nightshift.htm
Reggae, Dub and Groove.

Positive Vibrations *KDHX*
3504 Magnolia, St. Louis, MO 63118
PH: 314-664-3688 FX: 314-664-1020
Professor Skank pskank@kdhx.org
Michael Kuelker positivevibes_michael@kdhx.org
www.kdhx.org/programs/positivevibrations.htm
For the latest - and the greatest - in Reggae music.

The Rasta Experience *KVCU*
Campus Box 207, Boulder, CO 80309
PH: 303-492-1369 FX: 303-492-5031
ASKA rastaexperience@radio1190.colorado.edu
www.rastaexperience.com
*Culture words sounds & vibes. De wickedest ting
inna Colorado.*

Raw Roots Podcast
badgals-radio.com
*Interviews, reviews and great Reggae, Dancehall,
Funk and R&B.*

Reggae Rhythms *WAPS*
65 Steiner Ave. Akron, OH 44301
PH: 330-761-3098 FX: 330-761-3240
B. E. Mann theenergymanbe@yahoo.com
www.bemann.com/reggaerhythms.htm
Reggae music from the US and abroad.

The Reggae Ride *WDNA*
PO Box 558636, Miami, FL 33255
PH: 866-688-9362 FX: 305-662-1975
info@wdna.org
www.wdna.org
Authentic Reggae music from Ska (60's) to present.

The Reggae Train *KRBS*
PO Box #9, Oroville, CA 95965
PH: 530-534-1200
Buffalo DJ krbs@cncnet.com
www.radiobirdstreet.org
Classic Roots Reggae music.

Relentless Reggae *WHPK*
PH: 773-580-6137
Microphone Bill relentlessreggae@podomatic.com
www.relentlessreggae.com
*Running the roughest cuts from yard. With a moral
obligation to raise the consciousness with a groove.*

Rocket Ship Ska Trip *KFAI*
1808 Riverside Ave. Minneapolis, MN 55454
PH: 612-341-0980 FX: 612-341-4281
Capt. 2much Freetime capt2much@yahoo.com
www.kfai.org

Roots, Rock, Reggae *KUSP*
203 8th Ave. Santa Cruz, CA 95062
PH: 831-476-2800
Lance & Jeff kusp@kusp.org
www.kusp.org/playlists/rrr
The best from the Reggae world.

sakapfet.com
PO Box 66-9303, Miami, FL 33166
PH: 305-599-8060 FX: 305-599-1005
www.sakapfet.com
Your cyber-highway to Haiti.

Saturday's a Party *WUSB*
Stony Brook Union 266
Stony Brook, NY 11794-3263
PH: 631-632-6501 FX: 631-632-7182
Lister Hewan-Lowe music@wusb.fm
wusb.fm
The longest-running Reggae-politics mix (RPM) in the USA. Den de Dubwise playyyyyyy, it play, it play!!!

Ska's The Limit *KDHX*
3504 Magnolia, St. Louis, MO 63118
PH: 314-664-3688 FX: 314-664-1020
Paul Stark SkasTheLimit@kdhx.org
home.mindspring.com/~stlska/ska.htm
A weekly all-Ska radio show.

Tropical Reggae *KGLP*
200 College Dr. Gallup, NM 87301
PH: 505-863-7626 FX: 505-863-7633
Steve Buggie buggie@unm.edu
www.kglp.org
You'll hear the finest in Reggae music from the Caribbean, Africa or elsewhere.

Tunnel One *WNYU*
194 Mercer St. 5th Fl. New York, NY 10012
PH: 212-998-1660
DJ Mush1 tunnel.one@wnyu.org
www.wnyu.org
Old school, Rocksteady and third wave Ska.

Vibes of the Time *KRUA*
PO Box 20-2831, Anchorage, AK 99520
PH: 907-223-4531
Ras Jahreal dready@gci.net
reggaealaska.com/jahreal
Featuring Roots Reggae, Dancehall Dub and Lovers Rock.

West Indian Rhythms *WWUH*
200 Bloomfield Ave. West Hartford, CT 06117
PH: 860-768-4701 FX: 860-768-5701
wwuh@hartford.edu
www.wwuh.org
A blend of music and information straight from the Caribbean. A rich mixture of Calypso and Reggae.

Yard Vibes *WRUW*
11220 Bellflower Rd. Cleveland, OH 44106
PH: 216-368-2208
Empress Ajah empressajah@yardvibes.net
www.yardvibes.net
The best in Roots Reggae and conscious Dancehall music.

Canada

Caribbean Linkup *CJSW*
DJ Leo C cjswfm@ucalgary.ca
www.cjsw.com
Dedicated to the Caribbean - news, views and music. E-mail for address to submit.

Reggae in the Fields *CKCU*
U. Ctr. Rm. 517, 1125 Colonel By Dr.
Ottawa, ON K1S 5B6
PH: 613-520-2898
Junior Smith reggaeinthefields@canada.com
www.cyberus.ca/%7Eacdas/Reggae.html
The longest-running Reggae program in Canada.

reggaemania.com
djronnelson@rogers.com
www.reggaemania.com
Discover the pulse of the dancehall.

Scratch
scratch@azevedo.ca
www.azevedo.ca/scratch
Early-1960's Ska, through Rocksteady, Reggae and on to modern-day Dub.

Jamaica

IrieFM.net
Coconut Grove, Ocho Rios, St. Ann, Jamaica
PH: 876-974-5051
customerservice@iriefm.net
www.iriefm.net
24-hour all-Reggae station.

France

Dance Hall Style *Radio Mega*
DJ Prince Thierry princethierry@wanadoo.fr
www.dancehallstyle.net
All styles of Reggae with a little bit emphasis on Roots, Oldies and Dub.

Dub Action *Radio Canut*
24, rue Sergent Blandan 1er arrdt - BP 1101 - 69201
Lyon, France
PH: 04-78-39-18-15 FX: 04-78-29-26-00
Bassta bassta69@hotmail.com
regardeavue.com/radiocanut
Ici toute les composantes de la musique jamaïcaine sont d'actualité: du Mento, du Ska, du Rock Steady, du Reggae etc.

Germany

Freedom Sounds *Radio Flora*
Harenberger Straße 25, 30453 Hannover, Germany
Peter Roth info@freedomsounds.de
www.freedomsounds.de
Ska, Reggae and Rocksteady.

The Netherlands

Radio Bassculture
PH: 0(031)641295359
Marko de Pender Jahdepender@bassculture.nl
www.bassculture.nl
Crossovers binnen de underground muziek waar de bas een voorname rol speelt, denk aan Reggae, Dubstep, Funk, Dub, Soul, Jungle and Hip Hop.

United Kingdom

BBC Radio 1xtra *Dancehall*
www.bbc.co.uk/1xtra/dancehall
Home page of the BBC 1xtra's various Dancehall shows. Info, shows, contacts etc.

Dub Basement *BBC 6*
6 Music, Western House, 99 Great Portland St.,
London, W1A 1AA UK
PH: 08700-100-600
www.bbc.co.uk/6music/shows/dub_bashment
Brinsley brings you the best in Dub, selected by his own fair hand.

Israel

Reggae Power
Dr. Reggae drreggae@irielion.com
www.irielion.com/israel/reggae_power.htm
The best Reggae vibes from the best radio station!

Soul / R&B Radio

United States

African New Dawn *WRSU*
126 College Ave. New Brunswick, NJ 08901
PH: 732-932-8800 FX: 732-932-1768
Alvin Fair wrsu@wrsu.rutgers.edu
wrsu.rutgers.edu
Promotes new, unknown and un(der)exposed music artists and music companies.

blackmusicamerica.com
support@bossnetworks.com
www.blackmusicamerica.com
Music, information, culture and entertainment for the Black community.

BlakeRadio.com
PO Box 403, Massapequa Park, NY 11762
Neil Blake MusicMassage@BlakeRadio.com
www.blakeradio.com
R&B, Jazz, Soul and Reggae slow jams. Music for your mind, body & soul!

Chocolate City *KCRW*
1900 Pico Blvd. Santa Monica, CA 90405
PH: 310-450-5183
Garth Trinidad garth.trinidad@kcrw.org
www.kcrw.org
A progressive mix of Soul, Hip Hop and World Rhythms.

Chunk of Funk *KVCU*
Campus Box 207, Boulder, CO 80309
PH: 303-492-7405 FX: 303-492-1369
dj@radio1190.org
www.myspace.com/chunkoffunkradio
The baddest show on the radio. Bringing you Funk/Soul/rare groove.

City Sounds Radio
Dick Fairchild citysounds@citysounds.biz
www.citysounds.biz
Welcomes R&B, Smooth Jazz, Southern Soul and Blues for possible airplay. We will help to promote you however we can.

Coolarity Radio
PO Box 970389, Ypsilanti, MI 48197
PH: 734 572-9535
Thayrone X bcms@thayrone.com
www.thayrone.com
I give airplay to Soul and R&B artists that other radio stations won't touch. See my playlist pages ...and my mission statement on the 'LISTEN' page.

Etherbeat Radio
14781 Memorial Dr. #1791, Houston, TX 77079
PH: 713-344-1562
www.etherbeat.com
Funk, Soul, Jazz, Latin, World, Afro, Reggae. Charges a FEE for airplay.

Fusebox *WRSU*
14 Easton Ave. #250,
New Brunswick, NJ 08901-1918
PH: 732-932-8800 FX: 732-932-1768
DJ Fusion music@wrsu.org
wrsu.rutgers.edu
Supports new and un(der)exposed artists. Soul, Funk, R&B, Hip Hop etc.

The Half Show
PH: 206-600-4253
Me-saj mesaj@thehalfshow.com
www.thehalfshow.com
*Podcast featuring an undiscovered star on the rise
in genres such as music, comedy, acting and
literature.*

KBBG
918 Newell St. Waterloo, IA 50703
PH: 319-235-1515
www.kbbgfm.org
R&B, Jazz, Gospel, Blues etc.

KDTN Radio One Network
4881 Hwy. 86, Elizabeth, CO 80107-7441
Kenny Smith kdtnradio@sdcog.net
www.live365.com/stations/kdtn
Playing independent R&B since 1997!

KJLU
PO Box 29, Jefferson City, MO 65102
PH: 573-681-5301 FX: 573-681-5299
www.lincolnu.edu/pages/504.asp

KPOO
PO Box 423030, San Francisco, CA 94142
PH: 415-346-5373 FX: 415-346-5173
info@kpoo.com
www.kpoo.com
*Specializes in Jazz, Reggae, Salsa, Blues, Gospel
and Hip Hop.*

KPVU *Prairie View A&M U.*
PO Box 519, Prairie View, TX 77446-0519
PH: 936-261-5788 FX: 936-261-3769
kpvu_fm@pvamu.edu
www.pvamu.edu/kpvu

KTSU *Texas Southern U.*
www.ktsufm.org

Liquid Sound Lounge *WBAI*
120 Wall St., 10th Fl. New York, NY 10005
PH: 212-209-2800 x2931
radio@liquidsoundlounge.com
www.liquidsoundlounge.com
*Devoted to exposing Soul infused grooves of all
persuasions.*

**The Listening Lounge with
Alysia Cosby** *WEIB*
Alysia weibfm@aol.com
www.weibfm.com
*A hip and groovy mix of Chillout, Jazz, Soul,
Brazilian, Latin and World rhythms.*

Love Radio
Dr. Love tdavis@dr-love.com
www.dr-love.com
*We are looking for Soul, R&B, Hip Hop and Reggae
artists to play on our shows. We also offer
opportunities to play at our events in Atlanta.*

The Love Zone *WHCR*
PO Box 537, New York, NY 10018
PH: 917-545-2169
Maurice Watts maurice@mauricewatts.com
www.mauricewatts.com
*For over 23 years playing some of the best R&B
love songs of the past and present.*

LoveZone247.com
PO Box 537, New York, NY 10018
PH: 917-545-2169
Maurice Watts maurice@mauricewatts.com
www.lovezone247.com
*24 hour Old School, Soul and R&B station host by
legendary radio host Maurice "The Voice" Watts.*

The Michael Baisden Show / B-Side
106 W. Calendar Ct. #303, La Grange, IL 60525
Andrea Goodman ag@minglecity.com
www.MichaelBaisden.com
*Breaking new and undiscovered artists! Songs
MUST fit the Love, Lust and Lies format, Old
school, R&B and Neo Soul. No Hip Hop or Rap!
Check site for submission details.*

projectVIBE
projectvibe.net
*From Neo-Soul rhythms to Deep House, from Jazz
to Classic R&B. Visit our site for submission details.*

RadioBlack.com
www.radioblack.com
*A guide to radio stations around the world catering
to Urban America.*

RHYTHMflow Radio
PO Box 130, Bronx, NY 10467
www.rhythmflow.net/Radio.html
*We're always looking for R&B, Jazz, Gospel and
other neglected music genres (sorry, no Rap or Hip
Hop) to add to our playlist.*

The Smooth Groovers Review Podcast
www.smoothgroovers.com
*In addition to Smooth Jazz we love Jazz-Funk, Funk
and Soul.*

smoothbeats.com
www.smoothbeats.com
Streaming non-stop beats 24 hours a day.

Soul Music of The World Podcast
LRMC-CMR 402, Box 999, APO AE 09180
PH: 011-49-16091790264
DJ Come of Age djcomeofage@yahoo.com
www.myspace.com/djcomeofage2
*Features independent Soul artists from all over the
world.*

Soul Patrol Radio
PH: 609-351-0154
Bob Davis earthjuice@prodigy.net
www.soul-patrol.com
*A celebration of great Black Music from the ancient
to the future.*

Soul Sessions
soulsessionsradio@gmail.com
www.myspace.com/soulsessionsradio
*I'm looking for people with great music that needs
to be played on my station!*

Urban Landscapes
1138 Seaward St., San Luis Obispo, CA 93405
Velanche Stewart mail@urbanlandscapes.org
www.urbanlandscapes.org
*Funk & Soul (old school & new sounds),
Latin/Brazilian, Soulful House.*

WHCR *City College of New York*
138th & Convent Ave. Nac Building, Rm. 1/513
New York, NY 10031
PH: 212-650-7481
whcr903fm@whcr.org
www.whcr.org

WMOC
www.mocradio.com
R&B to Hip Hop to Old School to House music.

WNSB *Norfolk State U.*
700 Park Ave. Norfolk, VA 23504
PH: 757-823-8274
Douglas Perry dperry@nsu.edu
www.nsu.edu/wnsb
*A unique blend of R&B, Jazz, Hip-Hop, Gospel and
Reggae.*

World Dynamic Radio
1055 Lancashire Cir. #B4
Stone Mountain, GA 30083
Carla P. Jewel inquiries@WorldDynamicRadio.com
www.WorldDynamicRadio.com
Features Jazz, Pop, Sacred Gospel and R&B.

Canada

FLOW 93.5
211 Yonge St. #400, Toronto, ON M5B 1M4
PH: 416-214-5000 FX: 416-214-0660
info@flow935.com
www.flow935.com
*An Urban music mix that primarily includes R&B
and Hip Hop. We also feature Reggae, Soca and
Gospel music.*

The Grooveyard *CKIC*
W-106, 160 Princess St., Winnipeg, MB R3B 1K9
Diablo & Honey Brown heyeverybody@kick.fm
www.kick.fm
Blues, Trad R&B, Soul and Funk.

The X, Urban FM *Fanshawe College*
1460 Oxford St. E., London, ON N5V 1W2
PH: 519-453-2810 x201
contact106.9thex@gmail.com
www.1069fm.ca

France

Right On FM
contact@righton-fm.com
www.righton-fm.com
A melting pot of Jazz, Soul, Funk, DnB, NuJazz etc.

Touchofsoul
touchofsoul@free.fr
touchofsoul.free.fr
Afrobeat, Electro, Broken Beat, Soul and Funk.

The Netherlands

Fingerpoppin' Soul
PO Box 14876, 1001 LJ Amsterdam,
The Netherlands
Hans Diepstraten hans@fingerpoppinsoul.nl
Harry van Vliet harry@fingerpoppinsoul.nl
www.fingerpoppinsoul.nl
*Now in our 15th year we intend to keep on doing
what we do best: Play great Soul Music!*

Groove Inc.
PH: +31-6-54973521
info@grooveinc.nl
www.grooveinc.nl
*Soul, Funk, Disco, Electro, Swingbeat, Hip Hop &
Smooth Jazz.*

Royal Groove
www.royalgroove.org
*Starting with Funk and Soul and going from Jazz to
Bossa Nova, from Hip Hop to Latin, Afro-Beat and
everything in between.*

SaveOurSoul
crew@saveoursoul.nl
saveoursoul.nl
*Playing the best in today's R&B and Classic Soul.
We also review and interview some of the artists we
play.*

The Soul of Amsterdam Radio Show
2e Oosterparkstraat 59-D, 1091 HW Amsterdam,
The Netherlands
PH: +31-6-165-22229
Andreas Hellingh
andreas@thesoulofamsterdam.com
thesoulofamsterdam.com
*Show centers around Soul music. We also play R&B,
Urban, Disco, Funk, Gospel and Jazz.*

United Kingdom

Basic Soul
www.basic-soul.co.uk
*Syndicated show broadcasting through various
stations online.*

BBC Radio 1xtra *RnB*
www.bbc.co.uk/1xtra/rnb
*Home page of the BBC 1xtra's various RnB shows.
Info, shows, contacts etc.*

BBC Radio 2 *Blues, Soul and Reggae*
www.bbc.co.uk/radio2/r2music/blues
*Home page of the BBC Radio 2's various Soul and
Reggae shows. Info, shows, contacts etc.*

Beatnik Radio
beatnik.209radio.co.uk
*2 hours of broken beats, Bossa Jazz, Afro Beat,
international dance floor sounds, Hip Hop, Latin,
World Breaks and Nu Jazz Bizniz.*

Choice FM
PO Box 969, London, WC2H 7BB UK
PH: 0207 378 3969 FX: 0207 378 3911
www.choicefm.net
The future of Urban music radio & culture.

The Funk and Soul Show *BBC 6*
6 Music, Western House, 99 Great Portland St.,
London, W1A 1AA UK
PH: 08700-100-600
Craig Charles funk.6music@bbc.co.uk
www.bbc.co.uk/6music/shows/funk_soul
*The most comprehensive mix of Funk and Soul
records on the radio.*

Invincible Radio
#107, 203 Mare Studios, London, E8 3QE UK
PH: +44-0208-525-4131
www.invincibleradio.com
*The world's market-leading radio station for new
music, bringing you the future today.*

KEMET Radio
151-153 Alfreton Rd. Radford, Nottingham,
NG7 3JR UK
info@kemetradio.com
kemetradio.com
*Created to serve the needs of the African and
Caribbean communities of Nottingham and
surrounding areas.*

Solar Radio
PH: +44-870-949-0129
info@solarradio.com
www.solarradio.com
*The best in Soul, Jazz, Funk and other related
music.*

Soul Discovery *209 Radio*
Citylife House, Sturton St., Cambridge,
CB1 2QF UK
PH: 01223-488418 FX: 01223-488419
Mick O'Donnell souldiscovery@209radio.co.uk
www.209radio.co.uk
*The mixture of music styles played, the telephone
interviews with the artists and the guests in the
studio who are mainly collectors/DJs gives the show
a great feel and personality.*

Soul Real *209 Radio*
Citylife House, Sturton St., Cambridge,
CB1 2QF UK
PH: 01223-488418 FX: 01223-488419
Kelsey soulreal@209radio.co.uk
www.209radio.co.uk
*An exclusive show that plays music from the genre
classified as 'Neo Soul'.*

Starpoint Radio
46 Jasper Rd. Upper Norwood, London,
SE19 1SH UK
PH: +44 (0) 20-8659-7581
info@starpointradio.com
www.starpointradio.com
The real alternative for Soul music on the internet.

Women in Music Radio

North America

United States

Amazon Radio Show *WPKN*
PO Box 217, New Haven, CT 06513
Pamela S. Smith psmith@amazonradio.com
www.amazonradio.com
Welcomes music from women everywhere, all styles.

Assorted Women *WDIY*
301 Broadway, Bethlehem, PA 18015
PH: 610-694-8100 FX: 610-954-9474
info@wdiyfm.org
www.wdiyfm.org
*From Folk-Rockers to Jazz greats, from soul divas
to torch singers: It's not just chicks with guitars…*

Bread & Roses *KBOO*
20 SE. 8th Ave. Portland, OR 97214
PH: 503-231-8187 FX: 503-231-7145
www.kboo.fm
*Public Affairs radio produced and engineered by
women.*

Bunch of Betty's Podcast
Betty serafinafly@hotmail.com
www.bunchofbettys.blogspot.com
*My specialties of knowledge are: women vocalists,
current and past Folk music, Britpop and really
anything unique and strange …like ME!*

Church of Girl Radio
1405 SE. Belmont #65, Portland, OR 97214-2669
PH: 503-819-9201
Mary Ann Naylor radiogirl@churchofgirl.com
www.churchofgirl.com
*Featuring 14 different rotations of lady-made music.
Interviews too!*

Circle of Women *KBOO*
20 SE. 8th Ave. Portland, OR 97214
PH: 503-231-8187 FX: 503-231-7145
Annelise Hummel annelieseh99@yahoo.com
www.kboo.fm
Covering women's issues and all genres of music.

Diva Radio *KUSF*
2130 Fulton St., San Francisco, CA 94117
PH: 415-386-5873
kusfmusic@yahoo.com
www.kusf.org
A focus on women's independently produced music.

Divalicious
PO Box 15739, Boston, MA 02215
info@podgrrls.net
www.podgrrls.net/divalicious
*Amazing Ambient, tasty Trance and groovy Global
Beats. Please fill out our online release form.*

Dreamboat Radio *WRUW*
11220 Bellflower Rd. Cleveland, OH 44106
PH: 216-368-2208 FX: 216-368-5414
Monica Ionescu dreamboatradio@gmail.com
www.wruw.org
*Showcases the work of women artists in Old-Time,
Bluegrass and mostly traditional Acoustic music.*

The Eclectic Woman *WTJU*
PO Box 400811, Charlottesville, VA 22904-4811
PH: 434-924-0885 FX: 434-924-8996
Robyn, Blue, Sandy & Annette wtju@virginia.edu
wtju.net/cpages/musub
Showcases female singer-songwriters.

Eve Out Loud *WICB*
118 Park Hall, Ithaca, NY 14850
PH: 607-274-3217 FX: 607-274-1061
www.wicb.org
We're ALWAYS looking to promote new artists!

Every Womon Radio *WAIF*
1434 E. McMillan Ave. Cincinnati, OH 45206
PH: 513-961-8900
www.waif883.org
*We currently are accepting CDs for potential
airplay. Visit our site for more information.*

Face the Music *KZFR*
PO Box 3173, Chico, CA 95927
PH: 530-895-0131 FX: 530-895-0775
Terre Reynolds ponderosagal@yahoo.com
kzfr_facethemusic.tripod.com
*Tilts the scales in the opposite direction with music
performed, written and arranged by women.*

Female Focus Music Show *WMSE*
820 N. Milwaukee St., Milwaukee, WI 53202
PH: 414-799-1917
www.wmse.org
*Dedicated to playing a wide variety of female artists
including individual singers and female-fronted
bands.*

FemFrequency
PO Box 15739, Boston, MA 02215
info@podgrrls.net
www.podgrrls.net/ff
*Amazing, rocking musical talent from the women
your mother warned you about. Please fill out our
online release form.*

Feminist Magazine *KPFK*
3729 Cahenga Blvd. W.
North Hollywood, CA 91604
feministmagazine@yahoo.com
www.feministmagazine.org
*Public affairs show that eagerly spotlights the work
of women in all walks of life.*

La Femme Fatale *WBRS*
Shapiro Campus Ctr. 415 South St.
Waltham, MA 02453-2728
PH: 781-736-5277
music@wbrs.org
www.wbrs.org
Dedicated to dangerous women and their music.

Girls Rock Radio
PH: 608-831-0769
Tom (djMot) info@girlsrockradio.com
www.girlsrockradio.com
We feature contemporary Pop, Rock, and Alternative music performed by women artists - whether all-girl or girl-fronted.

Grrrlville *WIDR*
1511 Faunce Student Service Bldg.
Kalamazoo, MI 49008-6301
PH: 269-387-6305
Cait widr.music@gmail.com
www.widr.org
Delivering a diverse mix of female-fronted bands and singer-songwriters.

Global Women Radio Collective *Radio CPR*
radiocpr@riseup.net
www.radiocpr.com
Voices and music from women in our community and from around the world.

Her Infinite Variety *WORT*
118 S. Bedford St., Madison, WI 53703-2692
PH: 608-256-2001 FX: 608-256-3704
Sue & Steph musicdir@wort-fm.org
www.wort-fm.org
Showcases women in all genres/styles of music.

In Other Words *KUFM*
MPR, 32 Campus Dr. U. Montana
Missoula, MT 59812-8064
PH: 406-243-4931 FX: 406-243-3299
www.kufm.org
Women's program of music, international news…

Instrumental Women *KSDS*
1313 Park Blvd. San Diego, CA 92101
PH: 619-234-1062 FX: 619-230-2212
Janine Harty janineh@jazz88online.org
www.jazz88online.org
Highlights women in Jazz.

Into the Light *KMFA*
1406 Ridgecrest Dr. Austin, TX 78746
PH: 512-327-0004
Kathryn Mishell kmishell@intothelightradio.org
www.intothelightradio.org
Devoted to the music of Classical women composers.

Moving On *KBOO*
PO Box 10652, Portland, OR 97296
PH: 503-231-8187 FX: 503-231-7145
L.C. Hansen lchansen@spiritone.com
www.kboo.org
Political, feminist, Folk music.

Murphy's Magic Mess *KZUM*
941 "O" St., Lincoln, NE 68508
PH: 402-474-5086 FX: 402-474-5091
Nadine Murphy programming@kzum.org
www.kzum.org
Alternative spirituality, New Age and Women's music.

Musicwoman Live!
musicwoman08@yahoo.com
www.blogtalkradio.com/musicwoman
Women composers and performers, nationally and internationally.

Nette Radio
PO Box 35476, Los Angeles, CA 90035
Annette Conlon submit@netteradio.com
www.netteradio.com/submit.html
From Piano to Punk - it's great music by fab women artists. You MUST mail or fax our release form with your music.

Nowhere To Go Radio
814 N. 15th St., San Jose, CA 95112
admin@ntgradio.com
www.ntgradio.com
We play strictly women artists, both indie and mainstream. Please visit our website for submission details.

Other Voices *WORT*
118 S. Bedford St., Madison, WI 53703-2692
PH: 608-256-2001 FX: 608-256-3704
wort@wort-fm.org
www.wort-fm.org
Women composers, performers and conductors.

Rubyfruit Radio
Heather Smith rubyfruitradio@gmail.com
rubyfruitradio.com
Podcast featuring the best indie female artists. Mail me your MP3s!

Sing it Sister *KRZA*
528 9th St., Alamosa, CO 81101
PH: 719-589-8844
music@krza.org
www.krza.org
Music featuring women artists.

Sisters *KLCC*
136 W. 8th Ave. Eugene, OR 97401
PH: 541-463-6004 FX: 541-463-6046
Nanci LaVelle lavellen@comcast.net
www.klcc.org
Features the best of female performances in virtually every genre of music.

Sisters *KVSC*
720 4th Ave. S., 27 Stewart Hall
St. Cloud, MN 56301-4498
PH: 320-308-3126 FX: 320-308-5337
Laura & Emily music@kvsc.org
www.kvsc.org
Women's music Sundays from 2-5pm.

Something About the Women *WMFO*
PO Box 65, Medford, MA 02155
PH: 617-625-0800
info@satwomen.com
www.satwomen.com
Weekly radio show featuring the voices of woman artists in all genres.

The Sound Job *WNCI*
PO Box 4972, 270 Mohegan Ave.
New London, CT 06320
PH: 860-439-2850 FX: 860-439-2805
wcni_music@yahoo.com
www.wcniradio.org
All styles, all eras. Music by women only - so leave your dick at home.

Stroke the Goddess *WMHB*
Colby College, 4000 Mayflower Hill
Waterville, ME 04901
PH: 207-859-5450
Annie aandandy@somtel.com
www.colby.edu/wmhb
A show devoted to music by female artists.

T.G.I. Femmes *KZUM*
941 "O" St., Lincoln, NE 68508
PH: 402-474-5086 FX: 402-474-5091
Tad Frazier programming@kzum.org
www.kzum.org
An eclectic selection of women's music: Folk, Rock and fun.

Under the Skirt *WDBX*
224 N. Washington St., Carbondale, IL 62901
PH: 618-457-3691
wdbx@globaleyes.net
www.wdbx.org
Playing women vocalists (Jazz, Rock, Indie Rock etc.)

Venus Rising *KRBS*
PO Box #9, Oroville, CA 95965
PH: 530-534-1200
Marianne krbs@cncnet.com
www.radiobirdstreet.org
Music by women. Local and underplayed.

Vixen Vibrations *KLSU*
B-39 Hodges Hall, LSU, Baton Rouge, LA 70803
PH: 225-578-4620 FX: 225-578-1698
music.director@klsu.fm
www.klsu.fm
All female artists ranging from all girl bands to Country to Hip Hop to Jazz.

Voices of Women *WRIU*
326 Memorial Union, Kingston, RI 02881
PH: 401-874-4949 FX: 401-874-4349
Toni, Beth & Liza comments@wriu.org
www.wriu.org/voicesofwomen

Wild Women Radio *WNHU*
300 Boston Post Rd. West Haven, CT 06516
PH: 203-479-8807 01 FX: 203-931-6055
wildwomanradio@hotmail.com
www.myspace.com/wildwomanradio

The Wimmin's Music Program *KKUP*
933 Monroe St., PMB 9150, Santa Clara, CA 95050
PH: 408-260-2999
Laura Testa rinaldi@cruzio.com
www.kkup.com
Music by, about and for women.

The Wimmin's Show *KZUM*
941 "O" St., Lincoln, NE 68508
PH: 402-474-5086 FX: 402-474-5091
thewimminsshow@hotmail.com
www.kzum.org
WANTED: Recorded music by, for and about women.

Woman Song *KKFI*
PO Box 32250, Kansas City, MO 64171
PH: 816-931-3122 x106
Linda Wilson linda.kkfi@gmail.com
www.kkfi.org
Features music written and performed by women.

Womanotes *KBCS*
3000 Landerholm Cir. SE.
Bellevue, WA 98007-6484
PH: 425-564-2424
Mary & Tracey kbcsdj@ctc.edu
kbcs.fm
Enjoy Jazz music by women.

Women Hold Up Half the Sky *KALX*
26 Barrows Hall #5650, Berkeley, CA 94720-5650
PH: 510-642-1111
womens@kalx.berkeley.edu
kalx.berkeley.edu
Talk radio and music by and about women.

Women in the Arts *KALX*
26 Barrows Hall #5650, Berkeley, CA 94720-5650
PH: 510-642-1111
womens@kalx.berkeley.edu
kalx.berkeley.edu
Interviews, reviews, roundtables, music, artist spotlight segments.

Women In Music *NPR*
PO Box 15465, Boston, MA 02215
Laney Goodman WomenOnAir@aol.com
www.womenonair.com
Looking for exciting new female talent to add to our playlists!

Women in Music *KRVM*
1574 Coburg Rd. PMB 237, Eugene, OR 97401
PH: 541 687-3370
www.krvm.org
From Blues to New Wave to the most current to the obscure.

Women In Music *WTIP*
PO Box 1005, Grand Marais, MN 55604
PH: 218-387-1070 FX: 218-387-1120
Staci Drouillard info@wtip.org
wtip.org
A new perspective to women and their music, featured artists and interviews.

Women of Jazz *KEWU*
E. Washington U. 104 R-TV Bldg.
Cheney, WA 99004-2431
PH: 509-359-4282
jazz@mail.ewu.edu
www.kewu.ewu.edu
Three hours of music from dazzling divas.

Women of Rock *KUGS*
700 Viking Union MS 9106, Bellingham, WA 98225
PH: 360-650-2936
music@kugs.org
www.kugs.org
Weekly show for women that rock!

**Women on Wednesday /
One of Her Voices** *KMUD*
PO Box 135, 1144 Redway Dr.
Redway, CA 95560-0135
PH: 707-923-2513 FX: 707-923-2501
Kate Klein md@kmud.org
womenonweds.blogspot.com
Women's voices, women's issues and women's music.

Women on Women Music Hour *WLUW*
6525 N. Sheridan Rd. Chicago, IL 60626
PH: 773-508-9589 FX: 773-508-8082
wow@wluw.org
wluw.org
Focusing on female musicians from all genres.

Women Rock Radio
Stephanie stephanie@womnrockradio.com
www.womenrockradio.com
The premier showcase for women who simply rock, and rock hard!

Women's Blues and Boogie *KZUM*
941 "O" St., Lincoln, NE 68508
PH: 402-474-5086 FX: 402-474-5091
Carol Griswold cbluelf@aol.com
www.kzum.org
Legendary and contemporary female vocals.

Women's Collective *KVMR*
401 Spring St., Nevada City, CA 95959
PH: 530-265-9555 FX: 530-265-9077
womenscollective@kvmr.org
www.kvmr.org/programs/women
A group of broadcasters dedicated to bringing women's voices and women's experiences to the airwaves.

Women's Music *KMUN*
PO Box 269, Astoria, OR 97103
PH: 503-325-0010
Elizabeth Grant elizm@coastradio.org
www.kmun.org

Women's Music Hour *WXPN*
3025 Walnut St., Philadelphia, PA 19104
PH: 215-898-6677. FX: 215-898-0707
wxpndesk@xpn.org
xpn.org
Sixty minutes devoted to women's music.

Women's Music Show *KUMD*
130 Humanities Bldg. 1201 Ordean Ct.
Duluth, MN 55812
PH: 218-726-7181 FX: 218-726-6571
kumd@kumd.org
www.kumd.org
Music by women in all genres, with local interviews and information.

Women's Music Show *WTIP*
PO Box 1005, Grand Marais, MN 55604
PH: 218-387-1070 FX: 218-387-1120
info@wtip.org
wtip.org

Womens' Prerogative *KTOO*
360 Egan Dr. Juneau, AK 99801-1748
PH: 907-586-1670 FX: 907-586-3612
www.ktoo.org
Music by, for and about women with host Lise Paradis.

Women's Radio
2121 Peralta St. #138, Oakland, CA 94607
PH: 510-891-0004 FX: 510-891-0003
www.womensradio.com
The music of every woman artist your heart desires.

The Women's Show *WMNF*
1210 E. MLK Blvd. Tampa, FL 33603-4449
PH: 813-238-9663 FX: 813-238-1802
Arlene Engelhardt arlene@wmnf.org
www.wmnf.org
An eclectic feminist/womanist radio magazine.

Women's Voices *KUNV*
1515 E. Tropicana Ave. #240, Las Vegas, NV 89119
PH: 702-798-8797
kunv.unlv.edu
Want to hear some singing women? Hosted by Gerrie Blake.

Women's Voices *KZYX*
PO Box 1, Philo, CA 95466
PH: 707-895-2324 FX: 707-895-2451
musicdir@kzyx.org
www.kzyx.org

Women's Windows *WERU*
PO Box 170, 1186 Acadia Hwy.
East Orland, ME 04431
PH: 207-469-6600 FX: 207-469-8961
Magdalen & Linda info@weru.org
www.weru.org

Womenfolk *KFAI*
1808 Riverside Ave. Minneapolis, MN 55454
PH: 612-341-0980 FX: 612-341-4281
Ellen Stanley womenfolk@earthlink.net
www.kfai.org
Bringing you the best in women's Folk & Acoustic music.

Womansoul *KBOO*
20 SE. 8th Ave. Portland, OR 97214
PH: 503-231-8187 FX: 503-231-7145
Annelise Hummel annelieseh99@yahoo.com
www.kboo.fm
Women's music with rotating hosts.

Womyn Making Waves *WEFT*
113 N. Market St., Champaign, IL 61820
PH: 217-359-9338
music@weft.org
www.weft.org
Features live interviews and performances with local women as well as women from around the world. All genres of music are played.

World Woman *KOPN*
915 E. Broadway, Columbia, MO 65201
PH: 573-874-5676 FX: 573-499-1662
Leigh & Kay two89.5gals@yahoo.com
www.kopn.org
Playing local artists and women's music from around the globe.

Canada

Big Broad Cast *CFUV*
PO Box 3035, Victoria, BC V8W 3P3
PH: 250-721-8702
cfuvwoa@uvic.ca
cfuv.uvic.ca/women

Hersay *CKUT*
3647 U. St., Montreal, QC H3A 2B3
PH: 514-398-4616 FX: 514-398-8261
music@ckut.ca
www.ckut.ca
Transister radio.

Iron Maidens *CKCU*
Rm. 517 U. Ctr., 1125 Colonel By Dr.
Ottawa, ON K1S 5B6
PH: 613-520-2898
DD Rocker ddrocker@yahoo.com
www.ckcufm.com
Where female musicians of steely determination dare to challenge their male peers in the wide, wonderful world of music. From Roots to Heavy Metal, we cover it all.

A Madwoman's Underclothes *CFRU*
U.C. Level 2, Guelph, ON N1G 2W1
PH: 519-837-2378 FX: 519-763-9603
Lori info@cfru.ca
www.cfru.ca
Words and music made mostly by women.

The Neo Brideshead *CHLY*
#2-34 Victoria Rd. Nanaimo, BC V9R 5B8
PH: 250-716 3410
Elle J & Mel neobrideshead@chly.ca
www.myspace.com/theneobrideshead
Dedicated to female musicians that rock really hard!

Packin' Attitude *CKLN*
55 Gould St. 2nd Fl. Toronto, ON M5B 1E9
PH: 416-979-5251 FX: 416-595-0226
Sheila Chevalier music@ckln.fm
www.ckln.fm
This is girl-on-girl action! Queerness is not an adornment here, it's the engine that drives. Behold the female* genius in Punk, Indie, Electro, Darkwave, n Rawk grrls.

Venus Radio *CKUT*
3647 U. St., Montreal, QC H3A 2B3
PH: 514-398-4616 FX: 514-398-8261
www.myspace.com/venusradio
We are a collective show that's all about women in music.

Women on Air *CFUV*
PO Box 3035, Victoria, BC V8W 3P3
PH: 250-721-8702
cfuvwoa@uvic.ca
cfuv.uvic.ca/women
Music, news and interviews on diverse women's voices.

Womyn's Words *CHRY*
Rm. 413, Student Ctr. Toronto, ON M3J 1P3
PH: 416-736-5656 FX: 416-650-8052
www.yorku.ca/chry
International documentaries on women and feminism.

The XX Show *CIOI*
135 Fennell Ave. W., PO Box 2034
Hamilton, ON L8N 3T2
PH: 905-575-2175 FX: 905-575-2385
www.myspace.com/xx_show
Music written and performed by women.

France

Babes in Boyland *Clapas FM*
195 bd de l Aeroport Int. Le Polynice Bat B,
Appt 48, 34000 Montpellier, France
babes@babesinboyland.info
www.babesinboyland.info
Entirely dedicated to women in music, especially "Rock" but it nevertheless remains open to any digression. Feel free to send us stuff.

panx radio
BP 5058, 31033 Toulouse, France
PH: 33-0-561612145 FX: 33-0-561114895
infos@panx.net
www.panx.net
Hardcore, Punk, CyberThrash, Grindcore, TechnoBruit, Crades Mélodies.

The Netherlands

Radio Monalisa *Amsterdam FM*
Patricia Werner Leanse monalisa@dds.nl
www.radiomonalisa.nl
A weekly program of women's Classical music.

United Kingdom

Girls & Guitars *Forest of Dean Radio*
Rheola House, Belle Vue Ctr. Belle Vue Rd.
Cinderford, GL14 2AB UK
PH: 01594-820722
Sue Brindley contactus@fodradio.org
www.fodradio.org
Featuring female Singer/Songwriters.

Suck My Left One *Subcity Radio*
John McIntyre Bldg. University Ave. Glasgow,
G12 8QQ Scotland
PH: 0141-341-6222 FX: 0141-337-3557
www.myspace.com/suckmyleftoneradioshow
We play everything from 90s girl Grunge, Punk and Hardcore to 70s Girl-Punk, to post-millennial, post-queer, feminist-Electro-Disco-Trash.

Australia

3RPP Women's Music Programming
PO Box 602, Somerville, VIC 3912 Australia
PH: 03-5978-8200 FX: 03-5978-8551
programming@3cr.org.au
www.3rpp.asn.au
We feature a DOZEN shows that help to promote women artists.

Behind the Lines, Frock Off, Women with Attitude *2XX*
PO Box 812, Canberra, ACT 2601 Australia
PH: 02-6247-4400 FX: 02-6248-5560
info@2xxfm.org.au
www.2xxfm.org.au
Programs that endeavour to give a fair representation to performances by women.

Burning Down The House / Drastic On Plastic *RTR FM*
PO Box 842, Mt. Lawley, WA 6929 Australia
PH: +61-8-9260-9210 FX: +61 8-9260-9222
rtrfm@rtrfm.com.au
www.rtrfm.com.au
Women's issues and music from all genres.

Girly is Good *3CR*
PO Box 1277, Collingwood, Melbourne,
VIC 3065 Australia
PH: 03-9419-8377 FX: 03-9417-4472
Emily & Maria girlyisgood@yahoo.com
www.3cr.org.au
Featuring women musicians, visual artists ...basically any art form that is girly.

Hip Sista Hop *3CR*
www.myspace.com/hipsistahop
Ladies, we'd love to interview you, play your music and promote your work.

MegaHerz *4ZZZ*
PO Box 509, Fortitude Valley,
QLD 4006 Australia
PH: 07-3252-1555 FX: 07-3252-1950
info@4zzzfm.org.au
www.4zzzfm.org.au
Women's issues and music.

The Women Zone *JOY Radio*
PO Box 907, S. Melbourne, VIC 3205 Australia
PH: 61-03-9699-2949 FX: 61-03-9699-2646
onair@joy.org.au
www.joy.org.au
Female musicians take the spotlight.

New Zealand

Girl School *RDU*
PO Box 31-311, Ilam, Christchurch, New Zealand
PH: 03-348 8610 FX: 03-364-2509
Missy G. station@rdu.org.nz
www.rdu.org.nz
It's all about the ladies!

World Radio

United States

Afropop Worldwide
688 Union St. Storefront, Brooklyn, NY 11215
www.afropop.org/radio
Dedicated to African music and the music of the African Diaspora. Does CD reviews too.

alterNATIVE Voices *KUVO*
PO Box 2040, Denver, CO 80201-2040
producer@alternativevoices.org
www.alternativevoices.org
We entertain, educate and generally promote positive excellence and appropriate role models by and for, American Native people.

The American Indian Radio
1800 33rd St., Lincoln, NE 68503
PH: 402-472-3287
airos@unl.edu
airos.org
A national distribution system for Native programming to Tribal communities and to general audiences.

Café LA *KCRW*
1900 Pico Blvd. Santa Monica, CA 90405
PH: 310-450-5183 FX: 310-450-7172
Tom Schnabel cafe@kcrw.org
www.kcrw.com/show/cl
Emphasis on new Brazilian, European, African and Tropical Latin music. There are also frequent guests and live performances.

Culture Cafe *WWUH*
200 Bloomfield Ave. West Hartford, CT 06117
PH: 860-768-4701 FX: 860-768-5701
Brian Grosjean abgrosjean@earthlink.net
www.wwuh.org
Folk music from the rest of the world - African, Latin, Flamenco, Native American, Asian music and much more.

Earthsongs
818 E. 9th Ave. Anchorage, AK 99501
PH: 907-258-8880 FX: 907-258-8914
feedback@knba.org
www.earthsongs.net
Exploring the Native influences that help shape and define contemporary American music.

Folks of the World *KDHX*
3504 Magnolia, St. Louis, MO 63118
PH: 314-664-3688 FX: 314-664-1020
Harriet Shanas folksoftheworld@kdhx.org
www.kdhx.org/programs/folksoftheworld.htm
A wealth of old and new ethnic music from Asia, Europe and the Mid East.

Global JazzWire *KGOU*
Copeland Hall, Rm. 300, U. Oklahoma,
Norman, OK 73019-2053
PH: 405-325-3388 FX: 405-325-7129
Chad Mitchell chad@globaljazzwire.com
www.globaljazzwire.com
Our focus is primarily upon African and South American artists, with a generous helping of Reggae and the occasional Eastern or Celtic artist.

The Indestructible Beat *WITR*
32 Lomb Memorial Dr. Rochester, NY 14623-0563
PH: 585-475-2271 FX: 585-475-4988
witr.rit.edu
Devoted to World music. A wide range of sound, from early 20th Century field recordings to the latest cutting edge World fusions.

International Pulse! *WVKR*
Box 726, Vassar, 124 Raymond Ave.
Poughkeepsie, NY 12604
PH: 845-437-7178 FX: 845-437-7656
Michel Joseph msanonjoseph@hotmail.com
www.wvkr.org
*The rhythmic music of Afro-Caribbean,
South/Central America and Eurasia.*

Island Time *KMXT*
620 Egan Way, Kodiak, AK 99615-6487
PH: 907-486-5698 FX: 907-486-2733
Russ Josephson russ_josephson@yahoo.com
www.kmxt.org
*Polynesian, Caribbean, other islands traditional
music.*

KIDE *Hoopa Radio*
PO Box 1220, Hoopa, CA 95546
PH: 530-625-4245
www.hoopa-nsn.gov/departments/kide.htm
Tribally owned and operated community radio.

KILI
PO Box 150, Porcupine, SD 57772
www.lakotamall.com/kili
*Largest native owned and operated public radio
station in America.*

KNBA
3600 San Jeronimo Dr. #480, Anchorage, AK 99508
PH: 907-279-5622 FX: 907-793-3536
feedback@knba.org
www.knba.org
Native American music.

KUYI
PO Box 1500, Keams Canyon, AZ 86034
PH: 928-738-5525 FX: 928-738-5501
kuyihopiradio@yahoo.com
www.kuyi.net
Native American public radio.

KWRR
PO Box 396, Fort Washakie, WY 82514
PH: 307-335-8659 FX: 307-335-8740
admin@kwrr.net
kwrr.net
Native American radio at its best!

KWSO
PO Box 489, Warm Springs, OR 97761
PH: 541-553-1968 FX: 541-553-3348
kwso@wstribes.org
www.kwso.org
Native American radio.

**The Motherland Influence /
Ambiance Congo** *WRIR*
1311 Wentbridge Rd. Richmond, VA 23227
David Noyes davidn4010@yahoo.com
wrir.org
The best of African, Latin & Caribbean music.

Music of the World *KEUL*
Glacier City Radio, PO Box 29
Girdwood, AK 99587
PH: 907 754-2489
Karen Rakos keulkaren@hotmail.com
www.glaciercity.us
*Get ready to dance to the beat of the latest World
music.*

New World Buzz Radio
116 Farmcrest Dr. Oakdale, PA 15071-9332
info@newworldbuzz.com
www.newworldbuzz.com
*Provides a showcase to promote the composers,
artists and performers of music genres from all over
the world.*

Planet Waves *KZFR*
PO Box 3173, Chico, CA 95927
PH: 530-895-0131 FX: 530-895-0775
www.kzfr.org
Rhythmic music from around the planet and beyond.

Radio Afrodicia
PO Box 19866, Los Angeles, CA 90019
PH: 323-938-0720 FX: 206-279-3020
Nnamdi & Donna nnamdi@afrodicia.com
www.afrodicia.com
Afrobeat, Afropop, World and Fuji music.

Route 66 *WRUW*
11220 Bellflower Rd. Cleveland, OH 44106
PH: 216-368-2208
Carl md@wruw.org
wruw.org
*Features artists include 500 year-old rock bands,
Dub Ministers, Storytellers from Turtle Island. Get
yer kicks…*

Sound Travels *WERU*
PO Box 170, 1186 Acadia Hwy.
East Orland, ME 04431
PH: 207-469-6600 FX: 207-469-8961
Mark Boshko info@weru.org
www.weru.org
World music show.

Spin the Globe *KAOS*
CAB 301, Evergreen State College
Olympia, WA 98505
PH: 360-867-6896
Scott Stevens spintheglobe@earball.net
www.earball.net/spintheglobe
World music news and reviews.

Sunday Simcha *WFDU*
Metropolitan Campus, 1000 River Rd.
Teaneck, NJ 07666
Bill Hahn sundaysimcha@yahoo.com
www.wfdu.fm
Traditional & contemporary Jewish music.

World Fusion Radio
1452 Oak Ave. #2S, Evanston, IL 60201
worldfusionradio.com
*We play only certain genres of music that fit under
the "World Fusion" or "World Beat" umbrella.
PLEASE read our submission policy! Hosted by DJ
ProFusion.*

World Music Show *WBGU*
120 West Hall, BGSU, Bowling Green, OH 43403
PH: 419-372-8657 FX: 419-372-9449
David Sears davidsears@wbgufm.com
www.wbgufm.com
Weekly World music show.

World Party *KEWU*
E. Washington U. 104 R-TV Bldg.
Cheney, WA 99004-2431
PH: 509-359-4282
jazz@mail.ewu.edu
www.kewu.ewu.edu
*Music from around the globe: Latin, Brazilian,
African, European, Hawaiian, Reggae and others.*

Canada

CKMO
3100 Foul Bay Rd., Rm. 303 Young Bldg.
Victoria, BC V8P 5J2
PH: 250-370-3658 FX: 250-370-3679
Doug Ozeroff doug@village900.ca
www.village900.ca
*Our music programming is a format called Global
Roots, a contemporary mix of Folk, Roots and
World Beat music.*

Espace Musique *CBC*
Pierre Fortier pierre_fortier@radio-canada.ca
www.radio-canada.ca/folkalliance
*Canada's leading broadcaster of World music. We're
always on the look-out for new talent.*

WORLD FM
5915 Gateway Blvd. Edmonton, AB T6H 2H3
PH: 780-438-1017 FX: 780-437-5129
webmaster@cker.ca
www.worldfm.ca
*World music station that features shows in 22
different languages.*

United Kingdom

BBC Radio 3 *World Music*
www.bbc.co.uk/radio3/worldmusic
*Home page of the BBC Radio 3's various World
music shows. Info, shows, contacts etc.*

Front-ears *U. Radio York*
c/o Vanbrugh College, Heslington, York,
YO10 5DD UK
PH: 01904-433840 FX: 01904-433840
head.of.music@ury.york.ac.uk
ury.york.ac.uk/microsite/frontears
The absolute best in International music.

Australia

4EB
PO Box 7300, East Brisbane, QLD 4169 Australia
PH: 07-3240-8600 FX: 07-3240-8633
info@4eb.org.au
www.4eb.org.au
Sharing the World with you!

South Africa

Channel Africa
PO Box 91313, Auckland Park 2006 South Africa
PH: +27-11-7144541 FX: +27-11-7142072
David Moloto molotod@sabc.co.za
www.channelafrica.org
*Music from all the continents including exceptional,
underexposed artists.*

Radio Shows that Spotlight Local Musicians

"Local" is a relative term. For some stations, "Local" is defined as any artist who lives within the city limits. Others consider "Local" to be anyone that lives within the listening area. There are many shows that consider "Local" to be musicians from anywhere within the state, province or territory, while others consider "Local" to be artists from the host country. If you're not sure whether you qualify for airplay with a particular show, get in touch with the station (or host) and in most cases they will happily respond and clarify what they consider to be "Local" talent.

North America

United States

Alabama

WBHM *Tapestry*
650 11th St. S., Birmingham, AL 35294
PH: 205-934-2606 FX: 205-934-5075
info@wbhm.org
www.wbhm.org/Tapestry
Music magazine that has a segment featuring local musicians.

WVUA *Loud and Local*
PO Box 870152, Tuscaloosa, AL 35487
PH: 205-348-6461
wvuamusic@sa.ua.edu
www.newrock907.com
From garage bands to headliners, it's all local all the time.

Alaska

The ANC Podcast
Rob theancpodcast@gmail.com
www.theancpodcast.com
Featuring local Anchorage musicians and music.

KRUA *Locals Only*
PSB Rm. 254, 3211 Providence Dr.
Anchorage, AK 99508
Dave Waldron aykrua9@uaa.alaska.edu
PH: 907-786-6805
www.uaa.alaska.edu/krua
An eclectic mix of Anchorage-area and statewide music.

Arizona

AZXunderground
www.azxunderground.com
Showcases AZ's best local Christian bands. Please fill out our online submission form.

KEDJ *Local Frequency*
7434 E. Stetson Dr. #265, Scottsdale, AZ 85251
Gadger booking@theedge1039.com
www.myspace.com/localfrequency
Three songs from Arizona's best local bands every week night at midnight!

KXCI *Locals Only*
220 South 4th Ave. Tucson, AZ 85701
PH: 520-623-1000
www.myspace.com/kxci
Host Don Jennings features music and live performances from local artists.

Arkansas

KXUA *NW Arkansas Local*
A665 Arkansas Union, Fayetteville, AR 72701
PH: 479-575-5883
charts@uark.edu
www.kxua.com
Bringing you the best in local and regional music.

WXFX *Fox Consumer Guide to New Rock / Locals Only*
1 Commerce St. #300, Montgomery, AL 36104
PH: 334-240-9274 FX: 334-240-9219
Rick Hendrick thefox@wxfx.com
www.wxfx.com
Playing the best new Rock.

California

Black Swan's LA Music Pipeline
PO Box 33006, Granada Hills, CA 91394
Eleanor Academia bswanea@aol.com
www.myspace.com/eleanoracademia
Eleanor is dedicated to giving LA indie artists direct access to millions of new fans immediately! Please visit our site for submission details.

Buck City Podcast
N.L. Belardes contact@nlbelardes.com
nlbelardes.com/musicrev.html
Hear local music, get book talk and interviews from Bakersfield artists.

KALX *KALX Live!*
26 Barrows Hall #5650, Berkeley, CA 94720-5650
PH: 510-642-1111
kalxlive@kalx.berkeley.edu
kalx.berkeley.edu
Musicians of varied styles perform at the beginning of the show, then at around 10:30 PM, the will be a live broadcast from a local club.

KFOK *Local Motives*
PO Box 4238, Georgetown, CA 95634
PH: 530-333-4300
Jim & Wendy info@kfok.org
www.kfok.org
Weekly show featuring local artists.

KIOZ *Local and Loud*
9660 Granite Ridge Dr. San Diego, CA 92123
PHH 858-292-2000
Missi promotions@rock1053.com
www.kioz.com
San Diego bands, send us an e-mail and tell us about your band.

KKUP *Jazz Line*
933 Monroe St., PMB 9150, Santa Clara, CA 95050
PH: 408-260-2999
Afrikahn Jahmal Dayvs jzzline@yahoo.com
www.kkup.com
The evolution of the Blues from Bebop to Hip Hop featuring Bay Area Jazz and Blues artists.

KOZT *Local Licks*
110 S. Franklin St., Fort Bragg, CA 95437
PH: 707 964-7277 FX: 707-964-9536
thecoast@kozt.com
www.kozt.com/LocalLicksInfo.htm
Mendocino County musicians playing a variety of music.

KRCK
73-733 Fred Waring Dr. #201
Palm Desert, CA 92260
PH: 760-341-0123 FX: 760-341-7455
dave@krck.com
www.krck.com
We support local talent and encourage independent artists. Rock & Alternative format.

KRXQ *Local Licks*
5345 Madison Ave. Sacramento, CA 95841
PH: 916-334-7777 FX: 916-339-4293
Mark Gilmore mgilmore@entercom.com
www.krxq.net
The best local bands in Sacramento along with the occasional interview and special in-studio guest.

KSDS *Local Jazz Corner*
1313 Park Blvd. San Diego, CA 92101
PH: 619-234-1062 FX: 619-230-2212
Cynthia Hammond cynthiah@jazz88online.org
www.jazz88online.org
Host Cynthia Hammond features Jazz from local artists.

KXJZ *Blue Dog Jam*
7055 Folsom Blvd. Sacramento, CA 95826-2625
PH: 916-278-5299 FX: 916-278-8989
jazz@capradio.org
www.capradio.org
Contemporary music featuring local bands, live recordings, and artists heard on NPR.

KZFR *Chico Butter*
PO Box 3173, Chico, CA 95927
PH: 530-895-0131 FX: 530-895-0775
DJX wordgroove@yahoo.com
www.kzfr.org
Features music/poetry/sounds produced in the northern fertile Sacramento valley of CA.

KZFR *LA Sounds*
PO Box 3173, Chico, CA 95927
PH: 530-895-0131 FX: 530-895-0775
Señor Felipe DJSrFelipe@aol.com
www.kzfr.org
East LA Cholo. Soul, R&B, Blues, Latin, Folk and Gospel.

KZSU *Wednesday Night Live*
PO Box 20510, Stanford, CA 94309
PH: 650-723-9010 FX: 650-725-5865
music@kzsu.stanford.edu
kzsu.stanford.edu
In studio performances and interviews.

Neighborhood Public Radio
npr@conceptualart.org
www.conceptualart.org/npr
Our motto: If it's in the neighborhood and it makes noise ... we hope to put it on the air.

Nor Cal Local Roots
JP NorCal@LocalRootsRadio.com
www.myspace.com/NorCalLocalRoots
If you are from the Nor Cal area and want your music broadcast world wide then you need to hit us up. We also love having bands LIVE in studio to chat and/or play acoustic sets!

Sound Pollution Podcast
soundpollution@gmail.com
www.soundpollution.info
Music and interviews with local Fresno bands. We also rant, rave and review.

Sound Scene Revolution Podcast
Rich soundscenerevolution@gmail.com
www.soundscenerevolution.com
*Music and interviews with local bands in the SF Bay
Area. We also review new music.*

West Coast Live
2124 Kittredge Ave. #350, Berkeley, CA 94704
PH: 415-664-9500 x2
producers@wcl.org
www.wcl.org
*Music, ideas and humor from a rich mix of
musicians, writers and thinkers from the Bay Area
and around the country.*

XTRA *Loudspeaker*
9660 Granite Ridge Dr. San Diego, CA 92123
www.91x.com
*Our local show featuring bands from and in San
Diego.*

Colorado

The Colorado Wave
carmen@thecoloradowave.com
www.thecoloradowave.com
The original homegrown music showcase!

KCSU *The Local Loco*
Student Ctr. Box 13, Lory Student Ctr.
Fort Collins, CO 80523
PH: 970-491-7611 FX: 970-491-7612
kcsumusic@gmail.com
www.kcsufm.com

KRFC *Colorado Sound*
619 S. College #4, Fort Collins, CO 80524
PH: 970-221-5065
Chris K. pc@krfcfm.org
krfcfm.org
*Features the music of Colorado / Southern Wyoming
artists.*

KVCU *Basementalism*
Campus Box 207, Boulder, CO 80309
PH: 303-492-3243
us@basementalism.com
www.basementalism.com
*We are a strong supporter of the Colorado Hip Hop
Scene.*

KVCU *Local Shakedown*
Campus Box 207, U. Colorado, Boulder, CO 80309
PH: 303-492-5031 FX: 303-492-1369
dj@radio1190.org
www.radio1190.org

Connecticut

WCCC *Homegrown*
1039 Asylum Ave. Hartford, CT 06105
www.wccc.com/homegrown.php
*WCCC believes in local music. If you're in a band,
send your CD and band info to us.*

WKZE *Off the Beaten Track*
7392 S. Broadway, Red Hook, NY 12571
PH: 845-758-9811 FX: 845-758-9819
Todd Mack info@wkze.com
www.wkze.com
*The show spotlights artists residing within the
WKZE listening area.*

WPLR *Local Band Show*
PO Box 6508, Whitneyville, CT 06517
Rick Allison rick@thelocalbandsshow.com
www.thelocalbandsshow.com
*We listen to everything that comes from the WPLR
listening area.*

Delaware

WSTW *Hometown Heroes*
2727 Shipley Rd. PO Box 7492
Wilmington, DE 19803
Mark Rogers mrogers@wstw.com
www.wstw.com
*Spotlighting the best music from the Delaware
Valley! (Delaware, Southeastern PA, South Jersey
and Northern Maryland). We'll even bring some of
the artists into the studio to perform live on the air.*

Florida

97X *Local Motion*
11300 4th St. N. #300, St. Petersburg, FL 33716
localmotion@97xonline.com
97xonline.com/locals
*The best and brightest of our local music scene.
Check out who's been in the studio, who's playing
where, submit a gig…*

All Florida Indies Podcast
PO Box 560727, Orlando, FL 32856
Bing Futch bing@jobentertainment.com
allflorida.blogspot.com
*Here's to hoping that you'll discover what a diverse
music scene we have here in Florida.*

Sunday Blues *The Local Set*
WKPX, 8000 NW. 44th St., Sunrise, FL 33351
DAR dar@blueatheart.com
www.blueatheart.com
Local Blues bands, send in your CDs!

WJRR *Native Noise*
2500 Maitland Center Pkwy. #401
Maitland, FL 32751
PH: 407-916-7800
DJ dj@realrock1011.com
www.wjrr.com
*Join DJ as he brings you the best from the local
music scene.*

WLKF *Mayhem in the AM*
404 W. Lime St., Lakeland, FL 33815
Attn: Sarah
PH: 863-682-1430 FX: 863-683-2409
www.myspace.com/sarahsmiles321
*During my segment I will be promoting all of our
favorite local bands and local shows and events.
There will be amazing guests and different featured
artists every show.*

WMNF *Live Music Showcase*
1210 E. MLK Blvd. Tampa, FL 33603-4449
PH: 813-238-9663 FX: 813-238-1802
Bill & Chris livemusic@wmnf.org
www.wmnf.org
*Features live performances by local and national
musicians.*

WPBZ *Local Band Of The Month*
701 Northpointe Pkwy. #500,
West Palm Beach, FL 33407
PH: 561-616-4600
www.buzz103.com
*A local band from South Florida visits the Buzz
studios to perform.*

WRGP *Local Radiation*
11200 SW 8th St. GC-210, Miami, FL 33199
PH: 305-348-3575
wrgpmusic@gmail.com
www.wrgp.org
*Tune in for the lovely sounds of the Florida
underground.*

WUSF U. South Florida
4202 E. Fowler Ave. TVB100
Tampa, FL 33620-6902
PH: 813-974-8700 FX: 813-974-5016
info@wusf.org
www.wusf.usf.edu
Sometimes hosts live Classical performances.

WVFS *Hootenanny*
420 Diffenbaugh Bldg. Tallahassee, FL 32306-1550
music@wvfs.fsu.edu
www.wvfs.fsu.edu
Local music, interviews and live performances.

Georgia

Joe Stevenson Music / Homegrown
2536 Henry St. Augusta, GA 30904
PH: 706-364-7614 FX: 706-790-6857
info@joestevensonmusic.com
www.joestevensonmusic.com
*We produce 95 Rock's Homegrown radio program,
featuring the Southeast US's best up and coming
artists.*

WRAS *Georgia Music Show*
PO Box 4048, Atlanta, GA 30302-4048
PH: 404-413-9727
georgiamusicshow@gmail.com
www.myspace.com/gamusicshow
*If you "used" to live in Georgia and now live
elsewhere, you are no longer local.*

WREK *Live at WREK*
350 Ferst Dr. NW. #2224, Atlanta, GA 30332-0630
PH: 404-894-2468 FX: 404-894-6872
music.director@wrek.org
www.wrek.org
Music you don't hear on the radio.

Hawaii

The DoctorTrey.com Podcast
PH: 808-699-1297
podcast@doctortrey.com
www.doctortrey.com
Dedicated to the Hawaiian music industry.

KIPO *Aloha Shorts*
738 Kaheka St. #101, Honolulu, HI 96814
PH: 808-955-8821 FX: 808-942-5477
www.hawaiipublicradio.org
*A program of local literature, local authors, local
actors and local music.*

KTUH *Monday Night Live*
2445 Campus Rd. Hemenway Hall #203
Honolulu, HI 96822
PH: 808-956-5288 FX: 808-956-5271
live@ktuh.org
ktuh.hawaii.edu/shows.php?mnl
*Featuring occasional interviews with the band du
jour. At 10pm is Monday Night Live proper,
featuring an hour of original music from one of
Hawaii's best local bands.*

Illinois

Fearless Radio *Mac and Slater*
www.fearlessradio.com
*A Chicago based show hosted by Mac and Slater
that features local personalities.*

Radio Free Chicago
radiofreechicago@gmail.com
www.radiofreechicago.typepad.com
*Covering the local music scene. Also features live
reviews and interviews.*

WDCB *Folk Festival*
College of DuPage, 425 Fawell Blvd.
Glen Ellyn, IL 60137
PH: 630-942-4200 FX: 630-942-2788
Lili Kuzma KuzmaL@wdcb.org
wdcb.org
Music in the Folk tradition with live performances and interviews with local and regional artists.

WEFT *WEFT Sessions / Champaign Local 901*
113 N. Market St., Champaign, IL 61820
PH: 217-359-9338
music@weft.org
www.weft.org
Two shows featuring local artists.

WKQX *Local 101*
230 Merchandise Mart, Chicago, IL 60654
PH: 312-527-8348 FX: 312-527-8348
Chris Payne Chris@Q101.com
www.q101.com/local101
Airplay and reviews of Chicago artists.

WLUW *Radio One Chicago*
6525 N. Sheridan Rd. Chicago, IL 60626
PH: 773-508-9589 FX: 773-508-8082
Mike Gibson mike@lovehasnologic.com
wluw.org
Interviews, music and guests explore Chicago's independent music scene.

WONC *Local Chaos*
30 N. Brainard, PO Box 3063, Naperville, IL 60566
PH: 637-5965 x3 FX: 630-637-5900
localchaos@wonc.org
myspace.com/localchaos891
Local music every Sunday night.

WPGU *Inner Limits*
512 E. Green St., Champaign, IL 61820
PH: 217-244-3000 FX: 217-244-3001
music@wpgu.com
www.wpgu.com
One hour of local music.

WXAV *The A & J Show*
3700 W. 103rd St., Chicago, IL 60655
PH: 773-298-3376 FX: 773-298-3381
wxavmusic@yahoo.com
www.wxav.com
We've had several Chicago bands visit us in the studio over the years.

WXRT *Local Anesthetic*
4949 W. Belmont Ave. Chicago, IL 60641
PH: 773-777-1700 FX: 773-777-5031
www.wxrt.com
WXRT will only accept recorded materials that are clearly labeled as such. Any packages with hand written "send to" or "received from" information will not be accepted into the station.

Indiana

Fields of Bluegrass
Carey Allen Fields bluegrassindy@yahoo.com
www.fieldsofbluegrass.com
Bringing independent, high-quality Bluegrass programming to central Indiana's FM airwaves.

WFHB *The Local Show*
PO Box 1973 Bloomington, IN 47402
PH: 812-323-1200 FX: 812-323-0320
music@wfhb.org
www.wfhb.org

Iowa

Dirt Road Radio
4033 Fagen Dr. Des Moines, IA 50310
PH: 515-277-6329
www.brianjoens.com
Explores the wide world of regional, national and international music. It's still small town Iowa radio in some regards.

KAZR *Local Licks*
1416 Locust St., Des Moines, IA 50309
PH: 515-280-1350
Suzi suzi@lazer1033.com
www.lazer1033.com
If your band is releasing a CD, send me an e-mail with all of the info.

KIWR *Planet O!*
2700 College Rd. Council Bluffs, IA 51503
PH: 712-325-3254 FX: 712-325-3391
Kady & James planeto897@yahoo.com
www.897theriver.com
Omaha's longest running local music show! Accept NO substitute!!!!

KUNI *Live from Studio One*
U. Northern Iowa, Cedar Falls, IA 50614-0359
PH: 319-273-6400 FX: 319-273-2682
Karen Impola karen.impola@uni.edu
www.kuniradio.org/kustud.html
Unique weekly live broadcast featuring local and national artists.

Kansas

KJHK *Plow the Fields*
1301 Jayhawk Blvd. Kansas Union, Rm. 427
Lawrence, KS 66045
PH: 785-864-5483
kjhkpr@ku.edu
kjhk.org
Celebrate the area's fertile musical heritage. Indigenous harmonies from all genres. Local music submissions always accepted and appreciated as well.

Kentucky

WWHR *Local Shots*
College Heights, 1 Big Red Way
Bowling Green, KY 42101
PH: 270-745-5350
Koufax localshots@revolution.fm
www.myspace.com/localshots
Features artists from Bowling Green and the surrounding areas.

Louisiana

KBON
109 S. 2nd St., Eunice, LA 70535
PH: 337-546-0007 FX: 337-546-0097
dj@kbon.com
www.kbon.com
About 70% of the music on KBON is the music of Louisiana recording artists.

KLSU *Saturated Neighborhood*
B-39 Hodges Hall, LSU, Baton Rouge, LA 70803
PH: 225-578-4620 FX: 225-578-1698
music.director@klsu.fm
www.klsu.fm
Music and interviews with Louisiana bands of all styles.

New Orleans Radio
nospam@lagniappe.la
www.lagniappe.la
We've now built the site to allow for MP3 uploads of music or syndicated shows.

Rajun' Cajun Radio
11603 Hwy. 308, PO Drawer 1350
Larose, LA 70373
PH: 985-798-7792 FX: 985-798-7793
klrz@mobiletel.com
www.klrzfm.com
All Louisiana, All the Time!

Maine

WCLZ *Music From 207*
420 Western Ave. South Portland, ME 04106
Lara Seaver lseaver@portlandradiogroup.com
www.myspace.com/musicfrom207
Featuring live interviews and new music from the best local musicians.

WMPG *Local Motives*
96 Falmouth St., Portland, ME 04104-9300
PH: 207-780-4909
Jan Wilkinson localmotives@yahoo.com
www.wmpg.org
Every Friday night, we bring a the sounds of a local Portland band.

Maryland

98 Rock *Noise in the Basement*
3800 Hooper Ave. Baltimore, MD 21211
PH: 410-481-1098 FX: 410-467-3291
Matt David mattdavis@hearst.com
www.myspace.com/mattdavisdj
Baltimore's local music outlet. For airplay consideration send your material to the above address.

WWDC *Local Lix*
1801 Rockville Pike #405, Rockville, MD 20852
Roche roche@dc101.com
dc101.com
Devoted to the many great local bands in the DC metropolitan area.

Massachusetts

Exploit Boston! Radio
PO Box 1243, Allston, MA 02134
PH: 781-420-9660
contact@exploitboston.com
www.exploitboston.com
Regional and national acts coming to town should contact us.

Local Roots Music Showcase
PO Box 31, Elmwood, MA 02337
PH: 508-726-5471
Tree & Rich LocalRoots@LocalRootsRadio.com
www.myspace.com/localroots1
A local music internet radio on Bunkradio.com. Playing the best in local and indie music!

WAAF *Bay State Rock*
20 Guest St. 3rd Fl. Boston, MA 02135-2040
PH: 617-931-1112 FX: 617-931-1073
Carmelita baystaterocklistings@yahoo.com
www.baystaterock.com
Playing the music of bands from the Boston area. We feature 4 song acoustic sets from bands at 11:30 each Sunday night.

WAMH *Live @ WAMH*
AC #1907 Campus Ctr. Amherst, MA 01002-5000
PH: 413-542-2288
Zachary wamh@amherst.edu
wamh.amherst.edu

WATD *Tomorrow's Dreams*
Box 284, 1271-A Washington St.
Weymouth, MA 02189-2316
Steve & Bobbie Sands
tomorrowsdreams@comcast.net
www.tomorrowsdreamsshow.com
Spotlighting New England talent. No Heavy Rock or Rap. Most everything else goes.

WBCN *Boston Emissions*
83 Leo M. Birmingham Pkwy. Boston, MA 02135
PH: 617-746-1400
www.wbcn.com
Features local artists plus a band of the month.

WBRS *Watch City Coffeehouse*
Shapiro Campus Ctr. 415 South St.
Waltham, MA 02453-2728
PH: 781-736-5277
music@wbrs.org
www.wbrs.org

WFNX *New England Product*
25 Exchange St., Lynn, MA 01901
PH: 781-595-6200
fnxradio@fnxradio.com
www.myspace.com/newenglandproductfnx
Live in-studio performances and interviews. We focus on bringing you the best up-and-coming acts.

WICN *Jazz New England*
50 Portland St., Worcester, MA 01608
PH: 508-752-0700 FX: 508-752-7518
Tyra Penn tyra@wicn.org
www.wicn.org
Music from regional artists, conversations about their music.

WICN *The Contemporary Café*
50 Portland St., Worcester, MA 01608
PH: 508-752-0700 FX: 508-752-7518
Nick DiBiasio nick@wicn.org
www.wicn.org
The finest acoustic performances of Folk, Blues and Americana music by the biggest names in New England and around the world.

WMBR *Pipeline!*
3 Ames St., Cambridge, MA 02142
PH: 617-253-8810
pipeline@wmbr.org
wmbr.mit.edu
www.oscillations.org/pipeline
Proof that there are geographical solutions to emotional problems! Local bands and a live in-studio performance every single week.

WMVY *The Local Music Cafe*
PO Box 1148, Tisbury, MA 02568
PH: 508-693-5000 FX: 508-693-8211
local_musicafe@mvyradio.com
www.mvyradio.com/local_musicafe
Music from some of the best local musicians on Cape Cod and the Islands of Martha's Vineyard and Nantucket.

WPXC *Homegrown*
278 South Sea Ave. W., Yarmouth, MA 02673
PH: 800-445-7499 FX: 508-862-6329
Suzanne Tonaire rockbabe@pixy103.com
www.pixy103.com
Cape Cod's original local artists showcase. Includes band of the month.

WUML *Live from the Fallout Shelter*
1 University Ave. Lowell, MA 01854
livefromthefalloutshelter@wuml.org
www.wuml.org
A variety of Indie Rock, Punk, Alt-Country, Jazz and any and all other Underground music.

WZBC *Mass. Avenue and Beyond*
BC, McElroy Commons 107
Chestnut Hill, MA 02467
PH: 617-552-4686 FX: 617-552-1738
Tracey Stark wzbcmusic@gmail.com
www.wzbc.org
Local Rock, focusing on new music. Includes interviews from local musicians, artists etc.

Michigan

The Bush! Radio
PH: 989-400-6381
Charlie Kole thebushradio@yahoo.com
myspace.com/thebushradio
We are devoted entirely to local Michigan music!

Detroit Jazz Stage
jazzstage@gmail.com
jazzstage.us
A monthly podcast featuring the best talent from the Detroit Jazz scene.

Local, Loud & Proud with Unkle Bonehead
3435 Dietz Rd. Williamston, MI 48895
PH: 517-512-9259
Unkle Bonehead unkleboneheadshow@yahoo.com
www.myspace.com/unkleboneheadshow
A show on The Bush Radio showcasing the best indie music that Michigan has to offer. With news, reviews, interviews contests and more!

WCBN *The Local Music Show*
530 Student Activities Bldg.
Ann Arbor, MI 48109-1316
PH: 734-763-3501
localmusic@wcbn.org
www.wcbn.org/
A weekly 2 hour broadcast of music from Ann Arbor and the surrounding area.

WRIF *Motor City RIFFS*
Attn: Shaffee, 1 Radio Plaza, Detroit, MI 48220
PH: 248-547-0101 FX: 248-542-8800
Doug Podell doug@wrif.com
www.wrif.com/motorcityriffs
WRIF puts the local scene in the spotlight every Sunday night.

Minnesota

Independent Stream
PH: 206-338-5643
Gary Holdsteady
independentstream@podomatic.com
www.independentstream.podomatic.com
Podcast supporting the Minnesota music scene.

KMSU *Midwest Beatdown*
www.myspace.com/midwestbeatdown
Specializes in local Rock and Metal from the Minnesota, Iowa, Wisconsin, Illinois and the South Dakota area.

KTCZ *Minnesota Music*
1600 Utica Ave. S. #400, St. Louis Park, MN 55416
PH: 952-417-3000
Jason Nagle Jason@Cities97.com
www.cities97.com
In addition to playing local artists' tunes throughout the week, we dedicate a full hour to them Sunday nights.

KVSC *Monday Night Live*
720 4th Ave. S. 27 Stewart Hall
St. Cloud, MN 56301-4498
PH: 320-308-5337 FX: 320-308-5337
info@kvsc.org
www.kvsc.org
Every Monday it's an hour of live music from our studio featuring the best in Minnesota music.

KXXR *Loud & Local*
2000 SE. Elm St., Minneapolis, MN 55414
PH: 612-617-4000
www.93x.com
Send in info on your band.

KUOM *Off the Record*
610 Rarig Ctr. 330 21st Ave. S.
Minneapolis, MN 55455
PH: 612-625-3500 FX: 612-625-2112
music@radiok.org
www.myspace.com/otrhatesu
Local music and a live band in Studio K.

WHMH *MN Homegrown*
1010 2nd St. N. Sauk Rapids, MN 56379
Tim Ryan tim@rockin101.com
www.myspace.com/101mnhomegrown
If you have a band and want some exposure send CDs and bios to us.

Minneapoliscast
4044 13th Ave. S., Minneapolis, MN 55407
Tony Thomas truetone@gmail.com
www.minneapoliscast.com
A Podcast featuring independent Minnesota artists. Send me your CD and bio.

MPR *The Current*
480 Cedar St., Saint Paul, MN 55101
PH: 651-989-4893
Barb Abney babney@mpr.org
minnesota.publicradio.org/radio/services/the_current
Features performances by the outstanding artists of our region alongside recordings by the world's finest music makers.

MPR *The Local Show*
480 Cedar St., Saint Paul, MN 55101
PH: 651-989-4893
Chris Roberts mail@mpr.org
minnesota.publicradio.org/radio/programs/local_show
The show explores the Twin Cities local music scene, both past and present.

Missouri

KDHX *River City Acoustic*
3504 Magnolia, St. Louis, MO 63118
PH: 314-664-3688 FX: 314-664-1020
Johnny Fox rca@kdhx.org
www.kdhx.org/programs/rivercityacous.htm
Features local and regional musical acts performing original material in an acoustic setting.

KPNT *The Local Show*
800 Union Stn. Powerhouse Bldg.
St. Louis, MO 63103
PH: 314-231-1057 FX: 314-621-3000
www.kpnt.com
Get in on STL's bitchin' local scene and hear the indie bands that might become tomorrow's Rock superstars. Hosted by Cornbread.

Nebraska

Coffee Club Podcast
www.journalstar.com/media/podcast
Jeff Korbelik interviews Lincoln Singer/Songwriters and features their music.

KEZO *Z-92's Homegrown*
11128 John Galt Blvd. #192, Omaha, NE 68137
PH: 402-592-5300 x5316
Scott Murphy scott@z92.com
www.z92.com
Features the best music from local Rock bands every Sunday night.

KIBZ *Local Bandwidth*
4630 Antelope Creek Rd. Lincoln, NE 68506
PH: 402-484-8000 FX: 402-483-9138
Luna luna@kibz.com
www.kibz.com
Featuring the music of local acts.

KRNU *Heresy*
147 Andersen Hall, PO Box 880466,
Lincoln, NE 68588-0466
PH: 402-472-8277
Sam Morris krnu-music@unl.edu
krnu.unl.edu
My radio show is strictly for Metal and Hardcore music. The unsigned bands I play are from the Lincoln/Omaha area.

KZUM *Alive in Lincoln*
941 "O" St., Lincoln, NE 68508
PH: 402-474-5086 FX: 402-474-5091
Hardy Holm strawberry67@neb.rr.com
www.kzum.org
Variety of local artists of all genres.

KZUM *River City Folk*
941 "O" St., Lincoln, NE 68508
PH: 402-474-5086 FX: 402-474-5091
Tom May programming@kzum.org
www.kzum.org
Interviews and regional Folk artists.

Nevada

KTHX
300 E. 2nd, 14th Fl. Reno, NV 89501
PH: 775-333-0123 FX: 775-322-7361
info@globalstudio.com
www.kthxfm.com
We play local music every night at 10pm and have Acoustic performances on several of our shows.

LV Rocks *Sounds of Sin*
PH: 866-587-6257
www.myspace.com/localmusicmama
Host Miss Amber features interviews and live performances from some of Vegas' hottest musicians & bands.

New Hampshire

RAGEROCKRADIO.COM
562 Montgomery St., Manchester, NH 03102
ragerockradio.com
The heaviest place on the planet! Supporting New England's Underground music.

WSCA *Hear Us Out*
909 Islington St. #1, Portsmouth, NH 03802-6532
PH: 603-430-9722 FX: 603-430-9822
Steve & Paul
music@portsmouthcommunityradio.org
www.wscafm.org
Features New Hampshire artists.

New Jersey

WCBP - The Rock House
410 E. Center Ave. Maple Shade, NJ 08052
PH: 856-649-3351
Jim Santora radio@casabonitaproductions.com
www.casabonitaproductions.com
Freeform Rock station that plays local Rock, indie artists, unsigned and general Rock format. Please visit our website for our submission details before sending your material. Featuring artists from the Philly / South Jersey area.

WDVR *Heartlands Hayride*
PO Box 191, Sergeantsville, NJ 08557
PH: 609-397-1620 FX: 609-397-5991
Chris Val lcvillano@aol.com
www.wdvrfm.org/hayride.htm
Live Country music show. The show invites participation to new and upcoming local talent who would not ordinarily have access to performing on the radio.

WSOU *Street Patrol*
400 S. Orange Ave. South Orange, NJ 07079
PH: 973-761-9768 FX: 973-275-2001
wsoumusic@hotmail.com
www.wsou.net
Highlighting the area's top local Hard Rock acts. We also feature regular interviews and live performances.

New Mexico

NMbands.com
podcast@nmbands.com
www.nmbands.com/submit
A weekly music podcast devoted to New Mexico bands. Artists must have some connection to New Mexico. All styles of music accepted.

New York

Brooklyn Heights Radio
smetrick@aol.com
www.brooklynheightsradio.com
To those artists and musicians in Brooklyn, who struggle to have their efforts heard THIS IS FOR YOU.

Bumpskey.com
PH: 201-455-8379
jerry@bumpskey.com
www.Bumpskey.com
Live show featuring all independent music and in studio performances.

East Village Radio
19 1st Ave. New York, NY 10003
PH: 212-420-5908
Echo Danon echo@eastvillageradio.com
www.eastvillageradio.com
Dedicated to streaming and linking the music, art, culture and community of NYC's East Village into the world's conscience. We are supporters of free radio and are interested in providing a forum for obscure music as well as a platform for local DJs and personalities.

WBAB *The Homegrown Show*
555 Sunrise Hwy. West Babylon, NY 11704
PH: 631-587-1023 FX: 631-587-1282
Fingers fingers@cox.com
wbab.com/homegrown
For over 20 years WBAB has supported the local Long Island music scene, playing Long Island's best bands.

WBNY *The Local Show*
1300 Elmwood Ave. Buffalo, NY 14222
PH: 716-878-5104 FX: 716-878-6600
www.wbny.org

WCWP *Aural Fix Transmission*
PO Box 6054, North Babylon, NY 11703
PH: 631-943-3213
Mike Ferrari auralmail@aol.com
www.auralfix.com
Features artists from the Long Island, New York region. Don't ask for permission…just SEND YOUR MUSIC IN!

WICB *Home Brew*
118 Park Hall, Ithaca, NY 14850
PH: 607-274-3217 FX: 607-274-1061
www.wicb.org
Join Taz for local music news and in studio performances.

WLIR *Tri-State Sound*
3075 Veterans Memorial Hwy. #201
Ronkonkoma, NY 11779
info@wlir.com
www.wlir.fm
Host Harlan Friedman showcases the best up and coming musicians from Long Island, NYC, CT and NJ.

WUSB *Local Insomniac Music*
Stony Brook Union 266
Stony Brook, NY 11794-3263
PH: 631-632-6501 FX: 631-632-7182
music@wusb.fm
wusb.fm
The best in original local music from the Tri-State area, in a variety of genres.

WUSB *LOCAL LIVE*
Stony Brook Union 266
Stony Brook, NY 11794-3263
PH: 631-632-6501 FX: 631-632-7182
Bill Frey longislandmusiclive@yahoo.com
wusb.fm
Radio show featuring Long Island musicians in a live performance & interview format.

WVKR *Scene Unseen*
Box 726, Vassar College, 124 Raymond Ave.
Poughkeepsie, NY 12604
PH: 845-437-7178 FX: 845-437-7656
Sharon Panaro sharon@wvkr.org
www.wvkr.org
Featuring bands and music artists from the listening area. Local music news, interviews and live musical performances.

North Carolina

600 Southcast
Jeff Ayers jeff@600southcast.com
600southcast.com
Created to showcase area/regional artists in a live setting.

WEND *90 Minutes*
801 E. Morehead St. #200, Charlotte, NC 28202
PH: 704-376-1065
Divakar 90minutes@1065.com
www.1065.com/pages/90minutes.html
The ONLY place for local & regional music in Charlotte.

WGWG *Carolina Drive*
PO Box 876, Boiling Springs, NC 28017
Walter Hoyle info@wgwg.org
www.wgwg.org
Spotlighting artists of all styles across the Carolinas.
Rock, Country, Blues, Bluegrass, Gospel, Classical
and Jazz. Anything goes!

WPVM *Be Here Now*
75 Haywood St., Asheville, NC 28801.
PH: 828-258-0085 FX: 828-350-7853
music@wpvm.org
www.wpvm.org
Features new and exciting regional music.
Live in-studio performances each week.

WQDR *The PineCone Bluegrass Show*
3012 Highwoods Blvd. #201, Raleigh, NC 27604
www.wqdr.net
Plays the music of local Bluegrass artists.

Ohio

Audio Gumshoe
PO Box 41071, Dayton, OH 45441-0071
PH: 888-223-5108
podcast@audiogumshoe.com
www.richpalmer.com/podcasts
A Miami Valley podcast that features the people in
SW Ohio that keep music interesting.

Cool Cleveland Podcast
14837 Detroit St. #105, Cleveland, OH 44107
Events@CoolCleveland.com
www.coolcleveland.com
Featuring music, news and interviews with local
talent.

WAIF *Kindred Sanction / Live City Licks*
1434 E. McMillan Ave. Cincinnati, OH 45206
PH: 513-961-8900
www.waif883.org
Local, regional music and interviews.

WCSB *Blue Monday*
Rhodes Tower 956, 2121 Euclid Ave.
Cleveland, OH 44115-2214
PH: 216-687-3721 FX: 216-687-2161
John Veverka musicdirector@wcsb.org
www.wcsb.org
The finest local and national Blues artists are heard.

WRUW *Live from Cleveland*
11220 Bellflower Rd. Cleveland, OH 44106
PH: 216-368-2208
md@wruw.org
wruw.org
Features live local bands every Thursday night.

WYSO *Banks of the Ohio*
795 Livermore St., Yellow Springs, OH 45387
PH: 937-767-6420
Fred Bartenstein banksoftheohio@aol.com
www.wyso.org/banksohio.html
Features Bluegrass from Ohio artists.

Oklahoma

Festival City Radio
Tom, Travis, Will & Jeremy
festivalcityradio@gmail.com
festivalcityradio.libsyn.com
We aim to give you a quick look at new releases,
Norman bands, upcoming shows and whatever else
we like.

iROK Radio
PO Box 33141, Tulsa, OK 74153-1141
comingsoon@irokradio.com
www.myspace.com/iROKRadio
A podcast and web radio station focused on
Oklahoma's unsigned and emerging artists. Playing
only Oklahoma artists, all the time!

KMYZ *HomeGroan*
5810 E. Skelly Dr. #801, Tulsa, OK 74135
PH: 918-665-3131 FX: 918-663-6622
www.myspace.com/z1045homegroan
Featuring local and regional talent.

Oregon

JamminFM.com *Tha Undaground Show*
0234 SW. Bancroft, Portland, OR 97201
PH: 503-243-7595 FX: 503-417-7653
StarChile starchile@jamminfm.com
www.jamminfm.com
Portland'z #1 ALL Hip Hop show!!!! This is the
ONLY show that gives MAJOR LUV 2 Northwest
artists!!!

KBPS *Played in Oregon*
515 NE. 15th Ave. Portland, OR 97232-2897
PH: 503-916-5828 FX: 503-802-9456
Robert McBride robert@allclassical.org
www.allclassical.org
There needs to be some Oregon connection and it
needs to be "Classical" music.

KBVR *Locals Live*
210 Memorial Union E., Corvallis, OR 97331
PH: 541-737-6323 FX: 541-737-4545
oregonstate.edu/dept/kbvr/html
A 2 hour show that gives local musicians the chance
to perform live on KBVR.

KINK *Local Music Spotlight*
1501 SW. Jefferson, Portland, OR 97201
PH: 503-517-6000 FX: 503-517-6100
Beth Clyman bclyman@kink.fm
www.kinkfm102.com
Tuesday through Friday at 9:20 pm we spotlight a
couple of tracks from a local artist or group.

KLCC *Friends and Neighbors*
136 W. 8th Ave. Eugene, OR 97401
PH: 541-463-6004 FX: 541-463-6046
Kobi Lucas klcc@lanecc.edu
www.klcc.org
Very Acoustic Folk music. A focus on new releases
and local music, both recorded and live.

KLRR *Today's Homegrown Hit*
63088 NE 18th St. #200 Bend, OR 97701
PH: 541-389-1088 FX: 541-388-0456
Dori dori@clear1017.fm
www.clear1017.fm
Playing the music of a local artist each weekday
morning.

KLRR *Homegrown Music Showcase*
63088 NE 18th St. #200 Bend, OR 97701
PH: 541-389-1088 FX: 541-388-0456
Dori dori@clear1017.fm
www.clear1017.fm
A full hour of music you won't hear anywhere else.
If you are a musician or band from Oregon, we want
to hear from you.

KMHD *Home Grown Live*
26000 SE. Stark St., Gresham, OR 97030
PH: 503-661-8900 FX: 503-491-6999
Mary Burlingame burlingm@mhcc.edu
www.kmhd.org
Featuring the music of Oregon artists.

KNRK *Get Local*
0700 SW. Bancroft St., Portland, OR 97305
PH: 503-733-5470
www.knrk.com
Jaime Cooley plays local music every Wednesday
night.

KNRQ *Native Noise*
1200 Executive Pkwy. #440, Eugene, OR 97405
PH: 541-684-0979
Derrick dlau@nrq.com
www.myspace.com/nativenoise
Featuring the music of Oregon Rock bands.

Pennsylvania

Coal Cracker Radio
coalcrackerradio@gmail.com
www.coalcrackerradio.net
Music and interviews with some of NE
Pennsylvania's best independent artists.

Indie Band Radio *The Pennsylvania Rock*
Show
www.parockshow.info
Featuring the best unsigned Rock Pennsylvania has
to offer.

Local Support Podcast
www.citypaper.net/podcast
Philadelphia City Paper's bi-weekly local music
podcast.

Old School House Radio
PO Box 2224, Harrisburg, PA 17105
Crazy John Kerecz info@OSHRadio.com
www.oshradio.com
Reviews, interviews and you can also post your
MP3s. Several shows covering the Harrisburg
entertainment scene.

PaXposure Radio
320 Jackson St., Reynoldsville, PA 15851
www.myspace.com/paxposurenetradio
Playing PA's best indie artists. Send us a copy of
your CD. NO attachments!

The Phil Stahl Show *WXLV*
PO Box 231, Pennsburg, PA 18073
PH: 610-799-1145
Phil phil@philstahl.com
philstahl.indiegroup.com
Features unsigned local music acts only.

WBXQ *The Backyard Rocker*
PH: 814-944-9320
www.wbxq.com
A 2 hour weekly local music program.

WQXA *Under the Radar*
515 S. 32nd St., Camp Hill, PA 17011
Maria maria@1057thex.com
1057thex.com
Local and regional music. Send your music in. No
phone calls, please!

WRVV *Open Mic Night*
600 Corporate Cir. Harrisburg, PA 17110
PH: 800-724-5959 FX: 717-671-9973
Michael Anthony Smith
requestsomething@yahoo.com
www.river973.com
Join us every Sunday nights for 2 hours of the best
local and regional Rock n' Roll.

WXPN *Philly Local*
3025 Walnut St., Philadelphia, PA 19104
PH: 215-898-6677. FX: 215-898-0707
Helen Leicht phillylocal@xpn.org
xpn.org
*Each weekday at 1pm I put the spotlight on one
song from an up and coming local artist. Send in (2)
CDs. Please do not send your bios, demos etc. by
e-mail!*

WZZO *Backyard Bands*
1541 Alta Dr. #400, Whitehall, PA 18052-5632
PH: 610-720-9595 FX: 610-434-9511
Brother Joel wzzobyb@aol.com
www.wzzo.com
*Eastern PA's #1 radio showcase for regional
unsigned bands.*

Rhode Island

WBRU *Home BRU'd*
88 Benevolent St., Providence, RI 02906-2046
PH: 401-272-9550 FX: 401-272-9278
homebrud@wbru.com
wbru.com
*We play stuff hot off the local music presses, chat
about gigs around the area and dish out the latest in
local music news.*

WRIU *Vocalists & Localists*
326 Memorial Union, Kingston, RI 02881
PH: 401-874-4949 FX: 401-874-4349
jazz@wriu.org
www.wriu.org
*A showcase for the many talented Jazz artists who
call New England home.*

South Carolina

WUSC *Locals Show*
RHUU Rm. 343, 1400 Greene St.
Columbia, SC 29208
PH: 803-777- 9872
wuscmd@sc.edu
wusc.sc.edu
Featuring the music of SC artists.

WYBB *Local X*
59 Windermere Blvd. Charleston, SC 29407
Local_X@hotmail.com
www.myspace.com/localx
*A spotlight on all the best in local and regional Rock
& Roll.*

Tennessee

WDVX *Live At Laurel*
PO Box 18157, Knoxville, TN 37928
PH: 865-494-2020
Brent Cantrell cantrellb@netstarcomm.net
www.wdvx.com
*Performances recorded Live directly from the
historic Laurel Theater in Knoxville.*

WEVL *The Memphis Beat*
PO Box 40952, Memphis, TN 38174
PH: 901-528-0560
wevl@wevl.org
www.myspace.com/memphisbeat
*There are a lot of talented musicians in Memphis
and we love to show them off!*

WMTS *Fascination Street Radio*
Box 58, 1301 E. Main St., Murfreesboro, TN 37132
PH: 615-898-2636 FX: 615-898-5682
DJ Steve program@wmts.org
www.myspace.com/fascinationstreetradio
*I interview local artists and sometimes have them
play an acoustic song or two live on the air.*

WRLT *Local Lightning Spotlight*
1310 Clinton St. #200, Nashville, TN 37203
www.wrlt.com/music/local-lightning.cfml
*Features two different local artists each week. Send
in your music and bio. Please, no phone calls!*

XNRock *The Local Buzz*
1824 Murfreesboro Rd. Nashville, TN 37217
aljon@1029thebuzz.com
myspace.com/localbuzz
*We have been responsible for launching the careers
of many local artists.*

Texas

Austin Riffs
austinriffs@yahoo.com
www.austinriffs.com
*We bring you the best in Blues, Funk & Soul. From
well-known to not-so-well-known artists from (or
appreciated in) Austin, Texas. We hope you enjoy!!!*

KACV *TexTunes*
PO Box 447, Amarillo, TX 79178
PH: 806-371-5222
Jesica kacvfm90@actx.edu
www.kacvfm.org
*Sunday mornings, it's all about Texas music. Join
Marcie Lane for three hours of tunes from artists
who live and rock in the Lone Star State.*

KBXX
24 Greenway Plaza #900, Houston, TX 77046
latinagirl979@yahoo.com
www.kbxx.com
*#1 for Hip Hop and R&B. We meet with local
artists/labels on Monday's between 1p-3p at the
KBXX offices.*

KFAN *Texas Six Pack / The Texas Lady's
Spotlight*
PO Box 311, Fredericksburg, TX 78624
PH: 830-997-2197 FX: 830-997-2198
musicandprogramming@ctesc.net
www.texasrebelradio.com
*Daily segments featuring unsigned local and
regional Texas musicians.*

KISS *Texas Traxx*
8930 Four Winds Dr. #500, San Antonio, TX 78239
PH: 210-646-0105 FX: 210-871-6116
Randy Bonillas randy.bonillas@coxradio.com
www.kissrocks.com
*Weekly show featuring local music from the state of
Texas.*

KOOP *Around the Town Sounds*
PO Box 2116, Austin, TX 78768-2116
PH: 512-472-1369 FX: 512-472-6149
Charlie Martin charliemuz@aol.com
www.koop.org
*Covering the many genres and ethnic shades of the
contemporary local club scene.*

KPLX *The Front Porch*
3500 Maple Ave. #1600, Dallas, TX 75219
PH: 214-526-2400 FX: 214-520-4343
Justin Frazell Justin@995thewolf.com
www.995thewolf.com/porch.html
Proud and honored to play TEXAS MUSIC.

KSTV *Texas Style Saturday Night*
3209 W. Washington, PO Box 289
Stephenville, TX 76401
PH: 254-968-5788
Shayne Hollinger shayneholl@yahoo.com
www.kstvfm.com/shayne.htm
Music and interviews with local artists.

KSTX *Sunday Nite Session*
8401 Datapoint Dr. #800
San Antonio, TX 78229-5903
PH: 210-614-8977
David Furst sns@tpr.org
www.tpr.org/programs/sns.html
*Features interviews, live music and recordings of
contemporary musicians from San Antonio and
around Texas.*

KTRU *The Local Show*
PO Box 1892, Houston, TX 77251
PH: 713-348-KTRU
noise@ktru.org
www.ktru.org
Featuring the music of area artists.

KUT/KUTX *Live Set*
1 University Stn. A0704, Austin, TX 78712
PH: 512-471-2345 FX: 512-471-3700
Larry Monroe music@kut.org
www.kut.org
*Some of the best darned music you'll hear anywhere
on the planet!*

KVRX *Local Live*
PO Box D, Austin, TX 78713-7209
PH: 512-495-5879
local_live@kvrx.org
www.kvrx.org/locallive
*Handmade according to an ancient Austin recipe,
using only the choicest barley, hops and spring
water.*

Radio Free Texas
PO Box 167, Nederland, TX 77627
PH: 409-440-7192
radiofreetexas.org
Bringing Texas red dirt music to the world!

Texas Blues Cafe
texasblues.podomatic.com
*We promote the Blues featuring as many local and
regional independent blues artists as we can.*

Utah

provoPODCAST.com
submit@provopodcast.com
www.provopodcast.com
*Each week we pack up our gear and go hunting for
the coolest local Provo artists.*

Vermont

WBTZ *Buzz Homebrew*
255 S. Champlain St., Burlington, VT 05401
Attn: Homebrew Crew
mailbag@999thebuzz.com
www.999thebuzz.com
*A show for local acts to prove that good music
comes in all forms and genres.*

WEQX *EQX-Posure!!*
PO Box 1027, Manchester, VT 05255
PH: 802-362-4800
Jason Irwin eqx@capital.net
www.weqx.com
The BEST local/regional music!

Virginia

804Noise Solution *WRIR*
PO Box 4787, Richmond, VA 23220
noisesolution@804noise.org
www.804noise.org
*Invited guest hosts and DJs from the 804noise
community share their Experimental music
collections.*

WNOR *Homegrown*
870 Greenbrier Cir. #399, Chesapeake, VA 23320
PH: 757-366-9900 FX: 757-366-9870
Shelley shelley@fm99.com
www.fm99.com/homegrown.asp
Featuring local and regional bands, plus live interviews and performances.

WRIR *River City Limits*
PO Box 4787, Richmond, VA 23220
PH: 804-649-9737 FX: 804-622-1436
music@wrir.org
wrir.org
Featuring music from local artists.

WXJM Live!
983 Reservoir St., Harrisonburg, VA 22801-4350
PH: 540-568-3425
wxjm@jmu.edu
wxjmlive.com
Features live performances of local acts.

Washington

The KCDA Local Lounge
808 E. Sprague, Spokane, WA 99202
Scott Shannon scottshannon@clearchannel.com
www.1031kcda.com/pages/local_lounge.html
I hand the KCDA studio and the station over to a new band each week.

KCMS *Local Music Project*
19319 Fremont Ave. N., Seattle, WA 98133
PH: 206-546-7350 FX: 206-546-7372
Sarah Taylor sarah@spirit1053.com
www.spirit1053.com
Every weekday at 5:30 we feature the music of a local Puget Sound Christian artist.

KNDD *The Young & The Restless*
1100 Olive Way #1650, Seattle, WA 98101
PH: 206-622-3251
www.myspace.com/theyoung_therestless
Two hours of Northwest bands.

KPLU *Jazz Northwest*
12180 Park Ave. S., Tacoma, WA 98447-0885
PH: 253-535-7758 FX: 253-535-8332
Jim Wilke jwilke123@comcast.net
kplu.org/jandb/wilke.html
Focuses on the regional Jazz scene from Portland to Vancouver.

KUGS *Local Smorgasboard*
700 Viking Union MS 9106, Bellingham, WA 98225
PH: 360-650-2936
music@kugs.org
www.kugs.org

Rainy Dawg Radio
SAO 254, Box 352238, Seattle, WA 98195
PH: 206-543-7675
www.myspace.com/rainydawg
A wide variety of local music from the Northwest. From Punk, to Electronic and everything in between.

West Virginia

Bluegrass Preservation Society Radio Show
94 Beech St., Gassaway, WV 26624
Ewell Ferguson ewell@bluegrasspreservation.org
www.bluegrasspreservation.org
We only play what we record locally. You won't hear any slick, studio recordings here.

WAMX *Loud and Local*
134 4th Ave. Huntington, WV 25701
PH: 304-525-7788 x143 FX: 304-525-3299
Brandon Woolum
brandonwoolum@clearchannel.com
www.myspace.com/x1063local
The original local & regional Rock show.

WRZZ *Songwriter Night with Todd Burge*
PH: 304-422-4068
Todd songwriternight@hotmail.com
www.songwriternight.com
A live radio show which takes place at the Blennerhassett Hotel in Parkersburg, WV.

WWVU *The Morgantown Sound*
PO Box 6446, Morgantown, WV 26506-6446
PH: 304-293-3329 FX: 304293-7363
Orville Weale oweale@yahoo.com
www.wvu.edu/~u92
The exclusive source of live local music in the area.

Wisconsin

WJJO *The JJO Local Stage*
PH: 608-321-0941
www.wjjo.com
Our commitment to the Madison music scene.

WMSE *Midnight Radio*
1025 N. Broadway, Milwaukee, WI 53202
PH: 414-277-7247 FX: 414-277-7149
www.wmse.org

WWSP *Club Wisconsin*
1101 Reserve St. CAC Rm. 105
Stevens Point, WI 54481
PH: 715-346-3755 FX: 715-346-4012
Jon Quam jquam744@uwsp.edu
www.uwsp.edu/stuorg/wwsp
The best in Moo-town music. Local concert information and interviews of bands playing in the area.

Canada

All Axis Radio
PO Box 51073, RPO Beddington
Calgary, AB T3K 3V9
PH: 206-339-2947
AllAxisRadio@gmail.com
allaxisradio.com
100% Canadian music podcast. We feature great new indie music, a few anecdotes and the odd interview with Canadian musicians.

Bandwidth *CBC*
PO Box 3220, Stn. C, Ottawa, ON K1Y 1E4
PH: 613-562-8570
www.cbc.ca/bandwidth
Host Amanda Putz features an eclectic mix of Canadian music.

CIUT *Back To The Sugar Camp*
100 Bain Ave. 19 The Lindens
Toronto, ON M4K 1E8
PH: 416-465-9464
Steve steve@backtothesugarcamp.com
www.backtothesugarcamp.com
Weekly radio show featuring Canadiana music.

CKCU *Canadian Spaces*
Rm. 517, U. Ctr. 1125 Colonel By Dr.
Ottawa, ON K1S 5B6
PH: 613-520-2898
Chopper McKinnon chopper@nutshellmusic.com
www.ckcufm.com
Canada's most respected Folk and Roots music and interview show.

Confessions of a DJ Podcast
PH: 206-309-7031
confessionsofadj@gmail.com
confessionsofadj.libsyn.com
Playing the best Canadian independent music.

Definitely Not the Opera *CBC*
Box 160, Winnipeg, MB R3C 2H1
PH: 866-630-3686
www.cbc.ca/dnto
Host Sook-Yin Lee likes to play Canadian indie bands on the show and is always looking for new music.

Indie Night in Canada *CFOX*
#2000-700 W. Georgia, Vancouver, BC V7Y 1K9
PH: 604-280-2369 FX: 604-331-2722
webmaster@cfox.com
www.cfox.com
Independent bands from Vancouver and across the country plus interviews and special live performances.

IndieCan Radio
50 Cordova Ave. #2102, Toronto, ON M9A 4X6
Joe Chisholm info@indiecan.com
www.indiecan.com
This acclaimed syndicated podcast brings you up close and personal with the best emerging talent in Canada. IndieCan brings you backstage to learn the realities of indie music life in Canada.

Interactive Slam Jam *Slakrz Radio*
303 Whiteside Rd. NE, Calgary, AB TLY 2Z6
Mike mike@slakrz.com
www.slakrz.com/slakrzradio
Canadian artists get their music heard by a real record executive so they can get feedback on what you might or might not need to do to put the finishing touches on your music.

Mp3this/Breakthrough Windsor
4553 Hunt Club Cres. Windsor, ON N9G 2P6
PH: 519-250-0034
Jonathan Nehmetallah
john.nehmetallah@gmail.com
www.mp3this.blogspot.com
We are both a MP3 blog and radio show that is always interested in new Canadian indie music.

Roots Music Canada *CBC*
700 Hamilton St. PO Box 4600
Vancouver, BC V6B 4A2
PH: 604-662-6790 FX: 604-662-6594
info@rootsmusiccanada.com
www.rootsmusiccanada.com
Features Canadian Roots and Folk music.

Slakrz Radio
303 Whiteside Rd. NE, Calgary, AB TLY 2Z6
Mike mike@slakrz.com
www.slakrz.com/slakrzradio
Your home for Canadian independent music!

Sounds Like Canada *CBC*
Box 4600, Vancouver, BC V6B 4A2
PH: 604-662-6608 FX: 604-662-6025
www.cbc.ca/soundslikecanada
Our goal is to drench the airwaves with voices and sound from all over the country. Hosted by Shelagh Rogers

The Sunday Edition *CBC*
PO Box 500 Stn. A, Toronto, ON M5W 1E6
PH: 416-205-3700 FX: 416-205-6461
radio.cbc.ca/programs/thismorning/sunday.html
Here you will also find a particularly eclectic mix of music. Hosted by Michael Enright.

TheSoundRadio
#204 - 10138 81st Ave. Edmonton, AB T6H 1X1
PH: 780-702-2907
www.thesoundradio.com
A place for rising artists to host their MP3s and build a fan base.

Vinyl Café *CBC*
PO Box 500 Stn. A, Toronto, ON M5W 1E6
PH: 416-205-3700
www.cbc.ca/vinylcafe
Host Stuart McLean features music, both live and recorded.

Waxing Deep *CKUT*
235 Metcalfe Ave. #402, Westmount, QC H3Z 2H8
PH: 514-398-4616 FX: 514-398-8261
Daniel daniel.zacks@mail.mcgill.ca
www.waxingdeep.org
Specializes in Canadian and Quebecois Bossa, Jazz, Funk, Breaks, Soul, Disco, Latin and everything in between.

Alberta

CBC *Our Music*
PH: 403-521-6241
www.cbc.ca/ourmusic
Host Catherine McClelland presents the best of Alberta's many talented Classical musicians.

Key of A *CBC*
PH: 780-468-7472 FX: 780-468-7468
www.cbc.ca/keyofa
Host Katherine Duncan goes behind the scenes with performers from across Alberta.

British Columbia

CITR *Live From Radio Thunderbird Hell*
#233-6138 SUB Blvd. Vancouver, BC V6T 1Z1
PH: 604-822-8733 FX: 604-822-9364
citrmusic@club.ams.ubc.ca
www.citr.ca
Features live band(s) every week performing in the comfort of the CITR lounge. Most are from Vancouver.

CVUE *The All Canadian Show*
PO Box 2288, Sechelt, BC V0N3A0
PH: 604-885-0800
Mike oceanviewaudioworks@hotmail.com
www.civu.net
Fabulous Canadian music from 'then' & 'now' with lots of music by local musicians & other artists from around BC.

Music BC Radio
#530-425 Carrall St., Vancouver, BC V6B 6E3
PH: 604-873-1914 FX: 604-873-9686
info@musicbc.org
musicbc.org
Features the music of Music BC members.

North by Northwest *CBC*
Box 4600, Vancouver, BC V6B 4A2
PH: 604-662-6089
www.cbc.ca/nxnw
Host Sheryl MacKay presents creative people and what they create.

On the Island *CBC*
1025 Pandora Ave. Victoria, BC V8V 3P6
PH: 250-360-2227 FX: 250-360-2600
www.cbc.ca/ontheisland
Host Paul Vasey presents a lively blend of news, reviews and interviews.

Radio Bandcouver
#110-360 Columbia St., Vancouver, BC V6A 4J1
Mark Bignell mark@bandcouver.com
www.bandcouver.com
Artists & bands send your CDs and press kits in.

Transpondency.com
transpondency.com
Podcast with an earful of suburban culture and indie music from BC and beyond.

The Zone's Band of the Month
The Zone, Top Fl. 2750 Quadra St.
Victoria, BC V8T 4E8
PH: 250-475-6611
James Sutton james@TheZone.fm
www.thezone.fm
Our featured band will be highlighted in a mini audio bio that will air between five and seven times each day.

Manitoba

CKIC *HomeSpun*
W-106, 160 Princess St., Winnipeg, MB R3B 1K9
Rick rick@kick.fm
www.kick.fm
Featuring music made in Manitoba.

Weekend Morning Show *CBC*
PH: 204-788-3612 FX: 204-788-3674
www.cbc.ca/weekendmorning
Host Ron Robinson presents eclectic music, comedy and special features.

New Brunswick

Shift *CBC*
PO Box 2358, Saint John, NB E2L 3V6
PH: 506-632-7743 FX: 506-632-7761
www.cbc.ca/shift
Host Paul Castle connects people in NB with the events of the day and with each other.

Newfoundland

CHMR *Upon this Rock*
Box A-119 St. John's, NL A1C 5S7
PH: 709-737-4777 FX: 709-737-7688
Kevin Kelly thekmaster@yahoo.com
www.mun.ca/chmr
Two hours of the best in Newfoundland and Labrador music. From Traditional to Alternative.

MUSICRAFT *CBC*
PO Box 12010, Stn. A, St. John's, NL A1B 3T8
www.cbc.ca/musicraft
Host Francesca Swann presents musical events from across the province and discussions with the people who bring the music to life.

On the Go *CBC*
PO Box 12010, Stn. A, St. John's, NL A1B 3T8
PH: 709-576-5270
www.cbc.ca/onthego
Host Ted Blades presents a lively package of news, interviews and the best in local music.

The Performance Hour *CBC*
PO Box 12010, Stn. A, St. John's, NL A1B 3T8
www.cbc.ca/performancehour
Newfoundland's finest Singers and Songwriters recorded live at the LSPU Hall in St. John's.

Republic of Avalon Radio
PO Box 5851, St. John's, NF A1C 5X3
PH: 724-426-8176
Jim Fidler republicofavalonradio@gmail.com
www.republicofavalonradio.com
Newfoundland's first podcast. A bit of everything from the heart of Avalon.

Nova Scotia

All The Best *CBC*
PO Box 30000, Halifax, NS B3J 3E9
PH: 902-420-4426 FX: 902-420-4089
www.cbc.ca/allthebest
Host Shauntay Grant presents music ranging from Classical through classic Jazz to traditional.

Atlantic Airwaves *CBC*
PO Box 3000, Halifax, NS B3J 3E9
PH: 902-420-4426 FX: 902-420-4089
www.cbc.ca/atlanticairwaves
Host Stan Carew presents profiles of music makers from Canada's four Atlantic Provinces as well as national and international artists appearing throughout the region.

CIGO *East Coast Rising*
11 MacIntosh Ave. Port Hawkesbury, NS B9A 3K4
PH: 902-625-1220 FX: 902-625-2664
1015thehawk@1015thehawk.com
www.1015thehawk.com/ecr.asp
Tune in to get updates on the East Coast music scene!!

CIGO *Highland Fling*
11 MacIntosh Ave. Port Hawkesbury, NS B9A 3K4
PH: 902-625-1220 FX: 902-625-2664
1015thehawk@1015thehawk.com
www.1015thehawk.com/highland.asp
Committing to focus on Cape Breton fiddle, piano, Gaelic song and bagpipes.

CKDU *The One Inch Punch*
Dalhousie Stud. Union Bldg. 6136 U. Ave.
Halifax, NS B3H 4J2
PH: 902-494-6479
Derrick & Louie music@ckdu.ca
www.ckdu.ca
Punk focusing on the local scene.

CKDU *Saturday Morning Musical Box*
Dalhousie Stud. Union Bldg. 6136 U. Ave.
Halifax, NS B3H 4J2
PH: 902-494-6479
Walter Kemp music@ckdu.ca
www.ckdu.ca
Classical music. Interviews with local performers.

Connections *CBC*
PO Box 30000, Halifax, NS B3J 3E9
PH: 902-420-4248 FX: 902-420-4089
www.cbc.ca/connections
Host Olga Milosevich presents an uplifting mixture of music - largely Maritime and ranging from Classical to Folk, Jazz, Pop and World Beat.

MainStreet Halifax *CBC*
PO Box 3000, Halifax, NS B3J 3E9
PH: 902-420-4378 FX: 902-420-4357
www.cbc.ca/mainstreetns
Host Carmen Klassen brings you the latest on the news of the day ...and of course, some great music.

WEEKENDER
PO Box 3000, Halifax, NS B3J 3E9
PH: 902-420-4378 FX: 902-420-4357
www.radio.cbc.ca/programs/weekender
Host Peter Togni features music that's engaging, fun and played by the best in the business.

Ontario

All in a Day *CBC*
PO Box 3220, Stn. C, Ottawa, ON K1Y 1E4
PH: 613-562-8442 FX: 613-562-8810
www.cbc.ca/allinaday
In any given program, you're likely to hear Rock, Jazz, Pop, World Beat, Classical or Blues. Hosted by Adrian Harewood

CHUO *L'Express Country*
65 University Pvt. #0038, Ottawa, ON K1N 9A5
PH: 613-562-5967 FX: 613-562-5969
Robert Guindon webmestre@transcontinental.ca
groups.msn.com/RobertGuindonAnimateur
Musique Country francophone d'artistes connus dans la région.

CKCU *Ottawa Live Music*
Rm. 517 U. Ctr. 1125 Colonel By Dr.
Ottawa, ON K1S 5B6
PH: 613-520-2898
Charles Anthony
charlesanthony@ottawalivemusic.com
www.ottawalivemusic.com
Artists perform live on the air in the CKCU studios. Listeners call in with questions.

Fear and Loathing in Ottawa
fandlottawa1@gmail.com
www.fearandloathinginottawa.com
If you're looking for a unique take on the local entertainment, social and political scene, you've come to the right place.

Fresh Air *CBC*
PO Box 500, Stn. A, Toronto, ON M5W 1E6
PH: 416-205-3700
www.cbc.ca/freshair
Host Jeff Goodes presents a variety of music and stories. It's like sitting around the kitchen table with old friends.

The LiVE Indie Sessions
livelounge@livelifeLiVE.fm
www.livelifelive.fm
Every Friday night, catch The LiVE Indie Sessions at The LiVE Lounge as we showcase some of the best talent in Ottawa and beyond - and record the whole thing live!

Ottawa Morning *CBC*
PO Box 3220, Stn. C, Ottawa, ON K1Y 1E4
PH: 613-562-8442 FX: 613-562-8810
www.cbc.ca/ottawamorning
Kathleen Petty is your ear on entertainment and the local music scene.

Sunday night Soul *AM1430*
Johnny Max johnnymaxband@rogers.com
www.sundaynightsoul.com
I love promoting the amazing talent pool that the Toronto region has. Canadian Blues, Soul, Roots, whatever, I play the music that we love.

Toronto Independent Music Podcast
blogto.com/toronto_independent_music_podcast
If you are in a Toronto area band and would like to have a song considered for the show, please fill out our online form.

Prince Edward Island

Island Music Radio
PO Box 2000, Charlottetown, PE C1A 7N8
PH: 902-368-6176 FX: 902-368-4418
island@gov.pe.ca
www.gov.pe.ca/radio
Please fill out our online form and send it in with your CD.

Quebec

A Propos *CBC*
Box 6000, Montreal, QC H3C 3A8
PH: 514-597-6000 FX: 514-597-4423
www.cbc.ca/apropos
Host Jim Corcoran features the most popular tunes coming out of Quebec.

Saskatchewan

Morning Edition *CBC*
2440 Broad St., Regina, SK S4P 4A1
PH: 800-661-7540 FX: 306-347-9797
www.cbc.ca/morningedition
Host Sheila Coles features music and a good sprinkling of humour.

Online Marketing & Promotions for Emerging & Indie Artists!

Strategic Campaigns include:

- Social Network Marketing (Myspace, Facebook, YouTube, iLike & many other sites)
- Online press coverage in music webzines and blogs
- Online Tour Press, Promotions & Marketing
- Film/Music Placement Opportunities
- Online Media Buy Campaigns
- Guerilla & Viral Campaigns
- Contests/Sweepstakes
- Content Distribution
- Press Release Syndication
- Online Radio and Satellite Radio Promotions
- Customized Campaigns for your specific needs
- Street Team Basic Setup, Management & Maintenance
- Video Promotions (YouTube, AOL, Google and countless others!)

Recent Artist Campaigns include:

 Terence Blanchard

 Natalie Walker

 Rosey

 Deana Carter

 Jason Ricci & New Blood

 Emerson Hart (of Tonic)

 SwampDaWamp

 Steve Cole

 Kelly Sweet

 Anne Murray

Please call us today to set up a consultation meeting!
323. 806. 0400 or chip@mileshighproductions.com www.mileshighproductions.com

SECTION FOUR: PROMOTION AND MARKETING SERVICES

Mainstream

North America

United States

+1 Management & Public Relations
242 Wythe Ave. Studio 6, Brooklyn, NY 11211
PH: 718-599-3740 FX: 718-599-0998
Ashley Purdum ashley@plusonemusic.net
www.plusonemusic.net
If you have a demo you think we might like, send it with a bio and any press clips to our address.

928 Event Management
PO Box 292656, Sacramento, CA 95829
PH: 916-308-9647
www.928events.com
We offer event planning to promote a product, person or service, or to work in conjunction with a PR or marketing plan. Record release parties, concerts, movie premieres etc.

AlchemyHouse Productions
PO Box 202, Yellow Springs, OH 45387
PH: 937-523-0252
Tom Blessing tblessing@alchemyhouse.com
www.alchemyhouse.com
Our services are engaged in the creation of music, motion picture, broadcast and digital media. We are also heavily involved in talent management, legal and publicity/promotion.

Allure Media Entertainment
PO Box 275, 50 E. Wynnewood Ave.
Wynnewood, PA 19096
www.allureartists.com
Works with, counsels and advises artists to promote and advance their music careers.

The Almighty Institute of Music Retail
11724 Ventura Blvd. Ste. B, Studio City, CA 91604
PH: 818-752-8000
sales@almightyretail.com
www.almightyretail.com
Services record labels and youth culture companies looking to promote their product in record stores and other outlets that sell prerecorded music.

AlphaMusicGroup
1133 Broadway #706, New York, NY 10010
PH: 212-696-7934
info@alphamusicgroup.com
www.alphamusicgroup.com
A selective independent A & R company that strives to be the most reliable source for unsigned artists/bands looking for help in getting a record deal.

Already There Media
259 W. 30th St. #12FR, New York, NY 10001-280?
PH: 212-564-4611 FX: 212-564-4448
alreadytheremedia@yahoo.com
www.alreadytheremedia.com/services.html
We offer an extensive knowledge of radio and press promotion as well as national "brick & mortar" retail marketing.

American Voices
404 Cordell St., Houston, TX 77009
PH/FX: 713-862-7125
John Ferguson john.ferguson@americanvoices.org
www.americanvoices.org
Furthering the appreciation and understanding of American music, especially in developing countries.

AMP3 Public Relations
928 Broadway Ave. #801, New York, NY 10010
PH: 646-827-9594
info@AMP3pr.com
www.amp3pr.com
A boutique PR firm specializing in arts & entertainment publicity for lifestyle brands.

Ariel Publicity Artist Relations and Cyber Promotions
325 W. 38th St. #505, New York, NY 10018
PH: 212-239-8384 FX: 212-239-8380
Ariel Hyatt ah@arielpublicity.com
www.arielpublicity.net
Professional promotional services for indie artists.

This Indie Bible has thousands of PR opportunities (and we already know which ones will love your music)

CYBER PR
Customized publicity campaigns for musicians starting at under $500 a month

ArielPublicity.com
212 239-8384
contact@arielpublicity.com
Mention this ad for a discount

AristoWorks
1620 16th Ave. S., Nashville, TN 37212
PH: 615-269-7071 FX: 615-269-0131
Jon Walker contact@aristoworks.com
www.aristoworks.com
We provide a full range of new media services including web marketing, design and promotion.

Artspromo
PO Box 685, Shutesbury, MA 01072
PH: 413-259-1111
Jaime Campbell Morton artspromo@artspromo.org
www.artspromo.org
Support for nationally touring artists. $25 to send out your press release, MySpace support and other touring support. National references.

Art Attack Promotions
2414 Elmglen Dr.
Austin, TX 78744
PH: 512-445-7117
FX: 512-447-2493
Gigi Greco info@
artattackpromotions.com
www.
artattackpromotions.com
Marketing company specializing in grassroots marketing, online promotions, lifestyle campaigns and street team development.

ArtFRONT Presentations
1112 Liberty St.
Chattanooga, TN 37405
PH: 423-756-4827
Robin Merritt
Music@ArtFRONT.com
www.ArtFRONT.com
Produces the ArtFRONT Concert Series. Content provider for press and radio. Promoter/publicist.

Artistic Pursuit
16 Fiona Way
Brunswick, MD 21758
PH: 888-637-6512
FX: 301-834-7287
www.artisticpursuit.com
An online publishing company that accepts music content from artists, provides a professional review and pays artists selected for publication.

Baby G Publishing
17328 Ventura Blvd. #430, Encino, CA 91316
PH: 201-456-0349
Rachel Noelle babygmusic@gmail.com
www.babygmusic.com
An independent music publisher offering copyright administration, creative and licensing services to writers, producers and publishers.

bandpromote.com
PO Box 4102, Hollywood, CA 90078
PH: 323-276-1000 FX: 323-276-1001
Mike Galaxy mgalaxy@bandpromote.com
www.bandpromote.com
Distribute your music to thousands of record execs.

Beartrap PR
PH: 704-649-7128
Chuck Daley chuck@beartrappr.com
www.myspace.com/beartrappr
I can assist you with all your press needs; whether it's obtaining reviews / interviews, tour promotion, sending out press releases and news briefs or simply keeping the media updated with your every move, I'm all over it.

Bender Music Group
PMB 455, 835 W. Warner Rd. #101
Gilbert, AZ 85233
PH: 877-290-7536
Jon info@bendermusicgroup.com
www.bendermusicgroup.com
Our services include online/MySpace marketing, website & MySpace design, traditional/online distribution and band management. Years of label experience.

Big Noise Management
11 S. Angell St. #336, Providence, RI 02906
PH: 401-274-4770
Al Gomes al@bignoisenow.com
www.bignoisenow.com
We do artist development, A&R, music marketing, and film and TV licensing. We work with Pop, Rock, R&B, Hard Rock, Metal, Jazz, Acoustic, Dance and Blues artists. Currently seeking new artists. Please call or email first. We also run Big Noise Records. See our ad on Pages 223 and 233.

Big Top Music
2801 Meadow Lark Trail, Duluth, GA 30096
PH: 678-851-4282
Sean Owen bigtopmusic@yahoo.com
www.myspace.com/indiemusiccoaching
20+ years of artist management, promotion and production, provides coaching to indie artists

Bill Wence Promotions
PO Box 39, Nolensville, TN 37135
PH: 615-776-2060 FX: 615-776-2181
www.billwencepromotions.com
Hundreds of singles and albums have been charted for our clients.

Black & Blue Star
3554 Vinton Ave. #109, Los Angeles, CA 90034
PH: 310-924-5651 FX: 253-830-0840
Mindi Sue Meyer mindi@blackandbluestar.com
www.blackandbluestar.com
Independent record label giving talented artists an avenue to have their voices and masterpieces heard.

Broken Record Productions
PO Box 969, Katy, TX 77492
PH: 832-457-7790
Devon Mikeska info@brokenrecordproductions.com
www.myspace.com/brokenrecordproductions
We are an artist development company helping bands with radio, booking, PR and management.

Artist Representation - Professional booking agents provide dedicated service to represented artists.

Music Business Resources - Artist development, business and marketing plans that produce results.

CD/DVD Publishing - Full color CD/DVD & demos specializing in short runs and re-orders.

Promotional Products - Posters, fliers, stickers, buttons, band t-shirts are available at budget prices.

Contact information:
www.carnelianagency.com
360.752.9829

"The mission of Carnelian Agency is to provide musicians with the service products and resources they need with professionalism, integrity and an invested belief in the unlimited potential of our clients"

Broken Window Production
3501 Block Dr. Irving, TX 75038
PH: 214-507-1649
Glendon Guttenfelder
g2@brokenwindowproductions.com
www.BrokenWindowProductions.com
We are a multi-media promotional/marketing company that specializes in independent film and music.

Carnelian Agency
PH: 360-752-9829
www.carnelianagency.com
Our mission is to provide musicians with the services, products and resources they need with professionalism, integrity and an invested belief in the unlimited potential of our clients. Our vision is to offer a one stop artist's services and products company with several departments under one parent corporation. We provide exceptional customer service and nurture each client relationship with personal dedication.

CD Register
PO Box 180902, Utica, MI 48318
PH: 586-480-3000
Terrance info@cdregister.com
cdregister.com
Get your music in the hands of DJs, magazine writers, film & TV producers and A&R staff from around the world.

Celebrity Public Relations
49 E. 41st St. #449, New York, NY 10165
PH: 212-812-4427 x705 FX: 212-812-4427
Ruben Malaret ruben.malaret@celebrity-pr.com
www.celebrity-pr.com
A public relations agency providing artists and labels publicity services for their music launches. Some of our clients are Sony/BMG, Warner Music Group, A&M Records, Interscope, Motown and Capitol Records.

conqueroo
13351-D Riverside Dr. #655
Sherman Oaks, CA 91423-2450
PH: 818-501-2001
Cary Baker cary@conqueroo.com
conqueroo.com
A music industry publicity firm started up in 2004 by an ex label executive.

Countdown Entertainment
110 W. 26th St., New York, NY 10001-6805
PH: 212-645-3068 FX: 212-989-6459
submitmusic@countdownentertainment.com
www.countdownentertainment.com
Represents artists, composers, music producers and music managers to independent music labels and major recording labels for record deals, music licensing deals, film music deals, TV music deals, record distribution and music publishing.

Crash Avenue
120 Webster St. #217A, Louisville, KY 40206
PH: 502-583-4001
Jeffrey Smith jeffrey@crash-avenue.com
www.crash-avenue.com
An indie publicity and radio promotion company.

CTW Promotions
PO Box 40701, Redford, MI 48240
Mike Warden promotions@conquertheworld.com
www.conquertheworld.com/ctwpromotions.htm
We do MySpace promotion for labels, authors, bands and artists. Would you rather have your music profile blowing up daily or just sit there collecting dust?

Digital Bear Entertainment
PO Box 301090
Boston, MA 02130
PH: 888-844-2327
www.digitalbear.com
Devoted to the mission of artist development: finding gifted musical acts and helping them have a successful, sustainable career in music.

Entertainment Marketing & Promotions
PH: 309-826-8105
Jason Kaumeyer
jason@entertainment-mp.com
www.entertainment-mp.com
Creates name recognition for artists of all genres as well as offering marketing tools geared specifically to promote you.

Fanatic Promotion
135 W. 29th St. #1101, New York, NY 10001
PH: 212-616-5556
Josh Bloom info@fanaticpromotion.com
www.fanaticpromotion.com
Our goal is to turn on the world to talented new artists.

FeelingAnxious
Arien Rozelle arien@feelinganxious.com
www.feelinganxious.com
Marketing and public relations service. Our mission is to help artists build their audiences, develop a professional image, and move into the next level of their careers.

Foley Entertainment
PO Box 358, Greendell, NJ 07839
PH: 908-684-9400
Eugene Foley EugeneFoleyMusic@aol.com
FoleyEntertainment.com
Providing a wide range of music industry disciplines, including artist development, marketing, promotion, advertising, songwriting, composing, arranging, intellectual property, publishing, touring, distribution, producing and merchandising.

Fusent Entertainment
130 Church St. #166, New York, NY 10007
PH: 212-812-5432 FX: 212-812-5432
info@fusententertainment.com
www.fusententertainment.com
Artist management, development, promotions and creative concepts.

The Gate Media Group
1270 Springbrook Rd. Ste. H
Walnut Creek, CA 94597-3995
PH: 925-256-1770 FX: 925-256-1774
sales@gatemedia.com
www.gatemedia.com
Develops successful indie music promotional campaigns.

Genese Music and Entertainment Group
PO Box 245, Gambrills, MD 21054
PH: 410-514-8158 FX: 410-514-8158
Ralph Rogers info@genesemusic.com
www.genesemusic.com
Maintains a small studio, deals with artist development and works on marketing and product development.

Green Galactic
PH: 213-840-1201
Lynn Hasty lynn@greengalactic.com
www.greengalactic.com
A marketing and production media company specializing in youth culture.

Heatwave Entertainment
PO Box 777671, Henderson, NV 89077
PH/FX: 702-648-5401
Dennis McCummings heatwavedm1@cox.net
www.heatwavedbm.com
A booking agency looking for new talent.

The Hennessy Group
4236 Franklin Ave. Hollywood, CA 90027
PH: 323-371-2895 FX: 323-953-8592
Angela angela@thehennessygroup.net
www.thehennessygroup.net
Talent management for bands and solo artists. Management and promotions tailored to your needs.

Hire A Consultant
110 W. 26th St., New York, NY 10001-6805
PH: 212-645-3068
Ms. Lovie Jones
Lovie@CountdownEntertainment.com
www.CountdownEntertainment.com
We have a track record of representing multi-platinum & gold recording artists. If you have the "goods", we can provide industry contacts to listen to your music.

Hype-PR
PH: 407-797-1385
Aly M. Cleary AMCleary@hype-pr.com
www.hype-pr.com
Entertainment PR firm with a solid focus on the artist/band's needs.

InBlaze Entertainment
9225 W. Parmer Ln. #104-207, Austin, TX 78717
PH: 512-276-5199
www.InBlaze.com
We don't think you should sit around for months, maybe years, and wait for a label to pick you up. We think you should be heard by the masses now.

indie911.com
8949 Sunset Blvd. #201,
West Hollywood, CA 90069
PH: 310-943-7164 FX: 310-919-3091
Justin Goldberg justin@indie911.com
www.indie911.com
Label and management company. Helps indie musicians and labels sustain their livelihoods and increase their revenues by managing their most valuable asset, their own music.

The Industry Resource
101 W. 23rd St. #2152, New York, NY 10011
PH: 800-878-6113 FX: 800-878-6114
www.theindustryresource.com
Home to today's top industry professionals from management companies, booking agents, labels and publishing firms. These executives are actively seeking new and exciting talent.

IRL Music Group
31441 Santa Margarita Pkwy. #A366,
Rancho Santa Margarita, CA 92688
PH: 949-766-7979
Johnny Mendola jmendola@earthlink.net
www.johnnyrock.com/join
Get exposed to over 3,500 labels worldwide! Free online service. Join now!

Kari Estrin Artist Career Consulting
PO Box 60232, Nashville, TN 37206
PH: 615-262-0883
kari@kariestrin.com
www.kariestrin.com
Consulting, artist services and special projects.

Kacey Jones Consulting
PO Box 121253, Nashville, TN 37212
PH: 888-999-9975 FX: 615-321-2244
Kacey Jones kacey@kaceyjonesconsulting.com
www.kaceyjonesconsulting.com
Professional advice from a music industry veteran with 30 years experience. Record deals, promotion, publishing, radio and distribution.

Last Call Agency
26 Church St. #300, Cambridge, MA 02138
PH: 781-922-1238
Susan Scotti susan@lastcallagency.com
www.lastcallagency.com
Offers booking, publicity and promotional services.

Lenticular Productions
PO Box 1914, Hobbs, NM 88240
Dan Bryan info@lenticularproductions.com
www.lenticularproductions.com
A music and publication promotions and distribution company that focuses on developing independent artists and authors.

Luck Media & Marketing
8900 Olympic Blvd. Beverly Hills, CA 90211
PH: 310-860-9170
Steve Levesque steve@luckmedia.com
luckmedia.com
Our staff has a well-deserved and well-earned reputation as one of the most creative, productive and successful PR organizations.

Many Moods Production Company
41 Schermerhorn St. #135
Brooklyn, NY 11201
PH: 917-622-2694
mmp7@earthlink.net
www.manymoods.com
We offer assistance with music contracts, copyright formalities & registration, artist development, music production, songwriting, recording, CD and demo packages, music promotions and more.

Massive Music America
1227 Perry St.
Denver, CO 80204
PH: 720-221-8370
Randall Frazier
questions@massivemusicamerica.com
www.massivemusicamerica.com
Independent promotions company that offers radio, media/print, internet and tour support.

Mazur Public Relations
PO Box 2425, Trenton, NJ 08607-2425
PH: 609-448-7886 FX: 609-890-4556
www.mazurpr.com
Full service PR company that represents all genres.

MC-Input.com
499 N. Canon Dr. 4th Fl. Beverly Hills, CA 90210
PH: 310-926-7232
www.mc-input.com
Helps artists recognize their potential and assists them by giving useful tips and connections to succeed in the industry.

mediaHo publicity
Michelle Crispin michelle@mediahopublicity.com
www.mediaHopublicity.com
Internet marketing, publicity, promotion, artist development and more!

Mi2N PR Syndicate
www.mi2n.com/prsyndicate
We'll syndicate your press release across the web, getting your announcement in front of industry and friends.

Miles High Productions
6622 Delongpre Ave. Hollywood, CA 90028
PH: 323-806-0400 FX: 323-462-0829
mhpmanagement@mileshighproductions.com
www.mileshighproductions.com
Created to bridge the gap of companies working directly with music artists and entertainment based projects who are in need of additional marketing support. MHP also focuses on non-music ventures such as corporate brand building, cosmetics, gaming, sports and other industries. MHP's goal is to elevate your product or artist to a higher ground in an expedient timeframe by exposing them to new and existing online audiences. MHP also focuses on taking our campaigns one step further by cross-promoting all traditional methods of marketing with online opportunities for further outreach.

Missing Beat Music
290 Merrill Rd. Pittsfield, MA 01201
Keith khannaleck@missingbeat.com
www.missingbeat.com
Uses internet and traditional methods to gain exposure for our artists and helps them become successful.

Mixed Media Publicity & Promotion
PH: 401-942-8025 FX: 401-943-1915
Ginny Shea mixedmediapromo@cox.net
www.mixedmediapromo.com
We've built relationships with entertainment editors at every major magazine and prominent newspaper in the US and abroad. That can mean the difference between a one-line mention and a feature with a photo.

MLC PR
30423 Canwood St. #240, Agoura Hills, CA 91301
PH: 818-706-8080 FX: 818-292-8996
Mona Loring contact@monaloring.com
www.monaloring.com
We provide music publicity services to unsigned artists, music labels and anyone else in the music industry.

Montgomery Guns Productions
14131 SE 86 Ter. Inglis, FL 34449
PH: 352-447-2560
Troy "Gun" Montgomery
troygun@montgomerygunproductions.com
www.montgomerygunproductions.com
We have produced music and artists that have achieved worldwide recognition. From songwriting and publishing to artist development and representation, let Montgomery Gun Productions take you to the next level.

The MuseBox
205 Lexington Ave. 2nd Fl. New York, NY 10016
PH: 212-231-7439 FX: 212-231-7334
themusebox.net
A different kind of marketing company. We exist out of our love for music culture and want to expose it to you.

MusicianPromote
1313 Racquet Club N. Dr. D
Indianapolis, IN 46260
PH: 317-536-5637 FX: 317-536-8416
Fred Demming fd@musicianpromote.com
www.MusicianPromote.com
Markets artist songs at the online digital media iTunes store and connects artist and bands and musicians to online music resources with a provided free electronic press kit.

MusicSUBMIT
34 E. 23rd St, 6th Fl. New York, NY 10029
PH: 917-512-2958
support@musicsubmit.com
www.MusicSUBMIT.com
Promotes your music to the decision makers at internet radio stations, music blogs, online music magazines and more, AND we give you a full report of everything we do for you!

My Rockstar Killed Yours
PO Box 532, Manalapan, NJ 07726
PH: 917-548-0795
Karin Graziadei info@myrockstarkilledyours.com
www.myrockstarkilledyours.com
Represents artists of many genres and works very hard to get artists and bands the best promotion possible!

New Game Media
343 Colleen Pl. Costa Mesa, CA 92627
PH: 949-650-6229
Ken Tamplin ken@newgamemedia.com
www.NewGameMedia.com
A strategic entertainment marketing investment company focussing on talent with pre-exiting fan bases and taking them to the next level. We look for exceptional indie artists that we can help with corporate endorsements, TV, film etc.

Nightlife Productions Entertainment
630 9th Ave. #1200, New York, NY 10036
PH: 212-757-1669 FX: 212-757-1663
Bernadette Brennan nightlifeproductions@msn.com
www.nightlife-productions.com
We are a music marketing company that does online promotion and physical/digital distribution.

Nina Denny Public Relations
PO Box 1248, Ogdensburg, NY 13669
PH: 315-323-1058 FX: 877-349-0225
www.ninadenny.com
PR with a personal touch, affordable rates and music expertise.

Omni Entertainment/Caprice Records
3131 Turtle Creek Blvd. #1150, Dallas, TX 75219
PH/FX: 214-452-3726
Don Brooks info@omnicaprice.com
www.omnicaprice.com
A full service management, booking, marketing and promotions company.

On Target Media Group
6464 W. Sunset Blvd. #540, Hollywood, CA 90028
PH: 323-461-4230 FX: 323-461-4229
www.ontargetmediagroup.com
Internet marketing, publicity and promotion, music video and EPK editing as well as DVD authoring.

On That Note Entertainment
239 New Rd. Ste. A109, Parsippany, NJ 07054
PH: 973-486-0867 FX: 973-486-0875
Dan Balassone dan@onthatnote.net
www.onthatnote.net
A full service booking agency working with national and regional acts of all types and genres.

Outlandos Music
PO Box 415, Saugerties, NY 12477
PH: 202-316-1193
Kate Bradley Kate@outlandosmusic.com
www.outlandosmusic.com
Guided DIY artist consulting - an insider's view on what's what & who's who in the music business.

Paperwork Media
1658 Milwaukee St. #241, Chicago, IL 60647
Jill Katona jill@paperworkmedia.com
www.paperworkmedia.com
A one-stop music boutique that represents bands & artists. We remove the hassles of everyday business-related paperwork and allow clients to focus solely on their music.

Pavement PR
PO Box 2, Lake Geneva, WI 53147
PH: 262-903-7775
Tony Bonyata bonyata@wi.rr.com
www.pavementpr.com
Specializes in national and regional tour campaigns - offering artists the strongest press support where and when they need it most - while on the road. Our ongoing relationships with daily newspapers, weekly alternatives, monthlies, online entertainment sites and music blogs, radio and local TV help ensure that our client's regional shows and events get the exposure they need.

Phantom Power Promotions
3071 W. 107th Pl. Ste. G, Westminster, CO 80031
PH: 720-244-9599
Dave Goff info@phantompower.net
www.phantompower.net
Affordable, honest and knowledgeable DIY promotions for independent musicians. Radio, retail, press and web!

Planet Meridian Public Relations
5039 Old Waynesboro Rd. Hephzibah, GA 30815
PH: 201-521-9742
Lisa "Chase" Patterson & Hard Hittin Harry
planetmeridian@aol.com
www.planetmeridian.com
A national publicity, internet marketing/cyber promotions, event coordination, artist development company.

Platform-1 Entertainment
357 W. Chicago #3S, Chicago, IL 60610
PH: 312-266-9600 FX: 312-266-9579
Devin Buttner Dbuttner@platform-1.com
www.platform-1.com
We are a full service marketing and management company that brings years of success working with artists, labels, brands, publishing companies, entertainment lawyers, properties, major to small market PDs, MDs etc.

Posse Up Entertainment
24451 Lake Shore Blvd. #1601,
Cleveland, OH 44123
PH: 440-549-3779
Sarah Heuer Sarah@PosseUpEnt.com
www.PosseUpEntertainment.com
We are full service Management and publicity firm specializing in press kit design, radio promotion and more. We will get the "Buzz" going for up and coming talent and established artists.

PRLady
2520 Vestal Pkwy. E., Box 321, Vestal, NY 13850
www.publicitylady.com
An innovative website designed to teach the basics of music publicity through both email and phone consultations. Geared toward musicians who are not ready, or able, to hire a full time national publicist.

The Press House
302 Bedford Ave. #13,
Brooklyn, NY 11211
PH: 718-302-1522
FX: 718-302-1522
Dawn Kamerling
dawn@thepresshouse.com
www.thepresshouse.com
Full service media relations company specializing in music of all genres.

Promo Only
257 S. Lake Destiny Dr. Orlando, FL 32810
PH: 407-331-3600 FX: 407-331-6400
www.promoonly.com
The nation's largest provider of promotional content, offering music on CD and music video on DVD designed to meet the specific needs of music professionals and entertainment venues. Check our website for our Canadian and UK mailing address.

Promising Projects
201 W. Wall #900, Midland, TX 79701
PH: 432-618-0705 FX: 866-357-2247
Ronn Reeger indiebible@promisingprojects.com
www.promisingprojects.com
We provide young, growing indie bands with a combination of services such as artist and business management, booking and promotion.

PRThatRocks.com
197 Morning Sun Ave. Mill Valley, CA 94941-4116
PH: 415-381-8647 FX: 415-381-8682
Christopher Buttner rockme@prthatrocks.com
www.prthatrocks.com
PRWeek-recognized public relations agency serving music and entertainment talent.

Quickstar Productions
419 Greenlow Rd. Baltimore, MD 21228
PH: 443-552-7058 FX: 312-235-6598
admin@QuickstarProductions.com
www.quickstarproductions.com
Helping you with digital distribution, album mastering, getting merchandise made, comp CD, booking a tour, creating a music video, designing your logo, CD, and website, or anything else your band could need!

Sign up for
The Indie Contact Newsletter
www.indiebible.com

Randolphe Entertainment Group
738 Main St. #454, Waltham, MA 02451
PH: 781-983-4120
Serge Randolphe, Jr. serge@randolphe.com
www.randolphe.com
We work harder to connect artists to their fans!
College radio promotion, tour promotion,
distribution and more.

REDWING Management & Consulting
4712 Admiralty Way #536
Marina del Rey, CA 90292
PH: 323-272-3055
Liz@LizRedwing.com
www.lizredwing.com
Liz has successfully represented artists/songs at
MIDEM, has helped set up tour schedules and is
pursuing song/catalog representation for film/TV
placement.

Rockstar's Girlfriend Promotions
224 SW 153rd St. #264, Seattle, WA 98166
PH: 360-464-3042
Marcella de Lancret
Rockstars_Girlfriend@yahoo.com
www.myspace.com/princessbadkitty
Promote and represent artists/bands in an intense
way, including sending out demos to labels, radio,
print media and online publications.

Rooftop Promotion
1032 S. Orange Grove Ave. #3
Los Angeles, CA 90019
PH: 310-433-7997
Garo garo@rooftoppromotion.com
www.rooftoppromotion.com
We do press & radio promotion.

Serge Entertainment PR
PO Box 2760, Acworth, GA 30102
PH: 678-445-0006 FX: 678-494-9269
Sandy SergeEnt@aol.com
www.sergeentertainmentgroup.com
Internet publicity/marketing, CD release publicity,
sync licensing deals, radio promo and more!

Sevier Productions
1602 17th Ave. S., Nashville, TN 37212
PH: 615-500-4411
Chris Sevier severerecords7@yahoo.com
www.sevierproductions.com
Artist development and A&R outsourcing. We help
deserving artists make a record and build their team
for success.

Smash Publicity
683 S. Main St., Corona, CA 92882
PH: 951-737-3938
Michele Weber smashpublicity@sbcglobal.net
www.smashpublicity.com
A full service public relations firm for bands. We
also offer website design services at reasonable
prices.

Space 380
2008 Swindon Ave. Columbia, MO 65203-8985
PH: 573-446-7221 FX: 309-210-9037
www.space380.com
Creates name recognition for independent artists of
all genres.

Spinner PR
1745 No. Wilcox #437, Los Angeles, CA 90028
PH: 323-467-7633
Deborah Brosseau brosseaupr@aol.com
myspace.com/spinnerpr
PR, media relations, promotions, tour support,
branding, corporate bonding, music supervision
outreach and event booking. Our clients have
enjoyed placement with MTV, VH1, USA Today, The
Tonight Show and hundreds of local and regional
outlets in between!

Spygirl Productions
PO Box 583, Wilmington, NC 28402
PH: 910-431-4040 FX: 866-729-8212
Tracy Wilkinson thespygirl@spygirlproductions.biz
www.spygirlproductions.biz
Promotions, contract negotiations & drafting,
booking agent, publicity and marketing.

Stretch the Skies
770 Emerson St., Rochester, NY 14613
PH: 585-254-0420 FX: 585-787-4185
support@stretchtheskies.com
www.stretchtheskies.com
Retail distribution. Digital distribution. On-line
distribution. Your gateway to FYE stores coast to
coast!

Sydney Skyler Music
2402 17th St. S. #101, Fargo, ND 58103
PH: 701-526-0969
Ramon Gonzalez ramon@sydneyskylermusic.com
www.sydneyskylermusic.com
We are a music publisher. We promote aspiring
Singer/Songwriters to indie markets nationwide.

Talent 2K
13618 N. 99th Ave. Sun City, AZ 85351
PH: 800-499-6395 FX: 623-875-5827
demosubmissions@talent2k.com
www.talent2k.com
Independent A&R firm. We shop demos out to
different labels looking for recording contracts.

Tate Music Group
127 East Trade Center Ter. Mustang, OK 73064
PH: 888-361-9473 FX: 405-376-4401
www.tatemusicgroup.com
Partners with its artists to provide them with the
production, manufacturing, distribution and
promotion they need to succeed in today's music
industry. Regardless of the style of your music, we
are interested in hearing from you.

Team Clermont Promotion
191 E. Broad St. #310, Athens, GA 30601
PH: 706-548-6008 FX: 706-548-0094
prpeople@teamclermont.com
www.teamclermont.com
We get maximum exposure for the records we
promote.

Threshold Sound + Vision
2114 Pico Blvd. Santa Monica, CA 90405
PH: 310-571-0500 FX: 310-571-0505
Peter A. Barker Peter@thresholdsound.com
www.thresholdsound.com
A full service audio and video company. We provide
mastering, recording, production, and video services
for major and independent labels.

Tinderbox Music
3148 Bryant Ave. S., Minneapolis, MN 55408
PH: 612-375-1113 FX: 612-341-3330
Krista Vilinskis krista@tinderboxmusic.com
www.tinderboxmusic.com
Music promotions, radio, press & CD distribution.

True Music And Songs
7 Wild Flower Dr. Kings Park, NY 11754
PH: 631-896-9800
www.truemusicandsongs.com
Helps artists get their music to the right people in
the music industry.

twentyfourhustle.com
info@twentyfourhustle.com
twentyfourhustle.com
We can increase your song plays and/or profile/page
views on any social networking space that you're
on.

TwoShepsThatPass
396 Broadway Ave. #503, New York, NY 10013
PH: 646-613-1101 FX: 786-513-0692
Vera Sheps twoshepsthatpass@aol.com
www.twoshepsthatpass.com
Gives you a presence on and off the net.

Wavelength Music
PO Box 86723, Portland, OR 97286
PH: 503-928-6764
John Capo info@wavelengthmusic.com
www.wavelengthmusic.com
Professional promotion and consulting services for
musicians.

**Wendy Vickers Artist Assistance and
Promotion**
wendyv2941@aol.com
www.wendyv.com/promo.html
Music promotion, radio marketing, artist assistance
and more. Please see website for more information.

Wholeteam Enterprises
5588 Chamblee Dunwoody Rd. PMB #110
Dunwoody, GA 30338
PH: 888-755-0036
Kysii Ingram keyc@wholeteam.com
www.wholeteam.com
We specialize in resources for aspiring artists and
labels. We have the low cost solution to give your
company global exposure with impressive results.

Wiselephant
PH: 888-625-9258
www.wiselephant.com
Marketing tools geared specifically to promote you.

Workhouse Publicity
133 W. 25th St. #3W, New York, NY 10001
PH: 212-645-8006 FX: 212-645-1950
info@workhousepr.com
www.workhousepr.com
A one-stop shop whose value can be found in the
creation of publicity, marketing, advertising, design
and special events.

Canada

Absolutely Music
19 Cowdy St., Kingston, ON K7K 3V8
PH: 613-531-9685
njgreig@absolutelymusic.on.ca
www.absolutelymusic.on.ca
A full service entertainment agency dedicated to
serving the needs of Canadian musicians and to
providing public and corporate clients with quality
music for all occasions.

CatsAsk Music & Entertainment
PO Box 31029, Barrie, ON L4N 0B3
PH: 647-723-3085
www.catsask.com
Monthly music reviews, indie music eZine,
independent musician's community hub.

City Lights Entertainment
1845 Baseline Rd. #913, Ottawa, ON K2C 3K4
PH: 613-686-1179
Michael Wood mike@citylightsent.com
www.citylightsentertainment.com
We do not promote artists directly. We offer consultation and guidance services among other things.

Danie Cortese Entertainment & Publicity
14-3650 Langstaff Rd. #280
Woodbridge, ON L4L 9A8
PH: 905-857-2432
Danie Cortese daniecortese@rogers.com
www.daniecortese.com
Publicity representing all talent. Management & consulting. Radio releases. Film & music division.

Katcall PR
PO Box 44145, 6508 E. Hastings St.
Burnaby, BC V5B 4Y2
Kat B. info@katcallpr.com
www.katcallpr.com
Freelance Rock music publicist available to assist labels and indie musicians from Europe, the US and Canada with press/publicity; including tour publicity, CD releases, media relations and more.

Kindling Music
Attn: Demos, 411 Queen St. W. 3rd Fl.
Toronto, ON M5V 2A5
PH: 416-506-9696 FX: 416-979-0505
info@kindling.ca
www.kindlingmusic.com
Label for career artists: promotion, publicity, marketing, booking and tour support.

Last Tango Productions
29 Galley Ave. Toronto, ON M6R 1G9
PH: 416-538-1838 FX: 416-538-2633
Yvonne Valnea lasttango@rogers.com
www.lasttangoproductions.com
National publicity & radio tracking. Tour support and promotions.

LastJack Management
171-A Rink St. #235, Peterborough, ON K9J 2J6
PH/FX: 705-201-1143
info@lastjack.com
lastjack.com
Indie management firm looking to add Ontario bands & artists to their current roster.

MassiveRecordProductions.com
10 Royal Orchard Blvd. #53081
Thornhill, ON L3T 7R9
PH: 905-764-1246
Jerry Bader info@mrpwebmedia.com
MassiveRecordProductions.com
We produce and promote the music artists who want to take their fledgling careers to the next level.

MRPwebmedia
10 Royal Orchard Blvd. #53081
Thornhill, ON L3T 7R9
PH: 905-764-1246
Jerry Bader info@mrpwebmedia.com
mrpwebmedia.com
Providing artists with the promotional tools needed to create a buzz in the competitive music industry.

The MuseBox
360 Dufferin St. #105, Toronto, ON M6K 1Z8
PH: 647-436-8423 FX: 647-436-3174
themusebox.net
A different kind of marketing company. We exist out of our love for music culture and want to expose it to you.

Skylar Entertainment
PH: 416-413-9672
Diane Foy diane@ skylarentertainment.ca
www.skylarentertainment.ca
Specializes in Canadian indie music and entertainment publicity.

S.L. Feldman & Associates
200-1505 W. 2nd Ave.
Vancouver, BC V6H 3Y4
Attn: Watchdog
Sarah Fenton
fenton@watchdogmgt.com
www.slfa.com
Canada's leading full-service entertainment agency. Please note we do our best to listen to all demos we receive.

TEA South
101 Burlington St., Toronto, ON M8V 3W1
PH: 416-251-1501
www.teasouth.com
We provide radio tracking / promotions, live showcases, press kits and press releases. Always free consultations!

Tenoseven Entertainment
#8-5901 57th St., Taber, AB T1G 1P7
PH: 403-223-0844 FX: 403-223-0844
Sharla Bauschke sharla@tenoseven.com
www.tenoseven.com
Artist development & management services including booking, promotions, tracking and more.

Working Title Artists
18 Blong Ave. Toronto, ON M4M 1P2
PH: 416-999-6434
Brent Bain info@workingtitleartists.com
www.workingtitleartists.com
We are an artist development service provider. Artists retain 100% ownership of their material.

Europe

Germany

ES&L Entertainment
Strichweg 110, 37476 Cuxhaven, Germany
Oliver info@esl-entertainment.de
www.esl-entertainment.de
We offer promotion, marketing, distribution, booking and management.

Silverdome Entertainment
Goethestr. 56 - 69214 Eppelheim, Germany
PH: +49-06221/4304142 FX: +49-06221/4304142
Constantin Voujouklidis chief-manager@silverdome-rock.com
www.silverdome-rock.com
Artist promotion for live performing, record deals and distribution deals.

Italy

Your Indie CD.net
Via Casal De' Pazzi 20 - 1/C/19 - 00156, Rome, Italy
PH: +39-328-2748653 FX: +39-06-4073553
Luigi Nespeca info@yourindiecd.net
www.yourindiecd.net
Online store featuring independent music. We'd love to sell your music!

The Netherlands

Pro-Demo
Ploeglaan 28, 3755HT Eemnes, The Netherlands
PH: +31 (0)35-523-0514 FX: +31 (0)35-533-6875
Tom Pearce tom@pro-demo.com
www.pro-demo.com
Actively promotes new artists and composers in the entire media industry, including gaming and broadcast.

Spain

TheBorderlineMusic
PH: +34-958-52-24-55
promociones@theborderlinemusic.com
www.theborderlinemusic.com
If you have a group or CD that you want to promote, our service is an inexpensive and effective way to reach your goals.

Sweden

BorderBlaster International
Box 3271, S-103 65 Stockholm, Sweden
info@border-blaster.com
www.border-blaster.com
We provide music production & publishing, distribution, management & consulting and booking.

United Kingdom

The Black Label
4 Buckingham Rd. Doncaster, DN2 5DE UK
PH: +44 (0) 1302-811-631
info@theblacklabel.co.uk
www.theblacklabel.co.uk
Radio and retail promotion.

Delicious PR
PH: +44 7535 503544
Louise and Jane contact@deliciouspr.com
www.deliciouspr.com
A UK based PR and promotion agency that helps artists raise their public profile and enjoy increased media attention.

G Promo PR
PH: +44-7574-503544
Geraint Jones info@gpromopr.com
www.gpromopr.com
UK based firm that works with independent labels and self-released artists targeting print and online media in the United Kingdom & Europe. If it's interesting, we'd love to hear it!

Indie Distribution
Kevin info@indiedistribution.co.uk
www.indiedistribution.co.uk
Distribution company who are open to all kind of new artists.

Mosquito Records
PO Box 39375, London, SE13 5WP UK
PH: 442088520433 FX: 442088520433
mail@mosquito-records.com
www.mosquito-records.com
Indie label promoting bands and solo artists.

Pan Artists Agency
PO Box 45502, London, NW1 2AX UK
panartists.co.uk
A physical and digital music distribution service. We supply our physical catalogue to thousands of major retail and internet stores in the US, Canada and Europe.

S-a-N Agency
3rd Fl. 64 Colwyn Rd. Hartlepool, TS26 9AS UK
PH: 0044-429-864208
Garry Hutchinson
garry.hutchinson@s-a-nagency.com
www.s-a-nagency.com
A UK booking agency with an in-house promotion company. We work with over 50 UK and overseas artists and numerous record labels and management groups.

We Are Listening
www.wearelistening.org
Provides professional prospects for independent artists and a forum for discovering new talent. We initiate unique A&R campaigns in the form of songwriting, lyric writing, music video and performance contests, and assemble distinguished music professionals to lend their expertise as contest judges.

Zest PR Ltd.
32-34 Great Marlborough St.
London, W1F 7JB UK
PH: +44(0)207 734 0206 FX: +44(0)20-7734 4084
Tom Green tom@zestpr.com
www.zestpr.com
One of the most respected creative agencies in the UK . We specialize in full service public relations, marketing, event management and as creative consultants. Our team has worked successfully across the fields of Classical, Pop, Jazz, Indie and Alternative music and covering all areas of the arts including visual, literary, theatre and performance.

Australia

Apollos Lounge
PO Box 366, Collins St. W., Melborne,
VIC 8007 Australia
PH: 0407-365-215 FX: 03-9642-2573
Richard O'Brien richard@apolloslounge.com
www.apolloslounge.com
Consulting and assistance in developing and promoting of artists and their works, through advice, databases and all A&R aspects.

Australian Music Biz
PO Box 1042, Fortitude Valley, QLD 4006 Australia
PH: 07-3854-0945 FX: 07-3854-0734
mail@musicbiz.com.au
www.musicbiz.com.au
Promotes local indie labels on a national level.

Newsouthfolk Tour Management
17 Crest Cres. Moruya Heads, NSW 2537 Australia
PH: 61-2-44742736
Jim MacQuarrie marmac@newsouthfolk.com.au
www.newsouthfolk.com.au
A professional service for national & international musicians. Please contact us before sending any material.

Asia

KR International - Global Music Agents
The Green Factory Studio, Akasaka,
Tokyo 03-59485595
PH: (+81) 80-3415-3080
kr-international.com
Building Artists/Groups profiles worldwide, organising logistics for touring, showcasing, deal making, artists development and management, agents for work in Asia, licensing, publishing and direct wholesale in Asia.

Blues

Crossroads Blues Agency
PO Box 10168, 7301 GD Apeldoorn,
The Netherlands
PH: 31-55-5214757 FX: 31-55-5787815
crossroads@crossroads.nl
www.crossroads.nl
Specializes in European tours of Blues artists.

Just Roots PR
PO Box 6283, Jackson, MI 49204
PH: 517-414-2433 FX: 866-594-1824
Dave King dking@justrootspr.com
www.justrootspr.com
There is no arguing that a well written press release in the hands of the right people, can do more for you than advertising ever will. If you are a Blues or Roots musician, you can get your press release out there and into the hands of the people who would most help you achieve your musical ambitions. Contact us, and tell us what you would like to achieve. Your Friends at Just Roots PR "The web's only human optimized, human distributed, exclusively Roots music press release distribution site."

Christian

Black Gospel Promo
45 E. Cityline Ave. #303, Bala Cynwyd, PA 19004
PH: 215-883-1000 FX: 240-220-8694
Veda Brown info@blackgospelpromo.com
blackgospelpromo.com
The Gospels source for marketing & publicity.

The BuzzPlant
709 W. Main St., Franklin, TN 37064
PH: 615-550-2305
info@buzzplant.com
www.buzzplant.com
Marketing and internet & new media promotion for Christian music.

CLG Distribution
PO Box 21370, Minneapolis, MN 55421
PH: 612-208-0300 FX: 612-208-0301
David C. Coleman contact@clgdistribution.com
www.clgdistribution.com
We offer major worldwide distribution to indie Christian labels and artists.

Divine Design Creative Services
PH: 403-286-1235
www.divinepresskits.ca
Christian company offering administrative support for musicians including domain name research, custom website design and internet marketing services.

Fruition Artist Agency
PO Box 3721, Brentwood, TN 37024
PH: 615-300-3755
Carla Archuletta info@fruitionartistagency.com
www.fruitionartistagency.com
Turning vision into reality. We do review and consider each and every Artist Promotional Kit we receive based on the New Artist Inquiry Form located in the ROSTER section of our website.

M/I Productions
3737 Bales Ave. #200, Kansas City, MO 64128
PH: 816-921-3633
Terrell L. events@miproductions.org
www.MIProductions.org
Event production company concentrating on the creative development, project organization and implementation of concerts, release parties, special events and other Christian entertainment gatherings.

Ministry Networks
PH: 519-668-2517 FX: 519-668-3165
www.ministrynetworks.net
Digital Download and promotional programs available to get your song to Christian radio. Indie Bible subscribers can have their songs submitted to digital download to Christian radio stations in Canada and U.S for just $35.00 per song. Just let us know you found out about it through the Indie Bible.

Prodigal Son Entertainment
115 Penn Warren Dr. #300, Box 145
Brentwood, TN 37027
PH: 615-377-0057
www.prodigalson-entertainment.com
Artist management & development. indie & signed mainstream and Christian (no Rap/Urban).

Sapphire Entertainment and Management
1304 Kendall Dr. Durham, NC 27703
PH: 919-358-0056
Carol "Coco" Diggs
sapphire.entertainment@hotmail.com
www.sapphireem.com
Artist management, booking, promotion and career development services. Sapphire also provides event planning services for conferences, seminars, concerts and special events.

Classical

Jeffrey James Arts Consulting
45 Grant Ave. Farmingdale, NY 11735
PH/FX: 516-586-3433
jamesarts@worldnet.att.net
www.jamesarts.com
Management and PR for Classical artists.

ArtPro Artist Management
PO Box 22044, Tel Aviv 61220 Israel
PH: +972-9-9505816 FX: +972-9-9505817
UriZur@ArtPro.co.il
www.artpro.co.il
All artists are represented exclusively and worldwide.

Country

United States

Honky Tonkin Music
2334 CR 2265, Telephone, TX 75488
PH: 903-664-3741 FX: 903-664-3741
info@honkytonkin.com
www.HonkyTonkin.com
We offer a wide variety of independent music.

Miranda Promotions
733 Ruth St., Prattville, AL 36067
PH: 334-361-9060 FX: 334-361-9060
Miranda Leake
mirandap@mirandapromotionsinternational.net
www.mirandapromotionsinternational.net
Country and Gospel artist promotion and management. Radio distribution and bookings.

Payne County Line Promotions
3333 E. 68th St., Stillwater, OK 74074
Stan Moffat stan@paynecountyline.com
www.paynecountyline.com
We welcome all genres of music and accepts gladly your demos, press packets, band news, events etc.

Publicity House/Wildfire Publicity
PO Box 558, Smyrna, TN 37167
PH: 615-825-0019 FX: 615-825-0094
Laura Claffey laura@WildfirePublicity.net
www.wildfirepublicity.net
Schedules interviews & coordinates CD reviews with e-zines, print magazines, newspapers etc, and adds your music to various portals. Publicity House handles tour press for all genres.

Q-Note Productions
PO Box 462, Garden Valley, CA 95633
PH/FX: 530-333-1018
Cindy Hayden cindy@qnoteproductions.com
qnoteproductions.com
Publicity services for the touring artist including press and radio advance work, press release writing and launch. We also specialize in CD releases!

Red Haired Girl Publicity
PO Box 939, Cherryville, PA 18035-0939
PH: 484-221-1026
Liz Winchester rhgpublicity@yahoo.com
www.RHGPublicity.com
PR firm specializing in publicity for independent musicians and indie labels in the Americana & Texas music formats.

so much MOORE media
1819 Tula Pace Rd. Pleasant View, TN 37146
PH: 615-746-3994
Martha E. Moore martha@somuchmoore.com
www.somuchmoore.com
I am a full -time entertainment publicist working with indie artists in Country, Alt-Country and Americana genres for 19 years.

The Indie Link Exchange

A new, free and easy way to promote your website

www.indielinkexchange.com/ile

United Kingdom

Hotdisc
Friars Mount, Friars, Jedburgh, TD8 6BN Scotland
PH: +44 (0) 1835-864833 FX: +44 (0) 1835-864688
country@hotdisc.net
www.hotdisc.net
The leading promotional company for Country music in Europe.

Australia

NfS Publicity
PO Box 475, Morayfield, QLD 4506 Australia
PH: 07-5428-7167 FX: 07-5428-7168
nfs@nfspublicity.com.au
www.nfspublicity.com.au
Dedicated to the promotion of Country music in Australia.

Dance and Electronic

masspool Dj Assoc.
30 Revere Beach Pkwy. Revere, MA 02151
PH: 781-485-1901 FX: 781-485-1902
masspool.dj@verizon.net
www.masspool.com
One of the most highly regarded DJ record pools in the US.

Traffic Online
6 Stucley Pl. London, NW1 8NS UK
warden@trafficonline.net
trafficonline.net
Promotions, street teams and more for UK bands.

Experimental and Electronic

The Kitefishing Family
241 E. South Temple #4, Salt Lake City, UT 84111
PH: 801-637-2828
admin@kitefishingfamily.com
www.kitefishingfamily.com
Dedicated to the promotion of all forms of independent art.

Folk

Green Linnet
916 19th Ave. S., Nashville, TN 37212
PH: 615-320-7672 FX: 615-320-7378
publicity@greenlinnet.com
www.greenlinnet.com
Promotes new Celtic music.

Hip Hop

215 Execs Entertainment Consulting and Management
PO Box 4032, Capital Heights, MD 20743-9998
G. Mookie McClary gmcclary@215execs.com
www.215execs.com
Music consulting and management firm. Rap is something you do. Hip Hop is something you live!

artistpr.com
support@artistpr.com
www.artistpr.com
Music promotion company that can help you get the industry exposure you desire.

Buzzin' Bee Entertainment
3833 W. Ave. 42, #117, Los Angeles, CA 90065
PH: 323-381-0000
www.myspace.com/thebuzzinbee
All aspects of guerilla brand marketing, promotions, public relations, event planning/management and bookings.

CrackAudio.com
PH: 305-506-4738
Stun stun1og@gmail.com
www.crackaudio.com
Hip Hop music marketing and promotions, mix tapes & mix shows. Please don't attach any MP3s.

Crazy Pinoy
PO Box 46999, Seattle, WA 98146
PH: 206-860-4052
Gene Dexter Hiphop206@aol.com
www.CrazyPinoy.com
I can write and implement a national marketing plan, help create an artist's image and consult on their material, look and sound.

Cream Music Consultants
PO Box 416, Brice, OH 43109
PH: 614-579-6150 FX: 614-863-4953
Pamela Bennington creammusicgroup@yahoo.com
www.creammusicgroup.com
Consulting, career development, demo-shopping, artist management and promotions. Hip Hop, R&B, Gospel, Reggae and Pop.

Cwood56
4259 Macedo Pl. Santa Clara, CA 94035
PH: 408-230-9897 FX: 408-988-8833
Chris Underwood chrisunderwood@cwood56.com
www.Cwood56.com
We provide professional management and marketing to Hip Hop artists and producers.

djizm.com
PH/FX: 206-984-4357
info@djizm.com
www.djizm.com
We'll submit your single to our digital record pool consisting of DJs, radio and magazines that like to break new artists.

Heavyweights Record Pool
14731 Manecita Dr. La Mirada, CA 90638
PH: 888-998-2041
Truly OdD heavyweightsent@aol.com
www.heavyweights.org
An outlet for labels trying to get their records to the most predominant DJs who actually will play and promote your records.

HomeBase Promotions
PO Box 680784, San Antonio, TX 78268
PH: 210-764-4760 FX: 210-764-4761
info@homebasepromotions.com
www.homebasepromotions.com
Promotions company providing profile listings, press releases, reviews and event management. Specializing in Hip Hop and R&B music genres.

IndieStreet Entertainment
3620 Pelham Rd. PMB #317,
Greenville, SC 29615-5044
info@indiestreetent.com
www.indiestreetent.com
Provides a platform and opportunities to gain experience, exposure and knowledge. Our magazine features articles, photo galleries, music, interviews and event coverage.

Planetmeridian PR
5039 Old Waynesboro Rd. Hephzibah, GA 30815
PH: 201-521-9742
Chase or Harry planetmeridian@aol.com
www.planetmeridian.com
*Independent PR, Urban marketing and event
planning.*

Q-York Entertainment
PH: 818-243-4980
Steven Yassin contact@q-york.com
www.q-york.com
Hip Hop artists, music, videos, online store.

Richh Kiddz Entertainment
1st Ave. at Port Imperial #1202
West New York, NJ 07093
PH: 404-394-0365 FX: 201-430-3842
Russ Downs promotions@richhkiddz.com
www.richhkiddz.com
*A multifaceted entertainment and marketing
company. We help develop, expose and manage
independent artists who take the business of music
seriously.*

Thompkins Marketing
10101 SW Freeway #612, Houston, TX 77074
PH: 713-609-9607 FX: 281-431-8573
TC Thompkins
thompkins@thompkinsmarketing.com
www.thompkinsmarketing.com
*Urban promotions, distribution & entertainment
consultant.*

Unified Product Distribution
101 Marietta St. #1030, Centennial Tower
Atlanta, GA 30303
PH: 404-751-3400
Kevin Blackman Kevin_blackman@updonline.com
www.updonline.com
*The new face in distribution is here! We can fulfill
all of your Urban music needs. Suitable for any
budget small or large, major or independent.*

Jamband

Green Door Promotions
info@greendoorpromotions.com
greendoorpromotions.com
*Promoting Jamband music of Washington, Baltimore
and beyond!*

Soulever Music Corp.
16 Meahon Pl. Centerport, NY 11721
PH: 917-743-7690
info@soulevermusic.com
www.soulevermusic.com
*An artist management and music consulting firm.
While we concentrate primarily on the Jamband/
Groove genre, we are open to working with all
talented artists, no matter the genre. Please check
our submission policy.*

Jazz

Cheryl Hughey Promotions
811 Westrun Dr. Ballwin, MO 63021
PH: 314-660-1755
Cheryl Hughey cherylhughey@charter.net
cherylhugheypromotions.com
*We put music in motion. National press, CD
releases/marketing strategies, image shaping, tour
press and concert promotion. Get the word out!*

Jazz CD Promotional Campaign
8947 Washington Ave. Jacksonville, FL 32208
PH: 904-264-4642 FX: 904-264-4667
Rachelle Bivins mailbox@abyssjazz.com
www.abyssjazz.com
*A 12-month marketing tool offering just about
everything an independent Jazz artist needs to kick
start their promotion.*

Kari-On Productions
PO Box 436, Evans, GA 30809
PH: 706-294-9996 FX: 706-210-9453
Kari Gaffney karionprod@knology.net
www.karigaffney.com/publicity.html
*Publicity agency that represents, Jazz, Blues and
World artists to obtain reviews in music
publications.*

Playscape
64 Belleclaire Ave. Longmeadow, MA 01106
PH: 413-567-7967
www.playscape-recordings.com
Promotes Jazz artists and music.

Metal

Alkemist Fanatix Europe
Via Pacinotti 77, 51037 Montale (PT), Italy
PH: 0039 / 3402868918
Carlo Bellotti info@alkemist-fanatix.com
www.alkemist-fanatix.com
*Works with bands and record labels, for setting up
distributions, licences and contracts. The agency is
affiliated with important companies that are
integrating parts of the operations. These companies
carry out several activities like the shooting of
professional video clips, booking of European tours,
distribution and CD pressing.*

Fixion Media
43 Samson Blvd. #322, Laval, QC H7X 3R8
PH: 450-689-7106 FX: 450-689-7106
Rob sales@fixionmedia.com
www.fixionmedia.com
*Expose your band to 2 million monthly visitors! We
represent the leading Heavy music sites.*

Glass Onyon PR
PO Box 18254, Asheville, NC 28814
PH: 828-350-8158 FX: 828-350-0569
William James glassonyonpr@cs.com
www.ant-bee.com/glassonyonpr.htm
*A multi-faceted publicity company specializing in
the promotions of bands, labels, releases, tours and
gigs. Glass Onyon PR differs from most
commercial/AOR press agencies due to our
expertise in the promotions of alternate genres of
music including Hard, Classic and Progressive
Rock, Heavy Metal, Alternative, Avant-garde, Blues
and Country.*

JETT FOX Promotions
PH: 620-200-3437
Jett Fox jettfoxpromos@yahoo.com
www.myspace.com/rock07
*Works with Alternative bands. We are PR/publicist
affiliate of HollywoodMusic.tv.*

Just Rock PR
2976 Washington Blvd.
Cleveland Heights, OH 44118
PH: 216-453-0771
justrockpr.com
*We are media professionals that know how and why
things get into print.*

Risestar Promotion
Palmas de Mallorca #1126, La Reina,
Santiago, Chile
PH: +56-9-97899475
promotions@risestar.cl
www.risestar.cl
*Promotes Hard Rock and Heavy Metal bands
worldwide.*

Sick Productions
8508 89th Ave. #210, Fort St. John, BC V1J 6B6
PH: 250-787-8526
www.sickproductionsmusic.com
*We are the engine that can power your band online!
Diggin' through the trenches as musicians ourselves,
Sick has built an empire for independent artists to
make a stand and be heard.*

Sick Promotions
PO Box 2550, North Babylon, NY 11703
PH: 631-918-2641 FX: 631-665-5378
Meredith & Gina sickpromo@hotmail.com
www.myspace.com/sickpromotions
*Full service music promotions, specializing in
Metal, Rock and Hardcore. Books local and touring
acts mainly in the Northeast US.*

V.Q. Promotions
PH: 818-716-6670
Nancy B. Sayle creative@vqpr.com
www.vqpr.com
Promotions services for Indie Rock bands.

Punk

Earshot Media
Mike Cubillos earshotmedia@earthlink.net
www.earshotmedia.com
*Publicity company for Alternative, Indie Rock, Punk
and Metal music.*

Scrocca Entertainment Group
2572 Rte. 9, Ocean View, NJ 08230
PH: 609-425-7785 FX: 609-624-1500
Joe Scrocca Jr. j.scrocca@yahoo.com
*Artist Management focusing on Alternative and
Punk Rock (all genres are represented for
exceptional artists and bands). We work on
commission only - there are no up front or hourly
fees. We accept unsolicited material. Please include
bio, photo and any reviews written on you.*

Reggae

Black Style Production
Calandastrasse 6, CH-8048 Zürich, Switzerland
PH: 0041-78-856-18-01
www.blackstyleproduction.com
*Organization of concerts and some parties
throughout Switzerland, as well as the booking and
management of artists throughout Europe.*

Roots Garden Promotions
info@rootsgarden.com
www.myspace.com/rootsgarden
*We specialise in playing and promoting strictly
conscious Reggae and Dub music new and old.*

RoV Roots Creations
110 S. Church Ave. #4030, Tucson, AZ 85701
PH: 520-344-7200
James "Ras Jammie" Rouse
RouseYourSpirits@aol.com
www.rovrecords.com
*Our indie label specializes in original Reggae,
Reggaeton and other genres of Latin, Caribbean,
and African music.*

Soul/R&B

4Sight Media Relations
109 W. 38th St. #1200, New York, NY 10018
PH: 212-730-1177 FX: 212-730-1188
www.4sightmedia.com
A diversified public relations firm for projects that require unique music-based experience.

Bullseye Entertainment
www.myspace.com/bullseyeentertainmentinc
Committed to setting the standard of excellence and innovation in the world of Hip Hop and R&B.

Creativity in Music
PO Box 3481, Bridgeport, CT 06605
PH: 203-331-9982
Gi Dussault & Joe Kelley npsfunk@optonline.net
www.creativityinmusic.com
Promoting independent musicians - helping them in spreading the word.

The Chittlin Circuit
2403 N. L St., Pensacola, FL 32501
PH: 850-433-1842 FX: 850-454-0014
www.chittlincircuit.com
We offer exposure and promotions to independently owned record labels, authors, entertainers, dancers, comedians, movies and actors.

Genese Music and Entertainment Group
PO Box 245, Gambrills, MD 21054
PH: 410-514-8158 FX: 410-514-8158
Ralph Rogers infor@genesemusic.com
www.genesemusic.com
Maintains a small studio, deals with artist development and works on marketing and product development.

Lucky 7 Records & Entertainment
PH: 866-721-5825
Frank Wilson l7entertainment@att.net
www.l7recordsandentertainment.com
An entertainment consulting firm for R&B artists.

Sounds In The Key of Gee
26721 Berg Rd. #219, Southfield, MI 48033
PH: 313-549-7400
Gisele "Gee" Caver gisele@keyofgee.com
www.soundsinthekeyofgee.com
Entertainment and event consultants who specialize in the promotion of independent artists.

Taylor Entertainment Group
699 Ponce De Leon #239, Atlanta, GA 30308
PH: 404-685-8555 FX: 404-815-5222
taylordentertain@aol.com
www.taylordentertainment.com
Tour planning, booking agents, radio play, management, opening for headliners, major showcase performances and artist development.

Women in Music

Power of Pink Promotions
64 Central St., Ipswich, MA 01938
PH: 617-851-7298
Lynn 'JULIAN' Booking@CookieCutterGirl.com
www.cookiecuttergirl.com
Cookie Cutter Girl, "The Queen of Internet Promotion," will put *HER* skills to work for *YOU*! Who better than a Pop Superhero to make *your* business FLY?

Warrior Girl Music
12115 Magnolia Blvd. #200,
North Hollywood, CA 91607
PH: 818-442-9294
info@warriorgirlmusic.com
www.warriorgirlmusic.com
Recording, publishing and promotions company that is about developing artists.

World

Kongoi Productions *Norway*
www.kongoi.com
African music, PR and publishing company.

rock paper scissors
PO Box 1788 #137, Bloomington, IN 47402-1788
PH: 812-339-1195 FX: 801-729-4911
Dmitri Vietze music@rockpaperscissors.biz
rockpaperscissors.biz
Publicity and marketing in the U.S. for World music and Reggae labels, artists, websites etc.

Sign up for
The Indie Contact
Newsletter

www.indiebible.com

I Am Desiree' Bassett

"I have a natural power.
It was just in me from
the start, I guess.
— Desiree' Bassett, 15

I Am **Sonicbids.** Sonicbids.com/IAm

SECTION FIVE: VENDORS AND LABELS

Most of the online vendors listed in this section offer "non-exclusive" contracts. Non exclusive means you are allowed to sign up with as many of online vendors as you like without violating any agreement. The fees and/or commissions vary from site to site. I suggest you visit as many as you can to find out which sites you get a good feeling from. Be wary of large setup fees!

Mainstream

North America

United States

3000 Records
PO Box 180902, Utica, MI 48318
PH: 586-480-3000
Terrance go@3000records.com
www.3000records.com
We mostly release Co-Op CDs. We promote music to college radio, independent radio, satellite radio, internet radio, and magazines, along with other creative avenues of music promotion.

AB-CD
3306 S. Dixie Hwy. West Palm Beach, FL 33405
PH: 561-833-0633
www.ab-cd.com
We specialize in hard to find, rare and indie music and media.

Allegro Corporation
Attn: Label Submissions
14134 NE. Airport Way, Portland, OR 97230-3443
www.allegro-music.com
One of the largest independent distributors of music in the US. We work with labels that include no fewer than 12 artists and/or 25 titles.

ALLALOM Music
1604 S. Hwy 97, Ste. 2 #154, Redmond, OR 97756
PH: 541-350-1607
Samuel Aaron allalom@gmail.com
www.allalom.com
An independent music collective (record label / webzine / promotions and CD duplication) for serious music lovers.

AmazingCDs
1107 181ˢᵗ St. Ct. E., Spanaway, WA 98387
info@amazingcds.com
www.amazingcds.com
All CDs are accepted - all styles of music.

amazon.com Advantage Program
www.amazon.com/advantage
Lets millions of customers find, discover and buy what you're selling.

Ariana Records
PH: 520-790-7324
Mr. Jimmi jtiom@aol.com
www.arianarecords.net
Rockin' the Southwest for 25 years! Send me great music. No demos, finished masters only.

Arizona University Recordings
10700 E. Prince Rd.
Tucson, AZ 85749
PH: 520-749-9895
FX: 520-749-9893
William Penn
wpenn1@cox.net
www.AURec.com
A sophisticated catalog of music that is reflective through consistently high artistic quality and outstanding recording technology. It is intended that each release guarantees listeners that they have received a production that has been originally crafted and designed with painstaking, loving care. Jazz, Smooth Jazz, Swing, Blues, Bossa Nova, Latin Music, World Music, Sophisticated Pop, Classical Music and more.

Artist1Stop
3650 Osage St.
Denver, CO 80211
PH: 877-247-5046
FX: 303-433-8228
www.artist1stop.com
Brick and mortar store CD distribution, online distribution and digital distribution (iTunes, Napster etc.).

Azor Records
241-35 148ᵗʰ Rd. Rosedale, NY 11422
PH: 347-548-4545 FX: 347-548-4545
Chardavoine chardavoine@ azorrecords.com
www.azorrecords.com
Indie label looking for artists in all genres.

Back to Work Records
Warren Miller info@ backtoworkrecords.com
www. backtoworkrecords.com
Although still a fledgling label, we welcome the submission of all independent music for potential release.

backstagecommerce.com
700 Freeport Pkwy. #100, Coppell, TX 75019
www.backstagecommerce.com
Sell your music goods on your website, our store and your gigs.

BandMinusLabel.com
www.myspace.com/ bandminuslabel
Gathering talent from across the globe, providing listeners with as much unsigned talent as humanly possible.

Bathtub Music
23905 Clinton Keith Rd. 114-155
Wildomar, CA 92595
PH: 951-551-5502
Moses de los Santos
moses@bathtubmusic.com
www.bathtubmusic.com
Online store that sells independent artist CDs and DRM free downloadable music. We represent thousands of artists' albums from 27 countries. What are you waiting for? Get in the tub!

B&R Records
744 Boyd St., Santa Rosa, CA 95407
Cory Thrall bandrrecords@yahoo.com
www.brrecords.com
A net label with many different genres represented.

Bear Grass Records
Wayne Murphy
waynemurphy@beargrassrecords.com
www.beargrassrecords.com
An independent label dedicated to the preservation and integrity of Acoustic music and musicians.

BETA Records
PO Box 48, Hollywood, CA 90028
PH: 877-232-2382
Christian office@betarecords.com
BetaRecords.com
An online record company that offers a free web page with song hosting, photos and e-mail, plus a free ringtone widget.

Big Noise Records
11 S. Angell St. #336, Providence, RI 02906
PH: 401-274-4770
Al Gomes al@bignoisenow.com
www.bignoisenow.com
We work with Pop, Rock, R&B, Hard Rock, Metal, Jazz, Acoustic, Dance and Blues artists. Currently seeking new artists. Please call or email first. See our ad on Pages 223 and 233.

BinaryStar Music
PO Box 650246, Miami, FL 33265
PH: 888-457-2209 FX: 786-206-0657
Henry A. Otero info@binarystarmusic.com
www.binarystarmusic.com
A music production/indie record label that features Pop, Rock, Hip Hop and R&B.

Black Sea Records Group
PO Box 548, DeFuniak Springs, FL 32435
PH: 850-892-6275 FX: 850-892-5611
www.blacksearecords.com
We are an indie record label and distributor. Artists are welcome to sell their music with us. No setup fees!

Blue Monkey Records
2107 Starlight Ln. Independence, KY 41051
PH: 859-356-1918
Junette Gausman junettegausman@aim.com
www.myspace.com/blumonkeyrecords
We offer representation, distribution, promotion etc. We want to build long term, lasting relationships with our artists and their fans.

Boosweet Records
PO Box 451594
Los Angeles, CA 90045
PH: 310-613-3535
FX: 909-877-9199
Vernon Neilly info@boosweet.com
www.boosweet.com
Specializing in the recording and distribution of major acts as well as up and coming artists. We will promote and sell your products worldwide via the internet. We can get any artist's material into the major digital download stores as well.

buythiscd.com
buythiscd.com
There are great artists waiting to be heard. We want people to hear them!

Captiva Records
925 Hwy. 80 #195,
San Marcos, TX 78666
PH: 512-322-9293
FX: 512-479-1805
Chris Perez
cperez@captivagroup.com
www.captivarecords.com
Indie label with a focus on artist development.

CD Baby
5925 NE. 80th Ave.
Portland, OR 97218-2891
PH: 503-595-3000
FX: 503-296-2370
cdbaby@cdbaby.com
www.cdbaby.com
We will expose your CD to 10,000 customers a day. In addition we have an amazing digital distribution service that is available to all CD Baby members. CD Baby will also make your CD available to over 2400 CD stores worldwide (mostly US).

CD Networx
1837 Harbor Ave. Memphis, TN 381131
PH: 901-405-4109 FX: 901-737-9190
Craig Whitney artistservices@cdnetworx.net
www.cdnetworx.net
Independent CD distribution through networking and marketing. Offering unlimited potential.

CD Quest Music
feedback@cdquest.com
www.cdquest.com
Reaches farther into the independent world than any other site.

CDfuse.com
PO Box 4397, Austin, TX 78765
PH: 512-825-9108
Sal Silva III sal@cdfuse.com
cdfuse.com
We represent the next level for listening, reviewing and buying music online.

CDpulse.com
140 Island Way #290, Clearwater, FL 33767-2216
PH: 727-443-5111
Ryan Gans info@cdpulse.com
www.cdpulse.com
Online retailer of music for independent artists and labels. Also provides album reviews and Soundscan reporting.

CDreview.com
30 Compton Way, Hamilton Square, NJ 08690
PH: 609-689-1711
offices@cdreview.com
www.CDreview.com
Get 100% of your CD sale price. Type in the code "indiebible" to even waive the set up fee.

CDs-FROM-THE-ARTIST dot com
www.cdsfromtheartist.com
Harnesses the potential of the web to bring independent artists and music lovers from all over the world together.

Chaodic Records
PO Box 332, Pottstown, PA 19464
PH: 610-960-0659
Scott Marshall chaodicrecords@comcast.net
www.chaodicrecords.com
An independent label looking for new talent to sign, promote or work with.

Coach House Records
3503 S. Harbor Blvd. Santa Ana, CA 92704
PH: 714-545-2622 FX: 714-545-3490
www.coachhouserecords.com
Introduces indie releases into the retail market.

Crafty Records
75 Earley St., Bronx, NY 10464
Dan Treiber craftydan@craftyrecords.net
www.craftyrecords.net
An independent, artist friendly record label.

Darla Records
2107 Camino Cantera, Vista, CA 92084
PH: 760-631-1731 FX: 760-454-1625
webmaster@darla.com
www.darla.com
Sells indie CDs worldwide.

DigitalCuts.com
2940 Heather Stone Way, Lawrenceville, GA 30043
www.digitalcuts.com
Offers artists the opportunity to develop and promote their music .

Disgraceland Records
PO Box 10882, Knoxville, TN 37939
Paul Noe paul@disgraceland.com
www.disgraceland.com
Online record label.

Domaincleveland Records
6004 Middlebrook Blvd. Cleveland, OH 44142
PH: 216-376-0238
www.domainclevelandrecords.com
Dedicated to spreading quality music at an affordable price to as many people as possible.

EDGE Entertainment Distribution
11012 Aurora Hudson Rd. Streetsboro, OH 44241
PH: 330-528-0410
Jenni jlh@edgedistro.com
www.edgedistro.com
Our main focus is the distribution of audio and video physical goods to college bookstores, public libraries, mass merchants, independent music stores and jukebox operators.

Enexia
609 Corona Ave. Corona, CA 92879
PH: 951-858-0709
Anthony Pratt anthonypratt@enexiaent.net
www.enexiaent.net
A growing record label that also utilizes digital media. The company hangs its hat on artist development.

Evil Music Industry Records
929 S. Peoria #2-219, Aurora, CO 80012
PH: 720-690-4562
Jim Huddleston emi_ceo@yahoo.com
evillabel.musicdot.com
We help with all your recording, mastering &
distribution, promos ... everything!

EvO:R
www.evor.com
Online store. Works with indie musicians around the
world.

Fox on a Hill Productions
PO Box 568, 1513 Kilborn Dr. Petoskey, MI 49770
PH: 231-622-2333
Susan Fawcett susan@foxonahill.com
www.foxonahill.com
We do promotion, production and distribution of
film, art and music.

Friendly Fire Recordings
205 Lexington Ave. 2nd Fl. New York, NY 10016
info@friendlyfirerecordings.com
www.friendlyfirerecords.com
We like demos. In fact, we love demos. We listen to
everything we receive.

GEMM
PO Box 4062, Palm Springs, CA 92263
PH: 760-318-6251 FX: 760-318-6251
seller@gemm.com
www.gemm.com
Worlds largest music catalog. Submit your CD.

GoJangle.com
simon@gojangle.com
www.gojangle.com
Dedicated to fans of music who want a single source
solution for all new music.

Guitar Nine Records
8201 Hambledon Ct. Raleigh, NC 27615
PH: 561-423-0741 FX: 561-423-0741
www.guitar9.com
Guitar worship. New releases and demos wanted!

Halogen Records
1763 Main St., Montpelier, VT 05602
info@halogenrecords.com
www.halogenrecords.com
Grassroots promotion, marketing, distribution and
manufacturer.

Hammondbeat Records
11124 NE. Halsey #488, Portland, OR 97220
Kahlil Breithaupt hbinfo@hammondbeat.com
www.hammondbeat.com
International analog Funk, Soul, Jazz, Dance and
Library grooves featuring electronic organs and
vintage keyboards. Established 2002.

Independent Records
PO Box 510, Blairstown, NJ 07825
PH: 908-362-5524
Chris Midkiff customerservice@indierec.com
www.indierec.com
Imagine your CD sitting in your local record store
display window! Think it's impossible? WRONG!!!!

IndepenDisc Music Club
PO Box 183, North Haven, CT 06473
Gary Vollono info@independisc.com
www.independisc.com
We listen to every submittal for review,
representation, & promotion, regardless of genre.

Indie Star Search
2930 N. Delaware, Indianapolis, IN 46205
PH: 317-610-6656
info@indiestarsearch.com
www.indiestarsearch.com
Gathered here in one place, are hundreds of
independent musicians who are living their musical
dreams and letting their star shine.

Indie4Ever.com
www.indie4ever.com
Where you can sell your music without selling out!

Indiecentric
info@indiecentric.com
www.indiecentric.com
No major labels here...only new music from the best
new independent musicians.

IndiePro.com
PO Box 25, Monson, MA 01057-0025
Scott McElreath submissions@indiepro.com
www.indiepro.com
Submit your CD for review. Sell it online.
Submissions can be mailed in order done online
through Sonicbids www.sonicbids.com/indiepro

IndieRhythm
160 Aztec Way SE. Acworth, GA 30102
PH: 678-574-6310
James McCullough sales@indierhythm.com
www.IndieRhythm.com
A CD megastore that is dedicated solely to
independent music and the artists that create this
music. We've got room for all styles, genres and
categories!

IndieSolo.com
PH: 519-342-9526 FX: 519-342-9746
Johnny Ioannou johnnyi@indiesolo.com
www.indieSolo.com
Gives bands exposure in what has become a very
crowded and competitive online music world.

Insound
221 W. 17th St. 5th Fl. New York, NY 10011
PH: 212-777-8056 FX: 212-777-8059
patrick@insound.com
www.insound.com
Brings the best underground culture to the surface.

ItsAboutMusic.com
2167 Kimberton Rd. Phoenixville, PA 19460
PH: 610-415-1311
Dean Sciarra dean@itsaboutmusic.com
www.itsaboutmusic.com
Connects artist with fans worldwide.

Joseph Street Records
PH: 504-866-4103
Nathan Schwam info@josephstreetrecords.com
www.josephstreetrecords.com
Dedicated to exposing the world to exciting artists
who deserve to be heard - not ignored.

Kaos Records
demo@kaosrecordsllc.com
www.kaosrecordsllc.com
A vehicle for artists, musicians, producers and songwriters of any genre to display their ideas and talents by recording fresh, innovative music. We are dedicated to cultivating the best talent and giving our artists the opportunity to grow with us.

Lakeshore-Records
9268 W. 3rd St., Beverly Hills, CA 90210
PH: 310-867-8000 FX: 310-300-3038
info@lakeshore-records.com
www.lakeshore-records.com
Dedicated to finding and developing unique new talent in addition to releasing soundtrack albums not only from our films, but also from other independent films of merit and interest.

lala
support@lala.com
www.lala.com
We are taking the unprecedented action of giving artists 20% of our revenues from used CDs.

LightningCD Corporation
4707 Aurora Ave. N., Seattle, WA 98103
distribution@lightningcd.com
www.lightningcd.com
Supports indie artists with national distribution of their CDs.

Little Pocket Records
255 N. Yondota Rd. Curtice, OH 43412
PH: 419-460-0437
Steve Mohr littlepocketrecords@yahoo.com
www.littlepocketrecords.com
More of a music community than a label. No contracts, no meanies, just friends with hopes of playing a part in the greatness of music. In the summer we run the annual Toledo Indiepop Fest (myspace.com/toledoindiepopfest).

Locals Online
PH: 503-419-6402
sales@localsonline.com
www.localsonline.com/local.music
Global collection of local music.

LOL Records
PO Box 5148, Beverly Hills, CA 90209
PH: 310-790-5689 FX: 208-460-2903
Gerry Davies info@lolrecords.com
lolrecords.com
Releases music overlooked by commercial recording companies.

LOUiPiMPS
1217 Silver St., New Albany, IN 47150
andrew@louipimps.com
www.louipimps.com
Internationally distributed indie record label.

Lucky 7 Records & Entertainment
PH: 405-848-3885
Franklin Wilson
l7entertainment@att.net
www.platinumheaven.net
Record label and distribution company seeking artists from all music genres. If you are interested in being signed by a label or for distribution please submit the following: 3 - 4 song CD (complete mixed & mastered), professional photographs, a biography/EPK. We are looking for "Hits" only, so send us your very best. All submissions must be in MP3 format, and all photos must be in JPG format.

Marble Mountain Records
2493 Belvidere Rd. Phillipsburg, NJ 08865
PH: 908-884-9252
Walter Hnot sales@marblemountainrecords.com
www.marblemountainrecords.com
Provides a kaleidoscope of services. Music production, music video production & editing, engineering, mixing & mastering, CD artwork design & layout, worldwide marketing & sales outlets, website design and maintenance and copyrighting services.

MEI Records
PO Box 1661, Mineola, NY 11501-0904
www.meirecords.com
Everyone involved in the company has earned their ride through hard work as either an artist or as a professional in their field. The label is not focused on the current "trends" or "standard practices" that other companies follow.

Moozikoo
PO Box 50322, Nashville, TN 37205-0322
Anthony Bates artist_services@moozikoo.com
www.moozikoo.com
An online retail site and radio station with an international customer/listener base. Our reputation and business is built upon the premise that we play and sell ONLY THE BEST of today's indie music - which assures exposure within the U.S. and abroad.

Morphius Records
100 E. 23rd St., Baltimore MD 21218
PH: 410-662-0112 FX: 410-662-0116
Simeon Walunas simeon@morphius.com
www.morphius.com
Over 13 years of great Pop, Rock, Punk & Hip Hop releases. Sell your CDs and MP3s!

Music Distributors.com
2443 Fair Oaks Blvd. #126, Sacramento, CA 95825
PH: 916-338-6881 FX: 916-338-6882
info@themusicdistributors.com
www.musicdistributors.com
We cater to independent artists and labels.

Music Loft
1445 1st Ave. SE. Cedar Rapids, IA 52402
PH: 319-362-4208
www.music-loft.com
We will set up an individual page for your music which includes description and reviews, cover shot, audio clips and a link to your website. No setup fee!

music2deal.com
PO Box 30869, Seattle, WA 98113
usa@music2deal.com
music2deal.com
This international network gives you a unique possibility to be promoted in different foreign countries via the top 5 or the local newsletter.

My CD Party
1020 Music Row #8, Nashville, TN 37228
PH: 615-818-7871 FX: 615-329-9831
Bill McCleskey bill@myCDparty.com
www.myCDparty.com
Sells indie music worldwide and will administer digital distribution.

Navigator Records
1300 Division St. #105, Nashville, TN 37203
PH: 615-742-5581 FX: 615-742-8014
Chuck Thompson cthompson@missingink.com
www.navigatorrecords.com
For the new artist searching for a label deal, we have a loyal audience and a well-established touring base.

Net Spin
PO Box 6927, Folsom, CA 95763
www.netspin.com
The indie superstore for movies, music and more!

NETUNES.com
3183 Airway Ave. Bldg. E, Costa Mesa, CA 92626
PH: 949-498-3600 FX: 949-498-6900
www.netunes.com
You get a distribution agreement regardless of genre.

Neutral Habitat Records
PO Box 1662, Santa Monica, CA 90406
Samson Shulman info@neutralhabitat.com
www.neutralhabitat.com
We are an independent record label/music supervision company that is always actively looking to sign new talent.

New Artists Online
PO Box 21437, Philadelphia, PA 19141
PH: 215-696-0598 FX: 215-548-9216
newartistsonline@newartistsonline.com
www.newartistsonline.com
Dedicated to featuring, showcasing and selling the CDs of independent artists.

Nine 12 Records
6151 Strickland Ave. Los Angeles, CA 90042
PH: 805-368-2251
Sara sara@nine12records.com
www.nine12records.com
Independent record label based in LA area. Individualized contracts based on artist goals.

Not Lame
PO Box 2266, Fort Collins, CO 80522
FX: 970-407-0256
Bruce popmusic@notlame.com
www.notlame.com
A record label that focuses on 'Power Pop'/Melodic Rock and also an online record store dedicated to selling indie releases from other melodically driven bands.

Old House Records
Attn: A&R, 711 N. 4th Ave. Teague, TX 75860
www.oldhouserecords.net
Committed to the artist above all else, and encouraging creativity above marketability.

DOT ON SHAFT GUITARS

Manufacturer, Distributors and *now Franchise Retail Store.*
Opening in a city near you!

We are original in many ways.
We sell only OUR brand of Guitars and Strings.
When you buy a guitar from our store, we give you
STRINGS FOR LIFE! Ask us how:)

We distribute the following products in Canada:
- Snap Jack Cables (www.snapjackcables.com)
- Carparelli HandWound Pickups
- KahlerUSA
- Decarlo HandMade Guitars
- Carparelli Guitars
- DOS-WYRES hand wound Telfon Coated Strings

Fastest growing Guitar company in Canada

DOT ON SHAFT GUITARS
37 Livingstone Street West
Barrie, Ontario L4N 7J2
705-812-1061 or 416-628-1467

**DOT ON SHAFT GUITARS &
SCHOOL OF MUSIC**
5875 Highway & Units 5 & 6
Woodbridge, Ontario L4L 1T9
(SE Corner of Highway 7 and 27)
416-249-PLEK

www.dotonshaft.com

peermusic
3260 Blume Dr. #405
Richmond, CA 94806
PH: 510-222-9678
FX: 510-222-9676
www.peermusic.com
Promotion and development with a personal touch.

Peppermint CDs
581 Old Hwy. 8 NW.
New Brighton, MN 55112
PH: 800-633-7020
peppermintcds@gmail.com
www.peppermintcds.com
Wants full-time musicians with at least 2 CDs released.

Perris Records
PO Box 841533
Houston, TX 77284
PH: 281-550-0988
FX: 775-719-4768
Tom Mathers
perris@houston.rr.com
www.perrisrecords.com
80's Rock label, mail order & distribution company that sells worldwide. Perris is now accepting CDs for possible label consideration and distribution deals worldwide.

THE REC(o)RD LINK
PO Box 647, Orange, NJ 07051
mail@TheRecordLink.com
www.therecordlink.com
Will promote your recordings on the internet.

Revolver USA Distribution
2745 16th St., San Francisco, CA 94103
FX: 415-241-9009
order@midheaven.com
revolverusa.blogspot.com
Labels/bands interested in having us distribute their music can mail samples to the above address.

RiPPYFiSH Records
PO Box 1964, Salt Lake City, UT 84110
PH: 801-487-7302 FX: 801-487-7304
www.rippyfishrecords.com
We are an open genre independent record label.

ROA Records
6014 Chenango Ln. Orlando, FL 32807
Monica Rabino monica@roarecords.com
roarecords.com
Independent music label by artists for artists.

Rock Ridge Music
info@rockridgemusic.com
www.rockridgemusic.com
Offers national distribution and online marketing services.

SCREACHEN
PO Box 16352, Phoenix, AZ 85011-6352
Al Harbison president@screachen.com
www.screachen.com
Reviews, manages and produces local & national bands.

Shut Eye Records
1180 Vickers St. 2nd Fl. Atlanta, GA 30316
PH: 678-986-5110 FX: 404-584-5171
howdy@shuteyerecords.com
www.shuteyerecords.com
Record label, publicity firm, CD manufacturing and more.

SignHere Online, Inc.
contact@signhereonline.net
www.signhereonline.net
Provides artists with an opportunity to promote original MP3 music and solicit recording contract offers.

Silk City Recording Company
PO Box 704, West Paterson, NJ 07424
PH: 973-599-0236 FX: 973-599-0236
silkcity@silkcitycd.com
www.silkcitycd.com
An online retail site that sells indie products.

Sit-n-Spin Records
118-A Estes Dr. Carrboro, NC 27510
PH: 843-853-3084
www.myspace.com/sitnspinrecords
A record label that will change your life!

Six Nights Records
PO Box 400817, Las Vegas, NV 89140-0817
PH: 702-561-1249
Maribeth Lewis info@sixnightsmusic.com
www.sixnightsmusic.com
Independent music publishing company and record label. Currently accepting unsolicited submissions from artists and songwriters.

OneSource
PO Box 162, Skippack, PA 19474
PH: 215-661-1100 FX: 215-661-8959
onesource.pan.com
Distribution system for the online sale of e-CDs.

Online Rock
2033 Ralston Ave. #50, Belmont, CA 94002
PH: 650-649-2304 FX: 650-649-2304
info@onlinerock.com
www.onlinerock.com
Bands can promote, distribute and sell their music online.

The Orchard
100 Park Ave. 17th Fl. New York, NY 10003
PH: 212-201-9280 FX: 212-201-9203
info@theorchard.com
www.theorchard.com
Supplier of independent music on the internet.

Outstanding Records
PO Box 2111, Huntington Beach, CA 92647
PH: 714-377-7447
Earl Beecher Beecher@OutstandingMusic.com
www.outstandingmusic.com
We feel our mission is to provide a way talented artists can break into the music business. We encourage them to approach us.

Paradiddle Records
14 Bunkerhill Dr. Huntington, NY 11743
PH: 631-680-0544
www.paradiddlerecords.com
We showcase exciting new songwriters and musicians. We also develop projects that reach a very specific audience - projects that might not find an outlet elsewhere.

Pinnacle Music
PO Box 491808, Redding, CA 96049
PH: 775-232-2132
Steven "Bambino" Pearce
pinnaclemusic@yahoo.com
www.pmrev.com
We do it all, from artist marketing & development to worldwide distribution of your CD in stores and online.

Pop Sweatshop
PO Box 460954, Denver, CO 80246
PH: 303-525-5840
Chris Barber info@popsweatshop.com
www.popsweatshop.com
We work furiously, in sweatshop conditions, to make and distribute great indie releases for bands.

Poverty Records
PO Box 1155, Port Richey, FL 34673-1155
Billy James King info@povertyrecords.com
www.povertyrecords.com
Independent record label specializing in industry loop holes and questionable business practices.

Range Records
2730 E. County Line Rd. Ardmore, PA 19003
PH: 610-649-7100 FX: 610-649-7566
info@ rangeentertainment.com
www. rangeentertainment.com
Our expertise lies in artist development, recording, booking, management and promotion.

Reason Y
2871 Royal Bluff, Decatur, GA 30030
PH: 404-723-5098
Moe info@reasonyrecords.com
www.reasonY.com
Promotion and distribution for indie bands of all genres.

something sacred
PO Box 15533, San Luis Obispo, CA 93401
PH: 805-545-5887
info@somethingsacred.com
www.somethingsacred.com
Promotes indie artists. Submit your material.

sonaBLAST!
115 W. 28th St. #1102, New York, NY 10001
PH: 212-868-5233
Matt Parker matt@thegroupentertainment.com
www.sonablast.com
We are a label, management and publishing firm all wrapped into one.

SongRamp
1710 Roy Acuff Pl. Nashville, TN 37203
PH: 615-256-3354 FX: 615-256-0034
store@songramp.com
www.songramp.com
We offer independent artists an outlet to sell their CDs.

Sonic Wave International
415 S. Maple #603, Oak Park, IL 60302
PH: 708-445-8373 FX: 847-577-9528
www.sonicwaveintl.com
Our goal is to find, promote and release GOOD music that people want to hear.

Southbound Records
103 E. Main St., Willow, OK 73673
PH: 580-287-3589 FX: 580-287-3590
southboundrecordsusa@yahoo.com
www.southboundrecordsusa.com
Label featuring Southern music.

Sub Pop Records
PO Box 20367, Seattle, WA 98102
PH: 206-441-8441 FX: 206-441-8245
info@subpop.com
www.subpop.com
We don't listen to demos every day, but periodically we go through a bunch of them. Please don't call or e-mail to follow up.

Substantial Records
Management management@substantialrecords.net
www.substantialrecords.net
Offering the best new music in every genre from around the world. Send ONE MP3 to the above e-mail address.

Sunlight of the Spirit Music
PO Box 60097, Nashville, TN 37206
PH: 615-403-8587
www.sunlightofthespiritmusic.com
Offering only the highest quality music that has been created by artists in recovery. Please contact us via our website for approval before submitting CDs.

Terrestrial Records
2438 SE. Taylor St., Portland, OR 97214
PH: 503-232-3980 FX: 503-231-2475
Leslie Naramore les@terrestrialrecords.com
www.terrestrialrecords.com
Boutique label & production company with an in-house recording facility. We specialize in Jazz and cross-genre Rock including Jam, Shoegaze, Space-Pop and unclassifiable Pop.

Tomahawk Records
PH: 216-659-1513
Javon Bates tomahawkrecordsllc1@yahoo.com
www.myspace.com/tomahawkrecordsllc
We make hits and make musical moves. If you need duplication, music production or consultants.

Twee Kitten
1547 Palos Verdes Mall #213
Walnut Creek, CA 94597
PH: 925-947-2842
goldfish@tweekitten.com
www.tweekitten.com
Online vendor that focuses on music possessing beauty, melody, charm etc.

U & L Records
1617 Cosmo St. #310, Los Angeles, CA 90028
PH: 323-230-6592 FX: 323-924-2352
Jonathan Lazar jonathan@urbandlazar.com
www.urbandlazar.com
Let your music be heard!

Unfun Records
19144 Brookview Dr. Saratoga, CA 95070
PH: 408-344-0402
www.unfunrecords.com
We are not a genre label, nor are we against any types of music. Our main goals are to support bands in their search for their target audience, through the release of quality media, while undercutting mainstream pricing and keeping a DIY atmosphere in each project we are involved with.

United For Opportunity Music
133 W. 25th St. 5th Fl. New York, NY 10001
PH: 212-414-0505 FX: 212-414-0525
www.ufomusic.com
An organization of experienced, independent-thinking music industry activists that have come together to create a new model for a record label/music distribution company.

Wampus Multimedia
4 Weems Ln. #300, Winchester, VA 22601
Mark Doyon mail3@wampus.com
wampus.com
Record label, retail store, recording studio and marketing company.

Wednesday Records
PO Box 2501, Santa Barbara, CA 93120
PH: 805-456-3619
Tim Boris info@wednesdayrecords.com
www.wednesdayrecords.com
Purveyor of fine indie records.

Wyman Records
PO Box 46188, Los Angeles, CA 90046
PH: 323-848-7311
Tip Wyman twyman@wymanrecords.com
www.wymanrecords.com
Independent record label that focuses on career development as well as record sales.

Xact Records
PO Box 1832, Bangor, ME 04402-1832
info@xactrecords.com
xactrecords.com
Promotes unsigned bands and sells their merchandise.

xiie.net
PO Box 935, Angleton, TX 77516
PH: 979-849-1279 FX: 979-849-1278
John McNerney john@xiie.net
www.xiie.net
Offers original music by original artists via the web - selling around the world 7 days a week, 24 hours a day. Huge pay outs.

Zoomoozik.com
info@Zoomoozik.com
www.zoomoozik.com
Started by a bunch of guys sitting around and bitching about the way the music industry screws artists. After a few beers we decided to shut up and step up…

Canada

A-B-A-C-A Records / Entertainment Group
5790 Adera St. #1, Vancouver, BC V6M 3J2
PH: 604-731-8689
Debora Nortman info@abaca-music.com
www.abaca-music.com
A record label, music publishing company and record industry consulting firm offering distribution, publishing, record label deals and/or live performance (touring) opportunities for the acts we represent, in foreign territories.

BenT Music
32 Paul St., Toronto, ON M5A 3H3
bentmusic@bentmusic.ca
www.bentmusic.ca
Helps musicians get their music out to the public.

CANtunes.com
356 Ontario St. #311, Stratford, ON N5A 7X6
Stewart info@cantunes.com
www.cantunes.com
Sell your independent CDs in Canada the easy way!

Crony Records
290 Bridge St. W., Waterloo, ON N2K 1L2
Brad Weber brad@cronyrecords.ca
www.cronyrecords.ca
Community based record label helping musicians promote each other through the label.

Cyclone Records
PO Box 71550, Aurora, ON L4G 6S9
PH: 416-738-5022 FX: 905-841-7463
Brad Trew btrew@cyclonerecords.ca
www.cyclonerecords.ca
Producer of high quality CD compilations at a local, regional, national and international level.

gigzter.com
230 Hampton Heath Rd. Burlington, ON L7L4P3
PH: 905-631-8302
info@gigzter.com
www.gigzter.com
Your source for independent artist profiles, quality original music, profiles, charts, playlists and more!

High 4 Records
256 Major St., Toronto, ON M5S 2L6
PH: 416-561-1271
Darrin Pfeiffer darrin@high4records.com
www.high4records.com
We wanted to start a label where the bands have a lot of creative control, where they'd feel safe and where they could grow as artists.

Jack Kitty Records
981 Coxwell Ave. #1, Toronto, ON M4C 3G4
PH: 705-445-0200 FX: 705-445-0200
Tyler Flear jackkittyrecords@gmail.com
www.myspace.com/jackkittyrecords
An independent label that offers online radio, forum, gallery, artist profiles, downloads and more!

TuneVault.com
www.tunevault.com
Reviews, news, calendar, artist pages and more. Sell your stuff!

Voodoo Records
124 Crockford Blvd. Toronto, ON M1R 3C3
mike@voodoorecords.ca
PH: 416-939-8782
voodoorecords.ca
Catering to music ranging in styles from Japanese Taiko, R&B and Hip-Hop, to Rock, Punk, Metal and Alternative.

Europe

Austria

Flowing Records
Giesshueblerstrasse 6, 2371 Hinterbruehl, Austria
PH: 0043-6767048651
Florian Spitz office@flowingrecords.com
www.flowingrecords.com
A place for all kinds of audio productions. We support our artists from the recording procedure until the finished CD.

TON 4 Music Group
PH: +44 (0)20-81-33-63-33
Erwin Pitsch p@ton.cc
www.ton4music.com
We're an European label/publisher and have specialized in world-wide digital distribution and radio promotion. Contact us for our mailing address.

Belgium

Kinky Star Records
Vlasmarkt 9 9000 Gent Belgium
PH: +32-9-223-48-45
Sebbe d'Hose sebbe@kinkystar.com
www.kinkystar.com
Rock, Surf, Hip Hop, Electro and Experimental releases.

Czech Republic

Indies Records
Dolní Lou?ky 191, 594 55, Czech Republic
Premysl Stepanek premysl@indies.eu
www.indies.eu
Supporting many young talented artists.

France

MVS Records
15, Rue Des Immeubles Industriels (Nation)
F-75011 Paris, France
PH: 33329561942
Jose contact@mvs.fr
www.mvsrecords.com
Les artistes que nous produisons évoluent dans différents styles musicaux tels que Pop, Rock, Métal, Electro, Chanson Française, Variété Internationnale!

Ocean-Music
2, place du Foirail, 81220 St Paul Cap de Joux, France
www.myspace.com/oceanmusicrecords
We are a record label that listens to demos and promotes indie artists.

Germany

amazon.de
www.amazon.de
Sell your CD through our store.

CoArt-Music
Graf-Anton-Weg 10, 22459 Hamburg, Germany
PH: 0049-0-7646-913555
www.co-art-music.com
Offers non exclusive physical and digital distribution in Germany for independent music.

Dr. Music Direct Distribution
Intückenweg 13, 44289 Dortmund, Germany
Torsten doc@dr-music-distribution.de
www.dr-music-distribution.de
We'll bring your CD to the German division of Amazon & into our own online music shop, Dr. Music Mailorder and Wholesale.

European Music Group GmbH
Heilbronner Str.7, 70174 Stuttgart, Germany
PH: +49 (0)1805-09-04-04
Christian Schulze christian@emg-music.com
emg-music.com
Our aim is simply to release & promote great music we discover and believe in. Do you want a record deal? Do you want to be known internationally?

Music Marketing Service
c/o Arte Leon Ltd., Albinsuweg 5, 06679
Hohenmoelsen, Germany
PH: 0049-34441-21184 FX: 0049-941-59-92-21-184
info@arteleon.de
www.music-marketing-service.com
We offer bands distribution throughout Europe. CDs and digital distribution. We also do radio promotion!

NovaTune
Nürnberger Str. 15, 91126 Schwabach, Germany
PH: +49-9122-874-038 FX: +49-9122-873-902
info@orca-records.net
www.novatune.de
German fair-trade-label with reasonable prices and fair artist payments.

RockCity Hamburg
Neuer Kamp 32 / 2.OG, 20357 Hamburg, Germany
PH: 040-319-60-60 FX: 040-319-60-69
Claudia music@rockcity.de
www.rockcity.de
Resource for indie musicians.

Scales Records
Kleygarten 14, 59302 Oelde, Germany
PH: +49 (0)2522-838309
info@scales.de
www.scales.de
Label & distributor of Instrumental Electric Guitar music from Heavy Metal to Jazz and beyond.

Silverdome Entertainment
PH: (+49)06221/4304142 FX: (+49)06221/4304142
Constantin Voujouklidis chief-manager@silverdome-rock.com
www.silverdome-rock.com
Artist promotion for live performing, record deals and distribution deals.

track4.de
PH: +49 (0) 511-270-07-56
FX: +49 (0) 511-270-07-58
www.track4.de
MP3s, news, charts etc.

Gibraltar

Melodrift Productions
30 Halifax Ct. Gibraltar, Europe
PH: +34-636737428
Wesley contact@melodrift.com
www.melodrift.com
Offering artists promotional advertising and/or music distribution, licensing deals etc.

Italy

Alma Music
Via Marovich 5, 30030 Chirignago, Venezia, Italy
PH: 041-5441558 FX: 041-5441588
ossigeno@o2pub.com
www.almamusic.it a
Promotes and sells independent music from Italy and the rest of the world.

Millennium Music
Via le Mazzini 119, 00195 Rome, Italy
PH: 039-06-37-51-51-14 FX: 039-06-37-51-70-70
Toni Armetta toniarmetta@millennium-music.org
www.millennium-music.org
An independent label producing artists without any limitation of musical style.

OmOm World
Piazza Euclide 21, 00197 Roma, Italy
PH/FX: 39-06-8070486
Robert Ruggeri info@omomworld.com
www.omomworld.com
Italian independent label.

RES - Registrazioni e Suoni
PO Box 292, 31100 Treviso Centrale, Italy
PH: +39-335-8409306 FX: +39-0422-235743
Joachim Thomas info@res-net.org
www.res-net.org
A record label always looking for new music.

Tanzan Music Group
Piazzale Lugano, 6, 20158, Milano, Italy
PH: +393487261050 FX: +390377802606
Paolo Cornalba info@tanzanmusic.com
www.tanzanmusic.com
Music publisher & label featuring artists such as Mario Percudani, Marco Tansini & Blueville.

Luxembourg

LILI IS PI Records
Place du Marche no. 8, 4621 Differdange,
Luxembourg
PH (Europe): 352-621395551
PH (US): 201-204-9513
Remo Bei info@lili-is-pi.com
www.lili-is-pi.com
Small independent record label accepting demo submissions into Alternative Pop, Electro Rock, Electronica, Chill Out, Acoustic and Singer/Songwriter only.

The Netherlands

Mr. Kite Records
Van der Woudestraat 226, 1815 VZ, Alkmaar, Noord-Holland, The Netherlands
PH: +31648529427
Gerhardt Heusinkveld info@mrkiterecords.com
www.mrkiterecords.com
A record company that supplies an internet platform for authentic and willful music.

WM Recordings
PO Box 26, 6400 AA, Heerlen, The Netherlands
PH: +31 (0)45-850-3629 FX: +31 (0)84-724-5674
Marco Kalnenek info@wmrecordings.com
www.wmrecordings.com
An online record label that does not specialize in one style. We bring you exciting sounds that you're not likely to find anywhere else.

The Indie Link Exchange - *A new, free and easy way to promote your website*

www.indielinkexchange.com/ile

Slovakia

Vision Records
Pavla Horova 13, 841 07 Bratislava, Slovakia
PH: +421-907-47-22-33
Slavomir Bachraty sb@vision-sd.com
www.vision-sd.com
Music and film PR & promotion services for independent artists from around the world.

Spain

Anima Pop Productions
C Oso 9 Bis 4ºB 28012 Madrid, Spain
PH: 675415519
Victor Cobos victor.animapop@gmail.com
www.myspace.com/victorcobos
We develop new talents from bands with a Britpop sound & attitude. We also help international bands to licence music in Spanish market.

ATIZA
PH: 93-247-82-76
Juan info@atiza.com
www.atiza.com
Música, noticias, bares y conciertos en Barcelona.

INANNA NAKED
Apdo. de Correos 4233, 35080 Las Palmas de G.C.
Las Palmas (Canary Islands) Spain
PH: +34-928-25-65-93
Héctor Noble Fernández info@inannanaked.com
www.inannanaked.com
Offers a selection of emotional, intense, dark, sad, melancholic... music done with quality and personality, into all musical genres.

popchild.com
c/Joan Güell 184-188, 08028 Barcelona, Spain
PH: +34-93-444-17-69
postmaster@popchild.com
www.popchild.com
Promotes indie/unknown artists.

Sweden

Crazy Bear Records & Publishing
Nyponstigen 6. 578 31 Aneby, Sweden
Bjorn Andersson info@crazybear.se
www.crazybear.se
We are proud to present some of Sweden´s most gifted and innovative artists to the world.

Top Five Records
c/o Singfeldt, Rönnholmsgränd 41 BV, SE-127 42
Skärholmen, Sweden
Mattias Andersson info@topfiverecords.se
www.topfiverecords.se
We are a mail order company that is starting to release records. Send us your demo. Alt-Rock, Electro, Garage, Pop etc.

Turmic Records & Distribution
Hyllie Kyrkovag 51B, 21616 Limhamn, Sweden
Shane Doherty submissions@turmicrecords.com
www.turmicrecords.com
We have helped many unsigned artists and bands move to greater platforms and we hope to continually do so. Artists that are interested can send a press kit or send us a link to their web page.

Switzerland

Brambus Records
Berghalde, CH-8874 Mühlehorn, Switzerland
PH: ++41-55-614-10-77 FX: ++41-55-614-10-77
Paul Rostetter info@brambus.com
www.brambus.com
An excellent source for great Singer/Songwriter and Jazz/Blues CDs. Check it out!

United Kingdom

25 Records
PO Box 3006, Poole, BH12 2HU UK
info@25records.com
www.25records.com
Discovers new and exciting bands and brings them to the world's attention.

amazon.co.uk
www.amazon.co.uk
Simple, direct and profitable way for sell your music.

CD Unsigned
PO Box 4462, Worthing, West Sussex,
BN11 3YF UK
PH: 0871-8725324
www.cdunsigned.com
Specializing in CDs by new and emerging bands.

CD WOW! 'unsigned...AS YET!'
#2a, Gregories Ct. Gregories Rd. Beaconsfield,
Bucks, HP9 1HQ UK
PH: 44-0-1494-683500
unsigned@cd-wow.com
www.cd-wow.com/unsigned
Sell your music and gain exposure.

Collaborator Records
PH: 01225-404445
Paul Corket colaborator@clara.co.uk
www.collaboratorrecords.com
Specialising in producing limited edition EPs - which feature studio recordings, demos and live versions of songs that will be re-recorded for the artist's first albums.

CPL Records
www.myspace.com/cplrecords2004
An independent record label. Our genres include Pop, Pop/Rock, Classical Crossover and Dance music.

Ditto Music
Branston Ct. Branston St., Birmingham,
B18 6BA UK
PH: 0121-551-6624
Tony info@dittomusic.com
www.dittomusic.com
Primarily we are a distributor but we (uniquely) release unsigned artists' material under our own labels and distribute them through our networks. Artists can also sell their music downloads through The Ditto Music Shop www.dittomusic.net

drinkmilk
6 Rosebery Rd. Anstey, Leicestershire, LE7 7EJ UK
PH: +44 (0) 7966-586-848
hello@drink-milk.net
www.drink-milk.net
Record label specialising in tiny limited editions in hand made sleeves.

fierce panda records
PO Box 21441, London, N7 6WZ UK
ellie@fiercepanda.co.uk
www.fiercepanda.co.uk
Send all demos to the above address. The music should be tuneful, handsome and whacked-out.

Human Recordings
PO Box 3, Huntingdon, Cambs, PE28 0QX UK
www.human-recordings.com
We're sick of hearing bands that just don't make the grade and so our standards are very high. If we don't 100% fall in love with a band's music, we won't sign them.

HyperDIY Media
29 Somerfield Rd. PO Box 56255,
London, N4 9AA UK
PH: +44-20-7144-6367
Richard Godbehere info@hyperdiymedia.com
www.hyperdiymedia.com
Everything you would get from a record label, but pay a fixed fee and keep all your royalties.

iMusic Stage
4, Crosspost Industrial Pk. Cowfold Rd. Bolney,
W. Sussex, RH17 5QU UK
PH: +44 (0)1444-881300 FX: +44 (0)1444-881030
Customer.Service@iMusicStage.com
www.iMusicStage.com
We cater to bands of all genres who want to sell their merchandise online.

LoneBoyStore
3rd Fl. 727A Green Lanes, London, N21 3RX UK
PH: +44-20-8373-3265
team@loneboymusic.com
www.loneboystore.com
Regardless of stature, money spent on marketing - all artists get the opportunity to stock their goods here.

Mile High Records
1 Clover Grove, Telford, Shropshire, TF3 2AA UK
PH: 44-1952-275569
Lorenzo Cosco lorenzo@milehighrecords.com
www.milehighrecords.com
We are an independent online record label seeking new artists and new music to release on iTunes. Gigging bands preferred.

Mohican Records
99 Rochester Ave. Feltham, Middlesex,
TW13 4EF UK
davemohican@mohicanrecords.co.uk
www.mohicanrecords.co.uk
Be creative. Be inspired. Be part of Mohican Records.

Norman Records
#1 Armley Park Ct. Stanningley Rd. Leeds,
LS12 2AE UK
PH: 44-0113-2311114
phil@normanrecords.com
www.normanrecords.com
Features indie CDs from around the world.

On the Run Recordings
20b Westbourne Terrice Rd. Little Venice, London,
W2 6NF UK
PH: 07800-732-870
info@ontherunprod.com
www.ontherunprod.com
Indie label run by musicians for musicians. Features films, games and recording department. We're always looking for new acts to take on board!

Overplay
PO Box 11188, Sutton Coldfield, B76 1WX UK
PH: 0870-112-1382
service@overplay.co.uk
www.overplay.com
Provides a platform for artists/bands to get reviews and to sell their music.

RawRip
130 Shaftsbury Ave. London, W1D 5EU UK
PH: 020-7031-4288 FX: 020-7031-4302
Mark Sando Mark@corp.rawrip.com
www.rawrip.com/indiebible
A music distribution service making history as the first to give artists 100% of royalties earned from every downloaded track. In addition to pay as you go downloads, fans can stream music for free, store songs in their own personal music library, and explore new music using the 'The Rippler.' Artists can also sell their tracks through portable 'Raw Stores', a widget that allows them to earn 100% from sales to fans on websites such as their own band site, blogs, MySpace, or Facebook.

Real2Can.com
info@real2can.com
www.real2can.com
Produces cutting edge Underground records, books and films that will shake your world!

Rhythm Online
94 Catharine Street, Cambridge, CB1 3AR UK
nick@rhythmonline.co.uk
www.rhythmonline.co.uk
We specialise – very broadly speaking – in all things Alternative or 'independent' and pride ourselves on the size and comprehensive yet eclectic nature of our listings.

tap into MUSIC
www.tapintomusic.com
Stocking the best music from independent record labels, artists and bands.

Trend-Records
Greentrees, Glassel, Banchory, AB31 4DL UK
PH: 07846271921
Thomas Button thomas@trendrecords.co.uk
www.trendrecords.co.uk
An independent label located in Scotland. We specailse in Indie, Acoustic and Pop music.

Urban Angel Music
1st Fl. 126 Bloomfield Ave. Belfast, N. Ireland
PH: +44-870-4600-290 FX: +44-289-046-5591
Mark McAllister uaminfo@mac.com
www.urbanangelmusic.co.uk
We are accepting submissions from artists and songwriters for our record label and publishing divisions.

Vertical Recordings
info@verticalrecordings.com
verticalrecordings.com
An online CD retail shop. All our music is EXCLUSIVE to us and not available in physical music retail outlets or any other music sites online.

Australia

The CAN
5 Harper St., Abbotsford, VIC 3067 Australia
PH: +61-3-9412-3596
Stomp thecan@chaos.com
www.thecan.com.au
An online retail and distribution resource for independent artists.

CD Suite
14 Urquhart St., Hawthorn, VIC 3122 Australia
PH: +61398192954 FX: +61398192954
Nathan nathan@cdsuite.com
www.cdsuite.com
Online CD store distributing albums by independent artists. Get your album heard and distributed internationally.

Hardrush Music Corporation
GPO Box 2609, Canberra, ACT 2601 Australia
PH: +61-2-6112-8046 FX: +61-2-6296-1937
K. Fahey info@hardrushmusic.com
www.hardrushmusic.com
Recording label promoting indie artists across the nation and to the world.

Megaphone Records
PO Box 8446 Woolloongabba, QLD 4102 Australia
PH: +61738912577 FX: +61738911797
Cindy-Leigh Boske info@megaphonerecords.net
www.megaphonerecords.net
"The voice of the future"... Megaphone Records is an Australian indie label that promotes and markets new exciting artists.

Modern World Records
PO Box 422, New Lambton, NSW 2305 Australia
Craig Mitchell modernworld@hunterlink.net.au
www.modernworld.com.au
Online catalogue for Australian indie CDs.

One World Music
Ste. 7-10, Aero Bldg. 247 Coward St., Mascot, NSW 2020 Australia
Leigh leigh@oneworldmusic.com.au
www.oneworldmusic.com.au
Independent record label for Chill-Out/World Beat genres.

Pure Pop Records
221 Barkly St., St Kilda, VIC 3182 Australia
PH: 03-9525-5066
submit@purepop.com.au
www.purepop.com.au
Licenses and distributes Indie Pop CDs in Australia.

Asia

CDJam
2-18-1-501 Kusagae, Chuo-ku, Fukuoka, 810-0045, Japan
PH/FX: 81-92-716-8848
Jeffrey and Mutsumi Martin jeff@cdjam.jp
www.cdjam.jp
Helps artists promote and sell their music in the Japanese market. We not only will sell your music, we also promote it to local media.

Fish the Music
2-19-630 Mizusawa Miyamae, Kawasaki, Kanagawa 216-0012 Japan
Yamamiya info@fishthemusic.com
fishthemusic.com
Our "Artist's Explosion in Japan" package will help you to get exposure for your music in Japan.

RB Records
15-8-312 Sakuragaokacho Shibuya-ku, Tokyo 150-0031 Japan
info@rb-records.com
www.rb-records.com
Mixture, Rapcore, Rapmetal.

Blues

Alligator Records
New Material, PO Box 60234, Chicago, IL 60660
info@allig.com
www.alligator.com
We will NOT accept inquiries or phone calls regarding the receipt or status of submissions. Also, do not send song files. Send a CD with 4 songs max.

Blue Skunk Music
12400 Russet Ln. Huntley, IL 60142
PH: 847-275-8378
Joe Rutan jrutan@blueskunkmusic.com
www.blueskunkmusic.com
We encourage you to send us a press kit, including audio samples of your group.

Bluebeat Music
PO Box 1645, Boulder Creek, CA 95006-1645
PH/FX: 831-338-4784
www.bluebeatmusic.com
We have one of the largest selections of Blues CDs on the internet. Over 10,000 different Blues titles.

BluesandJazzSounds.com
134 Overlook St., Mt. Vernon, NY 10552
Bob Putignano info@bluesandjazzsounds.com
www.bluesandjazzsounds.com
Pays attention to detail and dedicates itself to its clients' success. We tailor each campaign to the project's specific requirements and the client's individual needs.

CrossCut Records
PO Box 106524, 28065 Bremen, Germany
PH: +49-4748-8216-55 FX: +49-4748-8216-59
blues@crosscut.de
www.crosscut.de
Our roster of artists is not limited to a certain Blues style or region. Most importantly, we believe in honest and heartfelt music.

NorthernBlues Music
225 Sterling Rd. #19, Toronto, ON M6R 2B2
PH: 416-536-4892 FX: 416-536-1494
info@northernblues.com
www.northernblues.com
I don't want just another shuffle - I want originality, I want crossover, I want exciting, I want different, and I want every NorthernBlues Music CD to be exceptional.

Silk City Records
PO Box 704, West Paterson, NJ 07424
PH: 973-599-0237 FX: 973-599-0236
Andy Allu silkcity@silkcitycd.com
www.silkcitycd.com
Provides recordings of the finest quality Blues, Folk, Jazz, New Age and Roots artists, both established and emerging.

Stony Plain Records
PO Box 861, Edmonton, AB T5J 2L8
PH: 780-468-6423 FX: 780-465-8941
info@stonyplainrecords.com
www.stonyplainrecords.com
Canada's prominent Roots music label.

Topcat Records
PO Box 670234, Dallas, TX 75367-0234
PH: 972-484-4141 FX: 972-620-8333
info@topcatrecords.com
topcatrecords.com
The primo Texas Blues indie label.

Children's

Kids' CDs and Tapes
Old Bank Chambers, 43 Woodlands Rd.
Lytham St. Annes, Lancashire, FY8 1DA UK
PH: 01253-731234
info@crs-records.com
www.kidsmusicshop.co.uk
Specialist producers of Children's music.

Kidsmusic
The Fairway, Bush Fair, Harlow, Essex,
CM18 6LY UK
PH: 44-01279-444707 FX: 44-01279-445570
enquiries@kidsmusic.co.uk
www.cypmusic.co.uk
Marketing and distribution of Children's audio.

Music for Little People
PO Box 1460, Redway, CA 95560
PH: 707-923-3991
customerservice@mflp.com
www.musicforlittlepeople.com
Producer of Children's music.

Music4Kids Online
220 SW. G St., Grants Pass, OR 97526
PH: 541-956-8600
mail@music4kids.com
www.music4kidsonline.com
Sells Children's indie music.

Rabbit Ranch Records
PO Box 5020, Champaign, IL 61825
info@rabbitranch.com
www.rabbitranch.com
A Christian Children's music company.

Christian

United States

Araunah Music
2 Oxley Square Rd. Gaithersburg, MD 20877
PH: 240-696-6051
www.araunah.com
*A Christian label that produces, promotes and
distributes the best Christian indies.*

Big Baby Music Group
PH: 626-533-4838 FX: 800-866-3454
Drew Strickland Drew@bigbabymusicgroup.com
www.bigbabymusicgroup.com
*A Christian record label looking for unsigned
artists. We specialize in Hip Hop and R&B.*

blackgospelmusic.com
2628 N. 23rd St. #32, Philadelphia, PA 19132
PH: 215-227-5026 FX: 215-893-4321
webminister@blackgospel.com
www.blackgospel.com
Resources for the Black Gospel music community.

Blastbeats.com
PO Box 863255, Plano, TX 75086
PH: 972-867-2720 FX: 484-204-4196
staff@blastbeats.com
www.blastbeats.com
Indie/Underground Christian music.

By Faith Records
2153 E. Main St. #C14-346
Duncan, SC 29334-9295
PH: 888-299-9730 FX: 888-299-9730
Anthony Frazier contact@byfaithrecords.com
www.byfaithrecords.com
We provide spiritual uplifting through music.

Chrematizo Label Group
PO Box 21370, Minneapolis, MN 55421
PH: 612-208-0300 FX: 612-208-0301
David C. Coleman dave@chrematizo.com
www.chrematizo.com
*We are a group of Christian record labels. We also
provide MAJOR distro for Christian indie artists.*

Christian Concert Authority
2234 Ahu Niu Pl. Honolulu, HI 96821
FX: 406-622-3845
Karla@ccauthority.com
www.ccauthority.com
Sells Christian CDs (all genres) online.

ChristianDiscs.com
2705 S. Pike Ave. Allentown, PA 18103
service@christiandiscs.com
www.christiandiscs.com
Sells indie and mainstream Christian CDs.

Gospel Artist Network
3913 Brainerd Rd. #106, Chattanooga, TN 37411
PH: 423-622-9867 FX: 423-622-9861
www.gospelmusicmart.com
A site developed for all Gospel and Christian artists.

Holy Hip Hop
PO Box 1023, Pine Lake, GA 30072
PH: 404-893-5752
holyhiphop.com
*Production, distribution and marketing for Christian
Hip Hop music.*

independentbands.com
4316 Main St. #130, The Colony, TX 75056
bandrelations@independentbands.com
www.independentbands.com
Site and service for Christian indie bands.

Indie Heaven
PO Box 1628, Franklin, TN 37065
www.indieheaven.com
Site for all indie Christian artists.

King Cat Music
17300 Gray Dr. Pleasant Hill, MO 64080
PH: 816-540-4197
info@kingcatmusic.com
www.kingcatmusic.com
*For Christian music listeners and music creators.
Come network and find out how to do your ministry
with excellence.*

OutBoundMusic.com
16506 FM 529 #115, PMB 145, Houston, TX 77095
PH: 281-859-6715
info@outboundmusic.com
www.outboundmusic.com
Distribution and promotion services for indie artists.

RAD ROCKERS
PO Box 207, Milan, MI 48160
PH: 734-439-7029
customer.service@radrockers.com
www.radrockers.com
Mothership of hard to find Christian music.

The Shepherd's Nook
316 McMahan Blvd. Marion, OH 43302
PH: 740-389-4000 FX: 740-389-6601
Tom Hypes tom@theshepherdsnook.com
www.shopthenook.com
Carries Christian indie CDs on consignment.

SLM Records (Saved by the LORD's Music)
1166 Glendale Blvd. Los Angeles, CA 90026
PH: 213-353-9780 FX: 213-353-9780
Erwin Cabalang erwin@slmrecords.com
www.slmrecords.com
*A Christian label trying to make a difference. Giving
Christian & Gospel artists a chance!!*

True Grace Promotions
PH: 862-262-9207
Homa Morrison admin@truegracepromotions.com
www.truegracepromotions.com
*Dedicated to promoting the word of God, through
the vehicle of Caribbean Gospel music.*

vineyardonline.com
5721 E. Virginia St., Evansville, IN 47715
PH: 800-578-7984 FX: 812-479-8805
info@vineyardonline.com
www.vineyardonline.com
Everything Christian.

worshipmusic.com
2432 W. Peoria Ave. #1182, Phoenix, AZ 85029
www.worshipmusic.com
*Before we can review your CD you must complete
the easy steps of our submission process.*

Wounded Records
1145 Stierley Rd. N., Wadesville, IN 47638
PH: 812-985-5969 FX: 812-985-5969
W. Bryant Duncan bryant@woundedrecords.com
www.woundedrecords.com
*Accepting demos with a positive message. All
genres. From recording to production of your
project, including distro and promotion, we are here
for you.*

Canada

House of James
2743 Emerson St., Abbotsford, BC V2T 4H8
PH: 604-852-3701 FX: 604-852-3734
info@houseofjames.com
www.houseofjames.com/departments/music.html
*Christian Bookstore with thousands of in-stock
books, music, videos and DVDs.*

Pro-CD & DVD
3779 154 A St., Surrey, BC V3S 0V4
PH: 604-628-2400
info@rocksolidmusic.com
www.rocksolidmusic.com
Contemporary Christian music of all styles.

Classical

North America

United States

Centaur Records
136 St. Joseph St., Baton Rouge, LA 70802
PH: 225-336-4877 FX: 225-336-9678
info@centaurrecords.com
www.centaurrecords.com
*Accepts unsolicited submissions of Classical
material.*

Cliff's Classics
www.cliffsclassics.com
*Supports independent Classical musicians. Looking
for positive uplifting music.*

Eroica Classical Recordings
584 Island View Cir. Port Hueneme, CA 93041
PH: 805-488-7490
Larry A. Russell cds@eroica.com
www.eroica.com
*The finest in music of all genres, performed by
world class artists on fully guaranteed CDs of the
highest quality that are not available elsewhere. We
are accepting new artists in all genres. Please send
your demo (preferably, a shrink wrapped market
ready CD) to the above address.*

Ivory Classics
PO Box 341068, Columbus, OH 43234-1068
PH: 614-761-8709 FX: 614-761-9799
michaeldavis@ivoryclassics.com
www.IvoryClassics.com
Independent Classical record label devoted to pianists.

Music & Arts
523 Coventry Rd. Kensington, CA 94707
PH: 510-525-4583 FX: 510-524-2111
info@musicandarts.com
www.musicandarts.com
Independent Classical and Jazz label.

Naxos of America
416 Mary Lindsay Polk Dr. #509
Franklin, TN 37067
PH: 615-771-9393 FX: 615-771-6747
naxos@naxosusa.com
www.naxos.com
Selling and distribution of Classical indie music.

New Albion Records
Box 25, Elizaville, NY 12523
PH: 415-621-5757 FX: 415-621-4711
ergo@newalbion.com
www.newalbion.com
Develops, records and releases for indie artists.

Phoenix USA
200 Winston Dr. Cliffside Park, NJ 07010
PH: 201-224-8318 FX: 201-224-7968
sales@Phoenixcd.com
www.phoenixcd.com
A label for recent Classical music.

Wildboar Records
2430 Bancroft Way, Berkeley, CA 94704
PH: 510-849-0211 FX: 510-849-9214
wildboar@musicaloffering.com
www.musicaloffering.com
Independent Classical CD store/label.

Telarc
23307 Commerce Park Rd. Cleveland, OH 44122
PH: 216-464-2313
artists@telarc.com
www.telarc.com
Submit your demo to sell music here.

Canada

early-music.com
7753, rue Tellier, Montréal, QC H1L 2Z5
PH: 514-355-1825 FX: 514-355-5628
info@early-music.com
www.early-music.com
Providing an international marketplace for world-class professionals involved in all aspects of Early Music.

Marquis Classics/Marquis Records
30 Kenilworth Ave. Toronto, ON M4L 3S3
PH: 416-690-7662 FX: 416-690-7346
info@marquisclassics.com
www.marquisclassics.com
Accepts submissions from independent musicians in several genres.

Naxos of Canada
3510 Pharmacy Ave. #3
Scarborough, ON M1W 2T7
PH: 416-491-2600 FX: 416-491-2621
naxos@naxoscanada.com
www.naxos.com
Selling and distribution of Classical indie music.

Europe

Denmark

Danacord Records
Norregade 22, DK-1165 Copenhagen, Denmark
PH: 45-33-15-17-16 FX: 45-33-12-15-14
distribution@danacord.dk
www.danacord.dk
Independent Classical record label.

Germany

FARAO Classics
Schwere-Reiter-Str. 35 Gbd. 20, 80797 Munchen, Germany
PH: 49-89-30777616 FX: 49-89-30777617
info@farao-classics.de
www.farao-classics.de
Founded by professional musicians for musicians!

Pink Tontraeger
Munstertaler Str. 23, D-79219 Stuafen im Breisgau, Germany
PH: 7633-7265 FX: 7633-50441
info@stieglitz-klassik-musik-label.de
www.pink-tontraeger.de
Sells CDs of Classical indie musicians.

Italy

Stradivarius
valeriaelli@stradivarius.it
www.stradivarius.it
The leading Italian Classical music label.

United Kingdom

Chandos
1 Commerce Pk. Commerce Way, Colchester, Essex, CO2 8HX UK
PH: 44-1206-225200 FX: 22-1206-225201
enquiries@chandos.net
www.chandos.net
Independent Classical record company.

Divine Art Record Company
8 The Beeches, E. Harlsey, N. Yorkshire, DL6 2DJ UK
PH: 44-0-1609-882062
Stephen Sutton info@divine-art.com
www.divine-art.com
We deal in Classical/Experimental/Nostalgia music.

Hyperion
PO Box 25, London, SE9 1AX UK
PH: 44-0-20-8318-1234 FX: 44-0-20-8463-1230
info@hyperion-records.co.uk
www.hyperion-records.co.uk
Independent Classical label.

tutti.co.uk
18 Hillfield Park, London, N10 3QS UK
PH: 44-0-20-8444-8587
www.tutti.co.uk
Source for independent Classical labels. Sell your music.

Australia

Move Records
1 Linton St., Ivanhoe, VIC 3084 Australia
PH: 03-9497-3105 FX: 03-9497-4426
Martin Wright move@move.com.au
www.move.com.au
Classical and Jazz CD label with own studio with grand piano.

Country

United States

Aspirion Records
1200 Division St. #206, Nashville, TN 37203
PH: 615-401-6994 FX: 615-401-6998
Steve Baker sbaker@aspirionrecords.com
www.myspace.com/aspirionrecords
We act as a service company / label to set up national distribution, radio promotion, video production, PR and other services for Country music artists & labels.

Bloodshot Records
3039 W. Irving Park Rd. Chicago, IL 60618
PH: 773-604-5300 FX: 773-604-5019
bshq@bloodshotrecords.com
www.bloodshotrecords.com
Insurgent Country label. We absolutely DO NOT accept demos from third party lawyers or promotion companies shopping stuff for clients.

CountySales.com
PH: 540-745-2001 FX: 540-745-2008
info@countysales.com
www.countysales.com
World's largest selection of Bluegrass music.

Flat Earth Records
6900 S. Gray Rd. Indianapolis, IN 46237
info@flatearthrecords.com
www.flatearthrecords.com
Indie label with a focus on Twang.

Miles of Music
11271 Ventura Blvd. #620, Studio City, CA 91604
PH: 818-284-6426 FX: 818-232-0199
info@milesofmusic.com
www.milesofmusic.com
More music to the gallon!

Old 97 Wrecords
1400 Lexington Ave. Greensboro, NC 27403
PH/FX: 336-275-7286
info@old97wrecords.com
www.old97wrecords.com
A cooperative label celebrating the diverse sounds of Southern String Band music.

Old-Time Music Home Page
20 Battery Park Ave. Asheville, NC 28801
PH: 828-285-8850 FX: 828-285-8851
david@lynchgraphics.com
www.oldtimemusic.com
Sells Old-Time (traditional Southern string band) music CDs.

Canada

Cedar Trail Music
Box 1139, TDC Postal Stn. 77 King St. W.
Toronto, ON M5K 1P2
Mike Belobradic contact@cedartrailmusic.com
www.cedartrailmusic.com
Indie label focussing on Country music. We also offer a full range of publicity, promotional, marketing and business planning services.

Germany

Glitterhouse Records
Gruner Weg 25 D-37688 Beverungen, Germany
PH: 49-0-5273-36360 FX: 49-0-5273-363637
info@glitterhouse.com
www.glitterhouse.de
The ultimate Mail-order for Americana, Roots, Alternative and Folk CDs.

Australia

Country Music Store
GPO Box 3000, Brisbane, QLD 4001 Australia
PH: 07-3221-3000 FX: 07-3221-3983
cmstore@countrymusic.com.au
www.countrymusic.com.au
Online resource for all your Australian Country music.

Dance and Electronic

Artificial Bliss Recordings
23 Stephens Close, Luton, Bedfordshire,
LU2 9AN UK
www.artificialbliss.com
An Electronic music based label and community focusing on innovation and creativity.

BangingTunes.com
4 Westbourne Grove, Hove, East Sussex,
BN3 5PJ UK
PH: +44-1273-208040
www.bangingtunes.com
The UK Dance music store.

Click Pop Records
1220 N. State St., Bellingham, WA 98225-5016
PH: 360-527-1150
Dave Richards dave@clickpoprecords.com
www.clickpoprecords.com
Specializing in Techno, House, Down Tempo and Alternative music.

ClickGroove
24 Old Steine, Brighton, East Sussex, BN1 1EL UK
www.clickgroove.com
The best in Underground House, Future Boogie and Dancefloor Soul.

DeanHil Promotions
Fussenich Str. 16a, 50126 Bergheim, Germany
www.deanhil-promotion.com
A pool for new beats of the music industry. Top DJ's from around the world evaluate your music.

Deepermotions Music
37 Leslie Rd. Essendon, VIC 3040 Australia
PH: +61411205395
Mike Gurrieri deepermotions@hotmail.com
www.deepermotions.com
We are a Deep House/Downtempo digital record label. We sell our music currently on Traxsource & Stompy & cater to the DJ market.

Freestylemusic.com
18565 SW. 104th Ave. Miami, FL 33157
PH: 305-234-8033
freestylemusic@mailcity.com
www.freestylemusic.com
Distribution network for independent artists and DJs.

Haywire
Studio A. 21 John Campbell Rd. London,
N16 8JY UK
PH/FX: +44 (0) 20-7503 3921
Amanda Burton amanda@haywire.co.uk
www.haywire.co.uk
We deal with artist management, live bookings & events. We also offer ALL the info on the local music scene.

Juno Records
PO Box 45557, London, NW1 0UT UK
www.juno.co.uk
The world's largest online Dance music store, with over 800,000 tracks on vinyl, CD and download.

Just Music / Absolute Zero / Just Publishing
Hope House, 40 St Peters Rd. London, W6 9BD UK
PH: +44 (0) 20-8741-6020
Serena Benedict justmusic@justmusic.co.uk
www.justmusic.co.uk
Offering the very best in cutting-edge Electronica, Acoustic, Ambient, Down-Tempo and Chill. We are specifically for tracks for that we can buy out all rights to (records and publishing rights).

Knob Records
216 E. 29th St. #3A, New York, NY 10016
PH: 917-449-5250
DJ Style style@knobrecords.com
www.knobrecords.com
Underground Progressive, Tribal House, Trance and Breaks.

Nilaihah Records
Attn: Demo Submission
PO Box 82614, Columbus, OH 43202
nilaihah@nilaihah.com
www.nilaihah.com
Indie record label for Dance music.

Phuture Sole Recordings
227 Madison Ave. Clifton, NJ 07011
PH/FX: 973-614-0302
Sweet Sarah SweetS@PhutureSoleRecordings.com
www.PhutureSoleRecordings.com
We are an independent label specializing in soulful House music.

Poposm Records
Thomas Coles shoeareyou@gmail.com
www.poposmrecords.com
Edinburgh, UK label that specialise in a unique Acid Psychedelic flavour, featuring far-out soundscapes and bassbin-blasting basslines. Breakbeats in your face, yo.

Real Estate Records
2544 W. North Ave. #2B, Chicago, IL 60647
PH: 773-862-9652 FX: 773-862-9662
Veronica Beckman info@elephanthaus.com
www.realestaterecords.com
Indie Electronic label.

Tweekin Records
593 Haight St., San Francisco, CA 94117
PH: 415-626-6995 FX: 415-626-5206
Manny info@tweekin.com
www.tweekin.com
San Francisco's premiere Dance record store.

Ubiquity Records
70 Latham Ln. Berkeley, CA 94708
PH: 949-764-9012 FX: 949-764-9013
Andrew Jervis andrewj@ubiquityrecords.com
www.ubiquityrecords.com
Send demos by mail only. Do NOT send MP3s!

Web-Records.com
Im Vogelsang 17, 71101 Schonaich, Germany
PH: 0180-5-555-701 FX: 0180-5-555-702
info@web-records.com
web-records.com
World's biggest internet shop for Club music.

Experimental

United States

Ambient.us
info@ambient.us
www.ambient.us
A positive energy Ambient music guide. Contact me by e-mail if you would like a review.

Arthropoda Records
1223 Wilshire Blvd. #812, Santa Monica, CA 90403
PH: 310-930-0990 FX: 310-315-8273
Craig Garner craig@arthropodarecords.com
www.arthropodarecords.com
Record label promoting original thinking.

Forced Exposure
219 Medford St., Malden, MA 02148
FX: 781-321-0321
mailorder@forcedexposure.com
www.forcedexposure.com
Sells Experimental, Techno, IDM and more.

Frog Peak Music
PO Box 1052, Lebanon, NH 03755
PH: 603-643-9037 FX: 603-643-9037
fp@frogpeak.org
www.frogpeak.org
An artist-run composers' collective dedicated to producing Experimental and unusual works by its members.

Helmet Room Recordings
1227 Perry St., Denver, CO 80204
PH: 720-221-8370
Randall Frazier info@helmetroom.com
www.helmetroom.com
Artist-owned label specializing in Psychedelic, Progressive, Experimental and Drone.

Hypnos
PO Box 6868, Portland, OR 97228
mg@hypnos.com
hypnos.com
Source for Ambient, Space and Experimental music.

Joyful Noise
PO Box 20109, Indianapolis, IN 46220
Karl joyfulnoiserecordings@hotmail.com
www.joyfulnoiserecordings.com
Spiritually focused Experimental/Noise/Improv label.

Sonic Space
Dmitry demos@sonicspacerecs.com
www.sonicspacerecs.com
Accepts instrumental music in all styles. We listen to all demos received. The best way to send us your MP3 along with your biography and contact information is via e-mail.

Squidco
160 Bennett Ave. #6K, New York, NY 10040
PH: 917-535-0265
sales@squidco.com
www.squidco.com
We sell Improvisational, Experimental, Progressive, RIO and otherwise unusual music.

Tract Records
PO Box 28705, Columbus, OH 43228-9998
Thomas Heath thomas@tractrecords.com
www.tractrecords.com
Label specializing in Underground Folk, Alt-Country and Experimental. We release compilations on a semi-yearly label. We accept demos.

Tzadik
200 E. 10th St. PMB 126, New York, NY 10003
info@tzadik.com
www.tzadik.com
Avant-garde and Experimental music.

Canada

Artoffact Records
PO Box 68039, Winnipeg, MB R3L 2V9
demos@artoffact.com
www.artoffact.com
Releasing and promoting Electronic music sounds.

ping things
rik@pingthings.com
www.pingthings.com
We sell CDs of Experimental and Electronic sounds.

Germany

dense
Reichenberger Str. 147, 10999 Berlin, Germany
PH: +49 (0)30-616-529-60
FX: +49 (0)30-616-529-46
www.dense.de
Promotion services to fit the needs of independent labels and artists releasing Experimental music.

SynGate.net
Eibenweg 10, 53894 Mechernich, Germany
PH: 49-2443-903609
Lothar Lubitz mail@syngate.net
www.syngate.net
The gate to Synthesizer based music.

The Netherlands

Weirdomusic.com
PO Box 26, 6400 AA, Heerlen, The Netherlands
PH: +31 (0)45-850-3629 FX: +31 (0)84-724-5674
Marco Kalnenek marco@weirdomusic.com
www.weirdomusic.com
We take you on a journey along the darkest corners of the musical universe. From Exotic to Experimental, you can find it on Weirdomusic.com.

Spain

FuckTheSystem Records
Crevantes 25 Santa Olalla, Toledo-45530, Spain
PH: 34-678627506
José Henriquez jose.henriquez@fts-records.com
www.fts-records.com
An Experimental and Rock independent music label.

United Kingdom

Sonic Arts Network
171 Union St., London, SE1 0LN UK
PH: 44-0-20-7928-7337 FX: 44-0-20-7928-7338
www.sonicartsnetwork.org
Worldwide events, education and information resource.

32,000 Live Music Venues in the US and Canada

www.IndieVenueBible.com

Film and TV

United States

5 Alarm Music
35 W. Dayton St., Pasadena, CA 91105
PH: 800-322-7879
info@5alarmmusic.com
www.5alarmmusic.com
The largest independent production music library in the US! With over 85,000 tracks online, as well as over 200 independent artists, original music and music supervision services, we truly are a one-stop shop for TV music, film music, trailer music, music for video, and music for commercials.

AudioSocket
PH: 206-701-7931 FX: 206-264-7916
www.audiosocketmusic.com
Licenses the best independent music to film, TV and new media in a fun, creative and efficient fashion.

Broadjam Deliveries
6401 Odana Rd. Madison, WI 53719
PH: 608-271-3633
www.broadjam.com/deliveries
Your chance to get placed in a film, commercial or TV show.

Countdown Entertainment
110 W. 26th St., New York, NY 10001-6805
PH: 212-645-3068 FX: 212-989-6459
James Citkovic
submitmusic@countdownentertainment.com
www.countdownentertainment.com
Represents bands, groups, singers, songwriters, musicians, composers, music producers and music managers to independent music labels and major recording labels for record deals, music licensing deals, film music deals, TV music deals, record distribution and music publishing.

Crucial Music
www.crucialmusic.com
Gives creators of original music a direct path to those important gatekeepers who place music in film, commercials and television shows.

dBE.Music
info@digitalbear.com
www.dbemusic.com
Specializes in placement of indie music in TV, film, advertising and other sound for picture uses.

Filmtracks
Christian Clemmensen tyderian@filmtracks.com
www.filmtracks.com
Get the score ...the true orchestral magic of Film music.

FlightSafe Music
Attn: Music Submission
17 Janet Way #2, Tiburon, CA 94920
info@flightsafemusic.com
www.flightsafemusic.com
Generates music synchronization licenses for placement in films, documentaries, commercials and TV shows.

Fresh Sounds Music Competition
c/o Dreaming Tree Films
4646 N. Ravenswood Ave. 2nd Fl. Chicago, IL 60640
www.fresh-films.com
A music platform to uncover local independent music talent across the nation.

Goodnight Kiss Music
10153 ½ Riverside Dr. #239
Toluca Lake, CA 91602
PH: 831-479-9993
www.goodnightkiss.com
You MUST be a subscriber to our newsletter before you do anything else. If you send in your music without your assigned "code" it will be thrown away.

Indie Film Composers
PH/FX: 208-730-8713
indifilm@earthlink.net
www.indifilm.com
Subcontracts compositions out to our worldwide affiliates.

indie911
PH: 310-943-7164
Gregg Allen gregg@indie911.com
www.indie911.com/aflp
One of the industry's leading independent music resources for music licensing for TV, films, video games and other new media.

Indy Hits
PO Box 4102, Hollywood, CA 90078
PH: 323-276-1000 FX: 323-276-1001
info@bandpromote.com
www.indyhits.com
Working with unsigned bands helping to secure record/publishing deals and film/TV placements.

INgrooves
539 Bryant St. #405, San Francisco, CA 94107
PH: 415-896-2100
info@ingrooves.com
www.ingrooves.com
Works with indie artists and labels to license your music to the TV & Film industry.

isynx
3422 Old Capitol Trail #700
Wilmington, DE 19808-6192
Peter Furst peter@isynx.com
www.isynx.com
Exists to help independent artists get promoted and paid through licensing their music for use in areas ranging from films to TV shows to computer games.

J2R Music
471 Old Eagle School Rd. Wayne, PA 19087
PH: 610-687-3553
info@j2rmusic.com
www.j2rmusic.com
Supplies high quality original music to clients in network and cable television and feature film production.

Jetset Sound
www.jetsetsound.com
Specializes in ongoing film and television music licensing of extremely talented, as yet unknown artists.

LicenseQuote.com
19049 Janisse Ln. Lake Elsinore, CA 92530
PH: 951-678-5725
Michael Borges contact@licensequote.com
www.licensequote.com
Provides music licensing solutions for independent artists, labels and music publishers. It enables publishers to license their songs, recordings and related assets directly from their own websites.

LoveCat Music
PO Box 548, Ansonia Stn.
New York, NY 10023-0548
FX: 646-304-7391
info@lovecatmusic.com
www.lovecatmusic.com
We offer film & TV placements, licensing and more.

Luke Hits
137 N. Larchmont Blvd. #555
Los Angeles, CA 90004
lukehits.com
*Links bands with high profile film/TV projects.
Please READ our online demo submission policy
BEFORE you send in your music.*

Mother West *The Vault*
37 W. 20th St. #1006, New York, NY 10011
PH: 212-807-0405 FX: 212-741-7688
info@motherwest.com
motherwest.com
A vast music licensing library.

Musync
PH: 415-282-3444 FX: 415-282-2099
info@musync.com
www.musync.com
*A catalog of real music with real librarians to help
you find what you need. The catalog consists of
16,573 tracks of real pre-cleared music from
established indie labels worldwide.*

myHitFactory
www.myhitfactory.com
*The leading professional music industry resource &
pitch sheet for music publishers, record labels and
professional producers/writers.*

Noteborn Music
PO Box 8171, Ann Arbor, MI 48107-8171
www.notebornmusic.com
*We hand pick quality music for use in movies, TV
shows, advertising campaigns and for music
producers. If you do not have a Sonicbids
membership, your submission can be mailed ($15
per submission/3 songs).*

OpTic NoISe
424 Duboce Ave. San Francisco, CA 94117
PH: 415-252-1180
info@optic-noise.com
www.optic-noise.com
*Offers the full scope of licensing and exposure
opportunities to its clients. Pop, Rock, Techno, Pop
Punk only. No instrumental tracks!*

The Orchard *Trackdown*
100 Park Ave. 2nd Fl. New York, NY 10017
PH: 212-201-9280 FX: 866-864-7305
www.orchardmusicservices.com
*Makes your music available to select music
supervisors and other industry professionals.*

PanoraManiacal Soundscapes
PH: 415-381-8647 FX: 415-381-8682
Christopher Buttner chris@panoramaniacal.com
www.panoramaniacal.com
*Features a massive library of original music
available for TV, film, advertising and electronic
gaming production.*

Play It For The Labels
5451 Independence Pkwy. #2603, Plano, TX 75023
PH: 972-841-6017
Tony Boswell Tony@playitforthelabels.com
www.PlayItForTheLabels.com
*A conduit through which artists and songwriters are
able to contact reps from music, TV/film and video
game industries.*

Position Soundtrack Services
PO Box 25907, Los Angeles, CA 90025
PH: 310-442-8170 FX: 310-442-8180
Tyler Bacon tyler@positionmusic.com
www.positionmusic.com
*Represents artists for the placement of their music in
film, television, soundtrack albums, advertising and
video games.*

Psychedelic Records
A&R Dept. PO Box 1247
Redondo Beach, CA 90278-0247
Chris Davis info@psychedelicrecords.com
www.psychedelicrecords.com
*We are currently seeking music to submit for Film
and TV Licensing deals, such as mainstream POP,
Alt Rock, R&B, Acid Jazz, Cinematic Orchestral,
Ambient, Instrumental, Piano, Acoustic Guitar, 30
second Jingles or Music Cues, and Holiday or
Christmas music.*

Pump Audio
Box 458, Trivoli, NY 12583
www.pumpaudio.com
We license your music to TV, film and advertising.

RipTide Music
4121 Redwood Ave. #202, Los Angeles, CA 90066
PH: 310-437-4380 FX: 310-437-4384
contact@riptidemusic.com
www.riptidemusic.com
*A boutique music shop providing one stop licensing
of world-class artists and composers for film,
television, games, trailers and advertising.*

Rumblefish
919 SW. Taylor St. #300, Portland, OR 97205
PH: 800-293-9102
info@rumblefish.com
www.rumblefish.com
*We handpick music from all over the world, across
all genres for our catalog. Our artist-members'
songs are pre-cleared and ready to license for film,
TV, internet, corporate, even samples and beats.*

Sandra Marsh Management
9150 Wilshire Blvd. #220, Beverly Hills, CA 90212
PH: 310-285-0303 FX: 310-285-0218
www.sandramarsh.com
*We have opened a music department devoted to
representing composers, music supervisors and
music editors in film, television and commercials.*

SirGroovy
www.sirgroovy.com
*Features over 10,000 pre licensed songs for music
supervisors who need music for their project.*

Song and Film
Josh Zandman songandfilm@gmail.com
www.songandfilm.com
Leading music placement company for film and TV.

TAXI
PH: 800-458-2111
www.taxi.com
Record and publishing deals, film & TV placement.

Transition Music Corporation
PO Box 2586, Toluca Lake, CA 91610
PH: 323-860-7074 FX: 323-860-7986
Todd Johnsen onestopmus@aol.com
www.transitionmusic.com
*Unsolicited submissions accepted. No more than 3
songs/tracks per submission. No tapes, CDs only.
Must be master quality.*

True Talent Management
9663 Santa Monica Blvd. #320
Beverly Hills, CA 90210
PH: 310-560-1290 FX: 310-441-2005
submissions@truetalentmgmt.com
www.truetalentmgmt.com
*I am available to help you achieve your goals.
Services range from TV and film pitching and
placement, marketing and brand consulting to
promotion and publicity.*

TruSonic
7825 Fay Ave. Ste. LL-A, La Jolla, CA 92037
PH: 858-362-2323 FX: 858-362-2324
artistsupport@trusonic.com
www.trusonic.com
*Music and messaging service used by various
businesses. We're always on the lookout for fresh
upcoming acts with artistic vision and control of
their own content.*

Urband & Lazar Music Publishing
1617 Cosmo St. #310, Los Angeles, CA 90028
PH: 323-230-6592
Jonathan Lazar jonathan@urbandlazar.com
www.urbandlazar.com
*A full service music publishing company with a
sister record label called U & L Records. We place
music into film, TV, advertisements, video games &
new media. Linking the finest compositions with
media is the core of Urband & Lazar.*

VersusMedia
556 S. Fair Oaks Ave. #245, Pasadena, CA 91105
PH: 877-633-8764 FX: 323-375-0430
www.versusmedia.com
*Provider of publicity services and film music
networking opportunities. Please contact us before
sending in your material.*

Visions From the Roof
1032 S. Orange Grove #3, Los Angeles, CA 90019
PH: 310-433-7997
info@visionsfromtheroof.com
www.visionsfromtheroof.com
We specialize in Film/TV placement.

Canada

dittybase
31 Bastion Sq. #102, Victoria, BC V8W 1J1
PH: 250-381-8780 x20 FX: 250-384-6761
sales@dittybase.com
www.dittybase.com
*Helps music directors find the perfect track for any
project.*

SongCatalog
(Canada) 400-601 W. Broadway
Vancouver, BC V5Z 4C2
PH: 604-642-2888 FX: 604-642-2889
(USA) 6255 Sunset Blvd. #1024
Hollywood, CA 90028
info@songcatalog.com
www.songcatalog.com
*Music management, marketing and licensing
initiatives.*

United Kingdom

The Beat Suite
Ste. 45, 7-15 Pink Ln. Newcastle, Tyne and Wear,
NE1 5DW UK
info@beatsuite.com
www.beatsuite.com
*Providing music for the multimedia, broadcast and
computer games industry. If you would like to
submit music tracks for our music library then
please visit the "Become a Composer" page and
follow our guidelines on music submissions.*

The Music Broker Network
The Studio, Homefield Ct. Marston Magna,
BA22 8DJ UK
support@themusicbroker.net
www.themusicbroker.net
*Pitches unsigned bands, artists & songwriters to
labels, publishers and film/TV studios.*

SongLink
23 Belsize Cr. London, NW3 5QY UK
PH: 44-0-207-794-2540 FX: 44-0-207-794-7393
www.songlink.com
Music contacts across the globe.

Toolshed Digital Marketing
45 Belcher Rd. Warwick, NY 10990
PH: 845-988-1799
dhuey@toolshed.biz
www.toolshed.biz
*Provides new media promotion, digital licensing,
online strategy services, and state-of-the-art digital
promotion tools to a select list of media and
entertainment clients.*

Toryumon
22 Upper Grosvenor St., London, W1K 7PE UK
PH/FX: +44 (0) 20-7495 3885
artistinfo@toryumon.co.uk
www.toryumon.co.uk
*Has licensed music for adverts fashion shows, film
soundtracks and virtual online DJ mixing.*

Triple Scoop Music
3727 W. Magnolia Blvd. #125, Burbank, CA 91505
PH: 818-459-3846
artists@triplescoopmusic.com
www.triplescoopmusic.com
*Licensing service built for photographers,
videographers and all other creative professionals!*

YouLicense
PH: 605-209-4701
admin@youlicense.com
www.youlicense.com
*A platform which enables music artists and music,
media & entertainment agents to conduct business
directly with one another in a safe and secure
environment. The online destination allows artists to
upload their musical content, bio and copyright
information free of charge.*

Folk

Acoustic Music Resource
PO Box 3518, Seal Beach, CA 90740
PH: 562-431-1608 FX: 562-598-5928
www.acousticmusicresource.com
*For most of the titles we list here, this is the only
place you will ever find them!*

Desert Highway Records
1015 Gayley Ave. #1115, Los Angeles, CA 90024
Ernest ernest@deserthighwayrecords.com
deserthighwayradio.com
*America needs its Roots music and it probably needs
your music.*

DIG Music
1831 V St., Sacramento, CA 95818
PH: 916-442-5344 FX: 916-442-5382
Ben Lefever ben@digmusic.com
www.digmusic.com
*Independent record label and artist management
company. AAA, Roots/Americana,
Singer/Songwriter.*

efolk Music
101 Evans Ct. Carrboro, NC 27510
PH: 919-434-8349
artists@efolkMusic.org
www.efolkmusic.org
Making indie music available to the world.

Firebird Arts & Music
PO Box 30268, Portland, OR 97294
PH: 503-255-5751 FX: 503-255-5703
firebird@firebirdarts.com
www.firebirdarts.com
*An online store which sells Celtic, Folk, Filk and
Native American music.*

FOLK TRAX
PO Box 250, Nairne, SA 5252 Australia
PH: 0418-852-173
manager@folktrax.com
www.folktrax.com
*If you have Acoustic music related merchandise that
you are prepared to consign to us, we will offer it
for sale on our site.*

Trad&Now Music Shop
PO Box 532, Woy Woy, NSW 2256 Australia
PH: +61-2-4325-7369 FX: +61-2-4325-7362
info@tradandnow.com
www.tradandnow.com/shopping
Supporting independent creativity.

Village Records
PO Box 3216, Shawnee, KS 66203
PH: 913-631-4199 FX: 913-631-6369
sales@villagerecords.com
villagerecords.com
*Folk discs, special orders, independent labels and
more.*

GLBT

Centaur Music
45 Main S. #707, Brooklyn, NY 11201
PH: 718-852-6777 FX: 718-852-8877
info@centaurmusic.com
www.centaurmusic.com
*Our products are sold in stores across the US and
Canada, from independent record stores to major
chains.*

Chainsaw Records
PO Box 11384, Portland, OR 97211
info@chainsaw.com
www.chainsaw.com
Queer/girl friendly record label.

StoneWall Society
info@stonewallsociety.com
www.stonewallsociety.com
*Presents a place to sell and buy GLBT music and
art. Submissions reviewed in the StoneWall Society
E-newsletter.*

Woobie Bear Music
woobiebearmusic@adelphia.net
www.woobiebearmusic.com
*Features music by bears, music for bears. The latest
news, reviews and happenings.*

Sign up for
The Indie Contact Newsletter
www.indiebible.com

Goth

Alfa Matrix
32 ave. Albert Jonnart, 1200 Brussels, Belgium
PH/FX: 0032-2-732-14-81
info@alfa-matrix.com
www.alfa-matrix.com
*We have become a trademark for innovative
Electronic music.*

DSBP *(Ditch Sex Buy Product)*
237 Cagua NE Albuquerque, NM 87108
PH: 505-266-8274
dsbp@dsbp.cx
www.dsbp.cx
America's Hard Elektro / Harsh Industrial label.

Final Joy Records
392 E. Harrison St. Chandler, AZ 85225
info@finaljoyrecords.com
www.finaljoyrecords.com
We specialize in Gothic music. Send us your demo!

Gore Galore
PO Box 87, Cynthiana, IN 47612
PH: 812-622-0088 FX: 309-410-2893
info@gore-galore.com
www.gore-galore.com
Submit your music for review.

IsoTank
526 S. 5th St., Philadelphia, PA 19147
PH: 215-861-0313 FX: 215-925-9075
isotank@aol.com
www2.mailordercentral.com/isotank
CDs, videos and merchandise.

Latex Records
info@latexrecords.com
latexrecords.com
Specializing in Goth/Industrial and related genres.

Metropolis Records
PO Box 974, Media, PA 19063
PH: 610-595-9940 FX: 610-595-9944
label@metropolis-records.com
www.metropolis-records.com
Home to Industrial, Gothic and Electronic artists.

MONSTAAR Records
1345 W. North Shore Ave. Chicago, IL 60626
PH: 773-343-9337
monstaar.com
*Purveyors of Noise, Experimental, Darkwave, Goth
and other cruel & unusual music.*

Musicwerks
612 E. Pine St., Seattle, WA 98122
PH: 206-320-8933
musicwerks@musicwerks.org
www.musicwerks.org
Complete selection of Gothic and Industrial CDs.

Planet Mu
Mike Paradinas mike@planet-mu.com
www.planet-mu.com
*Exposure for new and already established
musicians. Send links to your MP3s or MySpace
page.*

Tetragram Records
31 S. McLean Blvd. #16, Memphis, TN 38104
PH: 901-219-5509
www.myspace.com/tetragram
*Artist services and consulting covering the darker
side of indie. All genres with emphasis on Heavy
Metal, Gothic, Industrial, Psychobilly, Hellbilly,
Darkwave and Alternative.*

Van Richter Records
100 S. Sunrise Way #219, Palm Springs, CA 92262
PH: 415-235-3373
www.vanrichter.net
Your Aggro-Industrial record label!

Hip Hop

United States

ATAK Distribution
PO Box 1027, La Canada, CA 91012-1027
PH: 626-398-3229
www.truehiphop.com
Send a copy of whatever you want ATAK to sell. If it's the dopest thing EVER, it's in the catalog. If it's doo-doo, you might not ever hear from us again.

Anytime Records
455 E. Carson Plaza Dr. Ste. G, Carson, CA 90746
PH: 310-527-2647
DJ New York City Ken djnycken@gmail.com
www.anytimerecords.com
We are a Hip Hop, Rap and R&B record label. Grindin' 24-7 with music for the streets from the streets!

B Boy Records World
630 Woodsmill Rd. Gainesville, GA 30501
PH: 770-654-9191 FX: 678-450-3329
Chill-Bill bboyrecords@aol.com
www.bboyrecordsworld.com
We work with the music from the streets. Rap, Hip Hop, Dance, Reggaetron and Latin.

basically-hiphop
Max maxjeromeo@basically-hiphop.com
basically-hiphop.com
Playing Underground and mainstream Hip Hop.

Block Party Records
320 N. Canon Dr. Beverly Hills, CA 90210
PH: 310 927-9666 FX: 310 492-6111
Tony Hicks tony@blockpartyrecords.com
www.blockpartyrecords.com
Reviews all Hip Hop/Rap music of unsigned artists.

Boundless NY
143 Roebling St. 1B, Brooklyn, NY 11211
PH: 718-821-9690 FX: 718-821-7881
info@boundlessny.com
boundlessny.com
Promotes independent Hip Hop artists.

Brainstem Records
1001 34th Ave. NE, Minneapolis, MN 55408
Mike Hastert sixwontoo_eynk@hotmail.com
www.brainstemrecords.com
Bringing underground Hip Hop and all its elements to the forefront of the world. Counter-culture themed music and artwork to work toward the betterment of Hip Hop and its straying directions.

DJcity.com
4041 Sepulveda Blvd. Culver City, CA 90230
PH: 310-737-9200 FX: 801-340-7618
info@djcity.com
www.djcity.com
We specialize in both the party-jammin' major label Hip Hop and R&B, as well as all the underground label cuts blowin' up round the corner.

Empakk Familiar Records
PH: 216-441-1012
Orlando Divinchy
orlandodivinchy@empakkrecords.com
www.empakkrecords.com
We are a Hip Hop label open to new beats. We do commercial songs for franchise and gaming companies.

FTB Records
Cato Kelly
khato@ftbrecords.com
www.ftbrecords.com
Our goal and mission is to promote and give exposure to musicians and models all over the world. To find the best music from unsigned artist, DJ's, producers or independent record labels.

Get Real Records
PO Box 15194, Augusta, GA 30919-1194
PH: 706-414-3296
reelbigent@get-real-records.com
www.get-real-records.com
We help Hip Hop artists promote and distribute their music.

Headquarters Records
PMB 141, #102, 2200 Wilson Blvd.
Arlington, VA 22201
PH: 703-912-1720 FX: 703-995-4913
Al Clipper ac@headquartersrecords.com
www.headquartersrecords.com
About positive vibes that are not offensive.

HoodGrown Records
PO Box 733, Pocono Summit, PA 18346
info@hoodgrownrecords.com
www.hoodgrownrecords.com
We are focused on selling albums. As such we generally provide key singles off an album as free downloads in order to create a buzz for our artists.

JaThom Records
PO Box 1579, New York, NY 10025
thefamily@jathomfamily.com
www.jathomrecords.netfirms.com
Label and distributor that specializes in working with independent artists.

MixUnit.com
PO Box 340811, Hartford, CT 06134
Attn: Submissions
PH: 860-296-2922
www.mixunit.com
To submit your item for review, please send a minimum of 5 copies to the above address.

New West Music & Publishing, Inc.
PO Box 250670, Brooklyn, NY 11225
PH: 866-603-6874
Johnnie Newkirk Jr.
john@newwestmusicpublishing.com
www.newwestmusicpublishing.com
A R&B, Rap, Hip Hop and Pop record label and publishing company.

Mic Master Records
PO Box 1671, Clementon, NJ 08021
PH: 856-504-0911 FX: 856-504-3962
Cesar G. Gutierrez cesar@micmasterrecords.com
www.micmasterrecords.com
Booking agent and independent label.

Much Luvv Records
4930 Dacoma St. Ste. C, Houston, TX 77092
PH: 713-957-6991
Bobby Herring tre9@dasouth.com
www.realityrap.com
Our vision is to provide Hip Hop music that positively influences people. We are committed to maintaining standards above the norm, yet quality music that competes with the best the music industry has to offer.

New Experience Records
PO Box 683, Lima, OH 45802
PH: 419-371-5334
James Milligan just_chilling_2004@yahoo.com
www.newexperiencerecords.com
We are a Hip Hop and R&B record label, studio production company, music publisher and management firm.

Noc On Wood Records
300 Fairview Ave. N., Seattle, WA 98109
PH: 800-253-8009
www.noconwood.com
A new breed of record label run by a team of smart, enterprising young executives.

Nomadic Wax
486 Jefferson Ave. Brooklyn, NY 11221
info@nomadicwax.com
www.nomadicwax.com
African and international Hip Hop production company and label.

Rich Rapper
www.richrapper.com
Offers CD and MP3 online sales. We only carry underground Hip Hop projects from rappers that are determined to make a difference with their music.

Rotation Music Entertainment
Attn: A&R
PO Box 4807, Laguna Beach CA 92652
PH: 949-510-3188
Allan sales@rotationmusic.com
www.rotationmusic.com
Send your radio playable Hip Hop, R&B and Pop demos to this indie label with national distribution.

Sandbox Automatic
425 5th Ave. #603, New York, NY 10016
Attn: Submissions
sandbox@pobox.com
www.sandboxautomatic.com
We will check your stuff out and if we are interested, we will contact you back with more instructions. You do not need to follow up on your submission request.

Starfleet Music Pool
3521 Mallard Cove Ct. Charlotte, NC 28269
PH: 704-599-6645 FX: 704-599-1863
Ronnie Matthews rmatthews@starfleetmusic.com
www.starfleetmusic.com
Helping labels break their new releases in every night club in every city that Starfleet covers!

Stones Throw Records
2658 Griffith Park Blvd. #504
Los Angeles, CA 90039-2520
info@stonesthrow.com
www.stonesthrow.com
Indie record label. Calendar, news, sell CDs etc.

Thug Life Army Records
7672 Montgomery Rd. #270, Cincinnati, OH 45236
PH: 513-673-3144
info@ThugLifeArmyRecords.com
thuglifearmyrecords.com
There are many indie artists who deserve their shine and they are just sitting on their projects because of lack of direction in promotion and or distribution.

UndergroundHipHop.com
PH: 617-364-4900
www.undergroundhiphop.com
Do NOT mail us your CD. Read our online submission policy, then send us an E-MAIL with all the information that we request.

Canada

Camobear Records
21646-1424 Commercial Dr.
Vancouver, BC V5l 3X9
info@camobear.ca
www.camobear.ca
An indie record label distributing Hip Hop music to the people. We also book Hip Hop shows in the Vancouver area.

Mumbles Hip Hop
info@mumbleshiphop.com
www.mumbleshiphop.com
Record store with a small record pool. We have started this record pool as a free promotional service for independent artists and labels.

Saquan Entertainment
5845 Yonge St., PO Box 45027
Willowdale, ON M2M 4K3
PH: 905-266-9879
www.saquanent.com
A record label that specializes in Reggae and Hip Hop. We strive to create moments where our artists transform entertainment to a celestial plateau.

Soul Choice
info@soulchoice.ca
www.soulchoice.ca
Canada's premiere Urban record pool.

Germany

Rap.de
Köpenicker Str. 178, 10997 Berlin, Germany
PH: 030-695-972-10 FX: 030-695-972-40
Mischa Wetzel wetzel@styleheads.de
www.rap.de
Magazine, events calendar, online store & more.

The Netherlands

BusyR.com
shop@BusyR.com
www.busyr.com
Holy Hip Hop online store.

recordbuddy.com
Stationstraat 10, 9711 AS Groningen,
The Netherlands
PH: +31628336304
info@recordbuddy.com
www.recordbuddy.com
Our aim is to support the upcoming talents by selling CDs / tapes / LPs of Hip Hop talents.

Switzerland

hiphopstore.ch
General Guisan-Str.1 Ch-5000 Aarau, Switzerland
PH: 41-62-834-40-00 FX: 41-62-834-40-09
info@hiphopstore.ch
www.hiphopstore.ch
Online distribution of indie CDs.

United Kingdom

Don't Stop The Flow Records
PO Box 246 Manchester, M8 9WR UK
PH: 44-161-202-0035 FX: 44-161-202-0035
Steve Beer steve.beer@dontstoptheflow.co.uk
www.dontstoptheflow.co.uk
Recording label specialising in Hip Hop and Urban Pop.

Rap and Soul Mail Order
PO Box 60201, London, EC1P 1QZ UK
PH: 020-7713-0912 FX: 020-7833-2611
james@rapandsoulmailorder.com
www.rapandsoulmailorder.com
Will sell your CD online for a low cost.

Jam Band

Harmonized Records
6520 Oak Grove Church Rd. Mebane, NC 27302
PH: 919-304-9931
www.harmonizedrecords.com
Our goal is to team up with talented hard-working musicians and help them build their careers through a realistic record label/artist relationship.

Home Grown Music Network
PO Box 340, Mebane, MN 27302
PH: 919-563-4923
leeway@homegrownmusic.net
www.homegrownmusic.net
Promotes the best indie music being made today.

Sunshine Daydream CDs & Gifts
2027 E. Euclid Ave. Mt. Prospect, IL 60056
PH: 847-299-2622
customerservice@sunshinedaydream.biz
www.sunshinedaydream.biz
New & used CD retail store that specializes in Jam Band music.

Jazz

Abstract Logix
103 Sarabande Dr. Cary, NC 27513
PH: 919-342-5700
webmaster@abstractlogix.com
abstractlogix.com
The center of the new musical universe!

AppleJazz
10825 Wheaton Ct. Orlando, FL 32821
PH: 888-241-2464
info@applejazz.com
www.applejazz.com
Offering online sales of Jazz CDs for indie artists.

ArtistShare
info@artistshare.com
www.artistshare.net
Nominated for Record Label of the Year by the Jazz Journalists Association.

Blue Canoe Records
17 Timberlake Cove, Cartersville, GA 30121-5200
www.bluecanoerecords.com
If your music is Jazz, Jam Band, Progressive, Fusion, Avant-garde or fits under the "umbrella of Jazz", you should consider submitting your music to us. We only accept CDs from our staff producers and through our partnership with www.SonicBids.com

Counterpoint Music
PO Box 25093, Fresno, CA 93729-5093
PH: 559-225-7801 FX: 559-225-7801
info@counterpoint-music.com
www.counterpoint-music.com
Specialists in Jazz CDs!

InterJazz
9 Ridge Way, Purdys, NY 10578
PH: 914-277-7775
support@interjazz.com
www.interjazz.com
Your online connection to everything Jazz.

The Jazz Loft
14115 NE 2ⁿᵈ St., Bellevue, WA 98007
PH: 425-646-6406
www.jazzloft.com
Your online resource for truly independent Jazz!

Jazz 'n' Soul Music
jazz-n-soulmusic.com
Dutch online store featuring Jazz and Soul CDs.

JAZZCORNER.com
245 W. 25ᵗʰ St., New York, NY 10001
www.jazzcorner.com
News, reviews, interviews, web hosting.

ropeadope
andy@ropeadope.com
www.ropeadope.com
If you'd like to submit artwork, videos, audio mixes, editorial, e-mail them to us.

Utopia Records
PO Box 660-100, Flushing, NY 11366
PH: 718-418-7200 FX: 718-418-5696
Alfonzo Blackwell interns@UtopiaRecordings.com
utopiarecordings.com
Releasing promising Jazz artists that will bring great music and a legacy that will last a lifetime.

The Netherlands

Evil Rabbit Records
Van Spilbergenstraat 80hs, 1057 RL Amsterdam,
The Netherlands
PH: +31 20 6164558 FX: +31 20 6164558
Meinrad Kneer & Albert van Veenendaal
mail@evilrabbitrecords.eu
www.evilrabbitrecords.eu
Independent label for honest and authentic Improvised music and Contemporary Jazz, rooted in the European music tradition.

United Kingdom

Jazz CDs
Christine Allen christine@jazzcds.co.uk
www.jazzcds.co.uk
Many of our Jazz CDs are normally only available at gigs or at a limited range of specialist Jazz record stores.

Latin

Barrio Records
PO Box 230801, Boston, MA 02123
info@barriorecords.com
www.barriorecords.com
Source for Latin music. Accepts submissions.

DESCARGA.com
328 Flathbush Ave. #180, Brooklyn, NY 11238
PH: 718-693-2966 FX: 718-693-1316
info@descarga.com
www.descarga.com
The ultimate source for Latin CDs.

Discuba
50 Richmond St. E. 2nd Fl. Toronto, ON M5C 1N7
PH: 416-981-3334 FX: 416-981-3355
discuba@microlatin.com
www.discuba.com
Cuban music shop.

Latin Cool Records
PH: 973-571-0848
David Wasserman latincool2@aol.com
www.latincool.com
Supports/sells Latin indie music.

Luna Musik Group
227 Rosewood Dr. Calhoun, GA 30701
PH: 706-624-3468 FX: 706-262-2937
Homero Luna info@lunamusicgroup.com
www.lunamusicgroup.com
We are a Latino record label, We do marketing for independent artists.

MaraRecords
www.mararecords.com
Brazilian LPs, Groove, Bossa, Jazz, Soul, Funk and rare records.

Tejanoclassics.com
PH: 281-355-0777
tejanoclassics@worldnet.att.net
www.tejanoclassics.com
An online music vendor for classic and current titles.

Tumi
8/9 New Bond St., Pl. Bath, BA1 1BH UK
PH: 44-0-1225-464736 FX: 44-0-1225-444870
info@tumimusic.com
www.tumimusic.com
Website and record label for Latin American and Caribbean music.

Metal

United States

Apocrypha Records
PO Box 2570, San Francisco, CA 94126
PH: 503-616-3247 FX: 914-560-5343
John MacMurphy info@apocrypharecords.com
www.apocrypharecords.com
Metal only record company that provides label and distribution services for artists and other labels.

Beowolf Productions
PO Box 731, Phoenixville, PA 19460
Burt Wolf beowolfco@aol.com
www.myspace.com/beowolfproductions
Covers all styles of Extreme music.

Black Sheep Records
2220 NW Market St. Ste. L-11, Ballard, WA 98107
PH: 206-201-2520
LL elleelle@blacksheeprecords.us
www.blacksheeprecords.us
We are an Extreme Metal record label looking for talent.

Brutal Noise Music Co.
PO Box 6827, San Juan, Puerto Rico 00914-6827
PH: 787-525-4545 FX: 787-948-5851
www.brutalnoise.com
Promoting bands and creating awareness in the difficult world of music business.

Chunksofmeat Records CD Store
4640 Demaree Ct. House Springs, MO 63051
PH: 636-226-7032
Lee lees@chunksofmeat.com
www.chunksofmeatrecords.com
Online store selling CDs for independent musicians.

BlackMetal.Com Records
PO Box 12635, Casa Grande, AZ 85230
PH: 520-421-1208 FX: 520-421-1208
Elden M. support@blackmetal.com
www.blackmetal.com
Send promotional copies to the above address. For retail consideration (once the band or label's sample has been approved), our terms preferred are either consignment or trade against our label's own releases.

Metal Mayhem
32 Lanthorne Rd. Monroe, CT 06468
PH: 203-261-9536
info@metalmayhem.com
www.metalmayhem.com
Indie Bands, send us your CDs!

Nightmare Records & Distribution
7751 Greenwood Dr. St. Paul, MN 55112
PH: 763-784-9654 FX: 763-784-7914
www.nightmare-records.com
A label and distributor of indie based Melodic Hard Rock.

Screaming Ferret Wreckords
PO Box 56, Hillsboro, NH 03244
PH: 603-770-0648
info@screamingferret.com
www.screamingferret.com
Accepts all styles of Metal for review and sales.

Strictly Heavy Management
132 S. Harrison St., Easton, MD 21601
PH: 410-822-5074
Mark J. Burke mrmarkburke@hotmail.com
www.myspace.com/strictlyheavyptl
Our management team offers representation to up & coming artists in most genres (heavy music preferred). Our contracts are set up to support the artist's career goals, without "breaking the bank" (unlike management clearing houses.)

StrictlyRock.com
PO Box 909, Palm Desert, CA 92261-0909
steve@strictlyrock.com
www.strictlyrock.com
We're about selling Rock/Metal/Punk band's CDs to the WORLD!

Turkey Vulture Records
N2653 Millpond Rd. Brownsville, WI 53006
Jason Z. info@turkeyvulturerecords.com
www.turkeyvulturerecords.com
Metal, Hardcore and Rock record label.

Canada

Shrunken Head Records
PO Box 27014, Lakeport PO, 600 Ontario St.,
St. Catharines, ON L2N 7P8
James MacEachern
contact@shrunkenheadrecords.ca
www.myspace.com/shrunkenheadrecords
Even though we specialize primarily in Rock and Metal artists, you'll find excellent music from virtually every genre on our website. After all, great music is great music!

Cyprus

Pitch Black Records
PO Box 28522, Nicosia 2080, Cyprus
PH: +15302393055 FX: +15302393055
Phivos info@pitchblackrecords.com
www.pitchblackrecords.com
A Rock/Metal label driven by love and passion! Worldwide distribution and promotion.

Germany

Dr. Music Mailorder & Distribution
Intückenweg 13, 44289 Dortmund, Germany
Torsten Wohlgemuth doc@dr-music-mailorder.de
www.dr-music-mailorder.de
Rock & Metal distribution specialist for the European market. Cooperation with Omniamedi, CMS, Sony and DADC.

Limited Access Records
Intückenweg 13, 44289 Dortmund, Germany
Torsten Wohlgemuth contact@la-records.com
www.la-records.com
Stands for timeless Rock and Metal releases.

ZCM Records
Am Kesselhaus 9, 79576 Weil am Rhein, Germany
PH/FX: +49 (0) 76-21-1-67-79-50
www.zcmrecords.com
Independent Metal/Punk/Hardcore label, distro and mail order.

Spain

Inanna Naked
Apdo. de Correos 4233, 35080 Las Palmas de G.C.,
Las Palmas (Canary Islands), Spain
PH: 00-34-928-256593
Héctor Noble Fernández info@inannanaked.com
www.inannanaked.com
Promotion through our webzine and free compilation CDs network. Specialized in emotional, intense, dark, sad and melancholic music (all styles).

Mondongo Canibale
PO Box 27106, 28080 Madrid, Spain
info@mondongocanibale.com
www.mondongocanibale.com
Metal, Punk, HC and Rock distribution and record label. Please don't send MP3s!

United Kingdom

Rock Detector
PO Box 7556, Coalville, Leics, LE67 4WR UK
info@rockdetector.com
www.Rockdetector.com
If you have an independent CD you can now sell it here on the world's biggest Rock & Metal website.

Valley Of Death Records
13 Donald St., Abercanaid, Merthyr Tydfil,
Mid Glamorgan, CF48 1NX UK
Sean Jenkins sean0289@hotmail.com
www.valleyofdeath.co.uk
A d.i.y. label focusing mainly on Death Metal, Grindcore and other obscure genres.

Australia

Crusade Records
Level 8, 100 Walker St., North Sydney,
NSW 2060 Australia
PH: +61 (0)2-8404-4175 FX: +61 (0)2-8404-4170
Tom info@crusade.com.au
www.crusade.com.au
Houses Australian and international bands in Metal, Hardcore and Rock genres. Bands – head over to our Demos page to submit your demo via the online submission form.

New Age

A Cup of Music
PO Box 15197, San Diego, CA 92175
info@acupofmusic.com
www.acupofmusic.com
Relaxing music for the world!

GROOVE Unlimited
PO Box 2171, 8203 AD Lelystad, The Netherlands
PH: 31-0-320-219496 FX: 31-0-320-218910
info@groove.nl
www.groove.nl
We have a large diversity of New Age, Synth, Spacerock etc.

Hearts of Space
305 W. 71st St., New York, NY 10023
PH: 212-580-9200 FX: 212-580-9233
help@hos.com
www.hos.com
Submit material for the record label.

LuxMusica Records
5841 Overbrook Ave. Philadelphia, PA 19131
PH: 215-477-9985 FX: 215-879-1457
Jamey Reilly jreilly@virtualux.com
www.luxmusica.com
Peaceful heart, Quiet mind. Exceptional music from around the world that celebrates the light of eternal truth in its many forms.

Music "à la Carte"
1111 Coolamon Scenic Dr. Mullumbimby,
NSW 2482 Australia
PH: 61-2-66843143 FX: 61-2-66843144
www.musicalacarte.net
International indie music store for soothing sounds.

Music Design
Attn: New Title Dept.
4650 N. Port Washington Rd. Milwaukee, WI 53212
PH: 414-961-8380 FX: 414-961-8681
order@musicdesign.com
www.musicdesign.com
The premier wholesaler of music and self-help recordings into non-traditional markets.

NewAgeMusic.com
8033 Sunset Blvd. #472, Hollywood, CA 90046
PH: 323-851-3355 FX: 323-851-7981
info@newagemusic.com
www.newagemusic.com
Production, packaging, marketing and promotion.

The Night Cafe
PH: 0870-896-5779
questions@nightcafe.co.uk
www.nightcafe.co.uk
Distributor of relaxing late night music with a high "chill out" factor. We also sell CDs by independent artists covering most genres.

Silver Wave Records
PO Box 7943, Boulder, CO 80306
PH: 303-443-5617 FX: 303-443-0877
info@silverwave.com
www.silverwave.com
Independent label producing Native American, New Age and World music.

Progressive Rock

AOR Heaven
Landshuter Strasse 11, 84051 Altheim, Germany
PH: 49-8703-8517 FX: 49-8703-8568
Georg georg.siegl@aorheaven.com
www.aorheaven.com
If you have a demo feel free to contact us.

CD Inzane
PO Box 136, Albertville, MN 55301
www.cdinzane.com
Promotion is what makes a band "become" and we are here to help!!!

Kinesis CDs
PO Box 586, Hanover, MD 21076-0586
Larry Kolota info@kinesiscd.com
www.kinesiscd.com
A CD label and mail order specializing in Progressive, Symphonic and Art Rock.

InsideOut Music Europe
Landwehr 4-6, D-47533 Kleve, Germany
PH: +49 2821/979 12 0 FX: +49 2821/979 12 40
www.insideout.de
It would be helpful to e-mail us in advance including a link to your website and to MP3s.

New Horizons Music
4 Rosehill Close, Penistone, Sheffield, S36 6UF UK
PH: +44 (0)1226 762679
Rory Ridley-Duff music@roryridleyduff.com
www.newhorizonsmusic.co.uk
Independent label promoting and seeking Progressive Rock albums for worldwide physical and digital distribution channels.

Punk

United States

Blackened Distribution
PO Box 8722, Minneapolis, MN 55408
PH: 612-722-1134 FX: 612-722-1134
www.profaneexistence.com
Making Punk a threat again!

Double Crown Records
PO Box 4336, Bellingham, WA 98227-4336
Sean Berry records@dblcrown.com
www.dblcrown.com
Surf and Garage Rock label, with an online catalog.

Embryo Records
1655 S. Mojave Rd. Las Vegas, NV 89104
PH: 702-210-5081
www.embryorecords.net
A new breed has arrived. Metal - Hardcore - Rock - Industrial - Punk.

Epitaph Records
2798 Sunset Blvd. Los Angeles, CA 90026
PH: 213-413-7353
Hilary Villa publicity@epitaph.com
www.epitaph.
Post your link. Accepts demos. Keep it Punk!

Eyeball Records
70 E. Ridgewood Ave. 2nd Fl. Ridgewood, NJ 07450
Marc Debiak info@eyeballrecords.com
www.eyeballrecords.com
Please don't be afraid to send us any questions, but if they are stupid we're going to pass them around the office and make fun of you, so choose wisely.

Fall Records
PO Box 20886, Baltimore, MD 21209
info@fallrecords.com
www.fallrecords.com
An independent record label featuring Indie, Rock, Punk and so on.

Fat Wreck Chords
PO Box 193690, San Francisco, CA 94119
mailbag@fatwreck.com
www.fatwreck.com
Punk Rock record label features MP3s, videos, e-cards and more. Send demos to the above address.

Halogen Media Works
PO Box 128, Montpelier, VT 05602
Justin Hoy info@halogenmediaworks.com
www.halogenrecordsvt.blogspot.com
Record label, marketing, development and distribution.

Hill Billy Stew Records
PO Box 82625, San Diego, CA 92138-2625
Lee xhillxbillyx@hotmail.com
www.hillbillystew.com
Record label that puts out music by Indie Rock, Punk, Folk and Country artists.

Interpunk
PO Box 651328, Potomac Falls, VA 20165-1328
sales@interpunk.com
www.interpunk.com
Punk bands worldwide. Submit your CDs.

Lumberjack Mordam Music
5920 American Rd. E., Toledo, OH 43612
PH: 419-726-3930 FX: 419-726-3935
www.lumberjackmordam.com
We distribute labels. We don't work directly with artists.

Matchbox Records
198 E. Park Ave. Flushing, MI 48433
PH: 810-423-1711
info@matchboxrecords.com
www.matchboxrecords.com
An independent record label for Rock, Alt, Punk, Metal type genres.

Nightmare Records
2447 Tiffin Ave. #206, Findlay, OH 45840
info@nightmarerecords.biz
www.myspace.com/thenightmarerecords
An indie record label with offices in Hollywood, CA and Findlay, OH. Please e-mail us a link to you're MySpace along with your touring history. Please do not send us MP3s via e-mail.

Quote Unquote Records
info@quoteunquoterecords.com
www.quoteunquoterecords.com
A donation-based record label. We have simple goals which is to put out good music, put out fun music and help our artists get heard.

Radical Records
77 Bleecker St. #C2-21, New York, NY 10012
PH: 212-475-1111 FX: 212-475-3676
keith@radicalrecords.com
www.radicalrecords.com
NYC indie label seeks Punk, Hardcore bands and the like.

RevHQ.com
PO Box 5232, Huntington Beach, CA 92615-5232
PH: 714-842-7584
feedback@revhq.com
www.revhq.com
The best source for independent music.

Rumble Club Records
9 E. 15th St., Covington, KY 41011
PH: 859-491-2835
info@rumbleclubrecords.com
www.rumbleclubrecords.com
Independent record label specializing in Rockabilly, Psychobilly and Punk.

Slackertone Records
PO Box 5633, Salem, OR 97304
Casper Adams info@slackertone.com
www.slackertone.com
Focusing on Rock, Punk and Americana artists who aren't afraid to work and play hard. No slackers allowed!

Smartpunk
11783 Cardinal Cir. Garden Grove, CA 92843
PH: 714-638-7451 x406
www.smartpunk.com
Punk, Emo, Hardcore, Metal and Indie music store.

Takeover Records
PO Box 41070, Long Beach, CA 90853-4107
PH: 661-333-5461
www.myspace.com/takeoverrecords
A highly active/involved Rock/Pop Punk/everything & anything melodic record label.

Unfun Records
PO Box 40307, Berkeley, CA 94704
PH: 408-344-0402 FX: 408-253-1653
unfunrecords.com
Label dealing with mainly Rock, Punk, Hardcore and Electronica genres. We offer distribution for non-label artists as well.

Vagrant Records
2118 Wilshire Blvd. #361, Santa Monica, CA 90403
info@vagrant.com
www.vagrant.com
Indie and Punk Rock record label.

Vamped Records
17442 Apex Circle, Huntington Beach, CA 92647
PH: 714-552-4244
Herbie Headkick vampedrecords@yahoo.com
www.myspace.com/vampedrecord
Original Indie, Punk, Experimental, Gothic, Garage, Rock record label, management company, future web and television show. Original acts wanted.

Zero Youth Records
1975 S. Maple Tree Ln. Bolivar, MO 65613
PH: 417-326-8308
Matt Oldenburg info@zeroyouthrecords.com
www.zeroyouthrecords.com
Label that actively puts out CDs from bands in the Punk and Psychobilly genres ...but we're open to others.

Canada

Steel Capped Records
301-1670 Fort St., Victoria, BC V8R 1H9
PH: 250-514-8434
www.myspace.com/steelcappedrecords
Independent label focusing on the Punk/Oi/Streetpunk scene.

Year of the Sun Enterprises
3-304 Stone Rd. W. #520, Guelph, ON N1G 4W4
PH: 519-830-9687
Chris Benn contact@yearofthesun.com
www.yearofthesun.com
Punk, Alternative and Metal. We're always looking to expand our roster with new and exciting bands and artists.

France

Walked in line Records
B.P.04 - 60840 Breuil le Sec, France
PH: 03-44-50-23-63
www.wilrecords.com
The French Underground label.

Germany

Ebus Music
Bottenhorner Weg 37, 60489 Frankfurt, Germany
PH: +49 (0) 69-787-113 FX: +49 (0) 69-789-58-70
Carsten Mr. Ebu Olbrich Mr.Ebu@ebusmusic.com
www.ebusmusic.com
Established on earth since 1988 - label - broadcasting - mailorder - artist's club in Frankfurt.

unterm durchschnitt
PO Box 19 04 71, D-50501 Köln, Germany
PH: +0049 (0) 2234-91-45-95
info@unterm-durchschnitt.com
www.unterm-durchschnitt.de
A DIY Indie Rock, Stoner, Grunge, Garage, Punk label.

Wolverine Records
Im Huckinger Kamp 43a, 47259 Duisburg, Germany
PH: 0203-6082921 FX: 0203-6082923
sascha@wolverine-records.de
www.wolverine-records.de
Germany's finest independent Punk, Ska and Swing label.

Italy

For Monsters Records
Roberto formonstersrecords@yahoo.com
www.myspace.com/formonstersrecords
Obscure Garage Punk label from the island of Sardinia (Italy). Putting out raw vinyl for cavemen to dig on old records players.

Sweden

Zorch Productions
Klostergatan 7-9, s70361, Orebro, Sweden
www.myspace.com/zorchproductions
Scandinavia's finest Punk, Rock and Garage vinyl provider.

Switzerland

Lux.-NOISE Productions
Steinengraben 30, CH-4058 Basel, Switzerland
PH: 41-61-271-39-05
Michael Hediger info@luxnoise.com
www.luxnoise.com
Record label & promotion company. Alternative/Garage-Rock! NO ELECTRONIC-stuff.

United Kingdom

FFRUK.com
BCM Box 4664, London, WC1N 3XX UK
PH: 0207-100-3410 FX: 0870-199-2166
info@ffruk.com
www.ffruk.com
Online Punk record label promoting music, selling CDs and merchandise for Electronic and Punk Rock music.

ORG Records
19 Herbert Gardens, London, NW10 3BX UK
Sean organ@organart.demon.co.uk
www.organart.com
If your music is something that excites us then we'll be on the case. We're mostly interested in Punk, Metal, Alternative and Prog.

punkrockcds.com
PO Box 231, Dewsbury, WF13 4WW UK
www.punkrockcds.com
Punk, Oi and Hardcore.

Australia

Alien Punk Records
PO Box 113, Sanctuary Cove, QLD Australia 4212
PH: 0422463972 FX: 61-7-55778688
Tone Porno music@alienpunk.com.au
www.alienpunk.com.au
Indie record label and complete design service for music industry specialising in event promotions and band management. Actively seeking new talent.

Volume Overdose Records
126 Franklin Rd. Cherrybrook, Sydney, NSW Australia
C.J brokenheadboy@gmail.com
www.volumeoverdose.com
We are a record company that can sign you or do the artwork etc. for your music projects.

Reggae

Black Roots Online
The Basement, 301 Southend Ln. Catford, London, SE6 3ND UK
PH: 07050135444
www.blackroots.net
We have been producing and retailing Reggae music for over 25 years. Our online store is rapidly becoming the most stocked on the web.

Dubroom
www.dubroom.org
MP3s, reviews, forums and much more!

reggaeCD.com
229-19 Merrick Blvd. #237, Laurelton, NY 11413
PH: 718-362-1711 FX: 718-763-6241
www.reggaecd.com
Online Reggae CD, DVD, video, MP3, t-shirt and merchandise store.

Zionway Recordings
1027 Mahlon Ct. Lafayette, CO 80026
PH: 720-300-4264 FX: 303-443-8701
www.zionway.net
Record label, recording studio and producers of conscious Reggae and Hip Hop music.

Soul / R&B

United States

Dusty Groove America
Attn: Buyer
1120 N. Ashland Ave. Chicago, IL 60622
PH: 773-342-5800 FX: 773-342-2180
dga@dustygroove.com
www.dustygroove.com
We tend to only stock music we love and music that we feel fits into our rather narrow format.

Groove Distribution
346 N. Justine St. #202, Chicago, IL 60607
PH: 312-997-2375 x123 FX: 312-997-2382
Dirk van den Heuvel dirkv@groovedis.com
www.groovedis.com
The main thing is that you must fit our kind of music (Loungey Dance music—with a Jazz or Soul influence) AND we have to think we can sell you — which means you have to be REALLY good. Singles are FAR easier to pick up than a full CD (and by single I do mean a 12" VINYL single not a CD single).

It's Soul Time! Records
PO Box 572, Ridgewood, NJ 07451-0572
andy@itssoultime.com
www.itssoultime.com
Focusing on Soul and R&B.

Quinn Records
PO Box 771693, St. Louis, MO 63177
PH: 314-802-7550 FX: 314-802-7550
store@quinnrecords.com
www.quinnrecords.com
Label and distributor of Blues, Gospel, Jazz and Soul music.

Sound Mindz Entertainment
702 2nd Ave. N., Birmingham, AL 35203
PH: 205-252-5587 FX: 205-397-0320
Tony Gideon soundmindz@soundmindzmusic.com
www.soundmindzmusic.com
We are a record company interested in R&B, Blues and Black Gospel.

Voice Distributions
PO Box 537, New York, NY 10018
Maurice mauricewatts@mauricewatts.com
www.VoiceDistributions.com
Home of the best R&B, Soul and Classic music.

Canada

SoMuchSoul Records
2187 Birchleaf Ln. Burlington, ON L7L 6G8
PH: 905-334-2527
Alex Brans info@somuchsoul.com
www.somuchsoul.com
Promotes great music from talented artists. Funk, Jazz, Soul Grooves, Rock ...we cover it all!

United Kingdom

Acid Jazz Records
146 Bethnal Green Rd. London, E2 6DG UK
PH: 020-7613-1100
info@acidjazz.co.uk
www.acidjazz.co.uk
Acid jazz is the new Soul, anything with its head and mind in the history and the feet to the dance floor, eyes to the future. Send demos to the above address.

Crazy Beat Records
87 Corbets Tey Rd. Upminster, Essex, RM14 2AH UK
PH: 01708-228678 FX: 01708-640946
sales@crazybeat.co.uk
www.crazybeat.co.uk
Are you an artist or a distributor that has something hot that you think we should be promoting, then please get in touch or better still send us a sample. We carry Soul, Jazz, Funk, House, Garage, Dance etc.

Soul Brother Records
1 Keswick Rd. E. Putney, London, SW15 2HL UK
PH: 020-8875-1018 FX: 020-8871-0180
soulbrothers@soulbrother.com
www.soulbrother.com
We're specialists for new independent Soul and Jazz CDs as well as a good source for rare original vinyl LP's and 12" singles.

Japan

Totown Records
Tamari 30-1, Kakegawa City, Shizuoka Prefecture, Japan 436-0011
PH/FX: 81-537-23-7585
Malcolm W. Adams info@totown.net
www.totown.net/totownrecords.htm
Originators of the Nu-Jazz-Funk. Dedicated to producing and marketing the highest quality world-class entertainment products in the Asia Pacific region.

Women In Music

Angelic Music
PO Box 61, East Molesey, KT8 6BA UK
Janis Haves info@angelicmusic.co.uk
www.angelicmusic.co.uk
A recording, publishing and meeting place to promote female artists.

Benten Records
3F Ebisu West, 1-16-15, Ebisu-Nishi, Shibuya-ku, Tokyo 150-0021 Japan
benten@sister.co.jp
www.sister.co.jp/english
Japanese label specializing in female artists of many genres.

chicks on speed records
Rosenthaler Strasse 3, 10119, Berlin, Germany
PH: 0049-30-27-89-05-24 FX: 0049-30-27-89-05-25
promo@chicksonspeed-records.com
www.chicksonspeed.com
Promotes Electronic female musicians. Visit our site for submission details.

Daemon Records
PO Box 1207, Decatur, GA 30031
Attn: A&R
hello@daemonrecords.com
www.daemonrecords.com
Indie label covering Southeastern US.

Female Musician
www.femalemusician.com
Offering virtual performances and promotional opportunities for music-minded women.

Goldenrod Music
1310 Turner St., Lansing, MI 48906
PH: 517-484-1712 FX: 517-484-1771
music@goldenrod.com
www.goldenrod.com
Full service center for indie artists with a focus on women.

Harmony Ridge Music
123 Bonita, Moss Beach, CA 94018
PH: 650-563-9280 FX: 650-563-9266
hrmusic@hrmusic.com
www.hrmusic.com
Dedicated to female Singer/Songwriters.

Kill Rock Stars
120 NE. State Ave. PMB 418, Olympia, WA 98501
krs@killrockstars.com
www.killrockstars.com
Send us your demo tapes!!

Ladyslipper.org
PO Box 3124, Durham, NC 27715
PH: 800-634-6044 FX: 919-383-3525
info@ladyslipper.org
www.ladyslipper.org
Our purpose is to further new musical and artistic directions for women musicians.

On the Rag Records
PO Box 251, Norco, CA 92860-0251
PH: 909-273-1402 FX: 909-478-5208
Renae Bryant webmistress@ontherag.net
www.ontherag.net
Female owned and operated record label that puts out female fronted and all gal Punk and Hardcore bands. This is a diy operation...the little engine that could.

panx
BP 15058-31033 Toulouse, France
PH: 33-0-561612145 FX: 33-0-561114895
infos@panx.net
www.panx.net
Hardcore, Punk, CyberThrash, Grindcore, TechnoBruit, Crades Mélodies.

Sonic Cathedral
PO Box 8505, Baltimore, MD 21234
s.c.onlinesoniccathedral.com
www.soniccathedral.com
Specializing in female vocal Metal.

World

African Allstars
4325 Roosevelt Hwy. College Park, GA 30349
PH: 404-684-9955
www.panafricanallstars.com
We feature the best African music on the web.

Deep Down Productions
3-182 Wright Ave. Toronto, ON M6R 1L2
PH: 416-535-5247
info@deepdownproductions.com
www.deepdownproductions.com
Promotes Traditional music from around the world.

Earth Vibe Music
PO Box 5007, Brighton, BN50 9DS UK
PH: 0870-350-9407 FX: 0871-661-5556
contact@earthvibemusic.com
www.earthvibemusic.com
Promoting music from indie bands and musicians.

Fast Lane International
4856 Haygood Rd. Virginia Beach, VA 23455
PH: 757-497-2669 FX: 757-497-5159
info@fastlaneintl.com
www.fastlaneintl.com
Promotes shows and brokers for artists worldwide.
Worldbeat and Fusion, Reggae, Ska, Dance and
Alternative Rock.

Music Yogi
#98-98/1, 3rd Fl. S. P. Rd. Bangalore, India - 560 002
PH: 009-80-41224526
www.musicyogi.com/asp/independents.asp
Online Store that features indies from India. Users
can sample their music and buy their CDs.

New World Music
PO Box 3090, Ashland, OR 97520
PH: 800-771-0987
www.newworldmusic.com
We only release a very few carefully selected albums
every year. Please visit our site for submission
details.

Onzou Records
2444 Benny Cres. #110, Montreal, QC H4B 2R3
PH/FX: 514-485-0728
info@onzou.com
www.onzou.com
Producing traditional West African music.

Putamayo World Music
411 Lafayette St. 4th Fl. New York, NY 10003
Jacob Edgar info@putumayo.com
www.putumayo.com
Music of other cultures. Submit demos.

Rhyme Records
1 Jackson Dr. N., Poughkeepsie, NY 12603
PH: 845-462-3450 FX: 845-463-7664
Probir K. Ghosh probir@rhymerecords.com
www.rhymerecords.com
Our focus is to promote the rich musical heritage of
India.

World Music Store
56 Browns Mill Rd. Montpelier, VT 05602
PH: 802-223-1294 FX: 802-229-1834
support@worldmusicstore.com
www.worldmusicstore.com
Traditional and Contemporary World music.

Zook Beat
info@zookbeat.com
www.zookbeat.com
Check out up and coming artists and all time
favorites!!

Sign up for

The Indie Contact Newsletter

www.indiebible.com

PLANNING A TOUR?

32,000 Live Music Venues
in the US and Canada!!

Whether you're playing around town or planning a national tour, we can help you find the perfect fit! Thousands of venues in every major city and ALL points in between!

clubs   colleges   festivals   coffee shops   halls   bookstores
open mics   churches   record stores   community centers
restaurants   house concerts   jams   booking agents

www.IndieVenueBible.com

SECTION SIX: SITES THAT WILL ALLOW YOU TO UPLOAD YOUR MUSIC OR VIDEO FILES

Digital Music Distributors and Services

CD Baby Digital Distribution
5925 NE. 80th Ave. Portland, OR 97218-2891
PH: 503-595-3000
cdbaby@cdbaby.com
cdbaby.net/dd
You keep all the rights to your music. You just lend us the right to be your digital distributor: to get your music to legitimate music services like Apple iTunes, Rhapsody, Napster, MSN Music, MP3tunes, Yahoo MusicMatch and more!

FoxyMelody Digital Distribution
1610 W. 7th St. #312, Los Angeles, CA 90017
PH: 310-857-6686 FX: 408-676-0985
www.foxymelody.com
Digital distribution for indie labels/artists. Sell your music on the world's best online retailers.

HIP Video Promo
2 Draeger Pl., South River, NJ 08882
PH: 732-613-1779
Andy Gesner hipvideo@aol.com
www.hipvideopromo.com
We can get your video to the outlets most likely to share and appreciate your own musical and visual aesthetic.

Independent Digital Entertainment & Arts
IDEA
28 Locust St. #303, Brooklyn, NY 11206
Alfredo Cabeza contact@ideadistributors.com
www.ideadistributors.com
Music and video distribution to the leading online services such as iTunes, Napster, Rhapsody etc.

INgrooves
539 Bryant St. #400, San Francisco, CA 94107
PH: 415-896-2100 FX: 415-896-2220
submissions@ingrooves.com
www.ingrooves.com
Signing content from the best established and emerging artists from around the world and serving as their digital record company (distribution, marketing, promotion, licensing).

IODA
539 Bryant St. #303, San Francisco, CA 94107
PH: 415-777-4632
Vivek info@IODAlliance.com
www.iodalliance.com
We distribute music from independent labels, but typically don't work with individual artists. Artists signed to independent labels should have their labels contact us.

Musicadium
#4, 29/25 James St., Fortitude Valley, Brisbane, QLD, 4006 Australia
PH: +61-7-3252-9962
info@musicadium.com
www.musicadium.com
We supply music to digital download stores around the world including iTunes, eMusic and more.

One Stop Shop Media
Truman Brewery, 91 Brick Ln. London, E1 6QL UK
info@onestopshopsos.com
www.onestopshopsos.com
We're a one stop shop for digital services such as distribution, online marketing, viral campaigns, mobile licensing & distribution etc.

The Orchard
100 Park Ave. 17th Fl. New York, NY 10003
PH: 212-201-9280 FX: 212-201-9203
info@theorchard.com
www.theorchard.com
Supplier for North American digital music as well as the leading European DMS providers.

PassAlong Networks
230 Franklin Rd. Ste. 11-JJ, Franklin, TN 37064
PH: 615-425-5800
support@passalong.com
www.passalongnetworks.com
Building a foundation for the next wave of digital entertainment distribution, consumption and communication, while ensuring our infrastructure will be flexible enough to support future demands and trends.

RocMP3
PO Box 670718, Flushing, NY 11367
PH: 718-502-9134
info@rocmp3.com
www.rocmp3.com
We are an online music distribution site and we also provide the opportunity for artists to earn residual income by network marketing.

SongCast
2926 State Rd. #111, Cuyahoga Falls, OH 44223
info@songcastmusic.com
www.songcastmusic.com/promo
One of the World's largest distributors of independent music. We have deals with iTunes, Rhapsody, Amazon, Emusic and Napster, allowing us to put our artists' music in front of millions of music buying consumers. With SongCast, you can start selling your own music on these major retail sites right away. We also provide you with customized code to link your MySpace and other websites directly to the stores. Your fans will easily be able to find and purchase your music online. Combined with the power and social phenomenon of sites like MySpace and Facebook, it is no longer necessary to give away your musical freedom to a major record label. ENTER PROMO CODE 673

StreamerNet
PH: 800-930-8202
info@streamernet.com
www.streamernet.com
Enables content owners to distribute live performances in a uniquely branded delivery environment through revenue producing Virtual Ticket Sales.

Tone Box Digital
thedigital@toneboxdigital.com
www.toneboxdigital.com
Digital distribution and online marketing for indie bands and labels

TuneCore
20 Jay St. #7A2, Brooklyn, NY 11201
PH: 646-651-1060
info@tunecore.com
www.tunecore.com
Distribution service that gets music you created up for sale on iTunes and Rhapsody without asking for your rights or taking any money from the sale.

Vision Promotions
22 Upper Grosvenor St., London, W1K 7PE UK
PH: 44 (0)207-199-0101
vision@visionmusic.co.uk
www.visionmusic.co.uk
Music PR / promotional services: press / radio / DJ promotion for albums / singles / labels / events + artists digital / online marketing / podcast production / video + audio streaming / encoding video production / artwork / web design / online / mobile solutions through our sister company - www.commotionstudios.com dj / artist / remix booking agency / TV & film placement of music for sync licensing.

Digital Music Sites

Getting your music onto the sites listed in this section varies a great deal cost-wise. Many services will allow you to upload your files for free, while others charge a fee or percentage from each sale that you make. Be wary of large setup fees. Many of the Online Digital Stores deal only with Digital Distribution Services such as CD Baby or The Orchard to get their indie music. I have indicated which stores deal only with Distributors throughout this Section. There are also many MP3 Audioblog sites listed that will post your music (if they like it) for a week or two in order to help promote your music. You will also find many social networking sites in SECTION 7 – ONLINE COMMUNITIES that will allow you to upload your music and video files.

All Styles
North America
United States

1 Cubed
www.1cubed.com
Music video show with music news and features from around the World.

Acid Planet
PH: 608-256-5555 FX: 608-250-1745
www.acidplanet.com
Artist profile for uploading songs and writing reviews. Now featuring weekly podcasts.

AirSpun
3182 Campus Dr. #363, San Mateo, CA 94403
PH: 650-266-9254
info@airspun.com
www.airspun.com
Offers innovative online and offline marketing services for digital media artists.

Algeka
info@algeka.com
www.algeka.com
The home for unsigned Singer-Songwriters to post music videos. It's part singing competition, part online video site and home of the coolest emerging music videos in the world.

Amazon MP3
amazonmp3.com
Please note that Amazon MP3 is currently only available to US customers.

American Idol Underground
5813-A Uplander Way, Culver City, CA 90230
info@idolunderground.com
www.idolunderground.com
An online community where emerging artists get their music heard and fans discover new music.

Amie Street
Joshua Boltuch josh@amiestreet.com
www.amiestreet.com
Artists upload their music at no charge, which immediately goes up for sale in the marketplace. All songs start free on Amie Street and rise in price the more popular they become. This community based pricing model is designed to encourage members to discover new music and act as a promotional and marketing tool for artists.

Apple's iTunes Music
www.apple.com/itunes
Songs must be delivered through a Digital Music Distributor such as www.cdbaby.com or www.theorchard.com.

Apollo Tunes
feedback@apollotunes.com
www.apollotunes.com
A download site for unsigned musicians with higher yields as well as signed bands looking for a more profitable approach. Dedicated to promoting the unsung hero the local musician.

Artistopia
12955 Buck Board Ct. Woodbridge, VA 22192
www.artistopia.com
Professional presentation of the music artist to the music industry, with comprehensive profile and press kit building tools.

Artist Weekly
10740 N. 56th St. #195, Tampa, FL 33617
ArtistWeekly.com
Post as many original songs as you like for five bucks each and you will automatically be entered into our weekly contest.

ARTISTdirect
1601 Cloverfield Blvd. #400 S.
Santa Monica, CA 90404
listen.artistdirect.com
Showcases downloads from independent bands.

Artistic Pursuit
www.artisticpursuit.com
An online social-networking web venue for artists to display and get paid for their MP3s and videos.

ArtistServer.com
www.artistserver.com
Supporting independent music! ARTISTS, get involved, be heard, get feedback - we have the technology!

AT&T Wireless Ringtones
www.wireless.att.com/learn/ringtones-downloads/tones-graphics/ringtones.jsp
Songs must be delivered through a Digital Music Distributor www.theorchard.com.

Audio Lunchbox
1021 N. Sepulveda Blvd. Ste. R
Manhattan Beach, CA 90266
PH: 310-946-1004
support@audiolunchbox.com
www.audiolunchbox.com
We accept music from labels, distributors and individual unsigned artists.

AudioCandy.com
www.audiocandy.com
Song files are supplied through LiquidAudio.com

AudioStreet.net
5422 NW. 50th Ct. Coconut Creek, FL 33073
audiostreet.net
Offers MP3 hosting, full artist pages with bios, reviews, event listings and much more.

The Band Universe
www.banduniverse.com
A free promotion engine for artists. You can enter bio, roster, gigs, recordings and MP3 audio.

BandChemistry.com
info@bandchemistry.com
www.BandChemistry.com
A musician's network, where you can make your band and find your sound!

BearShare
www.bearshare.com
File sharing system that promotes solid independent artists.

BeatBuggy
info@BeatBuggy.com
www.BeatBuggy.com
A place where you can decide which musician will become tomorrow's hit. That means you have the real voice – because our review system eliminates cheaters. Musicians get a fair shot!

BestBuy.com Digital Downloads
www.bestbuy.com
Songs must be delivered through the CD Baby Digital Music Distributor www.cdbaby.com

BETA Records
Box 48, Hollywood, CA 90028
PH: 877-232-2382
Christian office@betarecords.com
www.BetaRecords.com
An online record company that offers a free web page with song hosting, photos and e-mail, plus a free ringtone widget.

Beyond.fm
44 W. Jefryn Blvd. Unit Y, Deer Park, NY 11729
content@beyond.fm
beyond.fm
Inspiring and well-timed concept for exposing digital content to the masses and allowing artists, musicians and photographers to create awareness and new-found revenue streams.

Bitmunk
bitmunk.com
You set the amount of money you want to receive for each sale of your music, then different sellers can sell it for whatever price they want on top of that.

Blinkx.com
One Market Plaza, Spear Tower, 19th Fl.
San Francisco, CA 94105
PH: 415-848-2986
feedback@blinkx.com
www.Blinkx.com
If you have video content on your website or blog, we will automatically keep an eye on your feed, picking up new videos when you create them and automatically indexing them.

blip.tv
blip.tv
content@blip.tv
Our mission is to support you by taking care of all the problems a budding videoblogger, podcaster or internet TV producer tends to run into. We'll take care of the servers, the software, the workflow, the advertising and the distribution. We leave you free to focus on creativity.

blogTV.com
www.blogtv.com
A leader in online video and live broadcasting. Create LIVE video shows and chat with your audience. All you need is a webcam and an internet connection.

The Blue Comet Café
info@bluecometcafe.com
www.bluecometcafe.com
A virtual showcase club for on-the-verge touring and recording artists. Videotaped live, the Blue Comet's "Main Stage" artists play the best traditional venues in the country with new songs and interview segments rotated on a regular basis.

Blue Pie USA
1009 NW 11th Ave. Battle Ground, WA 98604
PH: 360-600-5443 FX: 360-326-1527
Julian Tagg sales@bluepie.com.au
www.mybluepiemusic.com
The online digital music service run by Blue Pie, one of Australia's leading independent labels.

bMuze
www.bmuze.com
A service that allows musicians, podcasters and other artists that create audio to upload and share their works with the world. It doesn't cost any money to join, listen to music, upload tracks, tag songs and organize your favorites.

Bolt
bolthelp@boltinc.com
www.bolt.com
A place where you can store, organize and share all the media you create in the course of your digital life.

Are you in a band? Are you a songwriter?

SELL YOUR MUSIC
on iTunes™ & amazonmp3™!

BONXO
150 Delmar Rd. Rochester, NY 14616
PH: 585-314-2826 FX: 585-458-9611
Dan Regna dan@bonxo.com
www.bonxo.com
An alternative avenue for artists to get their music heard. Our goal is to create a sub-culture of music that is not tainted by the giant corporate spinning wheel.

BooMP3
boomp3.com
Upload your music and podcasts to place it at your website, MySpace page, LiveJournal page or any blog.

Break.com
www.break.com
Thanks to Break, you don't need to be famous to create entertaining videos and have them distributed to millions.

Broadjam Download Store
6401 Odana Rd. Madison, WI 53719
PH: 608-271-3633
www.broadjam.com
Exposure is everything and the more places you can sell your music the better, right?

BuyMusic.com
85 Enterprise #100, Aliso Viejo, CA 92656
www.buymusic.com
Great option for the independent community.

Can You Hear Me TV
info@canyouhearme.tv
www.canyouhearme.tv
Free competitions in various cities give bands a shot to be on this show.

CDFreedom.com
47 Mellen St., Framingham, MA 01702
FX: 508-820-7920
www.cdfreedom.com
We take a smaller cut than most online distributors!

Cdigix
www.cdigix.com
Digital media provider to colleges and universities. Songs must be delivered through a Digital Music Distributor www.theorchard.com.

CDTV.NET
67 Wall St. 22nd Fl. New York, NY 10005
PH: 212-696-7890
www.cdtv.net
Accepts demo CDs/music videos from all genres.

Clear Channel NEW Music Network
newmusicnetwork@clearchannel.com
clearchannelnewmusicnetwork.com
Share your music with your fans and music industry professionals who want to find new, promising acts.

CollegeMusicRadio.com
management@collegemusicradio.com
CollegeMusicRadio.com
Visitors decide which songs get played on the our station. We want our listeners to have total control of the music.

Cool Music Zone
coolmusiczone@gmail.com
coolmusiczone.com
One of our moderators will take a look at your song and make it available to everyone on the net.

CornerWorld.com
www.cornerworld.com
Online musical forum for both independent and record-labeled musicians.

CraveFest
PH: 905-660-3110 x264
FX: 905-660-3108
Jason Sukhraj jason@cravefest.com
www.cravefest.com
Allows artists to upload their videos for free where the public then votes on them. The most popular videos qualify for a music video festival.

culturedeluxe
www.culturedeluxe.com
News, views, reviews, abuse ...

The Current Fix
118 King St., San Francisco, CA 94107
PH: 415-995-8200 FX: 415-995-8201
info@current.tv
www.current.tv/fix
A weekly five minute music podcast on Current TV showcasing bands on the rise. Exclusive interviews and fan-focused experiences from all genres of music.

Current TV
118 King St., San Francisco, CA 94107
PH: 415-995-8200 FX: 415-995-8201
info@current.tv
www.current.tv
Most of the content that airs comes in the form of what we call Pods; non-fiction and satirical shorts about what's going on in your world, from your perspective, and in your voice. Please note that at this time we do not accept trailers for longer documentaries/films, music videos or PSA's.

CYBERMIDI.com
PO Box 120040, Staten Island, NY 10312
PH: 800-987-6434
cybermidi.com
We've got your favorite songs in MIDI the way they were meant to be heard. Feel free to send us some samples of your work and we can talk about including them at Shop CYBERMIDI.

Dailymotion
www.dailymotion.com
About finding new ways to see, share and engage your world through the power of online video.

DecentXposure.com
411@decentxposure.com
DecentXposure.com
An indie magazine chock full of ringtones, downloads and other ways for fans and bands to get together.

DigStation
info@digstation.com
www.digstation.com
Your music is made available from our site for free when you replicate CDs through Discmakers or Oasis.

DigitalSoundboard.net
www.DigitalSoundboard.net
*Delivers *paid-for* MP3s and FLAC digital music files.*

DigiFreq Music Promotion
www.digifreq.com/digifreq/music.asp
Aims to help independent musicians gain some added exposure for their work. The title being submitted must be available for sale from either Amazon.com or CDBaby.com.

Digimusic TV
1138 N. Germantown Pkwy. #101-225
Cordova, TN 38016
PH: 901-830-5258
www.digimusictv.com
Brings interviews, educational information, history and events spanning across all genres to keep you in tune with the music community.

DigiPie
22647 Ventura Blvd. #145
Woodland Hills, CA 91364
PH: 818-713-1510
support@digipie.com
digipie.com
Offers creators/artists powerful tools to profit from their digital creations from A-Z built into our model and software.

Digital Freakz
109 Poe Ave. Poteau, OK 74953
PH: 918-649-0429
Kerry Plummer kman@digitalfreakz.com
www.digitalfreakz.com
The perfect freakin' solution for selling your CDs and downloads. Build your online community of artists, labels, friends and freakz.

DiscRevolt
320 Prospect Pl. Alpharetta, GA 30005
PH: 678-381-2700 FX: 678-381-2705
info@discrevolt.com
Provides physical solutions for digital delivery of media. For artists, DiscRevolt is a way to deliver DRM-free digital music through artist-specific download cards.

DMusic
101 Greenwood Ave. #200, Jenkintown, PA 19046
PH: 215-885-3302 FX: 215-885-3303
www.dmusic.com
Get your music played on our broadcasts.

Download.com Music
music.download.com
A free artist upload and download site that is part of Download.com.

DreamMakersMP3.com
453 River Styx Rd. Hopatcong, NJ 070843
PH: 973-398-8540 FX: 973-398–8526
info@dreammakersmp3.com
DreamMakersMP3.com
Bridging the gap between your music and your fans by providing artist-friendly, professional services.

Drulz.com
PH: 404-993-7018
www.drulz.com
Web community for independent artists providing the outlet they need to be heard globally via the internet. Artists can sell their MP3s.

Echoingwalls Music
571 Rock Pillar Rd. Clayton, NC 27520
PH: 877-505-0476 FX: 877-907-1941
www.echoingwalls.com
Aimed at helping new and struggling artists by providing resources.

Echospin
333 Hudson St., New York, NY 10013
PH: 212-994-0307 FX: 800-786-7738
www.echospin.com
Enables artists to sell and deliver music directly to their customers via a wide variety of distribution channels.

Fake Science
PO Box 10823, Oakland, CA 94610
www.fakescience.com
We are dedicated to making independent music available digitally and affordably.

FileFactory
www.filefactory.com
Free unlimited file hosting. Your file will remain on our servers forever, provided it has been downloaded at least once in the past 15 days.

Finetune.com
www.finetune.com
Currently, we only support music coming to us directly from the major record labels, as well as two independent music distributors (CD Baby and The Orchard). We are not yet accepting submissions from private resellers or individual artists - though we may someday offer that type of service.

Flotones
support@flotones.com
www.flotones.com
Sell mobile content to your fans and build new fans.

funender.com
www.funender.com
Will review your songs and give you more plays.

Fuse
11 Penn Plaza, 15th Fl. New York, NY 10001
PH: 212-324-3400 FX: 212-324-3445
fuseinfo@fuse.tv
www.fuse.tv
Submit your music and band info.

Fuseboard
support@fuseboard.com
www.fuseboard.com
Exists to provide a platform for artists to expand their music through collaboration and networking with other artists.

Fuzz Artists
602 20th St., San Francisco, CA 94107
support@fuzz.com
www.fuzz.com
Engages artists and fans to promote, discover, share, review, influence, buy and sell music.

garageband.com
1617 Boylston Ave. Seattle, WA 98122
www.garageband.com
Rewriting the rules about how the music industry operates.

GetPlayed.com
admin@getplayed.com
www.getplayed.com
A music community dedicated to providing amateur musicians with the thing they need most (aside from gear), a listening audience.

Gigga Music.com
PH: 954-937-3769
Mike Lewitt newmusic@giggamusic.com
www.giggamusic.com
The search for new undiscovered music starts here! Our site is intended to introduce our visitors to the latest in our search for great artists.

Google Video
https://upload.video.google.com
In addition to televised content, we'll also host video from anyone who wants to upload content to us.

GorillaPop
lance@gorillapop.com
www.gorillapop.com
Artists, add your songs and find new fans.

GreatIndieMusic.com
1534 Pennsylvania Ave. Monaca, PA 15061
info@greatindiemusic.com
www.GreatIndie.com
MP3 digital downloads from great independent artists.

Griffdog Records
17442 Apex Cir. Huntington Beach, CA 92647
PH: 714-375-6162
info@griffdogrecords.com
www.griffdogrecords.com
We are actively looking for new talent. Register on our website and make your music available for download.

Groove Mobile
www.groovemobile.net
Supplies full-length track downloads to some of Europe's leading mobile music services. Songs must be delivered through The Orchard's distribution service www.theorchard.com.

Groupie Tunes
3100 Main St. #349, Dallas, TX 75226
PH: 214-760-9977 FX: 214-742-1245
customerservice@groupietunes.com
www.GroupieTunes.com
A mobile community dedicated to create a real-time, direct relationship for fans with their favorite artists.

Hear Me Out
Jeff Toms mainstpl@hotmail.com
www.hear-me-out.net
Bringing musicians and artists an honest platform in order to be heard the world over!

Hitmusiclink.com
PO Box 241, Clifton, TX 76634
Duke Machado duke@hitmusiclink.com
www.hitmusiclink.com
With a worldwide network of artist managers, promoters, and booking agents, you are sure to find what you are looking for in our site.

HitQuarters
www.hitquarters.com
An A&R, record label, music publishing, artist manager and music industry directory. The success of our artists is very important to us; therefore our A&R team consider every submission carefully and listen thoroughly to all songs, since it is in our strong interest to supply the industry with talented artists.

Hollywood Music
admin@hollywoodmusic.tv
www.hollywoodmusic.tv
We're here to help all motivated and talented artists get the visibility they deserve. We offer artists the ability to upload their profile to our website.

HouseOfGigs.com
12157 W. Linebaugh #211, Tampa, FL 33626
PH: 888-260-3138 FX: 888-260-3138
houseofgigs@gmail.com
www.houseofgigs.com
Artists can set up gigs, post songs, buy and sell equipment, check out the latest music news and much more.

i think music
ithinkmusic.com
We take care of hosting, credit card payments and delivery of download music on behalf of its users giving them 95% of the list cost of their music.

iamusic.com
44 Music Sq. E. #503, Nashville, TN 37203
PH: 615-335-3262 FX: 215-895-9672
www.iamusic.com/add_your_music.php
For Instrumental music only!

iJamr
6297 Ball Rd. Cypress, CA 90630
PH: 949-933 0800
Daniel Nicolas daniel@rocksnrolls.com
www.iJamr.com
Sell your music via our iJamr Music Grids carried by a network of music grid publishers. It's free!

iJigg
PO Box 9682, Chapel Hill, NC 27515-9682
help@ijigg.com
www.ijigg.com
Unlimited tracks; put up all your tracks - no limits, no cost. Superior music quality; unlike other websites that reduce your music quality, iJigg leaves your music in the same high quality you upload it in.

iLike
1605 Boylston Ave. #202, Seattle, WA 98122
alpha1.ilike.com
Designed to help consumers discover and share music together. Your music must be posted on www.garageband.com to use this service.

iManifest
27 N. Wacker Dr. #516, Chicago, IL 60606
Mark McFarland artists@imanifest.biz
www.imanifest.biz
Service for musicians to expose their demos to music industry people looking for new artists.

iMuzic.com
855-A Kifer Rd. Sunnyvale, CA 94086
PH: 408-735-6800 FX: 408-735-6805
Phil Peretz phil@cddvdnow.com
www.imuzic.com
Back-end tracking letting you know what the fans think of your music.

Independent Artists Company
admin@iacmusic.com
independentartistscompany.com
We combine the best features from the MP3 era with modern options such as digital singles sales.

Indie Charts
info@indiecharts.com
indiecharts.com
Indie music reviews, music charts, indie radio & free music downloads!

indieclectic
www.indieclectic.com
A community of like-minded artists who have come together to share their music in an environment unencumbered by mainstream music distributors.

Indiedrive
3048 Pine Tree Ln. Shakopee, MN 55379
PH: 952-426-9709
Steve steve@indiedrive.com
www.indiedrive.com
The world's first USB flash-drive album marketplace. It is absolutely FREE for indies to sell their albums here!

IndieKazoo.com
PO Box 201927, Austin, TX 78720-1927
PH: 917-553-5582
Kenneth Feldman support@indiekazoo.com
www.indiekazoo.com
Create your own music download store and most importantly, receive 100% of your sales. Oh, and it's totally FREE for the entire first month.

Indieloo.com
38782 Mt. Gilead Rd. Leesburg, VA 20175
PH: 703-777-6840 FX: 703-777-2544
Bill Hornbeck bhornbeck@indieloo.com
www.indieloo.com
Hosts complete "replay" performances and offers a revenue sharing program. This is a free service.

Indiepad.com
indiepad.com
Complete our artist registration form and we will upload your songs free of charge!

IndiependenceMusic
2855 Brookside Rd. Lake Oswego, OR 97035
PH: 520-818-0136
Jacqueline Murray
Jacqueline@IndiependenceMusic.net
www.IndiependenceMusic.net
A free music community website offering digital downloads. Upload your music, pictures and biographic information.

indieTunes
1162 St. Georges Ave. #294, Avenel, NJ 07001
support@indietunes.com
www.indietunes.com
We offer a very modest subscription fee and pay 100% from each sale back to the artist.

INDISTR
contact@indistr.com
indistr.com
Places all of the control, creativity, and financial gain back into the artists' hands by allowing you to sell your own music online. Artists take 75% of all income and get paid instantly!

IndyReview.net
artists@indyreview.net
www.indyreview.net
Our job is to attract visitors to the great variety of music online here!

Insound
221 W. 17th St. 5th Fl. New York, NY 10011
PH: 212-777-8056 FX: 212-777-8059
Patrick patrick@insound.com
www.insound.com
Bringing the best underground culture to the surface.

iSOUND.COM
3140 Dyer St. #1500, Dallas, TX 75275
PH: 877-757-6863 FX: 214-965-9007
www.isound.com
Free place for bands to upload their music and gain exposure to our music community of over 1,000,000 visitors per month!

ItsFun.com
info@itsfun.com
www.ItsFun.com
Fans and professionals alike can access, not only cutting edge music from up and coming artists, but also bios, pictures, performance schedules and promotional materials.

Jabbertones
105 Forrest Ave. #26, Los Gatos, CA 95032
PH: 408-340-1993 FX: 408-868-9803
www.jabbertones.com
Port your music in the form of ringtones to over 179 million US cellular customers! Paid revenue share per download.

JamLoad
PO Box 2826, Hollywood, CA 90078
www.JamLoad.com
We make high quality music available, talented artists accessible, and industry professionals easy to reach.

Jamster
jamster.com
Selling and marketing ringtones to mobile customers around the world. Songs must be delivered through The Orchard's distribution service www.theorchard.com.

Jamzilla
PO Box 1451, Elmhurst, IL 60126
Mario Mario@jamzilla.com
www.jamzilla.com
Featuring some of the finest undiscovered musical talent you'll find on the web.

JukeBoxAlive
311 Montford Ave. Asheville, NC 28801
PH: 828-232-0016
jukeboxalive.com
Our Advanced Jukebox Player protects your music from being digitally downloaded, yet allows fans to hear your music online. This creates exciting possibilities for you to present yourself to new audiences without being ripped off.

LEEPFrog.TV
info@leepfrog.tv
www.leepfrog.tv
An online music video destination site featuring a carefully chosen selection of emerging music artists. We focus on full-length music videos, sampling and direct music purchase geared toward tastemakers, who are looking for what's next in music.

Live Music Archive
www.archive.org/details/etree
A community committed to providing the highest quality live concerts in a downloadable format.

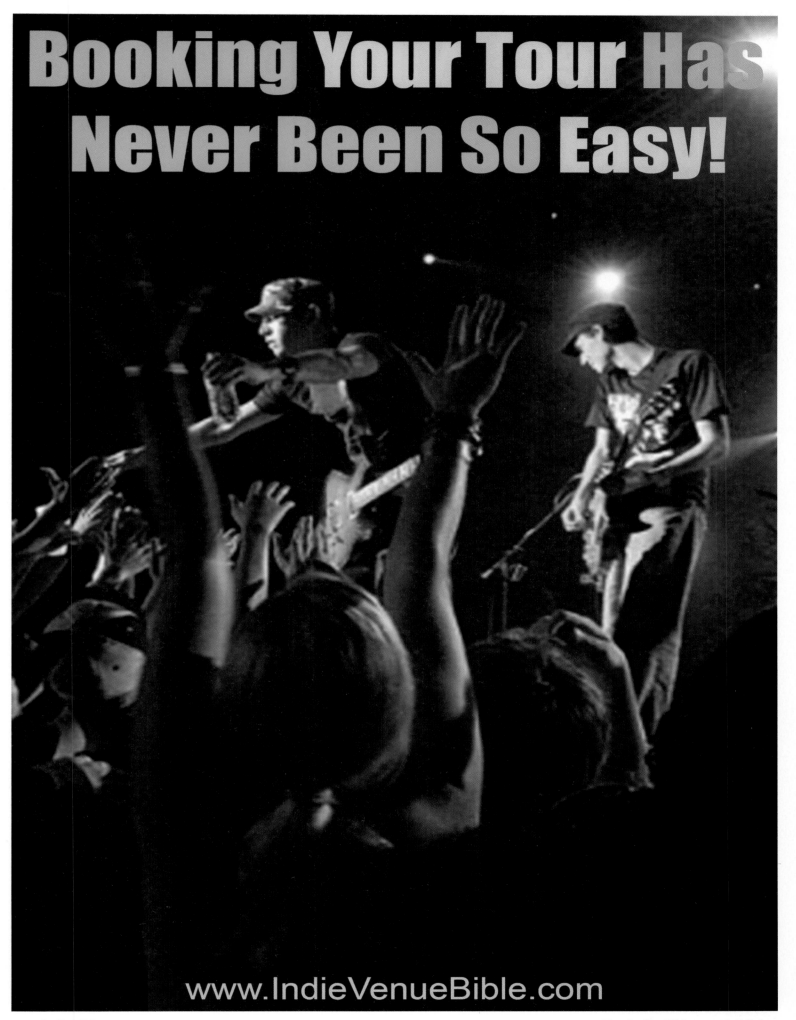

Booking Your Tour Has Never Been So Easy!

www.IndieVenueBible.com

Lulu.com
3131 RDU Ctr. #210, Morrisville, NC 27560
PH: 919-459-5858
support@lulu.com
www.lulu.com
*Upload your music, set your royalty, customize &
promote your Lulu storefront.*

Magnatune
2342 Shattuck Ave. #524, Berkeley, CA 94704
PH: 510-684-4175 FX: 510-217-6374
magnatune.com
*MP3 music and music licensing. Artists get a full
50% of the purchase price. We can also sell your
CD for you.*

MakeHitMusic.com
www.makehitmusic.com
*A community designed by musicians to help
independent artists and music producers succeed in
the music business, allowing them to collaborate,
promote, market and sell their music while keeping
the lions-share of the profit.*

ManiaTV
Submissions@ManiaTV.com
www.maniatv.com
*Expose your band to a worldwide audience via live
internet television.*

Mercora
PO Box 61539, Sunnyvale, CA 94088-1539
www.mercora.com
*A social music network that connects you to artists
and their music.*

MediaPal
6100 Hollywood Blvd. #305, Hollywood, FL 33024
PH: 954-889-5651
support@MediaPal.com
www.mediapal.com
*Makes selling any type of digital content fast, safe
and easy.*

The Mod Archive
modarchive.org
*Songs on this site are provided for free download by
the artists.*

MP3 Downloads at CD Baby
5925 NE 80th Ave. Portland, OR 97218-2891
PH: 503-595-3000 FX: 503-296-2370
cdbaby@cdbaby.com
www.cdbaby.com/mp3
*We've sold over $600,000 in MP3 downloads in the
last few months, with NO marketing or
announcements at all. That already puts CD Baby
ahead of Emusic, Yahoo Music, Sony Connect,
Verizon, MSN Music, Snocap and every company
except iTunes, Rhapsody and Napster.*

MP3.com
www.mp3.com
*Sign up for a free artist account and get exposed to
millions of fans.*

MP3charts.com
www.mp3charts.com
Offers bands the highest possible visibility.

MP3tunes
5960 Cornerstone Court W. 1st Fl.
San Diego, CA 92121
www.MP3tunes.com
*We use music from CD Baby's digital distribution
program. High rev-share to artists, with artists
keeping almost $6 of every CD sold and almost $.60
for each song.*

MP3.tv
www.mp3.tv
*Committed to creating an online community for
individuals with varied musical interests.*

MP3Unsigned.com
enquiries@MP3Unsigned.com
www.mp3unsigned.com
The best MP3s from new and unsigned artists.

MPTrax
www.mptrax.com
*The new face of music discovery! Gives artists and
fans a chance to work together to decide the future
of the music.*

MSN Music
music.msn.com
*Songs must be delivered through a Digital Music
Distributor such as www.cdbaby.com or
www.theorchard.com.*

MSSVision
542 W. University Pkwy. Baltimore, MD 21210
www.mssvision.com
Webcasts your indie music video.

mTraks
6440 Lusk Blvd. Ste. D210, San Diego, CA 92121
PH: 858-764-6910
artists@mtraks.com
www.mtraks.com
*A killer social music community and digital music
marketplace. mTraks is FOR musical artists and
their labels, promoting the equitable sale and
distribution of their independently produced music
throughout the entire universe. What a concept!*

MTV Indie Music Videos
www.mtv.com/music/indie
*Features streaming video premieres, online indie
radio and downloads.*

Music Forte
13400 S. Rt. 59, Ste. G #179, Plainfield, IL 60585
PH: 888-659-2867
Greg Percifield support@musicforte.com
www.musicforte.com
*Musicians - we're ready to start promoting your
band and music and it won't cost you a cent!*

Music Gorilla
12407 Mopac Expressway N. 100-312
Austin, TX 78758
PH: 512-918-8978 FX: 212-258-6394
Alexia info@musicgorilla.com
www.musicgorilla.com
*Exposure to major labels, indie labels, film studios
and publishers.*

The Music Oven Network
PH: 512-334-6270
editor@musicoven.com
www.musicoven.com
*Provides free promotional services to independent
artists. Submit your music ONLINE using our form.*

Musicane
support@musicane.com
www.musicane.com
*The do it yourself e-commerce solution that enables
artists and labels to sell digital downloads from
their own website.*

MusicBuilder.com
webmaster@musicbuilder.com
www.musicbuilder.com
*We want to make it easy for visitors to find your
music with our similar artist search, location search
and our searchable gig calendar.*

Music.com
6725 Sunset Blvd. #420, Los Angeles, CA 90028
PH: 323-769-9300 FX: 323-769-8303
Ithyle Griffiths ithyle@music.com
www.music.com
*Our mission is to expose the world's music and
make it universally accessible to passionate music
fans.*

MUSICFREEDOM.com
info@musicfreedom.com
www.musicfreedom.com
No monthly fee. We only make money when you do!

MusicGiants
926 Incline Way, Incline Village, NV 89451
musicgiants.com
*Combines a music player, a music store and your
music collection.*

MusicIP
766 E. Mariposa St. Ste. C, Pasadena, CA 91001
PH: 626-739-2143 FX: 626-359-9827
Frank Elliott frankii@musicip.com
www.musicip.com
*We will get your songs heard by listeners looking for
your music, without relying on genres, editorial
review, or other traditional search systems - all for
free!*

MusicNoyz.com
Falmouth, ME 04021
PH: 207-878-1722 FX: 207- 878-1723
info@musictoyz.com
www.musicnoyz.com
*Offers full service music hosting to artists who want
to share their artistic vision online.*

MusicSpawn.com
35 Village Walk, Covington, GA 30016
PH: 404-202-6344 FX: 770-786-2305
artistsupport@musicspawn.com
www.musicspawn.com
Downloads from new and upcoming artists.

MVine
www.mvine.com
*Members of our worldwide audience temporarily
download randomly assigned tracks (your music
cannot be stolen). They rate your music on a sliding
scale and post any further comments. Their recorded
responses tell us whether they – the ultimate
consumers – want to hear more. Our sophisticated
tracking system then uses a very wide range of
criteria to let us know exactly to whom your music
appeals.*

MyBandsMusic
290 Merrill Rd. Pittsfield, MA 01201
PH: 413-236-9800 x105
Keith Hannaleck khannaleck@missingbeat.com
www.mybandsmusic.com
*Allows new artists to launch a profile and bio page
including paid and free music downloads or sales of
their CDs. The fans can also create their own profile
and provide feedback to the artists on the site.*

myMPO
www.mympo.com
*Content for myMPO's main database must be
delivered through a Digital Music Distributor
www.theorchard.com.*

MyMusicSite.com
339 5th Ave. #405, New York, NY 10016
PH: 646-670-6611
Brad Turk bturk@mymusicsite.com
www.mymusicsite.com
An online music community helping independent artist sell, promote and create ringtones with their music.

MySongStore.com
PH: 323-650-7616
Larry Heller larry@mysongstore.com
mysongstore.com
Allows any musician to sell their downloads from any of their web pages - MySpace.com, PureVolume.com, HostBaby.com etc.

MySpace Ringtones
www.myspace.com/attstudio
MySpace and AT&T have teamed up to help unsigned artists on MySpace get their music closer to their fans by selling their ringtones.

MySpace Videos
vids.myspace.com
An online video streaming service similar to YouTube.

Myitracks.com
1809-A Linden Ave. Nashville, TN 37212
PH: 615-279-0322
www.myitracks.com
We only offer the best in Blues, Southern Rock, Jazz, R&B and some other small specialty genres.

myTracks
805 N. Milwaukee St. #401, Chicago, IL 60622
PH: 312-229-4430 FX: 312-229-4436
info@freshtracksmusic.com
www.mytracks.com
New music. No boundaries.

MyxerTones
George Vanderhoof artist@myxertones.com
www.myxertones.com
Artists can quickly and easily make their content available to mobile phones in the form of ringtones and wallpapers. All at no cost!

Napster
artistrelations@napster.com
www.napster.com
Contact us to get your music featured.

Nareos PeerReach
8350 Wilshire Blvd. #200, Beverly Hills, CA 90211
PH: 323-556-0666 FX: 323-556-0601
info@nareos.com
www.nareos.com
Enables legal music downloads on P2P networks. Songs must be delivered through www.cdbaby.com

Nexhit
www.nexhit.com
An online, digital media distribution and social networking community that currently hosts nearly 500,000 tracks of the best new and independent music - a number that we are constantly adding to.

NextRadio Solutions
www.nextradiosolutions.com
Streaming music to hundreds of thousands of users. Songs must be delivered through a Digital Music Distributor www.theorchard.com.

NewHotMusic.com
PO Box 2877, Palm Beach, FL 33480
PH: 561-775-4561 FX: 561-775-4562
www.newhotmusic.com
Take advantage of our promotional network.

Noisehead
todd@noisehead.com
noisehead.com
Upload up to 20 tracks - let us stream them for free - and we'll give you a place to sell your downloads (or anything else).

Number One Music
259 W. 30th St. #12FR, New York, NY 10001
reclabels@numberonemusic.com
www.NumberOneMusic.com
Creating a buzz for EVERY artist registered with us and turning 'potential' fans into committed fans.

Oddio Overplay
www.oddiooverplay.com
A catalog of neat-o websites that offer legal and free sharing of music. This website exists to spread some happiness all over the planet by connecting you with fantastic artists who deserve to be heard.

OneSource e-CD Distribution System
PO Box 162, Skippack, PA 19474
PH: 215-661-1100 FX: 215-661-8959
onesource.pan.com
Sell from your own website and get paid 100% of the sale.

OurStage
community@ourstage.com
www.ourstage.com
A brand new and exciting way for you to succeed as an artist. Our site is designed to leverage the power of the Internet to connect fans to emerging artists. You get exposure to new fans through our ranking and judging system. You can track fans with a fan club and comments. There is a monthly cash prize of $100 for the top entry in each channel and a $5,000 grand prize for music and a $1,000 prize for video. You may also get additional exposure and prizes through our partners, such as NEMO, CMJ, Noisepop, Paste, the DV Show and many others.

OurWorldMusic
ourworldmusic.com
Provides a platform and tools for artists and consumers to connect within a right business model, and provides an opportunity to discover, share, promote, and distribute content from around the world, and earn money and free music doing it!

passalong
www.passalong.com
Innovative p2pREVOLUTION™ platform and massive song catalog to build your own custom download store.

PayLoadz
295 Park Ave. S. #6B, New York, NY 10010
payloadz.com
It works seamlessly with your PayPal account, enabling you to offer digital music from your website or online auctions.

payplay.fm
244 Madison Ave. #357, New York, NY 10016
PH: 212-202-0220
hello@payplay.fm
www.payplay.fm
Online indie music download store. Visit our site to learn how to submit your music.

Pitchfork TV
eavvon@pitchforkmedia.com
pitchfork.tv
If you are an artist, label, or representative thereof, and would like to submit music videos, please send a query (links are acceptable, attachments are not) to our e-mail address.

Playgroundz.net
playgroundzmusic@yahoo.com
www.playgroundz.net
Free unlimited songs and video hosting. Dedicated artist page with networking tools. Live webcast services. Get your music reviewed. Concert & event bookings. Charts, rankings and so much more!

PocketFuzz
www.pocketfuzz.com
Allows you to incorporate a custom ringtone editor into your website or MySpace profile.

PostYourMusic.com
922 Santa Ana Blvd. Santa Ana, CA 92604
PH: 949-209-7233
postyourmusic.com
Working musicians (for hire) search engine. Upload your MP3s & videos. Download ringtones.

Project Overseer Productions
Chris Bishop projectoverseer@hotmail.com
www.projectoverseer.biz
Music hosting which starts for absolutely `FREE` with many VIP features and now includes the addition of `POP SPACE` …a blogger that's musically interlinked with POP's Artist section and is fast becoming very popular!

Prize Talent
www.prizetalent.com
Offers you the opportunity to get exposure to agents, producers and industry media.

promosquad
info@promosquad.com
home.promosquad.com
Our website is separated into five main areas: The Promosquad Jukebox (rate new music), Polls/Interactive, Get Famous, The Prize Store and the message boards.

Publik Music
PO Box 4076, Portland, ME 04101
PH: 207-772-6102 FX: 207-772-6106
info@publikmusic.com
www.publikmusic.com
Showcase artists in an intimate, interactive setting while cost-effectively reaching and growing their audiences.

pureVOLUME
c/o Virb Inc. 119 Braintree St. #603
Boston, MA 02134
labels@purevolume.com
www.purevolume.com
The place for rising artists to promote their music and shows.

QTRnote.com
PH: 901-487-0754
peter@qtrnote.com
www.qtrnote.com
Can work with accomplished composers.

Radio Radio
553 E. Main St., Jackson, TN 38301
PH: 615-986-9271 FX: 866-294-7843
RT Curtis webmaster@radioradio.us
www.radioradio.us
Create your own store to start selling music. All music that you upload will be played on our radio station.

RapidShare
www.rapidshare.com
Host your files with RapidShare for FREE!

RateMyCreation
www.ratemycreation.com
Developed for musicians who want to know what others think of their music.

RateSumMusic.com
www.ratesummusic.com
An opportunity to be heard, discovered and reviewed by the public and industry players.

ReadyToBreak.com
6725 Sunset Blvd. #420 Los Angeles, CA 90028
PH: 310-593-4172
Paula Moore management@readytobreak.com
www.ReadyToBreak.com
Comprehensive talent portal where emerging artists upload samples of work for signing consideration.

RedDotNet
1390 Decision St. Ste. B, Vista, CA 92081
PH: 760-936-0400 FX: 760-936-0401
info@reddotnet.com
www.reddotnet.com
Our content is drawn from the All Media Guide.

ResearchMusic
1550 NE Miami Gardens Dr. #305
Miami, FL 33179
PH: 305-926-1397 FX: 305-926-1397
www.researchmusic.com
We can publish your song or broker your master recording to a record label. Upload MP3 files for review by our A&R team.

ReverbNation.com
1123 Broadway #317, New York, NY 10010
PH: 212-367-0826
Lou Plaia LouPlaia@reverbnation.com
www.ReverbNation.com
Provides innovative online marketing solutions for artists, labels, managers and venues in a music community setting.

RHAPSODY
www.rhapsody.com
Songs must be delivered through a Digital Music Distributor such as www.cdbaby.com or www.theorchard.com.

Ruckus Network
feedback@ruckus.com
www.ruckusnetwork.com
A free, ad-supported subscription-model download service designed primarily for college and university students. Direct deals with large indies, otherwise catalogs must be delivered through a Digital Music Distributor such as www.cdbaby.com, www.iodalliance.com, www.irisdistribution.com, www.ingrooves.com, www.theonedigital.com or www.theorchard.com.

rVibe
www.rvibe.com
We realized there could be so much more to online music, and we wanted to be a part of it.

Shatterproof Studios
18 Mill St., Southbridge, MA 01550
PH: 508-764-3865 FX: 508-764-9501
Matt Soper matt.soper@shatterproofstudios.com
www.shatterproofstudios.com
Worldwide exposure. Live video production and internet broadcast partner. Broadcasts artist's performances LIVE to the world.

Showcase Your Music
info@showcaseyourmusic.com
www.showcaseyourmusic.com
Upload videos, songs, pictures and your bio for free.

SignHere Online
contact@signhereonline.net
www.signhereonline.net
Visitors listen to the available selections and provide feedback via electronic survey. These results are made available to interested record labels.

SizzleFizzle.com
17702 Mitchell N. #203, Irvine, CA 92614
PH: 949-222-2250 FX: 949-223-4277
customerservice@sizzlefizzle.com
www.sizzlefizzle.com
Features contests where visitors vote on their favorite song and videos in each genre.

SNOCAP
201 3rd St. 2nd Fl. San Francisco, CA 94103
www.snocap.com
Content registry and clearinghouse that enables record labels, publishers and individual artists to sell their entire catalogs through peer-to-peer networks and online retailers. Sell your music on MySpace and beyond!

SongCast.net
100 Cliffside Dr. Burleson, TX 76028
PH: 214-418-1544 FX: 817-447-4020
Richard Adams richard.adams@songcast.net
www.songcast.net
Free MP3 hosting, blogs and social networking.

SongCritic.com
J. Atkinson songcritic@comcast.net
www.SongCritic.com
A site where fans can download and listen to your song(s) and then post "reviews" of your tune.

Songfight.org
fightmaster@songfight.org
www.songfight.org
We post a title, people make songs for that title and compete.

SongPlanet.com
radioinfo@songplanet.com
www.songplanet.com
We offer free artist pages, forums and live chat.

Songsinc
www.songsinc.com
Accepted tracks are offered for download on the Songsinc TrackShop, and earn the TrackOwner no less than $2 (and up to $5!) per download in royalties – paid quarterly.

SonicJive.com
PO Box 7311, Villa Park, IL 60181
PH: 630-209-0630
www.SonicJive.com
Bands are able to sell MP3s, interact with fans, post webcasts, submit classified ads and get their music played on their online radio station, SonicJive Radio.

Sony Connect
www.sonyconnect.com
Songs must be delivered through a Digital Music Distributor such as www.cdbaby.com or www.theorchard.com.

Soundboard.com
mike@soundboard.com
www.soundboard.com
A 'soundboard' is like an audio album for all your favorite Mp3 soundbytes and audio clips. You can build a sound board for your own listening pleasure or upload your sound and share it with the world.

SoundClick
support@soundclick.com
www.soundclick.com
You can sell single songs as MP3 downloads or multiple songs as MP3 albums.

Soundmetro.com
PH: 714-777-2361
Greg Yancy daddysylem@soundmetro.com
www.soundmetro.com
A place for artists to get their faces seen and their music heard. Includes free web space, MP3 uploads and more!

SoundSauce
www.soundsauce.net
Write music? Play or Sing in a band? Join now and upload your MP3s for free!

Speakerheart
www.speakerheart.com
Enables you to upload your albums and tracks, set your prices and sell it all side-by-side in your own custom storefront.

SpiralFrog
content@spiralfog.com
www.SpiralFrog.com
We are always trying to expand our catalog of songs and video, and we'd love to include you. If you have content that you'd like to have us feature at SpiralFrog, please contact us.

Starbucks Music Download Service
www.starbucks.com
Songs must be delivered through a Digital Music Distributor www.theorchard.com.

stimTVnetwork
4347 Raytheon Rd. Oxnard, CA 93033
PH: 805-271-2759
info@stimtv.com
www.stimtvmusic.com
Hosts an endless stream of music video clips. Submit your band's videos.

SyncLive.com
app.synclive.com
Allows artists to stream their shows live to thousands of members for free from any location— including the concert hall, club, studio or living room—by using a simple computer interface.

Synchronicity Live
info@synchronicitylive.com
www.synchronicitylive.com
You can broadcast your live shows to thousands of new fans, create a band page and get live feedback for free.

The Indie Link Exchange

www.indielinkexchange.com/ile

Tarnius Music
PO Box 888, Addison, IL 60101
PH: 888-418-8637
info@tarniusmusic.com
tarniusmusic.com
We provide the tools for independent artists and labels to get their music heard.

TastyAudio
www.tastyaudio.com
An online music discovery system. Our goal is to promote artists and provide a new venue for listeners to hear your music.

Tap It
radio@tapitfame.com
www.tapitfame.com
A digital distribution and discovery engine for independent talent. Built for artists by artists.

TheBeat.fm
PO Box 17583, San Diego, CA 92177
PH: 858-869-3070
John L. Wilson admin@thebeat.fm
www.thebeat.fm/jamroom
Upload, listen, share your songs. Create your personal online store and earn money for your music.

TheTrackShack.com
1745 Markston Rd. Sacramento, CA 95825-4026
info@netmusicmakers.com
www.thetrackshack.com
Don't just sell songs for 99¢, sell them by the slice, too!

TouchTunes
740 Broadway #1102, New York, NY 10003
PH: 212-991-6521 FX: 646-365-0011
www.touchtunes.com
The largest out-of-home interactive entertainment network, providing innovative solutions to over 30,000 bars, restaurants, retailers and other businesses in North America. Also operates the largest network of interactive entertainment systems, playing over 1.5 million songs per day. TouchTunes maintains a digital music library covering more than two million licensed tracks from every major record label, plus independent music distributors and a host of independent labels.

Trackfinders.com
trackfinders.com
By creating a virtual retail warehouse online, we empower artists and songwriters to buy, sell and lease their compositions directly to the TV, film, and video gaming industries, without the hassles of expensive lawyer fees and lengthy negotiations.

tradebit
3422 Old Capitol Trail #717
Wilmington, DE 19808-6192
PH: 484-685-4535 FX: 480-275-3582
info@tradebit.com
www.tradebit.com
Sell music, photos and e-books using your own PayPal account or just host with us!

TuneFeed
www.tunefeed.com
Free, 100% legal music player. We pay royalties direct to the artist for every song played.

TVU Music Television
PO Box 1887, Westerville, OH 43086
PH: 614-890-9977 FX: 614-839-1329
www.tvulive.com
The music video channel that actually plays music videos!

Ultimate Band List
10900 Wilshire Blvd. #1400
Los Angeles, CA 90024
ubl.com
The ultimate online destination for independent bands, their fans and the music lovers who want to discover them.

UncensoredInterview.com
info@uncensoredinterview.com
www.uncensoredinterview.com
An online video platform for indie music artists and fans to be seen and heard in their truest form - uncensored and real. All music begins with a point of view and it's our mission to deliver to you a voyeuristic glimpse into the indie music world.

Unsigned Band Network
158 Wigwam Trail, Livingston, TX 77351-3551
PH: 936-465-7487
James Stetler unsignedbandnetwork@gmail.com
www.ubn2.com
Get the most plays and/or top rating and be our featured artist for the month.

UnsignedTube.com
www.UnsignedTube.com
The leader in online video and the premier destination to watch and share original videos worldwide through a web experience.

UpAudio
1333A North Ave. Box 613
New Rochelle, NY 10804
PH: 877-703-9084
support@upaudio.com
www.upaudio.com
We accept all artist submissions. We don't decide what's right for music fans to listen to. We just provide them with a way to find it.

Upto11.net
inform@upto11.net
www.upto11.net
Music lovers visit our site, type a band name into the search box, press "Get Recommendations" and we provide them with a list of recommended bands that they might like.

Veodia
1825 S. Grant St. #500, San Mateo, CA 94402
PH: 650-349-2100 FX: 650-349-2101
support@veodia.com
www.veodia.com
Our video broadcasting service makes it easy and inexpensive for businesses, universities, religious institutions, and even professional bloggers to broadcast high-quality live video and digitally archive content for on-demand viewing or podcasting.

Verizon Wireless V CAST
www.verizonwireless.com/music
Music catalog available for download on mobile phones. Songs must be delivered through a CD Baby's Digital Music Service www.cdbaby.com

The Video Load
PO Box 210328, St. Louis, MO 63121
contact@thevideoload.com
www.thevideoload.com
Designed for independent artists and other video content owners to create and sell video ringtones for mobile phones.

VideoMix TV
www.myspace.com/videomixtv
request@videomixtv.com
www.myspace.com/videomixtv
The future of music television!

Virgin Megastore Digital Downloads
VirginDigital.com
Songs must be delivered through a Digital Music Distributor such as www.cdbaby.com or www.theorchard.com.

Virtual Music Market
info@virtualmusicmarket.com
virtualmusicmarket.com
We want to be a bit more selective about what products are in our store and a bit more involved in helping aspiring artists and songwriters develop their careers, much like a record label would.

Vision 4 Music
9 Music Square S. Ste. 270, Nashville, TN 37203
PH: 615-405-9454 FX: 615-296-4228
Jeff M. Richfield info@vision4music.com
www.vision4music.com
Providing an efficient platform for artists, producers and labels to market their music in what we call V4Indies. We get your music heard to over 20 distribution channels globally (and growing).

vSocial
51 W. 3rd St. #101, Tempe, AZ 85281
PH: 480-967-6555 FX: 480-967-9575
www.vsocial.com
The fastest, easiest way to upload, watch and share your favorite video clips.

Wal-Mart Music Downloads
www.walmart.com/music
Artists must go through a distributor to get their music online www.theorchard.com.

Want2bdiscovered.com
PO Box 2119, Pahrump, NV 89041-2119
PH: 1-877-223-4726
Ron Link customerservice@want2bdiscovered.com
www.want2bdiscovered.com
We help artists get more exposure for their music and performance opportunities. This service is FREE to everyone!

We Music Store
8 N. Preston St., Philadelphia, PA 19104
PH: 215-387-3525
www.wemusicstore.com
A social network that allows all musicians to distribute their music online and keep 80 percent of each sale that they make.

World Music Service
Adrian Jones sellmusic@worldmusicservice.com
www.worldmusicservice.com
An online music marketplace where artists can sell their music for free and keep every cent with no copyright infringements.

Xrateit.com
4232 Balboa Ave. #9, San Diego, CA 92117
FX: 561- 431-0664
contact@xrateit.com
XrateIt.com
Upload your music for FREE! What's the catch? The music is rated which means, if it's BUNK, it's gone! If it's TIGHT it stays!

XYZMP3.com
3800 S. Congress Ste. C, Austin, TX 78704
PH: 512-535-6459 FX: 801-729-5122
Roland De Leon info@xyzmp3.com
www.xyzmp3.com
Sell your music from your website, our website and any of the social networking sites. You make 70% of the net wholesale for songs sold.

YOUMAKEMUSIC.COM
mail@youmakemusic.com
www.youmakemusic.com
Features a download shop (digital distribution) and an 'old fashioned' web shop (physical distribution).

YouTube
www.youtube.com
An online video streaming service that allows anyone to view and share videos that have been uploaded by our members. Broadcast yourself. Watch and share your videos worldwide!

ZeBox
no_spam@zebox.com
www.zebox.com
A great efficient music engine for indie artists.

Zulu Kangaroo
www.zulukangaroo.com
Helps music afficionados discover new music from the CD Baby catalog. By simply selecting a style and genre of music, you can enjoy a steady stream of great music from today's newest independent artists.

Canada

Apple iTunes Canada
www.apple.com/ca/itunes
Songs must be delivered through a Digital Music Distributor such as www.cdbaby.com or www.theorchard.com.

Bluetracks.ca
5074 de Lanaudiere, Montreal, QC H2J 3R1
info@bluetracks.ca
bluetracks.ca
We offer visitors an independent music catalogue that is varied, innovative and in constant evolution.

DIRT
Dave Lamoureux dirt-tv@hotmail.com
www.dirt-tv.com
Featuring independent music videos (of all styles) from around the globe! Airs across Canada on Express-Vu (Ch. 258) and Starchoice (Ch. 323).

DiscoverMeLive.com
736 The Queensway, PO Box 57095,
Etobicoke, ON M8Y 3Y2
contact@discovemelive.com
www.discovermelive.com
This site is free for all to use. You may upload all types of content from video, to music, to art, poetry and creative writing. You name it, if it is worth being discovered then this is the place you want to be!

MP3 Musicgrams
#5-7218 Progress Way, Delta, BC V4G 1H2
PH: 604-952-0400 FX: 604-952-0400
info@mp3musicgrams.com
www.mp3musicgrams.com
An interactive and viral promotional tool that allows artists to spread their music in a new format.

Mp3room.com
Ste. B-2306 Bedford Pl. Abbotsford, BC V2T 4A5
Jayson Lockyer jayson@mp3room.com
www.mp3room.com
Created to promote and showcase the music of independent bands.

Nextposure.com
#230-1122 Mainland St., Vancouver, BC V6B 5L1
PH: 604-261-5026 FX: 604-484-4965
Jan Cooper cooperjan@telus.net
www.nextposure.com
Online video network. We are seeking bands with good videos who want worldwide exposure.

NoWhere Radio
Box 42065 Southland Crossing PO
Calgary, AB T2J 7A6
artists@nowhereradio.com
www.nowhereradio.com
Here to help promote independent musicians around the world.

Puretracks
www.puretracks.com
Songs must be delivered through a Digital Music Distributor such as www.cdbaby.com or www.theorchard.com.

TouchTunes Canada
3 Commerce Pl. 4th Fl. Montreal, QC H3E 1H7
PH: 800-585-3021 FX: 514-762-6483
www.touchtunes.com
The largest out-of-home interactive entertainment network, providing innovative solutions to over 30,000 bars, restaurants, retailers and other businesses in North America. Also operates the largest network of interactive entertainment systems, playing over 1.5 million songs per day. TouchTunes maintains a digital music library covering more than two million licensed tracks from every major record label, plus independent music distributors and a host of independent labels.

Tzomé
26 Edgewood Ave. Brockville, ON K6V 1T6
info@Tzome.com
www.tzome.com
Features an online database of searchable music. Staffed by some incredibly talented indie artists.

zunior.com
283 Danforth Ave. #358, Toronto, ON M4K 1N2
Dave Ullrich dave@zunior.com
www.zunior.com
Artists pay only a 15% administrative fee to use zunior.com. The majority of this goes towards the merchant account, hosting and bandwidth fees.

Mexico

THOS3wires
those.wires@gmail.com
www.thos3wir3s.blogspot.com
Covers many styles of music.

South America

Search MP3
Av. Das America, 700 Bloco 03 Sala 112, Rio de Janeiro, Brazil 22640-100
PH: 55-21-2132-7757
www.searchmpthree.com
Register to create your own homepage containing your songs.

Europe

Austria

Trackseller
Hollandstrasse 8/4, A - 1020 Wien, Austria
PH: 0043-1-218-34-76-26 FX: 0043-1-218-63-00-63
Marc Muncke shop@trackseller.com
www.trackseller.com
Manages paid music downloads for musicians of any kind and all around the world directly off their website.

Czech Republic

Poslouchej.net
redakce@poslouchej.net
www.poslouchej.net
Czech music website (all genres) with online radios and MP3 downloads. 5000+ daily visitors.

Finland

Mikseri
PL 207, 00121 Helsinki, Finland
PH: 040-837-2758
Michka Hoffren michka.hoffren@mikseri.net
www.mikseri.net
Downloads covering all genres.

France

121 MusicStore
121 Rue du Caducée, 34000 Montpellier, France
www.121musicstore.com
A digital platform that sells only independent music with no DRM.

Apple iTunes France
www.apple.com/fr/itunes
Songs must be delivered through a Digital Music Distributor such as www.cdbaby.com or www.theorchard.com.

Deezer
78, Blvd. Sébastopol, 75003 Paris, France
FX: +33 (0)1-55-80-69-01
www.deezer.com
Free music on demand website. Come and discover more than 150.000 tracks. Create your playlists, upload your entire song library. No storage limit.

Germany

Amplify Music
Schoenblicker Str.10, 12589 Berlin, Germany
PH: +49 (0)30-641-69-287
FX: +49 (0)30-641-69-288
Oliver Meier support@amplify-music.com
www.amplify-music.com
We have developed a new conceptual approach that enables people who make music to market their songs without a need for the conventional distribution channels offered by the music industry.

Apple iTunes Germany
www.apple.com/de/itunes
Songs must be delivered through a Digital Music Distributor such as www.cdbaby.com or www.theorchard.com.

besonic.com
Hochstadenstr. 15, 50674 Koln, Germany
PH: 49-221-53097-51 FX: 49-221-53097-70
www.besonic.com
Music anytime, anywhere, tailored to the individual likes of users.

Kazzong
Nora Meyer nora.meyer@kazzong.com
www.kazzong.com
Empowers music artists to sell directly to fans anywhere on the web, including official artist websites and MySpace profiles.

MP3.de
Mozartstr. 35-37, 50674 Köln, Germany
PH: +49-221-71-60-77-20
FX: +49-221-71-60-77-11
info@mp3.de
www.mp3.de
Germany's largest MP3 site.

Music4u
www.music4u.cc
Free service. Upload your pics and MP3s to our database.

phonector Europe
Gleimstr.60, D-10437 Berlin, Germany
PH: +49 (0)30-44032480
service@phonector.com
www.phonector.com
We can help you sell your music via download distribution and burned audio CD distribution.

Open Music Source
Ickstattstr. 1, 80469 München, Germany
PH: 49-89-255-519-110 FX: 49-89-255-519-258
info@openmusicsource.net
www.openmusicsource.net
Database system which stores music and videos from bands around the globe.

Pooltrax
Brennerstr. 76, D-20099 Hamburg, Germany
PH: +49 (0) 40-539045-20
FX: +49 (0) 40-539045-22
info@tameco.eu
www.pooltrax.de
MP3 kostenlos downloaden, Charts, news, software für musik & MP3, uvm. bei POOLTRAX.

Songs Wanted
Willhelm-Dull-Str. 9, 80638, Munich, Germany
PH: 089-157-32-50 FX: 089-157-50-36
ellie@songswanted.com
www.songswanted.com
Helping artists get recognition.

Soundlift.com
www.soundlift.com
A music community open for musicians and music lovers from all over the world sharing their music and videos.

Soundtaxi
Nikolasustrasse 6a, 70190 Stuttgart, Germany
PH: +49 (0)711-4107147
Tim Rheinwald tim@soundtaxi.de
www.soundtaxi.net
Offers a continuously growing archive of excellent royalty free music.

web62.com
support@web62.com
www.web62.com
Internet television. Music coverage.

The Indie Link Exchange
A new, free and easy way to promote your website.

www.indielinkexchange.com/ile

Greece

S Music Show
Kaisarias 16, 17122 Nea Smyrni, Athens, Greece
PH: +30 2109358573
Karidakiss & Nancy info@smusic.gr
www.smusic.gr
Music show featuring videos, news etc. Send us your videos!

Italy

QOOB
qoob@mtvne.com
qoob.tv
A website where you can upload your audio and video contents, give them visibility and share them with other users.

Vetrina Musicale
PH: 39-081-896-9461
postmaster@vetrinamusicale.com
www.vetrinamusicale.com
Allows Independent artists to upload their music files at NO cost. We also offer contact information for Italian producers, record and publishing companies.

Latvia

Music is Here!
natalie@musicishere.com
www.musicishere.com
Songs must be delivered through a Digital Music Distributor such as www.cdbaby.com

Luxembourg

jamendo
contact@jamendo.com
www.jamendo.com
A community of free, legal and unlimited music published with Creative Commons licenses. Upload your music, share your favorite artists!

The Netherlands

MP3.nl
www.mp3.nl
Large database with information about tracks, albums and artists.

The Music Hall
van Marumstraat 10b1, 3112XV Schiedam,
The Netherlands
PH: +31-6-46406340
Feri Ascencion feri_ascencion@hotmail.com
www.themusichall.nl
3000+ music video clips. Watch or submit old & new music streaming clips.

Musicfan.fm
info@musicfan.fm
www.musicfan.fm
A social network based on music and entertainment!

Poland

MP3.pl
www.mp3.pl
Poland's largest MP3 site.

Russia

MP3.ru
www.mp3.ru
Russia's largest MP3 site.

RealMusic
realmusic.ru
Covers all genres of music.

Sweden

Digfi
Lars Jämtelid lars.jamtelid@digfi.com
www.digfi.com
Publicize your music on the site for free. Download our online application form.

Klicktrack
Box 1336, SE-621 24 Visby, Sweden
support@klicktrack.com
www.klicktrack.com
Provides ready-made, fully operational music download stores.

MP3Lizard.com
mp3lizard.com
Promote your band for free!

Musicbrigade
Box 30043, SE-104 25 Stockholm, Sweden
PH: +46-8-545 689 00
support@musicbrigade.com
www.musicbrigade.com
For a small fee we will take your video, digitize it to our high quality specifications and put it on our site.

Radio Sidekick
Bergsgatan 11b, 211 54 Malmö, Sweden
Martin Jönsson radiosidekick@gmail.com
radiosidekick.blogspot.com
Send us records, MP3s, promotion, cloths, magazines, tickets, posters etc.

Soundation
Halsingegatan 10b, 11323 Stockholm, Sweden
PH: 46-8-660-9910 FX: 46-8-661-8810
www.soundation.com
Sell your music directly from your website and MySpace pages (we don't take a percentage). Don't wait to be signed to a label - be your own e-label!

Switzerland

beatmaka.com
Manessestrasse 120, CH-8045 Zurich, Switzerland
www.beatmaka.com
Our review panel checks each incoming track and assures that only the best ones get online.

EuropaMp3.org
helpmusiciens@europamp3.org
www.europamp3.org
Boosts the launch of new labels and musicians by remunerating its subscribers for the essential work that they carry out for the distribution of your music!

United Kingdom

amazingtunes
9 Grey Street, Newcastle Upon Tyne, NE1 6EE UK
info@amazingtunes.com
www.amazingtunes.com
Upload your music. It's free and 70% of all profits go to the artist.

Amplifeye
Camborne, Cornwall, TR14 7QB UK
Dan Mitchell dan@amplifeye.com
www.amplifeye.com
An online organisation with the intention of helping promote unsigned artists and to help bridge the chasm between the artist and the industry.

Apple iTunes UK

www.apple.com/uk/itunes
*Songs must be delivered through a Digital Music
Distributor such as www.cdbaby.com or
www.theorchard.com.*

arkade

Fetcham Park House, Lower Rd. Fetcham, Surrey,
KT22 9HD UK
PH: +44(0)121-288-2727 FX: +44 (0)845-280-1928
www.arkade.com
*You set the price for your product and receive 100%
of the price you set. You also retain 100% of your
rights.*

Audigist

Studio Nyne, 75 Church St., Bonsall, Derbyshire,
DE4 2AE UK
support@audigist.com
www.audigist.com
Take your music to a wider audience.

BeatPick

Studio 8, 2nd Fl. East Wing, Oslo House,
Felstead St., London, E9 5LG UK
FX: +39-06-96708800
info@beatpick.com
www.beatpick.com
*FairPlay music label and music licensing (download
music and license pre-cleared indie music).*

contactmusic.com

Gate House, Iron Row, Burley in Wharfdale, Ilkley,
LS29 7DB UK
PH: 44-0-1943-865111 FX: 44-0-1943-865222
hello@contactmusic.com
www.contactmusic.com
*If you get a deal through our site, you'll get 100% of
the royalties.*

Cube-music

Albany Boathouse, Lower Ham Rd.
Kingston-upon-Thames, KT2 5BB UK
PH: 020-85471543 FX: 020-85471544
info@cube-music.com
www.cube-music.com
*Promote your video or audio tracks to UK
audiences.*

easyMusic.com

www.easyMusic.com
*Our "Copyleft" section features music from
unsigned artists, including music which can be
downloaded for free.*

eircom.net Music Club

www.eircom.net/music
*Irish download site. Songs must be delivered
through a Digital Music Distributor such as
www.theorchard.com.*

eListeningPost

PO Box 2290, Maidenhead, Berkshire,
SL6 6WA UK
info@elisteningpost.com
www.elisteningpost.com
*Allows the musicians to keep all the money
generated directly from download sales, providing
the musicians a return of as much as 94% of the
sale price as well as giving them the lions share of
advertising revenues associated directly to their
music.*

Epictunes

35 Orient Pl. Canterbury, Kent, CT2 8AW UK
customerservice@epictunes.com
www.epictunes.com
*Sell your music online through MP3 or CD format.
We also feature music podcasts and online radio.*

indiestore.com

Unit 1G, Zetland House, 5-25 Scrutton St., London,
EC2A 4HJ UK
PH: +44 (0) 207 099 7777
www.indiestore.com
*Do it yourself digital download store for
independent artists and labels.*

IntoMusic

support@intomusic.co.uk
www.intomusic.co.uk
Download music featuring independent musicians.

Kerascene Music Digital Distribution

16 Russell Ave. Dunchurch, Rugby, CV22 6PX UK
PH: +44 (0) 7790-957028
Stephen Parfitt info@kerascene.com
www.kerascene.com/business.htm
*Offers easy digital distribution, MySpace marketing,
music contracts, free ringtones setup, online artist
development and branding, FM quality radio and
Kerascene Music TV.*

Kerchoonz

www.kerchoonz.com
*Pays bands, artists, DJ's and songwriters when they
give their music to fans for free!!!*

Launch Music on Yahoo UK

uk.launch.yahoo.com
*Songs must be delivered through a Digital Music
Distributor www.theorchard.com.*

Letstalkmusic.com

Post House, Fitzalan Rd. Arundel, W. Sussex,
BN18 9JY UK
PH: 01273-424413
opps@letstalkmusic.com
www.letstalkmusic.com
*Upload your music for review, enter the showcase
CD and more.*

Mean Fiddler Music

www.meanfiddler.com
*Songs must be delivered through a Digital Music
Distributor www.theorchard.com.*

MP3Songs

www.mp3songs.org.uk
Help for unsigned artists.

MTV UK

www.mtv.co.uk
*Songs must be delivered through a Digital Music
Distributor www.theorchard.com.*

MyCokeMusic

mycokemusic.com
*Songs must be delivered through a Digital Music
Distributor www.theorchard.com.*

Napster.co.uk

artistrelations@napster.com
www.napster.co.uk
*Offers tracks by hundreds of independent and
unsigned artists.*

OIKZ.com

Pól pm@oIKz.com
www.oikz.com
*Gives bands and songwriters the opportunity to
easily sell their music.*

Orange Music

www.orange.co.uk/music
*Songs must be delivered through a Digital Music
Distributor www.theorchard.com.*

Packard Bell Music Station

www.packardbell.co.uk/products/playground/
music.html
*Songs must be delivered through a Digital Music
Distributor www.theorchard.com.*

Pocket Group

www.pocketgroup.co.uk
*The world's largest independent label mobile music
distributor. Songs must be delivered through a
Digital Music Distributor such as www.cdbaby.com*

Project Overseer Productions

www.projectoverseer.biz
*DJs & members play your music and add real time
comments.*

Rough Trade

130 Talbot Rd. London, W11 1JA UK
PH: 020-7229-8541 FX: 020-7221-1146
digital@roughtrade.com
www.roughtrade.com
Send us your music to make available for download.

Songstuff UK

www.songstuff.co.uk
*Post your songs for review, review other's songs,
discuss technical, creative and music business
issues, chat in our forum.*

SONY Connect Europe

www.connect-europe.com
*Songs must be delivered through a Digital Music
Distributor such as www.cdbaby.com or
www.theorchard.com.*

Soundlift.com

www.soundlift.com
*Open for musicians and music lovers from all over
the world sharing their music and videos.*

Stayaround.com

25 Barnes Wallis Rd. Segensworth East, Fareham,
PO15 5TT UK
PH: +44 (0)1489 889821 FX: +44 (0)1489 889887
info@stayaround.com
stayaround.com
*We offer the hottest, freshest and most up front
music around and let you decide how to listen.*

Tesco.com Downloads Store

www.tescodownloads.com
*Songs must be delivered through a Digital Music
Distributor www.theorchard.com.*

Tiscali Music

www.tiscali.co.uk/music
*Songs must be delivered through a Digital Music
Distributor www.theorchard.com.*

TuneTribe.com

50-52 Paul St., London, EC2A 4LB UK
PH: 020-7613-8200
unsigned@tunetribe.com
www.tunetribe.com
*Send your CD and we will prepare it for inclusion
on the site for free! You set the price per download.*

UKscreen

www.ukscreen.com
*A center for film and music making. From casting,
networking and crewing to broadcasting and
distribution.*

We7

www.We7.com
*Music downloads: free, safe, legal ...and artists get
paid!*

Australia

Apple iTunes Australia
www.apple.com/au/itunes
*Songs must be delivered through a Digital Music
Distributor such as www.cdbaby.com or
www.theorchard.com.*

Asylum TV
Peter Deske pd54@optusnet.com.au
www.asylumtv.com
*TV program focusing on independent artists.
Overseas submissions welcome.*

Blue Pie Australia
Unit 6 #11 Dudley St., Randwick,
NSW 2031 Australia
PH: 612-9310-0155 FX: 612-9310-0166
Julian Tagg sales@bluepie.com.au
www.bluepie.com.au
*The online digital music service run by Blue Pie,
one of Australia's leading independent labels.*

Boost Digital
Level 6 220 Pacific Highway CrowsNest,
NSW 2065 Australia
PH: +612-9460-1400 FX: +612-9460-0044
Graeme Logan graeme@boostdigital.com
www.boostindependentmusic.com
*MP3 music downloads store for independent &
unsigned artists & bands to sell, host, promote &
download all MP3 music online. A MP3 store to buy
& sell all independent & unsigned music online*

ChaosMusic
5 Harper St., Abbotsford, VIC 3067 Australia
PH: +61-3-9412-3596
info@chaosmusic.com
www.chaosmusic.com
Indie artists WANTED!!! Sell your CDs/sound files.

sanity.com.au
www.sanity.com.au
*Songs must be delivered through a Digital Music
Distributor www.theorchard.com.*

Show Off Recordings
355 Wellington St., Clifton Hill, Melbourne,
VIC 3068 Australia
www.showoffrecordings.com
*Selective digital distributing and marketing for
independent artists and labels.*

Soundbuzz
#1403 Level 14, Tower 2, 101 Grafton St.
Bondi Junction, NSW 2022 Australia
PH: 61-2-9387-7600 FX: 61-2-9387-8175
www.Soundbuzz.com
*A digital music service provider and the only
provider with a regional focus on the Asia-Pacific
markets.*

Voeveo
PO Box 24224, Wellington 6142, New Zealand
www.voeveo.com
*A site where producers can be recognised for their
quality mobile content and make money and buyers
can finally find unique content and buy it directly
from the creator themselves. Songs must be
delivered through a Digital Music Distributor such
as www.cdbaby.com*

Africa

Indieglobal.com
11 Sedgemoor Pl, Woodlands, Durban, KZN,
South Africa, 4004
PH: +27314691850 FX: +27314691850
www.indieglobal.com
*Website for independent artists, record labels etc.
Upload MP3s, images, profiles & links (for FREE).*

Asia

Gone Fishing for Blue Skies
2-2-4-503, Azuma, Kashiwa, Chiba, 277-0014,
Japan
PH: 81-80-3278-2862
Big Foot bigfoot@gonefishingforblueskies.com
www.gonefishingforblueskies.com
*On demand music streaming, introducing
independent music from around the globe.*

jammy.jp
www.jammy.jp
Japanese social networking service.

listen.co.jp
www.listen.co.jp
Specializes in indie/mainstream music.

Orientaltunes.com
admin@orientaltunes.com
www.orientaltunes.com
Follows the modern trends in Oriental music.

recommuni.jp
info@recommuni.jp
recommuni.jp
*Japanese social networking service with over
10,000 members.*

SessionSound
PO Box 182, Singapore 912307
PH: 65-91781920 FX: 65-64757237
Fadi Zeitoune contact@sessionsound.com
www.sessionsound.com
*Commission-free MP3 sales, CD on demand,
streaming audio, gig guides... all free!*

Sweet Basil
www.omega.co.jp/sb-i
Japanese site featuring overseas indie music.

PLANNING A TOUR?
32,000
Live Music Venues
in the US and Canada!!

www.IndieVenueBible.com

MP3 / Audioblogs

*MP3 / Audioblogs vary in what they have to
offer artists. Some do in-depth reviews of CDs
and will post a few MP3s of your songs, while
others simply post the songs with a few words
about the band. Some even do interviews. Your
songs are visible to visitors for up to 30 days.
After that, visitors of the blog would have to
search the archives to find your posts. Some
blogs also post videos. Many also feature
podcasts of music they like.*

*Many of these blogs feature what is called
"podsafe music". To find out what podsafe
music is, read the article in SECTION EIGHT of
this directory called "What is Podsafe Music?"*

North America
United States

3hive
PO Box 3778, Huntington Beach, CA 92605
suggestionbox@3hive.com
www.3hive.com
*Promoting MP3s in hope that people will hear
enough to buy the album, attend the live show, wear
the t-shirt ...*

365 Days Project
blog.wfmu.org/freeform/365_days_project
*WFMU blog featuring 365 days of cool and strange
and often obscure audio selections.*

4waystop
T3 4waystop@gmail.com
www.4waystop.com
*Helps new bands get exposure and exposes our
listeners to new music.*

5 Acts
PO Box 22618, Alexandria VA 22304
Jared Hoke 5actsblog@gmail.com
5acts.blogspot.com
A daily posting of music worthy of your ears.

52 Bands
Sammi Dittloff sammi.dittloff@b5media.com
www.52bands.com
Introducing you to new music, one week at a time.

52 Shows
info@52shows.com
www.52shows.com
A live music blog written by and for regular folks.

A Blog Soup
blogsoup@gmail.com
ablogsoup.blogspot.com
Blogging up a mess!

A Plague of Angels
Molotov mikarr785@aol.com
plagueofangels.blogspot.com
Music mandated by activist judges.

Advance Copy
kmhopkin@juno.com
advancecopy.blogspot.com
This is what you want, this is what you get.

Adzuki Bean Stash
Cchang cchang@math.utexas.edu
adzukipod.blogspot.com
*If you discover a musician/band on here that
happens to take your fancy, please read up on them.*

All the Peoples
allthepeoples@gmail.com
www.allthepeoples.com
We give you a taste of the new and hot music everyone's talking about. In our blog you can discover artists and music you've never heard of before and most important you can listen and download music.

All Things Go
Zack allthingsgoblog@gmail.com
allthingsgo.wordpress.com
Features music ranging from Hardcore to Hip Hop, Dance Rock to just plain adorable Indie.

The Alternakids
doctashock doctashock@gmail.com
thealternakids.wordpress.com
Updated daily, you'll find a bunch of kids talking about what they love most. Share your views with us, discover new music, be entertained!

An Idiot's Guide to Dreaming
farmerglitch@gmail.com
loki23.blogspot.com
The blogging equivalent of an acid tattoo scare.

Arjan Writes
arjanwrites@gmail.com
www.arjanwrites.com
Original interviews, music reviews and exclusive reports from behind the scenes.

Ashcan Rantings
Charles & Leah email.ashcan@gmail.com
ashcanrantings.blogspot.com
A blog about music and the arts.

asrestlessasweare
seandonson@gmail.com
www.arawa.fm
If you like what you see or hear, let me know! Leave a comment or send music, praise and insults to my e-mail address.

Attorney Street
PH: 917-512-5484
info@attorneyst.com
attorneyst.com
We post good. It look good. Oh, write good we too.

aurgasm
3 Ashford Ct. #1, Boston, MA 02134-2204
Paul Irish paul@aurgasm.us
aurgasm.us
An eclectic menagerie of aural pleasures. I scout out music you've never heard and deliver only the finest.

Banana Nutrament
nutramentmike@gmail.com
banananutrament.blogspot.com
Investigating new and old artists and music. We like to support artists making a living with their music.

Berkeley Place
ekalett@yahoo.com
We will listen to all submissions of entire albums (e-mail me to submit). Our preferred format is to receive a CD in the mail, but we also welcome .zip files. See our submission policy.

Between Thought and Expression
DJMonsterMo BTandE@gmail.com
djmonstermo.blogspot.com
An eclectic guide to life's musical journey. Features Indie Rock and Electronic MP3s, mash-ups and entertainment.

bigstereo
PO Box 5062. Portland, ME 04101
Travis promo@bigstereo.net
this.bigstereo.net
We try to work with artists and labels to provide content for our readers. Have a record we should hear?

The Big Ticket
mr.gilbert@mac.com
the-big-ticket.blogspot.com
News, opinions and MP3 reviews.

Both Sides of the Mouth
Alina & Brad bothsidesofthemouth@gmail.com
bothsidesofthemouth.blogspot.com
If you would like to be featured on this blog, send us an email. If we like what we hear, we'll post about it.

Bows + Arrows
555 Guava Ln. #9G, Davis, CA 95616
Brian Lum brian@bowsplusarrows.com
bowsplusarrows.com
I listen to absolutely everything I'm sent.

Brooklyn Heathen
brooklynheathen.com
Music and other good things in this wayward world.

Can You See the Sunset From the Southside?
Eric canyouseethesunset@gmail.com
www.canyouseethesunset.com
Daily MP3s and occasional podcasts. A little left of the mainstream and that's the way I like it.

Catbirdseat
catbirdseat.org@gmail.com
www.catbirdseat.org
MP3 blog with news and reviews.

Cause=Time
519 Galapago St., Denver, CO 80204
Julio Enriquez julio.enriquez@gmail.com
julioenriquez.blogspot.com
Slowly stumbling through life in the Mile High City...

The Cavedoll of it All
PH: 801-808-9269
Camden Chamberlain
camden@kitefishingfamily.com
www.cavedollband.blogspot.com
Focused primarily on Indie Rock, Pop and Electronic. If you think we'll enjoy what you're doing, send us a link to where we can hear your music.

clicky clicky
Jay jay.breitling@gmail.com
clickyclickymusic.com
News. reviews, opinion, fanboy excitation since 2003.

Cliptip
cliptip@gmail.com
cliptip.blogspot.com
Music news, reviews, videos etc.

Coffee Snorter
coffeesnorter@gmail.com
coffeesnorter.blogspot.com
Created by an over caffeinated coffee zealot with a slight case of A.D.D. in music.

COMBOPLATES
chef@comboplates.com
www.comboplates.com
Music is presented out of love and respect, not to profit or violate copyright.

Come Pick Me Up
Lizzy backtothesound@mac.com
cpmu.blogspot.com
I'm here to inform, not provide. If visitors dig the MP3s I post, I ask that they support the artist and purchase a CD.

Complicated Dance Steps
complicateddancesteps@gmail.com
complicateddancesteps.blogspot.com
Covering Indie music with MP3s and video clips.

Consequence of Sound
axyoung@gmail.com
consequenceofsound.net
A New York and Chicago based, worldly influenced music blog that seeks to cover the music world as it has never been covered before. Not only do we accept music submissions, we encourage them!

Copy, Right?
bigfatprettyface@yahoo.com
copycommaright.blogspot.com
Posts cover tunes.

Count Me Out
countmeoutblog@gmail.com
countmeoutblog.blogspot.com
Feel free to send a message with a link or MP3s for consideration. If you'd like to send an album through mail, please send an email as well.

Cover Songs
Jim Fusco admin@fusco-moore.com
www.laptopsessions.com
Free video blog featuring songwriters that do Acoustic Rock music videos, original music, cover songs and music reviews. Major and indie music versions of the best cover songs.

Crazed Hits
Alex William alex@crazedhits.com
www.crazedhits.com
A leading A&R tip sheet used by record labels, managers, booking agents, entertainment attorneys, publishers and various other people in the music industry to identify the best up and coming talent!

CRUD CRUD
Scott Soriano ss@s-srecords.com
crudcrud.blogspot.com
A tour through the stacks of records, demo tapes etc. that surround me.

Culture Bully
Chris chris@culturebully.com
www.culturebully.com
With album reviews and other posts ranging from Indie Rock to Hip Hop to Electronica, you never know what we'll bring.

Culturespill
gmanzione@culturespill.com
culturespill.com
We are hopeless music dorks who suffer from a neurotic compulsion to write about the music we love. The hope, of course, is to impose our tastes on the world, one city at a time.

Daytrotter.com
info@daytrotter.com
www.daytrotter.com
We're giving you exclusive, re-worked, alternate versions of old songs and unreleased tracks by some of your favorite bands and by a lot of your next favorite bands.

Dreams of Horses
Michael cassettetapes@gmail.com
dreamsofhorses.blogspot.com
If you'd like to see your band featured on my site, send me an MP3 and some info.

Each Note Secure
joe@eachnotesecure.com
www.eachnotesecure.com
MP3 blog created with the intent of promoting my favorite music.

EAR FARM
168 2nd Ave. #389, New York, NY 10003
Matt Tyson matt@earfarm.com
earfarm.com
If you send something to us and we like it, we'll feature it on our site.

Ear Taste
PO Box 1257 Sabinal, TX 78881
Rich Soos eartaste@gmail.com
www.eartaste.com
We listen to full CDs and write about 1 cut in particular.

EARVOLUTION
Jeff Davidson earvolutionsubmissions@gmail.com
earvolution.com
Music news, reviews, interviews and notes.

Elbows
elbo.ws
A collection of great music blog posts and is meant to provide you a snapshot of what's going on in this new genre of blogging.

Everybody Cares, Everybody Understands
everybodycares@gmail.com
everybodycares.blogspot.com
I'm rather obsessed with finding good (free and legal) music to share with everybody.

Exitfare
580 Harrison Ave. 4th Fl. Boston, MA 02118
Dany Sloan exitfare@gmail.com
exitfare.blogspot.com
New music, shows, interviews, TV and club night fun!

extrawack!
extrawack@gmail.com
extrawack.blogspot.com
Featuring reviews and quality MP3s of new music.

Fine Fine Music
mail@finefinemusic.com
www.finefinemusic.com
We link to MP3s of bands that we like.

Fingertips
letterbox@fingertipsmusic.com
www.fingertipsmusic.com
fingertipsmusic.blogspot.com
The ongoing heart of the site, featuring the three songs selected each week as the best free and legal MP3s found in my ongoing search for great free and legal MP3s.

Fluxblog
Matthew Perpetua fluxblog@gmail.com
www.fluxblog.org
Reviews music and posts MP3s. Send MP3s to my e-mail address. Contact me for instructions on sending your CD.

FreeIndie
mike@freeindie.com
www.freeindie.com
A blog that posts full albums from independent bands that you can download for free!

Fuzzy Lion
staff@fuzzylion.com
www.fuzzylion.com
If you would like to submit your music for possible review, get in touch.

Gather Round, Children
gabe.durham@gmail.com
gatherroundchildren.wordpress.com
E-mail me if you have a record, book, blog, or something you'd like me to check out.

The Glorious Hum
theglorioushum@yahoo.com
theglorioushum.blogspot.com
Generally the rule of thumb is pretty simple: if I like your music, I'll post on it. Please make sure you read our submission details.

Good Weather For Airstrikes
DerekDavies@aol.com
www.goodweatherforairstrikes.com
A place for me to share info about up and coming bands.

gorilla vs. bear
Chris chrismc99@hotmail.com
gorillavsbear.blogspot.com
We never have a bad thing to say about anyone, even if they are lame.

Hands Up!
handsuporlando@gmail.com
www.handsuporlando.com
If you're an artist and you'd like to get some of your work posted on Hands Up, email your tracks to us and we'll give them a listen!

Heart on a Stick
heartonastick@gmail.com
heartonastick.blog-city.com
News, photos, reviews etc.

He's a Whore
darren@darrenrobbins.com
hesawhore.blogspot.com
Hope you dig the blog. Feel free to drop me a note.

HIPSTER RUNOFF
carleser@gmail.com
www.hipsterrunoff.com
Please contact me if you want to be blogged about. I can basically blog about anything.

The Hood Internet
thehoodinternet@gmail.com
thehoodinternet.com
We receive an average of 6500 unique hits a day, and we've had over one million downloads of our tracks in the last year.

The House of Leaf and Lime
leafandlime@gmail.com
leafandlime.hobix.com
Updated several times weekly.

The Hype Machine
hype.non-standard.net
An experiment that keeps track of songs and discussion posted on the best blogs about music. Visitors listen, discover and buy songs that everyone is talking about!

I Am Fuel, You Are Friends
browneheather@gmail.com
www.fuelfriends.blogspot.com
Got something I should hear? E-mail me.

I Guess I'm Floating
contact.iguessimfloating@gmail.com
iguessimfloating.blogspot.com
Blog of the Rock n' Roll variety. If you're a band and would like to submit a demo, just e-mail us!

I Rock Cleveland
irockcleveland@gmail.com
irockcleveland.blogspot.com
Contact us if you want your band to be featured on our site.

Indie Rock Blog
www.bloggomite.com/indierock
All our content is provided by, and aggregated from some of the web's top indie music blogs.

indieMUSE.com
David david@indiemuse.com
indiemuse.com
A place where people who are as passionate about music as we are, can come together to listen and talk about music.

Indoor Fireworks
The Vicar indoorfireworksonline@gmail.com
indoorfireworks.blogspot.com
Music news and MP3s.

Jinners
missjinners@gmail.com
www.jinners.com
Music news, dates, video etc.

Kingblind
Martin Lee info@kingblind.com
www.kingblind.com
Music news, album & concerts reviews, MP3s, videos, art / entertainment and much more!

Largehearted Boy
boy@largeheartedboy.com
blog.largeheartedboy.com
Featuring daily free and legal music downloads as well as news from the worlds of music, literature and pop culture.

The Listen
2046 Hillhurst Ave. #22, Los Angeles, CA 90027
tips@thelisten.net
www.thelisten.net
We can't promise that we'll post your submissions, but we will do our best to give every song submitted a spin.

loudersoft
540 S. Mendenhall, #12-223, Memphis, TN 38117
ej@loudersoft.com
loudersoft.com
It's my pleasure to listen to anything you send me. Before you spend the postage or hard-earned cash you might want to review what's on my site for a while to see what I write about. I promise you I listen to everything you send, but I don't publish a review for every submission. PLEASE don't attach MP3 files to your emails!

Lunch of Champions
reviews@lunchofchampions.info
www.lunchofchampions.info
Send an email to with your name, contact info, bio and a link where we can hear your music.

marathonpacks
eric@marathonpacks.com
www.marathonpacks.com
I am very picky about what I post here, but you may make submission requests.

Missing Toof
PH: 310-574-2421
missingtoof@missingtoof.com
missingtoof.com
Knocking out dentals since 2006.

MOISTWORKS
moistworks@gmail.com
www.moistworks.com
We enjoy listening to new material and try to listen to everything sent our way.

Moroccan Role
hammmd@gmail.com
moroccanrole.blogspot.com
A totally killer music/MP3 blog.

Music For Ants
104 W. Irving #11, Normal, IL 61761
PH: 309-251-1258
Taylor Johnston musicforants@mac.com
musicforants.com
If you have music you'd like me to write about, e-mail me the MP3s or mail your CD.

music for robots
contact@music.for-robots.com
music.for-robots.com
Contact us if you think we'd be interested in your music.

Music Is Art
musicisart.ws
Focuses not only on excellent music, but on art, photography and writing and how they all intersect.

Music is My Boyfriend
angela@musicismybf.com
musicismybf.com
Notes and chords are sexy!

The Music Slut
themusicslut@gmail.com
musicslut.blogspot.com
We are based in New York City and outside of Edinburgh, Scotland. In an effort to save bands money, and hopefully save some trees along the way, our preferred method of submission is digital.

My Old Kentucky Blog
8565 Scarsdale Dr. E., Indianapolis, IN 46256
dodge77@gmail.com
myoldkyhome.blogspot.com
You can e-mail MP3s or send materials to our mailing address.

Needcoffee.com
wakeupyoubastards@needcoffee.com
www.needcoffee.com
You think you've got something that can keep us awake? Well? Do ya, punk? Bring that noise. We like it, we'll post it.

Noise for Toaster
noisefortoaster@gmail.com
www.noisefortoaster.com
We'll drag you through concerts, websites, new music reviews and the same shit you read everywhere else.

Obscure Sound
Mike Mineo mike@obscuresound.com
www.obscuresound.com
Provides reviews and information on relatively unknown bands that I think others will find enjoyable. We do not care if the band is unsigned or signed, just as long as we have an audio sample and a nice sound.

the of mirror eye
ofmirroreye@gmail.com
blog.ofmirroreye.net
The songs I'm posting are some of my favorites for one reason or another.

the oh so quiet show
roboppy@gmail.com
music.diskobox.net
Send me MP3s or real CDs (ask for my shipping address) but I'm not obligated to write about anything unless I like it.

Ohh! Crapp
hollywhore@gmail.com
www.ohhcrapp.net
News, reviews and interviews.

Out the Other
Janet Timmons outtheother@gmail.com
www.outtheother.com
A streaming archive of music to pay attention to. I also host a radio show on WRVU.

The Passion of the Weiss
Jeff Weiss jweiss24@yahoo.com
passionweiss.blogspot.com
Thoughts, MP3s and video clips.

The Plugg
www.theplugg.com
An arts & entertainment blog.

Pocket|Trax
135 Pleasant St. #11, Arlington, MA 02476
PH: 617-901-9822
Dave pockettrax@gmail.com
www.pockettrax.com
We do not review music. What we do is collect and share artist info and sample tracks and leave the reviewing up to the readers/listeners.

PolloxNiner
Sunny Pollox9@aol.com
polloxniner.blogs.com
I write and edit for magazines, newspapers, websites and TV.

PowerPop
Steve Simels ssimels@gmail.com
www.powerpop.blogspot.com
An idiosyncratic blog dedicated to the precursors, the practitioners and the descendants of Power Pop.

Powerpopulist
powerpopulist@yahoo.com
powerpopulist.blogspot.com
Comments and emails are more than welcome, as are submissions by bands and artists.

Radio Exile
radioexile.com
A work of love and devotion to this glorious, bloggy hype machine that can elevate the artists we love to stars.

Radio No. 1
radionoone@gmail.com
radionoone.blogspot.com
We like to hear new things! We like the old and the new, so send in your requests and tips to us!

The Rawking Refuses to Stop!
David Greenwald davideg@ucla.edu
rawkblog.blogspot.com
If you are in a band or work for a label, I'd love to hear your stuff. Link me some MP3s or drop me an e-mail and I'll let you know where can you send me promos.

The Rich Girls Are Weeping
Cindy & Pinkie elegantfaker@gmail.com
therichgirlsareweeping.blogspot.com
If you would like to send some material, drop us an e-mail to get our mailing address.

Ryan's Smashing life
therslweblog@gmail.com
ryanssmashinglife.blogspot.com
My goal is to provide exposure for fantastic music and art from around the world.

Scenestars
rachel@scenestars.com
www.scenestars.net
Send event info and MP3s for us to review!

scissorkick.com
8801 Ridge Blvd. Brooklyn, NY 11209
steve@scissorkick.com
www.scissorkick.com
A blog used for the purpose of cultivating interest in musicians and their music.

Shake Your Fist
shakeyourfist@gmail.com
shakeyourfist.blogspot.com
We encourage people to buy music, see shows and support the artists we feature.

shoes are for work
memo57 donmemo57@gmail.com
memo57.blogspot.com
If you would like to submit a file for posting, tell me...

Side One: Track One
12113 Metric Blvd. #1123, Austin, TX 78758
John Laird sideonetrackone@gmail.com
www.sideonetrackone.com
I post up songs here throughout the week and share my thoughts on them with the sugary sweet idea that those who stop by this place won't feel like I wasted their time.

Silence is a Rhythm Too
Michael djrez1@hotmail.com
siart.blogspot.com
I love music and I've always loved to share my favorite music. I like a lot of different things and hope you will too.

Single of the Day
Jody reviews@singleoftheday.com
singleoftheday.com
I choose a song a day to showcase to the world. Do not send MP3s as attachments!

Sixeyes
alanlwilliamson@gmail.com
sixeyes.blogspot.com
An MP3 blog that posts music news, reviews and interviews.

skatterbrain
Matthew mortigi_tempo@verizon.net
skatterbrain.org
Covering new and interesting indie music spanning just about all genres. We update daily with news, band spotlights and exclusive MP3 posts.

Slave to the Details
team@slavetothedetails.net
slavetothedetails.net
All MP3s are up for a limited time and are for sampling purposes only.

songs:illinois
629 Belleforte St., Oak Park, IL 60302
Craig Bonnell cbonnell@gmail.com
www.songsillinoismp3.blogspot.com
Mostly music musings on new and old releases, current favs and live shows. MP3 downloads updated several times a week for evaluation purposes.

Sonic Itch Music
2605 E. 3rd St., Austin, TX 78702
sonicitchmusic@gmail.com
www.sonicitchmusic.com
Our goal here is to share our thoughts, ideas, and experiences as they apply to the music that we feel to be interesting and exciting.

The Sound of Indie
kevin@thesoundofindie.com
www.thesoundofindie.com
One person's music collection laid forth for the world to hear.

STEREOB@!T
djgordonthomas@hotmail.com
www.stereobait.com
This blog is used to promote new music and artists. Not to steal from them. Please support the artists by buying their music.

The Suburbs are Killing Us
suburbs@christopherporter.com
www.christopherporter.com
MP3s are here to promote love. They are removed after one week.

These Rocks Pop
theserockspop@gmail.com
theserockspop.blogspot.com
If you are an artist and want your music on or off this blog, hit us up

Torr Blog
5908 Barton Ave. Los Angeles, CA 91604
Torr Leonard torrissey80@yahoo.com
torr.typepad.com/weblog
If you are interested in submitting music for plugging consideration, please send it to the above address.

Trigger Cut
Johnny Metro triggercut@crankautomotive.com
www.triggercut.com
Audio and video blog with occasional reviews.

Tuning
jayniemann@gmail.com
ggth.typepad.com/tng
Got a CD or band I should know about? Well then, why don't you flack yer tunes?

Two and 1/2 Pounds Of Bacon
fastbacker@haywoodnyc.com
fastbacker.blogspot.com
MP3 and video blog based out of Brooklyn.

Warped Reality
andrea@warpedrealitymagazine.com
www.warpedrealitymagazine.com
Covers lots of other interesting music that flies below the radar.

Wongie's Music World
wongiesworld@yahoo.com
www.wongiesmusicworld.blogspot.com
A blog focusing on music and videos that I'm into and would like to introduce to others. Whether it's hip bands or straight up Pop, it's all good here!

The Yellow Stereo
1993 Rick Dr. Auburn, AL 36830
theyellowstereo.blog@gmail.com
theyellowstereo.com
If you're interested in sending promotional material, please contact us.

Yeti Don't Dance
Jerry Yeti jerryyeti@gmail.com
noyetidance.blogspot.com
Blog posting music news and MP3s.

You Ain't No Picasso
matt@youaintnopicasso.com
youaintnopicasso.com
Blog with interviews with artists and reviews of MP3s.

You See The Sunset From The Southside
canyouseethesunset@gmail.com
www.canyouseethesunset.com
I like most styles of music. E-mail me for my mailing address.

Your Only Friends
youronlyfriends@gmail.com
blog.youronlyfriends.com
If you would like me to check out your material, e-mail it to me.

Canada

chromewaves.net
Frank frank@chromewaves.net
www.chromewaves.net
I write about stuff that I find interesting and noteworthy. Please check the site to see if your music fits before sending it in.

Condemned to Rock 'N Roll
anglopunk@hotmail.com
www.condemnedtorocknroll.blogspot.com
I'm a music fan with a heavy bias toward music produced in the UK and the rest of Europe.

herohill.com
herohill@gmail.com
www.herohill.com
Music interviews, news, reviews and tracks.

i (heart) music
1276 Wellington Ave. 2nd Fl. Ottawa, ON K1Y 3A7
info@iheartmusic.net
www.iheartmusic.net
All the latest news, views, reviews and MP3s. We'll accept anything and everything, but can't guarantee a review.

Indie Launchpad
Colin Meeks colin@indielaunchpad.com
www.indielaunchpad.com
Showcasing some of the best in independent music. We also have a podcast that features tracks from the music we review.

Kwaya Na Kisser
www.knkmusic.net
knk@knkmusic.net
Music blog cool moniker.

Mocking Music
RR 1, Mountstewart, PE C0A 1T0
Casey Dorrell mockingmusic@gmail.com
www.mockingmusic.blogspot.com
E-mail us to make arrangements and we'll gladly review your music.

Muzak for Cybernetics
Sean muzakforcybernetics@gmail.com
www.indierockblog.com
Features Indie Rock, Electro, Hip Hop and other cool music from all over the world.

Neiles Life
Styeiles neilesc@hotmail.com
www.neileslife.blogspot.com
The purpose this blog is to promote fantastic music.

Popsheep
popsheep@gmail.com
popsheep.com
Reviews of MP3s and live shows. Contact us if you want to invite us to your show.

Pregnant Without Intercourse
3647 Ave. Henri-Julien, Montreal, QC H2X 3H4
Keith Serry fatcitizen@gmail.com
www.pwithouti.com
What we taught the world is that you can suck and still rule.

Quick Before it Melts
quickbeforeitmelts@gmail.com
www.qbim.blogspot.com
QBiM believes that you should sample new artists freely, purchase new music wisely, support your favourites always.

Rock Snob
Miss Valerie sheswiththeband@hotmail.com
therocksnob.blogspot.com
Because we're better and we know it!

Said the Gramophone
Jordan Himelfarb jordan@saidthegramophone.com
www.saidthegramophone.com
A daily sampler of really good songs. All tracks are posted out of love.

Villains Always Blink
Kelly trillionmillion@hotmail.com
thetrainingground.blogspot.com
Indie music, reviews, hype, news, MP3s ...

Winnie Cooper
win.e.coop.r@gmail.com
winniecooper.net
If you are an artist and would like us to check out your skills, please feel free to email us with your choice tracks.

Europe

Czech Republic

Getecho
getecho@hotmail.com
getecho.blogspot.com
Send me info, you can! I also appreciate all suggestions/tips and label/band news. I'm specially searching for new bands!

Denmark

Hits in the Car
Stytzer hits_in_the_car@yahoo.dk
stytzer.blogspot.com
It's all about music!

France

alain finkielkrautrock
alainfinkielkrautrock@gmail.com
www.alainfinkielkrautrock.com
Support the music, buy records, read books, don't believe the hype.

La Blogothèque
www.blogotheque.net
Le premier MP3 blog, audioblog en France.

Germany

Almost Tropical
almost-tropical.blogspot.com
Audio and video blog from Berlin.

Indie Surfer
Ziggy gpanic@gmail.com
indiesurfer.blogspot.com
Intended to popularize the music of independent artists and to give you the latest info on their activity.

knicken
knickenberlin@googlemail.com.
knicken.blogspot.com
A Berlin-based blog about music, pop culture, entertainment and mainly things.

The Last Pop Song
thelastpopsong@gmail.com
thelastpopsong.blogspot.com
A passionate indie music blog.

Italy

Indie for Dummies
indiefordummies@gmail.com
www.indiefordummies.com
We help bands we like to be noticed in Italy.

Norway

For the Eardrums
Liljekroken 20, 3050 Mjöndalen, Norway
www.eardrumsmusic.com
A focus on new and interesting music. Alternative artists from the world of indie, Electronica, Experimental or Alt-Folk.

It's a trap!
PO Box 7064, Olympia, WA 98507-7064
avi.roig@itsatrap.com
www.itsatrap.com
Devoted to the promotion of Scandinavian music to an international audience. If it's not Scandinavian, we don't want it!

Sweden

24:hours
tunes@twentyfourhours.se
2-4-hours.blogspot.com
All about the music we love. We only post stuff that the artists and labels give us, which means no illegal files.

Swedesplease
cbonnell@gmail.com
www.swedesplease.net
The first daily MP3 blog devoted to Swedish music. Mostly Electronica, Indie Pop and Twee.

United Kingdom

Another Form of Relief
PO Box 756, Gillingham, Kent, ME8 6WW UK
scrunty@gmail.com
www.theclerisy.com/afor
We'll listen to everything that we are sent and will write about anything that we like.

Asleep on the Compost Heap
Gardenhead asleepontheheap@gmail.com
onavery.blogspot.com
Gardenhead is the salty air that whines through forgotten penny arcade machines on a November pier.

Black Country Grammar
jon@blackcountrygrammar.co.uk
grammardj.blogspot.com
If you have something for me to listen to, drop me a line.

The Devil Has the Best Tuna
kerr.thedevilstuna3@gmail.com
www.besttuna.blogspot.com
Dedicated to unearthing unknown, unheard, unseen, unheralded or downright unbelievable bands new or old, that have not yet hit the radars of the music papers, magazines and the British public in the UK. If you're in a new band, are unsigned and would like to be considered for inclusion on the site, please email me.

Get the Lot
www.getthelot.blogspot.com
Get your sounds heard here. If you're a musician or your in a band (preferably unsigned) and your looking for promotion, drop me a comment with a link to your music.

headphone sex
PO Box 204, Slough, SL2 2QE UK
James Woodley james@headphonesex.co.uk
www.headphonesex.co.uk
Tracks are posted for one week. Send me music!

Indie MP3 - Keeping C86 Alive!
www.indie-mp3.co.uk
Working hard to keep the Indie Pop scene alive.

mp3hugger
mp3hugger.com
The purpose of this site is to introduce music to people who may otherwise not get to hear it.

Music Liberation
musicliberation@hotmail.co.uk
www.musicliberation.blogspot.com
If you want to send me music, swap links, review a single or album, or just to chat about music, then contact me.

No Rock & Roll Fun
Simon simonb@gmail.com
xrrf.blogspot.com
Music news and reviews.

Nothing But Green Lights
Mike Smith mikesmithmikesmith@gmail.com
nothingbutgreenlights.net
Features fresh and exciting, legal MP3's from diverse artists and Pop acts from around the globe.

SPLENDIDA PROJECT
DJ durutti djdurutti@gmail.com
splendida.blogspot.com
An eclectic mix of sights and sounds provided by our contributors.

The Torture Garden
Shane thetorturegarden@gmail.com
thetorturegarden.blogspot.com
Downloads, news and interviews.

Australia

A Reminder
sean@a-reminder.org
www.a-reminder.org/music
If you are an artist and would like to have your music featured on this site feel free to e-mail me. I love actual CDs and I will provide you with a mailing address if you like. Emailing MP3s is cool too.

Joe.Blog
joe@hardy.id.au
joe.hardy.id.au/blog
Yep, yet another blog. This one belongs to Joe Hardy.

Twelve Major Chords
admin@twelvemajorchords.com
www.twelvemajorchords.com
We like to talk about music. We like to take photos of music. We like to talk to musicians about their music.

New Zealand

Einstein Music Journal
Sarah sarah@einsteinmusicjournal.co.nz
www.einsteinmusicjournal.co.nz
A Wellington based indie music blog. Showcasing Kiwi music to the world!

Africa

South Africa

another night on earth
Chris Keys cmint@axxess.co.za
www.anothernightonearth.blogspot.com
Audioblog covering a wide range of music.

Asia

Japan

Happy Oranges
www.xanga.com/munky_mp3
Check my website for details on how to upload your MP3s.

Blues

Cross Harp Chronicles

Dave King dking@crossharpchronicles.com
www.crossharpchronicles.com
With the tagline "Bringing the Blues Into the 21st Century," this free online quarterly helps today's Blues artist navigate the waters of a rapidly changing recording industry. Site includes in-depth interviews with both established Blues artists and promising "up-and-comings," both foreign and domestic; as well as provides the largest number of regularly updated news stories on the Blues on the web. Site includes forum, online video library, blog, etc. Accepts CDs for review consideration.

Children's

Mama Lisa's World Blog

Mama Lisa blog@mamalisa.com
www.mamalisa.com/blog
MP3 Blog featuring music and conversations about the languages and cultures of the world, especially the songs and traditions of children.

Planet KidVid

planetkidvid.blogspot.com
Blog featuring Children's music videos.

(sm)all ages

superclea@cox.net
smallages.blogspot.com
MP3 blog featuring Children's music.

Christian

316Muzik

2608 Valencia Grove Dr. Valrico, FL 33594
PH: 813-454-2464 FX: 813-944-2950
Casio Jones casio@316muzik.com
www.316muzik.com
The only place on the internet to watch full screen DVD quality Christian music videos. Free membership. No cost to the artist.

Christian/Gospel Show Local TV 33

Box 3318, Sierra Vista, AZ 85636
PH: 520-803-0675
Chuck Alton chuckalton@hotmail.com
I am developing a new music TV show featuring Christian/Gospel/Inspirational music. Please send your DVDs for consideration to the above address.

The Christian Jukebox

9900-E Greenbelt Rd. #208, Lanham, MD 20706
PH: 301-332-9239
Simone Henry info@thechristianjukebox.com
www.thechristianjukebox.com
A digital download store that is committed to spreading the gospel of Jesus Christ through great independent music!

Christian Music Fan

Jason Bean jason@b5media.com
www.christianmusicfan.com
Connecting with Christian music in a variety of ways. Christian, secular, worship, artists, songs, lyrics and more.

Gospel Music Channel

jbennett@gospelmusicchannel.com
www.gospelmusicchannel.com
We are currently seeking music videos from undiscovered and unsigned talent from churches and communities across all genres of Gospel and Christian music

Gospel Swap

PO Box 286261, Chicago, IL 60628
PH: 708-272-6640
Andr'e L. Carter alcarter@gospelsynergy.com
www.gospelswap.com
Your online home for independent Gospel music.

mypraisesong

www.mypraisesong.com
A social network where millions of Christians praise and worship music videos.

Classical

aworks

rgable.typepad.com/aworks
MP3 blog covering "new" American Classical music.

ChoralNet

4230 Mary Dr. Rapid City, SD 57702
www.choralnet.org
Extensive resources for Choral artists.

Classic Cat

webmaster@classiccat.net
www.classiccat.net
A directory with links to over 2000 free to download Classical performances on the internet, sorted by composer and work.

The Classical Music Archives

200 Sheridan Ave. #403, Palo Alto, CA 94306
PH: 650-330-8050
www.classicalarchives.com
Submit your music to get exposure.

Classical Music Mobile

Philippe Herlin classicalmusicmobile@yahoo.com
www.classicalmusicmobile.com
Download Classical music. Offers only high level interpretation.

Classical.com

55 Station Rd. Beaconsfield, Bucks, HP9 1QL UK
PH: +44-20-8816-8848
conductor@classical.com
www.classical.com
Online listening, downloads, custom CDs and more.

Dial 'M' for Musicology

Jonathan Bellman mmusicology@gmail.com
musicology.typepad.com
An academic blog, but it wants to be friends with everyone. Welcome to all critics, musicians, bedroom air-guitarists, louche aesthetes, prickly autodidacts, and random passers-by!

eClassical.com

Ö. Skansg. 32, SE-41302 Goteborg, Sweden
PH: +46-709-63-31-00
info@eclassical.com
www.eclassical.com
A completely virtual record label.

Impulse Classical Music

impulse@impulse-music.co.uk
www.impulse-music.co.uk
Provides personalized pages on performers and composers.

Musical Assumptions

Elaine Fine elainefine@gmail.com
musicalassumptions.blogspot.com
Music is a mystery for people who play it, write it, listen to it, and write about it. The only thing I can really do when I try to say something about music is assume.

NetNewMusic

netnewmusic.net
A portal for the world of NON-Pop/Extreme Indie/Avant-whatever music.

OnClassical

Via Ca'Petofi 13 - (36022) Cassola, Vicenza, Italy
PH: +39-0424-533137 FX: +39-0424-533137
info@onclassical.com
www.OnClassical.com
Distributing high quality Classical music in MP3 or CD quality files (WAV format). We are associated with kunstderfuge.com, the greatest resource of free MIDI files on the net. There are now entire tracks - streaming files - licensed under CC. Anyone may republish them on his site with no limits!

World Music Office

23 rue Nollet - 75017 Paris, France
PH: 01-47-70-38-68 FX: 01-47-70-39-71
annuaire@wmo.fr
www.wmo.fr
Classical music only! Worldwide digital distribution and synchronization opportunities. No fees. Non exclusive agreements.

Country

acousticfriends.com

feedback@acousticfriends.com
www.acousticfriends.com
Enables Acoustic musicians to be seen and heard by posting their music, video and upcoming performance information, increasing their fan base.

Digital Rodeo

www.digitalrodeo.com
An online community filled with fresh and exciting content for Country music artists and fans alike.

IndieHighway.com

www.indiehighway.com
This site was developed to help Americana artists gain international exposure and airplay.

Mandolin Cafe

eadg@mandolincafe.com
www.mandolincafe.com/mp3
Introduces new mandolin players.

Visual Image Marketing

PO Box 120576, Nashville, TN 37212
PH: 615-419-0886
Steve Baker steveb@visualimagemarketing.com
Bill Baker bill@visualimagemarketing.com
www.myspace.com/visualimagemarketing
We promote & market Country and Americana music videos to music networks & video outlets across the nation & around the world.

Dance and Electronic

North America

United States

7161.com

admin@7161.com
www.7161.com
We are a non profit site run by musicians. We have free web space for artists to add their music for streaming. We also offer free homepage creation and other free tools.

Beatport
support@beatport.com
www.beatport.com
Designed to service the evolution of the Digital music culture, redefining how DJs and enthusiasts acquire their music.

Curbcrawlers
curbcrawlers@gmail.com
thecurbcrawlers.com/blog
We're always looking for new music. If you're a label, producer or rmxer and want to submit music, please send us an email and we'll hook it up.

earwigs & wax
info@earwigsandwax.com
www.earwigsandwax.com
A music and culture magazine targeted on Electronic music and design.

Electric Zoo
electriczooblog@gmail.com
electriczoo.blogspot.com
All material featured is for evaluation purposes, aimed to help promote the artists/labels featured by encouraging others to buy and support their music.

Electronic Crack
electroniccrack@gmail.com
electroniccrack.blogspot.com
I'm currently trapped in the Midwest. Here you can read up on music [mainly Electronic, sometimes Hip Hop, Jazz and Funkadelic] that I find appealing.

Filter 27
filter@filter27.com
www.filter27.com
Music and video blog covering the world of Dance and Electronic music.

Find Voltorb, Catch Voltorb
jared.reyes@gmail.com
www.findvoltorbcatchvoltorb.blogspot.com
If you have any requests, comments, music, and the like that you feel inclined to share with me, hit me up.

Get Nice!
bashmentjack@gmail.com
getnice.net.au/blog
This is a blog to share the gems we find.

headstrong Dance music
info@headstrong-hq.com
www.headstrong-hq.com
Put your demos here to get exposure.

Honeybee Inn
honeybeeinn@gmail.com
honeybeeinn.blogspot.com
Catering to Disco House, Electro House and (good) Dance music. Send a song(s) my way and if it's totally awesome - we'll post it!

InternetDJ.com
Michael Bordash mbordash@internetdj.com
www.internetdj.com
Hosts and plays MP3s from independent musicians.

Knobtweakers
www.knobtweakers.net
The world's leading free and legal Electronic music MP3 blog, established to support and promote Electronic music culture.

Music V2
musicv2@musicv2.com
www.musicv2.com
Free MP3 hosting, artist pages, DJ sets, free music downloads.

Oh Death
oh.death.studio@gmail.com
oh-death.blogspot.com
I write about music, graphics and the occasional spill of randomness.

One More Disco
www.onemoredisco.com
Was originally thought out around 1000 BC, but it had only been made reality late 2007.

Outside Broadcast
DJ Roctakon roctakon@gmail.com
outsidebroadcast.blogspot.com
Audioblog featuring remixes, vinyl rips, mix CDs and other fun stuff.

Palms Out Sounds
palmsout@gmail.com
palmsout.blogspot.com
The music on this site is intended to inspire you to support the musicians who make it. If you have a question, submission, or complaint, please email us.

Panda Toes
pandatoes@gmail.com
pandatoes.blogspot.com
MP3 blog with news, reviews and interviews.

The Sexy Result
Tristan TheSexyResult@gmail.com
www.thesexyresult.blogspot.com
All about fabulous music for you to blast.

tribal mixes dot com
tribalmixes.com
Website for sharing live DJ mixes and live sets recorded in MP3 format.

Virgo Lounge
PO Box 4721, St. Louis, MO 63108
info@virgolounge.com
www.VirgoLounge.com
An online source for Dance music, industry networking and an event marketplace. Please send us your press release or info about your project or event.

Canada

Play it tonight
#23-1917 W. 4th Ave. Vancouver, BC V6J 1M7
FX: 208-246-4676
www.playittonight.com
If you would like to sell your music through our site, please contact us via e-mail.

Europe

Belgium

Boards of Electronica
boardsofelectronica.blogspot.com
Belgium blog with international coverage.

France

fluokids
fluokids@gmail.com
fluokids.blogspot.com
It has been almost 3 years ago now that fluokids have founded the bases of what a great European music blog should be.

I Was There
Nicolas iwasthereclub@gmail.com
i-was-there.blogspot.com
French audioblog with news and opinions on Dance and Electronic music.

Germany

This is Tomorrow
djblueprint@gmx.com
www.thisistomorrow.blogspot.com
If you have any promo material that you think we might like, feel free to e-mail your press kit and MP3s to us.

Greece

DJ SETS
6 Iliados Str. PC 54641, Thessaloniki, Greece
PH: +302310-843124
www.djsets.gr
A community where DJs can post their music files and have people rate them.

Spain

Muy Bastard
villadiamante@gmail.com
www.muybastard.blogspot.com
Intenta dilucidar la lógica del baile poniendo la pista como escenario principal, mostrar el Pop en su maxima expresión y arengar a artistas locales que estan haciendo cosas interesantes con la música.

Sweden

Groovegate
Simrishamnsgatan 20a, SE-214 23 Malmoe, Sweden
PH: +46-(0) 40-972 273 FX: +46-850-593-986
www.groovegate.com
A one stop store for DJ's and end users alike where they can find all the latest grooves for their listening pleasures.

United Kingdom

Audiojelly
80 Hadley Rd. Barnet, Herts. EN5 5QR UK
PH: +44 (0) 208-440-0710
FX: +44 (0) 208-441-0163
info@audiojelly.com
www.audiojelly.com
It's only a matter of time now before this becomes the norm and going into a record shop to buy a CD becomes unusual.

BLEEP
PO Box 25378, London, NW5 1GL UK
info@bleep.com
www.bleep.com
Warp Records selection of downloadable Electronica.

Creation Forge
www.creationforge.com
Net label that also features downloads of Breakbeat, Drum'n'Bass, Hip Hop, Dub, Techno, R&B and Reggae.

Scambler
www.scamblermusic.com
Features downloads of Electronic, Dance, Funk, Hip Hop etc.

Xpressbeats
Devonshire House, 223 Upper Richmond Rd.
London, SW15 6SQ UK
PH: +44 (0) 20-8780-0612
FX: +44 (0) 20-8789-8668
admin@xpressbeats.com
www.xpressbeats.com
We provide quality 'up front' Dance music and an extensive catalogue of tracks for music lovers.

Experimental

abop tv ... real music real arts television
PO Box 2478, New York, NY 10009
JB jb@aboptv.com
www.aboptv.com
Broadcasting some of the hottest music in the Avant-garde, Funk, Free-Style and Hard-bop scene today. Our mission is to free your mind!

experement.org
experement.org
A network buffer for contemporary art gathering music, photography etc. Every user gets 20 MB for their projects. So, get your shit ready for upload!

Music For Maniacs
Mr. Fab mail@m-1.us
musicformaniacs.blogspot.com
MP3 blog dedicated to extremes in music. "Outsider" recordings and utterly unique sounds reviewed.

PostClassic
www.artsjournal.com/postclassic
Blog focusing on beautiful new music from composers who've left the Classical world far behind.

tapegerm
1478 Stetson Cir. Salt Lake City, UT 84104
PH: 801-972-2441 FX: 801-972-2443
feedback@tapegerm.com
www.tapegerm.com
A new and vibrant center for music creativity.

Folk

Cantaria
www.chivalry.com/cantaria
A library of "bardic" Folk songs, mostly from Ireland, Scotland and England.

efolk Music
101 Evans Ct. Carrboro, NC 27510
PH: 800-516-2755
artists@efolkMusic.org
www.efolkmusic.org
Independent Folk MP3 and CD source.

ezFolk.com
Richard Hefner Richard@Hefner.com
www.ezfolk.com
Online community that offers artists unlimited upload of MP3s and videos.

FolkAlley Open Mic
1613 E. Summit St., Kent, OH 44242-0001
letters@folkalley.com.
www.folkalley.com
A place for developing and under-exposed singers, songwriters and musicians to post their music to share with Folk Alley listeners.

Woven Wheat Whispers
www.wovenwheatwhispers.co.uk
We work with artists and labels to provide Folk and related music as high quality, legal downloads.

GLBT

Dyke TV
PO Box 170-163, Brooklyn, NY 11217
PH: 718-230-4770
Elizabeth Maynard staff@dyketv.org
www.dyketv.org
Lesbian cable access show that airs nation-wide. We do occasionally solicit or welcome music submissions.

Hip Hop

33Jones
mrjones@33jones.com
www.33jones.com
Need your stuff promoted... leave me a message and I'll put it on the site or on the next mixtape.

88HIPHOP.COM
www.88hiphop.com
The world's first Hip Hop video channel, with diverse Hip Hop programming for multiple broadcast platforms.

Adam's World
adamsworldblog@gmail.com
adambernard.blogspot.com
Features interviews and an artist of the week.

Analog Giant
analoggiant@gmail.com
analoggiant.blogspot.com
Features Hip Hop, Reggaetron, Electronic, Jazz, Dub, R&B, Synthesism and a bit of Indie.

Beatsource
PO Box 40936, Denver, CO 80204
PH: 720-932-9103
https://www.beatsource.com
The world's first legal, online digital retailer specializing in the global sound of Urban music. Beatsource allows DJs and their fans access to premium-encoded formats that match the professional performance quality standards of the world's leading sound systems.

Biff's Hip Hop Section
Biff Reagle biffreagle@hotmail.com
biffhop.blogspot.com
Australia based MP3 blog with news, sound clips etc. I like to shine light on independent artists whenever I get the chance.

Brown Monkey Music
www.brownmonkeymusic.com
Gives musicians a central distribution point at which they can share their music with the world.

Canhead
canhead.wordpress.com
An all-purpose, one-stop and shop, Hip Hop digital hot spot.

Cocaine Blunts
cocaineblunts@gmail.com
www.cocaineblunts.com
Audio, video and reviews.

Da Nexx 2 Blow Video Show
3027 N. Talbott St., Indianapolis, IN 46205
PH: 317-332-0952
Mr. Bound mrbound1@yahoo.com
www.warbound.tv
Hip Hop independence on a national level.

Dopetracks
www.dopetracks.com
A Hip Hop collaboration community. The ultimate spot for emcees to collaborate with Hip Hop producers from around the world. Hook up a mic, pick a beat and start recording online. It's free!

Ear Fuzz
djmaru@earfuzz.com
www.earfuzz.com
A venue for music appreciation. Files are shared out of love and respect and is only meant to help expose and promote the featured artists.

eRiddims
PO Box 15532, Washington, DC 20003
Kiana Lewis eriddimsmusicsite@gmail.com
www.eriddims.com
Online music community targeted toward producers, artists, musicians and pure music lovers. This is a platform for producers to gain exposure and sell their beats for profit. It's free to browse around and free to become a member. It's also free to upload samples.

Givemebeats.com
PO Box 25822, Charlotte, NC 28229-5822
PH: 704-765-1911
www.givemebeats.com
If you make beats and you want to sell them on the internet, this is the beat place to do so.

GRANDGOOD
grandgood.com
News, reviews, interviews, audio and video.

The HardHead Show
PH: 888-839-2930 x81
www.hardheadshow.com
You can have your music videos played on our show. This means you can be seen by over 250,000 viewers (potential buyers) all over the country.

Hip Hop Palace.com
PO Box 158, Bowling Green Stn.
New York, NY 10274
hiphoppaletceceo@yahoo.com
www.hiphoppalace.com
Upload your music and be on our radio show.

Hip Hop Yaik
siouxlive@gmail.com
www.hiphopyaik.com
Webzine independiente de musica Hip Hop, con videos y video clips, MP3, maquetas, conciertos, discos, foro, chat y mucho mas.

Hit Makers
1115 N. Negley Ave. Pittsburgh, PA 15206
PH: 412-523-3021
Kyle Allen hitmakersinc@gmail.com
www.hmbeats.com
For Hip Hop music makers that want to sell their music over the internet.

Indie Planet Television
www.myspace.com/indieplanet
A 30 minute music video based format that features the top independent Hip Hop artists worldwide.

Indie Standard
PH: 954-302-1991 FX: 206-666-2337
Darryl Smith dasmith21@hotmail.com
www.indiestandard.com
*An online Urban artist showcase site. Downloads,
videos, bios and more!*

justrhymes.com
535 Robinson Dr. Tustin, CA 92782
www.justrhymes.com
*A place where artists can create profiles and sell
their music directly from the music player. Artists
can showcase their skills while listeners find the
urban music they like.*

MP3 Rap Hip Hop
info.rap.hiphop@gmail.com
www.reohiphop.com.ar
*Just good Latin Hip Hop underground indie artists.
MP3s, news, forums, photos ...*

Notes from a Different Kitchen
ian@differentkitchen.com
differentkitchen.blogspot.com
MP3 blog featuring news, reviews, music etc.

PassTheMic.com
4130 Heyward St., Cincinnati, OH 45205
PH: 718-213-4176
www.passthemic.com
*Community for independent Hip Hop artists, by
choice!*

RapSpace.tv
rapspace.tv
*Whether you have rhymes to record, beats to drop,
lyrics to blog or just want to check out the latest hot
indie rapper, RapSpace.tv is the digital voice for all
things Hip Hop.*

SpliffHuxtable
props@spliffhuxtable.com
www.spliffhuxtable.com
*Dedicated to droppin' classic and overlooked Hip
Hop, Soul, Funk ...whatever (as long as it's dope).*

UnderworldHipHop.com
PH: 416-333-2446
www.underworldhiphop.com
*A free MP3 uploading service for Hip Hop artists.
We also do reviews.*

Unlimitedtracks.com
922 Hwy. 81 E. Box 315, McDonough, GA 30252
PH: 678-432-1229
sales@unlimitedtracks.com
www.unlimitedtracks.com
*An online store for Urban musicians. Sell your
tracks online for .99 cents per track. You can also
sell your CD from our site.*

Ya Heard
yaheard.bet.com
*Unsigned artists upload your original songs and
create your own web page.*

Jam Band

bt.etree.org
bt.e@etree.org
bt.etree.org
*Provided by the etree.org community for sharing the
live concert recordings of trade friendly artists.
Please tell your friends and family about new bands
that catch your ear and support these artists by
going to see them live and buying their CDs!*

etree.org
wiki.etree.org
*An online community that uses an independent
network of file (FTP) servers that host and distribute
Shorten (SHN) audio files.*

Listen420
listen420.com
*Headies who enjoy an alternative lifestyle can find
and post music, videos, pictures and blogs.*

LIVEDOWNLOADS
www.livedownloads.com
*Offering an opportunity to listen to shows from a
current tour very soon after they've happened,
mastered directly from the soundboard.*

nugs.net
web1.nugs.net
*Artists can harness the demand for their live
performances and studio recordings.*

Jazz

be.jazz
mwanji@citizenjazz.com
www.be-jazz.blogspot.com
*Belgium MP3 blog. Can we handle this much
torque?*

Improvisos Ao Sul
antbranco@gmail.com
improvisosaosul.weblog.com.pt
Jazz MP3 blog based in Portugal.

Jazz&Archtops
jazzarchtops.wordpress.com
*Dedicated to Jazz music performed (mainly) on
archtop guitars.*

No Idle Frets
Nick Carver noidlefrets@gmail.com
noidlefrets.blogspot.com
MP3 blog. Dedicated to podsafe Jazz guitar music.

Rifftides
daramsey@charter.net
www.artsjournal.com/rifftides
*This blog is founded on Doug's conviction that those
who embrace and understand Jazz have interests
that run deep, wide and beyond Jazz.*

Latin

FaroLatino.com
Conesa 960 dpto 1, Ciudad de Buenos Aires,
BA 1426, Argentina
PH: +5411-4551-7527
administracion@farolatino.com
tienda.farolatino.com
*"La Cocina del Arte" is a virtual space dedicated to
promoting new bands. It offers an online space to
bands to promote their products.*

Latin Cool Now
www.latincoolnow.com
Sell your indie music here.

Latin Image Today TV
myspace.com/legendaryonline
Video show with news and interviews.

Metal

Black Death Metal
Daniel info@blackdeathmetal.com
www.blackdeathmetal.com
*Your Metal media website. Upload Death Metal /
Black Metal photos, videos, music and share them
with the community.*

Ear Assault
Jason admin@earassault.com
www.earassault.com
*A place for Metal bands to upload MP3s and gain
exposure.*

EarAche.com
43 W. 38th St. 2nd Fl. New York, NY 10018
PH: 212-840-9090 FX: 212-840-4033
Digby Pearson digby@earache.com
www.earache.com
Metal MP3s and videos.

Hardrock-tv.com
2709 15th St. S. #203, Fargo, ND 58103
"Metal Man" Dan mmd@hardrocksociety.com
www.hardrocksociety.com
Streaming Hard Rock/Metal video channel.

metalvideo.com
PO Box 86, Gold Hill, OR 97525
www.metalvideo.com
*Dedicated to Heavy Metal videos. I interview bands,
show their music videos and live concerts.*

Reality Check TV
danny@realitychecktv.com
www.realitychecktv.com
*Connect to the Metal underground world. We accept
submissions!*

The Rocking Ape
Leubeweg 91, D-89134 Blaustein, Germany
PH: +49 (0) 7304-929289 FX: +49 (0) 7304-929386
info@rockingape.de
www.rockingape.de
*Your independent music portal. Metal, Punk, Rock
and Rock n' Roll.*

Underground Video Television (UVTV)
Rich rich@uvtv.info
www.uvtv.info
Videos of Metal, Hardcore and Hard Rock bands.

New Age

Crystal Vibrations
crystalvibrations.blogspot.com
Audioblog featuring New Age and relaxation music.

Punk

altsounds.com
Unit 1 & 2, Royal Stuart Workshops,
Adelaide Place, Cardiff, Wales CF10 5BR UK
PH: +44-2920-161534
www.altsounds.com
*Free artist profiles allow you to host MP3s, WMA's
or OGG files, upload photos, news, gigs plus much
more.*

BlankTV
361 Vine St., Glendale, CA 91204
PH: 818-242-3107
info@blanktv.com
www.BlankTV.com
Free exposure for your videos to a worldwide audience of indie music lovers.

Download Punk
info@downloadpunk.com
www.DownloadPunk.com
We do accept submissions directly from unsigned artists, but we do request that they don't send demos, only pressed CDs.

Enough MP3s
PO Box 12 07 50, 68058 Mannheim, Germany
info@enoughfanzine.com
www.enoughfanzine.com
Feel free to upload your band's/label's MP3 files.

MegaPlatinum
www.megaplatinum.net
Home to the FIRST legitimate Rock and Punk peer to peer file sharing network.

PunkTV.ca
#307-11215 Jasper Ave. Edmonton, AB T5K3L5
punk@punktv.ca
punktv.ca
We offer an enhanced viewing experience and to enjoy the maximum quality, a codec download is required.

Rock n Roll TV
Share Ross info@rocknrolltv.net
www.rocknrolltv.net
If you are a Rock/Punk/Garage band and have a professionally produced video (no live videos), please drop us a line to find out how you can get it played on our show.

Reggae

Ghetto Bassquake
Boima Tucker ChiefBoima@gmail.com
ghettobassquake.blogspot.com
Audioblog featuring Reggae, Funk, Hip Hop etc.

The Heatwave Blog
PO Box 54688, London, N16 0YW UK
info@theheatwave.co.uk
www.theheatwave.co.uk/blog
Dancehall, Reggae, Bashment and more from the UK, the Caribbean and beyond!

Surforeggae
contato@surforeggae.com.br
www.surforeggae.com.br
Reggae MP3s, news, events and more.

Soul / R&B

A Hot Mess!
ahotmessblog@gmail.com
ahotmessblog.com
Our blog is an "Urban-geared" entertainment news and gossip site, though really we just update and report on anything that interests us. We also often post new music and videos from hot artists.

Captain's Crate
Captain Planet charlie@bywayof.net
bywayof.net/captains_crate
An MP3 blog featuring rare, funky and soulful music.

In Dangerous Rhythm
indangerousrhythm.blogspot.com
I am a writer who is dedicated to Keeping Soul Alive! My aim is to archive, collect and record information about all facets of Soul music. I have met and spoken to many people who have made Soul music.

Listen Think React
listenthinkreact@gmail .com
www.listenthinkreact.com
Summoning pure bliss, one beat at a time!

Soul-Sides
Oliver Wang soulsides@gmail.com
soul-sides.com
A Soul audioblog (and a darn fine one, we think).

uMusico.com
www.umusico.com
A fresh digital download store that allows artist and record labels to sell music.

Women In Music

blowupdoll
mordiblowupdoll@yahoo.co.uk
blow-up-doll.blogspot.com
MP3 blog featuring women artists.

International House Of Pussy
25 Woodhorn Farm, Newbiggin By The Sea, Northumberland, NE64 6AH UK
anfunny@theinternationalhouseofpussy.co.uk
www.theinternationalhouseofpussy.co.uk
MP3 blog featuring mostly female artists.

Schlocker
Bruno transistorrythm@yahoo.com
schlocker.blogspot.com
MP3 blog featuring audio and video of European female artists.

Womenfolk
robbie@womenfolk.net
womenfolk.net
The song blog dedicated to women in music.

World

Aduna
regcontact@free.fr
aduna.free.fr
Blog audio dédié à la musique Afro d'hier, d'aujourd'hui et de demain ...

Benn loxo du taccu
Matt Yanchyshyn letters@mattgy.net
bennloxo.com
MP3 blog featuring African music for the masses.

Calabash Music
249 Elm St., Somerville, MA 02144
PH: 617-459-4062 FX: 617-507-7769
techsupport@calabashmusic.com
www.calabashmusic.com
A global marketplace for independent World music. Our unique music service has downloads from the ever-expanding genres of Jewish music

OySongs.com
PH: 918-299-4112 FX: 918-299-4113
oy@oySongs.com
www.OySongs.com
Our unique music service has downloads from the ever-expanding genres of Jewish music.

WeLove Music
sue.miod@gmail.com
welove-music.blogspot.com
World music audioblog.

SECTION SEVEN: HELPFUL RESOURCES FOR MUSICIANS AND SONGWRITERS

"If you can achieve one successful thing a day to help your music career then you are on the right track. Pick one thing, just one and do it today! - **Chris Standring, Founder of A&R Online**

Resources - General

Animoto Productions
247 Centre St. #3B, New York, NY 10013
Rebecca Brooks rebecca@animoto.com
www.animoto.com
Produces MTV-style videos using the images and music our users choose. Well over half of our users choose the music we provide on our site (in lieu of uploading their own). Our videos have already been viewed millions of times on the web. People put these videos on their personal blogs, MySpace pages, and we even have a Facebook app, so it definitely offers the musicians we feature a way to get their music out there virally.

bandsforlabels.com
PH: 562-627-9251
info@bandsforlabels.com
www.bandsforlabels.com
A free band-label matchmaking site.

Clear Channel Music - NEW!
new@clearchannel.com
www.clearchannelmusic.com/new
Unsigned artists, please submit music to www.garageband.com. Every three months we'll pick 50 NEW! independent artists from the top of the Garage Band charts.

Denny's All Nighter
www.dennysallnighter.com
Features a change to become an "adopted" band as well as "Band of the Month."

House of Blues Entertainment *Ones to Watch*
Attn: Jesse Ervin / Ones To Watch,
6255 Sunset Blvd. 16th Fl. Hollywood, CA 90028
www.hob.com/artistfeatures/onestowatch
Introducing promising new talents that aren't even playing our stages yet. Send package to the above address (no calls or e-mails please).

indieFINANCIALnetwork
522 N. State Rd. #102, Briar Cliff Manor, NY 10510
PH: 914-762-2238 FX: 914-762-8670
Rick Kennell rick@indiefinancialnetwork.com
www.indiefinancialnetwork.com
Business management company providing financial and networking services for the independent music community.

iVideosongs
support@ivideosongs.com
www.ivideosongs.com
All about this new kind of musical experience. A personal connection that happens when you learn your favorite songs from the original artists who wrote and performed those songs.

Laughing Cat Films
PH: 707-321-3389
Louis Ekrem Louis@LaughingCatFilms.com
www.LaughingCatFilms.com
We produce professional quality EPKs and demo videos for performing artists.

LaunchALabel.com
PH: 407-745-1809
Karol karol@launchalabel.com
launchalabel.com
In the first year we will sign 5 bands to contracts of approximately $200,000 each. That includes advances, recording, marketing, and touring. This is not regular "indie" label money we're talking. These bands will be taken care of like they should be.

The League of Rockers & The Rolling RocHaus
13318 31st Ave. NE., Seattle, WA 98125-4411
PH: 206-367-3584
James II therollingrochaus@hotmail.com
www.theleagueofrockers.com
Each is a licensed recording, publishing, motion picture & concert promotion company all wrapped into one!

Linked Musicians
PH: +31-641256907
www.linked-musicians.com
Netherlands based resource that enables musicians, bands, orchestras, fans and product & service providers to register a very detailed live music related profile, to invite and link to their friends and business contacts and to link to other members.

MusiciansOnly.net
www.musiciansonly.net
A FREE musician classified system. The concept is similar to Craigslist but more tailored for musicians.

MyMusicJob.com
www.mymusicjob.com
Providing assistance to those who make their living in the music industry.

New Music Label
www.newmusiclabel.com
Where singers, musicians and artists meet record labels, music managers and scouts.

Operation Gratitude
16444 Refugio Rd.
Encino, CA 91436
cblashek@aol.com
www.opgratitude.com
Sends care packages and letters of support to soldiers deployed overseas. If you have excess inventory that you can donate to us, we would be delighted to include your CDs, DVDs, caps, t-shirts etc. in our packages.

RockSites
1543 Park Meadows Dr. #2, Fort Myers, FL 33907
PH: 239-313-6821
Summer Summer@rocksites.com
www.rocksites.com
Promotional resource for independent musicians. Free customizable full-featured "RockSite" to get your music heard now!

Savidetup Productions
PO Box 121626, Fort Worth, TX 76121-1626
PH: 817-737-3026
Tim Sisk tim@savidetup.com
www.savidetup.com
Services for the consumer, artist and business communities.

SellaBand
Hogehilweg 8-D, 1101 CC, Amsterdam,
The Netherlands
PH: +31-6-53933032 FX: +31-20-4529291
Dagmar Heijmans dagmar@sellaband.com
www.sellaband.com
Empowers unsigned artists to record a professional album, funded by fans.

Slicethepie
info@slicethepie.com
www.slicethepie.com
Enables artists to raise money directly from their fans to professionally record and release an album.

Sonicbids
500 Harrison Ave. 4th Fl. Boston, MA 02118
PH: 617-502-1300
www.sonicbids.com
Creator of the Electronic Press Kit (EPK™). It's an easy-to-use, web-based graphic interface that contains all the basic information of a musical act such as music, photos or date calendar.

Resources - CD Duplication

CD Poster Shop
PMB 349, 4676
Commercial St. SE.
Salem, OR 97302-1902
info@cdpostershop.com
www.cdpostershop.com
We focus on providing quality CD duplication, CD inserts and posters at affordable prices. We have a CD release package, which includes 100 retail ready CDs, 50 posters, with a free UPC-A barcode and CD Baby setup starting at $230.

SpotDJ
www.spotdj.com
Brings the voice of bands, DJs and fans directly to listeners, adding relevant audio clips while people listen to music.

StreetBlast.com
8018 Third St. Rd. #3, Louisville, KY 40214
PH: 502-366-8006
Jake A. Wheat jake@streetblast.com
www.streetblastradio.com
Providing 24/7 streaming radio, quality podcasts and fresh website content advertising indie music bands, fans, and services to communicate to indie artists and fans. We believe in the power of the artist.

StubHub's Spotlight Artist
www.stubhub.com
Every month, the world's largest ticket marketplace, prominently features a currently touring artist on the homepage of StubHub.com with an attractive endorsement that includes an exclusive interview, multimedia content, artist bio and links to purchase a current album and tickets for the tour.

Unknown Public
www.mvine.com
A creative music festival for the front room, covering all the most interesting areas of new music from around the world, including Jazz, Electronica, World Music, film scores, contemporary Classical and Sound Art. It's a free-flowing portal for everything worth hearing in the world of creative music: live, recorded, on disc or online.

Unsigned.com
www.unsigned.com
Providing artists an outlet to be heard globally on the internet. Just as important is our goal to provide you with a new revenue and distribution model for your music.

XR VOLUME
xrvolume@gmail.com
www.xrvolume.com
Features local, indie, and garage bands so artists can gain worldwide exposure and network with other artists and venues.

Sign up for
The Indie Contact Newsletter
www.indiebible.com

CD Rollout
4001 Pacific Coast Hwy. #104, Torrance, CA 90505
PH: 310-791-7624 FX: 310-406-2109
Mike Naylor info@cdrollout.com
www.cdrollout.com
We offer CD and DVD replication, manufacturing as well as a wide range of services to market and promote your project. It's our "one-stop-shop" convenience that sets us apart from other companies.

CDDVDNOW!
855-A Kifer Rd. Sunnyvale, CA 94086
PH: 408-735-6800 FX: 408-735-6805
info@cddvdnow.com
www.cddvdnow.com
An award winning design and manufacturing company serving the creative and corporate community providing CD duplication, CD replication (stamping and manufacturing), DVD duplication and DVD replication (stamping and manufacturing) plus an entire suite of services including printing, packaging and fulfillment.

Copycats Media
712 Ontario Ave. W., Minneapolis, MN 55403
PH: 612-371-8008 Fx: 612-371-8011
www.copycatsmedia.com
*For almost a decade, COPYCATS has helped clients produce professional DVD & CD Duplication and replication projects. Your single source solution, COPYCATS provides clients with a full suite of services: * CD/DVD Manufacturing * Short Run DVD & CD Duplication * Digital Download Cards - NEW! * CD Mastering * Graphic Design & Prepress Services * Silk Screen & Offset On-disc Printing * Print & Packaging Solutions * Assembly * Inventory & Fulfillment Services. Professional CD & DVD projects - delivered on time and in budget. Mention the Indie Bible or CODE "INDIE 08" when getting a quote.*

Cravedog
1522 N. Ainsworth St., Portland, OR 97217
PH: 503-233-7284 FX: 503-234-5305
info@cravedog.com
www.cravedog.com
Over the years, Cravedog has developed an international reputation for excellent service, manufacturing millions of discs for our clients. Whether you are a long standing corporation, a small company, an independent artist or record label or a filmmaker, we know how to meet your needs.

Creative Sound Corp.
PH: 818-707-8986 FX: 818-707-8164
info@csoundcorp.com
www.csoundcorp.com
CD/DVD replication, special packages include graphics / high quality color printing. Full Guarantee for Competitive Pricing & Premium Quality. Plant Locations: California and North Carolina. Mention that you saw us in The Indie Bible and we will match or beat any advertised price.

Crystal Clear Disc & Tape
10486 Brockwood Rd. Dallas, TX 75238
PH: 800-880-0073
Jim Cocke info@crystalclearcds.com
www.crystalclearcds.com
For over 35 years thousands of artists have trusted us to take their CD duplication projects from concept to finished product. We can do it all - from full-color art design and digital mastering and editing to professional "retail-ready" manufacturing and packaging.

DISC MAKERS
7905 N. Rte. 130, Pennsauken, NJ 08110-1402
PH: 856-663-9030 FX: 856-661-3458
www.discmakers.com
The nation's leading CD / DVD duplicator, replicator and printer. When you're ready to make CDs, we're ready to make it happen. We're musicians too, so we know what you need to make it in this business: The best-looking product, the hottest-sounding audio and the most valuable (and free) promotional tools, including free distribution, a free UPC bar code and much more!

Disc2Day
2113 S. 48th St. #103, Tempe, AZ 85282
PH: 602-438-4848 FX: 602-438-2929
www.disc2day.com
A CD DVD duplication and replication company that works closely with the customer to fulfill his or her individual needs. We offer high-quality, professional services with some of the fastest turnaround times in the industry. If CD replication or DVD replication is what you are looking for, we have your solution. With our state-of-the-art facility we can handle any size job, from one to a million or more.

Media Replication Services (MRS)
1 Woodborough Ave. Toronto, ON M6M 5A1
PH: 416-654-8008 FX: 416-654-3663
replication.services@MediaRS.com
mediars.com
For customers seeking an end-to-end replication services company, Media Replication Services provides dependable, complete replication services on all media platforms. Our services include pre-mastering, graphic lay-out services, packaging, fulfillment and distribution. At Media Replication Services, our mandate is to provide a very high level of service to our client-base, which includes companies from a range of different sectors including corporations, software developers, and the audio industry. Our process is fully documented and we are in the process of completing our ISO registration in compliance with ISO 9001:94 standards.

OASIS CD Manufacturing
7905 N. Crescent Blvd. Delair, NJ 08110
PH: 540-987-8810 FX: 540-987-8812
info@oasisCD.com
www.oasiscd.com/ib
We help you manufacture your CD or DVD project. We also help you package it creatively, promote and distribute it so it doesn't become just more clutter in your apartment.

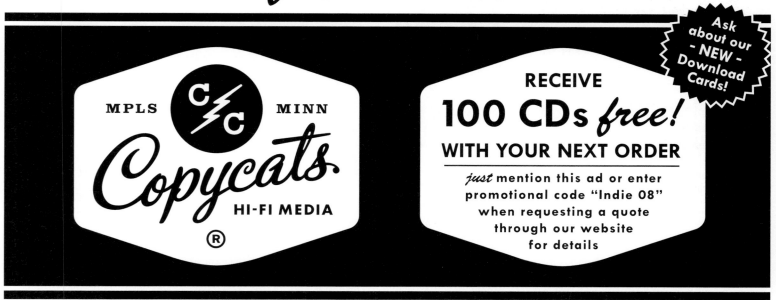
Play-It Productions
259 W. 30th St. 3rd Fl. New York, NY 10001
PH: 212-695-6530 FX: 212-695-4304
info@play-itproductions.net
www.play-itproductions.net
Founded in 1990 to provide local musicians and other content owners with a one stop solution for all of their duplication and graphic needs no matter the size of the project.

Progressive Media & Music
2116 Southview Ave. Tampa, FL 33606
PH: 813-251-8093 FX: 813-251-6050
info@progressivecds.com
www.progressivecds.com
For over a quarter of a century we have been manufacturing the highest quality duplicated media available. From compact discs, cd rom, audio cassettes, dvd's to vhs tapes we have been your trusted, one stop solution. If you can play it, hear it, or see it Progressive Media & Music has always been the first choice when the project really matters. Ask about getting a free custom printed full color t-shirt of your album art!!!

Vegas Disc / Hit Track
5320 Styers St., North Las Vegas, NV 89031
PH: 702-481-1663
Tom info@vegasdisc.com
www.vegasdisc.com
Provides CD and DVD manufacturing and duplication. Built by musicians for musicians!

Resources - Databases

All Media Guide
1168 Oak Valley Dr. Ann Arbor, MI 48108
www.allmusic.com
Massive database of CDs. Add yours!

allrecordlabels.com
324 8th St. E.
Saskatoon, SK S7H 0P5
Peter Scott
scottp@moondog.usask.ca
allrecordlabels.com
lights1.blogspot.com
A database of record label websites. I also announce new releases in my blog.

Bandname.com
Ryan Crowley
information@bandname.com
www.bandname.com
A worldwide database of band and artist name activity. The service notifies artists and labels where potential name conflicts exist.

ccMixter
www.ccmixter.org
This is a community music remixing site featuring remixes and samples licensed under Creative Commons licenses. Features an "Artist Spotlight."

Celebrity Access
2430 Broadway #200, Boulder, CO 80304
PH: 303-350-1700 FX: 303-339-6877
sales@celebrityaccess.com
www.celebrityaccess.com
A database with contact info on agents, managers, record companies, talent buyers and venues.

Coalition of Independent Music Stores
www.cimsmusic.com
A group of some of the best independent music stores in America. Contact the CIMS office to coordinate their efforts nationwide.

Daily Newspapers around the World
www.refdesk.com/paper.html
Links to hundreds of daily newspapers worldwide.

Discogs.com
www.discogs.com
A user-built database containing information on artists, labels and their recordings.

Festival Network Online
PO Box 18839, Asheville, NC 28814
PH: 800-200-3737 FX: 828-645-3374
info@festivalnet.com
festivalnet.com
Lists more than 10,000 events throughout the U.S. and Canada seeking performers, from local & regional to national & international.

FindSounds
www.findsounds.com
A free site where you can search the web for sound effects and musical instrument samples.

Resources - Education & Development

Arising Artist
50-52 Paul St.
London, EC2A 4LB UK
PH: +442077491980
FX: +442077298951
Ged Malone gedmalone@arisingartist.com
www.arisingartist.com
Online and offline A&R and music business advice from music industry professionals.

The Freesound Project
freesound.iua.upf.edu
A collaborative database of Creative Commons licensed sounds. Freesound focuses only on sound, not songs.

HitQuarters
www.hitquarters.com
Presents the world's top record company A&Rs, managers, publishers and producers, including their contact info & track records.

Indie Link Exchange
indielinkexchange@rogers.com
www.indielinkexchange.com/ile
Free service with listings of over 1500 music sites that wish to exchange links with other music related sites.

MusicBrainz
info@musicbrainz.org
www.musicbrainz.org
We are building an open-source database containing all the information you would ever want to know about songs, albums and artists.

MusicClassifieds.us
mcwebmaster03@musicclassifieds.us
www.musicclassifieds.us
Features instant posting of ads, over 80 music categories and much more.

Newspaper and News Media Guide
www.abyznewslinks.com
Database of HUNDREDS of international newspapers.

studiofinder.com
www.studiofinder.com
Search for a studio by name, location, equipment, price and/or area of expertise.

Technorati
www.technorati.com
The recognized authority on what's happening on the World Live Web, right now. The Live Web is the dynamic and always-updating portion of the Web. We search, surface, and organize blogs and the other forms of independent, user-generated content (photos, videos, voting, etc.) increasingly referred to as "citizen media."

Band Promotion 101
www.bloggomite.com/ bandpromo
Marketing tips for indie musicians.

Bandit A&R Newsletter
68-70 Lugley St., Newport, PO30 5ET UK
PH: +44-1983-524110
bandit.icb@aweber.com
www.banditnewsletter.com
Helping ambitious bands target their demos to labels, publishers etc.

CD Baby Podcast
5925 NE 80th Ave. Portland, OR 97218
Kevin Breuner info@cdbabypodcast.com
www.cdbabypodcast.com
Interview based talk show about how to be a successful musician without compromising your art. It's a perfect time to take advantage of the many opportunities for Do-It-Yourself artists that are springing up everywhere.

Digital Music News
www.digitalmusicnews.com
Technology news for music industry professionals.

Evolvor
1205 Woolen Way, Newark, DE 19711
PH: 856-498-9945
Eric Hebert eric@evolvor.com
www.evolvor.com
Music marketing and internet promotion for business, music and art. Our blog is updated regularly with tips and tricks on promoting yourself online.

Fear of Bad Music: New Marketing Models for Artists
9251 Sailfish Dr. Boerne, TX 78006-5338
PH: 210-693-0425 FX: 815-346-2465
Joachim Klehe jklehe@gmail.com
www.fearofbadmusic.com
Features new tactics for marketing your music.

getsigned.com
707 Miamisburg-Centerville Rd. #103
Dayton, OH 45459
Shawn Fields editor@getsigned.com
www.getsigned.com
EVERYTHING you ever wanted to know about the music biz.

Harris Institute
118 Sherbourne St., Toronto, ON M5A 2R2
PH: 416-367-0178 FX: 416-367-5534
info@harrisinstitute.com
www.harrisinstitute.com
A leader in music industry education since 1989. Students have come from over sixty countries and every province in Canada. A 68 member award winning faculty teaches the private college's 100 students.

How To Be Your Own Booking Agent
Jeri Goldstein jg@performingbiz.com
performingbiz.com
Get your step-by-step guide and begin to create your successful touring career...

HowToBand.com
4277 N. Shasta Loop, Eugene, OR 97219
PH: 503-421-2180
Eric C Smith eric@howtoband.com
www.howtoband.com
Free expert advice teaching indie bands how to make their bands great. Focused on helping bands build profits.

Indie Contact Newsletter
indiecontactnewsletter@rogers.com
www.bigmeteor.com/newsletter
Free monthly e-zine that lists radio shows, music magazines, labels etc. looking for new music.

Indie Music Biz Secrets Blog
Tom "Drummer" Likes tom@musicbizsecrets.com
www.musicbizsecrets.com/blog
Dedicated to helping you promote your music.

Market Wire
8th Fl. 48 Yonge St., Toronto, ON M5E 1G6
PH: 416-362-0885
www.marketwire.com
We post news released by small to large businesses worldwide.

Marketing Your Music
www.marketingyourmusic.com
An array of tips on how to call attention to your music.

MC-INPUT
c/o Poyel Music Entertainment
499 N. Canon Dr. 4th Fl. Beverly Hills, CA 90210
www.mc-input.com
An international online music consulting and coordination service that guides you through each step of the music business. Whether you are an artist, musician, engineer, producer, or if you are ready to launch your own venture, we have the proper tips and connections to assist you in reaching your goals in music.

Metalworks Institute
3611 Mavis Rd. #21, Mississauga, ON L5C 1T7
PH: 905-279-4000 FX: 905-279-4012
admissions@metalworksinstitute.com
www.metalworksinstitute.com
A dynamic, independent institution dedicated to providing an incomparable level of education in the areas of audio recording, live production and the business of entertainment. MWI prepares students for lifelong learning and leadership roles in the entertainment industry through innovative instruction techniques and exceptional learning resources. The Institute fosters investigation, research and creative professional activity by uniting faculty and students in the acquisition and application of technical, artistic and business knowledge in a qualified environment.

The Music Marketer Blog
A16 Mentari Court, 46150 Selangor, Malaysia
PH: 0(3)5630-1124 FX: 0(3)5630-1124
Jo Minor classicguitars@gmail.com
www.themusicmarketer.com
Blog and newsletter that helps independent bands and artists keep track of the world of indie music publishing.

Musician's Cyber Cooler
PH: 888-563-3228
Jammin Dave Jackson musicianscooler@gmail.com
www.musicianscooler.com
Features promotional tools, resources and an informative podcast for musicians.

Musicians Tip Sheet
Steve Veloudos zebra24@msn.com
www.zebramusic.com
This newsletter features information to help musicians with their musical career. The Tip Sheet includes industry contacts, web site reviews, interviews and many other items designed to advance a musicians musical career. Subscribe to the newsletter by visiting our website.

MusicPressReport.com
www.MusicPressReport.com
A daily weblog featuring headlines, articles, links and resources for the music press. We're constantly looking for useful content and skillful writers.

New Music Tipsheet
scott@sperrymedia.com
www.newmusictipsheet.com
We do everything we can to turn on readers to up & coming artists.

New Music Weekly Magazine
2530 Atlantic Ave. Ste. C, Long Beach, CA 90806
PH: 310-325-9997 FX: 310-427-7333
staff@newmusicweekly.com
www.newmusicweekly.com
Covers the radio and music industry with its 24+ page weekly magazine. Has become the standard for tracking radio airplay nationwide.

North by Northeast Music and Film Festival
189 Church St. LL, Toronto, ON M5B 1Y7
PH: 416-863-6963 FX: 416-863-0828
info@nxne.com
www.nxne.com
Canada's #1 showcase for new independent music, where fans can catch great local and international performers at intimate venues. An industry conference featuring celebrity interviews as well as panels and information exchanges for artists and music-biz professionals. NXNE has always been about the music. The festival gives 500 local, national and international artists the chance to rock the crowds and to showcase for agents, talent buyers, media, promoters, labels and management company heavies at a variety of essential downtown venues.

Pandora Podcast
Kevin Seal ks@kevinseal.com
blog.pandora.com/podcast
Educational podcasts that attempt to give you an inside look at the techniques musicians use to put their signature on the music they write and perform.

Press Release Writing Tips
315 Fruitwood Ln. Knoxville, TN 37922
PH: 865-671-8366 FX: 865-671-8437
info@press-release-writing.com
www.press-release-writing.com
Contains free tips on writing good press releases.

RockStar Machine
Patrick Silvestri rockstarmachine@gmail.com
www.rockstarmachine.com
A music promotion blog for musicians that want to learn to promote themselves.

spinme.com
www.spinme.com
Daily news, tools & tips for working musicians.

StagePass News
www.stagepassnews.com
Whether you need to find sponsorship money for your band's tour or how to handle intellectual rights, there is plenty to read here.

starpolish
1 Irving Pl. #P8C, New York, NY 10003
FX: 212-477-5259
info2@starpolish.com
www.starpolish.com
Resources include an extensive library of business advice, self-management tools and strong exposure opportunities.

Topica
www.topica.com/channels/music
Browse through hundreds of newsletters on music related subjects.

WikiMusicGuide
Anna Chua press@wikiwebguide.com
www.wikimusicguide.com
A wiki-based site wherein the contents are contributed and collaborated by the music lovers which include fans and artists themselves. We are also featuring new and upcoming artists, independent artists and bands every week. We'll be very glad to have you included on our ever growing number of pages.

Resources - Legal

American Bar Assoc.
www.abanet.org/intelprop
The home page of the ABA Section of Intellectual Property Law.

The Better Business Bureau
bbb.org
Find a local BBB in the US and Canada serving the consumers and businesses in their areas.

BitLaw
www.bitlaw.com
Contains over 1,800 pages on patent, copyright, trademark and internet legal issues.

Copyright & Fair Use
fairuse.stanford.edu
Stanford U. information on copyright law.

Copyright Infringement and Piracy Watch
www.copynot.com
Devoted to the protection of copyright works, anti-piracy and promotion of legitimate music sources.

Copyright Kit
www.indie-music.com/free2.php
Free download of Copyright Kit.

Copyright Law in the United States
www.bitlaw.com/copyright
A discussion on the copyright laws.

The Copyright Website
www.benedict.com
Copyright registration and information resource.

Copyright Your Song
www.copyright.gov/eco
File a copyright registration for your work through the Copyright Office online system.

Creative Commons
info@creativecommons.org
creativecommons.org
A nonprofit whose goal is to build a layer of reasonable, flexible copyright in the face of increasingly restrictive default rules.

Findlaw
www.findlaw.com
Provides information and links to resources on all areas of law, including copyright and entertainment law.

GS1 US *(Uniform Code Council)*
www.gs1us.org
Administers the U.P.C. bar code.

Independent Music Law Advice *UK*
Elliot Chalmers elliot@musiclawadvice.co.uk
www.musiclawadvice.co.uk
The first independent music law site for The UK. Providing accurate and up to date information on all issues related to music law.

Intellectual Property Law Firms
100 W. Cypress Creek Rd. #1050,
Fort Lauderdale, FL 33309
PH: 800-631-5158 x225
Joe Butch
webmaster@intellectualpropertylawfirms.com
www.intellectualpropertylawfirms.com
Enter your zip code or select your state, city and county to receive a free consultation from an attorney in your area.

Lawgirl.com
www.lawgirl.com
A free, interactive legal resource for those in the arts.

Music Law Offices
www.music-law.com
Free articles on copyright and music publishing.

Music Publishers Association
mpa.org
Features a listing of contact information for publishers, both domestic and foreign and copyright administrating offices.

Music * Technology * Policy
music-tech-policy.blogspot.com
Informative blog written by lawyer Chris Castle.

MusicContracts.com
help@jsrlaw.net
www.musiccontracts.com
Sells downloadable copies of the most widely used music business contracts.

RightsFlow
29 W. 17th St. 10th Fl. New York, NY 10011
PH: 917-509-8360 FX: 646-607-1492
info@rightsflow.com
www.rightsflow.com
Offers outsourced music publishing licensing and royalty systems to record labels, distributors, online music retailers and any other company engaged in distribution and sale of recorded music.

Songfile
711 3rd Ave. New York, NY 10017
PH: 212-370-5330 FX: 646-487-6779
www.songfile.com
The Harry Fox Agency online search and mechanical licensing tool. HFA represents the song catalogs of almost 28,000 publishers for their U.S. licensing needs.

Torrent Freak
torrentfreak.com
A weblog dedicated to bringing the latest news about BitTorrent, and everything that is closely related to this popular file sharing protocol.

Trademark Search
www.uspto.gov/main/trademarks.htm
Valuable information on trademarks in the US.

Traffic Control Group
Ste. 602 Albany House, 324-6 Regent St., London, W1B 3BL UK
PH: 0044-020-7637-3450
info@trafficcontrolgroup.com
www.trafficcontrolgroup.com
Have been providing immigration and visa services to the music and related industries since 1983.

T&S Immigration Services Ltd.
PH: 01557-339123 FX: 01557-330567
steve@tandsimmigration.co.uk
www.tandsimmigration.co.uk
We specialise in handling work permit applications, primarily for the entertainment industry. Most of our cases are for recording artists who are coming to the UK for performances and promotion.

United States Copyright Office
101 Independence Ave. SE.
Washington, DC 20559-6000
PH: 202-707-3000
copyinfo@loc.gov
www.loc.gov/copyright
Key publications and the homepages of other copyright-related organizations.

United States Patent and Trademark Office
TrademarkAssistanceCenter@uspto.gov
www.uspto.gov
The official website.

Volunteer Lawyers for the Arts
6128 Delmar, St. Louis, MI 63112
PH: 314-863-6930 FX: 314-863-6932
vlaa@stlrac.org
www.vlaa.org/resources.asp
A variety of programs and services.

Working in The UK
www.workingintheuk.gov.uk
Provides you with clear information about the various routes open to Foreign Nationals who want to come and work in the United Kingdom.

World Intellectual Property Organization
PO Box 18, CH-1211 Geneva 20, Switzerland
PH: +41-22-338-9111 FX: +41-22-733-54-28
www.wipo.org
Promoting the use and protection of works of the human spirit, through patents and copyright.

Resources - Mastering

Crazy Daisy Productions
4257 Barger Dr. #171, Eugene, OR 97402
PH: 541-517-1458 FX: 425-790-0630
Erik Veach info@crazymastering.com
www.crazymastering.com
Our state-of-the-art CD mastering provides high-quality professional sound at a price anyone can afford. Have all the tracks you can fit on a single audio CD (up to 80 min) mastered for less than $250.

DRT Mastering
20 Vine St., Peterborough, NH 03458
PH: 603-924-2277 FX: 603-924-4384
David Torrey davidt@drtmastering.com
www.drtmastering.com
Delivers a fat, high-impact sound, created with custom-built analog mastering gear. Recording artists and record labels worldwide rely on this competitive edge for their CD releases. Our website offers extensive commentary and techniques for artists recording their own albums.

Masterwork Recording
1020 N. Delaware Ave. Philadelphia, PA 19125
PH: 215-423-1022 FX: 215-423-6020
Albert Oon albert@masterworkrecording.com
www.masterworkrecording.com
We have been providing professional high resolution mastering services to major labels and artists of every kind for nearly three decades. Although we've seen tremendous changes in the music business and recording technology during that time, we're still doing what we've always done well – delivering results. In our business, that means a superior mastering experience, and superior product.

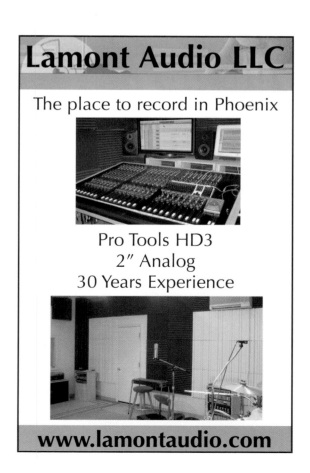

SongMastering.com

PO Box 217, Loveland, OH 45140-0217
PH: 513-833-9025
Jim Mason jimmason@songmastering.com
www.songmastering.com
I see songmastering.com as the final step in the recording process. It is a way to give yourself that extra bit of confidence before you post your tune on the net. I see my service as an audio Jiffy Lube, where you can get your song fine tuned for public consumption. I am an independent artist like you and know how important it is to have the best sounding recordings possible.

Sound Bites Dog

PH 310-621-1896
Hans hdekline@gmail.com
www.soundbitesdog.com
We are now offering high-quality and affordable mastering via the internet with minimal lead-time and great customer service. We deliver red book CD audio as well as the highest quality MP3/MP4s for internet sales and downloads. Whatever your needs, we are a reliable second pair of ears and a budget-friendly mastering solution.

Resources - Merch

ABC Pictures

1867 E. Florida St., Springfield, MO 65803-4583
PH: 417-869-3456 FX: 417-869-9185
www.abcpictures.com
Quality publicity picture reproduction, posters, 8x10's, head shots & composites for the entertainment industry.

Imprint Indie Printing

3449 Technology Dr. #212, North Venice, FL 34275
PH: 941-484-5151 FX: 941-484-5154
Walter walter@iloveimprint.com
www.iloveimprint.com
Since 1994 we've been helping people create projects to be proud of. We understand every step in the process of putting out records and CD's. From 7 inch covers to posters, CD replication to custom print work, we take as much pride in your project as you do. We are equipped to give you the best quality at great prices. No matter how big or small your project is, we handle them all with the same attention to detail and care.

Jakprints

3133 Chester Ave. Cleveland, OH 44114
PH: 216-622-6360 FX: 216-622-6361
www.jakprints.com
We continually strive to help each and every customer big or small, to expand and promote their passion with the highest quality service and merchandise. Take $50 OFF any order of $199 or more by using Promo Code ND2BBLE9WMB.

Rock Star Promotions

100 N. Federal Hwy. Ste. 1234
Fort Lauderdale, FL 33301
PH: 954-767-8385 FX: 801-740-6554
Aaron Schimmel servicedesk@rockstarpromos.com
www.rockstarpromos.com
Dedicated to helping everyone live like a rock star, even if you can't play a note!

Seatthole Shirts

PO Box 3137, Bellingham, WA 98227
PH: 360-733-2154
Django Bohren django@seatthole.com
seatthole.com
High-quality custom t-shirt screen printing and Rock n' Roll promotional items for your high-, medium-, low- or no-budget project.

Sinergy Merchandising Concepts *(SMC)*

PO Box 1908, Spring Hill, TN 37174
PH: 615-261-8592 (Nashville, TN)
PH: 714-989-8008 (Orange County, CA)
sales@smcincorporated.com
www.smcincorporated.com
SMC began as a distributor of merchandise for the entertainment industry in 2000. We targeted the music industry and specialized in the design and production of band & artist merchandise. SMC has always kept the end user in mind and never compromised our goal. This goal being: To provide the best product for the best price and deliver it on time. We have come a long way since 2000, but one thing has and will always remain the same, our passion for good design, excellent customer service, and most importantly, our attention to detail and superior quality.

Ultra Entertainment

4838 E. Baseline Rd. #121, Mesa, AZ 85206
PH: 602-334-4741 FX: 866-847-4508
www.ultraentertainment.com
Everything we do here at Ultra Entertainment is about artist development. Our mission is to provide bands affordable tools, products, and services. All of those tools, products, and services are designed to get your band to the next level. We talk about the "Next Level" a lot here at Ultra Entertainment. What this means is simply a development process of learning and growing as an artist while at the same time growing your fan base.

Resources - Music Equipment

ALLPARTS

13027 Brittmoore Park Dr. Houston, TX 77041
PH: 713-466-6414 FX: 713-466-5803
allparts@allparts.com
www.allparts.com
America's premier guitar and bass parts supplier.

Dot On Shaft Guitars

37 Livingstone St. W., Barrie, ON L4N 7J2
PH: 705-812-1061
dotonshaft.com
"The Dot On Shaft name is incredibly significant to us because it represents principles that are near and dear to our hearts and beliefs that we choose to live by. We strive to be independent from the rest, innovate in ideology, intelligent in thought and iconic in stature.

Entertainer's Secret

1119 3rd Ave. SW., Carmel, IN 46032
PH: 317-846-7452 FX: 317-846-1676
Gordon question@entertainers-secret.com
www.entertainers-secret.com
If you spend time speaking, singing, lecturing, selling, teaching, presenting, cheering telephoning, preaching, performing, announcing or you just talk a lot...we can help! Especially if you have overdone it and particularly if annoying allergies or other respiratory problems bring on those inevitable episodes of dry, sore throat, stress and hoarseness. Others do judge you by your voice. You owe it to your listeners and to yourself to sound and feel your very best.

The Hook Studios

PH: 818-759-4665
Mike Frenchik mike@thehookstudios.com
www.thehookstudios.com
Featuring one of the industry's premiere inventories of classic & contemporary microphones, The Hook offers affordable rental packages for tracking drums, guitars, and vocals. We cater to engineers, producers, labels, and production companies whose projects have limited budgets, yet demand the highest standards. Contact us today, and put "The Hook" in your recordings.

Sam Ash Music

PH: 800-472-6274 FX: 800-818-9050
www.samash.com
The only online musical instrument website backed by over 80 years of experience servicing the needs of musicians - from beginners to professionals. Every one of our sales associates are pros that can answer any question about the gear we sell. Yes, we actually have musicians, producers and DJs working in our call centers.

Sonic Distribution

PH: 617-623-5581 FX: 617-623-5857
info@sonicus.net
www.sonicus.net
We are the US Distributor for the sE Electronics line of microphones and accessories as well as the new Ghost Acoustics line. Located just outside Boston, MA, we handle anything and everything for sE and Ghost in the USA and Canada. If you'd like to purchase any of our products, please consult the dealer section of our website.

Superscope Technologies

1508 Batavia Ave. Geneva, IL 60134-3302
PH: 630-232-8900 FX: 630-232-8905
www.superscopetechnologies.com
Offers a line of innovative, easy-to-use music practice and recording tools for musicians and music educators worldwide. Superscope Technologies continues our legacy of providing high quality, reliable audio products under the Superscope brand. Superscope is rapidly gaining a reputation among a new generation of customers for providing high-quality products that address the needs of musicians and music educators. We like to think that today's Superscope embraces the best qualities of Superscope's rich 50-year heritage.

The Indie
Link
Exchange

www.indielinkexchange.com/ile

Tanager AudioWorks
17 Dolly Bridge Rd. Randolph, NJ 07869
PH: 973-895-1874 FX: 973-532-0821
info@tanageraudioworks.com
www.tanageraudioworks.com
A company founded on a basic mission-to provide indispensable tools for musical creation. We believe that today's powerful array of computer-based software aimed at writing and recording music could be made much more powerful and useful if only musicians had the right tools. In our experience, and as with many things, having the right tool makes all the difference.

WTSmedia
2841 Hickory Valley Rd. Chattanooga, TN 37421
PH: 888-987-6334 FX: 423-894-7281
Micah Boaz mboaz@wtsmedia.com
wtsmedia.com
CD & DVD recordable media, CD & DVD duplicators, blank audio cassettes, video tapes, labels, professional audio/video recorders and a variety of pro-audio products WTS Media offers the very best. We carry a full line of well-known, professional-grade audio equipment including: Microboards, Shure, Graff, Fender Audio, Verbatim, Sennheiser, Nady, Tascam, Rimage, Marantz, Sony, and many others.

Resources - Online Communities

12FRUITS.com
info@12fruits.com
12fruits.com
An online music-based networking site.

2ManProductions
11406 Sandrock St., Houston, TX 77048
PH: 713-386-9023 FX: 713-751-0906
Carlton info@2manproductions.com
www.2manproductions.com
Interactive web community for artists. Promote and upload your music, photos, videos, IM video conferencing and more! Upload your page today!

AMP
Terri Anderson pluginamp@gmail.com
www.pluginamp.com
A collective of artists networking together to build and support artists, create new art communities, and enhance those that already exist.

ArtistnArtists - The Artist to Industry Network
312 5ᵗʰ Ave. New Rochelle, NY 10553
PH: 914-374-3285 FX: 914-567-6609
Germaine Elvy artistnartists@a2inbox.com
www.artistnartists.com
An online social network that connects a variety of artists from the film, music and art platforms. Artists can create highly customizable web based portfolios where they showcase work, collaborate with fellow artists, and pitch directly to industry related companies.

Band Weblogs
Jenny May & Dave Tommo
info@bandweblogs.com
www.bandweblogs.com
Submit band press, reviews, links to MP3s, music videos, podcasts and more.

BandBUZZ
info@bandbuzz.com
www.bandbuzz.com
You have just stumbled on the only community driven music promotion platform where you can see the results. Sign up, build your profile and become one of our pioneering bands as you upload music that will be reviewed, rated and ultimately heard by thousands.

Bandwidth Discussion Group
launch.groups.yahoo.com/group/bandwidth
Discussion of web design as it relates to bands, labels and other music related sites.

bebo
142 10ᵗʰ St., San Francisco, CA 94103
www.bebo.com
The next generation social networking site where members can connect with friends, share photos, discover new music and just hang out.

Bizzy Connections
PO Box 631, New York, NY 10101
PH: 718-501-4191
Donald Murphy DM@BizzyConnections.com
www.bizzyconnections.com
If you are looking for new talent, a recording studio, beats, hooks, clothes, books, poetry or whatever you need to take you to the next level.

BlogExplosion
www.blogexplosion.com
A blogging community where people can find and read your blog, get your blog reviewed or even chat with other bloggers all around the world!

Buzznet
www.buzznet.com
Our integrated media and community platform allows our users to network like never before with leading bands, trendsetters and their peers through self-created content, videos, photos and journals.

CDInsight
cdinsight.com
Online community where you can post your CD releases, tour announcements etc.

Contrastream
team@contrastream.com
contrastream.com
A new way to find indie music. Anyone can hype or add a new album. The albums getting the most hype from the community will gain exposure.

Crunkbox
www.crunkbox.com
An electronic platform for independent music promotions and distribution.

Cyworld
support@cyworldinc.com
www.cyworld.com
A whole new way to connect with the people in your world. Here you'll find friends you know, new people to meet, clubs to join and special spaces for your photos, artwork, journals and more.

del.icio.us
del.icio.us
A social bookmarking website. The primary use of del.icio.us is to store your bookmarks online, which allows you to access the same bookmarks from any computer and add bookmarks from anywhere, too. On del.icio.us, you can use tags to organize and remember your bookmarks, which is a much more flexible system than folders.

Digg
feedback@digg.com
digg.com
A place for people to discover and share content from anywhere on the web. From the biggest online destinations to the most obscure blog, Digg surfaces the best stuff as voted on by our users. We're here to provide a place where people can collectively determine the value of content and we're changing the way people consume information online.

Doppelganger vSide
PH: 415-541 4955
www.doppelganger.com
Provides "next generation" social entertainment with our vSide product targeting the teen (taste maker) demographic where in-world activities and engagement focus on music, entertainment and fashion that complements their lifestyle.

eJamming
info@ejamming.com
www.ejamming.com
Enables musicians to play together in real time as if in the same room even if they're far away from each other. Also connects musicians and their fans through live performances from anywhere in the world.

epiTUNES
PO Box 1389, Los Angeles, CA 90078
www.epitunes.com
A music discovery portal that encompasses searchable directories for live music venues, music event listings, and artists and bands by genre, as well as podcasts, online radio and social networking.

Facebook
facebook.com
People use Facebook to keep up with friends, upload an unlimited number of photos, share links and videos, and learn more about the people they meet.

Face-Pic.com
5 Viewpoint Office Village, Babbage Rd. Stevenage, Herts, SG1 2EQ UK
PH: +44 (0)1438-356-764 FX: +44 (0)1438-724-115
www.face-pic.com
A UK social networking service (like MySpace) that allows unsigned acts to upload music.

Faceticket.com
www.faceticket.com
Create your own portal network, create profiles, connect with friends, upload videos, share photos.

finetune
www.finetune.com
Explore the finetune community - browse artists, users, playlists and more. Listen to professionally managed playlists spanning Todays most popular terrestrial radio formats.

Flickr
www.flickr.com
The best online photo management and sharing application in the world. We want to help people make their content available to the people who matter to them. We want to enable new ways of organizing photos and video.

Friendster

568 Howard St., San Francisco, CA 94105
FX: 415-618-0074
help@friendster.com
www.friendster.com
With more than 65 million members worldwide, Friendster is a leading global online social network. Friendster is focused on helping people stay in touch with friends and discover new people and things that are important to them.

Gaia

www.gaia.com
Our vision is to create a global community of like-minded people - a force for positive change.

GigShare

Jo Brew theindiemusician@gmail.com
theindiemusician.com/Gigshare.html
A free grassroots style directory for putting performing musicians in touch with other performing musicians in order to share and access gigs and resources.

Goombah

contact@goombah.com
www.goombah.com
An efficient way for artists and labels to reach individuals who already like their style of music.

Grooveshark

www.grooveshark.com
An online music community that rewards you for sharing, reviewing and discovering new music.

Haystack

haystack.com
A social music community connecting passionate fans to music through Tastemakers and friends.

Hi5.com

55 2nd St. #300, San Francisco, CA 94105
PH: 415-404-6094 FX: 415-704-3482
www.hi5.com
An international social networking community. Post your music!

imeem

www.imeem.com
A social network where millions of fans and artists discover new music, videos and photos, and share their tastes with friends.

IndabaMusic.com

info@indabamusic.com
www.indabamusic.com
Online collaboration site offering an advanced online production console for free. The site's goal is to create an online community both pro and amateur and show artists that they can work together regardless of geographical boundaries.

Jamglue

holla@jamglue.com
www.jamglue.com
A thriving online community for creating and personalizing audio. We let you upload and record music, remix it online, and share your hot mixes with everyone. On Jamglue, it's simple and fun for fans to get INVOLVED with the music they love!

Jamify.com

suppport@jamify.com
www.jamify.com
Lets you network with local musicians, recording studios, venues, and music industry experts to perform, record, produce, publish and market your talent with no contracts, no nonsense and no up-front fees!

JamNow

support@lightspeedaudiolabs.com
www.jamnow.com
Wanna broadcast your music live for the whole world? Jam with other musicians while your fans listen? Podcast a live discussion with friends all over the USA? You can do this and more by joining JamNow!

Just Plain Folks

5327 Kit Dr. Indianapolis, IN 46237
jpnotes@aol.com
www.jpfolks.com
Organization that networks, promotes and educates musicians.

Kompoz

collaborate@kompoz.com
www.kompoz.com
A social workspace for musicians and songwriters. Got an idea for a song? Record a track. Upload it. Then invite others to add drums, bass, vocals or anything else!

Laudr Underground Music

www.laudr.com
User submitted links to free music, broken down by genre, and ranked by community votes. Focused on non-mainstream artists.

LocaModa

www.locamoda.com
Now people in social places like bars or restaurants can connect with others in the venue as well as their online friends by engaging with interactive digital signs.

meteli.net

Tallberginkatu 1 C 125, FI-00180 Helsinki, Finland
info@meteli.net
www.meteli.net
A multi-channel music information database and end-user service targeting music fans. Featuring streaming radio, event calendars, discographies, music club information, ringtones, music community and much more.

The MODE

brew@theMode.com
www.themode.com
Find band mates and network with other musicians.

MOG

www.mog.com
With dedicated pages for artists, albums and songs, MOG is a springboard for delving deeper into the music you love.

Music Highway

15030 Ventura Blvd. #843
Sherman Oaks, CA 91403
PH: 818-785-7144
Sheena Metal sheenametal@onemain.com
www.music-highway.com
An organization that specializes in supplying invaluable industry contacts, promotional resources and a support network for aspiring artists.

Music Nation

support@musicnation.com
musicnation.com
Create an artist profile page. Upload videos, MP3s, photos, slide shows and anything else you like. Get the attention of the fans, and, well, we'll help you get the attention of the world.

Music Thoughts Discussion Group

musicthoughts-subscribe@egroups.com
launch.groups.yahoo.com/group/musicthoughts
All areas of music are discussed from promotion to tips on playing live.

MusicHawk

www.musichawk.com
A music community featuring tours, MP3s & videos, reviews and personalized news.

Musician's Crossroad

PH: 409-283-6935
Paul Winter cypher@musicianscrossroad.com
www.musicianscrossroad.com
Hosting a community of musicians, allowing them to promote their talent.

Muso City

info@MusoCity.com
www.musocity.com
A music oriented online community. We currently provide accounts designed for music fans, artists, musicians, music retailers and music venues.

My Indie Nation

www.myindienation.com
Online community featuring charts, events, streaming audio and more.

MySpace Music

www.myspace.com/index.cfm?fuseaction=music
Upload your music for exposure, reviews and more.

MyStrands

760 SW Madison #106, Corvallis, OR 97333
PH: 541-753-4426 FX: 541-754-6416
info@mystrands.com
www.mystrands.com
Be represented on MyStrands with information about your music, your songs and CDs, and links to hear your songs. Receive the same treatment as any mainstream artist.

NowLive

www.nowlive.com
A social broadcasting network that lets anyone create a live, interactive talk show.

Octopop

octopop.com
Enjoy the most interactive and easy to use social networking site on the Internet.

orkut

www.orkut.com
We are committed to providing an online meeting place for people to socialize, make new acquaintances and find others who share their interests.

OurStage

321 Billerice Rd. #202, Chelmsford, MA 01824
PH: 978-244-1440 FX: 978-244-1446
Anne-Marie Kennedy am@ourstage.com
www.ourstage.com
Fans rank (not rate) the best of the best. Every month one indie band or musician wins $5,000 in addition to exposure with industry tastemakers and influencers.

The Outer Post

www.theouterpost.com
After you create a profile, you will see the "Add/Edit Music" tab. Upload your songs and then wait for the admin (ahem, ME) to approve them.

Paltalk.com
Church Street Stn. PO Box 3454,
New York, NY 10008
PH: 212-520-7000
www.paltalk.com
Enjoy thousands of live video chat rooms and dozens of regularly scheduled video chat shows.

PerfSpot.com
www.perfspot.com
Social networking community. The Music section provides exclusive content, user reviews and song recommendations based upon the user's previous chosen songs. Upcoming features include postings of exclusive band interviews and live recordings in PerfSpot's studio.

Plugs Music Industry Network
dreamrow.ning.com
A music industry network for the professional or those offering professional services to the music industry.

Pro-Demo
Ploeglaan 28, 3755HT Eemnes, The Netherlands
info@pro-demo.com
www.pro-demo.com
A growing community of all the various creative and business elements of the media industry.

Project Opus
404, 329 Railway St., Vancouver, BC V6A 1A4
PH: 604-685-2454
David Gratton david.gratton@projectopus.com
www.projectopus.com
An online music community designed to support artists, fans and local music. It is a single point of contact for discovery of new music.

Second Life
secondlife.com
A 3-D virtual world created by its Residents. Since opening to the public in 2003, it has grown explosively and today is inhabited by millions of Residents from around the globe. It is becoming a popular promotional tool for independent musicians.

The Sims On Stage
thesimsonstage.ea.com
An online community from the people who make The Sims™ games. Here you can sing and record your favorite songs Karaoke-style as well as write and perform your own comedy sketches, poetry and stories.

Sound of Traffic
Adam Leonard mail@soundoftraffic.com
www.soundoftraffic.com
An online community of musicians trying to effectively promote their work. Members browse the pages of other members for credit that is used to send listeners to their own site. Other helpful tools are available to you as well.

Soundflavor
getfound@soundflavor.com
www.soundflavor.com
The easiest way to find music that you like, make and share great playlists, and meet people with similar musical tastes along the way. Search Soundflavor's extensive library of member-submitted playlists to find music to fit any mood, activity or event.

Soundshed.com
www.soundshed.com
A musicians classifieds service with over 10,000 registered members.

Splice
human@splicemusic.com
www.splicemusic.com
A community of wonderful musicians and music lovers who love to collaborate on various projects. Make music with the world's most advanced online sequencer, complete with real-time synths and DSP sound effects.

StudioTraxx
studiotraxx.com
A dedicated studio musician-for-hire resource. Our goal is to unite those who need music services with those that offer music services.

Sunnymead
PO Box 277, Waterloo, QC J0E 2N0
PH: 450-539-2098 FX: 450-539-5176
info@sunnymead.org
www.sunnymead.org
A virtual village of independent artists.

Tagged.com
PO Box 193152, San Francisco, CA 94119-3152
info@tagged.com
www.tagged.com
Provides a fun, safe, and exciting environment for people to showcase their personalities and talents, and to connect with friends and meet new ones.

TagWorld.com
PH: 310-394-5164 FX: 310-394-5167
www.tagworld.com
Join for free and view profiles, connect with others, blog, upload music and much more!

TalentMatch.com
ms@talentmatch.com
www.talentmatch.com
Designed to help aspiring and accomplished bands, singers, musicians and writers easily gain support, share their talents and gain worldwide exposure.

Talentplace.net
www.talentplace.net
We go outside the box by promoting all areas of talent, not just the music.

TalentScape.com
info@talentscape.com
www.talentscape.com
A platform to expose your talent to the world.

Top 40 Charts
www.thetop40charts.com
Worldwide jury of listeners who, each week, carefully evaluate each song based upon 5 tangible criteria: 1. The First 30 Seconds, 2. The Hook, 3. Uniqueness, 4. Performance, 5. Motivation to Own.

Trig
trig.com
A community for creative people with images, blogs, music, trends etc. Yeah, we could say all that. But what we really imagine is a place where people like their music loud, their opinions edgy and their life brave.

tumblr
www.tumblr.com
Post anything. Customize everything. Unlike blogs, tumblelogs aren't designed like a newspaper column. They're the easiest way to share everything you find, love, hate, or create — even if you're not wordy.

Twitter
164 South Park, San Francisco, CA 94107
twitter.com
A service for friends, family, and co-workers to communicate and stay connected through the exchange of quick, frequent answers to one simple question: What are you doing?

Ugly Bass Player
www.uglybassplayer.com
Whether you're a bass player or just one of the nameless, faceless musicians out there, you know that bass players have been left out of the mix for too long. We provide bassists with something of their own, a voice in a voiceless industry. We cater to a group of musicians who deserve it!

Unsigned Band Web
www.unsignedbandweb.com
Trade reviews, ideas, find answers, get feedback.

uPlayMe
www.uplayme.com
As you play music & videos on your computer we instantly show you who else is listening and watching. See someone who also loves that hard to find indie song? Send 'em a message!

Yahoo! Music Related Groups
launch.dir.groups.yahoo.com/dir/Music
Share photos & files, plan events, send a newsletter and more.

YourSpins
Office 408 Threshold House,
65-69 Shepherd's Bush Rd. London, W12 8TX UK
PH: +44(0)207 871 4227
talk2us@yourspins.com
yourspins.com
Online remixing community. Remix music. Make ringtones. Blog your mix. Share and meet other remixers.

Resources - Organizations

Creative Musicians Coalition
PO Box 6205, Peoria, IL 61601-6205
PH: 309-685-4843 FX: 309-685-4879
aimcmc@aol.com
www.creativemusicianscoalition.com
A fellowship of artists and labels that share and network.

Future of Music Coalition
1615 L St. NW #520, Washington, DC 20036
PH: 202-822-2051
Jenny Toomey jenny@futureofmusic.org
www.futureofmusic.org
A voice for musicians and citizens in Washington.

Guild of International Songwriters and Composers
Sovereign House, 12 Trewartha Rd. Praa Sands,
Penzance, Cornwall, TR20 9ST UK
PH: 01736-762826 FX: 01736-763328
songmag@aol.com
www.songwriters-guild.co.uk
International songwriters organization representing songwriters.

Indie Managers Assoc. *(IMA)*
554 N. Frederick Ave. #218
Gaithersburg, MD 20877
PH: 240-638-5060 FX: 240-597-1330
info@indiemanagers.com
www.indiemanagers.com
Exists to promote, educate and connect managers with artists seeking representation.

International Assoc. of African American Music
PO Box 382, Gladwyne, PA 19035
PH: 610-664-8292 FX: 610-664-5940
iaaam1@aol.com
www.iaaam.com
Promoting, perpetuating and preserving America's indigenous music.

International Songwriters Assoc. *Ireland*
jliddane@songwriter.iol.ie
www.songwriter.co.uk
Extensive information service for songwriters, lyric writers and music publishers.

LIFEbeat
630 9th Ave. #1010, New York, NY 10036
PH: 212-459-2590
info@lifebeat.org
www.lifebeat.org
Mobilizes the music industry to raise awareness and to provide support for the AIDS community.

MusiCares
3402 Pico Blvd. Santa Monica, CA 90405
PH: 310-392-3777 FX: 310-399-3090
Dee Dee deedee@grammy.com
www.grammy.com/musicares
A place to turn in times of financial, medical or personal crisis.

Musicians On Call
1133 Broadway, #630, New York, NY 10010-8072
PH: 212-741-2709 FX: 212-741-3465
info@musiciansoncall.org
www.musiciansoncall.org
Using music to complement the healing process for patients in healthcare facilities.

MusicPro Insurance Agency
135 Crossways Park Dr. #300, PO Box 9017
Woodbury, NY 11797
PH: 800-605-3187 FX: 888-290-0302
insurance@MusicProInsurance.com
www.musicproinsurance.com
Affordable and convenient insurance for musicians, including instruments, equipment, studio, tour, composer's liability, travel accident and health.

Positive Music Assoc.
4593 Maple Ct. Boulder, CO 80301
PH: 303-581-9083
www.positivemusicassociation.com
Established to promote positive music and those who create it and to establish a new musical genre called "Positive music." It's about making the world a better place through music.

Recording Industry Assoc. of America (RIAA)
webmaster@riaa.com
www.riaa.org
The trade group that represents the U.S. recording industry. Its mission is to foster a business and legal climate that supports and promotes our members' creative and financial vitality.

Society of Singers
15456 Ventura Blvd. #304
Sherman Oaks, CA 91403
PH: 818-995-7100 FX: 818-995-7466
www.singers.org
Helps professional vocalists, worldwide, in times of crisis.

Resources - Performing Rights Societies

AFM & AFTRA Intellectual Property Rights Distribution Fund
12001 Ventura Pl. #500, Studio City, CA 91604
PH: 818-755-7780 FX: 818-755-7779
Jo-Anne McGettrick royalties@raroyalties.org
www.raroyalties.org
Recording Artist Royalties Formed for the purpose of distributing royalties from various foreign territories and royalties established by government statute under U.S. Copyright Law.

American Federation of Television & Radio Artists (AFTRA)
5757 Wilshire Blvd. 9th Fl.
Los Angeles, CA 90036-3689
PH: 323-634-8100 FX: 323-634-8194
www.aftra.com
National labor union representing artists.

American Society of Composers, Authors and Publishers (ASCAP)
1 Lincoln Plaza, New York, NY 10023
PH: 212-621-6000 FX: 212-724-9064
info@ascap.com
www.ascap.com
A performing rights society that represents its members.

Australasian Mechanical Copyright Owners Society (AMCOS)
6-12 Atchison St., St Leonards, NSW 2065 Australia
PH: 02-9935-7900 FX: 02-9935-7999
apra@apra.com.au
www.apra.com.au
Represents music publishers in Australia and New Zealand.

British Academy of Composers & Songwriters
26 Berners St., London, W1T 3LR UK
PH: 020-7636-2929
www.britishacademy.com
Representing the interests of over 3,000 UK music writers.

British Music Rights
26 Berners St., London, W1T 3LR UK
PH: 44-0-20-7306-4446 FX: 44-0-20-7306-4449
britishmusic@bmr.org
www.bmr.org
Promotes the interests of composers, songwriters and music publishers .

Broadcast Music, Inc. (BMI)
320 W. 57th St., New York, NY 10019-3790
PH: 212-586-2000
www.bmi.com
Collects license fees on behalf of those American creators it represents.

GEMA
Postfach 30 12 40, 10722 Berlin, Germany
PH: 030-21245-00 FX: 030-21245-950
gema@gema.de
www.gema.de
German performing rights society.

Irish Music Rights Organization (IMRO)
Pembroke Row, Lower Baggot St., Dublin 2, Ireland
PH: 353-1-661-4844 FX: 353-1-661-3789
info@imro.ie
www.imro.ie
Collects and distributes royalties arising from the public performance of copyright works.

Mechanical Copyright Protection Society
Copyright House, 29-33 Berners St., London, W1T 3AB UK
PH: 020-7580-5544 FX: 020-7306-4455
www.mcps-prs-alliance.co.uk
Licenses the recording and use of music in the UK.

Phonographic Performance Limited (PPL)
1 Upper James St., London, W1F 9DE UK
PH: 020-7534-1000 FX: 020-7534-1111
info@ppluk.com
www.pamra.org.uk
A music industry organisation collecting and distributing airplay and public performance royalties in the UK on behalf of over 3,500 record companies and 40,000 performers.

RoyaltyShare
www.royaltyshare.com
We take care of the increasingly complex, tedious tasks of sales data consolidation and royalty reporting.

SESAC
55 Music Sq. E., Nashville, TN 37203
PH: 615-320-0055 FX: 615-329-9627
www.sesac.com
Performing rights organization in the US.

Societa Italiana Degli Autori Ed Editori
PH: 06-59902615 FX: 06-59902435
urp@siae.it
www.siae.it
Performing rights association of Italy.

Societe Des Auteurs Compositeurs et Editeurs De Musique (SACEM)
225 ave. Charles de Gaulle 92528 Neuilly-sur-Seine, France
PH: 01-47-15-47-15
www.sacem.fr
An advocate for French performers.

Society of Composers, Authors and music Publishers of Canada (SOCAN)
41 Valleybrook Dr. Toronto, ON M3B 2S6
PH: 416-445-8700 FX: 416-445-7108
www.socan.ca
We represent individuals who make their living creating music.

SoundExchange
1121 14th St. NW. #700, Washington, DC 20005
PH: 202-640-5858 FX: 202-640-5859
info@soundexchange.com
www.soundexchange.com
Distributes royalties from internet airplay (ie: XM, Sirius, Live365). If you have had airplay from any internet sources, you probably have some royalties waiting for you. Sign up today!

SoundScan
PH: 914-684-5525 FX: 914-684-5680
clientservices@soundscan.com
home.soundscan.com
An information system that tracks sales of music and music video products throughout the United States and Canada. Sales data from point-of-sale cash registers is collected weekly from over 14,000 retail, mass merchant and non-traditional (online stores, venues etc.) outlets.

Sweden Songs
Vanadisv 6, 113 46 Stockholm, Sweden
PH: 08-545-45065 FX: 08-34-46-30
info@swedensongs.se
www.swedensongs.se
Music publishing service.

Resources - Songwriting

Addicted-to-Songwriting
info@addicted-to-songwriting.com
www.addicted-to-songwriting.com
Your resource for songwriting information, articles, news, tips and more.

Circle of Songs
1223 Wilshire Blvd. #1610
Santa Monica, CA 90403
PH: 310-458-7664 FX: 310-458-7663
Jenna Leigh jenna@circleofsongs.com
www.circleofsongs.com
Learn to build a lifetime career in music.

Muse's Muse
96 William Curtis Cir. Newmarket, ON L3Y 8L6
jodi@musesmuse.com
www.musesmuse.com
Songwriting tips, tools, interactivities and opportunities to connect.

Ninety Mile Wind
ninetymilewind.blogspot.com
A blog for songwriters.

Pianocast - Anatomy of a Song Podcast
Todd Thalimer pianocast@gmail.com
www.thalimer.com
Creating a song from an idea so that listeners can hear how a song evolves as it created from the first musical notes, to the last lyric.

Singers U.K.
singers@singers-uk.org
www.singers-uk.net
Created to help promote professional singers on the internet.

The Singers' Workshop
4804 Laurel Canyon Blvd. #123
Valley Village, CA 91607
PH: 818-623-6668
Lis Lewis lis@thesingersworkshop.com
www.thesingersworkshop.com
Provides valuable articles that singers need to know.

SingerUniverse
11684 Ventura Blvd. #975, Studio City, CA 91604
Dale info@singeruniverse.com
www.SingerUniverse.com
Features valuable, comprehensive information for pros and newcomers alike. We don't accept unsolicited material. Please contact us before submitting your music.

Songbridge
79 Frank St., PO Box 370
Campbellford, ON K0L 1L0
PH: 705-653-2700 FX: 705-653-2709
Jana Lee Reid jana@thesongbridge.com
www.thesongbridge.com
Provides a weekly "pitch sheet" full of "song wanted" ads to its songwriting and publishing members.

SongQuarters
www.songquarters.com
Welcome to the world's most extensive tip sheet for songwriting leads to major & developing artists.

SongRights.com
PO Box 1441, Austin, TX 78767-1441
PH: 512-304-5275
RCarter154@aol.com
www.songrights.com
Dedicated to exploring and discussing legal issues facing songwriters.

Songs2Share
PO Box 580, Monee, IL 60449
PH: 708-534-1193 FX: 312-281-8622
Roberta Roberta@Songs2Share.com
www.Songs2Share.com
We sell original song licenses to artists worldwide 24/7 from our website and other media. If you want to earn residual income with your songs, or if you need original songs to sing, visit us.

Songsalive!
12115 Magnolia Blvd. #219
North Hollywood, CA 91607
PH: 310-238-0359
usa@songsalive.org
www.songsalive.org
Non profit organization supporting and promoting songwriters and composers worldwide.

Songstuff
www.songstuff.com
Articles, reference material, artist pages, news and forums.

Songwriter101.com
contact@songwriter101.com
songwriter101.com
Everything about the business side of the songwriter's profession - information, education, and the accumulated experience of music business professionals.

SongwriterPro.com
info@SongwriterPro.com
www.songwriterpro.com
Seeking to bring together like-minded songwriters, musicians, agents, producers, artists and music fans.

Songwriters Showcases of America
PH: 386-947-0997 FX: 775-249-3127
showstage@aol.com
www.ssa.cc
Creates showcases for songwriters and original bands.

Songwriters Resource Network
PO Box 135, 6327-C Capitol Hill Hwy.
Portland, OR 97239
Steve Cahill info@songwritersresourcenetwork.com
www.songwritersresourcenetwork.com
A free online news and information resource.

Songwriter's Tip Jar
Robert Cote robert@songwriterstipjar.com
www.songwriterstipjar.com
FREE weekly ezine focused on helping craft a better song.

Songwriting Contests
www.musesmuse.com/contests.html
Listing of all the best songwriting contests.

Songwriters Directory
201 N. Front St. #515, Wilmington, NC 28401
FX: 910-763-8703
swd@songwritersdirectory.com
www.songwritersdirectory.com
Listings database used by music fans and music industry executives.

USA Songwriting Competition
Eddie Phoon info@songwriting.net
www.songwriting.net
The world's leading international songwriting event honors songwriters, composers, bands and recording artists everywhere.

Resources - Studios

Lamont Audio
534 S. Honeysuckle Ln. Gilbert, AZ 85296
PH: 480-503-3004
Sandy Lamont sandy@lamontaudio.com
www.lamontaudio.com
Striving to provide cutting edge sound and service at affordable rates. Specializing in Country, Rock, Jazz, Old R&B, Gospel & New Age. Custom & vintage equipment. 30 years experience in recording and production. The studio provides digital, analog, and midi recording in a laid back relaxing setting.

Metalworks Studios
3611 Mavis Rd. Mississauga, ON L5C 1T7
PH: 905-279-4000 FX: 905-279-4006
paul@metalworksstudios.com
www.metalworksstudios.com
Recognized for an unprecedented Eleven consecutive years as "RECORDING STUDIO OF THE YEAR" at the CMW Canadian Music Industry Awards, Metalworks has become the undisputed leader in the recording studio business in Canada. It is little wonder that Gold & Platinum record awards line the corridors at Metalworks. Prince, Tina Turner, David Bowie, The Cranberries, D12, Guns and Roses, Bruce Springsteen, N'Sync and Christina Aguilera chose to make themselves part of the Metalworks legend.

Muzik Studio
14 Chesler Sq. Succasunna, NJ 07876
PH: 973-927-7250
info@muzikstudio.com
amuzikstudio.com
We do full production Recording in a friendly, relaxed environment. Our Engineer is Pro-Tools certified and experienced in every phase of the recording and production process. Whether your project is ready to go or in pre-production; MuZik Studio will help you achieve your dream. In-house musicians available including drums and percussion. We are a modern equipped results oriented studio!

Pasadena Rehearsal Studios
2016 Lincoln Ave. Pasadena, CA 91103-1323
PH: 626-296-0310
alan@pasadenarehearsal.com
www.pasadenarehearsal.com
Our philosophy is simple, supply the best rooms, equipment and customer service possible so all you have to worry about is being creative.

Virtuo Sound Studio
4894 Farm Valley Dr. Woodstock, GA 30188
PH: 770-367-2132
Josh contact@virtuosoundstudio.com
virtuosoundstudio.com
Audio recording, mixing & mastering, post-production/film audio (suitable for projects at all levels).

Resources - Tools

AudioSparx
140 Frontera Dr. St. Augustine, FL 32084
PH: 954-791-9795 FX: 954-252-2352
Lee Johnson lee@audiosparx.com
www.AudioSparx.com
The world's marketplace for Hollywood sound effects, stock music, loops and more!

Babel Fish Language Translator
world.altavista.com
Ever get a music review in a foreign country and have no idea what they're saying?

Bandzoogle
550 Jean d'Estrees #901, Montreal, QC H3C 6W1
info@bandzoogle.com
www.bandzoogle.com
Lets you build a band website without any web programming knowledge.

CCNow
www.ccnow.com
A low-risk way for small businesses to sell their product online.

CDstands.com
30 Compton Way, Hamilton Sq., NJ 08690
PH: 609-689-1711
info@cdreview.com
cdstands.com
We manufacture our own line of CD boxes for artists to sell their music at shows or in stores.

eStockMusic.com
www.estockmusic.com
An online community for royalty free music and stock music.

FATdrop
PO Box 5107, Brighton, BN50 9RG UK
www.fatdrop.co.uk
A web based delivery solution for creating stunning digital promos online. You can upload and send, both streaming and downloadable audio, copy and images in your own branded templates.

FeedBurner
www.feedburner.com
Tools for blogging and podcasting. Sends your blog updates every day at noon to all your subscribers.

Free Acid Loops
Daniel McCarthy admin@acidlabz.com
www.acidlabz.com
Download free acid loops, FL studio samples & more!

GetYourGrooveOn
www.getyourgrooveon.com
Every songwriter I know keeps a record of the songs they've written. These songs are usually accompanied by other information like chord progressions, tabs and sometimes a simple mp3 file. I wanted a way to organize this information myself, and figured there would be a lot of people in my exact situation. With that, the idea for GetYourGrooveOn was born.

Gracenote CDDB
2000 Powell St. #1380, Emeryville, CA 94608
PH: 510-547-9680 FX: 510-547-9681
GracenoteSupport@gracenote.com
www.gracenote.com
The industry standard for music recognition services. Seamless handling of soundtracks and other compilations, expanded album and track fields, credits, genres and ISRC code.

HitPredictor
www.hitpredictor.com
A little over five years ago we started testing songs before airplay. At first we didn't believe it ourselves, but now, after testing almost every release from the past five years, the HitPredictor has shown incredible accuracy in determining the hit potential of new songs prior to airplay.

Hostbaby
5925 NE. 80th Ave. Portland, OR 97218-2891
PH: 888-448-6369
hostbaby@hostbaby.com
www.hostbaby.com
The best place to host your website/domain!

Indie Artist Assistant
233 E. Magnolia Ave. Auburn, AL 36830
PH: 888-292-0847
Rob Slocumb rob@indieartistassistant.com
www.indieartistassistant.com
Your personal office manager created for today's DIY artist. Let us handle your daily workload so you can perfect your craft.

Indie Band Manager / Indie Office
620 Iroquois Dr. Fremont, MI 49412
PH: 215-825-6913
Charlie Cheney info@indiebandmanager.com
www.indiebandmanager.com
Database software for independent musicians.

International Country Calling Codes and World Time Zones
www.countrycallingcodes.com
Find the international dialing code or time zone for any country. Online tool will instantly show you ALL telephone prefixes needed to call from one area code to another.

LISTBABY: your email list mailer
5925 NE 80th Ave. Portland, OR 97218-2891
PH: 888-448-6369
hostbaby@hostbaby.com
hostbaby.com/features/listbaby
Instead of sticking everyone you know into "BCC:" field of your email program, an email list manager on your site will let you email some or all of your contacts, using their name right in the email itself.

LiveJournal
feedback@livejournal.com
www.livejournal.com
A journal community with powerful personal publishing (blogging) tool, built on open source software.

LiveWire Contacts
156 Hamilton St., Cambridge, MA 02139
support@LiveWireContacts.com
www.LiveWireContacts.com
A contact manager specifically designed for musicians.

mrTonePhone.com
62 N. Chapel St. #204, Newark, DE 19711
PH: 866-439-1634
Jeffery Hiester info@mrtonephone.com
www.mrtonephone.com
A telephone based companion to the artists already existing electronic press kit. We give you a telephone number of your choice, anywhere in the USA, that anyone can call from a touch tone phone.

Mievo
Leah Haynes leah@mievo.com
www.mievo.com
Stands for: MyEvolution. Online promotion site for musicians and artists that can help them maximize revenue from their work by employing Google page rank mechanisms.

Music Industry News Network (*mi2n*)
1814 Astoria Blvd. Astoria, NY 11102
PH: 718-278-0662
Eric de Fontenay editor@mi2n.com
www.mi2n.com/submit_top.html
Submit your press releases for free.

Music Stir
1810 Marlene Dr. Lincoln, NE 68506
PH: 970-988-6310
Chris McConnell chris@musicstir.com
www.musicstir.com
Combines three products into one site. Includes a revolutionary news service, the ability to easily and effectively release news to the masses and supporting community tools that will give new life to plain text news and features.

Muze
304 Hudson St. 8th Fl. New York, NY 10013
PH: 212-824-0300
info@muze.com
www.muze.com
Our products and services are designed to drive commerce, enhance the consumer experience and increase customer loyalty.

MyNewsletterBuilder
comments@mynewsletterbuilder.com
www.mynewsletterbuilder.com
A user-friendly, feature-rich, online newsletter management program for novices and professionals alike.

MyScoreStore - Publish & Download Written Music
Patrick Vergouwen info@myscorestore.com
www.myscorestore.com
A platform where composers and arrangers can publish scores online, making them available for immediate printing.

Onlinegigs
PO Box 6368, Delray Beach, FL 33482
PH: 888-595-3122 FX: 866-215-0034
Jay Flanzbaum support@onlinegigs.com
www.onlinegigs.com
Automates the administration of booking and promoting your band. It is a centralized database of nationwide venues, colleges, festivals and media contacts.

PayPal
www.paypal.com
The world's largest online payment solution. No start-up fees, no monthly fees.

The Patchbay
getconnected@thepatchbay.com
www.thepatchbay.com
Compare all the best quotes to manufacture vinyl records CDs, & CDRs. One click to email thousands of companies and announce your new music. Promo Page for secure distribution of your high resolution promotional materials. Mailing labels with cover letters for companies that don't respond to your email. Connections log of companies you contact so you can follow up with a call or fax. Radioactive widget to make fans an active part of your radio promotion.

PR Web
PO Box 333, Ferndale, WA 98248
PH: 360-312-0892 FX: 360-380-9981
www.prweb.com
We have helped over 4,000 companies distribute their press releases.

RockBandSites.com
support@rockbandsites.com
www.rockbandsites.com
Create your own design! The industry's best update tools. Sell audio tracks from your site. Private, band-only pages. Plus: video, photos, press kit, merch, blog, mailing lists and more... starting at just $4.95!

SoundRangers.com
PH: 206-352-8818 FX: 206-374-8109
www.soundrangers.com
Royalty free music and sound effects download site.

Stock Music Site
140 Frontera Dr. St. Augustine, FL 32084
PH: 954-791-9795 FX: 954-252-2352
Lee Johnson lee@audiosparx.com
www.StockMusicSite.com
The ultimate source for high-impact royalty free music - over 1,000 artists and 20,000+ tracks.

StudioTraxx
www.studiotraxx.com
Provides access to the largest and highest quality "virtual" musician-for-hire talent pool. Discover why so many working musicians have made StudioTraxx.com their online studio home!

TalkShoe
12300 Perry Hwy. #306, Wexford, PA 15090
PH: 724-935-8255
info@talkshoe.com
www.talkshoe.com
A service that enables anyone to easily create, join, or listen to live interactive discussions, conversations, podcasts and audioblogs.

Vista Prints
www.vistaprint.com
Get 250 free business cards.

Vontoo
7602 E. 88th Pl., Indianapolis, IN 46256
PH: 877-768-8183
Andrew Innes vontoosales@gmail.com
www.vontoo.com
A permission based voice messaging system that can send messages direct from bands to fans.

WordPress.com
wordpress.com
Express yourself. Start a blog!

youSENDit
www.yousendit.com
Allows you to e-mail files up to 100 mbs for free!

Blues

Barrelhouse Blues
www.barrelhouseblues.com
Our goals are to spread the beauty of the Blues to all who will listen. Features an "Artist Spotlight."

Blues FM
www.wnart.com/s/blues
Blues news and information hub.

The Blues Foundation
49 Union Ave. Memphis, TN 38103
PH: 901-527-2583 FX: 901-529-4030
www.blues.org
Encourages and recognizes the achievements of Blues artists.

CD of the Week / Cornbreads Parking Lot
11469 Olive Blvd. #163, St. Louis, MO 63141
Cornbread@STLBlues.net
www.stlblues.net/parking_info.htm
We get over 15,000 hits a day. A great way to promote your CD!

Children's

Children's Music Network
PO Box 1341, Evanston, IL 60204-1341
PH: 847-733-8003
office@cmnonline.org
www.cmnonline.org
Catalyst for education and community-building through music.

Children's Music Web
www.childrensmusic.org
Connecting families with great Children's music.

Children's Music Workshop
info@childrensmusicworkshop.com
www.childrensmusicworkshop.com
A music education resource for students, parents and teachers.

KiddieGifts
18 Tnuat Hameri St., Ramat Gan, Israel
PH: 972-3-6766122 FX: 972-57-7947115
Amos Barzel amos@kiddiegifts.co.il
www.kiddiegifts.co.il
A production company producing musical programs on CDs, DVDs and cassettes.

KidScreen
366 Adelaide St. W. #500, Toronto, ON M5V 1R9
PH: 416-408-2300 FX: 416-408-0870
www.kidscreen.com
Serving the information needs of children entertainers.

Pancake Mountain
PO Box 40128, Washington, DC 20016
bands@pancakemountain.com
www.pancakemountain.com
Syndicated Children's music TV show.

Parents' Choice Awards
201 W. Padonia Rd. #203, Timonium, MD 21093
PH: 410-308-3858 FX: 410-308-3877
info@parents-choice.org
www.parents-choice.org
Details and entry forms are available online.

Christian

The 5000 Music Group
PH: 402-327-9659
Chris McConnell chris@the5000music.com
www.the5000music.com
Offers Christian musicians and fans a variety of resources. Our mission is to see that promising Christian artists are not lost in a sea of noise. We want to make it possible for music lovers to discover the fusion of professional and independent music found on our site.

Band With a Mission
3800 S. 48th St., Lincoln, NE 68506
PH: 615-435-3017
Austin C. Cook austin@bandwithamission.com
www.BandWithaMission.com
We are a national Christian music talent search. We help Christian musicians harness their gifts and develop effective ministry tools.

Called2Music
www.called2music.com
A platform for experienced artists and church leaders to share insights, experiences and accumulated wisdom with the nation's music community.

Christian Country Music Assoc.
PO Box 101336, Nashville, TN 37224
PH: 615-742-9210 FX: 615-248-8505
www.ccma.cc
Promoting Christian Country music.

Christian Independent Alliance
www.cialliance.org
We believe artists of faith should be sent to the church and world by an organization who has a proven history of supporting independent Christian artists and musicians. It is time for a new movement in Christian music!

Christian Indies
1946 S. Powahatan Ct. Independence, MO 64057
www.christianindies.com
Bringing you the best of Christian indie bands including the most concise databases of band and venue information and resources.

Christian Music Monthly
PO Box 654, East Amherst, NY 14051
Mark Weber primopr716@juno.com
www.christianmusicmonthly.com
Promote your CD/event, post opinions ... get connected!

The Christian Pulse
www.thechristianpulse.com
Create a free profile and make new Christian friends. Use our forum, blogs, & photo album to share with others. Features interviews, artist spotlights and more!

Christian Radio & Retail Weekly
5350 N. Academy Blvd. #200,
Colorado Springs, CO 80918
PH: 719-536-9000 FX: 719-598-7461
Dave Koch dave@christianradioweekly.com
www.christianradioweekly.com
Publication featuring song rankings, news and information for various genres of Christian music.

Christian Songwriter's Network
PO Box 18895, Panama City Beach, FL 32417
FX: 206-279-1601
James Moore james@christiansongwriters.org
www.christiansongwriters.org
Our goal is to provide Christian songwriters the best resources available for ensuring success in their songwriting.

ChristianIndieForums.com
Michael Eshom oldiesmann@oldiesmann.us
www.christianindieforums.com
Artists can have their board hosted here, as well as ask for reviews and critiques on their music while meeting new fans and other artists.

ChristianTuner.com
PO Box 147, Power Springs, GA 30127
submissions@christiantuner.com
www.christiantuner.com
The most complete collection of live Christian radio and TV stations, programs, MP3 downloads and podcasting links on the internet.

Creative Soul
PH: 615-400-3910
Eric Copeland ec@CreativeSoulOnline.com
www.CreativeSoulOnline.com
Christian music resource designed for artists who need to reach the next level of music ministry.

FaithBase.com
www.FaithBase.com
Online Christian community where you can post your CD releases, tour announcements, MP3s etc.

Firestream.net
forums.firestream.net
An online community of Christians that enjoy heavy music, whether its Rock, Metal, Hardcore etc.

Gospel Music Assoc.
1205 Division St., Nashville, TN 37203
PH: 615-242-0303 FX: 615-254-9755
www.gospelmusic.org
Promoting the development of all forms of Gospel music.

Gospel Music Workshop of America
PO Box 34635, Detroit, MI 34635
PH: 313-898-6900
manager@gmwanational.com
www.gmwanational.org
Dedicated to the perpetuation of Gospel music.

Heaven's Metal
webmaster@heavensmetal.com
www.heavensmetal.com
Your CD is rated by visitors to the site.

HeavenSound
PH: 817-691-8840
info@heavensound.com
www.heavensound.com
Offers concert database services to Gospel artists, with the added benefit that music fans can easily find hundreds of concerts for their area.

HookUps
7233 Pioneers Blvd. Lincoln, NE 68506
PH: 402-327-9659
Chris McConnell info@cmcconnell.com
www.christianrecorddeal.com
An online resource that we call a "record label alternative" designed from scratch to provide Christian indie artists with the tools to create, distribute and promote their music on their own terms.

MyMusicMission.com
www.mymusicmission.com
Providing artists valuable career management/promotion tools, resources, guidance and support, as well as access to music industry buyers and service providers.

Push-It Online Newszine
PO Box 18126, Cincinnati, OH 45018
PH: 313-207- 5786
Bruce Knight bknight1229@yahoo.com
www.push-itnews.com
A one-stop shop for unsigned indie Gospel artists promoting sanctified Holy-Ghost filled independent talent!

Urban Gospel Alliance
PO Box 777, Lithonia, GA 30058
PH: 770-482-6849
www.urbangospelalliance.com
Broadening Gospel music's reach into the streets.

Classical

North America

United States

Adaptistration
www.adaptistration.com
During recent years, the environment of orchestra management has fundamentally changed. This weblog is designed to present ideas and create a forum to help accelerate that evolutionary process.

Afrocentric Voices in Classical music
www.afrovoices.com/futurevoices.html
Focusing on African American performers.

American Composers Forum
332 Minnesota St. #145E, St. Paul, MN 55101-1300
PH: 651-228-1407 FX: 651-291-7978
www.composersforum.org
Supporting composers and developing new markets for their music.

American Guild of Musical Artists
1430 Broadway, 14th Fl. New York, NY 10018
PH: 212-265-3687 FX: 212-262-9088
www.musicalartists.org
Labor organization that represents Operatic, Choral and Dance artists.

American Harp Society
PO Box 38334, Los Angeles, CA 90038-0334
www.harpsociety.org
National society that promotes harpists.

American Music Center
30 W. 26th St. #1001, New York, NY 10010
PH: 212-366-5260 FX: 212-366-5265
www.amc.net
Encourages the composition of Contemporary (American) music.

American Pianists Assoc.
www.americanpianists.org
Advancing the careers of American Classical and Jazz pianists.

American Viola Society
14070 Proton Rd. #100, Dallas, TX 75244
PH: 972-233-9107 x204
www.americanviolasociety.org
Promotion of viola performance and research.

Blognoggle New Music
www.blognoggle.com/classical.html
Shadowing the top 100 Classical music blogs.

Cadenza Musicians' Directory
PH: 206-202 3690
www.cadenza.org
Directory of performances and artists.

Center for the Promotion of Contemporary Composers
PO Box 631043, Nacogdoches, TX 75963
www.under.org/cpcc
An internet-based service organization for composers.

Chamber Music America
305 7th Ave. 5th Fl. New York, NY 10001
PH: 212-242-2022 FX: 212-242-7955
www.chamber-music.org
Promotes artistic excellence and economic stability within the profession.

classicOL.com
info@classicol.com
www.classicol.com
Get your free website specifically designed for Classical musicians.

ClassiQuest
29 Alscot Ln. Langhorne, PA 19047
PH: 215-891-0560 FX: 215-891-0561
David Osenberg Osenbergdd@aol.com
www.classiquest.com
FREE service for those in the music media.

Composers Concordance
PO Box 36-20548 PABT, New York, NY 10129
info@composersconcordance.org
www.composersconcordance.org
Created to increase awareness of the Concert music of our time.

Early Music America
2366 Eastlake Ave. E. #429, Seattle, WA 98102
PH: 206-720-6270 FX: 206-720-6290
earlymusic.org
Extensive resources for members.

earlyMusic.net
PO Box 854, Atlanta, GA 30301
PH: 770-638-7554 FX: 770-638-7554
www.earlymusic.net
Information and services about Early music.

Klassinen.fi
info@klassinen.fi
Klassinen.fi
A Finnish based comprehensive classical music information database.

hornplayer.net
www.hornplayer.net
Free classifieds and information archive.

International Horn Society
www.hornsociety.org
Preservation and promotion of the horn

International Society of Bassists
www.ISBworldoffice.com
Inspiring public interest in the double bass.

International Trombone Assoc. Journal
www.trombone.net
Trombone news, gigs and record reviews.

International Trumpet Guild
www.trumpetguild.org
Promotes communication among trumpet players around the world.

International Tuba and Euphonium Assoc.
www.iteaonline.org
Promotes performance of the euphonium and tuba.

Internet Cello Society
www.cello.org
An international cyber-community of cellists.

Meet the Composer
75 9ᵗʰ Ave. 3R Ste. C, New York, NY 10011
PH: 212-645-6949 FX: 212-645-9669
hhitchens@meetthecomposer.org
www.meetthecomposer.org
Increases opportunities for composers.

Musical America
400 Windsor Corp. Ctr. #200
East Windsor, NJ 08520
PH: 609-371-7877 FX: 609-371-7879
info@musicalamerica.com
www.musicalamerica.com
An industry standard for over a century. Our directory has facilitated lasting and important relationships with leading performing arts professionals.

Musical Chairs
features@musicalchairs.info
www.musicalchairs.info
List of worldwide orchestral jobs and competitions.

National Assoc. of Composers
PO Box 49256, Barrington Stn.
Los Angeles, CA 90049
www.music-usa.org/nacusa
Promotion and performance of American music.

New Directions Cello Assoc.
501 Linn St., Ithaca, NY 14850
PH: 607-277-1686
www.newdirectionscello.com
Newsletter, interviews, events and more.

Opera Base
www.operabase.com
Extensive online resource for Opera artists.

PostClassic
Kyle Gann kgann@earthlink.net
www.artsjournal.com/postclassic
So Classical music is dead, they say. Well, well. This blog will set out to consider that dubious factoid with equanimity, if not downright enthusiasm.

Society of Composers
PO Box 450, New York, NY 10113-0450
www.societyofcomposers.org
A professional society promoting new and contemporary music.

Viola Website
www.viola.com
Viola events and competitions, articles, resources and publishers.

Web Concert Hall
webconcerthall@usa.com
www.webconcerthall.com
Providing artist with a chance to gain exposure.

Young Artists International
2430 Apollo Dr. Los Angeles, CA 90046-1628
PH: 310-281-3303 FX: 323-969-8742
info@youngartists.org
www.youngartists.org
Develops the careers of exceptionally gifted young musicians.

Young Concert Artists
250 W. 57ᵗʰ St. #1222, New York, NY 10019
PH: 212-307-6655 FX: 212-581-8894
yca@yca.org
www.yca.org
Discovering and launching the careers of extraordinary young musicians.

Europe

France

ConcertoNet.com
67 rue St. Jacques, 75005 Paris, France
concertonet@yahoo.com
www.concertonet.com
Providing information about Classical music worldwide.

La Lettre du musicien
14 rue Violet, F.75015, Paris, France
PH: 33-01-56-77-04-00 FX: 33-01-56-77-04-09
info@la-lettre-du-musicien.com
www.la-lettre-du-musicien.com
News and information from the Classical music scene in Europe.

Italy

Operissimo
Via B. d'Alviano 71, IT-20146 Milano MI, Italy
PH: +39-02-415-62-26 FX: +39-02-415-62-29
pia.parisi@operissimo.com
www.operissimo.com
Add your information to our database.

The Netherlands

The International Society for Contemporary Music *(ISCM)*
www.iscm.org
An important international network of members from around fifty countries, devoted to the promotion and presentation of Contemporary music - the music of our time.

United Kingdom

Early music Network
3 Onslow House, Castle Rd. Turnbridge Wells, Kent, TN4 8BY UK
PH/FX: +44 (0)1892-511652
www.earlymusic.org.uk
Provides personalised pages on performers and composers together with entries for record labels and affiliated organisations.

International Assoc. of Music Information Centres
www.iaml.info
Network of organizations promoting new music.

Muso
4ᵗʰ Fl. 117-119 Portland St.
Manchester, M1 6ED UK
PH: 0161-236-9526 FX: 0161-247-7978
info@muso-online.com
www.muso-online.com
Designed for young professional musicians, students or music enthusiasts wanting to keep up with the latest news and gossip,

Country

All About Country
webmaster@allaboutcountry.com
www.allaboutcountry.com
THE website where Country labels & artists can reach radio decision makers. We carry the latest news and information.

Americana Music Assoc.
411 E. Iris Dr. Ste. D, Nashville, TN 37204
PH: 615-386-6936 FX: 615-386-6937
www.americanamusic.org
Promotes awareness of this genre.

The Euro Americana Chart
home.hetnet.nl/~noci48
Compiled by DJs, journalists, retailers, promoters and other people who are interested in Americana music from all over Europe. Every month they send in their top 6 CDs.

FiddleFork
PO Box 989, Chetwynd, BC V0C 1J0
PH: 250-401-303
info@fiddlefork.com
fiddlefork.com
One stop platform for anything fiddle related.

Indie World Country Record Report
PO Box 130, Brush Creek, TN 38547
PH: 615-683-8308
www.indieworldcountry.com
Designed to candidly alert the independent community, the general public and "major" industry about the growth development, aspirations and talents of new singers and songwriters worldwide.

International Bluegrass Music Assoc.
2 Music Cir. S. #100, Nashville, TN 37203
PH: 888-438-4262
www.ibma.org
Promoting and expanding the success of Bluegrass music.

Roots Music Association
13501 Ranch Rd. 12 Ste. 103-327,
Wimberley, TX 78676
PH: 512-667-6466
www.rootsmusicassociation.org
Dedicated to bringing "Roots" artists, the professional entertainment community, and their audiences together on a global level.

Society for the Preservation of Bluegrass Music of America
PO Box 271, Kirksville, MO 63501
PH: 660-665-7172 FX: 660-655-7450
www.spbgma.com
Preserves traditional Bluegrass music.

Western Music Assoc.
www.westernmusic.org
Promotes traditional and contemporary music of The Great American West.

Dance and Electronic

7161
info@7161.com
www.7161.com
Run by musicians for musicians! - 100% free indie music hosting on the www - It's free to join, make your own homepage, upload your original songs & deejay-mixes, create podcasts & blogs and more!

Buzzsonic.com
buzzsonic.dj
Covering news and products in the Electronic music industry.

DANCEBLOGGA
Dennis Romero chp@earthlink.net
dancemusic.blogspot.com
Blog covering the national Dance music scene. News that makes you move!

djmixed.com
BPM Magazine, 6725 Sunset Blvd. #320
Los Angeles, CA 90028
PH: 310-360-7170 x107 FX: 310-360-7171
feedback@djmixed.com
www.djmixed.com
DJ culture and the Electronic music lifestyle.

Electronic Music 411
www.em411.com
Giving Electronic musicians a place to discuss their tools and their craft.

FUSICOLOGY
2658 Griffith Park Blvd. #128
Los Angeles, CA 90039
PH: 800-980-3873
www.fusicology.com
A multifaceted media entity and national promotional vehicle for reaching trend setting, multicultural urbanites. We specialize in providing relevant information for early adopters and the musically forward.

junglescene.com
junglescene.com
D n' B community. News, events, audio etc.

littledetroit.net
www.littledetroit.net
Techno and Electro music community.

SPRACI
PH: +61 (0) 415-802-648 FX: +61-1300-300-374
www.spraci.com
A worldwide resource site for parties/clubs/festivals etc.

Experimental

clan analogue
clananalogue.org
Indie record label that assists with promotional materials.

Electronic Music Foundation
PO Box 8748, Albany, NY 12208
PH: 518-434-4110 FX: 518-434-0308
www.emf.org
Increasing the public's understanding of Electronic music.

The Gas Station
15a George St., Bath, BA1 2EN UK
PH: 44-0-125-442546
nick@sonicstate.com
www.the-gas-station.com
The Electronic musician's knowledge base and number one discussion site.

Hometapes
PO Box 7563, Boulder, CO 80306
info@home-tapes.com
www.home-tapes.com
Created to allow musical and visual artists a place to collaborate and experiment without the constraints, pressures and delays of traditional releases.

NetNewMusic
netnewmusic.net
A portal for the world of non-Pop, Contemporary Classical/Avant-whatever musics. We focus on the best living composer/performer sites.

Other Minds
www.otherminds.org
A global New Music community where composers, students and listeners discover and learn about innovative music by composers from all over the world.

shift!
Choriner Strasse 50, D-10435 Berlin, Germany
PH: 49-030-693-7814 FX: 49-030-693-7844
info@shift.de
www.shift.de
Invites artists to create without compromise.

Society for Electro-Acoustic Music
1 Washington Sq. San Jose, CA 95192-0095
www.seamusonline.org
Represents every part of the country and virtually every musical style.

STFU
contact@stfumusic.org
www.stfumusic.org
A network of groups and individuals who come together to make live Electronic music events happen.

Film and TV

Film Music Network / Film Music Magazine
27023 McBean Pkwy. #618, Valencia, CA 91355
PH: 310-645-9000 FX: 310-388-1367
www.filmmusicmag.com
Facilitates for networking among professionals in the film music business.

Film Music Weekly
editor@filmmusicweekly.com
www.filmmusicweekly.com
A weekly electronic magazine about the world of music for film, television and video games.

Film Score Monthly
6311 Romaine St. #7109, Hollywood, CA 90038
PH: 323-461-2240 FX: 323-461-2241
www.filmscoremonthly.com
Magazine about motion picture and television music.

Society of Composers & Lyricists
400 S. Beverly Dr. #214, Beverly Hills, CA 90212
PH: 310-281-2812 FX: 310-284-4861
www.thescl.com
Focuses on the creative and business aspects of writing music and lyrics for film and television.

SoundtrackNet
12011 Rochester Ave. #7, Los Angeles, CA 90025
www.soundtrack.net
Articles, news, interviews and resources about film and television music. We do NOT do music placement.

Folk

FOLKDJ-L
www.folkradio.org
An electronic discussion group for DJs and other people interested in Folk-based music on the radio.

folkjam.org
www.folkjam.org
This community site provides information on Acoustic Bluegrass, Old-Time, Irish, Fiddle, Roots and Acoustic jam sessions.

World Folk Music Assoc.
PO Box 40553, Washington, DC 20016
PH: 202-362-2225
wfma.net
Interviews with artists and songwriters, CD and tape reviews and more.

GLBT

Herland Sister Resources
2312 NW. 39th St., Oklahoma City, OK 73112
PH: 405-521-9696
www.herlandsisters.org
Womanist organization with a strong lesbian focus.

OutMedia
285 5th Ave. #446, Brooklyn, NY 11215
PH: 718-789-1776 FX: 718-789-8007
www.outmedia.org
Our mission is to increase the positive visibility of LGBTQQA people and promote inclusive multiculturalism through the arts.

Outmusic
PO Box 376, Old Chelsea Stn.
New York, NY 10113-0376
PH: 212-330-9197
www.outmusic.com
A network of gay, lesbian, bisexual and transgender musicians and supporters. Performers, producers, promoters and press/media.

OutVoice
PO Box 11135, Charleston, WV 25339
www.outvoice.net
Intersexed musician ranking chart and service network.

Goth

C8
stevvi@c8.com to
c8.com
Resource which posts articles, interviews, reviews etc.

darksites.com
www.darksites.com
Post information - views, articles, interviews, reviews etc.

HellWire Industrial Music Underground
www.hellwire.com
Music charts offering exposure to artists in the Electronic / Goth / Industrial genres. Includes area to post reviews.

Hip Hop

Blingd
www.blingd.com
A user-powered Hip Hop news site. You submit, You vote, You discuss.

BLOCK JAMS
www.blockjams.com
A premier direct-to-consumer mobile entertainment company. Grow your fan base, promote your music, videos, photos etc.

BuzzThis.net
234 Wegman Pkwy. Jersey City, NJ 07305
PH: 201-918-6337
Chuck Diesel buzzthis@gmail.com
www.BuzzThis.net
Provides an online forum for music labels, artists, DJs, producers, authors and all other 'creative types' to promote & market their product to key industry influencers and first movers. Through a tailored viral marketing campaign, BuzzThis.net digitally delivers your product to those who will most effectively enhance your buzz.

CrackSpace
8033 W. Sunset Blvd. #1038, Hollywood, CA 90046
crackspace@crackspace.net
hiphopcrack.com
The world's first Hip Hop social network.

Culture Universal
crew@cultureuniversal.com
www.cultureuniversal.com
Japanese based Hip Hop service offering intergalactic collaboration hook-ups for artists we support.

Hip Hop Press
Clyde Smith hiphoppress@netweed.com
www.hiphoppress.com
Free Hip Hop press release posting service.

HipHop-Network.Com
177 Stillman St., San Francisco, CA 94107
info@hiphop-network.com
www.hiphop-network.com
Represents Hip Hop and everyday life in the Hip Hop community.

HIPHOPDIRECTORY.COM
feedback@hiphopdirectory.com
hiphopdirectory.com
Largest directory of quality Hip Hop and Rap sites.

HipHopHotSpot.Com
PO Box 35534, RPO Strath Barton
Hamilton, ON L8H 7S6
www.hiphophotspot.com
Supports the growth of Hip Hop artists worldwide.

iHipHop
www.ihiphop.com
Social networking community with video, shows, message boards and more!

Mix Me Entertainment
PH: 877-732-7978
S. Jones webmaster@mixmeentertainment.com
www.mixmeentertainment.com
Your source for unique Rap and Hip Hop beats. We have a weekly promotion featuring producers and artists on the site! Enter the producer/artists of the week contest and get featured.

ProHipHop
Clyde Smith hiphoppress@netweed.com
www.prohiphop.com
Blog featuring Hip Hop marketing & business news.

Rap Coalition
3000 Old Alabama Rd. #119, Box 171
Alpharetta, GA 30022
PH: 404-474-1999
rapcoalition@aol.com
rapcoalition.org
Protects rappers, producers and DJs and provides artists with a place to turn when they need help or support.

RapChoice
PH: 360-556-8692
Jereme Manning diamond@rapchoice.com
www.RapChoice.com
An interactive forum based community designed to promote underground artists. Every new artist has the ability to sell their CDs and music in our store. We offer free homepage promotions to artists.

RapHead.com
www.raphead.com
Social networking for Urban music and entertainment.

Raptalk.net - Worldwide Rap and Hip Hop Music Network
PH: 626-443-3850
www.raptalk.net
We specialize in promoting independent music alongside of major acts. Hip Hop, Rap and R&B news, exclusive music and interviews.

SCREAM Star Entertainment
screamstar.com
We are giving you total control over your profile! Insert photos, music, movies and more!

SPATE Magazine
spatemag.ning.com
The hottest urban life style magazine in the world. It does not cost a thing to be a member. Join and upload pics and communicate with other members.

Spitkicker
www.myspace.com/spitkicker
A collective unit that, through the power and use of words, will set trends, unify cultures, and create positive standards for communities. Also features Spitkicker Radio.

SpitNow.com
nfo@spitnow.com
www.SpitNow.com
A social network for the global Hip Hop community.

That's Hip Hop
www.thatshiphop.com
News, honeys, friends, community, exclusive music, upload video, Hip Hop interviews.

TLA-PROnline.com
Robert administrator@tla-pronline.com
www.tla-pronline.com
A place where independent Rap, Hip Hop and Spoken Word artists are represented. We can help artists get noticed with interviews and press releases.

Urban Music Strategies
16781 Chagrin Blvd. #158
Shaker Heights, OH 44137
PH: 216-255-6558 FX: 208-723-3636
Martin Johnson martin@urbanmusicstrategies.com
www.urbanmusicstrategies.com/blog/
A website designed to help Rap, R&B and Urban Gospel artists with solid do-it-yourself strategies for independent music success.

Urban Network
3255 Wilshire Blvd. #815, Los Angeles, CA 90010
PH: 213-388-4155 FX: 213-388-0034
Arthur Mitchell amitchell@urbanetwork.com
urbannetwork.com
The premier entertainment industry publication, online portal and multi-media company bridging the Urban entertainment community.

Jam Band

Beginners B&P Instructions
14222 29th Ave. SE., Mill Creek, WA 98012
PH: 425-379-0592 FX: 425-316-0999
ed@mcnichol.com
www.mcnichol.com/bnp
Instructions for trading free live music on CD.

Coolmusicstuff.com
becky@coolmusicstuff.com
www.coolmusicstuff.com
A listing of hundreds of Jam Band tour dates and festivals. If I dig what a band is doing, then I just might put them on the schedule.

Jam Band Meetup
jambands.meetup.com
Post information about your band.

KindWeb
www.kindweb.com
A search engine, directory and online store specializing in music resources, band links and more.

TheJamZone
thejamzone.com
Press releases, band info, concert dates, classifieds and more!

Jazz

I Love Smooth Jazz
SmoothLee admin@smoothlee.com
www.ilovesmoothjazz.com
The most complete Smooth Jazz directory on Earth!

JazzPolice
Don Berryman editor@jazzpolice.com
www.jazzpolice.com
Extensive coverage of the local Jazz scene in ALL major US cities.

The Jazzserver
info@jazzserver.org
www.jazzserver.org
Add your group, venue, festival or concerts to earth's coolest Jazz website for free!

JazzWeek
info@jazzweek.com
www.jazzweek.com
The definitive Jazz and Smooth Jazz national radio airplay chart.

JazzWord
www.jazzword.com
News on Avant-garde, Free Bop, Energy Music, The New Thing and Contemporary Improvised Sounds.

The Polish Jazz Network
PO Box 40153, Long Beach, CA 90804
PH: 949-466-3517
info@polishjazz.com
www.polishjazz.com
The doorway to the world of improvised music from Poland. We offer the largest selection of material regarding Polish Jazz on the web.

Radio Jazz
www.radiojazz.com
Jazz news and information hub.

Third Stone Radio
spotlight@radiocave.com
www.radiocave.com/jazz.htm
A guide to Jazz on the internet. Be the next Jazz artist in our Spotlight. E-mail us your promo.

Latin

America Latina Jazz Network
www.americalatinajazznetwork.net
Promueve, interrelaciona y concentra músicos independientes, compositores, sellos discográficos, productores, clubes, festivales, organizaciones, y todo lo relacionado con el Jazz en América Latina para el estrechamiento de lazos e intercambio entre las diferentes naciones y su difusión al resto del mundo.

Bocada Forte
www.bocada-forte.com.br
Matérias, ultimas notícias, colunistas.

Latin Industry Connection
Angela Star angela@latinindustryconnection.com
www.latinindustryconnection.com
For artists, producers, DJs etc. We offer many industry opportunities as well as booking, management, publicity etc.

MySpace en Espanol
latino.myspace.com
Spotlights content, programming, artists and users relevant to the U.S. Hispanic MySpace population.

PuroRock.com
PH: 408-386-1500 FX: 650-254-8907
Gabriel Meza gabriel@purorock.com
www.purorock.com
The premier Spanish portal in the US.

Metal

Alterchatter
webmaster@alterchatter.com
www.alterchatter.com
Forums for Alternative music and lifestyle discussions. Metal, Rock, Punk, Emo, Goth or Alternative only.

Cyqo Music
www.cyqo.com
Each artist and fan is given a FREE web page with an easy to remember URL. Fans can come by and drop information about their band, show dates, fan pages etc. It's an open forum for music lovers, fans and artists alike.

Hard Radio
feedback@hardradio.com
www.hardradio.com
The Metal site with no Alternative aftertaste.

Heavycore.org
PO Box 4324, Bloomington, IL 61702
poserdisposer@heavycore.org
www.heavycore.org
Promotion for Heavy bands and musicians.

Metal Map of Europe
metalmap.czweb.org

Project Independent
PO Box 541, Torrance, CA 90508
www.myspace.com/projectindependent
A national touring, artist showcase program specifically designed for the discovery and development of independent metal artists.

ZRock.com
www.ZRock.com
Join our FREE online community of rockers and help bring back the music!

New Age

Nuevas Músicas
PO Box 5352, Barcelona, Spain
www.nuevasmusicas.org
Created to promote the music of New Age artists in Spain and the entire world. We also do CD reviews!

Progressive Rock

The Gibraltar Encyclopedia of Progressive Rock
www.gepr.net
Designed as a reference for visitors to discover bands that are unfamiliar and to broaden their listening horizons.

Heavy Harmonies
webmaster@heavyharmonies.com
heavyharmonies.com
Submit your CDs into our database.

Punk

Book Your Own Fucking Life
www.byofl.org
Guide for the Punk/Hardcore DIY community.

PunkRock.org
www.punkrock.org
News, upcoming gigs, blogs etc.

Punky Hosting
PO Box 773, Ipswich, IP1 9FT UK
Andrew Culture poo@beatmotel.co.uk
www.punkyhosting.com
We here at PunkyHosting.com got so pissed off with trying to find decent hosting that we decided to start a hosting company of our own.

Reggae

IREGGAE
www.ireggae.com
Promoting the sound of Reggae music.

Irielion
www.irielion.com
Irie Dutch/Belgian and Israeli Reggae/Ska concert agenda.

One Love Reggae
www.onelovereggae.com
West Coast calendar, clubs by state that do live music, festivals ...

Reggae Festival Guide Online
PO Box 50635, Reno, NV 89513
PH: 775-337-8344 FX: 775-337-6499
Kaati kaati@reggaefestivalguide.com
www.reggaefestivalguide.com
Find Reggae festivals around the world!

Skasummit.com
Ska Joe joe@ocska.com
www.skasummit.com
Great place for Ska bands from around the world to promote their shows and local scene.

Soul / R&B

Amplified
amplified@amplified-online.co.uk
www.amplified-online.co.uk
Our mandate has always been the support and promotion of Black Music not embraced by the mainstream yet loved by millions around the globe.

Do Your Art
www.doyourart.com
Our show format consists of concert performances and up-front interviews with popular artists whose music is featured on Do Your Art.com's top-trafficked music site. This enables viewers to discover today's most-talented, aspiring music artists.

Goldsoul
PO Box 909, Worksop, S80 3YZ UK
PH: +44 (0)1909-515150
sales@goldsoul.co.uk www.soulnight.co.uk
Our Northern Soul night calendar provides up to the minute information on a selection of top nights throughout the UK. Please submit your events for free!

RnBMusic.info
www.rnbmusic.info
Latest R&B news, songs, charts, music videos and more.

Soul Commune
www.soulcommune.com
This is the official portal to a growing community - the Soul community. This is a place where Soul lovers, organic Hip Hop lovers, soulful House lovers, and Jazz lovers can convene, connect, and cultivate friends, fans and business relationships.

Soul Daily
www.souldaily.com
Soul music news and information hub.

soulportal.dk
www.soulportal.dk
Danish site featuring interviews and music charts. Soul, Jazz, R&B and Hip Hop.

Soulful Kinda Music
Dave dave@soulfulkindamusic.net
www.soulfulkindamusic.net
The definitive major reference site for Soul artists discographies. If you have a discography that you would like to see on the site, let me have a copy.

Soulwalking
www.soulwalking.co.uk
General resource with gigs, news, articles and more.

Women in Music

Angelic Music
PO Box 61, East Molesey, KT8 6BA UK
info@angelicmusic.co.uk
www.angelicmusic.co.uk
A meeting place to promote female artists and to provide a place to make contact with each other for help, support and advice.

Chick Singer Night
www.chicksingernight.com
All singers are welcome to submit demos and perform. Check our website for the contact in your city.

Christian D.I.V.A.s Network
www.christiandivas.net
Female Christian artists from around the country who travel and perform in both secular and Christian venues.

DiscoverGirls
admin@discovergirls.com
www.discovergirls.com
Featuring talented women from around the world.

Drummergirl
drumsforgirls.ning.com
For women who drum. News, gigs, articles etc.

FEMALE PRESSURE
info@femalepressure.net
www.femalepressure.net
International database for female DJs and/or producers.

GirlBand.org
girlband.org
Dedicated to all female bands and artists. News, bios, videos, reviews etc.

Girls Rock Girls Rule / The Monthly Cycle
200 W. 15th St. #7G, New York, NY 10011
info@revolutionaryrecords.com
www.girlsrockgirlsrule.com
Covers news, tours, releases etc.

Indiegrrl
3682 Greensboro Rd. Ridgeway, VA 24148
PH: 276-224-0485
www.indiegrrl.com
A forum for information, networking and conversation about independent music from a female perspective.

International Women in Jazz
PO Box 230015, Hollis, NY 11423
PH: 212-560-7553
www.internationalwomeninjazz.com
Supporting women Jazz artists.

The Kapralova Society
info@kapralova.org
www.kapralova.org
Dedicated to promoting women in the field of Classical music.

Mamapalooza Festivals
PO Box 210, Hastings-On-Hudson, NY 10706
PH: 917-301-5635 FX: 914-479-5085
Joy Rose joy@mamapalooza.com
www.mamapalooza.com
An international organization with festival stages, tours, conferences, music publishing, a record label and Radio. Mamapalooza organizes events and opportunities for artists who are mothers, fathers and entrepreneurs year long.

Professional Women Singers Assoc.
PO Box 884, New York, NY 10024
www.womensingers.org
Our performing members specialize in a variety of Classical musical genres. Singers are selected by a jury of voice teachers, coaches and directors.

Rockin' Moms
PO Box 320988, Los Gatos, CA 95032
PH: 408-410-8487
Tiffany Petrossi submit@rockinmoms.com
www.rockinmoms.com
An organization that promotes and provides resources for moms in music.

SISTA Factory
sistafact@aol.com
www.sistafactory.com
Promotes and showcases diverse performing artists.

Social Networks for Musicians
PO Box 16940, Sugar Land, TX 77496-6940
Madalyn Sklar info@gogirlsmusic.com
www.socialnetworksformusicians.com
Social Network Confusion? Don't worry, we can help! With over 12 years internet marketing and promotion experience, we know their way around social networks like MySpace, Facebook, Twitter, Flickr, Blogger, Wordpress and more!

Women In the Arts
PO Box 1427, Indianapolis, IN 46206
PH: 317-713-1144
wiaonline.org
Produces and sponsors programs for women in the arts.

Women In Music National Network
1450 Oddstad Dr. Redwood City, CA 94063
PH: 866-305-7963 FX: 510-234-7272
www.womeninmusic.com
Supports the activities of women in all areas of music.

Women in Music UK
7 Tavern St., Stowmarket, Suffollk, IP14 1PJ UK
PH: 01449-673990 FX: 01449-673994
www.womeninmusic.org.uk
Supports, encourages and enables women to make music.

Women in Tune
23 High St., Lampeter, Ceredigion, SA48 7BH UK
PH: 01570-423-399
michele@womenintune.co.uk
womenintune.org.uk
A showcase for female musicians and a place of encouragement and inspiration where women could become involved in or learn about music with a supportive atmosphere.

World Music

Local World Music Guides
www.worldmusiccentral.org/staticpages/index.php/local_scenes
Guides for those who want to learn about the local World music scenes throughout the globe.

National Geographic World Music Page
worldmusic.nationalgeographic.com/worldmusic
News, videos, downloads, blogs etc.

SECTION EIGHT: ARTICLES THAT WILL HELP YOU TO SUCCEED IN THE MUSIC BUSINESS

"Don't forget to applaud the little steps, as well as the big." – **Janet Fisher, Goodnight Kiss Music**

While creating The Indie Bible I have been fortunate enough to have met many of the most knowledgeable people in the independent music industry. Successful authors, publicists, music reviewers, entertainment lawyers etc. I thought it would be a perfect fit if I presented several of their articles to help you gain insight on how to deal with the many twists and turns of this complicated industry. The articles in this section are sure to be helpful to musicians and songwriters, and especially to those that are just starting out. Every author I asked was kind enough to submit an article that will help you to move forward with your music career. Do yourself a favor, and put their experience to work for you!

o v e r v i e w

STAYING AHEAD OF THE CURVE: MUSIC MARKETING TRENDS YOU CAN COUNT ON

by Peter Spellman, MbSolutions.com
© 2009 All Rights Reserved. Used By Permission

The music biz stands at an historical crossroads – almost every aspect of the way people create, consume and listen to popular music is changing, dwarfing even the seismic shift in the 1880s when music lovers turned from sheet music and player pianos to wax cylinders and later, newfangled 78 rpm phonograph records.

The following highlights some of the most ground-shaking and, (in my opinion), enduring "metatrends" currently shaping the biz. The intent is to give guidelines to both musicians and industry careerists to help set their forward sails on this crazy ocean we call music.

METATREND 1: Empowered Music Consumers

Today may be the very best time to be a music fan, especially one looking for a connection to a favorite artist or guidance and access to the exotic or rare.

Be it the iPod, alluring satellite radio services such as XM, the fan-beloved minutiae posted on Web sites, the availability of live music performances on AOL, the esoteric music videos streaming off Launch.com or the self-tailored satisfaction of burning a homemade mix on CD at home, there is a singular zest to the modern fan experience today.

The public is now driving the market. The challenge to the industry is to respond positively in such a way as to secure the future of music while satisfying customer demand and providing choice.

It's becoming increasingly more difficult for companies to treat us like "mass market" ciphers. The trend is towards "mass customization" where consumers' unique needs are front and center. Some marketing gurus call this trend "The 1-to-1 Future" and the companies that can dance with this trend will prosper.

What You Can Do About It

- Get to know your fans. They are your chief asset going forward and the better you know them, the better you can communicate with them, build loyalty and enlist them in lending their support to you and your music projects.

- Involve them, empower them, mobilize them, let them co-create with you. None of us knows what all of us know. Build a community, a fan club, a subscription service and learn how to pool the wisdom of your following.

- Provide potential customers with as much choice as possible.

- Learn the technologies that will help you customize your communications with customers and fans.

METATREND 2: Music Product to Music as Service

Presenting music as a service, like radio or TV, would seem on the surface to be less profitable than selling millions of CDs, but actually, this change will be positive for the music industry. It will be able to sell more things associated with music. But the actual sale of music as a product will make less sense. It will be a move from transaction-based push to flat-fee pull.

Consumers have clicked, and they demand access to content by any means necessary. Just as AOL has gone from selling you five minutes of access to a take-whatever-you-want model, music too will move to a flat-fee model.

We're not there just yet. But in the next few years, the requisite technology will fall into place. Then most of us will carry a wireless Internet uber-gadget wherever we go – a unified cellphone/MP3 player/digital assistant/Blackberry/ camera/GPS locater/video recorder/co-pilot for life. This device will receive wireless Internet audio, a loose term I use to describe the various forms of streaming audio starting to appear on the Internet. With streaming audio, you can hear the music you love any time, anywhere.

The future isn't about a change in distribution, it's about the atrophy of distribution itself. Instead of distributing things, we'll get access. It's a critical difference.

The future isn't about downloading songs and burning CDs. It's about just-in-time customized delivery. Music as on-demand service not as industry-dictated product.

Just as in the early days of the record industry (c. 1900), music publishing will once again assume the primary role in the biz. Music will become available for diverse uses dictated by consumers and businesses.

How fast will the sun set on the compact disc? Quarter-size CDs that can float among compatible music players, computers, game devices, digital cameras and personal digital assistants are already developed.

Of course, a massive installed base of CD players means that the traditional recording industry markets are not going to disappear or even be impacted by digital distribution in the short term. But rising consumer interest in downloads and an increasingly multi-media business-to-business economy opens new opportunities for composers, editors, sound designers, and all forms of audio producer.

What You Can Do About It

- You should be figuring out how to distribute your work through digital music services now. The Net is your Open Mic to the world. Get yourself onto iTunes, Rhapsody and MusicNet. Learn the virtual ropes.

- As the industry moves away from physical product, it becomes increasingly important for musicians to learn the rules for licensing (read, 'renting') their music.

- Seek out users of music as well as buyers.

- Prepare for a multi-platform approach – value-added packages containing your music, artwork, DVDs, etc AND a container-less presentation using various online showcases, message boards and portals.

- Develop marketing plans for both your selected singles as well as for your full-length albums. 50% of current online music sales are in the singles format.

METATREND 3: The Next Music Companies

The writing is on the wall for traditional music companies. The record industry grew rapidly, matured, and is now in the throes of transformation. How successful this transformation will be depends on how creatively the musical industrial complex can dance with all the changes spiraling around it.

Unfortunately, so much of the music industry is beholden to corporate owners, itchy for quick profits, and driven by rigid corporate imperatives. This wreaks havoc with artist development; hell, it wreaks havoc with business development, and necessitates high turnover of both artists and employees. Major labels are also saddled with legacy problems regarding production and retail. Thus the geologic tempo of industry change.

But the same forces undoing the larger music companies are empowering individual musicians and micro-businesses.

As with most modern industries, a silent computer on a desk is the wildcard that makes so much tradition redundant. Perhaps the term "record company" itself is becoming outdated – "Music Services Company" might be more relevant. Many music biz execs echo the words of Steve Becket of Warp Records when he says, "I think we'll mutate into a new type of company – a mixture of artist management, publisher, marketing consultant, agent and promoter." "We're a communications company," agrees Marc Jones of Wall of Sound, "and that's what we're becoming more everyday. I don't think the model for a traditional record label will exist in this environment anymore."

But we don't have to solve the dilemma for the mainstream music business about which future to embrace. Indie artists are living the side-stream music movement that may inspire the majors but, God willing, will never be completely controlled by them.

Unlike mainstream commercial music, the farther you get out onto the fringes, the more helpful people become. The more participants, the greater the chances that something truly interesting will emerge from the collective rabble.

A new generation of music entrepreneurs is rising with a power in its corner it has never had before. The times are ripe for change and these creators are the spearhead.

What You Can Do About It

- The appetite for music only grows around the globe and you are the one who can satisfy it. You'll need to employ your maverick instincts over conventional "business rules", take fuller responsibility for your own success, and beware of "standard industry practices" that can chain your career.

- Concepts like "company", "work", "job" and "career" are morphing. The entire business economy is passing through a transition the likes of which haven't been seen since the industrial revolution. Rather than seeing your "career" as a ladder, think of it as a rouge wave full of rises, dips and switchbacks.

- It's time to think outside the normal channels of business and imagine new kinds of companies. Creative alliances and partnerships are the key. Combining good music, cheap, global distribution and business savvy almost guarantees success in today's music-hungry world.

METATREND 4: Segmenting Music Markets & Niche Music Cultures

I often hear musicians moaning about how consolidation and the monopolization of the media by companies like Clear Channel and Viacom threaten musical diversity, yet I can hear and obtain more interesting music today than I could ever hope to in the 1960s.

The menu of music choices and styles expands daily.

When the Grammys started in 1958 there were 28 categories of awards; last year there were 105. Check out the "Music Styles" page at the allmusic.com and you'll find over forty styles of music, each with a drop-down menu of several "sub-styles."

Even the pop charts, which have made room in recent months for PJ Harvey, Modest Mouse, Diana Krall and Franz Ferdinand, suggests there's an audience starving for something other than junk food.

The music market continues to segment and each segment is a "world", a portal, through which small companies can create value and success.

While good news for niche companies, this is bad news for the musical industrial complex. The major labels cannot justify going after these smaller markets because they are optimized instead for the larger, pop mainstream. These niche music cultures can't generate the sales needed to float the major label boat. While 20,000 unit sales are a cause to celebrate at a micro-label, they hardly register a blip on big company radar screens.

The times call for focus. Mass customization and a segmenting market encourage the development of products and services of a "niche" nature. Since few of us have the time, money or energy to mount national marketing campaigns, it is in our best interest to discover and concentrate on a niche, a segment, that we can explore towards successful enterprise. Whether your specialty is house, trance, bluegrass or neo-soul, learn to work that niche and scope out relationships and opportunities within it.

Micro-media targets the tributaries off the mainstream and if the artist occupies one of these "niche streams", they have an open and ready channel for exposure to their target audience. Each niche stream has its own burgeoning media culture and the smart combination of high-quality music, creative event-making, perseverance and strategic alliances gets people talking.

What You Can Do About It

- What is your niche? Maybe it's arranging music, or the history of rock, or the intricacies of music software. Whatever it is your niche will lie at the crossroads where your most compelling desires intersect with your background resources and current opportunities in the real world.

- What is your music's niche? If your music can be slotted into an established category, then master that area both musically and business-wise. Know the inlets and outlets for your music, become familiar with the influencers and tastemakers in that realm, and start communicating with them. If your music defies categorization then lead with that.

METATREND 5: The Next 'Big Thing' is Small

The analogy is television. 30 years ago, the three broadcast networks (ABC, CBS, and NBC) had a ninety percent share of the viewing audience. Today it's less than forty. Where's the other 50%? Watching cable channels. Though cable channels have miniscule ratings, they're profitable. Why? Because they've discovered and developed their niche.

And this is what smaller, indie labels do – the Americana sounds of New West Records, Red House Records' focus on singer/songwriters, the creative acid jazz of Instinct, and the deep reggae catalog of Trojan insures listeners they can expect quality discs from each company within their respective niche. Indie market share is on the rise!

Lacking vision beyond their own profit lines, major record companies fail to see that the revolution in music delivery occurred in reaction to the industry's mismanagement, not to mention its complicity in force-feeding the public a flavorless diet of sonic pabulum. With the increasingly conservative (read, "risk-averse") stance of the majors today, indie market niches become all the more important to the creative development of music.

The implosion of the musical industrial complex has also resulted in the availability of many formerly-signed artists and talented executives. The past ten years have seen veteran artists like The Pretenders, Rod Stewart, Foreigner, Aimee Mann, Sinead O'Connor, Carole King, Sammy Hagar, Dolly Parton, Hall & Oates, Hanson, Steve Vai, Sophie B. Hawkins and dozens of other either starting their own labels or signing on with smart indies.

What You Can Do About It

- The paternalisms of yesterday have given way to personal responsibility for your own success. The holy grail is NOT a record deal; it's waking up to your own power.

- Signing with a major label today in most cases is a career risk. These divisions-within-corporations are unstable and anti-art environments, and best avoided by aspiring recording artists.

- If you're up for it, start your own company and release your music through it. If you want to delegate the heavy lifting seek out a successful indie label to partner with. But only do so when you've achieved a level of success appealing to a business partner (that is, you're showing net profit for an extended period of time).

Record company bosses think society's top priority today must be restoring record-company revenue and profits. But music lovers and artists have a different perspective. They want to know how musicians can exploit the extraordinary technology of the Internet to expand the audience and enable more musicians to make a living doing what they love, and improve the quality of life of consumers.

In a sense musicians may be in a better place today than they've ever been before. Taking a cue from the cyber-bard John Perry Barlow, I believe we could be seeing a paradigm shift from the domination of the "music business" to that of the "musician business."

The more things go digital, the more we crave authentic, roots-based music; the more music that's available to us, the more we seek niches that provide meaning and navigation through all the choices; and the more worldwide radio shows through satellite radio, the more we desire shared cultural experience via local djs.

If we had to, all of these trends can be placed under one banner that reads: the larger the world economy the more powerful its smallest players.

Hey, we're talking about you.

Peter Spellman is Director of Career Development at Berklee College of Music, Boston and founder of Music Business Solutions, a training ground for music entrepreneurs. He's the author of The Self-Promoting Musician, Indie Power: A Business-Building Guide for Record Labels, Music Production Houses and Merchant Musicians and his newest, Indie Marketing Power: THE Guide for Maximizing Your Music Marketing. Find him at mbsolutions.com

r a d i o   a i r p l a y

GETTING RADIO AIRPLAY
by Lord Litter, host of Lord Litter's Radio Show
© 2009 All Rights Reserved. Used By Permission

It was the late 80's and I was doing freelance work for a commercial radio station. The first thing I discovered was an enormous heap of releases in the hallway. Here are some hints how to approach DJs. An important aspect of a release surely is that it can be used to promote the band/musician. If you don't take care of certain areas, your music *might* be on air, but no one will get to know who you are and where they can buy your music...so the whole promotional effect is lost.

Here are things that give me trouble and that I think may cause other DJs to NOT play the release:

1. Every item you send should have a clearly marked address. Info material will be separated from the CD, so if there is no address on the cover, then you'll get no play listing, your address will be not spread etc...

2. Since the CD became *the* medium of choice, some bands should send magnifying glasses with their releases. Sometimes covers look great but the writing is either much too small, or the use of colors make it impossible to read. Make sure it as *easy as possible* to identity the name of your band, the song order, and a contact address.

3. The more well known a DJ is, the better the promotional effect. It also means that a known DJ gets piles of releases every day. Therefore, the time to care about the individual release shrinks to almost seconds, leaving no time left to care about questions like: What the name of the band is, and what the title of the release is.

4. Give all of your material a professional approach. It is impossible to read ten pages to get the basic info about a band. Send a reduced informative version of your material with the offer to send more if interested. A link to your website is what I appreciate.

5. DJs are human beings - yes they are! Treat them like you want to be treated. No need to send endless letters, but a short "Hey, thanks - airplay really appreciated!" proves that you *care* about your music and about the one that *cares* about your music - the DJ.

6. The best way to get in touch is to check in before you send your music and say something like "We heard about your show from ... would you be interested in our music? If the DJ doesn't answer you

can forget him/her anyway. You might not even get playlist later. The basic idea here is to keep it somehow personal. You'll discover that it creates a very positive effect - in some cases you might even find a friend!

7. If you send CDRs (I do broadcast these!) make sure they really work! I have one CD player that doesn't take badly burned CDs. So, if your CD (in the running order of the show) must be played on that player and it doesn't work, it will not be played.

The basic idea is: make it as easy as possible to handle your material. Before you finish your material, take it to the printer, if the required aspects are not clear, change it. I know it's a lot of work, but the alternative would be: become rich, hire a professional promoter and watch how your release will be thrown away with the others. The answer is always "somewhere in the middle" as we say in Germany.

Lord Litter has earned the reputation for producing and delivering what is arguably one of the world's best independent music programs. Since the early 1990s, Lord Litter has known the pulse of independent music, and today, indie musicians from all over the planet know that his program is one of the ultimate destinations for their music. Website: www.LordLitter.de

♦

RADIO AIRPLAY 101 - COMMERCIAL AIRPLAY MYTHS
by Bryan Farrish, Bryan Farrish Radio Promotion
© 2009 All Rights Reserved. Used By Permission

When talking to people who are launching their first couple of projects, invariably the same misunderstood points come up concerning commercial regular-rotation airplay. *Here are some common myths:*

DJ's play the records
This only applies to non-commercial radio, and specialty/mixshow radio. The majority of people in the U.S. listen to commercial regular-rotation radio, and on these stations, the DJs have no say at all in what is going to be played (unless, in the case of a smaller station, the DJ is also the PD). So, the biggest pitfall to avoid is asking a DJ at a commercial station "Can I give you my CD for possible rotation?" The DJ is not allowed to say "No", and he/she is probably not going to explain that only the PD can approve regular rotation. The DJ is just going to say "OK".

Why do they play it?
Good songs do not mystically spread to other stations. Every single song you hear (or every syndicated program you hear) on commercial regular-rotation radio is on that station because of layers of promotion and marketing. The song you hear was the one that made it, it beat out the other 300 songs that were going for adds that week. What you don't hear are the endless phone calls, faxes, trade ads, personal meetings, consultant recommendations, call-out research, and other things which went into getting the station to add the record. The station owners make it a requirement that DJs make it sound like they picked the music themselves.

College or specialty/mix-show will expand to commercial
Just because you do well on non-commercial or specialty/mixshow radio, it does not mean anything will happen on commercial regular-rotation radio. Nothing at all will happen at commercial unless a separate, higher-level campaign is put into place to take the record into regular rotation. The pitfall here is that a listener will hear something on college, and then a month later hear it on commercial, and conclude that the college caused the commercial to happen. The listener did not know that both campaigns were in place simultaneously, and the college simply went for adds a month earlier.

You have to be signed
Untrue, being signed is only a signal to the stations that the basic marketing practices are going to be done right. If you have the budget, you can duplicate the marketing practices of larger labels, provided you know how.

The band *Creed* set a good example, of putting their $5 million marketing dollars into the right place.

Request calls will help

They won't hurt but your time is better spent doing other things, like inviting people to your gigs. Stations know which calls are real, and which are bands and their friends. Stations have consultants and seminars which cover this *one* topic.

I can't get airplay without distribution

It depends on the size of radio that you are going after. Smaller commercial regular-rotation stations in smaller markets won't make this too much of a sticking point, especially if you have a powerful radio campaign going, or if you are doing great gigs in their city, or if you have great college or specialty/mixshow results. But the larger stations... which you can't work anyway until you do the smaller ones... won't touch a project that has no distribution.

Airplay without gigs

Again, it depends on the size of radio that you are going after. Not being able to gig is a serious handicap at any station, but you can overcome it in smaller markets with intense radio promo, press, sales, and non-comm results.

Non-monitored stations are of no use

Non-monitored stations are of no use only on the *Billboard*, *R&R*, and the seven *Album Network* mag charts. But *FMQB*, *CMJ* and all specialty/mixshow charts are compiled manually. Since you need to start off on these smaller charts first, this works out just fine.

Bryan Farrish is an independent radio airplay promoter. He can be reached at 818-905-8038 or airplay@radio-media.com. Contact: and other articles found @ www.radio-media.com.

INDEPENDENT RADIO PROMOTER CHECKLIST

by Bryan Farrish, Bryan Farrish Radio Promotion
© 2009 All Rights Reserved. Used By Permission

If you are hiring a promoter to push your artist to radio, here are a few things you can consider which will help you have the greatest chance of success (and when I say promoter, I mean an airplay promoter, not a club or booking promoter). The big concern with this process is, if you choose the wrong person(s) to promote your artist and end up with bad results, you can't just go back and do it over again. That's it for that CD (at those stations). That CD is now "an old project" at those stations, and you can't go back to them until you have a new release.

Part One: Overview

Using a friend: Non-experienced friends sometimes offer to promote artists to radio for free, or "a few dollars". This is fine as long as you use them for the right tasks, like helping with the mailing. If you are working college radio, in the 20-30 station range, then they could make some calls too. If they try to call *commercial* radio, they will probably stumble after just a couple of weeks. And forget about any capacity of doing reports or trade charts.

Moonlighter: Staff promoters at major labels sometimes offer to "help you out on the side" for a fee. On their days off, or on the weekend, they say they will "make some calls for you". What happens is that their company finds out and disallows it, or the person gets tied up on their days off, and can't do it. Either way, it is a conflict of interest for them.

Publicity: Public relations people sometimes offer to work an artist to radio for airplay. But don't, however, confuse PR with airplay. A real radio campaign has nothing to do with publicity. They are two separate techniques, with different contacts, lead times, terminology, call frequency, and so on. A person who is good at one is usually terrible at the other. This is why they are always separate departments at labels.

Station People: Station employees are sometimes recruited to work an artist, and will tell you that "they know what stations want." This sounds convincing, but in reality, taking the calls (which they do/did at the station), and making the calls, are very different. Until station people are trained (at a label or indie), they make poor promoters.

Big clients: The most-often used sales technique of promoters is to tell you they have worked "some big artist", and that this would benefit you. Ask them what they mean by "worked". Were they solely responsible for charting that artist? Probably not, more than likely, the promoter was probably just partnered with a label or another promoter, or worse, was just an assistant or sidekick. Again, they will NOT tell you they were not the only promoter. You will *have* to ask the artist or the artist's management directly.

Part Two: What to look for in a Promoter

Making contact: Some Indies are always there when you call, others are never there. The ones who never answer that is usually a *bad sign*. If you thought it was difficult reaching them before you hire them, just wait until *after* they get your money. Also be wary, if they say they give clients (and potential clients) a different phone number to call than the one they give the stations. It is more likely you will never get that person on the phone when you do need them.

Reports: Reports are a requirement that well-organized promoters provide to you. Without a report, there is no other way you are going to be able to understand what is going on with your airplay each week... much less someone else such as stores, papers, clubs etc.

Office: If the promoter does not have an office (even a small one), then you will be competing with things like the promoter's sleep, TV, neighbors, dinner, etc.

Assistants: If a promoter handles more than one genre of music at the same time, or if the promoter does college radio at all, then assistants are mandatory. The phone calls have to be made, and no one person can call more than 150 stations a week, do reports, faxes, emails *and* talk to you when you call!

College Radio: College should be considered for every campaign, even if you are doing high-level commercial radio. College radio is relatively inexpensive, and will allow you to create some good looking charts and reports to show retail, press and clubs.

Faxes: Serious promoters use faxes. Faxing is simply the fastest way to get a one-page synopsis of info to the stations... with pictures if needed. They are not cheap, but a good promoter should still include these faxes.

Emails: While you may get excited about email, remember that since email is free, stations get them from every artist on the planet. And all the emails look the same. So, in order to build a solid project, you must use faxes and phone calls, because most artists can't afford them (and that is why you will stand out.)

References: Any promoter worth consideration will have a list of past clients. What you are looking for, is a promoter with projects that are on your (independent) level. A list of "big" clients, doesn't necessarily better, since a promoter used to having massive help from major label staff promoters, national tours, retail promotions, advertising etc., will not have these with your project. You need a promoter who is set up to work with indie projects like yours.

Do your Homework: The "major label" promoter was actually not the promoter that worked the major projects in the first place. They were probably just assistants in the office, or were mail people, or more often than not, they were just outright lying. It happens all the time. Ask the artist directly to find out.

Bryan Farrish is an independent radio airplay promoter. He can be reached at 818-905-8038, or www.radio-media.com. Email for event info: meet@radio-media.com

HOW TO SELECT A RADIO PROMOTER

by Peter Hay, Twin Vision
© 2009 All Rights Reserved. Used By Permission

As an independent record promoter, the most frequent question I get from artists is "How many projects are usually worked at one time?" This question is so intuitively perfect that it may be the most important way of evaluating whether to use one promoter or another.

I find that six to eight projects can be served effectively. For projects submitted to me that go over my limit, I usually try to schedule their campaigns for other times (which sometimes causes a loss of business).

The reason this number is manageable is because some campaigns are just starting, some are in the middle while others are winding down. These different stages create a flexible focus. Ultimately, the effort is to give every project their day in the sun and to ensure that their potential is fulfilled. It takes a bit of juggling, but that is what makes for a professional.

There are some promotion companies that are working fewer releases. They are usually ones that are still getting established. There is no real advantage to that smaller number. As a promoter, as long as you are conveying all that needs to be conveyed to create a positive impression, you are doing the job.

How am I assured that my project will remain a priority?

Some promoters have so many releases they just naturally start to emphasize the ones that are hot and neglect to give special emphasis to those that need the most help. When that happens, you need a promoter to promote the promoter. There are ways to make sure you don't end up in this position.

In order to assure that your project will not slip through the cracks, you must stay on top of the promoter. Ask them every question that occurs to you each week. Check to see what stations are priority targets in a particular period and make sure you get the details of their conversation with those stations. You should get a detailed report every week. Do not hire any promoter that does not provide a detailed report.

Make sure to keep your promoter up to date on developments such as upcoming gigs, mentions in the press and everything else related to your career. This will help bring some relevance to your release.

Don't worry about being a pest. You deserve face time at least once a week, if not with the head of the company, then the rep who is actually handling your project.

Another question that should be asked is "How many major label projects are you regularly working with?" Let your common sense tell you what the number should be while keeping in mind that major label clients are probably getting more attention.

Should you hire a promoter who has a list of "name" artists on their resume?

If they delivered for Norah Jones or Death Cab For Cutie, they must be good for you. Well, maybe. Of greater importance is how the promoter feels about your music. Listen closely to the tone and enthusiasm they convey about your project. This will give you a hint of what they will say to the stations about you.

Peter Hay is a 38 year veteran in the music business who is president of Twin Vision, an independent promotion company specializing in Triple-a, Americana and college radio. Contact him at TwinVision@aol.com, www.MySpace.com/twinvision www.twinvision.net

♦

PODCAST PRIMER: A MUSICIAN'S QUICK REFERENCE GUIDE

by Andre Calilhanna, Disc Makers
© 2009 All Rights Reserved. Used By Permission

What's a podcast?

Most simply, a podcast is the digital delivery of an audio or video file. In many ways, podcasts are to the internet what "on-demand" cable is to television. With podcasting, music and video content is available by subscription download. Once downloaded, it can be viewed or heard at the user's command.

A computer program, dubbed a "podcatcher," is required to listen to or view a podcast. Contrary to what the name suggests, podcasts don't have to be heard or viewed on an iPod. The iPod is the most popular digital audio player in the world, but various other players can be used, either portable or on a computer.

The technology that makes podcasts possible is cutting-edge, but the model is fairly basic. A podcaster will assemble a show – many resemble a radio show – and post it online with an RSS (Really Simple Syndication) file that enables it to be distributed via podcast. Users use software like iTunes to subscribe and download the content. Once downloaded, the files are ready to be listened to on the user's digital audio/video player of choice.

A majority of the content available as podcasts is free, and podcasting software makes it easy to keep up with the latest contribution from your favorite podcasters. In fact, the software is constantly seeking updates and new programs once you subscribe to a podcast.

Here's an example: Let's say you go online to the iTunes directory and subscribe to a free audio podcast from IndieFeed. You can then download any or all of the individual songs they've archived for podcasting. And since you're now a subscriber, iTunes will constantly (invisibly to you) check for new episodes from IndieFeed. When new songs are posted, they are automatically available for you to download.

This model is fairly consistent across the spectrum of material offered as podcasts, which is as varied as the internet itself. Business coaching, music videos, animated shorts, sermons, sporting events... it's all out there waiting to be podcasted. So is a ton of independent music.

Podcasting independent music

iTunes alone has over 150 different independent music podcasts available, and there are other directories out there that list hundreds more. If you're a user looking for indie music, the problem becomes, "How do I find the good stuff?" As an indie musician, the problem is, "How do I get my music heard?"

There are a number of independent music podcasts that solicit music from artists, including IndieFeed and Insomnia Radio. Browse through the directories included at the end of this article and you'll find dozens more. Most screen and hand-pick the songs for inclusion, so there's no guarantee your music will be podcasted. In many ways, these podcasts are analogous to college radio ten years ago: they are indie friendly, but getting in takes some luck and requires someone on the listening end appreciating your art.

Typically, all you need to submit for podcasting is an MP3 of your music, though many podcasters also ask for information about your act, like a short bio and URL to list in the event that they play your music.

Getting your music played on one of these podcasts is a viral means of reaching a fan base you wouldn't have reached before. As the medium gains momentum, more and more users are using podcasters as their gatekeepers. Landing a track on a popular podcast is almost like landing a song on a TV show or a soundtrack. It's all about getting more ears to hear your music.

Creating your own podcast

Another possibility is to create your own podcast. It can be just about anything you want it to, but for the sake of example, let's say you want to combine a music track with a voice-over. You can talk about the meaning or the inspiration for the song, go on a political rant, tell stories from the road – whatever you think might make your podcast more enjoyable and relevant.

It's fairly easy to do. You'll need:

- A computer
- An MP3 file to podcast
- Music editing/recording software
- Text-editing software
- An RSS text file
- Somewhere online to post your files

Let's assume you already have an original song saved as an MP3 file on your computer. You'll then want to add a voice-over track to complete the "show." With free audio software like Audacity, you can quickly record and edit voice-over elements right on your computer. If you have any kind of home studio, you can easily create a more elaborate recording.

Once compiled and edited, save the new file as an MP3 (if you're using Audacity, you'll need the LAME MP3 Encoder). To make your file ready to podcast, there is specific ID and naming protocol you need to follow. Yahoo! Has an easy tutorial at http://podcasts.yahoo.com/publish/1, and there's another great step-by-step explanation at www.podcastingnews.com/articles/How-to-Podcast.html. Then you need to FTP your file to your own web site, or use a hosting service like Yahoo! Geocities.

What sets podcasting apart from the simple hosting of MP3 files is that subscribers automatically get updates as soon as you post new shows. To make that possible, you have to create an RSS feed for your podcast. The RSS feed alerts subscribers' podcatchers to your updates and allows them to be downloaded immediately.

This article originally appeared in Disc Makers' Fast Forward monthly e-newsletter. Visit www.discmakers.com/music/ffwd to get a free subscription.

◆

PODCASTS AS A PROMOTIONAL TOOL
by Colin Meeks, IndieLaunchPad.com
© 2009 All Rights Reserved. Used By Permission

In their simplest form, podcasts are audio files created on a computer or portable media device that are subscribed to by people interested in the content of the Podcast. These audio files are then transported across the Internet to the users computer. This can be done automatically using one of a myriad of podcast aggregators like Juice, Doppler or WinPodder. Podcast comes from the amalgamation of two words, iPod and broadcast. This has led to the common misconception that an iPod is required to listen to them, this is not the case. You can listen to a podcast on any computer, MP3 player or CD player if the podcast has been written to an audio CD. The early genesis of podcasting is commonly attributed to Adam Curry and Dave Winer. With Adam's drive to make it happen and Dave's RSS (Really Simple Syndication) to act as the kind transport layer to get the podcast out to all subscribers. Talking of subscribers, another common misconception is that you need to pay for the podcasts you download, after all you are a subscriber. While there are a few paid for podcasts, the vast majority are totally free. Podcasts have grown at a phenomenal rate and their popularity was launched into the stratosphere, when Apple decided to jump on the podcast wagon and allow people to subscribe to podcasts through iTunes. Like music before it, suddenly podcasts were available to the regular person, without requiring complex knowledge of RSS feeds and aggregator software.

With podcasts coming into their own in the latter half of 2004, suddenly there was a medium that was inexpensive and could reach the world over. Creating a podcast can be relatively cheap, but once the bug catches hold, it's not long before podcasters outgrow their modest hardware and strive for perfection with a new microphone and mixer. Another big issue for podcasters is bandwidth. Having a few dozen people download your podcast is fine, even though the average music podcast is around 20-30 megabytes, but just imagine what happens when you have thousands of people downloading. Many people find themselves with an expensive bill from their Internet provider. There are many services that alleviate this problem for a small fee and it's these hidden costs that most people, especially listeners are not aware of.

Adam Curry had his own podcast called the Daily Source Code. At the beginning of each show and occasionally within, he would play music often referred to as mashups. This was the fusion of two or more different songs into one. This sometimes resulted in some great songs, but it was also in direct violation of copyright. While many didn't think it to be a real problem, it wasn't long before the powers that be came knocking on Mr. Curry's door and he was forced to stop. In the latter half of 2005 however an artist from NY, USA stepped into the breech and gave Adam full permission to play his song Summertime on the Daily Source Code. This artist was Brother Love and it was the beginning of something quite special. It wasn't long after this, that bands began to see the potential of podcasts and either gave permission to podcasts to feature their music or to sometimes create podcasts themselves.

There are now literally thousands of podcasts, featuring a multitude of new bands and artists. Bands are now finding new audiences from around the world. Hollow Horse, a band from Glasgow, Scotland are one of the many bands with positive things to say about podcasts. Kenny Little from the band says "If it wasn't for the medium of podcasting we would probably have split up. As it is, we are now in the middle of recording our third album and, the strange sideline to all of this, is we now have friends and fans from all over the world.". After being first featured in a couple of podcasts, Kenny said "We have sold more copies of the album in America than we have in Scotland. How amazing is that". Many bands now have no intention of seeking a record label, preferring to handle everything themselves. With Podcasts, MySpace and a Myriad of other services available in your arsenal, it's now quite a feasible thing to do.

Colin Meeks is host and produce of the Indie Launchpad Podcast www.indielaunchpad.com which showcases some of the best in independent music.

◆

WHAT IS PODSAFE MUSIC?
by David Wimble, The Indie Bible
© 2009 All Rights Reserved. Used By Permission

As you visit the hundreds of music podcast and MP3 blog sites you'll notice that most them feature something called PODSAFE MUSIC. For this article I have gathered information from various internet sites in order to help clarify what podsafe music is and how it can become another helpful tool to place into your marketing utility belt.

Definition of podsafe music (from Wikipedia en.wikipedia.org)
Podsafe is a term created in the podcasting community to refer to any work which, through its licensing, specifically allows the use of the work in podcasting, regardless of restrictions the same work might have in other realms. For example, a song may be legal to use in podcasts, but may need to be purchased or have royalties paid for over-the-air radio use, television use, and possibly even personal use.

The effective definition of "podsafe" for a given work depends entirely on the contract through which the podcaster licenses the work; there is no single podsafe license. The concept of podsafety, in its true form, greatly favors the artist and the profitability of the artist's product, in exchange for only very limited concessions to the podcasting community.

While some works such as public domain works or works under some Creative Commons licenses are inherently podsafe, the only actual requirement for a work to be podsafe is that any licensing requirements it has, if applicable, allow for the work's free use (typical broadcast use in its original form, if in no other form, depending on the specific license) in a podcast or web broadcast. This gives specific favor to podcasts only, allowing the artist to impose more traditional constraints on everyone else. Podsafe licensing can, for example, continue to require non-podcast consumers to pay for the work, require royalties on derivative works, and profit significantly from the work's use in traditional radio, television, or film.

The licensor of any podsafe work must be legally capable of making it so. An artist cannot distribute his or her own work through a podsafe license if doing so would break any laws or breach any standing agreements (e.g. with the RIAA). The creator of a derivative work may also not claim this work podsafe without express permission from the original copyright holders. (PMN has more specific and stringent terms to this effect in its agreement.)

Another point of contention is that not all podcasts are non-commercial works; in fact, an increasing number of podcasts are taking on sponsors and looking to make a profit. In general, no significant distinction is yet made between podsafe for non-commercial use and podsafe for commercial use, but it could easily arise at any moment.

Motives for the podcaster to use podsafe music (from Wikipedia en.wikipedia.org)
As podcasting grows more and more popular, illegal use of heavily licensed music (as through the RIAA) becomes increasingly difficult to hide. This is in general of greater concern to podcasters than to the typical sharer of music, because podcasters usually produce their shows for and promote them to the public—a far more overt and traceable action.

Including such licensed music legally has its own set of caveats. Indeed, under many jurisdictions it's currently impossible, but the message from those in the know is that many licensing agencies, if they do intend to allow the use of their music on podcasts, will require not only the payment of royalties but also the use of DRM on the shows. (DRM, because of its proprietary, system-specific nature, would be destructive to the general openness and system independence of podcasts.)

Use of podsafe music instead of more stringently licensed material allows a podcaster to continue to produce an inexpensive, legal program with little hassle. Not least important for an independent podcaster is the promise of being able to avoid the confusing maze of licensing organizations.

Motives for the artist to use podsafe music (from Wikipedia en.wikipedia.org)

Conventional radio (and television) can present a difficult, and not always logical, barrier of entry for a musician or other media artist involving large sums of money and often a great deal of surrender in both ownership and creative freedom.

In contrast, podcasting, an increasingly popular medium for audio programs, is as a whole very receptive, indeed thirsty for artists and input. This is due in part to the creative and economic nature of the largely independent podcasting community and further fueled by its need to avoid repetition. While a conventional radio show may be able to risk replaying a large part of its music selection from day to day, there would be little point in downloading a music podcast whose selection did not vary significantly from a previous show. Podcasting is thus a voracious medium. With a growing and international audience podcasting is now becoming an effective means for inexpensive artist promotion often aimed squarely at the people most like to be interested in that type of music.

What is The Podsafe Music Network?

The Podsafe Music Network (music.podshow.com) is a comprehensive source for podsafe music. It was founded in 2005 by ex MTV VJ and current podcaster Adam Curry (Daily Source Code www.dailysourcecode.com). PMN brings a large group of podcasters together with a wide variety of all-podsafe music and the artists who produce it.

According to PMN, podsafe music is music that meets all of the following conditions:

1. Works submitted to the Podsafe Music Network are the property of the artist, and all rights to these works, including lyrics and music, are the property of the artist.

2. All works contain no recordings, lyrics, copyrights, or other elements that are the copyright of any other artist, except under the limited provisions of the Creative Commons License Agreement www.creativecommons.org

3. Despite any recording contracts with RIAA, ASCA, BMI or other recording industry entity, the artist retains ownership of the works and is free to distribute, broadcast, license or sell these works at the artist's discretion.

The licensing agreement between the artist and PMN: music.podshow.com/music/artistTerms.htm

What are Creative Commons Licenses?

(from www.creativecommons.org)

Creative Commons Licenses help you publish your work online while letting others know exactly what they can and can't do with your work. When you choose a licence, we provide you with tools and tutorials that let you add licence information to our own site or to one of several free hosting services that have incorporated Creative Commons.

1. Standard License

License your song under your terms. Our set of standard licenses will let you share music with fans while protecting your song from limits you put in place.

Or, choose a prepared license for audio works.

2. Sampling License

People can take and transform pieces of your work for any purpose other than advertising, which is prohibited. Copying and distribution of the entire work is also prohibited.

3. Share Music License

This license is aimed at the musician that wants to spread their music on web and filesharing networks legally for fans to download and share, while protecting the music from commercial use or remixing of any kind.

How does a Creative Commons license operate?

Creative Commons license are based on copyright. So it applies to all works that are protected by copyright law. The kinds of works that are protected by copyright law are books, websites, blogs, photographs, films, videos, songs and other audio & visual recordings, for example. Software programs are also protected by copyright but, as explained below, we do not recommend that you apply a Creative Commons license to software code or documentation.

Creative Commons licenses give you the ability to dictate how others may exercise your copyright rights—such as the right of others to copy your work, make derivative works or adaptations of your work, to distribute your work and/or make money from your work. They do not give you the ability to restrict anything that is otherwise permitted by exceptions or limitations to copyright—including, importantly, fair use or fair dealing—nor do they give you the ability to control anything that is not protected by copyright law, such as facts and ideas.

Creative Commons licenses attach to the work and authorize everyone who comes in contact with the work to use it consistent with the license. This means that if Bob has a copy of your Creative Commons-licensed work, Bob can give a copy to Carol and Carol will be authorized to use the work consistent with the Creative Commons license. You then have a license agreement separately with both Bob and Carol.

Where are the forms that I have to fill out?

Creative Commons licenses are expressed in three different formats: the Commons Deed (human-readable code), the Legal Code (lawyer-readable code) and the metadata (machine readable code). You don't need to sign anything to get a CCL. Just select your license here: www.creativecommons.org/license

Hmmm ...what if I change my mind?

This is an extremely important point for you to consider. Creative Commons licenses are non-revocable. This means that you cannot stop someone, who has obtained your work under a Creative Commons license, from using the work according to that license. You can stop offering your work under a Creative Commons license at any time you wish; but this will not affect the rights with any copies of your work already in circulation under a Creative Commons license. So you need to think carefully when choosing a Creative Commons license to make sure that you are happy for people to be using your work consistent with the terms of the license, even if you later stop distributing your work.

Before you do anything, make sure you have the rights!

Before applying a Creative Commons license to a work, you need to make sure you have the authority to do so. This means that you need to make sure that the person who owns the copyright in the work is happy to have the work made available under a Creative Commons license.

Where do podcasters find podsafe music? (from Dave's Imaginary Sound Space soundblog.spaces.live.com)

Discovering new music and the ability to use it fairly without fear of copyright infringement is a key issue for podcasters and listeners alike. Artists, composers, producers and consumers can all benefit from clear, fair and flexible copyright licenses that embrace new technologies. 'Podsafe' means non-RIAA audio and video that can be used legally in podcast productions and freely distributed online for downloading.

Podsafe music can be found in many locations on the web including: artists websites, MP3 blogs, open source music communities, podcast directories, netlabels, P2P networks and BitTorrent hosts. A quick search for "podsafe" in a podcast directory like PodcastAlley.com reveals a rich and diverse array of productions featuring podsafe music. Unfortunately it becomes extremely time consuming for podcasters to source available music and listen to it. Recommendations by listeners and fans play an important part in the podcast production process.

The definitive list of podcasting safe music sites can be found here: www.soundblog.spaces.live.com/Blog/cns!1pXOS7l93k8mqeQ7FlEEmOS Q!907.entry

It's always about the music

For an artist just entering into the podcast/MP3 blog universe, the amount of information to take in can be overwhelming. It's not unlike a lifelong typist being plopped in front of a computer and asked to create a spreadsheet with colored charts.

As you watch the internet continue to explode with new technologies, it may feel like life has passed you by and left you lying in the dust. However, the truth is we're all still tightly bundled together. No one is *ever* left behind. The opportunity to move towards the cutting edge is available to anyone (my father-in-law has just learned how to use a computer at the age of 81). Don't let fear (and the excuses it can conjure up) lessen your attempts to succeed.

Remember, it has always been, and always will be about the music - that unique expression that *you* have to offer to the world. Podcasts, podsafe music, MP3 blogs, Creative Commons licenses and all that other bounce-off-the-head stuff is simply a collection of new and useful tools to help you get your music heard by more people.

Final thoughts

For the newbie, my suggestion would be to take it slow. Go to the Creative Commons site www.creativecommons.org and poke around. It's a very user-friendly website. They understand that musicians are not lawyers.

Once you're done that, then start checking out the various podcast and blog websites. You'll soon discover that bloggers and podcasters are simply human beings with a passion for music - a collection of music lovers that are ready and willing to help you get your songs heard by a new stream of potential fans.

The Indie Link Exchange
www.indielinkexchange.com/ile

KNOWING THE DIFFERENCE BETWEEN GOOD PR AND BAD PR

by John Foxworthy, Garage Radio Magazine
© 2009 All Rights Reserved. Used By Permission

Publicity and networking are the two most important parts of any successful music project. Unless you lack aspirations to venture beyond your local scene, your career risks stagnation without them. This is why it's important to get a handle on how to conduct yourself when interacting with radio, publications, labels or any other facet of the music business ... otherwise you chance snuffing your credibility before you even get out of the gate.

Whether you work PR for your own act or someone else's, your role seems simple ... create and maintain public interest; however, even the most marketable project and the most interesting press releases are hardly enough to achieve these goals. As with anything you do, there are unwritten laws of etiquette you must follow to function effectively as a publicist.

As the Chief Editor of a busy e-zine and Host of a widely listened radio show, bands, labels, publicists and other publications contact me regarding press and airplay on a regular basis. This correspondence is truly the backbone of what I do ... it keeps me in the know on many levels and provides me the opportunity to make new contacts. On the other hand, it also aggravates and frustrates me more often than not. I'm learning that better than half of the folks taking responsibility for public relations are most likely shooting themselves in the foot.

Do your research

This is a point I just can't stress enough. In fact, I could write this entire article on just that subject. It requires a lot of work, but the rewards will come back ten-fold. There are so many source guides and directories out there that it's virtually impossible to keep up and these are great tools, but used unwisely they can actually work against you. Here's a scenario based on my own experience:

I host a Rock/Punk/Metal radio show that's clearly described as such on my web site, as well as every directory in which it appears. Yet, almost daily I get press releases and requests for airplay from artists who play anything but Rock, Punk or Metal. This probably wouldn't annoy me as much if I didn't also get the same, exact emails to my e-zine inbox.

You may ask me, "What's the problem? Why not just delete the email?"

That's a simple solution and often times I do, but this is the symptom of a behavior that's sure to thwart the efforts of the sender. Think about it ... if they're doing it to me, they're doing it to their other contacts as well. It tells me that this is someone who uses the gum-at-the-wall approach and may not be worth looking into ... plus they tend to go onto my SPAM list. I also stay in regular contact with my other colleagues in the biz, so they may even end up on a "blacklist" and could even get stonewalled press-wise in the future.

The solution? Take some time to find out to whom your email is going by doing a simple search to check out their site, show, magazine or whatever. It's even acceptable to send a preliminary email to introduce yourself and get a better idea of what they're looking for (or if they even want your correspondence) before you fire off that request. This is also a great way to make first contact, which makes for an appropriate segue into our next topic.

First contact

I leave my email address publicly accessible to make it easy for people to contact me. This also contributes to the amount of SPAM I receive ... a necessary evil in my position ... so I spend an average of eleven hours a week sifting through my new messages in an attempt to separate the SPAM from the news. Why? First of all, most people don't know how to effectively title the subject of their message. Secondly, it's first contact ... I may not know who sent the email because I've never corresponded with them.

In the last eight years I've trained myself to tell the difference between South African bank scams and artists trying to get exposure for new releases. This doesn't mean I've trained myself to stop deleting messages based on the subject. Titles like, "WE REQUEST YOUR ATTENTION" or "THE NEXT BIG THING" equate to "GET THE LOWDOWN ON

THE SMALLEST CAPS" and will quickly prompt most of your potential contacts to hit the delete button.

First contact is the most important contact. The old adage that you never get a second chance to make a first impression holds very true … especially with the sensitive nature with which people have been conditioned regarding SPAM these days. So, the first lesson on the subject is to make sure your email says what it means before it's even opened.

"New Alternative Rock Band From NYC" is a simple, yet operative title for an email to a new contact. They'll get an idea of the message you're trying to get across and you'll notice it wasn't all capitalized, which could be another form of suicide!

Next, you'll want to make sure you tailor the body of your email to fit your expected recipient. Address them by name (if you have it), be cordial, introduce your act (or yourself) and get to the point. Proper grammar and punctuation play a big role here, so if you have no clue what I mean by that, you shouldn't be doing PR in the first place.

Your first email should be more of a request than a release. Remember, you're dealing with people that are busy, so summarizing a description of the music, adding a few stats (including CD sales) and press quotes is quite alright as long as you keep it to a minimum … 3 short paragraphs will suffice. Then, you can include links and contact info for your recipients to explore further if they're interested. DO NOT, and I reiterate, DO NOT email MP3 files or other attachments. This is annoying and will piss your target off in a heartbeat.

After you've made your first contact, it's wise to set a waiting period before following up. Again, these people are busy and prone to a lot of email, so there is a fine line between correspondence and SPAM.

Follow-up

I'm one to appreciate diligence and I'll be the first to admit that some of my attempts to create steady contacts have backfired on me more than once. Now, finding myself on the receiving end, I see what I was doing wrong. A beleaguered ally can quickly become a foe … and it's for this reason I find it essential to define the difference between follow-up and pestilence.

Let's disregard the preceding tips for a moment and imagine you've emailed your press release or a request for coverage to a few addresses. It's possible that a few of the folks you contacted have contacted you back, but there are some that haven't responded. Many of them may be preoccupied with current projects or might even be completely uninterested. You have no way of knowing where they stand, so how do you decide when (or if) to send a second email?

Five business days is a good rule, but hinges on when you sent your initial correspondence. Monday through Wednesday are the best days to get in touch with your potential outlets. Due to the fact that most schedules revolve around the standard workweek, it stands to reason that these are the best days to send your follow-ups. If you still get no responses, you'll be better to write these contacts off and continue your exchange with the responsive set.

Mailing lists

This falls more closely under the subject of "netiquette" than etiquette. Just because you have contact email addresses, doesn't mean you have contacts. The inventory of rules surrounding mailing lists is another that could be an entire handbook … and could be one of the single most contributors to death in the press/play world, but I'll try to emphasize the biggest no-nos.

Never, never, NEVER add arbitrary email addresses to your list. There's no negotiating this rule … here's why:

Out of hundreds of emails a day, only about 30% apply to my day-to-day dealings. Another 5%-10% are personal and the rest are just garbage. In my capacity, I have to consider every message as a possible contact … even though I have a "strict" policy that defines how I want to communications to be sent.

My standards are such that I never post uninvited news to other sources and with that, I avoid accepting the same. I personally don't have time to sift through everything I get, so a great percentage is deleted out of constraint. What does this mean? I'm flat-out not interested in getting updates from unsolicited suppliers. It also implies that I'd like permission from people to be added to their mailing lists … and I'm pretty sure there are a lot of people out there that feel exactly the same way.

Not separating your contact lists is another hugely horrific move. This is a chapter right out of "BE ORGANIZED!" Sending gig updates to radio shows or publications that specifically do CD reviews is a waste of time. Additionally, sending the next gig on the morning of your next gig is just plain stupid. Your fans may want to know this (even though they probably already do), but it does no good to inform anyone else that you'll be playing CBGB in seven hours. Plan out your itinerary and send a release with your calendar for the next month or so. If your target wants to announce it, they'll have time to get the word out.

It's best to separate the lists of publications, shows, and other entities by type … and tailor your announcements accordingly. You'll never ruin a contact faster than if you send a daily barrage of so-called updates and/or messages containing your personal agenda.

Last, but NOT least is how to send to your lists. Your email program or web-based mail will have the fields "To" "CC," and "BCC." Forget all about the "CC" field when sending to multiple recipients … and I mean FORGET IT! No matter your capacity in the biz, this line is bad MoJo. Every contact in this field can be seen by every other contact that receives the email. Use "BCC" and save yourself a bevy of pissed off contacts!

Is your news really news?

I get everything from updates on CD sales figures to reminders that bands will be playing venues … the same venues … several times a week. This goes back to a behaviorism, and a destructive one at that. I, and many in my position, are extremely turned off by this and are very likely to disregard further contact.

Constant updates are not a great way to keep your act in the forefront of our minds. We like to stay informed, but it's good form to save up the news. One release with the band's future happenings, or a retrospective of the last month or so will go a lot further than a daily barrage of minor occurrences … no need to desensitize your awaiting public.

Press kits

Press kits are arguably the meat and potatoes of exposure for any act. This is a pretty easy subject, as you won't likely get an address which to send them without permission. For those that make their mailing info readily available, it's a good idea to look further and find an email contact. Make your target privy of the impending envelope and allow a week for it to arrive, but DO NOT follow up in a week!

One thing you must understand is that many of these folks get quite a few of these packages every day. I myself get 30 per week, so I really don't have the time I need to properly distribute and/or review them in seven days. In this case a good follow-up rule is probably 2 weeks … even if you never heard back from your email.

These are the best tips I have without writing an entire book on public relations. My advice is a culmination of my experience and that of the professionals I work with every day. Following it can enhance your effectiveness as a publicist and help create your niche in the music world … not following it may greatly reduce your chances of success in this fickle world we call the music biz.

John "RoadRash" Foxworthy runs Garage Radio Magazine. From event and CD reviews to interviews and industry news, GR Magazine features all the best new music from the people that make it happen.
Contact: www.garageradio.com, roadrash@garageradio.com

getting your music reviewed

HOW TO SUBMIT MUSIC FOR REVIEW
by Jodi Krangle, The Muse's Muse
© 2009 Jodi Krangle. All Rights Reserved. Used By Permission.

Getting the attention of music reviewers can be almost as difficult as breaking into a bank - and let's face it - sometimes far less profitable. But a good review is worth its weight in gold. So how does one go about getting reviewers to give your particular package the time of day? I receive quite a few of these packages myself, so while I'm no expert, I do have a few suggestions:

Be polite when making first contact

1. This may sound like it's too obvious to mention, but trust me - if you contact a potential reviewer by demanding their submissions address because you are simply the best thing that has happened to music since the microphone and the reviewer would be out of their mind to pass you up, you're likely to be disappointed at the response you receive.

2. Your initial contact should be polite and brief. A simple, "Hello, my name is (so and so) and I'm interested in a possible review in your (publication/web site). Would you be able to supply me with the proper contact information so that I can send you my CD?" will be kindly received. Even if it takes the reviewer a little while to get back to you - whether it's by regular mail, e-mail or through the feedback form of a web site - their reply will usually be helpful.

3. One last word on the subject of first contact: PLEASE don't send an e-mail with your web site address and only a "Check this out!" line for clarification. You don't want to know how much spam e-mail I receive in a day and messages like that simply make me feel as if I'm being asked to check out the latest in cheesy porn. I delete such messages on sight and I honestly don't know many reviewers who pay them any attention either.

Presentation

1. The presentation of the CD itself is probably the most important element of your package. It's that CD that will give the reviewer their initial impression of your music. That doesn't mean you have to have spent thousands of dollars on your presentation, a huge CD insert, a gorgeous color cover, etc. That just means that your "look" should be consistent.

Note: if you're not getting a professional printing of anything, a color inkjet printer creating your own letterhead along with a similarly designed CD covering sticker, will work quite nicely.

2. Simplicity is often the best way to go. Above all, avoid sending in a blank recordable CD with black marker written on it. Your contact information should be on the CD and the insert and/or cover. No matter what you do, make sure your contact information is easy to find.

3. The insert certainly doesn't need to be in color but there should be one, if at all possible. The insert is the perfect place to put contact information, credits (the reviewer is often fascinated by who did and wrote what), anecdotal information, etc - the things that make you special and different from the other folks the reviewer will be listening to. If there is a chance the CD might become separated from the rest of your work, you want the reviewer to be able to contact you from that CD alone.

Things to include in your package

- A brief cover letter addressing the reviewer by name (a MUST)
- A bio (1 page!)
- A CD, with an insert of some kind.
- Up to 3 reviews if you really feel you need them (try to keep this on one or two pages)
- Make sure your contact information is on everything.

Note: Keep in mind that if your CD itself is a nice little package all on its own including inserts, you may not need the bio or the reviews and could probably get away with just sending in the CD and a cover letter. If you have a web site and include the URL to that site in your cover letter, the reviewer can find out tons more information on you should they wish to.

Be patient

Remember to be patient, not that you shouldn't ever re-contact the reviewer. Remind the reviewer you're around! Just don't do it every day. Wait a couple of weeks between contacts. Reviewers have a lot of demands upon their time and are frequently several weeks - or even months behind in their reviews depending on the publication(s) they write for.

Be professional

The way in which you treat people will reflect upon your professionalism even more so than the look of your CD. It takes years to build up a good reputation and only a few minutes to completely destroy it. As with anything in the music business, you never know when someone you were kind to will be in a position to return that kindness. It's all about relationships. Make sure you're the sort of person who fosters good ones and it'll all come back to you.

Be pleasant; don't demand to know why your CD wasn't chosen for a review and/or spotlight if you are told that it wasn't - not unless you actually want to hear what the reviewer has to say. And if that reviewer *does* let you know why, let it be a lesson and move on. Try to keep in contact with the reviewer. It might be that a future release of yours will be better received. I hope these hints have helped. Meanwhile, good luck with your music!

Jodi Krangle is Proprietress of The Muse's Muse Songwriting Resource www.musesmuse.com Visit Jodi@www.musesmuse.com, to find out more about her free monthly e-zine.

INSIDE THE HEAD OF A MUSIC REVIEWER
by Suzanne Glass, Indie-Music.com
© 2009 All Rights Reserved. Used By Permission

What to send? When to follow up? What to say? Should you keep bugging a writer to review your material? What makes writers chose one CD over another to review? And most of all can you increase your chances of getting a published review when you submit a CD? Answer: Absolutely! By understanding a writer's mind, and following a few simple guidelines, you will substantially increase the likelihood your music will be chosen for a review or feature.

Indie-Music.com recently asked our writers; Heidi Drokelman, Jennifer Layton, Les Reynolds, and Erik Deckers, a series of questions designed to let musicians see inside writers' heads, and get a unique look at how the behind-the-scenes process works. After the Q&A, we give a quick checklist for getting your music reviewed successfully.

Q. What impresses you about an artist/musician/band?

A. *Heidi Drokelman:* Number one; the biggest impression is always the music, and the talent (however sometimes hidden it is) of songwriting. The versatility of all the members is important, and having an appreciation for good songwriting, no matter the genre, will always shine through in someone's work. Sure, clean production always sounds nice and makes a big impression when you're only listening to something a few times for review.... but I've been doing this [reviewing] for a long time now, and if the material is there (even in raw form), the first thing I forgive is production quality. When your songs stand out, even if you've recorded on the worst machine you can possibly find, then that's what counts. Even the worst material can't surpass a production snow job.

A. *Jennifer Layton:* There's no one thing. I've been impressed by so many different things. I'm impressed when I hear a musician doing something new that I've never heard before. I'm impressed when I hear a poetic folk song that expresses something so true; I feel it tugging at my heart. No matter what the press kits look like or how fancy the web site is, none of it matters if I'm not touched by the music in some way.

A. *Les Reynolds:* Real talent in at least one area (vocal, instrumental, lyrical) and especially when all those elements come together. Also, if they've got their s*** together —correspond in timely manner, not pushy about reviews, answer questions coherently and communicate well (even if this is through an agent, having the right agent who can do those things is crucial).

Q. What impresses you in a promo pack submission?

A. *Erik Deckers:* "Is the press kit complete? Does it have a bio and headshot or group photo? Are there other articles from other reviewers? If the answer is YES to these questions, then I am impressed. If the press kit contains a three-line bio, or vague and airy generalities discussing the metaphysics of the universe in relation to their music, I am decidedly unimpressed."

A. *Heidi Drokelman:* "Oh, this is a completely relative thing. I look at this part of the packaging after I've already listened to the music. If getting signed by a label is your goal, I'd much rather receive bio materials, a dated letter (it's really hard to separate the volume of mail that some of us receive, so including a dated letter from a band representative is a nice touch), a simple photo that expresses the personality of an artist or band, and on occasion, I enjoy a good piece of gag swag. Taking that extra step, and coming up with a creative piece of swag can push a pack to the top of the pile. However, please refrain from the offensive, even if it's meant in jest."

A. *Jennifer Layton:* "I take a different route with promo packs. I know those materials are expensive, and I have a small office and can't hang on to all the press materials I get each month. Which means that if I don't absolutely love the artist, the promo pack winds up in the trash after I write the review. I feel really guilty about that. So when an artist contacts me about submitting material, I tell them they don't have to bother with headshots or elaborate press kits — just a simple bio sheet that includes the web site address, telling me whatever they want me to know about them. What I'm really interested in is the music."

A. *Les Reynolds:* "It looks like the artist/band took time and care in preparing it and it "fits" with the image and overall music style. Quality photos, if included, also get my attention. While I won't use the pix (except to decorate my pod at work!), it says something about the artist — I can get a "vibe" or feel off that. I am also just impressed with quality photography since I used to be a photographer."

Q. How can bands get your attention?

A. *Erik Deckers:* "Write a personalized note to me, not a generalized form letter."

A. *Heidi Drokelman:* "Bands can get my attention fairly easily, but holding it can be another story altogether. I am all about helping out quality bands and artists, and will take extra steps to make sure that I am doing all I can without showing blatant favoritism (although I AM known for that as well), so some of the ways to do this are: Be courteous: I should clarify because I despise kiss asses just as much as the repeat offender rudeness. I'm not asking for special treatment, just a bit of humanity. Don't be overly pushy. I don't mind the follow-up to check in on the status of a review, but DO NOT expect to get a review every time you send in material. Some pushiness is good, but use common sense to know where the line has been drawn."

A. *Les Reynolds:* "Contact me directly. Keep the lines of communication open, and don't tell me to just go to your MP3 site. I hate that! It's become the universal cop-out (besides — what if the computer is malfunctioning or the internet is down?) Also: if they can describe their music accurately in a sentence— that shows they know who they are and have read my Indie-Music.com bio blurb."

Q. What do bands do which wastes their money, when they send submissions?

A. *Erik Deckers:* "Send crappy press kits. If I don't have much background information on the band, I can't write a good review. If I can't write a good review, then it doesn't help the band much."

A. *Heidi Drokelman:* "If they're unsolicited, it's a huge waste of money in general. Don't just blindly send your discs out to everyone you think has an inkling of interest in your work. Make sure that you contact someone and at least use the proper procedure. I'm sure this may sound lame to you, but the procedure we use is built to enhance our reviews, not to bring you down. On another note, photos, postcards, stickers, bio write-ups, and discs are not a waste of money. Just plan your priorities and work up to the full packet."

A. *Jennifer Layton:* "I hate to see bands spend money by sending me glossy headshots and other expensive materials. While I'm impressed by their professionalism, I'm not a label rep or someone who will have a major influence on their career — I'm just an indie writer. Also, I tell

artists not to waste money by sending their submissions by Federal Express. Regular old mail will do fine.

A. *Les Reynolds:* Sending tons of press clippings - one sheet is enough. Sending all sorts of odd-shaped stickers and things that, by themselves — once away from the package — mean nothing. Most Press kits are guilty of overkill."

Q. How can bands improve their submissions?

A. *Heidi Drokelman:* "Solicit your submissions for review – it will ultimately benefit you more to do some research and look into different publications and specific writers, than it will to blindly send things out. Quality is key - you're looking for someone to thoughtfully review your material, to respect it, and cultivate new contacts for publicity and marketing purposes. Do what you can presently afford, and the rest will fall into place."

A. *Jennifer Layton:* "I think they can tone down their bios a little. I'm aware that most artists write their own bio sheets, so I have to laugh when I read stuff like "This is the most amazing rock band on the music scene today. No one has ever come close to matching their talent and energy." Also, be sure to run your press materials through a spell- checker! One of the funniest bio sheets I ever got was from a folk artist who called himself a great intellectual songwriter, and the word "intellectual" was misspelled."

A. *Les Reynolds:* "Unwrap those CDs - Pleeeze!!! Send quality materials that won't fall apart immediately. Send good quality CDs (occasionally defective ones or discs produced in an odd format is received, and they won't play.)"

Q. How do you deal with your personal music preferences when reviewing? Do you review styles you would not normally listen to/buy?

A. *Erik Deckers:* "It's actually a little harder for an artist to impress me when they're in a genre I already like, because I have some definite ideas about what I enjoy and what I don't. But that means that if an artist CAN impress me, then they've done an excellent job. I do review styles that I normally don't listen to, so if an artist can create something that I enjoy (i.e. country music), then they also get a good review."

A. *Heidi Drokelman:* "Actually, I may be one of the few reviewers that will instantly admit that I use my personal music preference as a barometer for my reviews. I believe that it is almost impossible to take that out of the mix, especially when considering first impressions and different "trends". But this can be a very positive tool, especially when considering things like generational preferences (determining who this music will appeal to), and regional trends."

A. *Jennifer Layton:* "That's been an interesting issue for me. Over the past three years, I've learned not to rule out styles of music I don't normally listen to. I thought I hated all folk music before I started writing for Indie-Music.com, and now I am completely in love with acoustic folk/rock music. The only thing I can't review is rap. I'm a middle-class white girl who still listens to Barry Manilow and the Carpenters occasionally – I have ZERO credibility when it comes to rap and hip- hop."

Q. What do you most enjoy about reviewing indie music?

A. *Erik Deckers:* "It's not the same old schlock I hear on commercial radio. In most cases, it's better.

A. *Heidi Drokelman:* I'm still amazed, after all these years, at the quality and talent that's out there. The best thing about reviewing indie music is the sheer unpredictability of it all."

A. *Jennifer Layton:* "I know this sounds dramatic, but writing about indie music for the past three years has changed my life. I'm a lot more open-minded about so many things because I've learned to be more open-minded about the music I listen to. I've met several of the artists I've reviewed and am so happy that I've been able to encourage them by contributing positive reviews to their press kits. I've become such a fan of indie music that I flew up to NYC for my birthday last year to see performances by some of the artists I'd written about."

A. *Les Reynolds:* "The fact that there's an unlimited amount of real talent out there and it keeps coming and won't ever stop. I've heard stuff I would have never heard otherwise, met musicians I'd never even dreamed existed. And the cream is when a real connection is made... that's worth everything."

Q. What most irritates you in writing reviews?

A. *Erik Deckers:* "Getting unsolicited reviews. I'm pretty busy to begin with, and so I have to be selective about whose reviews I undertake. When I get one that I didn't ask for, I don't look favorably upon that artist. If I do manage to get around to doing their review, they've got a bigger hurdle to clear in that I'm already annoyed with them."

A. *Heidi Drokelman:* "The only thing that ever gets me is the volume of the mailings that I get. Making the commitment to give advice, constructive criticism, and deliver it in a way that isn't cruel, disconcerting, or rude is never easy. I may have harped a little about bands realizing that the reviewers are human, but remembering how personal the work is to others keeps me in check when delivering my honest opinion about their work."

A. *Jennifer Layton:* "What drives me NUTS is when artists or labels put me on their mailing lists when I didn't ask them to. Some artists have even put me on their lists before they've even sent me the CD for review. The worst was after I wrote a positive review of one band, and then their label put me on the mailing list of every single artist on their roster. That's one of the reasons I don't deal with labels or PR people anymore. If I love an artist's work, I'll ask to be put on the mailing list. And I have done that many times."

A. *Les Reynolds:* "Bad (inaccurate/incomplete) information on liner notes (it happens) or if the info is not legible — that stuff is very helpful and often necessary (in my opinion) in writing reviews. That, and wishing I had nothing to do but write, because most of these artists deserve a timely review."

Review check list

1. Communicate professionally - Use standard grammar and punctuation, proofread, and use a spell checker. You don't have to write a business letter like you learned in 8th Grade Grammar class, the letter could be creative, but make sure it is identifiable as a business communication and not junk mail. Make sure to directly state you are looking for a review. Don't send mass mailings, it's obvious to the recipient. On the phone, leave useful messages designed to make it easy to call you back (spell your name, and repeat your phone number twice to make copying easy for the listener).

2. Follow submission guidelines - Guidelines exist for a reason, which is to help an organization handle a large flow of music submissions in an efficient manner. Each publication does it differently, but if you choose not to follow the guidelines, expect your submission to be late, lost, or worse.

3. Send a cohesive promo pack - Writers have differing preferences on what they like to receive as part of a promo pack. Most writers, though, like to read a band biography and a few press clips (it helps in writing a review to know more about an artist), and many also like to see a band photo. If you are unsure what a writer requires, err on the side of sending too MUCH rather than not enough. If you choose not to include photos and graphics, make sure they are easily available on your website, in case the reviewer plans to publish your review with pictures.

4. Give contact information - When your review goes up, nothing would be dumber than to make your CD hard to find. Many artists, though, forget to include full contact information including mailing address, phone, email, and website URL.

5. Identify your genre - When people read reviews, they want to know, upfront, whether it's their "style" or not. So even if you simply say "a cross of rock, folk, and punk", that is much better than saying "we cannot be categorized". Better to categorize yourself than let a writer do it for you. Many writers are not musicians, and do not know precisely how to describe your genre just by listening. Help them.

6. Write a meaningful bio - Drop the lines that say you are "incredible", "changing the face of music", or "talented beyond belief etc.,

7. Make the writer's job easy - Since writers are, at the basic level, just people doing their job, it only makes sense that if you can make their job easier, they will like you and try to return the favor. That's just human nature. Include everything the writer needs, be sensitive to their schedule, and provide graphics or answers to any questions promptly.

8. Follow up courteously - Writers vary greatly in how they respond to follow-ups. Some people will respond promptly, keeping you up to date at each step of the process. Other writers ignore follow- ups completely. Your best bet is learning each writer personally. As a general rule, follow up about 2-4 weeks after your submission should have arrived with a short note. If you hear nothing, try again in another two weeks. If you again hear nothing, try waiting a month. Don't threaten or chastise the writers, just ask if a decision has been made about your review yet.

9. Don't argue with the reviewer - You can't win. If you don't like the review, you can pass on that reviewer with your next CD. Or you can submit again and see if their opinion has changed. Either way picking a fight about something the reviewer wrote is a waste of your time. If there is a factual error, fine, ask the writer to correct it. But don't argue, "Our choruses are NOT boring! They are complex and emotive". Since the characterization of your choruses as "boring" is only the reviewer's opinion, you are not going to change it. You might, however, piss off the writer for life.

10. Keep the connection - You need to cultivate your relationships with writers. Check in with them periodically between CDs, read their other work, let them know if you have news, and send thank-you notes - even if you did not get reviewed. Your goal is to build a relationship. You never know when that relationship may help you out - but you can be sure it will work in your favor if you present yourself as nice, interested, and understanding.

Suzanne Glass is the founder of Indie-Music.com, All the reviewers featured in this piece write for Indie-music. For more information please contact: www.indie-music.com.

WHY MOST DEMO RECORDINGS ARE REJECTED
by Christopher Knab author of "Music Is Your Business"
© 2009 All Rights Reserved. Used By Permission

"Getting a deal" has long been the goal of many would-be artists and bands. For mostly naive reasons, most new talent feel that by securing a recording contract with a significant major or independent label, success will be guaranteed. (Talk about naiveté.) To get this 'belief system' up and running, many musicians figure all they have to do is send off their music to a label, and a recording contract will come their way shortly.

How to improve your odds
The following list of 10 Reasons Why Demo Are Rejected was gathered together after years of listening to comments made by Record Label A&R reps at music industry conferences and workshops, as well as from personal interviews with reps, and from many interviews A&R reps have given to the press. The purpose of providing you with this information is to at least improve the odds that your music will get listened to when you submit your demos. This list will look at the most common mistakes musicians make when either shopping for a record deal, or trying to get the attention of A&R Reps with their demo recordings.

10 reasons why demos are rejected

1. No Contact Information on CDR and/or CDR container: Put your name, address, email, and phone number on both.

2. Lack of Originality: Just because you can record, doesn't mean your music is worth recording.

3. The Music Is Good, But The Artist Doesn't Play Live: This applies to all genres of music except electronica and experimental music.

4. Poorly Recorded Material: So you bought Pro-Tools ... so what!

5. Best songs are not identified or highlighted on the CDR: Give the folks a break. For demos-send only 3 or 4 songs and highlight the best ones.

6. Sending Videos In Place Of CDRs: Keep it simple, in the demo mode. All anyone wants is to check out your songwriting and musicianship.

7. Sending Unsolicited Recordings: You sent them, but they never asked for them.

8. Sending The Wrong Music To The Wrong Label: You didn't do your research to find out what labels put out what kind of music.

9. Musicians Can't Play Their Instruments Competently: This is so basic, but you would be astounded at how incompetent most start-up musicians are.

10. The Music Sucks: This criticism is as old as music itself. You may think your music is the greatest thing since frappacinos, but most demo recordings the industry receives are as bad as the first round contestants on American Idol.

Christopher Knab is a music business Consultant, Author and Lecturer. He was recently honored by Seattle's Rocket magazine as "One of the Most Influential People in the Northwest Music Industry." Visit his website at: www.4frontmusic.com or contact him personally at: Chris@Knab.com

t o o l s

WHAT ARE PERFORMANCE RIGHTS ORGANIZATIONS?

by Jer Olsen, CEO MusicBootCamp.com
© 2009 All Rights Reserved. Used By Permission.

Performance rights organizations like BMI, ASCAP and SESAC all perform a similar task but in slightly different ways. Essentially, they all perform the duty of collecting royalties for non-dramatic performances of intellectual property. In simpler terms, they collect the income from radio stations, TV stations, programming companies, Internet marketers and any other entity where music and related intellectual property is used. These royalties are then, in turn, paid to the various publishers and authors associated with a particular recording or performance.

Why do we need them?
The fundamental reason behind the birth of these organizations is the simple fact that individual artists and song writers can't possibly devote the time, attention and research required to collect royalties from the plethora of companies that use their music, even though by law they are entitled to those royalties. Artists depend on these performance rights organizations to do the hunting and collecting for them—a small price to pay for a piece of a much, much bigger pie! There's a saying, "50% of everything is a whole lot better than 100% of nothing!" Well, we don't know exactly how much money these organizations charge for their services, but we can be certain it covers their time and energy (similar to how music publishers earn money for getting music played in movies, TV shows, or recorded by other artists, etc.) The truth is, performance rights organizations are a necessary and helpful tool for musicians and publishers. The toughest decision is choosing which one to align with.

Which one to choose?
Please visit the page of each organization to find on-line information about joining as well as a ton of other terrific resources. Compare and make a decision on which one best suits you. If you don't, you can practically assure yourself of never being paid for airplay.

United States
BMI—Broadcast Music, Inc (www.bmi.com)
ASCAP—The American Society of Composers Authors and Publishers (www.ascap.com),
SESAC (www.sesac.com)

Canada
SOCAN—The Society of Composers Authors and Music Publishers of Canada (www.socan.ca)
The UK
PAMRA—Performing Arts Media Rights Association (www.pamra.org.uk)
PRS—The Performing Right Society (www.prs.co.uk)
MCPS—The British Mechanical Copyright Protection Society Limited (www.mcps.co.uk)
France
SACEM—Societe Des Auteurs Compositeurs Et Editeurs De Musique (www.sacem.fr)
CISAC—Confédération Internationale des Sociétés d'Auteurs et Compositeurs (www.cisac.org)
Germany
GEMA—The German Society For Musical Performing Rights And Mechanical Reproduction Rights (www.gema.de)
Italy
SIAE—Societa Italiana Degli Autori ed Editori (www.siae.it)
Spain
SGAE—Sociedad General de Autores y Editores (www.sgae.es)
Sweden
STIM—Svenska Tonsattares Internationella Musikbyra (www.stim.se)
Australia
APRA-The Australasian Performing Right Association Limited (www.apra.com.au)
Note: If you are looking for information on how to start your own publishing company, inquire on each site or call each company on how to obtain membership as a publisher. Becoming a publisher is not as nearly as difficult as performing the duties of a publishing company since a publisher's main task is exposing compositions and recordings to as many profitable opportunities as possible. Many of the duties of publishing companies can be effectively performed through a membership with the *Harry Fox Agency* (www.harryfox.com).

Jer Olsen is the founder and CEO of MusicBootCamp.com, home of "Dirt-Cheap CD Replication and FREE Music Business Training!" This article is a sample of the many free resources available on the Web site. Jer is also an accomplished musician and producer with several top 20 Billboard hit remixes to his credit. www.MusicBootCamp.com

♦

UPC & BARCODES FOR PENNIES AND SENSE

by Lygia Ferra, LAMusicGuide.com
© 2009 All Rights Reserved. Used By Permission

With all the details that go into making a CD it is easy to put off making certain decisions, especially if there is cost involved or contradictory information.

So what exactly is a barcode?
Bar codes are also called UPC Symbols (generated by the Uniform Code Council (www.uc-council.org.) They are the small black and white lines that correspond to a unique 12 digit number used to track sales of CD's, while Sound scan correlates the information with your barcode in their database. Unless you are planning on starting a record label and putting out a number of releases with several artists, the $750 expense isn't really necessary.

Soundscan
Since Soundscan (www.soundscan.com) has a direct influence on placement in Billboard and CMJ music charts and other forms of recognition, payola has all been obliterated. It is a tracking system that did away with the potentially subjective reports of radio programmers and store managers prior to 1991. Sound Scan's records are not public, so the only way to access their data is open an account at a minimum price of several thousand dollars per year. The only ones checking are the larger labels and bigger companies. If you want to impress, you would need to sell more than 1,000 units to catch their eye.

Why do you need one?

One reason why you may need a barcode at all is that most stores and online retailers require an UPC code on every product they sell. So sparing the $750 expense, you can acquire one through Oasis or Discmakers for "free" when you replicate your discs, or through *CD Baby* for a modest $20 fee.

In the case of CD Baby the agreement does not bind you to the company in any way, other than having them listed as your "Parent Label" in Sound Scan's database. They provide you with the code as an electronic image, and you can include it in any cover art as appropriate.

How do you get credit for sales?

To ensure you are properly credited for all record sales as in the case of Discmakers you fax the necessary forms to Soundscan (914-328-0234), you will need a separate form for each release. Any independent artist or band can have their retail sales tracked through Sound scan, though only a label with two or more acts can take part in their Venue Sales Reporting Procedure. You must also have been in business two years or more, with a $500 fee.

It's never too late

You can always purchase one afterwards and have them printed on stickers. If you do it yourself make sure your printer is at least 720 dpi so they will read correctly. You can easily download a shareware barcode. A simple search for "UPC Barcode" @ http://shareware.cnet.com, or www.download.com will yield many results.

Alternatives

You can also go through a company (usually with a minimum order of 1,000 stickers) they will print them out for you, saving you the hassle of doing it yourself. If you are only going to sell your product at gigs or through alternative means, you really do not need a barcode at all. But for a mere $20, CD baby will save you all the worry and give you many more possibilities to sell your product.

Sources:

The Uniform Code Council: 1-800-543-8137 www.uc-council.org
Soundscan: (914) 684-5525 www.soundscan.com, clientservices@soundscan.com
Note: If you do decide to bite the bullet and purchase a barcode through the Uniform Code Council the process can take a number of weeks so allow for that extra time.
Independent Records: 1000 stickers Single Format Registration, Price: $55.00 - www.indierec.com/s-barcodes-register.html
Bar Codes Talk, Inc: 888-728-4009 Florida $30.00 shipping included.

Lygia Ferra is a Singer/Songwriter, Producer and Entrepreneur based in Los Angeles, Ca. In addition to helping with the IMB, she is actively involved with developing the La Music Guide site (where this article originally appeared) (www.lamusicguide.com). Please visit www.lygiaferra.com, for more info.

◆

BAND AND PRESS KIT ESSENTIALS

by Richard V. Tuttell, Daily News
© 2009 All Rights Reserved. Used By Permission

Destiny's Mother-in-Law may not be the best local band in town — or even the loudest, but they know how to attract attention. The heavy metal group's marketing plan included an obvious first contact for any promotion — their hometown newspaper. Many bands overlook this option when promoting their CDs and gigs. What may seem stuffy and low-tech, however, is a golden opportunity for getting publicity and building a local following.

In the case of Destiny, a power trio based in eastern North Carolina, the first step was a phone call to the editor to introduce the band, gauge interest and find out the preferred method of submitting information. A press kit containing, a press release, photo and CD followed this.

Press release

This is the most important piece of the promotion program. It should answer six questions: who (the name of the band and its members), what (the style of music, gigs, or recording being promoted), where (the location of the performance or where the recordings are available, when (the time and date of the show), why and how (is the show a benefit, then for whom, why should people want to hear the band and how can people get advance tickets or find the club or other venue?) Leave the detailed back-story, how the lead singer while working at the Citgo station met the guitarist when he drove in with a flat, for a later full-blown feature.

Format is just as important as content. A sloppy presentation reflects a lack of professionalism and reduces the chances the release will run as written, or at all. Type the release on standard letter-size sheets or submit it as a digital text file on diskette or by email. Use plain text, which is compatible with most computer programs and operating systems used by newspapers. Not everybody has a copy of Microsoft Word around. If you email your release, paste the text of the release into the body of the message because editors are wary of opening attachments from strangers. Write in narrative form with complete sentences (use both lowercase and uppercase letters) rather than sending a flyer, (because it gives the band a better shot at controlling how the information will be printed.) Be sure to include contact information (names, phone numbers and email addresses), just in case.

Photos

Destiny's Mother-In-Law sent a standard 8x10 black and white print, which was fine for our paper, but I would suggest sending color prints. It leaves open the opportunity of it being used on a feature front. If the image is to go on an inside page a color photo can still be scanned as grayscale. Many papers are using digital cameras and will accept digital images with a resolution of at least 2 MPs. Submit a jpeg or tiff file on a diskette or by email. It's helpful to provide a paper printout to show what the digital image looks like. You can also refer to a Web site from which the photo can be downloaded.

Don't print a digital image on your inkjet, submit it on a sheet of copy paper and expect it to be published. The quality just won't be acceptable. Also avoid Polaroids that usually have poor production quality. Spend a few bucks for a professional portrait or get a friend with a decent camera and an eye for composition to help you out. Keep the shot tight with members grouped closely together to avoid dead space. Filling the viewfinder to the max allows you to decide how the photo should be cropped rather than a photo editor.

Always attach caption information to the photo on a piece of paper taped the back or bottom of the print. Name everyone in the photo, identifying each person. Even if that information is already on the accompanying press release put in the caption. Photos and releases are often separated.

Recordings

Including a CD showcasing your talent is a nice touch with a press release, but is more important when requesting a music review or feature story. Some newspapers prefer to experience the band live and others may accept MP3 files. Do not send your only master copy of your sure-fire hit, because there's often no guarantee that it will be returned.

Don't be discouraged if the big metro paper rejects your submission. For every daily paper there are about nine weeklies or other non- daily publications, and they depend on local content

Daily newspaper editor Richard Tuttell is the author of Good Press: An Insider's Guide to Publicizing Business and Community News, available from Barnesandnoble.com, Amazon.com and other on-line booksellers. This article originally appeared in Disc Makers Fast Forward newsletter. For a free one-year subscription, call 1-800-468-9353, or visit www.discmakers.com.

SO, WHAT'S THE SCOOP WITH ELECTRONIC PRESS KITS?

by Panos Panay, CEO Sonic Bids

It seems that the big buzz out there in the music word today is all about Electronic Press Kits (EPK™). Should independent musicians use an EPK™ or a traditional press kit when approaching club promoters, festival organizers, radio programmers or record label A&R representatives? Do they work as well as regular press kits or should one stick with the tried and true method of snail mail kits? Are industry insiders even using them?

Electronic press kit, why is it important?

The answer is simple: like every other major innovation over the years ranging from the Compact Disc to the MP3, the industry was slow to initially accept it but it's fast becoming the ubiquitous standard that everyone from up-and-coming independent artists to word-renown festival directors is using to send and receive information about bands and artists from around the globe.

An EPK™ is like a virtual passport that you can use again and again to gain entry into hundreds of conferences, festivals, clubs, music competitions, colleges, or to even get your songs played on radio or reviewed by record companies or music producers. It contains everything your regular press kit contains and more: music samples, high-resolution photos, bio, press reviews, and even an up-to-date gig calendar (try that with a regular press kit). What's great about an EPK™ is that it takes literally 20 minutes to create one online and you can put it to use and start saving money almost immediately. For the cost of little more than sending out two regular press kits, you can sign up for an account, create an electronic press kit, and email it out to anyone, anywhere, at anytime. It not only communicates all the information that is found in your average press kit or web site, but it does so more quickly, more efficiently and far more effectively. Think how mind-blowing it is to be able to email someone everything they need to know about you or your band as soon as you get off the phone with them (or better yet, while you are even still talking with them).

Cost effective solution

Think of the implications of this innovation for the average up-and-coming artist. For the first time in history, there is no direct link between how many people you can reach and the cost of reaching them. For example, with a traditional press kit there is a vast cost difference between sending out 10, 100, or 1,000 of them. This means that even though today an independent artist has access to an unprecedented amount of information, the ability to take full advantage of this has, until now, been limited (consider the cost involved in sending a regular press kit to every single possible contact in this guide.)

The Electronic Press Kit has changed all this. Every day there are artists that are sending out their EPK™ to say, 100, or 200 college promoters at practically zero cost. These artists are receiving offers from people that normally they would have had to spend way too much money to reach (and often paying way more in reaching them than the actual fee they receive). The cost and effort of emailing an EPK™ to all these promoters is a small fraction of the corresponding investment in regular press kits – not to mention the benefits of the fact that communication is practically immediate (versus waiting for a week or so to get a press kit in the mail).

Conclusion

Does all this mean that you can go ahead and recycle all your physical kits right after you finish reading this article? Well, my prediction is that "hard" copy press kits are going the way of the vinyl and the cassette tape but like any other new technology, adoption takes a while — and there are still the technology laggards. Traditional press kits and CDs still have their place (for now) but my advice is to save your money and send them to the increasingly fewer people that specifically ask for them after they review your electronic press kit. Then you at least know that these are high prospects that are worth spending an extra $20 in trying to communicate with them.

Panos Panay is the founder and CEO of Sonicbids, the online pioneer of the Electronic Press Kit (EPK™) platform. The service currently has over 70,000 registered artist members and 6,000 active promoter members who actively use EPK's to connect and communicate with each other on a daily basis.

♦

WRITING A BAND BIO

by Suzanne Glass, Indie-Music.com

Having a little trouble coming up with a decent band bio? Check out these suggestions:

1. Don't worry about writing a book. One page or even a few paragraphs is fine. In fact, most people don't want to read any more than that.

2. Do emphasize your strong points while minimizing areas where you lack. If you have played gigs with well known bands, be sure to list it. If you haven't played many gigs, don't bother mentioning the fact. Go on to your recording, or your other musical experience. Also, while it's OK to "hype" a little bit, never tell any out-and- out lies or make a boast you might not be able to come through on. It will come back to haunt you, and then you will lose all credibility in the reader's eyes. Not to mention these music people talk to each other...and HOW!

3. Do use your band's letterhead to write it on. (You DO have a logo and letterhead, right?) Be consistent in your entire promo package with the image, logo, etc.

4. Don't say your band's music is "not able to be classified". Aside from the fact that a million other bands say the same thing, the music industry contact reading your bio wants and NEEDS to know who you are comparable to. For instance, if someone recommends a movie to you, you probably need to know if it's a horror flick, a romance or whatever before you decide if you want to see it.

5. Do use humor or slight sarcasm if it fits your band's image. But avoid the temptation to go overboard. A bit of humor can make a low budget press kit seem better. Too much is a loser. Also, some types of bands fit into a niche that is more open to humor. Just make sure what you say will not offend anyone.

6. Don't, repeat, DO NOT say you are the coolest, best, or greatest band around, or anything even remotely close to it. Music Industry people want to decide for themselves if you are good or not. Avoid the flowery adjectives.

7. Do list the band's major musical influences. This goes along with trying to give the person an idea of what you sound like. It can work great to come up with a unique description of your music. For instance, Indiana guitarist Michael Kelsey describes his music as "Progressive, aggressive acoustic music".

8. Unless your band has former members of Aerosmith and Van Halen in it, it's probably not a good idea to do one of those story bios. "John was playing in Joe's band until the singer quit. Then John met Steve, who was playing with the Nobodys. They formed a band called The Losers. When the drummer quit, they changed their name to The New Losers", etc. This is irrelevant and, well, boring. Not to mention it shows your lack of ability to keep a band together. It is OK to use an interesting line or two about how the band got started, or how songs are written. It's also OK to add any interesting facts, like maybe your band donates all proceeds from their cassette sales to charity.

9. Of course you want to list all your major accomplishments. Any recordings, awards, education, or whatever.

10. A quick concise listing of each member is good. Sometimes you can do fun things with this like a listing of each members' favorite drink, or other non-relevant stuff. But make sure it works. Nobody really cares what your favorite anything is, so it has to be part of a humorous image. If any members have played in well known bands, it's good to mention it here, but don't make a big deal out of it.

11. You may use a different version of your bio depending on who will be receiving it. For instance, a record label and a club booking agent

might need different info to decide if you interest them. A record label wants to know you have it all together: music, business, a fan base, songwriting, etc. A club agent is mostly concerned with whether you have a following that will bring paying business to his club.

12. Do make absolutely sure you have your address and phone number (and your e-mail and website URL, if applicable) listed prominently. This goes for all items in your press kit. Name, address, and number on EVERYTHING. (Demo tape included!)

13. Read other bands' bios. Compare and rewrite. Have other people read and comment on what you write. Make sure it is grammatically correct, with no typos. If you really feel yourself lacking in this area, consider hiring someone to write your bio for you. A good bio is part of the press kit that forms the first impression of your band. Don't mess it up.

Suzanne Glass is the founder of Indie-Music.com, an online magazine that reviews dozens of independent artists each month, includes music charts, audio & internet radio, and how-to-succeed articles for musicians, all at no cost. A paid members option gets your music in rotation with streaming audio, radio, multimedia advertising AND full access to our DIY music industry database with over 7000 venues.
www.indie-music.com

◆

HOW TO GET THE MOST OUT OF YOUR FAN LIST
by Mark Brooks, Fanbridge

Tips for your fan list

1.   Communicate Regularly
Some of our clients are able to write great newsletters each week for their fans. They aren't particularly long, but fans like hearing from the band and it keeps the band fresh in each fan's mind. Even if you can't find the time to do a weekly newsletter, you absolutely must send something, at the very least, once per month. If you wait longer than a month between messages, you are not going to maintain as strong a bond between the artist and fan as you could.

2.   Encourage Interaction
Many of our clients write their newsletters in a very 'one way' fashion. This is not a newspaper, it's the internet! Use the technology available and ask questions of your fans. Do surveys! Maybe pick a winner out of all the responses and give them a small token prize. Encourage your fans to interact and they will look forward to your email each week/month. They will want to open your message and be the first to reply. It will become an important event instead of just an afterthought.

3.   Include Links to Places You Want Fans to Go
This one seems obvious, but you'd be surprised at how many bands do not include a link to their website in each message. Not only should you be including a link to your website, but you should have a link to your MySpace/Facebook/etc. profile, your merch store, a place where they can download your music, your tourdates, and anything else that's important. You'll be surprised how much more traffic you get when you start including links.

4.   Create a Special Event in Each Message
This one ties in with #2. If you can create a special event in each message, fans will learn that your messages are important, and will not want to miss any message from you. Examples of special events could be: a limited time sale on CDs or other merchandise items, posting a list of upcoming tourdates just for newsletter subscribers before they are released to the general public, secret special downloads of live recordings or unreleased material, contests to win backstage passes or signed merchandise, or any other kind of special things your fans would crave.

5.   Ask for Help
Fans signed up for your list because they want to hear from you and that indicates a level of devotion to the band. Because of this, don't be afraid to

ask for their help. Ask them to forward the newsletter on to their friends (we automatically include a forward to a friend link in the footer of each email you send). You can also ask for help with street teaming (putting up posters in a town before a show), promoting online, looking for places to sleep, ideas of other bands to tour with, ideas of venues to play in a city you've never been to, and just about anything else. Your fans want to see you succeed, so let them help you!

We hope you think about these 5 simple tips and incorporate them into your fan communication strategy. They've worked for other artists, now start making them work for you!

FanBridge.com is the world leader in fan list management for bands. The company provides advanced email list and mobile messaging tools to bands, saving valuable time and effort for musicians. With advanced scheduling and targeting capabilities, the FanBridge platform enables bands to send relevant and timely communications to their fans, ending the ineffective practice of just blasting everyone at once. For more information or to signup for free, please visit www.FanBridge.com

◆

THE "T" IN TOUR MERCHANDISE STANDS FOR T-SHIRT
by Gigi Swanson, M.G. Incentives Inc.

When you think of tour merchandise you might envision major label artists playing large arenas and selling everything from tie-dye t-shirts, bumper stickers, embroidered baseball caps and in the case of the Rolling Stone's famed Voodoo Lounge tour—a custom motorcycle.

But even if you are an independent artist you can run your business like the big acts by utilizing an added revenue stream source—custom merchandise. As an artist/performer you are selling an experience and fans will buy a souvenir of that experience in the form of a CD, clothing, buttons, posters, etc. As music fans we have all come home with something more tangible than a ticket stub and it's usually something we can wear.

The custom wearables market has plenty to choose from, but let's focus on the long held wardrobe staple—-the t-shirt. What better promotion is there than a walking billboard to advertise who you are and what you do. It's generally inexpensive to produce and if made with good-quality materials it can last a very long time. But better than that, there is a healthy margin of profit in the sales of wearables, which can at least offset or even cover your travel expenses.

You can package CDs with a T –shirt for an "added value" sales incentive such as offering them "half off" with a CD purchase. You can use them as door prizes or as a thank you for the sound guy or the waitress at the clubs you play. The same applies for coffeehouse, church and house concert gigs. Even when you play for free you can earn money and build goodwill and name recognition.

Don't think selling T- shirts is for more visible and established acts. If you are playing out and selling CDs you can sell shirts. But before you jump in, here are a few pointers to make your promotional dollars work for you.

The most popular T- shirt is the basic crew neck. Not only is it low in cost, it's a style people are familiar with. As far as color options are concerned, the sky is the limit with the least expensive being the standard white, then the heathers/naturals, and then the darker colors. Besides the basic tee, you can branch out with different styles such as '70s retro ringer tees, baseball raglan tees and new styles made for women such as scoop necks, baby-doll tees, and the new layered looks.

I prefer 100% cotton heavyweight Tees in the 6.0 oz range for long term durability. Brands such as Gildan, Hanes, and Jerzees have been common favorites for years. Heavier fabric is knitted tighter which enables a better screen print, especially when using detail and four color process. Plus they are typically cut larger and hold up better with multiple washings. But you must think of the tastes of the end user and the image you are trying to promote. That's where fashion often comes in. Knowing your audience is key.

For example, one of my Rap group clients goes for the extra large size heavier weight tees, whereas a rock group client sells mostly light weight, smaller tight fitting "alternative" tees. They cost more but the look they achieve supports their brand image. Check out the on-line stores of different recording artists to get a sense of what fans are buying and to see what might work with your audience.

What makes your t-shirt sell isn't the style, its size or color but its logo design. Logo art needs to be readable and convey the image you want to promote, but keep in mind it should be something a person will want to wear.

When it comes to printing logos, you can opt for gel, sugar-glitter, suede, reflective, metallic, glow in the dark, and ink in one color and up to 12 colors.

Screen printing using one color ink in one position on the shirt is the most economical. You have to pay for an art screen with each color you use as well as for any extra handling of the shirt. That includes flipping it over to print on a different side. Some artwork may require added film screens to replicate more complicated designs. So keep it simple if you can. If you have to go with a certain "look" make sure you get a thorough quote before you proceed.

Your logo art needs to be in a graphic format generally saved as an eps file. Many imprinters charge an hourly rate to prepare art that isn't standard or isn't vector art for more complicated designs. Most printers carry standard Pantone Colors but also offer color-matching inks for an added charge.

How many T shirts should you buy? The real price breakpoints in the industry start at 144 units, but that amount isn't practical for everyone. You can find reasonable shirts at the 72-unit range or even less if you plan it right. Funds still short? I know of some bands that purchased co-op shirts with another band or with a sponsor such as a local nightclub. They basically sold space on the shirt to share or subsidize the cost and helped promote their partners at the same time.

If you can get your shirts for under $5 and sell them in the $10-15 range you will see a quick return on your investment. When I taught music business classes, I used to illustrate the power of selling tour merchandise to my students this way: A typical major label recording artist might make a little over $1 off the sale of a CD . He would have to sell five CDs or more to make the same margin off the sale of one basic T- shirt. That's why some of the major labels have affiliated merchandise companies as an added revenue stream for themselves.

Tour or gig merchandise can be incorporated in your overall marketing plan. It fits right in with preparing press kits, driving traffic to your website, getting people in the door and selling CDs. The right product will promote you long after the gig.

Keep an eye out for future articles on more promotional products. Trucker hats anyone?

Gigi Swanson started an entertainment division three years ago when she left her teaching and administrative duties as director of the music business program at McNally Smith College of Music located in the Twin Cities. She commutes between the company's Minneapolis and St. Petersburg offices and recently opened a satellite office in Nashville. M.G. Incentives, Inc., a company that specializes in promotional products. The company has worked with advertising firms and corporations for over 15 years.

♦

HOW TO MAKE THE MOST OUT OF A MUSIC CONFERENCE

by Valerie DeLaCruz, Musician/Songwriter
© 2009 All Rights Reserved. Used By Permission.

OK, so you've decided to take a positive step toward your goal as a songwriter or artist; you want to check out that music conference you keep getting brochures or email blasts about. It's time to take the plunge, whether you are a seasoned veteran and have attended them before, or a "newbie" hoping nobody at the conference notices!

How you get the most out of the experience

1. Review the promotional materials to determine what the main focus of the conference is; i.e.: songwriting, legal issues, performance, and make sure that this is an area you are interested in.

2. Define your goals. Are you going to strengthen some qualities you already have? Gain more knowledge about something technical or legal? To network with others at you're level and hopefully move up a notch in your field of expertise? Write them down and refer to them as you determine your schedule. Often, panels or workshops are taking place at the same time and you have to choose between them. If you go with a friend, you can split up and compare notes and resources later.

3. Figure out the overall cost including travel, accommodations, conference fees, etc. Start saving up and realize this is an investment in your profession. You may be able to interest a friend to go and share the expenses of a room.

4. There is almost always the opportunity to showcase at these events, and usually, if you are selected to showcase, you can attend the conference at a reduced fee or for FREE. This is certainly worth doing as you will get to show the industry professionals and potential collaborators what you can do. Be realistic about the costs involved in bringing your band to the conference. You may elect to do a solo or duo acoustic set to cut costs if that presents your material well. If not, again it may be a worthwhile investment to perform a showcase, always more fun than a bar gig and in a concert setting where people actually listen. We'll touch on the showcase preparation further on.

5. Send in the application. Many times there is a reduced "early bird" registration fee and this is great if you can take advantage of it. If you are also applying for a showcase slot, tailor your presentation materials to the theme of the conference to better your chances of being selected. Remember that professional presentations, or something that stands out, will cut through the many, many packages that the organizers will be receiving.

6. Reserve your room and travel arrangements. Often the conference will have blocks of rooms reserved for the conference at a reduced rate. It is always better to spend a little more and stay right at the hotel where the conference is taking place. A great deal of the networking and connections that take place are during casual times between seminars, and you don't want to waste time in a taxi getting back and forth. You may need to run back up to your room to get another package or CD to give out. They usually have special airfare rates, too. I use www.expedia.com for the best rates and schedules.

7. Now that you are set to go, you need to prepare the materials you will need. Make a checklist and give yourself a few weeks to gather them. Once I left printing out lyric sheets and bios 'til the last minute, and of course, the cartridge on my printer started to act up on a Sunday evening when there were no stores open! I also email things like the bio file and one-sheets to myself so that in a pinch, I can download them at Kinko's or forward them to someone I meet. They are up there in my virtual file cabinet wherever I go.

What's in a package?

Bring 5-10 full packages that include: Bios, photos, a one-sheet of several of your reviews and critics' quotations, photocopies of great press if you had a photo in print or if it is from a major publication like Billboard. Use the magazine's actual heading on your press sheet to get attention and gain credibility. Also don't forget your business card and CONTACT INFORMATION (the most important thing, seemingly obvious, right?)

The packages should be set up so that your name (or band name) and photo are on the front. If you have a CD, using the CD cover on the front of your folder looks very professional too. You want them to quickly identify you when they are digging through a huge pile of packages. Inside, have something visually compelling like a color copy or photo on one side and your bio immediately available on the other. Insert a CD or demo into one of the pockets. I hate to say this, but it's time to bite the bullet if you are still using cassettes and get a CD burner so you can make CD demos tailored to the audience you are trying to reach.

Note: Have extras of all of the above materials in case you need to throw together more packages or don't want the expense of handing out an entire package when selected materials will do.

Promotional tools

Have flyers of your performance time and venue if you are showcasing to hand out and leave all over the place. Have a stack of business cards. It is worth it to spend a little extra on these, as they are truly your calling card, and will remind someone of whom you are. I always like to have a photo on it, and color stands out. An unusual layout is important, and if you are a band, have a graphic designer (not your cousin's girlfriend) design a logo that will identify you. The most important thing here is to make it legible! A card that you need a magnifying glass to read already makes your contact frustrated.

Plaster your website on all of your materials. Everything you hand out should have all your contact information. This seems obvious, but how many CDs have ended up in the trash can because no one could find the envelope or cover it came in? A website is the most important business tool you can have. Busy industry people are inundated with wanna-be and would-be artists. They love to check out your site in the privacy of their own office/home and get the important info at their own leisure. Remember a slow-loading site is one that will not be viewed as they go on to the next one.

Check in

Take advantage of early check-in, arrive the night before so you are rested and don't have to fight a crowd. I always plan to stay one more day if possible, so that I can really enjoy the last day and night, which is when you are really feeling connected to the other participants and start making plans to get together for follow ups or collaborations. Get the materials upon registration and go back to your room and plot out your schedule. Leave time for regrouping; non-stop seminars can be exhausting.

Network

Networking is the name of the game. You will meet so many people that you won't remember them all when you leave, and the same for them remembering you. The single most important thing you can do is exchange and collects business cards. Write a note to yourself about what you talked about, and whether or not you told the person you would like to follow up. Don't just start handing out packages to the panelists after their presentation. Instead collect their card and ask if you can send it along in a week or two. This again separates out your stuff from the crowd. But use your judgment; seize the moment. If you have the opportunity to hand deliver a package to the producer you never thought you'd be lucky enough to meet, take it! Practice remembering names; it will go a long way to be able to address someone you met by their name. Everyone wants to feel valued.

Other important tips

1. Find out where everyone is hanging out after the sessions. Definitely go to the "mixers" to talk to people in a more casual atmosphere. Sometimes there are informal "jams" or guitar-pulls late into the night where you hear some of the most compelling music. I ended up booking someone to share a bill with me after being astonished at her beautiful song during one of these sessions.

2. In the question-and-answer session that normally follows a presentation, be conscious of not wasting the time of the panelists or other attendees with your personal request. (I heard recently and saw many eyes roll when a participant used his chance at the microphone to go into microscopic detail about the steps he had taken to get his demo played on radio). Ask yourself if the question you have would benefit everyone, or if it would be better to talk to the speaker later privately.

3. Take advantage of signing up for one-on-one critique sessions. These are invaluable and educational, not to mention making a personal connection with someone in the industry that may be able to help you. Even if there is an extra charge for this, sign up for at least one. Here is where you can pick the brains of the experts. And if you ask for a critique, take it graciously; don't challenge the reviewer's advice or become defensive. This is how we learn and progress. You may not agree entirely with them (it is, after all, one person's opinion), but there is probably a grain of truth in there.

4. If you showcase, prepare a great and tight set list that shows what you have that is different than everyone else. Better a fantastic five-song set than two hours in a bar where no one pays attention. Have only one ballad, and close with another fantastic up-tempo song.

5. If they can't get a flavor of your style, in five songs, then you have not focused on a genre, and you will have a lot of problems anyway. It's good to start with a strong, driving, up tempo song. Try for a smooth transition. Don't stand around onstage while you and the band are trying to decide the next song; this looks unprofessional. Be flexible though if you think a different song would maintain your momentum; just be well rehearsed and prepared for this possibility if you do it.

6. Have your cards and demo CDs at the stage readily available for people to take. You never know when Miles Copeland will be in the audience!

When you get home, the real work begins, unless you were signed to a recording contract right on the spot! Follow up with thank you notes to all your contacts. Start by organizing the business cards you collected and assign action steps to them. Put the packages together and send them within a week or ten days while it is still fresh. To stay organized, keep a log of your contacts, and what you did to follow up. Then call in about two weeks to follow up on the packages you sent out. Lastly schedule those co-writing or demo sessions, and order the publications and/or resources that you discovered.

Valerie is one of the 60 original Just Plain Folks members and her passionate career pursuit and professionalism has been a model for other grassroots artists. Through hard work and persistence (and talent!) she's continued to prosper in the industry. Contact: www.valeriedelacruz.com.

BUILDING A MUSIC SITE THAT SELLS: PROMOTE YOUR CD, NOT YOURSELF

by Mihkel Raud, author of "How to Build a Music Website that Sells"

Marketing your CD on the Internet isn't really that different from marketing any other product on the Net – be it some fancy million dollar mansion in the Hollywood Hills, a how-to-get-divorced-in-less-than-ten-days consulting service, a super-cheap DVD player, or a subscription to some kind of porno website...whatever....it's the same game. To play any game, you have to know the rules.

Break all the rules

When it comes to music, I encourage people to get as crazy as they can. Break all the rules you've ever heard of. Try new! Don't think just of radio! Forget about what anyone else may or may not think of your music! Be yourself! Do what you want to do! And do it now! You have to dare to do!

Still, marketing your music – be it on the Internet or offline – is a totally different ballgame. You need to use some rational sense if you want to see results.

I know that it's pretty uncomfortable to think of your CD as a piece of merchandise. After all, music is supposed to be art, right? It is. Tell the opposite and I'd be the first to protest. Your CD is just as much of a product as a bottle of beer. Your CD is a product that everybody should "need."

This concept of "need" is exactly what soooooo many musicians fail to understand. Almost every band or singer/songwriter website that I have seen concentrates on the artist.

Basic elements to a site

- Biography
- Photo gallery
- News
- Gigs
- Sound samples

Think outside the box

There are many possibilities of what to include on your site. Some bands post lyrics, or have discussion boards and chat rooms. The most commonly used concept in the music business is still to build the website around the artist.

So what's wrong with that approach? Nothing really, except that it's so common. And the artist approach will not sell your CDs. You ask... how is that true? Let's look at an example. Let's say you're planning to buy a Mesa Boogie amp. You want to get yourself the best full stack in the world. Visit Mesa (www.mesaboogie.com) and take a close look at what's on that site. Are you being bombarded by raves about just how great a guy Randall Smith is? He's the mastermind behind Mesa amplifiers. Do you see any Smith family snapshots on the front page? Or "better" yet, is there a guest book form asking you to leave Randall an "I love you" message? Nope. None of that "person" stuff is on the Mesa Boogie amp website. Why? Because it's the product you're after, not touchy feely with its inventor. Why on earth should your website be any different?

If you really want to succeed, you need to stand out. In order to beat that competition, you will have to use The Billion Dollar Baby Website Concept, as I have ironically titled the concept (if you know the Alice Cooper song, you know what I mean!) In other words, create a website that is solely focused on your product – the CD.

Your CD as the spotlight

That's right. The only hero of your movie should be your cool-sounding-Grammy-winning-absolutely-fabulous CD. Every other detail of your website has to serve the same master - your CD. Nothing is more important than that music that you want to sell. If you use The Billion Dollar Baby Website Concept, you can turn the whole internet music game upside down. And you will win. It's as simple as that! OK, this may hurt your ego a little bit. I understand perfectly. After all, you wrote the songs. You spent hours singing them in perfect tune. Heck, you may even have produced the CD all by yourself and that's no easy task. But now I'm asking you to spotlight the CD instead of yourself?

Remember this important point. I'm NOT telling you to shut down your existing artist website. On the contrary, it's smart to have one. In fact, you can have a bunch of them.... the more, the merrier. You can have your loyal fans create them for you. However, on your Billion Dollar Baby Concept Website you are going to play a supporting role. Your CD will be the main player.

A separate website?

It is absolutely essential to have a separate website for your CD only. And when the time comes, for your next CD.... plan a separate website for it too. Every time you put out a new CD, you will build a new website designed just for it. My concept demands a lot of time and dedication, and is directly from my own experience. It's loads of work, and is expensive, but is another way to be a success.

I found a medieval music band from Estonia and produced a record of Black Sabbath songs in the 14th Century style of music. "War Pigs" sung in Latin. "The Wizard" played on Gothic harp and a fiddle (www.sabbatum.com.) I sold well over 1000 copies in the first few months. I sold 1000 copies entirely on the Internet with no marketing funds whatsoever. I did it all from my small apartment in Tallinn, Estonia. Now, if I could do it, so will you.

Mihkel Raud is the author of "How To Build A Music Website That Sells." To order your copy, please go to: www.musicpromotiontips.com

legal

HOW TO COPYRIGHT YOUR MUSIC
by Nancy Falkow, Said So Public Relations

Sometimes musicians think every song written needs to be immediately copywritten, but this isn't always true! Copyrighting, registers your music so that if a situation arises that someone is stealing your music, your registration of copyright is on file, which protects you. So, if you're singing these songs in your living room for your family, you don't need to run to Washington, DC!

What can be copy written?

Literary works; musical works, including any accompanying words, dramatic works, including any accompanying music, pantomimes and choreographic works, pictorial, graphic, and sculptural works, motion pictures and other audiovisual works, sound recordings and architectural works.

Library of Congress

If you plan on distributing your music through the web you should copyright your songs. Go to the *US Copyright Registration site* and download the forms you need. Each situation is different, read all of the information, and figure out which best applies to you. Put your music and lyrics on tape or CD, fill out the appropriate forms and write the check. It takes up to 6 weeks to receive all the paperwork and registrations.
Internet: www.loc.gov/copyright
Phone: 202/707-3000 (this is NOT a toll-free number)
Write: U.S. Copyright Office, Library of Congress, 101 Independence Avenue, S.E, Washington DC 20559-6000

The forms

What you need is a properly completed application form, a nonrefundable filing fee ($30) for each application and a non returnable deposit of the work being registered (A tape, CD, and/or lyric). You can copyright more than one song on one tape or CD by sending it in as an anthology. In short, you put your songs on one format, give it a name like "Greatest Hits" and send it in. This is the best way to save money. Instead of copyrighting each song for $30, you're copyrighting an entire batch for $30. Remember it's always important to protect yourself and your songs. Good luck!

Nancy Falkow is the former President of Said So Public Relations www.nancyfalkow.com - an independent grassroots publicity firm.

HOW TO TRADEMARK YOUR BAND NAME
by Derek Sivers, CEO CD Baby

Anytime you are promoting, you are also promoting your name - so make sure it's yours!

I'm giving you some unofficial advice here from my own experience. There are attorneys and specialists that can help you much more. I recommend a book called "*Trademark Legal Care for Your Business & Product Name*" by Stephen Elias (Nolo Press). It covers everything, and even includes the forms you'll need to register. For basic trademark advice, go to my web page of reprints from Nolo Press: (www.hitme.net/useful/c.html)

Research to make sure no one else has your name

Check the PhonoLog at your nearest record store. If you can, check *Billboard's Talent Directory*. (It IS expensive to buy however). If you've got $$, hire a search firm (attorneys) - this is the most reliable, but it will set you back $300-$500. I also heard CompuServe has a trademark research center.

The library is free

Call the nearest largest Public Library and ask if they have a "*Federal Trademark Register CD-Rom*". (Each state has between 1-3 libraries that will have one). You can go in, and they'll even show you how to do a search. Search for your full band name, then each word individually. *Example*: my band "Hit Me": search "Hit Me" then search "HIT" then search "ME". The reason is there may be a band called "Kick Me" or "Hit Us" that could be a conflict. If you can think of other similar words to search, try those, too. You can also get a printout of all this. If there's nothing even remotely similar, you're doing OK. If someone, even a clothing company, is using your name, then you should consult an attorney.

Trademark & Servicemark

1. Make sure you search the Federal Register, then the Pending Register. These are for the names that have been applied for, but not completed yet. Call Washington, DC: (703)308-HELP and ask for the book "Basic Facts about Registering a Trademark".

2. Trademark covers a product, while a Servicemark covers a service. As a musical act, we are a service. If ALL you do is make CDs and tapes, but never play live, maybe your name only applies to a product. For most of us, it's a service first, then a product second. It's all the same form, just a technicality. Note: You can still use the ® [little (R) in a circle] when you are registered.

3. You can start using "TM" or "SM" after your name now. It means you have *intent* to register, or are claiming legal ownership of that name. You can use the ® *after* and only after the whole registration is complete.

How much does it cost?

Each registration class costs $245. When I called the office help line, they said if you register your Servicemark, that's plenty of protection for now. That is until you start selling loads of t-shirts, hats, action figures! Make sure you get the new forms, since the older forms have $200. A Servicemark for a musical act, you will want to file a "CLASS 41". The description of product/services is: "Entertainment Services in the nature of Musical Performance." Don't forget to do this NOW, or all the work you're doing to promote your act will be wasted.

Derek Sivers was the founder and president of the extremely popular online music store, CD Baby. Derek has sold CD Baby and is now developing new projects to help independent artists to succeed. For his free e-book on how to be more successful promoting your music, visit www.sivers.org

◆

TRADEMARKING YOUR LOGO
by Vivek J. Tiwary and Gary L. Kaplan, StarPolish.com
© 2009 All Rights Reserved. Used By Permission

A good logo is an invaluable tool in the imaging and marketing of a developing artist. That is why it's important to design a logo immediately after you have settled on your name. But unlike your name, it's more acceptable to change your logo over the years without losing or confusing fans. *311* and *The Rolling Stones* are great examples of bands that have either changed or modified their logos to adapt with changing times or the themes of certain albums or tours.

Not every artist has a logo, but a logo can only help. Remember that your name simply and consistently printed in a certain standard font can be a fine logo (e.g. Cheap Trick). I personally like logos that are minimal, easy to remember, tied into the artist's name, and easily reproduced. Like your name, your logo should somehow also be in line with the vibe of your act.

How do you get one?

A band member or friend designing your logo may assure a genuine and intimate connection between the logo and the band. If no one you know is talented in the visual arts, you can seek help from local design companies. Be careful though, as some of these companies can be expensive. Alternately, you can solicit help from local design schools, whose students may be willing to design a logo for free in order to gain working experience and build up their own design portfolios. Try putting flyers/posters up in the schools or posts on school bulletin boards announcing that you are a local band/songwriter looking for a logo designer.

Be seen

Once you have a logo that you are satisfied with, put it on everything— all over your website, your merchandise, your CD, your letterhead, etc. Make stickers and always keep a small stack of your logo stickers on hand. Stick them on everything and everywhere. Consistency and repetition are critical marketing keys. The more times people see the same logo, the more they will remember it and your act.

Register your logo

Register with the *U.S. Patent and Trademark Office* (or comparable body if you are based in another country). Much like with your name, you acquire rights to your logo when it is publicly used in commerce. This means that when you sell your merchandise, or play a show where your logo is displayed, you automatically obtain some common law rights in that logo. Registering your logo as a trademark, however, will provide you with important additional rights:

Do a search

Assuming that you are the first to use this logo, registering your logo will help secure your right to use it, and prevent others from using the same or a similar logo. Because of the extremely subjective nature of the trademark analysis for logos, it might not be worthwhile to perform a search. It is not with certainty you will discover the same or similar logo being used by another band. If you choose to perform a search, you can try *Thomson & Thomson*, or the folks at (*www.tradename.com*) A lawyer can take care of the whole thing, since the analysis is so touchy, that only an experienced trademark attorney will be able to offer sound advice.

The good news is it's not quite as disastrous, if you are forced to change your logo. It might not be what you'd ideally like to do, but it pales comparison to having to change your name. If you can afford to hire an attorney to assist you, go ahead and trademark your logo. If your problem is that you're strapped for cash, try to register your trademark yourself by using the website of the U.S. Patent and Trademark Office (www.uspto.gov.)

Vivek J. Tiwary is the founder and President/CEO of both StarPolish and The Tiwary Entertainment Group, a multi-faceted entertainment venture focusing on artist management, marketing consultation, and project production. Vivek has 10 years experience in the arts and entertainment industries, Prior to joining StarPolish.com, Gary L. Kaplan spent three years at Skadden, Arps, Slate, Meagher & Flom, one of the world's preeminent law firms. Gary was a member of Skadden's Intellectual Property Department, focusing on patent litigation. Contact: www.starpolish.com

◆

ENTERTAINMENT INDUSTRY LAWYERS: WHO, WHERE AND HOW MUCH?!
by Wallace Collins, Entertainment Lawyer
© 2009 All Rights Reserved. Used By Permission.

As a creative artist in the entertainment industry you do not need to know everything about the business in order to succeed, but you should hire people who do. When I was a teenage recording artist back in the late 70's, I can remember being intimidated by the "suits". Now that I am on the other side of the desk, I have a broader perspective. I am here to tell you that those "suits" can help you; provided, however, that like any other aspect of your life, you use your instincts in making your selection.

The team

The best place for you to start building your "team" of representatives is with a competent lawyer who specializes in entertainment law, which is a combination of contract, intellectual property (copyright, trademark and patent) and licensing law. Eventually, your team could possibly include a personal manager, a booking agent and a business manager/accountant. Your lawyer can assist you in assembling your team. He may then function as the linchpin in coordinating the activities of your team and insuring that these people are acting in your best interests.

The lawyer

A good lawyer will navigate you safely through the minefield that is the entertainment industry. Record contracts, publishing agreements and licensing arrangements can be extremely complicated. Proper negotiating and drafting requires superior legal skills as well as knowledge of entertainment business and intellectual property practice. Your lawyer can explain the concepts of copyrights, trademark and patents to you and assist you in securing proper protection for your work. In addition to structuring and documenting a deal to maximize the benefits to you, some lawyers also actively solicit deals for their clients.

What to look for

When looking for a lawyer take the time to interview a few before retaining one. Some lawyers are with large firms, but many are solo practitioners. Lawyers have various personalities and legal skills and you should seek out a situation where the "vibe" is right. It is not necessary that your lawyer like or even understand your creation. It is more important that you feel he or she is a trustworthy and competent advisor.

When do I pay?

Keep in mind that a lawyer with other big name clients is not necessarily the best lawyer for you; if it comes down to taking your calls or those of a superstar, which do you think will get preference? A lawyer, much like a doctor, is selling services, so if you go to him for advice you should expect to pay. With the odds of success in this business being what they are, very few lawyers will agree to work for you and wait for payment until you are successful and can pay your bills. You may also find someone who will work on a contingency basis.

The cost

1. A lawyer specializing in the entertainment field usually charges an hourly fee or a percentage of the money value of your deal. Hourly rates generally run from $200 and up. Percentages are based on the "reasonable value of services rendered" and generally run around 5% of the deal. A few lawyers may charge a set fee, such as $1,000 or $1,500, to review and negotiate certain documents. Check around to see if the fee arrangement proposed is competitive.

2. Most lawyers will require a payment of money in advance or "retainer", which can range anywhere from $1,000 to $10,000. Even those who take a percentage of the deal as a fee may require that you pay a retainer. In addition to the hourly fee or percentage, you are usually required to reimburse your lawyer for his out-of-pocket costs, including long distance telephone calls, photocopies, postage, fax, etc.

3. You should realize that in retaining a lawyer you are making a contract even if your agreement is not written. In return for a fee, the lawyer promises to render legal services on your behalf. However, some lawyers may want a fee arrangement in writing (specifically in connection with a percentage deal) and/or a payment direction letter. A cautious lawyer will advise you that you have the right to seek the advice of another lawyer as to the propriety of a percentage fee arrangement.

As a general rule

You need a lawyer if you are asked to sign anything other than an autograph. Too many aspiring creative artists want to get a deal so badly they will sign almost anything that promises them a chance to do it. Even successful careers have a relatively short life span, especially in the music, movie and television business. Therefore, it is important for you to get maximum returns in the good years and not sign away rights to valuable income.

Never sign anything without having your own lawyer review it first! Do not rely on anyone else (or even their lawyer) to tell you what your contract says. Do not let anyone rush you or pressure you into signing any agreement. There is really no such thing as a standard "form" contract. Any such contract was drafted by that party's attorney to protect that party's interests; your lawyer can help negotiate more favorable terms for you.

Wallace Collins is an entertainment lawyer with the New York law firm of Serling Rooks & Ferrara, LLP. He was a recording artist for Epic Records before attending Fordham Law School. Contact: (212) 245-7300, www.wallacecollins.com

ROYALTIES IN THE MUSIC BUSINESS
by Joyce Sydnee Dollinger, Entertainment Lawyer
© 2009 All Rights Reserved. Used By Permission

What is a royalty? In the real world, the word royalty is the power or rank of a king and queen. In the music wo royalty is synonymous with *money*. Royalties are the most important entitlements of the musician. These entitlements warrant them to receive money from their craft - the craft of MAKING MUSIC.

Royalties

There are many types of royalties. The list is constantly growing because of the new technology, but here are some to name a few: Artist Royalties, Mechanical (Publishing) Royalties, US Performance Royalties Synchronization Royalties, Grand Rights Royalties, Foreign Royalties for record sells and performances, Lyric Reprint Royalties.

General definition

Artist Royalties, in a nutshell, are monies paid to the recording artist from the record company. They are the share of the proceeds from the sale of the artist's records paid directly to the artist after the artist records material for the record company. This, in turn, gives the record company permission to exploit the musical work in the marketplace.

Recording contracts

In artist recording contracts, artist royalties are usually negotiated in points. When record label business affairs attorneys use that terminology, they are referring to the percentage points the record company will pay an artist on each album sold. For example, if an artist gets 10 points, it usually means that the artist receives 10% of the retail cost of each record sold.

1. **Superstar Deals**
   Royalties usually are:
   - 16%-20% of retail of top-line records plus escalations
   - 18-20% is quite high and the artist must sell a lot of records - usually more than 5 million
   - 100% CD rate and can receive new configuration royalties
   - 12-14% of singles + escalations receive increased royalties when contract options are exercised

2. **Mid-Level Deals**
   Royalties usually are:
   - 14%-16% of retail top-line records plus escalations (escalations usually based on genre)
   - 16% is high and the artist must sell a lot of records
   - 85-90% CD rate and new configurations
   - 12-13% of singles or 3/4 of LP rate receives increased royalties when contract options are exercised

3. **New Artist Deals**
   Royalties usually are:
   - 11%-13% of retail top-line records
   - 75-85% CD rate and new configurations
   - 10-11% of singles

When to renegotiate

If the artist sells a ton of records, the artist can usually re-negotiate with the record label and try to receive increased royalty rates.

- Increase net royalty rates on remaining LPs in the contract increase rate for each successive LP include escalations for attaining sales plateaus

- Receive the increase royalty rate on future sales of past LPs improve the royalty computations increase foreign rates, the CD rate, the new technology rate, licensing fees and free goods

- Reduce the recoupment percentages

Record royalty formula

The record royalty formula is usually based upon a percentage of records that are sold. In using the formula, the record company looks to the retail price of the commercial top-line records and standard deductions that every record company takes from the gross income from the sales of those

.Some of the deductions are: recording costs of the records, ʌaging, returns and reserves, discounted military sales, video costs, tour ₌pport, promotional records and free goods. Please note: records on which royalties are paid are quite different from deductions from gross royalties.

Joyce Sydnee Dollinger is an attorney admitted in New York and Florida. She is also the Vice President of 2 Generations SPA Music Management, Inc., and involved with 2generations.com and SPA Records, Inc. Contact: www.sparecords.com.

ARTIST-MANAGEMENT CONTRACTS
by Richard P. Dieguez, Entertainment Lawyer
© 2009 All Rights Reserved. Used By Permission.

Next to a record label deal, the artist management contract is the most exciting agreement an artist will sign. As with any legal document, a contract shouldn't be signed without the advice of a music attorney. Let your lawyer take the blame for "asking too much" or for being such a "tough negotiator" that is what they are being paid to do. Here are the fine points to negotiate:

- How long will the agreement be in effect?

- How much will the manager get paid during the agreement?

- How much will the manager get paid after the agreement has ended?

The art of negotiation

1. It is likely you and your manager are each likely to have a legitimate difference of opinion as to the amount of time for which the contract will be binding. Whatever the reason, you don't want to get locked in with a loser for the next seven years. On the flipside nothing can be more frustrating for a manager than to have her budding artists go to another manager, where they then make it to the big time.

2. Depending on the particular circumstances of the parties, the negotiation will center on a contract term ranging from as short as six months to as long as several years. What length of time is fair really depends on what you and your manager are each bringing to the relationship you wish to form. For example, let's say that neither of you has too much experience in the music business. In this situation, you're both probably better off with a short-term contract, (6-12months) so that you can check each other out without getting locked in. You can always enter into another agreement if it turns out, at the end of the contract, that you have a future together.

The time and money equation

What happens if you can't agree to a fixed amount of time? Well, to satisfy both parties, the attorneys can always try to hammer out a compromise: a short-term contract with the potential of being converted into a long-term contract. For example, the parties could agree to a one-year contract. Part of the agreement, however, would be that the manager must meet certain conditions during this one-year period — such as getting you a record deal, a publishing deal or even guaranteeing that you earn a minimum amount of income. If the manager fails to meet the conditions, then the contract ends when the year is up. If, however, the manager is successful in meeting the conditions, then he has the right to automatically extend the contract for an additional period of time, say for another year.

Commission

The custom is for the manager to work on a commission. In other words, the manager gets compensated for his efforts by taking a percentage of whatever income you earn as an artist. Obviously, your attorney is going to try to negotiate for as small a percentage as possible. You'll argue that the manager simply manages, and without your talent, there is nothing to sell to the labels or to the publishers. The manager's attorney is going to negotiate for as high a commission as possible. Their position will be that there is a lot of talent out there — especially in the major music centers like California and New York.

Money talks

So what's the range of the amount of the commission? It can generally be anywhere from 10% to 25% of your gross income. The amount that is settled on may very well depend on the circumstances. Again, the art of compromise may bring new life to a negotiation that is at a deadlock on the issue of the commission amount. Regardless of the particulars, the concept here is that the lower percentage rate should be satisfactory to you, while the manager is also given an incentive to make a bigger percentage if he can get you to earn in excess of a certain amount of gross income. And, of course, getting you over that amount, whether it's $25,000.00 or whatever, will be to your benefit as well.

The manager

Your manager will likely try to apply their commission to every conceivable entertainment-related activity from which you could possibly earn an income. Examples of such money-making activities would be live performances, record sales and the sale of promotional merchandise such as t-shirts, posters, buttons, programs and pictures. If you feel that the commission rate the manager is asking for is too high, you can try to compromise by proposing that you'll accept the commission rate, but only if certain activities are excluded from the commission.

After the contract ends

Another touchy subject is whether the commission on gross income earned by the artist continues after the contract has ended. Your response will probably be "of course not!" After all, once the contract is over, neither party has any further obligation to the other. Once the contract is over, there should be a clean break, but it is not always so clear-cut

You may be fortunate enough to have signed some money-making deals. As agreed, the manager gets his percentage and you keep the rest. But it may be that your money-making contracts will still be in effect for quite some time after your management contract has ended. Since you will continue to profit from a deal he helped you obtain, the manager may feel that he should also continue to profit even after the artist-manager relationship legally ends.

When you get a new manager

If you enter into a contract with a new manager, that new manager will probably be no different from your former manager on the question of compensation. The new manager's attorney will probably demand that the commission apply to every conceivable entertainment- related activity from which you could possibly earn an income. And this would include the money pouring in from deals your former manager obtained! You wouldn't want to be stuck paying two commissions on the same money.

Conclusion

There are many aspects of the artist management contract that will be subject to negotiation. An issue may be made of as to who collects the income: the manager, you or maybe a third party like a business manager or accountant. Another traditional sticky point is the extent of the manager's authority to sign contracts on your behalf. There may even be some negotiating points that to you and the manager don't seem crucial, but to the attorneys seem to mean everything. The personal circumstances surrounding any given artist management contract can be so unique, that the art of compromise expands the parameters of the so-called "standard" contract.

An NYU Law graduate, Richard P. Dieguez has over 16 years experience in entertainment law. He has represented hundreds of clients across the U.S. and several nations in music, film, television, publishing etc., Mr. Dieguez is also the founder of The Circle, a monthly music industry seminar held in New York City. Contact: www.RPDieguez.com

THE WRITTEN AGREEMENT AMONGST BAND MEMBERS
by John Tormey III, Entertainment Lawyer
© 2009 All Rights Reserved. Used By Permission

AABM
I have seen references to the above-mentioned document as both "Inter-Band Agreement", and "Intra-Band Agreement". Rather than initiate any argument with grammarians as to which term is correct -let's simply call this all-important document the "Agreement Amongst Band Members"; or, "AABM", for short. If one is a musician playing in a multi-member band, is an AABM needed? *Absolutely*, yes!

The agreement
There are some parallels to an agreement amongst band members, and a pre-nuptial agreement between prospective spouses. But I actually find the case for having an *AABM* more compelling than a pre-nup. A marriage should be a function of love. A band formation, on the other hand, is often a commercial exercise.

Written agreements should be required for any collaborative commercial endeavor between 2 or more people. Maybe it seems easier NOT to make it official, but no band member should skip the *AABM*, if the band member takes his or her band or career seriously. It may not be realistic to operate on blind trust, in place of a good written agreement.

If the band formation is not viewed as a commercial exercise, then I suppose the band members can simply agree on a handshake, and then gig for free in the subways. However, the majority of bands that I hear from, are concerned about their financial, as well as their artistic, futures. Many are trying to find a way to become economically self- sufficient on music alone, while preparing to quit their "day jobs". It is best to have an agreement in hand, rather than, to put it off.

When to begin?
No one wants to be required to negotiate and close the AABM once the band is already successful, or once the band has already been furnished with a proposed recording agreement. The optimal time to close the *AABM* is while the band is just being formed or while it is still struggling. A good *AABM* should also be flexible enough to contemplate future changes, such as changes in personnel and, Artistic direction. It is also likely one of the members may have more of a hand in the writing of the words or the music of the band's original songs, all the more reason for creating the *AABM* as early as possible.

Band members
In the average 4-person band, each member may play a different instrument. Some may have been in the band longer than others, or more experienced in the business of music. Maybe one of you has "connections" to clubs and labels, or more free time to invest in the running of the band's business. Each member can perform a different function in business.

Why a contract?
The real value of a contract - any contract, including the *AABM* - is as a dispute-resolution and dispute-avoidance tool. By dealing with things ahead of time, it may be best to discuss things now; and put the results on paper. Resolve things before having to pay litigators thousands upon thousands of dollars to do it in the courts later.

What happens if...
All of those "what if" questions, may not be the focus at the beginning. Band members may not want to think about, what *may* happen if the bass player departs to raise kids in Maui, or the singer-songwriter front man decides to join the Air Force. If all the other band members all value their investment of time, sweat and money in the band, then they should know and have fully thought through - in advance - the answers to these types of questions. Who owns and administrates the copyrights in the songs? Who is responsible for storing the masters? Who has final say in the hiring and firing of a manager? If the band breaks up, which member or members, if any, may keep using the band's name? And these are just *some* of the questions that should come up.

When to get a lawyer
Every band's situation is different, and the lists of questions to consider will be as different as there are different band personalities and different band members. The band may be better off, if a lawyer prepares the AABM. In a perfect world, all band members would be separately represented by a different attorney, but that is not realistic.

Should all these considerations prevent a band from creating a good AABM? Absolutely not, the band should at least try to resolve amongst its own members, the answers to all of the "what if" questions that will likely come up in the life cycle of any band. The band can try to resolve these questions on paper. Thereafter when affordable, one of the band members may decide to consult with an attorney to review and revise the band's starting-point document - (typically, this turns out in practice to be the band member with the most at stake in the outcome).

Be aware that one attorney may well not be able, or be allowed to represent all band members simultaneously. This is due to concerns about possible conflicts of interest, (especially if different band members have different percentage investments at stake in the band's commercial endeavors.)

It is best to draft some kind of written agreement between band members, since doing so now can save a lot of heartache and expense down the road in the future.

John Tormey III is a New York lawyer who handles general commercial, transactional, and corporate matters. John is also admitted to practice law in California, and in Washington, D.C. John's focus is in the area of entertainment, arts, and media, including endeavors to market artistic material to professional entertainment industry recipients. Please contact: www.tormey.org

♦

HOW TO LEGALLY SELL DOWNLOADS OF COVER SONGS
by Derek Sivers, CD Baby
© 2009 All Rights Reserved. Used By Permission.

Please note that the below is not official legal advice. It is ONLY for the U.S.A. We are not your lawyers, and you should always contact your attorney before entering into any contract such as a license.

If you have recorded a cover version of someone else's song, and you plan to make that recording available over the Internet, the following information applies to you. You must follow these steps BEFORE you make your recording available for distribution to the public!

If you record a cover version of a song, (meaning your performance of a song that has been released in the U.S. with consent of the copyright owner), you are entitled by law to release your recording commercially, and the owner of the copyright to the song cannot prevent you from doing so.

The Copyright Act provides for what is called a "Compulsory License" for downloads and CD sales, which means that if you follow the steps set forth by statute, you can distribute your recording of that song on a CD or over the internet. This Compulsory License is only available for sales in the United States. Other uses of masters, such as streaming, conditional downloads, and the like, are not subject to a Compulsory License. A separate license from the publisher is needed in those cases.

The following details the procedure for individuals to obtain a compulsory license to digitally distribute cover songs over the Internet to end users in the United States.

Identify the Copyright Owner - the publisher
The first step is to identify the owner(s) of the copyright to the song. The publisher. The easiest way to do this is to search the songwriter/publisher databases, here:

BMI (bmi.com)
ASCAP (ascap.com)
SESAC (sesac.com)
Harry Fox (songfile.com)
U.S. Copyright Office (copyright.gov)

Keep in mind that the owner of these rights is typically a publisher, and that the owner of the rights in the song is not the same as the owner of the rights to any particular recording of the song. In other words, Record Labels are almost never the owners of the copyright to the musical composition - they typically own only sound recordings. You should be looking for the name of a publisher (or in some cases an individual).

Be careful to identify the exact song you want, as there are many songs with the same names. If you cannot find the owner through these websites, search the records of the Copyright Office online.

If you cannot find the copyright holder(s) after a thorough search, you can send the letter to the Copyright Office, along with a small filing fee, currently $12.00. See the Copyright Office website for the proper address and current filing fees if you are going to be sending the letter of intent to them.

Instructions on how to do that are on "Circular 73" from the U.S. Copyright Office, on a PDF file, here: copyright.gov/circs/circ73.pdf

WE STRONGLY RECOMMEND DOWNLOADING AND READING THIS FILE, because it carries the essence of this entire article.

Send a Letter of Intent - EXACTLY like this

You must send one letter for each song for which you seek a compulsory license 30 days before you begin distribution of your downloads. The letter must be sent by registered or certified mail and contain the following:

1. A clear subject line/title that says "Notice of Intention to Obtain a Compulsory License for Making and Distributing Phonorecords"

2. Your full legal name

3. All fictitious/assumed names (stage name, band name) used

4. The names of each individual owning a 25% interest or more in the distribution of the song (band members, if you split your sales income)

5. Your fiscal year (usually January 1st - December 31st)

6. Your full physical address - P.O. boxes are unacceptable, unless that is the only option for addresses in your geographic region

7. The title of the song

8. Name(s) of the author(s) of that song

9. The type of configuration expecting to be made (a music file distributed over the Internet is called a "Digital Phonorecord Delivery" (DPD))

10. The expected first date of distribution

11. The name of the performer/band doing the cover

12. Your signature.

If there is more than one publisher listed, sending a letter to one of them is sufficient for the compulsory mechanical license; however, if one or more of the copyright holders is not from the United States, it is best to send the notice to all copyright holders.

Send royalty statements and pay royalties

Once you begin distributing the song over the Internet, you must send monthly statements of royalties on or before the 20th of each month, and pay the royalties.

The monthly statement must be sent by registered or certified mail and include:

1. A clear title that says "Monthly Statement of Account Under Compulsory License for Making and Distributing Phonorecords"

2. The period (month and year) covered by the statement

3. Your full legal name

4. All fictitious/assumed names (stage name, band name) used

5. The names of each individual owning a 25% interest or more in the distribution of the song (band members, if you split your sales income)

6. Your full physical address - P.O. boxes are unacceptable, unless that is the only option for addresses in your geographic region

7. The title of the song

8. Name(s) of the author(s) of that song

9. the name of the performer/band doing the cover

10. The playing time (length) of your recording of the song (minutes:seconds)

11. The number of DPDs made, i.e. how many times your recording was downloaded

12. The number of DPDs that were never delivered due to a failed transmission

13. The number of DPDs that were retransmitted in order to complete/replace an incomplete/failed delivery

14. The total royalty payable (number of total DPDs, not counting ones never delivered multiplied by the statutory royalty rate (see below))

15. The following statement: "I certify that I have examined this Monthly Statement of Account and that all statements of fact contained herein are true, complete, and correct to the best of my knowledge, information, and belief, and are made in good faith"

16. Your signature

You must also send an Annual Statement of Account at the end of each calendar year, which is virtually identical in content to the Monthly Statements, but must be certified by a licensed Certified Public Accountant (CPA).

Statutory royalty rates

The current (2006) statutory rate for royalties is 9.1¢ for every copy sold if the playing time for the song is under five minutes. If the playing time for the song is longer than five minutes, the rate is 1.75¢ per minute, rounding up to the next minute.

under 5 minutes = 9.1¢ per copy
5 to 5:59 minutes = 10.5¢ per copy (6 minutes x 1.75¢)
6 to 6:59 minutes = 12.25¢ per copy (7 minutes x 1.75¢)
7 to 7:59 minutes = 14¢ per copy (8 minutes x 1.75¢) etc.

The Copyright Office can always keeps the most up to date information concerning statutory royalty rates at this link: www.copyright.gov/carp/m200a.html

IMPORTANT notes

The publisher may tell you to that they don't deal with compulsories, and that you should contact the Harry Fox Agency. Though the Harry Fox Agency can handle mechanical licenses for DPDs for most publishers, you still have right to obtain a compulsory license by following the directions, above.

Remember the law is on your side. You are entitled to a compulsory license by law. You have permission - (a compulsory license) - as soon as you send the notice, described above, to the proper publisher. As long as your notice complies with Copyright Section 115, (described above), the publisher need do nothing other than receive the royalty payments. You don't even need to wait for their reply.

Other notes

You may be able to negotiate a better deal for yourself, either with lower royalty rates or less frequent statements of account. If terms are negotiated which deviate from the standard Section 115 then a mechanical license will be issued by the publisher or HFA.

If you wish to distribute physical copies (e.g., CDs) of a cover song, you must obtain a similar compulsory license, available for most popular songs through the Harry Fox Agency at harryfox.com. If you plan on distributing between 500 and 2500 physical copies, you can obtain a compulsory license through the Harry Fox Agency online at songfile.com.

For more information on compulsory licenses for all forms of distribution, please refer to the Copyright Office's web site, at copyright.gov, and contact your attorney.

Helpful publications available through the Copyright Office include Circular 73 (Compulsory License for Making and Distributing Phonographs), Circular 75 (The Licensing Division of the Copyright Office), and M-200 (Checklists under Section 115 of Title 17).

If you have been distributing a cover song without a compulsory license or an agreement with the copyright owner, you are ineligible to obtain a compulsory license for that recording (!), and you may be subject to civil and/or criminal penalties for copyright infringement.

Be careful to follow the steps exactly as described above, in order to be legal.

Download and print/save these files

How to Investigate the Copyright Status of a Work
www.copyright.gov/circs/circ22.pdf

Compulsory License For Making and Distributing Phonorecords
www.copyright.gov/circs/circ73.pdf

Notice of intention to obtain a compulsory license
www.loc.gov/cgi-bin/formprocessor/copyright/
cfr.pl?&urlmiddle=1.0.2.6.1.0.175.17&part=201&section=18&prev=
17&next=19

Royalties and statements of account under compulsory license
www.loc.gov/cgi-bin/formprocessor/copyright/
cfr.pl?&urlmiddle=1.0.2.6.1.0.175.18&part=201&section=19&prev=
18&next=20

Checklists of Required Information
www.copyright.gov/carp/m-200.pdf

These and more available at the U.S. Copyright Office website:
www.copyright.gov

Derek Sivers was the founder and president of the extremely popular online music store, CD Baby. Derek has sold CD Baby and is now developing new projects to help independent artists to succeed. For his free e-book on how to be more successful promoting your music, visit www.sivers.org

marketing and promotion

CREATING AN INDIE BUZZ

by Daylle Deanna Schwartz, author of "I Don't Need a Record Deal! Your Survival Guide for the Indie Music Revolution"
© 2009 All Rights Reserved. Used By Permission

People won't buy your music or come to shows if they don't know about it. By working the media, you can create a foundation for your career. Artists ask, "Why would someone write about an unknown artist or play their music?" Lose that mentality if you want to create a buzz around you and your music! If you've got THE GOODS, the potential is there. Once you believe your music is worthy of media exposure, you can work to inform others.

Build your story one press clip and one radio show at a time. Take baby steps up the ladder from teeny publications and local radio stations to larger ones. As your story builds, so will opportunities to increase it even more! According to Dalis Allen, producer of the Kerrville Folk Festival, "Having your record reviewed in [local magazines] may not propel your career to the degree that you want it to end up. But every one of those things adds up. If I see a review of someone's record in Performing Songwriter and then hear their name somewhere else and then see their package, I've seen their name over and over again. It doesn't matter if it's not the most important thing that you're going to do. It's one more step in what you're going to do."

Let people know about you and your music through the media. It may feel useless if your hard work doesn't pay off immediately. Don't lose hope! Every CD that goes out is another chance for progress. Indie artist Jennie DeVoe says, "I give CDs to radio and anyone else who should have it. It's like planting seeds." Plant your own seeds once you have something to pass out. It takes time, but if your music moves people, your career can sprout by means of reviews, radio play and other exposure that builds your foundation.

If you plant enough, you have a better chance for a lovely blooming garden. Indie artist Canjoe John says, "The business of music requires public awareness and major marketing in order to sell. Major labels have major money to market with. Independents must get publicity in order to survive. I send well-written press releases out on a regular basis. I look for every opportunity to get in the news, TV, radio, newspapers, magazines. If I'm in a new town, I call newsrooms to try and get a story. I've been very successful at this and consider getting major free press as much an art as performing major stages." Exposure builds your story!

Start by creating what's known as a one-sheet. It should be a summary of your story on one sheet of paper. Include whatever ammo you have – a short bio, a track listing, tour dates and past venues, radio play, short press quotes and any other notable info. Design the info on your one-sheet in an organized way. Send your one-sheet with a CD to publications for reviews, radio for airplay, venues, potential agents, managers, distributors and almost anyone else you want to get interested in you and your music. Call first to see if they want a full press kit or just a one-sheet with a link to your website.

Check out daily and weekly papers, alternative publications, trade magazines and even papers from schools. Be creative about where you can fit it into publications. If you have a good story or technique relating to your guitar playing, pitch a guitar magazine. If you've made savvy business moves, pitch a business magazine or the biz section of a local paper. Do research at stores with big magazine sections. Find an angle about you or your music and look for music and general publications that might write about it.

Create a good electronic press kit on your website that people can go to for more info and a selection of photos (least 300dpi in quality) that they can download without having to deal with you. Include a private page with full songs and send media people the URL so they can hear your music. Organize a street team of fans who can help you create your buzz. They can make follow-up calls to press and radio stations in their regions. Fanpower combined with your own hard work can create a buzz that will get you to bigger publications and radio stations, which leads to better venues. This can lead to the day you quit your day job because you've created a full time income from your music!

Daylle is the best-selling author of Start & Run Your Own Record Label and The Real Deal: How to Get Signed to a Record Label. She also presents music industry seminars, does phone consulting for musicians and record labels and publishes Daylle's News & Resources, a free industry newsletter. daylle@daylle.com www.daylle.com

♦

HOW TO BE YOUR OWN PUBLICIST

by Ariel Hyatt, Ariel Publicity
© 2009 All Rights Reserved. Used By Permission

For this article, I interviewed several entertainment writers from across the country. Their comments and advice are included throughout. Writers who will come up throughout are: Mike Roberts (*The Denver Westword*), Jae Kim (*The Chicago Sun Times*), Silke Tudor (*The SF Weekly*).

MYTH: A Big Fat Press Kit Will Impress a Writer.

TRUTH: Writers will only become exasperated by a press kit that is not succinct and to the point. A bio, a photo and 6-8 articles double-sided on white paper is a good sized kit. If a writer wants to read more than that he will contact you for further information. If you don't have any articles, don't worry, this will soon change.

The first step in your journey is to create a press kit, which consists of four parts — the Bio, the Photo, the Articles and the CD.

Jae Kim: "The ultimate press kit is a very basic press kit which includes: a CD, a photo with band members' names labeled on it — not a fuzzy, arty photo — a clear black and white, a bio, and press clips — 10 at most, one or two at least. 40 are way too much."

PART 1: The bio

Write a one-page band bio that is succinct and interesting to read. I strongly advise avoiding vague clichés such as: melodic, brilliant harmonies, masterful guitar playing, tight rhythm section, etc. These are terms that can be used to describe any type of music. Try to make your description stand out. Create an introduction that sums up your sound, style and attitude in a few brief sentences. This way if a writer is pressed for time, she can simply take a sentence or two from your bio and place it directly in the newspaper. If you try to make a writer dig deeply for the gist, that writer will most likely put your press kit aside and look to one of the other 30 press kits that arrived that week.

TIP: Try to create a bio with the assumption that a vast majority of music writers may never get around to listening to your CD (500 new releases come out in the United States each week). Also, writers are usually under tight deadlines to produce copy — so many CD's fall by the wayside.

Q. Whose press materials stand out in your memory?

A. *Jae Kim:* "Action shots of bands. Blur has had a few great photos, and Mariah's are always very pretty. Also, Mary Cutrufello on Mercury has a great photo — enigmatic with a mysterious quality. Her picture was honest and intelligent, just like her music."

A. *Silke Tudor:* "The Slow Poisoners — a local SF band who are very devoted to their presentation. They have a distinct style and everything leads in to something else. Photos are dangerous. If the band looks young and they're mugging you have a pretty safe idea of what they're going to sound like."

PART 2: The photo
It is very tough to create a great band photo. In the thousands that I have encountered only a few have had creativity and depth. I know it can seem cheesy to arrange a photo shoot but if you take this part seriously you will deeply benefit from it in the long run.

Create a photo that is clear, light, and attention grabbing. Five musicians sitting on a couch is not interesting. If you have a friend who knows how to use PhotoShop, I highly recommend you enroll him or her to help you do some funky editing. Mike Roberts tends to gravitate towards: "Any photos that are not four guys standing against a wall. Also, a jazz musician doesn't always have to be holding a horn."

MYTH: Photos Cost a Fortune to Process in 8 x10 Format.

TRUTH: Photos do not have to be expensive. There a few places to have photos printed for a great price. My personal favorite is ABC Pictures in Springfield, MO. They will print 500 photos (with layout and all shipping) for $80. Click the link to check out their web site or telephone 888.526.5336. Another great resource is a company called 1-800-POSTCARD, (www.1800postcards.com) which will print 5000 full-color, double-sided postcards for $250. Extra postcards not used in press kits can be sent to people on your mailing list, or you can sell them or give them away at gigs

PART 3: The articles
Getting that first article written about you can be quite a challenge. Two great places to start are your local town papers (barring you don't live in Manhattan or Los Angeles), and any local fanzine, available at your favorite indie record store. Use this book as a resource for CD reviews. Find music that is similar to your band's type of music and then send your CD's to those reviewers. As your touring and effort swell, so will the amount of articles written about your band.

PART 4: The CD
The CD artwork, like the press kit, must be well thought out. You should customize your press kits so that they look in sync with your CD. This way when a writer opens up a package the press kit and the CD look like they go together. Put your phone number and contact info in the CD so if it gets separated from the press kit, the writer knows how to contact you. I asked Eric Rosen, the VP of Radical Records, how he oversees the development of product. He had a few things to say about stickering CD's (placing an extra sticker on the cover to spark the interest of a writer).

"If you are going to sticker your product, be unique in the way you present it — try to be clever about it — plain white stickers are boring." He went on to say that "Recommended Tracks" stickers are great for the press (suggesting no more than two or three selections). Eric does not think

that stickers are too advantageous in CD stores, because then "You are just covering up your artwork."

TIP: Don't waste precious CD's! Keep in mind that 500 new CD's come out every week in the United States. Unless you are sure a writer actually writes CD reviews (many are not given the space to run them) don't waste your hard-earned dollars sending that writer a CD. Again, ask the promoter which writers like to receive CD's for review and which ones don't need them.

Q. What do writers like?

A. *Silke Tudor:* "When people personalize things and use casual words. If an envelope is hand-addressed, I will notice it right away and I always open things that people put together themselves. Hand-written stuff gets read first . . .The bands that do PR for themselves are the ones that stand out for me"

A. *Mike Roberts:* "Include the name, show date, time, ticket price, place, and who you are playing with. If I don't see the contact number I have 69 other kits to get to."

Q. What do writers hate?

A. *Jae Kim:* "I hate those padded envelopes that get gray flaky stuff all over you — I feel like its asbestos." She also dislikes "When I get a package with glitter or confetti in it — it gets all over my desk." "I [also] don't like Q & A sheets" — She prefers to come up with questions herself rather than receive answers pre-fabricated for her and spoon-fed.

A. *Silke Tudor* similarly reports: "I never open anything over my computer."

A. *Mike Roberts:* "I don't have much interest in gimmicks like hard candy. If I tried to eat it, it might kill me. Also you can't expect a writer to shove something in the paper at the last minute. Please give as much lead time as possible."

Q. What do writers throw in the garbage immediately?

A. *Mike Roberts:* "Anything past deadline."

A. *Jae Kim:* "Pictures of women's butts or profanity that is degrading to women."

A. *Silke Tudor:* "If I already know the band and I know that I don't like it."

Getting your press materials out there
Once you have a press kit together try to start planning PR for any tour 6-8 weeks before you hit the road. As soon as a gig is booked, ask the promoter for the club's press list (most clubs have one.) Promoters are dependent on this local press to help sell tickets. Have the list faxed or e-mailed to you. Don't be shy — you are working with the promoter to make the show happen and promoters love it when the show is well publicized. Also be sure to ask the promoter who his or her favorite writers are and which ones will like your style of music. When you do call those writers, don't be afraid to say which promoter recommended them and invite them to the show.

If the local promoter has a publicist, let that publicist do his or her job. Pack everything up and mail it to the promoters. Make sure you ask the promoters how many posters they would like and send them along with the press kits. After a few days it's best to call and verify that the material was received. If you can't afford to send kits to everyone, ask the promoters in each area which three or four writers would most likely cover a band that plays your style of music. Also, ask the promoters where the clubs run strip ads (these ads will be in the papers that cover music and inform people in the area about club happenings.)

Publications
If you are servicing press yourself, and the club does not have a press list, pick up The Musician's Atlas, or The Musician's Guide To Touring. Both of these guides are packed with a wealth of information on publicity outlets across the country, as well as venues, record stores, labels, etc. I recommend sending materials 4-6 weeks prior to the gig. Beware of

monthly publications — if you are not at least six weeks out, don't bother sending to them.

Call the writers

Most of the time you will be leaving messages on voice mail. Be polite, get right to the point, and be brief!! 9 times out of 10 writers will not call you back.

Persevere

If you are a totally new band and you are worried because a paper did not cover you the first time around, keep sending that paper information every time you play in the area. I have never met a writer that ignores several press kits from the same band sent over and over again. It may take a few passes through in each market, but the more a writer sees over time, the more likely he will be to write about you.

Don't let all that all that voice mail discourage you

I have placed hundreds of articles, mentions, and photos without ever speaking to the writer.

Writers are more responsive to e-mail

It's free for them and does not take too long to respond to. If you are sending e-mail follow-ups, put a link to your site, or the club's site if you don't have one. You can also send a sound clip if you have the capability. IMPORTANT NOTE: Don't bother sending out materials a few days before the gig. Writers are usually way past their deadlines by then and they won't be able to place your band.

Posters

Posters are a great form of PR and they don't have to cost you a fortune. The most cost-effective way to make posters is to buy 11x17 colored paper from your local paper store (approx. $7 per ream of 500) and run off copies at the copy shop (approx. 7 cents each). Make several white copies and include these with your colored posters — this way the promoter can make extras, if needed. For higher quality posters, I recommend a copy process called docutech. These cost a penny or so more apiece, but they are computer-generated and look better than regular copies. Have whoever designed your poster also design small lay-ups to send out as fliers and ad-mats. Make sure your logo is included on them so the promoter can use them for strip or display advertising.

Have patience

The first few times you play a market, you may not get any press. PR is a slow moving vehicle that can take time to get results. I have worked with some bands that have needed to go through a market 3-4 times before any results started showing up in the press. When sending materials on repeated occasions, include a refresher blurb to remind the writer of your style. Always include the following information: date, show time, ages, ticket price, club name and address, time, and who is on the bill. Don't make writers hunt around for the event info. Make their job as easy as possible by providing as much information. Also keep in mind that some writers will probably not write about you over and over again. If you hit the same markets continually, a great tactic is to change your photo every few months and write "New Band Photo" on the outside of the envelope.

Field staff

Try to enroll a fan to be on your field staff in each market you visit. In exchange for a few tickets to your show, have this person put up posters, hand out fliers, and talk to the college newspaper about writing a feature or the local radio station about spinning your CD. To get a field staff started, include a sign up column on your mailing list and on your web site. If they sign up, they are the people for you! With a bit of planning and focus, you can spin your own publicity wheel. All it takes is foresight and organization. A band that plans well is a band that receives the most PR.

Your website

If you don't already have one — get on it!! Websites can be easy and inexpensive to design — you can buy software that can take you through it step by step. Better yet, have a friend or a fan help you design a site. Your site should include your upcoming tour dates, as most people will visit it to find out when you're coming through town. Another great place to post all

of your dates is tourdates.com it's free, and you can also put your bio and photo up as well. More advanced sites include merch as well as CD sales. This is a great idea if you are at the point where you're selling a lot of merchandise. If you're for your own site, at least be sure to link your site to a place where fans can order your CD.

Ariel Hyatt is the President of Ariel Publicity, Artist Relations, and Cyber Promotions, in NYC. For the past five years she has worked closely publicizing a diverse family of touring and developing indie bands including Sally Taylor, Leftover Salmon, K-Floor, and The Stone Coyotes. Contact: www.arielpublicity.com

♦

TOP 10 MUSIC PR TIPS
by Mona Loring, MLC PR
© 2009 All Rights Reserved. Used By Permission

Publicity is a huge driving force when you're looking at success in the music industry. Although it's definitely beneficial to retain a publicist once you have your music career in gear, you can still manage to create a little buzz on your own in the meantime. Below are the top ten tips for generating your own publicity as a music artist.

1. Make sure you have a press kit that includes a well-written bio, an 8X10 photo, CD and contact info.

2. Go local. Local press is by far the easiest press to get. Let them know your story and send in a CD. Shoot for the music editor or columnist and if they don't have one assigned specifically, contact the entertainment editor.

3. Social networking sites are all about music these days. For example, MySpace's reach is incredible for gaining new fans. Where else can you find people to listen to your music in the convenience of their own home? Make sure you are updating your music, adding friends, keeping them all posted, and updating the tour dates. There are magazines on MySpace looking for music to feature all the time.

4. Radio is a great way to share your music with the masses. You don't have to approach the big ones-you can see success with air play on smaller stations as well. Send in your CD to local DJs and look up college radio shows nationally and see if they'll spin your music. Online radio is picking up these days too… USA4Real.com is a great option… it doesn't cost much and it gets your music heard.

5. Music licensing is a great way to make money and get publicity. Try contacting some music supervisors on TV shows for a start. Send them an inquiry with your information and a link to your music. If you get placed, you can use it for press-and it becomes a story!

6. Music websites and e-zines are always looking for music to review. Look up their websites and send emails to their editors. Tell them why you're a fit for their magazine and ask if you can send in a CD. Again, try to make contact first… sending in a random package may be useless.

7. Youtube.com and Stickam.com are wonderful outlets to share your music. When done right, you can really start gaining a fan base. Try to do something charismatic and original. Reaching out to people online can do wonders. Create a music video, a video blog, sing an acoustic set, take a stab at some comedy— anything… Just remember, first impressions are everything.

8. Be philanthropic. Charity does wonders for publicity outreach. Find something you believe in and offer to play at their event or donate proceeds to their cause. Not only does it get you out there and give you a story angle… but it feels good to help out.

9. Send your CDs to appropriate magazines for your music's genre. Make sure you call ahead and find out the right contact, unsolicited packages get lost in the shuffle. A good rule of thumb is to look up specific writers you feel would enjoy your music and find out how to reach them.

10. Try to book shows in different towns, that way you can easily label the cluster of shows as a tour and contact local newspapers and radio stations and offer them merch in exchange for promotions/articles.

Note that PR is about being smart and creative. It's about finding a reason for people to care about you and your music. Sure, great music and a good look are helpful, but you also need to reach out to the public and come up with stories. Think outside of the box and you'll really benefit from the results in no time. Good luck!

Mona Loring, president of MLC PR, brings forth solid experience in public relations, freelance writing, copywriting, marketing, and business development. Specializing in creative thinking and promotional development, Loring has successfully combined her passion for communications and creativity to establish a PR career that is both mentally stimulating and captivatingly diverse. For more information visit www.monaloring.com

♦

MUSIC MARKETING STRATEGIES
by Derek Sivers, CEO CD Baby
© 2009 Derek Sivers. Reprinted with permission.

Call the destination, and ask for directions
Work backwards. Define your goal (your final destination) - then contact someone who's there, and ask how to get there. If you want to be in Rolling Stone magazine, pick up the phone, call their main office in New York City, and when the receptionist answers, say "Editorial, please." Ask someone in the editorial department which publicists they recommend. Then call each publicist, and try to get their attention. (Hint: Don't waste Rolling Stone's time asking for the publicist's phone number. You can find it elsewhere; get off the phone as soon as possible.)

If you want to play at the biggest club in town, bring a nice box of fancy German cookies to the club booker, and ask for just 5 minutes of their advice. Ask them what criteria must be met in order for them to take a chance on an act. Ask what booking agents they recommend, or if they recommend using one at all. Again, keep your meeting as short as possible. Get the crucial info, and then leave them alone. (Until you're back, headlining their club one day!)

I know an artist manager of a small-unsigned act, who over the course of a year, met with the managers of U2, REM, and other top acts. She asked them for their advice, coming from the top, and got great suggestions that she's used with big results.

Put your fans to work
You know those loyal few people who are in the front row every time you perform? You know those people that sat down to write you an Email to say how much they love your music? The guy that said, "Hey if you ever need anything - just ask!" Put them all to work!

Often, people who reach out like that are looking for a connection in this world. Looking for a higher cause. They want to feel they have some other purpose than their stupid accounting job. You may be the best thing in their life. You can break someone out of their drab life as an assistant sales rep for a manufacturing company. You might be the coolest thing that ever happened to a teenager going through an unpopular phase. You can give them a mission!

Gather a few interested fans for pizza, and spend a night doing a mailing to colleges. Anyone wanting to help have them post flyers, or drive a van full of friends to your gig an hour away. Have the guts to ask that "email fan" if she'd be into going through the *Indie Contact Bible* and sending your press kit to 20 magazines a week. Eventually, as you grow, these people can be the head of "street teams" of 20 people in a city that go promote you like mad each time you have a concert or a new CD.

Go where the filters are
Have you been filtered? If not, you should start now. People in the music biz get piles of CDs in the mail everyday from amateurs. Many of them aren't very good. How do you stand out? Filters allow the best of the best pass through. It will also weed out the "bad music", or the music that isn't ready. I worked at Warner Brothers for 3 years. I learned why they never accept unsolicited demos: It helps weed out the people that didn't do enough research to know they have to go meet managers or lawyers or David Geffen's chauffeur *first* in order to get to the "big boys. If you *really* believe in your music, than have the confidence to put yourself into those

places where most people get rejected. (Radio, magazines, big venues, agents, managers, record labels, promoters...)

Have someone work on the inside
I prefer to ignore the music industry. Maybe that's why you don't see me on the cover of Rolling Stone. One of my only regrets about my own band was that we toured and got great reviews, toured and got lots of air play, toured and booked some great-paying gigs. BUT... nobody was working the inside of the music business. Nobody was connecting with the "gatekeepers" to bring us to the next level. We just kept doing the same gigs. Maybe you're happy on the outside of the biz. (I know I am.) But if what you want is to tour with major-label artists, be on the cover of *Spin*, heard on the airwaves, or get onto MTV, You're going to have to have someone working the inside of the biz, Someone who loves it. Someone persuasive who gets things done 10 times faster than you ever could, and who's excited enough about it, that they would never be discouraged. Find someone who's passionate about the business side of music, and particularly the business side of YOUR music.

Be a novice marketer not an expert
Get to the point of being a novice marketer/promoter/agent. Then hand it to an expert. Moby, the famous techno artist, says the main reason for his success was that he found experts to do what they're best at, instead of trying to do it himself. (Paraphrased:) "Instead of trying to be a booking agent, publicist, label, and manager, I put my initial energy into finding and impressing the best agent.... I just kept making lots of the best music I could."

If you sense you are becoming an expert, figure out what your real passions in life are and act accordingly. Maybe you're a better publicist than bassist. Maybe you're a better bassist than publicist. Maybe it's time to admit your weakness as a booking agent, and hand it off to someone else. Maybe it's time to admit your genius as a booking agent, and commit to it full- time.

Reach them like you would want to be reached
Reach people like *you* would want to be reached. Would you rather have someone call you up in a dry business monotone, and start speaking a script like a telemarketer? Or would you rather have someone be a cool person, a real person?

When you contact people, no matter how it's done (phone, email, mail, face-to-face) - show a little spunk. If it sounds like they have a moment and aren't in a major rush, entertain them a bit. Ask about their day and expect a real answer. Talk about something non-business for a minute or two. If they sound hectic, skip the long introduction. Know what you want to say ahead of time, just in case.

Every contact with the people around your music (fans and industry) is an extension of your art. If you make depressing, morose, acoustic music, maybe you should send your fans a dark brown-and-black little understated flyer that's depressing just to look at. Set the tone. Pull in those people who love that kind of thing. Proudly alienate those that don't. If you're an in your face, tattooed, country-metal-speedpunk band, have the guts to call a potential booking agent and scream, "Listen you fucking motherfucker. If they like that introduction, you've found a good match. Don't be afraid to be different.

What has worked on you?
Any time you're trying to influence people to do something, think what has worked on YOU in the past. Are you trying to get people to buy your CD? Write down the last 20 CDs you bought, then for each one, write down what made you buy it. Did you ever buy a CD because of a matchbook, postcard, or 30-second web sound clip? What DID work? (Reviews, word-of-mouth, live show?) Write down your top 10 favorite artists of all time, and a list of what made you discover each one and become a fan.

This goes beyond music. Which TV ads made you buy something? What anonymous Emails made you click a link and check out a website? Which flyers or radio ads made you go see a live show by someone you had never heard?

Have the confidence to target
Bad Target Example: Progressive Rocker Targeting Teeny Bopper. On CD Baby, there is a great musician who made an amazing heavy-progressive-

metal record. When we had a "search keywords" section, asking for three artists he sounds like, he wrote, "britney spears, ricky martin, jennifer lopez, backstreet boys, MP3, sex, free" What the hell was he thinking? He just wanted to turn up in people's search engines, at any cost. For what, and who? Did he really want a Britney Spears fan to get "tricked" into finding his dark-progressive-metal record? Would that 13-year-old girl actually spend the 25 minutes to download his 10 minute epic, "Confusing Mysteries of Hell"? If she did, would she buy his CD? I suggested he instead have the confidence to target the REAL fans of his music. He put three semi-obscure progressive artists into the search engine, and guess what? He's selling more CDs than ever! He found his true fans.

If you don't say whom you sound like, you won't make any fans

A person asks you, "What kind of music do you do?" Musicians say, "All styles. Everything." That person then asks, "So who do you sound like?" Musicians say, "Nobody. We're totally unique. Like nothing you've ever heard before." What does that person do? Nothing. They might make a vague promise to check you out sometime. Then they walk on, and forget about you! Why??? You didn't arouse their curiosity! You violated a HUGE rule of self-promotion! Bad bad bad!

What if you had said, "It's 70's porno-funk music being played by men from Mars." Or... "This CD is a delicate little kiss on your earlobe from a pink-winged pixie. Or... "We sound like a cross between *AC/DC* and *Tom Jones*." Any one of these, and you've got their interest.

Get yourself a magic key phrase that describes what you sound like. Try out a few different ones, until you see which one always gets the best reaction from strangers. Have it ready at a moment's notice. It doesn't have to narrow what you do at all. Any of those three examples I use above could sound like anything. And that's just the point - if you have a magic phrase that describes your music in curious but vague terms, you can make total strangers start wondering about you.

Touch as many senses of theirs as you can

The more senses you touch in someone, the more they'll remember you. BEST: a live show, with you sweating right on top of someone, the PA system pounding their chest, the smell of the smoky club, the flashing lights and live-in-person performance. WORST: an email, a single web page, or a review in a magazine with no photo.

Whenever it is possible, try to reach as many senses as possible. Have an amazing photo of yourself or your band, and convince every reviewer to put that photo next to the review of your album. Send videos with your press kit. Play live shows often. Understand the power of radio to make people hear your music instead of just hearing about it. Get onto any TV shows you can. Scent your album with patchouli oil. Make your songs and productions truly emotional instead of merely catchy.

Be an extreme version of yourself

Define yourself. Show your weirdness. Bring out all your quirks. Your public persona, the image you show to the world, should be an extreme version of yourself.

A good biz plan wins no matter what happens

In doing this test marketing you should make a plan that will make you a success even if nobody comes along with his or her magic wand. Start now. Don't wait for a "deal". Don't just record a "demo" that is meant only for record companies.

You have all the resources you need to make a finished CD that thousands of people would want to buy. If you need more money, get it from anyone except a record company. And if, as you're following your great business plan, selling hundreds, then thousands of CDs, selling out small, then larger venues, getting on the cover of magazines... you'll be doing so well that you won't need a record deal. If you get an offer you'll be in the position of taking it or leaving it. There's nothing more attractive to an investor than someone who doesn't need his or her money. Make the kind of business plan that will get you to a good sustainable level of success, even without a big record deal.

Don't be afraid to ask for favors

Some people *like* doing favors. It's like asking for directions in New York City. People's egos get stroked when they know the answer to something

you're asking. They'll gladly answer to show off their knowledge.

One bold musician I know called me up one day and said, "I'm coming to New York in 2 months. Can you give me a list of all the important contacts you think I should meet?" I ended doing a search in my database, E-mailing him a list of 40 people he should call, and mention my name.

Maybe you need to find something specific: a video director for cheap, a PA system you can borrow for a month, a free rehearsal studio. Call up everyone you know and ask! This network of friends you are creating will have everything you want in life. Some rare and lucky folks (perhaps on your "band mailing list") have time on their hands and would rather help you do something, than sit at home in front of the TV another night. Need help doing flyers, or help getting equipment to a show? Go ahead and ask!

Keep in touch!

Sometimes the difference between success and failure is just a matter of keeping in touch! There are some AMAZING musicians who have sent a CD to CD Baby, and when I heard it, I flipped. In a few cases, I've stopped what I was doing at that moment, picked up the phone and called them wherever they were to tell them I thought they were a total genius. (Believe me - this is rare. Maybe 1 in 500.) Often I get an answering machine, and guess what... they don't call back!! What success-sabotaging kind of thing is that to do? 2 weeks later I've forgotten about their CD as new ones came in.

The lesson: If they would have just called back, and kept in touch, they may have a fan like no other at the head of one of the largest distributors of independent music on the web. A fan that would go out on a limb to help their career in ways others just dream of. But they never kept in touch and now I can't remember their names. Some others whose CDs didn't really catch my attention the first time around, just keep in touch so well that I often find myself helping them more as a friend than a fan.

A short description - 10 Seconds or less

Most of the world has never heard your music. Most of the world WON'T hear your music, unless you do a good job describing it. It's like a Hollywood screenplay. You not only have to write a great screenplay, but you have to have a great description of it that you can say in 10 seconds or less, in order to catch people's attention. Find a way to describe your music that would catch anyone's attention, and describe it accurately.

Read about new music

Go get a magazine like CMJ, Magnet, or Alternative Press. You'll read about (and see pictures of) dozens of artists who you've never heard of before. Out of that whole magazine, only one or two will really catch your attention. WHY? I don't have the answer. Only you do. Ask yourself why a certain headline or photo or article caught your attention. What was it exactly that intrigued you? Adapt those techniques to try writing a headline or article about your music.

Derek Sivers was the founder and president of the extremely popular online music store, CD Baby. Derek has sold CD Baby and is now developing new projects to help independent artists to succeed. For his free e-book on how to be more successful promoting your music, visit www.sivers.org

♦

100 MILLION COMPELLING REASONS TO USE MYSPACE.COM
by Andre Calilhanna, Discmakers
© 2009 All Rights Reserved. Used By Permission

The indie music universe is constantly waning and expanding: new bands emerge, old ones dissolve, conferences come and go, new web sites pop up as older ones fall out of fashion. As with any other industry or business model, these indie music offerings fail and succeed with their ability to create and meet market demand for their service.

Enter MySpace.com. Incorporating successful elements of MP3.com and IUMA, and eclipsing PureVolume and Friendster as the place to be online, MySpace is the epitome of what an online community can be. In it's short life it has adapted and evolved to meet the evolving needs of its user base, and it has expanded to a network of over 43 million users in the process. Thanks, in large part, to the bands.

Billionaire Boys Club, from Jersey City, NJ, boast the distinction of being the first band ever to grace the front page of MySpace. Through good timing and good tunes, BBC caught the attention of MySpace co-founder Tom Anderson and ushered in a new wrinkle in the MySpace universe. The band is still listed as one of Anderson's MySpace favorites.

Fireflight, from Orlando, FL, recently signed to Flicker Records, and attribute a lot of their growing fan base to their efforts and presence on MySpace. Through their page on MySpace, the band sees continuous growth and interest, which should only increase as they release their album in July and start playing a full regimen of shows.

We sat down with these two indie music veterans and gleaned some insights into the finer points of MySpace marketing. Here's our list of five phenomenal reasons to use MySpace!

1. Super-targeted viral marketing.
2. Communication runs both ways.
3. Motivated fans.
4. Crossover marketing opportunities.
5. Free marketing is the best marketing ever!

Super-targeted viral marketing

One of the tenets of good marketing is to target your market. You wouldn't pitch your Crunk Speed-Metal band with an ad in Today's Grandparent magazine. The idea is to figure out who your market is, find out where they are, develop your message, then figure out how to get that message in front of the people who might want to buy what you're selling.

MySpace delivers this in spades. Pockets and niches of users, called "friends," gather around each other and share info on bands they like. For instance, let's say you like My Chemical Romance. You can go check out their site, listen to their music, and read their blog. Then, if you want to find bands with a similar sound, you can check out the band's friends, which include a host of other bands. Presumably, these are bands that have something in common with My Chemical Romance, so you go and check them out.

There are also fans listed as friends, and they typically have a bunch of bands on their pages. So someone into My Chemical Romance will have a number of other bands posted. You might be interested in checking some of them out. It's viral marketing in its purest form, and the friend network is what really sets MySpace apart from other band sites.

It's also why Isac Walter, who does marketing and programming for MySpace, says major labels are clamoring to get their bands on the site. "With 43 million users, it's almost better than going to TV, what with the way people watch TV nowadays. People come to this site to discover new music, and what better way to expose an artist than to leak a band to this audience?"

As a band, this works the other way, too. Once you start developing a fan base, you can communicate to them when you have a show or a news event to broadcast. MySpace provides a service where you can target the friends you contact by region.

Billionaire Boys Club, from Jersey City, NJ

"They added this feature," says Leigh Nelson of BBC, "where you can set up an event, and you can say I want to invite all my friends in a radius of x number of miles from this zip code. So we'll do a show in New York and set up an invitation and invite all of our friends within 50 or 100 miles of the city. So we're directly targeting that audience, where with email you end up sending show announcements to people in Germany. These are things that get added one little bit at a time. Tom really seems to get how people are using MySpace and what they want to do with it, and they're always adding functionality based on that."

Communication runs both ways

The internet has completely changed the way we communicate, particularly in terms of marketing. Take something as simple as a band mailing list, for instance. In the early 90's, that meant printing post cards, labeling them, putting stamps on them, and lugging it all to the post office weeks before the gig. It sounds like the Dark Ages, doesn't it? It cost a

bunch of money, and fans could only communicate by seeing you at a show or writing a letter. Email changed all that. Now it's free to email your announcement, fans can immediately reply, and you don't need to plan your promotion months in advance.

MySpace has taken that even further. MySpace not only allows you to communicate with your fans quickly and cost effectively, but it allows them to communicate with you and each other.

Fans can tell you what they think of everything on your page – a picture, a song, a blog entry – and their response is posted immediately. They can then spread your news to their friends with a couple of keystrokes. It's an amazing development, and there are many ways to take advantage of it to create drama and stir up a buzz.

Fireflight, from Orlando, FL

"We started leaking the news about our signing to Flicker on MySpace because we knew people were going to be reading our blog," says Justin Cox of Fireflight, "but we got way more response than we thought we would. That generated more interest in our page than anything had in a long time. You could see us singing a contract but you didn't know with who, and that blog is the most visited we have. We put it on our regular site, too, but we don't have it set up where people can comment, so it's cool to know that so many people were keeping track and were genuinely interested."

There are examples of bands booking shows to meet the demand of their MySpace fans, tells Walter. "There's this band Cut Copy from Australia who did the Franz Ferdinand tour, and when they played Los Angeles they had enough people on MySpace saying, 'Oh I wish you were playing your own show!' So they booked a show at a smaller club called The Echo and gave discounts to their MySpace friends and sold the place out. Bands like that who keep in contact and get a little more personal with their audience can really have success."

And Nelson explains that opportunities are coming to them by way of MySpace. "We used to get a decent amount of fan email, but now all those comments are pretty much coming exclusively from MySpace. Also coming in are show offers, booking people who are interested, soundtracks who are interested in songs… a lot of that comes via MySpace. It makes us more likely to follow up, too, because we can get a better idea of who these people are by looking at their page."

Motivated fans who find you and help promote you

Indie bands need help. It's a lot of work to do promotion, book gigs, sell merch, rehearse, write, and do the hundreds of little details involved with a band. Street teams and helpful fans have been the solution to much of that, though not always easy to assemble and coordinate. MySpace, with its younger demographic and infectious network qualities, makes it easier to find folks ready to jump on and paint your bandwagon. Sometimes, the band doesn't even know it happening.

"We have this banner on our MySpace page," explains Cox. "I was surprised to find that people who were our friends were taking it and posting it on other people's MySpace pages, trying to drive traffic to us. So let's say there was no MySpace and you had a web site, and you had that same banner. It's cool, but what are people going to do with it? Now that we've got MySpace, they take those banners and post them as comments on other people's pages and blogs, and people read the blogs and then automatically they're going to your site for no other reason than that it's there."

Finding where your MySpace fans are coming from can lead to unexpected market research, like expanding your gig radius based on fan input. "I can search for BBC across the whole site and see how many people have added us and said we're one of their favorite bands," says Nelson. "It's really cool to see fans crop up in markets we've never even been to. All of a sudden we see there are a lot of friends in upstate New York, we get in touch with them and find out where we should play and then go do some shows. In the past there was no way to find that kind of information."

Crossover marketing

At its best, one marketing endeavor feeds another, and spills into your other efforts. As Walter says, "The bands who promote their MySpace pages become the biggest bands on MySpace, hands down." By linking from your regular web site, adding your MySpace URL to all your stickers, t-shirts, etc., you drive people to your site, and more likely broadcast to all those MySpace users that you're on there, too.

It also works in reverse. MySpace traffic drives traffic to your regular web site, and people to your shows. "Traffic on our site has increased drastically as well," says Cox, "and I'm sure that has something to do with MySpace because it's been a steady ramp since we've been on there.

"I can also remember instances specifically where people have come up to me at a show and say they heard us on MySpace and decided to come check us out, which to me is the best. It's just a big network and a big word of mouth kind of thing and you can't get that kind of exposure unless you're playing shows every night. It's just been this awesome marketing tool."

Free marketing is the best marketing ever!

Sounds obvious, and it is! But it can't be understated or undervalued. Many of the band web sites out there offer great services, and there's no reason not to be on every site you can get to. MySpace has the unique distinction, though, of offering just about everything you could imagine wanting all under one roof: a potential fan base, an opportunity to broadcast your music, a place to hang your photos, a web presence with a decent amount of customization… the list goes on. Not to mention the features and functions that allow you to be a smart marketer.
"The thing that sets MySpace apart from sites that are just for bands," touts Nelson, "is people sign onto MySpace every day, just to check their messages, read, and communicate. I use it every day, to check in and see what's going on, look for any bulletins from bands, figure out what's going on tonight in the city. So just by putting your journal or show dates or advertisements and songs up there, you're simply going to get a lot more exposure than people just randomly checking your web site. People spend more time on it than anywhere else. I guess credit to Tom there, for setting it up in such a way that makes it so addictive!"

This article originally appeared in Disc Makers' Fast Forward monthly newsletter. Visit www.discmakers.com/music/ffwd to get a free subscription.

HOW TO LEAD PEOPLE TO YOUR MUSIC IN A DIGITAL AGE

by Bill Pere, President of the Connecticut Songwriters Association
© 2009 All Rights Reserved. Used By Permission

With the maturity of digital delivery and a proliferation of websites that allow easy uploading and legal downloading of music, the old models of making and marketing CDs are gone. The shift from an album-based economy to a track-based economy spawns many new considerations for the Indie artist when the time comes to go into the studio and record.

In the old days, the typical strategy was to record an album, release a featured "single" and people would then purchase the whole album, never having heard the other songs. Albums often contained several 'filler' tracks of songs which never would have stood alone.

Today, anyone can easily hear up to 2-minute samples of tracks before purchasing, so the notion of using filler tracks is essentially useless – ALL the tracks have to be good or the consumer will just bypass them and download the ones they want. More than ever before, the quality of the songs is important helping your music rise above the baseline of filler tracks that are out there on CD Baby, i-Tunes, and other internet music stores. If you spend the time and money to record a filler track, it's not going to give you the return on your investment in a track-based music economy as it might have in the old album-based economy.

This leads to the obvious question, is the concept of an "Album" even valid anymore? Should an artist spend time and money making a physical CD, when CD sales are rapidly declining and digital sales are increasing? If you are a touring artist, you'll still (for now) want physical CDs to sell at gigs, but remember that the ultimate goal is always to be able to generate income without having to be physically present.

Content is king

Consider how a typical listener comes to find new music. As an Indie artist, it's fair to assume that most people have never heard of you. How will they find your songs? The most likely path to your music will come from consumers doing Internet searches on topics which have nothing to do with you. However, if your website contains content that might be of

interest to particular groups of people, they will find you and then discover your music. For example, I have lots of website content about hunger and homelessness, and also about songwriting techniques. I've had lots of folks around the world find me and my music because they were searching on those topics, and now they've become fans. Think of the content on your website as a net to catch Internet searchers.

Another way to increase the effectiveness of your net is to put the lyrics to all your songs online as a separate page for each song. If you write songs about various topics, people searching those topics will be more likely to find your content. Again, the importance of the songwriting comes to the fore. If you just write generally about love and how you broke up or got together, you're going to be lost in an ocean of similar content. If however, you want to write about those things and use some interesting metaphors, like "your love is kryptonite" (a Superman reference) or "My heart is as parched as the desert of Tatooine" (a Star Wars reference), you're now providing potential hooks for people with specific interests. In this age of niche marketing, specificity is always going to be a big plus. Over the years, I've been commissioned to write songs about a submarine, a river, a statue, horseback riding, Special Olympics, and various other unusual but specific things. These songs get found by people searching for related content. As an example, my submarine song about the USS Connecticut is often mentioned on websites of Navy personnel.

In a track-based digital music world, there are some things we've lost from the album-based model. Concept albums like the "Days of Future Past" (Moody Blues) , or "The Who Sell Out" (The Who) don't translate well to a track-based model. The order of tracks and the transitional content between them were essential to making concept albums work as a whole. With individual digital tracks available in any order, the artist can no longer control how the listener will hear the content. Each song will have to be able to stand alone, and transitional material between songs is meaningless, and complicates where to place the track markers. If you want to do a concept album with transitional material, it is a good idea to submit a different version for digital download, where any inter-song transitional material is omitted. With most sites giving a 30-second clip to preview the song, it's important to limit the length of musical introductions and get right into the song, unless you can specify the section to use for the preview clip.

Critical mass
Similar to a concept album, but more in tune with today's market is the themed-album. This is a collection of individual songs, each of which could stand alone, but all of which relate to some common and specific theme e.g., high school life, baseball, rural life, spirituality, boats, etc. This serves two purposes. It makes it much easier to identify a target audience, enabling you to focus your promo efforts. It also provides a critical mass of content on the Internet, making a much bigger net for catching Internet searches about that topic. The more specific the theme, the better.

What's in a name?
One of the most important things to think about in a digital world is the song title. Typically the title of a song going to be a phrase in the first or last line of the chorus, as that is the most easily remembered part of the song. But it might not be the most unique phrase as far as search keywords go. So you can use the technique of double-titling, where the song has one primary title, followed by a second in parentheses. An example would be Rupert Holmes' song "Escape (The Pina Colada Song). In the aftermath of hurricane Katrina, I produced a song by a fellow writer called "Daydream" about memories of growing up in New Orleans. I suggested that it would be advisable to double-title the song calling it "Daydream (The Levees of New Orleans)". You can see the difference that would make in number of search hits the song receives.

If you can come up with a title which is similar to some word or phrase which is commonly searched, it will be a big help to you. Before there was the "High School the Musical" phenomenon, I released my CD and song "High School My School". This gets many hundreds of hits each day from people searching "High School Musical". If you can generate high web traffic, you only need to convert a small portion of that into sales to start seeing meaningful royalties.

To summarize
In today's world of individual tracks and search engines, make it a part of your overall planning to think about how you can maximize the web traffic that each of your songs can generate. Think of lyrics, titles, and subject matter as web content. Make sure each song is truly strong enough to stand on its own as if it were a featured single. Learn how search engines like Google work and optimize your website content to draw people to you. Cast a well-thought-out net, and you'll be well-rewarded.

Bill Pere is President of the Connecticut Songwriters Association and author of "Songcrafters' Coloring Book: The Essential Guide to Effective and Successful Songwriting."

◆

BRINGING YOUR MUSIC TO LIFE ON YOUTUBE
by Daylle Deanna Schwartz, author of "The Real Deal"

YouTube is a community that allows people to watch and share original videos on the Internet. With a camera and creativity, you can post a video on YouTube that can get people excited about your music. Jennifer Nielson, marketing manager at YouTube, says, "People have the opportunity to upload and share videos with people around the world and connect with a new audience." Like MySpace, the competition for attention is fierce. But if you have great music and can make an interesting video, it's worth taking advantage of this expanding promotional tool.

In November, the winners of YouTube's Underground music video contest were announced on Good Morning America. Four bands (Ostrich Head, Maldroid, Greenland and Pawnshop Roses) with limited media coverage were put in the spotlight of a national TV show. All felt hopeful that exposure on YouTube will help them get a lot further. You too can take advantage of YouTube. With creativity and hard work, you can maximize opportunities for getting your music to more fans.

Why do a video?
Because you can! YouTube gives you tools and a site to post and promote a video. Ryan Divine of Maldroid says, "Musicians now have the capacity to get themselves out there without anybody's help." And it's FREE! The price is the work you put into it. Calmentz of Ostrich Head adds, "It's the easiest way for a humongous audience to see our video and get exposure to the entire world fast." A video gives you a platform for your music that can reach people around the world.

What makes a video appealing?
It should be interesting and catch the viewer's eyes with your concept, look or performance. Nielson says, "Videos that make you laugh out loud or that are bizarre or simply brilliant get the most attention on YouTube. There is no real formula for a video to go viral, but original content and opinions are popular, as well as videos that express emotion and tell it like it is." Before doing a video, visit and look at the ones that are most popular to get ideas. The Channels area of the site has the most popular content and users with the largest audiences.

What was special about the winners of the contest?
Ostrich Head (Most Creative) made their video colorful and exciting, with a freak shows concept that alternates characters between normal and freaky. Maldroid (Best Video) used animation as a hook. Divine did it himself. Patrick Rickelton of Greenland (Best Song) says that the exuberance in their song and video makes people happy to watch it. Pawnshop Roses (Best Live Performance) filmed an edgy performance video.

Can you make a low-budget video?
Think creatively! Low budget doesn't mean poor quality. Kevin Bentley of Pawnshop Roses warns, "If you want to represent your band on YouTube, have something good. Don't just put anything on there." Film something professional looking that's worthy of your music. Nielson advises, "You don't need a slick and expensive music video to have success on YouTube. All you need is a little creativity and a camera to create something truly original." Michael Green of Greenland says they made their video with a small, borrowed camcorder, adding, "You need time and creativity. We definitely put in the work."

Can you make a video without experience?

Learn! Divine encourages, "I learned as I went. If you're willing to put the work in - it's very time consuming - you can learn how to put a video together. Take the time to learn how to do it right. You don't need a budget but you have to make it something desirable." Try to find someone to help if you have no experience. Post a notice in colleges that you're looking for someone to film your video. There are enough resources available to get a video done if you look. A video can be worth the effort of learning how to do it. Tres Crow of Greenland adds, "If people see a good video, they pay attention and think the band has something if they could put it together." You don't need a big budget to get creative and work hard!

How can you promote a video?

Let everyone know about it with emails and announcements at gigs. Encourage fans to forward it. Rickelton warns that people rarely find you accidentally, as there are so many. "You've got to tell them where it is and promote it as much as you can." Nielson recommends becoming part of the YouTube community to better understand what's happening on the site. You can watch videos, subscribe to your favorite channels, participate in discussions and upload content. She adds, "This is the best way to become a part of the community and help yourself rise up." Like with MySpace, you can go to videos for musicians in your genre that have a lot of comments and invite people who might enjoy yours to view it, one at a time.

Making use of your video

YouTube has become a live calling card. When you're booking gigs, send promoters to your video so they can see you in action. Calmentz recommends, "Instead of handing out DVDs to everyone, send them to YouTube." You can also embed the video on your MySpace page so friends can put links on their own pages. Make sure to include contact info so you're easy to reach. If you get a camera and are super creative, you can post a video on YouTube that gets people excited about your music. http://www.youtube.com Nielson advises, "Just get on the site and start creating videos that express your creativity and personality. You never know what will become a viral hit." Why not yours?

Ostrich Head (Calmentz aka Zach Arnet, Nowonder aka Steve Montez, Loreaxe aka Jaime Jorn, Mess E Recspin aka James Morgan, Say What aka Lyndsay Haldorson) http://www.youtube.com/watch?v=fGm-gwHwgcQ

Maldroid (Rasmus, Ryan Divine, I.Q., Todd Brown, Cpt. Sean Shippley) http://www.youtube.com/watch?v=FHGvh3i35Uk

Greenland: (Tres Crow, Matt Goetz, Michael Green, Evan James, Patrick Rickelton) http://www.youtube.com/watch?v=2P9EonMpzlM

Pawnshop Roses: (Paul Keen, Kevin Bentley, Justin Monteleone a.k.a Blaze, Rich "Figgs" Fogg) http://www.youtube.com/watch?v=5Gx6CGvDj74

Daylle Deanna Schwartz www.daylle.com is best-selling author of 8 books, including I Don't Need a Record Deal! Your Survival Guide for the Indie Music Revolution and Start & Run Your Own Record Label (Billboard Books). She does phone coaching/consulting for musicians and record labels, presents seminars, and publishes 2 free newsletters (music industry and self-empowerment). To subscribe send your name and city/state to daylle@daylle.com

♦

20 STEPS TO CREATING A SUCCESSFUL BLOG FOR YOUR BAND

by Lance Trebesch, TicketPrinting.com

Blogs prove to be a tricky field to conquer, especially when it comes to gaining an initial reader-base. However, once you get that reader base, great potential for increasing your online reputation is created. Successful blogs keep their status by following these 20 rules from the start and throughout their blog's lifetime.

1. Focus the topic

Thousands of different blogs exist on the web. Only the well-established ones can post general news and see success. Instead, focus your blog around a niche. The more narrow the subject, the more likely you will get a steady reader base.

2. Search similar blogs and subscribe

Because there are so many blogs on the internet, chances are somebody somewhere will also be talking about your subject. Find these sites and subscribe to them so you get instant updates. The best action to take is to read up on these blogs and know what they talk about regularly.

3. Create business relationships

By helping out someone else and their blog in some way, they will in return help you and your blog out. One good example is devising a list of online radio stations you can submit your music to and give them the list so they can use it for their benefit as well. By becoming business friends, you can promote each other by talking about one another's web page, music, blog etc.

4. Make quality content

Just writing a blog is not enough. You have to make sure what you are writing is good content. No one will comment or read your blog if the content seems worthless and poorly written. Also, write grammatically. Misspellings are one of the most painful things to witness in blogs.

5. Work on the title

The title is a necessity. The first thing people look at and what makes them read your blog is the title. Titles that hint of content with lists and bullets also draw people in due to the pleasing layout and more white space of lists. If the title perks their interest, they will click on your blog to continue reading. Take the time to think about an interesting title and log which titles draw more readers.

6. Submit to directories

After creating a good content-and-keyword-rich blog, submit it to different directories. Top Blog Area and BlogFlux are two good sites to submit blogs to according to category of blog. Another option is to write just one blog for an established blogging site in the rock music industry and tell them why they should feature your blog on their site. If they choose to put the blog on their site, you will see greatly increased traffic.

7. Get a friend to submit your blog to Digg, StumbleUpon, Technorati, Netscape, and Reddit

These search sites generate a ton of traffic to your site if viewed frequently (or "digged," "thumbs up" "favored," etc). However, people view down on you if you constantly submit your own content to these sites, so instead, make a buddy submit your blogs, videos, or podcasts to these sites one or two times a week. Eventually, your good content will make it to the homepage of these content-search sites, generating an unimaginable amount of traffic to your blog.

8. Ping every site

Some submission sites allow you to 'ping' them, which means they get an automatic update when you post a new blog. This is good so they always have your latest posts in their records. These sites also allow you to put in key tag terms. By inputting a tag term, your blog will pop up if someone searches for the term you used. For instance, if you are writing about electric guitar comparisons (tag terms) and the searcher inserts "compare guitars," your blog will show as a result. You must utilize pings and tags to increase your blog popularity.

9. Write regularly and stand out

The only way to gain a steady reader base is if you write a blog regularly. The best blogs update their content daily or sometimes several times a day. As an upcoming artist, though, weekly will suffice if you write on a consistent day around the same time every week. In addition, you need to stand out from other bloggers. Write properly, but use your personality. Personality keeps the blog interesting and keeps readers coming back. In addition, the readers like to be treated as humans, so drop the business lingo. Blogs are for entertainment, so engage your audience. Write for them.

10. Host your blog on your website domain

Using a different host for your blog not only confuses your readers, but also reduces the amount of quality traffic to your site. The only smart way to host a blog is through your own website. If readers like what they read,

...ing about your music in the blog, they can easily ...site to find out more information. Creating a blog ...of promoting your music online, which you can only do ...easily access your website from your blog.

...e to subscribe
...ow users to subscribe to your blog and receive an update when ...d new blogs. This makes it convenient for readers so they do not need to check for blog updates. An alternative is to send the updated blog through email, so having both an email subscription and a RSS feed is necessary. Also, make the sign-up process simple and prominent. Display the RSS button everywhere and occasionally mention it in your posts to sign-up. The simpler the process to sign-up, the more chance the reader will go through with the process.

12. Offer a bribe to sign-up
Take an example for Marketing Pilgrim, by offering a $600 cash giveaway by signing-up for a RSS feed. The code to register for the money is in an RSS-only message. Receiving $600 free is pretty convincing to sign-up. Other options to get people to sign up are free e-books related to your topic ("How to Get a Record Deal"), or send a personalized autographed picture of you or the band to those who sign-up.

13. Comment on forums. Comment on blogs. Comment on chats. And comment by providing a link back your blog
By injecting your opinion and showing your personality through these comments, people will notice you and want to find out more. Make sure the comments are meaningful and not just some form of spam to create a link back to you. People appreciate when an expert adds their knowledge, so write truthful comments that will help the audience. Comments are the biggest promotion of your blog in the beginning months of the blog.

14. Leave blogs open for discussion
If compiling a list, ask for comments to add their suggestions for the list. The 5 Rules of Social Media Optimization (SMO) blog by Influential Marketing Blog became instantly popular by people linking to it, posting comments and recommending the blog. After writing a general blog that does not include a list, ask a question at the end to encourage comments and blog discussion. The more, interesting discussion, the more people will link to your blog, promoting it.

15. Respond to comments
Read your comments daily and respond when someone asks a question to you through the comments. Once you start getting a steady reader base that begins posting comments, do not discourage them by never responding back. Respond rapidly to make your reader happy.

16. Start a podcast
A podcast is a great way to promote both your blog and your music. Podcasts are an audio blog, but you should not update it as often as your blogs (unless you just want to run an audio blog exclusively). On the podcast, talk about interesting subjects related to your blog and mention your music often. Play a fraction of your music just prior to and just after your podcast, promoting both your music and your blog.

17. Invite guest bloggers. Be a guest blogger
Your blog gains interest if you occasionally - monthly, quarterly - invite guest bloggers to write. Your business pals become a good place to start when thinking about guest bloggers. The guests then feel flattered by your interest in them and in return promote your blog or music. On the other hand, ask your business friends to guest blog for them, which immensely promotes your music or blog through their site. Whenever you get an opportunity to guest blog, take it.

18. Add videos, pictures, MP3s etc.
Just having words on every blog gets boring. Perk reader's interest by putting a funny YouTube video in your blog, adding a unique MP3 or taking a snapshot of the website you mention in the blog. Any item out of the norm to create a change will boost your blog's appeal. Every once in awhile, make your blog a video-blog through YouTube where you narrate the blog (and act as well). You can also create a music video for you or the band and advertise it through your blog.

19. Use tracking software and analyze
Find out how many people are visiting your blogs and which ones generate the most traffic. You should re-create titles and content that receives many views. The tracking software can also tell you how people are hearing about your blog, through Digg, Google, etc. It can give you a great insight on your viewers and many other marketing hints if you are creative.

20. Build a brand
You want people to recognize your blog as an object, not just another blog. Make your blog worthwhile to the reader. Promote the blog with any sources you have. Tell your friends, family and strangers about it. On your website, promote your blog and on your blog promote your website. Do the same with social networking sites, YouTube videos, podcasts, live performances, etc. By marketing in a bunch of different places, you spread your name and have more sources to promote your blog and music.

Your blog will only see success if you follow all these steps and promote it as often as possible. Blogging takes a lot of dedication but pays off in the end with increased music sales. Never stop blogging and remember, you are writing for your audience.

Lance Trebesch, CEO of TicketPrinting.com , has a successful 18 year track record of technology and early-stage experience. TicketPrinting.com is the leader in affordable online ticket printing for small-to-medium size organizations, companies, venues, non-profits, schools, associations, and clubs. Over the past 10 years, TicketPrinting.com has designed and printed millions of tickets for thousands of events, fundraisers, performances, concerts, plays, sporting events, raffles, parties and more. TicketPrinting.com has hundreds of ticket templates - just put in your event or raffle information and we print and ship in 24 hour. Or, our Design-Your-Own ticket online tool enables you to customize your ticket.

♦

WHAT IS THE KEY TO GETTING YOUR MUSIC INTO FILM, TV etc?
by Brent McCrossen, Audiosocket

Know the project
Many different films and TV shows have various musical themes running through them. A car driving down the street in a LA beach scene might have some hip-hop or a club scene may have some electronica and big beats blasting in the background. Still, common sense tells you that a movie taking place during the turn of the century isn't going to be using alternative industrial music and you probably won't be hearing any punk music either. There are certain times where there maybe an exception, but for the most part this rule is pretty reliable.

Have the goods
Increase your odds of placement by having good songs that are WELL recorded. Creating a great song is no easy task. It's takes taste, musicianship and sensibility. However, once you've done that, you need to assure that it's recorded well. Levels, the use of digital sounds, and mastering are all important parts of creating a well rounded product. You could have the best song in the world, but if it isn't well recorded it's not getting placed.

It's all in the Packaging
Music supervisors are busy people but they DO listen to music that is sent to them. However, you need to make their job easier. Put a post it note on the outside of the CD and list the feel and subject matter of the tracks.

for example....

Track 1. Style- Upbeat pop rock / Keywords- surfing beach life
Track 2. Style- Heavy driving rock / Keyword- loosing a loved one

Additionally, make sure the spine of your CD has your band (artist) name and defines your style. If you're a composer with a large catalog send a couple of CD's that showcase the different styles you've crafted, each CD in a certain genre.

Last but not least, remember to put your contact info on the post it note, and on the CD itself, or at least the liner notes. One sheets get lost. By assuring music supervisor can access all the information they need in one location you increase your odds of placement.

Grant it, this is just a snap shot of the process but the above listed are easy "keys" to successful music placement. By providing great songs that are well recorded, and packaging the material in away that is easy to reference you're well on your way to success.

Brent McCrossen is President of Audiosocket, a music licensing agency that represents music for placement in Film, TV, Advertising, Video Games and Web / Mobile media. For more info visit www.audiosocketmusic.com

distribution

PREPARING FOR DISTRIBUTION
by Daylle Deanna Schwartz, author of "The Real Deal"
© 2009 Revenge Productions. Reprinted with permission.

People who want to press up their music in order to sell it are most concerned about getting distribution. Your focus if you want to make money from your music, is to first take yourself seriously as a business. Whether you like it or not, outside of your circle of fans, you and your music are looked upon as products. If you prefer being idealistic, create and perform music for fun. But, if earning a living from your music is an eventual goal, developing a *business attitude* is critical.

What's necessary?
Read books on the biz and attend seminars if you can. Get a good picture of how the music industry operates. Network as much as possible to create a support system of folks you can call on for resources, advice and encouragement. While you shouldn't negotiate your own contracts, you should know enough to discuss the terms of one with your lawyer. Don't be one of those musicians who tell their lawyer, publisher, manager, etc., "Whatever you say." Gather enough knowledge so you can make informed decisions based on input from your representatives. Think of yourself as a professional. Even if you're only pressing up your own music, you're a record label. Act like one! Being responsible will max your chances of others wanting to work with you.

Getting distribution
Getting distribution isn't always a guarantee. You can ship 500 pieces and get them all back if you haven't been able to promote your product to a target audience. Distributors get records into stores. Most don't promote them. Stores tell me that records sell because people know the artist. Before taking in your product, distributors need to see that you have a market already interested in buying it. Creating a demand is what sells records. Distributors want you to have a handle on promotion before they work with your label. Once you have that, they'll want your product.

Do the groundwork
Until you identify your potential market and develop strategies for letting them know about your music, having distribution won't sell CDs. The most important thing you can do first is to target the group who might buy your product and figure out how to reach them. Distributors want product that will sell, and will *want* to work with labels that have artists with a buzz going. They don't care how good the music is if nobody knows about it.

It still amazes me how many folks come to me for consultations and aren't sure who is most likely to buy their music. They tell me since it's good music, everyone will buy. That usually means they have no clue and don't want to bother to figure it out. If you can't target your audience, play your music for people who work in record stores or other music related folks and ask for their honest feedback.

Your audience
Anyone may buy your CD, but promote it to the group more likely to appreciate it. Is it college students? Young adults? Teens? Baby boomers? Once you know that, what kinds of promotion will you do to make them want to buy your record? Figuring this out sounds simple at first but if it was, there would be a lot more records making big money independently. It is more than the music being great, for people to buy your CD. They need to hear your music to be enticed to buy it. How will you reach their ears? What will make them buy it? Figuring out a marketing plan can be the hardest part of putting out your music. Distribution is easy once you get this in place.

Create a demand
The best way to get your product into stores is to develop a story around your act first. Focus your energy on getting reviews, getting radio play (college and public radio are best to start with), selling product on your own, and increasing your fan base by touring. Create a demand, and then put together a one-page synopsis of the artist's story, known as a one-sheet. This has the artist's story - reviews and stories in the media (include quotes), radio play, gigs, direct sales, internet presence, etc, as well as details about the record itself. Include anything that shows the act is marketable, concisely on one sheet of paper. A small photo of the act and/or the album cover should be on the sheet too.

How to get in stores
Send you're one-sheet to potential distributors. Don't send a sample of the music until they request it. The story is more important than the music. Some distributors take calls if you want to try that first. But if their interest is piqued, they'll ask you to fax them a one-sheet. Be prepared. Don't approach distributors until you have a good foundation. Make them take you seriously the first time! Distributors are in the business of selling records. If they think yours will sell, they'll carry it. It's that simple. Start with a local distributor until your buzz gets stronger and you prove you can sell product on a wider scale. Then work your way up to larger ones.

Daylle is the best-selling author of Start & Run Your Own Record Label and The Real Deal: How to Get Signed to a Record Label. She also presents music industry seminars, does phone consulting for musicians and record labels and publishes Daylle's News & Resources, a free industry newsletter. daylle@daylle.com www.daylle.com

♦

25 THINGS TO REMEMBER ABOUT RECORD DISTRIBUTION
by Christopher Knab, author of "Music Is Your Business".
© 2009 All Rights Reserved. Used By Permission

1. Distributors will usually only work with labels that have been in business for at least 3 years, or have at least 3 previous releases that have sold several thousand copies each.

2. Distributors get records into retail stores, and record labels get customers into retail stores through promotion and marketing tactics.

3. Make sure there is a market for your style of music. Prove it to distributors by showing them how many records you have sold through live sales, internet sales, and any other alternative methods.

4. Be prepared to sign a written contract with your distributor because there are no 'handshake deals' anymore.

5. Distributors want 'exclusive' agreements with the labels they choose to work with. They usually want to represent you exclusively.

6. You will sell your product to a label for close to 50% of the retail list price.

7. When searching for a distributor find out what labels they represent, and talk to some of those labels to find out how well the distributor did getting records into retailers.

8. Investigate the distributor's financial status. Many labels have closed down in recent years, and you cannot afford to get attached to a distributor that may not be able to pay its invoices.

9. Find out if the distributor has a sales staff, and how large it is. Then get to know the sales reps.

10. What commitment will the distributor make to help get your records into stores?

11. Is the distributor truly a national distributor, or only a regional distributor with ambitions to be a national distributor? Many large chain stores will only work with national distributors.

12. Expect the distributor to request that you remove any product you

have on consignment in stores so that they can be the one to service retailers.

13. Make sure that your distributor has the ability to help you setup various retail promotions such as: coop advertising (where you must be prepared to pay the costs of media ads for select retailers), in-store artist appearances, in-store listening station programs, and furnishing POP's (point of purchase posters and other graphics).

14. Be aware that as a new label you will have to offer a distributor 100% on returns of your product.

15. You must bear all the costs of any distribution and retail promotions.

16. Furnish the distributor with hundreds of 'Distributor One Sheets' (Attractively designed summary sheets describing your promotion and marketing commitments. Include barcodes, list price, picture of the album cover, and catalog numbers of your product too.

17. Distributors may ask for hundreds of free promotional copies of your release to give to the buyers at the retail stores.

18. Make sure all promotional copies have a hole punched in the barcode, and that they are not shrink-wrapped. This will prevent any unnecessary returns of your product.

19. Don't expect a distributor to pay your invoices in full or on time. You will always be owed something by the distributor because of the delay between orders sent, invoices received, time payment schedules (50-120 days per invoice) and whether or not your product has sold through, or returns are pending.

20. Create a relationship that is a true partnership between your label and the distributor.

21. Keep the distributor updated on any and all promotion and marketing plans and results, as they develop.

22. Be well financed. Trying to work with distributors without a realistic budget to participate in promotional opportunities would be a big mistake.

23. Your distributor will only be as good as your marketing plans to sell the record. Don't expect them to do your work for you, remember all they do is get records into the stores.

24. Read the trades, especially Billboard for weekly news on the health of the industry, and/or the status of your distributor.

25. Work your product relentlessly on as many fronts as possible… commercial and non commercial airplay, internet airplay and sales campaigns, on and offline publicity ideas, and touring…eternally touring!

Christopher Knab is a music business Consultant, Author and Lecturer. He was recently honored by Seattle's Rocket magazine as "One of the Most Influential People in the Northwest Music Industry." Contact: www.4frontmusic.com, Chris@Knab.com

♦

SUCCEEDING WITHOUT A LABEL

by Bernard Baur, Music Connection Magazine
© 2009 All Rights Reserved. Used By Permission

DIY

Music Connection set out to see how realistic the independent route is, and if artists can find success on their own. We found that independent artists are very popular with music fans; and, that acts like *The Dave Matthews Band*, *Godsmack*, *Nickelback* and *The White Stripes* didn't depend on a record company to break them. They did it themselves and sold thousands of records, which naturally attracted hundreds of labels. Moreover, those who enjoyed independent success negotiated deals that were superior to the average deal most artists are offered.

To find out what it takes, MC contacted a variety of artists who took the "Do It Yourself" approach and are making it work. They are self-sufficient artists who found that they didn't need a label to live their dream. They prove that the DIY option is not only viable; it may also be the best

course of action. After all, who wouldn't like to call their own shots in a market that's up for grabs?

Choosing the road less traveled

Sitting in a label president's office suite can be surreal, especially when he's explaining what an artist needs to do to get signed. The list is so long (covering a variety of areas) so, you can't help but ask, " If an artist did all of that, why the hell would they need you?"

Well, some artists don't think they need an established label at all. Award winning artist, Aimee Mann, has had three major record deals but now says, "I can't recommend signing a label deal. Why should you give them all the power? Really, it's frustrating. You think labels are supposed to sell records, but they don't always do what they're supposed to so, why deal with them?" In response, Mann formed her own company, *Super Ego Records*, and became a poster girl for DIY success thanks to her Oscar-nominated song from the film *"Magnolia"* and the 200,000 units sold of her *"Bachelor No. 2"* album. Today, she claims to be happier than she ever was at a major. "Now, I have the freedom to do what I want, when I want. And, if any mistakes are made, I get to make them myself rather than have someone make them for me."

The independent mindset

It seems simple. You don't have to be signed to release a record. In fact, if you wait to be signed it could be a very long time according to Tim Sweeney, a consultant who specializes in independent artists. He not only presents workshops on DIY, but has also written books about it. Sweeney maintains, "Less acts are being signed nowadays, and of those that do get a deal only 1-3% will make it beyond a record or two before they get dumped."

DIY avoids that scenario, but artists need to be a special breed to do it right. According to Pat McKeon, former owner of *Dr. Dream Records* and general manager at *Ranell Records,* states, "An independent artist will have to wear more than one hat. When they first start out, they'll probably be doing everything themselves, and not every artist can handle that."

It is also important to understand how much work DIY truly is. K.K. Martin, an indie artist who survived several label deals intimated, "You have to learn about the business and pay attention to it. If you can't do that, find someone you trust, or you'll never progress."

Keeping' it real

If you want DIY success, you have to have realistic expectations. Nearly every artist dreams of playing The Forum or appearing on MTV. Unfortunately, that doesn't even happen to major label acts unless they have a hit and are extremely successful. Most independent artists have to set their sights a little lower. That's not to say it could never happen, because it does. But, the fact is you'd have to have fantastic connections or enjoy phenomenal success to reach that level.

"Keeping your goals realistic is essential for all independents," Moon points out. "If you don't do that, you're going to be disappointed." Moon suggests keeping it real and at a level you can achieve. "Set up small goals on a monthly, quarterly and yearly basis. Then, evaluate the results. If you reached your goals, move on – if not, figure out why."

Perhaps the greatest state of mind independent artists need is patience. Angus Richardson, of the band Brother, has known phenomenal success, selling over 150,000 records and playing almost 250 dates a year. Nevertheless, even Brother had to suck it up. " When we didn't get a quick record deal, it would have been easy to get discouraged," Richardson reveals. "But, we believed in our music, our fans and ourselves. And, the fact is," he stresses, "if you get hurt every time you're rejected in this business, you're going to have a lot of scars. Just look around at all the bands that have disappeared"

Touring is key

The most important part of the plan is playing live. Everything, including radio, promotions, distribution and marketing, should revolve around that, it's the way you sell records. Of course, you're going to need a recording, but according to Moon, it need not be up to industry standards. "Even a live recording will do," she says. "Your fans want to hear your songs, not the production."

Most artists have booked themselves before, so this area should be familiar. The difference is that you have to book gigs beyond your backyard. Sweeney suggests that artists should start by looking 2-3 hours in each direction. "That will only cost $30-40 in gas, and you should be able to make that in sales," he says. "If an act is based in Los Angeles, they can look as far as San Diego and Santa Barbara. Eventually, increase the drive time and even look at neighboring states. But, he warns, "don't try to do it all at once."

Naturally, when it comes to touring solo artists have it the easiest. Moon, Malone and Martin only occasionally bring a full band along. "It's a matter of economics as well as personal dynamics," Martin maintains. "Traveling in a van with five other guys can challenge your patience." To cut costs, Malone, who toured eight times across the country in three years, established a network of musicians he hires in each city. "That way," he says, "I only have to pay them for the gig."

Expenses on the road
If you're a real band, expenses become a concern. Tina Broad, Bother's manager, relates that their merchandise table is a critical part of their financial success. "If we didn't have product to sell we couldn't do it. Our merchandise sales (CDs and goods) have a dramatic impact on our ability to tour. Traditionally, we make 2 to 3 times more from our merchandise than we do from tour guarantees or ticket sales." Broad also advises bands to take a serious look at their hospitality riders. "Include things that you need (towels, water, food, backline, etc) so that you have fewer things to deal with, and insist on a 50% deposit so that you're not shouldering all the cash flow until the performance check clears."

Your bank
Touring, recordings, and merchandise obviously require money, and artists should be ready to dip into their own pockets. Sweeney contends that if artists aren't willing to invest in themselves, he questions how serious they are about a career. "However, if resources are severely limited, you just have to start smaller and think smarter," he says. "Find a sponsor to help with costs. Play free shows for them and put their name on your CD. " Moon suggests doing your own artwork or finding a friend who's talented. In fact, every independent artist who is successful uses a network of resources to help them defray costs.

Some, such as *Skywind*, a Minneapolis band who tours over 100 days a year and plays before 1000 or more fans, got their family and friends to loan them seed money. Bill Berry, their manager, indicates, "Everyone got paid back in just over a year. And since then," he relates, "We've been able to pick up sponsorships and lines of credit." Each band member contributes to pay off loans and, by doing this; Skywind has been able buy a van and tour three states.

The bottom line is that you're going to need a budget, so that you know what you can do. Indeed, Brother's manager, Broad advises artists to be realistic about costs. "If you don't know what your real expenses are," she informs, " you're going to be operating in a vacuum."

Art meets commerce
If you want to be an independent artist who's self-sufficient, don't deceive yourself: you are in business, and there are two parts to business – the legal side and the practical side. Legally, you must protect your interests and follow the law. Everyone agrees that you should consult with counsel when setting things up. You may need a band contract, a business license, and an assortment of other things that make you a legal entity.

On the practical side, keep accurate records of all your sales and income. Sweeney informs us that you can simply pay the tax on your sales, to obtain a verifiable record. These figures are all important if you hope to convince anyone – including a label, a distributor or a lender – to work with you. Indeed, Broad says it still makes her guts churn to think that Brother neglected to register the sales from their 2001 Summer Tour. "That was 15,000 unverifiable sales," she sighs. "We've got manufacturing records, but it's not the same."

Marketing & promotion
Mann contends that marketing and promotion is always a challenge, whether you're on a label or not. "It was my biggest cause for concern with every deal I had," she reports. "At least, now, I have the freedom and control to do it the way I want." But, when you're independent, you have to think outside the box. You cannot compete with the majors, so you have to do things differently.

McKeon points out, "All independent promotions must revolve around live gigs. That has to be your focus because it's your moneymaker. After booking gigs, you can contact press, radio and retail." Of all of them, radio is usually the most difficult, but persistence pays off.

Skywind's Berry relates that they maintained a two-year relationship with a local station before their songs were played. "We bought advertising time late at night because it's cheaper and played radio events for free. After they got to know us, they put our songs in rotation." Sweeney suggests attending station concerts and handing out free CDs. "It gets your music to their audience," he says.

Artists should also learn to cooperate with each other. Sweeney advises, "Artists should work towards a common goal, book shows together, share expenses and even buy commercial time on cable TV. Cable companies will sell 30-60 seconds for less than $100 and you can promote your act on MTV. If you run a few commercials a week before your show, you'll see tremendous results."

The distribution monster
Distribution is one of the biggest issues facing all independent artists. You need to stock your CDs wherever you play, but getting distribution isn't easy. For some artists, consignments may be the way to go. Many record stores will accept your CDs on spec and if they sell, will order more. "You might start with only 10-20 in a store, but if they move the orders will increase," Martin explains. "The only problem with consignment is that you have to keep on top of it on a regular basis."

Other artists, like Nashville songwriter, Hal Bynum, have found alternative markets. He reveals, "I've been a songwriter for 50 years, and it's still not easy to get distribution." So, Bynum created a unique package – a book and CD – that Barnes & Noble will carry. "I agreed to make in-store appearances and they agreed to promote me."

Start an organization or join one
Some artists set up their own organization. With the help of her New York manager, Michael Hausman, Aimee Mann founded *"United Musicians,"* a sort of cooperative for artists. Hausman explains, "We found that distributors don't like to work with a single artist. They want product every few months, so we set up *United Musicians* for other artists who may be in the same boat. *R.E.D.* agreed to distribute our records and we're sharing our contacts with artists."

If you're not quite to that stage yet, there are services to meet your needs. The independent network is full of companies that cater to independent artists, and one of the newest and most intriguing *is 101 Distribution.* Damon Evans, 101's executive director, describes his company as an alternative solution to traditional distribution. "We service over 2100 retail stores across the country and into Europe." Essentially, 101 take the work out of consignments. They give stores product on consignment, collect revenue and pay artists every 30 days. Their split with artists is generous (70-80% of wholesale) and they will handle promotions and marketing, unlike other distributors.

The ultimate reward
Of course, for some, whose music may not be mainstream, independence is their only choice; while for others it's by design. But, regardless of whether you're a maverick or an act still seeking a deal, the same rules apply. If you want success, you have to work for it. While DIY may be a lot of work, it can be very rewarding. "It is time consuming and takes a lot of patience but," Gilli Moon concludes, " there's nothing quite like having control over your own destiny. You can be as big or as small as you want and go at your own pace."

Ten steps to success for the independent artist
(All the artists profiled are self-sufficient. They make a living "solely" with their music. This list was compiled from their interviews.)

1. **Believe in yourself**
   You must believe in yourself. Realize that you don't need a label to be a success. Don't be egotistical, but be confident. Be optimistic – believe you are good enough and can get what you want. If you don't have faith in yourself – no one else will.

2. **Be realistic**
Do research – Get objective opinions - Identify your market. Know that you're going to have to tour. Know when to ask for help. Accept the fact that you probably won't become a star or get on MTV, but that you can make a living playing music.

3. **Make a wish list**
Create a Wish List – What do you ultimately want and how do you plan to get it? What are the things you need to do and how long will it take? Set reasonable goals and break your Plan into phases: 3 months – 6 months – 1 year – 3 years, etc…

4. **Know your budget**
If you're serious about a career, you're going to have to invest in yourself. Itemize your expenses and add 20%. Approach Sponsors with a detailed plan. Negotiate deals that take care of the basics: travel, food, lodging, backline, etc... And, don't forget manufacturing and promotional costs.

5. **Take care of business**
Remember – it is the music "business." Network as much as possible; organize a team, with each person responsible for a specific area. If you're solo, manage your time wisely. Get your own Bar Code. Seek professional advice to set up your business entities. Pay attention to licenses and tax implications. When you tour, get insurance.

6. **Market yourself**
Think creatively. Make time for "personal appearances" before your gigs. Set up cross-promotions with radio stations, sponsors, venues, and retail stores. Make sure you have enough products to sell – both CDs and merchandise. Offer promotional contests. Play Special Events. Work your mailing list and keep in touch with your fans at least once a month.

7. **Keep records**
Keep books that reflect income and expenses. Accurately account for sales. Register and report to SoundScan. Maintain tax records. Record your draw – note the venue/locale that draws best. Keep updating your mailing list.

8. **Adapt & adjust**
Evaluate results: What works – What doesn't? Revise your plan and adjust your approach accordingly. Find ways to increase your fan base and make a profit. What can be done better?

9. **Keep the faith**
No matter how hard you work, there will be frustrating times. Keep the faith and don't let it deter you. Everyone experiences setbacks. Those that persevere will prevail.

10. **Make it fun**
If it's not fun anymore – don't do it. Reward yourself (and your team) whenever possible. Acknowledge a job well done. Take a break – enjoy life – then, get back to work.

Bernard Baur is the Review Editor & Feature Writer for Music Connection Magazine. Contact: www.musicconnection.com, Tel: 818-755-0101 Ext.519 EqxManLtd@aol.com

the music business

10 KEY BUSINESS PRINCIPLES
by Diane Rapaport, author of "A Music Business Primer"
© 2009 Reprinted with permission.

Given two bands (or two businesses) that have equal talent, the one that incorporates the business principles below will often have a competitive edge.

Business principles to follow

1. Get to know the people you work with personally. Go out of your way to meet them.
2. Make it easy to for people to associate with your business.

- Show up for gigs and appointments on time
- Keep promises you make
- Phone people back in a timely manner
- Have a positive attitude
- Pay your bills on time. If you cannot, call people up and explain your situation.
- Be nice to secretaries and receptionists. Often the "gatekeepers" for access to their bosses.
- Develop long-term relationships with service vendors.
- Key business people have few minutes to listen. State what you want succinctly and politely.
- Say thank you. Forgive easily. Anyone can make a mistake.

3. Treat your employees courteously, pay them a fair wage, be appreciative of their good work, and when you can afford it, reward them with bonuses and other benefits. They'll repay you with loyalty and good work. Retraining a new employee costs time and money.

4. Listen to the needs of the people and businesses you work with. Find out what is important to them.

5. Do every job and every gig as though it mattered.

6. Provide value added to people you do business with. This can mean everything from playing an extra encore, having special prices for CDs for fans who buy them at gigs; sending out a free newsletter once a month; providing one free CD for every ten a customer buys; and sending favored vendors free goods.

7. Keep track of your money. Negotiate for better rates. Keep business debt to a minimum. Pay your loans on time.

8. Cultivate a good reputation. Be principled in your dealings. Leadership in ethics and good conduct will be rewarded many times over in loyalty, in people speaking well of your business, and, perhaps most importantly, of people you do business with dealing fairly and ethically with you. If you examine the histories of people who are constantly being taken advantage of or stolen from, you will almost invariably find that their business conduct invited it.

9. Good advice is invaluable, and, often freely given. Learn to invite advice. Feedback is important, even when it is negative. Receive criticism with neutrality and graciousness.

10. When you are successful, give something back to the industry that has served you. Share information with other bands. Donate time or profits to a nonprofit organization.

This article is from Diane Rapaport's book, "A Music Business Primer", published by Prentice Hall (Pearson Education). Diane Rapaport is also the author of How to Make and Sell Your Own Recording. Her company, Jerome Headlands Press, designs and produces The Musician's Business and Legal Guide; and The Acoustic Musician's Guide to Sound Reinforcement and Live Recording by Mike Sokol. Contact: jhpress@sedona.net

♦

WHAT MAKES A WINNING MUSIC BUSINESS STRATEGY?
by Kavit Haria, Music Business Consultant
© 2009 All Rights Reserved. Used By Permission

I asked myself this crucial question when writing my latest e-book, "What are the important skills and practices required to create a winning and profitable music business apart from good music?"

The answer rests in being a good leader of your ship, having a well-designed and communicated strategy and a good marketing plan that can be executed to promote your music in a structured way.

If you re-read that last paragraph, you'll see how much I emphasize the idea of strategy and structure. It is with this careful planning and well-understood principles that your music business will become profitable.

Strategy
A strategy comes to life through its ability to influence hundreds and thousands of decisions, both big and small, made by anyone from the

director level to the street team level. It is, at its core, a guide to how you behave and provides an external reflection of your music business.

A good strategy fuels and ignites your fire to more compelling actions and results. It leads you to a destination that is clear in your mind. A bad strategy on the other hand leads you to a less competitive, less differentiated position. It is simply a waste of time and energy as it does not move you forward; instead, it keeps you where you're already at.

The word "winning" is important in this context. An average strategy plan, when executed, gets you mediocre results and may not be a fair reflection of your true talent. A winning strategy plan on the other hand transforms your current situation into monster success through developing the right tools, people, techniques and street teams to share your art with the wider world.

As musicians, we are explorers. As explorers, our job is to explore the depths of our hearts and souls to share the music that feels most at home to us. Our job is to experiment, and experimentation takes time before it is successful.

Your music business needs a framework for achieving results that can be built upon to achieve your specific goals in your specific music genre. When you start to put together a puzzle, you would start by finding the corners and the edge pieces before building and assembling the inner pieces. It is the same with putting together the framework for your music business.

Constructing a music business plan is the first step in gaining clarity and direction in what you'll do, how often you'll release an album, how you'll market your music and how you'll make money. The framework of your music business is what holds it all together - the operations, the marketing, the management and the finances. Let's look at each one separately.

Operations plan
Your business operations is the activities your music business will do in order to share your music. These are usually gigs (what type of gigs?), recording (how often? when?), distribution (whom? how?), sponsorship, and other avenues of generating revenue.

Marketing plan
The activities and tactics you will undertake to promote your music through your music business. These may include PR, social networking on Facebook, Myspace, etc, blogging, podcasting, video blogging, flyer and poster marketing, etc.

Management plan
Who will form your core team for your music business and what will they do? Regardless of whether you have the capacity to get these people involved, knowing what you want is core to getting a framework to build your music business.

Finance plan
Knowing what money goes out and what comes in is crucial to understanding how your music business can be successful. My accountant often tells me that the success of my business is equal to how well I can understand the numbers on my cash flow sheet. He is right and I pass this advice on to you.

Kavit Haria is founder and consultant at Inner Rhythm, a London-based music business consultancy providing workshops, courses and consulting to musicians looking to develop better strategies, marketing and music business success. He writes a free weekly Musicians Development Newsletter to over 10,000 musicians worldwide. For more information visit: www.innerrhythm.org

STOP BURNING BRIDGES…OR YOUR CAREER MIGHT GO UP IN FLAMES!
by Sheena Metal, Music Highway
© 2009 All Rights Reserved. Used By Permission

Hey, nobody said the music business was going to be easy. It truly is a jungle out there filled with: snakes, rats, rabid carnivores, sharks…well, you get the picture. In the course of your musical journey, there will be confrontations, arguments, misunderstandings, and miscommunications. You'll get jerked around, screwed over, ripped off and disrespected. So, you want to be a rockstar? Welcome to your nightmare.

But this is also a business of good people, who'll give you opportunities and chances and help you out when you least expect it. That's why it's so important that you, as musicians and as a band, act professionally and respectfully regardless of the behavior of those you encounter. You don't have to be a pushover and of course, you have a right to defend yourself against the questionable actions of others, but the music community can be a very small town and the behavior you exhibit will follow you throughout your musical career.

On the flipside of that, there are musicians out there who, either knowingly or unknowingly bring negativity on themselves through their own actions. Short temperedness, egocentricism, brazen entitlement, compulsive lying and just plain old psychotic behavior can brand your band as troublemakers and deprive you of important opportunities that you need to move forward in this business.

So, how can you make sure that you're doing onto others as you wish they would do onto you? What can you, as musicians do, to eliminate aspects of your personality that may be causing bad blood between you and the people you run across on your way to superstardom?

The following are a few tips that may help you to make sure you're exhibiting professional behavior at all times.

Be timely and courteous
Whether you're playing out live or emailing booking inquiries from home, there is never a substitute for courteously or timeliness. At gigs, show up when you're supposed to, be friendly, treat others with respect, set up quickly, end your set on time, break down quickly, be mindful of other bands on stage, compliment those around you and don't forget simple things like, "please" and "thank you." When you leave a positive impression in people's minds, you'll be high on their list when it comes time to fill an open booking slot, recommend a band for a review, etc.

Make sure your actions match your words
It's such a simple thing but you'd be surprised how many musicians seem incapable to doing what they say they're going to. If you book a gig, show up and play. If you say you're going to bring twenty friends and fans to your gig, do it. If you reserve an ad in a local music magazine, pay for it. If you write a check, make sure that it doesn't bounce. If you say you're going to send out a press package or a CD, mail it. It is true that many people in the music business are distrustful of bands that they don't know, and with good reason in many instances. Build your good reputation in the industry by proving that you will do what you've promised. Start small. Once you've gain people's trust, you'll see more and more doors opening up for your band.

Take the high road
It may be tough but there's nothing to be gained from returning someone's improper behavior with a heap-load of your own. That doesn't mean that you need to let every industry slime-bag from New York to LA ride roughshod all over your music project but there are ways to deal with the negative behavior in this business without branding yourself with a label equally as negative. Sending firm yet professional letters, making intelligent and informed phone inquiries and, if need be, taking legal action against those who have acted inappropriately are ways to handle unpleasant situations without drawing negative attention to yourself. Public scenes, yelling and screaming, long-winded and ranting emails, threats and accusations and spiteful actions may make you feel vindicated but it may chase away the good people as well as the bad and that just sets your band back.

You can't undo what you've already done

It's much harder to undo past bad behaviors, or reverse negative reputations than it is to foster positive ones. It's best when starting out to avoid acting rash as a rule. If you have a band member that is incapable of keeping his or her cool, perhaps it's time to rethink his or her place in your group. The entertainment industry has a long memory and a spiteful tongue. Make sure when people speak of you, they're speaking well.

This may all seem like such common sense that it isn't even worth mentioning but you'd be surprised how many shows, interviews, tours, and record deals have never materialized because of burned bridges. You may have talent and great tunes, but if your attitude sucks you'll get passed over time and again. No one wants to work with rage-aholics, egomaniacs or crazies. Don't let anyone think that's what your band is about. Sure it's important to be creative geniuses but if no one likes you, you'll be performing your masterpieces in the garage for grandma and her Pomeranian. Get smart and treat people right and you may find yourself rockin' all the way to the bank.

Sheena Metal is a radio host, producer, promoter, music supervisor, consultant, columnist, journalist and musician. Her syndicated radio program, Music Highway Radio, airs on over 700 affiliates to more than 126 million listeners. Her musicians' assistance program, Music Highway, boasts over 10,000 members. She currently promotes numerous live shows weekly in the Los Angeles Area, where she resides. For more info: www.sheena-metal.com

♦

FINDING A SPONSOR
by Bronson Herrmuth, author of "100 Miles To A Record Deal"
© 2009 All Rights Reserved. Used By Permission

Success in the music business is about separating yourself from the pack. One of the quickest and most effective ways to do this as an artist is to find sponsors. Unless you live in some unpopulated remote region of the world, then you are probably surrounded by plenty of potential sponsors for your music. Basically any individual, company or corporation doing business in your area is a possible sponsor. All it really takes is them wanting to sponsor you, and then you feeling good about promoting whatever the product is that they make, sell, or distribute. In a nutshell that is how a sponsorship works. Your sponsor "supports" you and in return you promote their product.

How does a sponsor support?

A sponsor can support you in many different ways, depending on their product and how active they are in promoting it. To give you a real-life example, my band once had a sponsorship with Budweiser through a regional distributor who we met through a club owner friend after we played his club. We were invited to this distributors warehouse where we were given t-shirts, ball caps, fancy mugs, stickers, etc., all kinds of Budweiser merchandise including several cases of their beer. They paid to have a big banner made with our logo on it, done very professionally and to our satisfaction. We would hang it up behind us whenever we performed. In one corner of the banner it said "Budweiser presents" with their logo and then our logo, much bigger and more prominent. None of this cost us a dime and being sponsored by Budweiser definitely gave us an edge up on our competition when it came time to get gigs in the clubs.

How do you find a sponsor for your music?

1. Target the businesses that actively promote their product on your local radio stations or TV, the ones that are already showing their desire and ability to promote their product effectively in your area, city or town.

2. Call or just stop by their location and meet them. Do your homework first to find out who are in charge, then make an appointment and go meet them. Chances are you may already know them if you live in a small town or city. Maybe someone you know, like a friend or a family member, already has a relationship with him or her. Use any and all connections you have to get started.

3. If they run radio spots and you have original music already

professionally recorded, see if they are open to using your music for the background music "bed" in their radio promotions.

4. If you are a songwriter, write them a song. This can be tremendously effective as a starting point to approaching a potential sponsor. Walk in and play them a song you wrote about them and their product.

5. Car dealerships are great places to start looking. Many bands are riding down the road right now in a vehicle that was provided by their sponsor. Good chance that there name or logo is professionally painted on that vehicle too, along with their sponsor's. Car dealerships also do lots of promotions and events where they have live music for their customers. Even if you approach them for a sponsorship and they decline, making them aware of you and your music can turn into some great paying gigs on a consistent, long-term basis.

6. Radio stations can be awesome sponsors. Many radio stations produce and promote concerts and in most cases use local or area talent to open these concerts, not to mention all the free radio exposure you can get if they sponsor you, or even if they just like you. If you have a record out, having a radio station for a sponsor can really help you get exposed in your immediate area quickly. Approach the ones that play your style of music.

Bronson Herrmuth is author of the new book "100 Miles To A Record Deal". For more details please visit him @ www.iowahomegrown.com, or www.songrepair.com

m o t i v a t i o n a l   a r t i c l e s

BE COMMITTED!...YOU'LL NEVER BE FAMOUS IF YOU DON'T SHOW UP!
by Sheena Metal, Music Highway Radio
© 2009 All Rights Reserved. Used By Permission.

Everyone wants to be famous: live in a mansion, drive a sports car, tour the world in your private plane, date a model, float around in the pool while collecting royalties for CD sales, and drink beer right out of your private tap. But not everyone is aware that, with any career that has the potential to end in a bounty of riches and beautiful babes, climbing your way to rock stardom is very hard work.

So, how does your average musical genius go from penniless Pop Tart-eater to Lifestyles of the Rich and Famous? How do you move on up from mom's garage to a deluxe apartment in the sky? What's your first baby step on the Yellow Brick Road to fame and fortune? That's simple…be committed!

It sounds silly, but many a musical boat has sailed with a crestfallen unsigned artist standing confused on the dock, for lack of nothing else but follow-through. Commitment to your deeds and plans is the single most essential skill towards achieving your goal of Ultimate Superstardom. Entertainment is a fickle business and chances don't come along every day. One missed opportunity now could have spiraled into dozens even hundreds of opportunities down the line.

It may be true that talent is a gift you carry with you from birth, but commitment is a learned skill that you need to hone every day. So, how can you make sure that you've got what it takes to gather up your supreme musicality and conquer the universe with it continuously?

The following are a few tips that may help you to make sure that you're truly committing yourself to your musical career on a daily basis:

Follow up on all leads

No matter how insignificant they may seem at the time, it's important to follow up on every musical lead that's thrown your way. Letters, calls and emails should be answered politely and in a timely fashion. New contacts should be logged in your address book for future correspondence. Opportunities should be taken, invites accepted, and chances to network relished. By starting out with just these simple rules you'll watch your resources and mailing list grow. Suddenly you'll have music community friends with which to share your leads and ideas, ask advice, trade experiences, and combine talent and energies. Through these friends, you'll meet new friends and fans and from them even more new connections. Soon, you'll have so many opportunities that your concern will change from lack of opportunity to lack of time in the day to pursue each new chance.

Just show up

Sounds so simple it's stupid, but you'd be surprised how many talented people have fallen by the wayside because they were unable to simply show up. Cancelled gigs, forgotten meetings, and missed auditions say to the Musical Powers That Be, "I'm a huge flake who doesn't think your opportunity is worth a half-hour of my precious time." This is a really bad thing. Entertainment is a small town with a huge memory. Don't give people any reason to think that you're not the person they want to work with, give the job to, book for the gig, sign to their label, write about, talk about, and help any way they can. Remember there are tens of thousands of musicians waiting to take your place, so step up to the plate and seize each chance with optimism and enthusiasm.

Take initiative

Don't wait for opportunities to come to you. The world is a virtual cornucopia of information, so reach out and nab yourself some chances at stardom. Comb the internet, join music communities, visit open mic nights, take classes and workshops…put yourself out there where there are cool musical happenings and let others know that you can be relied upon and want to be involved. By going out and seizing your own opportunities, you may double, triple, etc. your resources and chances, and expedite your journey to success.

Do the best job you can

As important as it is to show up, it is also essential that you come off efficient, talented, and professional when faced with a new opportunity. Being there is half the battle but the other half is being the best that you can be and impressing industry, press, clubs and your fellow musicians enough to make them want you to be involved in anything and everything they do. Make a commitment to put on the best live show possible, to have a terrific CD, to make a professional presskit, and to spread the word about your music. Be punctual, be courteous, be positive and be fun. Don't give anyone any reason not to work with you again and you'll see that it becomes easier and easier to get what you want for your artistic career.

It really is as easy as simply showing up, following up and giving it your all. Making it in music is not impossible; it's just a lot of elbow grease, a little organization, a bit of strategy, and the simple sculpting of your talent into a marketable commodity. There are thousands of chances offered every day to musicians…reach out and grab them by the handful, make every opportunity your own, get everything you want from this business and when you're richer than Oprah and more famous than Madonna, remember that it was you who made it happen. You were a pro. You showed up. You committed.

Sheena Metal is a radio host, producer, promoter, music supervisor, consultant, columnist, journalist and musician. Her syndicated radio program, Music Highway Radio, airs on over 700 affiliates to more than 126 million listeners. Her musicians' assistance program, Music Highway, boasts over 10,000 members. She currently promotes numerous live shows weekly in the Los Angeles area, where she resides. For more info: www.sheena-metal.com

♦

LEAVE YOUR DRAMA AT HOME: MORE ROCKIN' AND LESS SQUAWKIN'!

by Sheena Metal, Music Highway Radio
© 2009 All Rights Reserved. Used By Permission

No matter how we, as human beings, live our lives ... drama happens. And the average musician has more drama than the crazy cat lady down the block has bags of used litter on her porch. At every turn, your average wannabe rockstar has a crazy squeeze, a crazier ex, a harem of would-be lovers, and a gaggle of insane stalkers. Then there's the band drama, manager drama, club drama, fan drama, gear drama, and let's not even get

started on the online drama potential. Before you know it, your band makes "Desperate Housewives" look like 60 Minutes.

Certainly, no one ever said that music was going to be a safe, secure and solid profession to get into. Any industry that pays buckets of money to young, pretty people for jumping around and showing off is bound to inspire zaniness to some degree or another. And the creative process often brings with it a certain amount of tortured genius that fuels the seeds of drama like miracle grow on weeds. Plus, there are more than twenty million musicians around the world that are clamoring for maybe a thousand record deals like contestants on "Survivor" running obstacles courses for a single meager chicken wing. If there was a country built on drama, a musician would be its queen.

However, as much as the music biz is filled with glitz and glamour and the stuff that tabloid headlines are made of, it is also a business. And if there's one thing you don't want in the middle of your business, it's drama. There's a reason why doctors don't fight over dying patients about their golf scores, pilots don't announce to a plane full of passengers that they've been dating the stewardess, and the chef doesn't come to tell you he forgot to wash his hands before he cooked your four-star meal…drama does not belong in business. Whether you're aspiring to get a record deal or searching for a cure for cancer, leave your drama at home!

The following are a few tips that will help you to navigate the gossip and erratic turbulence of life in the music industry without becoming a slave to your own drama:

Don't let the internet suck you in

Every since the invention of the internet, there's been more drama in cyberspace than at a convention for bipolar drag queens. It's easy to gossip and backbite while you can stay anonymous, so the internet has becoming a breeding ground for anyone and everyone with an agenda, an out-of-control jealousy problem, an axe to grind, or an unbelievable ego. Angry, upset, small-minded people with inferiority complexes like size of Shamu will use the internet to poke at your band with a cyber stick. As hard as it may be, you need to learn to let it all roll off your back. As long as they're posting about you, it means they're listening. Removing their inflammatory posts, or replying with similar negativity, feeds the drama until your entire message board is about the trouble-maker on your web site and not your music. What if a potential magazine reviewer or an interested label rep is perusing your page with interest only to find more info about your fight with some internet psycho than about your band? It's not worth risking a loss of opportunity to engage in drama.

Drama doesn't belong at your gigs

When you're at a show, your goal is to make music, engage the audience, sell CDs, and win the club over so that you can play there again and again. People make room in their schedules, pay for gas, and fork out cash for a cover charge and bar priced drinks, just to hear you play your songs for them. They want to be entertained; to get away from the pressures of their real lives and escape into the safety and excitement of your music and lyrics. What they don't need is more drama at your gigs then they get from their office co-workers, their wacky neighbors, and bully at their kids' school combined. Whatever problems you're having in your personal and professional life, keep it away from your fans and your industry contacts or they'll start to remember your shows more for the drama than for the music.

Your manager is not your therapist

Although a manager's professional duties make them almost like the band's parent, don't cry to mommy every time the drummer calls you a name or your girlfriend decides she wants to play the field. There is too much music industry drama that your manager has to deal with every day, to add to his/her troubles by piling a heap of your personal woes on top of his/her already overburdened shoulders. If a club owner stiffs you at the door, tell your manager. If another band records one of your songs without permission, tell your manager. If your wife compulsively flashes her breasts at your shows, send her to a therapist, but leave your manager out of it.

Take the crazymakers off your mailing list

A lot of damage control can be done simply by eliminating from your mailings the nuts that show up and bring their own boatload of drama. If you know that your ex has never gotten over you, that she's off her meds and that she likes to show up and start swinging at every girl she thinks is catching your eye…why would you invite he to your shows? Comb your address book with a big, black sharpie pen and ink out the stalkers, crazies, attention-getters, and overblown drunkards that will turn each and every one of your gigs into a three-ring circus of drama that you're forced to ringmaster from the stage during your set.

Once you remove the drama from your musical career, you'll find that your gigs go smoother, your website is a more positive place for fans to hang in cyber space, and the industry is less wary about getting behind what you're doing. It may seem silly, but too much drama can often be a warning sign that something is really wrong with a band and you may find that industry types will become gun shy around your band if they're worried that your reputation as drama queen will be more trouble than it's worth. Working in the music business is hard enough. Don't give anybody any reason not to work with you. Be smart. Leave your drama at home and show the industry that your music is what's most important to you and your band.

Sheena Metal is a radio host, producer, promoter, music supervisor, consultant, columnist, journalist and musician. Her syndicated radio program, Music Highway Radio, airs on over 700 affiliates to more than 126 million listeners. Her musicians' assistance program, Music Highway, boasts over 10,000 members. She currently promotes numerous live shows weekly in the Los Angeles area, where she resides. For more info: www.sheena-metal.com

◆

DEALING WITH REJECTION IN THE MUSIC BUSINESS
by Suzanne Glass, Indie-Music.com

Being a musician, by and large, is a rewarding thing. We get to indulge our muse, spend time with other artistic types, and hear a lot of great sounds. When it comes to jobs, being a musician is great work if you can get it. Unfortunately, it's not all roses. The tremendous amount of competition makes it likely that we will sometimes lose a gig, get fired from a band, or be turned down for a songwriting award. Most of us handle the rejections pretty well most of the time. However, problems can start to occur if you have a run of too many rejections in too short a time. Musicians may begin to doubt their talent, commitment, and even sanity when repeatedly slapped with "no's".

Tips to help you through the hard times:

1. Believe in your music and yourself. People tell you this all the time, and you need to take it seriously. Many mega-hit songs were repeatedly rejected before someone decided to release them to become #1 hits. Believe that your talent is unique, and continue to pursue your own musical path.

2. If you hear the same type of rejection often, ("You need to pick up your choruses" or "Work on your pitch"), you may want to look into the criticism. Having an open mind may help you improve your craft.

3. If you get down on music, take some time out. Go to the beach, the mountains, or your backyard, and do something enjoyable that has nothing to do with music.

4. Give yourself the freedom to quit. This may sound contradictory, though by giving you a mental "out", it can help diffuse the pressure when nothing is going right. Chances are you won't quit, but you will know you have a choice.

5. Go jam with some musician friends who do it just for fun, and forget the business. People who strictly do music as a hobby sometimes have a positive energy that will help your jaded, negative energy slip away, and bring you back to the joy of playing music.

6. If you are in a situation where you can't find a band to jam with, and have excess creative energy, consider another type of art or craft. Doing something creative, even though it's not music, will keep your

creative juices flowing. Painting, carving, candle making - activities like these may also open your creative flow and inspire you musically.

7. If the problem is due to a conflict in your band, talk it out honestly with the people involved instead of keeping it to yourself and becoming cynical. Conflicts are common in bands (and every other kind of group), and surviving them means the difference between success and failure, since most bands will break up if the unresolved conflicts are not addressed. It will NOT be a pleasant experience.

8. Write a song about it. Who knows, it might be a masterpiece.

9. Think back on all your successes and good times in music, and focus on that energy. Try to balance the current bad times by realizing it's all part of the flow.

10. If you can't kick the down feelings in a few weeks, don't hesitate to talk to your doctor. Artists are known to have high rates of depression and stress-related illnesses, and today there are many new treatments. Make sure you follow a healthy diet and get some exercise.

Getting through those periods when "music sucks" is an experience all musicians have been through at one time or another. Those that master the down times go on to have productive musical careers. Those that get bogged down in the problems and become bitter are doomed to less happy - and maybe less musical - futures.

Suzanne Glass is the founder of Indie-Music.com, one of the Internet's premier musician websites. The company offers thousands of resources and contacts to achieve success in the music industry, including venues, labels, radio, media, studios, and band listings, plus articles, interviews, and reviews of indie music. Contact: www.indie-music.com

◆

BABY STEPS AND THE ROAD TO SUCCESS
By Chris Standring, A&R Online

"If you can achieve one successful thing a day to help your music career on the right path then you are on the right track".

It's very easy to sit at home and get frustrated with the apparent lack of forward movement in your music career. Especially when you know in your heart that you have what it takes to succeed. It's very easy to get discouraged, for the simple reason that it seems "you are only as good as your last event". Musicians and actors are similar in that we like the highs that our performances give us. We thrive on the exhilaration. It's like a drug. When it goes away we want it again.

All about perception
Gearing up to a live event is exciting. We can talk it up to friends and fans, promote it the best way we know how and enjoy the thrill of the performance itself. Then it is over and there may be a lull between events. It can seem like your career is going nowhere. It's very easy to feel that. However, other people's perception may be entirely different and probably is.

The music business is all about perception. It is based on hype and salesmanship ability. I wish it was different but it is not and will never ever be. If your band is perceived to be doing well then people will talk. If your band is perceived to be on the way out then people will also talk. If your band is doing nothing, nobody will talk! It is therefore extremely important that you keep the hype factor up. This is one of the things you need to be focusing on between events. Sit back and think about what you clearly have achieved so far in your career. Think about the things that were absolutely in your control.

Take baby steps
We are constantly bombarded with new creative marketing ideas, most of them excellent, inventive and effective. However, the ideas that you personally will primarily adopt are those ideas that you are totally comfortable with. These are the things that you will make a priority. It's too easy to get overwhelmed with new promotional ideas so we put them off

and resort to the things we know we can do. I have two words to give you. BABY STEPS.

How not to get overwhelmed

It's just too damn hard to do every new promotional idea to get your band to the next level at the same time. This is especially true, if you don't have a team of people working with you. Start by doing just one thing today. If you can achieve one successful thing a day to help your music career on the right path then you are on the right track. So the key is to pick one thing, and do it today!

Increase your fan-base

The only way you can get successful as an independent artist is by letting people know you exist. So ask yourself for example, "What can I do today to expand my fan-base?" Well, there are infinite possibilities. Let's say you want to increase your e-mail database. Think about the most effective ways you can do that. The most effective ways to build a database, (but more importantly get those people to be fans and come to shows), is to personally get to know them. So start with friends, have them refer their friends, and so on. Hand out flyers and sample CD's or tapes to everyone you know. (Make sure you have a good stack in your car.) Grab business cards of all the people you meet and get their e-mail addresses. Send them a very personal e-mail asking them if they would be interested to know about your band.

An overview

Be creative, DO something that you know you can personally do, to expand other people's awareness of you. It takes a good amount of time but you can help yourself by really being active and productive.

Read everything you can about promoting your own shows and do the things that you are most comfortable doing, the things that you know you can be effective at. Then, step out and try something new.

Do one thing a day to help get to where you want to be, and at the end of each week think about what you have achieved. There is nothing that fuels drive, more than drive itself. There's nothing that fuels lethargy more than sitting at home wishing you were successful and doing little about it!

It can be extremely overwhelming when there seems such a long way to go. So take it one step at a time. That's all truly successful people ever did.

Chris Standring is the CEO and founder of A&R Online www.aandronline.com). He is also a contemporary jazz guitarist presently signed to Mesa/Bluemoon Records. The music is marketed at NAC and Urban AC radio. For more info visit Chris @ www.chrisstandring.com

♦

SO HOW DO WE MAKE OUR DREAM BECOME REALITY?

by Janet Fisher, Director of Goodnight Kiss Music
© 2009 All Rights Reserved. Used By Permission

Define the dream

What is it you are actually trying to do? Be the world's best writer? Become a megastar performer? Lead the church choir? Own a record label that records other acts? You would not believe how many writer/artists come to me, saying they just want to do "something" in the Music Industry. Sorry, you have to specialize a bit more than that!

Sit down with paper and pen. Define EXACTLY what it is in your heart that you dream of. (Hint, the bigger the dream, the harder to achieve... but as long as you are prepared to give what it takes, you'll find a place in the scheme of things.

Research the dream

Let's say you decided that you want to be a great writer, who is successfully cut on the charts, and makes a lot of money. Do you know what the real charts are? Who's on them currently? What labels are consistently charted? What are the styles of the top ten successes been in the last two years?

Do you know what the actual elements of a great standard song are?

Can you name the top sellers of all time in your genre, or the top sellers of the current year? How did they attain success? Do you hone your skills and knowledge whenever you have a chance? Can you make the presentation of your art a commercial reality? Not just WILL you, CAN you?

Practice the dream

Go do 150 sit ups without practice. Go write a great song without practice. You have to practice (i.e., actually write) everyday, just like you would with any improvement program. If the newest song you are showing is old, you are not competing as a writer.

Rewrite the dream

If something doesn't go the exact direction you thought it should have, rewrite the situation. If it's the song that has flaws, rewrite it until they are gone. If it's the voice, get some training.

If it's the gig, create one that works for you (when I was playing gigs in KCMO, I went to the Plaza, to nice places that DIDN'T have entertainment. I'd offer the owner a free evening of music, if he liked it, I'd work X amount of weekends for X amount per night. I almost always got the gig, partly because I was prepared, partly because few can resist something for nothing and not sense some obligatory return. (Most wanted entertainment, but had no idea they could afford it. For me, it was a way to go).

If you find that you thought you wanted the big dream, but then you realize that your dream didn't include all the nonsense that goes along with one of those in exchange for your "other dream(s)", (perhaps your family or job?), it is TOTALLY alright to adapt your dreams to accommodate each other. Unfortunately, some dreams require 24 hour dedication to maintain (ask any professional who is a megastar in their field.)

Pursue the dream

Don't give up. That's the first thing anyone successful who is giving advice says, so it MUST be true. Take advantage of all opportunities, work, work, and work at it!

Live the dream

Remember that each time you sing, play, write, perform, discuss, pitch, etc., you are creating a reality that supports your dream. Don't forget to applaud the little steps, as well as the big. You write a birthday song for your sister-in-law, and it makes her cry with your kindness. Your song is used in a campaign for adoption, and though it didn't earn a dime, it was perfect, and said so much to so many. A peer complimented your writing at a recent song pitch. You were the hit of the community musical. It all matters. All these things make us more professional, and give us the reasons for doing the work. They are as important as the royalties, and enrich our life of music. Don't overlook them.

Appreciate your dream

Did you know that most of your little steps are someone else's big dream? Some people would give a great deal to have the opportunity to perform ONE karaoke song in front of an audience, or have anyone use a song for any reason. Appreciate the skills and opportunities you have been blessed with, and that you might even have a dream.

Janet Fisher is Managing Director of Goodnight Kiss Music (BMI) www.goodnightkiss.com, along with its sister company, Scene Stealer Music (ASCAP). Both are Music Publishers dedicated to supplying the Entertainment Industries with perfect material for any musical need. Janet is also an author in, and the editor of "Music horror Stories", a collection of gruesome, true tales as told by innocent victims seeking a career in the music business". Contact: janet@goodnightkiss.com

We don't just make CDs. We kick-start your career.